Biographical Companion to Literature in English

Antony Kamm

The Scarecrow Press, Inc.
Lanham, Md., & London
1997

SCARECROW PRESS, INC.

Published in the United States of America
by Scarecrow Press, Inc.
4720 Boston Way
Lanham, Maryland 20706

The author acknowledges the advice and technical assistance of Adrian Bukkers of Rowland Phototypesetting in the preparation of the text of this edition.

British Library Cataloguing in Publication Information Available

Library of Congress Cataloging-in-Publication Data

Kamm, Antony.
    Biographical companion to literature in English / Antony Kamm.
      p. cm.
    Rev. and updated ed. of: Collins biographical dictionary of English literature. © 1993.
    Includes bibliographical references.
    ISBN 0-8108-3319-0 (alk. paper)
    1. Authors, English—Biography—Dictionaries. 2. Authors—Biography—Dictionaries. 3. English literature—Dictionaries.
I. Kamm, Antony. Collins biographical dictionary of English literature. II. Title.
PR106.K35 1997
820.9'0003—dc21   97-11819
[B]   CIP

ISBN 0-8108-3319-0 (cloth : alk. paper)

CONTENTS

TO THE READER

This is a revised and updated version, primarily for the North American market, of my *Collins Biographical Dictionary of English Literature*, published in the United Kingdom in 1993. It comprises brief outlines of the lives and principal literary achievements, and indicates the links between the life and art, of 1544 authors: 744 from Britain and Ireland, 249 from the United States of America (of whom 43 are new to this edition), 264 from past and present members of the Commonwealth, 246 from other nations, and 41 from the ancient classical world.

The intention has been to include a representative selection of authors who have made a significant contribution to literature in English or to their national literature, or to both. Writers in languages other than English are included whose works are widely read in English or have influenced the development of literature in English.

The identification of an author as Irish, Scottish, or Welsh has both literary and national significance. Those born in England who flourished before the union of the English and Scottish parliaments in 1707 are designated English; those whose writing was done after that date are identified as British.

This is a work of biography. It must therefore be expected that more space is given to authors who have led varied and interesting lives as well as to those whose literary achievements, influence, or versatility have been the greater. Virgil is not necessarily a more significant poet than Homer; it is just that more is known about him and a wider variety of works are attributed to him.

By writing half as much about each author, it would theoretically have been possible to include twice as many, but that would have made it a different book. As it is, I have endeavoured to maintain an appropriate balance between various literary genres, and between the nations, regions, and cultures represented, while still including writers whose personal individuality or eccentricity has enriched the history of literature in English.

TO THE USER

CROSS-REFERENCES

A name in small capitals indicates that there is an entry for that person to which reference can be made; the surname only is given except where there is more than one entry with that name (e.g. AUSTEN; CHARLOTTE BRONTË).

Several additional categories of headword are included in the main alphabetical sequence: significant authors and editors to whom reference is made in the course of an entry but who have no separate entry of their own; pseudonyms and pen names; names of which there are alternative ways of being represented as headwords.

BIBLIOGRAPHICAL REFERENCES

Italic type indicates that the work was published in volume form, or was performed in public, under that title. It should generally be clear from the context whether the date cited for a play is that of its first performance or first publication; often the two are the same.

Titles in Latin, French, German, Italian, Portuguese, Spanish, and Dutch are given in the original language as well as in that of the published translation. Square brackets are used to indicate English equivalents of titles in other languages. Italic type (or roman type in quotation marks) within square brackets indicates the title under which the work has been published or performed in an English translation.

Dates within the main text of an entry are, unless otherwise stated, those of first publication. In the case of a translation, the date is of first publication in the USA, where appropriate. The date and details of a work's first translation into English are given where these may be of historical interest.

In the 'See . . ' references at the end of an entry, the date in each case is that of the latest recorded edition of the work. Discrepancies can occur where a book has been imported from its country of origin.

The term 'new edn' usually, but not exclusively, indicates the publication of a subsequent paperback or softcover edition of the work. Many books from university presses and other academic publishers are now issued simultaneously in hardcover and paperback editions. The terms 'rev. edn' (revised edition), '2nd edn', etc. are self-explanatory.

Books cited within or at the end of an entry for reference, or for background or additional reading, have been chosen as far as possible for their accessibility to the ordinary reader and for their general availability.

General Notes

Inherited titles are incorporated in the headwords of an entry in bold type; conferred titles (other than those which are part of an author's usual designation) are in the text face.

Alternative names in the headwords of an entry are enclosed in light brackets.

In so far as it is possible to apply the distinction, 'pen name' denotes the name under which a person writes, 'pseudonym' that by which they are or were generally known in everyday life.

The term 'sizar' is defined in the entry for George Farquhar, where it first appears.

It should be clear from the context whether the academic title of 'professor' is used in its American sense of a university teacher or lecturer, or in its British sense of principal lecturer in a field of learning or the holder of a university chair.

Abbreviations

AB	Bachelor of Arts
AC	Companion of the Order of Australia
AM	Member of the Order of Australia
ANC	African National Congress
AO	Officer of the Order of Australia
b.	born
BA	Bachelor of Arts
BBC	British Broadcasting Corporation
BCh	Bachelor of Surgery
BD	Bachelor of Divinity
BL	Bachelor of Law
BLitt	Bachelor of Letters

BM	Bachelor of Medicine
BSc	Bachelor of Science
c.	*circa*, about
CB	Companion of the Order of the Bath
CBE	Commander of the Order of the British Empire
CH	Companion of Honour
CMG	Companion of the Order of St Michael and St George
d.	died
DBE	Dame Commander of the Order of the British Empire
DCL	Doctor of Civil Law
DD	Doctor of Divinity
DLitt	Doctor of Letters
DPhil	Doctor of Philosophy
DSO	Distinguished Service Order
ed.	editor, edited by
edn	edition
edns	editions
eds	editors
fl.	*floruit*, flourished
GBE	Knight Grand Cross of the British Empire
HMS	His (*or* Her) Majesty's Ship
Hon.	Honourable, Honorary
INLA	Irish National Liberation Army
IRA	Irish Republican Army
KBE	Knight Commander of the British Empire
KCB	Knight Commander of the Bath
KCMG	Knight Commander of St Michael and St George
KCVO	Knight Commander of the Royal Victorian Order
KGB	State Security Committee (in former USSR)
LittD	Doctor of Letters
LLB	Bachelor of Law
LLD	Doctor of Law
LRCP	Licentiate of the Royal College of Physicians
MA	Master of Arts
MB	Bachelor of Medicine
MBE	Member of the Order of the British Empire
MD	Doctor of Medicine
MI5/6	Military Intelligence, Section 5/6
MP	Member of Parliament
MRCS	Member of the Royal College of Surgeons
NCO	non-commissioned officer
n.d.	no date [printed in the book]

OBE	Officer of the Order of the British Empire
OM	Order of Merit
PhD	Doctor of Philosophy
QC	Queen's Counsel
RA	Royal Academician
rev.	revised
tr.	translated, translated by, translator
trs	translators
USSR	Union of Soviet Socialist Republics
VC	Victoria Cross
vol.	volume
vols	volumes

A

ABÉ KOBO (1924–93) Japanese novelist and dramatist, was born Abé Kimifusa in Tokyo and was brought up in Mukden, Manchuria, where his father was doctor to the Japanese occupying forces. In 1933, shocked by the treatment of the local population, he changed his name to its Chinese equivalent. On his return to Japan, where he felt equally that he did not belong, he studied medicine at Tokyo University. He failed his examinations, but was given a face-saving pass on condition that he never practised. His first novel, [*The Road Sign at the End of the Road*] (1948), set in Manchuria, contains in its study of alienation and isolation the key to much of his work. The setting of [*The Woman in the Dunes*] (1962; tr. E. Dale Saunders, 1964; with an introduction by THWAITE, 1987), the sand dunes where an entomologist disappears and survives in an underground community, is sufficiently indefinite to give the book a universality which is unusual in Japanese fiction—the film, the script of which he was co-author, won the jury prize at the Cannes Film Festival in 1964. In [*The Face of Another*] (1964; tr. Saunders, 1966), the isolation is of a research scientist whose face has been horrifyingly scarred in a laboratory explosion; in [*Secret Rendezvous*] (1978; tr. Juliet Winters Carpenter, 1979) it is of a salesman whose wife has mysteriously been consigned somewhere in the nightmare underground complex of a hospital. *Beyond the Curve*, tr. Carpenter (1991), is a collection of short stories which further illustrate his disquiet about family responsibilities, identity, and oppressive conditions in the workplace.

He published his first play in 1955, and in 1973 began to produce his own work (mainly collages of different forms of visual images) in a theatre built for him by its owner on the ninth floor of a department store—see *Three Plays by Kobo Abe* (1993). He was the first writer to introduce Western concepts of absurdity and nihilism into Japanese literature, and though his fiction has been compared to that of BECKETT, KAFKA, and ROBBE-GRILLET, he himself acknowledged the influence rather of CARROLL and POE. His motif of isolation was reflected in his own life: he never opened his mail or answered the telephone.

ABÉLARD, PETER (or **PETRUS ABAELARDUS**) (1079–1142) French theologian and philosopher, was born in Le Pallet, near Nantes. He renounced his birthright as the eldest son to study logic in Paris under William of Champeaux (*c.*1070–1121), whom he defeated so often in disputation that it was advisable to move on to the schools at Melon and Corbeil, where he lectured to packed audiences. After a spell at home for his health, he studied theology at Laon, and in 1115 became a canon of Notre-Dame and a professor of philosophy, in which capacity he is said to have instructed one future pope, 19 cardinals, and over fifty bishops. Attracted to Héloïse, the 17-year-old 'reputed niece' of Canon Fulbert, he became her private tutor. They had an intense affair, of which a son, Astralabe, was born. Though they secretly married in Brittany, Héloïse refused to acknowledge that she was his wife so as not to prejudice his preferment in the Church. A furious Fulbert had Abélard castrated, as he slept, by a thug with a razor.

Héloïse retired to a nunnery at Argenteuil. Abélard became a monk of the abbey of St Denis, but after his teaching and his book *Introductio ad Theologiam* had been condemned as heretical, he went into hermitage near Nogent-sur-Seine. His disciples promptly besieged the place, and built him a stone chapel, dedicated under the name of Paraclete. In due course, when Abélard was appointed Abbot of St Gildas de Rhuys in Brittany, it became a convent, of which Héloïse was put in charge. A philosophical conceptualist and a theological rationalist, Abélard died at Cluny, where he had stopped on his way to Rome to answer further charges—a selection of his writings is in *Ethics*, ed. and tr. D. E. Luscombe (1971). For the more romantically minded is the cache of four letters between the former lovers, hers more ardent than his, written in Latin in about 1132 and first published in 1616—see *The Letters of Abelard and Heloise*, ed. and tr. Betty Radice (1974), which includes 'Historia Calamitatum' [The Story of His Misfortunes], his own account of his life up to 1132, and other documents. Héloïse died in 1163/4 and was buried beside him at Paraclete. Their remains are now in Paris, in the cemetery of Père La-chaise.

ABRAHAMS, PETER (b. 1919) South African novelist, was born in Vrededorp, near Johannesburg, and educated at the Diocesan Training College, Grace Dieu, and St Peter's Secondary School, Rosettenville. In his late teens he read right through the American negro literature section of the library in the Bantu Men's Social Centre, becoming what he termed a 'colour nationalist', and had a book of verse printed, *A Blackman Speaks of Freedom*. In 1941, having served for two years as a stoker in the Merchant Navy, he settled in England. He was on the staff of the Communist newspaper, the *Daily Worker*, and published a book of short stories, *Dark Testament* (1942), and a minor novel, *Song of the City* (1945). *Mine Boy* (1946) established him as what Michael Wade, in *Peter Abrahams* (1972), calls 'South Africa's first proletarian writer'. *Wild Conquest* (1950) is an artistic view of the collision between Boer and Matabele at the time of the Great Trek. His revealing personal reports on South Africa, written for the *Observer*, were published as *Return to Goli* (1953). In 1955 he and his family moved to Jamaica, where he was Editor of the *West Indian Economist* and Controller of 'West Indian News' broadcasts 1955–64, and Chairman of Radio Jamaica 1977–80. His divorce from the South African scene forced him now to take a broader look at contemporary black issues. *A Wreath for Udomo* (1956) looks at the implications of an African country's independence. *The View from Coyaba* (1985) is a historical novel which re-creates black experience in Africa, the Caribbean, and the American South. See *Tell Freedom: Memories of Africa*, 1954 (autobiography).

ABSE, DANNIE (b. 1923) Welsh poet, novelist, and dramatist, was born in Cardiff and educated at St Illtyd's College, Cardiff, the University of South Wales and Monmouthshire, and King's College, London, qualifying as a physician in 1950, and becoming a chest specialist. His poetry, which began with *After Every Green Thing* (1949) and which he has continued to write—a recent volume is *Remembrance of Crimes Past* (1990)—is rooted in his Welsh and Jewish backgrounds and in his own day-to-day experience, being reflective, often amusing, and usually readily accessible. His plays are extensions of his poetic impulse rather than departures into a different genre. Those regarded as his best are the one-act *Gone* (produced 1962) and *In the Cage*, both published in *Three Questor Plays* (1967); the latter is a revised version in prose of his verse play *Fire in Heaven* (produced 1948, published 1956), a study of the dilemmas of pacifism and of how violence can escalate. *Ash on a Young Man's Sleeve* (1954) is a sharply-etched semi-autobiographical novel

of a Jewish family in Cardiff before World War II; *There Was a Young Man from Cardiff* (1991) is a companion volume. See *White Coat, Purple Coat: Collected Poems 1948–1988*, new edn 1992; *Selected Poems*, 1994; *A Poet in the Family*, new edn 1984 (autobiography); *Intermittent Journals*, 1995 (medical and literary reminiscences, and personal experiences); Joseph Cohen (ed.), *The Poetry of Dannie Abse: Critical Essays and Reminiscences*, 1983.

ACHEBE, CHINUA (b. 1930) Nigerian novelist, poet, and critic, was born Albert Chinualumogo into a Christian family in the prominent village of Ogidi, Eastern Nigeria, in which 'the old had not been completely disorganized . . . and the festivals were still observed'. He was educated at Government College, Umuahia, and on a scholarship at University College, Ibadan. 'When I left school I didn't really know what I wanted to do and medicine was very glamorous, but I soon discovered that it was not really my cup of tea, so I changed.' He graduated as BA in English literature in 1953, and after a few months as a teacher joined the Nigerian Broadcasting Corporation as a talks producer in Lagos, becoming Controller, Enugu, in 1958, and Director of External Broadcasting in 1961. He began thinking about a novel at university, and started to write it in 1956, when he decided to make two books out of the story, and to 'blow up the first part'. *Things Fall Apart* (1958), whose theme is the mutual incomprehension between tribal communities and white officials in the 1890s (with more than a glance at changing attitudes within the tribe), is overlaid with colourful detail, and with insights into traditions, strange rituals, and taboos. One such taboo catalyses the downfall of the chief character in *No Longer at Ease* (1960), the civil servant who is the grandson of the stubborn tragic hero of *Things Fall Apart*. *Arrow of God* (1964) reverts to an earlier phase of colonial intervention, and explores in greater depth the conflict between African spirituality and British authority. *A Man of the People* (1966) is a searing indictment of post-colonial political corruption in an African state.

In 1966, because of the political situation, Achebe gave up his job in Lagos and returned to his eastern homeland, serving Biafra during the civil war of 1967–69 as a roving ambassador. Out of the war itself came a collection of strong poems, *Beware, Soul-Brother and Other Poems* (1971), which in a revised edition (1972) was joint winner of the inaugural Commonwealth Poetry Prize. During the 1970s he concentrated on teaching: as Director of African Studies at the University of Nigeria, Enugu (where in 1971 he founded and began his sojourn as Editor of *Okike: an African Journal of New Writing*), and then as Professor of English, Nsukka; and as a visiting professor in American universities. He was also writing critical essays—see *Morning Yet on Creation Day: Essays* (1975), in which appeared 'The African Writer and the English Language' and 'The Novelist as Teacher'. He extended the role of the novelist as an educator of society by writing fiction for children, *The Flute* (1977) and *The Drum* (1977). *Anthills of the Savannah* (1987) was his first novel for 22 years. More complex than his others in that the action is seen from several points of view, it follows the tragic course of events, fomented apparently out of nothing, which unstabilizes the military government of the state of Kangan (representing Nigeria). While bleakly demonstrating the pitfalls of government by those who have not been educated for it, the novel ends on a note of challenge, and hope.

Achebe has explained that his novels are 'all related' and that he has tried 'to look at the story of Africa in the modern world'. The inevitable conflicts are rooted in what he sees as 'the mark on the face that sets one people apart from their neighbours'. He supports an African literature in English where, as in Nigeria, English functions as a supra-regional *national* language. He has won many honours and honorary degrees. His 60th birthday in 1990 was marked by a three-day international symposium at Nsukka, at which, it was reported, 'he sat silent through all the sessions, his face a mask as he listened to the praises of the many academics who analysed his writings from every possible angle'. While returning to Lagos to catch a flight to New York, he was badly injured in a car crash, and spent six months in Stoke Mandeville Hospital in the UK. He recovered sufficiently to fulfil a teaching engagement in the USA, in a wheelchair. See *Hopes and Impediments: Selected Essays 1965–87*, 1990; C. L. Innes, *Chinua Achebe*, new edn 1992 (critical study); Simon Gikandi, *Reading Chinua Achebe: Language and Ideology in Fiction*, 1991; Kirsten Holst Petersen and Anna Rutherford (eds), *Chinua Achebe: a Celebration*, 1991.

ACKROYD, PETER (*b.* 1949) British novelist and biographer, was born in London, the only child of working-class Catholic parents, and was brought up on a council estate in Acton—his father, with whom he has subsequently corresponded but not met, left the family home when Ackroyd was a baby. He went (on a scholarship) to St Benedict's School, Ealing, and then to Clare College, Cambridge, after which he was a Fellow of Yale University 1971–73. He then became, at 23, Literary Editor of the *Spectator*. His first published works were two volumes of verse, reissued together as *Diversions of Purley* (1987), but he 'found the urge to write poetry stopped—poetry is an act of intransigence; prose offers a social interaction'. In his first novel, *The Great Fire of London* (1982), Dicken-

sian London and the characters in *Little Dorrit* have their parallels in the 1980s. In *The Last Testament of Oscar Wilde* (1983) he explores the mind of the writer in the form of a confession by the dying man. In the darkly brooding *Hawksmoor* (1985) two Londons, of the 17th century and of today, dissolve into each other in a hunt for a bizarre killer. He employs a similar artifice, involving three eras, in *Chatterton* (1987), in which the poet's death is linked with the marriage of MEREDITH and with curious events and characters in modern times. *Hawksmoor* was the second leg of a remarkable double, for it won the Whitbread Award for fiction the year after his *T. S. Eliot* (1984) gained the Whitbread Award for biography. The latter, which centres on the poet's creative years, is all the more impressive in that permission was not forthcoming to quote from any of Eliot's published or unpublished work. CHATTERTON, WILDE, and T. S. ELIOT reappear, as does Ackroyd himself, in the occasional fictional dialogues introduced into *Dickens* (1990), a biography in which the novelist's characters receive fuller treatment than his family. The technique is extended in *English Music* (1992), a novel of the 1920s in which a boy visionary, in alternate chapters, meets classic English writers and painters and moves through their works, the whole forming a lyrical panorama of English culture. Fiction and fact, present and past, are amalgamated, too, in the sinister narratives of London, *The House of Doctor Dee* (1993) and *Dan Leno and the Limehouse Golem* (1994). *Milton in America* (1996) is an alternative and satirical excursion into the life of the poet. *Blake* (1995) is a straight and distinguished critical biography of the the poet, engraver, and mystic—see BLAKE.

ACORN, MILTON see PURDY.

ADAM, VILLIERS DE L'ISLE see MAETERLINCK.

ADAMS, HENRY (BROOKS) (1838–1918) American prose writer, the great-grandson of the second President of the USA, grandson of the sixth President, and son of Charles Francis Adams (1807–86), congressman and diplomat, was born in Boston 'under the shadow of Boston State House'. After graduating from Harvard College in 1858 and travelling and studying in Italy and France, he was from 1860 to 1868 private secretary to his father, who was appointed Minister in England in 1861. In 1870 he became Editor of the *North American Review* and also, reluctantly, an assistant professor of medieval history at Harvard. He resigned from both posts seven years later to undertake historical research in Washington for biographies of the former Secretary of the Treasury, Albert Gallatin (1879), and the colourful Virginian congressman, John Randolph (1882). He also published (anonymously) *Democracy: an American Novel* (1880), an attack on political corruption, and (as Frances Snow Compton) *Esther: a Novel* (1884), a study of a woman's conflict of mind; and worked on his nine-volume *The History of the United States of America During the Administrations of Thomas Jefferson and James Madison* (1889–91). The suicide of his wife in 1885 led to a restless period of extended travel and little creativity, from which he emerged to write *Mont-Saint-Michel and Chartres* (privately printed 1904; trade edition 1913), a travelogue of the imagination which he saw as 'a study of 13th-century unity'. In *The Education of Henry Adams* (privately printed 1907; trade edition 1918), 'a study of 20th-century multiplicity', he decried his failure as a useful member of society and projected that the quickening pace of scientific advance would dehumanize the world and reduce it to chaos. His contribution to literature as a social philosopher outweighs anything he might have achieved in the political field during his lifetime. See Ernest Samuels, *Henry Adams*, new edn 1989, rev. edn in one volume, 1995 (biography); R. P. Blackmur, *Henry Adams*, ed. Veronica A. Makowsky, new edn 1984 (critical study).

ADAMS, RICHARD (*b.* 1920) British novelist, was born in Newbury, Berkshire, and educated at Bradfield College and, after wartime service in the Royal Army Service Corps, at Worcester College, Oxford. He became a civil servant, being Assistant Secretary, Department of the Environment 1968–74, with special responsibilities in air-pollution research. He was elected President of the Royal Society for the Prevention of Cruelty to Animals in 1980, but resigned in 1982. His first novel, *Watership Down* (1972), having been turned down by several major publishers, was published as a children's book and swiftly, and deservedly, became a classic. Whether read as a political or an environmental allegory, or simply as a quest story, it is especially remarkable for the creation of a complete world, and of characters and convincing language for the rabbit community which inhabits it. In *Shardik* (1974), set in a shadowy but ably-delineated mythical past, a great bear is unwittingly the moving force behind clashes between primitive cultures. *The Plague Dogs* (1977) reverts to modern times, as two dogs escape from an animal research station. Subsequent novels about human characters, *The Girl in a Swing* (1980) and *Maia* (1984), met with less critical acclaim. After *Traveller* (1989), in which events in the American Civil War are seen through the eyes of General Robert E. Lee's horse, and a seven-year gap, came *Tales from Watership Down* (1996), stories and rabbit mythology of the original community which he had been accumulating over the years. See

The Day Gone By: an Autobiography, new edn 1991.

ADCOCK, FLEUR (*b.* 1934) New Zealand poet, the elder sister of the novelist Marilyn Duckworth (*b.* 1935), was born in Papakura, and between 1939 and 1947 went to numerous schools in England, where her Manchester-born father was then lecturing for the Workers' Educational Association. Back in New Zealand, she went to Wellington Girls' College, married ALISTAIR CAMPBELL in 1952 (they had two sons, and were divorced in 1958), and graduated in classics at Victoria University. From 1958 she taught and did library work, and then in 1963 emigrated to the UK—'Stewart Island' expresses her ambivalent feelings about New Zealand at this time. She was Assistant Librarian, Foreign and Commonwealth Office Library, until 1979, when she became a full-time writer. A number of poems from her first book, *The Eye of the Hurricane* (1964), published in Wellington, were reprinted in *Tigers*, published in London in 1967. *Selected Poems* (1983; reissued 1991) includes the pamphlet *Below Loughrigg* (1979). Subsequent collections are *The Incident Book* (1986) and *Time Zones* (1991), in which she applies her crisp approach and precise use of language to personal, communal, and international issues, weaving past experience into the expression of present concerns and future uncertainties. She has also written English versions of *The Virgin and the Nightingale: Medieval Latin Poems* (1983), from manuscripts she studied while she was Northern Arts Fellow at the universities of Durham and Newcastle from 1979 to 1981; translated from the Romanian the poetry of Grete Tartler (1989) and Daniela Crasnaru (1991); and compiled *The Oxford Book of Contemporary New Zealand Poetry* (1982). She was made MBE in 1996.

ADDISON, JOSEPH (1672–1719) British essayist, critic, poet, dramatist, and statesman, was born in Milston, Wiltshire, the son of Rev. Lancelot Addison (Dean of Lichfield 1683–1703), and was educated at Charterhouse (where he first met and became a close friend of STEELE) and The Queen's College, Oxford. His precocity at Latin verse led to his transfer to Magdalen College, where he was a Fellow 1698–1711—'Addison's Walk' along the River Cherwell still bears his name. His interest in politics brought him a Treasury grant to travel in Europe for five years and the commission to write a celebratory poem on the victory of the Duke of Marlborough (1650–1722) at Blenheim, published to great acclaim in 1705 as *The Campaign*. With a succession of government posts in prospect, he was able to lend Steele money for his theatrical ventures. In 1708 he was elected a Member of Parliament, which he remained for the rest of his life. While Chief Secretary in Ireland, he contributed essays anonymously to Steele's *Tatler*. When the Whigs fell in 1710, leaving him out of office, he and Steele founded, edited, and became chief contributors to the daily periodical the *Spectator*, which like the *Tatler* consisted of a single sheet printed on both sides. In two bursts (March 1711 to December 1712 and June to December 1714) it had great success, and was also published in book form (1712–15). Addison's verse tragedy *Cato* was performed in 1713, its popularity being due partly to its political implications and partly to the fact that it is a good play of its kind. A comedy, *The Drummer*, flopped in 1715, but in that year, with the return of the Whigs after the accession of George I, he was reappointed to the Government and to his former Irish post, and published his own political journal, the *Freeholder*, which ran for 55 issues. In 1716 he married the Dowager Countess of Warwick, and in the next year he was appointed one of the two secretaries of state under the Crown. His health was failing, though, and he retired in 1718, to die of 'asthma and dropsy'. He was just 46.

The periodical essay, which particularly flourished in the 18th century, reached its acme as a vehicle of critical, philosophical, and political opinion, and of cultured amusement, in the hands of Addison and Steele. The aim of the *Spectator*, propounded by Addison in issue 10, was 'to enliven morality with wit, and to temper wit with morality'. The wit was enhanced by the introduction of experiences of members of the fictitious Spectator Club, notably Sir Roger de Coverley. Addison's series of essays 'On the Pleasures of the Imagination' (issues 411–21) and his 18 weekly essays on Milton beginning in issue 267—also published in book form as *Notes Upon the Twelve Books of Paradise Lost* (1719)—are admirable in the context of the attitudes of the times, and stand among the most elegant examples of early 18th-century literary criticism. See *The Spectator*, ed. Donald F. Bond, 5 vols, new edn 1987; Peter Smithers, *The Life of Joseph Addison*, 2nd edn 1968.

ADE, GEORGE (1866–1944) American fabulist and dramatist, was born in Kentland, Indiana, the son of an English immigrant. He had a school essay, 'A Basket of Potatoes', published in the local *Gazette* in 1881. In 1883, because of his aversion to farming as a career, he was sent to Purdue University, Lafayette, from which he graduated in 1887 with a commencement oration on 'The Future of Letters in the West'. He became a journalist and was taken on by the Chicago *Morning News* (later *Record*), for which he began in 1893 a daily double column, 'Stories of the Streets and of the Town', illustrated by his college friend, John T. McCutcheon (1870–1949). From this he extracted sketches of three characters, each of whom he made the subject of a book:

Artie (1896), *Pink Marsh* (1897), and *Doc' Horne* (1899). As a further outlet for his aptitude for the representation of colloquial speech and for his lightning humour, he invented his own brand of fable, of which the first appeared in the *Record* in 1897. A collection followed, *Fables in Slang* (1899), whose text, liberally sprinkled with capital letters, evoked American types and regional and cultural quirks. He was still writing them in 1939. His career as a dramatist was as spectacular but much shorter, effectively consisting of a musical, *The Sultan of Sulu* (produced 1902), and two comedies: *The County Chairman* (1904), about local politics, and *The College Widow* (1904), a satire on university life (the climax is a football game and the pace and noise of the production impressed even audiences in London, who were thoughtfully provided with a glossary of Americanisms). See Lee Coyle, *George Ade*, 1964 (critical study).

AESCHYLUS (525–456 BC) classical Greek dramatist, was born in Eleusis, near Athens, and first entered the annual dramatic festival of Dionysius in 499, without success. He fought against the Persians at the battle of Marathon (490), in which he took more pride than anything else. He won the prize for tragedy in 484, and again in 472, but after losing to SOPHOCLES in 468, he left Athens in disgust for the court of Syracuse. He returned later, and won his last prize in 458 with his trilogy, the *Oresteia* (*Agamemnon*, *Choephoroi*, and *Eumenides*), the themes of which are respectively retribution, punishment, and reconciliation. He died in Gela, it is said when an eagle, looking for a rock on which to smash the shell of a tortoise, dropped it on his bald head. Four other tragedies survive of the ninety plays he wrote—*The Suppliants*, *The Persians*, *Seven Against Thebes*, and *Prometheus Bound*, in the last of which especially he developed his idea of a supreme ruler who is working towards perfection rather than being perfection itself. Aeschylus is regarded as the founder of Greek tragedy; the poetry in his plays is dramatic, intense, and often lyrical. By introducing a second actor and reducing the role of the chorus, he effectively invented dramatic dialogue. See *Plays*, tr. Kenneth McLeish and Frederic Raphael, 2 vols 1991; *Oresteia*, tr. Michael Ewans, 1995 (includes acting directions).

AESOP see HENRYSON; LA FONTAINE.

AGATE, JAMES (1877–1947) British dramatic critic and novelist, was born in Pendleton, Lancashire, and educated at Manchester Grammar School, after which he joined his father's business of agent to the cotton trade. From 1907 he was also writing dramatic criticism for the *Manchester Guardian*. During World War I, in which his main function in

France was to buy hay for horses, he wrote an epistolary novel, *L. of C.* [Lines of Communication] (1917). After the war he set up, briefly, as manager of a general store in London, published a further novel, *Responsibility* (1919), and was then appointed Dramatic Critic first of the *Saturday Review* and then, in 1923, of the *Sunday Times*, which he remained until his death. He produced two more novels and several volumes of essays and criticism, but his chief work is a day-to-day diary, published in nine volumes as *Ego* (1935–48), which describes wittily and often caustically the cultural and social life of London. As a critic he was sometimes obstinate in his reluctance to detect any greatness in contemporary dramatists or actors, but he was always respected and entertaining. He is also to be remembered for his advice to aspiring journalists, quoted by his godson Paul Dehn in *For Love and Money* (1956): 'Spend three times as long on your first paragraph as you spend on the rest of your article. Then cut the first paragraph.'

AGEE, JAMES (1909–55) American novelist and journalist, was born in Knoxville, Tennessee, and educated at Exeter Academy and Harvard, after which he became in 1932 a staff writer on *Fortune*. He published a book of verse, *Permit Me Voyage*, in 1934. A series of articles (with photographs by Walker Evans) on the conditions of the poor white tenant-farmers in Alabama, was commissioned in 1936 by *Fortune*, and then rejected. The resulting book, *Let Us Now Praise Famous Men* (1941; in UK 1965), is a masterpiece of discreet documentary reportage. In 1939 he moved to *Time*, for whom he reviewed books and films, while also being Film Critic of the *Nation* from 1943 to 1948—see *Agee on Film: Reviews and Comments* (1958). He also wrote film scripts, among them that of FORESTER's *The African Queen* (1951). *The Morning Watch* (1951), his first novel, covers a traumatic day in the life of a boy at a Catholic boarding school. *A Death in the Family* (1957), published posthumously and awarded the Pulitzer Prize for fiction, is a semi-autobiographical study of a boy, and his family, coping with the death of his father in a car accident. Agee's experimental approach to marriage is described by his second wife, Alma Mailman (1912–88), in Alma Neuman, *Always Straight Ahead: a Memoir* (1993), edited by their son Joel. See Laurence Bergreen, *James Agee: a Life*, 1984.

AGNON, S(HMUEL) Y(OSEF) (1888–1970) Israeli novelist, was born Samuel Josef Czaczkes in the Galician town of Buczacz, the son of a fur merchant, and adopted his pseudonym as his official name in 1924. He was privately and broadly educated, studying German and the Talmud with tutors, and

Hasidic literature at the synagogue. He published about seventy prose and verse pieces in Yiddish and Hebrew before going to Palestine in 1907, after which he wrote only in Hebrew. In 1913 he settled in Germany, where he published three collections of stories (1921–22). He returned to Jerusalem in 1924, having that year lost most of his manuscripts in a fire at his home, including that of a semi-autobiographical panoramic novel of modern Jewish history. His principal oeuvre is the series of five novels which he wrote between then and his death: [*The Bridal Canopy*] (1931; tr. I. M. Lask, 1937), [*A Simple Story*] (1935), [*A Guest for the Night*] (1939; tr. Misha Louvis, rev. edn 1968), [*Yesteryear*] (1945), and the unfinished *Shira* (1971; tr. Zeva Shapiro, 1989), in each of which a wandering, tormented soul searches futilely for a mate. Conscious of his mastery of shorter fiction—see *Twenty-One Stories*, ed. Nahum N. Glatzer (1970)—he often published extracts from his novels as separate works. An author in the European tradition of Jewish literature, he was awarded the Nobel Prize for Literature in 1966, the first writer in Hebrew to receive it.

AIDOO, (CHRISTINA) AMA ATA (*b.* 1942) Ghanaian dramatist, novelist, and short-story writer, was born in Abeadzi Kyiakor and educated at Wesley Girls' High School, Cape Coast, and the University of Ghana, Legon, where her first play, *The Dilemma of a Ghost* (published 1965), was performed by the Students' Theatre in 1964, during her last year as an undergraduate. Basically about traditional responses to modern attitudes, it was produced in Lagos, Nigeria, later that year and published in 1965. As Research Fellow at the Institute of African Studies, University of Ghana, she studied contemporary Ghanaian drama, after which she travelled in East Africa, England, and the USA, where she was Creative Writing Fellow at Stanford University. Her second play, *Anowa* (1970), is her interpretation of a tale of the Gold Coast in the late 19th century, told to her by her mother in the form of a song. The short stories of contemporary Ghana in *No Sweetness Here* (1970) are the work of a critical, involved observer, and are 'written to be heard, primarily'. In her novel, *Our Sister Killjoy: or, Reflections from a Black-eyed Squint* (1977), the critical eye is directed at European attitudes to black visitors, expressed by a girl from Ghana who concludes that Africa, 'crazy old continent', is 'home with its unavoidable warmth and even after these thousands of years, its uncertainties'. Aidoo, who taught African literature at the universities of Cape Coast and Nairobi, before settling in Zimbabwe, has also published two collections of verse, *Someone Talking to Sometime* (1985) and *Angry Letter in January* (1992).

AIKEN, CONRAD (1889–1973) American poet, fiction writer, and critic, was born in Savannah, Georgia, the son of a New England couple, a physician and the daughter of the Minister of the First Congregational Society, New Bedford. He was reading POE when he was ten, 'and scaring myself to death. Scaring my brothers and sisters to death, too.' He was 11 when he heard two pistol shots, and made the discovery that his father had killed his wife and then himself after an argument. He was subsequently brought up by an elderly relative in New Bedford, and was educated at Middlesex School, Concord, and Harvard, where he was President of the *Advocate* and 'saw a great deal' of T. S. ELIOT. He graduated in 1912, and married (the first of three wives) a few days later. He honeymooned in Europe, and then began writing poems for *Earth Triumphant and Other Tales in Verse* (1914), the first of eight volumes of poetry he published in the next ten years, and of 42 books in all which appeared during his lifetime. After several extended trips abroad, and three years in England, living in Sussex, where his daughter, the British novelist and children's writer Joan Aiken was born in 1924, he settled in Brewster, Massachusetts. Initially compared with MASEFIELD, he went on to be influenced by FREUD, and to investigate musical forms, from 'symphonies' to 'preludes'— see *Collected Poems 1916–1970* (1971). He wrote five experimental novels, beginning with *Blue Voyage* (1927), which he alternated with volumes of short stories—see *The Collected Short Stories* (1960). *Collected Criticism* was published in 1968. His most lasting prose work is *Ushant: an Essay* (1952), a partly-fictional, third-person narrative in which he explores his life and describes his literary acquaintances.

AINSWORTH, WILLIAM HARRISON (1805–82) British novelist, was born in Manchester and educated at Manchester Grammar School, which he left at 16 to be articled to a local solicitor. After having had stories printed in several periodicals, he published anonymously *Sir John Chiverton* (1826), a novel of chivalry in the style of WALTER SCOTT, who read it on publication and noted the debt to him in his journal. After getting married and having a brief career as a publisher, Ainsworth wrote, according to him in 'less than twenty-four hours', *Rookwood* (1834), a novel glamorizing the highwayman Dick Turpin (1706–39). He continued this genre with *Jack Sheppard* (1839), whose eponymous anti-hero was hanged in 1724 at the age of 22. The critics were outraged; the public was delighted. He followed these Gothic-style romances with a string of historical novels, many with local associations, of which *The Tower of London* (1840), *Old St Paul's, a Tale of the Plague and the Fire of London* (1841), for

which the *Sunday Times* paid him £1000, and *The Lancashire Witches* (1849) are still readable for the sense of solid horror which they evoke. He was Editor of *Bentley's Miscellany* 1840–42 and 1854–68, *Ainsworth's Magazine* 1842–53, and the *New Monthly Magazine* 1845–70.

AKHMATOVA, ANNA, pseudonym (from her grandmother's name) of Anna Andreevna Gorenko (1889–1966) Russian poet, was born in Bolshoi Fontan, a suburb of Odessa, the daughter of a retired naval engineer, and spent her early years near St Petersburg, where she went to secondary school. 'We didn't have any books in the house, not a single book. Only Nekrasov [1821–77, Russian editor and poet of peasant life], a thick, bound volume. My mother used to let me read it on feast days. . . . [It] was a present to Mama from her first husband, who shot himself.' She began a course in law at the college for women in Kiev, but returned to St Petersburg. In 1910 she married the poet Nikolai Gumilev, with whom and MANDELSTAM she was a founder member of the Acmeist movement, which gave more attention to sound and meaning than was the habit of the Symbolists. They were divorced in 1918 (he was executed in 1921 for allegedly plotting against the Bolsheviks). She subsequently remarried twice, and in between times lived in a creative relationship with a composer and an actress. After the appearance of several volumes of verse and a collected edition, *Anno Domini* (1923), she was persecuted for her former husband's connections and banned from publishing any new poems— there were times when she feared even to write them down. It was now that she met Lydia Chukovskaya (1907–96), who would memorize poems Akhmatova had written on scraps of paper, and hand them back to be burned—see Lydia Chukovskaya, *The Akhmatova Journals 1938–1941* (1976, Paris; tr. Milena Michalski and Sylva Rubashova, poetry tr. Peter Norman, 1994).

Freedom to write during World War II, part of which she spent in central Asia, was followed by a clampdown on writers such as Akhmatova, whose favoured themes of love and religion were not regarded as serving the interests of the state. In 1946 she was expelled from the Writers' Union, of which ultimately, in the only comparatively relaxed atmosphere following the denunciation of Stalin in 1956, she was elected President in 1964. The supreme Russian lyric poet of the 20th century, whose reputation antedates the Revolution of 1917, she was a firm believer in Christianity whose work also reflects the physical torment and private suffering of families who were persecuted in the name of Communism, particularly *Requiem*, tr. D. M. Thomas with *Poem Without a Hero* (1979). See

The Complete Poems, ed. Roberta Reeder, tr. Judith Hemschemeyer, 2nd enlarged edn 1993; *Selected Poems*, tr. Stanley Kunitz with Max Hayward, new edn 1989; *Selected Poems*, tr. Richard McKane, 1989; *My Half Century: Selected Prose*, ed. Ronald Meyer, 1992; Amanda Haight, *Anna Akhmatova: a Poetic Pilgrimage*, new edn 1990 (biography); Roberta Reeder, *Anna Akhmatova: Poet and Prophet*, new edn 1995 (biography); Konstantin Polivanov (ed.), *Anna Akhmatova and Her Circle*, tr. Patricia Beriozkina, 1994; David Wells, *Anna Akhmatova: Her Poetry*, 1996.

ALAIN-FOURNIER, pen name (from 1907) of Alain Henri Fournier (1886–1914) French novelist, was born in La Chapelle d'Angillon in the valley of the Cher, and grew up in Epineuil-le-Fleuriel, where his father was the village school teacher. After two years at the Lycée Voltaire, Paris, he transferred of his own volition to the naval training school in Brest, which he left after a short time to return to the Cher. He went to the Lycée Lakanal, Paris, in 1903; spent the summer holidays of 1905 in Turnham Green, London, translating letters for Sanderson's, the wallpaper manufacturer; and twice failed his entrance to the École Normale Supérieure. He did his statutory military service from 1907 to 1909, when he found work as a journalist on *Paris-Journal*; in 1910–11 he gave French lessons to T. S. ELIOT, who recommended English books for him to read and gave him a copy of the works of JOHN FORD. *Le Grand Meaulnes* (1913; tr. Françoise Delisle as *The Wanderer*, 1929; tr. Frank Davison as *The Lost Domain*, 1959), a Symbolist novel of youthful aspirations whose structure is akin to that of STEVENSON's *Kidnapped*, first appeared as a five-part serial in *Nouvelle Revue Française*, and controversially just failed to win the Prix GONCOURT. Early on in World War I he was shot in the head while leading his company on a reconnaissance in the woods of Saint-Remy, shortly after the battle of the Marne. He was a devoted admirer and lover of the actress Simone (Pauline Casimir-Perier), whose husband was killed in action in 1915. She died in 1985 in her 109th year.

ALASDAIR MACMHAIGHSTIR ALASDAIR see MACDONALD, ALEXANDER.

ALBEE, EDWARD (FRANKLIN) (*b.* 1928) American dramatist, was born in Washington, D.C., and was at two weeks old adopted by Reed and Frances Albee, members of a theatrical family. He was named after his adoptive grandfather, Edward Franklin Albee (1857–1930), who owned or had an interest in several hundred coast-to-coast vaudeville theatres. It is said that he wrote his first play, *Aliqueen*, a three-act sex farce, when he was 12. He was educated at Valley Forge Military Academy, Choate School, and Trinity College, Hartford, which he left in his sophomore year after failing to attend classes. In 1950, against his parents' wishes, he went to live in Greenwich Village, New York, where for eight years he wrote poetry and supplemented the $50 a week from his grandmother's will trust by working as an office boy, sales assistant, luncheonette counterman, and messenger for Western Union. Just before his 30th birthday he typed out a one-act play, *The Zoo Story*, a park bench confrontation piece. First produced in Berlin in 1959, it was followed by other short dramas—see *The Zoo Story and Other Plays* (1962)—and then by his first full-length play (and first Broadway production), *Who's Afraid of Virginia Woolf?* (1962). This new-style battle of the sexes, in which, during the course of the early hours of one morning, a marriage disintegrates and then, through a symbolic sacrifice, is made stronger than before, won awards and plaudits, and is still his most significant work. *A Delicate Balance* (1966), in which a couple face up to responsibilities to friends, won the Pulitzer Prize, but in other plays dramatic intensity has often given way, as it does in *Tiny Alice* (1963), to surrealism. In *Three Tall Women* (1994), which won the Pulitzer Prize and is, according to Albee, about his adoptive mother, who lived into her nineties, the familiar alienated protagonist becomes, in the second act, a synthesis of three, at different ages. He has also adapted for the stage novels of CAPOTE, MCCULLERS, and MELVILLE. Often involved in, and provoked by, controversy, he has stated that his influences are 'Sophocles and Noël Coward'. See Richard Amacher, *Edward Albee*, rev. edn 1982 (critical study); Gerry McCarthy, *Edward Albee*, 1987 (critical study).

ALCOTT, LOUISA MAY (1832–88) American novelist, was born in Germantown, Pennsylvania, the youngest of four daughters. Her father was the educationist and social reformer Amos Bronson Alcott (1799–1888), whose Utopian schemes and general unworldliness put the burden of supporting the family first on his wife—see Cynthia H. Barton, *Transcendental Wife: the Life of Abigail May Alcott* (1996)—, who did social work, and then on his daughter. In between times the family subsisted on what the four girls called the 'Alcott Sinking Fund' (handouts from charitable neighbours). Louisa was taught by her father at home, and by friends, including EMERSON, HAWTHORNE, and THOREAU, and worked as a servant, seamstress, and teacher, before establishing herself as a writer. She was writing seriously at least from 1849: *Flower Fables* (1854) was her first published book. She also wrote at this time, anonymously or as A. M. Barnard, Gothic romances, thrillers, and sensation novels of violence, rape, incest, and drug abuse—see *Louisa May Alcott Unmasked: Collected Thrillers*, ed. Madeleine Stern (1995). As ardent an abolitionist as her father, but more practical, she volunteered as a nurse in the Civil War and, until struck down by typhoid after six weeks, served in the Union Hospital, Georgetown, an experience which she re-created in *Hospital Sketches* (1863). Having written, unsuccessfully, a psychological study of married love, *Moods* (1864), she was persuaded by an editor to write a girls' story, though she complained in her journal: 'Never liked girls or knew many, except my sisters; but our queer plays and experiences may prove interesting, though I doubt it.' *Little Women: or, Meg, Jo, Beth and Amy* (1868) and its second volume (1869), later called *Good Wives*, succeeded because of their truth and warmth, and in doing so became the forerunners of the modern family story for children. The saga of the March family was extended by *Little Men: Life at Plumfield with Jo's Boys* (1871) and *Jo's Boys and How They Turned Out* (1886), and complemented by other domestic tales. Latterly Alcott lived in Boston, where she campaigned for temperance and women's rights, her concern for which is reflected in several later novels, extracts from which, with representative samples of her other lesser-known writings, are in *Selected Fiction*, ed. Daniel Shealy, Madeleine B. Stern, and Joel Myerson (1991). See *The Selected Letters of Louisa May Alcott*, ed. Joel Myerson and Daniel Shealy, 1995; Madeleine B. Stern, *Louisa May Alcott*, new edn 1996 (biography); Martha Saxton, *Louisa May Alcott: a Modern Biography*, 1995.

ALDINGTON, 'RICHARD' [EDWARD GODFREE] (1892–1962) British poet, novelist, critic, biographer, and translator, was born in Portsmouth and educated at Dover College and University College, London, which he left for financial reasons without taking a degree. With POUND and DOOLITTLE, whom he married in 1913, he was a leading exponent of Imagist poetry; his first book of verse, *Images 1910–1915*, was published in 1915. He served in France from 1916 to 1918, being gassed and shell-shocked; out of his traumatic experiences he wrote his first work of fiction, *Death of a Hero* (1929; rev. edn 1930), the most violently anti-war English novel to come out of World War I. He separated from his wife soon after the war and from 1928 until his death lived in France and, during World War II, the USA. Publicity of his messy love life, his rather too frank revelations about NORMAN DOUGLAS published in 1954, and the furore over his findings in his biography of T. E. LAWRENCE (1955) made him so unpopular with the literary establishment that at one time all seventy of his books were out of print. He continued to publish poetry until 1937 and novels until 1946. He wrote a notable biography of the Duke of Wellington (1946) and influential studies of D. H. LAWRENCE. He was also a gifted transla-

tor of the Greek and Latin poets, and of Italian and French literature. Latterly, after the failure of his second marriage, the friendship with his first wife was revived—see *Richard Aldington and H. D.: the Later Years in Letters*, ed. Caroline Zilboorg (1995). See *The Complete Poems*, 1948; *Selected Critical Writings 1928–1960*, ed. Alister Kershaw, 1970; Norman T. Gates (ed.), *Richard Aldington: a Biography in Letters*, 1992; Charles Doyle, *Richard Aldington: a Biography*, 1989.

ALDISS, BRIAN (*b.* 1925) British novelist and short-story writer, was born in East Dereham, Norfolk, and educated at Framlingham College and West Buckland School, where he first began to write science fiction and other stories—a cache of risqué tales, buried in a biscuit tin to avoid punishment, was discovered by boys at the school fifty years later. He served in the Royal Signals in the Far East during and after World War II. After a spell in bookselling, he was Literary Editor of the *Oxford Mail* 1958–69. His reputation as one of the most respected and creative writers of science fiction has less to do with any conscious attempt to extend the boundaries of the genre than with a preoccupation with the forces of time and change. This, he himself suggests, has inspired most of his many novels. They range from *Non-Stop* (1958), a conventional space-disaster story, through *Barefoot in the Head: a European Fantasia* (1969), a linguistically innovative study of the effects of a brain poison on the thought processes, and through the three sagas of the sexual self-education and progress of Horatio Stubbs—*The Hand Reared Boy* (1970), *A Soldier Erect* (1971), *A Rude Awakening* (1978)—, to the 'Helliconia Trilogy' (1982, 1983, 1985), for which he created a solar system with its own history, culture, and religions to be a metaphorical image of our own society, and *Somewhere East of Life* (1994), a futuristic novel of personal and political conscience. Collections of short stories include *The Canopy of Time* (1959), *Best Science Fiction of Brian Aldiss* (1965), *Seasons in Flight* (1984), and *The Secrets of This Book* (1995) with linking commentary. Poetry is in *At the Caligula Hotel* (1995). He has edited many science-fiction anthologies, and written *Billion Year Spree: a History of Science Fiction* (1973) and *The Detached Retina: Aspects of SF and Fantasy* (1995). See *Bury My Heart at W. H. Smith's*, new edn 1991 (literary reminiscences).

ALEICHEM, SHALOM see SHALOM ALEICHEM.

ALEXANDER, WILLIAM (1826–94) Scottish novelist, was born in Chapel of Garioch, Aberdeenshire, and went to the parish school. He became a farm labourer, but an accident on the land when he was in his twenties resulted in his losing a leg. He moved to Aberdeen, to try to earn a living by writing. The breakthrough came only after many years, with the serialization in the *Aberdeen Free Press* in 1869–70 of a novel, *Johnny Gibb of Gushetneuk* (1871). This vivid, episodic evocation of events, controversies, and conflicting loyalties in a country parish during and after the Disruption (1843), which split the Church of Scotland and caused the establishment of the Free Church of Scotland, is narrated in literary English, with the dialogue of the country folk represented in the local Buchan dialect of Scots. Written only thirty years after the events it depicts, it is a significant social document as well as a literary landmark. Alexander went on to edit the *Aberdeen Free Press*.

ALFRED, 'THE GREAT' (849–99) King of Wessex, translator, and prose writer, was born in Wantage, Berkshire. He succeeded his brother Æthelred in 871, and successively defeated, or forced the submission of, the Danes who occupied the rest of England, until ultimately he achieved supremacy over the whole land. His early education was rudimentary, consisting mainly of what he learned from two journeys to Rome before he was seven. He was unable to read English until he was 12, or Latin until he was nearly forty. Then, with the help of a monk called Asser (*d.* 909), later Bishop of Sherborne, who wrote a biography of him—see *Alfred the Great*, tr. and ed. Simon Keynes and Michael Lapidge (1983)—Alfred began to read passages of Latin and to turn them into English. This was the beginning of English prose, and part of Alfred's design that English (in the form now known as Old English or Anglo-Saxon) rather than Latin should be the medium of instruction in schools. Between 892 and his death he worked on English translations of five major works: *Cura Pastoralis* [Pastoral Care] of Pope Gregory (*c.*540–604); a history of the world by the 5th-century Christian cleric Orosius; *Historia Ecclesiastica* of BEDE; *De Consolatione Philosophiae* of BOETHIUS; and a curious work which he called *Blostman* [Blossoms], in which a translation of the first book of the *Soliloquies* of St Augustine (*d. c.*606), Archbishop of Canterbury, forms an introduction to his own philosophical arguments and thoughts on immortality. In a preface, he likens his literary endeavours to those of a man collecting wood in a forest, where others may follow and find the means of constructing all manner of buildings. The claim, first made in 1964, that Asser's life is a medieval forgery, has exercised scholars ever since. See Alfred P. Smyth, *Alfred the Great*, 1995 (biography); David Sturdy, *Alfred the Great*, new edn 1996 (biography).

ALGER, HORATIO, JR (1832–99) American writer of fiction for boys, was born in Chelsea, Massachusetts, the son of a Unitarian minister who in 1844 defaulted on his debts and moved his family and pulpit to Marlborough. He was educated there at Gates Academy, and at Harvard. He then vacillated between teaching, writing— *Bertha's Christmas Vision: an Autumn Sheaf*, stories and verses, appeared in 1856—, and the ministry before opting to study at Cambridge Divinity School, from which he graduated in 1860. After a hurried European tour, he returned to Massachusetts, and published stories and poems in journals, breaking into the juvenile market with *Frank's Campaign* (1864). In 1864 he accepted the post of Minister of the Unitarian Society of Brewster. He resigned 15 months later 'and hastily left town on the next train for parts unknown', according to the parish standing committee, after being charged with 'the abominable and revolting crime of unnatural familiarity with *boys*'. He settled in New York, where he interested himself in the plight of vagrant boys and with the efforts made on their behalf by the Newsboys' Lodging House, and began to write, as expiation as well as for employment, moral tales in which virtue and industry are rewarded. *Ragged Dick: or, Street Life in New York with the Boot-Blacks* (1868), the first of a series of eight volumes including *Mark, the Match Boy* (1869) and *Ben, the Luggage Boy* (1870), began a personal literary crusade which continued with numerous similar books throughout his life, and beyond—*Out for Business* (1900) was completed by Edward Stratemeyer (1863–1930), his successor in the field of popular juvenile fiction, who as Laura Lee Hope wrote 'The Bobbsey Twins' series, and as Carolyn Keene the original 'Nancy Drew Mysteries'. Alger retired to South Natick, Massachusetts, in 1896, broken by overwork, having been a noted traveller, personal tutor to prominent families, and a respected member of the Harvard Club, New York. See Gary Scharnhorst and Jack Bales, *The Lost Life of Horatio Alger, Jr*, new edn 1992; Gary Scharnhorst, *Horatio Alger, Jr*, 1980 (biographical/critical study).

ALGREN, NELSON (1909–81) American novelist and journalist, was born Nelson Ahlgren Abraham in Detroit, the son of working-class Jewish immigrants with Swedish antecedents. He was brought up in Chicago, graduated from the University of Illinois in 1931, took a qualification in journalism, and rode the railroads in the South, picking up copy from the vagrants of the Depression, which he used in his first novel, *Somebody in Boots* (1935)—see also *The Texas Stories of Nelson Algren*, ed. Bettina Drew (1995). In his second, *Never Come Morning* (1942), of which HEMINGWAY remarked, 'You should not read [it] if you cannot take a punch', a doomed Polish teenage boxer is sentenced to death in Chicago for murder. Algren worked for the Chicago Venereal Disease Program in 1941–

42, and served in the US Army Medical Corps from 1942 to 1945. *The Neon Wilderness*, a collection of short stories, appeared in 1947. A meeting with BEAUVOIR at a literary party in 1947 was the beginning of an intense affair, which ran into problems when in the early 1950s the State Department withdrew his passport for suspected un-American activities. *The Man with the Golden Arm* (1949), the murky career and messy suicide of a Chicago gambling-den card dealer and morphine addict, won the National Book Award and was filmed (1955). Of his contribution to the script Algren commented later: 'I went out there for a thousand a week, and I worked Monday, and I got fired Wednesday. The guy that hired me was out of town Tuesday.' After the poor reception for *A Walk on the Wild Side* (1956), a reworking of aspects of his first novel, he gave up fiction. See Bettina Drew, *Nelson Algren: a Life on the Wild Side*, new edn 1991.

ALLEN, ROLAND see AYCKBOURN.

ALLENDE, ISABEL (*b.* 1942) Chilean novelist, was born 'by chance' in Lima, Peru. Her father 'disappeared without leaving any traces behind', and her mother subsequently married a diplomat; 'so we were always going round the world and that gave me a permanent horror of travelling . . .'. She has worked since she was 17, usually as a journalist. With her husband and two children, she left Chile for Venezuela 18 months after the military coup which toppled the government and was responsible for the death of her uncle, Salvador Allende (1908–73), the country's President. After receiving a death-threat she went to California. Her first novel, *La Casa de los Espíritus* (1982; tr. Magda Bogin as *The House of the Spirits*, 1985), parts of which are autobiographical, covers four generations against a background of national events in Chile leading up to the political persecution of the 1970s; she treats the same theme with even more brutal realism in *De Amor y de Sombra* (1984; tr. Margaret Sayers Peden as *Of Love and Shadows*, 1987). In *Eva Luna* (1987; tr. Peden, 1988) and *The Stories of Eva Luna* (1989; tr. Peden, 1991) romantic love and love play act as a counterpoise to pain, hardship, and images of terror. She and her second husband now live in California, the setting of the intertwined stories of the present generation over the past thirty years in *El Plan Infinito* (1991; tr. Peden as *The Infinite Plan*, 1993). She still writes in Spanish: 'Fiction is something in my belly: it's organic. In order to write in English, I would have to process it in my mind, and that would be a barrier for me.' And she begins a book always on the same date, 8 January. *Paula* (1994; tr. Peden, 1995) is a confessional autobiography which began as a series of letters to her

daughter, who died in 1992 after months in a coma.

ALLINGHAM, WILLIAM (1824–89) Irish poet, was born in Ballyshannon, Donegal, and educated at a local school where only Latin was taught, and at a boarding school in Co. Cavan, which he left at 14 to work initially in the Ballyshannon branch of the Provincial Bank, of which his father was then manager. After seven boring years of banking, he became a customs officer (the job was offered first to his brother, who was too young to accept it), in Ireland, then in London, and finally in Lymington, Hampshire. In London in 1849 he met HUNT, to whom he dedicated his first book, *Poems* (1850), and PATMORE, who introduced him to TENNYSON, for whom Allingham retained a lifelong admiration, for all Tennyson's occasional brusqueness to him. Other London friends were the BROWNINGS, CARLYLE, CLOUGH, and the ROSSETTIS. *Day and Night Songs* (1854) was followed by *Laurence Bloomfield in Ireland: a Modern Poem* (1864), a long work (2300 heroic couplets) in the vein of CRABBE in that it paints a realistic picture of country life and the wretched conditions of tenants under an absentee landlord. Allingham gave up the customs in 1870 to be a sub-editor and then (1874–9) Editor of *Fraser's Magazine*. In 1874 he married Helen Patterson (1848–1926), the water-colourist and illustrator. The illness which caused his death was brought on by a fall from a horse. The frequency with which 'The Fairies' ('Up the airy mountain / Down the rushy glen . . .') has been reprinted belies his considerable ability as a composer of short poems deftly expressing atmosphere or an emotional moment. See *Songs, Ballads, and Stories*, new edn 1977; *A Diary*, ed. Helen Allingham and D. Radford, new edn 1985; Alan Warner, *William Allingham: an Introduction*, 1971.

AMADO, JORGE (*b.* 1912) Brazilian novelist, was born in Ilheus, Bahia, and studied at the Federal University, Rio de Janeiro. A social and political critic whose literary territory is usually the northeastern part of the country where he was born, he was imprisoned and also temporarily exiled for the socialist principles he expressed in his early novels, the first of which was *O País do Carnaval* (1932). The first to be published in English was *Terras do Sem Fim* (1942; tr. Samuel Putnam as *The Violent Land*, 1945), about the effect of the cacao phenomenon on the exploited populace. *Gabriela, Cravo e Canela* (1958; tr. James L. Taylor and William L. Grossman as *Gabriela, Clove and Cinnamon*, 1962) is less polemical and more subtle in its amusing exploration of conflicts between traditional values and social change. More satirical still is *Os Velhos Marinheiros* (1961; tr. Harriet de Onis as *Home is the Sailor*, 1964).

AMICHAI, YEHUDA (*b.* 1924) Israeli poet and novelist, was born in Germany in Wurzburg, and in 1936 emigrated with his parents to Palestine, where they settled in Jerusalem and he subsequently went to the Hebrew University. He served with the Jewish Brigade during World War II and in the infantry during the War of Independence (1948–49). With his first volume of verse (1955) he introduced into Hebrew poetry modern terms from technology, law, and war, as well as English forms and manners of expression such as irony and understatement—['My father . . .'] is the opening poem of a sonnet sequence. He was thus in the forefront of those who have created a new idiom reflecting the radical changes which have occurred in the Hebrew language. [*Not of This Time, Not of This Place*] (1963; tr. Schlomo Katz, 1973) is a novel in which the Israeli protagonist seeks to exact retribution from the Germans who have destroyed his native town—see also *The World is a Room and Other Stories*, preface by Elinor Grumet (1984). See *Yehuda Amichai: a Life of Poetry 1948–1994*, ed. and tr. Barbara and Benjamin Harshav, new edn 1995 (substantial collection); *The Selected Poetry of Yehuda Amichai*, rev. edn with 40 new poems, tr. Chana Bloch and Stephen Mitchell, 1996.

AMIS, (Sir) **KINGSLEY** (1922–95) novelist, critic, and poet, was born in London and educated at City of London School and St John's College, Oxford. He was a lecturer in English at University College, Swansea 1949–61, and a Fellow of Peterhouse, Cambridge 1961–63, from which he resigned largely because of the backbiting he found there. Two volumes of poetry—see *Collected Poems* (1979)—were followed by his novel *Lucky Jim* (1954, dated 1953), which describes the tribulations of Jim Dixon, lecturer in history at a new university. Though not the first of the wave of novels which gave their authors (and the dramatist OSBORNE) the sobriquet 'Angry Young Men', it was the one which did most to suggest the existence of such a movement. Amis's fiction is comic in that, especially in the early novels, heroes tend to be accident-prone and set pieces are farcical. In the later, more socially aware novels—notably *The Anti-Death League* (1966), *Ending Up* (1974), *Jake's Thing* (1978), and *The Old Devils* (1986), which won the Booker prize for fiction—comedy gives way to satire of a fiercer kind, which in *The Folks that Live on the Hill* (1990) and *The Russian Girl* (1992) is tempered by sporadic injections of sympathy. He used, however, a variety of forms to express what he wanted to say: *The Green Man* (1969) is a ghost story based on local folklore; *The Riverside Villas Murder* (1973) is in the form of a detective mystery. He was a writer essentially of comedies of morals rather than of manners, whose penultimate novel, *You Can't Do*

Both (1994), set in the 1930s to 1950s, has autobiographical parallels. *Collected Short Stories* (1980) was followed by *Mr Barrett's Secret and Other Stories* (1993), six pieces which are mainly variations on literary or historical themes.

What Became of Jane Austen (1970) contains a revealing and readable selection of personal and critical essays on literary and other topics—see also *The Amis Collection: Selected Nonfiction 1954–1990* (1990). *Memoirs* (1991) is not so much an autobiography as an acerbic, often amusing, sometimes bawdy collection of character sketches and anecdotes. After a divorce in 1965 he married the novelist Elizabeth Jane Howard (*b.* 1923). They divorced in 1983, after which until his death he lived in Hampstead, London, with his first wife and her third husband. He was knighted in 1990. His eldest son, Martin (*b.* 1949), was Literary Editor of the *New Statesman* 1977–79, and has written several powerful and often satirical novels including *Dead Babies* (1975), *London Fields* (1989), and *The Information* (1995) for which he is regarded as one of the leading novelists of his particular generation—see James Diedrick, *Understanding Martin Amis* (1995). See Eric Jacobs, *Kingsley Amis: a Biography*, new edn 1996; John MacDermott, *Kingsley Amis: an English Novelist*, 1988 (critical study); Paul Fussell, *The Anti-Egotist: Kingsley Amis, Man of Letters*, 1996 (biographical/critical study).

AMIS, MARTIN see AMIS.

ANACREON (560–476 BC) classical Greek lyric poet, was born in Teos, Ionia, from which he emigrated to Thrace when the Persians invaded the territory. He lived in Samos at the court of Polycrates until the latter's assassination and subsequent crucifixion in 522 at the hands of the Persians. He then accepted an invitation from Hipparchus, younger brother of the tyrant of Athens, to join his literary coterie. Hipparchus was murdered in 514 by a homosexual couple, the sister of one of whom he had insulted after the youth had rejected his advances. Anacreon is said to have ended his days in Thessaly, and to have choked to death on a grape pip. Only a few fragments of his verse survive, graceful evocations of wine and love in metrical forms largely of his own invention, but the publication in Paris in 1554 of a spurious collection of sixty later imitations began a vogue for the composition of 'anacreontics'. The tradition spread to England, where it influenced DRAYTON, JONSON, HERRICK, and COWLEY, and caused Alexander Brome (1620–66) to be dubbed the 'English Anacreon'. LANDOR's *Imaginary Conversations* . . . contains a dialogue between Anacreon and Polycrates. See in *Seven Greeks*, tr. Guy Davenport, 1995.

ANAND, MULK RAJ (*b.* 1905) Indian novelist and critic, was born in Peshawar, the son of an army subadar, and was educated at Khalsa College, Amritsar, and at Punjab University, after which he went to London to continue his studies, keeping himself by working in Indian restaurants. He was in England for 21 years, becoming PhD at London University, spending a year at Cambridge, and interesting himself in Marxism. He also wrote several of the books for which he is regarded as a founder of the Indian novel in English, notably *Untouchable* (1935), *The Coolie* (1936; rev. edn 1972), and the trilogy, *The Village* (1939), *Across the Black Waters* (1940), and *The Sword and the Sickle* (1942), in all of which his chief characters are victims of the system, and *The Big Heart* (1945; rev. edn, ed. Saros Cowerjee, 1980), in which the traditional coppersmiths demonstrate their response to industrialization. In 1946 he became Editor of the quarterly arts journal *Marg*, in Bombay. He was Tagore Professor of Fine Art, Punjab University 1963–66, and Fine Art Chairman, National Academy of Art 1965–70. *Seven Summers: the Story of an Indian Childhood* (1951) became in due course the first of an autobiographical novel sequence, continued with *Confession of a Lover* (1976) and *The Bubble* (1984). *Selected Short Stories*, ed. M. K. Naik (1977) is a distillation of forty years of publishing volumes in this medium. His numerous non-fiction works include studies of literature, art, humanism, and curry. See *Pilpali Sahab: the Story of a Childhood under the Raj*, 1985; *Conversations in Bloomsbury*, new edn 1996 (reminiscences).

ANDERSEN, HANS CHRISTIAN (1805–75) Danish novelist, dramatist, and children's writer, was born in Odense, the son of a shoemaker and of an illiterate, alcoholic washerwoman, and at 14 set out for Copenhagen to be an actor. He became associated with the Royal Theatre, and came to the notice of Frederick VI, at whose instigation he was put through grammar school, where he remained until he was 22. His earliest writings were verse, travelogues, and plays (including an adaptation of WALTER SCOTT's *The Bride of Lammermoor*). Travel grants out of the royal purse enabled him to broaden his experience, and to write his first novel, *Improvisatoren* (1833); in a translation by Mary Howitt (1799–1888) as *The Improvisatore: or, Life in Italy* (1845), it was called by E. B. BROWNING, in a letter to her future husband, 'a book full of beauty [which] had a great charm to me'. In 1835 he published, as a 64-page booklet containing four stories, the first of his collections of *Eventyr* [Fairy Tales], of which only the initial six were advertised as 'Told for Children'. Unlike the GRIMMS, he was a creator rather than a collector of tales; even those for which he had a source, such as ['The Tinder Box'], are enriched from his

own experience and with his own personality. No less than four collections of his stories appeared in Britain in 1846, of which *Wonderful Stories for Children* was translated by Howitt, who changed the opening of 'Tommelise' (Thumbelina) to obscure the fact that the wife in the tale was seeking an aid to fertility. He published a further four volumes of [New Fairy Tales] (1843–47), and continued to write plays and novels, while remaining an inveterate traveller—see *The Diaries of Hans Christian Andersen*, ed. and tr. Patricia Conroy and Sven H. Rossel (1990)—if not always an entirely welcome guest. DICKENS, with whom he stayed at Gad's Hill in 1857, put up a card above a mirror: 'Hans Andersen slept in this room for five weeks, which seemed to the family AGES!' See Elias Bredsdorff, *Hans Christian Andersen: the Story of His Life and Work*, new edn 1994.

ANDERSON, SHERWOOD (1876–1941) American novelist and short-story writer, was born in Camden, Ohio, the third of seven children of a harness maker, as a result of whose search for work and general instability the boy had only a year of high school in Clyde (the setting of *Winesburg, Ohio*), to which the family moved in 1844. When his mother died in 1895, he went to Chicago. After serving briefly in the US Army (he enlisted to fight in the Spanish–American War of 1898 but arrived in Cuba after it was over), he completed his high school education in one year at Wittenberg Academy, Springfield, and then went into advertising. He married into a wealthy family in 1904, and in 1907 started his own business, selling building materials in Elyria, Ohio, where he was known as the 'Roof-Fix Man'. He was also, in his spare time, writing the two novels later published as *Windy MacPherson's Son* (1916) and *Marching Men* (1917), and two others. In 1912 he had a brainstorm, walked out of his office, and woke up several days later in a Cleveland hospital. He left his family and went to Chicago, where he associated with DREISER, MASTERS, and SANDBURG, and wrote the stories and character sketches which became *Winesburg, Ohio* (1919). He called his protagonists 'grotesques', but in depicting the natural frustrations and passions underlying the outward ordinariness of their lives, he was revealing an America in the grip of a social order which was inherently damaging. He wrote further novels of an even more experimental nature but less literary significance, and several volumes of short stories, including *Horses and Men* (1923), in which genre is the best of his later writing. In 1925 he purchased a farm near Marion, Virginia, and two years later bought the two politically-opposed weekly newspapers, to each of which he contributed regular columns. He married for the fourth time in 1933, and became a roving champion of the working man.

He died of peritonitis, from a broken tooth-pick, in Colon, Panama, en route to South America as a goodwill envoy for the State Department. *A Story Teller's Story* (1924), *Tar: a Midwest Childhood* (1926), and the unfinished *Sherwood Anderson's Memoirs* (1942) are fictionalized autobiography. See Kim Townsend, *Sherwood Anderson: a Biography*, 1987; Irving Howe, *Sherwood Anderson*, 1951 (critical study).

ANDREEV, LEONID NIKOLAE-VICH (1871–1919) Russian novelist, short-story writer, and dramatist, was born in Orel in central Russia, and after his father's early death studied law at St Petersburg University. Poverty and hopelessness led to a third attempt at suicide in 1894, after which, and a lapse into debauchery, he obtained a degree at Moscow University. He became a police court reporter, and in 1898 a story attracted the attention of GORKY, who became a friend, patron, and, briefly in 1905, fellow prisoner after a revolutionary exploit. Andreev's early stories and novels, such as [*The Seven Who Were Hanged*] (tr. Herman Bernstein, 1909), tended to be unashamedly sensational in theme but progressive in intent. Latterly he verged toward Symbolism, as in his best-known play, [*He Who Gets Slapped*] (tr. Gregory Zilboorg, 1921), in which a circus clown represents the oppressed intellectual. He did not support the Revolution in 1917, and retired to Finland, where he had built a house for himself and his family.

ANDREW OF WYNTOUN (c.1350–c.1422) Scottish poet and cleric, was a canon of St Andrews, being elected Prior of the monastery of St Serf's Inch, an island in Loch Leven. There he wrote in rugged couplets for his patron, Sir John of Wemyss, a verse history of Scotland from the Creation to 1408, shortly after the boy king JAMES I had been captured by the English. *The Orygynale Cronykil of Scotland* survived in manuscript form and was first published in 1795. It is significant in that it is written not in Latin, but in the dialect of northern English which became Scots. The chronicler is on safer ground when writing about events nearer his own time, but he recognized the value of a chronological account. In the seventh book is quoted the earliest example of Scottish verse, the lament for Alexander III, an eight-line stanza which begins 'Quhen Alexander our Kynge was dede / That Scotland lede in luve and le . . .', and was probably written shortly after the King's death in 1286.

ANDREWES, LANCELOT (1555–1626) English cleric, was born in Barking, Essex, the son of a well-to-do merchant, and was educated at Merchant Taylors' School and Pembroke Hall, Cambridge, of which he became a Fellow in 1567. He was ordained in 1580, and was Master of the college 1589–1605. He was also Dean of Westminster 1601–05. When in London he used to walk to Chiswick for recreation, always accompanied, according to a contemporary cleric, by two students, 'and in that wayfaring Leisure, had a singular dexterity to fill those narrow Vessels with a Funnel'. Under James I he received royal advancement, and became successively Bishop of Chichester (1605), Ely (1609), and Winchester (1618), besides being the leading light of the committee responsible for the portion of the Old Testament from Genesis to Kings, and for the Epistles in the New Testament, in the 'Authorized Version' of the Bible (1611). A pillar of the Anglican Church, and also (according to T. S. ELIOT) its 'first great preacher', his *XCVI Sermons* (1629) was edited by two bishops and published by command of the King. A more personal book in every sense is *Preces Privatae* [Private Devotions], originally written in Latin, Greek, and Hebrew, part of which was first published in 1647. See *Selected Writings*, ed. P. E. Hewison, 1995; 'Lancelot Andrewes' in *Selected Prose of T. S. Eliot*, ed. Frank Kermode, 1975.

ANDRÉZEL, PIERRE see BLIXEN.

ANGELOU, MAYA (b. 1928) American poet and dramatist, was born in St Louis, Missouri, and was brought up by her grandmother in Stamps, Arkansas. She went to public schools in Arkansas and California, and studied music, dance, and drama, beginning her stage career in 1954–55 on an international tour of *Porgy and Bess*, the opera by George Gershwin (1898–1937). She performed off-Broadway in several shows, including the revue, *Cabaret for Freedom* (1960), of which she was co-author. At the request of Martin Luther King (1929–68), she served as Northern Coordinator of the Southern Christian Leadership Conference in 1958–59. She spent the years 1963–66 in Ghana, where she was an adminstrator of the School of Music and Drama, University of Ghana Institute of African Affairs, and also wrote for the *Ghanaian Times* and for radio. She has said: 'The only two things I've ever loved in my life are dancing and writing . . . but by twenty-two my knees were gone so there was no chance of achieving the best I had to give in [dancing]. . . . I started to write when I was mute. I always thought I could write because I loved reading so much. I loved the melody of Poe and I loved Paul Laurence Dunbar.' The basis of her poetry, of which she has published several volumes since *Just Give Me a Cool Drink of Water 'fore I Diiie* (1971), is rhythm, with its changes and breaks reflecting her manifold moods.

As national laureate in 1993, Angelou became the first poet since FROST to be invited to participate in the inauguration of the President of the USA. In 1996 she made a literary pilgrimage to Scotland, recorded in a television documentary directed by herself, to celebrate the bicentenary of the death of BURNS: he 'wrote about my people without ever having left Scotland'. Her dramatic writings include *Ajax* (produced 1974), from SOPHOCLES, *And Still I Rise* (1976, published 1978), a musical, and *All Day Long* (1974), a film which she also directed. She was a visiting lecturer at several universities before taking up an appointment as Reynolds Professor of American Studies at Wake Forest University, North Carolina. In five volumes of autobiography from *I Know Why the Caged Bird Sings* (1969) to *All God's Children Need Traveling Shoes* (1987), she covers her life as both black activist and feminist, from her traumatic childhood and adolescence to her time in Ghana, where she hoped, but failed, to find a rooted existence. *Wouldn't Take Nothing for My Journey Now* (1994) is a slim volume of essays reflecting on social essays.

ANGUS, MARION (1866–1946) Scottish poet, was born in Aberdeen and spent her childhood and youth in Arbroath, where her father was a minister. She did not begin to write seriously until after World War I; her first book of verse, *The Lilt and Other Poems* (1922), was followed by five others. She spent most of her adult years in Aberdeen, returning to Arbroath the year before she died, and her ashes were at her own request scattered in the sea at Elliot's Point. Much of her poetry was written in Scots, and she is the best of the poets of northeast Scotland who presaged the Scottish Renaissance which was spearheaded by MACDIARMID. She often took her inspiration from the ballads, within a few lines developing a romantic situation with depth and insight, as in 'Mary's Song', 'Think Lang', and 'The Lilt'. In 'Alas! Poor Queen', written in English in irregular rhyming stanzas, she applies the same technique to the predicament of Mary, Queen of Scots. See *Selected Poems*, ed. Maurice Lindsay, 1950.

ANOUILH, JEAN (1910–87) French dramatist, was born in Cérisole, Bordeaux, of French Basque parents, his father being a craftsman tailor's cutter and his mother a violinist. He was educated at the École Colbert, Bordeaux, and Collège Chaptal, Paris, after which he studied law for two years at the Sorbonne. He spent two years as an advertising copywriter for products ranging 'from noodles to automobiles', and when he was 19 wrote in collaboration a one-act farce. *L'Hermine* (produced 1932; tr. Miriam John as *The Ermine*, 1955) and *Le Voyageur Sans Bagage* (1937; tr. John Whiting as *Traveller Without Luggage*, 1959) are naturalistic dramas of a kind he later called 'pièces noires'. By contrast, *Le Bal des Voleurs* (published 1938; tr. Lucienne Hill as *Thieves' Carnival*, 1952) is a 'pièce

rose'. *Antigone* (1946; tr. Lewis Galantière, 1946), from SOPHOCLES, was first staged in 1944 in a Paris still under German occupation, which gave an additional dimension to a dramatic confrontation between idealism (resistance) and realism (collaboration). *L'Invitation au Château* (1948) is a light fantasy which was adapted for the British stage by FRY as *Ring Round the Moon* (1950). His 'pièces costumées' include *L'Alouette* (1953; tr. Christopher Fry as *The Lark*, 1955), a study of the mythology of Joan of Arc (c.1412–1431), and *Becket: ou, L'Honneur de Dieu* (1959; tr. Hill as *Becket: or, The Honor of God*, 1960). His craftsmanship extended to his work for the cinema as director and scriptwriter—he wrote *Monsieur Vincent* (1947), *Anna Karenina* (1948), and *La Ronde* (1964). See *Five Plays*, 1987; *Plays*, 1992, *Plays: Two*, 1993.

APOLLINAIRE, GUILLAUME (1880–1918) French poet, dramatist, novelist, and critic, was born in Rome, where he was baptized Guillelmus Apollinaris Albertus de Kostrowitsky. He was the son of Angelica (de) Kostrowitsky (1858–1919) and probably of her Italian lover, Francesco Flugi d'Aspermont. A few months later his mother made a formal act of recognition of him as her natural son, with the name of Guillaume Albert Wladimir Alexandre Apollinaire. He was educated at Collège Saint-Charles, Monaco, Collège Stanislas, Cannes, and for two terms at the lycée in Nice, which he left in 1897 either having failed or without taking his baccalaureate. In 1901, having had some political and financial articles and two poems published, and having resorted to writing pornographic novels to earn some money, he went as tutor to the daughter of a German–French family in Honnef, in the Rhineland. He fell for the English governess, Annie Playden, whom he pursued to London. For consolation after her and her family's final repudiation of him in 1904, he pieced together the narrative poem, 'Le Roman du Mal-Aimé', in which the essence of modernism finds expression. In 1911, now also an art critic and a leader of the artistic avant-garde (he is credited with coining the term 'surrealism'), he was arrested on a charge of receiving two stolen statues and of colluding in the theft of the 'Mona Lisa', but was provisionally freed after spending a fortnight in jail. The experience was traumatic, but during the following year he managed to write some of his most lasting poems, including 'Le Pont Mirabeau' and 'Zone' (English translation by BECKETT, 1972).

His collection of critical articles, [*The Cubist Painters*] (1913), led people to expect something rather more futuristic than was the case with the only collection of verse published in his lifetime, *Alcools* (1913; tr. Anne Hyde Greet, 1965), which comprised largely older material from which at proof stage he had removed the punctuation. War service and two concurrent love affairs inspired some fine poems on both topics—see *Calligrammes: Poems of Peace and War (1913–1916)*, tr. Greet, ed. Greet and S. I. Lockerbie (bilingual edn 1980). In March 1916 he was posted to the front line, where, while relaxing in his trench after the main attack was over, he was hit in the head by a piece of shrapnel which pierced his helmet. He recovered sufficiently to deliver in 1917 his famous lecture defining 'l'esprit nouveau', the new spirit in art and life. He succumbed to the epidemic of Spanish flu in Paris, shortly after marrying Jacqueline Kolb. Fiction is in *The Wandering Jew and Other Stories*, tr. Rémy Inglis Hall (1967). See *Selected Poems*, ed. and tr. Oliver Bernard, 1986; Margaret Davies, *Apollinaire*, 1964 (critical biography).

APOLLONIUS OF RHODES (*fl. c.*250 BC)

Hellenistic narrative poet, was born in Alexandria, and while young wrote an epic poem, *Argonautica*, which was derided by the public and by other poets. He retired to Rhodes in pique, and either there, or later, when he was director of the royal library at Alexandria, he produced a revised version, which was such a success that he was granted the freedom of Rhodes. His rendering of the legend of Jason is the fullest that we have of his epic journey in search of the golden fleece, and includes the story of the love for Jason of the princess Medea, from which VIRGIL took elements for his account of Dido and Aeneas. See *The Voyage of the Argo*, tr. E. V. Rieu, 2nd edn 1971.

APULEIUS, LUCIUS (*fl. c.*160)

novelist, who wrote in Latin, was born in Madaura in the Roman province of Africa, the son of a wealthy provincial magistrate of ancient Greek stock. He was educated in Carthage, Athens, and Rome, where he studied oratory, at which he later made a living. He married a rich widow in Oea (now Tripoli), whose family took him to court for sorcery. He wittily conducted his own defence (it survives as 'Apologia'), and was acquitted. His novel, *Metamorphoses* (or *The Golden Ass*), the bare plot of which derives from a Greek story, is a rollicking tale of the supernatural, told in the first person, of how Lucius dabbles in magic, is given the wrong ointment by the serving maid who is his bed-mate, and is turned into an ass. Several good stories are spliced into the action, including an excellent version of the Cupid and Psyche legend. It is also a religious novel in that it surprisingly culminates in the conversion of Lucius to the cult of Osiris. Apuleius himself, as well as being a priest of Osiris and Isis, was a devotee of Asclepius, god of medicine, which he found compatible with organizing gladiatorial shows. See *The Golden Ass*, tr. Robert Graves, 1950; tr. P. G. Walsh, new edn 1995.

ARDEN, JOHN (*b.* 1930)

British dramatist and novelist, was born in Barnsley, Yorkshire, and educated at Sedbergh School and King's College, Cambridge, after which he studied architecture. A Victorian period comedy, *All Fall Down*, was staged by students in Edinburgh in 1955, but it was a radio play, *The Life of Man* (1953), which brought him to the notice of the English Stage Company. In contrast to the bleak realism of JOHN OSBORNE and WESKER, his earlier plays, *The Waters of Babylon*, which did not survive beyond a single experimental performance, *Live Like Pigs*, and *The Happy Haven*—see *Three Plays* (1964)—appeared to be amoral social fantasies. *Serjeant Musgrave's Dance: an Un-Historical Parable* (1960) introduced an effective theatrical technique, repeated in *Armstrong's Last Goodnight: an Exercise in Diplomacy* (1965), whereby contemporary issues are interpreted in terms of the past, and poetic prose is interspersed with snatches of verse which hark back to traditional ballad forms and themes. Subsequent plays, some in collaboration with his wife, the actress Margaretta D'Arcy, have met with less critical acclaim, though *The Island of the Mighty: a Play on a Traditional British Theme* (1974), a poetic amalgam of the mythical and the political King Arthur, which had been many years gestating, is memorable. *Silence Among the Weapons* (1982), is a rich, complex, adventure novel of the later Roman republic, with a theatrical background. The four stories in *Cogs Tyrannic* (1991) feature in historical terms aspects of communication by mechanical means. *Jack Juggler and the Emperor's Whore: Seven Tall Tales Linked together for an Indecorous Toy Theatre* (1995) is a multi-layered historical thriller with theatrical overtones. He has also published *To Present the Pretence: Essays on the Theatre and Its Public* (1977). See *Plays*, 2 vols, new edns 1994; Frances Gray, *John Arden*, 1982 (critical study).

ARIOSTO, LUDOVICO (1474–1533)

Italian poet and dramatist, was born in Reggio Emilia, the eldest of ten children of a minor nobleman in the service of the Estes of Ferrara, and studied law at Ferrara University, though his preference was for classical literature. Having to provide for the family after his father's death in 1500, he became an ambassador for Cardinal Hippolytus, but left him in 1517 to be court poet to the Cardinal's brother, now Duke d'Este. Ariosto had written two comedies and published the first edition of his narrative poem, *Orlando Furioso* (1515), when in 1522 the Duke sent him to be governor of the turbulent Este region of Garfagnana. After his return in 1525 he built himself a modest house in Ferrara and returned to his writing: two further comedies, including *Lena* (performed 1528; tr. Guy Williams in *Five Italian Renaissance Comedies*, 1978), a witty denunciation of ducal administration in Ferrara; seven satires (published 1534); and the third, definitive edition of *Orlando Furioso* (1532) in 46 cantos, each comprising a hundred or more stanzas in *ottava rima*. Towards the end of his life he secretly married Alessandra Benucci Strozzi, now a widow, who had been his mistress for over fifteen years. He had two children by other women.

Orlando Furioso (tr. Guido Waldman into prose, 1974; tr. Barbara Reynolds into verse as *The Frenzy of Orlando*, 2 vols 1975), was originally intended as simply a complete version of the unfinished verse romance of the French hero and Christian knight Roland (Orlando) by Matteo Maria Boiardo (*c*.1430–94), itself an elaboration of an earlier version by Luigi Pulci (1432–84). It became an epic poem of chivalry in its own right, which VOLTAIRE described as 'the *Iliad* and *Odyssey* and *Don Quixote* all rolled into one'. The first English translation, into 'heroical verse', was by Sir John Harington (1561–1612) in 1591. William Stewart Rose (1775–1843) produced a later version (8 vols 1823–31), of which, at one of ROGERS's celebrated breakfasts, the host, according to WALTER SCOTT (*Journal*, 19 October 1826), 'made us merry with an account of some part; proposed that the Italian should be printed on the other side for the sake of assisting the indolent reader to understand the English; and complained of his using more than once the phrase of a lady having "voided her saddle", which would certainly sound extraordinary at Apothecaries' Hall'! See also *Cinque Canti/Five Cantos*, tr. Alexander Sheers and David Quint, (bilingual edn 1966).

ARISTOPHANES (*c*.450–*c*.385 BC) classical Greek comic dramatist, was probably born in Athens, but was taken as a boy to his father's estate in the island of Aegina, thus later laying himself open to a charge of not being a genuine Athenian. He won a second prize in 427 with a lost satirical play. *The Acharnians* (425), a plea for the cessation of the Peloponnesian War, won first prize at the Lenaea, under a pseudonym. So, under his own name, did *The Knights* (424), a satire on the defects and misuses of democracy and in particular on the ruthlessness of the demagogue, Cleon (*d*. 422). As the war continued, his fantasies grew wilder and his targets broader—the new learning in *The Clouds* (423), and the legal system in *The Wasps* (422). *Peace* (421) and *The Birds* (414) are more directly in his anti-war vein, while in *Lysistrata* (411) he plays his ultimate card, that the women of Athens should deny their husbands their conjugal rights and stage a sit-in at the seat of government. By contrast, in 405, the disastrous year of the final defeat of Athens by the Spartans, he produced *The Frogs*, an extended joke involving a contest in Hades for supremacy between AESCHYLUS

and EURIPIDES which incorporates a good deal of social and political, as well as literary, criticism. See *Plays*, tr. Kenneth McLeish, 2 vols 1993.

ARISTOTLE (384–322 BC) Greek philosopher, was born in Stagira, the son of the physician to the King of Macedonia. He went to Athens in 367 and was a pupil of PLATO, after whose death in 347 he went to Asia Minor. He was tutor to Alexander (the Great) until the latter's accession to the throne of Macedonia in 335, when he returned to Athens. Here he established in the gymnasium in the Lyceum his own school of philosophy, known as Peripatetic, from his habit of teaching while walking round the shady paths of the sacred grove. In the anti-Macedonian backlash after Alexander's death in 323, he left Athens for Chalcis in Euboea, where he died. He wrote particularly formative works in ethics, natural philosophy (in his classification of which he was followed by BACON)—see *Physics*, tr. Robin Waterfield, introduction by David Bostock (1996)—, and politics—see *The Politics*, tr. Ernest Barker, rev. and ed. R. F. Stalley (1995). His treatise on poetics (in which he includes drama)—see in *Classical Literary Criticism*, tr. T. S. Dorsch (1965)—is cited frequently by writers from the Elizabethan era onwards, and was the authority on which 17th-century French classical drama was based, even if he did not specifically postulate all the dramatic unities of action, time, and space which are attributed to him.

ARMAH, AYI KWEI (*b*. 1939) Ghanaian novelist, was born of a Fante-speaking family in Sekondi Takoradi, and was educated at Achimota School, Groton School (Massachusetts), Harvard (where he read sociology), and the Graduate School of Fine Arts, Columbia University. He worked as a French translator in Algiers, a television scriptwriter and an English teacher in Ghana, and for the Parisian news journal *Jeune Afrique*. An inscription on a bus seen by the anonymous protagonist is the title of his first novel, *The Beautyful Ones Are Not Yet Born* (1968), a metaphysical study of corruption in Ghana. *Fragments* (1970) continues the theme. In 1970 he settled in East Africa, learned Kiswahili, and wrote. He travelled south to teach African literature and creative writing at the National University of Lesotho, and back again to the College of National Education of Chang'ombe, Tanzania. During this period he wrote *Why Are We So Blest?* (1972), a surrealist account of three lost souls in a North African capital; *Two Thousand Seasons* (1973), an excursion into a thousand years of history and folk myth; and *The Healers* (1978), a plea for unity through the creative force of inspiration, set in the 19th century during the second Ashanti war. After teaching at the University of Wisconsin, Armah returned to

West Africa to live in Dakar, Senegal. Unlike most authors, he consistently declines to be interviewed about, or to discuss, his work. See Robert Fraser, *The Novels of Ayi Kwei Armah: a Study in Polemical Fiction*, 1980.

ARNOLD, MATTHEW (1822–88) British poet and critic, was born in Laleham, Middlesex, and educated at Rugby School, where his father, Dr Thomas Arnold (1795–1842), the celebrated educational reformer and religious leader, was Headmaster, and Balliol College, Oxford, where he won the Newdigate Prize for poetry with a poem about Cromwell (1843). Otherwise his academic studies took second place to his social life; a disastrous final result was partly compensated for by an appointment as a Fellow of Oriel College. Here he joined his close friend and literary 'mate', CLOUGH, in commemoration of whose death he later wrote 'Thyrsis' (1866), one of the best of his shorter poems and a neat blend of the classical and the colloquial. In 1847 he became secretary to the Marquis of Lansdowne (1780–1863), Lord President of the Council, and in 1851, the year of his marriage, he was appointed an inspector of schools, in which capacity he trailed round elementary schools, conscientiously upholding his faith in the need for a humane and efficient system of state education. He retired in 1883 on a Civil List pension, and immediately undertook an arduous American lecture tour to repay money he had borrowed to settle his son's gambling debts at Oxford. He was Professor of Poetry at Oxford 1857–67.

Most of his poetry was written in the 1850s. *The Strayed Reveller and Other Poems* (1849) and *Empedocles on Etna and Other Poems* (1852) were published as by 'A'. *Poems* (1853) included the famous 'The Scholar Gipsy', which reflects his unease with contemporary society, and the narrative poem 'Sohrab and Rustum', whose lush style and sometimes jerky rhythm are redeemed by splendid touches of detail and an ending whose image of still night and a gently flowing stream recurs often in Arnold's verse. *Poems, Second Series* (1855) contained 'Balder Dead', based on Norse mythology. The meditative 'Dover Beach', though first published in *New Poems* (1867), was written much earlier, along with other poems expressing despair, and it was the feeling that poetry can only record experiences, not effect reforms, that led him to concentrate on prose.

Arnold's literary criticism influenced his attitude to the state of society, for which he saw a remedy in culture (including religion), with literature as the key. This and his natural bent towards the classics led him to favour works which had 'high seriousness', a quality which he found lacking in CHAUCER; for all that he was a sound, innovative, and eloquent critic. In *Essays in Criticism, First Series*

(1865) and *Second Series* (1888) he drew together recently published studies on the nature of criticism and religion, and on MILTON and the Romantic poets. *Culture and Anarchy* (1869) is his central statement on bringing the forces of culture in its widest sense to bear on the ills of society, represented by Barbarians (the aristocracy), Philistines (the middle classes), and Populace (the working classes). See *Poems*, ed. Kenneth Allott, new edn 1985; *Selected Poems and Prose*, ed. Miriam Allott, new edn 1995; Park Honan, *Matthew Arnold: a Life*, new edn 1983; Nicholas Murray, *A Life of Matthew Arnold*, 1996; Lionel Trilling, *Matthew Arnold*, new rev. edn 1979 (critical biography); Stefan Collini, *Matthew Arnold: a Critical Portrait*, new edn 1994.

ASCHAM, ROGER (1515–68) English prose writer and teacher, was born at Kirby Wiske, near Northallerton, Yorkshire, and educated at St John's College, Cambridge, where in about 1538 he became Reader in Greek. Hoping for royal patronage, he dedicated to Henry VIII a part-philosophical, part-instructional handbook on archery, *Toxophilus* (1545), cast in the form of a dialogue between archer and sage, for which he was rewarded with a pension of £10 a year. A recurrence of a serious illness moved him to petition the Archbishop of Canterbury for permission to eat meat instead of fish on fast days: by whatever cure, he was fit enough in 1546 to become Public Orator of the university. When in 1548 the private tutor of Princess Elizabeth (later Queen Elizabeth I) died of the plague, he got himself appointed to the post, from which he resigned the following year after a tiff with her steward. On the accession of Mary Tudor, he became her Latin secretary, in spite of his Protestant leanings, and throughout her bloody reign remained on friendly terms with Elizabeth. In *The Scholemaster*, published posthumously in 1570, he outlines his theory and practice of teaching. Ascham was a most unusual man, who combined great learning with a passion for sport, and whose masterly English style is a model of both simplicity and balance. He died of a chill caught while sitting up too late writing a poem to Queen Elizabeth. See Lawrence V. Ryan, *Roger Ascham*, 1963.

ASHBERY, JOHN (b. 1927) American poet, was born in Rochester, New York, and educated at Deerfield Academy, Massachusetts, and Harvard, and then took a further degree at New York University. In 1955, after four years in publishing, he went to France as a Fulbright scholar; he returned there in 1958 and spent seven years as an art critic, foreign correspondent, and arts magazine editor. He was then Executive Editor of *Art News*, New York, and became a professor of English in the creative writing course at Brooklyn College in 1974. A writer whose interest in art has influenced his work and who has suggested that 'any one of my poems might be considered to be a snapshot of whatever is going on in my mind at the time', he published his first book of verse in 1953. *Some Trees* (1956) was chosen by AUDEN for the Yale series of books by younger poets. *The Tennis Court Oath* (1962) largely concludes his period of experimenting with the collage medium of verse. The starting point of the title poem of *Self-Portrait in a Convex Mirror* (1975), which won both the National Book Award and the Pulitzer Prize, is the painting of that title by the Italian Mannerist, Parmigianino (1503–40). A long poem in loose iambic pentameters, it explores the feelings of and relationship between artist and poet, within a complex web of sensibilities. He has continued to publish collections of a kind of which David Shapiro in *John Ashbery: an Introduction to the Poetry* (1979) argues that 'the "difficulty" is more imaginary than real. . . . Like Gertrude Stein, James Joyce, and others who have attempted to ensnare the psychic processes we so carefully suppress, Ashbery focuses hard on the way the mind deals with the random stuff that drifts into it.' *Flow Chart* (1991) is a long poem about making poetry among the distractions of modern life. See *Selected Poems*, ed. Donald Allen, 1994; John Shoptaw, *On the Outside Looking Out: John Ashbery's Poetry*, 1995.

ASHFORD, 'DAISY' [MARGARET MARY JULIA] (1881–1972) British story writer, was born in Petersham, Surrey, and educated at home until she was 17, and then for a year at the Priory, Hayward's Heath. In 1889 the family moved to Lewes, where she dictated two stories and then wrote in her own hand *The Young Visiters, or Mr Salteena's Plan* and other stories, including 'The Hangman's Daughter', all before she went to school. After her mother's death the manuscripts resurfaced and *The Young Visiters*, as the most hilarious, was offered to Chatto & Windus and published in 1919 with a foreword by BARRIE. Its rapturous reception was due not just to the child's view of high society and romantic love, the unintentional humour, and the erratic spelling, but also to the magic of the story line, which accounts for its continued success—there was a play (1920), a musical (1968), a film (1984), and a second illustrated version (1984). Ashford married in 1920, had four children, and with her husband ran a farm, and for a year a hotel, in Norfolk. Though all her surviving childhood stories have been published, it was as though, when she put away childish things, she abandoned her literary ambitions, for she wrote nothing more. See R. M. Malcolmson, *Daisy Ashford: Her Life*, 1984.

ASHTON-WARNER, SYLVIA (1908–84) New Zealand novelist, was born in Tara-

naki, one of nine children of an invalid father and a working primary school teacher, and was educated at Wairarapa High School and Auckland Teachers' Training College. In 1932 she married Keith D. Henderson, a fellow teacher, and went with him to a remote sole-charge school. After the birth of their second child she returned to teaching, and for twenty years took the infant class in the predominantly Maori schools of which her husband was head. She developed her revolutionary 'key vocabulary' reading scheme, which the New Zealand Department of Education consistently declined to recognize. *Teacher*, her account of her methods, to which was appended a diary, 'Life in a Maori School', was completed in 1953 but failed to find a publisher. She rewrote the classroom experiences into a novel, *Spinster* (1958), whose plot and construction are linked by references to sonnets and other poems by HOPKINS. Her indelicate wit and the lifestyle of her flamboyant French heroine in *Incense to Idols* (1960) 'weeded out my fans overnight', she observed. *Teacher* was finally published in 1963. In *Myself* (1968), her fifth novel, based on her own diaries, she re-creates aspects of her marriage and her struggles to find effective conditions under which to write. After her husband's death in 1969 she satisfied her ambition to escape abroad; she taught at Aspen (Colorado) Community School from 1970 to 1971, and then lectured in education at Simon Fraser University, Vancouver, until 1973. *Three* (1971), set in London, is a further excursion into fictional autobiography. Her actual autobiography, *I Passed This Way* (1980), won the New Zealand Book Award for non-fiction. In retirement she lived in New Zealand, still largely unappreciated, and devoted herself to painting and music. See Lynley Wood, *Sylvia!: the Biography of Sylvia Ashton-Warner*, 1988.

ASIMOV, ISAAC (1920–92) American novelist, prose writer, and editor, was born in Petrovichi, Russia, the son of a rabbi, and in 1923 emigrated with his parents to the USA, of which he became a citizen in 1928. He went to Columbia University, New York, becoming PhD in chemistry in 1948. He taught biochemistry at Boston University School of Medicine from 1949, becoming Professor in 1979. He taught himself to read English at five, and pored over the science-fiction magazines in his family's candy store. His first short story, 'Marooned off Vesta', was published when he was 18. In his first book of stories, *I, Robot* (1950), he promulgated his three 'laws of robotics'. As well as publishing 467 books, he claimed to have contributed to 'about three thousand publications'. His fiction includes a number of science-fiction novels, of which the trilogy, *Foundation* (1951), *Foundation and Empire* (1952), and *Second Foundation* (1953), has lasted best; he published a second group of 'Foundation' novels in the 1980s, and rounded off the whole with a seventh, more personal, volume, *Forward the Foundation* (1993). *The Complete Stories: Volume 1* (1993) contains 48 of his earlier pieces, many of them prophetic; *Volume 2* was published in 1994. His non-fiction embraces a host of titles ranging from the academic to the popular: *Asimov's Guide to Shakespeare* (2 vols 1970) and *Asimov's Guide to the Bible* (2 vols 1968–69), as well as *Asimov's New Guide to Science* (1984), *Exploring the Earth and the Cosmos* (1982), and *Asimov's Biographical Encyclopaedia of Science and Technology* (rev. edn 1982). He also published rude verses, such as *Lecherous Limericks* (1975). The unenviable, or enviable, distinction of being the most prolific author of modern times is a justification of his skill as a communicator (to which children as well as adults can testify), and of his sympathy with the aspirations of his readers. After recovering from a heart attack in 1977, and a triple bypass operation two years later, he ceased to be gloomily pessimistic about the future of the world: 'If I can pull myself up by my own bootstraps, then so can the human race.' See *In Memory Yet Green: the Autobiography of Isaac Asimov 1920–1954*, 1979, and *In Joy Still Felt: the Autobiography of Isaac Asimov 1954–1978*, 1980; Michael White, *Asimov: the Unauthorized Life*, new edn 1995; James Gunn, *Isaac Asimov: the Foundations of Science Fiction*, rev. edn, 1996 (critical study).

ASTLEY, THEA (*b.* 1925) Australian novelist, was born in Brisbane and educated at All Hallows Convent and Queensland University. After her marriage to E. J. Gregson in 1948, she taught in schools in New South Wales. She was appointed Senior Tutor in English, Macquarie University, Sydney, in 1968, subsequently being a Fellow until her retirement in 1980. Her first two novels, *Girl with a Monkey* (1958) and *Descant for Gossips* (1960), are studies of what she refers to as 'the misfit' in a small town society, a milieu to which she returns in *A Kindness Cup* (1974), based on a real incident of racist brutality, and *Reaching Tin River* (1990), whose protagonist, after an unsettled childhood and unhappy marriage, searches for a meaningful existence through an obsessive piece of local research. *It's Raining in Mango* (1988) takes in aspects of the history and social tragedies of Queensland over four generations of a family. In *An Item from the Late News* (1982), feelings are fomented by an anti-nuclear protest. A Pacific hurricane resolves the fates of a mixed set of characters in *A Boat Load of Home Folk* (1968), and an island revolution of those in *Beachmasters* (1985). *The Well Dressed Explorer* (1962) and *The Acolyte* (1972) are portraits of egotism. Astley is a witty, sometimes savage, but essentially compassionate writer, who delights in plunging the reader into the action, as she

does ingeniously in the title story of her collection, *Hunting the Wild Pineapple* (1979). She has won the MILES FRANKLIN Award three times. She was made AO in 1992.

ASTLEY, WILLIAM see WARUNG.

ATWOOD, MARGARET (*b.* 1939) Canadian novelist, short-story writer, poet, and critic, was born in Ottawa, the second child of an entomologist whose research into forest insects took him, and his family, on extended sojourns in the bush country of northern Ontario and Quebec. Her Canadian roots are deeper than most, going back, through American, Scottish, Irish, Welsh, and French ancestors, to the 17th and 18th centuries. She was educated at home by her mother, and at Leaside High School, Toronto, and Victoria College, Toronto University, graduating in 1961, when she published a book of verse, *Double Persephone*, which was awarded the E. J. PRATT Medal. Her first substantial collection, *The Circle Game* (1966), won the Governor General's Award. She did postgraduate study at Radcliffe College, Massachusetts, and Harvard; has taught English at several Canadian universities; and delivered the Clarendon Lectures at Oxford in 1991, on the theme of 'Strange Things'. Her marriage in 1967 ended in divorce in 1973, after which she went to live with the Canadian novelist Graeme Gibson (*b.* 1934).

Atwood's first two novels, *The Edible Woman* (1969) and *Surfacing* (1972), are basically studies of survival, a theme which runs through her fiction and informs her major critical work, *Survival: a Thematic Guide to Canadian Literature* (1972). Of her subsequent novels, *Bodily Harm* (1981) reflects her concern about modern political oppression and humanitarian issues; *The Handmaid's Tale* (1985), which won the Governor General's Award for fiction, imagines a future north America as a bleak, misogynist dystopia. On the blighted childhoods which underlie the sinister events of *The Robber Bride* (1993) she commented: 'The percentage of the total population of Canada that was sent to the war is pretty high. . . . A lot of people of my age were dislocated by it. And it's the central fact of our century. . . . Most Canadians are here because their ancestors got kicked out of somewhere else.' She picked up originally from MOODIE's *Life in the Clearing* an account of a sensational murder case in the 1840s, which in *Alias Grace* (1996) she reworks into a psychological study of Grace Marks, convicted at the age of 16.

In *Dancing Girls and Other Stories* (1977), the first of several collections, she uncovers some of the madnesses affecting modern society: the stories in *Wilderness Tips* (1991) are cautionary tales in which private lives are explored in Canadian contexts. *Murder in the*

Dark: Short Fictions and Prose Poems (1983) is a predominantly experimental work in which she investigates the craftiness as well as the craft of the writer. *Good Bones* (1992) is a pocket-size writer's sketchbook of images, ideas, and stories. Her poetry, sharp, often ironic, sometimes personal, has continued to reflect similar preoccupations to those in her fiction, notably the place of women in society—see *Poems 1965–1975* (new edn 1990 of *Selected Poems*, 1976), *Poems 1976–1986* (new edn 1991 of *Selected Poems 2*, 1986), and *Morning in the Burned House* (1995). She has also published *Second Words: Selected Critical Prose* (1982); *Conversations*, ed. Earl G. Ingersoll (1992), a series of dialogues on the Canadian literary tradition and other topics related to her own writing; and *Strange Things: the Malevolent North in Canadian Literature* (1995). She edited *The New Oxford Book of Canadian Verse in English* (1982). Canada's most distinguished contemporary literary figure, and one of the most versatile writers on the international scene, Atwood was made Companion, Order of Canada, in 1981. See Barbara Hill Rigney, *Margaret Atwood*, 1987 (critical study); Coral Ann Howells, *Margaret Atwood*, 1995 (critical study).

AUBREY, JOHN (1626–97) English folklorist and antiquary, was born at Easton Piers near Malmesbury, Wiltshire. His studies at Trinity College, Oxford, were interrupted first by the Civil War and then by smallpox. His father died in 1652, leaving Aubrey (by his own account) £2800 of debts. A series of lawsuits led to his bankruptcy in 1670, after which, largely to avoid his creditors, he did the rounds of his friends in London and in the country. In 1649 he had discovered the significant megalithic archaeological site at Avebury, and in 1663 his literary and scientific interests won him election to the Royal Society. His itinerant existence was good for research but bad for collating and writing up the results. The only work published in his lifetime was *Miscellanies* (1696), a compendium of superstitions and supernatural experiences. His literary fame, however, rests on the mass of notes which he offered to his cantankerous friend, Anthony Wood, otherwise à Wood (1632–95), for a dictionary of lives of Oxford writers and bishops, *Athenae Oxonienses* (1691–92), and which, having quarrelled with Wood, he deposited in the Ashmolean Museum in 1693. The edited versions of *Brief Lives* reveal an eye for descriptive detail, a nose for gossip, a lively wit, and an appreciation of the biographer's art—much of the information he assiduously collected was from first-hand accounts. See *Brief Lives*, ed. Richard W. Barber, new edn 1993; *Brief Lives*, ed. Oliver Lawson Dick, new edn 1996; Anthony Powell, *Aubrey and His Friends*, new rev. edn

1988; David Tylden-Wright, *John Aubrey: a Life*, 1991.

AUCHINCLOSS, LOUIS (*b*. 1917) American novelist and short-story writer, was born in Lawrence, Long Island, New York, the son of a Wall Street lawyer descended from a Scot who arrived in 1803 and founded a profitable textile business. He was educated at Groton School, Massachusetts, and Yale, from which, having had a novel rejected by a New York publisher, he dropped out after three years to study at the University of Virginia School of Law; he graduated in 1941 and was admitted to the New York Bar. He began work with a New York law firm before serving in World War II, in which he saw action in the Atlantic and Pacific as a naval lieutenant. He returned to the practice in 1946. *The Indifferent Children*, a novel with autobiographical elements, appeared in 1947, in deference to his mother's wishes under the name of Andrew Lee. The stories in *The Injustice Collectors* (1950) are thematically linked and had previously been published in magazines. After the publication of *Sybil* (1951), he resigned from the firm to be a full-time writer; only to look for a job again in 1954, having discovered that he did not write more, or better, without one. He was taken on by Hawkins, Delafield and Wood, of which he was a partner from 1958 until his retirement in 1986, and published a novel or a volume of short stories virtually every year from 1956 to 1990. As an author of the novel of manners to whom fiction is an exploration of character, and a conscious descendant of HENRY JAMES and WHARTON (of both of whom he has written literary studies), Auchincloss writes about the stratum of society in which he was brought up as an 'insider'. The most highly regarded novels among nearly forty volumes of fiction are *Portrait in Brownstone* (1962), a family saga, *The Rector of Justin* (1964), a study of a single-minded headmaster of a private preparatory school, and *The Embezzler* (1966), the basis of which is an actual financial scandal. The eponymous narrator of *The Education of Oscar Fairfax* (1995) suitably begins his account of his times in 1908, where HENRY ADAMS left off; each chronological episode of the novel centres on his involvement with a different character. *The Collected Stories* (1994) is Auchincloss's own selection of what he considers his best short fiction. *Reflections of a Jacobite* (1961), *Life, Law and Letters* (1979), and *Style's the Man: Reflections on Proust, Fitzgerald, Wharton, and Others* (1994) are collections of essays and reviews. *La Gloire: the Roman Empire of Corneille and Racine* (1997) is a critical study of the two French classical dramatists. *A Writer's Capital* (1974) is an autobiography of his literary development, concluding with his return to Wall Street. See David B. Parsell, *Louis Auchincloss*, 1988 (critical study); Vincent Piket, *Louis Auchincloss: the Growth of a Novelist*, 1991 (critical study).

AUDEN, W(YSTAN) H(UGH) (1907–73) poet, dramatist, and critic, was born in York, the son of a doctor, and was educated at Gresham's School, Holt, and Christ Church, Oxford, where he was unofficial leader of a number of young poets such as BETJEMAN, DAY LEWIS, MACNEICE, and SPENDER—see *Juvenilia: Poems 1922–1928*, ed. Katherine Bucknell (1994). He was a schoolmaster for several years, then travelled in Europe and China. In 1935, at the instigation of ISHERWOOD, he married Erika Mann (1905–69), the eldest child of MANN and herself a writer, whom he had never met, to enable her to have a British passport. With other like-minded intellectuals he served in the Spanish Civil War, as an ambulance driver on the Republican side. He emigrated to the USA in 1939 and became an American citizen in 1946. He was Professor of Poetry at Oxford 1956–61.

While Auden acknowledged the influence of such diverse poets as WYATT, HARDY, and ELIOT, and the inspiration of TOLKIEN's lectures on Anglo-Saxon and Middle English poetry, he says in 'Dichtung und Wahrheit' (1959), '. . . of any poem written by myself, my first demand is that it should be genuine, recognizable, like my handwriting, as having been written, for better or worse, by me'. The energy and objectivity of his verse, combined with a sharp sense of humour, a delight in pastiche, a penchant for popular speech and everyday images, and a sympathy with the feelings of ordinary people, distinguish his work throughout the two main phases of his life and poetic progress, variously called 'the English Auden' and 'the later Auden', or 'the Marxist Auden' and 'the Christian Auden'. His first book, *Poems* (1930; rev. edn 1933), displayed an extraordinary variety of moods and verse forms, and included 'On Sunday Walks' and 'This Lunar Beauty'. With other contemporaries, he was in the 1930s concerned with the need for social, political, and spiritual reform, which he expressed with growing bitterness and anger, though to this period also belong 'In This Island', 'Lullaby', 'Night Mail', and the tripartite 'In Memory of W. B. Yeats', as well as 'Spain 1937' and several sardonic cautionary-ballads, such as 'James Honeyman'. His re-conversion to Christianity in the 1940s introduced a religious tone and religious themes to his canon, notably with 'Horae Canonicae'—in the collection *The Shield of Achilles* (1955)—and the Christmas oratorio, *For the Time Being* (1945). His increasing fear of loneliness is reflected in *The Age of Anxiety: a Baroque Eclogue* (1947). *Homage to Clio* (1960) contains a greater proportion of lighter verse.

Auden was associated with many stage performances. As adapter or librettist he often collaborated with his homosexual partner, Chester Kallman (1921–75), whom he had first met in April 1939, when Kallman attended a poetry reading in Manhattan by Auden, ISHERWOOD, and MACNEICE—see also Thekla Clark, *Wystan and Chester: a Personal Memoir of W. H. Auden and Chester Kallman* (1995). He also wrote the verse play, *The Dance of Death* (1933), his most extreme statement of Marxism, and, with Isherwood, *The Ascent of F6* (1937) and two other plays. Some of his criticism is collected in *The Dyer's Hand, and Other Essays* (1962). See *Collected Poems*, ed. Edward Mendelson, new edn 1994 of rev. edn 1991; *Selected Poems*, ed. Edward Mendelson, 1979 (100 poems); *As I Walked Out One Evening: Songs, Ballads, Lullabies, Limericks and Other Light Verse*, ed. Edward Mendelson, 1995; *The English Auden: Poems, Essays, and Dramatic Writings 1927–1939*, ed. Edward Mendelson, new edn 1986 (includes all the poems he wrote in the 1930s); *Auden's Complete Prose 1926–1938*, ed. Edward Mendelson, 1996 (includes his two travel books); Humphrey Carpenter, *W. H. Auden*, new edn 1992 (biography); Charles Osborne, *W. H. Auden: the Life of a Poet*, new edn 1995; Richard Davenport-Hines, *Auden*, new edn 1996 (biography); Stan Smith, *W. H. Auden*, 1985 (critical study); Anthony Hecht, *The Hidden Law: the Poetry of W. H. Auden*, new edn 1994 (critical study).

AUGUSTINE, ST (354–430) was born in Thagaste, Numidia, the son of a local official and of a devout Christian, and was educated in Madaura and then in Carthage, where he had a son, Adeodatus (*d*. 389), by a mistress. After teaching oratory and literature in Carthage and Rome, he was in 384 appointed municipal professor in Milan, where through the influence of Bishop Ambrose (*c*. 340–397) he and his son were baptized in 387. He returned to Africa, where initially he lived a monastic life. In 397 he was made Bishop of Hippo, where he dealt firmly and energetically with heretics and schisms, and died during the Vandal invasion. He wrote in Latin. *Confessions* (tr. Henry Chadwick, 1991), is the spiritual and instructional autobiography of a philosopher and scholar who, after studying the ways of Manicheism and Neoplatonism, found truth and perfection in Christianity. Among many other philosophical, polemical, and religious treatises, the most inspirational is *De Civitate Dei* [The City of God], a considerable work of persuasive prose, written to combat the theory that Christianity had contributed to the fall of Rome in 410. See John M. Rist, *Augustine: Ancient Thought Baptized*, 1994.

AUROBINDO, SRI (1872–1950) Indian philosopher and poet, was born in Calcutta and educated in England at St Paul's School and King's College, Cambridge. On his return to India he was a civil servant and then a university lecturer in Baroda, after which he turned to journalism. In 1910 he went into seclusion in Pondicherry, where he continued his contemplation of the spiritual revelations of the Hindu philosopher, Swami Vivekananda (1863–1902), and delivered himself of a considerable body of prose and verse which only hovers on the borders of literature and lucidity. See *Collected Poems and Plays*, 1942; *On Himself*, new edn 1985.

AUSTEN, JANE (1775–1817) British novelist, was born in the rectory of Steventon, Hampshire, the seventh of eight children, and apart from being at boarding school in Oxford, Southampton, and Reading between the ages of seven and nine, was educated by her father and elder brothers. The family home, in which she lived all her life, moved to Bath (1801), to Southampton (1806), and to the Hampshire village of Chawton (1809), her father having died in 1805. She was the first of six brothers and two sisters to die, which she did from a form of anaemia at 42, tragically young for a novelist. Two of her brothers rose to the rank of admiral in the Navy. Though she never travelled outside the south of England, and never married, her family and social life was not uneventful, and she had the right environment and upbringing to write, which she did from childhood—see *Catharine and Other Writings*, ed. Margaret Anne Doody and Douglas Murray (1993). All the novels published during her lifetime appeared anonymously, though her brother Henry (1771–1850), who acted as her literary agent, disclosed the authorship of *Pride and Prejudice* from what she calls in a letter 'the warmth of his Brotherly vanity & love'. The six novels, in the order in which they were first published, are:

Sense and Sensibility: published 1811 by Thomas Egerton (of the Military Library, Whitehall) with a revised edition in 1813. It was rewritten in 1797 from an earlier story in epistolary form called *Elinor and Marianne*, and further revised in 1809.

Pride and Prejudice: published January 1813 by Egerton, with a second edition in November 1813. As *First Impressions*, it had originally been offered in 1797 to Thomas Cadell, who turned it down.

Mansfield Park: finished in June 1813 and published May 1814 by Egerton at the author's expense, a second edition being published in 1816 by John Murray. It was written between February 1811 and June 1814.

Emma (dated 1816): published by Murray in December 1815, and written between January 1814 and March 1815.

Northanger Abbey and *Persuasion* (dated 1818): published together in four volumes by Murray in December 1817, after the author's death. *Northanger Abbey* had originally been written between 1798 and 1799 as *Susan*, and

was accepted in a revised form in 1803 by Crosby and Co. of Bath, who paid £10 for the copyright, but never published the book. The author wrote to them in 1809 under an assumed name, demanding action and offering to supply a copy if the original manuscript had been lost. Crosby said that they were under no obligation to publish, but offered to return the manuscript if they could have their money back. Nothing was done until 1816, when Henry Austen retrieved the copyright from the unsuspecting publisher, who was unaware of the author's identity. It was now revised for publication as *Catherine*. *Persuasion* was written under the title of *The Elliots* between the summer of 1815 and August 1816. The final titles of both books were chosen by Henry.

Other significant contributions to the canon are: *Love and Freindship*, a short burlesque in letters, written when she was 16; *Lady Susan*, a longer epistolary novel, and the beginning of *The Watsons*, written in about 1806, which Q. D. Leavis (1906–81) argues in *Scrutiny* Vol. X (1941–42) were subsequently reworked into *Mansfield Park* and *Emma* respectively (if this theory is correct, it would account for the years during which the author appears to have written virtually nothing); and *Sanditon*, 12 chapters of which were written between 27 January and 18 March 1817.

Jane Austen can claim to be the most frequently re-read of all novelists in English literature, a distinction which calls for qualities far beyond those required merely to delineate characters, depict settings, develop plots, and devise dialogue. In a letter to her nephew (16 December 1816) she describes her medium as 'the little bit (two inches wide) of Ivory on which I work with so fine a Brush, as produces little effect after much labour'. It is the depth, drama, and selection of detail with which she invests her society and its manners, the acuteness and deadly precision of her observation, the deftness with which she develops a situation and displays her characters and their changing relationships with each other, and her devastating wit, whether she is writing in a vein of comedy or parody, which bring the reader back to her again and again. She also freed the English novel from its predominantly episodic or epistolary form, and set new boundaries in literary style and narrative art. See *The Complete Novels*, biographical sketch by Nigel Nicolson, introductions by V. S. Pritchett, Patrick O'Brian, Loreto Todd, and others, 1994; *Jane Austen's Letters*, ed. Deirdre Le Faye, 3rd edn 1995; *Selected Letters*, ed. R. W. Chapman, 1985; Park Hoffman, *Jane Austen: Her Life*, rev. edn 1997; Mary Lascelles, *Jane Austin and Her Art*, new edn 1995; Marilyn Butler, *Jane Austen and the War of Ideas*, new edn 1988 (critical study); Jocelyn Harris, *Jane Austen's Art of Memory*, 1989 (critical study).

AUSTIN, ALFRED (1835–1913) British poet, novelist, and journalist, was born in Headingley, Leeds, and educated at Stonyhurst College and Oscott College. He was called to the Bar, but in 1858, having received a family legacy, he abandoned the law for literature. His novels and verse were coolly received, and he bolstered his apparent corpus of poetry by incorporating earlier work in each new publication. In *The Poetry of the Period* (1870) he was wide of the mark, and unnecessarily rude, in his criticism of ARNOLD, ROBERT BROWNING, and TENNYSON. He was joint Editor and then Editor (1887–95) of the *National Review*. In 1894 he published *The Garden That I Love*, prose jottings on the charms of his Kentish home, which proved popular with a certain kind of reader. It was either because of this or his support as a political journalist of the party of the Marquis of Salisbury (1830–1903), Prime Minister at the time, that he was appointed Poet Laureate in 1896. His official poems vary between the tolerable and the awful—that on the Jameson Raid in 1896, includes the couplet: 'They went across the veldt / As hard as they could pelt'. He was on safer ground with nature poetry, even if we learn, in 'Primroses', 'Now that mid-March blows and blusters, / Out you steal in tufts and clusters'. A lapsed Catholic, he was convinced to the end that it was spite on the part of the critics which prevented him from receiving his proper due. See Norton Barr Crowell, *Alfred Austin: Victorian*, 1955.

AVISON, MARGARET (b. 1918) Canadian poet, was born in Galt, Ontario, the daughter of a minister, and was brought up in the Canadian west. She graduated in 1940 from Toronto University, to which she returned in 1964 for postgraduate studies in English. She also attended courses in creative writing at the universities of Indiana and Chicago between 1955 and 1957. Her poetry dates from 1940 and appeared in Canadian anthologies long before her first collection, *Winter Sun* (1960), which won the Governor General's Award. A profound spiritual experience in 1963 converted her from a metaphysical to a predominantly religious poet, whose new faith is expressed in the title and other poems of *The Dumbfounding* (1966)—the two books were combined as *Winter Sun/ The Dumbfounding: Poems 1940–66* (1982). *No Time* (1989) also won the Governor General's Award. She worked for the Canadian Broadcasting Corporation Archives Division from 1973 to 1978, and became involved in Presbyterian missionary work in Toronto in 1968, joining the staff of the Mustard Seed Mission in 1978. She has also translated poems from the Hungarian. See *Selected Poems*, 1992; David A. Kent, *Margaret Avison and Her Works*, 1985.

AWOONOR, KOFI (b. 1935) Ghanaian poet and critic, was born in his mother's town of Wheta; 'grew up in a typical African community of relatives, aunts, uncles, some who came as far afield as Togo'; and was educated at a Catholic mission school in Dzodze, a German Presbyterian mission school in Keta, and Achimota School. He went on to the University of Ghana, Legon, where he won the creative writing prize and, with the encouragement of a lecturer, began to translate into English the Ewe folk songs of his childhood, to which he added compositions of his own. He lectured in English and then African literature at the University of Ghana, before becoming Managing Director of the Ghana Ministry of Education Film Corporation, and a founder member of the Ghana Playhouse. He studied on a fellowship at London University in 1967–68, and in 1968 established a course in African literature at the State University of New York, Stony Brook, where he was Chairman of the Department of Comparative Literature. After his return to Ghana in 1975 to teach at Cape Coast University, he was arrested during the political crisis and spent a year in solitary confinement for allegedly helping the organizer of a coup against the military government. He went back to his post, and was Professor of Literature and Dean of the Faculty of Arts 1977–82. Subsequently he was Ghana's Ambassador to Brazil and to Cuba, and then Permanent Representative to the United Nations. He published (as George Awoonor-Williams) *Rediscovery and Other Poems* in Nigeria in 1964. *Night of My Blood* (New York, 1971) incorporates some of the poems from the earlier collection, with others redolent of the African speaking voice. His American experiences and American traditions and speech rhythms are reflected in *Ride Me, Memory* (1973). The title of *The House by the Sea* (1978) is an ironic reference to Ussher Fort Prison, where he was confined in 1975; the volume includes poems written while he was there. *This Earth My Brother* (1971) is a prose poem/novel of a symbolic quest for the reunification of the African self. *The Latin American and Caribbean Notebook* (1992) is a collection which reflects his diplomatic travels. *Comes the Voyager at Last: a Tale of Return to Africa* (1992) is a novel. He has also written *The Breast of Earth: a Survey of the History, Culture and Literature of Africa South of the Sahara* (1975), and translated *Guardians of the Sacred Word: Ewe Poetry* (1974). See *Until the Morning After: Selected Poems 1963–1985*, 1987; in Gerald Moore, *Twelve African Writers*, 1980; and in Jane Wilkinson (ed.), *Talking with African Writers*, 1992.

AYCKBOURN, (SIR) ALAN (b. 1939) British dramatist and theatre director, was born in London. His father, a violinist, left home when he was six, and his mother, a writer, subsequently married a Sussex bank manager, with whom he did not get on. He was educated at Haileybury College, and at the age of 17 rescued his mother from her now deteriorating marriage, and was taken on as a stage manager by (Sir) Donald Wolfit (1902–68) for his touring company. The other great influence on his career was the stage director and advocate of the theatre 'in the round', Stephen Joseph (1921–67). He acted in Joseph's productions from 1961 to 1964 and succeeded him as Artistic Director of the Stephen Joseph Theatre in Scarborough, where he has written all his more than forty plays, which have been performed in fifty countries, in thirty languages. Of his association with his theatre he has said: 'I've been lucky in the combination of pressures. . . . I've had to write plays that decent actors would cut their salaries in half to come and work in. . . . On the other hand I've had to write plays that the local audience will come and see—that's sort of meant comedy. . . . A comedy is just a tragedy interrupted. You stop the action at the point where they lived happily ever after.' From his first success, *Standing Room Only* (as 'Roland Allen'), produced in Scarborough in 1961, he has tended to develop an unusual situation, with dazzling dramatic ingenuity, often exploring the variables as well; as he has done with the same events seen from three interlocking viewpoints in the *Norman Conquests* trilogy (1975), the four versions of *Sisterly Feelings* (1979), and the multiple endings of *Intimate Exchanges* (1982). Though his plays are outwardly comedies, often with farcical elements, he takes a pessimistic view of human nature, which he presents in all its nastiness in *Absurd Person Singular* (1972) and *Man of the Moment* (1988), and with a dash of bitterness in *The Revengers' Comedies* (1991). The device of 'Time: past, present and future' in *Time of My Life* (1993), his 44th play, is developed further in *Communicating Doors* (1995), his 49th, a comedy thriller in which the main character is able to alter the course of events. He was made CBE in 1987, and was Cameron

Mackintosh Professor of Contemporary Theatre at Oxford 1992–93. He was knighted in 1997. A new Stephen Joseph Theatre, with two auditoriums, opened in Scarborough in 1996. See Michael Billington, *Alan Ayckbourn*, 2nd edn 1990 (critical study).

AYTOUN, WILLIAM EDMONSTOUNE (1813–65) Scottish poet and satirist, was born in Edinburgh, the son of a lawyer, and went to Edinburgh Academy and Edinburgh University, where he read law, which he later confessed he 'followed but could never overtake'. He published *Poland, Homer and Other Poems* in 1832. From 1836 until his death he contributed articles and poems to *Blackwood's Edinburgh Magazine*. He was elected Professor of Belles Lettres at Edinburgh University in 1845, and appointed Sheriff and Lord Admiral of Orkney and Shetland in 1852. Some of his parodies of traditional ballads and of contemporary poets were included in *The Bon Gaultier Ballads* (1845), written with Sir Theodore Martin (1816–1909). His reputation was made by *Lays of the Scottish Cavaliers* (1849), in which 'The Execution of Montrose', 'The Burial March of Dundee', and 'The Widow of Glencoe', in particular, have fine feeling and resounding rhythms, while reflecting and helping to popularize the more romantic aspects of the grim history of the Scottish Highlands. His most audacious literary exploit was to publish in *Blackwood's* (1854) a spoof review (with extracts) of 'Firmilian' by 'Percy Jones', a poet of the 'Spasmodic school'. Neither the poem nor its author existed, and the Spasmodic school was an invention of Aytoun to describe the ramblings of some contemporary poets, notably Sydney Dobell (1824–74) and ALEXANDER SMITH, who were attempting to write in the style of BYRON and GOETHE. He then extended the joke by writing and publishing the complete work, in the form of a burlesque, as *Firmilian, or The Student of Badajoz: a Spasmodic Tragedy* 'By T. Percy Jones' (1854). See *Stories and Verse*, ed. W. L. Renwick, 1964; *Essays*, ed. John Pitcher, 1985.

B

BABEL, ISAAK (1894–1940) Russian novelist, short-story writer, and dramatist, was born in Odessa, the son of a Jewish shopkeeper, who set him to study Yiddish, the Bible, and the Talmud while also attending Nicholas I Commercial Institute. He graduated from Saratov University and in 1915 settled in St Petersburg, where Jews were banned from living. In 1916 he met GORKY, who printed his first stories (for which Babel was arrested), and encouraged him to go out and experience life. In 1919 he took part in the defence of the city against the White forces, after which he returned to Odessa and married. When Poland invaded Russia in 1920 he signed up as a war correspondent, but served as an officer in the First Cavalry—see [*1920 Diary*] (1990; ed. Carol J. Avins, tr. H. T. Willetts, 1995). He published a volume of stories in 1925; further volumes, of linked tales, contained childhood impressions (1926, including ['The Story of My Dovecot']), and sketches of a Jewish gangster in Odessa (1931)—see *Collected Stories*, tr. David McDuff (1995). In his novel, [*Red Cavalry*], (tr. Nadia Helstein, 1926), he used the film techniques which fascinated him to build up, by means of 35 situations, a picture of a Jewish intellectual involved in battle. He was secretary of a village soviet in 1930. After an abortive attempt at a cycle of stories about collective farming, he wrote *Marya* (1935), 'a play in eight scenes', a realistic but fragmented drama of Petrograd in 1920 which offers modern audiences a small slice of Soviet history. He came under attack in 1934 during the First Congress of Soviet Writers, at which he commented that he was a 'grand master' at the art of silence—see Nathalie Babel (ed.), *Isaac Babel: the Lonely Years 1925–1939, Unpublished Stories and Private Correspondence* (1964). He was arrested on 15 May 1939, and shot on 27 January 1940. The 27 folders of confiscated manuscripts have never been seen again. For an account of his interrogation see Vitaly Shentalinsky, *The KGB's Literary Archive* (in USA as *Arrested Voices: Resurrecting the Disappeared Writers of the Soviet Regime*), tr. John Crowfoot (1995). See also A. N. Pirozhkova, *At His Side: The Last Years of Isaac Babel* (1996).

BACHMAN, RICHARD see KING.

BACON, (Sir) FRANCIS (1561–1626) English prose writer, essayist, and jurist, was born in York House, the Strand, London, the youngest son by his second marriage of Elizabeth I's statesman, Sir Nicholas Bacon (1509–79). He was educated at home and at Trinity College, Cambridge, which he had to leave when he was 14 because of an outbreak of plague. After learning diplomacy in France, he studied law, graduating in 1582, and was elected to Parliament in 1584. After some years in subordinate posts, he was knighted by James I in 1603, and appointed successively Solicitor General (1607), Attorney General (1616), and Lord Chancellor (1618), becoming Baron Verulam in 1618 and Viscount St Albans in 1621. In that year he was accused of taking bribes from three suitors while their cases were being tried in his court. Though he had found against them, he was adjudged guilty of corruption in the House of Lords, dismissed from all his offices, and fined £40,000. He spent the rest of his life writing.

Throughout the whole of his professional career Bacon wrote legal and political works which, with his frequent speeches in Parliament, form a sizable literary output on their own. Yet this extraordinary man, of whom POPE said in *An Essay on Man* (IV, 281–82), 'If Parts allure thee, think how Bacon shin'd, / The wisest, brightest, meanest of mankind', also produced several major philosophical and scientific treatises in Latin (the lingua franca of scholarship), including the unfinished *Instauratio Magna* (1620), and four literary works in English which are unique in his age. The first volume of his essays (containing ten) was published in 1597, and an enlarged edition in 1612. The definitive edition (1625) contains 58 essays, including extended versions of ones already published. Didactic, aphoristic, incisively and clearly written, and often having striking openings, they also present a shrewd and objective picture of the manners and morals of the time. 'The Advancement of Learning'—*The Twoo Bookes of Francis Bacon: Of the Proficience and Advancement of Learning, Divine and Humane* (1605)—is a wide-ranging and systematic investigation into the knowledge of his era. *The Historie of the Raigne of King Henry the Seventh* (1622) is a landmark in English historical writing in that Bacon departs from the unselective chronicle approach to produce a coherent and balanced narrative, while bringing psychological insight to bear on his characters. *New Atlantis*, left unfinished and first published with *Sylva Sylvarum: or a Naturall Historie* (1627), is a philosophical, scientific and, in some respects, prophetic fable of the construction and methodology of society.

Bacon's enquiring mind was the cause of his death. Keen to try refrigeration as a means of preserving food, he left his coach to buy a chicken, which he stuffed with snow. He developed a sudden chill and died in the house of a friend. See *The Essayes or Counsels, Civill and Morall*, ed. Michael Kiernan, 1985; *Essays*, ed. John Pitcher, 1985; [*Selection*], ed. Brian Vickers, 1996; Brian Vickers, *Francis Bacon and Renaissance Prose*, 1968; Anthony Quinton, *Francis Bacon*, 1980 (introduction).

BAGEHOT, WALTER (1826–77) British economist, political philosopher, literary critic, and journalist, was born in Langport, Somerset, the son of a banker and shipowner, and was educated in Bristol and at London University, where he excelled at mathematics, philosophy, and political economy. After studying for and being called to the Bar, he joined his father's business, while contributing articles to literary and economic journals and, in 1855, becoming joint Editor of the *National Review*. In 1858 he married a daughter of James Wilson (1805–60), founder of the *Economist*, whom he succeeded as Editor in 1860, holding the post until his death. Bagehot's *The English Constitution* (1867; rev. edn 1872) is a classic, often-cited study of government in which, among other recommendations, he advocated life peerages. In *Physics and Politics* (1872) he applied DARWIN's theory of 'natural selection' to world politics; and in *Lombard Street* (1873) he examined the current financial market. Collected volumes of literary, economic, and biographical studies were published 1879–81, after his death. His article 'Wordsworth, Tennyson and Browning, or Pure, Ornate and Grotesque Art in English Poetry' (1864) is much quoted, and contains the coinage of 'literatesque' to describe 'that perfect combination in the *subject-matter* of literature, which suits the *art* of literature'. See *The Best of Bagehot*, ed. Ruth Dudley Edwards, 1993; Norman St John-Stevas, *Walter Bagehot: a Study of His Life and Thought, with a selection from his political writings*, 1959.

BAILLIE, LADY GRISELL (1665–1746) Scottish poet, was born at Redbraes Castle, Berwickshire, the eldest of nine children of Sir Patrick Hume (1641–1724), later 1st Earl of Marchmont. At 12, she was secret messenger between her father and Robert Baillie, imprisoned in Edinburgh for his Covenanting principles. After Baillie's execution in 1684,

Hume took refuge in a hide-out known only to his wife and Grisell, who supplied him with food. After he had fled to Holland, the family joined him. Grisell made all the arrangements and then returned to Scotland to fetch her sick sister, whom she had to carry on foot for twenty miles when they reached the Dutch shore. On the accession of William and Mary, she was invited to be Maid of Honour to the Queen, but preferred to return to Scotland to marry her childhood sweetheart, George Baillie (1664–1738), whom she had first met when she took the messages to his father. Her meticulous domestic accounts, with menus and instructions to servants, were published as *The Household Book of Lady Grisell Baillie*, ed. Robert Scott-Moncrieff (1911). She was the first of a line of women poets who adapted traditional forms to their own views of pastoralism and nationalism. Her best-known song, 'Werena My Heart Licht I Wad Dee' was, like others of her poems, published in RAMSAY's *The Tea-Table Miscellany*.

BAINBRIDGE, BERYL (*b.* 1933) British novelist, was born in Liverpool to a family in which (according to her story, 'The Longstop') 'Mr Baines, who was my maternal grandfather, was a lover of cricket. Mr Bainbridge, my father, didn't care for the game. He cared even less for my grandfather.' She was educated at Merchant Taylors' School and then at a ballet school in Hertfordshire, after which she acted in repertory, married a painter (in 1954), had three children, and divorced (in 1959). From 1961 to 1973 she worked for the firm which became her publisher in 1972, with a curious interlude in 1970 when she was a cellar woman in a bottle factory, a milieu which recurs in *The Bottle Factory Outing* (1974). Her first novel to be published was *A Weekend with Claude* (1967; rev. edn 1981); the one she wrote first was *Harriet Said . . .* (1972)—reissued in *A Bainbridge Omnibus* (1989) with *The Dressmaker* (1973) and *The Bottle Factory Outing*. She claimed (in 1976), 'I am not very good at fiction. It is always me and the experiences I have had': she has nevertheless invested bizarre themes with grim humour, as in *Young Adolf* (1978), and treated domestic situations with irony, as in *A Quiet Life* (1976). *Watson's Apology* (1984) is based on an actual murder by a clergyman of his wife in Victorian times. In *An Awfully Big Adventure* (1989), involving a time lock, the drama develops during rehearsals for a Christmas performance of BARRIE's *Peter Pan* in Liverpool in the 1950s. She employs a similar device in *The Birthday Boys* (1991), an account of the Antarctic exploration in 1910–12, the starting point of which was a letter written to Barrie by the dying Captain Scott (1868–1912). After a gap of five years, she published *Every Man for Himself* (1996), a novel of the doomed maiden voyage of the *Titanic*. 'People like Scott and the builders of the *Titanic* knew that the First World War was coming, but they did not want to look over the horizon. The ship is like a symbol of all the great endeavours that were doomed to strike icebergs within a couple of years, whether it had survived or not.' *Collected Stories* (1994) contains the novella *Filthy Lucre* (1986), which she began writing when she was 13, the 12 stories from *Mum and Mr Armitage* (1985), and six uncollected pieces.

BALDWIN, JAMES (1924–87) American novelist, dramatist, and essayist, was born in Harlem, New York. He was illegitimate. Two years later his 24-year-old mother married, as his second wife, David Baldwin, the son of a slave, who was a lay preacher with 'a job on Long Island' and terrorized his family. At 14, 'afraid of the evil within me and afraid of the evil without', he 'fled into the Church', an experience which he described later in the *New Yorker* in his celebrated indictment of social prejudice (and also of separatism as a solution), 'Letter from a Region of My Mind' (1962)—reprinted in *The Fire Next Time* (1963). He was for three years a boy preacher, described as 'very hot', until one day he walked out of church during a service to go to a Broadway matinée, and never returned. He graduated from DeWitt Clinton High School in 1942, and at first worked as an elevator boy to help his now widowed mother raise her eight other children, the last of them born on the day of the death of his stepfather, who had become insane with paranoia. He went to live in Greenwich Village, where he attempted to become a writer, and to come to terms with his homosexuality and with being a black American. His first published piece was an article in the *Nation* on GORKY. He sold a story ('Previous Condition') and began to get commissions for reviews and essays. In 1948, having failed to reconcile any personal identity with prevailing political and social attitudes, and being determined to find his own way of protesting, he followed RICHARD WRIGHT to Paris, where initially he 'lived mainly among *les misérables*'. He returned briefly in 1952, but 'when my first novel was finally sold, I picked up my advance and walked straight to the steamship office and booked passage back to France'.

That novel, *Go Tell It on the Mountain* (1953), which critics regard as his best, is autobiographical in that its point of resolution is the mystical conversion to religion of a Harlem lad on the night of his 14th birthday (in the story in 1935), and that Baldwin's family circumstances are reflected in those of his characters. But it also incorporates, through flashbacks, aspects of the owner/slave, black/white issues such as had brought about the current situation. The title of his collection of essays written between 1948 and 1955, *Notes of a Native Son* (1955), refers to the novel by Wright, whose sacrifice of art to the message of social protest is a central criticism of a work which established Baldwin's credo. Ignoring his publisher's suggestion that he should set his second novel in the black community, he wrote *Giovanni's Room* (1956), which has no black characters and in which race plays no part, as an American in Paris is torn between his responsibilities to his homosexual lover and his moral instincts. The only black male in *Another Country* (1962) dives off a bridge to his death early on, leaving his sister and white friends to resolve their lives and loves as best they can. With *Tell Me How Long the Train's Been Gone* (1968) and *If Beale Street Could Talk* (1974) Baldwin is firmly back in the world of black unrest and social injustice in which he grew up. In his last novel, *Just Above My Head* (1979), the death in London of a homosexual gospel singer sparks off a train of reminiscences on the part of his brother, whose relationship with the former Harlem child preacher, Julia, is a continuing theme. It is, however, in Africa that Julia, forced as a child into incest with her father, and then into prostitution to earn money for herself and her brother, finally finds liberation. He also wrote two notable plays. *The Amen Corner*, first produced in 1955 in a black college in Washington, D.C., and in 1965 in New York, London, and Edinburgh (published 1965), explores through the character of a woman minister the conflict between human understanding and the rigid observance of God's law. In *Blues for Mr Charlie* (1964), based on two actual incidents of racial injustice, a secondary theme is the collapse under provocation of the determination to effect social improvement by peaceful protest.

Baldwin spent much of the 1960s in Istanbul, and latterly lived mainly in the south of France. He died of cancer. His short stories were collected in *Going to Meet the Man* (1965). *Nobody Knows My Name: More Notes of a Native Son* (1961) was a second volume of essays—see also *The Price of a Ticket: Collected Nonfiction 1948–1985* (1986). See David Leeming, *James Baldwin: a Biography*, new edn 1995; James Campbell, *Talking at the Gates: a Life of James Baldwin*, new edn 1992 (critical biography); Louis H. Pratt, *James Baldwin*, 1978 (critical study).

BALE, JOHN (1495–1563) dramatist, was born of poor parents near Dunwich, Suffolk. At an early age he went to the Carmelite convent in Norwich, and was educated there and at Jesus College, Oxford. Abandoning his vows, he became a Protestant, got married, and was appointed to the living of Thorndon, Suffolk. He was imprisoned in 1536 for making anti-Catholic statements, and removed from his living the following year. In 1552 he became Bishop of Ossory, in Ireland; with misgivings, as the Irish Parliament had not accepted the new form of consecration. When

Mary Tudor came to the throne, he hurriedly left his post, and after a near-shipwreck and several spells in prison en route, arrived in Holland. He returned in 1556. Not feeling up to his bishopric again, he became a canon of Canterbury Cathedral. All his five surviving plays were written in one burst, under the patronage of Thomas Cromwell (c.1485–1540), the Protestantizing Lord Chancellor, after his ejection from Thorndon. In the trilogy known as *The Chief Promises of God, John the Baptist's Preaching*, and *The Temptation of Our Lord*, he departed from the form of the traditional morality play to present dramatized sermons projecting the new doctrine. *The Three Laws of Nature, Moses and Christ*, the first English play in five acts, is a vitriolic satire. *King John*, written in most irregular verse and only discovered and published in 1838, is the first English historical drama. He also compiled the first dictionary of English literature (1548). See Peter Happé, *John Bale*, 1996 (critical study); and in F. P. Wilson, *The English Drama 1485–1585*, new edn 1990.

BALLANTYNE, R(OBERT) M(I-CHAEL) (1825–94) Scottish novelist, was born in Edinburgh, the son of the younger brother of the two Ballantynes with whose printing and publishing companies WALTER SCOTT was so disastrously involved. He was educated by his mother and briefly at Edinburgh Academy, and was then an apprentice clerk with the Hudson's Bay Company in Canada from 1841 to 1847. On his return he was a railway clerk, and then a partner in a printing firm, before becoming a full-time writer. Encouraged by the interest in his first book, *Hudson's Bay: or, Every-Day Life in the Wilds of North America* (1848), a factual account based on his diaries, he produced for boys *Snowflakes and Sunbeams: or, The Young Fur-Traders* (1856), the unmanly first part of the title being dropped in subsequent editions. After *Ungava: a Tale of Esquimeaux Land* (1857) came the story for which he is best known, *The Coral Island: a Tale of the Pacific Ocean* (1857). This is more than a jolly survival tale, with some horrific incidents and a strong Christian message, being also an introduction to 'valuable information' about geography and natural history. The response to the formula was such that he repeated it with endless variations, though an error in *The Coral Island* in describing the coconut in the wild, which he had never seen, determined him wherever possible to get firsthand experience of an environment. The morality in his works slows up the narrative, but he echoes the imperialistic ideals of his times. He did for geography what HENTY was to do for history, and he was a strong influence on STEVENSON. See Eric Quayle, *Ballantyne the Brave: a Victorian Writer and His Family*, 1967.

BALLARD, J(AMES) G(RAHAM) (b. 1930) British novelist and short-story writer, was born in Shanghai, the son of the owner of a cotton mill ('I spent a lot of time alone in the house, with about nine servants, all Chinese, except for a punitive White Russian nanny . . . who used to make me sit uselessly on a wooden lavatory seat for hours—the 1930s' equivalent of television, and probably far more educational.'). In 1942 the family was interned by the Japanese in a prison camp at Lunghua, 'absolutely the reverse of everything that I had ever known', the experience of which he re-creates in *Empire in the Sun* (1984), to which *The Kindness of Women* (1991) is a highly-charged sequel. After World War II he was educated at the Leys School and King's College, Cambridge. When his wife died in 1964 he brought up his children in the 1930s' suburban semi-detached house in Shepperton into which they had moved in 1960. He himself has accepted the tag of writer of science fiction, but it is an inner, rather than outer, space which he reflects, and present, often surrealist, nightmares, not the future. Such in particular are the themes of *The Drowned World* (1962), his first novel, and *Crash* (1973); *The Drought* (1965), *The Crystal World* (1966), and *Concrete Island* (1974) offer more, if still bizarre, entertainment. *Rushing to Paradise* (1994) is a dystopian vision of feminism run disturbingly wild; *Cocaine Nights* (1996) is a futuristic whodunnit set in a nightmare Spanish holiday resort. His short stories are often topical and can be ferociously satirical—his obsession with Ronald Reagan (President of the USA 1981–89), who recurs in the collection *War Fever* (1990), resulted at one time in his being temporarily banned from American bookshops. Other collections since *The Best of J. G. Ballard* (1977) include *The Venus Hunters* (1980) and *Myths of the Near Future* (1982). *A User's Guide to the Millenium* (1996) collects the best of his reviews and essays. See Roger Luckhurst, *The Angle Between Two Walls: the Fiction of J. G. Ballard*, 1996.

BALZAC, HONORÉ DE (1799–1850) French novelist, was born in Tours and was in 1807 sent away to board at the Oratorian College, Vendome, where his mother visited him just twice in six years. In 1814 the family moved to Paris, where he briefly attended two schools and in 1816 was articled to a lawyer. In 1819 (the year his uncle was guillotined for the murder of a maid he had seduced) the family acceded to Balzac's wish to become a writer, and set him up initially in an unheated garret near the Bastille. During the next ten years he wrote pseudonymous novels, lost money on unwise publishing and printing ventures, and had his first serious affair, with Mme Laure de Berny (d. 1836), 22 years his senior, who also gave him inspirational and financial assistance. With *Le Dernier Chouan* (1829; rev. edn as *Les Chouans,* 1834; as *The Chouans,* tr. George Saintsbury, 1890; tr. Marion Ayton Crawford, 1972), a historical novel of 1799 whose stimulus was the vogue for WALTER SCOTT, he at last received literary recognition. *La Peau de Chagrin* (1831; tr. as *The Magic Skin,* 1888; as *The Wild Ass's Skin,* tr. Ellen Marriage, 1901; tr. Herbert J. Hunt, 1977), a philosophical fantasy, also brought success and fame, which he further justified with *Eugénie Grandet* (1833; tr. 1859; tr. Sylvia Raphael, 1990) and *Le Père Goriot* (1834; tr. as *Daddy Goriot: or, Unrequited Affection,* 1860; tr. A. J. Krailsheimer as *Père Goriot,* 1991).

Balzac now conceived his grand, but impossible, design of presenting in fiction a complete social, philosophical, and analytical study of modern French civilization, with recurring characters. The ninety novels and stories which he completed of 'La Comédie Humaine', as it was called from 1842 (and in translation as 'The Human Comedy', ed. George Saintsbury, tr. Clara Bell, Ellen Marriage, James Waring, and R. S. Scott, 40 vols 1895–98), have a cast of two thousand characters, and include, in addition to the earlier works, *Les Illusions Perdus* (2 vols 1837–39; tr. Hunt as *Lost Illusions,* 1971) and *La Cousine Bette* (1848; tr. Raphael as *Cousin Bette,* 1992). See also *Selected Short Stories,* tr. Raphael (1977). In spite of his enormous creative energy and ambition, Balzac was usually in debt (he went into hiding from his creditors in 1835), and from 1841 he was also in poor health. In May 1850 he was married in Polish Ukraine to his long-term mistress, Countess (Evelina) Hanska (*d.* 1882), whom he had first met in 1833 after she had written him anonymous fan letters—her husband had died in 1841. By the time the couple reached Paris, after a nightmare journey by coach, Balzac was dying. He had a daughter in 1834 by Mme Maria du Fresnay (*d.* 1892), the original dedicatee of *Eugénie Grandet,* and a son in 1836 by a further mistress, the English wife of Count Guidoboni-Visconti. See V. S. Pritchett, *Balzac,* new edn 1992 (biography); Graham Robb, *Balzac: a Biography,* new edn 1996.

BANIM, JOHN (1798–1842) and **MICHAEL** (1796–1874) Irish novelists, were born in Kilkenny, the sons of a farmer who doubled as a sports' outfitter. Michael was educated locally and at 16 chose the law as his career. John went to Kilkenny College and then studied art at the Royal Dublin Society, becoming a drawing teacher in Kilkenny. After the death of his fiancée, he returned to Dublin, to be a writer. The success of a tragedy, *Damon and Pythias,* staged at Covent Garden, London in 1821, encouraged him to suggest to Michael, who had in the meantime had to give up the law to sort out the family

businesses, that they should write a number of Irish national novels and stories of Irish life together. This they did, initially in the form of two series of *Tales, by the O'Hara Family* (1825 and 1826). Of the 24 novels written by them, Michael claimed after John's death that he was responsible for $13^1/_2$, but the true number may be nearer twenty, with John taking ultimate editorial responsibility. They range from the historically-based tales, such as *The Boyne Water* (1826), *The Croppy* (1828), and *The Denounced* (1830), through those which are a blend of realism and folklore— *Croohore of the Bill Hook* (1825), *The Fetches* (1825), in which there is an account of Kilkenny College, and *The Ghost Hunter and His Family* (1831)—to studies of situation, such as *The Nowlans* (1826), in which a Catholic priest breaks his vows and marries.

BANNATYNE, GEORGE see MAITLAND; SCOTT, ALEXANDER.

BARAKA, AMIRI (*b.* 1934) American poet and dramatist, was born Everett LeRoy Jones in Newark, New Jersey, of middle-class parents. He was educated at Barringer High School, Newark, and Howard University, Washington, D.C., by which time he had adopted the spelling LeRoi. Dishonourably discharged from the US Air Force in 1956, he settled with his first (white) wife in Greenwich Village, where he founded and edited a postmodernist literary journal, *Yugen* (1958–62). He also produced a volume of Beat poetry, *Preface to a Twenty Volume Suicide Note* (1961), followed by *The Dead Lecturer* (1964). *Blues People* (1963) was a pioneering historical and sociological study of Afro-American music. In the plays *Dutchman* and *The Slave* (published together 1964), the struggle for black cultural liberation is represented as a source of continuing violence. In 1965 he left his wife (they were divorced that year) and two daughters, and founded the short-lived Black Arts Repertory Theatre in Harlem. He then returned to Newark to regroup the black arts movement, married a black woman, and became actively involved in nationalist politics. *Black Magic: Collected Poetry 1961–1967* (1969), comprising three sections, 'Sabotage', 'Target Study', and 'Black Art', was published as by LeRoi Jones, though he had now changed his name to Ameer (later Amiri) Baraka, to which he appended the title Imamu [Spiritual Leader]. As a further mark of his dedication to the policy of separation, he established locally what amounted to a new Afro-American culture. In 1974 he abandoned cultural nationalism for Third World Marxism, and in 1980 became a member of the teaching staff of the African Studies department, State University of New York, Stony Brook. See *The LeRoi Jones/Amiri Baraka*

Reader, ed. William J. Harris, 1991; *Funk Lore: New Poems 1984–1995*, 1996; *The Autobiography of LeRoi Jones*, 1996.

BARBAULD, ANNA LETITIA (1743–1825), née Aikin, British poet, essayist, and critic, was born in Kibworth, Leicestershire, the eldest child of Rev. John Aikin (1713–80). It is said that she could read fluently when she was two, and that her early progress at Italian and French was such that her father reluctantly agreed to teach her Greek and Latin. In 1758 he was appointed classical tutor at the new Nonconformist academy at Warrington, Lancashire, to which the family moved. Her first publications were *Poems* (1773), which included 'The Mouse's Petition' and 'Corsica' (an effusion in blank verse which was admired by MONTAGU), and *Miscellaneous Pieces in Prose* (1773), written jointly with her brother John (1747–1822), later a physician, prose writer, and translator. In 1774 she married Rev. Rochemont Barbauld, the son of a Church of England cleric of Huguenot descent, who was studying at the academy. They settled in Palgrave, Suffolk, where he led a congregation and established a boys' school, but his instability took them in 1785 to the Continent for a year; subsequently they lived in Hampstead and then Stoke Newington, near her brother. They had no children, but adopted her nephew, Charles Rochemont Aikin (1775–1847), later a distinguished doctor, for whom she wrote *Lessons for Children, from Two to Three Years Old* (1777), *Lessons for Children, from Three to Four Years Old* (1778), and *Hymns in Prose for Children* (1781). She campaigned in prose and verse against slavery, war, and prohibitions limiting the participation of Nonconformists in politics, and for freedom of worship and speech. She edited the correspondence of SAMUEL RICHARDSON (6 vols, 1804), for which she wrote a life of the novelist. After her husband died, insane, in 1808, she undertook the editing of *The British Novelists* (50 vols 1810). Her last work, *Eighteen Hundred and Eleven* (1812), a long poem of social criticism, caused offence for its pessimism and was savaged by SOUTHEY in the *Quarterly Review*. Her *Works* (2 vols 1825) were edited by her niece, Lucy Aikin (1781–1864), a poet, critic, and historical writer. See *The Poems of Anna Letitia Barbauld*, ed. William McCarthy and Elizabeth Kraft, 1994.

BARBOUR, JOHN (*c.*1320–95) the earliest known Scottish poet, was probably born in or near Aberdeen. He is first mentioned in 1357, when as Archdeacon of Aberdeen (a post he held until his death) he was granted a pass by Edward III of England to accompany three scholars to Oxford. In that year, too, he was the Bishop's proxy at the council in Edinburgh to raise the ransom for the release of David II from England. He held various posts in the royal household and was auditor of the exchequer in 1372, 1382, and 1383. Two lost poems are attributed to him, *The Brut* and *The Stewartis Original*. His surviving work, *The Bruce*, 13,550 lines long, and written in rhyming couplets of iambic tetrameters, is a patriotic panegyric of Robert I (Robert the Bruce) and his successful fight to free Scotland from English domination (culminating in the battle of Bannockburn in 1314), and also of the ordinary people of Scotland who played their part in the struggle. It is remarkable for its attention to detail, its attempt to present an authentic record, and its narrative power and insight. In 1377 Robert II (grandson of the Bruce and the first Stewart King of Scotland) granted Barbour £10 for writing the poem and a pension of 20 shillings a year, which the poet made over to the cathedral for a mass for him and his parents to be said each year on his birthday, which was done until the Reformation. Two 15th-century transcripts of *The Bruce* survive: the first printed edition was in 1571. See *The Bruce*, ed. and tr. George Eyre-Todd, new edn 1996 (prose); in Kurt Wittig, *The Scottish Tradition in Literature*, new edn 1978; and in R. D. S. Jack (ed.), *The History of Scottish Literature Volume 1: Origins to 1660*, new edn 1989.

BARKER, GEORGE (1913–91) British poet, was born in Loughton, Essex, the son of a former soldier in the Coldstream Guards and of an Irish Catholic from Drogheda, and was brought up in a cramped London tenement. He went to Marlborough Road London County Council School, Chelsea, and Regent Street Polytechnic, which he left at 15, having realized that he was a poet and begun to dress acccordingly, in cloak and huge hat. *Thirty Preliminary Poems* and a novel, *Alanna Autumnal*, were published in 1933. With *Poems* (1935) he was made welcome at Faber & Faber by T. S. ELIOT, who persuaded five friends anonymously to pay Barker £4 a week. He was in 1936 the youngest poet to be included by YEATS in *The Oxford Book of Modern Verse*, but it was not until *Lament and Triumph* (1940) that a sense of assurance entered his poetic canon. He was Professor of English Literature at Imperial Tohoku University, Japan 1939–41, after which he spent several years in the USA. Subsequently he lived in Rome for five years, and held visiting professorships at American universities. A prolific writer, with a sensual streak, his work abounds with elegies for lost friends and memories of love, with lyrical poems, celebrations, satirical excursions, personal observations, and expressions of disgust, most of which are present in various guises in the sardonic *The True Confession of George Barker* (1950; rev. edn 1965). A further novel was *The Dead Seagull* (1950). His affair with the Canadian writer, Elizabeth Smart (1913–86), who had four children by him, inspired her cult novel, *By Grand Central Station I Sat Down and Wept* (1945). Through her, he met Elspeth Barker (*b.* 1943), née Langlands, sister-in-law of MASSIE, whose first book, *O Caledonia* (1991), is a 20th-century Gothic novel in the Scottish tradition. They had five children, and married in 1989. See *Collected Poems*, ed. Robert Fraser, 1987; *Street Ballads*, 1992 (posthumous collection); *Selected Poems*, ed. Robert Fraser, 1995.

BARLOW, JOEL (1754–1812) American poet and political journalist, was born in Redding, Connecticut, and went to Yale, from which he took time off to fight for the American revolutionary army at Long Island in 1776. After taking a further degree in theology, he founded a newspaper, the *American Mercury*, and opened a bookshop in Hartford, where he was a member of the Connecticut Wits. He also qualified as a lawyer (1786), and published *The Vision of Columbus* (1787), an epic poem in heroic couplets on America's greatness, whose re-publication in an expanded version as *The Columbiad* (1807) brought him late fame as a patriot but little as a poet. In 1788 he and his wife went to Europe, where they spent much of the next seventeen years. He became an ardent supporter of the French Revolution, and wrote *Advice to the Privileged Orders in the Several States of Europe . . .* (1792), a response to BURKE's *Reflections on the Revolution in France*, and *A Letter to the National Convention of France on the Defects in the Constitution of 1791 . . .* (1792), for which he was made an honorary French citizen. While campaigning in Savoy in 1793 as a candidate for the National Assembly, he expressed his delight at being served for breakfast a Gallic version of an American recipe by writing *The Hasty Pudding* (1796), a mock heroic on which his poetic reputation largely depends. He was American consul in Algiers in 1795. In 1811 he was appointed Minister in France, to negotiate a trade treaty with Napoleon. He followed the Emperor to Poland, only to witness the terrible retreat from Moscow, on which he composed the bitter 'Advice to a Raven in Russia' (December 1812). Before he could himself turn back, he died of pneumonia, and was buried in a village near Cracow.

BARNARD, A. M. see ALCOTT.

BARNARD, MARJORIE (1897–1987) Australian novelist and critic, was born and educated in Sydney, graduating in 1920 from Sydney University with a first in history. When the family refused to let her take up a scholarship at Oxford, she trained as a librarian, and worked at Sydney Technical College from 1920 to 1932. After publishing a book of children's stories, *The Ivory Gate* (1920), she began a collaboration with Flora Eldershaw (1897–1956), later an industrial consultant. As M. Barnard Eldershaw they wrote five novels, of which the first, *A House is Built* (1929), the saga of a family business, shared first prize with PRICHARD's *Coonardo* in a competition sponsored by the *Bulletin*, in which it was serialized as 'The Quartermaster'. *Tomorrow and Tomorrow* (1947), a futuristic political novel incorporating vivid descriptions of Sydney in the 1930s and 1940s, was reissued in 1983 in an uncut version with the original title of *Tomorrow and Tomorrow and Tomorrow*. Their *Essays in Australian Fiction* (1938) was especially significant for its time. Barnard returned to librarianship in 1942, working at the Commonwealth Scientific and Industrial Research Organization until 1950. On her own account she published historical works, including the popular *A History of Australia* (1961), a critical study of MILES FRANKLIN (1967), and *The Persimmon Tree, and Other Stories* (1943). She was made AO in 1980.

BARNES, DJUNA (1892–1982) American novelist and dramatist, was born in Cornwall-on-Hudson, New York, into a bizarre home in which her numerous siblings, also with outlandish names, were born synchronously of two mothers. There she received a curious education from her eccentric grandmother and her indigent father, and afterwards studied at the Pratt Institute, Brooklyn, and the Arts Students' League. She began work as a journalist on the Brooklyn *Daily Eagle* in 1913, and in 1915 had a volume of poems and drawings, *The Book of Repulsive Women*, privately printed in Greenwich Village. Three avant-garde one-act plays were produced by the Provincetown Players in 1919. In 1920, having left her husband of two years, Courtenay Lemon, she went to Paris, where she lived with an American sculptress. She lampooned the local lesbian coterie in the privately-printed *Ladies Almanack . . . As Well as a Full Record of Diurnal and Nocturnal Distempers Written and Illustrated by a Lady of Fashion* (1928), in which RADCLYFFE HALL appears as Lady Buck-and-Balk. *Ryder* (1928) is a satirical work in the form of a family chronicle. *Nightwood* (1936), a densely plotted sexual roundabout, much of which is narrated through a haze of booze by a superannuated transvestite doctor, had a certain *succès d'estime*, prompted by an introduction by T. S. ELIOT, who was a director of the firm which originally published it in Britain—see *Nightwood: the Original Version and Related Drafts*, ed. Cheryl J. Plumb (1995) for an account of its complicated history. In 1937 she settled in Greenwich Village, where she lived largely in seclusion and devoted herself to her writing, the only tangible manifestation of which was the latter-day Jacobean drama in blank verse, *Antiphon*, published in 1958 but first performed in 1961 in Stockholm, in a Swedish translation—the sentence in Eliot's draft blurb for the original edition, 'Never has so much genius been combined with so litle talent', was not appreciated by Barnes. *Spillway* (1962) is a collection of short stories extracted from *A Book* (1923; rev. edn as *A Night Among the Horses*, 1929). See *Collected Stories*, ed. Phillip Herring, 1996; Phillip Herring, *Djuna: the Life and Work of Djuna Barnes*, new edn 1997.

BARNES, JULIAN (*b.* 1946) British novelist, was born in Leicester, the younger son (his brother is a classicist and philosophy don) of two teachers of French, and was educated at City of London School and Magdalen College, Oxford, where he read modern languages. After working in Oxford dating coinages and usages for the supplement to the *Oxford English Dictionary*, he started reading for the Bar, but instead became a journalist and television critic. The French connection is apparent from his first novel, *Metroland* (1980), in which the conflicting lifestyles of two friends are analysed and found not to be quite so satisfactory/unsatisfactory as had appeared. Marital, pre-marital, and extra-marital relationships feature in *Before She Met Me* (1982) and in *Talking It Over* (1991), in which three protagonists, locked in a love triangle, offer different angles on the proceedings. His distinctive, epigrammatic approach particularly informs *Flaubert's Parrot* (1984) and *A History of the World in 10½ Chapters* (1989), zany fictional studies from respectively a literary and a biblical starting point. *The Porcupine* (1992) is a political parable in a contemporary Eastern European setting, in which an old-style Communist and a new-style democrat clash in court. *Cross Channel* (1996) is a collection of stories, in a variety of literary styles, about the British in France at different points in history. *Letters from London 1990–1995* (1995) comprises articles written as London correspondent of the *New Yorker*. He has also, as Dan Kavanagh, written thrillers about a bisexual detective. For his literary links with France (he has won both the Prix Médicis and the Prix Femina) he was made Chevalier de l'Ordre des Arts et des Lettres in 1989 and Officier in 1995.

BARNES, WILLIAM (1801–86) British poet and philologist, was born in Rushay, Dorset, the son of a tenant farmer, and was educated at Mullett's school in Sturminster until he was 14, when he became a solicitor's clerk. In 1820 he saw Julia Miles, an excise officer's daughter, alighting from a stagecoach in Dorchester. They married in 1827—see *Love Poems and Letters 1820–1827*, ed. Charlotte H. Lindgren (1986). By this time he had his own school; was having verses published in local periodicals; had learned woodengraving; and was studying French, Italian, Welsh, Russian, Hebrew, and Hindustani. His first poems in the Dorset dialect were published in the *County Chronicle* in 1833. In 1838 he registered with St John's College,

Cambridge, as a ten-year student. He was ordained in 1847 and graduated as BD in 1850. *Poems of Rural Life, in the Dorset Dialect* was published in London in 1844: 'To write in what some may deem a fast out-wearing speech-form may seem as idle as the writing of one's name in the snow of a spring day. I cannot help it. It is my mother tongue, and is to my mind the only true speech of the life that I draw'. After the death of his wife in 1852 (see the elegy 'The Wife A-Lost') and the failure of his school, he got into chronic financial difficulties, in spite of his growing reputation as a poet (*Hwomely Rhymes* was published in 1859), literary journalist, and antiquary, and as the author of a comparative philological grammar (1854). The situation was saved by the award in 1861 of a Civil List pension at the instigation of the Prime Minister, Lord Palmerston (1784–1865), and the offer of the living and rectory of Winterbourne Came. HARDY edited his *Select Poems* (1908). Barnes was a good pastoral and romantic poet in both Standard English and in Dorset dialect; his appeal is freshened by his use of dialect and enhanced by his instinct as a self-trained linguist for apposite combinations of terms, such as featured also in the work of another of his admirers, HOPKINS. See *The Poems of William Barnes*, ed. Bernard Jones, 2 vols 1962; *William Barnes: a Selection of His Poems*, ed. Robert Nye, new edn 1988; *Selected Poems*, ed. Andrew Motion, 1994; Alan Chedzoy, *William Barnes: a Life of the Dorset Poet*, 1985.

BARRETT, ELIZABETH see BROWNING, ELIZABETH BARRETT.

BARRIE, (Sir) **J(AMES) M(ATTHEW)** (1860–1937) Scottish dramatist, novelist, and journalist, was born in Kirriemuir, Angus, third son and ninth child of a handloom weaver. After the death of the second son in a skating accident in 1867, Barrie went to live with Alick, his eldest brother by 18 years, who paid for him to go to Glasgow Academy, where he was a teacher. When Alick became one of Her Majesty's inspectors of schools and moved to Dumfries, he paid for the boy to go to Dumfries Academy and then to Edinburgh University. Barrie was a leader writer on the *Nottingham Journal* from 1882 to 1884, after which he returned home to write articles for London periodicals. In 1885 he moved permanently to London, and in 1894, encouraged by Alick, embarked on a disastrous marriage with a young actress, Mary Ansell—there was a distressing divorce in 1909, after which she married her lover, the novelist and dramatist Gilbert Cannan (1884–1955). Barrie's Scottish pieces, published as *Auld Licht Idylls* (1888) and *A Window in Thrums* (1889), give him the dubious distinction of being the earliest member of the Kailyard school of novelists, who tended to present cosy as well as rosy portraits of Scottish rural life. *The Little Minister* (1891) was hugely successful as a novel and then (1897) as one of Barrie's earliest plays. He was the first major Scottish-born playwright, and *The Admirable Crichton* (1902), *Dear Brutus* (1917), and *Mary Rose* (1920) are still remembered if not often performed. There is more of Barrie—his closeness to his mother, his nostalgia for childhood, and his love for the five boys for whom he cared after the deaths of both their parents, for which see Andrew Birkin, *J. M. Barrie and the Lost Boys* (1979)—in the perennially popular children's play about the boy who never grew up, *Peter Pan* (1904), which he rewrote as a story, *Peter Pan and Wendy* (1911). (A special provision in the British Copyright Act of 1988 ensures that royalties from the play shall continue in perpetuity to go to the Great Ormond Street Hospital for Sick Children, London.) Barrie was created a baronet (1913), awarded the OM (1922), and elected Chancellor of Edinburgh University (1930). See *Peter Pan and Other Plays*, ed. Peter Hollindale, 1995; Leonée Ormond, *J. M. Barrie*, 1987 (critical study); R. D. S. Jack, *The Road to the Neverland: a Reassessment of J. M. Barrie's Dramatic Art*, 1991.

BARTH, JOHN (*b.* 1930) American novelist, was born in Cambridge, Maryland, and after graduating from high school studied briefly at the Juilliard School of Music before entering Johns Hopkins University, initially to major in journalism, 'because it sounded easy'. He graduated in creative writing in 1951, and obtained a further degree the following year on the basis of an unpublished novel, 'Shirt of Nessus'. He was appointed a professor of English at the State University of New York, Buffalo, in 1965, and in 1973 returned to Johns Hopkins as Centennial Professor of English and Creative Writing. The protagonist of *The Floating Opera* (1956; rev. edn 1967), who after a day of vacillation decides against suicide, explains the title: 'It's a floating opera, friend, chock-full of curiosities, melodrama, spectacle, instruction and entertainment, but it floats willy-nilly on the tide of my vagrant prose', which could be applied to Barth's work as a whole. The chief character in *The End of the Road* (1958; rev. edn 1967) appears at its close to be taking an opposite course, thus initiating a creative philosophy whereby Barth often refutes in the second of a pair of novels the position he has taken in the first. In his two major works, the sprawling variety of themes and tones of *The Sot-Weed Factor* (1960; rev. edn 1967) gives way to a measure of structural and mythological unity in *Giles Goat-Boy: or, The Revised New Syllabus* (1966). *Letters* (1979) and *Sabbatical: a Romance* (1982) are experiments in autobiographical fiction. *Lost in the Funhouse: Fiction for Print, Tape, Live Voice* (1968), *Chimera* (1972), and *On with the Story: Stories* (1996)

represent cunning attempts to elucidate the confusion between life and art. The Scheherazade legend which features in the latter recurs as the starting point of the frolicsome *The Last Voyage of Somebody the Sailor* (1991). The voyage in the partly factual, partly fictional *Once upon a Time: a Floating Opera* (1994) is the basic myth of quest and perilous journey, leading to an eternal return, undertaken in this instance by the author and his second wife, 'a middle-aged, uninnocent Adam and Eve'. *The Friday Book: Essays and Other Nonfiction* (1984) and *Further Fridays: Essays, Lectures, and Other Nonfiction 1984–1994* (1995) contain material on Barth's academic rationale. See Charles B. Harris, *Passionate Virtuosity: the Fiction of John Barth*, 1983; E. P. Walkiewicz, *John Barth*, 1986 (critical study); Heide Ziegler, *John Barth*, 1987 (critical study).

BARTHELME, DONALD (1931–89) American fiction writer, was born in Philadelphia, the eldest child of an architect who designed the house ('wonderful to live in but strange to see on the Texas prairie') to which the family moved in 1933. Brought up as a Roman Catholic, he went to local schools, wrote for and edited school magazines, and studied journalism at Houston University. He was drafted into the US Army in 1953, and served in Japan and Korea, after which he was a reporter on the *Houston Post*, founded the university literary journal, *Forum*, and was Director of the Houston Contemporary Arts Museum 1961–62. He then went to New York, edited the magazine *Location* from 1962 to 1964, and in 1963 published his first story, in the *New Yorker*. Of the terms characterizing current modes of American fiction, in which he is a key figure, he favoured 'post-modernism' as 'the least ugly'. In *Come Back, Dr Caligari* (1964) and *Unspeakable Practices, Unnatural Acts* (1968), his first books of short stories, he applied to social issues what have also been called techniques of 'metafiction', which, broadened into irony in *City Life* (1970) and *Sadness* (1972), and with the addition of parody, are a feature of the non-fiction pieces in *Guilty Pleasures* (1974)— see also *Sixty Stories* (1981). His novels include *Snow White* (1967), a modern version in which the heroine is never rescued by anyone, *The Dead Father* (1975), a verbal collage incorporating techniques from other creative arts, and *The King* (1990), in which he applies his principle of overlapping unrelated frames of reference to the court of King Arthur fighting World War II. See Lois Gordon, *Donald Barthelme*, 1981 (critical study); Maurice Couturier and Régis Durand, *Donald Barthelme*, 1982 (critical study).

BARTHES, ROLAND (1915–80) French critic, was born in Cherbourg a year before his father's death in a naval battle. In 1924 he went to Paris with his mother, with whom he lived until her death in 1977. His education at the Sorbonne and his subsequent academic career until 1948 were interrupted by bouts of tuberculosis. After teaching at the Institut Français in Bucharest, he was Reader at the University of Alexandria until 1950, when several of his articles on literary criticism appeared in the leftist journal, *Combat*. These became the basis of his first book, *Le Degré Zero de l'Écriture* (1953; tr. Annette Lavers and Colin Smith as *Writing Degree Zero*, 1967) in which he introduced his theory of *'écriture'* as a function of language and as the formal sign of literature. Between 1952 and 1959 he was engaged in research into lexicology and sociology at the Centre National de Recherche Scientifique. He transferred to the École Pratiques des Hautes Études in 1960, becoming Director of Studies in 1962. He published his essay on 'The Structuralist Activity' in 1963. In *S/Z* (1970; tr. Richard Miller, 1975) he postulated a change in the structuralist 'science of reading' to accommodate the effect of an immediate rereading of a text. In the articles republished as *Mythologies* (1957; ed. and tr. Lavers, 1972) he analysed contemporary images of mass culture. *Roland Barthes* (1955; tr. Richard Howard, 1977) is an autobiographical/critical study of his theories. See *A Roland Barthes Reader*, ed. Susan Sontag, new edn 1993; Louis-Jean Calvet, *Roland Barthes: a Biography*, tr. Sarah Wykes, new edn 1996.

BASHŌ (or MATSUO BASHŌ) (1644–94) Japanese poet and prose writer, was born Matsuo Munefusa in Ueno, the fourth of seven children of a minor samurai, and was called Kinsaku as a child, and then Toshichiro when he came of age. At nine he entered the service of the Todo family, as companion to the 11-year-old Yoshitada, after whose death in 1666 he ran away to Kyoto, where he studied and wrote verse. In 1672 he moved to Edo (Tokyo), near which an admirer built him an isolated house at Fukajawa in 1680. He took his ultimate pen name of Bashō from another gift, a stock of the species of banana tree which has that appellation. The house burned down in 1682, but though a new one was built for him, in 1684 he began a spectacular series of travels, about which he wrote several works of prose interspersed with verse. He died of dysentery in Osaka, having determined on this occasion to reach the southern tip of Japan. From *haikai*, the traditional sequence of linked verses, he formulated *haiku*, the three-line form of five, seven, and five syllables, complete in itself, which became the representative poetic medium of the Tokugawa (or Edo) period (1603–1868). See *The Narrow Road to the Deep North and Other Travel Sketches*, tr. Nobuyuki Yuasa, 1970; *Basho's 'Narrow Road': Spring and Autumn Passages*, tr. Hiroaki Sato, 1996; *The Narrow Road to Oku*, tr. Donald Keene, 1997 (bi-

lingual edn); *On Love and Barley: the Haiku of Bashō*, tr. Lucien Stryk, new edn 1986.

BAUDELAIRE, CHARLES(-PIERRE) (1821–67) French poet, critic, and translator, was born in Paris. He was the son by his second marriage of Joseph-François Baudelaire (1759–1827), a former priest, after whose death his 35-year-old widow married an army officer, who entered the boy as a boarder at Collège Royal, Lyons, in 1832. He went on to Collège Louis-le-Grand, Paris, from which he was expelled in 1839 for a minor misdemeanour—he obtained his degree later that year after private tuition. After a year at law school during which he attended no lectures, led a bohemian existence, and contracted both syphilis and debts, he was dispatched on a sea voyage to India. He left the ship at Réunion, returned to Paris, and after coming into his inheritance from his father, settled in a hotel on the Ile Saint-Louis. He mixed in literary circles, had liaisons with a stunning black whore and a refined, but sensually emancipated, society courtesan, both of whom were inspirations for his verse, and had his financial affairs, at his family's insistence, put in the hands of a trustee. He published reviews of the annual art exhibition in 1845 and 1846, and started several novels, of which only *La Fanfarlo* (1847) was ever finished.

At about this time he first came across the stories of POE, on the translation of whose fiction he worked for fifteen years, publishing five volumes of it (1856–65) as well as several lengthy critical essays. *Les Fleurs du Mal* (1857; tr. James McGowan, ed. Jonathan Culler, as *The Flowers of Evil*, bilingual edn 1993), an accumulation of lyric verses which are romantic in their essence, realistic in their attention to the carnal, criminal, and spiritual problems of his age, and apocalyptic in their anticipation of Symbolism, was withdrawn after a court had found six poems indecent, though he was acquitted of attacking religion. In the second edition (1861), the six were replaced by 32 new poems. During his last years (he was stricken with paresis in 1866), as well as poetry he produced both art and literary studies, and a discussion of narcotics, *Les Paradis Artificiels* (1859–60), which incorporates his translation and adaptation of DE QUINCEY's *Confessions of an English Opium Eater*. See *Complete Verse*, tr. Francis Scarfe, 2 vols 1985–87; *Selected Poems*, tr. Joanna Richardson, 1975; *Intimate Journals*, tr. Christopher Isherwood, new edn 1990; tr. Norman Cameron, new edn 1995; Claude Pichois and Jean Ziegler, *Baudelaire*, tr. Graham Robb, new edn 1991 (biography); Joanna Richardson, *Baudelaire*, 1994 (biography).

BAXTER, JAMES K(EIR) (1926–72) New Zealand poet and dramatist, was born in Dunedin, the son of a small farmer of Scottish descent who for his pacifism suffered physically in World War I and socially during World War II, and of a somewhat pushy, Cambridge-educated daughter of a university professor. He spent much of his childhood in the rural township of Brighton, where community life was minimal and culture non-existent outside the Calvinistic atmosphere of his own home—'It seems to me that the negative aspects of my growth were in the long run of most help to me as a writer.' He spent the years 1937–39 at boarding school in England and on the Continent with his parents. He began composing verse when he was seven, and at 13 was writing 'four or five' poems a week. In 1944 he enrolled at Otago University, where 'Aphrodite, Bacchus, and the Holy Spirit were my tutors, but the goddess of good manners and examination passes withheld her smile from me.' After having had a book of verse accepted for publication, *Beyond the Palisade* (1945, dated 1944), he dropped out, and 'after much apparently useless experience in various factories, farms, dens, bedrooms, pubs and hovels', went to Christchurch, where he underwent Jungian therapy, edited a literary page for *Canta*, and associated with CURNOW and GLOVER. In 1948 he married J(acquie) C. Sturm (*b.* 1927), who during the ensuing chaos of his life brought up their two children, achieved a first-class degree in philosophy, and made a reputation for herself as a short-story writer. He graduated from Victoria University in 1955, having also trained as a teacher and earned some money by working in an abattoir and subsequently as a postman, losing that job for 'being asleep dead-drunk with my head on a full satchel of letters'. He joined Alcoholics Anonymous in 1954. In 1958 *In Fires of No Return: Selected Poems* was published by Oxford University Press in London and New York and brought him international recognition; his first play, *Jack Winter's Dream*, was nationally broadcast; he became a Roman Catholic; and he undertook a Unesco mission to Japan and India to study school publications, an experience which also brought him face to face with poverty.

During much of the 1960s he wrote prolifically—prose plays including *The Band Rotunda* (produced 1967) and two with themes from Greek mythology, *The Sore-Footed Man* (1967) and *The Temptations of Oedipus* (1970), as well as poetry. He was Robert Burns Fellow at Otago University in 1966 and 1977: 'A Varsity person, with an office / Just round the corner—what nonsense! / If there is any culture here / It comes from the black south wind . . .'. In a dream in 1968 he had a call, 'Go to Jerusalem!' (a Maori settlement and mission station on the Wanganui River). With only a change of clothes and a Maori Bible, he set out alone. He arrived in Jerusalem in September 1969, having en route worked in

Auckland among junkies, drop-outs, and the homeless, such as now flocked to him. A further commune, in Wellington, lasted for only a few weeks in 1971. In an interview in 1972 he said: 'I do not favour chemical solutions for spiritual and psychological problems. . . . But I do recognize that smashed myths have somehow to be replaced or reconstructed. That is why I have become a Christian guru, a barefooted and bearded eccentric, a bad smell in the noses of many good citizens.' *Jerusalem Sonnets* (1970), a series of poems of seven unrhymed couplets, and *Jerusalem Daybook* (1971) record his way of life there. So does the posthumously-published *Autumn Testament* (1972), which, as well as the title-sequence, includes 'He Waiata mo Te Kare', affectionately addressed to his long-suffering wife.

In addition to his considerable corpus of poetry, and his plays, he wrote several notable critical works, including *Aspects of Poetry in New Zealand* (1967) and *The Man on the Horse* (1967), a collection of lectures—see also *James K. Baxter as Critic: a Selection from His Literary Criticism*, ed. Frank McKay (1978). See *The Essential Baxter*, ed. John Weir, 1994; *Collected Poems*, ed. John Weir, new edn 1996; *Selected Poems*, ed. John Weir, 1983; *Collected Plays*, ed. Howard McNaughton, 1983; Frank McKay, *The Life of James K. Baxter*, new edn 1993; Charles Doyle, *James K. Baxter*, 1976 (critical study).

BAYNTON, BARBARA (1862–1929) Australian short-story writer, was, according to her grandson, born in Scone, the Castlereagh region of New South Wales, the youngest child of Captain Robert Kilpatrick, lately Bengal Light Cavalry, and Penelope Ewart, whom he seduced from her husband on board ship on the way to Australia—they married in 1859, after Ewart's death. Self-educated, she read the Bible and her father's books, mainly DICKENS, POE, and the Russian novelists. In 1880 she married a local grazier, Robert Frater; he eloped in 1887 with one of her own cousins, who was staying in the house. She moved to Sydney with her three children, and in 1890, the day after her divorce came through, married Dr Thomas Baynton, a leisured gentleman with a circle of literary acquaintances. To make a name for herself, she began to write, and a story, 'The Tramp', was printed in the *Bulletin* in 1896. After Baynton died in 1900, leaving her a wealthy woman, she went to England, where 'The Tramp' (retitled 'The Chosen Vessel') was published with five other uncompromising stories of outback life in *Bush Studies* (1902)—later reissued, with two additional stories, as *Cobbers* (1917). She filled a succession of fine houses with antiques, and on visits to Australia bought black opals. During World War I her home in Great Cumberland Place, London, was open house for Australian servicemen. In 1921, liking the idea of a title, she married the colourful 5th Lord Headley (1855–1935), who to her disappointment turned down the offer of the throne of Albania. They parted after a few years. Latterly she lived in a house she built in Toorak, Melbourne. Her economic prose style and grim realism, with studied flashes of humour, give a distinction to her stories which is not matched in her bush novel, Human Toll (1907).

BEAUCHAMP, KATHLEEN MANSFIELD see MANSFIELD.

BEAUMARCHAIS, (CARON, PIERRE AUGUSTIN) DE (1732–99) French dramatist, was born in Paris, the son of a watchmaker called Caron, whose trade he followed with some skill, being recognized by the Academy of Sciences and at the court of Louis XV, to whose daughters he taught the harp. He took his title in 1756, from the estate of his first wife, a wealthy court widow who died the following year. Speculation and a further prudent marriage paid handsome dividends. In a series of satirical Mémoires (1774–78), which represented him as a champion of the rights of the people, he turned the tables on those who in the course of a lawsuit (which he lost) accused him of corruption. He ran arms to the American insurgents during the War of Independence in 1775, but had to take refuge in London and Holland from 1792 to 1796 after being accused of doing the same for the émigrés of the French Revolution, during which he lost his fortune. Recent research has revealed his part in the publication of the 172 volumes of the Kehl edition of the works of VOLTAIRE (1785–89), and his association from 1776 to 1788 with Courier de l'Europe, a journal reporting British affairs (including parliamentary debates), printed in London until the Government banned its export, and then in Boulogne from copy smuggled across the Channel. He had several farces produced during the 1760s, but nothing then or later compared with the success of his two comedies of intrigue and social comment, Le Barbier de Séville: ou, La Précaution Inutile (1775; tr. as The Barber of Seville, 1776) and La Folle Journée: ou, Le Mariage de Figaro (1783; tr. as The Follies of a Day: or, The Marriage of Figaro, 1785), which became the basis respectively of the operas by Gioacchino Antonio Rossini (1792–1868) and Wolfgang Amadeus Mozart (1756–91). See The Figaro Plays, tr. Graham Anderson, 1994.

BEAUMONT, FRANCIS (1584–1616) English dramatist, was born at Grace Dieu, Leicestershire, the son of a judge, on whose death in 1598 he and his two elder brothers had to leave Oxford without finishing their degree courses. He enrolled as a law student in London, was accepted by JONSON and his circle, and met JOHN FLETCHER, with whom he struck up such a rapport that they shared the same lodgings and, according to AUBREY, 'one wench between them'. The only play generally regarded to be by Beaumont alone is The Knight of the Burning Pestle (c.1608), a boisterous burlesque in which a grocer and his wife take their apprentice to the theatre and get hilariously involved in the plot and in the action of the play on the stage. Between 1607 and 1613, when Beaumont married a Kentish heiress, he and Fletcher collaborated on some ten plays, usually marked by complex plots and surprising revelations. They knew their market and the poetry in their plays suffers only in comparison with that of their more famous contemporaries. Phylaster (c.1609) is a tragicomedy of frustrated love. In The Maides Tragedy (c.1611) Amintor is forced by his king to break off his engagement and marry Evadne, who reveals on their wedding night that she is the royal mistress. The destinies of the main characters are resolved by violent deaths, but the play is notable for its initial situation and for the conflicts of loyalty which it depicts. See W. W. Appleton, Beaumont and Fletcher: a Critical Study, 1956.

BEAUMONT, GUSTAVE DE see TOCQUEVILLE.

BEAUVOIR, SIMONE DE (1908–86) French novelist and critic, was born in Paris; her mother was a devout Catholic and her father a sceptic. She was educated at the Institut Saintes-Marie, Neuilly, and the École Normale Supérieure, where she graduated in philosophy in 1929 at the same time as SARTRE. With him she 'signed a two-year lease', which lasted until his death in 1980 and developed into a relationship of unimaginable complexity and bisexual ramifications—see, for example, Bianca Lamblin, A Disgraceful Affair: Simone de Beauvoir, Jean-Paul Sartre, and Bianca Lamblin, tr. Julie Plovnik (1996)—, in the course of which she abandoned her job as a lycée philosophy teacher in 1943 after being formally accused of corrupting a minor—see Letters to Sartre, ed. and tr. Quentin Hoare (1991) and Witness to My Life: the Letters of Jean-Paul Sartre to Simone de Beauvoir, ed. de Beauvoir, tr. Lee Fahnestock and Norman McAfee (1992). On her first visit to the USA in 1947 she encountered ALGREN, her 'only true passionate love'. Her private life belied the militant feminist stance she took in public, the nature of which she expounded in Le Deuxième Sexe: les Faits et les Mythes and L'Expérience Vécue (2 vols 1949; tr. H. M. Parshley as The Second Sex, 1953), a seminal text; DRABBLE has described the effect of reading it at 20 as 'both already familiar and deeply shocking. . . . It was the unknown known.' Her fourth novel, Les Mandarins (1954; tr. Leonard M. Friedman as The Mandarins, 1956),

which won the Prix GONCOURT, accurately reflects the situation, and society, in Paris in 1944–47. An intellectual whose career was her writing, and whose conviction was the primacy of personal decisions, she poured much of her artistic endeavour into five volumes of autobiography, from *Mémoires d'une Jeune Fille Rangée* (1958; tr. James Kirkup as *Memoirs of a Dutiful Daughter*, 1959) to *Toute Compte Fait* (1972; tr. Patrick O'Brian as *All Said and Done*, 1974). See Deirdre Bair, *Simone de Beauvoir: a Biography*, new edn 1991; Mary Evans, *Simone de Beauvoir*, 1996 (critical study).

BECKETT, SAMUEL (1906–89) Irish dramatist, novelist, translator, and critic, was born in Foxrock, near Dublin, the son of a quantity surveyor, and was educated at Portora Royal School, Co. Fermanagh, and Trinity College, Dublin, where he got a first in French and Italian literature and excelled at sport. After teaching in Belfast and Paris, and at Trinity College, Dublin, he settled in Paris, where he had previously met and become closely associated with JOYCE. In the 1930s he published two volumes of verse, *Whoroscope* (1930) and *Echo's Bones and Other Precipitations* (1935); a collection of short stories, *More Pricks Than Kicks* (1934); a critical study of PROUST (1931); and a novel, *Murphy* (1938). In 1936–37 he spent several months in Germany, where he was made aware of the dangers of Nazism. Early in 1938 he was stabbed in a Paris street after going to the cinema with friends. He was visited in hospital by a former tennis partner, Suzanne Deschevaux-Dumesnil, who shared the rest of his life—they married in 1961. At the outbreak of World War II he returned to Paris from Ireland and joined the Resistance. When his intelligence-gathering cell was betrayed, he and Suzanne escaped to Provence. There he worked as a labourer, wrote a second novel, *Watt* (not published until 1953), and rejoined the Resistance—he was awarded the Croix de Guerre in 1945.

In Paris after the war, between 1945 and 1950 he wrote (all in French) three novels—*Molloy* (English translation by himself, 1955), *Malone Meurt* (*Malone Dies*, 1956), *L'Innomable* (*The Unnamable*, 1959)—and the play *En Attendant Godot*, which was performed in Paris in 1953 and made his reputation. In his own translation as *Waiting For Godot*, it was staged in New York in 1954 and London in 1955, and published in the UK in 1956. Between 1956 and 1961, after a fallow period following the death of his mother, he wrote in English *All That Fall: a Play for Radio* (1957); *Embers* (a piece for radio) and the one-act play *Krapp's Last Tape*—published together as *Krapp's Last Tape and Embers* (1959); and the two-act stage play *Happy Days* (1962). His other most significant drama in English is *Not I* (1973), first performed in New York in 1972. He was awarded the Nobel Prize for Literature in 1969.

Even if one includes *Waiting for Godot* and the one-act play *Endgame* (translated by himself from *Fin de Partie* and first published in the UK in 1958), Beckett's total contribution to literature in English comprises two slim volumes of verse, a book of short stories, five novels (of which three were originally written in French), a handful of short plays, and some even briefer pieces; and the concessions that he made to his readers tended to decrease in inverse proportion to the growth of his reputation. (*A Dream of Fair to Middling Women*, written when he was just 27, has autobiographical elements and marks the original appearance of Belacqua Shuah; it was first published posthumously, ed. Eoin O'Brien and Edith Fournier, in 1992.) His poetry has an innocence underlying the bitterness, and an Anglo-Irish linguistic ring. Belacqua (the name is that of a Florentine musical instrument maker and friend of DANTE, who uses him in *Divina Commedia* as a symbol of indolence) appears in all the tales in *More Pricks Than Kicks*, among which 'Dante and the Lobsters' stands out not only as a remarkable story in its own right, with an unforgettable and thought-provoking ending, but as descriptive prose at its tautest and most expressive. All these stories are set in Dublin. The protagonist of *Murphy* lives, and in the oddest way imaginable dies, in London, having just found the mental contentment towards which he has been blundering. With *Watt*, Beckett returns to Ireland. Watt himself is the archetypal fall guy, whose route to mental salvation ends in a lunatic asylum, not as a nurse, as Murphy is briefly, but as an inmate. The experimental style had now become mannered and, as though he had reached his particular philosophical periphery in narrative prose, Beckett now turned to French as his medium for the novel, and to drama, whose intellectual limits he redefined even more profoundly than JOHN OSBORNE was to change the direction of its subject matter.

Beckett's relentless theme is depression, often verging on despair. With *Waiting for Godot*, he proved that it was possible dramatically to project the desolation and meaningless protraction of existence through characters who represent just these states in their actions and dialogue. In *Endgame* and *Not I*, he abandoned movement and other normal stage conventions even more radically. In *Happy Days*, his only moderately optimistic piece, the main character is immobilized up to the waist in sand in the first act and to the neck in the second: her husband, the only other character, is hardly seen. Though the theatrical presentation of *Krapp's Last Tape* is enhanced by visual devices built into the script, Beckett's economy and manipulation of timing as well as of language make the piece just as effective on radio. See *The Complete Dramatic Works*, new edn 1990; *The Beckett Trilogy*, new edn 1994; *Collected Shorter Prose 1945–1988*, enlarged edn 1996; *As the Story Was Told: Uncollected and Late Prose*, 1990; *Collected Poems 1930–1989*, new edn 1997; Deirdre Bair, *Samuel Beckett: a Biography*, new edn 1991; James Knowlson, *Damned to Fame: the Life of Samuel Beckett*, 1996; Lois Gordon, *The World of Samuel Beckett 1906–1946*, 1996 (biography); Anthony Cronin, *Samuel Beckett: the Last Modernist*, 1996 (critical biography); A. Alvarez, *Beckett*, 2nd rev. edn 1992 (critical study); John Calder, *The Philosophy of Samuel Beckett*, 1996; Hugh Kenner, *Reader's Guide to Samuel Beckett*, 1996; John Pilling (ed.), *The Cambridge Companion to Beckett*, 1994.

BECKFORD, WILLIAM (1759–1844) British novelist and prose writer, was born at the family seat of Fonthill Abbey, Wiltshire, the son of a wealthy alderman of the City of London, and educated by a private tutor, Rev. Dr Lettice. At 21, he inherited the family fortune (amassed largely from Jamaican plantations) of £1m, plus £100,000 a year. At 22, in one sitting of three days and two nights, he drafted in French *Vathek, an Arabian Tale*. A pirated translation of the finished work was published in 1786, and an authorized English edition (tr. Samuel Henley) and the original French version in 1787. Though frequently abroad and from 1796 a virtual recluse, Beckford was elected to Parliament, for various constituencies, for the years 1784–94 and 1806–20. He had Fonthill rebuilt by James Wyatt (1746–1813) in 1796 as a half-ruined Gothic monstrosity, with a 275-foot tower which collapsed shortly afterwards and was as promptly replaced. Here he devoted himself to scandalous pursuits and the collection of books and objets d'art. In 1822, his fortune now reduced to a mere £80,000, he sold out and retired to Bath. *Vathek* is a fantasy-adventure, written with enormous gusto, of a sadistic caliph who sells himself to Eblis, the Devil, in whose underground halls, lit with flaming pyramids, Vathek's heart and those of the newly damned finally burst into eternal fire. Beckford also wrote the satirical *Biographical Memoirs of Extraordinary Painters* (1780) and some witty and perceptive accounts of his travels. See *Vathek and Other Stories*, ed. Malcolm Jack, 1995.

BEDDOES, THOMAS LOVELL (1803–49) British poet and dramatist, was born in Clifton, the son of the physician and physicist Dr Thomas Beddoes (1760–1808) and Anna Maria (*d.* 1824), the youngest sister of EDGEWORTH, and was educated at Charterhouse and Pembroke College, Oxford. An undergraduate of eccentric temperament, he published two works while he was up, *The Improvisatore* (1821), three Gothic tales in verse

which he later tried to suppress, and *The Bride's Tragedy* (1822), a verse drama of some merit much in the vein of WEBSTER. The latter met with little critical response, and after taking his degree he went to Gottingen and Wurtzburg to study, qualifying as MD in 1831, having made a name and an unfortunate reputation for himself as a political agitator. He spent the rest of his life mainly in Germany and Switzerland, pursuing his medical career, studying German literature (and writing prose and verse in German), and producing two dramatic fragments, 'Torrismond' and 'The Second Brother'. He was also forever revising *Death's Jest Book* (1850), a revenge drama in a mixture of verse and prose, with Jacobean, Gothic, and German Romantic elements, which he had begun in 1825. This extraordinary, unfinished work may be presumed to be the ultimate manifestation of his philosophical and anatomical preoccupation with death, which is hardly absent even from his short poems and lyrics, a handful of which are still sometimes praised. His death was self-inflicted and appropriately morbid. Beddoes's papers were left by his executor to BROWNING, after whose death, and his son's death, the box containing them was lost. Authentic copies, however, materialized in the 1930s. See *Plays and Poems*, ed. H. W. Donner, 1950; *Selected Poems*, 1980.

BEDE (or **BÆDA**), known as 'Venerable' (*c.*673–735) prose writer, historian, and cleric, was probably born in Northumbria within the lands granted to Benedict Biscop (628–90) in which to found a monastery at Wearmouth. At the age of seven, he was put into the care of Benedict, and in 682 was transferred to the new sister institution at Barrow, under Abbot Ceolfrid (642–716). He was made a deacon at 19, six years earlier than the usual age, and a priest 11 years later. By his own account, his main task for the rest of his life was to compose commentaries on the scriptures for the benefit of his fellow monks, but he was also able to write (in Latin) scientific treatises on natural history and chronology, critical and grammatical studies, and biographies of the three abbots of the monastery, as well as the work for which he is justly regarded as the 'Father of English History'. His last days are graphically and movingly described in a letter to a friend from Cuthbert, one of Bede's pupils who was later Abbot of Wearmouth and Jarrow. The five books of *Historia Ecclesiastica Gentis Anglorum* [The Church History of the English People] cover the period of massive change between the arrival of CAESAR in 55 BC to AD 731 in his own time, written with a scholar's eye for colourful detail and an experienced expositor's attention to the broader sweeps of his subject. See *A History of the English Church and People* tr. and with an introduction by Leo Sherley-

Price, new edn revised by R. E. Latham, 1968; Benedicta Ward SLG, *The Venerable Bede*, 1990 (study of his Christian thought and writings).

BEERBOHM, (Sir) **MAX** (1872–1956) British essayist, critic, broadcaster, parodist, and caricaturist, was born in London and educated at Charterhouse and Merton College, Oxford, without taking a degree. Dubbed by G. B. SHAW in 1898 'the incomparable Max', he lived outwardly as a leisurely dandy, while at the same time doing many things very well. It was a sign of his impish and paradoxical nature to call his first book *The Works of Max Beerbohm* (1896), and his next two volumes of essays *More* (1899) and *Yet Again* (1909). In 1898 he succeeded Shaw as Dramatic Critic of the *Saturday Review*, a post he held until 1910. Then, having married the actress Florence Kahn (*d.* 1951), he retired to Rapallo, Italy, where except for the two world wars he remained for the rest of his life. His only novel, *Zuleika Dobson: or, an Oxford Love Story* (1911), describes delicately but uproariously the effect on undergraduate passions of the beautiful and predatory niece of the head of an Oxford college. *A Christmas Garland* (1912) is a collection of devastating parodies of notable authors of the time (including HENRY JAMES, KIPLING, HARDY, and CONRAD) on the theme of Christmas, which are as incisively observed and executed as his pictorial caricatures of the famous, including members of the Royal Family—a new edn (1993) is illustrated with related Beerbohm caricatures and has an extensive introduction by N. John Hall. *Seven Men* (1919), later published as *Seven Men, and Two Others* (1950)—actually only eight—is a volume of short stories, among them ' "Savonarola" Brown', which incorporates a memorable skit on Elizabethan drama, with a few sly digs at ROBERT BROWNING. See also *Collected Verse*, ed. J. G. Riewald, 1994. He was knighted in 1939. See David Cecil, *Max*, new edn 1983 (biography); Lawrence Danson, *Max Beerbohm and the Act of Writing*, new edn 1991 (critical study).

BEHAN, BRENDAN (1923–64) Irish dramatist and novelist, was born in Dublin while his father (a house painter) was in prison for Republican activities. He was educated at the French Sisters of Charity School. He joined the junior branch of the IRA when he was 14, and wrote prose and verse for its journal. In 1939, anxious for a piece of action, he crossed to Liverpool, where he was arrested, convicted of possessing dynamite, and committed to Borstal for two years. In 1942 he was sentenced to 14 years for firearms offences, but was released in 1946. O'FAOLAIN published his article, 'I Became a Borstal Boy', in *The Bell* in 1942. In between further spells in prison Behan wrote some lyrics in Irish, several short stories, and a crime novel which was serialized in the *Irish Times* in 1953 and

published as *The Scarperer* (1966). *The Quare Fellow*, published in 1956, the year of its production in London, revolves around the execution of a condemned prisoner, who is never seen, the process being realized through the dialogue and responses of others who are affected, from the Governor, warders, and hangman, to the man's fellow convicts. In *The Hostage* (1958) Behan explores, with a mixture of violent language, high drama, and tenderness, the predicament of a British solider captured by the IRA. *Borstal Boy* (1958) is one of the most unusual and readable of literary autobiographies. Behan's outward persona tended to obscure his original talent, which his expansive way of life had frustrated even before it killed him. In 1955, after a brief courtship conducted mainly in pubs, he married an artist, Beatrice ffrench-Salkeld (1931–93), who displayed the same dignity in widowhood as she had during their stormy marriage, and wrote *My Life with Brendan Behan* (1973). See *The Complete Plays of Brendan Behan*, ed. Alan Simpson, 1978; Ulick O'Connor, *Brendan Behan*, new edn 1993 (biography); Colbert Kearney, *The Writings of Brendan Behan*, 1977.

BEHN, MRS APHRA (or **AYFARA**) (1640–89), née Johnson, English dramatist and novelist, was born in Wye, Kent. Her early life is an enigma. She may have visited Surinam with a member of her family or with a lover. If so, she then married a Dutchman who died soon afterwards. She was certainly employed as a spy by the English government in 1666 to obtain information from a former lover about English dissidents in Holland, but was left high and dry, and penniless, by her employers. Consequently, in about 1670 she needed to earn a living: in doing so she became the first English professional woman writer. Her comedies tend to be derivative and faintly indecent. *The Rover* (1677), an anonymous picaresque play about the amorous adventures in Europe of a band of Cavaliers, was her first major success; she wrote a second part in 1681 under her own name. *The City Heiress* (1682) is more typical of Restoration drama, and has a political message—the Commonwealth sympathizer is bested by his Tory nephew. She also wrote fiction, of which *Oroonoko: or the Royal Slave* (1688) is regarded as the first English philosophical novel, in that within an adventure story of love and treachery is an expression of what nobleness and honour mean to those in whom the society of the time allowed there to be none, and an indictment of the people who ran, or merely tolerated, the slave trade. See *The Rover and Other Plays*, ed. Jane Spencer, new edn 1995; *Oroonoko and Other Writings*, ed. Paul Salzman, 1994; *Oroonoko, The Rover and Other Works*, ed. Janet Todd, 1992; *The Poems: a Selection*, ed. Janet Todd, 1994; Maureen Duffy, *The Passionate Shepherdess:*

Aphra Behn 1640–1689, new edn 1989 (biography); Janet Todd, *The Secret Life of Aphra Behn*, 1996 (biography); Susan Wiseman, *Aphra Behn*, 1996 (critical introduction).

BEITH, JOHN HAY see HAY, IAN.

BEKERDEREMO, J. P. CLARK see CLARK.

BELL, ACTON see BRONTË, ANNE.

BELL, CURRER see BRONTË, CHARLOTTE.

BELL, ELLIS see BRONTË, EMILY.

BELLAMY, EDWARD (1850–98) American novelist and political philosopher, was born in Chicopee Falls, Massachusetts, the third of four sons in an ancient New England family of ministers, and had his statutory 'emotional experience of a religious conversion' when he was 14. Having failed his fitness test for West Point, he studied for a year at Union College, Schenectady, New York, and then in Germany, after which he read for the Massachusetts Bar examinations, passing with such distinction that he was offered a partnership by a Westfield lawyer. He preferred to open his own office in his home town, but closed it in disgust after his first case, which involved evicting a widow for arrears of rent. He became a journalist, and also published *Six to One: a Nantucket Idyl* (1878), and *Dr Heidenhoff's Process* (1880), one of the earliest American psychological novels. In 1880 he founded, with his younger brother Charles, the triweekly Springfield *Penny News*, whose success encouraged them to transform it into the *Daily News*. Hitherto a confirmed bachelor, in 1882 he married Emma Sanderson, ten years his junior and his father's adopted daughter; his deep friendship towards her had become 'an absurd passion' when she got engaged to someone else. Marriage convinced him of the need to campaign for a better world in which their two children might live, and in 1884 Charles persuaded him to retire from their now troubled newspaper to write 'fresh essays in romance'. After another psychological study, *Miss Ludington's Sister: a Romance of Immortality* (1884), he redeployed in *Looking Backward: 2000–1887* (1887; rev. edn 1888) the dream-visitation technique of some of his short stories. The narrator wakes from a hypnotic trance in the year 2000, and learns of the new socialist order which has resolved many of the political and economic problems of his own time. Its success all over the world was dramatic, and in 1889 the Boston Bellamy Club, the first of many such societies, was inaugurated. Bellamy secured the subscription list of its short-lived journal, the *Nationalist*, for his own *New Nation*, which first appeared in January 1891. Through this he promoted the principles of Nationalism, advocating nationalization. In *Equality* (1897), a second Utopian novel, he answered critics of the first and enlarged upon and clarified some of the ideas it propounded. He was now suffering from tuberculosis, of which he died. See Sylvia E. Bowman, *Edward Bellamy*, 1986 (critical study).

BELLOC, (JOSEPH) HILAIRE (1870–1953) British poet, novelist, travel writer, and journalist, was born in St Cloud, France, of Anglo-French Catholic parentage, and was educated at the Oratory School, Birmingham. He did military service in the French army before being helped by his sister, the mystery story writer and dramatist Mrs (Marie) Belloc Lowndes (1868–1947), to go to Balliol College, Oxford. He was a Liberal Member of Parliament 1906–10, but did not seek re-election after making an anti-Semitic remark in the House. He was Literary Editor of the *Morning Post* 1906–10, and founded the journal *Eye-Witness* in 1911. He was a prolific writer: he had to be, for his wife died in 1914 leaving him with five children to support. His more lasting works include his cautionary tales for children (e.g. 'The chief defect of Henry King / Was chewing little bits of string . . .'); some lyrics, among them 'Tarantella' ('Do you remember an inn, Miranda? . . .'), 'Ha'nacker Mill', and 'The South Country'; numerous epigrams (including 'When I am dead, I hope it may be said / His sins were scarlet and his books were read.'); *The Path to Rome* (1902), a personal account of a journey on foot; biographies of Wolsey (1930), Napoleon (1932), Cromwell (1934), and Louis XIV (1938); *The Servile State* (1912), an attack on both socialism and capitalist industrial society; and some light novels, of which *Belinda* (1928) was the most notable in his time. See *Complete Verse*, new edn 1991; A. N. Wilson, *Hilaire Belloc*, new edn 1986 (biography).

BELLOW, SAUL (*b*. 1915) American novelist, was born in Canada in the Lachine Jewish ghetto in Montreal, the fourth child of Russian Jews who had emigrated from St Petersburg two years before. Here he learned English, French, Hebrew, and Yiddish, and had a near-fatal bout of pneumonia, before the family moved to Chicago. He went from Tuley High School to Chicago University, where he was 'a contrary undergraduate' and after two years transferred to Northwestern University, Illinois, where he read sociology and anthropology. In 1937 he enrolled at the University of Wisconsin on a graduate scholarship, but dropped out ('In my innocence, I had decided to become a writer') and returned to Chicago, where he married a social worker. Over the next ten years, during which he published two sombre novels, *Dangling Man* (1944) and *The Victim* (1947), he worked as a tutor at the Pestalozzi-Froebel Teachers' College, and with the 'Great Books' editorial team of *Encyclopaedia Britannica*, and served in the US Merchant Marine. In 1948, having now taught English for two years at the University of Minnesota, he gained a Guggenheim Fellowship, on which he lived in Paris, saw Europe, and began his third novel. He had already, as MALCOLM BRADBURY notes in *The Modern American Novel* (1983), displayed 'a sceptical view both of realism and modernism that would prove characteristic of a number of his contemporaries': he now 'moved towards an exuberant comedy—a mode which would reach from the comedy of suffering to the ideal of aspiration towards human grandeur'. Or as Bellow himself put it in an interview: 'Obliged to choose between complaint and comedy, I chose comedy, as more energetic, wiser, and manlier.'

The Adventures of Augie March (1953) is an extravagant, picaresque novel which follows its narrator from his origins in a Chicago slum through all parts of America to Africa and Europe, with his goal of discovering his *raison d'être* always beyond his grasp. The protagonist of the title novella of *Seize the Day, with Three Short Stories and a One-Act Play* [*The Wrecker*] (1956), the culmination of which is a single moment of truth, is comic also in the oddity of his being an abject Jewish failure, whose catalogue of disastrous decisions has just been increased. The seeker after a purpose in *Henderson the Rain King* (1959) is a disillusioned millionaire whose wanderlust takes him to a metaphorical Africa, where he finds a use for his innocence but learns that the ways to nobility are fraught with violence. The suffering of the Jewish scholar in *Herzog* (1964), written shortly after and reflecting the circumstances of the break-up of his second marriage, is in the mind, detailed in a voluminous series of letters addressed to the living and the dead, but never sent. The survivor in *Mr Sammler's Planet* (1970) is an elderly Jew who has escaped death in the Holocaust only to experience a form of living death in New York's West Side, whose society he cannot fathom. Death is a theme, too, of *Humboldt's Gift* (1975), in which the legacies of a flamboyant but failed poet ultimately offer a salvation to an overwrought intellectual. In *The Dean's December* (1982) preoccupations in Chicago and Bucharest cause an academic to accept final defeat in his search for a key to social disorder. *Him with His Foot in His Mouth and Other Stories* (1984) returns to the ambience of the Jewish family, such as he immortalized in *The Adventures of Augie March*. The two chief characters in *More Die of Heartbreak* (1987) are each searching for the revelation which will illuminate dilemmas faced at a turning point in life. *A Theft* (1989) and *The Bellarosa Connection* (1989) are novellas in which the powers respectively of faith and

memory have a restorative effect. They were reissued in *Something to Remember Me By* (1992), whose title story is a witty but profound statement about relations with parents, prefaced with a foreword in which Bellow defends his new-found Chekhovian brevity. *The Actual* (1997) is about a high-school love that survives everything. *It All Adds Up: From the Dim Past to the Uncertain Future* (1994) is a collection of wide-ranging essays and reminiscences, including his Nobel lecture.

To Jerusalem and Back: a Personal Account (1975) is a reflective record of a trip to Israel in 1967 to report on the Ten Days' War. Bellow's plays, of which the only full-length one is *The Last Analysis* (1965), a comedy of self-psychoanalysis with farcical elements, have attracted little public response. In 1962 he was appointed to the Committee on Social Thought at Chicago University, and he was Chairman from 1970 to 1976. He was awarded the Nobel Prize for Literature in 1976, 'for the human understanding and subtle analysis of contemporary culture that are combined in his work'. In his Romanes Lecture at Oxford in 1990, he pleaded for an 'aesthetic bliss' through which one may understand 'essences permanently associated with human life', and which may be communicated by the novelist who has a distinctive and individual voice. In 1994, aged 79, he was rushed from the Caribbean into intensive care in Boston, suffering from a further attack of pneumonia and a rare form of poisoning, which he survived thanks also to attentions of his fifth wife, Janis (*b.* 1958), an academic and former student of his. See Peter Hyland, *Saul Bellow*, 1992 (biographical/critical study); Robert B. Dutton, *Saul Bellow*, rev. edn 1982 (critical study); Malcolm Bradbury, *Saul Bellow*, 1982 (critical study); and in George Plimpton (ed.), *Writers at Work: Third Series*, new edn 1977.

BELY, ANDREI, pseudonym of Boris Nikolaevich Bugaev (1880–1934) Russian poet, novelist, and critic, was born in Moscow, the son of a teacher of mathematics, and studied science and philology at Moscow University. Under the influence of the philosopher Vladimir Soloviev (1853–1900), he came to regard himself as a philosopher whose search for the ultimate fusion of art with music and religion led him to proclaim symbolism as a way not only of life but also of foreseeing the future; as he claimed to have done in his novels [*The Silver Dove*] (1909) and [*Petersburg*] (1913–14; definitive version 1922; tr. Robert A. Maguire and John E. Malmstad, 1978). In 1912 he met Rudolf Steiner (1861–1925), founder of the spiritual science of anthroposophy, with whom he travelled in Europe and whose principles he propounded in Russia after the Revolution of 1917. Three times married, and at one time the well-publicized lover of BLOK's wife, he became as disappointed in the direction of the new Russia as the new Russia was in the complexity of his works. After an equally disheartening stay in Berlin from 1921 to 1923, he returned to Moscow, was reconciled to the regime, and became a Marxist. The volume of verse he published in 1921 has been translated by Gerald Janáček as *The First Encounter* (1979); see also *Complete Short Stories*, ed. Ronald Peterson (1979). See Roger Keys, *The Reluctant Modernist: Andrei Belyi and the Development of Russian Fiction 1902–1914*, 1996.

BENNETT, (ENOCH) ARNOLD (1867–1931) British novelist, short-story writer, dramatist, and journalist, was born in Hanley, Staffordshire, one of the five towns of the 'Potteries', the setting of many of his novels and stories. He was educated locally and given a sound background in the arts at home. In 1893 he gave up his solicitor's training in London to be Assistant Editor of the weekly journal, *Woman*, becoming Editor in 1896. His first novel, *A Man from the North*, was read in manuscript by BUCHAN, on whose advice it was published in 1898, followed by *Anna of the Five Towns* (1902). He then spent ten years in Paris, where he got the inspiration for *The Old Wives' Tale* (1908), an intricate saga of two sisters from the Potteries whose inclinations take them in separate directions, but who live out their final years together. *Clayhanger* (1910) has the same regional and social background, but its quality is not matched in its sequels, *Hilda Lessways* (1911) and *These Twain* (1915 in USA, 1916 in Britain). During World War I, Bennett gave valuable service to the Ministry of Information. The postwar years, during which he lived in London in some style, were ones of increased activity but waning creativity, though the grim story of a London bookseller, *Riceyman Steps* (1923), won him his first literary award. He was a tireless patron of the arts, and introduced many people to new and often unknown writers through his reviews in the London *Evening Standard*. His lasting contribution, however, is as a regional novelist who reflected magnetically and in meticulous detail a whole way of life. His own doings are similarly recorded in *Journals*, of which that for 1929 was published in 1930, and those from 1896 to 1928 in three volumes, ed. Newman Flower (1932–33); the whole in one volume, ed. Frank Swinnerton (1954). See Margaret Drabble, *Arnold Bennett*, new edn 1985 (biography).

BENNETT, LOUISE (*b.* 1919) Jamaican dialect poet, was born in Kingston and educated at Excelsior High School. She performed her own poems in Creole when she was in her teens, having as a schoolgirl begun 'to wonder why none of our poets and writers were not taking more of an interest in the kind of language usage and the kind of experience of living which were all around us'. She went to London in 1945 on a British Council scholarship to study at the Royal Academy of Dramatic Art, after which she worked with provincial repertory companies and in intimate revue. She returned to Jamaica in 1955 to teach drama to adult and youth groups, and was a lecturer in drama and Jamaican folklore, University of the West Indies Extra Mural Department 1959–61. Far more than a mere entertainer, she has resuscitated the oral tradition and has developed the language of Jamaica into a valid medium of literature and a vehicle for social satire as well as social revelation: 'Miss Jane jus hear from 'Merica, / Her daughta proudly write / Fe sey she fail her exam, but / She passin' dere fe wite!' She has been made MBE. See *Jamaica Labrish*, introduction and notes by Rex Nettleford, 1966; *Selected Poems*, ed. Mervyn Morris, 1982.

BENSON, E(DWARD) F(REDERIC) (1867–1940) British novelist and prose writer, was born at Wellington College, Berkshire, of which his father, Edward White Benson (1829–96), a future (and singularly unpopular) Archbishop of Canterbury, was the first Master. Two of his brothers, A. C. (1862–1925), Master of Magdalene College, Cambridge, and R. H. (1871–1914), a Church of England cleric who converted to Catholicism, were also writers—A. C.'s verse includes 'Land of Hope and Glory', words to be sung to the music by (Sir) Edward Elgar (1857–1934). E. F. was educated at Marlborough College, where he edited the school magazine, and King's College, Cambridge, where he got a first in classics, after which he worked for the British School of Archaeology in Athens, and for a year in Egypt for the Society for the Promotion of Hellenic Studies. He became a full-time writer in 1895, living much of the time in HENRY JAMES's house in Rye, of which he was Mayor 1934–37. He published over a hundred books, a quarter of which were non-fiction, mostly popular biography and history, sport, and well-observed (and sometimes malicious) family and personal reminiscences. The rest, apart from a handful of plays, were novels, of which the first, *Dodo* (1893), a light society tale, was successful enough to lure or lull him into trying to reproduce too much of the same thing—see also *Desirable Residences and Other Stories*, ed. Jack Adrian (1992). Only in his novels about Lucia, beginning with *Queen Lucia* (1920), and of *Miss Mapp* (1922)—two small-town comic characters who come together in *Mapp and Lucia* (1931)—does the particular pre-war society that he tried to portray, and satirize, survive with complete assurance. Of equal significance are his tales of the supernatural. See Brian Masters, *The Life of E. F. Benson*, new edn 1993.

BENTHAM, JEREMY (1748–1832) British philosopher and political economist, was born in Houndsditch, London, of a prosperous family (his great-grandfather was a pawnbroker, and his grandfather and father were barristers). He was educated at Westminster School and The Queen's College, Oxford, after which he studied law, but could not be bothered to practise it, preferring to use his knowledge of it to rethink the principles upon which government and man's conduct were based. He opened his public campaign with the anonymous *A Fragment on Government* (1776). *An Introduction to the Principles of Morals and Legislation* was published in 1789. While staying in Russia with his youngest brother, the naval engineer (Sir) Samuel Bentham (1757–1831), he had developed an idea for an imaginative penal system which was printed for circulation to government officials as *Panopticon: a Series of Letters* (1791). His personal philosophy was 'utilitarianism', broadly the greatest happiness of the greatest number of people, which he certainly practised when in 1814 he moved the parents, brothers, and sisters of the young MILL from their overcrowded quarters in Newington Green to Queen Square, where he lived, paying half their rent and giving the children the run of his garden. In 1823 he established at his own expense the *Westminster Review*, as a radical response to the conservatism of the *Quarterly Review* (founded 1809) and the literary exclusiveness of the *Edinburgh Review* (founded 1802). In the event, Bentham was not so much himself a reformer as one who influenced the development of society through his followers, among the most prominent of whom was Mill himself. He is also credited with the coinage of the words 'international', 'codify', and 'minimize'. He left his body to science. After dissection, the skeleton was dressed in his clothes and deposited in University College, London, where it is on view 9am–5pm daily. See John Dinwiddy, *Jeremy Bentham*, 1989 (introduction to his thought).

BENTLEY, E(DMUND) C(LERIHEW) (1875–1956) British poet and novelist, was born in London and educated at St Paul's School and Merton College, Oxford. He was called to the Bar in 1901, but became a journalist the following year, being a leader writer on the *Daily Telegraph* from 1912 to 1934. At school, by his own account when he was 16, but probably a year or two later, he invented a new verse form by writing the first known clerihew—the first collection, composed by Bentley and his school friends and written out by him in a notebook, with illustrations by CHESTERTON, is dated September 1893. His own first published collection was called *Biography for Beginners* (1905). From *More Biography* (1929) comes this literary example of the form (two rhyming couplets of

lines of any length): 'On one occasion when Browning / Saved a débutante from drowning / She enquired faintly what he meant / By that stuff about good news from Ghent.' *Trent's Last Case* (1913), regarded as the prototype of the modern, realistic detective story, was a conscious and successful attempt to give readers of the genre a substitute for the eternal infallibility of DOYLE's Sherlock Holmes. See *The Complete Clerihews of E. Clerihew Bentley*, introduction by Gavin Ewart, 2nd edn 1983; *Those Days*, 1940 (autobiography); Nicolas Bentley, *A Version of the Truth*, 1960 (son's reminiscences).

BÉRANGER, PIERRE JEAN DE (1780–1857) French poet, was born in Paris and brought up by an aunt in Péronne, where he worked in a printer's shop. After a final quarrel with his father, who wanted him to enter a respectable trade, he set himself up in 1802 in a Paris garret, where he tried to write for a living. Poems he sent to Lucien Bonaparte (1775–1840), brother of Napoleon, resulted in a small pension and, in 1809, a clerical post at the university. The satirical 'Le Roi d'Yvetot' was one of the lively verses in *Chansons* (1815). After the fall of the Empire in 1815 he turned to glorifying the Napoleonic age and to ridiculing the Bourbon regime. The collections published in 1821 and 1828 earned him respectively three and nine months in jail; on the latter occasion the accompanying fine was paid by public subscription. After the revolution of 1848 he was elected a member of the Assembly, but resigned on the grounds that making speeches was not his métier. On his death, Napoleon III ordered a lavish state funeral in his honour. DICKENS is attributed with observing that his work 'is most popular with our enlightened working class'. Editions of his songs in English appeared from 1837 (in America 1844), the most noteworthy of them being *Songs of Béranger*, 'done into English verse by William Young' (1878), revised from the fourth American edition and published by Blackwood's.

BERKELEY, GEORGE (1685–1753) Irish philosopher and cleric, was born at Dysart Castle, Co. Kilkenny, and educated at Kilkenny College and Trinity College, Dublin, of which he became a Fellow in 1711. In 1707 he began a series of commonplace books (now referred to as *Philosophical Commentaries*) in which he incorporated his beliefs about existence and perception. His first published works were *An Essay towards a New Theory of Vision* (1709) and *A Treatise concerning the Principles of Human Knowledge* (1710). He was in England in 1713, where he joined the circle of ADDISON, POPE, and STEELE, and then travelled abroad until 1721, when he returned to Trinity College. In 1724 he was appointed Dean of Derry. A reformer as well as a visionary, he sailed for America in 1728 with the promise of government sponsorship for a college in Bermuda 'for the Christian civilisation of America'; only to return in 1731 when the grant failed to materialize. While he was there, he wrote *Alciphron: or, The Minute Philosopher* (1732), a dialogue which is Platonic in both form and thought. He was created Bishop of Cloyne in 1734, retiring in 1752 because of ill health, which had earlier moved him to write *Siris* (1744), a treatise on the medical properties of tar-water. The basis of his philosophy is immaterialism: the belief that objects do not exist except in the mind, and that knowledge is confined to what can be perceived. His works are marked by clarity and dignity of style as well as of thought. See A. A. Luce, *The Life of Berkeley*, 1949; J. O. Urmson, *Berkeley*, 1982 (introduction to his thought).

BERMANT, CHAIM (*b.* 1929) British novelist, essayist, and critic, was born in Breslev, Poland, and brought up in Glasgow. He was educated at Queen's Park School, Glasgow Rabbinical College (he describes himself as a 'rabbi manqué'), and Glasgow University, with two years in between at the London School of Economics. He was a television scriptwriter before being Features Editor of the *Jewish Chronicle* 1964–66. His first novel, *Jericho Sleep Alone* (1964), a genuinely funny study of growing up, is both Jewish and Scottish in its humour. In his many subsequent novels, punctuated by *Diary of an Old Man* (1967), a short, moving acount of a month in the life of an elderly man, he has unerringly and in an often richly comic vein dissected metropolitan and provincial Jewish and upper-class English attitudes, notably in *Now Dowager* (1971) and *The House of Women* (1983). His commitment to an understanding of Jewish assimilation is reflected in several sociological works, including *Troubled Eden: an Anatomy of British Jewry* (1969) and *The Cousinhood: the Anglo-Jewish Gentry* (1971). *What's the Joke: a Study of Jewish Humour through the Ages* (1986) brings into focus this widely-appreciated but seldom fully understood literary genre. For over thirty years Bermant has contributed a regular column to the *Jewish Chronicle*, with its circulation of a hundred thousand. *Murmurings of a Licensed Heretic* (1990) is a collection of essays which are typical of his trenchant, passionate, and compassionate style of journalism.

BERRINGTON, JOHN see BROWNJOHN.

BERRYMAN, JOHN (1914–72) American poet and critic, was born John Smith in McAlester, Oklahoma, the elder son of a banker who shot himself outside the boy's window in 1926. His mother married John Berryman, whose name he took. He was educated at South Kent School, Connecticut, and Colum-

bia College, from which he graduated in 1936 (after being suspended for one semester for failing a course) and won a fellowship to Clare College, Cambridge, where he was Oldham Shakespeare Scholar in 1937. His life was fraught with personal, professional, and creative turmoil. He was three times married (1942, 1956, 1961), on the last occasion to a young woman 25 years his junior, who out of deference to his wishes legally changed her first name from Kathleen to Kate. Though professing himself a scholar who only 'masquerade[d] as a writer', and in spite of his dedication as a teacher, his insecurity was such that even after having been a staff member at the University of Minnesota since 1954, and given the title of Regents' Professor of Humanities in 1969, he could in 1971 place an anguished personal ad. in the *New York Review of Books* offering to 'contribute radiance & the facts to an occasional change of scene'.

Berryman wrote his first serious poetry (four sonnets for his mother) when he was 'about nineteen', had an elegy published in the *Nation* in 1935, and was in *Five Young American Poets* (1940). *Poems* (1942) owed much to the influence of YEATS and AUDEN, but in *The Dispossessed* (1948) his own experimental style emerged to reflect a dual concern with being 'put out of one's own' and relieved of misery. His preoccupation with the sufferings of the Puritan poet BRADSTREET and with what he saw as the inhibitions which prevented her from voicing her truest, wildest instincts, led him to compose a 50-line ode, which became the 57 stanzas of a dramatic dialogue between them: *Homage to Mistress Bradstreet* (1959). In about 1955 he began to write his 'Dream Songs', informed by 'an imaginary character . . . named Henry, a white American in middle age sometimes in blackface [who] has a friend, never named, who addresses him as Mr Bones and variants thereof'. A first collection of these semi-autobiographical, colloquially phrased, unique poetic fragments was published as *77 Dream Songs* (1964), and a second as *His Toy, His Dream, His Rest: 308 Dream Songs* (1968)—combined as *The Dream Songs* (1969; in UK 1990).

In January 1972 he committed suicide by jumping off a bridge in Minneapolis on to the frozen bank of the Mississippi below. The compulsive, self-destructive energy which he lavished on his critical biography of STEPHEN CRANE (1950), on an unpublished edition of SHAKESPEARE's *King Lear*, and on *Recovery* (1973, with a preface by his friend BELLOW), his unfinished novel ('It will have the greatest number of technical details about alcoholism ever to appear in a book. I *know*. I'm an expert.'), stifled his creative output as much as did his fate in the matter of literary awards: 'Somehow the prizes / come at the wrong times to the proper people / & vice versa'

(Dream Song 361). *The Freedom of the Poet* (1976), a collection of critical essays and stories, was finally put together by Robert Giroux. See *Collected Poems 1937–1971*, ed. Charles Thornbury, new edn 1991; John Haffenden, *The Life of John Berryman*, 1982; J. M. Linebarger, *John Berryman*, 1974 (critical study).

BESANT, (Sir) **WALTER** (1836–1901) British novelist, historian, and critic, was born in Portsea, Hampshire, and educated at St Paul's Grammar School, Portsea, King's College, London, and Christ's College, Cambridge. He began to study for the Church, but instead became Senior Professor, Royal College of Mauritius 1861–67. On his return to London he was Secretary, Palestine Exploration Fund 1868–86, after which he became a full-time writer. An altercation over an article he had submitted to *Once a Week* ended amicably with Besant and its editor, James Rice (1843–82), collaborating on a series of popular novels which began with *Ready-Money Mortiboy* (1872) and continued until Rice's death. Besant went on to produce a novel a year, of which *All Sorts and Conditions of Men* (1882), a thinly disguised plea for the regeneration of London's East End, succeeded in its purpose in that the fictional 'Palace of Delight' actually materialized as the People's Palace, opened by Queen Victoria in 1887. In 1894 he began a multi-volume, systematic survey of the history and topography of London, which remained unfinished at his death. As a critic, his most influential contribution is probably the paper on the art of fiction delivered at the Royal Institution in 1884, which inspired HENRY JAMES to respond with his classic essay, 'The Art of Fiction' (1884). Besant was an energetic advocate of the rights of authors and a tireless propagandist against the iniquitous practices of publishers. He was a founder of the Society of Authors in 1884, Chairman of its Management Committee 1884–85 and 1887–92, and was knighted in 1895. See *Autobiography*, 1902.

BETJEMAN, (Sir) **JOHN** (1906–84) British poet and sage, was born in Highgate, London, the only child of a successful furniture manufacturer. He was educated at Marlborough College and Magdalen College, Oxford, where he antagonized his tutor, C. S. LEWIS, and was sent down after failing his preliminary examinations. An early interest in architecture became a lifetime's preoccupation with the Gothic revival, churches, and the social history of urban and rural England as it is illustrated by buildings large and small; it inspired many elegantly written and effectively argued architectural and topographical works from *Ghastly Good Taste* (1933; rev. edn 1970) to *London's Historic Railway Stations* (1972). His first book of verse, *Mount Zion* (1932), comprised just 11 short poems: *Continual Dew* (1937) was more substantial. His poetry was regarded by some critics at the time as facile, with its jaunty rhymes and rhythms, suburban middle-class settings, muscular maidens, and expressions of innocent love. It was, however, hugely enjoyed by the public for its accessibility and wit, and for its evocation of places, past times, and situations. Betjeman is a poet of compassion, whose fear of ultimate infirmity and death was counter-balanced by his Christian belief, and whose insight into such a range of themes repeatedly causes the reader to respond with recognition, and often with surprise. 'How to Get on in Society', published in *A Few Late Chrysanthemums* (1954), anticipated the 'U/non-U' controversy stirred up by NANCY MITFORD. He was knighted in 1969, and appointed Poet Laureate in 1972. See *Collected Poems*, ed. Earl of Birkenhead, new edn 1989; *The Best of Betjeman*, ed. John Guest, 1978 (includes prose); *Summoned by Bells*, new edn 1989 (verse autobiography); *Letters*, ed. Candida Lycett Green, *Volume 1 1926–1951*, new edn 1995; *Volume 2 1951–1984*, new edn 1996; Bevis Hillier, *Young Betjeman*, new edn 1989 (early biography).

BHATTACHARYA, **BHABANI** (1906–88) Indian novelist, was born in Bhagalpur, Bihar, the son of a civil servant who later became a judge. While at Patna University he wrote articles on world literature for a Bengali journal, literary criticism and sketches in English for Calcutta newspapers, and translated into English poems of TAGORE, who gave him personal encouragement as a writer. After being coolly received by the English department at London University, he switched to history, in which he became PhD in 1934. Having in the meantime travelled widely in Europe, he now settled in Calcutta, embarked on an arranged (but creatively inspirational) marriage, and worked as a journalist. The great famine in Bengal in 1942–43 stimulated him to begin his fictional account of human suffering and national aspirations, *So Many Hungers*; the collapse at the time of Partition of the investments he had inherited from his father spurred him to finish it for publication in Britain in 1947. It sold in many countries and languages. *Music for Mohini* (1952), begun soon after his own marriage, is a celebration of what can be achieved through just such an arrangement. *He Who Rides a Tiger* (1960) is a social satire on caste and wealth in a rural setting. After two more novels of comment on the Indian scene, he ventured farther afield with *A Dream in Hawaii* (1979), an exploration of religious fervour and integrity in a setting he knew from having spent a year teaching at the University of Hawaii. Latterly he lived in the USA, where he was Visiting Professor, University of Washington, Seattle. See Dorothy Blair

Shimer, *Bhabani Bhattacharya*, 1975 (critical study).

BIERCE, AMBROSE (1842–1914) American short-story writer, satirist, and journalist, was born in Meigs County, Ohio, the tenth of 13 children, and grew up on a farm in Indiana, from which he walked to school in Warsaw. Having been a printer's devil on an anti-slavery paper for two years, he spent a year at Kentucky Military Institute. At the beginning of the Civil War in 1861, he enlisted as a private in the Union Army, in which he served throughout the hostilities, even after being wounded in the head at Kennesaw Mountain, Georgia, and became a lieutenant—see *Ambrose Bierce's Civil War*, ed. William McCann (1996). He then trained himself to be a writer while working in the Sub-Treasury in San Francisco, and contributed to the *News Letter*, whose editor he became in 1868. He spent the years 1872–75 in England, where he published, as Dod Grile, *The Fiend's Delight* (1873) and two other collections of journalism. Back in America, he was briefly associated with the new *Argonaut*, dabbled disastrously but not fatally in a mining operation in Dakota, and in 1887 began writing his 'Prattle' column for the *San Francisco Examiner*, founded by William Randolph Hearst (1863–1951), while also contributing regularly to the *New York Journal*. In 1888 he left his wife after finding compromising letters to her from an admirer; in 1889 his 16-year-old son was killed in a gunfight over a girl. These calamities nettled him into writing, between 1888 and 1891, a series of admirable short stories of passion, terror, and tragedy, some of which, such as 'An Occurrence at Owl Creek Bridge' and the disturbing 'Chickamauga', reflect his Civil War experiences.

In 1900, having spent most of the previous decade in places in California for his asthma, he moved to Washington, where he was cared for by his Girl Friday, Carrie Christiansen, whom he had known as a schoolgirl. *The Cynic's Word Book* (1906), later called *The Devil's Dictionary*, is a glossary of timeless aphorisms: e.g. 'APOLOGISE, To lay the foundation for a future offence'; 'INSURANCE, An ingenious modern game of chance in which the player is permitted to enjoy the comfortable conviction that he is beating the man who keeps the table'; 'MARRIAGE, The state or condition of a community consisting of a master, a mistress and two slaves, making in all, two'. After spending several years preparing *The Collected Works of Ambrose Bierce* (12 vols 1909–12), he expressed a wish to visit his old Civil War battlefields, and then cross the border from Texas into Mexico, which was in the throes of a rebellion. His last letter (26 December 1913) states his intention of going the next day to Ojinaga, on the Rio Grande. The town was besieged by the rebel forces from 1 January to 11 January 1914,

when it fell. The 71-year-old journalist is believed to have died in battle. See M. E. Grenander, *Ambrose Bierce*, 1971 (biographical/critical study).

BINYON, LAURENCE (1869–1943) British poet and art critic, was born in Lancaster of a Quaker family and educated at St Paul's School and Trinity College, Oxford, where he won the Newdigate prize for poetry and, with MANMOHAN GHOSE, contributed to *Primavera: Poems by Four Authors* (1890). He became a member of the staff of the British Museum in 1893, and was Keeper of Oriental Prints and Drawings 1913–33. He wrote studies of the watercolourists Thomas Girtin (1900) and John Sell Cotman (1903), and several works on the art and followers of BLAKE, in addition to *Landscape in English Art and Poetry* (1931). While he was at Oxford he had been introduced by BRIDGES to the as yet unpublished poetry of HOPKINS, whose influence can be detected in much of Binyon's subsequent variations on traditional forms of verse, notably in 'For the Fallen' in *The Four Years* (1919). While he also wrote poetical dramas and narratives, his most lasting contribution is in the form of lyrics and short elegies, of which 'The Little Dancers', 'The Burning of Leaves', 'O Summer Sun', and 'In Misty Blue' are fine examples. His *Collected Poems* was published in 1931. When Binyon's publisher, Macmillan, refused to allow T. S. ELIOT, Poetry Editor at Faber, to publish a 'Selected Poems', Eliot proposed that he print a new collection instead. It appeared as *North Star and Other Poems* (1941). Before he died Binyon remodelled, with Eliot's *Quartets* in mind, a wartime sequence, 'The Ruins', as *The Burning of the Leaves* (1944). He also did a pleasing translation of the *Inferno* of DANTE (1933–43) into the original metre, which took him 12 years to complete. He was made CH in 1932. See John Hatcher, *Laurence Binyon: Poet, Scholar of East and West*, 1996 (critical biography).

BION see THEOCRITUS.

BIRNEY, (ALFRED) EARLE (b. 1904) Canadian poet, novelist, and critic, was born in Calgary of Scottish descent (see 'Tea at My Shetland Aunt's'), the only child of a farmer who after war service set up in 1916 as a fruit rancher at Erickson, British Columbia. Here, at 15, Birney 'jotted down the substance' of 'Kootenay Still-Life', the only poem to survive the bonfire of his juvenilia which he made in 1940. After high school he worked as a bank clerk, farm worker, and national parks' labourer before going to the University of British Columbia to read chemistry. He switched to English in his second year, and edited *Ubyssey*, the student journal. His further education was fraught by financial problems, which he alleviated by teaching in

Utah and by working in New York for the Trotskyite branch of the Communist Party. He was thus able to do postgraduate study at the universities of Toronto and California, and at Queen Mary College, London, where he completed a dissertation on CHAUCER's irony—see his *Essays on Chaucerian Irony*, ed. Beryl Rowland (1985). He then lectured in English at Toronto University, and was Literary Editor of *Canadian Forum* 1936–40. His first volume of poetry, *David and Other Poems* (1942), won the Governor General's Award; as did his second, *Now Is Time* (1945). Having been an army reservist, he was posted to Europe in 1943 (see 'Conference of Heads'), serving in England ('Invasion Spring', 'D-Day') and in action in Europe ('The Road to Nijmegan'), and being responsible (with the rank of major) for personnel selection in Belgium and Holland in 1944–45. Some of his army experience is reflected in his novel, *Turvey: a Military Picaresque* (1949; rev. edn 1976), the efforts of an innocent Canadian in the face of the absurdities of the army command, which won the Stephen LEACOCK Medal for humour. After the war he edited *Canadian Poetry Magazine* (1946–48), and taught medieval literature at the University of British Columbia, where he established the Department of Creative Writing, of which he was Chairman 1963–65. Subsequently he was until 1984 writer-in-residence at several Canadian universities.

In *The Creative Writer* (1966) he suggests: 'The effective writer is one who is inwardly sure of the entire naturalness of his creative art. For instance, he must be aware that he is writing not merely because he is neurotic.' His 'naturalness' has generated poems of outrage, poems of compassion and guilt ('David', 'Arrivals—Wolfville . . .', 'For George Lamming', which recalls a convivial party in Jamaica in 1962), poems of commentary on his travels in Europe, the Pacific, the Caribbean, South America, Australia, New Zealand, India, and the Far East, and latterly—see *Last Makings* (1991)—tender and erotic love poems. It has also enabled him effectively to ignore conventions (the device of substituting spaces for punctuation occurs as early as 1940), and playfully to experiment with language, concrete forms, and sounds, in his belief that 'poetry is both an oral entertainment and a visual notation'. His other critical works include *Spreading Time: Remarks on Canadian Writing and Writers 1: 1926–1949* (1980). He has also published a second novel, *Down the Long Table* (1955), based on his Trotskyite days, *Big Bird in the Bush: Selected Stories and Sketches* (1978), and *Words on Waves: Selected Radio Plays*, ed. Howard Fink (1985). He was made Member, Order of Canada, in 1970, and Officer in 1981. See *Collected Poems*, 2 vols 1975; *The Rugging and the Moving Times: Poems New and Uncollected*, 1976; *Fall by Fury and Other Makings*, 1978; Peter Ai-

chinger, *Earle Birney and His Works*, 1985; Elspeth Cameron, *Earle Birney*, 1995 (critical study).

BISHOP, ELIZABETH (1911–79) American poet, was born in Worcester, Massachusetts, of Canadian descent on both sides. After her father's death when she was eight months old, she and her mother lived with her maternal grandparents in Great Village, Nova Scotia, the scene of several of her short stories. In 1916 her mother became permanently insane and was institutionalized. Bishop never saw her again. She was brought up by her other grandparents in Worcester, and then by a married but childless aunt in Boston, and suffered an accumulation of diseases which included asthma, bronchitis, eczema, and irregular spasms. She also had to come to terms with her lesbianism, which she felt isolated her: 'I feel about as much at home as an elephant in a negligée,' she wrote to a college friend while staying with relatives. At 16 she was able to board at Walnut Hill School, Natick, after which she went to Vassar. She graduated in English literature in 1934, having begun a friendship with MARIANNE MOORE, whose poetic protégée she became, in much the same way as from 1946 ROBERT LOWELL was hers. Between 1935 and 1938 she travelled in Europe, and for most of 1943 she lived in Mexico, where she met NERUDA. Her first volume of verse, *North and South*, was published in 1946. In 1951, on a visit to Brazil at the start of a South American tour, she had a violent allergic reaction to cashew fruit. She was invited to recuperate at the home of Lota de Macedo Soares, a Brazilian aristocrat, who became the love of her life, and on whose estate at Petropolis she was when she heard, from a newsman in the American embassy, that she had won the Pulitzer Prize for her second collection, *Poems: North & South—A Cold Spring* (1955), which incorporated her first volume. She stayed in Brazil for 15 years, only returning permanently to the USA after Lota committed suicide in 1967 in New York. She settled in Lewis Wharf, Boston, in 1974, and taught full time at Harvard until 1977. She died of a stroke.

Questions of Travel (1965) contains a sequence of poems initiating the traveller into the life and traditions of Brazil. The title of *The Complete Poems* (1969), which won the National Book Award, was a misnomer, for it was followed by *Geography III* (1976), which included the crucial 'In the Waiting Room', in which she identifies the source of her interest in observed detail, and other poems which epitomize her poetic philosophy. She translated Brazilian poetry, and also the prose work, *Minha Vida de Menina—The Diary of 'Helena Morley'* (1957)—written by a teenager in the 1890s. See *The Complete Poems 1927–1929*, new edn 1991 of rev. edn 1983; *Collected*

Prose, ed. Robert Giroux, new edn 1994; *One Art: the Selected Letters*, ed. Robert Giroux, new edn 1996; Brett C. Millier, *Elizabeth Bishop: Life and the Memory of It*, new edn 1995 (biography); Gary Fountain and Peter Brazeau, *Remembering Elizabeth Bishop: an Oral Biography*, new edn 1996; David Kalstone, *Becoming a Poet: Elizabeth Bishop with Marianne Moore and Robert Lowell*, ed. Robert Hemenway, new edn 1991 (biographical study); Thomas J. Travisano, *Elizabeth Bishop: Her Artistic Development*, new edn 1989.

BLACKMORE, R(ICHARD) D(OD-DRIDGE) (1825–1900) British novelist, was born in Longworth, Berkshire, the son of the curate of the parish. Three months after his birth, his mother died in a typhus epidemic. Educated at Blundell's School, Devon, and Exeter College, Oxford, he was called to the Bar in 1852, but gave up the law in 1855 because of attacks of epilepsy. He was briefly a schoolmaster, but with a legacy from an uncle was able in 1858 to build a country house in Teddington, Middlesex, where he devoted the rest of his life to writing and to market gardening. In 1855 he had two volumes of poetry published anonymously, *Poems by Melanter* and *Epullia*. A verse translation of the first two books of VIRGIL's *Georgics*, infelicitously entitled *The Farm and Fruit of Old*, appeared in 1862, and convinced him that there was no money in poetry. He then wrote 15 novels, of which the first, *Clara Vaughan* (1864), was published anonymously, and *The Maid of Sker* (1872) was his favourite. His literary distinction, however, rests entirely on his third, *Lorna Doone* (1869), a regional novel somewhat in the vein of WALTER SCOTT, set on and around Exmoor and covering the events and aftermath of the rebellion of the Duke of Monmouth in 1685. It was not well received by the critics, but it soon won enormous and continuing popular acclaim for its melodramatic plot and for the lyrical intensity with which he evokes the romance between John Ridd and Lorna Doone, the blood feud between their families, and the rugged Devon landscape. See Kenneth Budd, *The Last Victorian: R. D. Blackmore and His Novels*, 1960.

BLACKWOOD, ALGERNON (1869–1951) British novelist and short-story writer, was born in Shooters Hill, Kent, the second son of (Sir) Arthur Blackwood, later Secretary of the Post Office, and Sydney, widow of the 6th Duke of Manchester. He was educated at the Moravian school in the Black Forest, at Wellington College, and at Edinburgh University, after which he was dispatched to Canada to live on a small allowance. He describes the next ten years, during which he had many different jobs and experienced desperation and poverty until he became a journalist in New York, in *Episodes Before Thirty* (1923). Back in England, he felt able to give up working in the dried-milk business after the publication of his book of stories, *The Empty House* (1906). This was the first of a number of collections in which he explores the border between reality and the supernatural to evoke a response of terror. This line, continued in *Strange Stories* (1929) and *The Tales of Algernon Blackwood* (1938), proved his most effective, but he extended his range beyond the ghost story to the psychological mystery, and to novels of fantasy and of mystical communion with the past. He was made CBE in 1949. See *Tales of the Mysterious and Macabre*, new edn 1989; *The Empty House and Other Ghost Stories*, 1993.

BLAIR, ERIC see ORWELL.

BLAIS, MARIE-CLAIRE (*b.* 1939) French-Canadian novelist, was born in Quebec City and educated at the Pensionnat St Roch, which she left at 16 to work in a shoe factory, determined to be a writer. She had eight other jobs during the next three years, and attended courses in French literature at Laval University. She was just 20 when she published her first novel, *La Belle Bête* (1959; tr. Merloyd Lawrence as *Mad Shadows*, 1961), which, like her less lurid second, *Tête Blanche* (1960; tr. Charles Fullman, 1961), is about a troubled adolescent. A Canada Council Fellowship enabled her to spend a year in France, and a Guggenheim Fellowship, sponsored by EDMUND WILSON, to go to Cambridge, Massachusetts. She lived in New England until 1971, and in Brittany until 1975, when she returned to Quebec. Her constant experimentation with form is a feature of her novels, of which the earlier ones especially reflect a bleak outlook on life and on underlying strands of Montreal society. Among her more notable works are the trilogy, *Les Manuscrits de Pauline Archange* (1968), winner of the Governor General's Award, *Vivre! Vivre!* (1969)—translated together by Derek Coltman as *The Manuscripts of Pauline Archange* (1969)—, and *Les Apparences* (1970; tr. David Lodbell as *Durer's Angel*, 1974); *Les Nuits de l'Underground* (1978; tr. Ray Ellenwood as *Nights in the Underground*, 1979), an exploration of lesbian love; and *Le Sourd dans la Ville* (1979; tr. Carol Dunlop as *Deaf to the City*, 1987), for which she won her second Governor General's Award. *Visions d'Anna* (1982; tr. Sheila Fischman as *Anna's World*, 1983) offers a society in which loving relationships and a will to survive can exist. Blais was made Member, Order of Canada, in 1980. See Mary Jean Green, *Marie-Claire Blais*, 1995 (biographical/critical study).

BLAKE, NICHOLAS see LEWIS, C. DAY.

BLAKE, WILLIAM (1757–1827) British poet, painter, illustrator, and engraver, was born in London, the son of a hosier. He attended a drawing school and at 14 was apprenticed to James Basire (1730–1802), engraver to the Society of Antiquities, after which he studied at the Royal Academy. At an early age he was given to visionary experiences, some of which he expressed in verses included in *Poetical Sketches* (1783). For *Songs of Innocence* (1789) he devised a novel method of book production by etching text and illustration into a plate, and colouring the printed sheets by hand, with his wife as helper. In 1794 he added further poems so that the book could demonstrate 'the two contrary states of the human soul', and published it as *Songs of Innocence and Experience*. Only 24 copies of the original edition are recorded. In opposition to the radical thinking of the day, he had begun to issue his 'Prophetic Books', including *The French Revolution* (1791), *Visions of the Daughters of Albion* (1793), and *America: a Prophecy* (1793), in all of which the different forces of revolution are interpreted in moral and cosmic terms; in *The First Book of Urizen* (1794), *The Book of Ahania* (1795), *The Book of Los* (1795), and *The Song of Los* (1795), the tone and the vision become even more turbulent. The years 1799–1803 were spent on the estate of the minor literary figure, William Hayley (1745–1820), at Felpham, Sussex, and were frustrating rather than fruitful, culminating in Blake being unsuccessfully prosecuted for sedition on the evidence of a drunken soldier whom he had removed from his garden. Between 1804 and 1808 he wrote and etched *Milton*, a complex work inspired by and related to *Paradise Lost*. In the preface occurs the hymn 'And did those feet in ancient time . . .'. *Jerusalem: the Emanation of the Giant Albion* was written and etched between 1804 and 1820. In 1809, having been thwarted by the Royal Academy, where he had exhibited since 1780, and which now refused to exhibit what he termed his 'portable frescos' (done in a water-based medium), he held his own show, 'At No 28, Corner of Broad Street, Golden Square. . . . Admittance to the Exhibition 1 Shilling'. The enterprise was a financial failure, but *A Descriptive Catalogue of Pictures, Poetical and Historical Inventions*, 'Price 2s6d', is a fine example of evocative and expository prose.

In *Jerusalem* (I. 5, 17–19) Blake writes, '. . . I rest not from my great task! / To open the Eternal Worlds, to open the immortal Eyes / Of Man inwards into the Worlds of Thought . . .'. An early and particularly intense but largely unheeded Romantic, his personal satisfaction came from the knowledge of his own eccentric, mysterious, and mystical genius, which he displayed in his early lyrics ('The Little Black Boy', 'The Chimney Sweeper', 'The Tyger') as clearly as he did, with enhanced symbolism and a mythology based on a dual vision of God and man, in his later works. See *Complete Poetry*

and Prose, ed. Geoffrey Keynes, new edn 1989; *Selected Poetry*, ed. Michael Mason, 1996; *Poems of William Blake*, ed. Peter Ackroyd, 1995; Mona Wilson, *The Life of Blake*, ed. Geoffrey Keynes, new edn 1978 of 3rd edn, 1971; James King, *William Blake: His Life*, new edn 1992; Peter Ackroyd, *Blake*, 1996 (critical biography); Martin K. Nurmi, *William Blake*, 1975 (critical study).

BLIND HARRY (or **HARRY THE MINSTREL**) (*fl. c.*1475–92) Scottish poet, is described as a blind wandering minstrel in the *Historia Majoris Britanniae* (1521) of the Scottish historian John Major (1469–1550); is possibly the 'Blin Hary' listed as having died, in DUNBAR's 'Lament for the Makaris' (printed 1508); and disappears from the treasury accounts of Scotland in 1492. Whoever he was, and if he was blind this is something which is more likely to have happened to him later in life, he is regarded as the author of *The Actis and Deidis of the Illuster and Vailyeand Campioun, Schir William Wallace, Knicht of Ellerslie*, of which a manuscript of 1488, written by a John Ramsay, survives. It was first printed in 1508. Violently anti-English, as befits the times in Scotland and thus his Scottish audience, this 12,000-line historical romance of the life of Sir William Wallace (1274–1305), presents its hero not only as a lusty fighter but also as a ladies' man, who in one of the out-and-out fictitious episodes makes a considerable impression on the Queen of England. There is a great deal of violence, but also tenderness, as in Wallace's lament for Sir John Graham, a historical personage who was killed at the battle of Falkirk in 1298, and in the joyful panegyric on Wallace's all-too-brief marriage. Possibly the first example of the use of the heroic couplet in Scottish literature, it is also an early blood-and-thunder adventure story, with a hero whose cliff-hanging exploits parallel those of IAN FLEMING's James Bond, five centuries later. See in Roderick Watson, *The Literature of Scotland*, 1984.

BLIXEN, KAREN (1885–1962), née Dinesen, Danish novelist (as Isak Dinesen) and prose writer in English, was born on the estate of Rungstedlund, near Rungsted, and was educated at home and at the Royal Academy, Copenhagen, with a further period studying painting in Paris. When her love for a dashing cousin was not reciprocated, she accepted a proposal from his twin brother, Baron Bror Blixen-Finecke, and followed him to Kenya, where they were married in Mombasa in 1914. They settled on a farm near Nairobi, intending to produce maize and coffee, and raise cattle, but he preferred hunting, and after a year she went home for treatment for syphilis, which she had contracted from him. They were divorced in 1921: he died in a car accident in 1937. With the help of money from her family, she continued to try and run the farm, and fell in love with Denys Finch-Hatton, a cultured safari conductor. She was forced to sell up in 1931, only weeks before Finch-Hatton died when his light plane went out of control and crashed. She returned to Rungstedlund, where slowly she began to write: first *Seven Gothic Tales* (1934); then *Out of Africa* (1937), an account of her struggles with the farm which is also a story of double love, for Africa and for Finch-Hatton. The manuscript of *Winter's Tales* (1942) was smuggled out of the country during the Nazi occupation in World War II, when she also published in Copenhagen in Danish, under the pseudonym of Pierre Andrézel, a thriller, *Gengældelsens Veje* (1944; as *The Angelic Avengers*, 1946). *Last Tales*, a further collection of stories out of an essentially romantic, but intellectual, imagination, was published in 1957, when she was nominated for the Nobel Prize for Literature, which went instead to CAMUS. See Judith Thurman, *Isak Dinesen: the Life of a Storyteller*, new edn 1995.

BLOK, ALEXANDER (1880–1921) Russian poet, was born in St Petersburg, the son of a scientist, and studied law and then philology at St Petersburg University. When he graduated in 1906 he had already published a volume of eight hundred romantic songs 'About the Beautiful Lady', an idealistic charmer with some of whose attributes, especially wisdom, he invested his wife, the daughter of the chemist Dimitri Ivanovich Mendeleyev (1834–1907), whom he married in 1903. The confusion and gloom he experienced after the failure of the 1905 Revolution is apparent in the poetry of his next period, during which he also wrote a trilogy of plays bitterly and satirically reflecting on his own early mysticism. He briefly returned to romanticism after the successful Revolution of 1917; in its aftermath he wrote ['The Twelve'] (1918), in which a band of marauding Red soldiers become the Apostles, with Christ as their leader, and ['The Scythians'] (1918), an acceptance of the passing of the old world. Thereafter, though he held minor posts in cultural affairs, he wrote no more poetry. See *Selected Poems*, tr. Jon Stallworthy and Peter France, 1974; Nina Berberova, *Aleksandr Blok: a Life*, tr. Robyn Marsack, 1996.

BLUNDEN, EDMUND (1896–1974) British poet and critic, was born in London, though the family shortly afterwards moved to Yalding, Kent. He was educated at Christ's Hospital. His first book, *Poems, 1913 and 1914*, was privately published in 1914, the year he joined the Army. He served as a lieutenant at the front from 1916 to 1918, winning the Military Cross. After the war he spent a year at The Queen's College, Oxford, and was Professor of English Literature, Tokyo University 1924–27. He was appointed a Fellow of Merton College, Oxford, in 1931. In 1943 he joined the editorial staff of *The Times Literary Supplement*, but returned to the Far East after World War II, first as a special Foreign Office cultural envoy in Japan, and then as Professor of English at Hong Kong University 1953–64. He was elected Professor of Poetry at Oxford in 1966, but resigned two years later because of ill health. Blunden's quiet and reflective nature is mirrored in his work. Even in his classic prose account, *Undertones of War* (1928), his personal reminiscences of the ghastly business conducted in Flanders, and in his war poems written at the time and afterwards, there is more expression of pity and ironic observation than of anger or outrage. Much of his poetry is occasional, or pastoral, as is suggested by the titles of some of his earlier volumes: *Pastorals* (1916), *The Waggoner* (1920), *The Shepherd* (1922). His experiences in World War I, during which he probably spent longer in the trenches than any other recognized war writer, continued throughout his life to colour his poetic impulse and to haunt his imagination. He was a fervent cricketer, whose *Cricket Country* (1943) is a notable and noble attempt to assess the nature and appeal of the game. He wrote deft critical biographies of HUNT (1930), LAMB (1932), and P. B. SHELLEY (1946), and nearly a thousand articles and reviews in *The Times Literary Supplement* alone. See *Poems of Many Years*, ed. Rupert Hart-Davis, 1957; *Selected Poems*, ed. Robyn Marsack, 1982; *Overtones of War: Poems of the First World War*, ed. Martin Taylor, 1996; Barry Webb, *Edmund Blunden: a Biography*, 1990.

BLUNT, WILFRED SCAWEN (1840–1922) British poet and traveller, was born at Petworth House, Sussex, and educated at Stonyhurst College and Oscott College, after which he joined the Diplomatic Service, officiating in several countries as secretary of legation. In 1869 he left the service and married Lady Anne Isabella Noel (1837–1917), a granddaughter of BYRON. Three years later he inherited the family estates, and he and his wife went travelling in the Middle East by out-of-the-way routes, and then visited India. Out of his experiences came a conviction of the iniquities of imperialism and of Britain in particular, and several books, including *The Future of Islam* (1882) and *Ideas about India* (1885). He also actively supported the Irish cause, and was arrested in Galway and imprisoned for two months in 1887, on which he reflected in a sonnet sequence, *In Vinculis* (1889). He lived partly in Sussex, where he entertained leading literary and political figures and bred racehorses from the stock he had acquired on his travels from the Emir of Hail, and partly on his estate in Egypt, where he dressed as an Arab and spoke the Bedouin language. *Sonnets and Songs, by Proteus* (1875) included 'A Woman's Sonnets', written by GREGORY, with whom he had an affair. It was revised several times, and the interest in that and in a second poetic sequence, *Esther* (1892), is in individual poems rather than in the whole. He also had an affair, in about 1884, with Jane, wife of MORRIS. Blunt was a poet of love, and also of country pursuits (especially riding), tragic experience and desolation, and sometimes of politics, too. *My Diaries* (1919–20) is considerably less reliable than two books about their travels by his wife: Lady Anne Blunt, *The Bedouin Tribes of the Euphrates* (1879) and *A Pilgrimage to Nejd* (1881). See *The Poetical Works*, 1914; Elizabeth Longford, *A Pilgrimage of Passion: the Life of Wilfred Scawen Blunt*, 1979.

BLY, ROBERT see WRIGHT, JAMES.

BLYTH, OLIVER see MACNAMARA.

BLYTON, ENID (1897–1968) British children's writer, was born in East Dulwich, London, and educated at St Christopher's School, and afterwards in Froebel and Montessori methods of teaching. She contributed verses, stories, and articles to *Teachers' World* and to literary journals; wrote and edited the magazine *Sunny Stories*; and by the beginning of World War II had become a respected and popular author of children's adventure, mystery, and school stories. The priority given during the war to new books by established authors worked to her advantage, and her unchanging formulae, ability to appeal to children at all levels of reading attainment, and phenomenal output (she wrote every word of her books herself, straight on to a portable typewriter), helped her to an unassailable position. Ten years after her death, and in spite of or because of the fact that many public libraries would not buy her books, her English-language sales were (according to her literary agent) increasing at the rate of five million copies a year, and after Lenin (1870–1924), MARX, and VERNE, she was the fourth most translated author in the world. Her popularity with children, though not with adults, is due to her innate understanding of childish tastes, which she was able to exploit by her ability to think like a child (and in some ways she was permanently childlike), while writing with the skill and experience of an adult. The very predictability of her plots panders to the child's need for security. In 1996 the residual copyrights in the more than seven hundred books that she wrote were purchased by a British property/leisure company for £14.25m. See Sheila G. Ray, *The Blyton Phenomenon: the Controversy Surrounding the World's Most Successful Children's Writer*, 1982 (critical study).

BOCCACCIO, GIOVANNI (1313–75) Italian prose writer and poet, was born in either Paris or Florence, the illegitimate son of a merchant, Boccaccio di Chellino da Certaldo, who married shortly afterwards. He was brought up in Tuscany, and sent to Naples in 1327 to learn business, which he gave up in 1331 with his father's consent to study canon law. He returned to Florence in 1341 after the collapse of his father's business, and set about finishing the several literary works he had begun, all inspired by 'Fiammetta', the Neapolitan lady of noble birth with whom he was utterly smitten: 'Filocolo', a prose romance; 'Filostrato', a poem in *ottava rima* which is the source of CHAUCER's *Troilus and Criseyde*; and 'Teseida', a verse epic which Chaucer used in both 'Anelida and Arcite' and 'The Knight's Tale'. To these he added 'Ameto', an allegorical romance; 'Ninfale Fiesole' (tr. Daniel J. Donne as *The Nymph of Fiesole*, 1960), a pastoral; and 'Fiammetta', a prose work with affinities to the psychological novel, in which the heroine recounts her passion for a lover who betrays her. The real Fiammetta, it appears, went off with another man, and died in 1348 in the Black Death, the terrors of which Boccaccio graphically describes from first hand experience in the introduction to *Decameron*. The work comprises one hundred stories, ten each told by ten young protagonists (seven female, three male) during the ten days that they shelter from the plague on a hillside estate near Florence. Though Chaucer also used the format of 'tales within a tale' for *The Canterbury Tales*, it is unlikely that he knew *Decameron*, whose realistic stories are all rooted in the contemporary world of professional people as well as of princes, priests, and peasants.

In about 1350 Boccaccio became a civic diplomat for Florence, in which capacity he invited PETRARCH to visit the city. This was the beginning of a long friendship and correspondence, and to his abjuring fiction and the vernacular for solid works of reference in Latin: *De Genealogia Deorum Gentilium* [Genealogies of Pagan Gods], a section of which (tr. C. G. Osgood) has been issued as *Boccaccio on Poetry* (1930); *De Claris Mulieribus* [Famous Women]; *De Casibus Virorum Illustrium* [The Downfalls of Famous Men], the source of LYDGATE's *The Falle of Princis* and the inspiration for the enormously popular *A Myrroure for Magistrates* (1559). In 1373 Boccaccio was elected to the first chair of DANTE studies in Florence, but after delivering lectures on the first 17 cantos of *Inferno* he fell ill and had to return to Certaldo, where he died. The first English translation of *Decameron* was in 1620, probably by John Florio (1553–1625), translator of MONTAIGNE. DRYDEN translated three tales into verse in *Fables Ancient and Modern*. KEATS took his *Isabella* from *Decameron*, and planned with his friend John Hamilton Reynolds (1796–1852) a complete volume of narrative poems based on it. GEORGE ELIOT turned one of its stories into rhymed verse: TENNY-

SON wrote a play (*The Falcon*) from another. See *The Decameron*, tr. G. H. McWilliam, 2nd edn 1995; *The Decameron*, tr. Guido Waldman, ed. Jonathan Usher, 1993.

BOECE (or **BOETHIUS**), **HECTOR** (*c.*1465–1536) Scottish historian, was born in Dundee and educated at St Andrews University and at the university in Paris, after which he was until 1498 a teacher at the constituent Collège Montaigu, where he was a contemporary of ERASMUS. He then assisted William Elphinstone (1431–1514), Bishop of Aberdeen, in the establishment of King's College, Aberdeen, of which he was the first principal. His major literary work, for which he received from James V a pension, from the university a doctorate, and from the city of Aberdeen the offer of a tun of wine or £20 (Scots) with which to buy bonnets, was *Historiae Gentis Scotorum*, printed in Paris in 1527. Written in Latin in the style of LIVY, with emphasis on direct speech and vigorous action rather than on historical accuracy, it was translated into Scots at the King's request by John Bellenden (1495–*c.*1550), Archdean of Moray and a minor court poet, as *The Hystory and Croniklis of Scotland* (1536); and from Scots into English for HOLINSHED's *Chronicles*, where it was the source of the story of SHAKESPEARE's tragedy, *Macbeth*.

BOETHIUS, ANICIUS MANLIUS SEVERINUS (*c.*480–524) Roman scholar, was of high birth, and was taken on the staff of Theodoric the Ostrogoth, who ruled Italy from 493 to 526. He was appointed consul in 510, and head of legal and other services in 520. In this capacity he undertook the defence of a senator accused of being in contact with the ruler of the eastern empire, was himself charged with treason, and died under torture after a period of imprisonment. *De Consolatione Philosophiae* [The Consolation of Philosophy] (tr. V. E. Watts, 1969), written in prison, is a beautiful work in prose and verse, in which the philosopher who was also a Christian argues, through an examination of good and evil, towards the existence of an omniscient being. It was one of the first books to be translated into English, by ALFRED. Subsequent translators include CHAUCER and Elizabeth I, who took time off in her sixties for the self-appointed task. Boethius also wrote doctrinal and mathematical commentaries and treatises, and translated ARISTOTLE into Latin.

BOETHIUS, HECTOR see BOECE.

BOGAN, LOUISE (1897–1970) American poet and critic, was born in Livermore Falls, Maine, of Irish descent on both sides, and went to the Girls' Latin School, Boston. She left Boston University after a year and married army officer Curt Alexander (*d.* 1920), from whom she separated after the birth of

their daughter in 1917. She left the child with her parents and settled in Greenwich Village, New York. Her first collection, *Body of This Death* (1923), largely a selection from what she had published since the age of 18, confirmed her as a lyric poet beneath whose emotions lurked a sense of tragedy. Of her chosen poetic form, she explained in a letter (1969): 'Lyric poetry is the most difficult gift there is: the most *exigent*. And it cannot be *faked*, like a good deal of other writing.' In 1925 she married Raymond Holden (1894–1972), poet and novelist. *Dark Summer*, a more metaphysical volume bulked out by ten poems from the earlier book, was published in 1929. Later that year, while they were away, fire destroyed their house in Hillsdale, with all their possessions and manuscripts. This tragedy, compounded by Holden's losses in the Wall Street crash, was instrumental in a loss of creativity and an increase in mental instability, though in 1931–35 she had short stories of a psychological nature published in the *New Yorker*, and established herself as a critic—see *Selected Criticism: Poetry and Prose* (1955). She and Holden separated in 1933 (divorced 1937). Bogan managed to put together enough poems for her last collection of new verse, *The Sleeping Fury* (1937). Subsequent volumes were *Poems and New Poems* (1941), *Collected Poems 1923–1953* (1954), and *The Blue Estuaries: Poems 1923–1968* (1968). She was Consultant in Poetry to the Library of Congress 1945–46. Her main influences were AUDEN, RILKE, and YEATS, while those who benefited from her inspiration included ROETHKE, with whom she had a close relationship. See Ruth Limmer (ed.) *Journey Around My Room: the Autobiography of Louise Bogan, a Mosaic*, 1980; Jacqueline Ridgeway, *Louise Bogan*, 1984 (critical study); Elizabeth Frank, *Louise Bogan*, new edn 1986 (critical biography).

BOGAN OF BOGAN, MRS see NAIRNE.

BOIARDO, MATTEO MARIA see ARIOSTO.

BOILEAU, NICOLAS (1636–1711) French poet and critic, was born in Paris, where he was educated at Collège de Beauvais and then studied law, being called to the Bar in 1656. In 1666 he began publishing his 'Satires' (which were admired, and translated or imitated, by ROCHESTER and other wits of the court of Charles II), and in 1670 his 'Epistles', some of which were addressed to Louis XIV, who appointed him Historiographer Royal in 1677. The mock heroic *Le Lutrin* [The Lectern] (1674–83), which DRYDEN said had 'the majesty of the heroic, finely mixed with the venom of the other', was translated into English by ROWE (1708). *L'Art Poétique* (1674), a poetic sketch in four cantos of the literary aesthetics of neoclassicism, was influential on

English letters, its precepts being respected by ADDISON, POPE, RYMER, and others, as well as by Dryden.

BOLDREWOOD, ROLF, pen name (from the Introduction to Canto I of WALTER SCOTT's *Marmion*) of Thomas Alexander Browne (1826–1915) Australian novelist, was born in London and in 1831 was brought by his father to Sydney, where he was educated at T. W. Cape's 'Sydney Academy' and Sydney College. At 18 he set himself up as a squatter (grazier) on a station in the Port Fairy district of Victoria, which he called Squattlesea Mere (also from Scott). In 1862 he moved to Swan Hill, and from there to Narrandera, New South Wales, where he wrote his earliest sketches. These were published in *Cornhill Magazine*, and later reprinted, with other pieces including 'How I Began to Write', in *In Bad Company and Other Stories* (1901). The drought of 1869 finally forced him off the land, and in 1871 he became Police Magistrate, and later also Goldfields' Commissioner and District Coroner, in Gulgong, New South Wales. He subsequently held similar posts in Armidale and Albury until 1895, when he retired to Melbourne. He wrote to supplement his income, and he came to writing late. Of 16 romances and adventure novels, his second, *Robbery Under Arms* (1888; rev. edn 1889), survives for its vigorous telling and re-creation of sensational events, as a bushranger narrates the circumstances which finally landed him in the condemned cell.

BOLINGBROKE, (SAINT-JOHN, HENRY), 1ST VISCOUNT (1678–1751) British historian, political philosopher, and statesman, was born in Battersea and probably educated at Eton, after which he spent several dissolute years, visited the Continent, and acquired excellent French. In 1701 he was elected Tory Member of Parliament for the family borough of Wootton Bassett, Wiltshire. His able mind and considerable eloquence secured for him the posts of Secretary for War (1704), Secretary of State for Foreign Affairs (1710), and in 1711 the leadership of his party in the House of Commons when Robert Harley (1661–1724) was made Earl of Oxford. He was himself elevated in 1712, becoming Viscount Bolingbroke, and in 1713 was largely instrumental in securing the Treaty of Utrecht, which ended the War of the Spanish Succession. He appears to have been in communication with James Edward Stuart (1688–1766) about the succession to the throne of Britain when Queen Anne should die. When George I succeeded in 1714, Bolingbroke was dismissed from office. Believing that his life was in danger, he fled in disguise to France, where he became Secretary of State to James. For this he was impeached in his absence, and lost his peerage.

He was eventually pardoned and returned to England in 1723, though he was not allowed to take his seat in the House of Lords. He intrigued unsuccessfully for power by bribing the King's mistress, and had to be satisfied with contributing, to the journal *Craftsman*, letters attacking the government of Robert Walpole (1676–1745), which were reprinted as *A Dissertation upon Parties* (1735). He spent the years 1735–42 in France and then returned to Battersea, where he wrote *Letters on the Spirit of Patriotism: on the Idea of a Patriot King . . .* (1749). Written in France but only published posthumously in 1752 was *Letters on the Study and Use of History*, in which he delved rather more deeply than had been done before in English into the causes of changes in the 'scales of power' and the precise points at which their effects were felt. He was twice married, in 1700 to Frances Winchcombe, heir to a Berkshire estate, who died in 1718 leaving nothing to him; and in 1720 to the 42-year-old Mme de Villette (*d.* 1750), with whom he had been on terms of some intimacy for several years. See Harry T. Dickinson, *Bolingbroke*, 1970 (biography).

BÖLL, HEINRICH (1917–85) German novelist and short-story writer, was born in Cologne of devout Catholic parents, and was educated at Kaiser Wilhelm Gymnasium, after which he was apprenticed to a book dealer until his compulsory labour service. Shortly after enrolling at Cologne University he was called up for a military training course, on which he was when World War II began. By a variety of subterfuges he survived the war, in which he was wounded four times, and returned to a devastated Cologne and to his wife, to try and build a career as a writer—the manuscripts of some six novels, written before the war, had been destroyed in the bombing. The sales of a novella (1949), a volume of stories (1950), and a novel, *Wo warst du, Adam?* (1951; tr. Mervyn Savill as *Adam, Where Art Thou?*, 1955), all three dealing with the war, were so unpromising that his publisher let him go—between 1949 and 1950 he attempted a longer narrative about rebuilding a life after World War I, first published in 1992 as *Der Engel Schwieg* (tr. Breon Mitchell as *The Silent Angel* 1994). A new publisher vigorously and successfully promoted *Und sagte kein einziges Wort* (1953; tr. Richard Graves as *Acquainted with the Night*, 1954), the first of several novels exploring problems of postwar economic restoration. In *Haus ohne Hüter* (1954; tr. Savill as *Tomorrow and Yesterday*, 1957) and *Billard um Halbzehn* (1959; tr. Patrick Bowles as *Billiards at Half Past Nine*, 1962) the concern is with ways of living with the past. Satire is the medium of social criticism in *Ansichten eines Clowns* (1963; tr. Leila Vennewitz as *The Clown*, 1965), and irony in *Ende einer Dienstfahrt* (1966; tr. Vennewitz as *End of a Mission*,

1968). The publication of *Gruppenbild mit Dame* (1971; tr. Vennewitz as *Group Portrait with Lady*, 1973), in which he aimed 'to describe or to write the story of a German woman in her late forties who had taken upon herself the burden of history from 1922 to 1970', may have influenced his award of the Nobel Prize for Literature in 1972. A variety of narrative techniques are used in *Die verlorene Ehre der Katharina Blum* (1974; tr. Vennewitz as *The Lost Honor of Katharina Blum*, 1975) to piece together the background to a murder which is symptomatic of the defamatory tactics of the contemporary press. Short stories are collected in *Absent Without Leave and Other Stories* (1963) and *Children Are Civilians Too* (1973), both tr. Vennewitz. With his wife he translated many authors into German, including BEHAN, MALAMUD, SALINGER, G. B. SHAW, and SYNGE.

BOLT, ROBERT (1924–95) British dramatist, was born in Sale, Manchester, and educated at Manchester Grammar School, after which he worked as an office boy before going to Manchester University. He completed his degree in history in 1949, having in the meantime served in both the Royal Air Force and the Royal West African Frontier Force. He was Head of the English Department at Millfield School, Somerset 1952–58. His first stage play, *The Critic and the Heart*, a conventional drama with affinities with MAUGHAM's *The Circle*, was produced in 1957, followed by *Flowering Cherry* (published 1958), which was Chekhovian in its theme and more poetic in its language. *A Man for All Seasons* (1961, but originally a radio play, broadcast in 1954), about the predicament, imprisonment, and death of THOMAS MORE, has strong stylistic echoes of BRECHT, but Bolt's linking character, the Common Man, plays several parts, and the obvious stage devices are used deliberately to enhance the atmosphere of the artificial and to act as a contrast to the historical reality. He returned to Tudor politics and to conflicts of character as well as of conscience and power with *Vivat! Vivat Regina!* (1971), in which Elizabeth I and Mary, Queen of Scots, are the protagonists. The balance between the romantic and the melodramatic is neatly maintained, even if the colourful climax is not so much theatrical gesture as historical fact. Bolt also wrote screenplays, including *Lawrence of Arabia* (1962) and *Dr Zhivago* (1965), for both of which he won Oscars. After a divorce in 1967 he married the actress Sarah Miles, who was 17 years younger than he was. They separated in 1973 and were divorced in 1976. Having partially recovered from a severe stroke, he was briefly married to Ann Zane, formerly Marchioness of Queensberry. He and Miles remarried in 1988—her account of their marriages is in her third autobiographical vol-

ume, *Bolt from the Blue* (1996). See Ronald Hayman, *Robert Bolt*, 1969 (critical study).

BOND, EDWARD (*b.* 1934) British dramatist, was born in Holloway, London, was evacuated during World War II, and was afterwards educated at Crouch End Secondary Modern School. He used to go to music hall shows (one of his sisters worked as the girl sawn in half by the magician) and at the age of 14 saw (Sir) Donald Wolfit (1902–68) as Macbeth, which inspired his ambition to write for the stage. Two years' National Service in the army focused his dramatic creativity, and in 1958 he submitted two plays to the Royal Court Theatre, which invited him to join its Writers' Group. After *The Pope's Wedding* had been performed successfully in 1962, the theatre commissioned a new play. *Saved* fell foul of the Lord Chamberlain, whose cuts Bond refused to accept. In 1966 it was put on at the Royal Court, which was convicted of presenting an unlicensed play. *Early Morning*, having been conclusively banned by the Lord Chamberlain, was performed before members of the English Stage Society in 1968; two months later *Narrow Road to the Deep North* opened in Coventry, with amendments to which Bond had agreed. The new Theatres Bill became law on 28 September 1968, and in 1969 all three plays were publicly performed at the Royal Court in repertory. With *The Sea* (1973) he rounded off his original plan for a series of extremely dark and often violent comedies whose main theme is coming to terms with reality. *Bingo: Scenes of Money and Death* (performed 1973) and *The Fool: Scenes of Bread and Love* (1975) began another, in which social problems of the past are used to highlight disorders of the present. It has been followed by a range of war parables—see *The War Plays: a Trilogy* (1985). He has also published *Poems 1978–85* (1985). See *Plays*, 6 vols 1977–97; Tony Coult, *The Plays of Edward Bond: a Study*, 2nd rev. edn 1980.

BORGES, JORGE LUIS (1899–1986) Argentinian short-story writer, poet, and critic, was born in Buenos Aires. His father was a lawyer of an ancient family; his mother was the daughter of a colonel who died in action during civil war in 1874, and of an English woman who was born in Staffordshire. As a child he read KIPLING and STEVENSON, and 'at about ten or eleven' GEORGE DOUGLAS's *The House with the Green Shutters*. He grew up in Spain and Switzerland, where he attended Collège de Génève, and in 1921 returned to Buenos Aires, where he edited and contributed to literary and intellectual journals, and by the end of the decade had published several volumes of verse and critical essays. *Historia Universal de la Infamia* (1935; tr. Norman Thomas di Giovanni as *A Universal History of Infamy*, 1973), his first collection of stories, was written in the style of fantasy which became known as 'magic realism'.

In 1946, having publicly expressed doubts about the democratic principles of the newly elected President, Juan Perón (1895–1974), Borges was transferred from his post as a third assistant in a municipal library to that of inspector of poultry and rabbits in a local market. On Perón's removal from power in 1955 he was appointed Director of the National Library. After he had shared with BECKETT the inaugural Prix Fomentor (awarded by an international publishing group) in 1961, his reputation abroad was further confirmed by the publication in English of *Ficciones* (1944; tr Anthony Kerrigan, 1963) and *El Aleph* (1949; tr. di Giovanni as *The Aleph and Other Stories 1933–1969*, 1970). He held his post at the National Library until 1973, while also teaching English literature at the University of Buenos Aires, intensifying his study of Old English and Old Norse, lecturing to audiences in the USA and Europe, and continuing to write: all this despite the onset in 1955 of a congenital eye condition which made him virtually blind. For thirty years until her death in 1975 at the age of 99, he lived with his mother in a small sixth-floor apartment in downtown Buenos Aires. Maria Kodama (*b.* 1945), who had been his companion for several years, became his third wife eight weeks before he died. He was awarded an honorary doctorate at Oxford in 1971, and was appointed Honorary KBE. *Selected Poems 1923–1967*, ed. di Giovanni (1972), contains translations by several poets. See also *Labyrinths: Selected Stories and Other Writings*, ed. Donald A. Yates and James E. Irby (1972). See James Woodall, *The Man in the Mirror of the Book: a Life of Jorge Luis Borges*, 1996 (biography); Beatriz Sarlo, *Jorge Luis Borges: a Writer on the Edge*, ed. John King, 1993 (critical essays); Norman Thomas di Giovanni (ed.), *The Borges Tradition*, 1995 (critical essays).

BORROW, GEORGE (1803–81) British linguist, prose writer, and traveller, was born in East Dereham, Norfolk, the son of a regimental staff officer, and was educated at the High School of Edinburgh and Norwich Grammar School. He was articled to a solicitor, but went to London on his father's death and worked as a publisher's editor and hack writer. Disillusioned, he spent the years 1825–32 wandering through England, often with gypsies as companions. In 1833 he became an agent of the British and Foreign Bible Society, and for two years travelled to Russia, Spain, Portugal, and Morocco, gratifying his gift for languages—while he was in St Petersburg in 1835 he published *Targum: or Metrical Translations from Thirty Languages* and the first English translation of PUSHKIN. On his return in 1835 he married a widow whom he had met in Spain, and settled with her in Oulton Broad, Norfolk. He began his full-time literary career with *The Zincali, or an Account of the Gypsies of Spain* (1841). He then used the letters he had written to the Bible Society as the basis of *The Bible in Spain* (1843), which was an instant success. This led him to write two accounts of his earlier life: *Lavengro* (1851)—the Romany for 'wordmaster'—and a sequel, *The Romany Rye* (1857)—*rai* means 'gentleman'. More profitably read as picaresque fiction than as autobiography, they are discursive, racy, often comic, with sharp dialogue. Borrow's attitude to gypsies was overromantic, but he influenced later Romany scholars such as John Sampson (1862–1931) and Dora Yates (1879–1974). See David Williams. *A World of His Own: the Double Life of George Borrow*, 1982.

BOSMAN, HERMAN CHARLES (1905–51) South African journalist and short-story writer, was an Afrikaner born in Kuils River, near Cape Town, and had an English education in Johannesburg. He was a teacher when in 1926 he was condemned to death after a shooting incident in which his stepbrother was killed. He was reprieved and did 4¹/₂ years' hard labour. His unfailing sense of humour, as well as his courage, are reflected in his account of prison, *Cold Stone Jug* (1949). On his release he was a journalist in Europe and South Africa. He wrote essays and sketches, romantic verse (as Herman Malan), and two novels. His place in South African literature is due to his rural short stories narrated by the Afrikaner, Oom Schalk Lourens. Collected in *Mafeking Road* (1947) and *Unto Dust* (1963), they present sympathetically and wittily a whole range of passions and human circumstances. See *Collected Works*, new edn 1992.

BOSWELL, JAMES (1740–95) Scottish prose writer and biographer, was born in Edinburgh, the son of a barrister, who in 1754 became a judge of the Court of Session with the courtesy title of Lord Auchinleck. He was educated at Mundell's School, Edinburgh, and by private tutors, before going to Edinburgh University, where he took an arts degree and indulged his passions for poetry and the theatre. His subsequent free living led to the first of several breaches with his father and to his being enrolled for a course in law at Glasgow University, from which he quickly escaped to London in 1759. After failing to get a commission in a Guards regiment, he was persuaded to renew his law studies in Edinburgh. In 1762, having attained his majority, he left again for London, where for the first time he met his literary idol JOHNSON—see *Boswell's London Journal 1763–64*, ed. F. A. Pottle (1950) for a full account of this momentous incident. After further studies in Utrecht and making the Grand Tour of Europe (including Corsica), he was called to the Scottish Bar in 1766, and in

1768 published *An Account of Corsica*, an admirable descriptive work and an eloquent justification of Corsican nationalism. After numerous rebuffs, changes of heart and mind, and several torrid affairs, he married in 1769 Margaret Montgomerie, a cousin two years his senior, whom he had known for some years—she died in 1789, having borne him four children. Also in 1769, he bought an interest in the *London Magazine*, to which as 'The Hypochondriack' he contributed a regular series of essays on popular philosophical and practical issues between 1777 and 1785.

In 1773 he managed to persuade Johnson, who was notoriously averse to anything Scottish, to accompany him on an exhausting but successful three months' trip, taking in Edinburgh, Aberdeen, and Glasgow, as well as the Western Isles, which he wrote up in a classic travelogue, *The Journal of a Tour to the Hebrides, with Samuel Johnson, LL.D.* (1785), a much superior account to that of his travelling companion. After Johnson's death, Boswell left his family in Scotland in 1786, and went to London to prepare his friend's biography. He was admitted to the English Bar, at which he performed with even less success than he had in Scotland. His monumental *The Life of Samuel Johnson* was published in 1791, and reflects not only his dedication to his task and to his subject, but his brilliant eye for a telling detail, his skill as an interviewer, his recall of dialogue and ability to reconstruct a conversation, and his flair for the dramatic situation. Boswell's death was hastened if not caused by his compulsive concupiscence. He was a failure at the law and was consistently rejected in his pursuit of public office; yet through his books, journals, and other writings, many of which were only discovered in Ireland and Scotland between 1926 and 1950, he is the most vivid personality of his age. See *The Journals of James Boswell 1761–1795*, ed. John Wain, new edn 1994; Iain Finlayson, *The Moth and the Candle: a Life of James Boswell*, 1984.

BOUCICAULT, DION (1820 or 1822–90) Irish actor, dramatist, theatre manager, and director, was born Dionysius Lardner Boursiquot in Dublin, nominally the son of a wine merchant and his wife (a sister of DARLEY), but more probably of the wife and Dionysius Lardner (1793–1859), the academic and encyclopedist. He was educated in and near London (for two years at University College School), and became an actor in 1838, when he also had a melodrama performed in Brighton. *London Assurance*, a realistic comedy of contemporary metropolitan life, was produced at Covent Garden in 1841 and was a brilliant success (it ran for an unprecedented 360 nights). In America between 1853 and 1860 he wrote and produced a number of popular melodramas notable for their sensational climaxes. *The Colleen Bawn: or, The Brides of Garryowen*, the first of his Irish dramas, opened in London in 1860. This, *Arrah-na-Pogue: or, The Wicklow Wedding* (1864), and *The Shaugraun* (1874), constitute his most original and significant contributions to the stage and had some influence on SYNGE, G. B. SHAW, and O'CASEY. The initial success of *The Colleen Bawn* encouraged him to establish his own touring company, an innovation which revolutionized the American provincial theatre. He was a prolific dramatist whose aim was to satisfy the taste of the public; he also adapted many comedies and thrillers from the French, as well as novels by AINSWORTH, DICKENS, IRVING, READE, and WALTER SCOTT. Boucicault was said to have by various means acquired, and by ill-judgment and extravagance lost, several fortunes. He was married three times, his second wife being Agnes Robertson (1833–1914), the Scottish-born actress, who starred in most of his plays. In 1885, he married in Australia a young member of his company, Louise Thorndyke, claiming that he and Agnes had never legally been married. Agnes obtained a formal divorce in England in 1889, thus re-legitimizing their six children, the eldest of whom, Dion (1859–1929), was also an actor, dramatist, and director. See Robert Hogan, *Dion Boucicault*, 1969 (critical study).

BOWEN, ELIZABETH (1898–1973) Irish novelist and short-story writer, was born in Dublin, spent her early summers at the family estate of Bowen's Court, Co. Cork, and was educated at Downe House, Kent. Of Anglo-Irish descent, she is regarded as combining the subtle observation of manners of AUSTEN and the class-awareness of EDGEWORTH, with the Irish social comedy of the cousins SOMERVILLE and Ross. The carefully built-up and sustained situations and settings of her novels span both milieus. *The Last September* (1929) centres on a big house in Ireland during the 1920 'Troubles'. Wartime London and the blitz are the background to *The Heat of the Day* (1949), a highly intelligent novel of romantic love and suspected treachery. The loneliness and vulnerability of the young are recurrent themes, a reflection of her own insecurity caused by her father's mental illness and her mother's death when she was 13. These are most evident in *The House in Paris* (1935), *The Death of the Heart* (1938), and *Eva Trout: or, Changing Scenes* (1969). Her first book was the volume of short stories, *Encounters* (1923), and throughout her career she invested her short stories with similar themes and settings to those of her novels, with the added dimension of the supernatural. She was made CBE in 1948. See *Collected Stories*, new edn 1994; *Bowen's Court*, new edn 1984 (early autobiography and family history); *Pictures and Conversations*, 1975 (unfinished autobiography); Victoria Glendinning, *Elizabeth Bowen: Portrait of a Writer*, new edn 1993; Edwin J. Kenney, *Elizabeth Bowen*, 1975 (critical study); Phyllis Lassner, *Elizabeth Bowen*, 1991 (biographical/critical study).

BOWERING, GEORGE (*b.* 1935) Canadian poet, novelist, and critic, was born in Penticton, British Columbia, and educated at South Okanagan High School, Oliver, and for a year at Victoria College, after which he was an aerial photographer in the Royal Canadian Air Force. He then studied at the University of British Columbia, becoming BA in history (1960) and MA in English (1963); with four others he founded in Vancouver in 1961 the west-coast literary magazine, *Tish*, which survived until 1969. He taught English at the University of Calgary and Sir George Williams University, going on to Simon Fraser University in 1972. He was founder-Editor of the journal *Imago* 1964–74. His first of over thirty books of verse was *Sticks and Stones* (1963). He won the Governor General's Award for *Rocky Mountain Foot: a Lyric, a Memoir* (1969) and *The Gangs of Kosmos* (1969); he was awarded another for his third novel, *Burning Water* (1980), about the exploration of the Northwest Passage by Captain Vancouver (1758–98), who is the subject, too, of Bowering's long poem, *George Vancouver* (1970). He has also published several books of short stories, a study of PURDY (1970), and *Imaginary Hand: Essays by George Bowering* (1988). See *Particular Accidents: Selected Poems*, ed. Robin Blaser, 1980.

BOWLES, JANE see BOWLES.

BOWLES, PAUL (*b.* 1910) American novelist, short-story writer, poet, translator, travel writer, and composer, was born in New York City, the son of a dentist who had a passion for golf. After high school and a taste of art school, he went to the University of Virginia (because of POE), from which he disappeared during his first year to Paris, where he had had poems published in the journal *transitions*. He returned to the USA to finish the college year, then studied music under the composers Aaron Copland (1900–90) and Virgil Thomson (1896–1989). In spite of discouragement from STEIN, he continued to write verse—see *Next to Nothing: Collected Poems 1926–1977* (1981). He was Music Critic for the New York *Herald-Tribune* 1942–46. Since then he has lived mainly in Tangier, Morocco. His musical compositions comprise operas, including *The Wind Remains*, performed in New York in 1943 with a libretto by GARCÍA LORCA, ballets such as *Pastorella* (1941), chamber music, orchestral works, songs, and incidental music for plays and films. His novels, beginning with *The Sheltering Sky* (1949), are particularly concerned with conflicting cultures in North African set-

tings. *Collected Stories 1939–1976* was published in 1979. His first translation was SARTRE's *Huis Clos* for Broadway (published 1946). Latterly he has concentrated on editing and translating works by contemporary North Africans. His wife Jane Bowles (1917–73), née Auer, whom he married in 1938, was a novelist, short-story writer, and dramatist, whose explorations of female mysteries and realities have earned her a following since her death. See *Without Stopping: an Autobiography*, 1972; *In Touch: the Letters of Paul Bowles*, ed. Jeffrey Miller, new edn 1995; Simon Bischoff (ed.), *Paul Bowles: Photographs—'How could I send a picture into the desert?'*, 1995 (visual record of his life in Morocco with introduction and interview).

BOX, EDGAR see VIDAL.

BOYD, MARK ALEXANDER (1563–1601) Scottish poet, was born in Galloway, the son of Robert Boyd of Penkill Castle, Ayrshire. He was educated by his uncle, James Boyd, Archbishop of Glasgow 1572–81, and at Glasgow University, where he attacked his teachers, burned his books, and refused to study. After fighting a duel at court, he was advised to become a mercenary on the Continent, which he did in intervals between the serious study of literature and law at various academic centres of excellence. In 1592 he published in Antwerp a volume of elegant Latin verses, *Epistolae Heroides, et Hymni*, dedicated to JAMES VI, to which was added a selection of his letters, written on his travels. He returned to Scotland in 1595. Among the papers he left to the Advocates' Library, Edinburgh, is his only surviving poem in Scots, the love sonnet 'Fra banc to banc, fra wod to wod, I rin . . .', as significant for its time in its directness and simplicity of language as it is in its intensity and expression of personal feeling.

BOYD, MARTIN (1893–1972) Australian novelist, was born in Lucerne, Switzerland. He came of a distinguished colonial family on both sides, and was the third of three artistic sons of Arthur Merric Boyd (1862–1940), the watercolour landscapist, and E(mma) M(innie) Boyd (*d.* 1936), née a'Beckett, painter of landscape and genre. He was educated at Trinity Grammar School, Kew, Victoria, and St John's Theological College, Melbourne, after which he trained in an architect's office. He travelled to England in 1915 to enlist as an officer in World War I, and served at the front in the Buffs, before transferring to the Royal Flying Corps, in which he became a pilot. After the war he returned for a time to Australia, where he published a book of poems, *Retrospect* (1920), at his own expense. He then travelled in Europe, and joined, on impulse, a somewhat chaotic Franciscan community in Dorset, which provided the setting for his first novel, *Love Gods* (1925). This, *Brangane: a Memoir* (1926), and *The Montforts* (1928; rev. edn 1963), an ambitious novel based on family history which won the inaugural Australian Literary Society Gold Medal, were published under the pen name of Martin Mills.

He was now living in London, where he wrote under his own name four novels with which he was later dissatisfied, 'because I did not know the sort of people I was writing about'. *Nuns in Jeopardy* (1940) was written as 'a symbol of the transmutation of the human soul, told in physical terms'. In Cambridge during World War II he wrote *Lucinda Brayford* (1946), a quadripartite expression of his attitude towards the British Establishment, of his support of 'the landed gentry, the creative artist and the Christian religion', and of his pacifism. The years 1948–51 were spent restoring and living in his maternal grandfather's country house near Berwick, Victoria, which he gave up after falling ill in England. During his recovery he began *The Cardboard Crown* (1952), which, with *A Difficult Young Man* (1955), *Outbreak of Love* (1957), and *When Blackbirds Sing* (1962), constitute the 'Langton tetralogy', a further but more striking excursion into family history in England and Australia. In 1958 he settled in Rome. See *A Single Flame*, 1939, and *Day of My Delight*, new edn 1986 (autobiography); Brenda Niall, *Martin Boyd: a Life*, new edn 1989.

BOYD, NANCY see MILLAY.

BOYLE, KAY (1903–94) American novelist, short-story writer, and poet, was born in St Paul, Minnesota. She was educated at home and in Europe while travelling with her parents, and at schools in the USA. She then attended the Cincinnati Conservatory of Music and studied architecture at the Ohio Mechanics Institute. In 1922 she married Richard Brault, a French graduate in engineering, with whom she went to live in France. In Paris she mixed with what STEIN called the 'Lost Generation' of expatriate writers— Boyle added a memoir to the 1968 edition of *Being Geniuses Together 1920–1930*, an autobiographical study of that milieu by Robert McAlmon (1896–1930). She also wrote poetry for little magazines, published her first book, *Short Stories* (1929), and made a remarkable recovery from tuberculosis shortly before having her first child. After a divorce in 1931, she married Laurence Vail, an American expatriate writer and painter, with whom she bought a house in the French Alps. While bringing up children, she continued to write: poetry, both of a personal nature and out of a political and social consciousness which manifested itself also in her activities—see *Collected Poems* (1991); short stories, of which there were four further volumes between 1932 and 1940—see also *Fifty Short Stories* (1980); and novels with strong characters (American, German, or French) and tragic overtones, reflecting settings and situations from her own experience, such as *Plagued by the Nightingale* (1931), *Year Before Last* (1932), and *Death of a Man* (1936). In 1941 the family (including six children) was airlifted by Clipper from Lisbon to the USA. In 1943, having obtained a divorce, she married Baron Joseph von Franckenstein (*d.* 1963), an Austrian refugee working in the USA. As a foreign correspondent for the *New Yorker*, Boyle accompanied him to his posting in occupied Germany in 1945—her experiences are reflected in *The Smoking Mountain: Stories of Post War Germany* (1951) and her novel *Generation Without Farewell* (1960). In 1953 they returned to the USA, where she taught English at San Francisco State University 1963–80, being appointed Professor Emerita on her retirement. In the 1960s she was twice imprisoned for protesting against the Vietnam War, as is the protagonist of her last novel, *The Underground Woman* (1975). *Words That Must Somehow Be Said: Selected Essays of Kay Boyle 1927–1984*, ed. Elizabeth S. Bell (1985) illustrates both her political and her artistic sensibilities. See Sandra Whipple Spanier, *Kay Boyle: Artist and Activist*, new edn 1987 (biography).

BRACKENRIDGE, HUGH HENRY (1748–1816) American novelist, prose writer, and poet, was born Hugh Montgomery Breckenridge in the western Highlands of Scotland, near Campbeltown, Kintyre. He was the son of an impoverished farmer, who in 1753 sailed with his family to Philadelphia, from which they walked most of the way to the Scottish settlement of the Barrens, York County. He went to the county school, and at 15 offered himself as a pupil teacher at the free school at Gunpowder Falls, Maryland, after which he made a similar arrangement with the College of New Jersey, Princeton. He graduated as BA in 1771, having with FRENEAU written a fantastic adventure story, 'Father Bombo's Pilgrimage to Mecca', possibly the first prose fiction written in America. In 1772 he was appointed head of an academy at Back Creek, Maryland, for whose students he wrote a verse drama, *The Battle of Bunkers-Hill* (1776). In 1776 he joined the army of George Washington (1732–99) as a chaplain, in which capacity he delivered political sermons to the troops, published in *Six Political Discourses Founded on the Scripture* (1778). After the British evacuation of Philadelphia in 1778, he founded and edited the *United States Magazine*. He was admitted to the Philadelphia Bar in 1780, and then set out for the frontier town of Pittsburgh, where he practised, married, and was instrumental in the establishment in 1785 of the *Pittsburgh Gazette*, having persuaded two printers to bring a press over the mountains. He used the paper to promote his political career, and also to campaign for civic cultural and educational amenities, including a bookshop and a lending library. In 1786 he was elected to the State Assembly of Pennsylvania, where he obtained a land endowment for the Pittsburgh Academy (University of Pittsburgh). After failing to be re-elected in 1788, he gave vent to satire, first with a (wisely) unfinished attempt to apply the technique of SAMUEL (HUDIBRAS) BUTLER to American politics, and then with the first two volumes of a more happily inspired comic novel, somewhat after CERVANTES, *Modern Chivalry* (1792). Volume III, published in Pittsburgh, was the first literary work to be written, printed, and issued west of the mountains. There followed Volume IV (1797) and Part II (1804), with a definitive edition of the whole in 1815.

After an unfortunate attempt to mediate in the Whiskey Rebellion of 1794, Brackenridge returned to politics in 1798 as leader in western Pennsylvania of the Republican party of Thomas Jefferson (1734–1826); in 1799 he was appointed a judge of the Pennsylvania Supreme Court. He wrote some poems in Scots, addressed in kind to David Bruce, a fellow Scottish-American poet and country storekeeper, and also 'An Epistle to Walter Scott' (1811), in puerile imitation of the prosody of *The Lady of the Lake*. His eccentricities included propping up his bare feet on the bar of justice, and riding naked in the rain with his only suit under his saddle, because it would otherwise be spoiled. Shortly after the death of his first wife, being attracted to the girl who brought his horse round to the door after a stop to have it fed, he offered her father $10 a year for someone else to clear his meadow, married her, and promptly dispatched her to Philadelphia to have her manners polished and her rustic ways removed. See *A Hugh Henry Brackenridge Reader 1770–1815*, ed. Daniel Marder, 1970.

BRADBURY, MALCOLM (*b.* 1932) British novelist and critic, was born in Sheffield, spent his early years in Harrow, Middlesex (his father worked for the London and North Eastern Railway Company), and in 1941 returned with his parents to Sheffield, where he suffered 'terror by night and disturbance by day' during the Blitz in World War II. Born with a hole in the heart, for which there was no treatment until he was 26, he could not play games, 'so I was always told to go to read in the library. It's why I became a writer.' He was educated at West Bridgford Grammar School, Nottingham, and University College, Leicester, continuing his studies at the universities of London, Indiana, and Manchester, before teaching at Hull and (with DAVID LODGE) at Birmingham. He became a lecturer in English at the University of East Anglia in 1965, and was Professor of American Studies 1970–1994. In his essay 'Campus Fictions', he explains, of his arrival at university: 'I had little expectation of the strange world I was entering, and little confidence in my right to be there. Even so, I had had some glimpses of what to expect, and these came from what can be called university novels. . . . I had not yet grasped the spaces which exist between fiction and fact . . .'. Into the 'spaces' he inserted three of his first four novels, *Eating People is Wrong* (1959), largely written while he was a student, *Stepping Westward* (1965), set in the 'moral supermarket' of a new American university, and *The History Man* (1975), in which the comedy is now harsher and tensions deeper. A similar psychological approach informs *Rates of Exchange* (1983), in which the exchanges are linguistic as well as economic, in an Eastern European setting. *Doctor Criminale* (1992) opens at a Booker fiction award dinner and continues with a literary quest which is also an academic satire on the 1990s and an investigation into the essence of history. His short stories have been published as *Who Do You Think You Are?: Stories and Parodies* (rev. edn 1984). His critical works include *The Modern American Novel* (1983; 2nd edn 1992), *The Modern British Novel* (1993), and *Dangerous Pilgrimages: Trans-Atlantic Mythologies and the Novel* (1995). He edited *Classwork* (1995), a collection of stories by those who took the MA course in creative writing which he established with ANGUS WILSON at the University of East Anglia in 1970 to complement the programmes which had been taught in the USA since the 19th century. He was made CBE in 1991. See in John Haffenden, *Novelists in Interview*, 1985.

BRADBURY, RAY(MOND) (*b.* 1920) American short-story writer and novelist, was born in Waukegan, Illinois, the son of a telephone linesman, who in search of work in 1934 moved his family to Los Angeles. While at Los Angeles High School ('the unhappiest years of my life') he established himself as a theatrical all-rounder, and discovered the Los Angeles Science Fiction League. After graduating in 1938, he worked as a newspaper boy, published four issues of his own science-fiction magazine, and attended HEINLEIN's weekly writing classes. He sold one story in 1941, two in 1942, and 11 in 1943, when he gave up the newspaper job to write full time. In 1947 he published his first collection of weird stories, *Dark Carnival*, won an O. HENRY prize, and celebrated his literary coming of age by burning 'a million words of bad writing' the day before his wedding. With *The Martian Chronicles* (1950), a structured tapestry of fictional pieces about the colonization of Mars, and the futuristic novel, *Fahrenheit 451* (1953), he crossed the divide between pulp magazine maestro and writer of mainstream novels, in which category are also his autobiographical fantasies, *Dandelion Wine*

(1957), *Something Wicked This Way Comes* (1962), and *A Graveyard for Lunatics* (1990), and his imaginative memoir of a trip to Ireland in 1953, *Green Shadows, White Whale* (1992). His major effort, however, has gone into the production of short stories, latterly of a realistic nature, as well as fantasy and science fiction—see *The Stories of Ray Bradbury* (1980). He has continued to write for the stage—see *The Wonderful Ice-Cream Suit and Other Plays* (1972)—and has also published books of verse, collected in *The Complete Poems of Ray Bradbury* (1982), which has an appeal to Bradbury buffs. See David Mogen, *Ray Bradbury*, 1987 (critical study).

BRADDON, MARY ELIZABETH (1835–1915) British novelist and dramatist, was born in London of a talented family— her elder brother, (Sir) Edward Braddon (1829–1904), became Prime Minister of Tasmania. She was educated privately, and made some appearances on the stage. In 1854, a printer in Yorkshire, where she was then living, offered her £10 to write a 'dramatic' serial, but went bankrupt before it could be published. The story, 'Three Times Dead' (published in 1861 as *The Trail of the Serpent*), laid the ground for her later reputation. *Garibaldi, and Other Poems* was published in 1861, and her first play, *The Loves of Arcadia*, was staged in 1860. In that year she went to live with the publisher John Maxwell (1825–95), whose wife was in an asylum, and to look after his five children—they married in 1874 after the wife's death. She responded to his urgent request for a serial for a new magazine by producing *Lady Audley's Secret*. It was transferred to another periodical when the first one folded, and then published in three volumes (1862). This archetypal novel of sensation (some contemporary critics regarded it rather as a 'shocker'), with its thoroughly poisonous, blonde heroine, so impressed the public (and other critics) that she produced 13 further novels in the next six years—the play of *Lady Audley's Secret* followed in 1863, written not by herself but by the comedian and writer of farces, C. H. Hazlewood (1823–75). In all, she wrote over eighty novels (some with lurid titles)—she was still writing them in her seventies—and nine plays; she also edited periodicals, including *Temple Bar* and *Belgravia*. See Robert Lee Wolff, *Sensational Victorian: the Life and Fiction of Mary Elizabeth Braddon*, 1979.

BRADSTREET, ANNE (1612–72), née Dudley, the first published American poet, was born in England, the second of six children by his first wife of Thomas Dudley (1576–1653), steward to the Earl of Lincoln and later Governor of Massachusetts, who ensured that she had the best education that tutors could provide. In 1628, when she was 16, she had smallpox, and married Simon

Bradstreet (1603–97); with him and her parents and a shipload of other Puritans she sailed for Massachusetts in 1630, in the wake of the Pilgrim Fathers, who had made the journey ten years before. After a terrible three-months' voyage, the couple moved in quick succession from Salem to Boston to Cambridge to Ipswich, and finally to Andover, where in 1640, after 'a long time without a child, which was a great greif to me, and cost mee many prayers and tears before I obtained one', she had the first of her eight children, all but one of whom survived her. Her sister Mercy (1621–91), who also wrote verse, had in 1639 married John Woodbridge (1613–96), who was ordained in Andover in 1645 and in 1647 returned to England, where he was chaplain to the Parliamentary commissioners who treated with King Charles I in the Isle of Wight. He took with him a manuscript of Bradstreet's poems, which were published in London, without her permission and much to her embarrassment, as *The Tenth Muse lately sprung up in America. . . . By a Gentlewoman in those parts* (1650). Indeed, 'Thy visage was so irksome in my sight; / Yet being mine own, at length affection would / Thy blemishes amend, if so I could' ('The Author to Her Book', written in about 1666). So she set about revising the poems, which were posthumously reprinted in Boston in *Several Poems compiled with great variety of Wit and learning. . . . By a Gentlewoman in New England* (1678), with others that she had composed in the meantime. Among these is 'Contemplations', in which she expresses, as many American poets did later, her trust not so much in theology as in the evidence of her own eyes: 'If so much excellence abide below, / How excellent is He that dwells on high, / Whose power and beauty by his works we know'. Otherwise, her devotional verse is of less immediate appeal than her occasional verses: to her husband, often 'absent upon Public Employment'; on family bereavements or recoveries from illness; on her children; and '. . . Upon the Burning of Our House, July 10th 1666'. Her prose 'Meditations Divine and Morall', written down in 1664 at the request of her eldest son, were printed in full in the 1867 edition of her works. She died of consumption. Her husband married again, was twice Governor of Massachusetts (1679–86 and 1689–92), and lived to the ripest of old ages. See *The Works of Anne Bradstreet*, ed. Jeannine Hensley, 1981; Elizabeth Wade White, *Anne Bradstreet: 'The Tenth Muse'*, 1971 (critical biography).

BRADY, NICHOLAS see TATE, NAHUM.

BRAINE, JOHN (1922–86) British novelist, was born in Bradford, Yorkshire, and educated at St Bede's Grammar School, Bradford, and Leeds School of Librarianship. With a break of three years as a freelance writer, he rose in the library world to the post of Branch Librarian at Darton, Yorkshire, from which he resigned in 1957 on the publication of his first novel, *Room at the Top*. This iconoclastic story of the opportunist Yorkshire lad from a working-class background who makes it (in both senses) to social acceptance and material prosperity was, with the help of a television feature, an instant success, though the publisher to whom the paperback rights were first offered rejected it as amoral. *The Vodi* (1959; rev. edn 1978), a novel of supernatural possession, was not well received (it was probably written before *Room at the Top*). He returned to his original formula and characters with *Life at the Top* (1962), in which, and in a number of subsequent novels including *Stay with Me till Morning* (1970) and its sequel, and *One and Last Love* (1981), he dissects middle-class married life. *The Jealous God* (1964) investigates the personal conflicts which can affect the Catholic priesthood. *The Pious Agent* (1975) and *Finger of Fire* (1977) are spy stories in which the rights are questioned of those who control the agents. In *Writing a Novel* (1975) Braine discusses the craft of the novelist.

BRASCH, CHARLES (1909–73) New Zealand poet and editor, was born in Dunedin and educated at Waitaki School and St John's College, Oxford. After three seasons as a trainee archaeologist in Egypt and much travel, he taught at Little Missenden Abbey, a progressive school. He visited New Zealand in 1938–39, and when he returned to England, via the USA, he left with GLOVER the manuscript of a book of verse, *The Land and the People* (1939), to be published in his absence. Unfit for war service, much to his surprise, because of a lung complaint, he was a fire watcher in London, and then did intelligence work for the Foreign Office at Bletchley Park. He returned to New Zealand in 1945, having written an allegorical mime in verse, *The Quest* (1946), and a number of poems which appeared in *Disputed Ground* (1948), including 'Word by Night', which came to him complete during a storm on the night of the German capitulation. In 1947 he founded the quarterly literary and arts review, *Landfall*, which he edited until 1967, and in which honesty compelled a youthful C. K. STEAD to give a lukewarm reception to Brasch's third book of poetry, *The Estate* (1957)—further volumes appeared in 1964, 1969, and 1974. He was a notable patron of the arts, who left a valuable collection of books and paintings to the Hocken Library, Dunedin. See *Collected Poems*, ed. Alan Roddick, 1984; *Indirections: a Memoir 1909–1947*, 1980.

BRATHWAITE, EDWARD KAMAU (b. 1930) Barbadian poet and critic, was born in Bridgetown and educated at Harrison College, from which, having elected to pursue history and English language on his own, he won an island scholarship to Pembroke College, Cambridge. Rather than return home, he took an appointment as an education officer in Ghana, of which he wrote in his autobiographical essay, 'Timehri' (1970): 'Obscurely, slowly but surely, during the eight years that I lived there, I was coming to an awareness and understanding of community, of cultural wholeness, of the place of the individual within the tribe, in society.' *Rights of Passage* (1967), *Masks* (1968), and *Islands* (1969), reissued as *The Arrivants: a New World Trilogy* (1973), were revolutionary in poetic content as well as form and shape. The reader is taken from the West Indies to the USA, then to the Afro-Caribbean roots in West Africa, and finally on an exploration of meaningful existence in the Caribbean. *Other Exiles* (1975) contains poems written during the previous 25 years, and illustrates the development of his poetic language. *Mother Poem* (1977), *Sun Poem* (1982), and *X-Self* (1987) comprise a further trilogy, in which first the voices of women, then male rituals, and then impressions from an intellectual autobiography mark the confrontation between the cultures of Europe and Africa. *Middle Passages* (1992) is both a selection and a rearrangement into a sequence, including newer visual poetry created with the help of a computer. Brathwaite taught at the University of the West Indies from 1962, being appointed Reader in 1976, and Professor of Social and Cultural History in 1983. His prose works include *The Development of Creole Society in Jamaica 1770–1820* (1971) and *History of the Voice: the Development of National Language in Anglophone Caribbean Poetry* (1984). See Stewart Brown (ed.), *The Art of E. K. Brathwaite*, 1996; and in Bruce King (ed.), *West Indian Literature*, 2nd edn 1995.

BRAUTIGAN, RICHARD (1935–84) American poet and novelist, was born in Tacoma, Washington, and published his first book of verse, *The Return of the Rivers*, in San Francisco in 1957. Through his epigrammatic verse—*The Pill Versus the Springhill Mine Disaster: Poems 1957–1968* was published in 1968—he developed a prose style for fiction ('I used poetry as a lover but I never made her my old lady') which he first exhibited in *A Confederate General from Big Sur* (1965), *Trout Fishing in America* (1967), and *In Watermelon Sugar* (1968), becoming in the process the literary spokesman of the Woodstock generation. His experimental style appealed for the simplicity of its language (though not of its thought), the comedy, the literary and other allusions, and the quest imagery. Subsequent novels include *The Hawkline Monster: a Gothic Western* (1974) and his last, *So the Wind Won't Blow It Away* (1982). In the meantime, a trip to Japan satisfied an early preoccupation and inspired two significant works.

At 17 he had begun to read BASHŌ and other Japanese *haiku* poets: 'I liked the way they used language concentrating emotion, detail and image until they arrived at a form of dew-like steel', which is reflected in his last volume of verse, in the form of a poetic diary, *June 30th, June 30th* (1978). In the novel *The Tokyo–Montana Express* (1980), a Bashō-like spirit of Zen Buddhism underpins the philosophy 'I spend a lot of my time interested in little things, tiny portions of reality.' He died from a self-inflicted gunshot wound.

BRECHT, BERTOLT (1898–1956) German dramatist and poet, was born in Augsburg, where he attended the gymnasium. He entered Munich University in 1917 to study medicine and natural science, only to be called up for service as a medical orderly in World War I, after which he worked as *dramaturg* (dramatic adviser and editor) in Munich and Berlin. Morally an anarchist, but politically a supporter of Communism as the only valid alternative to Fascism, he had had several reactionary plays produced when he hit upon a public success, *Die Dreigroschenoper* [*The Threepenny Opera*] (1928), adapted from GAY's *The Beggar's Opera*, with music by Kurt Weill (1900–50); in the context of it he later wrote, 'Complex seeing must be practised. . . . Thinking above the flow of the play is more important than thinking from *within* the flow of the play.' Public performances of *Die Mutter* [*The Mother*] (1932), based on GORKY's novel, were banned, as were many of his books, and in 1933 he fled the country, not to Russia, as might have been expected, but to Denmark, from which he went to Sweden in 1939, and then Finland in 1940. In 1941 he arrived (via the USSR) in Los Angeles, USA, on immigration papers arranged by émigrés to Hollywood. There he worked on and contributed to the screenplay of *Hangmen also Die* (1943), though sole credit as writer was awarded to John Wexley (1907–85) after an enquiry by the Screen Writers Guild.

During the years 1937–41 he wrote *Mutter Courage und ihre Kinder* [*Mother Courage and her Children*] (produced Zürich 1941), *Leben des Galilei* [*The Life of Galileo*] (Zürich 1943), *Der gute Mensch von Sezuan* [*The Good Woman of Setzuan*] (Zürich 1943), and in 1944–45 *Der kaukasische Kreidekreis* [*The Caucasian Chalk Circle*] (Potsdam 1949). These were the plays which most firmly established his reputation abroad, and reflected his proposition: 'The illusion of the theatre must be only partial, so that it can always be recognized as an illusion. Reality, in all its perfection, must be changed through the fact of artistic presentation, so that it may be recognized and treated as changeable.' Thus his 'epic' (or 'open') theatre shows men and women producing themselves and their situations, rather than discovering them. In 1949 Brecht settled in East Berlin, where he established the theatre company, the Berlin Ensemble, which his second wife, the actress Helene Weigel (1900–72), continued after his death. He acquired an Austrian passport in 1950. His verse, the first commercially published volume of which appeared in 1927, and which contains much of lasting value, is in *Poems 1913–1956*, ed. John Willett, one volume edn 1987—see also *Bad Time for Poetry: Was It? Is It? 125 Poems and Songs*, ed. John Willett, tr. Michael Hamburger and others (1995) and *Everything Changes: Essential Brecht Poems*, ed. John Willett (1995). See *Collected Plays*, ed. John Willett and Ralph Manheim, 1970– ; *Collected Stories*, ed. John Willett and Ralph Manheim, new edn 1992; *Brecht on Theatre: the Development of an Aesthetic*, ed. and tr. John Willett, new edn 1994; Hans Otto Münsterer, *The Young Brecht*, tr. Tom Kuhn and K. J. Leeder, 1992 (reminiscences of 1917–22); John Fuegi, *The Life and Lies of Bertolt Brecht*, new edn 1994 (biography).

BRENNAN, CHRISTOPHER (1870–1932) Australian poet and critic, was born in Sydney, the eldest son of Irish immigrant parents, and was educated at St Ignatius College, Riverview, and Sydney University, where he graduated in classics. Intended by his family for the priesthood, he suffered a change of heart through his study of philosophy, in pursuit of which he went to Berlin University in 1892 on a scholarship. Instead he fell in love with Anna Werth, his landlady's daughter, and, discovering the poetry of MALLARMÉ, decided to 'go in for verse'. He became a cataloguer in the State Library in Sydney in 1895. In 1897 he issued for his friends eight copies of *XVIII Poems*, which he incorporated in *XXI Poems: Towards the Source* (1897), prefaced with an elegy projecting his emotions at meeting Anna, and published shortly before she arrived to marry him. In 1908, after many applications, he was appointed to teach French and German at Sydney University. 'Towards the Source' comprised the first of five parts of *Poems* (dated 1913), which he had devised during the years 1897–1902 as a single, Symbolist poetic cycle. He became Associate Professor of German and Comparative Literature in 1920. In 1922 he began an association with Violet (Vie) Singer, a lively 34-year-old, with whom he went to live and to whom he wrote some tender lyrics. She was killed by a tram in 1925, three months before he was deprived of his university post, mainly because of revelations about the affair which came to light during Anna's divorce suit against him. His remaining years were dogged by alcoholism and poverty, partly relieved in 1931 by a grant of £1 a week from the Commonwealth Literary Fund. In the development of Australian literature Brennan's poetry is significant for its intellectual aims and technical innovation, and his lasting position owes more to his critical sense than to his bohemian life-style and unconventional attitudes. See *Christopher Brennan*, ed. Terry Sturm, 1984 (compendium); *Selected Poems*, ed. G. A. Wilkes, 1973; *The Prose of Christopher Brennan*, ed. A. R. Chisholm and J. J. Quinn, 1962; Axel Clark, *Christopher Brennan: a Critical Biography*, 1980.

BRENT OF BIN BIN see FRANKLIN.

BRETON, ANDRÉ (1896–1966) French poet and critic, was born in Tinchebray and educated at Collège Chaptal, Paris, and the Faculté de Médecine, after which he served in World War I as an assistant in army psychiatric units. *Les Champs Magnétiques* (with Philip Soupault, 1920), an experiment in poetry by means of automatic writing, was a precursor of the Surrealist movement, whose manifesto he published in 1924. He edited *La Révolution Surréaliste* (1925–29), and *Le Surréalisme au Service de la Révolution* (1930–33). As well as poetry—see *Poems*, tr. Jean-Pierre Cauvin and Mary Ann Caws (1983)—he wrote narrative works in a poetic prose, of which *Nadja* (1928, tr. Richard Howard, 1960) caused a controversy for its denunciation of the use of psychiatry as an aid in enforcing bourgeois standards of conformity. See *What Is Surrealism?: Selected Writings*, ed. Franklin Rosemont, new edn 1990; Mark Polizzotti, *Revolution of the Mind: the Life of André Breton*, 1995 (biography).

BRIDGES, ROBERT (1844–1930) British poet and critic, was born in Walmer, Kent, the eighth of nine children of a landowning farmer. His father died when he was nine, but left provision for his education at Eton and Corpus Christi College, Oxford, where he rowed, played soccer, and narrowly missed a first in Greats. After travelling and studying in the Middle East and Europe, he determined to practise medicine until he was 40, and then retire to write poetry. He began his medical studies at St Bartholomew's Hospital in 1871. He brought out his first volume of verse in 1873, qualified as MB in 1874, and published three more books of poetry in the next six years, while also working as a hospital physician—he estimated that in 1877 he examined 30,940 casualty patients for an average of 1.28 minutes each. In the end illness forced him to give up his profession when he was 37. Two years later, in 1884, he married 21-year-old Monica Waterhouse, the daughter of the architect of the Natural History Museum, London. His *Collected Shorter Poems* was published in four books in 1890, with a fifth in 1894. In 1907 the couple moved to a house he had built on Boar's Hill, Oxford, where they lived quietly and contentedly—their third child and only son, Edward (1892–1969), became a distinguished civil servant and was created Lord Bridges in 1957.

Bridges aimed poetically to use form and words to create an object of beauty. He continually experimented with metre and line stress, employing poetic diction to enhance linguistic precision. He was the first to publish poems in 'sprung rhythm', a form developed by his friend HOPKINS, which particularly suits his topographical poems, notably 'London Snow' and 'The Downs'. His lyrics, especially 'The Linnet', 'Cheddar Pinks', and 'Christmas 1913', reveal his command of simple language as a medium of melody. His last major work, *The Testament of Beauty* (1927–29), is a long poem 'in loose Alexandrines' in which he attempts to reconcile idealistic philosophy with modern scientific thought and to relate beauty to reason. His criticism is best represented by the essay 'Milton's Prosody' (1893; rev. 1921). He was appointed Poet Laureate in 1913 on the death of AUSTIN, and was awarded the OM in 1929. See *A Choice of Verse*, ed. Lord David Cecil, 1987; Catherine Phillips, *Robert Bridges: a Biography*, 1992.

BRIDIE, JAMES, pseudonym of O. H. Mavor (1888–1951) Scottish dramatist, was born in Glasgow, the son of an engineer, and was educated at Glasgow Academy and Glasgow University, where he read medicine and generally had a good time. He qualified as a doctor in 1913, and served in the Royal Army Medical Corps from 1914 to 1919, as he did again in World War II. After World War I, he was a consulting physician to the Victoria Infirmary, Glasgow, and then Professor of Medicine at Anderson's College. His life changed dramatically with the performance in 1928 of *The Sunlight Sonata*, a preliminary excursion into what was to become his main motif, the morality play in modern terms. *Tobias and the Angel*, the first of several plays with biblical themes, was staged in London in 1930, and *The Anatomist*, about the early 19th-century body-snatchers, Burke and Hare, and their enigmatic master Dr Knox, in 1931. He wrote 42 plays, of which *Mr Bolfry* (1943) and *Daphne Laureola* (1949) were probably the most popular. His works are intricate and witty, with several layers of meaning. He was the first genuinely Scottish playwright and, like many Scottish writers, was preoccupied with questions of good and evil, with the Presbyterian Church in its various forms, and with the contradictions of contemporary life. He was Chairman of the Glasgow Citizen's Theatre and in 1950 founded the first Scottish college of drama. He was made CBE in 1946. See *One Way of Living*, 1939 (autobiography); Ronald Mavor, *Dr Bridie and Mr Mavor*, 1988 (biography); J. T. Low, *Devils, Doctors, Saints and Sinners*, 1980 (critical study).

BRINK, ANDRÉ (*b.* 1935) South African novelist, critic, and translator, was born in the village of Vrede, Orange Free State, and educated at Lydenburg High School and Potchef-stroom University. He joined the teaching staff of Rhodes University, Grahamstown, in 1963, becoming Professor and Head of the Department of Afrikaans and Dutch Literature in 1980. As a counterblast to Afrikaans novels which he called 'a literature of drought and poor whites', he wrote between 1958 and 1967 six novels in Afrikaans in which he experimented with modern narrative techniques. *Kennis van die Aand* (1973), for its outspokenness on many issues, including apartheid, was banned in South Africa, and published in the UK in his own translation as *Looking on Darkness* (1974). He has translated into English all his subsequent novels, of which *Rumours of Rain* (1978), a study of the morality of Afrikaner nationalism, and *A Chain of Voices* (1982), a powerful historical story of a slave revolt, are the most highly regarded. In the short novel (an original paperback), *The First Life of Adamanter* (1993), CAMÕES provides the starting point, and RABELAIS the basis, of an allegorical tale of the original encounter between Europe and southern Africa. *Imaginings of Sand* (1996) is a post-apartheid novel exploring an Afrikaner past. His most influential critical work, written in English, is *Mapmakers: Writing in a State of Siege* (1983), an expression of his views on literary freedom. His many translations into Afrikaans include works by CAMUS, CHEKHOV, COLETTE, GRAHAM GREENE, HENRY JAMES, SHAKESPEARE, SIMENON, and SYNGE; and children's books of CARROLL, GRAHAME, C. S. LEWIS, and WILDE.

BRITTAIN, VERA see HOLTBY.

BRODSKY, JOSEPH (1940–96) Russian-born poet and critic, was born in Leningrad, left school at 15, and then studied literature on his own, reading FAULKNER and KAFKA first in Polish. Repeatedly hauled up before the authorities as a 'social parasite', he was in 1964 sentenced to five years' exile with hard labour in the Arkhangelsk region in the north. He served 20 months, during which he read AUDEN, T. S. ELIOT, STEVENS, DYLAN THOMAS, and YEATS with a dictionary, making literal translations of the first and last verses and then imagining what came in between. In 1972, having been asked to leave the country, he went to the USA, of which he became a citizen in 1977, and where he taught at Columbia and New York universities, and latterly at Mount Holyoke. Before he left the USSR he had enjoyed the friendship and patronage of AKHMATOVA, and had already written some significant poems, including 'Elegy for John Donne' and 'Verses on the Death of T. S. Eliot' (composed while in exile within 24 hours of hearing the news). *Selected Poems*, tr. George L. Kline with a foreword by AUDEN, was published in 1973, and *A Part of Speech*, tr. Anthony Hecht and others, in 1980.

A further collection, *On Grief and Reason* (1996), was published just before his death from a fourth heart attack. He wrote poetry primarily in Russian, often translating his own work into English, and latterly prose in English. An admirer particularly of Latin poetry, the Metaphysicals, HARDY, and AUDEN, he acknowledged the 'moral purity and firmness' of Russian poetry, while making skilful use of Greek mythology in his own. Though he never went back to Russia, and his parents were refused permission to visit him, he became eventually a best-selling author there, being regarded as one of the final links with poets such as Akhmatova, MANDELSTAM, and TSVETAEVA; his collection of essays, *Less than One* (1986), includes masterly studies of them, as well as two autobiographical pieces. He was awarded the Nobel Prize for Literature in 1987, and named US Poet Laureate in 1991. See *To Urania: Selected Poems 1965–1985*, new edn 1997; *So Forth: Poems*, 1996 (final collection); *Less than One: Selected Essays*, new edn 1987; David M. Bethea, *Joseph Brodsky and the Creation of Exile*, 1994 (critical study).

BROME, ALEXANDER see ANACREON.

BRONTË, ANNE (1820–49) British novelist and poet, the youngest sister of CHARLOTTE and EMILY BRONTË, was born at Thornton Vicarage, Yorkshire, and educated at home at Haworth, and for two years at Miss Wooler's school at Dewsbury Moor. She became a governess in 1839 but was forced to leave her second post in 1845, probably because of an impending scandal in which her brother Branwell, tutor in the same household, was involved. She died of consumption during a trip to Scarborough. Her first novel, *Agnes Grey* (1847), written under the pen name of Acton Bell, appeared as the third volume of a publication whose first two consisted of Emily's *Wuthering Heights*. *The Tenant of Wildfell Hall* was published on its own in 1848. Charlotte wrote: 'Anne's character was milder and more subdued [than Emily's]; she wanted the power, the fire, the originality of her sister . . .'. Anne was unable to invest her limited experience of life with the imagination required of a great novelist, and though *Agnes Grey* portrays faithfully and vividly the tribulations of a governess, and *The Tenant of Wildfell Hall* the degeneration of an alcoholic (based on her observation of Branwell), her place in fiction is largely founded on her being one of a remarkable family trio. The same is true of her poetry. Her religious verse reveals the extent to which Calvinism disturbed her consciousness, and how she tried to reconcile the notion of retribution with that of compassion. See *Poems*, ed. Edward Chitham, 1979; Edward Chitham, *A Life of Anne Brontë*, new edn

1992; Elizabeth Langland, *Anne Brontë: the Other One*, 1989 (critical study).

BRONTË, CHARLOTTE (1816–55) British novelist and poet, was born at Thornton Vicarage, Yorkshire, the third child of Rev. Patrick Brontë (1777–1861), an Irish-born, Cambridge-educated, Church of England minister with genuine literary pretensions— see Juliet R. V. Barker, *The Brontës* (1994). In 1820 he was appointed to Haworth. Mrs Brontë died of cancer in 1821, and the children, of whom there were now six, were looked after by her sister. In 1824 Charlotte and EMILY joined their elder sisters, Maria and Elizabeth, at the Clergy Daughters' School at Cowan Bridge. The following year Maria and Elizabeth were sent home with tuberculosis and died. Charlotte and Emily were removed from the school and stayed at home until 1831, when Charlotte went to Miss Wooler's school at Roe Head for eighteen months—see Barbara Whitehead, *Charlotte Brontë and Her 'Dearest Nell': the Story of a Friendship* (1994)—, then came home to teach her two sisters. A year after the death of his two eldest children, Mr Brontë had brought home, for his son Branwell (1817– 48), a box of wooden soldiers, which were the immediate inspiration for a fantasy world called the Glass Town Confederacy, documented in prose, drama, and verse, and developed later by Charlotte and Branwell as the kingdom of Angria—see Fannie E. Ratchford, *The Brontës' Web of Childhood* (1941), and *Charlotte Brontë's High Life in Verdopolis: a Story from the Glass Town Saga*, ed. Christine Alexander (1995). Charlotte returned to Roe Head (the school moved to Dewsbury Moor in 1837) from 1835 to 1838, when she came home, ill and dispirited. In the next two years she had two posts as governess and turned down two proposals of marriage. She then took the momentous step of going with Emily to Madame Heger's boarding school for young ladies in Brussels, where she developed a profound but unrequited passion for the proprietor's husband, Constantin (1809– 96). Back at Haworth, she discovered in 1845 some poems by Emily, which gave her the idea of offering for publication a book of verse by the three sisters. *Poems by Currer, Ellis and Acton Bell* (1846), subsidized by the authors, got three reviews and sold two copies.

Meanwhile they were each finishing a novel. Emily's and ANNE's were accepted for publication together, but Charlotte's *The Professor* (an attempt to reconstruct her Brussels' experience of love with the roles reversed) was rejected seven times. In 1847 she sent another manuscript to Smith, Elder and Co., the publisher who had been most constructive about *The Professor*; it was published as *Jane Eyre. An Autobiography. Edited by Currer Bell* (1847). This emotional story, with the now

classic ingredients of penniless orphan, appalling schooldays, lonely mansion, enigmatic and brooding hero, mad wife, a legacy, and a providential fire, was an immediate success. By the time Charlotte had finished her next book, *Shirley* (1849), Anne, Emily, and Branwell were dead. In 1850 she first met GASKELL, which led to a close friendship with her ultimate biographer. When Smith, Elder again refused to bring out *The Professor* (it was finally published posthumously in 1857), she began *Villette* (1853), a further reworking of her romance, incorporating characters drawn from real life, which virtually exhausted her remaining materials for realistic fiction. In a depressed state, she accepted a proposal of marriage from her father's curate, Arthur Bell Nicholls (1818–1906). Mr Brontë, furious at an impecunious parson marrying his now famous daughter, refused to attend the wedding in June 1854. Later that year, Charlotte wrote two chapters of *Emma*, which her husband feared might be criticized as repetitious—the fragment was published in 1860 in *Cornhill Magazine* with an introduction by THACKERAY. On 31 March 1855, already weakened by a chill caught on the moors, she died of excessive pregnancy sickness.

Charlotte Brontë's failings as a writer outnumber but do not outweigh her virtues— Professor Lord David Cecil in *Early Victorian Novelists* (new edn 1964) describes her as a 'freak genius'. Her range was constricted by her own experience, except in *Shirley*, where the Luddite episodes are drawn from her father's recollections. The development of the dramatic action is frequently broken, and the plot often turns on the most improbable coincidences. Yet she succeeds through the very vigour of her storytelling, the way she brings opposites into conflict and also into relationship with each other, the depth with which she explores feelings, and the dramatic unity imposed, as it is to such advantage in *Jane Eyre*, by concentration on the experiences of the main character. As a poet she lacked the intensity of feeling and expression of either of her sisters, and she was inhibited by the restrictions of the verse forms she used as a child and as an adult. See *Complete Novels of Charlotte and Emily Brontë*, biographical sketch by Loreto Todd, introductions by Eileen Dunlop, A. Norman Jeffares, Hilary Mantel, and others, 1993; Winifred Gérin, *Charlotte Brontë: the Evolution of Genius*, new edn 1987 (biography); Rebecca Fraser, *Charlotte Brontë*, new edn 1989 (biography); Lyndall Gordon, *Charlotte Brontë: a Passionate Life*, new edn 1995 (biography); Helen Moglen, *Charlotte Brontë: the Self Conceived*, new edn 1984 (critical study).

BRONTË, EMILY (1818–48) British novelist and poet, younger sister of CHARLOTTE BRONTË, was born at Thornton Vicarage and educated briefly at Cowan Bridge, then at home by her father, and for three months in 1835 at Roe Head, where the restrictions made her so ill that she was brought home. The freedom that she enjoyed at Haworth was embodied in the moors, over which she roamed and ran, while the dramatic terrain and skyscapes, and the companionship of animals and birds in the wild, were immediate sources of inspiration in her childhood literary pursuits and a formative influence on her adult writing. By the time Charlotte went to Roe Head in 1831, Emily and ANNE had abandoned any further development of the Glass Town saga for their own creation, the kingdom of Gondal. Emily contributed throughout her life to the growth of its mythology, and the main characters, notably the strong, wilful, passionate, criminally-inclined heroine, Augusta Geraldine Almeda, frequently recur in her verse. Her re-establishment at home after Roe Head coincided with the ignominious return of Branwell from London, where he had gone in hopes of making a mark in the arts, and he was a stimulus to her reading and writing—see also Christine Alexander and Jane Sellars, *The Art of the Brontës* (1995), a study of the family as artists. In 1837–38 she spent a few depressing months as a teacher at Law Hill, Halifax. Her unhappiness, homesickness, and continuous search for freedom of mind and body are reflected in the poems she wrote at the time or soon after, such as 'I'll come when thou art saddest', 'Gleneden's Dream', 'Loud without the wind was roaring', and 'A little while, a little while . . .'.

In 1841, with Branwell in the unlikely job of clerk to the railways, and Charlotte and Anne unsettled as governesses, it was proposed that the three sisters should open a school. The scheme was abandoned, or postponed, in favour of Charlotte and Emily's educational sojourn in Brussels, which was cut short by the death of their Aunt Branwell in October 1842. Charlotte returned to Brussels as pupil-teacher; Emily remained at Haworth to look after their father. The discovery by Charlotte in 1845 of Emily's poems and her decision to get them published along with hers and Anne's must be seen also in the light of the family financial circumstances. Mr Brontë was going blind; Branwell, having lost his job on the railways, had now also been dismissed from his post as tutor to the family to which Anne had been governess, and was showing signs of disintegration. Emily wrote *Wuthering Heights* between the autumn of 1845 and July 1846, but it was a year before it was accepted for publication by T. C. Newby. Even so, Charlotte's *Jane Eyre*, which was then not even finished, was published before *Wuthering Heights*. *A Novel by Ellis Bell* appeared in two volumes, with Anne's *Agnes Grey* making the third. They were full of misprints, and *Wuthering Heights*

got such a bad press that Newby decided to boost his sales by encouraging the prevailing rumour that all three novels were work of a single author. While Emily stayed at home, hoping to retain her anonymity, Charlotte and Anne caught the night train to London and resolved the confusion in person. These circumstances contributed to Emily's decision to abandon, and probably to destroy, a second novel. Branwell died in September 1848. Emily, easily the most athletic and usually the healthiest of the family, caught a cold at his funeral. On 19 December she died of consumption.

Wuthering Heights is an extraordinary book by any criteria. That it was written by a young woman of just 27 whose life was constricted even by Victorian standards makes it arguably the most powerfully imaginative novel in the English language. From its brooding opening scenes, which are remarkable for their realistic domestic detail, it moves inexorably through the present and the dark and stormy past to the ghostly reunion of Heathcliff and the lost and ill-used love of his youth. The mystical vision which enabled Emily to write it, and the strange passions, conflicts, and forces which motivate its characters, are easier to comprehend in the light of her poetry, much of which is concerned with these elements in the mythical world of Gondal. Heathcliff's and Catherine's death-wish has its parallel, too, in many of her finest poems, notably 'No coward soul is mine . . .' and 'Silent is the House . . .' (sometimes called 'The Prisoner'), both written while she was working on *Wuthering Heights*. See *Wuthering Heights*, ed. Ian Jack, 1981; *The Complete Poems*, ed. Janet Gezari, 1992; *The Complete Poems of Emily Jane Brontë*, ed. C. W. Hatfield, new edn 1996; *The Poems*, ed. Derek Roper and Edward Chitham, 1996; Katherine Frank, *Emily Brontë: a Chainless Soul*, new edn 1992 (biography); Edward Chitham, *A Life of Emily Brontë*, new edn 1992.

BROOKE, FRANCES (1724–89), née Moore, British novelist, was born in Claypole, Lincolnshire, the eldest daughter of the vicar. She was orphaned when young, and was brought up by relatives. In the 1750s she was living as a writer in London; in November 1755 she founded and, as 'Mary Singleton, Spinster', wrote most of a weekly periodical with a feminist slant, the *Old Maid*, which ran for 37 issues. About this time she married Rev. John Brooke (1709–89)—she appears as 'Mrs Brooke' on the title page of *Virginia* (1756), a verse tragedy with 'Odes, Pastorals and Translations'. He sailed for Canada, where he was a military chaplain in 1757. In 1760 she published her translation from the French of the popular novel, *Letters from Juliet, Lady Catesby, to Her Friend, Lady Henrietta Campley*, by Marie-Jeanne Riccoboni (1714–92). Her own sentimental epistolary novel,

The History of Lady Julia Mandeville, appeared in 1763, the year she sailed with her son to join her husband in Quebec, seen off fondly, it was reported, by JOHNSON. The whole family returned in 1768, by which time she had written *The History of Emily Montague* (1769), a romance with three sets of lovers. Set mainly in Canada in the 1760s, and incorporating in its 228 letters informed comment on Anglo-French relations, it is the first Canadian novel. A further Canadian novel, the anonymous *All's Right at Last: or, The History of Miss West* (1774) may or may not be by her. In the 1770s she jointly managed the Opera House, Haymarket, with the actress Mary Ann Yates (1728–87), who played the lead in her *The Siege of Sinope: a Tragedy*, staged at Covent Garden Theatre in 1782. She also had two comic operas performed, *Rosina* (1783) and *Marian* (1788). Her picaresque novel of an innocent country girl set loose in London society, *The Excursion* (1777), contained a lampoon of the actor-manager David Garrick (1717–79), who had rejected two of her plays: she inserted an apology in an expurgated second edition (1785). See Lorraine McMullen, *Frances Brooke and Her Works*, 1983.

BROOKE, RUPERT (1887–1915) British poet, was born in Rugby and educated at Rugby School, where his father was a housemaster, and King's College, Cambridge, of which he then became a Fellow. His first book, *Poems* (1911), revealed a sardonic wit as well as a lyrical bent. While in Berlin in May 1912 he wrote, or according to some sources 'dashed off', a series of nostalgic octosyllabic couplets which appeared the following month in the Cambridge journal, *Basileon H*, as 'The Old Vicarage, Grantchester', with the final lines: 'Stands the Church clock at ten to three / And is there honey still for tea?' It was also published in *Georgian Poetry 1911–1912*, the first of five anthologies edited by (Sir) Edward Marsh (1872–1953), civil servant and literary patron, to whom Brooke had suggested the idea—the 'Georgian Poets' were not so much a movement as a group of younger poets whose work needed a forum. In 1913 Brooke went on a world tour and in Tahiti wrote some love poems, notably 'Retrospect' and 'Tiare Tahiti', which rank among his best. On the outbreak of war, he was commissioned in the Royal Naval Volunteer Reserve and saw action at Antwerp in October 1914, after which he wrote five jingoistically-inspired war sonnets. The last of these, 'The Soldier' ('If I should die, think only this of me . . .'), earned him immortality as a poet-figure. In 1915 his division was posted to the Dardanelles, but he died en route at Scyros, of blood poisoning. He was a fine prose writer—see especially *Letters From America*, preface by Henry James (1916)—and also wrote a one-act play, *Lithuania* (1915). See *Collected Poems*, with a memoir by Edward Marsh and introduction by Gavin Ewart, new edn 1992; *Selected Poems*, ed. Ian Hamilton, 1995; Christopher Hassall, *Rupert Brooke: a Biography*, new edn 1972.

BROOKNER, ANITA (b. 1928) British novelist, was born in London of a Jewish family from Poland (her father changed his name from Bruckner). She was educated at James Allen's Girls' School, Dulwich, then studied French literature at King's College, London, and the history of art at the Courtauld Institute, where she was appointed Lecturer in 1964 and was Reader from 1977 until her retirement in 1988. She was Slade Professor of Fine Art at Cambridge 1967–68, the first woman to hold the post. She had written several works on art, including *Watteau* (1968), *The Genius of the Future: Studies in French Art Criticism* (1971), and *Jacques-Louis David* (1980), before she began, in her mid-forties, to write novels, initially as a way of discovering how it was done. *A Start in Life* (1981) is also partly a mirror of her own experience at the time; as a result of writing it she concluded, 'self-analysis . . . leads nowhere—it is an art form in itself'. Since then, in a series of stories of blighted female lives, of which *Hôtel du Lac* (1984) won the Booker prize for fiction, she has subtly and gracefully, and with a perceptive eye for detail, analysed feminine experience and the search for intellectual and physical fulfilment in an ordinary world. In *A Private View* (1994), the protagonist is male, and the perspective subtly different. The heroine of *Incidents in the Rue Laugier* (1995), which Brookner had said was her last novel, is a displaced woman from Dijon, trying to make sense of her own life through piecing together the story of her parents' marriage. In *Altered States* (1996), the image and the reality of a man's past affair return to haunt him. See John Skinner, *The Fictions of Anita Brookner: Fictions of Romance*, 1992; and in George Plimpton (ed.), *Writers at Work: Eighth Series*, 1988.

BROOKS, CLEANTH see WARREN.

BROOKS, GWENDOLYN (b. 1917) American poet, was born in Topeka, Kansas, of parents who encouraged her poetic talent. She was educated in Chicago, transferring from Hyde Park to Phillips to Englewood high schools, after which she graduated from Wilson Junior College in 1936. She married Henry Blakely in 1939 (they separated in 1969). She attended a writers' workshop at the South Side Community Art Center, and in 1945 the New York firm of Harper responded to her bombardment of 'negro poems' by publishing *A Street in Bronzeville*. With her second volume, *Annie Allen* (1949), she became the first black writer to win the Pulitzer Prize for poetry. In her earlier verse—see also *Selected Poems* (1963)—she used traditional forms (often the sonnet) to capture the essence of black urban life. In the volatile atmosphere of the Second Black Writers' Conference at Fisk University in 1967, at which BARAKA was in particularly provocative form, she experienced a revelation, which she has explained as the wish to send a SOS to 'all black people in taverns, alleys, gutters, schools, offices, factories, prisons, the consulate, pulpits, mines, farms, thrones—to teach, to entertain, to illumine'. The new Brooks speaks to black readers about issues especially of identity, often in free verse; and as a measure of her commitment she switched her allegiance from Harper to Broadside Press, Detroit, which exists to encourage young black writers, for the publication of *Riot* (1970) and subsequent collections. On the death of SANDBURG, she was in 1968 named Poet Laureate of Illinois. In 1985–86 she was the first black woman to be Poetry Consultant to the Library of Congress. See *Report from Part One: an Autobiography*, 1973; *Report from Part 2*, new edn 1993 (autobiography); Harry B. Shaw, *Gwendolyn Brooks*, 1980 (critical study).

BROWN, CHARLES BROCKDEN (1771–1810) American novelist, was born in Philadelphia to Quaker parents, and was educated at Friends' Latin School until he was 16, when he was apprenticed to a law firm. At 21 he persuaded his parents of the dubious morality of defending a wrong cause, and was instead allowed to pursue a literary career. His first novel, 'Sky-Walk', was finished in 1797 but never appeared, owing to the sudden death of the publisher. With *Alcuin: a Dialogue* (1798), America's first professional novelist began an astonishing burst of creative activity. *Wieland: or, The Transformation. An American Tale* (1798) was published in New York during the yellow fever epidemic in which the radical Elihu Hubbard Smith, Brown's closest friend, died. He then published in quick succession *Ormond: or, The Secret Witness* (1799), *Arthur Mervyn: or, Memoirs of the Year 1793* (1799–1800), *Edgar Huntly: or, Memoirs of a Sleep-Walker* (1799), *Clara Howard: In a Series of Letters* (1801; in Britain as *Philip Stanley: or, The Enthusiasm of Love*, 1807), and *Jane Talbot: a Novel* (1801). All his major writing had now been done. For the rest of his literary life he largely confined himself to political pamphleteering. As a novelist he used accepted forms such as the Gothic romance and the tale of seduction as the basis for the exploration of intellectual ideas and psychological factors. See Donald A. Ringe, *Charles Brockden Brown*, rev. edn 1991 (critical study).

BROWN, CHRISTY (1932–81) Irish novelist and poet, was born in Dublin, one of 13 of 21 children of a bricklayer who lived to be adults. Almost totally paralysed from birth by cerebral palsy, through his own and his mother's determination, and the encouragement and teaching of the dramatist Dr Robert Collis (1900–75), he managed to type, with his little toe, *My Left Foot* (1954), a classic autobiography which is all the more moving for the restraint of its feeling and its spare prose. *Down All the Days* (1970) is a fictional, more elaborately-written, version of the same events. His verse, first published in *Come Softly to My Wake* (1970), has flashes of inspiration. See *Collected Poems*, new edn 1990.

BROWN, GEORGE DOUGLAS see DOUGLAS, GEORGE.

BROWN, GEORGE MACKAY (1921–96) Scottish poet, novelist, short-story writer, and dramatist, was born in Stromness, Orkney, the son of a postman, and was educated at Stromness Academy, going outside the island for the first time when he was 25. Illness prevented him from continuing his education until 1957, when he went to Newbattle Abbey College (of which MUIR was then Warden), and again until 1962, when he went to Edinburgh University. The rest of his life was spent in Stromness, visiting England just once, in 1989, when he saw the sights of London and Oxford, witnessed the election of HEANEY as Professor of Poetry, and visited some of the haunts of Cardinal NEWMAN. He wrote: 'Most islands . . . have a rich tradition of song and music. This is not so in Orkney. . . . Art in Orkney has devoted itself in the main to the production of stories: the noises and sounds come from the grave mouth of the storyteller.' Orkney belonged to Norway until 1468, and its unusual Pictish/Viking history and folklore, its communal and religious life, its rugged landscape and changeful skies, and the continual presence of the sea which is both friend and enemy, provided the themes for his four novels, *Greenvoe* (1972), *Magnus* (1973), *Vinland* (1992), and *Beside the Ocean of Time* (1994), for two novellas, published together as *The Golden Birds* (1987), for a book of essays, *An Orkney Tapestry* (1969), and for many of his short stories and poems—his first volume of verse was appropriately called *The Storm* (1954) and a later one *The Wreck of the Archangel* (1989). Much of his poetry is concerned too with the rituals and rhythms of life, death, and resurrection—he became a Catholic in 1961. He was made OBE in 1974. See *Selected Poems 1954–1992*, new edn 1996; *Following a Lark: Poems*, 1996 (final collection); *Winter Tales*, new edn 1996 (stories).

BROWNE, FRANCES (1816–79) Irish poet, novelist, and children's writer, known as 'the blind poetess of Donegal', was born in the mountain village of Stranorlar, the seventh of 12 children of the postmaster. Blinded by smallpox in infancy, she bribed her siblings to read out their school work to her, in return for doing their share of the housework. In this way she also listened to the novels of WALTER SCOTT, POPE's *Iliad*, and BYRON's *Childe Harold*. In 1840, after hearing a book of Irish songs, she composed a poem, 'The Songs of Our Land', which was published in the *Irish Penny Journal*. Subsequent poems appeared in the *Athenaeum*, *Hood's Magazine*, and *Lady Blessington's Keepsake*, with a complete volume, *The Star of Attéghéi, the Vision of Schwartz, and Other Poems* being published in London in 1844. With her earnings, she educated a sister to become her reader and scribe. Having been awarded a small Civil List pension, she went in 1847 with her sister to live in Edinburgh, where *Lyrics and Miscellaneous Poems* (1848) was published, and where she mixed in the same literary circles as JOHN WILSON. In 1852 she moved to London, and received a gift of £100 from the 3rd Marquis of Lansdowne (1780–1863). Though she wrote historical novels and short stories, and a sentimental novel of struggle and ultimate disillusionment, *My Share of the World: an Autobiography* (1861), she is rightly remembered for *Granny's Wonderful Chair, and Its Tales of Fairy Times* (1857), which incorporates eight original fairy stories. These present Christian morals in such an imaginative and compelling fashion that in 1887 BURNETT reproduced much of them from memory in an American magazine as 'Stories from the Lost Fairy Book as Retold by the Child Who Read Them'.

BROWNE, (Sir) **THOMAS** (1605–82) English prose writer, was born in London, the only son of a silk dealer. He was educated at Winchester College and Pembroke College, Oxford, then studied medicine on the Continent, becoming MD of Oxford University in 1637. He set up practice in Norwich, where he remained for the rest of his life, being knighted by Charles II in 1671 as the most distinguished citizen of the town. His major work, *Religio Medici*, which he wrote in about 1636, attempts to reconcile science with religion, and other apparently contradictory elements with each other. It was published in an authorized version in 1643. *Pseudodoxia Epidemica: or Enquiries into Very many received Tenets And commonly presumed Truths* (1646), more commonly referred to as 'Vulgar Errors', ranges widely in science, medicine, ritual, and biblical history. *Hydriotaphia: Urne-Buriall* (1658) is a treatise on cremation, inspired by the discovery in Norfolk of some ancient funerary urns. It was published with *The Garden of Cyrus*, an extraordinary speculation about the existence of the 'quincunx, lozenge, or net-work' pattern in heaven and on earth, using as a starting point the pattern in which Cyrus the Great is said to have planted his trees in the 6th century BC. The distinction of Browne's writing is not only in the breadth of thought and learning, but in the prose itself: clauses are skilfully fashioned like linguistic bricks and built up into resounding periods. His blend of English and classical (especially Latin) usage, in the exercise of which he coined 'electricity' and other useful terms, represents the ultimate in 17th-century intricacy of style. See *The Major Works*, ed. C. A. Patrides, 1977; *Selected Writings*, ed. Sir Geoffrey Keynes, 1968; Joan Bennett, *Sir Thomas Browne: 'a Man of Achievement in Literature'*, 1962 (critical study).

BROWNE, THOMAS ALEXANDER see BOLDREWOOD.

BROWNING, ELIZABETH BARRETT (1806–61), née Moulton Barrett, British poet, was born at Coxhoe Hall, Co. Durham, the eldest of 11 children of an autocratic owner of West Indian plantations, whose wife died in 1827. Initially educated alongside her brother, she became a proficient classicist and acquired several modern languages. Some of her early verse was privately printed. The publication of *Poems* (1844), written at home in London during a period of seclusion caused by ill-health, led to a correspondence with BROWNING—see Daniel Karlin, *The Courtship of Robert Browning and Elizabeth Barrett* (1985). Fearing a confrontation with her father, the couple married secretly in 1846 and eloped to Italy, where they settled in Florence—see Julia Markus, *Dared and Done: the Marriage of Elizabeth Barrett and Robert Browning* (1995). There she took a strongly partisan interest in the struggle for the unification of the Italian states, which took poetic form in *Casa Guidi Windows* (1851) and *Poems Before Congress* (1860). Admired as a poet in her lifetime, when she was more highly regarded than her husband, she has suffered a decline in reputation, although the case for a reappraisal is well argued in Alethea Hayter, *Mrs Browning: a Poet's Work in Its Setting* (1962). *Aurora Leigh* (1856), a lengthy romantic novel in verse, has received attention as a feminist work, but her reputation rests mainly on *Sonnets from the Portuguese*—in *Poems* (1850); first published separately under this title in 1886—a technically near-perfect celebration of her love for Browning, and some late lyrics, notably 'A Musical Instrument' and 'Bianca among the Nightingales'. See *Aurora Leigh and Other Poems*, ed. J. R. G. Bolton and J. B. Holloway, 1995; *Selected Poems*, ed. Margaret Forster, new edn 1996; Margaret Forster, *Elizabeth Barrett Browning*, new edn 1990 (biography); Peter Dally, *Elizabeth Barrett Browning; a Psychological Portrait*, 1989; Dorothy Mermin, *Elizabeth Barrett Browning: the Origins of a New Poetry*, 1989 (critical study).

BROWNING, ROBERT (1812–89) British poet, was born in Camberwell, London, and educated at Peckham School until he was 14, and later at London University, from which he dropped out after six months. His father, a mild man who had become a Bank of England clerk after being unable to stomach administering plantations in St Kitts with slave labour, gave him a firm grounding in classics and literature and the run of his library of six thousand volumes; his mother, to whom he was deeply attached, instructed him in religion and music. Until he was 34, he lived at home, supported by his father. In 1833 his family's faith in his poetic destiny was justified by the publication of *Pauline*, a piece of romantic soul-baring, parts of which he later regretted. *Paracelsus* (1835), a series of dramatic dialogues in which he used settings in medieval Europe for an exposition of the conflict between love and knowledge, was admired by the critics. His passion for Italy inspired *Sordello* (1840), an excursion into the philosophy of the poetic soul against a background of the wars of the Guelphs and Ghibellines. That the poem is obscure is due to Browning's conviction that his audience was as widely read as he was and to his reluctance to reveal his inner self. In the meantime his play *Strafford* (1837) had run for only five nights. Two more historical dramas were rejected by the actor-manager W. C. Macready (1793–1873), who accepted *A Blot in the 'Scutcheon* with misgivings. It was performed just three times in 1843 and marked Browning's end as a dramatist (*Colombe's Birthday*, written at the same time, had a week's run in 1853), but not as a dramatic poet.

Between 1841 and 1846 he published eight books of verse under the series title of *Bells and Pomegranates*. *Pippa Passes* (No. I) comprises four Italianate scenes in which evil plots are contrasted with the innocence of the silk-worker, Pippa, who appears on the scene but does not intervene in the action. *Dramatic Lyrics* (II), which marked his greatest change of attitude and form, included the monologues, in different metres and rhythms, 'My Last Duchess' and 'Soliloquy of the Spanish Cloister'; 'The Pied Piper of Hamelin' (written to amuse Macready's son Willy when he was ill); the allusive dialogue 'In a Gondola'; and the grim story-poem 'Porphyria's Lover'. *Dramatic Romances and Lyrics* (VII) contained the fine religious monologue 'The Bishop Orders His Tomb at St Praxed's Church'; the lyrics, 'Home-Thoughts from Abroad' and 'Meeting at Night'; and the galloping but wholly imaginary 'How They Brought the Good News from Ghent to Aix'. After his marriage in 1846 (see E. B. BROWNING), he and his wife lived in Florence until her death in 1861; during this time, in spite of the distraction of the hyperactive childhood of their son, the sculptor Robert 'Pen' Browning (1849–1912)—see Maisie Ward, *The Tragi-Comedy of Pen Browning* (1972)—it was she who was the

more productive. Apart from *Christmas-Eve and Easter-Day* (1850), which vividly explores the threefold choice of worship then exercising Christians, his only new work was *Men and Women* (1855), comprising 50 poems (plus 'One Word More: to E. B. B.') which include his most outspoken statements of sexual love, as well as 'Fra Lippo Lippi' and 'Andrea del Sarto', and the romance, 'Childe Roland to the Dark Tower Came'. After Elizabeth died, he returned with Pen to London, where on his father's death in 1866 his only sister, Sarianna, came to keep house for him—his proposal of marriage to Lady Ashburton in 1871 was couched so undiplomatically that it could only be refused. *Dramatis Personae* (1864) contained the last of his shorter poems of quality, but *The Ring and the Book* (1868–69) placed him in popular acclaim second only to TENNYSON among living poets. Through dramatic monologues in blank verse, it retells the case of Count Guido Franceschini, accused in 1698 of murdering his teenage wife. Browning found the lurid and the legal details in a 'square old yellow book' he had picked up on a Florentine market stall in 1860. He died in Venice on the day his last book, *Asolando: Fancies and Facts* (dated 1890) was published, and was buried in Westminster Abbey.

Just as the speaker in a Browning monologue masks the poet from the reader, so Browning's outer persona obscured a character which puzzled his contemporaries. He was concerned to use grotesque as well as conventional subjects, and broken rhythms, discordances, and colloquialisms, as well as passages of beauty, to demonstrate the devious workings of the mind, particularly when it is under stress. In doing so he brought Victorian poetry into the 20th century. See *The Poems*, ed. John Pettigrew and Thomas J. Collins, 2 vols 1981; Donald Thomas, *Robert Browning: a Life Within Life*, new edn 1989; Philip Drew, *The Poetry of Robert Browning: a Critical Introduction*, 1970; John Woolford and Daniel Karlin, *Robert Browning*, 1996 (critical study).

BROWNJOHN, ALAN (*b*. 1931) poet, was born in Catford, southeast London, and educated at Brockley County School and Merton College, Oxford. His first book of verse, *The Railings*, for which he devised the descriptive legend, 'Poems concerned with love, politics, culture, time', was published in 1961. He was a borough councillor for Wandsworth from 1963 to 1965, during which time he stood for Parliament as Labour candidate for Richmond, Surrey. He was Senior Lecturer in English, Battersea College of Education 1965–79, and Tutor in Poetry, North London Polytechnic 1981–83. He was Poetry Critic for the *New Statesman* from 1968 to 1976, and has been a member of the Arts Council Literature

Panel and Chairman of the Greater London Arts Association Literature Panel. ADCOCK has described him as having 'a narrative gift and a social conscience', who 'can be a fierce satirist', and his poems as being 'elegantly and ingeniously made'. Of the two longer poems which are the framework of a recent collection, *The Observatory Car* (1990), 'Sea Pictures' illustrates his narrative technique, and 'The Automatic Days' the social commentary, through a year in the existence of a department store. In *the Cruel Arcade* (1994) contains reflections on childhood as well as on current events and the anomalies of life. A novel, *The Way You Tell Them: a Yarn of the Nineties* (1990), is a jestful, quasi-political, fantasy of the future. He has also written for children a book of poems, *Brownjohn's Beasts* (1970), and (as John Berrington) a novel, *To Clear the River* (1964). See *Collected Poems 1952–1988*, 1988.

BRUTUS, DENNIS (*b.* 1924) South African poet, was born in Salisbury, Southern Rhodesia (Zimbabwe), both his parents being teachers. He was brought up as a 'coloured' in Port Elizabeth, South Africa, and graduated from Fort Hare University College. After being dismissed from his teaching post at Government High School, Port Elizabeth, in 1962, he studied law at Witwatersrand University. His active opposition to apartheid, particularly in sport, led to his arrest, to his being shot while trying to escape, and to his being sentenced to 18 months' hard labour, during which his first book of verse, *Sirens, Knuckles, Boots* (1963) was published in Nigeria. He has explained that 'every poem [in it] was written for a particular person or to serve a particular function', in much the same way as most of those in *Letters to Martha and Other Poems from a South African Prison* (1968) were written as letters, since he was banned from writing poetry. He left for England on a Rhodesian passport in 1966, and became closely and vigorously involved with anti-apartheid organizations, being instrumental, as President of the South African Non-Racial Open Committee for Olympic Sports (SANROC), for South Africa's exclusion from the Games. In 1971 he went to the USA, where he taught English at Northwestern University, Evanston. He became Chairman of the Department of Black Community Educational Research and Development at Pittsburgh University in 1986. His poetry reflects his personal conflict with apartheid, and has its own inner tensions, with elements of laughter, for as he admitted in an interview, 'I enjoy the fight.' Later verse, as in *Stubborn Hope* (rev. edn 1991), reflects a broader view of Third World problems—see also *Still the Sirens: Poems* (1994). See *A Simple Lust: Selected Poems*, 1973; and in Alastair Niven (ed.), *The Common-*

wealth Writer Overseas: Themes of Exile and Expatriation, 1976.

BRYAN, MICHAEL see MOORE, BRIAN.

BRYANT, WILLIAM CULLEN (1794–1878) American poet and newspaper editor, was born in Cummington in the backwoods of Massachusetts, the son of a classically-minded, Calvinist physician. He had a poem printed in the Hampshire *Gazette* when he was 13, and in 1808 his father printed his political lampoon, *The Embargo, or Sketches of the Times: a Satire*. He entered Williams College in 1810, but left after a year to go to Yale, only to find that his father could not raise the fees. Instead he studied law, which he began to practise in Great Barrington in 1816. 'Thanatopsis', a reflective dialogue with Nature in blank verse, was published in 1817 in the *North American Review*, whose editor pressed him for more. He replied: 'I may perhaps, some time or other, venture a little collection in print—for I do not write much—and should it be favourably received—it may give me more courage to do something more.' He duly came up with a very slim volume, *Poems* (1821; enlarged edn 1832), published in the year of his marriage. In 1825 he made a move to New York, where he edited the *New York Review and Athenaeum Magazine*, after whose failure in 1826 he joined the staff of the *Evening Post*, of which he became part owner and Editor-in-Chief in 1829. The business prospered, and he went travelling, about which he wrote *Letters of a Traveller: or, Notes of Things Seen in Europe and America* (1850), and subsequent volumes (1859, 1869). He published just two more collections of poetry (1846, 1864), incorporated in *The Poetical Works of William Cullen Bryant* (1878), a work which marks the transition between the traditionalists and the emergence of the new schools of poetry. He had a distinguished public life and unbounded energy—in his seventies he embarked on a verse translation of the whole of HOMER (1870–72). He was a millionaire when he died from the effects of a fall after speaking in Central Park at the unveiling of a statue to the Italian patriot, Giuseppe Mazzini (1805–72).

BRYHER see DOOLITTLE.

BUCHAN, JOHN (1875–1940) Scottish novelist, biographer, and statesman, was born in Perth, the son of a Free Church minister, and was educated at Hutcheson's Boys School and Brasenose College, Oxford, where he won the Stanhope historical essay prize and the Newdigate prize for poetry, was President of the Union, and got a first in Greats. He was called to the Bar, worked in South Africa on the staff of the High Commission and, on his return, became a journalist. In 1927 he was elected Conservative Member of Parliament for the Scottish universities, a seat he held until 1935, when, as Lord Tweedsmuir of Elfield, he was appointed Governor General of Canada. (The annual Governor General's Awards for Literature, of which there are now 14, were established in Canada in 1937 with his approval and encouragement.) He wrote his first novel, *Prester John* (1910), because he was 'appalled by the dullness of most boys' books'. His subsequent success as a writer of adventure stories, the first of which, *The Thirty-Nine Steps* (1915), was written while he was confined to bed by illness, was due not only to his plots and settings, but also to the realistic detail with which he delineates his various heroes—see *The Complete Richard Hannay* (1992). These books have tended to obscure his influence in other fields of literature. *Poems, Scots and English* (1917; rev. edn 1936) contains some good nature poetry in Scots—see also *John Buchan's Collected Poems*, ed. Andrew Lownie and William Milne (1996)—, while his anthology of Scottish verse, *The Northern Muse* (1924), was the first of its kind. He wrote several fine biographies, of which that of MONTROSE (1928) is the classic study, and *Sir Walter Scott* (1932) contains precise, if sometimes unnecessarily apologetic, criticism. His sister, Anna Buchan (1877–1948), wrote an autobiographical study of the family, *Unforgettable, Unforgotten* (1945), and (as O. Douglas) several novels of which the romantic *Penny Plain* (1920) is still remembered. See *The Complete Short Stories*, ed. Andrew Lownie, 3 vols 1996; *Memory Hold-the-Door*, new edn 1984 (autobiography); Andrew Lownie, *John Buchan: the Presbyterian Cavalier*, 1995 (biography).

BUCHANAN, GEORGE (1506–82) Scottish humanist and historian, was born in the parish of Killearn, Stirlingshire, and educated at the local school until he was 14, and then for two years in Paris. After serving with the French troops in the Borders, keeping the English at bay, he studied under the historian John Major (1469–1550) at St Andrews University, and then returned to Paris as a student and then teacher. In 1536 he came back to Scotland and was appointed tutor to an illegitimate son of James V, who also commissioned him to write some satires against the Franciscans. He wrote these, as was usual for him, in Latin, the normal medium of academic communication in Scotland until the 18th century, and their appeal to the learned element resulted in his having to escape to Europe to avoid conviction for heresy. He came back some twenty years later as Latin tutor to Mary, Queen of Scots, on her return to her country, his claims as a scholar outweighing his Protestant inclinations; these he openly declared by his support of the new General Assembly of the Church of Scotland,

of which he was elected Moderator in 1567. His relationship with Mary went sour after the murder of her husband, Lord Darnley, in 1567, and even sourer when in 1568, after she had been imprisoned in England, he published a vicious attack on her, *Detectio Mariae Reginae Scotorum*, in which he quoted from some of the notorious 'Casket Letters'—see in *The Tyrannous Reign of Mary Stewart*, ed. and tr. W. A. Gatherer (new edn 1978). He was tutor to JAMES VI until the boy King was 12. *De Jure Regni apud Scotos* (1579), his most significant political work, is a treatise on monarchy and a justification of James's accession in place of his mother, a theme which recurs in Buchanan's 20-volume history of Scotland, published in 1582. He also wrote, in Latin, two classical dramas (translated into Scots by GARIOCH), original poetry, and metrical versions of the Psalms. His only notable work in the vernacular of the time is *The Chamaeleon*, an appropriately-titled prose attack on the ex-Queen's unfortunate secretary, William Maitland of Lethington (*c*.1525–73). See I. D. Mcfarlane, *Buchanan*, 1981 (biography).

BUCK, PEARL S(YDENSTRICKER) (1892–1973) American novelist and non-fiction writer, was born in Hillsboro, West Virginia, while her missionary parents, Absalom and Caroline Sydenstricker, were on leave from China, where she was taken a few months later. She was educated at mission schools and had a private tutor in Chinese language and culture, before going to a boarding school in Shanghai in 1909, and then to Randolph-Macon Women's College, Virginia. After graduating in 1914 she returned to China to look after her sick mother, and in 1917 married John Lossing Buck, an American agriculturist employed by the Presbyterian Mission Board. Between 1921 and 1931 she taught at universities in Nanking, and wrote two novels, one of which was destroyed when soldiers entered her home during the revolution in 1926–27. The other, *East Wind: West Wind*, the first of many with a Chinese background, was published in 1930 after she had, at the publisher's request, revised the literary style. *The Good Earth* (1931), a saga of a peasant family in a narrative style which is basically Chinese, won the Pulitzer Prize. In 1934 she took up permanent residence in the USA, and, after a divorce, married in 1935 Richard J. Walsh (*d.* 1960), President of the publisher John Day, with whom she adopted eight children. In 1936 she published *The Exile* and *Fighting Angel*—in one volume as *The Spirit and the Flesh* (1944)—biographies respectively of her mother and father. These were the decisive factor in her being awarded the Nobel Prize for Literature in 1938. Her subsequent output of fiction and non-fiction was as vast as it was uneven in quality—she also wrote several novels on American themes as John Sedges. She founded the East and West Association for international understanding in 1941, Welcome House, an adoption agency for Asian-American children, in 1949, and the Pearl S. Buck Foundation, to care for Asian children of half-American parentage, in 1964. See Peter Conn, *Pearl S. Buck: a Cultural Biography*, 1996; Paul A. Doyle, *Pearl S. Buck*, rev. edn 1980 (critical study).

BUCKLER, ERNEST (1908–84) Canadian novelist, was born in Dalhousie West, Nova Scotia, and educated at Dalhousie and Toronto universities. After a few years working for a Toronto insurance company in the 1930s, he returned to rural Nova Scotia, which is the setting of many of his short stories—see *The Rebellion of Young David and Other Stories*, ed. Robert D. Chambers (1975). His first novel, *The Mountain and the Valley* (1952), also set in the Annapolis Valley, is primarily a study of artistic development and unfulfilment. The protagonist of *The Cruelest Month* (1963) is a recluse whose awkward personality is ultimately purged through a forest fire. The pleasant rural sketches and reminiscences which make up *Ox Bells and Fireflies* (1968) are largely re-creations of Buckler's own childhood. See John Orange, *Ernest Buckler and His Works*, 1990.

BULGAKOV, MIKHAIL (1891–1940) Russian novelist and dramatist, was born in Kiev, qualified as a doctor at Kiev University in 1916, served at the front, and then practised in Kiev. In 1921 he gave up his career and moved to Moscow, where for several years he flourished as a journalist, writer of comic stories, and dramatist. He adapted [*The White Guard*] (1927–29; tr. Michael Glenny, 1971), a non-Bolshevik civil war novel reflecting the experiences of his own family, for the stage as [*The Days of the Turbins*] (tr. in *Early Plays*, ed. Ellendea Proffer, 1972). In 1930, by which time none of his works were being published or performed any more, he wrote to Stalin asking to be expelled with his wife from the USSR. The response was an enigmatic phone call from Stalin himself, with the suggestion of a job at the Moscow Art Theatre. Though *The Days of the Turbins* was restored to the theatre's repertoire, and put back again at Stalin's request after being dropped, the ban on his work continued and further appeals to Stalin were ignored. Bulgakov now worked intensively on his philosophical fantasy of the Devil's visit to contemporary Moscow, [*The Master and Margarita*], a recurring motif of which is the postulation, 'manuscripts don't burn'. In 1939, shortly before he went blind and died, he wrote in a letter, 'nothing has ever worked out as I wished'. *The Master and Margarita* was finally serialized in the journal *Moskva* in 1966–67, and appeared in English (tr.

Glenny) in 1967, two years before its full publication in its original language.

BULWER-LYTTON, EDWARD (GEORGE) (1803–73) British novelist, dramatist, poet, and politician, was born in London, the third son of General William Bulwer (1757–1807) and Elizabeth Lytton, on whose death in 1843 he succeeded to her ancestral home of Knebworth, Hertfordshire, and took the additional surname of Lytton. After a disjointed early education, he entered Trinity College, Cambridge, but persuaded his mother to let him transfer to Trinity Hall, where he did not have to attend lectures, on the grounds that a tutor had insulted him. In 1827 he published his first novel, *Falkland*, and much against his mother's will married Rosina Wheeler (1802–82), an Irish woman of exceptional beauty. They were legally separated in 1836, after which each persecuted the other. The need for money drove him to diversify and stretch his literary talents. *Pelham* (1828) takes a light-hearted look at fashionable society; *Paul Clifford* (1830) and *Eugene Aram* (1833) are psychological stories of crime; *The Last Days of Pompeii* (1834), virtually the only novel for which he is now remembered, is the first of several in which history and romance tend to alternate rather than coalesce. Later he branched into the supernatural with *Zanoni* (1842), into realistic stories of contemporary life with *The Caxtons: a Family Picture* (1849), and even into Utopian satire with *The Coming Race* (1871). *King Arthur* (1848–49), an epic poem, is best forgotten, but two of his three plays are really rather good: *Richlieu* (1839), a historical melodrama in blank verse, and *Money* (1840), a contemporary comedy of manners and changes of fortune.

He was a Member of Parliament 1831–41 and 1852–66, being appointed Secretary for the Colonies in 1858 and created Lord Lytton of Knebworth in 1866. The Dramatic Copyright Act of 1833, which finally granted to the author, for a limited period, the right to authorize a performance, is known as Bulwer-Lytton's Act. In 1856 and 1858 he was elected Lord Rector of Glasgow University, the first Englishman to hold the office twice. He died in the arms of his son Edward Robert Bulwer Lytton (1831–91), who was Viceroy of India from 1876 to 1880, when he was created Earl of Lytton. As Owen Meredith, the Earl of Lytton wrote some rather derivative poetry and several verse-novels, of which the posthumously published *King Poppy* (1892) is the most original and amusing.

BUNIN, IVAN (ALEKSEIEVICH) (1870–1953) Russian novelist, poet, and translator, was born in Voronezh of a 'noble but impoverished family', had a private tutor, studied briefly at Moscow University, and published his first poems in 1887 and his first stories shortly afterwards. He served his literary apprenticeship as a provincial journalist, and in 1903 won the PUSHKIN Prize for his poetry and for his translations of BYRON's *Cain* and LONGFELLOW's *The Song of Hiawatha*. His popularity as a short-story writer and novelist was founded on his pseudo-realistic treatments of contemporary rural life, such as [*The Village*] (1910; tr. Isabel Hapgood, 1923). He travelled in Europe, North Africa, and the Middle East, fled from Moscow to Odessa after the Revolution of 1917, to which he was firmly opposed, and finally escaped to France. His first appearance in English was *The Gentleman from San Francisco and Other Stories*, translated by D. H. LAWRENCE, S. S. Koteliansky, and LEONARD WOOLF (1922). The first part of his autobiographical novel of the pre-revolutionary era was published in 1930 (tr. Glebe Struve and Hamish Miles as *The Well of Days*, UK 1933, USA 1934; ed. Andrew Baruch Wachtel, with Book 5 tr. Heidi Hillis, Susan McKean, and Sven A. Wolf as *The Life of Arseniev: Youth*, 1994). He was awarded the Nobel Prize for Literature in 1933, the first Russian to receive the award, 'for the strict artistry with which he has carried on the classical Russian traditions in prose writings'. He and his wife, whom he had married in 1922 after she had been his companion for 16 years, escaped to further exile in the south of France when the Nazis occupied Paris during World War II. He died in Paris in virtual obscurity, a last volume of stories, *Dark Avenues*, tr. Richard Hare, having appeared in 1949. See Thomas Gaiton Marullo (ed.), *Ivan Bunin: a Portrait from Letters, Diaries, and Fiction*, 2 vols, *Russian Requiem 1885–1920*, 1993, and *From the Other Shore 1920–1933*, 1995.

BUNTING, BASIL (1900–85) British poet, was born in Scotswood on Tyne, Northumberland, the son of a doctor, and was educated at Newcastle Royal Grammar School, Ackworth School, Yorkshire, and Leighton Park School. In 1918 he was jailed as a Quaker conscientious objector to military service. He was at the London School of Economics from 1919 to 1922, without taking a degree. In 1923 he assisted FORD MADOX FORD to edit the *transatlantic review* in Paris, where he met POUND, and he was for a time music critic of *Outlook*. In the 1930s he lived in the USA, the Canary Islands, and Italy, where *Redimiculum Matellarum* (1930) was published. His conscience allowed him to serve in World War II, during which he became a Persian interpreter in the Middle East—see 'The Spoils' (1951). He returned there afterwards as Persian correspondent for *The Times*, but for 12 years from 1952 he worked as a subeditor for the *Newcastle Chronicle*, and wrote nothing. His recognition as a poet followed the publication of the autobiographical *Briggflatts* (1966), after which he was President of the Poetry Society 1972–76, and held various

teaching posts in the USA, without ever managing to make a comfortable living. In the Preface to *Collected Poems* (rev. edn 1978), he wrote: 'I have set down words as a musician pricks his score, not to be read in silence, but to trace in the air a pattern of sound that may sometimes, I hope, be pleasing.' In with the sounds are allusions to and echoes of older poets, including HORACE, DANTE, VILLON, SPENSER, WORDSWORTH, WHITMAN, and POUND. See *The Complete Poems*, ed. Richard Caddel, 1994; Peter Makin, *Bunting: the Shaping of His Verse*, 1992 (critical biography); Victoria Forde, *The Poetry of Basil Bunting*, 1991.

BUNYAN, JOHN (1628–88) English preacher and prose writer, was born in Elstow, near Bedford, the son of a travelling tinker, and learned to read and write at a local school. He was conscripted into the Parliamentary army in 1644, serving mainly on garrison duty until he was discharged in 1647. In 1655 he became a full member of the Nonconformist church at Bedford, shortly before the death of its founder, John Gifford (a former royalist officer in the Civil War), and from 1656 he was preaching and publishing tracts and pamphlets. His first wife died in 1658, leaving him with four children, the eldest of whom was blind. He married again in 1659. At the Restoration of the Monarchy and the return of the bishops in 1660, he was charged with preaching illegally, and was offered the choice of stopping his religious activities or going to jail. He chose the latter, and was sentenced to 12 years, during which he wrote a spiritual autobiography, *Grace Abounding to the Chief of Sinners* (1666), and much if not all of the first part of *The Pilgrim's Progress, From This World to That Which is to Come* (1678). This rehearses Bunyan's own spiritual struggles in allegorical form, as Christian, in the author's dream, sets out from the City of Destruction, having failed to convince his family to accompany him. He extricates himself from the Slough of Despond, and journeys through various hazards, including the Valley of the Shadow of Death, Vanity Fair, and Doubting Castle, to the Gates of Heaven, meeting on the way Obstinate, Pliable, Mr Worldly Wiseman, the monster Apollyon, Giant Despair, Ignorance, and others, and being helped along by sundry more pleasing qualities. *The Pilgrim's Progress* is more than just an allegorical quest romance or even an expression of Puritanism. It is a statement, founded on the author's experience as well as on his beliefs, of support for the English poor, written in a straightforward, basically monosyllabic but beautifully expressive prose which the English labouring man, and his wife, could readily appreciate.

The rest of Bunyan's life was one of heavy pastoral duties (he was elected to lead the congregation in 1671), but included a further short term of imprisonment in 1677 and periods spent hiding from arrest. In 1685, fearing a further term or perhaps even a sentence of death, he made over his meagre property to his wife. He still found time, however, for several further literary works. These included *The Life and Death of Mr Badman, Presented to the World in a Familiar Dialogue between Mr Wiseman and Mr Attentive* (1680), which can almost be classed also as a realistic novel of social life; *The Holy War* (1682), in which the field of battle is a town rather than the mind of man; and the second part of *The Pilgrim's Progress* (1684), in which Christian's aged wife and her children make their own journey. He probably died from pneumonia, caught while preaching in London. Of his posthumously published works, *Of Antichrist and His Ruin* (1692) is the most notable. See *The Best of John Bunyan*, ed. Robert Backhouse, 1996; Christopher Hill, *A Turbulent, Seditious and Factious People: John Bunyan and His Church*, new edn 1989; Roger Sharrock, *John Bunyan*, new edn 1984 (critical study).

BURGESS, ANTHONY, pseudonym of John Anthony Burgess Wilson (1917–93) British novelist and critic, was born in Manchester, and educated at Xaverian College and Manchester University. He was in the Army Education Corps from 1940 to 1946, becoming a sergeant major, and serving in Gibraltar, the setting of *A Vision of Battlements*, his first novel (not published until 1965). After several teaching posts in English and phonetics, he was Senior Lecturer in English at the Teacher Training College in Malaya 1954–57, from which experience he wrote his serio-comic *The Malayan Trilogy* (1964), the individual titles being published 1956–59. While working for the Brunei Department of Education in 1959, he collapsed in the classroom. An inoperable brain tumour was diagnosed, and he was given one year to live, during which he wrote 5¹/₂ novels, to leave to his widow, Llewela (Lynne) Isherwood Jones, whom he had married in 1942. He lived; she died in 1968. He was now contacted by a young Italian woman of aristocratic descent, Liliana Macellari, whose four-year-old son had been conceived as a result of a bout of amorous dalliance during an interview with Burgess about his writing. They married, and spent several years travelling Europe by van, before settling in Monaco. Of the novels he wrote while under sentence of death, the half, when completed and published as *Inside Mr Enderby* (1963), by 'Joseph Kell' (so as not to glut the market), introduced a neurotic poet, whose unusual adventures continue in *Enderby Outside* (1968) and *The Clockwork Testament: or, Enderby's End* (1974)—see also *The Complete Enderby* (1995). Of many other inventive novels, the futuristic *A Clockwork Orange* (1962)—the original version published in England had an additional final chapter—achieved distinction for its dazzling manipu-

lation of language and notoriety for the violence of its theme. *Napoleon Symphony* (1974) has a musical structure, befitting an author who was also a composer.

The posthumously published *Byrne* (1995)—it was to have been called *The Hunters Are Up in America*—is a panoramic novel of the 20th century in more than six hundred stanzas, modelled on BYRON's *Don Juan*. His critical works include an introduction to JOYCE (rev. edn 1982) and a study of his language (1973), and a biography of SHAKESPEARE (1970). *Urgent Copy* (1968) is a selection from his numerous reviews. *A Mouthful of Air: Language and Languages, Especially English* (1992) is a lively introduction to linguistics and phonetics. See *Little Wilson and Big God*, new edn 1988 (autobiography to 1959); *You've Had Your Time: Being the Second Part of the Confessions of Anthony Burgess*, new edn 1991.

BURKE, EDMUND (1729–97) Irish political philosopher, was born in Dublin (his father was a Protestant attorney and his mother a Catholic), and was educated at a Quaker school in Co. Kildare and at Trinity College, Dublin. In 1750 he began studying law in London, but gave it up for literature against his father's will. His first two books were published anonymously. *A Vindication of Natural Society* (1756) is an ironic attack on the views of BOLINGBROKE. In *A Philosophical Enquiry into the Origin of our Ideas of the Sublime and Beautiful* (1757) he distinguishes between the sublime (which can be born of mystery or even of horror) and beauty (which is founded on love). He entered Parliament in 1765, and was a leading light of the Whigs until his retirement in 1794. A halting delivery made him a poor speaker, but there is little wrong with his eloquence or his ideals when cast in print. He believed in the constitutional right of Parliament to govern—see *Thoughts on the Cause of the Present Discontents* (1770); in a unified America; in free trade with Ireland and toleration of Catholicism; in reform of the Indian administration—with SHERIDAN he formulated and presented the case for the impeachment of the Governor General, Warren Hastings (1732–1818); and in peace and change, not revolution, in France, which he advocated in *Reflections on the Revolution in France* (1790). See Conor Cruise O'Brien, *The Great Melody: a Thematic Biography and Commented Anthology*, new edn 1994; Stanley Ayling, *Edmund Burke: His Life and Opinions*, new edn 1990.

BURNETT,   FRANCES   (ELIZA) HODGSON (1849–1924) novelist and children's writer, was born in Manchester, the eldest daughter of Edwin Hodgson, a hardware wholesaler. After his death in 1854, the business was looked after by his widow until 1865, when she took the children to her brother's log cabin in Knoxville, Tennessee. After a failure at running a private school, 'Fanny' turned to writing for a living. In 1873 she married Dr Swan Moses Burnett. With *That Lass o' Lowrie's* (1877) and *Haworth's* (1879), novels of industrial Lancashire with a fair sprinkling of local dialect, she achieved a considerable following as a serious novelist. *Little Lord Fauntleroy* (1886), the characteristics and outfits of whose hero were based on those of her second son, Vivian (1876–92), changed the course of her career and the source of her reputation. After a divorce in 1898, she married, apparently on impulse, Stephen Townsend, a young English physician with aspirations towards the stage, with whom she had collaborated in writing two plays from her own novels. They were divorced in 1901. She became an American citizen in 1905, and travelled in style between the USA and England, where for some years she maintained a house in Kent. She finally settled in Long Island, where she was known to her friends as 'Fluffy' and sported a Titian wig. *The Secret Garden* (1911), which made little impact during her lifetime, has become a classic for its depiction of real children, in a real world, achieving worthwhile aims. Her effective action to prevent an unauthorized dramatization in England of *Little Lord Fauntleroy* was instrumental in changes to the law in the Copyright Act (1911) to give protection to American authors, the USA not being a signatory to the international Berne Convention. See *The One I Know Best of All: a Memory of the Mind of a Child*, new edn 1980 (early autobiography); Ann Thwaite, *Waiting for the Party: the Life of Frances Hodgson Burnett*, 2nd rev. edn 1994.

BURNEY, FANNY [FRANCES] (1752–1840) British novelist and diarist, was born in King's Lynn, the third of six children of a distinguished musical scholar, whose wife died in 1761—see Roger Lonsdale, *Dr Charles Burney: a Literary Biography* (1965). She was largely self-educated at home in Norfolk and London through reading, writing, and meeting her father's acquaintances. *Evelina: or, The History of a Young Lady's Entrance into the World* (1778), written in the form of letters and set in the social climate which its author had so acutely observed, was highly praised and enormously successful. She was invited to join the formidable literary coterie of both sexes, the Blue Stocking Circle, about whose members she wrote a satirical play, 'The Witlings', which her father refused her to allow to be performed—over the years she wrote at least eight plays, of which only *Edwy and Elgiva* (1795) was performed. By contrast with *Evelina*, the heroine of *Cecilia* (1782) starts as an heiress, but achieves her true love only after some extraordinary adventures. More dramatic and less comic than *Evelina*, it was equally well

received. Fanny had a position at court from 1786 to 1791, and in 1793 she married a French refugee, General Alexandre d'Arblay (1753–1818). *Camilla* (1796) revealed that she had lost her touch as a novelist, but earned her enough to build a cottage for them and their son, Alexander (1794–1837). In 1801 d'Arblay returned to France to try and recover some of his possessions. She followed with their son in 1802, and stayed for ten years, during which her husband worked as a clerk in a government office. They returned in 1812 in an American ship, which was captured at sea by British officers, war between Britain and the USA having broken out. *The Wanderer* (1814), enormously long and unevenly written, which she had been working on since leaving England, was savagely treated by the critics but made her some welcome money. *The Diary and Letters of Madame d'Arblay 1778–1840* (1842–46), edited by her niece Charlotte Barrett, and *The Early Diary of Frances Burney 1768–78* (1889), ed. Annie R. Ellis, demonstrate her discerning eye and command of dialogue. See *Selected Letters and Journals*, ed. Joyce Hemlow, new edn 1987; Margaret Anne Doody, *Frances Burney: the Life in the Works*, 1989; Evelyn Farr, *The World of Fanny Burney*, 1993.

BURNS, ROBERT (1759–96) Scottish poet, was born in Alloway, Ayrshire. The eldest son of a poor farmer, he went to school at the age of six, and was later educated at home by a teacher hired by the families in the district. At 15 he was the farm's chief labourer. He supplemented his education with voracious reading, wrote poetry, and indulged enthusiastically in the rural pursuits of drinking, dancing, and fornication. When his father died in 1784, he and his brother Gilbert rented a farm at Mossgiel, which failed. By 1786 he had so many financial and domestic problems that he seriously considered going to Jamaica—two girls were pregnant by him, and the father of one of them, while refusing to let him marry his daughter (Jean Armour), was bent on retribution. Burns managed to raise the money from potential purchasers to have some of his poems printed. This Kilmarnock edition (from the place where it was printed) of *Poems, Chiefly in the Scottish Dialect* (1786) changed his life. He gave up the idea of emigrating, and became the toast of Edinburgh—it is to this period of his life that the celebrated correspondence with Mrs (Agnes) MacLehose (1759–1841) belongs. He also married Jean Armour (1767–1834), though not before she had borne him two sets of twins. Mere fame, however, did not pay the bills, and after trying farming again, Burns became a customs official in Dumfries. His main literary task from 1787 until his death from rheumatic fever was to contribute to and edit (unpaid) two compendia of songs, *A Select Collection of*

Original Scottish Airs (published from 1793) and *The Scots Musical Museum* (1787–1803). In 1790, to oblige a friend, he wrote a version of a scary folktale, 'Tam o'Shanter'. This narrative poem of sustained intensity is today recited at celebrations all over the world on Burns's birthday.

Burns is a poet of simple concepts, simply expressed. He employed a variety of metres to suit different poetic forms. His range is as prodigious as his output: satire ('Holy Willie's Prayer'); scenes of rustic life ('The Holy Fair', 'Poor Mailie's Elegy'); epistles to friends; epigrams; nature poems ('To a Mouse'); and songs—love songs ('A Red, Red Rose', 'O, Wert Thou in the Cauld Blast', 'Ye banks and braes o' bonny Doon'), and songs of the countryside ('The Birks of Aberfeldy'). He was concerned not only with Scottish themes and with promoting his area of the country as a source of poetry, but with the Scottish language, in which he was influenced by reading FERGUSSON, whom he followed in developing a composite, poetic Scots, employing words from different Scottish dialects. Unlike Fergusson, Burns wrote equally well in English and Scots, and even uses both in the same poem ('The Cotter's Saturday Night', 'To a Mountain Daisy'). He is one of the few major poets in any language to have overcome the handicap of an indigent upbringing—he was called 'the ploughman poet'. He was also an outspoken opponent of hypocrisy and a champion of the rights of the poor. See *Poems: in Scots and English*, ed. Donald A. Low, new edn 1996; *Selected Poetry and Prose*, ed. Donald A. Low, 1995; *Poems and Songs*, ed. with a glossary by James Kinsley, 2nd edn 1971; *The Letters of Robert Burns*, 2nd edn, ed. G. Ross Roy, 1985; Ian McIntyre, *Dirt and Deity: a Life of Robert Burns*, new edn 1997 (the poet in his historical context); Hugh Douglas, *Robert Burns: the Tinder Heart*, 1996 (women and song); David Daiches, *Robert Burns*, new edn 1994 of 3rd edn 1981 (critical biography); Richard Hindle Fowler, *Robert Burns*, 1988 (critical study).

BURROUGHS, WILLIAM S(EWARD) (*b.* 1914) American novelist, was born in St Louis, Missouri, a grandson of the adding machine tycoon, and was educated at Los Alamos Ranch School and Harvard, where he read anthropology. At various times he was a private detective, pest exterminator, and barman. He was discharged from the US Army in 1942 on psychiatric grounds. He lived in Mexico, Tangier, London, and Paris, before returning to the USA in 1974. In 1951 he shot his wife of six years in a 'William Tell' game that went wrong, and served 13 days in a Mexico jail; of which he said, 'I am forced to the appalling conclusion that I would never have become a writer but for Joan's death.' In 1944 he had become addicted to heroin, from which he was cured in London

in 1957. In the meantime he published, as William Lee, *Junkie: Confessions of an Unredeemed Drug Addict* (1953). *The Naked Lunch* (Paris 1959; in USA as *Naked Lunch*, 1962) was the last book to be censored by the US authorities. Created from hundreds of pages of notes made while he was addicted, and put together by the technique of 'cut-up', a kind of linguistic collage (of which BECKETT remarked, 'That's not writing, it's plumbing'), it received serious critical attention as a landmark in surrealist fiction. Bits left over from the process were recycled as a trilogy: *The Soft Machine* (1961, USA 1966), *The Ticket That Exploded* (1962, USA 1967), and *Nova Express* (1964). Subsequent fiction is more accessible to the general reader. *Cities of the Red Night: a Boy's Book* (1981) and *The Place of Dead Roads* (1984) reflect his satirical bent and his interest in science fiction and the western. See (with Daniel Odier) *The Job: Topical Writings and Interviews*, 1984; *The Letters of William Burroughs 1945–1959*, ed. Oliver Harris, new edn 1994; Ted Morgan, *Literary Outlaw: the Life and Times of William S. Burroughs*, new edn 1991.

BURTON, (Sir) RICHARD FRANCIS (1821–90) British traveller, orientalist, anthropologist, poet, and prose writer, was born in Hertfordshire, the eldest son of a colonel in the 36th Regiment, and had an irregular education, mainly in places on the Continent at which his parents stopped. He was destined for the Church, and entered Trinity College, Oxford. After five terms he rebelled against the regimen and joined the army in India, where he spent seven years without seeing action, but acquired several more languages and his lifelong passion for Orientalism. In 1853, in disguise, he penetrated the forbidden city of Mecca, and kissed the holy Black Stone itself, an exploit which he describes flamboyantly in *Personal Narrative of a Pilgrimage to El-Medinah and Meccah* (1855–56). *First Footsteps in East Africa* (1856) was written while recovering from being speared through both cheeks in an attack on his camp on the Somalian coast. He was head of the expedition in central Africa during which in 1858 the true source of the River Nile was first sighted. In 1860 he studied the Mormons in Salt Lake City. In 1861 he married Isabel Arundell (1831–96), who shared as many of his subsequent postings and travels as were thought fit for her. He was British consul for four years over a long stretch of the West African coast, from which came several books and numerous learned papers, and for another four years in South America. In 1872 he was appointed to Trieste, where he spent the rest of his life, with intervals for further travel. He wrote *The Book of the Sword*, a historical study, of which only the first volume appeared (1884). He translated *The Lusiads* of CAMÕES (1880) and, for private circulation, the Arabic classic, *The Thousand and One*

Nights (1885–88), unexpurgated and copiously annotated. The latter, which depended to some extent on the earlier English translation (1882–84) by John Payne (1842–1916), was reissued 'for household reading' (1887–88) in a version edited by his wife. After his death she destroyed the annotated complete translation of the 15th-century manual of Shaikh al-Nafwazi, *The Scented Garden*, on which he was working, and other unpublished manuscripts. He was made KCMG in 1885. See Frank McLynn, *Burton: Snow upon the Desert*, new edn 1993 (biography).

BURTON, ROBERT (1577–1640) English prose writer, was born at Lindley Hall in Leicestershire, and educated at the Free School in Sutton Coldfield, Nuneaton Grammar School, and Brasenose College, Oxford. In 1599 he was elected to a Fellowship at Christ Church, Oxford, where he lived a bachelor existence for the rest of his life, though after taking a degree in divinity in 1614 he became Vicar of St Thomas's, Oxford, and in 1630 was given the living of Seagrave, Leicestershire, by his patron, Lord Berkeley (1601–58). An excellent classicist, he wrote a satirical verse comedy in Latin, *Philosophaster*, which was performed in Christ Church hall in 1617. His life's work, *The Anatomy of Melancholy*, first published in 1621 and meticulously revised by him for four subsequent editions, has all the eccentricity traditionally associated with learned men at his university. It contains almost as much wit as wisdom, while reflecting his enormous learning in science and medicine, as well as in literature and philosophy. The first part covers the nature and causes of his subject, including 'Misery of Scholars', 'Windy (or flatuous) Melancholy', and 'Maids', Nuns', and Widows' Melancholy'; the second deals with its cures; the third is a treatise on love-melancholy and religious-melancholy, incorporating stories from classical authors and from CHAUCER, SPENSER, JONSON, and SHAKESPEARE. Many sections take a classical allusion or quotation as their starting point and can stand as plainly-stated essays in their own right. BOSWELL quotes SAMUEL JOHNSON as saying that it 'was the only book that ever took him out of bed two hours sooner than he wished to rise'. It influenced writers as diverse as MILTON and STERNE, and is the source of JOHN FORD's *The Lover's Melancholy* and KEATS's 'Lamia'.

BUTLER, GUY (*b.* 1918) South African poet and dramatist, was born in Cradock, Cape Province, and educated at the local high school and at Rhodes University, Grahamstown. During World War II he served in the South African Army in the Middle East and Italy, afterwards taking a further degree at Brasenose College, Oxford. He taught at Witwatersrand University before being Pro-

fessor of English at Rhodes University 1952–86. He sees English, 'the chosen language of literature of millions of blacks', as a unifying element, and much of his poetry, first published in *Stranger to Europe: Poems 1939–1949* (1952; enlarged edn 1960), describes African experiences in European, as well as English, ways, or Europe from the viewpoint of a South African. He has a broad metrical range and manifold poetic interests. His verse plays are particularly concerned with contemporary issues in a multiracial society. See *Selected Poems*, rev. edn 1989; *Essays and Lectures 1949-1991*, ed. Stephen Watson, 1994; *Karoo Morning: an Autobiography 1918–1935*, new edn 1983; *Bursting World: an Autobiography 1936–1945*, 1983; *A Local Habitation: an Autobiography 1945–1990*, 1991.

BUTLER, SAMUEL (1612–80) English poet, was born in Strensham, Worcestershire, the son of a well-to-do farmer, and was educated at King's School, Worcester. He is said to have served in various aristocratic households. By his own account, he met a colonel of the Parliamentary army and his clerk in London during the Civil War, and used them as the basis for the pedantic Presbyterian knight and the argumentative Nonconformist squire of his mock-heroic poem, *Hudibras*. After the Restoration of the Monarchy in 1660, Butler became secretary to the Lord President of Wales, and Steward of Ludlow Castle. The first two parts of *Hudibras* were published in 1662 and 1663 (dated 1663 and 1664). Between 1667 and 1669 he wrote his 'Characters', a series of satirical sketches on the failings and foibles of the times, which were not published until 1759. *Hudibras* Part III was published in 1678, earning him £100 from Charles II and a pension, which belies the poet's own claim that his reward for supporting the King with his satire was penury. *Hudibras*, written in rough-hewn octosyllabic couplets, has every claim to be ranked among the great English satirical poems, but where DRYDEN and POPE take a rapier, Butler employs a pikestaff. Those of the persuasion of Hudibras, for instance, 'Call fire, and sword, and desolation / A godly, thorough reformation'. His images are deliberately base, too: 'And like a lobster boil'd, the morn / From black to red begins to turn.' See *Hudibras Parts I and II and Selected Other Writings*, ed. John Wilder and Hugh de Quehen, 1973.

BUTLER, SAMUEL (1835–1902) British novelist, prose writer, poet, philosopher, and painter, was born in the rectory of Langar, Nottinghamshire, the son of a future canon of Lincoln and a grandson of the Bishop of Lichfield and Coventry. After accompanying his parents in 1843 on a tour of Europe by train (a new phenomenon), he was educated at Shrewsbury School and St John's College, Cambridge. Religious doubts, expressed in a correspondence with his father which is accurately but not fully reproduced in *The Way of All Flesh*, led him to abandon his family's intention that he should study for the ministry. When they opposed his ambition to become a painter instead, he emigrated to New Zealand in 1859. There he made a fortune breeding sheep—his accounts of his experiences, edited by his father, were published in 1863 as *A First Year in Canterbury Settlement*. In 1864 he returned to England, settled in London, and studied painting, later exhibiting on several occasions at the Royal Academy. While he was in New Zealand, he had contributed to the *Christchurch Press* a witty article on 'Darwin and the Machines', which became the basis of *Erewhon, or Over the Range* (1872), published anonymously. The state which the traveller finds (Erewhon is an anagram of 'nowhere') is not so much Utopia as a parody of Victorian society. It was his only book which enjoyed any success in his lifetime. *The Fair Haven: a Work in Defence of the Miraculous Element in Our Lord's Ministry* (1873), 'by the late John Pickard Owen', was based on a pamphlet privately printed in 1865, and is in point of fact a cleverly presented and amusing argument *against* the Resurrection.

Unwise investments in Canadian stocks led to several visits there to try and recover his funds, on one of which (1875) he composed 'A Psalm of Montreal', with the immortal refrain 'O God! O Montreal!', satirizing the treatment afforded by the local museum to the statue of a Greek discus-thrower. In 1877 he published *Life and Habit*, the first of several works in which he questioned the line of reason of DARWIN. The breadth of his interests is demonstrated also by two Alpine travel books, two published oratorios, prose translations of the *Odyssey* and *Iliad*, and two bizarre critical studies, *The Authoress of the Odyssey* (1897) and *Shakespeare's Sonnets Reconsidered* (1899). *The Way of All Flesh*, on which he worked for thirty years, was published posthumously in 1903. Technically a novel, it is also a blend of autobiography (particularly describing an unhappy childhood and rebellious youth, of which genre it is a forerunner), social satire, and eccentric interpretation of the scientific, psychological, and religious theories of the age. His own views on evolution were inspired by the French naturalist, Chevalier de Lamarck (1744–1829), and these, his stance on religious matters, and his attitude to money and wealth, influenced G. B. SHAW, who refers to his debt in the Preface to *Major Barbara*. See Peter Raby, *Samuel Butler: a Biography*, 1991.

BUZO, ALEXANDER (*b.* 1944) Australian dramatist, was born in Sydney, the son of an Albanian civil engineer and his Australian wife, and was educated at Armidale School, for a year at the International School, Geneva, and at the University of New South Wales. He had jobs as a salesman, messenger, publisher's storeman-packer, and civil service clerk until 1968, when *Norm and Ahmed* was performed in Sydney. When this street conversation piece between a Pakistani and an Australian was staged in Brisbane in 1969, the actor playing the latter was convicted of using obscene language (the play's final line), but the verdict was quashed by the Supreme Court of Queensland. Significant silences, action without words, light imagery, and the non-appearance of the motivating character are features of *Rooted* (1969), a study of middle-class disintegration. In the satirical *The Roy Murphy Show* (1973), the final mortification of the TV sports show anchorman is in public. As Resident Playwright for the Melbourne Theatre Company 1972–73, Buzo wrote *Macquarie* (1972), in which the situation of the Governor of New South Wales from 1808 to 1821 counterpoints that of a history lecturer in the 1970s. *Coralie Lansdowne Says No* (1974), *Martello Towers* (1976), and *Makassar Reef* (1978) are biting comedies of modern Australian manners; with *Big River* (1980) he returned to history, and extended his range to concerns of national identity. *The Search for Harry Allway* (1988) and *Prue Flies North* (1991) are satirical detective/adventure stories. See *Norm and Ahmed, and Other Plays*, 1993; and in Leslie Rees, *A History of Australian Drama, Vol. 2*, 1987.

BYATT, A(NTONIA) S(USAN) (*b.* 1936), née Drabble, British novelist and critic, was born in Sheffield, the elder sister of DRABBLE; rivalry and tension between sisters are recurring features in her fiction, notably in her second novel, *The Game* (1967), which followed *Shadow of a Sun* (1964), the growing up to an independent sensibility of a Cambridge undergraduate. She was herself educated at Sheffield High School, The Mount School, York, and Newnham College, Cambridge, after which she spent a year at Bryn Mawr College, Pennsylvania, and one at Somerville College, Oxford, where her research grant was terminated in 1959 when she married Ian C. R. Byatt, an economist. She lectured at the Central School of Art and Design, London, from 1965 to 1969, and at University College, London, from 1972, where she was Senior Lecturer in English 1981–83. *The Virgin in the Garden* (1978), dedicated to the memory of her 11-year-old son, who was run over and killed by a car in 1972, and *Still Life* (1985) constitute the first two parts of a projected quartet of novels, beginning in 1952, in which the symbolism (in the first) of English literary culture and (in the second) of art holds together the complex strands of relationships within a family. *Babel Tower* (1996), the third part, set in the 1960s, culminates in three sets of court proceedings involving a divorce and an 'obscene' publication. *Possession: a Romance* (1990), which won the Booker prize for fiction, is in essence a dual quest into Victorian literature, bolstered both by pastiche and by genuine scholarship. *Angels and Insects* (1992) takes the form of a pair of linked novellas in Victorian settings, whose themes are entomology and spiritualism. *The Matisse Stories* (1994) comprises three stories about articulate middle-aged heroines, with an undertext suggested by the work of the French painter Henry Matisse (1869–1954). *The Djinn in the Nightingale's Eye* (1995) is five intellectual fairy tales. Her critical works include *Degrees of Freedom: the Novels of Iris Murdoch* (1965), *Wordsworth and Coleridge in Their Time* (1970), and *Passions of the Mind: Selected Writings* (1991). After a divorce in 1969 she married Peter J. Duffy. She was made CBE in 1990. See Richard Todd, *A. S. Byatt*, 1997 (critical introduction).

BYRON, (GEORGE GORDON), 6TH LORD (1788–1824) poet, was born in London but spent his childhood in Scotland with his mother, the former Catherine Gordon of Gight (*d.* 1811), and inherited the title from his great-uncle in 1798. He was educated at Harrow, where a club foot did not hamper his athletic pursuits, and Trinity College, Cambridge. A selection of poetic juvenilia, *Hours of Idleness* (1807), was not unjustifiably savaged in the *Edinburgh Review*, which nettled Byron into responding with *English Bards and Scotch Reviewers* (1809). Between 1809 and 1811 he travelled in and around the Mediterranean, on one occasion swimming the Hellespont, and wrote the first two cantos of a spiritual travelogue, *Childe Harold's Pilgrimage*, which were an immediate success when published in 1812. He promptly turned out four dramatic tales—*The Giaour* (1813), *The Bride of Abydos* (1813), *The Corsair* (1814), and *Lara* (1814)—which contain some passages of fine poetry. He also indulged in two spectacular affairs: with Lady Caroline Lamb (1785–1828), the wife of the future Prime Minister Lord Melbourne (1779–1848); and with Augusta Leigh (1783–1851), his own half-sister, the daughter of his profligate father by a first marriage to Lady Carmarthen. The daughter born to Mrs Leigh in 1814 is generally regarded as Byron's. In 1815 he embarked on a disastrous marriage with Annabella Milbanke (1792–1860), who walked out on him soon after the birth of their daughter Ada (1815–52), claiming he was insane—see Joan Pierson, *The Real Lady Byron* (1992) for the rest of her life and that of her daughter. In 1816, hounded by creditors and ostracized by society, Byron left England, for good.

For a few months he lived on Lake Geneva, next door to P. B. SHELLEY and his mistress, Mary Godwin (MARY SHELLEY), and Mary's stepsister Claire Clairmont (1798–1879), with whom Byron resumed an affair which had begun in London—a daughter, Allegra (*d.* 1822), was born in 1817. During this time he wrote Canto III of *Childe Harold*. Canto IV was finished in Venice in 1817. In the Italian burlesque poetry of Luigi Pulci (1432–84) Byron now found the form and metre (*ottava rima*, stanzas of eight iambic pentameters rhyming *abababcc*) for the kind of epic satire he was contemplating. He experimented with *Beppo* (1817), a slender tale of technical infidelity. The 16 cantos of his unfinished masterpiece, *Don Juan*, were published in parts from 1819. In 1819 he met Teresa Countess Guiccioli in Venice, and moved to Ravenna to be near her. She left her husband for him in 1821. Through her brother he was introduced to the Carbonari, a secret society for the liberation of Italy, which inspired two Venetian dramas, *Marino Faliero* (1820) and *The Two Foscari* (1821). The former was staged at Drury Lane in 1821 against his wishes, and failed, much to his annoyance. *Don Juan* was attacked in 1821 in the preface to SOUTHEY's elegy on the late King George III, *A Vision of Judgement*. Never one to suffer fools, or critics, gladly, Byron produced his own version, *The Vision of Judgement* (1822), 'By Quevedo Redivivus', a satire so fierce that the publisher was fined £100 for 'calumny'. In 1823, bored with Teresa and suspecting a falling-off in his poetic reputation, Byron went to Greece, offering his services, and money, to the local freedom fighters against the Turks. He saw no action, and died of malaria at Missolonghi in April 1824.

For many years the more romantic and notorious aspects of Byron's life and character overshadowed his poetic reputation. He wrote some memorable short poems, including 'When We Two Parted', 'So, We'll Go No More A-Roving', 'She Walks in Beauty' and 'The Destruction of Sennacherib'—both published in *Hebrew Melodies* (1815)—, and 'The Isles of Greece', which appears in *Don Juan* Canto III. His true métier, however, was satire. *Don Juan* is also the most genuinely funny major poem in the English language. Its picaresque hero is sent abroad at 16, having been discovered flagrante delicto in a married woman's bed. After a dramatic and romantic odyssey to Greece, Constantinople, and Russia, he is sent by the Empress Catherine to England as her special envoy. The tale is cut short at the intriguing point at which a ghostly friar materializes in Juan's bedroom in a Gothic mansion, and is revealed as one of his fellow guests: 'In full, voluptuous but *not o'er*grown bulk, / The phantom of her frolic Grace—Fitz-Fulke'. The form and metre gave Byron the appropriate medium to digress on all manner of topics, and to use outrageous rhymes and familiar, often down-to-earth, diction and images; while the couplet at the end of each stanza invited the pithy epigram which had been such a feature of the satire of DRYDEN and POPE. See [*Works*], ed. Jerome J. McGann, 1986; *Selected Poetry and Prose*, ed. Donald A. Low, 1995; [*Selected Verse*] ed. Jerome J. McGann, 1994; *Selected Poems*, ed. Susan Wolfson and Peter Manning, 1996; *Byron: a Self-Portrait*, ed. Peter Quennell, 1990 (letters and diaries 1798–1824); *Selected Letters and Journals*, ed. Leslie A. Marchand, new edn 1993; Leslie A. Marchand, *Byron: a Portrait*, new edn 1993; Peter Quennell, *Byron: the Years of Fame*, new edn 1988, and *Byron in Italy*, new edn 1977 (biography); Andrew Rutherford, *Byron: a Critical Study*, 1961; Leslie A. Marchand, *Byron's Poetry: a Critical Introduction*, 1965.

C

CABELL, JAMES BRANCH (1879–1958) American novelist, was born in Richmond, Virginia, of a notable Southern family. He had a brilliant career at the College of William and Mary, during which he taught French and Greek while an undergraduate, published poems in the college monthly, some of which reappeared in his collection, *From the Hidden Way* (1916), and wrote a paper on CONGREVE which was later published in the *International* (1901). After graduating in 1898 he had newspaper staff jobs in Richmond and New York, and then embarked on a career as a professional genealogist, the fruits of which were several sumptuous privately-printed volumes. There was a surprising break in his activity in 1911–13, when he worked for a coal-mining concern in the mountains of West Virginia. In 1913 he married Priscilla Shepherd (1874–1949), a widow with five children, the eldest of whom was severely handicapped from infantile paralysis. They lived in comfort, first in the Shepherd farmhouse, 'Dumbarton Grange', and then in Richmond (with a summer retreat on Mountain Lake). Cabell had in 1902 begun to contribute romances to popular magazines, which reappeared in volume form under titles such as *The Eagle's Shadow* (1904), *The Line of Love* (1905), *Gallantry* (1907), and *Chivalry* (1909). When asked by his main publisher, Harper, to tone down the more fleshly aspects, he refused, and was dropped.

He now began the ambitious fictional sequence, 'Biography of the Life of Manuel', the history and legend of his mythical French province of Poictesme. Ultimately reissued in 18 volumes (1927–30), it incorporates revised versions of all his early romances, of which *The Soul of Melicent* (1913) became *Domnei* (1920). *Jurgen: a Comedy of Justice* (1919), having reached its third printing, was prosecuted for obscenity in 1922, and acquitted on the direction of the judge on the fourth day of the trial. After completing his vast work, Cabell announced that James Branch Cabell would write no more. Instead, he began to write as Branch Cabell, before reverting to his full name, the last element of which he said, when nettled by public criticism, was pronounced as rhyming with 'rabble'. Later fictional works include the satirical trilogy, *Smirt: an Urbane Nightmare* (1934), *Smith: a Sylvan Interlude* (1935), and *Smire: an Acceptance in the Third Person* (1937). See Joe Lee Davis, *James Branch Cabell*, 1962 (critical study).

CABLE, GEORGE WASHINGTON (1844–1925) American novelist and short-story writer, was born in New Orleans, the fifth child and eldest son of a businessman, on whose death in 1859 he left high school to work in the customhouse. He enlisted in the Confederate Army cavalry in 1863 and served until the end of the Civil War in 1865, being twice wounded. He married in 1869, and in 1870 began writing a column, signed 'Drop Shot', for the New Orleans *Picayune*, which ran for eighteen months. While holding down accountancy jobs with three organizations in the cotton industry to support his growing family, he began to write stories, which Edward King (1848–1896), gathering material for his book on the post-Civil War South, recommended to his publisher. 'Sieur George' was printed in *Scribner's Monthly* in 1873, and others followed. A collection, *Old Creole Days* (1879), was only published at the intervention of Hjalmar H. Boyesen (1848–1895), the academic and critic, who guaranteed Scribner's against loss. In 1879, after his family had weathered the yellow fever epidemic, Cable's novel, *The Grandissimes: a Story of Creole Life* (1880) began serialization; in 1881 he finally felt able to become a full-time writer. *Dr Sevier* (1884), a strong novel with a social message, the historical study *The Creoles of Louisiana* (1884), and two polemical essays, 'The Convict Lease System in the Southern States' and 'The Freedman's Case in Equity—published together in *The Silent South* (1885)—made him so unpopular in the South that he moved with his family to Northampton, Massachusetts. He published little further significant fiction, but he was now a celebrated author, who toured with TWAIN in 1884, and subsequently travelled thousands of miles (with a visit to England in 1898) giving platform readings. In 1886 he instituted the Home Culture Clubs, for inter-racial reading groups and educational improvement. The organization, to which Andrew Carnegie (1835–1919) donated $50,000 in 1903 for a headquarters, was renamed the

People's Institute in 1909. See Philip Butcher, *George W. Cable*, 1962 (biographical/critical study).

CAEDMON (fl. c.660–70) Anglo-Saxon poet, is described by BEDE in chapter 24 of his 'Church History' as being an unlearned and unsociable farm worker who was inspired by a vision while he slept in the stables to 'sing about the Creation'. In one of the manuscripts of Bede the nine lines of what he sang are written in the Northumbrian style of English which he would have used, and these qualify Caedmon to be the first known English poet. He reported his literary revelation to the farm manager, and was taken to the famous abbess Hild (*d*. 680), who admitted him to her community as a monk. Here he composed a great corpus of religious verse on themes which Bede describes, but which has not survived. The Genesis poems in the Bodleian Library manuscript known as 'Junius II' are stylistically of a later date and are regarded as of the school of Caedmon.

CAESAR, (GAIUS) JULIUS (102–44 BC) Roman statesman and historian, was born in Rome, and by the age of 30 had squandered his wife's fortune and his own. He used his oratorical powers to campaign for public office, becoming a praetor in 63, in which capacity he nabbed also the post of *pontifex maximus* and discovered (in Spain) a military talent which enabled him to amass enough booty to pay off his debts. As consul in 59 he set up the ruling triumvirate, and obtained the governorship of Gaul for ten years, during which, by brilliant but punitive tactics, he became master of the whole region west of the Rhine. He also made two expeditions to Britain, which had been unknown to the Roman world. In 49, when Pompey (106–48 BC) made his bid for power, Caesar crossed the river Rubicon at the head of his troops, signifying that he came as an invader. Pompey was defeated and pursued to Egypt, where Caesar then spent a fruitful holiday with Cleopatra. He returned with his troops via Asia Minor, where he annihilated the army of Pharnaces and sent the senate his celebrated piece of telegraphese: 'Veni vidi vici [I came, I saw, I conquered].' The Pompey faction having finally been stamped out, he was in 47 appointed dictator for ten years, and in 45 for life. A year less two days later, he was stabbed to death by a band of senatorial conspirators led by Marcus Junius Brutus (*d*. 42 BC). The judgment of history is that he tried to make too many changes too quickly. He was deified in 42. His own description of his campaign in Gaul, *De Bello Gallico* (tr. Carolyn Hammond as *The Gallic War*, 1996), is the earliest surviving record of contemporary events, and a distinguished army commander's account of his actions in a clear, no-non-

sense style. See Christian Meier, *Caesar*, tr. David McLintock, new edn 1996 (biography).

CAHAN, ABRAHAM (1860–1951) American novelist and journalist, was born in Vilna, Russia, went to Vilna Teachers' Institute, and in 1882 emigrated to the USA, of which he later became a citizen. He attended law school in New York, but was never admitted to the Bar. He wrote articles on Jewish subjects for New York papers, and stories in Yiddish. Almost his initial venture into fiction in English was *Yekl: a Tale of the New York Ghetto* (1896), the first American Jewish novel. It was followed by *The Imported Bridegroom and Other Stories of the New York Ghetto* (1898). He was a staff journalist on the New York *Commercial Advertiser* from 1897 to 1901, after which he edited the phenomenally successful Yiddish newspaper, the '*Jewish Daily Forward*' until he was in his eighties. *The Rise of David Levinsky* (1917) is the archetypal novel of the Jewish immigrant who achieves tangible success without any sense of moral achievement. Cahan's autobiography, written in Yiddish and published in five volumes 1926–31, was translated by Leon Stein, Abraham P. Conan, and Lynn Davison as *The Education of Abraham Cahan* (1969).

CAIN, JAMES M(ALLAHAN) (1892–1977) American novelist, was born in Annapolis, Maryland, and educated at Washington College, Chestertown, of which his father had become President in 1903. After trying several jobs, and taking instruction in singing, he decided to become a writer, and taught at Washington while studying for a further degree. He enlisted as a private in the US 79th Division in 1918, and served in France, where he edited the division's weekly paper, the *Lorraine Cross*. He was a reporter on the Baltimore *Sun*; taught journalism for a year at St John's College, Annapolis; then moved to New York, where he wrote editorials and articles for journals, a series of satirical dialogues for the *American Mercury* being published as *Our Government* (1930). In 1931 he went to Hollywood, where he stayed for 17 years, writing film scripts. *The Postman Always Rings Twice* (1934) was the first of his pacey stories of criminal love, which earned him the sobriquet, 'the twenty-minute egg of the hard-boiled school'. He wrote 'Double Indemnity' in 1936 to help finance the run of his stage version of *The Postman Always Rings Twice* (1936); it was published in *Three of a Kind* (1943), with 'Career in C Major' and 'The Embezzler'. In *Serenade* (1937), *Mildred Pierce* (1941), *The Moth* (1948), and *The Root of His Evil* (1951) are predominantly studies of character. Short stories are in *The Baby in the Icebox and Other Short Fiction*, ed. Roy Hoopes (1981). In an attempt to redress the imbalance in rewards between producers and writers of films, he proposed in 1946 the establishment of the American Authors' Authority, which foundered on the difficulty of writers to reach consensus. Of his four marriages, the shortest, to an ex-film star, ended in divorce after 18 months, and the longest, to a former opera singer, lasted for 19 years until her death in 1966. See David Madden, *James M. Cain*, 1987 (critical study).

CALDERÓN DE LA BARCA, PEDRO (1600–81) Spanish dramatist, was born in Madrid, where he attended a Jesuit school until he was 13. After a year at Alcala University, he went on to Salamanca University, where until 1620 he studied canon law, with theology, philosophy, and logic as subsidiary subjects. He then spent several riotous years in the company of two of his brothers, took part in poetic contests in honour of St Isadore, and had his first play performed in 1623. He became court dramatist in 1635 after the death of VEGA, and was in 1637 made a knight of the Order of Santiago, with whom he served in Catalonia in 1640–41 during the revolt against Spain, and was wounded. He returned to Madrid in 1642 with a monthly pension. In 1651, following the death of his two brothers and of a mistress by whom he had a son, he was ordained priest and became a chaplain to the King. He now restricted his literary activities to court plays and to two *autos sacramentales* (one-act religious pieces) a year for the city of Madrid. Calderón and his school of dramatists developed the *comedia* of Vega, and in more than a hundred secular plays he demonstrated a variety of types and moods. cloak-and-sword (or comedies of manners), national legends, historical dramas, tragedies of honour—see especially *El Medico de su Honra* (tr. Roy Campbell as *The Surgeon of His Honour*, 1960) and *El Pintor de su Deshonra* (tr. David Johnston and Laurence Boswell as *The Painter of Dishonour*, 1995)—and mythological and philosophical plays. Four *partes* (volumes), each of 12 plays, were published 1636–72, with a fifth, containing ten (of which Calderón disowned four), in 1677. Juan de Vera Tassis y Villarroel (1631–c.1701) published nine volumes of the dramatic works (1682–91), but died before he could bring out the tenth. English Restoration comedy owes a general debt to Calderón: Charles II encouraged Sir Samuel Tuke (*d.* 1674) to adapt *Los Empeños de Seis Horas* as *The Adventures of Five Hours* (1663), and *El Maestro de Danzar* is the source of WYCHERLEY's *The Gentleman Dancing-Master*. EDWARD FITZGERALD's *Eight Dramas of Calderón* (1853), of which *Life is a Dream* was first performed in 1926, are not now regarded as giving a fair impression of Calderón's art. See *Plays, Vol. 1*, tr. Gwynne Edwards, 1991.

CALDWELL, ERSKINE (1902–87) American novelist and short-story writer, was born in Coweta County, Georgia, 'in a place so remote it had no name', the only child of a Presbyterian minister whose peripatetic existence meant that the boy only had a year in high school, in Wrens. He attended Erskine College in 1920–21, and then the universities of Virginia and Pennsylvania until 1926 without finishing any course. In 1926, newly married, he gave up his job on the Atlanta *Journal* to go and write in the comparative sanctuary of Maine. He had published two tough-guy city novellas and a collection of stories, *American Earth* (1931), when he managed to encapsulate in *Tobacco Road* (1932) the desperation which had for years been the lot of the poor Southern white. Its modest reception was instrumental in the rejection of his next novel, about a family in Maine, which was finally published as *A Lamp for Nightfall* in 1952. Another publisher took his second seamy slice of rural low life and earthy sex, *God's Little Acre* (1933). Its acquittal in a New York Court of a charge of obscenity, and the success of the stage production of *Tobacco Road* (1934), which almost closed after a fortnight but went on to run for over six years, helped to project him into being a best seller. These two books, and the best of his economically worded short stories—see *The Complete Stories of Erskine Caldwell* (1941)—effectively represent his genuine contribution to American literature, though he published some twenty more novels. With his second wife, the photographer Margaret Bourke-White (1906–71), he produced several photographic essays, of which *You Have Seen Their Faces* (1937), a Southern study, is an especially noteworthy example of the genre. See *With All My Might: an Autobiography*, 1987; *Deep South: Memory and Observation*, new edn 1995; *Call It Experience: the Years of Learning How to Write*, new edn 1996; James E. Devlin, *Erskine Caldwell*, 1984 (critical study); Wayne Mixon, *The People's Writer: Erskine Caldwell and the South*, 1995 (critical study).

CALISHER, HORTENSE (*b.* 1911) American novelist and short-story writer, was born in New York City and educated at Hunter College High School and Barnard College, to which she went on money scraped together by her parents and earned by herself in a restaurant. She graduated in philosophy, did social work, and married in 1935. Her first story, which she composed while walking a child to school, was published in 1947. A collection of stories, *In the Absence of Angels* (1951), was followed ten years later by her first novel, *False Entry* (1961), an American chronicle which has links with her fifth, *The New Yorkers* (1969). Her range of forms is as wide as are her themes and settings. *Journal from Ellipsia* (1965) is an interplanetary version of SAMUEL BUTLER's *Erewhon* and SWIFT's *Gulliver's Trav-*

els; the character revelations in *Mysteries of Motion* (1983) are made during the first civilian space shuttle service; the unashamedly ribald reflections in *The Bobby-Soxer* (1986) are told with the hindsight of maturity. Critics regard her best medium as the short story, which she has defined as 'an apocalypse, served in a very small cup'—see *The Collected Stories of Hortense Calisher* (1975). *Herself* (1972) is an autobiographical study of a writing life, which includes critical articles and commentary on the writer as feminist, teacher, and parent—see also *Kissing Cousins: a Memoir* (1988).

CALLAGHAN, MORLEY (1903–90) Canadian novelist and short-story writer, was born in Toronto of Irish Catholic descent, and was educated at St Michael's College, Toronto University, and Osgoode Hall Law School. He was called to the Ontario Bar in 1928 but never practised. During summer vacations he had been a cub reporter on the Toronto *Daily Star*, where he came across HEMINGWAY, who encouraged him to write and arranged the publication of some of his stories in an American magazine in Paris. His work was also spotted by F. S. FITZGERALD, whose publisher issued his first novel, the lurid gangster tale, *Strange Fugitive* (1928). On an extended honeymoon in Paris in 1929, he mixed with the expatriate literary set, and caused a sensation by taking on the much heavier and more experienced Hemingway in a boxing match, and knocking him out. Callaghan's modest account of the exploit is in *That Summer in Paris: Memories of Tangled Friendships with Hemingway, Fitzgerald and Some Others* (1963): Hemingway wrote a splenetic version of the incident in *A Moveable Feast* (1964). After a brief stay in the USA, Callaghan returned to Toronto, where he spent the rest of his life as a full-time writer. During World War II he was with the Royal Canadian Navy on assignment for the National Film Board, and was anchorman of the peripatetic current affairs radio programme, 'Of Things to Come'. He also wrote two plays which, according to an obituarist, 'when produced, pleased neither him nor the public'. EDMUND WILSON, in an essay reprinted in *O Canada* (1965), compared him to CHEKHOV and TURGENEV. His impressionistic short stories—see *Morley Callaghan's Stories* (1959)—are regarded by some critics as of a higher order than his 14 novels and one novella, *No Man's Meat* (Paris, 1931). Most agree that his two novels which most powerfully represent society are both from the middle period of his development: *The Loved and the Lost* (1951), part thriller, part love story (winner of the Governor General's Award), and the one which followed, *The Many Colored Coat* (1960), a moral, Christian tale of human nature in crisis. He was made Companion, Order of Canada, in 1983. His son, the writer

and critic Barry Callaghan (*b*. 1937), has edited *The Lost and Found Stories of Morley Callaghan* (1985). See Gary Boire, *Morley Callaghan: Literary Anarchist*, 1994 (biography); Gary Boire, *Morley Callaghan and His Works*, 1990.

CALVIN (or **CAUVIN**), Jean (1509–64) French theologian, was born in Noyon, the son of an ecclesiastical lawyer, and was at 14 sent, with two young noblemen of the region, to Paris, where he became MA in 1529. Instead of going on to study theology at the Sorbonne, he decided to read law in Orleans and Bourges, after which, his father having died in 1531, he settled in Paris and produced a commentary on SENECA's *De Clementia* (1532). Formally associated with the doctrines of the *évangéliques*, he was forced to leave the country in 1533, and, in Basle, wrote and published in Latin *Institutio Christianae Religionis* (1535), the first complete vindication of Protestantism and the cornerstone of Calvinist theology. His own translation of it into French (1541) is a landmark in the use of the vernacular for serious prose. In 1539 he settled in Strasbourg where, in deference to his dictum that if he took a wife 'it would be in order to devote my time to the Lord, by being the more relieved from the worries of daily life', he consented to marry the widow of an Anabaptist whom he had converted. In 1541 he was persuaded to go and bolster the establishment of the Reformed faith in Geneva, where he reorganized the Church and aided its branches abroad, and in 1559 founded the Academy. His differences of opinion with Michael Servetus (1511–53) resulted in the latter being burned at the stake, though Calvin pleaded for a less painful method of execution. His success in grouping the Reformed communities of Europe into a coherent unity led to the religious wars which followed his death. His theology was inspirational in the development of Protestantism, and his ideas on Church government are the basis of Presbyterianism. His doctrines influenced English literature of the 16th and 17th centuries, and their effect is apparent in Scottish and Canadian literature into the 20th century. See François Wendel, *Calvin: the Origins and Development of His Religious Thought*, tr. Philip Mairet, new edn 1987.

CALVINO, ITALO (1923–85) Italian novelist and critic, was born in Santiago de las Vegas, Cuba, and grew up in San Remo, where his father was curator of the botanic garden. From his experience of service with a brigade of Communist partisans in 1943–45 during World War II, he wrote his first novel, *Il Sentiero dei Nidi di Ragno* (1947; tr. Archibald Colquhoun as *The Path to the Nest of Spiders*, 1957); it was reissued in 1964 with a preface (tr. Gwyn Morris in *Italian Writing Today*, 1967) in which he discusses neo-realism. He graduated from Turin University in 1947, when he joined the editorial staff of the publisher Einaudi; he edited the controversial literary magazine, *Il Menabò*, from 1959 to 1967. The structure and form of *I Nostri Antenati* (1960; tr. Colquhoun as *Our Ancestors*, 1980), a trilogy of novels of fantasy and high adventure in historical settings (originally published 1952–59), were developed from the narrative techniques of the storytellers among the partisans; further study led to *Fiabe Italiane . . .* (1956; tr. George Martin as *Italian Folktales*, 1982). In several collections of stories, some realistic, some verging on science fiction, a link is provided by a narrator, who in *Se Una Notte d'Inverno un Viaggiatore* (1979; tr. William Weaver as *If on a Winter's Night a Traveller*, 1981), which begins in a railway station, is bent on romancing the elusive Ludmilla, who represents the reader—see also *Numbers in the Dark and Other Stories*, tr. Tim Parks (1995), a posthumous collection of stories written in 1943–84. *Six Memos for the Next Millennium*, tr. Patrick Creagh (1992), comprises five out of the six lectures on specific literary values which he completed but did not live to deliver at Harvard University in 1985. *The Road to San Giovanni*, tr. Parks (1993) is a collection of five autobiographical essays written 1962–77.

CAMBRIDGE, ADA (1844–1926) Australian novelist and poet, was born in Norfolk, England. She was educated by governesses, and at 24 had published two books of religious verse and three moral tales. In 1870 she married Rev. George Cross (1844–1917), with whom she sailed to Australia. They lived in six country parishes in Victoria before settling in Williamstown in 1893. In 1874 she offered a serial to the *Australasian*, which printed nine of her stories during the next 12 years. In 1887 she published anonymously in London *Unspoken Thoughts*, a collection of poems some of which expressed religious doubts or raised questions about sexuality and marriage: it was quickly withdrawn. *A Marked Man* (1890), originally serialized as 'A Black Sheep', was the first of a dozen novels with Australian backgrounds to achieve success. Her plots are romantic and usually conventional, though she is an advocate of second marriages, achieved by providential means, when the first is unhappy; and her descriptions of rural social life and the terrain are vivid and valid. When Cross retired, they left for England, but she returned shortly after his death, and 'found a tiny home' in Malvern, Victoria, near her only daughter. Her autobiographical *Thirty Years in Australia* (1903), to which *The Retrospect* (1912) is a complement, is a valuable study of conditions and a revealing account of her life. See Margaret Bradstock and Louise Wakeling, *Rattling the Orthodoxies: a Life of Ada Cambridge*, 1991; Audrey Tate, *Ada Cambridge: Her Life and Work 1844–1926*, 1991.

CAMERON, NORMAN (1905–53) Scottish poet, was born in Edinburgh and educated at Fettes College and Oriel College, Oxford, where he read English, had several poems published in *Oxford Poetry*, and met GRAVES, who became a lifelong friend. In 1929 he accepted a post as an education officer in Nigeria, from which he resigned in 1932 to be near Graves in Majorca, and to write. The plan lasted only a few months, for he discovered that he also needed a paid job, and had a violent, but petty, quarrel with the American poet, Laura Riding (1901–91), with whom Graves was living. He worked in London as an advertising copywriter until World War II, in which he served in a political warfare capacity with the Eighth Army in Africa and Italy—the poems 'Black and White' and the often-quoted 'Green, Green is El Aghir' reflect his experiences. Afterwards he returned to advertising, and increased his literary output with some scrupulous but also technically outstanding verse translations of poems by RIMBAUD and VILLON, and English versions of the prose of BALZAC and VOLTAIRE; it was a measure of his dedication to his craft that he would not use a word which was unknown to the original author's English contemporaries. His life was fraught with domestic upheavals (he was married three times), and he suffered from hypertension. Graves, in *The Collected Poems of Norman Cameron* (1957), describes him as 'a divided character—alternately a Presbyterian precisian and moralist; and a pagan poet and boon companion'. See *Collected Poems and Selected Translations*, ed. Warren Hope and Jonathan Barker, 1990.

CAMÕES (or **CAMOËNS**), **LUIS DE** (1524–80) Portuguese poet and dramatist, was born, probably in Lisbon, of an ancient but impoverished house, and was educated at Coimbra University until about 1542. In 1544, in church, he saw a lady, identified by some as Caterina de Ataide (d. 1559), with whom he fell in love and in whose honour he composed a body of lyric poetry. At about this time, too, he wrote three plays: an adaptation from PLUTARCH, an imitation of PLAUTUS, and *Filodemo*, a comedy which was first performed in Goa when he was there in 1555. In 1546 he got into trouble at court (another critical faction has identified his inamorata as the Infanta Maria), and was banished up the Tagus river, from which he was sent to serve in Ceuta on the African coast, where he lost an eye in action. He returned to Lisbon in 1549, and in 1552 ended up in jail after a carnival brawl in which a courtier died. He was pardoned eight months later and sailed for India. From the Portuguese base of Goa he went on a military expedition to Ormiz, on the Persian Gulf, and spent an uncomfortable few months in Guardafui, at the tip of the Horn of Africa. In 1556 he was appointed to Macao, the Portuguese possession opposite Hong Kong, to oversee the effects of all people dead or absent. Having amassed a fortune, he was returned to Goa in 1559 to be tried for professional misconduct. The ship was wrecked near the mouth of the Mekong, Cambodia, and though he got safely to shore with the precious manuscript of *Os Lusíadas*, which he had conceived in the 1540s, he lost all his money and, it is said, a Chinese concubine. When he finally reached Goa, he was thrown into prison, released with his charges quashed, and then imprisoned again, for debt. He did not return to Lisbon until 1570, having en route spent two penniless years in Mozambique. In 1571 he was granted a ten-year copyright in *Os Lusíadas*, and in 1572 a pension of 15,000 reis. It was paid only irregularly, and he died in poverty. *Os Lusíadas* [The Lusiads, i.e. Lusitanians] (tr. Richard Fanshaw, 1655; tr. Leonard Bacon, 1950) is the national epic of Portugal, a personal and historical, as well as a mythological, odyssey in ten books of eight-line stanzas, which uses the explorations of Vasco da Gama (*c*.1469–1525) as its framework.

CAMPBELL, ALISTAIR (*b.* 1925) New Zealand poet, novelist, and dramatist, was born in Rarotonga, Cook Islands, of a Scottish father and a Polynesian mother, both of whom died when he was a child. He was brought up in New Zealand and was educated at Otago Boys' High School, Otago University (for a year, during which he was a classmate of BAXTER), Victoria University, and Wellington Teachers' College. *Mine Eyes Dazzle: Poems 1947–1949* (1950; rev. edns 1951 and 1956) contained lyrical evocations of nature and landscape and reflections on his uprooted childhood; later work recalls aspects of his first marriage, to ADCOCK, which finished in divorce after five years, and his remarriage. He was Editor, Department of Education School Publications Branch 1955–72, and Senior Editor, New Zealand Council for Educational Research 1972–87. *Sanctuary of Spirits* (1963), originally written for radio, is a poetic sequence from Maori history: ancestral elements feature in a further sequence, *The Dark Lord of Savaiki* (1980). *Stone Rain: the Polynesian Strain* (1992) contains significant poems on Polynesian themes. In a trilogy of novels, *The Frigate Bird* (1989), *Sidewinder* (1991), and *Tia* (1993), he has explored the effect on mental stability of cultural disconnection such as he himself experienced. See *Collected Poems 1947–1981*, 1981; *Island to Island*, 1984 (autobiography to 1950); Peter Smart, *Introducing Alistair Campbell*, new edn 1985 (biographical/critical study).

CAMPBELL, DAVID (1915–79) Australian poet, was born at Ellerslie, an old family property near Adelong, New South Wales. He was educated at King's School, Parramatta ('We all scoffed at poetry and thought sport was everything') and Jesus College, Cambridge, where he was encouraged by a fellow Australian to read some contemporary poetry. He was a rugby football internationalist, being capped as a flanker for England against Wales in 1937. During World War II he served in the Royal Australian Air Force—see his vivid poem about fighting in the jungle, 'Men in Green' (1943)—and was awarded the Distinguished Flying Cross and Bar. After the war he farmed, and wrote. His earlier books of verse, beginning with *Speak with the Sun* (1949), reflect his rural upbringing and interests, with excursions into Australianized lyrics and ballads, often with the expression of wry humour. The title sequence of *The Branch of Dodona and Other Poems 1969–1970* (1970) is drawn from Greek mythology, and the volume also contains a series of modern georgics, 'Works and Days'. Autobiographical poems are a feature of *Devil's Rock and Other Poems 1970–1972* (1974) and *Deaths and Pretty Cousins* (1975). He also published two books of short stories, *Evening under Lamplight* (1959), in which he recaptures images of his childhood, and *Flame and Shadow* (1976). See *Collected Poems*, ed. Leonie Kramer, 1989.

CAMPBELL, GEORGE (*b.* 1916) Jamaican poet, was born George Constantine Campbell Boyd in Colon, Panama, and was brought by his mother to Jamaica when he was five. He was educated at St George's College, Kingston, and later studied in the USA at the Dramatic Workshop of the New School for Social Research. He worked as a journalist on the *Daily Gleaner* and *Public Opinion*, as Editor of *Welfare Reporter*, the government journal for social services, and latterly as Publications Consultant, Institute of Jamaica. He was discovered as a poet by the wife of the statesman, Norman Manley (1893–1969), who, for such poems as 'Emancipation', 'I was Negro', and 'History Makers', called him 'Poet of the Revolution', and for the launching of whose People's National Party in 1938 Campbell wrote 'On This Night'. *First Poems* (1945) was also a landmark in that it broke away from Victorian conventions and used free verse as a medium for Caribbean poetry. See *First Poems: a New Edition, with Additional Poems*, introductory poem by Derek Walcott, 1981; *Earth Testament*, 1983 (subsequent collection).

CAMPBELL, JOSEPH (1879–1944) Irish poet, was born in Belfast, the son of a nationalistic building contractor married to a cultured Gael. In 1902 he went to Dublin, where the Irish Literary Revival caught his imagination. He published articles and poems, and wrote words for Donegal airs collected by the musician Herbert Hughes (1882–1937), which appeared as *Songs of Uladh* (1904). He worked and wrote a play for the Ulster Literary Theatre, but moved to London in 1906, where he taught, was involved with Irish literary organizations, and married a London woman. By the time they returned to a farm in Wicklow, he had had five volumes of verse published in Ireland, comprising in the main tightly-knit but often too tightly-expressed evocations of traditional Irish themes. *Irishry* (1913), with its character studies (notably 'The Old Woman'), and *Earth of Cualann* (1917) marked the highest points in, as well as the culmination of, his collections of poetry, but not the end of his promotion of Irish culture. After being arrested and imprisoned during the Civil War of 1922–23, he went to the USA, where he founded successively the School of Irish Studies in New York, the Irish Foundation, and the *Irish Review*. He returned to Wicklow in 1939 and lived there in solitude until his death, without ever completing the work on his 'Collected Poems'. See *The Poems of Joseph Campbell*, ed. Austin Clarke, 1963.

CAMPBELL, ROY (1901–57) South African poet and translator, was born in Durban of Scottish descent on both sides. He was educated at Durban High School, which he left at 16 to go to the Royal Military Academy, Sandhurst, spending a year at National University College to fill in time. He sailed for England in December 1918, having decided instead to go to Oxford. There, while studying for his entrance, he met an even younger poetry enthusiast, the composer (Sir) William Walton (1902–83), who introduced him to the SITWELLS and T. S. ELIOT. Realizing he would not achieve the necessary standard in Greek, he went to London, and then spent eighteen months in Provence. Back in London in 1921, he met the stunning, liberated Mary Garman (1898–1979). They were married five months later, and lived for a year in a rudimentarily converted cowshed in Wales, where he drafted *The Flaming Terrapin* (1924), whose subject is 'a great machine, / Thoughtless and fearless, governing the clean / System of active things . . .'. This vigorous philosophical poem, which T. E. LAWRENCE recommended to its publisher as 'a riot of glorious imagery and colour', startled the Georgian literary establishment.

As 'local boy makes good' he returned to South Africa, where he wrote the memorable African poems 'The Serf', 'The Zulu Girl', 'Tristan da Cunha', the symbolic 'Making of a Poet', and the satirical 'Poets in Africa'. These were published in his most significant collection, *Adamastor* (1930), with poems of Provence, notably 'Mass at Dawn' and 'Horses on the Camargue'. He was appointed Editor of a new review journal, *Voorslag*, on which he was assisted by PLOMER and VAN DER POST. After two issues he threw up the job, drafted *The Wayzgoose* (1928), a hilarious skit on the Durban cultural scene, and hastily returned to England, where he was lent the gardener's cottage of the NICOLSONS' house at Long Barn. Near catastrophe, caused by Mary's affair with SACKVILLE-WEST, was averted; the couple were reconciled and went to Provence. Campbell revenged himself on the Nicolsons and their literary circle in a heavy-handed satirical poem, *The Georgiad* (1931). When money grew scarce the Campbells moved to Spain, and were received into the Catholic Church, the twin inspirations of the poems in *Mithraic Emblems* (1936). His support of Franco in the Spanish Civil War, demonstrated not in action but with a propaganda poem 'from the Battlefield', published as *Flowering Rifle* (1939), made him even less popular in England.

He volunteered for the British Army in 1941 and served in East Africa. The immediate postwar years were spent in London, where he published his last collection, *Talking Bronco* (1946), redeemed almost entirely by his magnificent translation of 'En una Noche Oscura' of JOHN OF THE CROSS—see also his *The Poems of St John of the Cross* (1951). He was drinking heavily, and was now so argumentative that he fought with MACNEICE in a pub, threatened GRIGSON in the street, and punched SPENDER on the nose during a poetry reading. In 1952 he and his wife went to live in Portugal, where he did translations of Spanish and Portuguese writers, mainly for the BBC. In 1957, on the way back from the Holy Week celebrations in Seville, a worn tyre on their car burst while Mary was driving. Campbell died in the crash. See *Collected Poems*, 3 vols 1949, 1957, 1960; *Broken Record*, 1934, and *Light on a Dark Horse*, 1951 (autobiography); Peter Alexander, *Roy Campbell: a Critical Biography*, 1982; and essay by PATON in Christopher Heywood (ed.), *Aspects of South African Literature*, 1976.

CAMPBELL, THOMAS (1777–1844) Scottish poet, was born in Glasgow, the 11th child of a 67-year-old retired merchant, and was educated at Glasgow University. In 1794 he walked to Edinburgh and back to attend the trial for treason of the political reformer Joseph Gerrald (1763–96), whose address to the court made a lasting impression on him. He sprang into the public eye with his philosophical study in heroic couplets, *The Pleasures of Hope* (1799). Based on the method of ROGERS's *The Pleasures of Memory*, its first part takes political freedom (especially as applied to Poland) as a theme, and the second the imagination. In 1880 he visited Germany, where he wrote the rousing 'Ye Mariners of England'. A distant view of the battle of Hohenlinden inspired the narrative poem of that name, published with 'Lochiel's Warning', which combines the Scottish second sight tradition with the romantic view of the '45 Rebellion, and concludes that the latter was a mistake. In 1803 he married a cousin and moved to the London area. *Gertrude of Wyoming* (1809), an attempt at an American topic in Spenserian stanzas, moved WALTER SCOTT to suggest to IRVING that the poet was 'afraid of the shadow that his own fame casts before him'. In the same volume appeared 'The Battle of the Baltic' and the popular 'Lord Ullin's Daughter'. *Specimens of the British Poets* (1819) contained some good criticism and impressed even CARLYLE, but subsequent prose works were largely hackwork. He was nominally editor of the *New Monthly Magazine* (the real work was done by a colleague and, until her death in 1830, by Mrs Campbell) from 1820 to 1831, when he started the *Metropolitan Magazine*, which only lasted a short time. In 1843 he retired to Boulogne, where he died. He was buried in Westminster Abbey. He never lost his Scottish accent, and his popularity was such that between 1827 and 1829 he was three times in succession elected Lord Rector of Glasgow University, on the last occasion defeating Sir Walter Scott.

CAMPION, EDMUND see HOLINSHED; STANYHURST.

CAMPION, THOMAS (1567–1620) English poet and musician, was born in London and educated at Peterhouse, Cambridge. He then studied law at Gray's Inn, and medicine in France, qualifying as a doctor in 1606. Poems by him were included in a pirated edition of SIDNEY's *Astrophel and Stella* in 1591 (see also DANIEL). *Poemata* (1596) contained elegies and epigrams in Latin, in which, and in his English lyrics, he demonstrated the influence of CATULLUS and MARTIAL. Beginning with *A Book of Ayres* (1601)—he defines an air as the musical equivalent of a poetic epigram—he published six volumes of songs with music. There are some fine religious lyrics, deft classical parallels, and unconventional and witty plaints of love, notably 'Mistris, since you so much desire' and 'Come you pretty false-eyed wanton', as well as 'There is a Garden in her face' ('Cherry-Ripe'). In *Observations in the Art of English Poesie* (1602) he argued for a return to the rhythm of classical metres at the expense of rhyme.

In 1607 he composed a masque for the marriage of the King's Scottish-born favourite James Hay (d. 1636), later Earl of Carlisle. He was chosen to write the spectacular entertainment for the wedding night in 1613 of the Princess Elizabeth (later known as the 'Winter Queen') to Frederick V, Elector Palatine,

from whom the Hanoverian monarchs of Britain and the House of Windsor descended. In the same year two further masques by him were performed: *The Caversham Entertainment* for the Queen; and *The Somerset Masque* for the wedding of Robert Carr (d. 1645), created Earl of Somerset for the occasion, and Frances Howard, ex-wife of the Earl of Essex. The uneasy tone of the latter may reflect the seamy circumstances of the marriage, after which the couple were convicted of the murder of Sir Thomas Overbury (1581–1613), who had opposed the match—see David Lindley, *The Trials of Frances Howard: Fact and Fiction at the Court of King James* (1993). Campion's patron, Sir Thomas Monson (1546–1641), was for a time imprisoned as an accessory to the crime. See *The Essential Campion*, 1988; *Ayres and Observations: Selected Poems and Prose*, ed. Joan Hart, 1976; David Lindley, *Thomas Campion*, 1986 (critical study).

CAMUS, ALBERT (1913–60) French novelist, dramatist, and critic, was born in Mondovi, Algeria, where he was brought up by his mother, an illiterate charwoman, after his father's death in 1914 in the battle of the Marne. He was educated at the Lycée of Algiers on a scholarship, and at the University of Algiers, from which he received the *diplôme d'études supérieures* in philosophy in 1936, after tuberculosis had interrupted his studies and put paid to his becoming a college teacher—he still managed to play in goal for his university and for the Algerian national team at soccer. He founded the Théâtre du Travail, in which he was actor, director, and playwright, and published *L'Envers et l'Endroit* [Betwixt and Between] (1937), a collection of essays exploring a reconciliation between the states of happiness and suffering. Shortly after the publication in Paris of his novel *L'Étranger* (1942; tr. Stuart Gilbert as *The Outsider*, 1946), he left Algeria to join the French Resistance, for whom he edited the underground newspaper *Combat*.

In *Le Mythe de Sisyphe* (1943; tr. Justin O'Brien as *The Myth of Sisyphus*, 1955) Camus expounded his views on the contemporary human situation in terms of the destruction of beliefs: 'This divorce between man and his life, the actor and his setting, truly constitutes the feeling of Absurdity.' The disharmony is at the heart of the Theatre of the Absurd, to which his initial contribution was *Caligula* (1945; tr. Gilbert, 1948). A second cycle of works comprised *La Peste* (1947; tr. Gilbert as *The Plague*, 1948), a narrative of the descent of pestilence on Oran in the 1940s; *Les Justes* (1950; tr. Gilbert as *The Just Assasins*, 1958), a play inspired by the terrorist attack on the Tsar's uncle in 1905; and *L'Homme Révolté* (1951; tr. Anthony Bower as *The Rebel: an Essay on Man in Revolt*, 1953). He adapted for the French stage plays by CALDÉRON (1953) and VEGA (1957), and also FAULKNER's *Re-*

quiem for a Nun (1956). He died in a car accident, having been in 1957 the youngest winner of the Nobel Prize for Literature after KIPLING. In a briefcase found at the scene of the crash were 144 pages of scribbled, unpunctuated manuscript, the basis of his epic autobiographical novel inspired by the French–Algerian conflict (1954–62). With the addition of punctuation, it was published as *Le Dernier Homme* (1994; tr. David Hapgood as *The First Man*, 1995). See *Selected Essays and Notebooks*, ed. Philip M. W. Thody, new edn 1989.

CANETTI, ELIAS (1905–94) Bulgarian-born novelist and critic, was born in Russe of Sephardic Jewish parents. As a child he spoke Ladino, but his parents spoke to each other in German, which he always insisted was his mother tongue. The family moved to England in 1911. A year later his father died, and his domineering and possessive mother took him to Vienna. He was educated there, in Zurich, and in Frankfurt, finally obtaining a doctorate in chemistry at Vienna University in 1929, though he had no intention of being a scientist. *Die Blendung* (1936; tr. C. V. Wedgwood as *The Tower of Babel*, 1947), a story of personal paranoia with prophetic political implications, was published shortly before he settled in England. *Masse und Macht* (1960; tr. Carol Stewart as *Crowds and Power*, 1962; rev. edn 1973) is a sociological study. From his research notes for it he largely drew the aphorisms which are the basis of *Die Provinz des Menschen* (1973; tr. Joachim Neugroschel as *The Human Province*, 1978)—a further collection was published as *The Secret Heart of the Clock*, tr. Joel Agee (1991). Three volumes of autobiography, covering the years to 1937, appeared as *The Tongue Set Free* (tr. Neugroschel, 1988), *The Torch in My Ear* (tr. Neugroschel, 1989), and *The Play of the Eyes* (tr. Ralph Manheim, 1990). He was awarded the Nobel Prize for Literature in 1981. In 1934 he married Venetia Toubner-Calderon (d. 1963), whose stories of a Viennese street, written during the 1930s, were published as *Die Gelbe Strasse* (by Veza Canetti, 1990; tr. Ian Mitchell as *Yellow Street*, 1990). His second wife died in 1988. See Thomas H. Falk, *Elias Canetti*, 1993 (biographical/critical study).

ČAPEK, KAREL (1890–1938) Czech novelist, dramatist, and journalist, was born in Male Svatonovice, Bohemia, the son of a physician, and was educated at the universities of Berlin, Paris, and Prague, where he was awarded a doctorate in philosophy in 1915. An advocate of the Czech language, and a supporter of the new state of Czechoslovakia which was created after World War II, he wrote for *Lidové Noviny*, which supported the government, and established the Vinohradsky Arts Theatre in Prague in 1921. His futuristic play, *R. U. R. (Rossum's Universal Robots)*

(1920; tr. Paul Selver, 1923), was a warning of the dangers of treating humans like machines, and gave to the world the word 'robot'. In the satirical *The Insect Play* (1921; tr. Selver, 1923), written with his brother Josef (1887–1945), the habits of insects are tellingly applied to the human race. He wrote several science fantasies, notably [*War with the Newts*] (1936; tr. M. and R. Weatherall, 1937) and a philosophical novel trilogy, beginning with *Hordubal* (1933; tr. Weatheralls, 1934). He propounded the validity of the fairy tale as a genuine branch of literature ('Fairy stories originate in life . . .'), and demonstrated his belief by writing exuberant examples of this genre—see *Nine Fairy Tales and One More Thrown in for Good Measure*, tr. Dagmar Herrmann (1990). He succumbed to pneumonia, in despair at the Munich agreement, which effectively handed over Czechoslovakia to Hitler. When the Nazis entered Prague, the Gestapo called at his home to arrest him, not knowing he was dead. Josef was taken off to Belsen concentration camp, where he died just before the end of World War II.

CAPOTE, TRUMAN (1924–84) American novelist, short-story writer, and journalist, was born Truman Streckfus Persons in New Orleans, the son of a travelling salesman and a 16-year-old former Miss Alabama (they were divorced four years later). He lived with relations in rural Alabama until 1939, when he was adopted by his mother's second husband, Joseph Capote, a Cuban businessman. He boarded at St John's Academy and Trinity School, New York, and at Greenwich High School, Connecticut. He then worked for two years for the *New Yorker*, one version of his dismissal being that he had offended FROST. Having already had short stories published, he now returned to Alabama, where he began a novel. By the time *Other Voices, Other Rooms* (1948), the lyrical quest of a 13-year-old for a father figure, was finished and published, he was already, at 24, a notable figure on the literary scene. The critics were discouraging; he left New York for Haiti and France, and settled for a time in a villa in Sicily, and continued to write. After *A Tree of Night and Other Stories* (1949) came his second, and only other, novel, *The Grass Harp* (1951), in some ways another portrait of his own boyhood, which he also wrote as a play (1952). His novella, *Breakfast at Tiffany's*, the uninhibited New York exploits of the zany Holly Golightly, with which he claimed 'my second career began', was published in 1958 with three stories, of which 'A Diamond Guitar', set in a prison farm, illustrates the darker side of his work.

From 1959 to 1965 he worked almost exclusively on *In Cold Blood: a True Account of a Multiple Murder and Its Consequences* (1966). Variously called 'a non-fiction novel' and 'creative reporting', it is an exhaustive and gripping investigation into the motiveless murder of a Kansas family, the perpetrators of which he finally accompanied on their way to the gallows several years after their conviction. True to his public reputation, he celebrated his release from the strain of writing the book by throwing in New York what *Life* called 'the party of the century'. A review of the book by KENNETH TYNAN in the London *Observer* (13 March 1966) was the cause of bitter personal enmity between the two. A much longer feud, with VIDAL, started in 1948 and developed into a libel suit. Capote survived a car smash in 1969 and a cancer operation in 1971, between which he served three days in the Orange County Jail for failing to appear as a witness in the murder trial of a man he had been interviewing. 'Hand Carved Coffins', which he claimed was a reconstruction of a gruesome series of murders but has since been shown to be mainly fiction, was included in a collection of pieces, *Music for Chameleons* (1980). Only parts were ever published of 'Answered Prayers', his big novel, for which he first signed a contract in 1966. See *Capote Reader*, new edn 1993; Gerald Clarke, *Truman Capote: a Biography*, new edn 1993; Kenneth T. Reed, *Truman Capote*, 1981 (critical study).

CARDUS, (Sir) **NEVILLE** (1889–1975) British journalist, cricket writer, and music critic, was born in Rusholme, Manchester, the illegitimate son of Ada Cardus (*d.* 1954), who with her two sisters, he claims, graced 'the oldest of professions and became an adornment to it'. Information about his childhood is elusive, if not conflicting, but he attended a Board school, steeped himself in Western culture in the public library, haunted the music halls, and was passionately interested in music. In 1912 he became assistant cricket professional at Shrewsbury School, from which he made the unusual switch to headmaster's secretary in 1914. His eyesight prevented his being called up, and in 1916 he joined the staff of the *Manchester Guardian*. So it was that, having been instructed by the News Editor to recuperate from a chest illness with a few days in the sun at Old Trafford watching his beloved Lancashire, he became in 1920 the paper's cricket correspondent, in which capacity he developed his unique style of evocative reportage. At the same time he was assistant to the Music Critic, whom he succeeded in 1927. He spent World War II in Australia, writing on music and broadcasting, and in 1951 became the *Guardian* London music reviewer. In his music criticism—see especially *Ten Composers* (1945; rev. edn 1958 as *A Composers' Eleven*)—as in his cricket writing, he was more concerned with examining the essence of the art and recapturing the aesthetic pleasure of the audience than with techniques or technicalities. His selective autobiographies,

Autobiography (1947), *Second Innings* (1950), and *Full Score* (1970) may be read in the same light. He was made CBE in 1964 and was knighted in 1967. See Christopher Brookes, *His Own Man: the Life of Neville Cardus*, new edn 1986.

CAREY, PETER (*b.* 1943) Australian novelist, was born in Bacchus Marsh, Victoria, the son of a garage owner, and was educated at Geelong Grammar School and, for a year, at Monash University, after which he worked in advertising in Melbourne, London (1968–70), and Sydney. Two volumes of short stories, *The Fat Man in History* (1974) and *War Crimes* (1979), marked a distinctive debut in that though the characters are drawn realistically and cleverly, the situations are often surreal—see also *Collected Stories* (1995), comprising these two collections with four new tales. His first novel, *Bliss* (1981), which won the MILES FRANKLIN Award, is a blackly but not bleakly humorous account of an advertising executive's resuscitation from death and his subsequent lives. *Illywhacker* (1985) explores, through the reminiscences of a 139-year-old trickster, the myth of Australian national self-sufficiency. *Oscar and Lucinda* (1988), an elegant fantasy period piece, won the Booker prize for fiction. *The Tax Inspector* (1991) savages the mores of modern Sydney. *The Unusual Life of Tristan Smith* (1994) audaciously sets a physically disadvantaged protagonist in an alternative world of opposites whose principles, cultures, and colonial patterns are recognisable from the histories of the USA and Australia. *The Big Bazoohley* (1995) is an imaginative novel for children. Carey gave up his partnership in a New South Wales advertising agency in 1989, and moved to Greenwich Village, New York, with his second wife, a theatre director. See Karen Lamb, *Peter Carey: the Genesis of Fame*, 1992 (critical study); Anthony J. Hassall, *Dancing on Hot Macadam: Peter Carey's Fiction*, 1994 (critical study).

CARLETON, WILLIAM (1794–1869) Irish novelist and short-story writer, was born in Prillisk, Co. Tyrone, the youngest of 14 children of a small farmer. Bilingual, he had a rudimentary hedge-school education, but enjoyed a rich background of songs and stories from his parents. He was destined for the priesthood, but instead, after trying various jobs, he began writing for the Protestant paper, the *Christian Examiner*, in 1828. Two series of *Traits and Stories of the Irish Peasantry*, which had appeared in a number of journals, were published in book form in 1830 and 1833. The pieces deal with a variety of aspects of rural life—funerals, wakes, weddings, folklore, religion, sports, fights—and considering that he had no literary tradition from which to work, they are remarkable for their exuberance, wit, descriptive power, and dialogue. They are also the first genuine accounts of peasant life in Ireland before the Famine of 1845–48. *Tales of Ireland* followed in 1834. Subsequently he wrote more than fifteen novels, of which *Fardorougha the Miser* (1839) is the most notable. *The Black Prophet* (1847), *Red Hall, or the Baronet's Daughter* (1852), afterwards published as *The Black Baronet*, and *The Squanders of Castle Squander* (1852) deal gloomily and in lurid detail with the effects of the Famine. They are not as appealing as his shorter stories and pieces, and are written as though didactically directed to an audience who would know nothing of the background. See *Autobiography*, 1896 (published with his letters); Benedict Kiely, *Poor Scholar: a Study of the Works and Days of William Carleton*, new edn 1972.

CARLYLE, THOMAS (1795–1881) Scottish historian, biographer, critic, translator, and thinker, was born in Ecclefechan, Dumfriesshire, the eldest son of a stonemason by his second marriage, and was educated at Annan Academy and Edinburgh University. Having given up the idea of the ministry, he taught for several years, took up and then abandoned the law, studied German literature, and wrote *The Life of Friedrich Schiller* (1825). In 1826 he married Jane Baillie Welsh—Jane Welsh Carlyle (1801–66)—a woman of considerable intellect and owner of the small, remote estate of Craigenputtock, near Dumfries, where they lived from 1828 to 1834. Here he wrote *Sartor Resartus*, first published in *Fraser's Magazine* (1833–34), a witty 'symbolic myth' in the form of a philosophical treatise on clothing. In 1834 the couple moved to Cheyne Row in London. *The French Revolution* (1837)—the manuscript of the first volume was inadvertently burned by MILL's housemaid and had to be rewritten from memory—plants the reader vividly in the midst of the events described. *On Heroes, Hero-Worship and the Heroic in History* (1841), and a six-volume biography of Frederick the Great (1858–65), enabled Carlyle to pursue his favourite intellectual pastime of transcendentalism: finding precedents in the past to explain events and characters in recent history, which in turn offer pointers to the future.

Apart from his breadth of vision, Carlyle's appeal lay in the distinctive style he developed in mid-career, which has been called 'ejaculatory': a vast vocabulary backs conventional speech patterns. Critics differ as to how far, or whether, being married to him stifled his wife's creative abilities; it is probable that, realizing her limitations, she chose instead to use her critical faculties to help him, as she did other authors of their wide acquaintance. After her death, he wrote little. In 1874 DISRAELI, as Prime Minister, wrote to Carlyle, then 79, offering to recommend to Queen Victoria the award to him of the Grand Cross of the Bath and a pension 'equal to a good fellowship'. He replied, with great dignity and humility, declining both. See *A Carlyle Reader*, ed. G. B. Tennyson, 1984: *Jane Welsh Carlyle: a New Selection of Her Letters*, new edn 1959, and *Thomas Carlyle: Letters to His Wife*, 1953, ed. Trudy Bliss; Fred Kaplan, *Thomas Carlyle: a Biography*, new edn 1993; Simon Heffer, *Moral Desperado: a Life of Thomas Carlyle*, new edn 1996; A. L. Le Quesne, *Carlyle*, 1982 (introduction to his thought); and in Douglas Gifford (ed.), *The History of Scottish Literature Vol. 3: Nineteenth Century*, new edn 1989.

CARMAN, (WILLIAM) BLISS (1861–1929) Canadian poet, was born in Fredericton, New Brunswick, the eldest son of a barrister, and, through his mother, a first cousin of ROBERTS and related to EMERSON. He was educated at Fredericton Collegiate School, the University of New Brunswick, and for an unhappy year at Edinburgh University. He was a teacher, private tutor, and articled clerk in Fredericton before going on to Harvard, where he met the American poet, Richard Hovey (1864–1900). Between 1890 and 1900 he was on the editorial staff of various American journals, including the religious *Independent*, and *Atlantic Monthly*. The title poem of *Low Tide on Grand-Pré: a Book of Lyrics* (1893) typifies his initial elegiac tone which, in and after the publication (with Hovey) of *Songs from Vagabondia* (1894), became more boisterous. In 1896 he met Mary Perry King (1861–1939); he lived with her family in New York from 1897 to 1907, and settled near her in Connecticut in 1908. He reverted to classical themes in five volumes, reissued together as *The Pipes of Pan* (1806), and in *Sappho: Lyrics* (1902)—also *Sappho: One Hundred Lyrics* (1904). And as an expression of his further search for a poetic philosophy he wrote (with King) *Daughter of the Dawn: a Lyrical Pageant . . .* (1913) and *Earth Deities and Other Rhythmic Masques* (1914), reflecting the prevailing doctrine of Unitrinitarianism—Truth, Beauty, and the Good. In 1921, now regarded by the press as national poet laureate, he undertook after a serious illness the first of several poetry-reading tours of Canada; on his return from one of them he died in Connecticut. The most popular of the four Confederation Poets, the others being LAMPMAN, Roberts, and D. C. SCOTT, he gave a lead to Canadian writers to reflect their own culture. He never married. See *Windflower: the Selected Poems*, ed. Raymond Souster and Douglas Lochhead, 1985.

CARMI, T., pseudonym of Charmi Charny (1925–94) Israeli poet and editor, was born in New York, 'next to Bronx Zoo', of a Hebrew-speaking family. He graduated from Yeshiva University in 1946. In 1947, after spending a year in France in a relief unit working among

Jewish orphans, he settled in Palestine and joined the Haganah, the underground Jewish army, becoming, rather to his surprise, a hero of the War of Independence (1948–49). He then served as an officer in the Israeli air force. He was a co-editor of the literary journal *Massa* from 1952 to 1954, and children's books' editor of the publisher Am Oved from 1963 to 1970, after which he held visiting professorships in American universities. In 1978 he was appointed Visiting Professor of Hebrew Literature at the Hebrew Union College, Jewish Institute of Religion, Jerusalem. His verse, of which the first volume was published in 1950, combines traditional elements and modern conversational expressions, often with sensuous undertones. Collections in English are *The Brass Serpent* (1961; tr. Dom Moraes, 1964), *Somebody Like You*, tr. Stephen Mitchell (1971), and *At the Stone of Losses*, tr. Grace Schulman (1983), a selection. He translated plays by BRECHT, SHAKESPEARE, and SOPHOCLES into Hebrew, and edited and translated *The Penguin Book of Hebrew Verse* (1981). He was three times married, and had a child by each wife.

CARPIO, LOPE DE VEGA see VEGA CARPIO.

CARROLL, LEWIS, pseudonym of Charles Lutwidge Dodgson (1832–98) British children's writer and mathematician, was born in Daresbury, Lancashire, the son of the future Archdeacon of Richmond, and was educated at Rugby School and Christ Church, Oxford, where he then became a lecturer. Diffident and shy, he was best able to communicate with children. A story first told on the river to the daughters of the Dean of Christ Church was published in 1865 as *Alice's Adventures in Wonderland*; and for its wit, weird logic, linguistic fun, and wild rhymes, has remained popular with children and adults ever since. *Through the Looking-Glass and What Alice Found There* (1871) is slightly more contrived (as though the mathematician had influenced the storyteller), but in Humpty Dumpty, Tweedledum and Tweedledee, the White Knight, and the Red Queen, it is host to characters as memorable as any in the earlier book. His other venture into fiction, *Sylvie and Bruno* (1889) and a sequel, was not much appreciated even by his contemporaries, unlike *The Hunting of the Snark* (1876), a sustained nonsense-poem, many of whose witty allusions are just as valid today. Of a number of mathematical treatises, *Euclid and His Modern Rivals* (1879) was the most influential, and LUCAS records: 'Scattered up and down it were many jokes, which would have been more numerous but for the criticisms of friends.' Dodgson was an accomplished photographer, especially of little girls, of whom he started taking pictures in 1856 and ultimately claimed to have en-

joyed the friendship of over two hundred. See *The Selected Letters of Lewis Carroll*, ed. Morton N. Cohen, new edn 1996; Derek Hudson, *Lewis Carroll*, new edn 1995 (biography); Morton N. Cohen, *Lewis Carroll: a Biography*, new edn 1996; Donald Thomas, *Lewis Carroll: a Portrait with Background*, 1996.

CARTER, ANGELA (1940–92), née Stalker, British novelist, short-story writer, critic, and journalist, was born in Eastbourne, Sussex, the daughter of a Scottish journalist, and spent her early childhood in south Yorkshire. After going to a direct-grant school in Balham, south London, she was apprenticed to the *Croydon Advertiser*. She married Paul Carter, an industrial chemist, in 1960, and went with him to Bristol where, failing to get a job as a local newspaper reporter, she read English literature at Bristol University, specializing in the medieval period. After a trial run with a rather violent thriller, *Shadow Dance* (1966), she established the bounds of her particular territory with *The Magic Toyshop* (1967), a study of tyranny in a bizarre setting, which won the John Llewellyn Rhys Award for a work by an author under 35. With the proceeds of the Somerset MAUGHAM Award for her third novel, *Several Perceptions* (1968), she left her husband (they divorced in 1972) and spent two years in Japan, which, she claimed, gave an impetus to her feminism. The more immediate manifestations of this were the novel, *The Passion of New Eve* (1977), and her study, *The Sadeian Woman: an Exercise in Cultural History* (1979), one of the first books commissioned by Virago Press. *Nights at the Circus* (1984) is regarded as a classic of 'magic realism'. *The Bloody Chamber and Other Stories* (1979) contains imaginative, and disturbing, reworkings of traditional tales, an aspect of her intellectual curiosity which, with her penchant for inventiveness and broad comedy and her conviction of the indomitable nature of womanhood, inform her last novel, *Wise Children* (1991). Critical, often also disrespectful, pieces are in *Nothing Sacred: Selected Writings* (enlarged edn 1992) and *Expletives Deleted* (1992), which includes constructive essays on CHARLOTTE BRONTË, DE LA MARE, and STEAD. *The Virago Book of Fairy Tales* (2 vols 1990–92) contains her selection of orally transmitted stories which give substance to her ideological assumptions. *American Ghosts & Old World Wonders* (1993) is a posthumous collection of stories and sketches which she had suggested for publication in this form—see also *Burning Your Boats: Collected Short Stories* (1995) and *The Curious Room: Collected Dramatic Works* (1996). She died of cancer, having in 1984 had a son by her second husband. See Lorna Sage, *Angela Carter*, 1994 (critical introduction).

CARTER, MARTIN (*b.* 1927) Guyanese poet, was born in Georgetown and educated there at Queen's College. He was a civil servant for four years until forced to resign because of his involvement with the People's Progressive Party. He was already a published poet when, on Britain's imposition of direct rule in 1953, he was held for three months in a detention camp. *Poems of Resistance from British Guiana*, the contents of which he had written shortly before his arrest, was published in the UK in 1954. 'Black Friday 1962', recalling the use of British troops in the streets to support the suspension of the constitution, was published locally in *Jail Me Quickly* (1963). After independence in 1966 he became Minister of Public Information and Broadcasting, and represented Guyana at the United Nations. *Poems of Succession* (1977) contains poems from previous collections, including the philosophical 'Conversations' and those such as 'Listening to the Land' and 'Under a Near Sky', in which the past obtrudes on the present. He extended his range with *Poems of Affinity 1978–1980* (1980). See *Selected Poems*, 1989.

CARY, JOYCE (1888–1957) Irish novelist and short-story writer, was born in Londonderry, but spent most of his life in England. He was educated at Clifton College and (after two years studying art) at Trinity College, Oxford. He served with the Red Cross in the First Balkan War (1912–13), and was from 1913 to 1920 a member of the Nigerian Political Service—he saw action with the Nigerian Regiment in the Cameroons in 1915. Beginning with *Aissa Saved* (1932), he wrote four novels with African settings, of which the most notable, and memorable, is the tragicomic *Mister Johnson* (1939). *Charley is My Darling* (1940) echoes his own youth; *A House of Children* (1941) is an autobiographical evocation of a childhood holiday in Ireland. *Herself Surprised* (1941), *To Be a Pilgrim* (1942), and *The Horse's Mouth* (1944) are novels about the world of the artist which are designed as a trilogy—in each, the narrative is told and the other characters observed by a different one of the three main protagonists. He deals in the same way with aspects of politics in *Prisoner of Grace* (1952), *Except the Lord* (1953), and *Not Honour More* (1955). In these six works in particular, he is concerned with the place, and problems, of the creative individual trying to make his own world out of, and his own way through, the repressions and contradictions of a changing contemporary society. See Barbara Fisher (ed.), *Joyce Cary Remembered: in Letters and Interviews by His Family and Others*, 1988; Alan Bishop, *Gentleman Rider: a Biography of Joyce Cary*, new edn 1989; Barbara Fisher, *Joyce Cary: the Writer and His Theme*, 1980.

CASANOVA DE SEINGALT, GIACOMO GIROLAMO (1725–98) Italian adventurer and prose writer, brother of Francesco (1727–1805), the landscape painter, and of Giovanni Battista (1728–98), Director of the Academy of Fine Arts, Dresden, was born in Venice of parents who were both actors. After his father's death in 1733, his mother went to act in Dresden, and at the age of eight he was sent to Padua University. He returned to Venice as a graduate, took minor orders, and embarked on a lifetime of escapades, seductions, espionage, and questionable dealings, which took him, often pursued by the police, to France, Germany, England, and Spain, in all of which he moved in literary and theatrical circles and mixed with the great. He published a volume of plays in 1752. In 1755 he was sentenced to five years in the notorious 'Piombi' in the roof of the Doge's Palace in Venice for a variety of offences against the law and morality. His daring escape in October 1756 was the subject of his *Histoire de Ma Fuite . . .* (1788; tr. Arthur Machen as *Casanova's Escape from the Leads*, 1925). He was ultimately pardoned, and became an adviser on subversive literature. From 1785 he was nominally librarian to the Count of Waldstein at Dux in Bohemia, where he concentrated on his autobiography. Written in French and published in Leipzig as *Mémoires Écrits par Lui-même* (12 vols 1826–38), it was until the 1960s available only in expurgated versions, the first edition in English from the original manuscript being *History of My Life*, tr. William R. Trask (6 vols 1967–72).

CASTIGLIONE, BALDASSARE (1478–1529) Italian courtier and prose writer, was born on his father's estate of Casatico, Mantua, and studied at Milan University. He worked for aristocratic families and in 1504 joined the court of the rulers of Urbino, whom he served until in 1516 Francesco Maria della Rovere (1490–1538) was ousted by the troops of Pope Leo X, and retired to Mantua. Castiglione, who accompanied him, now married, settled down, and revised and polished his study of Renaissance manners, *Libro del Cortegiano* [*The Book of the Courtier*]. In 1519 he returned to diplomatic duties, becoming Mantuan ambassador to Rome and (in 1524) papal nuncio to Spain, where he spent the rest of his life and where he died. The threat of a pirated edition of his book galvanized him into sending an authorized manuscript to the famous Aldine Press in Venice, from whom he purchased half the printing of one thousand copies and a limited edition of 30 copies on fine paper for his friends. Published in 1528, this conversation piece in four books, consciously written in what he saw as an Italian national, rather than regional, vernacular, with frequent references to classical Roman writers, had less influence in Italy, where its ambience was somewhat passé, than in England, where it was translated in 1561 by Sir Thomas Hoby

(1530–66) and became the courtly ideal of the Elizabethan era. See *The Book of the Courtier*, ed. Virginia Cox, 1994; Peter Burke, *Fortunes of the Courtier: the European Reception of Castiglione's 'Cortegiano'*, 1996 (critical survey).

CATHER, WILLA (1873–1947) American novelist and short-story writer, was born Wilella, in Back Creek Valley, Virginia, the eldest of seven children of an easy-going son of a landed family, the head of which remained loyal to the North during the Civil War. In 1883 her father sold up his farm and moved to Nebraska, where 'we had very few American neighbours; they were mostly Swedes and Danes, Norwegians and Bohemians'. After a year, he sold up again, and moved into Red Cloud, where she attended high school. She went on at 17 to the University of Nebraska, Lincoln. Outspoken in her opinions and unusual in her style of dress (she favoured masculine cuts and cropped hair), she wrote in her first year a class essay on CARLYLE, which her teacher sent to the *Nebraska State Journal* without her knowledge. The sight of it in print determined her on a career as a writer, rather than in medicine, and when the *Journal* invited her to write a Sunday column and theatre criticism, she accepted enthusiastically. Her first published story, 'Peter', appeared in 1892 in the Boston magazine, *Mahogany Tree*, to which another teacher had sent it, and later that year, with changes, in the student journal, *Hesperian*, which Cather was now editing. After graduating, she became in 1896 Editor of *Home Monthly*, Pittsburgh, on the sale of which the following year she joined the telegraph desk of the *Pittsburgh Daily Leader*. In 1901 she went into teaching, and two years later became a member of the American literature department of Allegheny High School. She was now living with the family of Isabelle McClung, the daughter of a Pittsburgh judge and the great love of her life, on whose marriage in 1916 she was devastated, and on whose death in 1938 she felt she could not go on living.

In 1903 she published a book of verse, *April Twilights*, and had a telegram from S. S. McClure (1857–1949), the ebullient editor and publisher, whose journal, *McClure's Magazine*, had already rejected some of her stories. At a meeting in New York, he undertook to publish anything she wrote, beginning with a collection of stories, *The Troll Garden* (1905). In 1906, when the senior staff of *McClure's* walked out after a row, she accepted his invitation to become an editor. In 1908 she became managing editor, in which capacity she went on a scouting trip to London, where she attended the funeral of MEREDITH, met GOSSE and WELLS, and sat with GREGORY in YEATS's box to see the Abbey Theatre's production of SYNGE's *The Playboy of the Western World*. In 1909 she took an apartment in Washington

Place with Edith Lewis, with whom she lived for the rest of her life—see Edith Lewis, *Willa Cather Living: a Personal Record* (1953).

The London theatre world provided part of the background, and the collapse in 1909 of a new bridge over the St Lawrence at Quebec the denouement, of her first novel, *Alexander's Bridge* (1912). That year she visited Nebraska again, gave up her job, and, now almost 39, settled in New York to begin her life's work. She explained later: 'I began to write a book entirely for myself; a story about some Scandinavians and Bohemians who had been neighbours of ours when I lived on a ranch in Nebraska. . . . Here there was no arranging or "inventing"; everything was spontaneous and took its own place, right or wrong.' This was *O Pioneers!* (1913); in *The Song of the Lark* (1915) and *My Ántonia* (1918) she further explored pioneering themes and the place of the talented, and courageous, woman. In *One of Ours* (1922) a maladjusted hero from the plains ultimately meets an ironic death on the Western Front in World War I. To Cather, 'The world broke in two in 1922 or thereabouts.' With that feeling, and her reception into the Episcopal Church, her writing took a new direction. *A Lost Lady* (1923), based on the circumstances of someone she had known, the wife of a former governor of Nebraska, and *The Professor's House* (1925) are predominantly about conflicting values in life. The novella, *My Mortal Enemy* (1926), is a deeply felt study of disillusionment. *Death Comes for the Archbishop* (1927) and *Shadows on the Rock* (1931) are evocations of historical situations in New Mexico and Quebec respectively. Personal tragedies, a hand and a wrist injury, and the worsening international situation dogged the writing of her last novel, *Sapphira and the Slave Girl* (1940), for which she returned to the Virginia of her childhood, and to the circumstances of her own family 17 years before her birth. Among her numerous correspondents was the first president of the Czechoslovak Republic, T. G. Masaryk (1850–1937). See *Early Novels and Stories*, 1987, *Later Novels*, 1990, *Stories, Poems, and Other Writings*, 1996, ed. Sharon O'Brien; James Woodress, *Willa Cather: a Literary Life*, new edn 1989; Mildred R. Bennett, *The World of Willa Cather*, new edn 1995 (critical study); Sharon O'Brien, *Willa Cather: The Emerging Voice*, new edn 1997.

CATULLUS, GAIUS VALERIUS (c.85–53 BC) Roman lyric poet, was born in Verona and in about 62 came to Rome, where he was one of the 'new poets', who reacted against their elders. He had a blazing affair with a woman he calls Lesbia in his poems, who may have been the emancipated and profligate wife of Metellus Celer, consul in 60. In 57 Catullus went to Bithynia, Asia Minor, as a guest or camp follower of its governor, Memmius (to whom LUCRETIUS dedicated *De Rerum Natura*). He died soon after his return. The 116 complete poems that we have vary from two to 408 lines. As well as the love/hate poems to Lesbia, there are bitingly observant cameos of friends and enemies (including CAESAR), and accounts of chance meetings and alfresco sexual encounters, in which he is often coarse but always amusing. Others, including his longest work, a description of the wedding of Peleus and Thetis, have mythological themes, but still show depth of poetic emotion. His family had a villa at Sirmio, which inspired TENNYSON's lyrical 'Frater Ave atque Vale'. See *The Poems of Catullus*, tr. James Michie, new edn 1990 (includes Latin texts).

CAUSLEY, CHARLES (*b.* 1917) British poet and anthologist, was born in Launceston, Cornwall, and educated locally. He served in the Royal Navy in World War II, returning afterwards to his career as a local primary school teacher, which he remained until his retirement. His first book of verse was *Farewell, Aggie Weston* (1951); his reputation was confirmed by his third, *Union Street* (1957). Causley excels at the ballad form, taking his images from things he knows well—the sea, the Cornish countryside and folklore, Christianity, children. He often uses popular diction and reworks traditional rhythms and rhymes to create effects of intensity and surprise, as in 'Innocent's Song': 'Watch where he comes walking / Out of the Christmas flame, / Dancing, double-talking: / Herod is his name.' (Innocence is a recurring motif in his poetry.) His narrative poems, outwardly artless but constructed and finished with precision, often reveal disturbing truths, particularly 'The Ballad of Charlotte Dymond', 'Mother, get up, undo the door', and 'Ballad of Jack Cornwell'. Much of his verse is also accessible to children, for whom he has compiled several anthologies, the first of which, *Dawn and Dusk* (1962), broke new ground in that it comprised exclusively contemporary poetry originally written for adult audiences. Causley has also written poetry and plays especially for children. He was awarded the Queen's Gold Medal for Poetry in 1967 and was made CBE in 1986. See *Collected Poems 1951–1992*, 1992; *Collected Poems for Children*, 1996.

CAVAFY, C(ONSTANTINE) P(ETROU) (1863–1933) Greek poet, was born in Alexandria of a Phanariot family, and was educated in England until the collapse of the family export business—throughout his life he spoke Greek with a faint English accent. In 1892 he obtained a clerical post in the 'Third Circle' of the British-run Irrigation Department, for which he worked for thirty years, living in an overfurnished flat in a street haunted by prostitutes. He began to publish poetry in periodicals in 1886, and in the early 1900s issued two privately-printed pamphlets of his verse. From about 1911, which he regarded as the beginning of his mature period, he distributed single poems to a chosen circle of readers as offprints or in the form of broadsheets, to be collected into a folder. Some of them reflected aspects of the Hellenistic age which followed the death of Alexander the Great in 323 BC; others were outspoken evocations of homosexual love. FORSTER, who first met him in 1917, introduced him to English readers in an essay, 'The Poetry of C. P. Cavafy', in *Pharos and Pharillon* (1923). See *Collected Poems*, tr. Edmund Keeley and Philip Sherrard, rev. edn 1992; Robert Liddell, *Cavafy: a Critical Biography*, 1974; Edmund Keeley, *Cavafy's Alexandria*, 2nd rev. edn 1996 (biographical/critical study with extensive quotations).

CAXTON, WILLIAM (*c.*1420–91) English prose writer, translator, and printer, was born in Kent, and was apprenticed to a London mercer. He became a prominent merchant, trading between England and the Low Countries, and was Governor of the English Nation of Merchant Adventurers, based in Bruges, between about 1462 and 1470. He then branched into literature, as a translator and a printer, a craft he had studied in Cologne. In 1475 (or maybe in the previous year) he produced in Bruges, in his own translation from the French, *The Recuyell of the Historyes of Troye*, which was the first book to be printed in English. In 1476 he set up his press in London in a shop which he rented from Westminster Abbey, and from then until his death he printed and distributed a distinguished, but also catholic, list of translations of classical and European literature, and original works in English which included the first editions of CHAUCER, GOWER, LYDGATE, and (in a version edited by himself) MALORY. His own contribution as a translator comprises over twenty considerable works in Dutch, French, and Latin, for which he employed an English literary language which he calls 'not over rude, ne curyous, but in such termes as shall be understanden by goddys grace'. See N. F. Blake, *William Caxton and English Literature*, 1991.

CELAN, PAUL see HAMBURGER.

CELLINI, BENVENUTO (1500–71) Italian sculptor and prose writer, was born in Florence, the eldest surviving son of an architect who wanted him to be a musician but finally acceded to his request to be apprenticed to a goldsmith. Expelled from the city for six months for rioting, he got experience in Bologna and (having left town again after a row with his father) in Pisa. In 1519 he arrived in Rome, where he soon, by his own account, obtained commissions, and was also employed by Pope Clement VII as a court musician and, during the sack of Rome in 1527, as a gunner. He opened his own business and led a lively and varied life. In 1545 he returned to Florence, where he was elevated to the nobility in 1554. He was imprisoned two years later for an assault on another goldsmith, and again in 1557 for a homosexual act with one of his apprentices. He married late in life, but having no legitimate or illegitimate son who survived childhood, in 1560 he adopted his model's son as his heir, and then later disinherited him. His chief plastic memorials are the bronze Perseus and its elaborate base, and the massive silver salt cellar made for Francis I of France. His literary bequest to posterity is his autobiography, which he began in his own hand in 1558 and then dictated to a boy 'of about fourteen who was in a poor state of health'. The original manuscript was discovered in 1805; a printed edition from another source appeared in Naples in 1728, and was translated into English in 1771 by Thomas Nugent (1700–72). It is a vivid account of a man and his craft, of the nobility and the ordinary men and women of the times, and of the times themselves. See *The Life of Benevenuto Cellini*, tr. John Addington Symonds, new edn 1995.

CERVANTES (SAAVEDRA), MIGUEL DE (1547–1616) Spanish novelist, was born in Alcala de Henares, the fourth of seven children of an impoverished hidalgo whose ancestors probably converted from Judaism. The family moved to Valladolid, Cordoba, and Seville, where he went to the Jesuit college, and then to Madrid, where he probably attended the City School. After going to Italy in the train of Cardinal Acquaviva, he enlisted in the Spanish army, fought heroically at Lepanto in 1571 in the naval victory of Don John of Austria (1545–78) over the Turks, in which he permanently lost the use of his left hand, and then took part in expeditions against Tunis and the fortress of La Golita. In 1575, the galley in which he was travelling back to Spain was captured by Turkish pirates, and he spent five years as a slave in Algiers before being ransomed by Trinitarian monks. Unable to find a suitable job, he tried to make a living in Madrid by writing, but neither his plays nor a pastoral novel, *La Galatea* (1584), had any success. Already the father of an illegitimate daughter (Isabel Saavedra), in 1584 he married 19-year-old Catalina de Salazar y Palacios. They lived for a time in Esquivias, a village of La Mancha, where she had a farm, but soon separated. In 1587 he became a roving quartermaster for the Armada, the Spanish fleet, but was jailed in Seville in 1597 when a financier with whom he had deposited state funds went bankrupt. Continuously passed over for better posts (in 1590 he had even applied to be sent over-

seas), and again in jail in 1602, he finally managed to publish *El Ingenioso Hidalgo Don Quixote de La Mancha* (1605; tr. Thomas Shelton as *The History of the Valorous and Wittie Knight-Errant, Don-Quixote of the Mancha*, 1612). His pleasure in its immediate critical success (he had sold the rights for a pittance) was dampened when the police, investigating the circumstances in which a man had died in a street duel outside his home, discovered that Cervantes's sister and daughter were using the place for immoral purposes.

Late in life he wrote *Novelas Ejemplares* (1613; as *Exemplary Stories*, tr. C. A. Jones, 1972; as *Exemplary Novels*, tr. B. W. Ife, R. M. Price, Michael and Jonathan Thacker, John Jones, John Macklin, and others, 4 vols 1992); a second part of *Don Quixote* (1615), after the appearance the previous year of a pirated edition of an incomplete version; and *Los Trabajos de Persiles and Sigismunda* (1617; tr. from the French as *The Trauels of Persiles and Sigismunda*, 1619), a dream-like novel of adventure which he only just managed to finish before he died of dropsy. The complete *Don Quixote*, regarded as the first modern novel, is a work in the Spanish tradition whose wit, characterization, and imaginative exploration of illusion have given it a universal appeal. Among several 18th-century translations are those by Charles Jarvis or Jervas (*c.*1675–1739), painter and friend of POPE, whose version (1742) has been reissued many times, most recently (ed. E. C. Riley) in 1992, and SMOLLETT (1755). There were no less than four critical commentaries published in England in the 18th century, the first annotated edition, *Pleasant Notes upon Don Quixote* by Edmond Gayton (1608–66), having appeared in 1654.

CHALMERS, THOMAS (1780–1847) Scottish cleric, was born in Easter Anstruther, Fife, and educated at St Andrews University, becoming Minister of Kilmany, Fife, in 1803. In 1815 he was translated to the Tron Kirk, Glasgow, where his oratory was much admired as a reaction against the new unimpassioned pulpit liberality. His public weekday sermons were published in 1817 as *A Series of Discourses on the Christian Revelation Viewed in Connection with the Modern Astronomy*, which, according to HAZLITT, 'ran like wild-fire through the country'. The *Christian and Civic Economy of Large Towns*, a pamphlet published in 1819, was the first of a number of works in which he addressed social and economic, as well as religious, concerns. In 1820, having turned down a chair at Edinburgh University, he exchanged his influential parish for that of St John's, which the Town Council was establishing in the poorest part of Glasgow. He became Professor of Moral Philosophy at St Andrews in 1823, and Professor of Theology at Edinburgh in 1827. In

1843, at the head of 470 ministers, he literally walked out of the Church of Scotland, in protest against State interference in what they regarded as the prerogative of the Church, and founded the Free Church of Scotland, of which he was the first Moderator. He was more preacher than writer, who, according to the critic Rev. George Gilfillan (1813–78), 'always threw his heart, but not always his artistic consciousness, into what he wrote', but at a time when two-thirds of all Scottish books were of a religious nature, 'Astronomical Discourses' was the first to cross the line between the religious and the literary markets. He is also to be remembered in that, having blazed out of his publisher in a fury, he instigated an alternative outlet for his publications by lending £1600 of his own money at 5 per cent interest to his brother Charles (c.1790–1864) and William Collins (1789–1853) to found what became the house of Collins, now HarperCollins. See Stewart J. Brown, *Thomas Chalmers and the Godly Commonwealth*, 1982.

CHAMBERS, ROBERT (1802–71) Scottish prose writer and editor, was born in Peebles, the son of a cotton merchant, through whose copies of *Encyclopaedia Britannica* the boy 'roamed like a bee' at the age of ten. A drop in fortunes necessitated the family's removal to Edinburgh, where he attended a classical academy. At 16, having tried and failed at several jobs, he set up a stall, at the suggestion of his brother William (1800–83), from which he sold his own schoolbooks, pocket bibles, and old books from their home. The venture prospered, and in 1819 he went into the bookshop business proper with William (who had now finished his apprenticeship); from this beginning there soon emerged the publishing house of W. & R. Chambers. Robert's antiquarian and literary interests led him to compile *Traditions of Edinburgh* (1824; rev. edn 1868) and *Popular Rhymes of Scotland* (1826; rev. edns 1841 and 1869), which have remained standard works. He was still a young man when he published *History of the Rebellion in Scotland 1745–6* (1828) and began to write *A Biographical Dictionary of Eminent Scotsmen* (1832–34); in 1833 he became joint Editor with his brother of the literary, philosophical, and scientific periodical, *Chambers's Journal*. He was elected a member of the Royal Society of Edinburgh in 1840, after which he retired to St Andrews for two years to write *Vestiges of the Natural History of Creation* (1844). Published anonymously, for he did not want the expected furore to damage his literary reputation or that of their firm, this vivid exposition by a brilliant communicator prepared the ground for DARWIN and others to present similar views on evolution. See Milton Millhauser, *Just Be-*fore Darwin: Robert Chambers and 'Vestiges', 1959.

CHANDLER, RAYMOND (1888–1959) American novelist, was born in Chicago, the son of a railway engineer who one day disappeared, leaving his wife, an Irish immigrant, to look after the boy. He was educated in England at Dulwich College 'It would seem that a classical education might be rather a poor basis for writing novels in a hard-boiled vernacular. I happen to think otherwise. [It] saves you from being fooled by pretentiousness.' After a year in Europe, he became a British citizen, sat the civil service examination, in which he passed third out of six hundred candidates, and was appointed an assistant naval stores officer. He quit after six months, was taken on the staff of the *Westminster Gazette*, and wrote critical essays for the *Academy*. He returned to the USA in 1912, and studied bookkeeping. He enlisted in the Canadian Army in 1917, fought in France, and transferred to the Royal Flying Corps after recuperating from a shell blast which killed everyone else in his unit. After going back to Los Angeles, he married Cissy Pascal, 18 years his senior, and became an executive, and later vice president, of an oil company, which fired him in 1932 for absenteeism, dalliance, and drunkenness. Without a job, he studied pulp magazines, took a correspondence course in writing fiction, and had a story 'Blackmailers Don't Shoot' (on which he had worked for five months) published in *Black Mask* in 1933. With his first novel, *The Big Sleep* (1939), he turned crime fiction into an art form, and introduced his private detective, Philip Marlowe, a man of sentiment, humour, and a code of morality. In between the publication of *Farewell My Lovely* (1940) and *The Lady in the Lake* (1943) he spent time in Hollywood, initially to write the film of CAIN's *Double Indemnity* (1944). He wrote *The Long Goodbye* (1953) while Cissy was dying, and revised it to make Marlowe's character consistent with earlier books. After her death in 1954, he began to threaten suicide, went back to the bottle, and spent his last years commuting between London and La Jolla, California. He became an American citizen again in 1956. A genuine craftsman, he wrote to an associate (1945): 'All I wanted when I began was to play with a fascinating new language, and trying, without anybody noticing it, to see what it would do as a means of expression which might remain on the level of unintellectual thinking and yet acquire the power to say things which are usually only said with a literary air.' This is another way of putting what he said to *Atlantic Monthly* in 1948: 'Would you convey my compliments to the purist who reads your proofs, and tell him or her that I write in a sort of broken-down patois which is something like the way a Swiss waiter talks, and that when I split an infinitive, God damn it, I split it so it will stay split.' See *Stories and Early Novels*, 1995; *Later Novels and Other Writings*, 1995; Frank Mac-Shane, *The Life of Raymond Chandler*, new edn 1986; Tom Hiney, *Raymond Chandler: a Biography*, 1997; William H. Marling, *Raymond Chandler*, 1986 (biographical/critical study); and also HAMMETT.

CHAPMAN, GEORGE (1559–1634) English poet, dramatist, and translator, was born near Hitchin, Hertfordshire, and probably studied at Oxford or Cambridge, without taking a degree. He is mentioned in the 1590s as a writer of comedies, but his first known published work, *The Shadow of Night* (1594), consists of two poems of obscure meaning. *Ovids Banquet of Sence* (1595), however, demonstrates the qualities which enabled him gracefully to finish MARLOWE's *Hero and Leander* (1586). His translation of seven books of HOMER's *Iliad* was the first instalment of *The Whole Works of Homer* (1616), the *Iliad* in rhyming lines of 14 syllables, the *Odyssey* in heroic couplets. His grasp of Greek was tenuous, and his interpolations inappropriate, but this was a monumental achievement which thrilled his contemporaries and inspired one of KEATS's most quoted sonnets, beginning, 'Much have I travelled in the realms of gold . . .'. Chapman's comedies, of which *All Fools* (1599) still reads well, are largely based on Roman or continental models, with a dash of ethics and topical satire—*Eastward Hoe* (1605), written with JONSON and MARSTON, resulted in Jonson being jailed for insulting the Scots. His tragedies *Bussy D'Ambois* (1607) and its sequel (1613), and the two parts of *The Conspiracie and Tragedie of Charles Duke of Byron* (1608), are based on near-contemporary figures from French history. As a dramatist, though, Chapman is regarded as a gifted intellectual whose works lacked commercial instinct.

CHATEAUBRIAND, FRANÇOIS-RENÉ DE (1768–1848) French novelist, prose writer, and statesman, was born in Saint-Malo. After college, he spent a short time in the army, tried his hand at being a writer in Paris, and then left for America to avoid the French Revolution. He returned on hearing of the arrest of Louis XVI, joined the ranks of the émigrés, and was wounded and left for dead; he recovered and took refuge in England, where he gave French lessons for a living. *Essai . . . sur les Révolutions* (1797) is an apprentice work. He returned to France in 1800 and joined the Diplomatic Service. *Génie du Christianisme* (1802; tr. Frederic Shoberl as *The Beauties of Christianity*, 1813) is an emotional apologia for the Catholic faith, to which he had been converted. He extracted from it two short fictional narratives based on his experiences and research in America, *Atala* (1801; tr. Caleb Bingham, 1802) and *René* (1802; tr. 1813; with *Atala*, tr. Irving Putter, 1952), which are in the Romantic tradition. He was created Vicomte in 1815, and served as ambassador in Berlin, London, and Rome, being Minister of Foreign Affairs in 1822. Latterly he enjoyed the company of Mme Récamier (1777–1849). His most lasting work is *Les Mémoires d'Outre-Tombe* (1849–50), the story of his life in the context of the events and philosophies of his times, written and often rewritten over thirty years and published posthumously; the definitive text did not appear until 1948—see *Memoirs*, ed. and tr. Robert Baldick, new edn 1965 (selection).

CHATTERTON, THOMAS (1752–70) British poet, was born in Bristol shortly after the death of his father, a schoolmaster. His mother, then 21, earned a living by keeping a dame school and taking in sewing. The boy was educated at a charity school, and in 1767 was apprenticed to a lawyer. He had begun to write verse when he was ten, and soon afterwards he forged a 'medieval' poem which he presented to his teacher. He sold further forgeries of ancient documents to local worthies, including a verse tragedy, *Aissa*, purporting to be by a priest called Sir Thomas Rowley. Chatterton now invented a complete corpus of medieval poetry for Rowley, in which he tried unsuccessfully to interest HORACE WALPOLE. In 1770 he broke his indentures by threatening to commit suicide, and went to London to earn his living as a writer. He succeeded for only a few weeks. On 24 August, exhausted and near starving, he poisoned himself in his lodgings. He was not yet 18. His own verses, mainly satirical, are largely of a juvenile nature. The 'Rowley' poems, however, though written in a pseudo-medieval English, with many spurious or misused archaisms, contain much of genuine lyrical excellence, and it is these and the circumstances of his death which led to his being regarded as one of the forerunners of the Romantic poets, and inspired WORDS-WORTH's reference in 'Resolution and Independence' to 'Chatterton, the marvellous boy, / The sleepless soul, that perished in his pride . . .'. See *Complete Works*, ed. D. S. Taylor and B. B. Hoover, 1971; *Selected Poems*, ed. Grevel Lindop, 1986; Linda Kelly, *The Marvellous Boy: the Life and Myth of Thomas Chatterton*, 1971.

CHATWIN, BRUCE (1940–89) British travel writer and novelist, was born in Sheffield and went to Marlborough College, after which he took a job as a porter at Sotheby's. Having pronounced a Picasso watercolour in the saleroom a fake, on the strength of which he was appointed to a post of responsibility, he gave up the art world for archaeology, which he read at Edinburgh University. He had now acquired a taste for travel, which he satisfied as a nomadic journalist, setting out with just a knapsack wherever his fancy took him. *In Patagonia* (1977) revealed his eye for the telling as well as the eccentric detail; *The Viceroy of Ouidah* (1980), a study of the slave trade in Napoleonic times based on his travels in Dahomey and Brazil, demonstrated his ability convincingly to fictionalize his observations and research. A sense of location also informs *On a Black Hill* (1982), a novel expressive of life on a Welsh hill farm. He wrote two further novels, *The Songlines* (1987), basically a philosophical meditation on the nomadic way of life, and *Utz* (1988), a brief but profound exploration of character. He died in France of an AIDS-related illness, having personally put together the posthumous selection of pieces, *What Am I Doing Here* (1989)—see also *Photographs and Notebooks* (1993) and *Anatomy of Restlessness: Uncollected Writings*, ed. Jan Borm and Matthew Graves (1996). See Susannah Clapp, *With Chatwin: Portrait of a Writer*, 1997; Nicholas Murray, *Bruce Chatwin*, 1994 (critical study).

CHAUCER, GEOFFREY (c.1343–1400) English poet, public servant, and courtier, was the son of a prosperous London wine merchant. He may have attended St Paul's Cathedral School, and he almost certainly studied law between 1361 and 1367. The earliest record of him is in 1357 as a page in the household of Elizabeth, Countess of Ulster, the wife of Lionel, third son of Edward III. He served with the army in France in 1359, being taken prisoner and then released for a ransom, £16 of which was paid by the King, in whose service he appears in 1367 as valet. In this capacity he undertook the first of many diplomatic missions to the Continent which continued into the reign of Richard II. In 1372–73 and 1378 he was in Italy, where the physical and intellectual environment did much to inspire his poetic imagination. In about 1366 he married Philippa (d. c.1378), the daughter of Sir Payne Roet and sister of Katherine Swynford (1350–1403), mistress and, later, the third wife of John of Gaunt. Chaucer was Controller of Customs and Subsidy of Wools, Skins, and Hides in the port of London 1374–86, and Clerk of the King's Works 1389–91. His last public office was Deputy Forester of the royal forest of North Petherton in Somerset. On 4 December 1399, he took out a 53-year lease on a house in the garden of Westminster Abbey, where Henry VII's chapel now stands; he was buried in the Abbey on his death the following year—his monument was set up in 1555 in what later came to be known as Poets' Corner. From internal evidence, the order in which he wrote his main poetical works is as follows:

The Book of the Duchess: written in octosyllabic couplets to commemorate the death of Blanche, the first wife of John of Gaunt, in 1369; first printed in 1532 in Chaucer's works, ed. William Thynne (d. 1546).

The House of Fame: an entertaining, unfinished dream poem in octosyllabic couplets, written between 1374 and 1385, and first printed in 1477/8 by CAXTON.

The Life of St Cecilia: written in rhyme royal soon after 1373 and afterwards incorporated in *The Canterbury Tales* as the 'Second Nun's Tale'. It marks the beginning of the Italian influence on his work.

The Parlement of Foules: an imaginative treatment in rhyme royal of the dream poem, the Old French device of argument among birds, and the courtly disputation on questions of love, probably written for St Valentine's Day 1383. It is unusual and all the more lively in that the birds represent different strata in the human social hierarchy of the time, and the debate assumes the trappings of the English Parliament. First printed by Caxton in 1477/8 as *The Temple of Bras*.

Troilus and Criseyde: Professor F. N. Robinson in his edition of the works calls this 'Chaucer's supreme example of sustained narration . . . unsurpassed in its kind in later English poetry'. Written in rhyme royal not before 1385, it has more characterization, tragic passion, and feeling for plot and setting than its immediate source, *Filostrato* of BOCCACCIO. First printed by Caxton in about 1482. (See also HENRYSON.)

The Legend of Good Women: unfinished accounts of famous legendary and historical women, written between 1382 and 1394 and first printed in Thynne's edition. It marks the first use in English of the decasyllabic (heroic) couplet, in which *The Canterbury Tales* is mainly composed.

The Canterbury Tales: originally projected in about 1386. Less than a fifth of its tales were completed, and they were never put into any proper order. Even so, the result is one of the most sublime and enjoyable works in English literature, and though there are precedents for the format, Chaucer's treatment is unique in that the storytellers represent a wide variety of social classes, they interact with each other, and their characteristics are developed through their stories. The first printed edition was by Caxton in 1477/8. There are good modern verse translations by Nevill Coghill (1951) and DAVID WRIGHT (1985).

The Romaunt of the Rose is only attributed to Chaucer, but may partly be his. He wrote two prose works, *Boece*, a translation of *De Consolatione Philosophiae* of BOETHIUS, and *A Treatise on the Astrolabe*, a simplified translation from the Latin made in 1392 for a boy who may have been his own son. It is significant that he always wrote in English, and in the London speech of his time, rather than French, which was the language of the court and of many of his originals. In doing so, he developed the English language as a literary medium, while contributing to the dominance of the South-East Midland dialect on its way to becoming standard English. See *The Works*, ed. F. N. Robinson, new edn 1957: *The Riverside Chaucer*, ed. Larry D. Benson, 3rd edn 1987; Derek Pearsall, *The Life of Geoffrey Chaucer: a Critical Biography*, new edn 1994; S. S. Hussey, *Chaucer: an Introduction*, 1981; H. S. Bennett, *Chaucer and Fifteenth-Century Verse and Prose*, new edn 1973, reissued 1990 (overall study); Beryl Rowland (ed.) *Companion to Chaucer Studies*, 2nd edn 1979; Peter Brown, *Chaucer at Work: the Making of the Canterbury Tales*, 1994; Helen Cooper, *The Canterbury Tales*, 2nd rev. edn 1996 (critical study).

CHEEVER, JOHN (1912–82) American short-story writer and novelist, was born in Quincy, Massachusetts, of a troubled, genteel family. He was expelled from Thayer Academy, an experience which he used in his first short story, published in the *New Republic*. He lived in impoverished circumstances in New York, about which he wrote stories, principally for the *New Yorker*. His marriage in 1941, of which there were three children, survived until the end of his life, in spite of his alcoholism and bisexual escapades. His first collection of stories, *The Way Some People Live*, was published in 1943, while he was serving in the US Army, from which he was proud to receive an 'honourable discharge' at the end of World War II. He returned to being a full-time writer of fiction, and as he moved from New York, to Scarborough, to an expansive house in Ossining (built in 1799), so he became a chronicler of suburban American life. He worked for twenty years on his first novel, *The Wapshot Chronicle* (1957), which won the National Book Award. Its sequel, *The Wapshot Scandal* (1964), is a descent into the less edifying features of contemporary American mores, a theme to which he returned, with even more bite, in *Bullet Park* (1969). In *Falconer* (1977), the appalling experience of prison, which the protagonist somehow survives, represents the degradation of society itself. *The Stories of John Cheever* (1978) won the Pulitzer Prize. His daughter Susan Cheever wrote a memoir, *Home Before Dark* (1984); his son Ben Cheever's first novel, *The Plagiarist* (1992), is about a novelist whose father bears a close resemblance to him. See *The Journals of John Cheever*, ed. Robert Gottlieb, new edn 1993; *The Letters of John Cheever*, ed. Benjamin Cheever, new edn 1992; Scott Donaldson, *John Cheever*, 1988 (biography).

CHEKHOV, ANTON (PAVLOVICH) (1860–1904) Russian dramatist and short-story writer, was born in Taganrog, a dull provincial town on the Sea of Azov, the third of six children of a feckless shopkeeper whose father, a former peasant-serf, had become an estate bailiff. He stayed on at the local grammar school when in 1876 his father went bankrupt and left town, rejoining the family in Moscow three years later, when he entered the university medical school. He qualified in 1884, having supported the family in the meantime by writing humorous stories and sketches for weekly magazines. While in practice in Moscow he continued to write, more seriously, in that he spent longer on the 12 stories that were published in 1888 than on the 129 which appeared in 1885, and he was tackling more serious themes—see *Early Stories*, tr. and ed. Patrick Miles and Harry Pitcher (1994). While still at school he had written three plays. When he could not find a theatre for *Platonov* (1881), his first attempt to present a broad spectrum of the social forces which were moulding Russian life, and [*On the Highway*] (1884) failed to pass the censor, he turned to 'vaudevilles', the success of which encouraged a theatre proprietor to commission a full-length play. *Ivanov* (1887), written in ten days, was not the expected comedy, but a play of direct action, which Chekhov rewrote for its even more successful premiere in St Petersburg in 1889. [*The Wood Demon*] (1889), a morality play written under the influence of the teachings of TOLSTOY, failed, and he withdrew it. He wrote no further play for several years, during which he made an epic trip across Asia to the convict settlement on Sakhalin Island—see *A Journey to Sakhalin*, tr. Brian Reeve (1993)—went on a European tour, and acquired a small estate near Moscow at Melikhovo, where he continued his medical practice until 1899.

[*The Seagull*] (1896), 'a comedy, three female parts, six male, four acts, landscape (view of lake); a great deal of talk about literature, little action, five tons of love', in which he admitted 'sinning against the rules of the stage', was put on in St Petersburg after only nine rehearsals, and was taken off after a few performances. In 1897 Chekhov was diagnosed as tubercular. When he returned to Russia the following year after wintering in the south of France, he was persuaded to let the new Moscow Art Theatre include *The Seagull* in its repertoire. Though he felt that the actor-director Constantine Stanislavksy (1863–1938) had misinterpreted the play, and commented, 'Your acting is excellent, only you are not playing my character', the production was a resounding success, and the company adopted a seagull as its emblem. Contemporary critics reckoned that the public was not yet attuned to the new form of his drama when [*Uncle Vanya*] (1899), a reworking of *The Wood Demon*, was first performed; but the company's tour in the Crimea, where Chekhov was wintering for his health, encouraged him to write [*The Three Sisters*] (1901), 'a drama in four acts' with three (if not four) heroines, in which a chorus element reinforces the indirect action. In 1902 he married Olga Knipper (1870–1959), a leading actress with the Moscow Art Theatre, who took the part of the landowner, Mme Ranevskaya, at the opening performance of [*The Cherry Orchard*] (tr. Robert Brustein and George Calderon, 1995) in 1904, and was still playing it in 1943. This, Chekhov's last play, of which he was too ill to write more than 'about four lines a day', and which he designated a 'comedy', without 'a single pistol shot' (or a love triangle), is peopled by essentially comic characters but has often been played as a tragedy. He died in his bed less than six months later, having just, at his doctor's suggestion, downed a glass of champagne. He was a dramatist whose purpose was to be performed, and who altered a play to suit the actor or actress whom the management finally chose for the part. His short stories possess the essential elements of drama: structure (which he called 'architecture'), plot development, and action.

The Seagull was first performed in English at the Glasgow Repertory Theatre in 1909, and *The Cherry Orchard* (1911) and *Uncle Vanya* (1914) by the Stage Society in London. G. B. SHAW prefaced his *Heartbreak House* (1919) as 'not merely the name of the play. It is cultured, leisured Europe before the war . . . [of which] Chekhov had produced four fascinating dramatic studies.' Constance Garnett (1861–1946), mother of GARNETT, translated *The Tales* (1916–22) and *The Plays* (1923). Chekhov's version of naturalism, incorporating psychological expressionism, much influenced the development of Western fiction as well as drama. See *Five Plays: Ivanov, The Seagull, Uncle Vanya, The Three Sisters, The Cherry Orchard*, new edn 1980, *Twelve Plays*, 1992 (includes *Platonov, The Wood Demon*, and comic plays), tr. Ronald Hingley; *Chekhov Omnibus: Selected Stories*, tr. Constance Garnett, ed. Donald Rayfield, rev. edn 1994; Ronald Hingley, *A Life of Anton Chekhov*, new edn 1989; Andrei Turkov (ed.), *Anton Chekhov and His Times*, tr. Cynthia Carlile and Sharon McKee, 1995.

CHESNUTT, CHARLES W(ADDELL) (1858–1932) American short-story writer and novelist, was born in Cleveland, Ohio, the eldest child of freeborn negroes. His father, who had served with the Union army in the Civil War, moved his family to Fayetteville, North Carolina, in 1866; after his wife's death, he married again. When the boy, who had had a story serialized in a local negro weekly in 1872, explained to the Principal of Howard School that he must leave to help support the family, he was employed as a pupil teacher. He graduated to becoming Principal of the State Colored Normal School in 1880, but gave up a promising career to 'go North, where, although the prejudice sticks . . . yet a man may enjoy . . . privileges if he has the money to pay for them'. Having obtained the necessary proficiency in shorthand, he went to New York in 1883, and then

to Cleveland, where he passed the Ohio Bar examination in 1887 and opened an office as a court reporter. His story, 'The Goophered Grapevine', was published in *Atlantic Monthly* in 1887. His ethnic background was not publicly revealed until 1899, which saw the publication of *The Conjure Woman*, a collection of dialect tales of Uncle Julius, and *The Wife of His Youth and Other Stories of the Color Line*, in which he highlighted 'certain aspects of the race question which are quite familar to those on the unfortunate side of it'. When his three novels, *The House Behind the Cedars* (1900), *The Marrow of Tradition* (1901), and *The Colonel's Dream* (1905), failed to gain acceptance from a predominantly white reading public, he gave up creative literature for less subtle means of campaigning for equality for all underprivileged citizens. A man who could have passed for white but refused to do so, he confided in his journal (1881) that in the South 'I occupy a position similar to that of Mahomet's Coffin. I am neither fish, flesh, nor fowl.' See *Collected Stories*, 1996; *The Journals*, ed. Richard Brodhead, 1993; *To Be an Author: Letters 1889–1905*, ed. J. R. McElroth and R. C. Leitz, 1997; Sylvia Lyons Render, *Charles W. Chesnutt*, 1980 (critical study).

CHESTERFIELD, (STANHOPE, PHILIP DORMER), 4TH EARL OF (1694–1773) British statesman and prose writer, was born in London and educated privately and, for a year, at Trinity Hall, Cambridge, before doing the Grand Tour of Europe. He was elected to Parliament while still only 20, and succeeded to his father's title in 1726. He was Ambassador to Holland 1728–32, from where he returned with his mistress, Mlle du Buchet. She bore him a son soon afterwards, called Philip, to whom from the age of five Chesterfield addressed a voluminous series of letters of elegant exhortation. On Philip's death in 1768, he transferred his epistolary attentions to his godson and heir, a distant cousin who was also called Philip. Chesterfield had a long and distinguished political career. In 1733, much to the displeasure of King George II, he married the Countess of Walsingham (1693–1778), the illegitimate daughter of the Duchess of Kendal, mistress of George I. It was a business arrangement: the couple lived in separate houses next door to each other in Grosvenor Square. Apart from his journalistic and political writings, Chesterfield allowed little to be published in his lifetime. *Miscellaneous Works* (including 'Letters to His Friends') appeared in 1777, as did *Characters of Eminent Personages of His Own Time*, which included George I and Queen Caroline. Among the coinages and dicta in his letters to his illegitimate son (published in 1774) are: 'An injury is much sooner forgotten than an insult' (1746); 'Take care of the minutes, for the hours will take care of themselves' (1747); 'I should be sorry if you were an egregious fop; but I profess that, of the two, I would rather have you a fop than a sloven' (1749); '. . . a chapter of accidents . . .' (1753). See *Lord Chesterfield's Letters*, ed. David Roberts, new edn 1992; Colin Franklin, *Lord Chesterfield: His Character and 'Characters'*, 1993.

CHESTERTON, G(ILBERT) K(EITH)

(1874–1936) British novelist, poet, critic, and journalist, was born in London, the elder son of a prominent estate agent, and was educated at St Paul's School and the Slade School of Art. After a spell in publishing, he became a journalist, a designation he never abandoned even at the height of his fame. His first book, a volume of verse called *The Wild Knight*, appeared in 1900, and his first novel, *The Napoleon of Notting Hill*, a fantasy of the future, in 1904. In *The Man Who Was Thursday: a Nightmare* (1908), regarded as the best of his novels, fantastic and sinister plots are hatched by a band of anarchists, none of whom are what they seem. At the same time he was writing critical studies of ROBERT BROWNING (1903), DICKENS (1906), and G. B. SHAW (1909), while also contributing to a number of journals. He was associated with BELLOC and his ideas on the nature and efficacy of medieval society—so closely, indeed, that SHAW coined for them the name 'Chesterbelloc'. Chesterton became a convert to Catholicism in 1922, as had been presaged in his critical articles and in the controversial *Orthodoxy* (1909). *The Innocence of Father Brown* (1911) was the first of five collections of detective stories about that unassuming priest, whose character was based on Chesterton's Yorkshire friend and confidant, Father O'Connor—see *Father Brown: a Selection*, ed. W. W. Robson, 1995. As a poet, he has a fine command of rollicking rhythm, which he exploits to good effect not only in 'Lepanto' and 'The Rolling English Road', but also in more reflective poems such as 'The Secret People' and 'A Song of Gifts to God'. See *The Essential G. K. Chesterton*, introduced by P. J. Kavanagh, new edn 1986; *Poems for All Purposes: Selected Poems*, ed. Stephen Medcalf, 1994; *Autobiography*, new edn 1986; Michael Coren, *Gilbert: the Man Who Was G. K. Chesterton*, 1990; Joseph Pearce, *Wisdom and Innocence: a Biography of G. K. Chesterton*, 1996.

CHILDERS, ERSKINE (1870–1922)

novelist and Irish politician, was born in London, the second son of an eminent orientalist, who died in 1876, and of an Irishwoman from Co. Wicklow. He was educated at Haileybury and Trinity College, Cambridge, and was a clerk in the House of Commons from 1895 to 1910. He took time off to serve in the Boer War of 1899–1902, about which he wrote a personal record (1900). Out of his hobby of sailing, which he did single-handed or with just one or two crew (crossing the North Sea many times), came the milieu of his politically-motivated thriller, *The Riddle of the Sands* (1903). Two Englishmen, on a Baltic sailing holiday, become entangled with, and ultimately thwart the traitorous objectives of, a former British naval officer who is preparing for a German invasion of Britain. The story has humour and characterization as well as suspense. Childers's devotion to the cause of self-government for Ireland was surreptitiously demonstrated in 1914 when he and his American wife (who was crippled) ran a cargo of arms in his own yacht to the Irish National Volunteers. During World War I he served as a lieutenant commander in naval intelligence, winning the Distinguished Service Cross. On his demobilization, he moved with his family to Dublin, and was elected to and appointed as a minister in the self-constituted Dail Eireann. He did not support the treaty of 1921 with the British Government, and fought for the Republican army in the Civil War. In November 1922 he was captured at his mother's old home by soldiers of the Irish Free State, and was executed by firing squad a fortnight later, after a court martial which he refused to recognize. His son, Erskine Childers (1905–74), was President of the Irish Republic 1973–74. See Jim Ring, *Erskine Childers: a Biography*, 1996.

CHOPIN, KATE (1851–1904) American

novelist and short-story writer, was born Catherine O'Flaherty in St Louis, Missouri, the third child by his second marriage of an Irish immigrant (and prosperous businessman), and of a French-American, with whose family she lived after her father's death in 1855. She graduated from St Louis Academy of the Sacred Heart in 1868. In 1870 she married Oscar Chopin, went with him to New Orleans, and produced five sons and a daughter in quick succession. In 1879 they moved to Cloutierville, Louisiana, where, after his death of malaria, she kept up his business and conducted a semi-public affair with a caddish planter, who became the model for the lovers in her fiction. In 1884 she returned with her children to St Louis, and in 1889 her first published story, 'A Point at Issue', appeared in the *St Louis-Post Dispatch*. *At Fault* (1890), a novel, was published at her own expense, but her crisp, exotic stories of Creole life in rural Louisiana found a ready magazine market and were collected in *Bayou Folk* (1894) and *A Night in Acadia* (1897). The hostile reception of *The Awakening* (1899), whose message of sensual emancipation shocked a public not yet attuned to social, economic, or political equality for women, demoralized her as a writer. She died of a brain haemorrhage. See *Kate Chopin's Private Papers*, ed. Emily Toth, Per Seyersted, and Marilyn Bonnell, 1997; Emily Toth, *Kate Chopin: a Life*, 1991; Peggy Skaggs, *Kate Chopin*, 1985 (critical study).

CHRÉTIEN DE TROYES (*fl.* 1160–85) French poet, served from about 1160 to 1172, possibly as herald-at-arms, at the court in Troyes of his patron, Marie (*d.* 1198). She was the wife of the Comte de Champignon and the daughter of Louis VII and Eleanor of Aquitaine (*c.*1122–1204), who in 1152 immediately after her divorce married the future King of England, Henry II. Subsequently Chrétien was in attendance on the Count of Flanders. 'Erec et Énide' (composed between 1160 and 1170; tr. Burton Raffel, afterword by Joseph J. Duggan, 1997) is the oldest surviving Arthurian romance. In 'Cligès' (*c.*1176) the heroine suffers manifold discomforts and uses all her feminine wiles to keep herself for her lover. 'Lancelot' and 'Yvain', which is the direct source of the early 14th-century English Arthurian romance 'Ywain and Gawain', were both composed towards the end of the 1170s. The unfinished 'Perceval' (*c.*1181) features the symbolic Grail. Chrétien wrote for the most part in limpid, gliding octosyllabic couplets. Attributed to him in addition by some scholars are 'Philomena', 'Guillaume d'Angleterre', and two short Arthurian romances, 'Le Chevalier à l'Épée' and 'La Mule sans Frein'. See *The Complete Romances of Chrétien de Troyes*, tr. David Staines, new edn 1993; *Arthurian Romances*, tr. D. D. R. Owen, new edn 1991.

CHRISTIE, AGATHA (1890–1976), née Miller, British novelist and dramatist, was born in Torquay, and educated herself by reading at home until she went to Paris at 16 to study singing and the piano. She married Colonel Archibald Christie, Royal Flying Corps, in 1914, and during the war years served as a Voluntary Aid nurse in Torquay, and then in a dispensary, where it is probable that the seeds of her later career are to be found—see Michael C. Gerald, *The Poisonous Pen of Agatha Christie* (1993) for an exhaustive account of instances of poisoning in her works. Her first detective story, *The Mysterious Affair at Styles* (1920), introduced the retired Belgian policeman, Hercule Poirot. He, or the amateur sleuth Miss Marple, who first appears in *Murder at the Vicarage* (1930), feature in most of her novels, right up to *Curtain: Hercule Poirot's Last Case* (1975) and *Sleeping Murder* (1976), both written during World War II but kept back to complete the canon when the time came. In 1926 she precipitated a mystery of her own, when the breakdown of her marriage and other stresses led to her disappearance. She was discovered in a Harrogate hotel, registered in the name of her husband's mistress. In 1930 she married (Sir) Max Mallowan (1904–78), the archaeologist, in whose work she enthusiastically involved herself. She adapted some of her novels and short stories for the stage, *Witness for the Prosecution* (1953) being dramatically the most effective, and *The Mousetrap* (1952), which was

still running in 1997, financially the most successful. The fact that her books have been translated into more than a hundred languages is as much a reflection of her negative as of her positive qualities as a novelist. The upper-middle-class rural settings of much of her work are so quaint to modern readers as to be universal, and the lack of depth of characterization means that no understanding of racial, social, or environmental factors is required of the reader. She does provide a perpetual mental challenge, and justice is always done. She wrote romantic novels as Mary Westmacott. She was made CBE in 1956 and DBE in 1971. See *An Autobiography*, 1996; Janet Morgan, *Agatha Christie*, new edn 1985 (biography).

CHRISTINE DE PISAN (1363–*c.*1430) French poet and prose writer, was born in Venice and at the age of five was taken by her mother to Paris, where her father was court astrologer to Charles V. At 15 she married Étienne de Castel, a gentleman from Picardy who became the King's secretary. On her husband's death in 1389, with three children to support, she took to writing: lyrical verses, sometimes to order, sacred and scientific poems, romantic fiction in a mixture of prose and verse, and educational and sociological treatises. In *L'Épître au Dieu d'Amours* (1399) she launched a spirited counter attack on MEUNG and his *Roman de la Rose* on behalf of her sex. *La Cité des Dames* (1405; tr. Bryan Anslay as . . .*the Cyte of Ladyes*, 1521) is a collection of portraits drawn from BOCCACCIO. *Le Livre des Trois Vertus* (1406) is a handbook for women. She retired to a nunnery in about 1418, where in 1429 she wrote a celebration of the early successes of Joan of Arc (*c.*1412–31). Anthony Woodville, or Wydeville (*c.*1442–83), Earl Rivers, translated *Proverbs of Christine de Pisan*, 'set in metre', which was printed by CAXTON in 1478. There is a manuscript illumination in the British Library depicting her presenting a volume of her poems to Isabel of Bavaria, the wife of Charles VI and Queen of France. See *The Selected Writings*, tr. Kevin Brownlee, ed. Renate Blumenfeld-Kosinski, 1997.

CHURCHILL, CHARLES (1732–64) British poet and political journalist, was born in Westminster, the son of a clergyman, and was educated at Westminster School. He was admitted to St John's College, Cambridge, in 1748 to read for the Church, but was disqualified from continuing, probably because of his clandestine marriage. He still became a clergyman, succeeding to the curacy of St John's, Westminster, on his father's death. Improvidence, to which his wife contributed her share, led to bankruptcy, from which he extricated himself by writing *The Rosciad* (1761), a verse satire on the contemporary stage which echoes both DRYDEN and POPE. The

Critical Review, edited by SMOLLETT, treated it unfavourably: Churchill replied with *The Apology, addressed to the Critical Reviewers* (1761). A friendship with the radical politician John Wilkes (1727–97)—see Peter D. G. Thomas, *John Wilkes: a Friend to Liberty* (1996)—led to his adopting a political stance in much of his subsequent verse, beginning with the anti-Scottish *The Prophecy of Famine* (1763), and to their establishing the periodical *North Britain* in direct opposition to Smollett's *Briton*. Churchill separated from his wife in 1761, and his behaviour led to his resignation from St John's in 1763. Further complications ensued. He eloped with a young woman whose family threatened to assassinate him. Wilkes was involved in a duel over an issue of their journal which the House of Commons denounced as a seditious libel, expelled from Parliament, convicted of obscene libel for *An Essay on Woman* (privately printed before 1763), and had to take refuge in France. Churchill wrote *The Author* (1763) and *The Duellist* (1764) as spirited defences of his friend, and travelled to Boulogne to see him. He died there of a fever which in his general condition he was unable to survive—in 1762 he had, by his own account, been diagnosed as severely suffering from a venereal disease. See *The Poetical Works of Charles Churchill*, ed. Douglas Grant, 1956.

CHURCHILL, (Rt Hon. Sir) **WINSTON S(PENCER)** (1874–1965) British statesman, historian, and biographer, was born at Blenheim Palace, the elder son of the politician Lord Randolph Churchill (1849–95), and was educated at Harrow. From 1895 to 1900 he combined the functions of army officer and war correspondent, performing both with distinction in Cuba, India—about which he wrote *The Story of the Malakand Field Force* (1898)—, Sudan (where at Omdurman he took part in the last great cavalry charge of the British Army and won a second medal for bravery), and South Africa (during the Boer War of 1899–1902). He was elected to Parliament in 1900, in which year he published a loosely autobiographical adventure novel, *Savrola*; a biography of his father followed in 1906. From then until his death he was both politician and author. His posts included First Lord of the Admiralty 1911–15, Chancellor of the Exchequer 1924–29, and Prime Minister 1940–45 and 1951–55. Notable books are *The World Crisis* (1923–31), *Marlborough: His Life and Times* (1933–38), *The Second World War* (1948–54), and *A History of the English-Speaking Peoples* (1956–58). If his history of World War II is somewhat one-sided, that is because there was so much to be written about his conduct of it. He was able to use his own wide experience to illuminate his studies of people and events, and it is a measure of the quality of his prose that it almost demands to be read aloud. He was awarded

the Nobel Prize for Literature in 1953. See the official biography, begun (1966–67) by his son Randolph, and completed (1971–88) by Martin Gilbert, and Gilbert's one-volume study, *Churchill: a Life*, new edn 1992; Keith Aldritt, *Churchill the Writer: His Life as a Man of Letters*, 1992.

CIBBER, COLLEY (1671–1757) British actor, dramatist, theatrical manager, and poet, was born in London, the son of a Danish sculptor, and was educated for six years at the free school in Grantham, Lincolnshire. He became an actor in London. Frustrated at only playing small parts, he wrote one for himself, the foppish Sir Novelty Fashion in *Love's Last Shift*, a sentimental comedy performed in 1696. Other plays followed. He was a dramatic manipulator rather than an original dramatist, whose success depended on his wits rather than his wit; he was also an effective adaptor, his *Richard the Third* (1699), 'as I alter'd it from Shakespeare', being the standard performing text for some two hundred years. In 1704 he became actor-manager at Drury Lane. During the 1720s he generated quarrels not only with POPE, as did so many, but also with HENRY FIELDING, but his public standing, if not his literary reputation, was enhanced when in 1730 he was for some reason appointed Poet Laureate. *An Apology for the Life of Colley Cibber, Comedian* (1740) is a readable autobiography of a man who knew, if he would not publicly admit, his limitations, and a valuable first-hand account of the stage at the time. His son Theophilus (1703–58), also an actor and dramatist, wrote *Lives of the Poets of Great Britain and Ireland* (1753) and married, as his second wife, Susanna (1714–66), a notable singer and actress, the sister of Thomas Arne (1710–86), the composer. See *An Apology for the Life of Colley Cibber*, ed. B. R. S. Fone, 1968; Richard H. Barker, *Mr Cibber of Drury Lane*, 1939 (biography).

CICERO, MARCUS TULLIUS (106–43 BC) Roman statesman and prose writer, was born near Arpinum and studied in Rome. In 80 he successfully defended Roscius, charged with patricide on the evidence of a favourite freedman of the dictator, Sulla. He then prudently went abroad for his health. He returned after Sulla's death in 78, and helped by forensic triumphs ascended the political ladder, being elected consul for 63, and dealing firmly with Cataline's conspiracy against the state. In 58, having refused to join CAESAR's triumvirate and criticized its right to govern, he spent a year in exile. He returned reluctantly, and was governor of Cilicia in 51–50. After Caesar's assassination in 44, he delivered or published his 'Philippics', attacking Mark Antony (*c*.82–30) and urging the senate to grant an amnesty to the conspirators. When Antony and the second triumvirate came to power, Cicero was tracked down and murdered. His head and hands were cut off and sent to Rome, where they were nailed up in the forum. His speeches and philosophical works class him as a master of rhetoric and style. To students of Roman life, the four collections of letters, 'To his Brother Quintus', 'To his Friends', 'To Brutus' (the conspirator), and 'To Atticus' (his closest friend), edited shortly after his death, are of greater interest. See Elizabeth Rawson, *Cicero: a Portrait*, new edn 1994.

CLARE, JOHN (1793–1864) British poet, was born at Helpstone, near Peterborough, the son of a barely literate countryman. Though he attended school, he was taught to read and write by a local farmer's son. The education which inspired his poetry was his observation of nature and of the daily routines of country life. A bookseller in Stamford published his *Poems Descriptive of Rural Life and Scenery* in 1820, the year the poet married not the love of his youth, whom he never forgot, but a girl he had made pregnant. *The Village Minstrel* (1821) and *The Shepherd's Calendar* (1827) were published in London but were financial disasters. The latter had been subjected to drastic and unsympathetic editing by the publisher, John Taylor (1781–1864): the original version, ed. Eric Robinson and Geoffrey Summerfield (published 1964) reveals the true spirit of a village community. *The Rural Muse* (1835) earned Clare £40, but by now his resilience and mind were broken by poverty and privation—his wife had given birth to their seventh child in 1833. In 1837 he entered a private asylum, from which he ran away four years later. He was then committed to the Northampton county asylum, where he spent the rest of his life, kindly treated and still writing: the asylum register recorded laconically that he died 'after years addicted to Poetical prosing'. His poetry, which he never learned to punctuate and left unrevised, is shot through with penetrating insights and happy choices of phrase. His bird poems alone represent a corpus of nature poetry which is unique. See [*Works*], ed. Eric Robinson and David Powell, 1984; *Autobiographical Writings*, ed. Eric Robinson and Geoffrey Summerfield, new edn 1986; J. W. and Anne Tibble, *John Clare: a Life*, rev. edn 1972; John Lucas, *John Clare*, 1994 (critical introduction).

CLARK, JOHN PEPPER (*b.* 1935) Nigerian dramatist and poet, was born in Kiagbodo in the Niger delta, and was educated at Warsi Government College, Ughelli, and Ibadan University, where he founded the student poetry magazine, the *Horn*. He became a journalist, first as a government information officer, and then as Features Editor of the *Daily Express*, Lagos. *Song of a Goat* (1961), an African verse tragedy whose tone and structure echo Greek classical drama, was per-

formed throughout Africa and in Europe. Like *Poems* (1962), first published in Nigeria, it was reissued internationally in *Three Plays* (1964), with *The Masquerade* and *The Raft*; in the latter the unity of place is represented by a craft adrift on the Niger, and the denouement is its destruction. Experiences while on a fellowship at Princeton University in 1962–63 are the subject of *America, Their America* (1964), described by SALKEY as 'the first of its kind from any living negro author . . . polemical journalism . . . quality reportage . . . also a distinguished travel book'. Several poems incorporated in it, with some from *Poems*, were included in *A Reed in the Tide* (1965), the first collection by an individual African poet to be published internationally. In 1965 he became a lecturer at Lagos University, where he was later appointed Professor of English. *Casualties: Poems 1966–1968* (1970) comprises his reflections on the Biafran war—see also *A Decade of Tongues: Selected Poems 1958–1968* (1981). Further collections of plays are *The Ozidi Cycle* (1975), which he collected and translated from the Ijo of Okabou Ojobolo, and (as J. P. Clark Bekerderemo) *The Bikoroa Plays* (1985). His collection of critical essays on African literature, *The Example of Shakespeare* (1970), includes 'The Legacy of Caliban', a study of the language spoken by Africans and other 'natives' in English literature from SHAKESPEARE to ACHEBE.

CLARK, WALTER VAN TILBURG (1909–71) American novelist and short-story writer, was born in East Orland, Maine, eldest of four children of Walter Ernest Clark (*d.* 1955), President of the University of Nevada 1917–37. He was educated at Reno High School and the University of Nevada, where he studied literature and philosophy. While a teaching assistant at the University of Vermont, he wrote a master's thesis on JEFFERS, of whom he became a close friend—there are echoes of the Jeffers home in the symbolic title poem of Clark's first, and only, collection of verse, *Ten Women in Gale's House and Other Poems* (1932). In 1933 he married, and for the next ten years taught English and drama, and coached basketball, in high schools in Cazenovia and Rye, New York. At the age of 27 he wrote *The Ox-Bow Incident* (1940), a study of mob violence which is also a classic western novel. It is rooted in its author's feeling for the land itself: 'The desert does not move either. It does not stir or make a sound. It has no rhythm but the visible, static rhythm of its shapes. . . . [Nevada] is a region of extremes that exist at the same time' (1957). A second novel, *The City of Trembling Leaves* (1945), betrayed a youthful lyricism. Clark returned with his family to Nevada in 1946. A black panther is both the real and a mythic quarry in *The Track of the Cat* (1949), a second western of memorable dimensions. His last published work was *The Watchful Gods and Other Stories* (1950), the 'other stories' having been published in various journals 1940–46. He resigned as a member of his university in 1953 in protest at 'autocratic administration'. He taught creative writing at the University of Montana 1954–56, and San Francisco State College 1956–61, before returning to the University of Nevada as Writer-in-Residence.

CLARKE, ARTHUR C. (*b.* 1917) British scientific writer, novelist, and short-story writer, was born in Minehead, Somerset. When he was 13, his father died of the effects of being gassed in World War I. He was educated at Huish's Grammar School, Taunton, entered the civil service as an auditing clerk in 1936, and served in the Royal Air Force during World War II as a radar specialist with the rank of flight lieutenant. In an article in *Wireless World* in 1945, for which he was paid £15, he propounded the notion of geostationary satellites for global communications, which he further predicted, in a short story in 1960, would be employed also for disseminating pornography. After getting first-class honours in physics and mathematics at King's College, London, in 1948, he was for a time an assistant editor of *Physics Abstracts*, before publishing his first science-fiction novel, *Prelude to Space* (1951), and becoming a full-time writer. A Fellow of the Royal Astronomical Society, and Chairman of the British Interplanetary Society 1946–47 and 1950–53, his interest also in underwater exploration and photography took him in 1956 to Sri Lanka, which he decided to make his home, and where in 1975 he installed the only privately-owned Earth satellite station in the world and the only television set in the country. He is a realist who uses fiction as a medium for extrapolating from known data, and also, as in *2001: a Space Odyssey* (1968, from his own screenplay), *The Fountains of Paradise* (1979), and *3001: The Final Odyssey* (1997), for conducting a search for meaning. A recent non-fiction work, *How the World Was One: Beyond the Global Village* (1992), is partly a historical account of the 19th-century pioneers of transatlantic telegraphy and partly autobiography. In addition to *Ascent to Orbit: a Scientific Autobiography* (1984) and Neil McAleer, *Odyssey: the Authorised Biography of Arthur C. Clarke* (1992), there exists, by his own account, a private journal of 'four to five million words' which no one has seen. He was made CBE in 1989.

CLARKE, AUSTIN (1896–1974) Irish poet, novelist, and dramatist, was born in Dublin and educated at the Jesuit Belvedere College and University College, Dublin. In two early books of verse, *The Vengeance of Fionn* (1917) and *The Sword of the West* (1921), he attempted to re-create the Celtic ethos. *The Cattledrive in Connaught* (1925) is a more

lively representation of Ireland past. Clarke worked as a journalist in England from 1929 to 1937, when he returned to Co. Dublin. *Pilgrimage* (1929) and *Night and Morning* (1938) still reflect the past, but are concerned, too, with matters of the present, in particular the conflicts between asceticism and natural desire, and between faith and reason. His defiance of artistic censorship both motivated and provided the subject of his first novel, *The Bright Temptation* (1932). With Robert Farren (1909–84) he founded the Dublin Verse-Speaking Society in 1940 and the Lyric Theatre in 1944; for a time he concentrated on writing verse drama. In *Ancient Lights* (1955) he returned to his commitment to poetry and to speaking out loud about the various deprivations of life in Dublin. *Mnemosyne Lay in Dust* (1966) is a disturbing collection which recalls his incarceration in an asylum in his youth. He is essentially a national poet because of his concern about (and latterly satire on) the contradictions of modern Irish life and because he used, adapted, and breathed fresh life into traditional poetic forms. See *Selected Poems*, ed. Hugh Maxton, new edn 1992; *Reviews and Essays of Austin Clarke*, ed. Gregory A. Schirmer, 1995; *Twice Round the Black Church*, 1962, and *Penny in the Clouds*, new edn 1990 (autobiography); Gregory A. Schirmer, *The Poetry of Austin Clarke*, 1983 (critical study); Maurice Harmon, *Austin Clarke: a Critical Introduction*, 1989.

CLARKE, AUSTIN C(HESTER-FIELD) (*b.* 1934) Barbadian novelist, was educated at Harrison College and Toronto University, and became a freelance broadcaster and producer in Canada. His first two novels, *The Survivors of the Crossing* (1964) and *Amongst Thistles and Thorns* (1965), are studies respectively of Barbadian agricultural conditions and childhood. From 1968 to 1974 he taught literature and creative writing in the USA as a visiting university lecturer. *The Meeting Point* (1967), *Storm of Fortune* (1973), and *The Bigger Light* (1975) are distinctive for their theme of the West Indian, predominantly working-class, immigrant in Toronto, as well as for his even-handed treatment of this specific culture clash. The stories in *When He Was Free and Young and He Used to Wear Silks* (rev. edn 1973) are extensions of this theme, while in those in *When Women Rule* (1985) the immigrants are also from Europe; *In This City* (1992) and *There Are No Elders* (1993) are about settled immigrants and their children who are first-generation Canadians, and assimilation rather than conflict. He was Cultural and Press Attaché to the Barbados Embassy, Washington 1974–75, and then spent a year as General Manager, Caribbean Broadcasting Corporation, before returning to Canada. *The Prime Minister* (1977) is a novel about reverse isolation, in which a West Indian returns from Canada to his homeland to take up a political appointment. See *Growing Up Stupid Under the Union Jack*, 1980, and *Colonial Innocency*, 1982 (autobiography); Stella Algoo-Baksh, *Austin C. Clarke: a Biography*, 1994.

CLARKE, MARCUS (1846–81) Australian novelist and journalist, was born in Kensington, London, the son of a Chancery lawyer, and was educated at Highgate School (where he was a friend of HOPKINS). His father's sudden death left him not with an expected fortune of £70,000, but with only £800, with which in 1863 he was shipped off to Victoria, where an uncle was a provincial judge. He was dismissed from his job in a Melbourne bank for dilettantism, and spent two tough years in the Wimmera area before returning to the 'civilised attire, cigars, claret, and a subscription to the Union Club Balls' of Melbourne, and to the prospect of the journalistic career which his sketches and stories seemed to offer. As a writer he prospered, especially with his weekly articles in the *Australasian* as 'The Peripatetic Philosopher' (1867–70). His attempts to be an editor were disastrous, though *Colonial Monthly*, during his brief time there, serialized his first novel, *Long Odds* (1869), an English melodrama with a horseracing climax and an Australian ending. While employed by the *Australian Journal* he offered to write a new serial for £100. In researching it he studied the State Library of Victoria's records on transportation, and visited the former Port Arthur settlement in Tasmania, where he interviewed people with memories of it. The first monthly instalment of *His Natural Life* appeared in March 1870; the last was published in June 1872, by which time it is said many readers had lost the thread, and that he used to have to be locked up until he delivered another instalment. On the advice of (Sir) Charles Gavan Duffy (1816–1903), Irish editor and Prime Minister of Victoria in 1871, he radically revised the novel for book publication in 1874, in particular cutting and altering the beginning and end. It was reissued in 1885 as *For the Term of His Natural Life*. (The complete original version was first published in book form in 1970, ed. Stephen Murray-Smith.) In whatever form, it is the major 19th-century Australian contribution to the English novel, a graphic record of a penal system which had disappeared only twenty years before, and, for all the grim accounts of degradation (including homosexual gang rape and cannibalism) and barbaric floggings, a genuine attempt at a study of the psychological as well as physical effects of such punishment.

Clarke married an actress in 1869, and in 1870 parted with his 'birthright of free speech for a mess of official pottage' to be secretary to the Trustees of State Library of Victoria, becoming Assistant Librarian in 1876. This did not prevent him from writing two more novels, several volumes of short stories, and five dramatic pieces—including the popular pantomime, *Twinkle, Twinkle, Little Star . . .* (1873), and *The Happy Land* (1880), a political lampoon based on GILBERT and transferred to the current situation in Victoria—while regularly contributing to critical journals, newspapers, and miscellanies; or from being declared bankrupt in 1874 and 1881. Shortly after the second occasion he contracted pleurisy, of which he died in a house bereft of furniture, with a pencil in his hand. A bill in the Victorian Parliament to provide his destitute widow and six children with a pension was defeated. See *Stories*, ed. Michael Wilding, 1983; *A Colonial City: High and Low Life*, ed. Laurie T. Hergenhan, 1972 (journalism); Brian Elliott, *Marcus Clarke*, 1958 (biography).

CLAUSEWITZ, CARL VON (1780–1831) German military philosopher, was born in Burg and became an ensign in the Prussian army at the age of 12. He studied at the Military School, Berlin, from 1801 to 1803. In 1806 he was wounded and taken prisoner by the French, returning at the end of the war to work on the reorganization of the army. He entered Russian service in 1812, being in 1814 appointed Chief of Staff of the Russo-German Corps. He rejoined the Prussian army in 1815, becoming in 1818 Major General and Director of the Military School, and in 1830 Inspector of Artillery at Breslau and then Chief of Staff to the Army of Observation on the Polish border. He died of cholera. The nine volumes of his seminal study of war, especially in relation to politics, *Vom Kriege* [*On War*], was published by his wife in 1832. See *On War*, ed. Anatol Rapoport, tr. Col. J. J. Graham, new edn 1982; *Historical and Political Writings*, ed. and tr. Peter Paret and Daniel Moran, 1992; Peter Paret, *Clausewitz and the State: the Man, His Theories, and His Times*, 1985.

CLELAND, JOHN (1710–1789) British novelist and miscellaneous writer, was born in Kingston-on-Thames, Surrey, the first son of a Scot, Major William Cleland (c.1675–1741), Commissioner of Taxes and a friend of POPE. He went to Westminster School for two years and later joined the East India Company in Bombay. He returned in 1741, but after his father's death fell out with his mother (who controlled the family budget) and into considerable debt, for which he was in 1748 committed to the Fleet prison for a year. After the publication of the second of two parts of *Memoirs of a Woman of Pleasure* (1748–49), he was rearrested and, with his publisher, briefly imprisoned again for issuing an obscene publication. Cleland then himself produced an expurgated version, published in 1750 as *Memoirs of Fanny Hill*. The novel which brought him notoriety and, since a series of lawsuits in the 1960s, literary respectability, did nothing to make his fortune. For the rest of his long life he tried desperately to keep himself by writing: reviews for the *Monthly Review* (including perceptive articles on HENRY FIELDING and SMOLLETT); a disappointingly mild novel, *Memoirs of a Coxcomb* (1751); four romances, published together as *The Surprises of Love* (1764); medical treatises; translations from both Italian and French; stage comedies and tragedies, some of which were published but none performed; and satirical verses. BOSWELL described him in 1779 as a disappointed and lonely figure, living in shabby chaos, 'drinking tea and eating biscuits. . . . There was something *genteel* in his manner amidst this oddity.' And to cap it all, he was even suspected of being homosexual. *Memoirs of a Woman of Pleasure* is a witty and genuinely erotic work. His heroine, Fanny, has affinities with both SAMUEL RICHARDSON's Pamela and Fielding's Shamela, while having much more fun than either. See William H. Epstein, *John Cleland: Images of a Life*, 1974.

CLEMENS, SAMUEL see TWAIN.

CLOUGH, ARTHUR HUGH (1819–61) British poet, was born in Liverpool and stayed in England when his parents emigrated to America. He was educated at Rugby School, where he excelled at everything, and Balliol College, Oxford, where he did less well. In 1848 he resigned a fellowship at Oriel College rather than take holy orders, which religious doubts, implanted when he was an undergraduate, now made unthinkable. After two years as head of a college in London and three in America, he married and took a job with the Education Office in London. He died in Florence after a bout of malaria. *The Bothie of Tober-na-Voulich* (the revised title of a verse novel in hexameters, first published in 1848) is an amusing and tender account of a Highland holiday romance between an English undergraduate and a local girl, with a happy ending. 'Amours de Voyage', published in an American journal in 1858, is told in letters. Claude, who cannot crystallize his attitude to the short-lived Republic of Rome, dithers across Europe after the object of his affections, only to lose her in the end. Clough's other long poem, 'Dipsychus' (a reference to someone of a double-sided nature), is a drama in a variety of metres, comprising a dialogue with a tempting spirit. The best-known of his shorter poems are 'Say Not the Struggle Naught Availeth' and his skit on the Ten Commandments, 'The Latest Decalogue'. It was unusual for a poet of his time to express personal doubts and intellectual tussles, which he does with a sense of humour and a refreshing air of enquiring innocence. See *The Poems*, ed. F. L. Mulhauser, translations ed. Jane Turner, 2nd edn 1974; *Selected Poems*, ed. Jim McCue, 1991; *The Oxford Diaries of Arthur Hugh Clough*, ed. Anthony Kenny, 1990; Robindra Biswas, *Arthur Hugh Clough: Towards a Reconsideration*, 1972.

COBBETT, WILLIAM (1763–1835) British prose writer and political journalist, was born in Farnham, Surrey, the son of a small farmer, and had little formal education. He enlisted in the Army in 1784, and during a year at Chatham absorbed the contents of a local circulating library and taught himself grammar. He was a sergeant major in Nova Scotia and New Brunswick between 1785 and 1791. After his discharge he accused his former officers of embezzlement, as a result of which he and his wife took refuge in France and then in America, where, as Peter Porcupine, he wrote fierce criticism of the local Democrats. After two prosecutions for libel, he prudently returned to England before the publication of *Porcupine's Works* (1801)—see *Peter Porcupine in America: Pamphlets on Republicanism and Revolution*, ed. David A. Wilson (1994). In 1802 he began the weekly *Political Register*. His views veered from Tory to Radical, and in 1810 he was jailed for an article on army flogging. He repeatedly stood for Parliament, and was finally elected in 1832. A farmer as well as a writer, he toured southern England in 1822 to observe agricultural conditions. His accounts were published in volume form as *Rural Rides* (1830), an eccentric but engaging blend of autobiography, rural impressions, polemic, and lexical digressions. Other works include *Cottage Economy* (1822) and *Advice to Young Men, and, incidentally, to Young Women* (1829). HAZLITT wrote of him in *The Spirit of the Age*: 'He is not only unquestionably the most powerful political writer of the present day, but one of the best writers in the language.' See Daniel Green, *Great Cobbett: the Noblest Agitator*, 1985; Raymond Williams, *Cobbett*, 1983 (introduction to his thought).

COCTEAU, JEAN (1889–1963) French novelist, dramatist, poet, and critic, was born in Maisons-Laffitte of a family of lawyers. He was educated at the Lycée Condorcet, Paris, and at 18 had published two books of verse, which he later disowned. *Le Potomak* (1919), a prose fantasy, had been put aside during World War I; *Le Cap de Bonne-Espérance* (1919) comprised poetry reflecting his war experiences; *Ode à Picasso* (1919) gave notice of the direction of his attention towards modernism. His monstrous, or magnificent, egotism led him, with recourse to such restoratives to the imagination as the Catholic Church, opium, and solitude, into almost every artistic field, including the ballet and graphic arts, each of which he enlivened with his eccentric individualism. *Les Enfants Terribles* (1929; as

Enfants Terribles, tr. Samuel Putnam, 1930; as *Children of the Game*, tr. Rosamond Lehmann, 1955), written in three weeks, is a classic novel of adolescence. Of his plays, *La Machine Infernale* (1934; tr. Carl Wildman as *The Infernal Machine*, 1936) is based on the legend of Oedipus; the dramatic monologue *Le Bel Indifférent* (1941) was written for his friend, the popular singer (Edith) Piaf (1915–63), who died on the same day as he did; the costume romance *L'Aigle a Deux Têtes* (1946; tr. Ronald Duncan as *The Eagle Has Two Heads*, 1948) had a long London run. Films which he wrote and directed include *Orphée* (1949), from his own play (1926), and *La Belle et la Bête* (1945). See also *Tempest of Stars: Selected Poems*, tr. Jeremy Reed (bilingual edn 1992).

COETZEE, J(OHN) M(ICHAEL) (*b.* 1940) South African novelist, was born in Cape Town and graduated from Cape Town University in 1963, and as PhD (with a thesis on BECKETT's prose style) from the University of Texas in 1969. He was a computer programmer before teaching literature and linguistics at State University of New York and then at Cape Town University. The two novellas in *Dusklands* (1974, in USA 1985) are studies of the psychological and social conditioning of races by other races, which is at the heart of his work, whether the setting is allegorical, as in *Waiting for the Barbarians* (1980), or South Africa. His postmodernist technique is clearly illustrated in *In the Heart of the Country* (1977), in which the fantasies of the narrator are open to several interpretations. *Life and Times of Michael K* (1983), which won the Booker prize for fiction, and *Age of Iron* (1990) embody fables if not portents of the political future of his country. At the centre of *The Master of St Petersburg* (1994) is a part-factual, part-fictional DOSTOEVSKY, through whose preoccupations Coetzee combines ideological argument with magic realism. *White Writing* (1991) comprises critical essays exploring the mind and myths of South Africa through its writing—see also *Doubling the Point: Essays and Interviews*, ed. David Attwell (1992). *Giving Offense: Essays on Censorship* (1996) is a significant collection which illustrates how censorship in the USSR and South Africa deformed the work even of the most heroic opponents of the system.

COHEN, LEONARD (*b.* 1934) Canadian poet, novelist, composer, and singer, was born into a Jewish family in the plush Westmount district of Montreal, and went to McGill University. He abandoned his postgraduate studies at Columbia University, New York, after three weeks, and returned to Montreal, where he read his poetry in nightclubs; sampled the family clothing business; wrote an unpublished novel ('Ballet of Lepers'); and published a book of verse, *Let Us Com-*

pare Mythologies (1956), which draws on both Jewish and Christian themes and traditions, and whose feeling, simple forms, and graphic imagery made a considerable impact. A Canada Council award took him to England, where he worked on his first published novel, *The Favorite Game* (1963), in which a rich Jewish boy from Montreal comes to self-realization and embarks on a career as a folk singer. From England he went to the Greek island of Hydra, the source of much of his subsequent creativity. He has since divided his time between Greece, Montreal, and the demands of being an international singer with a distinctive style of delivery and a repertoire of idiosyncratic lyrics. *Beautiful Losers* (1966), his second novel, achieved cult status for its modernist technique, bizarre symbolism, and eroticism. *Selected Poems 1956–1968* (1968), chosen from his first and three further collections, was an international public success, and won him the Governor General's Award, which he declined, explaining: 'Much in me strives for this honor but the poems themselves forbid it absolutely.' See *Stranger Music: Selected Poems and Songs*, new edn 1994; Ira B. Nadel, *Various Positions: a Life of Leonard Cohen*, 1996; Linda Hutcheon, *Leonard Cohen and His Works: Fiction*, 1992, and *Leonard Cohen and His Works: Poetry*, 1992.

COHEN, MATT(HEW) (*b.* 1942) Canadian novelist and short-story writer, was born in Kingston, Ontario, of Jewish parents, and was brought up in Ottawa, where he went to Fisher Park and Nepean high schools. After graduating from Toronto University, he spent several months in Europe, where he wrote, while living alone in a barn, an epic poem, and part of a novel, for which he then received an offer from a London publisher. Feeling 'really scared' and 'unready for it', he returned to Toronto, took a postgraduate degree in political science, and subsequently burned the novel together with everything he had written before he was 25. He became a full-time writer in 1968, having spent a year teaching the sociology of religion at McMaster University. After two short novels whose protagonists have destructive dual consciousnesses, *Korsniloff* (1969) and *John Crackle Sings* (1971), he worked 'intensely' to complete *Columbus and the Fat Lady and Other Stories* (1972), in which fantasy or symbolism are often imposed on everyday situations—see also *The Expatriate: Collected Short Stories* (1981). In subsequent novels he has used the exploration of time in the elucidation of his themes, notably in *The Disinherited* (1974) and *The Sweet Second Summer of Kitty Malone* (1979). Time and the astronomical exploration of space inform *Nadine* (1986), in which a Jewish orphan of World War II searches for a professional and personal destiny. See George Woodcock, *Matt Cohen and His Works*, 1994.

COLERIDGE, SAMUEL TAYLOR

(1772–1834) British poet, philosopher, and critic, was born in Ottery St Mary, Devon, the tenth and youngest child of the vicar (he was also the grammar school master) and his second wife. A precocious boy who read and was deeply influenced by *Arabian Nights' Entertainments* at the age of six, he was educated at Christ's Hospital, which he found a traumatic experience, and Jesus College, Cambridge, where in 1791 he first took opium, for rheumatism. During his final year he got into debt and disappeared for four months to be an ineffective trooper in the Dragoons under the assumed name of Silas Tomkyn Comberbache, and finished without a degree. He had already begun publishing his poems in newspapers, when on a vacation walking tour in 1794 he was introduced to SOUTHEY in Oxford. A close friendship was forged, founded on the idea of establishing a 'Pantisocracy' in a remote part of America. The scheme did not materialize, but led to Coleridge marrying Sarah Fricker (1770–1845), the younger sister of Southey's fiancée. In 1796 he started a political journal, *The Watchman*, which survived for ten issues, and published *Poems on Various Subjects*, the second edition of which (1797) contained poems by LAMB, a friend from Christ's Hospital days, and Charles Lloyd (1775–1839). The next few years were momentous and productive. He wrote a play, *Osorio*, which was rejected by SHERIDAN but ultimately staged in 1813 as *Remorse*. A friendship with WORDSWORTH had in 1797 grown into such a bond that the poet and his sister moved to Alfoxden House, Somerset, to be near the Coleridges in Nether Stowey. Between November 1797 and May 1798 Coleridge wrote the three works on which his reputation as a major poet is founded: the first part of the weird ballad, 'Christabel' (the second was composed in 1800, and the rest never at all); the opium-inspired fragment, 'Kubla Khan'; and 'The Rime of the Ancient Mariner', which was included in *Lyrical Ballads* (1798). This joint publication with Wordsworth expressed the theory of poetic sensation towards which they had been working, and spearheaded the Romantic Movement. With the Wordsworths, he then undertook a study tour in Germany, after which they moved north and he spent some months in London as a journalist on the *Morning Post*. In 1800 he took his family to Greta Hall, in the Lake District, into which the Southeys also moved.

Coleridge was now addicted to opium and emotionally entangled with Sara Hutchinson (1775–1835), Wordsworth's sister-in-law—the poem 'Dejection: an Ode' was, in its original form, written for her under the title 'A Letter to . . .'. In 1804 he went to Malta for his health, and successfully took on the post of temporary Public Secretary of the island, only to return to England in 1806 more addicted to drugs than before—see Alethea Hayter, *A Voyage in Vain: Coleridge's Journey to Malta in 1804* (1973, reissued 1993). In 1808 he separated from his wife, and in 1810 he broke with the Wordsworths. He earned some fame, and some money, by giving courses of literary lectures, some of which have been reconstituted in *Shakespearean Criticism*, ed. Thomas M. Raysor (2 vols, new edn 1960). In 1816 he put himself in the hands of Dr James Gillman (1782–1839), into whose house in Highgate, London, he moved for what was intended to be a month. He stayed for 18 years until his death. The control of his addiction enabled him to attract a wide circle of disciples and friends, and to complete *Biographia Literaria* (1817), a critical study of poetry and philosophy with autobiographical digressions. He also published a new book of verse, *Sibylline Leaves* (1817), and a collected edition of his poetry (1828); he continued to write prose, though more discursively than before, and poetry, which by contrast was tighter and had lost its power to surprise—the discovery of three hundred unknown poems was announced in February 1995.

Of his three children who survived infancy, Hartley (1796–1849), referred to in the poems 'Frost at Midnight' and 'The Nightingale', both written in 1798, had poetical talent, but, having been sent to Oxford by Southey, lost his subsequent fellowship through drunkenness, failed as a school proprietor, and died a literary vagrant. Derwent (1800–83) became the first head of St Mark's College, Chelsea, and edited some of his father's and brother's works. Sara (1802–52), a notable scholar and translator, as well as a beauty, married her cousin Henry Coleridge (1798–1843). William Collins, father of WILKIE COLLINS, met her at the Wordsworths in 1818, and painted her as 'The Highland Girl', which was exhibited in London to great acclaim and much impressed her father, who had not seen her since she was a child. Her fantasy *Phantasmion* (1837) is interspersed with pleasant lyrics.

See [*Selected Works*], ed. H. J. Jackson, 1985; *Coleridge's Verse: a Selection*, ed. William Empson and David Pirie, 1972 (critical edition of the best poetry), reissued as *Selected Poems*, 1989; *Coleridge: Selected Poems*, ed. Richard Holmes, 1996; *Selected Letters*, ed. H. J. Jackson, 1987; Molly Lefebure, *Samuel Taylor Coleridge: a Bondage of Opium*, 1974 (biography), and *The Bondage of Love: a Life of Mrs Samuel Taylor Coleridge*, new edn 1988; Richard Holmes, *Coleridge: Early Visions*, new edn 1990 (biography to 1804); Rosemary Ashton, *The Life of Samuel Taylor Coleridge: a Critical Biography*, 1996; John Livingstone Lowes, *The Road to Xanadu: a Study in the Ways of the Imag-*

ination, new edn 1986 (critical study of 'The Ancient Mariner' and 'Kubla Khan'); Richard Holmes, *Coleridge*, 1982 (introduction to his thought and works).

COLETTE, (SIDONIE-GABRIELLE CLAUDINE) (1873–1954) French novelist, was born in Saint-Saveur-en-Puissaye, the daughter of a one-legged war veteran, and was educated at the local school until she was 16. At 20 she married a friend of the family, the 34-year-old Henri Gauthier-Villars ('Willy'). He introduced her to the cultural life of Paris and to his distinctly paedophiliac sexual tastes, in pursuit of which he encouraged her to write spicy schoolgirl stories in collaboration with him. The literary partnership ran for four books, beginning with *Claudine à L'École* (1900; as *Claudine at School*, tr. Janet Flanner, 1930; tr. Antonia White, 1963), and ending when they divorced in 1903. She now branched out on her own: as a novelist, with a succession of sensuous, exhilaratingly written, semi-autobiographical or aspiratory novels and stories evoking *la belle époque* and deep, sometimes ambiguous passions, of which *Chéri* (1920; tr. Flanner, 1930) and its sequel (see *Chéri and The Last of Chéri*, tr. Roger Senhouse, 1954), *Le Blé en Herbe* (1923; tr. Phyllis Mégroz as *The Ripening Corn*, 1931; tr. Senhouse as *Ripening Seed*, 1959), and the title story of *Gigi et Autres Nouvelles* (1944; tr. Senhouse as *Gigi*, 1953) are celebrated examples—see also *The Collected Stories of Colette*, ed. Robert Phelps (1984); as the lover of the Marquise de Belbeuf; and as an actress, in a lesbian sketch with the Marquise at the Moulin Rouge (the audience pelted them with cushions), and with more success on tour in a steamy bodice ripper called *The Flesh*, in the course of which her bodice was nightly ripped. In 1912 she married Henry de Jouvenal, Editor of *Le Matin*, by whom she had a daughter in 1913, and whose 19-year-old son she seduced. The marriage ended in 1925, and after ten years of nominal spinsterhood she married Maurice Goudeket, the son of a Jewish diamond merchant, whom she hid in her flat in the Palais-Royal from 1942 until the end of the war, having secured, through her Nazi friends, his release from incarceration. After her death, her coffin lay in state in the courtyard of the Palais-Royal, with the trappings of a Grand Officer of the Legion of Honour at its head. The refusal of the Archbishop of Paris to grant her a Catholic burial was attacked by many, including GRAHAM GREENE, who wrote an open letter to *Le Figaro Littéraire*. See Diana Holmes, *Colette*, 1991 (critical study); Dana Strand, *Colette: a Study of the Short Fiction*, 1995.

COLLINS, TOM see FURPHY.

COLLINS, WILKIE (1824–89) British novelist and dramatist, was born in London, the elder son of William Collins RA (1788–1847), the landscape painter, and was named after the Scottish painter, (Sir) David Wilkie (1785–1841). At the age of 12 he accompanied his parents for two years to Italy, where he later claimed to have lost his virginity to an older woman in Rome. On their return he went as a boarder to Mr Cole's school in Highbury Place. While working as a clerk with a London tea importer, he had a signed story published in the *Illuminated Magazine* (1843), wrote 'Iolani', a novel about the South Seas, and began *Antonina: or, The Fall of Rome*. In 1846 his dying father entered him for the law at Lincoln's Inn (he was called to the Bar in 1852). Collins's biography of his father appeared in 1848. He had a painting exhibited at the Royal Academy in 1849. *Antonina* was published in 1850, two days after the charity performance of his melodrama, *A Court Duel*, adapted without acknowledgment from the French—all his subsequent plays, several of them from his own books, are original works. In 1851 he met DICKENS, to whose magazine, *Household Words*, he regularly contributed stories while also writing novels, which included *Hide and Seek* (1854), featuring a profoundly deaf girl, and *The Dead Secret* (1857), a study of character depending on 'expectation rather than surprise' with a peripheral theme of blindness. His links with his editor, who was also sometimes his literary collaborator and on several occasions his travelling companion, were strengthened when in 1860 his brother, the painter Charles Collins (1828–73), married Dickens's second daughter, Kate (1839–1929), later Mrs Carlo Perugini.

The Woman in White (1860), first published as a serial in *All the Year Round*, is a sensational mystery novel, with a complex plot, several secrets, and two villains. It sold out on the day of publication and was reprinted six times in six months, the 1861 one-volume edition incorporating, in the light of criticisms by the reviewer in *The Times*, corrections to the intricate sequence of dates on which the denouement depends. Collins wrote in all over thirty novels, of which the most famous, and best, is *The Moonstone* (1868), in which Sergeant Cuff is the first detective in English fiction to play a major role in the action. The story is told from several points of view and thus has a depth unusual in novels of this genre, though characterization is secondary to plot, suspense, and revelation. In 1873–74 he spent six months touring the USA, where he read to audiences an expanded version of his story 'The Dream Woman'. With *The Law and the Lady* (1875), which has a female investigator bent on clearing her husband of killing his first wife, he moved even closer to the modern detective novel. Collins never married, but by 1858 was living openly with a widow, Elizabeth ('Caroline') Graves (1830–95) and her seven-year-old daughter. He acquired a second mistress, Martha Rudd (alias 'Mrs Dawson'), whom he had met in 1864 when she was 18 or 19 and was working in an inn in Great Yarmouth. Her presence in London in 1868 precipitated a crisis with Caroline, who upped and married the 27-year-old son of a distiller, only to return two years later when her marriage failed. He had three children by Martha (the first in 1869), all of whom he acknowledged and provided for. See Catherine Peters, *The King of Inventors: a Life of Wilkie Collins*, 1993.

COLLINS, WILLIAM (1721–59) British poet, was born in Chichester, the son of a hatter who was twice mayor of the city, and was educated at Winchester College and The Queen's College, Oxford, transferring to Magdalen as a scholar in 1741. In 1742 he published anonymously *Persian Eclogues*, four short extravaganzas in heroic couplets. His father died in 1744, and Collins, in debt and without a job, visited his uncle, Colonel Martin, serving in Flanders, who concluded that he was 'too indolent even for the army'. *Odes on Several Descriptive and Allegorical Subjects* (1746, dated 1747), his most substantial work, albeit only 12 poems, was neglected by the public. A plan sponsored by JOHNSON, who got him a commission to translate ARISTOTLE's 'Poetics', foundered in 1749 when Colonel Martin died, leaving the poet £2000; whereupon he repaid his debts and abandoned the project. His last known poem, 'An Ode on the Popular Superstitions of the Highlands of Scotland', was written in 1749. In the final years of his life depression became insanity. After his death his sister destroyed his surviving manuscripts. As befits his feckless way of life and his mercurial nature, true poetry flashes only intermittently in his works, of which the deeply-felt lyric, 'Ode: Written in the Beginning of the Year 1746' ('How sleep the brave . . .') and the unrhymed 'Ode to Evening' are regarded as his most accomplished. See Edward G. Ainsworth, *Poor Collins: His Life, His Art and His Influence*, 1937. See also THOMAS GRAY.

COLUM, PADRAIC (1881–1972) Irish poet, dramatist, and novelist, was born in Longford in the workhouse of which his father was at the time manager, and was educated at Glasthule National School, Sandycove. He worked as a railways' clerk until he was 22, when, with his poetry now beginning to be published, he was the recipient of a five-year scholarship from an American benefactor to further his literary studies and career. He was a founder member of the Abbey Theatre, for which he wrote *The Land* (1905), *The Fiddler's House* (1907, originally produced in 1903 as *Broken Soil*), and *Thomas Muskery* (1910), plays in which country folk are revealed as being more resilient and of a more worthwhile nature than people of the towns.

His poetry, much of the best of which appeared in *Wild Earth* (1907), was popular for its simple, nostalgic evocations of rural Ireland, as in 'A Ballad-Maker', 'A Cradle Song', 'The Plougher', and 'She Moved Through the Fair'—the later 'Monkeys' demonstrates a philosophical outlook but the same powers of observation. In 1914 he and his wife Mary (1884–1957), née Maguire, emigrated to the USA, where she became a respected literary critic and collaborated with him to write a volume of literary reminiscences, *Our Friend James Joyce* (1958). He continued to write poetry, and also made a name for his children's stories and retellings of Irish and classical legends, through which he was commissioned by the local administration to research and write up the folklore of Hawaii (1937). His novel *The Flying Swans* (1957) is a detailed reconstruction of life and the conflicts of class in rural Ireland in the late 19th century. See *The Poet's Circuits: Collected Poems of Ireland*, new edn 1981; *Selected Poems of Padraic Colum*, ed. Sanford Sternlicht, 1989; Zack Bowen, *Padraic Colum*, 1970 (critical study).

COMPTON, FRANCES SNOW see ADAMS, HENRY.

COMPTON-BURNETT, IVY (1884–1969) British novelist, was born in Pinner, Middlesex, the eldest of seven children of a crusading homeopathic doctor and his second wife—his first wife died in 1882, leaving five children who did not get on with their stepmother. She was educated at Addiscombe College, Hove, and the Royal Holloway College, where she took a degree in classics. After *Dolores* (1911), a heavy novel in Victorian style which she later claimed was largely written by her brother Noel (1887–1916), she wrote nothing until *Pastors and Masters* (1925). This established the distinctive ethos and literary style which pervade 18 further novels—*The Last and the First* (1971) was published posthumously. All are set at the end of the Victorian age and depict an enclosed community, such as a decayed country house or a school. In each, a tyrant, male or female, dominates the lesser characters (teachers, servants, companions or, most often, children), while a subsidiary group of hangers-on (solicitors, doctors, friends, relations) make up the complement. Casual revelations of crimes, carnal sins, and human failings (especially jealousy and acquisitiveness) motivate the plots, and the villains are more often condemned out of their own mouths than suffer at the hands of society or of their fellows. The actions are carried through almost entirely in dialogue, sometimes overheard through a keyhole or by a similar device, giving full play to the author's brilliant but austere wit. Especially recommended are *A Family and a Fortune* (1939), *Manservant and*

Maidservant (1947), and *Mother and Son* (1955). She was made CBE in 1951 and DBE in 1967. See Hilary Spurling, *Ivy When Young: the Early Life of Ivy Compton-Burnett 1884–1919*, 1974, and *Secrets of a Woman's Heart: the Later Life of Ivy Compton-Burnett 1920–1969*, 1984, one volume edn as *Ivy: the Life of Ivy Compton-Burnett*, 1996; Kathy Gentile, *Ivy Compton Burnett*, 1991 (critical study).

CONAN DOYLE, ARTHUR see DOYLE.

CONGREVE, WILLIAM (1670–1729) British dramatist, was born in Bardsey, Yorkshire, the son of an army officer who was soon afterwards appointed commander of the garrison at Youghal in Ireland. He was educated at Kilkenny College and Trinity College, Dublin (at both of which he was a contemporary of SWIFT), and then studied law in London, for which he had little inclination. His first published work was a novel, *Incognita, or Love and Duty Reconcil'd* (1692), by 'Cleophil', according to him 'written in the idler hours of a fortnight's time'. A comedy, *The Old Batchelour*, written four years earlier to amuse himself 'in a slow recovery from a fit of sickness', was put on in 1693 and ran for 14 days, a very successful run at that time—DRYDEN declared it to be the best first play he had ever seen. *The Double-Dealer*, performed later the same year and published in 1694, though also termed 'a comedy', has a darker side, which may account for its failure. *Love for Love* (1695), his best-constructed piece, restored his reputation and has remained the most frequently performed of his plays. *The Mourning Bride* (1697) is an out-and-out tragedy, but still packed the houses in its day.

In 1698 there appeared an attack on the prevailing spirit of theatrical comedy, *Short View of the Immorality and Prophaneness of the English Stage*, by a Nonconformist minister, Jeremy Collier (1650–1726). Congreve replied with *Amendments of Dr Collier's False and Imperfect Citations* (1698), but by general consent he got the worst of the argument. *The Way of the World* (1700) contains some of the most dazzling wit and repartee in Restoration drama, scenes of brilliant inventiveness, and cleverly drawn and contrasted characters, notably the two pairs of lovers, Mirabell and Millamant on the one hand, and the scheming adulterers, Fainall and Marwood, on the other. Though it was not quite the total failure often ascribed to it, and it reads the best of all comedies of manners, its initial reception was such that Congreve gave up writing for the stage at the age of 30. He was for a time VANBRUGH's colleague in the management of the new Haymarket Theatre, built in 1705, but his masque, *The Judgement of Paris* (1701), was published but never performed. The rest of his life was spent enjoying a series of near sinecures (he was Commissioner for Licensing Hackney Coaches until 1705, when he became Commissioner of Wine Licences, and he was appointed Secretary for Jamaica in 1714), and delighting in his many friends—unlike the main body of wits of the time, he is said never to have given offence to anyone. Latterly he suffered from blindness and gout, but basked in the regular company, and favours, of Henrietta, Duchess of Marlborough (*d.* 1733), to whom he left the bulk of his estate on the understanding that it would ultimately go to her (and supposedly his) daughter, Lady Mary Godolphin. See *Complete Plays*, ed. Hubert Davis, 1967; David Thomas, *William Congreve*, 1992 (critical study).

CONNOLLY, CYRIL (1903–74) British critic and editor, was born in Coventry, the only child of a regular army officer from a military family and his Irish wife, whom he had met and married when his regiment was posted to Ireland. The boy was taken to Ireland, South Africa, Corsica, and Tangier, before being sent to a preparatory school in Bath and then to St Wulfric's, where he was a contemporary and friend of ORWELL. He won scholarships to Eton and to Balliol College, Oxford, where his eclectic and hedonistic tastes informed his critical acumen and his prose style but affected his studies—he finished with a third in modern history. He developed as a writer with the encouragement of the American-born man of letters, Logan Pearsall Smith (1865–1946), whose secretary and travelling companion he was for a time. After marrying the first of his three wives in 1930, he travelled Europe in comfort, and wrote his only novel, *The Rock Pool* (1936), a satirical, semi-autobiographical study of life and character on the French Riviera. It was published in Paris, having been regarded as rather too daring for publication in Britain, where it finally appeared in 1947. *Enemies of Promise* (1938; rev. edn 1949) began as a 'didactic enquiry into the problem of how to write a book which lasts ten years', and developed into a series of critical insights into social and literary topics whose third part, 'A Georgian Boyhood', is a classic account of childhood. In 1939 he founded, with SPENDER, the prestigious literary monthly, *Horizon*, which he edited for the whole of its existence until 1950.

The Unquiet Grave (1944; rev. edn 1945), 'A Word Cycle by Palinurus' (the navigator in VIRGIL's *Aeneid* who fell asleep and went overboard), is a philosophical investigation into the mind of a writer, with many supporting literary quotations. From 1951 until his death he contributed a regular literary column to the *Sunday Times*. He published four volumes of articles and reviews (1945–73). His second wife, whom he married in 1950 and from whom he was divorced in 1956, was Barbara Skelton (1915–96), whose memoirs of her amorous life, *Tears Before Bedtime* (1987) and *Weep No More* (1989), are both amusing and scurrilous about him. He was made CBE in 1972. See *Selected Essays*, ed. Peter Levi, 1992; Clive Fisher, *Cyril Connolly: a Nostalgic Life*, new edn 1996 (biography); Jeremy Lewis, *Cyril Connolly: a Life*, 1997.

CONQUEST, ROBERT (*b.* 1917) British poet, critic, editor, and historian, was born in Great Malvern, Worcestershire, and educated at Winchester College, Magdalen College, Oxford, and Grenoble University. During World War II he served in the Oxfordshire and Buckinghamshire Light Infantry. He was then for ten years a member of the Diplomatic Service, and subsequently held various research and teaching fellowships at American universities. *Poems* (1955) expressed his avowed preference for themes illustrating 'the poet's relationship to the phenomenal universe—in particular to landscape, women, art and war', and for forms which are 'usually, though not always, traditional'. His anthology, *New Lines* (1956), brought together for the first time the poetry of nine emerging poets, including AMIS, ENRIGHT, THOM GUNN, JENNINGS, LARKIN, and WAIN, as well as himself, collectively representing what for the sake of convenience was briefly dubbed the Movement, whose work had the quality of control, combined with clarity and a certain wit. *New Lines 2* was published in 1963. Conquest's interest in science fiction has inspired several poems, as well as his compilation *Spectrum: a Science Fiction Anthology* (5 vols 1961–65), in collaboration with Amis, with whom he wrote *The Egyptologists* (1965), a comic mystery story with an antiquarian theme. He is the author of political and historical studies of the USSR, including *The Great Terror: Stalin's Purge of the Thirties* (1968; rev. edn 1973) and a biography of Stalin (1991).

CONRAD, JOSEPH (1857–1924) novelist and short-story writer, was born Teodor Josef Konrad Korzeniowski, near Mohilow in Poland. His father, a member of a landed family and a literary personality who had translated SHAKESPEARE and HUGO into Polish, brought his family to Warsaw in 1862 to start up a literary periodical, though this was a front for his political activity against Russian rule, for which he was exiled to the Urals. His wife accompanied him with the child, but she died in 1865. Father and son were allowed to leave Russia in 1867; on his father's death in 1869, the boy became the ward of his uncle, and studied classics and German at St Anne High School in Cracow. When he was 16 he persuaded his guardian to let him go to sea; he served in various French ships based at Marseilles, including one involved in gun-running for the Spanish Carlist cause. Ashore, he seems to have lost money by gam-

bling, and on one occasion he attempted suicide. In 1878 he joined the British ship, *Mavis*, bound for Constantinople, and returned with it to Lowestoft, Suffolk, hardly knowing a word of English. Yet he now determined to become a British seaman. He learned English while serving on a coastal ship plying between Lowestoft and Newcastle, and then worked his way in other vessels, having adventures which later reappeared in his novels. He qualified as third mate in 1880, mate in 1883, and master in 1886, when he changed his name and took British citizenship.

His first command lasted from January 1888 to March 1889, after which, while waiting around on shore for another ship, he had the breakfast table cleared earlier than usual one day, and began to write a novel, as he describes in *Some Reminiscences* (1912): 'The necessity which compelled me was a hidden, obscure necessity, a completely masked and unaccountable phenomenon. . . . Till I began to write that novel I had written nothing but letters. . . . The conception of a planned book was entirely outside my mental range.' (It would have spoilt an otherwise perfectly reasonable record to have revealed that in 1886 he wrote a story for the magazine *Tit Bits* which was not printed.) The unfinished manuscript of the novel accompanied him on subsequent voyages, including a traumatic trip on a Congo steamer which broke his health and almost his spirit. In January 1894 he resigned from the Merchant Navy, finished his novel, which was based on his experiences in and off the Malayan Archipelago in 1887–89, and submitted it to T. Fisher Unwin, whose reader, Edward Garnett (see GARNETT), recommended it for publication—it appeared as *Almayer's Folly* (1895)—and encouraged him to write more. *An Outcast of the Islands* (1896) and *The Nigger of the 'Narcissus'* (1897; in USA as *The Children of the Sea*, 1897) were followed by several further novels, notably *Nostromo* (1904), *The Secret Agent* (1907), and *Under Western Eyes* (1911), a psychological and political study in the ironical strain which runs through most of his work, and by volumes of short stories—'Heart of Darkness' first appeared in *Youth: a Narrative and Two Other Stories* (1902) and 'The Secret Sharer' in *'Twixt Land & Sea: Tales* (1912).

Conrad married a typist (the daughter of a warehouseman) in 1896 and they had two children. Family life in London was made more difficult by illness, despondency, and money problems. His fortunes changed with the publication in the USA of *Chance* (1913), in which he deliberately employed his craft to appeal to a wider public with a story, in two parts ('The Damsel' and 'The Knight'), of strange passion and remorse, with a happy ending. In *Victory* (1915) he pursued a similar theme of the redemption of a young woman abused by fate, but paradoxically, now that his reputation was assured and his financial position relieved, the inspirational and innovatory vein that had distinguished his work began to fade.

Conrad was a depressive nihilist whose attempts to find an identity and to express his views on the nature of human existence, though written in a language which he only consciously began to learn when he was 21 and never spoke clearly, took the English novel out of the Victorian age and gave it new dimensions. The exotic or romantic settings, the horrors, and many of the situations are real, and as is particularly exemplified in *Lord Jim* (1900), which was originally intended as a short story, he uses techniques entirely his own to build up the story line in such a way that complex designs and ambiguous motives are most vividly revealed. See *The Complete Short Fiction, Vol. 1: The Lagoon and Other Stories, Vol. 2: The Informer and Other Stories, Vol. 3: Heart of Darkness and Other Tales, Vol. 4: The Duel and Other Tales*, ed. Samuel Hynes, 1992–94; Jeffrey Meyers, *Joseph Conrad: a Biography*, 1991; Jocelyn Baines, *Joseph Conrad: a Critical Biography*, new edn 1993; John Batchelor, *The Life of Joseph Conrad*, new edn 1996 (critical biography); Gavin Young, *In Search of Conrad*, new edn 1992 (travelogue-cum-biographical study); C. B. Cox, *Joseph Conrad: the Modern Imagination*, 1976; Cedric Watts, *A Preface to Conrad*, 2nd edn 1993; J. H. Stape (ed.), *The Cambridge Companion to Joseph Conrad*, 1996; and in J. I. M. Stewart, *Writers of the Early Twentieth Century*, 1963, reissued 1990.

CONSTANT (DE REBECQUE), BENJAMIN (HENRI) (1767–1830) novelist, prose writer, and politician, was born in Lausanne, Switzerland, of refugee Huguenot descent; his mother died a fortnight later. He was educated by private tutors and travelled with his father, an army officer in the service of the Netherlands, to Belgium, Holland, and England (London and Oxford), after which he attended the universities of Erlangen (1782–83) and Edinburgh (1783–85). He then settled in Paris, where he immediately indulged his lifelong passions for gambling and women. In 1787 he met Mme de Charrière (1740–1805), with whom he began a close relationship and a correspondence, and at whose home at Colombier in 1788 he fought the first of several duels in his life—the last (seated) was in 1822. He was employed at the court of Brunswick from 1788 to 1795. He married in 1789 and was divorced in 1795, having in 1794 fallen madly in love with STAËL (the daughter born in 1797 was probably his). The stormy on/off affair lasted for 17 years, whereupon he transferred his affections and attentions to Mme Récamier (1777–1849), who was later to be the confidante of CHATEAUBRIAND. Having published several political tracts, he became a French citizen in 1798 and a member of the Tribunate

in 1799, his opposition to the policies of Napoleon resulting in his being expelled, with twenty others, in 1802. He left France with Staël, who was severely displeased at his secret marriage in 1808 (as her third husband) to Charlotte von Hardenburg, with whom he had first had an affair in 1794. Though he published an anti-Napoleonic treatise among other writings in 1814, he advised the Emperor during the 'Hundred Days' in 1815 between Napoleon's return to France from Elba and the battle of Waterloo, after which he wrote an apologia for his actions and had his exile revoked by Louis XVIII. His short novel *Adolphe*, a stylish exploration of personality, on which he had been working for ten years, was published in London and Paris in 1816 (tr. Alexander Walker, 1816). *Cécile*, a fictional version of his tangled relationships with Staël and Charlotte, which he never finished, turned up in 1948 and was published in 1951 (tr. Norman Cameron, 1952). In 1819 he was first elected to the Chamber of Deputies, in which as a liberal leader of the opposition he represented successively Sarthe, Paris, and the Lower Rhine until his death. He was given a state funeral. He also published *De la Religion Considérée dans Sa Source, Ses Formes et Ses Développements* (1824–31). See *Political Writings*, ed. Biancamaria Fontana, 1988; Dennis Wood, *Benjamin Constant: a Biography*, 1993.

COOK, GEORGE CRAM see GLASPELL.

COOKE, JOHN ESTEN (1830–86) American novelist, was born near Winchester of a prominent Virginia family, and was educated at Charlestown Academy. He then studied law and was admitted to the Virginia Bar in 1851, but preferred to be a writer. *Harper's Magazine* printed several of his stories; he also published historical romances of Virginia society, of which *The Virginia Comedians: or, Old Days in the Old Dominion* (1854), set just before the American War of Independence (1775–83), is regarded as having most merit. In the Civil War (1861–65) he rose quickly from private to captain in the Confederate army, and was in charge of a cannon at Bull Run. In *Surry of Eagle's Nest: or, The Memoirs of a Staff-Officer Serving in Virginia* (1866), 'Edited from the MSS of Colonel Surry', to which *Mohun: or, The Last Days of Lee and His Paladins . . .* (1868) is a sequel, he combined accurate historical action, bolstered by footnotes, with melodrama and romance. The revised edition of his life (1863) of General Thomas ('Stonewall') Jackson (1824–63), under whom he served, was published as *Stonewall Jackson: a Military Biography* (1866). After the Civil War he married, and settled on an estate in Clarke County, where he wrote further romances and historical studies.

COOPER, ANTHONY ASHLEY see
SHAFTESBURY.

COOPER, JAMES FENIMORE (1789–
1851) American novelist and social critic, was
born James Cooper (he added the middle
name, that of his mother's family, later) in
Burlington, New Jersey, the son of Judge William Cooper (1754–1809), who in 1790 moved
his family to his frontier settlement of Cooperstown, New York. The boy was educated
locally, and then for two years at the home of
a rector in Albany in preparation for Yale,
from which he was expelled in 1805 for playing pranks. He served before the mast at sea,
and was in 1808 commissioned as a midshipman in the US Navy. Having inherited his father's fortune, he resigned from the service in
1811 to marry Susan De Lancey, a member of
a patrician family which had retained some
of its lands after siding with the British during the American War of Independence
(1775–83). The couple had two sons and five
daughters, and lived in Mamaroneck and
then Cooperstown, before building a house
at Angevine Farm, near Scarsdale. To settle a
bet with his wife, Cooper wrote (anonymously) *Precaution* (1820), an English novel
of manners in the style of one he had been
reading to her. Having now discovered a talent (and a potential source of income without
having to rely on the De Lanceys to maintain
his social position while his father's estate
was still circumvented with legal obstruc-
tions), he wrote *The Spy: a Tale of the Neutral
Ground* (1821), a historical romance involving
a double agent, which is the first significant
novel about the War of Independence. He
now moved into New York City, where he
founded the exclusive literary and artistic
Bread and Cheese Club. While his initial literary pretentiousness matched the social affectation he displayed all his life, he was conscious of the need to exploit to the full the
new nation's 'poverty of materials' as a
source of literature. Before sailing with his
family for Europe in 1826, he published *The
Pilot* (1823), with which he virtually invented
the sea story; with *The Pioneers* (1823) and *The
Last of the Mohicans* (1826) he established the
foundation of his grand design and created,
in the character of Natty Bumppo, the quint-
essential frontiersman. The five 'Leather-
Stocking Tales', in which Bumppo appears in
various guises, are (in chronological order)
The Deerslayer (1841), *The Last of the Mohicans*,
The Pathfinder (1840), *The Pioneers*, and *The
Prairie* (1827).

His seven years in Europe included two extensive stays in Paris, where he met the reformer, the Marquis de Lafayette (1757–
1834), at whose request he wrote *Notions of
the Americans* (1828), designed to redress European misconceptions. He also wrote two
more notable sea stories, *The Red Rover* (1827)
and *The Water Witch* (1830), and three Euro-

pean historical romances. Among the latter
was *The Bravo: a Venetian Story* (1831), whose
reception in the American press moved him
to counter with *A Letter to His Countrymen*
(1834), in which he announced that he would
write no more novels; a resolution he shortly
broke. Back home at Cooperstown, he further
embroiled himself in controversy by refusing
public access to a point on Otsego Lake
which was a favourite picnic spot. When the
press attacked him, he responded with a series of libel suits. In *The American Democrat*
(1838) he defended a political stance which
upheld both democracy and the preservation
of the status of the gentleman. This brought
further attacks, which were intensified in the
form of objections to aspects of his *The History of the Navy of the United States of America*
(1839). The three 'Littlepage Novels', *Satans-
toe* (1845), *The Chainbearer* (1845), and *The
Redskins: or, Indian or Injin* (1846), constitute a
family saga which culminates in the Anti-
Rent disturbances of 1839–46, with whose
supporters he was in sympathy. The judgment of history, and the continuing popularity of his principal works as nostalgic evocations of a pioneering society, run counter to
the wickedly funny critique by TWAIN—'Fenimore Cooper's Literary Offenses'—in *The
Writings of Mark Twain*, Vol. XXII (1911)—in
which he claims: 'In one place in *Deerslayer*,
and in the restricted space of two-thirds of a
page, Cooper has scored 114 offenses against
literary art out of a possible 115. It breaks the
record.' See James Grossman, *James Fenimore
Cooper*, 1949 (biography); Alan Taylor, *William Cooper's Town: Power and Persuasion on the
Frontier of the Early American Republic*, new
edn 1996 (sociological/historical study);
Donald A. Ring, *James Fenimore Cooper*, 1988
(biographical/critical study); George Dekker,
James Fenimore Cooper: the Novelist, 1967 (critical study).

COOPER, WILLIAM, pseudonym of
Harry Summerfield Hoff (*b.* 1910) British
novelist, was born in Crewe, the son of two
schoolteachers, and was educated at Crewe
County Secondary School and Christ's College, Cambridge. He taught in Leicester from
1933 to 1940, and did war service in the Royal
Air Force, after which he became an assistant
commissioner with the Civil Service Commission, subsequently acting as a personnel
consultant to various national bodies. Beginning with the 'lightly romantic and poetic
and funny' *Trina*, set in Yugoslavia, to which
he had never been, he published four forgotten novels as H. S. Hoff between 1934 and
1946. The assumption of the pseudonym for
Scenes from Provincial Life (1950), whose setting had affinities with Leicester, was done to
protect real identities; as well as giving him a
new literary life, it heralded a new literary
form, in which the aspirations, fears, and activities of the young provincial intellectual

class are refreshingly and incisively captured and analysed. What was planned as a sequel, *Scenes from Metropolitan Life*, was for legal reasons not published until 1982; in *Scenes from Married Life* (1961) the personal problems of Joe Lunn are happily resolved, while in *Scenes from Later Life* (1983) the characters are brought face to face with the new problems inherent in the age in which they live. In several other novels Cooper brings his sense of humour to bear on his acute observation of familiar experiences. *From Early Life* (1990) is a series of 89 numbered fragments recalling his life until he went to university.

COOVER, ROBERT (LOWELL) (b. 1932) American novelist, short-story writer, and dramatist, was born in Charles City, Iowa, and graduated from Indiana University in 1953. He served as a lieutenant in the US Naval Reserve until 1957, then took a further degree at Chicago University. He held a series of university teaching posts between 1966 and 1976, and became Writer-in-Residence at Brown University in 1979. He began writing seriously in 1957, and had a series of five poems published in *Fiddlehead* in 1960, and his first fiction in *Noble Savage* in 1961. In 1962 he began his first novel, *The Origin of the Brunists* (1966), a conscious mixture of genres and narrative techniques. The postmodernist strain continued with *The Universal Baseball Association, Inc., J. Henry Waugh, Prop.* (1968). In *Pricksongs and Descants* (1969) he collected his earlier stories (seven 'exemplary fictions', after CERVANTES, and three under the title of 'The Sentient Lens') with further retellings from new perspectives of traditional tales (from the Bible and OVID as well as from folklore) and other pieces exploring the multiple possibilities of fiction. *The Public Burning* (publication delayed until 1977 because of possible legal objections), a bizarre sequence of treatments of the execution in 1953 of the spies Ethel and Julius Rosenberg, with Richard Nixon, then Vice-President, as circus ringmaster and narrator, began as a play and was finally expanded from a novella published in *TriQuarterly* 26. Subsequent fictional works have included *Spanking the Maid* (1982), variations on a sexual fantasy which challenge concepts of reality and exposition, and *In Bed One Night and Other Brief Encounters* (1983) and *A Night at the Movies: Short Fictions* (1987), further experiments in form and language. In *John's Wife* (1996) the nature of fiction itself allegorizes life in 'a quiet prairie town'. See Lois Gordon, *Robert Coover: the Universal Fictionmaking Process*, 1983 (critical study); Jackson Cope, *Robert Coover's Fictions*, 1986 (critical study).

CORELLI, MARIE (1855–1924) British novelist, was brought up as Minnie Mackay, and was almost certainly the daughter of Charles Mackay (1814–89), a journalist and minor Scottish poet, and Mary Elizabeth Mills (1830–76), a widow whom he married in 1861, a year after the death of his first wife. She never publicly acknowledged either of her parents (she claimed to be adopted) and always lied about her age. When she was 14 she was sent to a convent, after which she had a brief career as a concert pianist, under the name of Signorina Marie Corelli, which she retained permanently. After some poems and a story had been published, *A Romance of Two Worlds* (1886) was accepted for publication, followed the same year by the more melodramatic *Vendetta: or, The Story of One Forgotten*. They, and several more novels, were greeted politely by prominent individuals and with hostility by the critics, on whom she tried unsuccessfully to turn the tables with an anonymous satire, *The Silver Domino* (1892). *Barabbas: a Dream of the World's Tragedy* (1893), an overblown account of the Crucifixion and Resurrection, launched her into the bestseller class. *The Sorrows of Satan: or, The Strange Experience of One Geoffrey Tempest, Millionaire* (1895), aided by being one of the earliest novels to be published in a single volume at 6 shillings, achieved the highest sales on and immediately after publication of any English novel up to that time. In 1899 she moved from London to Stratford-upon-Avon, where her tactlessness and her belief in her own destiny outweighed her attempts at generosity. Local friction was intensified by a libel action in 1903 (she was awarded a derisory farthing's damages), and by her conviction during World War I for hoarding sugar. Her writing was genuinely felt and unashamedly sensational, with mystical undercurrents or pseudo-religious wrappings, and reflected the tastes of the public for the comparatively short time she was in vogue. She never married (though she indulged in some embarrassing flirtations), her faithful companion from 1876 being Bertha Vyver (1856–1942), who edited her posthumous *Poems* (1925).

CORNEILLE, PIERRE (1606–84) French dramatist and critic, was born in Rouen, the elder brother of the dramatist Thomas Corneille (1625–1709), and (his father being a magistrate) was educated there for the law, which he was licensed to practise in 1624. *Mélite*, a comedy of romantic intrigue which had been performed in Rouen, was in 1630 played in Paris, where he produced more of the same kind and was briefly a member of the stable of dramatists sponsored by Cardinal Richelieu (1585–1642), who in 1634 established the Académie Française to regulate linguistic and literary standards. *Médée* (1635; tr. 1639), a tragedy from Greek legend, gave notice of a deeper talent. It was confirmed by *Le Cid* (1637; tr. J. Rutter as *The Cid*, 1637), a tragicomedy based on a Spanish piece, which offended members of the Académie for its apparent disregard of their own interpretation of the dramatic unities of ARISTOTLE. In spite of the plaudits of the public, Corneille was sufficiently discouraged to go into temporary retirement, from which he emerged with the Roman tragedies *Horace* (1640), *Cinna* (1641), and *Polyeucte Martyr* (1643; tr. William Lower as *Polyeuctes*, 1655), in the last of which the personal predicaments inherent in the conflict between Christianity and paganism are played out in heroic manner. *La Mort de Pompée* (1643) was performed in Dublin (1663) in a version by KATHERINE PHILIPS, and in London (1664) in an adaptation by 'certain persons of honour', who included SEDLEY and WALLER. *Le Menteur* (1643; tr. as *The Mistaken Beauty: or, The Liar*, 1685) looks forward, in its comic invention, to MOLIÈRE. After a failure in 1652, he produced nothing for the stage until *Oedipe* (1659), after which he continued writing tragedies until 1674. His influence on the development of 17th-century English heroic drama was considerable, particularly in his use of rhyming couplets for tragedy, and he is cited continuously by DRYDEN in *Of Dramatick Poesie*. There are modern translations by John Cairncross (1975, 1980).

CORNFORD, FRANCES (1886–1960), née Darwin, British poet, was born in Cambridge, the only child by his second marriage of Sir Francis Darwin (1848–1925), the third son of DARWIN. She was privately educated. After her mother's death when she was 17, she lived in Cambridge for the rest of her life, marrying Francis Cornford (1874–1943), later Professor of Ancient Philosophy. RUPERT BROOKE was a frequent visitor to the house and gave her critical advice and encouragement. Her first book, *Poems*, was published in 1910. Her better verse is distinctive rather than distinguished, and often reflects a sudden observation, revelation, or experience: not only the bizarre 'To a Lady Seen from the Train' ('O why do you walk through the field in gloves . . .'), but also 'Pre-Existence', 'Childhood', and 'All Souls' Night'. Her eldest son, John Cornford (1915–36), enlisted in the International Brigade in the Spanish Civil War and was killed in battle. He had had poems published in literary journals and wrote several about the action in Spain. Frances Cornford was awarded the Queen's Gold Medal for Poetry in 1959. Her half-brother, Bernard Darwin (1876–1961), was a notable journalist and writer on golf, and compiled *The Oxford Dictionary of Quotations* (1941). See *Collected Poems*, 1954; *Selected Poems*, ed. Jane Dowson and Hugh Cornford, 1996.

CORNWELL, DAVID see LE CARRÉ.

CORTÁZAR, JULIO (1914–84) Argentinian novelist and short-story writer, was born in Brussels, Belgium, and returned to Buenos Aires with his parents in 1918. He qualified as a teacher, and in 1938 published a book of verse as Julio Denís. He worked as a high school teacher in Bolivar and Chivilcoy, and then taught French literature at the University of Cuyo, from which he resigned after being briefly imprisoned for protesting against the Perón regime in 1945. He then worked for the Argentine publishers' association while studying for a degree as a public translator. In the same month in which he published his first collection of stories, *Bestiario* (1951), he left Argentina for Paris, where he became a freelance translator for Unesco, and in 1981 a French citizen. His penchant for investing ordinary situations with mystery and phantasmagoric elements of fear was apparent in his first novel, *Los Premios* (1960; tr. Elaine Kerrigan as *The Winners*, 1965), in which the winners of a free cruise return having been nowhere. In *Rayuela* (1963; tr. Gregory Rabassa as *Hopscotch*, 1966), the illogicalities of life and the random actions of the protagonists are reflected in the structure of the narrative. See also *End of the Game and Other Stories*, tr. Paul Blackburn (1967), and *A Change of Light and Other Stories*, tr. Rabassa (1980). See Ilan Stavans, *Julio Cortazar: a Study of the Short Fiction*, new edn 1994.

COUVREUR, JESSIE see TASMA.

COWARD, (SIR) NOËL (1899–1973) British dramatist, actor, and songwriter, was born in Teddington, Middlesex, of a musical family, and had an irregular formal education before beginning his professional acting career in 1911 in a fairy play, *The Goldfish*; after this he regularly played child parts. By 1917 he had written several plays, of which one, the naturalistic *The Rat Trap*, was produced in 1924. He wrote and acted in *I'll Leave It to You* (1920), but his first real success was the comedy, *The Young Idea* (1922). *The Vortex* (1924), about drug addiction, created a sensation and ran for seven months, which was as long as he allowed himself to stay in one part. He directed, but did not act in, his comedy of manners, *Hay Fever* (1925), which ran for 337 performances. After a nervous breakdown and three failures, he came back with the operetta, *Bitter Sweet* (1929), and the romantic comedy, *Private Lives* (1930), while also writing revues. The patriotism which inspired the production, *Cavalcade* (1931), resurfaced in *In Which We Serve* (1942), the famous war film which he wrote and co-directed, and in which he starred. *Blithe Spirit* (1941), his most lasting comedy, is written with the poise and grace of a master. To ensure his financial stability in the light of the huge earnings from his cabaret performances in London and Las Vegas in the 1950s, he went to live permanently abroad, in Switzerland as well as Jamaica, where he built a house in 1948, and later a retreat on the hill above it. He directed *Hay Fever* at the National Theatre in 1964, and made his last appearance on the London stage in 1966. The ultimate all-rounder, as well as in person the epitome of the modern wit, he wrote a novel, *Pomp and Circumstance* (1960), short stories—see *The Collected Short Stories* (1962)—, and several volumes of reminiscences and diaries. He was knighted in 1970. See *Plays*, introduction by Raymond Mander and Joe Mitcheson, 5 vols 1979–83; *Autobiography*, introduction by Sheridan Morley, new edn 1992; *The Noël Coward Diaries*, ed. Graham Payn and Sheridan Morley, new edn 1991; Clive Fisher, *Noël Coward*, 1992 (biography); Philip Hoare, *Noël Coward: a Biography*, new edn 1996.

COWLEY, ABRAHAM (1618–67) English poet and essayist, was born in London, the posthumous son of a bookseller, and was educated at Westminster School and Trinity College, Cambridge, having already published *Poetical Blossomes* (1633). He became a Fellow of Trinity in 1640 but, like his friend CRASHAW, was expelled by the Puritans. He went to royalist-held Oxford, from where he joined the King's supporters in Paris. He was some kind of special agent, and on a mission to England was imprisoned in 1655, but with an assurance of £1000, put up by a friend, was released on bail. Between then and the Restoration of the Monarchy in 1660, he studied medicine, qualified as a doctor, and published *Poems* (1656). This considerable volume included an unfinished religious epic ('Davideis'); 'Pindarique Odes' (in rhyming free verse); *The Mistress* (appeals to or complaints about an unresponsive, and unknown, lady, originally published separately in 1647); and 'Miscellanies', mainly elegies and lyrics. Cowley's contemporary popularity as a poet must be measured against his closeness in time to SPENSER, JONSON, and DONNE, and the fact that his Pindarics became a vogue. At the Restoration he did not receive the preferential treatment he felt he had earned, but his fellowship was restored and the Crown gave him a favourable lease on an estate at Chertsey, Surrey. Here he retired to write, not so much poetry (except in Latin), as a series of lucid and graceful essays in the manner of MONTAIGNE on such general subjects as obscurity, liberty, solitude, and the garden. They are the work of a contented bachelor and professed Epicurean, who had declared in 'Anacreontics', 'After death I nothing crave, / Let me alive my pleasures have. / All are Stoics in the grave.' A biographical study was included in his *Works* (1668), edited by his friend, Thomas Sprat (1635–1713), Dean of Westminster. See *Poetry and Prose, with Sprat's Life*, ed. L. C. Martin, new edn 1988.

COWPER, WILLIAM (1731–1800) British poet, was born in Great Berkhamstead, Hert-

fordshire, the son of the rector of the parish. His mother, a descendant of DONNE, died when he was six, and he was sent to a local boarding school, where he was bullied, and then to Westminster School, after which he studied law. In 1750 he fell in love with his cousin Theodora (to whom, as 'Delia', he addressed several poems), but was forbidden to marry her because of his incipient madness. In 1763, unable to face the interview for a clerkship at the House of Lords, he attempted suicide, and was for a time confined in an asylum. On his discharge, and with a pension from friends and family, he lodged with a clergyman and his wife, Morley and Mary Unwin. On Morley's death in 1767, Cowper set up house with Mary (1724–96) in Olney, Buckinghamshire, and would have married her but for recurring fits of madness. Here, with the local rector, John Newton (1725–1807), he wrote *Olney Hymns* (1779); among the 66 which he contributed are 'God moves in a mysterious way . . .', 'Hark, my soul! It is the Lord . . .', and 'Sometimes a light surprises . . .'. *Poems* (1782) was indifferently received.

In 1781 he had met Lady Austen (d. 1802), a lively young widow, with whom he struck up such a rapport that for a time she lived in the unoccupied portion of their house—she is referred to as 'Anna' or 'Sister Ann' in his poems. In 1783 she suggested he write a poem in blank verse about a sofa. At the end of a year's work, it had become a 5200-line paean on country life, with comments on topical issues, in six books: 'Not having the music of rhyme, it requires so close an attention to the pause and cadence . . . as to render it . . . the most difficult species of poetry I have ever meddled with.' It was included, with the hilarious song 'John Gilpin' (the story of which he had heard from Lady Austen), in *Poems II* (1785), which made him famous. He was a most versatile poet, who left a mass of occasional poems, the last of which, 'The Castaway', reflects the turmoil of his illnesses. His poetry was exactly right for his time in that it was direct and often raised everyday sights and activities to genuine poetic levels, while speaking also for the Methodist and Evangelical movements. His letters—see *Selected Letters*, ed. James King and Charles Ryskamp (1989)—especially those on domestic and literary matters, are as felicitously written as any in the language. See *The Task and Other Selected Poems*, ed. James Sambrook, 1994; David Cecil, *The Stricken Deer*, new edn 1988 (biography).

COYLE, WILLIAM see KENEALLY.

COZZENS, JAMES GOULD (1903–78) American novelist, was born in Chicago, which his parents were visiting from Rhode Island, and was brought up in Staten Island, New York, where he went to Staten Island

Academy until he was old enough to be sent away to school. He graduated from Kent in 1922, having already had work printed in *Atlantic Monthly*. He was a sophomore at Harvard when his first novel, *Confusion* (1924), was published, which 'went to my head, and I took a year's leave of absence to write [*Michael Scarlett* (1925)]'. He never returned. Instead he went for a year to Cuba to teach the children of American engineers at a sugar mill, which provided the background for two more novels, *Cock Pit* (1928) and *The Son of Perdition* (1929). He then spent some months during 1926–27 in Europe as tutor to the poliomyletic son of travelling Americans, an experience which he later used in *Ask Me Tomorrow* (1940). In 1927 he married the head of the manuscript department of his literary agent. With *The Just and the Unjust* (1942), his first really major novel, he laid out his distinctive territory, to which he returned in *By Love Possessed* (1957), in which a lawyer whose family has long held a privileged position in a small community is the focal point of dramatic disorder within it. From Cozzens's service as a major in the US Army Air Force during World War II derived his Pulitzer prize-winning novel, *Guard of Honor* (1948)—three days on an air base during which the ramifications of a near miss between aircraft landing on the runway are played out.

CRABBE, GEORGE (1754–1832) British poet, was born in Aldeburgh, Suffolk, the eldest child of a salt-tax collector. A bookish boy, he went to school in Stowmarket, was apprenticed to a surgeon, worked in a warehouse while studying, and, in about 1777, set up practice himself. He had in 1774 published a didactic poem, 'Inebriety', and in 1780, engaged to be married and unable to make medicine pay, he went to London to try to sell his manuscripts. Though his poem 'The Candidate' was published in the *Monthly Review*, he was almost destitute when BURKE responded to a plea for help, secured a publisher for *The Library* (1781), had the poet to stay, advised him to take holy orders, and found him a job as chaplain to the Duke of Rutland, in whose castle he finished *The Village* (1783). This anti-romantic survey of rural life ('. . . I paint the cot, / As truth will paint it, and as bards will not') earned him literary fame, and he was able to marry at last. He got several livings, but after *The News-paper* (1785), a satirical poem, he published nothing until *Poems* (1807), having made periodic bonfires of much that he had written in the meantime. *The Borough* (1810) is a series of unlinked poetic sketches, one of which, 'Peter Grimes', is the source of the opera by Benjamin Britten (1913–76). In *Tales of the Hall* (1819) two half-brothers meet after a separation and exchange experiences. Most of Crabbe's verse is in heroic couplets. He

took a realistic, moral, lower-middle-class view of life, writing with compassion and wit, and using his verse form in an original way. *The Voluntary Insane* (ed. Felix Pryor, 1995), which first came to light in a notebook discovered in 1989, is in eight-line stanzas such as VILLON employed in his 'Testament' and which he himself had used for an earlier study of madness, 'Sir Eustace Gray' (1807). Written in about 1820, its dreamlike vision of degradation involves a woman who has killed a baby in her care and is tormented by a loss of faith. See *The Complete Poetical Works*, ed. Norma Dalrymple-Champneys and Arthur Pollard, 3 vols 1988; *Selected Letters and Journals*, ed. Thomas C. Faulkner, 1985; Tony Bareham, *George Crabbe*, 1977 (critical study); Frank Whitehead, *George Crabbe: a Reappraisal*, 1996.

CRAIK, (DINAH MARIA), MRS (1826–87), née Mulock, British novelist, was born in Stoke-upon-Trent, the daughter of a minister. She was educated privately, and went to London in 1846 to support her invalid mother and two younger brothers by writing. With the help of influential friends she was able to place the novels *The Ogilvies* (1849) and *Cola Monti: or, the Story of a Genius* (1849), which were the beginning of a stream of books for children and impressionable adults. *John Halifax, Gentleman* (1856) was the novel by which she was best known in her time (and has continued to be best known); on the title pages of her subsequent books the provenance was attributed to 'The authoress of John Halifax, Gentleman'. Its hero rises from turner's apprentice to wealthy mill owner by heroic qualities and a social and moral temperament which enables him to make a successful match with someone outside his class, a rarity in Victorian fiction. Contemporary events feature again in *A Life for a Life* (1859), in which real public figures also appear. In 1864 she married George Lillie Craik, of the publishing house of Macmillan. In that year, too, she was awarded a Civil List pension of £60, which she handed over for the use of poor authors. She published two volumes of verse (1859 and 1881), from which 'Douglas, Douglas, tender and true' found its way into *The Oxford Book of Victorian Verse* (1919). In *A Woman's Thoughts about Women* (1858) Mrs Craik demonstrates a similar attitude to that so often expressed by YONGE: 'Men and women were made for, and not like one another.'

CRANE, (HAROLD) HART (1899– 1932) American poet, was born in Garrettsville, Ohio, the child of a divided marriage which ended in divorce shortly after his father became a candy manufacturer in Cleveland, where the boy attended public schools, and was writing poetry at 13. After a visit in 1916 with his mother to his grandfather's fruit farm on the Isle of Pines, south of Cuba, which gave him his first taste of the sea, he settled in New York on his own. Ostensibly he was to be tutored for college, but the pull of the literary and bohemian life of the city prevailed. On the entry of the USA into World War I in 1917, he returned to Cleveland, where he worked in a munitions plant and a shipyard. As a compromise between his fascination for machinery and having the leisure to write, he then went to work in the factory owned by his father, who determined instead to 'drive the poetry nonsense' out of him. He went back to New York, where he lived precariously and wrote 'Chaplinesque', 'My Grandmother's Love Letters', 'At Melville's Tomb', the sequence 'Voyages', and other poems which were included in *White Buildings* (1926). Thanks to the personal financial support of a banker, he was able to write *The Bridge* (1930), a sequence inspired by the sea and harbour commanded by Brooklyn Bridge, in which he offered a cosmic and a personal view of American destiny. A Guggenheim fellowship took him to Mexico with the idea of planning a long poem on that country's history. On the return voyage from what had developed into lucid intermissions between bouts of alcoholism and homosexual debauchery, he took off his coat and jumped from the stern of the ship into the sea. See *The Complete Poems of Hart Crane*, ed. Marc Simon, new edn 1993; John Unterecker, *Voyager: a Life of Hart Crane*, new edn 1987; Warner Berthoff, *Hart Crane: a Re-Introduction*, 1989 (critical study).

CRANE, STEPHEN (1871–1900) American novelist, short-story writer, and journalist, was born in Newark, New Jersey, the 14th and last child of a Methodist minister who died in 1880. He was brought up by his mother in Asbury Park, and was sent to a military prep school at Claverack, New York, in 1888. He went on in 1890 to study engineering at Lafayette College, and immediately failed his course. He was accepted by Syracuse University, from which he dropped out after two semesters, having done well in English and distinguished himself as a baseball catcher. For two years he lived in his brother's house at Lake View and friends' lodgings in New York, where he had a few abortive newspaper jobs and a serious affair of the heart. In 1893 he privately published *Maggie: a Girl of the Streets*, 'By Johnston Smith', a short, naturalistic novel of New York tenement life; not even the active support of HOWELLS could make it move from the bookshops. He also began *The Red Badge of Courage*, for which he finally found a syndicate, owned by Irving Bacheller (1859–1950), prepared to arrange serialization. Bacheller also commissioned him to write a series of reports from the West and Mexico. Before he left he managed to sell a book of verse, *The*

Black Riders and Other Lines (1895), and the volume rights of *The Red Badge of Courage: an Episode of the American Civil War* (1895), which he revised while he was in New Orleans. This study of the pressures of battle on a young, untried volunteer to the Union cause, incorporating both realistic and impressionistic techniques (its author was not yet 24 and his combat experience was in the future), made him a celebrity, and was acclaimed also in England. While 1896 saw the commercial publication of *Maggie*, two more novels (*George's Mother*, a grim portrait of East-Side society, and the semi-autobiographical *The Third Violet*), and *The Little Regiment: and Other Episodes of the American Civil War*, it also marked the beginning of a spate of largely self-imposed calamities. Either through naivety or an over-passionate nature (the evidence is conflicting), Crane allowed himself to become involved with some rather unsuitable ladies, one of whom he saved from a charge of soliciting by appearing in court as a witness. The press made a meal of the episode. In Jacksonville, Florida, where he was en route to cover (as a participant) a gunrunning expedition to the Cuban revolutionaries, he met and established a permanent ménage with Cora Stewart (1865–1910), née Taylor, madam of the Hotel de Dream, who was still married to an English army officer whom she had abandoned.

The gunrunning exploit was a fiasco in that the ship sank and Crane and a few survivors had to make land in a dinghy, though he extracted from the incident some useful publicity and an outstanding story, 'The Open Boat'. He now went to Greece to report on the Turkish war, with Cora in tow—under the name of Imogene Carter she was the first woman war correspondent. He returned via England, where he deposited her. In 1898, having tried to join the US Navy to fight in the Spanish–American War and been rejected, he went all the same as a correspondent. He was closely involved in the action in Cuba, from which he filed over twenty vivid reports, and was mentioned in dispatches by the Marines for bravery as a volunteer signalman, before being forcibly evacuated with malaria to add to his inherent tuberculosis. In 1899 he travelled back to England, where Cora had rented, as 'Mrs Crane', Brede Place, a derelict 14th-century manor house in Sussex. Here he wrote compulsively, in an ultimately unsuccessful attempt to pay the bills. Shortly after a grand Christmas party for his English literary friends, he had a violent haemorrhage. On 31 March 1900, he had two more. Cora got him to Badenweiler in the Black Forest, where he died on 5 June. See *Prose and Poetry: Maggie, A Girl of the Streets, The Red Badge of Courage, Stories, Sketches, Journalism, and Poetry* 1984; *The Portable Stephen Crane*, ed. Joseph Katz, 1969; Christopher E. G. Benfrey, *The Double Life of Stephen*

Crane, new edn 1994 (biography); Edwin H. Cady, *Stephen Crane*, rev. edn 1980 (biographical/critical study); David Halliburton, *The Color of the Sky: a Study of Stephen Crane*, 1989.

CRAPSEY, ADELAIDE (1878–1914) American poet, was born in Brooklyn Heights, New York, third of nine children of Rev. Algernon Sidney Crapsey (1847–1928), a socially aware Episcopalian clergyman who was in 1906 deposed from the ministry at his own request after being suspended by the ecclesiastical court for 'heresy'. She was brought up in Rochester, New York, and educated at Kemper Hall, a boarding school in Wisconsin, and Vassar, where she graduated with honors, managed basketball teams, and was Editor-in-Chief of the *Vassarion*. Her roommate, and later her closest friend, was a great-niece of TWAIN, Jean Webster (1876–1916), the heroine of whose famous romantic novel *Daddy-Long-Legs* (1912) is partly based on Crapsey. After two years teaching at Kemper Hall, Crapsey spent a year studying at the School of Archaeology, Rome. She was forced to give up her post as instructor of history and literature at Miss Lowe's School, Stamford, Connecticut, because of exhaustion. She returned to Europe, spending some time in the British Museum, London, working on the 'application of phonetics to metrical problems'. In 1911 she was appointed instructor in poetics at Smith College; later that year her condition was diagnosed as tuberculin meningitis. *Verse* (1915), was, according to the publisher's wife (described by her husband as a 'Delphic Woman'), prepared by Crapsey from the grave. Also published posthumously was the unfinished *A Study in English Metrics* (1918). Her prime influences were KEATS and LANDOR: 'Ah, Walter, where you lived I rue / These days come all too late for me; / What matter if her eyes are blue / Whose rival is Persephone?' (Fiesole, 1909). From her study of the Japanese *haiku* and *tanga* in translation, she invented her 'cinquain': 'Sea-foam / And coral! Oh, I'll / Climb the great pasture rocks / And dream me mermaid in the sun's / Gold flood.' ('Laurel in the Berkshires'). See *The Complete Poems and Collected Letters of Adelaide Crapsey*, ed. Susan Sutton Smith, 1977.

CRASHAW, RICHARD (c.1613–49) English poet, was born in London, the son of a Puritan clergyman, and was educated at Charterhouse and Pembroke Hall, Cambridge, becoming a Fellow of Peterhouse. In 1644 he and five colleagues were dismissed for refusing to take the oath of the Solemn League and Covenant accepting uniformity of worship according to the Reformed Church. Having formally converted to Catholicism, he spent some time in Paris before becoming an attendant to Cardinal Palotta in Rome. He died in rather suspicious circumstances while on a pilgrimage to Loreto. From an early age Crashaw wrote poetry of an occasional and celebratory nature, and his first book of verse (in Latin) was published in 1634. *Steps to the Temple: Sacred Poems; with other Delights of the Muses* (1646) is in two parts, religious and secular. Crashaw has been classified as a Metaphysical poet because of his figurative language and extravagant comparisons. His religious verse is unusual in English literature in that it is written from a Catholic standpoint, and in his use of rhyme and rhythm, recurrent verbal motifs, and resounding climaxes, he demonstrates a keen ear for music and makes a conspicuous contribution to the cultural counter-Reformation. Most typical of his technique are 'The Flaming Heart' and other odes to St Teresa, especially those written in his favourite metre of octosyllabic couplets, and 'The Weeper' (to Mary Magdalene), in which the extravagant conceits are typically baroque. 'In the Holy Nativity of Our Lord God' takes the form of a Greek pastoral sung by shepherds and chorus. A memorable secular poem is 'Wishes to his Supposed Mistress', beginning 'Whoe'er she be—/ That not impossible She'. See *The Poems*, ed. L. C. Martin, 2nd edn 1957.

CRAWFORD, ISABELLA VALANCY (1850–87) Canadian poet, was born in Dublin, one of only three of the 12 or 13 children of Dr Stephen D. Crawford to survive childhood. In 1858 she came with her parents via Wisconsin to Canada, where her father was the first doctor in Paisley, Canada West. They moved on to Lakefield in about 1865, after his conviction for misappropriation of funds as municipal treasurer; from there they went to Peterborough, where he died in 1875, and her only surviving sister in 1876. She must have persuaded her mother that they should go to Toronto, where she might find outlets for her writing, which was the only means of supporting them both. She contributed stories to Canadian and American magazines; some of those which have been traced are in *Selected Stories of Isabella Valancy Crawford*, ed. Penny Petrone (1977). The only book published during her lifetime, and that at her own expense, was *Old Spookses' Pass, Malcolm's Katie, and Other Poems* (1884), of which only fifty copies were sold out of an edition of 1000, despite favourable notices in English and Canadian journals. A romantic poet of only moderate accomplishment, she nevertheless demonstrated that English poetic forms could be adapted to pioneer themes, native legend, and the natural features and landscapes of Canada. She died of heart failure. See Robert Burns, *Isabella Valancy Crawford and Her Works*, 1994.

CREELEY, ROBERT (*b.* 1926) American poet and critic, was born in Arlington, Massachusetts, and was brought up in a family of women after the death of his father, a doctor, when he was four. After Holderness School, New Hampshire, he went in 1943 to Harvard, from which he dropped out after a year and served as an ambulance driver with the American Field Service in India and Burma during the last months of World War II. Having in the meantime 'found' the poetry of w. c. WILLIAMS, he returned to Harvard, but left without taking a degree and farmed in New Hampshire. In 1950 an attempt to establish an alternative literary magazine foundered but brought him into contact with OLSON. Their *Complete Correspondence*, ed. George Butterick (1983–84) comprises six volumes and writing to each other could occupy a whole working day. After living in Aix-en-Provence and Mallorca, Creeley joined the staff of Black Mountain College, which awarded him the degree of BA in 1956, and founded and edited the *Black Mountain Review* 1954–57. After the college closed in 1956, he taught in a boys' school in Albuquerque, and as a visiting professor at the University of New Mexico. He joined the faculty of the State University of New York, Buffalo, in 1967 and was Gray Professor of Poetry and Letters from 1978 to 1989, when he became Capen Professor of Poetry and the Humanities. He was New York State Poet 1989–91.

Creeley's first volume of poetry was published in 1952, his first substantial collection being *For Love: Poems 1950–1960* (1962), dedicated to his second wife, whom he married in 1957 (divorced 1976). In a lecture (1967) he stated: 'I'm *given* to write poems. I cannot anticipate their occasion. . . . To begin with, I was shy of the word "poet" and all its associations in a world I was then intimate with. It was not, in short, a fit attention for a young man raised in the New England manner, compact of Puritanically deprived senses of speech and sensuality. Life was real and life was earnest, and one had best get on with it. The insistent preoccupation with words did begin for me early, just that I did want so much to know what people were saying, and what, more precisely, they meant by it.' His verse has an economy of language and style, and aims to achieve the breakthrough of the philosophical mind which will result in an often unexpected discovery. He has also published an autobiographical novel, *The Island* (1963), and *The Gold Diggers and Other Stories* (1965). See *The Collected Poems of Robert Creeley 1945–1975*, 1982; *Selected Poems*, new edn 1996; *The Collected Prose*, new edn 1988; *The Collected Essays*, new edn 1992; *Autobiography*, 1991; *Tales out of School: Selected Interviews*, 1993.

CROCE, BENEDETTO (1866–1952) Italian philosopher and critic, was born in the mountain village of Pescaseroli, Abruzzi, of a landowning family, and was brought up in Naples, where he went to a boarding school run by priests for the children of the gentry, and, encouraged by his mother, avidly read novels, especially those of WALTER SCOTT. When he was 17, his parents and sister were killed in an earthquake on the island of Ischia, from which he was rescued after being buried for twelve hours. He and his two younger brothers were taken in by a cousin, a statesman who lived in Rome. Croce studied law at Rome University, but withdrew in 1886 without a degree and returned to Naples, where he attended to the family estate and supported his own study and publication of research into Neapolitan culture and folklore. After toying with socialism and concluding that Marxism was without philosophical significance, he developed his own doctrine, outlined in *Estetica come Scienza dell 'Espressione e Linguistica Generale* (1902; tr. Douglas Ainslie as *Aesthetic as the Science of Expression and General Linguistic*, 1909), and elaborated in volumes on logic, economics and ethics, and historiography. In 1902 he established the bimonthly review, *La Critica*, which he ran until 1943, initially with the idealist philosopher Giovanni Gentile (1875–1944), who went on to be a spokesman for Fascism. After being appointed a life senator in 1910 and briefly serving as Minister of Education before Mussolini established his dictatorship in 1922, Croce joined the Italian Liberal Party. Though he was allowed to continue to publish, his name was banned from being publicly mentioned and Fascist thugs broke into and damaged his library. During World War II, he was in 1943 taken into safety on British orders; after the fall of Mussolini he became leader of the Liberals (to the exposition of whose aims his historical writings had contributed) and the first official spokesman of the political assembly established with the approval of Allied Command. His body of considerable literary criticism includes a study of ARIOSTO, SHAKESPEARE, and CORNEILLE (tr. 1921), and works on popular and literary poetry (tr. 1933) and poetics (tr. 1936). See *Philosophy, Poetry, History: an Anthology of Essays*, tr. Cecil Sprigge, 1966.

CROKER, THOMAS CROFTON (1798–1854) Irish folklorist, was born in Cork, the son of an army major, and was at 16 apprenticed to a firm of Quaker merchants, having had little formal education. A preoccupation with old traditions and a talent for sketching took him wandering through southern Ireland, after which he sent some 'ancient airs' to THOMAS MOORE, who invited him to London. In 1818 he moved there permanently, and obtained through John Wilson Croker (1780–1857)—no relation but Irish born and a man of letters as well as a Member of Parliament—a clerical post in the Admiralty, where he remained until 1850. *Re-*

searches in the South of Ireland (1824) was followed by *Fairy Legends and Traditions of the South of Ireland* (1825). This impressive and influential work, which was translated into German by the GRIMMS (1826), and was the first collection of oral tales from the British Isles, originally appeared anonymously. (It transpired that Crofton had lost the manuscript, which had to be rewritten with the help of his friends, who remembered many of the stories.) Further volumes, entirely his own work and under his name, were published in 1828. He was a distinguished member of numerous British and European antiquarian societies. Among his other publications are *Legends of the Lakes: or Sayings and Doings at Killarney* (1829) and *The Popular Songs of Ireland* (1839). Two light novels published under his name in 1832 were actually the work of his wife, the artist Marianne Nicholson (*d.* 1854). Croker breakfasted with WALTER SCOTT in October 1826, who described him in his journal as 'little as a dwarf, keen-eyed as a hawk, and of very prepossessing manners. Something like Tom Moore.' Three days later Croker returned with 'a present of a small box of curious Irish antiques'.

CRONIN, A(RCHIBALD) J(OSEPH)

(1896–1981) Scottish novelist, was born in Cardross, Dunbartonshire, and went to live with his mother's family after the death of his father when he was seven. He was educated at Dumbarton Academy (he won a national historical essay prize when he was 13) and Glasgow University, where his medical studies were interrupted by war service as a surgeon in the Royal Naval Volunteer Reserve. He qualified in 1919, and married a doctor in 1921. He practised in a mining district in Wales, and was Medical Inspector of Mines 1924–26, after which he went into private practice in London until 1930, when his health broke down. Recuperating at a farm near Inveraray, in the West Highlands, he wrote, in three months, *Hatter's Castle* (1931), like almost all his subsequent novels an extension of his observation of actual people. Its immediate international success enabled him to give up medicine to write. The publicity for his fourth novel, *The Citadel* (1937), in which he used his experience of private practice to expose some of its more lurid aspects, was cleverly orchestrated by his publisher, the crusading Victor Gollancz (1893–1967). He worked for the British Ministry of Information in the USA during World War II, after which he settled permanently in Switzerland. He uses well-described settings and well-realized predicaments—such as that of the Catholic priest in *The Keys of the Kingdom* (1942)—and his enormous appeal to a middlebrow audience was enhanced by 'Dr Finlay's Casebook', his television and radio adaptations of his Scottish novels based on his

experiences as a doctor. *Adventures in Two Worlds* (1952), ostensibly an autobiography, is useful as a guide to links between fiction and fact.

CROWFIELD, CHRISTOPHER see STOWE.

CULLEN, COUNTEE (1903–46) American poet, was probably born in Louisville, Kentucky, and was brought up in New York before being adopted in 1918 by Rev. and Mrs Frederick Cullen, of the Salem Methodist Episcopal Church, Harlem, and going to DeWitt Clinton High School. While at New York University he won national prizes for poetry, of which he published a collection, *Color*, in 1925, the year he went on to Harvard to do a MA degree. In 1927 he published a further collection, *Copper Sun*; *The Ballad of the Brown Girl: an Old Ballad Retold*, into which he introduced racial overtones for which there are no equivalents in the original; and *Caroling Dusk: an Anthology of Verse by Negro Poets*. His much-trumpeted marriage in 1928 to Yolande, the daughter of DU BOIS, ended in divorce after two years. In 1934 he became a teacher of English and French at Frederick Douglass Jr High School, New York City. He died of uremic poisoning, having published two further collections of verse, and a novel, *One Way to Heaven* (1932). He saw his contribution to the Harlem Renaissance of the 1920s as being to introduce the black experience to white readers through the medium of traditional poetic forms. See Alan R. Shucard, *Countee Cullen*, 1984 (biographical/critical study).

CUMMINGS, E(DWARD) E(STLIN)

(1894–1962) American poet, dramatist, and painter, was born in Cambridge, Massachusetts, the son of a Harvard lecturer who later became a Unitarian minister. He had an intellectual upbringing, drew and wrote poems freely, and was educated at Cambridge Latin School and Harvard, from which he graduated *magna cum laude* in 1915. Having gone to New York to study painting, in 1917 he volunteered as a driver in the Norton Harjes Ambulance Corps of the American Red Cross, and was sent to Paris to wait for his uniform, and then to the front. He was arrested by the French authorities for injudicious remarks made by him and a friend in letters home, and spent three months in an internment camp—his first book, *The Enormous Room* (1922), is an impressionistic account of his experiences. On his release and return to the USA, he was drafted into the Army as a private, and for the remainder of World War I was in a camp in Massachusetts. He spent the rest of his life between his studio in Greenwich Village, the family home of Joy Farm in New Hampshire (which he inherited and where he died), and France, with occasional trips to other parts of the world, including the Soviet Union, about which he published a journal, *EIMI* [Greek, 'I am'] (1933).

The titles of his four books of verse in the 1920s range from the traditional, *Tulips and Chimneys* (1923) and *XLI Poems* (1925), to the more original & (privately printed, 1925) and *is 5* (1926)—followed later by *1 × 1* (1944). The untitled work (1930) is an illustrated collection of surreal satirical tales. His intense individualism manifested itself especially in the creation of visual forms, for which he used line breaks (or lack of them), lower case (he signed himself 'e. e. cummings'), hyphens, unconventional punctuation, and spacing to enhance his effect. Within such a framework, his message is often simple, satirical, or tender (as in his love poems). He was married three times, on the first occasion to Elaine Orr, by whom he had had a daughter in 1919—his verse play, *Santa Claus: a Morality* (1946) reflects his loss of the child after her mother remarried. He published his Charles Eliot Norton Professor of Poetry talks at Harvard as *i: six nonlectures* (1953). See *Complete Poems 1904–1962*, ed. George J. Firmage, rev. and expanded edn, 1994; *Selected Poems*, ed. Richard S. Kennedy, 1994; *AnOther Cummings*, ed. Richard Kostelanetz, 1996 (avantgarde poetry and prose); Richard S. Kennedy, *'Dreams in the Mirror': a Biography of E. E. Cummings*, new edn 1994; Richard S. Kennedy, *e. e. cummings*, new edn 1995 (biographical/critical study); Cary Lane, *'I Am': a Study of the Poems of E. E. Cummings*, 1976.

CUNNINGHAM, E. V. see FAST.

CUNNINGHAME GRAHAM, R. B. see GRAHAM, R. B. CUNNINGHAME

CURNOW, ALLEN (*b.* 1911) New Zealand poet, was born in Timaru, the son of an Anglican clergyman, and was educated at Christchurch Boys' High School. He became a trainee journalist on the Christchurch *Sun*, but gave that up in 1931 to study for the Anglican ministry at St John's College, Auckland. Instead of being ordained, he returned to journalism, and worked as a reporter and subeditor for the Christchurch *Press* from 1935 to 1948, while graduating from Canterbury University in 1938. Three books of youthful verse were followed by *Not in Narrow Seas* (1939), a 'contribution to the antimyth about New Zealand'. In 1949 he worked for the *News Chronicle* in London, re-

turning to become a lecturer in English at Auckland University, of which he was Associate Professor 1967–76. Regarded as the poet who has most effectively represented New Zealand's upsurge in literary nationalism, until his career was well advanced he voiced public rather than personal issues, projecting an image in keeping with his advice 'To an Unfortunate Young Woman Who After Attending Six Public Readings by Thirty Poets Asked, Does Anyone Care?' ('. . . Does anyone care? / One man's rhubarb is another man's / artichoke and that's the reason why / the poetry of earth is never dead / dead dead'). In the impressive sequences *Trees, Effigies, Moving Objects* (1972), and *An Incorrigible Music* (1979), in which he sets against each other images of New Zealand and Italy, past and present, he explores more private concerns in terms of attitudes to real objects and events. *The Axe: a Verse Tragedy*, finished with the encouragement of MARSH, was produced in 1949, and is one of several plays which are concerned with cultural conflicts—see *Four Plays* (1972). Satirical verses on topical subjects, which he wrote weekly for forty years as a journalistic assignment, are collected in *The Best of Whim-Wham* (1959). His introductions and selections for *A Book of New Zealand Verse 1923–1945* (1945; rev. edn 1951) and *The Penguin Book of New Zealand Verse* (1960) demonstrated the existence of an established tradition. He won the Commonwealth Poetry Prize (1989) and the Queen's Gold Medal for Poetry (1990), and was made CBE in 1990. See *Selected Poems 1940–1989*, 1990; *Continuum: New and Later Poems 1972-1988*, 1988; *Look Back Harder: Critical Writings 1935–1984*, ed. Peter Simpson, 1987; Alan Roddick, *Allen Curnow*, 1983 (critical study).

CYNEWULF 8th- or 9th-century Anglo-Saxon religious poet, was the first English poet to sign his work, which he did by weaving his name in runic characters, acrosticfashion, into his verses. It appears towards the end of the four didactic poems: 'The Fates of the Apostles'; 'The Ascension', the second part of an eloquent sermon; and two lives of female saints, 'Juliana' and 'Elene' (St Helena, mother of the Roman emperor Constantine). Of the school of Cynewulf, or possibly even adapted by himself from an earlier version, is the magnificent 'The Dream of the Rood', the earliest example of English mystical poetry, and the forerunner of the 'dream' or 'vision' poem.

D

DAHL, ROALD (1916–90) British short-story writer, novelist, and children's writer, was born in Llandaff, Glamorgan, of Norwegian parents. His father was a shipbroker, after whose death when he was four, he was brought up by his mother. He was educated at Repton School, where he excelled at sport but was recorded as being 'quite incapable of marshalling his thoughts on paper'. He worked for Shell Oil in East Africa from 1937 to 1939, and in the early years of World War II flew Royal Air Force fighters in action in Libya (where he survived a crash-landing), Greece, and Syria. Invalided home and posted to Washington with the rank of wing commander, he worked for the British security organization. A press interview by FOR-ESTER led to his contributing articles and stories to American quality magazines. In his first adult book, *Over to You: 10 Stories of Flyers and Flying* (1946), the ghastly twists which characterize many of his stories, and which were to be reflected also in his personal life, are already apparent, but the wicked meet the roughest of desserts as often as do the innocent the perversities of fate. Subsequent collections include *Kiss, Kiss* (1960), *Switch Bitch* (1974), and *Tales of the Unexpected* (1979). The enormous success of his children's stories with the readers themselves is due not just to the situations which his weird imagination was able to devise and the cheerful manner with which his child characters outwit or take revenge on their antagonists, but also to his penchant for the repellent but appropriate descriptive detail, of a kind which other children's authors eschew. He wrote his books in pencil on a board across his knees, sitting in an old wooden shack at the bottom of his garden. In 1953 he married the American actress Patricia Neal (b. 1926). They were divorced in 1983. In her autobiography, *As I Am* (1988), she describes the triple tragedy which profoundly affected the early years of their marriage. See *The Collected Short Stories of Roald Dahl*, new edn 1992; *'Boy' and 'Going Solo': an Autobiographical Account 1916–1941*, new edn 1992.

DAHLBERG, EDWARD (1900–77) American novelist, poet, and critic, was born in a charity hospital in Boston, the illegitimate son of Saul Gottdank, an itinerant barber, and 'Lizzie' Dalberg (he added the 'h' in 1928). He was brought up by his mother, who opened the Star Lady Barbershop in Kansas City in 1905, and in 1912 put him into the Jewish Orphan Asylum, Cleveland, where he remained until after his confirmation in 1917—Lizzie features particularly in his autobiographical study, *Because I Was Flesh* (1964). After several vagabond years he enrolled at the University of California, transferring to Columbia University, where he graduated in philosophy in 1925. After teaching for a year, and travelling in Europe, he worked his childhood into a novel, *Bottom Dogs* (1929), which had a preface by D. H. LAWRENCE, with whose interpretation of the book Dahlberg disagreed. *From Flushing to Calvary* (1932), a sequel, is a more sophisticated work. *Those Who Perish* (1934) is an early anti-Nazi novel whose target is the complacency of American Jews at the time. *Do These Bones Live* (1941), a collection of critical essays in which he analyses the roots and development of American literature, was reissued in London as *Sing, O Barren* (1947), with a preface by HERBERT READ, and later in a revised edition as *Can These Bones Live* (1960). *The Flea of Sodom* (1950) is an enigmatic study of the role of the artist. *The Sorrows of Priapus* (1957), which Dahlberg described as 'a little book on whether a man should have a phallus or not', and its second part, *The Carnal Myth* (1968), are redolent with classical learning. *The Confessions of Edward Dahlberg* (1971) is allegorical autobiography. His poems were collected as *Cipango's Hinder Door* (1965). From 1950 almost perpetually on the move, he was in 1965 appointed a professor of English literature at the University of Missouri.

DAICHES, DAVID (b. 1912) British critic and prose writer, was born in Sunderland, the son of a rabbi, and was brought up in Edinburgh, as he describes with humour and tenderness in *Two Worlds: an Edinburgh Jewish Childhood* (1956). He was educated at George Watson's College and Edinburgh University, and afterwards at Balliol College, Oxford. He was Assistant Professor, Chicago University 1937–43, Second Secretary at the British Embassy in Washington 1944–46, and Professor of English, Cornell University 1946–51; his impressions and experiences of America are described in *A Third World* (1971). Back in Britain, he taught at Cambridge and was then Professor of English and American Literature at Sussex University from 1961 until his retirement in 1977, when he returned to Edinburgh. He has written *The Novel in the Modern World* (rev. edn 1960) and *A Critical History of English Literature* (4 vols, rev. edn 1969), but of even more lasting worth than these are his studies of the Scottish scene, especially *The Paradox of Scottish Culture: the Eighteenth Century Experience* (1964) and *Robert Burns* (rev. edn 1966), and his 1983 Gifford lectures, *God and the Poets* (1984). He has also written illustrated biographies of WALTER SCOTT (1971), BURNS (1972), STEVENSON (1973), and BOSWELL (1975), as well as *Charles Edward Stuart: the Life and Times of Bonnie Prince Charlie* (1973), and the historical guides, *Glasgow* (1977) and *Edinburgh* (1978). He was made CBE in 1991.

DALY, RANN see PALMER.

DANA, RICHARD HENRY, JR (1815–82) American prose writer and lawyer, was born in Cambridge, Massachusetts, the second of four children of Richard Henry Dana (1787–1879), poet, critic, and editor. After the death of his mother in 1822, he was sent to private schools in the Boston area, at one of which he was taught by EMERSON. He enrolled at Harvard College in 1831, was suspended in 1832 on a point of honour, and dropped out in his third year because of eye trouble after measles. His love of adventure, hatred of inactivity, and the attraction of novelty led him to sign aboard the brig, *Pilgrim*, bound for California round Cape Horn. His eye problem cleared up during the first week, and after two years and one month he arrived back in Boston, having made the return journey in *Alert*, and spent 285 days in all at sea. The title of his classic account, *Two Years Before the Mast* (1840), written from his journal, is thus author's licence, forgivable in the light of its influence both on reading tastes and on the introduction of seagoing reforms (he revised it for the final time in 1876). Having graduated from Harvard in 1837, he joined the Episcopal Church, opened a law office, and married in 1841. An able lawyer who specialized in maritime law, lectured effectively on its workings and on social issues, and was District Attorney for Massachusetts from 1861 to 1866, he preferred public service to the further exploitation of his literary talents. In 1866 he was sued for plagiarism by the deposed editor of *Henry Wheaton's Elements of International Law*, a revised edition of which Dana had been persuaded to prepare in his place. The proceedings dragged on until 1879, when Dana was largely vindicated. The damage was already done, however, and in 1876 his nomination by President Ulysses S. Grant (1822–85) as US Ambassa-

dor to Britain was blocked in the Senate. He retired to Paris in 1878, and died in Rome. See Robert L. Gale, *Richard Henry Dana*, 1969 (biographical/critical study).

DANIEL, SAMUEL (1562/3–1619) English poet and historian, was born in Somerset and educated at Magdalen Hall, Oxford, without taking a degree. His translation in 1585 of an Italian work on heraldic emblems is dedicated to Sir Edward Dymoke, hereditary Queen's Champion, in whose service he was for a time and with whom he visited Italy. In 1591, 28 of his love sonnets were printed, without his permission, by Thomas Newman (*c*.1562–*c*.1600) in a pirated edition of SIDNEY's *Astrophel and Stella*, with a preface by NASHE. Shortly afterwards he went to Wilton, Wiltshire, as tutor to William Herbert (1580–1630), the son of the Earl of Pembroke by his third wife, Mary (see SIDNEY). To the Countess he dedicated *Delia* (1592), containing the full sequence of 50 sonnets 'To Delia', which are in the main beautifully turned and phrased examples of the genre, and the narrative poem, 'The Complaint of Rosamond'. The second edition (1594) included also *Cleopatra*, a verse closet drama in classical style for which the Countess was the inspiration. Some domestic catastrophe then caused him to seek new patronage, which was forthcoming from GREVILLE and Charles Blount (1563–1606), Lord Mountjoy, to whom Daniel dedicated the first four books of his (ultimately unfinished) historical poem, *The Civile Warres between the Two Houses of Lancaster and Yorke* (1595).

He now became tutor to Lady Anne Clifford (1590–1676), the daughter of the Countess of Cumberland, who had houses in Northamptonshire and London. *A Defence of Ryme* (1603) was a direct answer to CAMPION and a blatant attempt to curry favour with the new King. James (JAMES VI) obviously had other things on his mind, but more subtle approaches led to Daniel's masque, *The Vision of Twelve Goddesses*, being presented in 1604 with the Queen herself taking a part, and to his accepting the poisoned chalice of the appointment as licensor of entertainments presented by the Children of the Queen's Revels. When he gave up the post a year later he was also in trouble for the company's performance of his *Philotas* (1605), which appeared to comment on the trial and execution of the Earl of Essex in 1601. His protestations of innocence were accepted, and *The Queenes Arcadia*, an adaptation of the Italian form of pastoral drama, was presented before the court at Oxford in 1605. In about 1610 he retired to a farm at Beckington, Somerset, and here and at court, where he had been a groom of the Queen's Privy Chamber since 1609, he devoted himself to *The Collection of the Historie of England*; the first part was privately printed in 1612, and the whole, up to the death of

Edward III, published in 1618. It is notable in that he upholds medieval culture and refuses to accept historical legend as fact. See *Poems and A Defence of Ryme*, ed. Arthur Colby Sprague, new edn 1965; Joan Rees, *Samuel Daniel: a Critical and Biographical Study*, 1964.

D'ANNUNZIO, GABRIELE (1863–1938) Italian novelist, poet, dramatist, and adventurer, was born in Pescara, the youngest of five children of a provincial councillor, and went to Ciognini College, Prato. He became a celebrated poet at the age of 16, when a commercial publisher reissued his privately-printed *Primo Vere* [Early Spring] (1879), with the omission of the more licentious verses. He published a further volume in 1881, before going to Rome, where he enrolled for, but did not pursue, several university courses, became a man about town, and in 1883 seduced and then married Donna Maria Hardouin (1865–1954), the daughter of the Duke of Gallese. Four years later he virtually abandoned wife, home, and three children, and began a period of astonishing literary fertility and passionate living. *Laudi . . .* [Praises . . .] was the overall title of a series of volumes of verse (1903–12) inspired by the 'enchantment of the sun', which he had begun to write in Florence after an apocalyptic visit to Greece. For the most spectacular of his many mistresses, the actress Eleonora Duse (1858–1924), he wrote the plays *La Città Morta* (1898; tr. Professor G. Mantellini as *The Dead City*, 1902), *La Gioconda* (1899; tr. Symons as *Gioconda*, 1901), and *La Figlia di Iorio* (1904; tr. Charlotte Porter, Pietro Isola, and Alice Henry as *The Daughter of Iorio*, 1907), which became a national drama but precipitated the end of the affair, as Duse was passed over for the lead. *Il Piacere* (1889; tr. Georgina Harding as *The Child of Pleasure*, 1898), which reflected the decadence of his own lifestyle, set the tone for further fin-de-siècle novels, *L'Innocente* (1892; tr. Arthur Hornblow as *The Intruder*, 1898), and *Trionfo della Morte* (1894; tr. Hornblow as *Triumph of Death*, 1896), the starting point of which was another well-publicized affair—the English translations were even more heavily bowdlerized than the French, on which they drew. In the Venetian novel *Il Fuoco* (1900; tr. Kassandra Vivaria as *The Flame of Life*, 1900; tr. Susan Bassnett as *The Flame*, 1991) he rehearsed his affair with Duse, most unfairly.

In 1910, plagued by debts caused by his own extravagances, he took refuge in Paris, where he continued much as before. He returned to Italy in 1915 to make impassioned overtures to the country to enter World War I on the Allied side. Once it had done so, he played an active role as an airman, dropping bombs and leaflets even after losing an eye, the result of a crash-landing in a seaplane. In 1919 he entered Fiume (Rijeka) at the head of a column of seven irregular battalions,

claimed it for Italy, installed himself as dictator, and remained there for 16 months, even after it had been declared a free city—when Fiume was finally annexed to Italy in 1924, he was on Mussolini's recommendation created Prince of Monte-Nevoso. A mysterious accident in 1922 marked his departure from the political scene, but in the extraordinarily decorated villa on Lake Garda to which he had retired he continued to write and to make assignations.

DANTE ALIGHIERI (1265–1321) Italian poet and political philosopher, was born in Florence, and had a classical education while also, according to his biographer BOCCACCIO, studying poetry, music, and painting. In 1289 he fought in the front rank of the Florentine cavalry against the Tuscan Ghibellines at the battle of Campaldino. At the age of nine, Dante says, he first set eyes on Beatrice Portinari, the eight-year-old daughter of a prominent Florentine citizen: he spoke to her for the first time nine years later when they passed in the street. His intense romantic passion for her was such that after she died in 1290, he collected the poems he had written about her into *La Vita Nuova* [*The New Life*] (tr. Mark Musa, 1992; tr. Dino S. Cervigni and Edward Vasta, bilingual edn 1994), with a linking prose commentary, and dedicated his life to improving himself in order to be able to write 'of this blessed one . . . more worthily', to which end he systematically studied philosophy, theology, and science. In 1294 he married Gemma di Donati, of a noble family, by whom he had several sons and a daughter, who assumed the name of Beatrice when she became a nun. He entered public life in 1295, having joined the guild of the physicians and apothecaries in order to regain the franchise from which nobly-connected citizens had been barred since 1284. In 1300 he was elected for two months to serve as one of the six ruling priors, who confirmed the sentences of banishment on the leaders of both the Black and White Guelph factions in the city. While he was on an embassy to Rome to oppose the Pope's invitation to Charles of Valois, brother of the King of France, to take a 'peacekeeping' force of twelve thousand men into Florence, Charles entered the city, the Blacks took over, and Dante was in his absence condemned to death. He never returned.

When in 1310 Henry, Count of Luxemburg, announced his intention of receiving the imperial crown of the Roman Empire, Dante openly supported him in a series of political letters written in Latin, and in *De Monarchia* [On Monarchy] outlined the philosophy of government which is inherent in *The Divine Comedy*. When Henry died of a fever in 1313, he resigned himself to the status quo and gave his full attention, latterly in Ravenna, to the completion of his life's work. The three great sections of *Divina Commedia, Inferno, Purgatorio, Paradiso,* represent an allegorical journey of man, who obtains reward or punishment for acts committed in the exercise of his own free will. Written in *terza rima* in the Italian vernacular, which he explained that even women can understand, it is also an epic spiritual and cosmological autobiography, in the course of which the poet himself is conducted by VIRGIL and by his beloved Beatrice, and meets and converses with the souls of historical figures. Dante's works have influenced many English poets from CHAUCER to MILTON, TENNYSON ('Ulysses', *In Memoriam*), D. G. ROSSETTI (who was named after him, translated him, and took inspiration from him for his painting), ROBERT BROWNING, and T. S. ELIOT, much of whose symbolism derives from Dante, and whose essay on the poet (1929) is central to his literary criticism. See *Inferno*, 1984, *Purgatory*, 1985, *Paradise*, 1986, tr. Mark Musa; *The Divine Comedy*, tr. Charles H. Sisson (blank verse), new edn, ed. David H. Higgins, 1993; *The Divine Comedy*, tr. Allen Mandelbaum (unrhymed pentameters), new edn, with notes by Peter Armour, 1995; *The Inferno of Dante: a New Verse Translation*, tr. Robert Pinsky (*terza rima*), foreword by John Freccero, notes by Nicole Pinsky, new edn 1996 (bilingual edn); *Hell*, tr. Steve Ellis (irregular blank verse), new edn 1995; George Holmes, *Dante*, 1980 (introduction to his thought).

DARK, ELEANOR (1901–85), née O'Reilly, Australian novelist, was born in Burwood, Sydney, the only daughter of Dowell O'Reilly (1865–1923), politician, poet, and fiction writer. She was privately educated and in 1922 married Dr Eric Payten Dark, general practitioner and writer on medical subjects. From 1921 for many years she contributed articles, poems, and stories to various magazines as Patricia O'Rane. Her first novel, *Slow Dawning* (1932), a study of a woman doctor, was nine years finding a publisher. It was followed by *Prelude to Christopher* (1934) and four other contemporary novels in which she employed experimental narrative techniques and psychological themes. *The Timeless Land* (1941), *Storm of Time* (1948), and *No Barrier* (1953) comprise a trilogy of which the first in particular, covering the early years of European settlement and treating with imaginative insight and historical veracity the conflict between Governor Arthur Phillip (1738–1814) and the Aboriginal Bennelong, is regarded as a landmark in Australian historical fiction. She was made AO in 1977.

DARLEY, GEORGE (1795–1846) Irish poet, critic, and mathematical writer, was born in Dublin, the eldest of seven children (one of whom became the mother of BOUCICAULT) of well-off parents who went shortly afterwards to America, leaving him with his paternal grandfather. Affected all his life by a crippling stammer, he was educated by a tutor and at Trinity College, Dublin, where he read classics and mathematics. He graduated in 1820 and, having given up working for a fellowship because of the strain, went to London to try and earn a living as a writer. He became a regular contributor to the *London Magazine* after submitting some pieces as 'Peter Patricius Pickle-Herring', and in 1822 published, partly at his own expense, *The Errors of Ecstasie: a Dramatic Poem, with Other Pieces*. Thereafter John Taylor (1781–1864), KEATS's publisher and Editor of the *London Magazine*, became his publisher. Through him Darley brought out *The Labours of Idleness: or, Seven Nights' Entertainments* (1826) 'by Guy Penseval', a collection of fictional prose, mainly about love, interspersed with lyrics; *A System of Popular Geometry* (1826), the first of five mathematical textbooks; and *Sylvia: or, The May Queen. A Lyrical Drama* (1827), the work by which he was best known in his time. He spent the years 1830–35 on the Continent studying the paintings and sculpture, and became a regular art critic for the *Athenaeum* on his return. He printed at his own expense in 1835 a small edition for his friends of his unfinished long poem, *Nepenthe*; he also had two verse chronicle plays published (1840 and 1841). Though he had friends, and admiring young female cousins, he wrote in a letter (1845): 'I never kept much of any person's society without in the end feeling myself far less liked than when I entered it first.' His anonymous imitation of a Cavalier lyric, 'It is not beautie I demande' (1828), was printed as genuine in F. T. Palgrave, *The Golden Treasury . . .* (1861), but was omitted from the 1896 edition after its provenance had been revealed. It has since been restored, properly attributed, to the 17th-century section. See *Selected Poems*, ed. Anne Ridler, 1979.

DARWIN, CHARLES (1809–82) British naturalist, the son and grandson of physicians, was born in Shrewsbury and educated at Shrewsbury School and Edinburgh University, before transferring to Christ's College, Cambridge, to read for the Church. He became more interested in zoology, and in 1831 was recommended by the Professor of Botany as official geologist and naturalist (unpaid) to HMS *Beagle*, which was sailing to South America and India on survey duties. The round-the-world excursion lasted five years, during which Darwin was in constant misery at sea because of seasickness and suffered severe hardships on land in pursuit of the objects of his research. The results were published in diary form as Volume III of Captain Robert Fitzroy's *Narrative of the Surveying Voyages . . .* (1839)—see also *Charles Darwin's Beagle Diary*, ed. R. D. Keynes (1988) and

Keith S. Thomson, *H. M. S. Beagle: the Story of Darwin's Ship* (1995). Darwin was now working on his theory of evolution through 'natural selection' of the fitter species, which he presented in 1858 with Alfred Wallace (1823–1913), who had come to similar conclusions, and published in 1859 as *On the Origin of Species by Means of Natural Selection.* Equally contentious theologically, but quite acceptable in biological terms, was *The Descent of Man* (1871), which traces human origins to the same ancestors as those of the higher apes. He also wrote various scholarly works on plants and on earthworms. His prose is a model of scientific exposition. His investments made him rich: so much so that when in 1880 he decided to visit his son at Cambridge, he hired a railway carriage from Bromley, which was shunted round from Victoria Station to King's Cross to avoid his having to change trains. See *The Origin of Species*, ed. Gillian Beer, 1996; *Charles Darwin's Letters: a Selection 1825–1859*, ed. Frederick Burkhardt, foreword by S. Jay Gould, 1996; Charles Darwin and T. H. Huxley, *Autobiographies*, ed. Sir Gavin de Beer, new edn 1997; Adrian Desmond and James Moore, *Darwin*, new edn 1992 (biography); Michael White and John Gribbin, *Darwin: a Life in Science*, new edn 1996; Janet Browne, *Charles Darwin: a Biography, Volume One: Voyaging*, new edn 1996; Daniel Dennett, *Darwin's Dangerous Idea: Evolution and the Meaning of Life*, new edn 1996 (study of his thought).

DAUDET, ALPHONSE (1840–97) French novelist, was born in Nîmes, Provence, from which in 1849 the family was forced to move to Lyons owing to the collapse of his father's silk business. For lack of funds he had to leave the lycée at 16 to work as an usher at a school in the Cévennes, a hateful task which he abandoned in 1857 and went to Paris to seek the financial support of his journalist brother Ernest (1837–1921). His book of verse, *Les Amoureuses* (1858), was admired by the wife of Napoleon III, whose half-brother, the Duc de Morny (1811–65), took him on as a secretary. He was now able to pursue his literary ambitions, which were first directed towards the stage, for which he wrote five unsuccessful plays, and also to follow his instincts (according to Ernest) 'to enter every low haunt of Bohemia', where he caught syphilis, which in the form of locomotor ataxia ultimately killed him. In 1866 his Provençal sketches began to appear in *L'Événement*, the first five, under the pseudonym of Marie-Gaston, being written with Paul Arène (1843–96). In 1867 he married Julia Allard (1845–1940), herself a minor poet, whom he took to Provence 'to show her my windmill'. He now began a second series of *Lettres de Mon Moulin* in *Le Figaro*, the whole collection being published in volume form in 1869 (tr. Mary Carey as *Letters from My Mill*, 1880; tr.

Frederick Davies, 1978). The ridiculous protagonist of *Les Aventures Prodigieuses de Tartarin de Tarascon* (1872; tr. C. Roland as *The New Don Quixote . . .* , 1875) and its sequels epitomizes the traditional temperament of southern France. The dichotomy between south and north, which is the essence of his work, is highlighted in the novel about a politician, *Numa Roumestan* (1880; tr. Mrs Granville Layard, 1884), which HENRY JAMES called 'a masterpiece . . . really a perfect work'. Daudet was by then the most successful writer of his day, but from 1882, when he had to rely on a full-time secretary, he was in continuous and intense pain, and at HUGO's funeral in 1885 he was already unable to sign his name.

DAVENANT (or **D'AVENANT**), (Sir) **WILLIAM** (1606–68) English dramatist and poet, was born and went to school in Oxford. His father was a well-respected innkeeper, and the boy was said to be SHAKESPEARE's godson (AUBREY suggests he may have been his son). He became a page, first to the Duchess of Richmond (*d.* 1639) and then to GREVILLE. He married, for the first time, in 1624, became a hanger-on at court, wrote two gruesome dramas—*The Tragedy of Albovine, King of the Lombards* (printed 1629) and *The Cruell Brother* (1630)—and caught a terrible dose of syphilis from a whore in Axe Yard, Westminster, as a result of which he lost much of his nose, to the endless amusement of the humorists of the time. *The Witts*, a comedy, was performed in 1633, and his first court masque in 1635. The publication of *Madagascar, With Other Poems* (1638), which inspired a congratulatory poem by his friend SUCKLING, was instrumental in his appointment later that year to succeed JONSON as official laureate. He was active in the royalist cause, being knighted in 1643, and spent much of the latter part of the decade in Paris. Here he began his long (and ultimately unfinished) poem, *Gondibert*; the appearance in 1651 of the first two parts was preceded by the publication of his critical essay on heroic poetry, *A Discourse on Gondibert* (1650), and of an 'Answer' by HOBBES. In 1650, while en route to Maryland on a mission for the exiled royal family, he was captured by the Parliamentary forces and only escaped the death penalty, it is said, on the intervention of MILTON. He was instead imprisoned in the Tower of London, released in 1652, and pardoned in 1654. He was the only person during the Commonwealth regime to be authorized to present theatrical entertainments, which he was probably able to arrange by claiming that they were musical performances. He presented his own *The Siege of Rhodes* (1656), which marked the inauguration of the tradition of English opera and of the regular use of scenery, and the first appearance of English actresses on the dramatic stage. At the

Restoration of the Monarchy in 1660, he received from Charles II one of the two patents to establish theatrical companies, which enabled him to present several of his own musical adaptations of Shakespeare.

DAVIDSON, DONALD see DICKEY; RANSOM; SPENCER.

DAVIDSON, JOHN (1857–1909) Scottish poet, dramatist, novelist, and journalist, was born in Barrhead, Renfrewshire, the son of a minister of the Evangelical Union, against whose Calvinistic principles he reacted strongly—'A Ballad in Blank Verse of the Making of a Poet' is regarded as autobiographical. He was educated at the Highlanders' Academy, Greenock, which he left at 13 to work in a laboratory. He returned there as a pupil teacher for four years, after which he spent a year at Edinburgh University. Between 1878 and 1889 he taught unenthusiastically at a succession of reputable schools. Then, having had four plays and a novel—*The North Wall* (1885)—published in Scotland, he set out for London, with his pregnant wife and infant son, to earn a living as a writer. He became appreciated by the critics and his literary friends for his contemporary urban poems (T. S. ELIOT [1888–1965] regarded 'Thirty Bob a Week' as a 'great poem' which was useful to him in his development as a poet) and his topographical, narrative, and lyrical verses, variously published in *In a Music Hall and Other Poems* (1891), *Fleet Street Eclogues* (1893), *Ballads & Songs* (1894), and other volumes, but was ignored by the public.

Though he also did some journalism and other hackwork, his income was so low that he would have been in financial distress even if he had not also to send money to his mother and sister in Edinburgh, and to support a brother who was certified insane. His angry pride and uncertain temperament surface particularly in his series of blank verse 'Testaments', notable only for his attempt to express poetically scientific ideas and language. Contributions by the Royal Literary Fund and a Civil List pension gave some relief, but his self-esteem was further damaged by a well-meant gesture by G. B. SHAW, who gave him £250 as expenses and encouraged him to write a play which would project his personal philosophy. Nothing performable emerged. In March 1909 Davidson left the house in Penzance to which he had recently moved, to post a manuscript to his publisher. The manuscript arrived at its destination: Davidson's decomposed body was fished out of the sea six months later. In his will he directed, 'No one is to write my life now or at any time.' See *The Poems of John Davidson*, ed. Andrew Turnbull, 2 vols 1972–73; *Selected Poems and Prose*, ed. John Sloan, 1995; John

Sloan, *John Davidson: First of the Moderns*, 1995 (critical biography); Mary O'Connor, *John Davidson*, 1987 (biographical/critical study); J. Benjamin Townsend, *John Davidson: Poet of Armageddon*, 1961 (critical study).

DAVIES, (WILLIAM) ROBERTSON (1913–95) Canadian novelist, dramatist, critic, and journalist, was born in Thamesville, Ontario, the son of a newspaper magnate of modest means but considerable ability, and undertook his first journalistic assignment at the age of 11, for which his father paid him 25 cents. The family moved to Renfrew and then Kingston, and he was educated at Upper Canada College, Toronto, Queen's University, Kingston, and Balliol College, Oxford, where he made an impact as a stage manager and actor, wore (as befitting his status as a mature student of 22) pince-nez and enormous hats, and wrote as a BLitt thesis *Shakespeare's Boy Actors* (1939). On the strength of his knowledge of Shakespeare, he got a job as assistant to (Sir) Tyrone Guthrie (1900–71), Administrator of the Old Vic Theatre, at which he also acted and taught in the theatre school.

In 1940 Davies married a former Old Vic stage manager and returned to Canada, and to journalism. He was Literary Editor of *Saturday Night*, Toronto, until 1942, when he joined his father's Peterborough *Examiner*, of which he became joint owner (with his two brothers) and Editor in 1946—the witty columns he wrote as Samuel Marchbanks were collected in three books (1947, 1949, 1967) and reissued as *The Papers of Samuel Marchbanks* (1985). He was also writing plays of an intellectual nature: in one act, of which the first to be staged was *Overlaid* (1947)—included in *Eros at Breakfast and Other Plays* (1949); see also *Fortune My Foe and Eros at Breakfast: Two Plays* (1994)—, and full-length dramas—see *Hunting Stuart and Other Plays*, ed. Brian Parker (1972). 'They were performed in Canada but it meant very little,' he commented in an interview in 1991; so he turned more seriously to fiction. *Tempest-Tost* (1951), *Leaven of Malice* (1954), and *A Mixture of Frailties* (1958), reissued as *The Salterton Trilogy* (1986), explore the quirks and manners of the inhabitants of a Canadian university town. He himself assumed academic life in 1963, when he became Master of Massey College, Toronto University, where he also taught English and drama studies (he was made Master Emeritus on his retirement in 1981).

Two further trilogies followed: 'I don't intend to write [them] but I get interested in the characters. I could go further, but unless you're Marcel Proust, you need to know when to put the cork in.' A misdirected snowball triggers off the worldly and otherworldly events which inform *Fifth Business*

(1970), *The Manticore* (1972), which won the Governor General's Award, and *World of Wonders* (1975)—*The Deptford Trilogy* (1983). The academic world, art, mysticism, and a reassessment of the gender roles (symbolically represented by the legend of Arthur) feature in the 'Cornish Trilogy': *The Rebel Angels* (1981), *What's Bred in the Bone* (1985), and *The Lyre of Orpheus* (1988). He suggested that few authors of consequence die without leaving behind at least one ghost story. To *High Spirits: a Collection of Ghost Stories* (1982) he added *Murther and Walking Spirits* (1991), whose narrator is bludgeoned to death on page one. Autobiographical overtones enhance the richness of many of the characters in *The Cunning Man* (1995), his final novel, in which a physician comes to know himself through recalling the theatrical features of life. It was said that his efforts in his novels to publicize the exploration of the Jungian 'Search for Self', and those of some critics to go to lengths to find it there, obscured his mastery of the comedy and satire with which he exposed pretentiousness in modern society. Critical essays are in *A Voice From the Attic: Essays on the Art of Reading* (rev. edn 1990) and *The Enthusiasms of Robertson Davies*, ed. Judith Skelton Grant (1979). He had honorary doctorates from 18 Canadian and two American universities, was twice shortlisted for the Nobel Prize for Literature, and was made Companion, Order of Canada, in 1972. See J. Madison Davis (ed.), *Conversations with Robertson Davies*, 1989; Judith Skelton Grant, *Robertson Davies: Man of Myth*, new edn 1995.

DAVIES, W(ILLIAM) H(ENRY) (1871–1940) British poet, was born in Newport, Monmouthshire, and was adopted by his grandparents after his father's death and mother's remarriage. After leaving school he was apprenticed to a picture framer, but at 22, with an advance of £15 from a small allowance left him by his grandmother, he sailed for New York. He spent the next few years as an exceptionally mobile tramp, returned to Britain, left again for the Klondike goldfields, lost a foot in an accident on the railways (he smoked his pipe while waiting for a doctor), had the leg amputated to the knee, and came back to Newport. He ended up in London, where he peddled pins and trinkets, sang hymns in the street, and, when he was 34, started writing poetry. *The Soul's Destroyer, and Other Poems* (1905) was admired by many, including G. B. SHAW and EDWARD THOMAS, who found Davies a cottage in Kent and, with other fans, paid the rent, heat, and light. Here he wrote *The Autobiography of a Super-Tramp* (1908). *The Collected Poems* (1928) contained 431 lyrics, songs, and short narrative poems, comprising 'all I care to remember, and a number of others that I would like to forget': *The Complete Poems*

(1963) has 749, and includes the fifty in *Love Poems* (1935), celebrating his marriage in 1923 to a farmer's daughter considerably younger than himself. He wrote four novels, of which *The True Traveller* (1912) and *The Adventures of Johnny Walker, Tramp* (1926) are semi-autobiographical. His poetry has an air of artless innocence, especially when it evokes the joys of nature: exemplified by 'Leisure' ('What is this life if, full of care, / We have no time to stand and stare . . .'). There is a sense of grimness elsewhere, among the enormous range of themes, many of which reflect his earlier itinerant existence. See *Selected Poems*, ed. Jonathan Barker, new edn 1992; *Later Days*, new edn 1985 (autobiography); Richard J. Stonesifer, *W. H. Davies: a Critical Biography*, 1963.

DAVIN, DAN(IEL) (1913–90) New Zealand novelist and short-story writer, was born in Invercargill into a closely-knit Irish Roman Catholic community. He was educated at Marist Brothers School, Invercargill, Sacred Heart College, Auckland, and Otago University, from which he won a Rhodes Scholarship to Balliol College, Oxford, where he got a first in Greats. During World War II he served in the New Zealand Division in Greece and Crete, where he was wounded; and then as a staff officer with the rank of major in North Africa and Italy. He was three times mentioned in dispatches, and made MBE in 1945. After the war he joined the staff of the scholarly wing of Oxford University Press, of which he was Deputy Secretary to the Delegates 1970–78, and Academic Publisher 1974–78. He was elected a Fellow of Balliol in 1965. In 1939 he had projected a sequence of novels each linked with his Southland background. Beginning with *Cliffs of Fall* (1945), and continuing with *For the Rest of Our Lives* (1947; rev. edn 1965), a notable narrative of the fighting in the Middle East in World War II, and further titles, it concludes, according to him, with *Not Here, Not Now* (1970). *Brides of Price* (1972) is a sophisticated departure into contemporary comedy. *Selected Stories* (1981) draws on two earlier volumes; *The Salamander and the Fire* (1987) brings together all his published stories of the war, with some new ones. *Crete* (1953), his official New Zealand war history, has been admired by literary critics as well as by historians. He also wrote *Katherine Mansfield in Her Letters* (1959) and (with W. K. Davin) *Writing in New Zealand: the New Zealand Novel* (2 vols 1956), and edited several anthologies, including *Short Stories from the Second World War* (1982). He was made CBE in 1987. See *Closing Times*, reissued 1986 (memoirs); Keith Ovenden, *A Fighting Withdrawal: the Life of Dan Davin; Writer, Soldier, Publisher*, 1996; James Bertram, *Dan Davin*, 1973 (critical study).

DAVIOT, GORDON see MACKINTOSH.

DAVIS, ARTHUR HOEY see RUDD.

DAVIS, REBECCA HARDING (1831–1910), née Harding, American novelist, was born in Washington, Pennsylvania, to which she returned from Wheeling, West Virginia, at 14 to live with an aunt and go to the female seminary. In 1861 *Atlantic Monthly* printed her first story, anonymously (by custom and at her request) and unaltered, except in respect of the more saleable title of 'Life in the Iron-Mills'. Based on conditions in Wheeling, it was revolutionary in its uncompromising exposé of the underside of industrial development. Her first novel, *Margaret Howth* (1862), which began as the serial 'A Story of Today', has a similar background and a romantic plot. In 1863 she married L. Clarke Davis (1827–1904), a Philadelphia lawyer with a connection with the downmarket *Peterson's Magazine*, whom she had agreed to meet after he had sent her a fan letter. Though she was under contract to *Atlantic Monthly*, he persuaded her to write for *Peterson's*, with the result that her subsequent serious fiction was essentially confined to the flawed *Waiting for the Verdict* (1868), a preview of post-slavery problems, and *John Andross* (1874), a study of political corruption. Her literary reputation was also somewhat unfairly eclipsed by that of her son, Richard Harding Davis (1864–1916), a talented journalist, and publicist, who led a glamorous life and wrote popular novels which matched the flamboyance of his wardrobe as well as of his exploits. See *A Rebecca Harding Davis Reader: Life in the Iron Mills, Selected Fiction and Essays*, ed. Jean Pfaelzer, 1995.

DAVISON, FRANK DALBY (1893–1970) Australian novelist and short-story writer, was born Frederick Douglas Davison in Glenferrie, Victoria, but chose the alternative first names in 1931 to distinguish him from his father, Fred(erick) Davison (1868–1942), editor and publisher. After some years abroad and service with the British cavalry in France during World War I, he spent four years trying to establish a soldier settlement farm near Injune, Queensland. The terrain was the background of his first novel, *Man-Shy*, a tale of a wild red heifer, which his father serialized in *Australia* (1923–25), and then printed and bound in 1931 in a rudimentary form, in which it won the Australian Literary Society's Gold Medal. Other novels include *The Wells of Beersheba* (1933), a short but epic account of the charge of the Australian Light Horse in Palestine in 1917, and *Dusty* (1946), about a dog whose mixed breeding results in divided instincts. He now embarked on 'the [novel] I had been wanting to write since I was a young fellow'. *The White Thorntree* appeared 22 years later, in 1968, initially in a limited edition of 500 copies. Long, and often tedious, it is a deep study of sexuality in which none of the protagonists appear to have much fun. *The Road to Yesterday* (1964) is a collection of his shorter fiction, of which the animal and bush stories in particular have considerable merit. He was made MBE for services to literature.

DAY-LEWIS, CECIL see LEWIS, C. DAY.

DEFOE, DANIEL (1660–1731) British journalist and novelist, was born Foe (he added the 'De' in about 1703) in Cripplegate, London, the son of a Nonconformist butcher, and was educated as a Dissenter at Stoke Newington Academy. He married in 1684, played a part in 1685 in the rebellion of the Duke of Monmouth (1649–85), went into business as a hosiery agent, and was made bankrupt in 1692. *An Essay upon Projects* (1697), written shortly after this experience, contains sound economical, social, and educational proposals, and places him among the forward thinkers of the day. Many political pamphlets followed, some in verse, including the popular satire, *The True-Born Englishman* (1701). *The Shortest Way with the Dissenters* (1702), however, an ironic attack on the 'high-flyers' in the Church, misfired and a warrant was issued for his arrest. After four months in hiding, he was taken, tried, and sentenced to prison indefinitely, a heavy fine, and three consecutive days in the pillory. The last part of the ordeal was eased by the crowds; instead of hurling bricks and ordure, they garlanded the scaffold with flowers, drank the prisoner's health, and bought copies of 'Hymn to the Pillory', which he had courageously composed for the occasion. Though he was released from Newgate after five months, and his fine was paid by the Crown, he had lost his decorative roof-tile business, he was bankrupt again, and he had a wife and six children to support. He now responded to an approach from Robert Harley (1661–1724), Secretary of State and later Tory head of the Government, to act as a secret negotiator in various ploys of state, and also to produce a journal, entirely written by himself, *A Weekly Review of the Affairs of France, Purged from the Errors and Partiality of News-Writers and Petty-Statesmen of All Sides* (more often and later known simply as the *Review*), which from 1704 to 1713 came out three times a week. This was all the more extraordinary a journalistic feat in that he was also active, and often away, on his other business (which included arrangements for the union of the Scottish and English parliaments), and that his comments on the various issues of the war were invariably shrewd. Though de facto he was no longer politically untainted and in particular had to submerge his Whig principles, he was using the experience to forge a vivid and popular prose style, which he was able to employ to advantage and sustain in longer works, while still continuing to the end of his life indefatigably to write political, topical, and instructional tracts.

The first manifestation of Defoe the novelist was the moral adventure story, *The Life and Strange Surprising Adventures of Robinson Crusoe, of York, Mariner* (1719), followed the same year by *The Farther Adventures of Robinson Crusoe*, and in 1720 by *Serious Reflections During the Life and Surprising Adventures of Robinson Crusoe*—all inspired by the experiences of the Scottish seaman, Alexander Selkirk (1676–1721). The genre of the desert island story had now been created. Encouraged by his success, Defoe published two further novels of action, known by their short titles of *Memoirs of a Cavalier* (1720) and *Captain Singleton* (1720), and then his second masterpiece, *The Fortunes and Misfortunes of the Famous Moll Flanders* (1722). The lengthy, titillating, and often reproduced subtitle of this romance tends to obscure the fact that this first-person narrative of a streetwise adventuress, in the words of Professor Bonamy Dobrée in *English Literature in the Early Eighteenth Century 1700–1740* (1959), 'marks the birth of the modern novel, if . . . the peculiar mark of the novel as an art form distinct from other literary forms is that it shows the interplay of the individual and society'. *A Journal of the Plague Year* (1722) began as a piece of opportunist journalism in the form of a pamphlet warning the public of the dangers of the plague, which was raging in Marseilles. It became a reconstruction of the actual epidemic in London in 1665, graphically and dramatically told as if by an eyewitness.

Defoe's powers of observation as well as of descriptive prose, and his energy, are also demonstrated in *A Tour thro' the Whole Island of Great Britain* (1724–27). While the original notes for this essential source book of geography and social and economic history were made years before, he undertook several visits to Scotland between 1724 and 1726 to check his original impressions, and he makes some prophetic as well as perceptive comments. See Paula Backscheider, *Daniel Defoe: His Life*, new edn 1992; Ian Bell, *Defoe's Fiction*, 1985.

DE GRAFT, JOE [JOSEPH] (1924–78) Ghanaian dramatist and poet, was born in Cape Coast and educated at Achimota School and the University College of the Gold Coast, where he was one of the first to take an honours degree in English. He established a drama programme at Kumasi University of Science and Technology, and was in 1961 seconded to be Director of the Ghana Drama Studio. Subsequently he developed diploma courses in drama and theatre studies at the universities of Ghana and Nairobi, where he was remembered also for his notable stage and television performance in the name role of SHAKESPEARE's *Othello*. His first play was produced in Accra in 1962 as *Visitor from the Past*. Published in a refined form as *Through a Film Darkly* (1970), it is a study of racial attitudes, with a strong situation and, almost inevitably, a violent conclusion. The main conflict in *Sons and Daughters* (1964) is the differing perceptions by young and old of the purpose of education. The poems in the collection *Beneath the Jazz and Brass* (1975) are in a variety of moods, from the grim political awareness of 'The Rock Behind the Fort' and 'Deaths: Seventeen April Nineteen Sixty-Seven', to the amusing irony of 'Un-African Breakfast', and the social satire of 'Platinum Lou'.

DEIGHTON, LEN (*b.* 1929) British novelist, was born in London and educated there at Marylebone Grammar School, St Martin's School of Art, and the Royal College of Art. He had had a range of semi-skilled and creative jobs, and was contributing a regular series of cookery comic strips to the *Observer*—see *Action Cook Book: Len Deighton's Guide to Eating* (1965)—when he burst on to the literary scene with *The Ipcress File* (1963), a Cold War spy thriller which was dryly witty, as well as tough and refreshingly unromantic (it appeared in the same year as LE CARRÉ's first spy novel). While also using his intricate background knowledge to effect in novels about the war in the air—see *Bomber* (1970) and *Goodbye Mickey Mouse* (1982)—his main preoccupation has been the dissection of the twilight world of espionage, most elaborately in the trilogy *Berlin Game* (1983), *Mexico Set* (1984), and *London Match* (1985), with its ultimate unmasking of the (female) traitor. The ensuing fortunes of the main characters are followed in a second trilogy, the climax of the third book, *Spy Sinker* (1990), being the collapse of the German Democratic Republic and the pulling down of the Berlin Wall as a result of the infiltration of a Western agent, whose identity turns the apparent outcomes of both trilogies upside down. He reverted to World War II in *City of Gold* (1992), a desert thriller with a classic opening. A further spy trilogy began with *Faith* (1994) and continued with *Hope* (1995) and *Charity* (1996). *Blood, Folly and Tears* (1993) is a critique of the conduct of World War I, in which his father fought, and World War II.

DEKKER, EDUARD DOUWES see MULTATULI.

DEKKER, THOMAS (1572–1632) English dramatist and prose writer, was a Londoner probably of Dutch origin, whose life was punctuated by prison sentences for debt. He collaborated variously with JOHN FORD, MASSINGER, MIDDLETON, and WEBSTER to write a total of some sixty plays, of which 17 survive.

He appears in ridiculous guise in JONSON's play *The Poetaster*, to which he retaliated with *Satiro-Mastix, or the Untrussing of the Humorous Poet* (1602). The first two plays under Dekker's single authorship (both performed in 1599) were *Old Fortunatus*, a pleasant poetical piece, and *The Shoemaker's Holiday*, a sound, realistic comedy whose aim is purely to entertain. The latter has some excellent scenes, carefully-studied characters (snobbish dignitaries, loyal craftsmen, star-crossed lovers), stock deceptions, and neat comparisons and contrasts, with racy dialogue and clever rhyming exchanges. The only other play known to be entirely his own work is the second part of *The Honest Whore* (1630), an uneven Italianate drama of morality and social class. Dekker was a chronicler of London life at all levels. *The Wonderfull Yeare* (1603) was the first of a series of pamphlets in which busy portraits of London provide a background to social comment and the grimmest of reports of the plague—see *The Plague Pamphlets*, ed. F. P. Wilson (1925). *The Gull's Hornbook* (1609) is a satirical vade mecum addressed to the rural gallant on how to disport himself most destructively in the city. See *Dramatic Works*, ed. Fredson Bowers, 1953–61; Julia Gasper, *The Dragon and the Dove: the Plays of Thomas Dekker*, 1990.

DE LA MARE, WALTER (1873–1956) British poet, novelist, children's writer, and critic, was born in Charlton, Kent, the sixth child of a Bank of England official, and was educated at St Paul's Cathedral Choristers' School. At 16 he joined the Anglo-American Oil Company, for which he worked until 1908, when NEWBOLT, then Literary Editor of the *Monthly Review*, obtained for him a Civil List grant of £200. His first book, written as Walter Ramal and prophetically entitled *Songs of Childhood* (1902), was followed by a literary fantasy, *Henry Brocken* (1904), by *The Return* (1910), a stunning novel of possession, and by his first books for children, *The Three Mulla-Mulgars* (1910) and *Peacock Pie: a Book of Rhymes* (1913). The basis of all his subsequent work had now been realized, but his popular success began only with *The Listeners, and Other Poems* (1912); it was confirmed by *Memoirs of a Midget* (1921), a classic incursion into microscopic fantasy. *Come Hither: a Collection of Rhymes and Poems for the Young of All Ages* (1923), arranged thematically and with additional material by way of commentary and parallels, possibly still is the most inspirational anthology for children. Most of de la Mare's work has undertones of sadness, mystery, and danger, especially where there is a confrontation with or absorption into the other world. His hold on reality, combined with his attention to detail and to precision of language and, in his poetry, with command of rhythm and rhyme, has ensured his appeal to the child in the adult as well as to

the adult in the child. *Pleasures and Speculations* (1940) contains essays on TENNYSON and RUPERT BROOKE. He was made CH in 1948 and awarded the OM in 1953. See *Collected Poems*, new edn 1979; *Short Stories*, 3 vols 1996; Theresa Whistler, *Imagination of the Heart: the Life of Walter de la Mare*, new edn 1995 (biography); Leonard Clark, *Walter de la Mare*, 1960 (on his writing for children).

DE LA RAMÉE, MARIE LOUISE see OUIDA.

DE LA ROCHE, MAZO (1879–1961) Canadian novelist, was born Maisie Roche in Newmarket, Ontario, of Irish parentage. She was educated at Parkdale College, Toronto, and spent some of her earlier years in rural surroundings. Her devoted companion (and secretary) was her cousin and adoptive sister, Carolyn Clement, with whom she adopted two children. They lived in England in Windsor during the 1930s, returning permanently to Toronto in 1939. A struggling journalist for many years, de la Roche published a book of unremarkable stories, *Explorers of the Dawn* (1922), followed by two novels in which realism and characterization intrude upon sentimentality, and then by *Jalna* (1927). This colourful 1920s' romance of the rurally gentrified, English colonial Whiteoaks family won the first *Atlantic Monthly*–Little Brown prize of $10,000. More significantly, it ensured by its literary as well as popular success a market for 15 sequels, six of which precede the events described in *Jalna*. *Ringing the Changes: an Autobiography* (1957) is deficient in its exposition of her creative process and misleading in respect of some of the facts, including her age. See Joan Givner, *Mazo de la Roche: the Hidden Life*, 1989.

DELEDDA, GRAZIA (1872–1936) Italian novelist, was born in the Sardinian mountain village of Nuoro, the eldest of seven children of an attorney and his illiterate wife. She attended the local elementary school until she was ten, after which she had some private tuition in French and Italian, and read Russian fiction in translation and French novelists. She had a story printed in a Rome fashion magazine when she was 15, and in 1892 she published the first of a considerable canon of novels about Sardinian life. On her father's death she managed the family winery, which she handed over to a brother after getting an unexpectedly large sum of money from the French translation of her second novel. On a visit to the capital, Cagliari, in 1899 to see the editor of a journal to which she contributed, she met Palmiro Modesani, an official in the Ministry of Finance. They married in 1900; when she accompanied him to Rome, where he had been posted to the Ministry of War, it was her first trip outside the island. In Rome she raised two children, and continued to write about the land and people of Sardinia. *Elias Portolu* (1903; tr. Martha King, 1992), which she began in 1900, is one of several of her novels whose theme is incest; *Cenere* (1904; tr. Helen Hester Colvill as *Ashes*, 1908) is about a young mother's sacrifice for her illegitimate child; in *La Madre* (1920; tr. Mary G. Steegman as *The Woman and the Priest*, 1922) a mother suffers for her son, a priest who has fallen in love. In all she wrote some 35 novels and 18 volumes of stories— *Chiaroscuro and Other Stories*, tr. Martha King (1994) was first published in 1912, the year after she visited Nuoro for the last time. Deledda was awarded the Nobel Prize for Literature in 1927 for her 'idealistically inspired writings which with plastic clarity picture the life on her native island and with depth and sympathy deal with human problems in general'; she was the second woman, after LAGERLÖF, to win it, and the second Italian.

DELONEY, THOMAS (?1543–c.1600) ballad maker and prose fiction writer, was probably born and educated in East Anglia, and is referred to by NASHE in 1596 as 'the Balletting Silke-Weaver, of Norwich'. The local knowledge of Berkshire which he displays in his novels suggests that at one time he was involved in the silk industry there. He was certainly living in London in 1586, where his son was baptized, and for the next ten years or so he was a leading, and notorious, composer of topical ballads (the Elizabethan equivalent of the popular journalist). *The Garland of Good Will*, a collection of his verses first registered in 1593, is largely composed of historical ballads and lyrics of a rough and ready nature. *Strange Histories* . . . , featuring 'The Dutchesse of Suffolkes Calamitie', of which the earliest known edition is dated 1602, comprises metrical versions, in chronological order, of several of the more sensational episodes in HOLINSHED's *Chronicles*. Deloney might well be termed the originator of the sponsored novel: *The Pleasant Historie of Jacke of Newburie* (registered in 1597) celebrates the weaving industry, *The Gentle Craft* (1597), from which DEKKER took elements for *The Shoemaker's Holiday*, the shoemakers, and *Thomas of Reading* (1600) the clothing trade. When compared with other forms of Elizabethan literature, these collections of loosely-linked and sometimes fanciful tales of the bourgeoisie have little distinction except for their lively dialogue and the fact that they provided an obviously popular alternative to the euphuisms of ROBERT GREENE, LYLY, and others.

DE MILLE, JAMES (1833–80) Canadian novelist, was born in St John, New Brunswick, and educated at Horton Academy and Acadia College, Wolfville. After a tour of Europe with his brother, he went to Brown University, Rhode Island, after which he opened a bookshop in St John, which did not survive long. In 1859 he married the daughter of the first President of Acadia College, where he taught classics from 1860 to 1864, when he went as a professor of English and history to Dalhousie University. He was a prolific novelist whose academic literary insight enabled him to produce, or parody, popular genres at will, and to indulge in linguistic jokes. His first real success was *The Dodge Club: or, Italy in MDCCCLIX* (1869), sketches of travel-wise American tourists. He wrote, too, a series of 'Brethren of the White Cross' archetypal Canadian holiday adventures for boys. His most ingenious story, *A Strange Manuscript Found in a Copper Cylinder* (1888), was published posthumously and also, to avoid loss of copyright, anonymously. A dystopian novel within a novel, a form which enabled him to satirize the vacuous academic discussions among the party which picks up the manuscript at sea, it describes the adventures of a seaman among the Kosekin of Antarctica, whom De Mille supplies with a complete vocabulary as well as with a culture.

DEMOSTHENES (383–322 BC) Athenian orator and statesman, the son of a wealthy arms dealer, was orphaned when he was seven. In 363, having come of age and been cheated by his guardians, he prosecuted them, and got the verdict, though not the money. Determined now on a career as a forensic and political speaker, he improved his diction and presentation by stringent training, and the style of his oratory by assiduous study. Of the sixty orations that survive, his 'Philippics' and other speeches against the aggressive policy of Philip of Macedon are the most eloquent and significant. Of these, none was more effective than 'On the Crown', delivered in 330 in response to a vicious personal attack on his credibility as a national hero, for which it had been proposed that he be publicly awarded a golden crown. Demosthenes was imprisoned in 325 for what was probably no more than gross negligence in the case of the plea by the Macedonian royal treasurer for asylum and for backing against his former ruler. He escaped into exile, to return in short-lived triumph on the death of Alexander (the Great) in 323. After the defeat of the Greek confederacy, he was for his earlier political activity declared an enemy of Macedonia by the new ruler, whose agents pursued him to a temple in the island of Calauria, where he took poison.

DENHAM, (Sir) JOHN (1615–69) English poet, was born in Dublin, his father being at the time Chief Baron of the Exchequer in Ireland. After three years (which he is said to have spent dreaming and gaming) at Trinity College, Oxford, he entered Lincoln's Inn in 1634. He allayed his family's horror at his gambling by writing and printing an essay decrying the habit, by attending to his studies (he was called to the Bar in 1639), and by translating into rhyming couplets the second book of VIRGIL's *Aeneid*. After his father's death in 1638 he returned to the gaming tables and lost all the cash, and plate, which he had inherited. *The Sophy* (1642), a verse tragedy in which a father orders the blinding of his son, who takes revenge by murdering his own daughter, on whom his father doted, earned him some notoriety. *Coopers Hill* (1642; first authorized edn 1655), by contrast, if not, as JOHNSON contends, the original example in English of 'local poetry, of which the fundamental subject is some particular landscape', is regarded as the first in which philosophical speculation is inspired by looking at the view.

For a time at the beginning of the Civil War Denham was High Sheriff of Surrey and Governor of Farnham Castle, and after being deprived of some of his property by Parliament he continued to support the royal cause in France and England. At the Restoration of the Monarchy in 1660 he was appointed Surveyor of Works; he was knighted after the coronation of Charles II in 1661 for his contribution to the organization of the occasion. He was elected Member of Parliament for Old Sarum in 1661, and to the Royal Society in 1663. In 1665 he married, as his second wife, the 18-year-old Margaret Brooke, whom PEPYS records the following year as being the mistress of the Duke of York (later James II). She died in January 1667, it is said from eating poisoned chocolates. At about this time Denham exhibited symptoms of insanity, from which he recovered enough to write an elegy praising the originality of the deceased COWLEY, beside whom he was buried in Westminster Abbey two years later. *Poems and Translations* was published in 1668. DRYDEN acknowledged his influence as a poet, and Johnson concluded: 'He is one of the writers that improved our taste, and advanced our language, and whom we ought therefore to read with gratitude, though, having done much, he left much to do.'

DE QUINCEY, THOMAS (1785–1859) British prose writer and critic, was born in Manchester, the son of a prosperous merchant, who died when the boy was seven. He was educated in the West Country before being sent in 1801 to Manchester Grammar School, from which he promptly ran away. With a small allowance from his mother, he wandered in Wales, and when the money was exhausted, ended up in London, subsisting on charity. In 1803 his guardians entered him for Worcester College, Oxford, where he remained intermittently for five years, but left without a degree, having felt unable to face his final viva. In 1804 a well-meaning acquaintance prescribed opium for a toothache: by 1813 he was an addict. In the meantime he

had come into his inheritance and settled in the Lake District. In 1817 he married a local farmer's daughter, by whom he had eight children; in 1821, to earn a living, he turned his talents and wide interests to writing. *Confessions of an English Opium Eater*, signed 'X. Y. Z.', appeared in the *London Magazine* in two parts in 1821, and thereafter he contributed articles to various journals, especially *Blackwood's Edinburgh Magazine*. He and his family moved to Edinburgh in 1830. Unable to work except in solitude, when his wife died in 1837 he took a cottage in neighbouring Lasswade, where he settled the children, while he lived in lodgings in the city. When the place got so snowed up with papers that he had no room to move, he locked the door and set up elsewhere; on his death he was paying rent on six sets of lodgings. Later works in which the materials of his waking dreams are superimposed on autobiography are *Suspiria de Profundis* (1845) and *The English Mail-Coach* (1849); the latter includes 'The Vision of Sudden Death' and 'Dream Fugue', in which there are passages of particular graphic and poetic power. His interest in the psychology of crime, on which he used to compile reports for the *Westmoreland Gazette*, inspired the penetrating critical essay, 'On the Knocking at the Gate in *Macbeth*', and the three parts of 'On Murder Considered as a Fine Art' (1827, 1839, 1854), of which the first two are a brilliant blend of parody and black comedy. See *The Confessions of an Opium-Eater: and Other Writings*, ed. Grevel Lindop, 1985; Grevel Lindop, *The Opium Eater*, new edn 1993 (critical biography).

DESAI, ANITA (*b.* 1937), née Mazumdar, Indian novelist, was born in Mussoorie of a Bengali father and a German mother, and was educated at Queen Mary's Higher Secondary School and Delhi University. She married in 1958, the year after she graduated in English literature, and has had four children. Her first novel was *Cry the Peacock* (1963). An accomplished stylist, she is concerned with analysing the Indian character in the context of the current Indian situation. In *Fire on the Mountain* (1977), which won a clutch of awards, the failure of different generations to understand each other leads to a disaster. In *Clear Light of Day* (1980) a Delhi family comes to terms with its past, and for some of its members there is an escape. *In Custody* (1984) is a study of a country town, and of the insecurity of a temporary college lecturer whose preoccupation with Urdu poetry leads to his manipulation by the unscrupulous. In *Baumgartner's Bombay* (1988) Desai gives rein to the expression of her own dual cultural heritage which came through her parents. *Journey to Ithaca* (1995) centres on a quest to discover the background of an eastern mystic. In *Games at Twilight and Other Stories* (1978) she runs through her elegant repertoire of humour, perception, and pathos. *The Village of the Sea* (1982) won the *Guardian* children's fiction award. She is a member of both the Royal Society of Literature and the Indian National Academy of Letters.

DESCARTES, RENÉ (1596–1650) French philosopher and mathematician, was born in Touraine of a family of lawyers and spent eight years at the Jesuit college of La Flèche, Anjou, after which he may have taken a law degree at Poitiers. In 1618 he enlisted in Breda as an officer cadet in the army of the Dutch Prince, Maurice of Nassau (1567–1625). The following year he set out for Copenhagen by a roundabout route, which took him in November near Ulm, Bavaria. Here, in a room heated by a stove, he claimed to have had a vision of his part in the elucidation of knowledge, by employing a unified science which could be applied to discoveries in any subject. In the course of his further research and contemplation he formulated his celebrated proposition: *Cogito ergo sum* [I am thinking, therefore I am], the cornerstone of his metaphysics. He returned to France in 1622, set off again for Italy the next year, and finally installed himself in Paris in 1626; only to move on to Holland in 1629, where he lived at various addresses and in 1635 had an illegitimate daughter called Francine, who died of fever when she was five. In 1649, having failed to get a post in the service of Louis XIV, he rather reluctantly accepted a pressing offer to join the court of Queen Christina of Sweden. The routine (she liked to have philosophy lessons at 5 am) and the winter climate proved too much for his health. He expounded his Cartesian philosophy in the quasi-autobiographical *Discours de la Méthode* (1637), and more fully in *Meditationes de Prima Philosophia* (1641) and *Principia Philosophiae* (1644). See *Discourse on Method* and *Meditations of the First Philosophy*, tr. John Veitch, 1989; Stephen Gaukroger, *Descartes: an Intellectual Biography*, 1995; Tom Sorell, *Descartes*, 1987 (introduction to his philosophy).

DE VERE, AUBREY (THOMAS) (1814–1902) Irish poet, was born at the family seat, Curragh Chase, Co. Limerick, the third son of Sir Aubrey de Vere (1788–1846), a minor poet who wrote in the manner of WORDSWORTH, and a younger brother of Sir Stephen de Vere (1812–1904), politician and translator of HORACE. He was educated by tutors at home—for this and other periods of his life see *Recollections of Aubrey de Vere* (1897)—and at Trinity College, Dublin. He raised no objection to his father's proposal that he should take orders in the Anglican Church, but instead of studying theology he read literature and philosophy, and travelled. In London he met TENNYSON, who spent five

comfortable and mentally recuperative weeks as his guest at Curragh Chase in 1848; he met Wordsworth, whose regular guest he became at Rydal Mount and whose grave he afterwards regularly visited until he was in his eighties; and he met COLERIDGE's delightful daughter Sara, with whom he became firm friends and to whom he wrote in 1851 to explain his conversion to Roman Catholicism. Poetry was more than just a natural extension of his cultured, leisurely, bachelor existence, though his first published work was a treatise on the Irish situation, *English Misrule and Irish Misdeeds* (1848). In *May Carols* (1857), written at the suggestion of the Pope, he applied his talent for religious poetry to composing hymns to the Virgin Mary and the saints. *Inisfail, a Lyrical Chronicle of Ireland* (1863) is a prophetic treatment of Irish legend and history. *The Foray of Queen Maeve* (1882) is regarded as the most impressive and interesting of his other poetical works. He also wrote verse dramas and literary criticism.

DEVLIN, DENIS (1908–59) Irish poet, translator, and diplomat, was born in Greenock, Scotland, the eldest child of nine in a well-to-do, cultured family, with whom he returned to Ireland when he was 12. He was educated at Belvedere College, Dublin, for a year at a seminary, and then, having decided against becoming a priest, at University College, Dublin, where he excelled at languages and he and his friend (and literary executor), Brian Coffey (1905–95), privately printed a very slim volume, *Poems* (1930). After further studies in Munich and Paris, he joined the Irish Department of External Affairs, for which he worked until his death from leukaemia, holding among several posts that of First Secretary to the Legation in Washington (1940–47), and Minister Plenipotentiary (1950) and then the first Irish Ambassador (1958) to Italy. *Intercessions* (1937) comprised 15 poems through which shines his study of French writers from VILLON to Paul Éluard (1895–1952). In the title piece in particular of *Lough Derg and Other Poems* (1946) he demonstrates his intellectual and poetic vision whereby the resolution of modern problems may lie in a religious response. He was as much a European as an Irish poet, whose philosophical attitude and poetic craft may also be sampled in such poems as 'The Passion of Christ', 'Ank'hor Vat', 'The Colours of Love', and in his sequence, 'The Heavenly Foreigner'; his versions of French, German, and Italian poetry are in *Translations into English*, ed. Roger Little (1992). See *Collected Poems*, ed. J. C. C. Mays, 1989.

DE VRIES, PETER (1910–93) American novelist, was born in Chicago of immigrant parents who were pillars of the Dutch Reformed Church. He was educated at the Chicago Christian High School and Calvin College, Michigan, where he began mildly to react against the inhibitions of his upbringing and cured his stutter by going in for a speaking contest. A candy vending machine operator and a radio actor in the early 1930s, he became in 1938 an editor of the influential Chicago-based *Poetry: a Magazine of Verse*, through which he met his wife, when he won a prize in one of the journal's competitions. Through THURBER, to whom he showed some of his humorous writing, he got a job with the *New Yorker*, for which he worked from 1944 to 1986, initially as poetry editor and then as cartoon editor. He settled in Westport, Connecticut, the ethos of which is shared by his fictional Avalon. An unashamedly comic writer, his oeuvre, in his view, begins with the farcical *The Tunnel of Love* (1954) rather than with any of the three novels published in the early 1940s. His range also incorporates parody, both linguistic—*The Tents of Wickedness* (1979)—and thematic—*Slouching Towards Kalamazoo* (1983); satire—*The Mackerel Plaza* (1958); and social comedy—*The Vale of Laughter* (1967)—and social comment—*The Blood of the Lamb* (1962). As well as more than twenty novels, he published *Without a Stitch in Time: a Selection of the Best Humorous Short Pieces* (1972).

DICKENS, CHARLES (1812–70) British novelist and editor, was born in Landport, Portsmouth, the second of eight children of a Navy pay clerk. His father's postings and inability to maintain a suitable style of living for his family, culminating in his imprisonment for debt, meant that the boy had 14 moves of home in as many years, several months' labour in Warren's Blacking Warehouse, and only two short periods of formal education. These were at William Giles's school in Chatham when he was nine, and at Wellington House Academy, Hampstead, from 1824 to 1827, when he started as a solicitor's clerk. In 1829, having learned shorthand, he became a newspaper reporter. In 1832 he applied for an audition at Covent Garden Theatre but missed it through illness. He abandoned the idea of the stage when in 1833 his first story, 'A Dinner at Poplar Walk' (later reprinted as 'Mr Minns and his Cousin'), was published in the *Monthly Magazine*, followed by eight more in January–February 1834. Subsequent series of pseudonymous sketches appeared in various journals, and were collected and published as *Sketches by Boz* (1836)—see *Dickens' Journalism: Sketches by Boz and Other Early Papers 1833–1839*, ed. Michael Slater (1994). *The Posthumous Papers of the Pickwick Club, edited by 'Boz'* (1837) had begun serialization in March 1836, a few days before his marriage to Catherine Hogarth (1815–79). All Dickens's novels were written and originally appeared as serials, the first 24 instalments of *Oliver Twist: or, the Parish Boy's Progress* (1838) being published

in *Bentley's Miscellany*, of which he was himself Editor from 1837 to 1839. In May 1837, the sudden death, literally in his arms, of his wife's 17-year-old sister Mary, who had come to live with the couple soon after their wedding, proved particularly traumatic, and she became a perpetual embodiment for him of youth and innocence. The tragedy also caused the suspension for a month of his writing of *Pickwick* and of *Oliver Twist*. Early in 1838 he went to Yorkshire to investigate reports of brutality in boarding schools for unwanted boys. On his return he began *The Life and Adventures of Nicholas Nickleby* (1839), the first episode being published on 31 March 1838.

This became the established pattern of his career: an almost incessant round of writing (only halted by his death from a cerebral haemorrhage after finishing six instalments of *The Mystery of Edwin Drood*), punctuated by frequent fact-finding, publicity, and family journeys, and by miscellaneous literary works. In 1842 he and his wife spent six months in the USA where, amid the fêting, he gave addresses on international copyright and inspected conditions in jails. From 1850 to 1858 he edited *Household Words*, where several of his novels were serialized, starting with the satirical *Hard Times* (1854), which doubled the journal's circulation even though his normal style had suffered because of the constrictions of space. In December 1853 he gave a public reading of his works, for charity. This became such a welcome diversion for the public, and such a preoccupation with himself, that in 1858 he started doing it regularly, for his own financial benefit—that year he toured 44 centres in Britain, and in 1867–68 a dozen American cities, in spite of continuous ill-health. His theatrical bent manifested itself also in his arrangement of and participation in amateur productions at Tavistock House, his home in London from 1851 to 1860, and at other places in England. For a tour in 1857 he engaged, with her mother and sister, the young actress Ellen Ternan (1839–1914). His relationship with her was the ultimate cause of his separation from his wife in 1858, after she had borne him ten children—see Claire Tomalin, *The Invisible Woman: the Story of Nelly Ternan and Charles Dickens* (rev. edn 1991). When the proprietors of *Punch*, who also had a substantial share in *Household Words*, refused to print a notice justifying the separation, he shut down *Household Words*, and in 1859 started in its place *All the Year Round*, which he edited until his death.

Dickens wrote two historical novels, *Barnaby Rudge* (1841) and *A Tale of Two Cities* (1859). The rest, excluding his shorter excursions into the supernatural, notably *A Christmas Carol* (1843), are stories of contemporary life. They range from the broad fun of Mr Pickwick, the lighter comedy surrounding

Nicholas Nickleby, and the black humour of *Bleak House* (1853), to the tear-jerking demise of Nell in *the Old Curiosity Shop* (1841), the darkness of *Little Dorrit* (1857), and the depth and suspense of *Great Expectations* (1861). The perennially popular *The Personal History of David Copperfield* (1850) contains elements from his own childhood and early career. Essentially he was a comic writer of genius and a remarkable student of character, with a highly-developed sense of drama and of dramatic speech, and a perception of the exact image and most telling descriptive detail. He was less of a social reformer (being too inconsistent in his arguments) than a great novelist who used social conditions to enhance his effects. See Peter Ackroyd, *Dickens*, new edn 1994 (biography); Grahame Smith, *Charles Dickens: a Literary Life*, 1996 (biographical/critical study); John Carey, *The Violent Effigy: a Study of Dickens' Imagination*, new edn 1991; John Butt and Kathleen Tillotson, *Dickens at Work*, 1957 (critical study); Nicolas Bentley, Michael Slater, and Nina Burgis, *The Dickens Index*, new edn 1990.

DICKEY, JAMES (LAFAYETTE) (*b.* 1923) American poet, novelist, and critic, was born and brought up in a suburb of Atlanta, the son of an attorney whose family had moved to the city from the northern Georgian hills. Tall and strong, he was a football star at high school but preferred athletics—see his essay 'Night Hurdling'. After a year at Clemson College, North Carolina, he enlisted in the air force and flew more than a hundred missions in the Pacific—'My values were formed by the service or military life.' To the rest periods he owes his initial acquaintance with modern poetry; to living 'with life and death every day and every night' can be attributed his portrayal as a writer of survival, often in heroic circumstances. After World War II he graduated *magna cum laude* in English from Vanderbilt University, where he was taught by the poet-critic Donald Davidson (1893–1968). His poetry was published in magazines while he was an instructor in technical English and report writing at Rice Institute, a stint interrupted by service as a flying instructor during the Korean War 1951–52. After a further year teaching at the University of Florida, he went into advertising, 'a fascinating and exciting way to live'. Known as 'Jingle Jim', he worked on the Coca-Cola account among others, and wrote his first book, *Into the Stone and Other Poems* (1960), in odd moments during company time. A Guggenheim fellowship enabled him to visit Europe, after which he returned to teaching. *Helmets* (1964) included several war poems: *Buckdancer's Choice* (1965) won the National Book Award. *Poems 1957–1967* (1967), his first major collection, included two significant new poems, 'Falling' and 'May Day Sermons', which he described (1981) as 'the one

the hallucinated version of a girl's fall from an airliner and the other an equally hysterical improvisation on a folk theme from north Georgia, both poems of madness, death, and violent affirmation'. He was Consultant in Poetry to the Library of Congress 1967–69.

In 1968 he became First Carolina Professor and Poet-in-Residence at the University of South Carolina. *Deliverance* (1970), a novel about a canoe voyage (a form of transport at which he is adroit) which he has described as 'a story where under the conditions of extreme violence people find out things about themselves that they would have no other means of knowing', had lain in a drawer for several years before he revised and finished it. It was a best seller and became a film (1972) for which he wrote the screenplay. After the death in 1976 of his first wife, by whom he had two sons, he married Deborah Dobson, a 23-year-old former student of his. *Puella* (1982), a collection celebrating the 'fragility and mystery' of young womanhood, was published on their daughter's first birthday. *The Central Motion: Poems 1968–1979* was published in 1983. Dickey's poetry is written in what he calls 'unrhymed, irregular verse', a longer poem going through 150 to 175 drafts. His criticism is outspoken but witty, honest, and often profound. He has translated a collection by his friend YEVTUSHENKO, *Stolen Apples* (1971), without necessarily approving of what he calls 'using poetry as a pretext for making bohemian speeches'. His critical works include *Babel to Byzantium: Poets and Poetry Now* (1968). See *Self-Interviews*, ed. Barbara and James Reiss, new edn 1984; Ronald Baughman, *Understanding James Dickey*, 1986 (critical study).

DICKINSON, EMILY (1830–86) American poet, was born in Amherst, Massachusetts, the second of three children of Edward Dickinson (1803–74), lawyer, civic leader, state senator, and member of Congress, and Emily Norcross (1804–82). She was educated at Amherst Academy and for a year as a boarder at Mount Holyoke Female Seminary, South Hadley, about eight miles from home. Of a number of early romantic friendships, the most intense was with Susan (Sue) Gilbert (1830–1913), who in 1856 married Emily's brother, Austin Dickinson (1829–95). In 1855 she was persuaded to accompany her younger sister Lavinia (1833–99) to Washington, and then to Philadelphia, where she may have heard a sermon at the Arch Street Presbyterian Church by Rev. Charles Wadsworth (1814–82). She later referred to him as 'my shepherd from little girl-hood', but only two meetings are recorded, when he visited her unexpectedly ('Why did you not tell me you were coming, so I could have it to hope for?') in 1860, and again in 1880. Though her bread won second prize at the local fair in 1856, the following year she served on the Cattle Show committee, and in 1864–65 she made two trips to Boston for eye treatment, in 1869 she could write, 'I do not cross my Father's ground to any House or Town.' In spite of the fact that latterly her seclusion bordered on the eccentric (she conducted interviews from upstairs through a half-closed door), her family saw nothing odd in her desire for solitude. According to Mabel Loomis Todd (1856–1932), the wife of an Amherst professor, who, as Austin's mistress, was often in the house (he lived next door to the family home), 'All the far-fetched and imaginative reasons for Emily having become a recluse, a white-draped and spectacular household ghost, are as unnecessary as they are false. It was merely a normal blossoming of her own untouched spirit.'

In 1862 she reacted to an article in *Atlantic Monthly*, 'Letter to a Young Contributor', by the critic Thomas Wentworth Higginson (1823–1911), by sending him four poems and a brief note, beginning, 'Are you too deeply occupied to say if my Verse is alive?'. Her response to his intrigued enquiries was a longer, but even more enigmatic letter, and three more poems. Though they only met twice, in 1870 and 1873 ('I never was with anyone who drained my nerve power so much,' he confessed to his wife), they corresponded regularly. She died of Bright's disease, and at her funeral he read EMILY BRONTË's 'No coward soul is mine . . .'.

Only seven of her poems were published in her lifetime, all anonymously. One of them (in 1878) was at the instigation, and insistence, of JACKSON, who in 1886 went to live in the same literary boarding house as the Higginsons, and who wrote to her in 1876: 'You are a great poet—and it is wrong to the day you live in, that you will not sing aloud.' She left, in all, 1775 poems, some threaded together in little packets, some jotted down on whatever was to hand, others sent to friends in letters or with gifts—see *The Manuscript Books of Emily Dickinson*, ed. R. W. Franklin (1981). Lavinia discovered the cache of packets in her room after her death, and took them to Todd, who transcribed them and, with Higginson, chose 115 for publication in 1890—with rhymes smoothed, metres regularized, and diction altered to suit what they regarded as the sensibilities of the public. Further collections continued to appear, with *Bolts of Melody: New Poems of Emily Dickinson* (1945), for which texts prepared by Todd were put together by her daughter, completing the canon. The first scholarly edition of all the poems was that of Professor Thomas H. Johnson, *The Poems of Emily Dickinson* (3 vols 1955), 'Including variant readings critically compared with all known manuscripts', which established a chronology for them— see also the one-volume (reading text) edition as *The Complete Poems of Emily Dickinson* (1960). Dickinson is now recognized as America's finest woman writer, and one of its greatest poets of either sex. Her compressed lyrics contain a wealth of emotions, presented in simple metre patterns and rhyme schemes which often reflect the hymns of the time, with idiosyncratic punctuation and an abundance of dashes, which she employed as a musical device. See *Selected Letters*, ed. Thomas H. Johnson, new edn 1985; Richard B. Sewall, *The Life of Emily Dickinson*, 2 vols new edn 1994; Jerome Loving, *Emily Dickinson: the Poet on the Second Story*, 1986 (critical study).

DICKINSON, PATRIC (1914–94) British poet, dramatist, and classical translator, was born in Nasirabad, India, only three months before his father, an officer in the British Army in India, was killed by the Turks at the battle of Tel-el-amara. At a prep school in Kent he 'learnt a lot'; at King's School, Bruton, he taught himself out of classroom hours 'a bit more Greek and Latin and a *lot* more English', by reading on his own. As a result, he won an exhibition to St Catherine's College, Cambridge, where his tutor was T. R. Henn (1901–74), the Irish poet and academic. He taught up to the beginning of World War II, and served in the Artists' Rifles in 1939–40, after which he worked for the BBC until 1948, first as a producer and then as Acting Poetry Editor. He was Gresham Professor of Rhetoric, City University 1964–67. His first collection of verse, *Theseus and the Minotaur, and Poems* (1946), reflected aspects of wartime and also the attitude of someone who had grown up in the prewar years to the shattering change brought about by the impact of nuclear fission. He was, however, primarily a lyricist and poet of the countryside, to whom the paradoxes of life were an essential part of his poetic expression. He wrote verse plays for BBC radio (including an adaptation of PLAUTUS) and for the stage; *The Durable Fire*, about the conflict between King John, Pope Innocent III, and Archbishop Langton at the beginning of the 13th century was commissioned for performance in the chapter house of Canterbury Cathedral in 1962. His translations include *The Aeneid of Virgil* (1961) and *The Complete Plays of Aristophanes* (2 vols 1971). See *Selected Poems*, 1968; *Shadow of the Earth: Poems from Forty Years*, 1992; *The Good Minute: an Autobiographical Study*, 1965.

DIDEROT, DENIS (1713–84) French philosopher and prose writer, was born in Langres, the son of a master cutler, went to the local Jesuit college, and graduated as MA in Paris in 1732. Destined for the Church, and then for the law, he chose instead to be a man of letters, which infuriated his father, who in 1742 had him shut up in a monastery to try to prevent his marriage. He was commissioned by a bookseller/publisher in 1746 to edit, with the mathematician Jean D'Alembert (1717–83), what was intended as a French translation of the fourth edition of *Cyclopaedia: or, An Universal Dictionary of Arts and Sciences* (1728) by Ephraim Chambers (1680–1740); it developed into an original work comprising over sixty thousand articles, many of them written by himself. *Encyclopédie: ou, Dictionnaire Raisonné des Sciences, des Arts, et des Métiers,* 'an endeavour,' wrote CARLYLE in the *Foreign Quarterly Review* (1833), 'to which only the Siege of Troy may offer some faint parallel', and which stands as a monument of the Enlightenment, was published 1751–72; the later volumes were issued unofficially after Parliament had in 1759 outlawed the work as a destabilizing influence on the Church. Diderot had already been imprisoned in 1749 in the Château de Vincennes for a pornographic novel, *Les Bijoux Indiscrets* (1748; tr. Sophie Hawkes as *The Indiscreet Jewels,* 1993) and a subversive tract, *Lettre sur les Aveugles* [Letter on the Blind] (1749).

To circumvent the regulations against unauthorized art criticism, he managed in 1759 to get himself appointed art critic to the *Correspondance Littéraire,* a handwritten journal with a tiny circulation, mainly to foreign potentates—*Diderot on Art,* ed. and tr. John Goodman (2 vols 1995) covers the exhibitions at the Salon Carré of 1765 and 1767 respectively. During the 1760s he wrote several works unpublished during his lifetime, including a satire, *Le Neveu de Rameau* [*Rameau's Nephew*], which GOETHE translated into German from a manuscript; a sequence of three philosophical dialogues, *Le Rêve de d'Alembert* (tr. Leonard Tancock as *D'Alembert's Dream* with *Rameau's Nephew,* 1966); *La Religieuse* (tr. Tancock as *The Nun,* 1974; tr. Frances Birrell as *Memoirs of a Nun,* rev. edn with preface by P. N. Furbank, 1992), a fictional memoir which began as a joke; and *Jacques le Fataliste et son Maître* (as *Jacques the Fatalist and His Master* tr. Tancock 1979; tr. Wesley D. Camp, 1984), a comic extravaganza whose starting point is STERNE—see also *This Is Not a Story and Other Stories,* ed. and tr. P. N. Furbank (1993). In 1765, to raise a dowry for his daughter, he sold his library to Catherine the Great of Russia, retaining the use of it during his lifetime. In 1773 he travelled to St Petersburg to thank her. Letters he wrote to Sophie Volland (1716–84), with whom he fell in love in 1755, constitute a philosophical autobiography—see *Letters to Sophie Volland,* tr. Peter France (1972). See *Selected Writings on Art and Literature,* tr. Geoffrey Bremner, 1994; P. N. Furbank, *Diderot: a Critical Biography,* new edn 1993.

DINESEN, ISAK see BLIXEN.

DISRAELI, BENJAMIN (1st Earl of Beaconsfield) (1804–81) statesman and novelist, was born in London of Jewish parentage, and

educated privately. When he was 13, his father, Isaac D'Israeli (1766–1848), a minor literary figure with private means who wrote *Curiosities of Literature* (6 vols 1781–1834), was in disagreement with his synagogue and had all his children baptized. Disraeli studied law, but abandoned it for politics and literature. Between 1826, when he published anonymously the first part of *Vivian Grey,* whose cynical hero manipulates his way to political power (and disaster), and 1837, when, after several unsuccessful attempts, he was elected to Parliament, he wrote ten novels of varying genres. The most notable of these are *Contarini Fleming* (1832), 'a psychological autobiography', and *The Wondrous Tale of Alroy* (1833), an oriental romance with a Jewish hero. The subsequent trilogy, *Coningsby* (1844), *Sybil* (1845), and *Tancred* (1847), highlights the duties of Church and Crown, the dichotomy between rich and poor, and the differences which affect relations between Christians and Jews. When he had become a senior political figure, he returned to fiction with *Lothair* (1870), a quest novel in which the hero is torn between (and tempted by) three women and the conflicting claims of Anglicanism, Catholicism, and Italian patriotism. *Endymion* (1880) is a reflection of his own early political career. In 1852 he served the first of three terms as Chancellor of the Exchequer, and he was Prime Minister in 1868 and again from 1874 to 1880. He was created Earl of Beaconsfield in 1876. He was the first British political novelist and the first major novelist in English who was of Jewish origin and wrote about Jewish themes. His considerable verbal and literary wit, however, was of the flamboyant English kind rather than of the more deprecatory nature usually associated with Jewish humour. See Stanley Weintraub, *Disraeli: a Biography,* 1993; Paul Smith, *Disraeli: a Brief Life,* 1996; Daniel Schwarz, *Disraeli's Fiction,* 1979; John Vincent, *Disraeli,* 1990 (study of his ideas and writings).

DOBSON, ROSEMARY (*b.* 1920) Australian poet, granddaughter of the Victorian poet and critic, Austin Dobson (1840–1921), was born in Sydney and educated at Frensham, Mittagong, New South Wales, and Sydney University. While at school she wrote, designed, and printed *Poems* (1937), a foretaste of the interest in art which informs much of her verse. During World War II she worked for the publisher Angus and Robertson. Her first commercial publication was *In a Convex Mirror* (1944). The title poem of *The Ship of Ice and Other Poems* (1948) dramatically recalls the discovery in the Antarctic in 1860 of a ship and its crew, preserved in the ice. In 1951 she married the editor and publisher Alec Bolton (*b.* 1926), during whose assignment in London between 1966 and 1971 she visited cultural and artistic centres in Europe. *Over the Frontier* (1978) has a section 'Poems for Pausanias', directly inspired by the 2nd-century AD Greek travel writer and including the sequence of four-line epigrammatic observations, 'Greek Coins'. *The Continuance of Poetry* (1981), incorporated in *Three Fates and Other Poems* (1984), contains a series of poems in memory of DAVID CAMPBELL, with whom she translated *Moscow Trefoil* (1975) and *Seven Russian Poets* (1979), including poems by AKHMATOVA and MANDELSTAM. She was made AO in 1987. See *Collected Poems*, 1991.

DOCTOROW, E(DGAR) L(AWRENCE) (*b.* 1931) American novelist, was born in New York City and recalls that at ten, 'Whenever I read anything I seemed to identify as much with the act of composition as with the story.' He went to the Bronx High School of Science, Kenyon College (where he studied poetry texts under RANSOM), and for a postgraduate year to Columbia University, after which he did two years with the US Army in Germany. He was an airport reservations clerk and reader for a film company before becoming an editor at New American Library in 1959, and then Editor-in-Chief (1964) and Publisher (1969) of Dial Press, New York. He resigned to write full time in 1971, since when he has also taught at Sarah Lawrence College, New York; he became an adjunct professor of English at New York University in 1982. *Welcome to Hard Times* (1960; in UK as *Bad Man from Bodie*, 1961) and *Big as Life* (1966), are postmodernist reinterpretations of the Western and of the science-fiction novel. *The Book of Daniel* (1971) is a study of the collective American consciousness during circumstances based on the Rosenberg affair, which culminated in 1953 with the execution of a middle-aged couple for spying for the USSR. A serious political writer, even when at his most entertaining, as in *Ragtime* (1975) and *World's Fair* (1985), or most compelling, as in *Billy Bathgate* (1989), he offers a revisionist view of American history, in which historical figures often play fictional parts. The individual elements of *Lives of the Poets: Six Stories and a Novella* (1984) differ in form but contain images and ideas which recur through the book. *The Waterworks* (1994) is largely a pastiche of POE. See also *Jack London, Hemingway, and the Constitution: Selected Essays 1977–1992* (1993). See Paul Levine, *E. L. Doctorow*, 1985 (critical study).

DODGSON, CHARLES LUTWIDGE see CARROLL.

DOMETT, ALFRED (1811–87) statesman and poet, was born in Camberwell Grove, Surrey, was educated at St John's College, Cambridge, without taking a degree, and studied law at the Middle Temple, being called to the Bar in 1841. He published a book of verse in 1833, and a long poem on Venice in 1839. In 1842 he purchased land in New Zealand, and emigrated there, to the consternation of his friend ROBERT BROWNING, of whose 'What's become of Waring / Since he gave us all the slip . . .' he is the subject. Nevertheless he prospered, being Member of the New Zealand House of Representatives for Nelson 1855–63, and Premier 1862–63, after which he held prominent positions in land administration. He retired to England in 1871. Neither *Ranolf and Amohia: a South-Sea Day Dream* (1872; rev. edn 1883), a philosophical poetic romance in which East, in the person of a Maori princess, meets and ultimately mates with West, nor *Flotsam and Jetsam: Rhymes Old and New* (1877) draw on the practical experience in New Zealand of this able administrator and politician, who was made CMG in 1880. His diaries of 1872–85—see *The Diary of Alfred Domett*, ed. E. A. Horsman (1953)—include a delightful picture of Browning buttering up 'a rather finely dressed lady' at an exhibition of his son's work, not recognizing her to be his own cook.

DONLEAVY, J(AMES) P(ATRICK) (*b.* 1926) Irish novelist and dramatist, was born of Irish parents in Brooklyn, New York, and was educated at a private school. He served in the US Navy during World War II, after which he went to Trinity College, Dublin. His first novel, *The Ginger Man*, whose protagonist was drawn from a college drinking companion, was published in Paris and London in 1955, but in its unexpurgated form not until 1963. By this time his stage adaptation had been performed (1959), and in Dublin withdrawn, and *Fairy Tales of New York* (1961) had also been staged. In 1967 Donleavy became an Irish citizen, in which capacity he has continued to bring Irish gusto (as well as an American flavour) to his novels. *The Beastly Beatitudes of Balthazar B.* (1968) has a mainly Irish setting, while the three in the Darcy Dancer sequence—*The Destinies of Darcy Dancer, Gentleman* (1977), *Leila* (1983), and *That Darcy, That Dancer, That Gentleman* (1990)—re-create a largely fictitious rural Ireland in which the hunt features strongly but not all the hunted are animal. Donleavy's colourful and eccentric characters, his relish for the bawdy, his rich, idiosyncratic prose, and his stylistic devices, notably the tailpiece haiku, make him one of the most distinctive as well as unusual modern Irish writers. *The History of the Ginger Man* (1994) is a rich autobiographical study of Dublin (including sketches of BEHAN) and New York, and of the problems of getting and being published. Since the early 1970s he has lived in a 250-year-old country house in the Irish midlands. He confessed in an article (1996): 'There I am, the squire and pasha, often bereft, lonely, and having again and again been left in the lurch by one beautiful woman after another.'

DONNE, JOHN (1572–1631) English poet, prose writer, and cleric, was born in Bread Street, London, of a prominent Catholic family. He studied at both Oxford and Cambridge, though prevented by his faith from taking a degree. He and his brother Henry entered Lincoln's Inn in 1592, but in 1593 Henry was arrested for harbouring a priest, and died in jail before coming to trial. From this period come 'Satire III', an agonized expression of the doubts that led to Donne's apostasy, and the half-bantering prose 'Paradoxes and Problems', as well, no doubt, as some of his secular songs and elegies. After two years serving with the fleet (see his poems 'The Storme' and 'The Calme') he became in 1597 secretary to the Lord Keeper of the Great Seal, Sir Thomas Egerton (c.1540–1617), in which capacity he was elected to Parliament in 1601. Unfortunately for his career prospects, he had fallen in love with, and in 1601 secretly married, Egerton's 16-year-old niece, Ann, whose father had him imprisoned and dismissed from his post. A fairly miserable period followed. Donne spent much time looking for patronage or a job. He was also writing such works as *Biathanatos*, a treatise on suicide (not intended for publication); many of the 'Holy Sonnets' and other religious poems; and verses to order, including the erotic St Valentine's Day 'An Epithalamion . . . on the Lady Elizabeth and Count Palatine Being Married', and the diplomatic 'Epithalamion' for the Earl of Somerset and his 'virgin' bride, the former wife of the Earl of Essex (see also CAMPION). 'A Funerall Elegie' (for Elizabeth Drury, died 1610) and its two *Anniversaries* so pleased the girl's father that he pressed for their publication, embarrassing the poet, who did not want his praise of the subject to offend two female patrons he was courting. Definitely intended for publication was *Pseudo-Martyr* (1610), an argument in favour of Catholics taking the Oath of Allegiance to JAMES VI, a copy of which he astutely presented to the King in person. James's response was equally shrewd. He turned down all Donne's requests for political and other posts, and insisted that he enter the Church, which he did in 1615 after a terrible year in which he was ill, his wife miscarried, and two of his children died.

The King now appointed him a royal chaplain, and obtained for him a Cambridge doctorate and several benefices. Donne also became Reader in Divinity at Lincoln's Inn in 1616, which entailed giving fifty sermons a year to an influential and intelligent congregation. In 1617 Ann died giving birth to their 12th child. Donne's grief is apparent from the sonnet 'Since she whom I loved . . .', which begins as a conventional hymn to the goodness of God and then breaks down: 'But though I have found thee, and thou my thirst has fed, / A holy thirsty dropsy melts mee

yett . . .'. In 1619 he was chaplain to Viscount Doncaster's mission of mediation between the Protestant Bohemians and the Emperor of Germany. The summit of his ambitions and the culmination of years of assiduous soliciting came in 1621 with his nomination as Dean of St Paul's Cathedral. Though he was required to preach only three times a year, he did so frequently. It was as a preacher rather than as a poet that he expected to be remembered, with some justification, in the light of his powers of imagery, rhetoric, and frequent economy of thought. The first volume of his sermons was published in 1622, and eight more before 1633. He died a few weeks after preaching his own death sermon before King Charles I at Whitehall, and having acted as model for his own effigy in St Paul's.

While many of his poems were circulated in manuscript in his lifetime, the first published edition of his poetry was in 1633, and included both secular and divine works. His apparent lack of melody and the doubts sparked off in DRYDEN's *A Discourse Concerning Satire* (1693), 'He affects the metaphysics . . . where only nature should reign' (from which came the term 'Metaphysical poets'), hindered his recognition. It is the very depth, allusiveness, and above all revelation of experience that distinguish his work and influenced 20th-century poetry, especially that of T. S. ELIOT. These qualities are to be found particularly in his poems of love, such as 'Loves Infiniteness', 'The Sunne Rising', 'A Lecture upon the Shadow', 'Elegie XIX: Going to Bed', 'Elegie XII: His Parting from Her', and the songs 'Goe, and catch a falling starre . . .' and 'Sweetest love, I do not goe . . .'. His poetry is also distinctive for the way in which conceits graphically yoke together heterogeneous elements. See [*Works*], ed. John Carey, 1990 (comprehensive selection); *Selected Poems*, ed. Richard Gill, 1990; *Selected Poetry*, ed. John Carey, 1996; *The Divine Poems*, ed. Helen Gardner new edn 1982; *Love Poems*, ed. Charles Fowkes, new edn 1989; *Selected Prose*, ed. Neil Rhodes, 1987; R. C. Bald, *John Donne: a Life*, new edn 1986; John Carey, *John Donne: Life, Mind and Art*, new edn 1990.

DOOLITTLE, HILDA (H. D.) (1886–1961) American poet, was born in Bethlehem, Pennsylvania, the eldest child by his second marriage of Charles Leander Doolittle (1834–1919), who in 1896 was appointed Flower Professor of Astronomy and Director of the Observatory, University of Pennsylvania. She went to the Friends' Central School, Philadelphia. When she was just 15 she met POUND at a Halloween party, and became his protégée and, at one point, his fiancée. She entered Bryn Mawr in 1904, but dropped out two years later because of illness. In 1911 she went to Europe with friends for a holiday, and did not return, having settled, with her parents' approval, in England, where Pound was now ensconced. In 1913 he placed in the fourth issue of the Chicago-based *Poetry: a Magazine of Verse* three poems signed 'H. D., Imagiste', thus establishing her as the most representative member of the Imagist movement. Later that year she married ALDINGTON, with whom she studied classical Greek literature, the main influence in her first collection of 27 poems, *Sea Garden* (1916). Aldington's war service was a factor in the breakdown of their marriage. The baby, Perdita, born shortly after they separated in 1919 (they divorced in 1938), was not his. H. D. was rescued from these and other tribulations by Winifred Ellerman (1894–1983), the novelist 'Bryher', who had sent her a fan letter after reading *Sea Garden*, and who became her lover, close friend, and patron, and later adopted Perdita.

H. D. now published translations of choruses from EURIPIDES (1916, 1919), further collections of verse, *Hymen* (1921) and *Heliodora, and Other Poems* (1924), and, as solid evidence of her craftsmanship, *Collected Poems* (1925). She settled in Switzerland, and in 1933–34 underwent analysis in Vienna by FREUD, a process which released several autobiographical and semi-autobiographical studies, notably *Tribute to Freud* (1956), *Bid Me to Live* (1960), *The Gift* (1969), and *HER-mione* (1981). While suffering the bombing in London during World War II, she wrote three linked poems in free verse couplets, inspired by a spiritual conviction that war can be endured: *The Walls Do Not Fall* (1944), *Tribute to the Angels* (1945), and *The Flowering of the Rod* (1946), published together as *Trilogy*. *Helen in Egypt* (1961) is a poetic reworking of the Trojan legend, told in the form of a dramatic monologue by Helen, whom she translates from Greece to Egypt. *End to Torment* (1979) is an account of her relationship with Pound, and also (during World War I) with D. H. LAWRENCE and his wife. See *Selected Poems*, ed. Louis L. Martz, new edn 1988; Janice S. Robinson, *H. D.: the Life and Work of an American Poet*, 1982.

DORRIS, MICHAEL see ERDRICH.

DOS PASSOS, JOHN (1896–1970) American novelist, was born in a Chicago hotel, the illegitimate son of a wealthy Portuguese-American attorney and a Maryland widow, by whose surname of Madison he was called until 1912, after his parents' marriage on the death of his father's wife. He had an uprooted childhood before going to Choate School, Connecticut, and Harvard College, where he wrote stories for and edited *Harvard Monthly*, and graduated *cum laude* in 1916, shortly after the death of his mother. Though he was one of the contributors to *Eight Harvard Poets* (1917), he has said of this juncture in his life, 'I never wanted to

be a writer.' Having signed up for ambulance service overseas, he was persuaded by his father, who had fought in the American Civil War, to go to Spain instead, to study architecture, his main interest at the time. On his father's death in 1917, he returned to the USA, enlisted in the ambulance service again, and served in France and Italy, being drafted into the Medical Corps when the USA entered World War I. *One Man's Initiation—1917* (1920; reissued as *First Encounter*, 1945) is an observer's fictional view of the war; *Three Soldiers* (1921) is a pacifist interpretation of the combat itself. In *Manhattan Transfer* (1925) he used techniques similar to those of the film editor to weave numerous characters into the fabric of his novel, which is essentially a study of frustration and failure in a depersonalized society. The same techniques, intensified by the use of sketches of real figures, collages of news headlines and snatches of songs, and impressionistic interludes, inform his major trilogy, *The 42nd Parallel* (1930), *1919* (1932), and *The Big Money* (1936), published together as *U.S.A.* (1938; new edn, ed. Townsend Luddington and Daniel Aaron, 1996), a historical and social, as well as a personal, vision of America's evolution from 1900 to the onset of the Great Depression in 1929, from a radical 1930s' point of view.

In common with other radical writers, he supported the cause (and in 1927 published a defence) of the two anarchists in the Sacco–Vanzetti affair, who were convicted of murder in 1921 and executed in 1927. Between 1926 and 1934 he was active in Communist affairs, without being a member of the party, but became disillusioned. After World War II he saw socialism as a greater threat to personal freedom than free enterprise, a philosophy reflected in a further trilogy: *Adventures of a Young Man* (1939), in which the protagonist's experience of Communism reflects his own, *Number One* (1943), and *The Grand Design* (1942)—published together as *District of Columbia* (1952). *Mid-Century: a Contemporary Chronicle* (1961) reverts to the format of *U.S.A.* A journalist, travel writer, and historian, he also wrote three plays in which the individual's place in society depends on coming to grips with time. *Chosen Country* (1951) is an autobiographical novel which follows his early life and his romance with his first wife, who was killed in 1947 in the car crash in which he lost an eye. See *The Best Times: an Informal Memoir*, 1968; Linda W. Wagner, *Dos Passos: Artist as American*, 1979 (critical study).

DOSTOEVSKY, FYODOR (MIKHAILOVICH) (1821–81) Russian novelist, was born in Moscow in the hospital for the poor where his father was resident doctor. He entered the military engineering school in St Petersburg in 1838, the year after his mother died. In 1839 his father, who had retired to a country estate, was murdered by his peasant-serfs. Dostoevsky was commissioned as a 2nd lieutenant in 1842 and joined the engineering department of the War Ministry, from which he resigned two years later for a literary career. He published the short novels [*Poor People*] and [*The Double*] in 1846, the year he began to have epileptic fits. In 1849 he was arrested for alleged participation in a socialist conspiracy, sentenced to death, led to the scaffold, and then reprieved. Two days later, in mid-winter, he was taken in irons to Siberia by sled. After four years in a labour camp he was transferred to Semipalatinsk, on the Mongolian border, to serve as a common soldier. He was promoted to ensign in 1856, and in 1857 he married Marya Dmitrevna Isaeva, née Constant, a widow, in Kuznetsk. In 1859, having been discharged from the army, he returned to St Petersburg and began writing again. [*Memoirs from the House of the Dead*] (tr. Marie von Thilo as *Buried Alive: or, Ten Years of Penal Servitude in Siberia*, 1881; tr. Jessie Coulson, 1983) was printed in full in his elder brother Mikhail's journal, *Vremya* [Time], in 1861. After the magazine was suppressed in 1863 he embarked on a trip to France and Italy with a female companion, Apollinaria Suslova—she later married the critic V. V. Rozanov (1856–1919). They returned via Homburg, where he gambled compulsively. Marya died in April 1864, Mikhail in July, shortly after the demise of their new journal, *Epokha* [The Age], through lack of funds.

[*Crime and Punishment*] (tr. 1886; tr. Coulson,, ed. Richard Peace, 2nd edn 1995), the first of his really significant novels, with a depth that belies its romantic theme of murder and remorse, was serialized throughout 1866, during which he dictated [*The Gambler*] (1866) to Anna Grigorevna, whom he married in 1867. They spent the next four years in Germany, where he gambled and worked on [*The Idiot*] (serialized 1868; tr. F. Whishaw, 1887; tr. David Magarshack, 1955); in Switzerland, where they had a daughter who died; in Italy; and in Germany again, where they had a second daughter, who survived. They returned to St Petersburg in 1871, eight days before the birth of a son. He now completed [*The Possessed*] (tr. Constance Garnett, 1913; tr. Magarshack as *The Devils*, 1953), which began serialization later that year. A second son died in 1878 of epilepsy at the age of two. With [*The Brothers Karamazov*] (serialized 1879–80; tr. Garnett, 1912; tr. Magarshack, 1958; tr. Richard Pevear and Larissa Volokhonsky, 1992; tr. David McDuff, 1993; as *The Karamazov Brothers* ed. and tr. Ignat Avsey, 1994) he confirmed his reputation as a religious and political spokesman as well as an interpreter of character and a skilful narrator of strong plots. He died two days after a lung haemorrhage.

The judgments of English critics during the fifty years after his death were mixed. STEVENSON, who read *Crime and Punishment* in French, was enthusiastic, as were WILDE, GISSING, BARING, and BENNETT; not so CONRAD, HENRY JAMES, GALSWORTHY, and D. H. LAWRENCE, who read *The Brothers Karamazov* three times and concluded: 'Each time I find it more depressing because, alas, more drearily true to life. At first it had been lurid romance.' Subsequently he has become recognized as one of the founders of the modern psychological novel, who had a profound insight into the human condition and into human behaviour. *A Writer's Diary* (tr. Kenneth Lantz, two vols; *1873–1876*, 1993, and *1877–1881*, 1994), which began as a weekly journal column and by 1876 had become a periodical in its own right, was the medium through which he shared his thoughts on literature and topical and social issues with the Russian public. See Frank Joseph, *Dostoevsky: The Seeds of Revolt 1821–1849*, new edn 1979; *The Years of Ordeal 1850–1859*, new edn 1986, *The Stir of Liberation 1860–1865*, new edn 1988, *The Miraculous Years 1865–1871*, 1995.

DOUGHTY, CHARLES MONTAGUE
(1843–1926) British poet and traveller, was born at Theberton Hall, Suffolk, the son of a landowning cleric, and was educated for the Royal Navy at Beach House School, Portsmouth. After failing his medical, he went to Gonville and Caius College, Cambridge, to read geology. Finding the teaching uncongenial, he transferred to Downing College, spending nine months during 1863–64 alone in Norway, examining glaciers. His consuming interest, however, was medieval and Elizabethan literature, and his aim was to write poetry which would recapture its flavour and language. As a start, he visited European cultural and historical centres, and by degrees reached Damascus. Here, having been refused help by the Royal Geographical Society, failed locally to get permission to join a pilgrim caravan to Mecca, and been disowned for his initiative by the British Consul, he spent a year learning Arabic. Then in 1876 he set out, on his own, dressed as an Arab but with no attempt to hide the fact that he was Christian. Even when writing up his astonishing and dangerous two-year personal pilgrimage, *Travels in Arabia Deserta* (1888), he remained true to what he regarded as his literary predestination. The literary style which he invented for it, with its admixture of Arabic and archaic terms and usages, ensured that what would otherwise just have been a masterpiece of travel writing and anthropology is also a linguistic curiosity, rather than the philological milestone he intended. Nothing daunted, he spent the rest of his life turning out epic poems in which he played out his personal theories of language and prosody, beginning with *The Dawn in Britain* (1906).

DOUGLAS, GAVIN (*c.*1474–1522) Scottish poet and cleric, was born at Tantallon Castle, the third son of Archibald 'Bell-the-Cat', 5th Earl of Angus (*c.*1449–1514), and was educated at St Andrews University and probably in Paris. He was much at the court of James IV, in whose honour he wrote an allegorical poem in courtly Italianate style, *Palice of Honour*. After the disaster of the battle of Flodden and the death of the King in 1513, Douglas's nephew, the 6th Earl (*c.*1489–1557), married James IV's widow (Margaret Tudor). She proposed the poet unsuccessfully for the vacant archbishopric of St Andrews and then successfully as Bishop of Dunkeld, which he became in 1516. For the rest of his life he was much in demand as a promoter of causes and a dealer in political intrigue, but he was finally exiled, and died in London of the plague. His position in literary history is very properly founded on *Eneados*, his translation into Scots rhyming couplets of the 12 books of VIRGIL's *Aeneid*, plus a 13th book from an original composed in 1428 by the Italian humanist Maphaeus Vegius, all of which he completed by 1513. It is regarded as the best translation of that epic until DRYDEN's, and livelier and more in tune with its readership in that the climate, landscapes, treatment of the supernatural, and the battles and ship sequences, are rendered in terms of the contemporary Scottish experience. See Priscilla Bawcutt, *Gavin Douglas: a Critical Study*, 1976.

DOUGLAS, GEORGE, pseudonym of George Douglas Brown (1869–1902) Scottish novelist, was born in the village of Ochiltree, Ayrshire, the illegitimate son of an independent-minded local farmer and the daughter of an Irish labourer. He was educated at Ayr Academy and Glasgow University, where he got a first in classics and an exhibition to Balliol College, Oxford. His mother's illness and his own ill-health contributed to a poor final result, and on her death in 1895 he went to London, where he became a freelance journalist and wrote a boy's adventure story, *Love and Sword* (1899), under the name of Kennedy King. He was encouraged by reactions to a story to expand it into a novel, which he did in a cottage retreat he rented in Haslemere. *The House with the Green Shutters* (1901) by 'George Douglas', written much on the lines of a Greek tragedy (complete with 'chorus' of village gossips) and with deliberate intent to counter the sentimentality of the Kailyard novelists, was very well received in the USA as well as in Britain, for all that its power genuinely to disturb the reader is not fully carried through to its end, which slides into melodrama. He now began to write up notes he had made on the craft of the novelist and to begin another novel, to be called 'The Incompatibles'. He died of pneumonia in a friend's house in London, having been taken ill during his return from a visit to Scotland, and was buried in his mother's grave in Ayr.

DOUGLAS, KEITH (1920–44) British poet, was born in Tunbridge Wells, Kent, and could read and write excellently, and also draw, when he went to boarding school at six. When he was eight, his father left home, and he never saw him again. He was educated at Christ's Hospital, where he impressed with his personality and energy and had a poem accepted by GRIGSON for *New Verse*, and for two years at Merton College, Oxford, where BLUNDEN was his tutor. As a member of the Officers' Training Corps (which he joined for the chance to get some free riding) he was liable for early call-up in World War II. After being commissioned, he was selected for attachment to the Indian Army, but found himself instead in the Middle East. As he recounts in his vivid war journal, *Alamein to Zem Zem* (1946; ed. Desmond Graham, illustrated by the author, 1992), he walked out of a staff post to rejoin his companions, fought in a tank across the desert from Egypt to Tunisia, and survived being blown up by a mine. He returned to England in 1943 to be trained for the invasion of Europe. He was killed on his third day in Normandy, after an information gathering exploit for which he was mentioned in dispatches. The ending of his last complete poem, 'On a Return from Egypt', expresses his premonition: 'The next month, then, is a window / and with a crash I'll split the glass. / Behind it stands one I must kiss, / person of love or death / a person or a wraith, / I fear what I shall find.' Some of his poems were published in wartime collections, and he was preparing a volume of his own just before he died. *Collected Poems* (1951) was the basis of a further edition (1966). See *Complete Poems*, ed. Desmond Graham, 2nd edn 1987; Desmond Graham, *Keith Douglas 1920–1944*, new edn 1986 (biography).

DOUGLAS(S), (GEORGE) NORMAN (1868–1952) British novelist and travel writer, was born in Thuringen, Austria, the son of a Scottish cotton mill manager and a Scottish–German mother, and spoke German as his first language. After his father's death in 1874 in a climbing accident, he was brought up in Scotland (his paternal grandfather was a Deeside laird) and England, and was educated at Uppingham School until his rebellious behaviour caused his removal to Karlsruhe Gymnasium in Germany. He joined the Foreign Office in 1893 and was on the staff of the British Embassy in St Petersburg from 1894 to 1896. He resigned after forming an indiscreet liaison with a highborn Russian lady, and bought a villa in Italy. His interest in natural history and related sciences had already enabled him to contribute to zoological journals and to write *Report on the Pumice Stone Industry of the Lipari Islands* (1895). He now devoted his time to further travel and to literature, publishing (under the joint pseudonym of Normyx) *Unprofessional Tales* (1901), written with his wife, the former Elsa Fitzgibbon, whom he married in 1878 and from whom he was divorced in 1903. *Siren Land* (1911; rev. edn 1923), about Sorrentino, and *Old Calabria* (1915) gained him a literary reputation for their grace, entertainment value, and erudition. In *South Wind* (1917), his first novel of four and easily the most distinguished, a thinly-disguised Capri is the background to a series of conversation pieces in which his own hedonism is reflected and the effect of Italy upon foreigners is explored. He lived most of his life abroad, and wrote two excursions into autobiography, *Looking Back* (2 vols 1933) and *Late Harvest* (1946). See Mark Holloway, *Norman Douglas: a Biography*, 1976.

DOUGLASS, FREDERICK (1817–95) American political and social philosopher, was born into slavery as Frederick Augustus Washington Bailey, near Easton in Talbot County, Maryland, the son of a white man whose identity he never knew, and of Harriet Bailey, from whom he was parted in infancy. By devious means he learned to read and write, and in 1836 forged passes for himself and several others, but the escape failed. He finally escaped in 1838 while working as a ship's calker in Baltimore, and reached New York. He went on to New Bedford, Massachusetts, where he changed his name and became a labourer. Persuaded to speak at a convention of the Massachusetts Anti-Slavery Society in Nantucket in 1841, he made such an impression that he was invited on the spot to be an agent and speaker for the society. *Narrative of the Life of Frederick Douglass, an American Slave* (1845), 'Written by Himself', a dignified, almost understated account of his experiences from childhood to freedom, confirmed and further publicized the current position in the South. He lectured throughout Britain and Ireland in 1846–47. During the Civil War of 1861–65 he campaigned for blacks to be eligible for service in the Union army, and then fought for them to have equal rights and pay; he was a champion of equal rights for everyone, black or white, male or female. He served in several official positions, being US Federal Marshal (1877–81) and Recorder of Deeds (1881–86), District of Columbia, and US Minister to Haiti 1888–91. After the death of his wife in 1882, he married a white woman who had been his secretary. *Life and Times of Frederick Douglass* (1881; rev. edn 1892) incorporates his original autobiography, which he expanded as *My Bondage and My Freedom* (1855). See *The Oxford Frederick Douglass Reader*, ed. William L. Andrews,

1996; William S. McFeely, *Frederick Douglass*, new edn 1996 (biography).

DOVE, RITA (*b.* 1952) American poet, was born in Akron, Ohio, and educated at Miami University, graduating *summa cum laude*, after which she studied modern European literature at the University of Tübingen, Germany, and took a further degree at the University of Iowa. After teaching creative writing at Arizona State University she was appointed Commonwealth Professor of English, University of Virginia, in 1989. From her first collection, *The Yellow House on the Corner* (1980), incorporating poems deeply resonant of adolescence, she has treated difficult subjects, often from more than one point of view, with quiet confidence. *Thomas and Beulah* (1986), which won the Pulitzer Prize, is a verse cycle, based on her grandparents' marriage, in which a black couple's experience illuminates the social history of the times. *Mother Love* (1995), her sixth collection and a further sequence, reflects her cosmopolitan experience as well as attitude, and her conviction that poetic form can be a 'talisman against disintegration': Demeter's grief-stricken pursuit of her daughter, abducted by Hades, is the mythical framework for a modern sociological odyssey. Dove has also published a volume of short fiction, *Fifth Sunday* (1985), and a novel, *Through the Ivory Gate* (1992). She was US Poet Laureate 1993–94. See *Selected Poems*, 1993.

DOYLE, (Sir) ARTHUR CONAN (1859–1930) British novelist and short-story writer, was born in Edinburgh of an artistic Irish Catholic family, and was educated at Stonyhurst College and Edinburgh University. He qualified as a doctor in 1881, and practised in Southsea from 1882 to 1890. During the Boer War (1899–1902) he volunteered as a senior physician in the field and was knighted for his services. His first full-length work, *A Study in Scarlet*, in which the detective Sherlock Holmes is introduced, was published in *Beeton's Christmas Annual* in 1887. A second Holmes novel, *The Sign of Four*, appeared in 1890, and stories about the private detective and his worthy henchman Dr Watson, including the longer tale *The Hound of the Baskervilles*, were published regularly in *Strand Magazine* from 1891 to 1893, at which point Conan Doyle killed off his hero by having him fall off a precipice. Popular opinion prevailed and Holmes was miraculously resuscitated for *The Return of Sherlock Holmes* (1905)—see *Complete Sherlock Holmes and Other Detective Stories*, introduction by Owen Dudley Edwards (1994) and *Sherlock Holmes: the Major Stories, with Contemporary Essays*, ed. John A. Hodgson (1994). Another creation was the scientist Professor Challenger—in *The Lost World* (1912) and *The Poison Belt* (1913). Doyle also adapted his easy, narrative style to historical romance with *The White Company* (1891), *Sir Nigel* (1906), and the stories about the Napoleonic Brigadier Gerard, beginning with *The Exploits of Brigadier Gerard* (1896)—see *The Collected Brigadier Gerard Stories* (1995). He was a vigorous campaigner for causes in which he believed—notably that of Oscar Slater, condemned to death (commuted to life imprisonment) in 1909 and finally pardoned in 1928. He also developed a strong interest in spiritualism, while retaining his love of boxing, the theme of *Rodney Stone* (1896). See *Memories and Adventures*, new edn 1994 (autobiography); Owen Dudley Edwards, *The Quest for Sherlock Holmes*, 1982; Michael Coren, *Conan Doyle*, new edn 1996 (biography).

DRABBLE, MARGARET (*b*. 1939) British novelist and critic, was born in Sheffield, younger sister of BYATT, and was educated at the Mount School, York, and Newnham College, Cambridge. Her first two novels, *A Summer Bird-Cage* (1962) and *The Garrick Year* (1964), clearly draw on her experience as a recently graduated young mother who was married to an actor. Subsequently she broadened her field of vision to encompass many personal and moral issues which exercise women of her generation and her times, while often linking her themes with English literary tradition, as she does particularly in *The Waterfall* (1969) and *The Middle Ground* (1980). *The Radiant Way* (1987), *A Natural Curiosity* (1989), and *The Gates of Ivory* (1991) constitute a trilogy about contemporary relationships which breaks new ground for its author in the third book, involving the unravelling of the mystery of a novelist's disappearance in the Far East. Mystery, and tension, resurface in *The Witch of Exmoor* (1996), written after a five-year gap. Her critical works include a study of WORDSWORTH (1966), a biography of BENNETT (1974), and *A Writer's Britain: Landscape in Literature* (1979); she edited and compiled the fifth edition of *The Oxford Companion to English Literature* (1985). She was Chairman of the National Book League 1980–82, and was made CBE in 1980. She is now married to Michael Holroyd CBE (*b*. 1935), the biographer of STRACHEY and G. B. SHAW. See Joanne V. Creighton, *Margaret Drabble*, 1985 (critical study); Valerie Grosvenor Myer, *Margaret Drabble: a Reader's Guide*, 1991.

DRANSFIELD, MICHAEL (1948–73) Australian poet, was born in Sydney, dropped out of university, tried being a government clerk and a journalist, considered becoming a monk, and succumbed to the drug culture. Latterly he travelled round, haphazardly but profitably, buying and selling old properties; his romantic interest in them is reflected in the 'Courland Penders' sequence in his first book, *Streets of the Long*

Voyage (1970). While cult status attaches to his poems expressing the predicament of the addict—see *Drug Poems* (1972)—he was also a mature poet of protest, with a lyrical bent. In 1972 his motorcycle was forced off the road. He never recovered mentally or physically from his injuries, though he continued to write feverishly, and he died a year later. *Memoirs of a Velvet Urinal*, which he had prepared for press, was published posthumously in 1975. He left six hundred poems in manuscript. See *Collected Poems*, ed. Rodney Hall, 1987; Livio Dobrez, *Parnassus Mad Ward: Michael Dransfield and the New Australian Poetry*, 1990.

DRAYTON, MICHAEL (1563–1631) English poet, was born in Hartshill, Warwickshire, the son of a tanner. According to his epistle to Henry Reynolds (1627), he determined to be a poet when he was ten, while serving as a page at Polesworth House, the seat of Sir Henry Goodere (*d*. 1595), who became his first patron. He did not rush into print. *Idea: the Shepheards Garland*, in the manner of SPENSER, appeared in 1593 under the pseudonym of 'Rowland'. *Ideas Mirrour* (1594), a sonnet sequence, includes 'Since ther's no helpe, come let us kisse and part . . .'; it was inspired by Sir Henry's daughter Anne (later Lady Rainsford), for whom he had a lifelong infatuation. *Poly-Olbion* (1612) was retitled *A Chorographicall Description of Great Britain* (1622), which better describes this patriotic panorama of the topography, traditions, and antiquities of England and Wales. He composed thousands of lines of chronicle verse, from *Englands Heroicall Epistles* (1597), in which 12 famous pairs of lovers address each other, to *The Battaile of Agincourt* (1627), employing a variety of forms. He made frequent revisions, entirely rewriting *Mortimeriados* (1596) as *The Barrons' Wars* (1603), and changing the metre from rhyme royal to *ottava rima*. While his history poems brought him success in his time, his reputation is founded largely on his pastoral poetry, notably the mock-heroic *Nimphidia* (1627) and *The Muses' Elizium* (1630). He was a convivial person; according to the notebooks of Rev. John Ward, Vicar of Stratford-upon-Avon from 1662 to 1681, the drinking at a 'merrie meeting' he had in 1616 with JONSON and SHAKESPEARE contributed to the latter's death. He never married, and the night before he died he was still penning lines to his beloved friend Anne, who had been a widow for nine years. See *Complete Works*, ed. J. William Hebel, Kathleen Tillotson, and Bernard H. Newdigate, 5 vols, rev. edn 1961.

DREISER, THEODORE (1871–1945) American novelist, was born in Terre Haute, Indiana, the 11th of 12 children of a domineering German-Catholic weaver, who the year before had lost his mill in a fire, his mobility and hearing in an accident, and his money through fraud. The family was reared in itinerant poverty, and the boy was educated in parochial schools and at a high school in Warsaw, which he left in 1887 to fend for himself in Chicago. He was rescued from his job as a hardware stockboy by a former teacher from Warsaw, who paid for him to attend the University of Indiana, Bloomington; he left after a year in frustration at his treatment by other students. He became a reporter in Chicago and then St Louis, and in 1895 settled in New York as a magazine editor. His first novel, *Sister Carrie*, a powerful story of rags to riches on the part of a young woman who follows instinct rather than propriety, was accepted by Doubleday, Page. The firm then had second thoughts, and having published an expurgated version in 1900 with minimal publicity and maximum reluctance, promptly withdrew it from sale. Disheartened and suicidal, Dreiser was encouraged by his brother, the songwriter Paul Dresser (1857–1906), with whose help he got further editorial posts, culminating in his being (very successfully) Editor-in-Chief of Butterick Publications from 1907 to 1910.

In the meantime he had worked on *Jennie Gerhardt* (1911), another story of an outwardly amoral woman, but this time with a heart. With the reissue of *Sister Carrie*, and the publication of *The Financier* (1912), the first of a 'Trilogy of Desire' based on the career of a notorious Chicago speculator—the others being *The Titan* (1914) and the posthumous *The Stoic* (1947)—his career was revivified and his reputation assured. *The 'Genius'* (1915) is partly autobiographical. The epitome of his philosophy is *An American Tragedy* (1925), in which he used an actual murder case, intensified by detail and supported with evidence, to argue that society is at fault for allowing the environment of the slums to breed the criminal instinct which comes from material ambition. His short stories were collected in *The Best Short Stories of Theodore Dreiser* (1956), with an introduction by J. T. FARRELL. *Dreiser Looks at Russia* (1928) and *Tragic America* (1931) are expressive of his socialist convictions. After the death in 1942 of his wife, from whom he had been separated since 1909, he married his cousin, Helen Richardson, with whom he had lived since 1920, after meeting her in 1919 and pursuing her to Hollywood, where she had a brief career as an extra and starlet. See *Newspaper Days*, new edn (ed. T. D. Nostwich) 1991 of *A Book about Myself*, 1922; Richard Lingeman, *Theodore Dreiser: At the Gates of the City, 1891-1907*, 1986 and *Theodore Dreiser: an American Journey, 1908-1945*, 1990, abridged edn 1993 (biography); Philip L. Gerber, *Theodore Dreiser*, 1964 (critical study).

DRUMMOND, WILLIAM, OF HAWTHORNDEN (1585–1649) Scottish poet, was born at Hawthornden, near Edinburgh, and educated at the High School of Edinburgh and Edinburgh University, after which he studied law on the Continent. On his father's death in 1610 he became Laird of Hawthornden, and retired into his library of 552 volumes, which included contemporary poetry in several languages. The first fruits of his self-imposed course of lifelong study was a conventional epitaph on Prince Henry, *Teares on the Death of Meliades* (1613). *Poems, Amorous, Funereall, Divine, Pastorall in Sonnets, Songs, Sextains, Madrigals* was published in Edinburgh in 1614, with a revised edition in 1616. The triumphal return to Edinburgh in 1617 of James I (and VI) occasioned his panegyric, 'Forth Feasting', which enhanced his reputation in the south. He now corresponded warmly with DRAYTON, and in 1618 he was for two weeks host to JONSON, who had done the journey from London on foot and whose recollections and views Drummond recorded for posterity. The sonnets and songs in *Flowres of Sion* (1623) reflect his loneliness and personal melancholy; the volume included 'A Cypresse Grove', a masterly prose essay on death and the nature of the soul. In 1627 he was granted patents for 16 mechanical inventions, most of which had military applications. Circumstances led him to sign the Covenant in 1639, while supporting (but not being afraid openly to criticize) the King and corresponding with MONTROSE. In the 1630s he became involved in a genealogical controversy reflecting on the legitimacy of Robert III, who had married Drummond's ancestress, Annabella Drummond. (There certainly was some mystery about the marriage of Robert's parents, but their children's legitimacy was established by papal dispensation in 1347.) Drummond waded in with voluminous correspondence and a treatise addressed to the King, which grew into a full-blown history of Scotland (published 1655), covering the years 1424–1542. Drummond's dearly loved fiancée died in 1615; he married in 1630, having in the meantime enjoyed the comforts of a mistress, who bore him three children. See *William Drummond of Hawthornden: Poems and Prose*, ed. R. H. Macdonald, 1976.

DRUMMOND, WILLIAM HENRY (1854–1907) Canadian poet, was born in Ireland at Currawn House, Co. Leitrim, and came to Canada with his parents and three younger brothers in about 1864. He was educated at Montreal High School, McGill University, and Bishop's University, Lennoxville, where he qualified as MD in 1884, after which he went into practice in Montreal. During the six summer vacations after he was 15 he worked as a telegrapher at Bord à Plouffe on the Rivière des Prairies, near Montreal, where he mixed with the French-Canadian habitants. The fractured English that he heard there he later re-created as the language of his popular ballads and lyrics, first collected as *The Habitant and Other French-Canadian Poems* (1897), followed by several more volumes. He died of a stroke in Cobalt, where he had gone to deal with an outbreak of smallpox in his brothers' mining camps. See *Habitant Poems*, ed. Arthur L. Phelps, new edn 1970.

DRYDEN, JOHN (1631–1700) English poet, dramatist, critic, and translator, was born in Aldwinckle, Northamptonshire, into a landowning Puritan household. He was educated at Westminster School and Trinity College, Cambridge, after which he settled in London. His first published work was a contribution, 'Heroique Stanzas . . .', to a volume of three complimentary poems commemorating the death of Oliver Cromwell (1599–1658). He greeted the Restoration of the Monarchy in 1660 in the person of Charles II with two equally effusive renderings, 'Astraea Redux' and 'To His Sacred Majesty', a demonstration of inconstancy which JOHNSON justifies in *The Lives of the Poets*; 'if he changed, he changed with the nation'. He was elected to the newly-established Royal Society in 1662, and in 1663 married a daughter of the Earl of Berkshire, Lady Frances Howard (*c.*1638–1714), who felt that she had wed beneath her. He now began a career as a dramatist which lasted until 1694, during which he published over thirty tragedies, tragicomedies, and comedies. In *Annus Mirabilis: the Year of Wonders* (1667), he describes in rhyming quatrains the Great Fire of London and celebrates, with some irony, the war against the Dutch and the glories of the Royal Society. In 1668, the year in which he published his critical study, *Of Dramatick Poesie*, he was appointed the first Poet Laureate, and he became Historiographer Royal in 1670.

In the political upheavals and long-running personal animosities of the time he now found the perfect outlet for his talents, and in the heroic couplet the ideal medium. With *Mac Flecknoe: or a Satyr upon T. S.*, largely written in 1678 but not published until 1682, he rounded on his former friend and now political enemy, SHADWELL, and silenced him and his cronies. *Absalom and Achitophel* (1681)—a second part by NAHUM TATE, with a long insertion by Dryden, was published in 1682—is overtly political, using the biblical story as a parallel in order to discredit the Earl of Shaftesbury (1621–83) in his support of the Duke of Monmouth (1649–85), the illegitimate son of Charles II, against future claims on the Crown by the Catholic James, Duke of York, the King's brother (later James II). In 1682 Dryden published *Religio Laici: or, A Layman's Faith*, a poem in which he defends the compromise between Catholicism and deism offered by the Anglican Church. After the accession of James II in 1685, Dryden became a Catholic, and wrote *The Hind and the Panther* (1687), a political and religious allegory from the standpoint of Catholicism, to which he remained faithful, even though on the accession of William and Mary in 1689 he lost his official posts and his steady income. He now turned to verse translation, including the satires of JUVENAL (1693) and the whole of VIRGIL (1697)—see *Dryden's Aeneid*, ed. Robin Sowerby (1986). *Fables Ancient and Modern* (1700), for which he was best known throughout the following century, contains tales from CHAUCER as well as from HOMER, OVID, and BOCCACCIO.

Dryden was a consummate craftsman. Many of the songs and lyrics sprinkled through his plays are justly memorable, as are his odes on the deaths of John Oldham (1684), Charles II (1685), and Anne Killigrew (1686), and *A Song for St Cecilia's Day, 1687* (1687) and *Alexander's Feast* (1697), both of which were set to music. Of his many plays, the best are the tragicomedy, *Secret-Love: or, The Maiden-Queen* (1667), and the tragedy *All for Love: or, The World Well Lost* (1677). For this deliberate attempt to emulate rather than copy SHAKESPEARE's *Antony and Cleopatra*, he abandoned rhyme for blank verse, and by restricting the action to events after the battle of Actium and the setting to Alexandria, succeeded in observing the classical unities of time and space. His value and significance as a critic, an art which he practised throughout his career in the form mainly of prefaces, lie in his incisive mind, his ability to appreciate different (and often divergent) literary traditions, and his prose style. These qualities are as apparent in his last piece, the preface to the *Fables*, as they are in his essay, *Of Dramatick Poesie*; if he is contradictory it is because he was able to change his mind. With his command of language (which became accepted poetic diction), his wit, his technical skill, and the control which led him to perfect the heroic couplet, he founded a school of satirical verse in which his follower, and his only equal, was POPE. See [*Selected Works*], ed. Keith Walker, 1987 (poetry and prose); *Selected Poems*, ed. Donald Thomas, new edn 1993; [*Selected Verse*] ed. Keith Walker, 1994; *Of Dramatic Poesy and Other Critical Essays*, ed. George Watson, 2 vols 1962; Charles E. Ward, *Life of John Dryden*, 1961; Paul Hammond, *Dryden: a Literary Life*, 1991; David Hopkins, *John Dryden*, 1986 (critical study).

DU BELLAY, JOACHIM (1522–60) French poet, was born in Liré of a noble Anjou family. Orphaned early on and afflicted with deafness, he studied law and the humanities at Collège de Coqueret, Paris, with his second cousin RONSARD. He became a member of Ronsard's group, the 'Brigade', the manifesto of whose inner circle, the 'Pléiade', he wrote as *La Deffence et Illustration de la Langue Françoyse* (1549). The second (1550) edition of his first book of verse, *L'Olive* (1549), a series of love sonnets in the style of PETRARCH, was prefaced with a further exposition of national literary aspirations. From 1553 to 1557 he was in Rome as secretary to his cousin, the ambassador Cardinal Du Bellay (1492–1560). On his return to Paris he published *Les Antiquitez de Rome* (1558), 32 sonnets which SPENSER translated as 'Ruines of Rome' in *Complaints*, and *Les Regrets* (1558), a longer sequence, more personal and meditative. Later translators have included LANG (see especially 'Winnower's Hymn to the Winds') and CHESTERTON ('Sonnet of Exile').

DU BOIS, W(ILLIAM) E(DWARD) B(URGHARDT) (1868–1963) American prose writer and novelist, was born in Great Barrington, Massachusetts, and educated at the local, predominantly white, high school, at Fisk University, and at Harvard, where in 1895 he became the first black to be awarded the degree of PhD, for his dissertation, *The Suppression of the African Slave Trade to the United States of America 1638–1870* (1896). He taught sociology at Atlanta University from 1897 to 1910, when, having been a founder member of the Niagara Movement agitating for black civil rights, he became Director of Research and Publications of the new National Association for the Advancement of Colored People, in New York. The patient tone of *The Souls of Black Folk* (1903), a skilful blend of essay material exploring his conviction that 'the problem of the Twentieth Century is the problem of the color line', gave way to the exasperation reflected in *Darkwater: Voices from within the Veil* (1920). In 1934 he returned to Atlanta as Chairman of the Sociology Department, from which he was unwillingly retired in 1944. He travelled the world in the interests of peace when allowed to do so by the US authorities, and in 1959 was awarded the Lenin Peace Prize from the USSR. He joined the American Communist Party in 1961, and settled in Ghana, of which he became a citizen in 1963. *The Quest of the Silver Fleece* (1911), his first and most successful novel, into which he blended a feminist strain, centres on the effects of the Northern control of the cotton trade at the turn of the century. *The Philadelphia Negro* (1899) was one of the first works in social science to incorporate urban ethnography, social history, and descriptive statistics. See *W. E. B. Du Bois: a Reader*, ed. David Levering Lewis, 1995; *The Oxford W. E. B. Du Bois Reader*, ed. Eric J. Sundquist, 1996; David Levering Lewis, *W. E. B. Du Bois: Biography of a Race*, new edn 1994;

Jack B. Moore, *W. E. B. Du Bois*, 1981 (biographical/critical study).

DUDEK, LOUIS (*b*. 1918) Canadian poet and critic, was born in Montreal of Polish immigrant parents, and was educated at Montreal High School and McGill University, after which he worked as a freelance journalist. He went to New York in 1943, where he graduated in history at Columbia University in 1946, and completed his studies in 1955 with a thesis published as *Literature and the Press: a History of Printing, Printed Media, and Their Relation to Literature* (1960). He taught English at City College, New York, from 1946 to 1951, when he returned to McGill. He was appointed Greenshields Professor of English in 1969, and established and largely financed the McGill Poetry Series, whose first volume was LEONARD COHEN's *Let Us Compare Mythologies*. In 1952 he founded, with LAYTON and SOUSTER, Contact Press, Toronto, which until 1967 published significant works of poetry; and he was founder-Editor of the literary journal *Delta* from 1957 until he closed it down in 1966. His own first book of verse was *East of the City* (1946). Subsequently, book-length philosophical poems, such as *Europe* (1954) and *En México* (1958), alternated with collections of lyrical and metaphysical verses. His critical works include *Selected Essays and Criticism* (1978), *In Defence of Art: Critical Essays and Reviews* (1980), and *Paradise: Essays on Art, Myth and Reality* (1992); he has also published (1974) his correspondence with POUND during the 1950s. See *Cross-Section: Poems 1940–1980*, 1980; *Continuation I*, 1981; *Continuation II*, 1990; *Notebooks 1960–1994*, 1994; Terry Goldie, *Louis Dudek and His Works*, 1985.

DUGGAN, EILEEN (1894–1972) New Zealand poet, was born in Tua Marina, the youngest of four daughters of an Irish immigrant railway worker, and won a scholarship to Marlborough High School. After being a pupil teacher, she graduated in history from Victoria University College in 1918. She taught briefly in high school and at Victoria University College before ill health forced her into retirement in Wellington, where she lived with her widowed sister and a close friend, and from 1927 until her death wrote the woman's page of the *Tablet*, New Zealand's Catholic journal. In *Poems* (1921) she confessed that 'Song comes to me / But haltingly . . .', but in that slim volume and two others, *Poems* (1937) and *New Zealand Poems* (1940), she successfully fused Maori terms and traditions with national history in pursuit of a corporate identity, and she was the first New Zealand poet to gain international recognition. A deeper experience, bordering on the metaphysical, is reflected in *More Poems* (1951). She was made OBE in

1937. See F. M. McKay, *Eileen Duggan*, 1977 (critical study).

DUGGAN, MAURICE (1922–75) New Zealand short-story writer, was born in Auckland, left his Catholic boarding school at 13, and four years later had a leg amputated because of osteomyelitis. He began to write stories as a form of compensation for his inability to participate in the action: 'Anyone I'd ever known, or so it seemed, was making or preparing for the journey to a war.' He was conscripted into industry, manhandling a metal press. In 1945, the year his first story was published, he married a young woman from the North Shore, where he had spent his earliest years. He was admitted to Auckland University in 1947, and in 1948 edited its literary annual, *Kiwi*. In 1950 he went to Europe, having published nine stories which he later referred to as 'juvenilia', and also 'Six Place Names and a Girl' (*Landfall* 1949), which appeared in his first collection, *Immanuel's Land* (1956), most of which was written in London. After two years he returned to New Zealand precipitately with tuberculosis ('In Spain I brightly and voluminously coughed'), and spent much of the rest of the decade as a semi-invalid. During this time he finally abandoned a novel, 'Along the Poisoned River', and wrote a children's story, *Falter Tom and the Water Boy* (1958), which he had devised to tell his son. After being Robert Burns Fellow at Otago University ('my best writing year'), he went in 1961 into advertising, in which he remained until his death. *Summer in the Gravel Pit*, which included three stories from the earlier volume, was published in 1965, and *O'Leary's Orchard and Other Stories* in 1970. The 'other stories' were 'An Appetite for Flowers' and 'Riley's Handbook', a monologue whose riotous use of language constituted, in the opinion of C. K. STEAD, 'surely an important new development in the history of our fiction'. By 1973 Duggan had managed to conquer his alcoholism, only to be diagnosed as suffering from cancer, of which he died. He destroyed all his unpublished fiction except an unfinished novel, 'Miss Bratby', on which he had worked sporadically for years. His published output comprises 30 pieces, the form and style of which dictated the length. Characters recur in a reassuring way that belies the bleakness of his vision and the sometimes disturbing depth of his imagination. See *Collected Stories*, ed. C. K. Stead, 1981; and in *Beginnings: New Zealand Writers Tell How They Began Writing*, ed. Robin Dudding, 1980.

DUMAS (DAVY DE LA PAILLETERIE), ALEXANDRE (known as Dumas *père*) (1802–70) French novelist and dramatist, was born in Villers-Cotterets, the son of a general whose mother was a Haitian negress. His father died in 1806 and he was brought up by his mother, the daughter of an innkeeper. Having been articled to a local solicitor and dismissed in 1822 for going hunting in office hours, he went to Paris, where through his father's old contacts he got a job in the secretariat of the Duc d'Orléans (Louis Philippe, King of the French 1830–48), whose assistant librarian he became after the success of his play, *Henri III* (1829). In *Antony* (1831) he brought the setting of the Romantic drama into modern times. With no let up in his flow of plays, he turned in 1835 to historical sketches, and in 1838 to novels, his output centring on the services of an equally inexhaustible supply of willing collaborators, none of whom ever achieved anything on his own—in 1845 he successfully sued for libel the author of a pamphlet accusing him of plagiarism, who was sentenced to 15 days in jail. His chief collaborator was Auguste Maquet (1813–88), with whom he wrote *Les Trois Mousquetaires* (1844; tr. W. Barrow as *The Three Musketeers*, 1846) and *Le Comte de Monte-Cristo* (1844–45; tr. Emma Hardy as *The Count of Monte Cristo*, 1846), which followed the novels of WALTER SCOTT in genre but exceeded them in popularity largely because they were created for serial format. A prodigious lover as well as writer and traveller, he is said to have remarked in his sixties: 'I need several mistresses. If I only had one she would be dead within a week'; his last serious fling, in 1866–67, was with Adah Isaacs Menken (1831–68), the American actress and poet. In 1840 he married Ida Ferrier (*d.* 1859), a minor actress (real name Marguerite Ferrand) who had been for several years one of his mistresses: they parted in 1844. The most notable of his children by several women was the first: the dramatist, novelist, and critic Alexandre Dumas *fils* (1824–95), author of *La Dame aux Camélias* (1848) from his own novel, who was the son of Catharine Labay (1794–1868), a dressmaker. Dumas *père* died at Alexandre's house in Puys, with his financial affairs in chaos, leaving unfinished his final *chef-d'oeuvre*, *Grand Dictionnaire de la Cuisine* (1873).

DU MAURIER, DAPHNE (1907–89) British novelist and short-story writer, the daughter of the actor-manager, (Sir) Gerald du Maurier (1873–1934), and granddaughter of GEORGE DU MAURIER, was born in London and educated privately and in Paris. She married (Lieutenant General Sir) Frederick Browning (1896–1965) in 1932, the year after the publication of her first novel, *The Loving Spirit*. Many of her novels and stories have a background of Cornwall, where they bought the old mansion of Menabilly. Though primarily regarded as a writer who provided entertainment, and suspense, qualities readily found in the Gothic romanticism of *Rebecca* (1938), to which Susan Hill, *Mrs de*

Winter (1993) is an adequate sequel, she wrote some fine historical novels, including *Jamaica Inn* (1936), *Frenchman's Creek* (1941), *The King's General* (1946), and *The Glass-Blowers* (1963), which features her family's history and former occupation. Her central characters are often interestingly treated, as in *The Parasites* (1949), a study of complex sibling relationships, *My Cousin Rachel* (1951), and many of her short stories, and she can compellingly develop unusual situations, as in *The Flight of the Falcon* (1965) and *Rule Britannia* (1972). She also wrote an extremely readable (if iconoclastic) theatrical biography of her father, *Gerald: a Portrait* (1934), composed in four months after his death; the scholarly *The Infernal World of Branwell Brontë* (1960); and three plays, including the stage version of *Rebecca* (produced 1940). *Letters from Menabilly: Portrait of a Friendship*, ed. Oriel Malet (1993) is valuable as a record of a correspondence with another writer which continued until her death. Latterly du Maurier lived in seclusion. She was made DBE in 1969. See *Myself When Young: the Shaping of a Writer*, new edn 1993 of *Growing Pains*, 1977, and its continuation *The Rebecca Notebook and Other Memories*, new edn 1993; Margaret Forster, *Daphne du Maurier*, new edn 1995 (biography).

du MAURIER, GEORGE (1834–96) British novelist and illustrator, was born in Paris, the eldest son of a French father and an English mother who came to England when he was five, but returned to France later. He was educated at the Pension Froussard, Paris, and University College, London, where he read chemistry. He then worked for two years as an analytical chemist in his own laboratory, provided by his father, who died in 1856. In the meantime du Maurier, whose heart was not in science, had gone back to Paris to study art. He then went to Antwerp, where in a drawing session he suffered a sudden detachment of the retina, and permanently lost the sight of one eye. In 1860 he settled in London, where he began to work as an illustrator, and married an English woman. In 1864 he became a member of the elite editorial board of *Punch*. From 1863 for the next twenty years he illustrated for *Cornhill Magazine* works by such novelists as MEREDITH, HARDY, GASKELL, and HENRY JAMES. The technical transition from wood engraving to block-making by photography enabled him to retain and sell his originals, giving him an extra source of income at a time when he had no idea how long his single eye would hold out. This led him to discuss with Henry James, his close friend, the possibility of becoming an author; the outcome was an offer from the American publisher Harper to produce *Peter Ibbetson* (1892), a dream-related novel based on his youth in Paris. *Trilby* (1894), which first appeared in instalments in

Harper's Magazine, with its innocent heroine under the mesmeric influence of the sinister Svengali, is one of the most famous Victorian melodramas; it is notable also for its description of bohemian life and for its view of the changing position of the artist in society. *The Martian* (1897) was published posthumously.

DUNBAR, WILLIAM (*c*.1460–*c*.1520) Scottish poet, was probably born in East Lothian, of the family of the earls of Dunbar and March, and almost certainly studied at St Andrews University from 1473 to 1479. By his own account, he became an itinerant Franciscan friar, but renounced the calling, and was employed by James IV on diplomatic assignments abroad. In 1500 his name appears as being granted a royal pension for life, or until promoted to a benefice. In 1501 he was one of a mission to London (a city with which he was much impressed) to arrange James's marriage to Margaret Tudor, the eldest daughter of Henry VII, about which he wrote 'The Thrissill and the Rois' [The Thistle and the Rose]. He composed a celebration of Aberdeen for the Queen's visit there in 1511. His name disappears from the records after 1513, which may suggest that he got his benefice in the end, for it is improbable that he followed the King to Flodden and participated in the disastrous defeat of the Scots at the hands of the English. In the meantime he seems to have been much around the court, writing religious poems, satirical poems, love poems, autobiographical poems, rude poems, moral poems, and poems of admonition and petition to the King, while continually complaining about his pension, grousing about the weather and his health, and harping on about his benefice.

Not until BURNS, who was also Scottish, is there a poet whose range of themes is matched by such versatility in the use of metrical forms, nor one so confident in his art that in true Scottish fashion he can imbue it with such frankness of tone. At its best, which is often, his poetry has a plangent rhythm, enhanced by alliteration and internal as well as end-rhymes. These qualities are apparent even when he is addressing the King about his entourage ('Schir, ye have mony servitouris . . .') or the Queen about her wardrobe-master ('The wardraipper of Venus house . . .'). His revelations about court life are as colourful and comic as those about female sexuality in his alliterative satire on the epic of courtly love, 'The Twa Mariit Wemen and the Wedo'; nor is he averse to ending a blessing for the practical skills of tailors and shoemakers ('Betuix twell houris and ellevin . . .') with a quiet dig at their honesty in business matters. There is, too, a strong imagination at work in visionary poems such as 'The Goldyn Targe' and 'The Dance of the Sevin Deidly Synnis', and an honest depth of feeling in his divine poems, especially that on the Nativity, 'Rorate celi desuper . . .', and the resounding hymn to the Resurrection, 'Done is a battell on the dragon black . . .'. While the sheer panic of 'I that in heill wes and gladness . . .' (known also as 'Lament for the Makaris'), with its Latin refrain every fourth line, 'Timor mortis conturbat me', makes it one of the most engagingly sympathetic of poems about death.

Six of Dunbar's poems were printed in 1508, and 24 (in adapted versions) by RAMSAY in *The Ever Green* (1724). The first edition proper of his works was in 1834. See *The Poems of William Dunbar*, ed. W. Mackay Mackenzie, new edn 1990; *Selected Poems*, ed. Priscilla Bawcutt, 1996; Priscilla Bawcutt, *Dunbar the Makar*, 1992 (critical study).

DUNCAN, ROBERT (1919–88) American poet and critic, was born Edward Howard Duncan in Oakland, California. After the death of his mother (in childbirth or from flu), he was adopted by a couple who were theosophists and who chose him for his astrological configuration. He was brought up as Robert Edward Symmes, under which name he published about twenty poems before reverting to Duncan in 1942. From his adoptive parents he received the grounding of hermetic lore and fairy tales, which, together with dreams, were integral to his poetic vision. A fall when he was three permanently affected his sight: 'I had the double reminder always. . . . One image to the right and above the other. Reach out and touch. Point to the one that is really there' (1964). Having 'recognized in poetry my sole and ruling vocation', he left the University of California, Berkeley, after two years to move east with a male lover. He was for a time associated with the circle of NIN, which then included HENRY MILLER, DURRELL, and BARKER. After a marriage in 1943 which only lasted a few months, he published in *Politics* (August 1944) a signed essay, 'The Homosexual in Society'. In 1946 he returned to Berkeley to study medieval and Renaissance culture; the following year he visited POUND in his Washington asylum and spent two days with him—'Homage and Lament for Ezra Pound' is in *The Years as Catches: First Poems 1939–1946* (1966). Duncan was for some time embarrassed by his first book, the poem *Heavenly City, Earthly City* (1947), only latterly recognizing it as an accepted part of his canon. In 1950 he met and established a permanent relationship with the painter and collagist Jess (Collins), which influenced the subsequent work of both men.

The First Decade: Poems 1940–1950 (1968) juxtaposed a series of 'Domestic Scenes' with *Medieval Scenes* (1950), and included 'The Venice Poem', a key work in the development of his poetics. Duncan taught at Black Mountain College for five months in 1956, after which he helped to found and was Assistant

Director of the Poetry Center, San Francisco State College 1956–57. *The Opening of the Field* (1960) is regarded as his most accessible collection. At about this time he started to write an extended critique of the poetry of DOOLITTLE, *The H. D. Book*, of which individual chapters were published in various journals 1963–85. *Bending the Bow* (1968) had a message that was 'political' in the sense of 'concerned with true citizenship'. In his despair at his inability to confront the enormity of current events, he publicly announced in the preface to the new edition (1972) of *Caesar's Gate: Poems 1949–1950 with Paste-ups by Jess* that he would publish no major book of poetry until 1984. *Ground Work: Before the War* (1984), comprising poems written largely between 1968 and 1975, was reproduced in wide format from his own typescripts; *Ground Work II: In the Dark* (1987) was published the year before his death from kidney failure. His poetry looks back to many traditions, including the occult, Celtic mythology, and Jewish mysticism, and to the work of poets, novelists, philosophers, linguists, and painters from classical through medieval to modern times; it also suggests avenues of meaning beyond the words themselves. In 1985 he was given the National Poetry Award, created in his honour by three hundred other writers. See *Selected Poems*, ed. Robert J. Berthoff, 1993; *The Truth and Life of Myth: an Essay in Essential Autobiography*, new edn 1973; *Fictive Certainties: Five Essays in Essential Autobiography*, new edn 1986; Ekbert Faas, *Young Robert Duncan: Portrait of the Poet as Homosexual in Society*, new edn 1984 (biography to 1950); Mark Andrew Johnson, *Robert Duncan*, 1988 (critical study).

DUNN, DOUGLAS (b. 1942) Scottish poet and short-story writer, was born in Inchinnan, Renfrewshire, where he grew up, and was educated at Camphill Senior Secondary School, Paisley, and the Scottish School of Librarianship. After working as a librarian in Glasgow and at the Akron Public Library, Ohio, he read English at Hull University, where he went on to be an assistant librarian (under LARKIN) in the Brynmor Jones Library from 1969 to 1971, when he became a freelance writer. His first book of verse, *Terry Street* (1969), deals honestly and compassionately with urban working-class life. Subsequent volumes, in which the range of subject matter is much wider, met with less enthusiastic critical acclaim, but with *Barbarians* (1979) and *St Kilda's Parliament* (1981) his elegiac vision of ordinary people was presented precisely and with technical expertise. The poems in *Elegies* (1985), written after and about the death of his wife from cancer in 1981, and recalling their life together, perform the miracle of preserving the privacy of the person in the public place of print, and the volume won the accolade of Whitbread Book of the Year. *Dante's Drum Kit* (1993) is a comparatively substantial collection in five parts. *Secret Villages* (1985) is a collection of short stories, most of which reflect in an elusive fashion the traditionally closed communities of rural Scotland; the stories in *Boyfriends and Girlfriends* (1995) are more wideranging in setting and situation. He lives in north Fife with his second wife, whom he married in 1985, and their children. He was 1991 appointed a professor in English at the University of St Andrews, where he is also Director of the St Andrews Scottish Studies Institute. See *Selected Poems 1964–1983*, 1986; Robert Crawford and David Kinloch (eds), *Reading Douglas Dunn*, 1992.

DUNSANY, (PLUNKETT, EDWARD JOHN MORETON DRAX), 18TH LORD (1878–1957) Irish short-story writer, dramatist, and novelist, was born in London and educated at Eton, from which he went to Sandhurst via a crammer, being commissioned in the Coldstream Guards in 1899, the year he succeeded to his grandfather's title. He fought in the Boer War, after which he assumed the family estates near Tara, Co. Meath. He exercised his passion for sport with cricket, shooting, and big-game hunting, and for romantic adventure by writing, which he did at terrific speed, dictating to his wife or standing at his desk with a quill pen. His first book of stories, *The Gods of Pegana* (1905), was published at his own expense; in this and subsequent collections he showed how to combine humour with the fabulous. *The Glittering Gate*, a play with a celestial setting, was written for the Abbey Theatre, where it was performed in 1909. *The Gods of the Mountain*, a short, equally imaginative play, staged in London in 1911, was the beginning of an especially productive line. In World War I he served in France in the Royal Inniskilling Fusiliers, with an interval while on Easter leave in 1916, when he went to Dublin to observe the Rising, and was shot in the head and taken to hospital, which was then besieged by the rebels. Between the wars he was an international chess player, wrote more plays, poetry, and stories, extended his range into novels—notably *The Curse of the Wise Woman* (1933) and *My Talks with Dean Spanley* (1936)—and invented Joseph Jorkens. This engaging character, whose exploits and fanciful effusions mirror his own, occupies several volumes from *The Travel Tales of Mr Jorkens* (1931) to *Jorkens Borrows Another Whiskey* (1954). See Mark Amory, *Lord Dunsany*, 1972 (biography).

D'URFEY, THOMAS (1653–1723) English dramatist and poet, better known as Tom Durfey, was born in Exeter of Huguenot descent on his father's side. He was, by his own account, intended for the law, but instead began a long writing career with *The Siege of Memphis: or, The Ambitious Queen* (1676), a rhyming heroic tragedy. *Madam Fickle: or, The Witty False One* (1677) and *The Fool Turn'd Critick* (1678), both with much farcical action and first performed in the same month in 1676, were more to the public taste. A third comedy of sexual ongoings, *A Fond Husband: or, The Plotting Sisters*, so pleased Charles II when it opened in 1677 that he attended three of the first five nights. (It was also chosen in 1713 for a benefit performance for its author, who was at that time down on his luck.) In subsequent plays, notably *Love for Money: or, The Boarding School* (1691), a sentimental streak emerged, such as was to dominate 18th-century drama. The obscenities in the several parts of *The Comical History of Don Quixote* (1694–96), from CERVANTES, caused him to be included in the vitriolic attack on the contemporary stage in 1698 by Jeremy Collier (1650–1726), and he was in fact prosecuted for profanity. He wrote a ponderous Pindaric ode on the death of Queen Mary in 1695, and he was still writing plays in the reign of her sister, Queen Anne, who was the fourth British monarch to show him favour. He was also a notable writer of songs, which he sang in public with great gusto, though he stammered in his normal speech. Various collections of these appeared, with a definitive edition, called *Wit and Mirth: or Pills to Purge Melancholy*, in six volumes (1719–20).

DURRELL, LAWRENCE (1912–90) British poet and novelist, was born in Julundur, India, and educated at St Joseph's College, Darjeeling, and St Edmund's School, Canterbury. He lived in Corfu from 1934 to 1940; for an amusing acount of this period, see *My Family and Other Animals* (1956) by his brother, the zoologist Gerald Durrell (1925–95). He was attached to the British Information Office in Cairo and Alexandria in World War II, after which he held government public relations' posts in Greece, Argentina, Yugoslavia, and Cyprus. His first novel was *Pied Piper of Lovers* (1935); *The Black Book: an Agon* was published subterraneously in Paris in 1938, and not in the UK and USA until 1977. His poetry began with *Quaint Fragment: Poems Written Between the Ages of Sixteen and Nineteen* (1931) and continued into the 1970s. Quiet, sometimes humorous, often lyrical, and especially effective when evoking places, it is his poetry, with his three so-called 'travel books', *Prospero's Cell* (1945), about Corfu, *Reflections on a Marine Venus* (1953), about Rhodes, and *Bitter Lemons* (1957), about Cyprus, which many British critics regard as his most lasting work. Durrell's international reputation, however, is based on his 'Alexandria Quartet' of novels, *Justine* (1957), *Balthazar* (1958), *Mountolive* (1958), and *Clea* (1960). The first three, in the author's words, 'interlap, interweave in a purely spatial relation', while the last is a sequel in time. Multi-layered patterns of sexual involvements and intrigues, with the action and characters seen from different viewpoints, illuminate an inherently dramatic, at times romantic, plot. In the five novels which make up *The Avignon Quincunx* (1974–85), the Knights Templar of old and their lost treasure represent a means of survival in the modern world. See *Collected Poems 1931–1974*, ed. James A. Brigham, 3rd rev. edn 1985; Gordon Bowker, *Through the Dark Labyrinth: a Biography of Lawrence Durrell*, 1996; G. S. Fraser, *Lawrence Durrell: a Study*, rev. edn 1973.

DÜRRENMATT, FRIEDRICH (1921–90) Swiss dramatist and novelist, was born in Konolfingen, Bern, the son of a Protestant clergyman of a notable family. Originally intended for the Church, he studied literature, philosophy, theology, and the history of art at the universities of Zurich and Bern, abandoned any claims to faith, and determined to be a writer. His first short story was published in 1945, and *Der Richter und sein Henker* (1952; tr. Cyrus Brooks as *The Judge and His Hangman*, 1955), a detective novel, was serialized in 1950. Having had a controversial play about religious revivalism performed in 1947, he turned seriously to the stage with *Romulus der Grosse* [*Romulus the Great*] (performed 1949), 'an unhistorical comedy' in mock-heroic style. He became in the 1960s the most frequently performed playwright (after SHAKESPEARE and BRECHT) in the German-speaking theatre, and a leading exponent of black comedy, which he imbued with a disturbing, often nihilistic, message. Two plays have been particularly effective on the British and American stage: *Der Besuch der alten Dame* (published 1956; tr. Patrick Bowles as *The Visit*, 1958), in which the richest woman in the world returns to the depressed village of her birth and offers to save it, at a price; and *Die Physiker* (1962; tr. James Kirkup as *The Physicists*, 1964), a strong discussion-piece on the use and abuse of nuclear power, set in a lunatic asylum—published, with *Romulus the Great*, *The Marriage of Mr Mississippi* (first produced 1952), and *An Angel Comes to Babylon* (1953), in *Four Plays* (1964), which also includes his study, [*Problems of the Theatre*] (1955), originally a series of lectures given in Switzerland and West Germany.

DUTTON, GEOFFREY (*b.* 1922) Australian poet, novelist, historian, travel writer, critic, and editor, was born and brought up on the family property of Anlaby, Kapunda, South Australia: 'My mother longed for London, as her equivalent in Chekhov longed for Paris. My father, stifled by the boredom of Adelaide, hid himself away in the country or by the sea, and drank himself to death.' He was at Geelong Grammar School and for two years at Adelaide University. He served as a flying instructor in Australia in World War II, during which he published his first book of verse, *Night Flight and Sunrise* (1944). After three years at Magdalen College, Oxford, and several more in London, where he became friends with ROY CAMPBELL and ALDINGTON, and in France, he returned to Australia and was Senior Lecturer in English, Adelaide University 1954–62. After then being Editor of Penguin, Australia, he co-founded in 1965 the paperback publisher, Sun Books, of which he was Editorial Director until 1983. He helped to establish and edited the journals *Australian Letters* (1957–68) and *Australian Book Review* (1961–70), and inaugurated and edited the quarterly literary supplements which appeared in the *Bulletin* from 1980 to 1985, and then in the *Australian* from 1985 to 1990. Much of his verse—see *Findings and Keepings: Selected Poems 1940–1970* (1970), *New Poems to 1972* (1972), and *New and Selected Poems* (1993)—is autobiographical and informed by travel, particularly to the USSR, in which he travelled in the late 1960s with YEVTUSHENKO, whose poetry he has translated into English.

Innocence, usually that of Australians in the face of the experience of 'outsiders', is the motivating feature of his fiction, which he began publishing with *The Mortal and the Marble* (1950). *Tamara* (1970), in which an unsophisticated Australian scientist is enmeshed in contemporary Soviet literary politics, is a particularly thoughtful social comedy. The innocence in *Queen Emma of the South Seas* (1976), a historical novel of the late 19th century, is that of the Samoans, one of whom transcended the influences of 'civilization' to build her own trading empire. Dutton's oeuvre also includes biographies, notably *The Hero as Murderer: the Life of Edward John Eyre* (1967), and critical studies of PATRICK WHITE (rev. edn 1971) and WHITMAN (1960) and of the artists S. T. Gill (1962) and Russell Drysdale (rev. edn 1981). *Snow on the Saltbush* (1984), an analysis of the growth of an indigenous literary culture in the context of British attitudes, includes an account of the Ern Malley affair (see MCAULEY). *The Innovators* (1986) is a study of the modernist movements in art and literature in Sydney. He edited *The Literature of Australia* (rev. edn 1976), the first popular critical study of the subject, and was one of those most instrumental in the lifting of censorship restrictions in 1972. Dutton was married in 1944. In 1983 he left his wife for a woman considerably younger than himself. His autobiography, *Out in the Open* (1995), was criticized for its frankness about his relations with people who were still alive: his wife's book, *Firing: an Autobiography* (1995)—the title refers to her artistic calling as an enameller—, makes no reference to his more sensational revelations. He was made AO in 1976.

E

EAST, MICHAEL see WEST, MORRIS.

EASTAWAY, EDWARD see THOMAS, EDWARD.

EBERHART, RICHARD see LOWELL, ROBERT.

ECO, UMBERTO (*b.* 1932) Italian critic and novelist, was born in Alessandro and was Reader in Aesthetics at Turin University before becoming Professor of Semiotics at Bologna University. He came into prominence as a critic in 1962 with a volume of essays on electronic music, television, the cinema, and literature, which included a study of JOYCE. His seminal work in his particular field is *Semiotics and the Philosophy of Language* (1984). In the essays in *The Limits of Interpretation* (1991) he focuses on bringing under control the vagaries into which post-structuralism had been verging—see also *The Search for the Perfect Language*, tr. James Fentress (1995). MALCOLM BRADBURY, in an article in *The Times Literary Supplement* (1990), refers to him as 'an important contributor to contemporary hermeneutic and semiotic discussion, a radical voice now placed by current developments in a position more resembling conservatism', whose novels 'show the ripe benefits of a modern hermeneutic self-awareness as well as an ability to reach a wide contemporary audience'. Further essays and occasional pieces are in *Misreadings*, tr. William Weaver (1993), *How to Travel with a Salmon and other Essays*, tr. Weaver (1994), *Apocalypse Postponed*, ed. Robert Lumley (1994), and *Six Walks in the Fictional Woods* (Charles Eliot Norton Lectures, 1994). *Il Nome della Rosa* (1980; tr. William Weaver as *The Name of the Rose*, 1983) is a metaphysical search for truth and meaning in the form of a thriller set in a medieval monastery, some keys to whose interpretation are in *Postillo a Il Nome della Rosa* (1983; tr. Weaver as *Reflections on The Name of the Rose*, 1984). *Il Pendolo di Foucault* (1988; tr. Weaver as *Foucault's Pendulum*, 1989), which he told people he wrote 'because one novel could have been an accident', is by contrast an experimental novel featuring computer science and Rosicrucianism. His third, *L'Isola del Giorno Prima* (1994; tr. Weaver as *The Island of the Day Before*, 1995),

set in 1643 in a ship wrecked on the International Date Line, is a rich amalgam of language, learning, and philosophical speculation. See *Reading Eco: an Anthology*, ed. Rocco Capozzi, 1997.

EDGEWORTH, MARIA (1767–1849) Irish novelist, was born in Oxfordshire, the eldest daughter of the educationist and inventor Richard Lovell Edgeworth (1744–1817) and his first wife. She was educated in England. In 1782 she accompanied her father and his third wife to the family estate of Edgeworthstown, Co. Longford, where she lived for the rest of her life, and where she died in the arms of her father's fourth wife. Her first published works were *The Parent's Assistant* (1795), a series of didactic and moral tales for children which by its 1800 edition had grown to six volumes, and *Practical Education* (1798), written with her father, who was until his death a fervent supporter of her literary endeavours, and whose *Memoirs*, written by them jointly, appeared in 1820. *Castle Rackrent* (1800), published anonymously, was a literary milestone in that it was the first regional novel in English. Narrated by a servant, it follows the fortunes of a family through several generations; the speech is the English which was used in Ireland. In its historical detail and spirit, it also looks forward to WALTER SCOTT, who repaid Maria's visit to Abbotsford in 1823 with one to Edgeworthstown in 1825, after which they toured Ireland together, fêted wherever they went. *Tales of Fashionable Life* (1809–12) includes 'Ennui' and 'The Absentee', which present accurate impressions of Irish contemporary life for a predominantly English readership. *Patronage* (1814), one of her four novels about English society, is unusual for its discussion of how to get a job; another, *Harrington* (1817), written partly as reparation for anti-Semitic attitudes in earlier books, contains (in the person of Mr Montenero) the first in-depth, sympathetic study of a Jew in English fiction. In *Ormond* (1817), a novel of Gaelic and ascendancy Ireland which is also the first to explore the effects of fictional characters on young people, the orphan hero's behaviour is influenced by the protagonists of HENRY FIELDING's *Tom Jones* and SAMUEL RICHARDSON's *Sir Charles Grandison*. He finally sobers up and acts responsibly. See Marilyn Butler, *Maria Edgeworth: a Literary Biography*, 1972.

EDWARDS, JONATHAN (1703–58) American theologian and Puritan divine, was born in East Windsor, Connecticut, fifth child and only son of Rev. Timothy Edwards and Esther Stoddard Edwards, who lived to the ages of 89 and 98 respectively, and grandson of Rev. Solomon Stoddard (1643–1729), for 57 years minister to the congregation at Northampton, Massachusetts. The boy was educated at home and at Yale College, where from the age of 15 he wrote philosophical and scientific papers. He graduated first in his class in 1720, staying on to read theology. In 1721 he underwent a form of self-induced conversion—see 'Personal Narrative' (1765). After a year as minister to a Scottish Presbyterian church in New York, he was in 1723 offered a tutorship at Yale. That year he made a note of a 13-year-old girl in New Haven, Sarah Pierrepont, 'of a wonderful sweetness, calmness and universal benevolence of mind'. In 1727, having become assistant to his grandfather, he was ordained, and married Sarah; they had 11 children.

On Stoddard's death, Edwards succeeded him. His powers of communication were soon evidenced by the publication, by popular demand, of *God Glorified in the Work of Redemption* (1731), a public lecture; *A Divine and Supernatural Light* (1734), a sermon; and *A Faithful Narrative of the Surprising Work of God in the Conversion of Many Souls in Northampton* (London 1737, Boston 1738). Though his philosophy was influenced by NEWTON and LOCKE, he aimed to offer a refined version of the theology of CALVIN. The arrival in Boston in 1740 of the English Methodist, Rev. George Whitefield (1714–70), increased the momentum of the Great Awakening, a state of religious fervour marked by extreme emotionalism, one of those affected being Sarah herself. Edwards's sermon at Enfield, Connecticut, *Sinners in the Hands of an Angry God* (1741), was about as much hellfire as congregations could take, and the movement subsided. Drawn-out arguments about a fixed salary, his public condemnation of young congregants for reading and distributing a 'bad book' (it turned out to be called *The Midwife Rightly Instructed*), and his final refusal to accept as full church members those who had not publicly professed to having been saved, resulted in 1750 in his dismissal (by 200 votes to 20). For seven years, during which his writings included *Freedom of the Will* (1754) and *The Nature of True Virtue* (1765), he was missionary to two hundred Housatonic Indians, to whom he preached through an interpreter, and pastor to a handful of settlers in the outpost village of Stockbridge. In 1757, he was chosen as President of the College of New Jersey (Princeton) on the death of the incumbent, who was his son-in-law. He was inducted in February 1758, and died a month later from a smallpox inoculation. His daughter Esther died in Philadelphia four days after him, probably from the same cause; Sarah went to look after Esther's children, and died six months later, of dysentery. See *A Jonathan Edwards Reader*, ed. John E. Smith, Harvey S. Stout, and Kenneth P. Minkema, 1995; David Levin, *Jonathan Edwards: a Profile*, 1969; M. X. Lesser, *Jonathan Edwards*, 1988 (biographical/critical study).

EKWENSI, CYPRIAN (*b.* 1921) Nigerian novelist, was born of an Ibo family in Minna, Northern Nigeria, and was educated at Government College, Ibadan, Yaba Higher College, Lagos, and the School of Forestry, Ibadan, after which he joined the government Forestry Department. 'In the days in the forest I was able to reminisce and write': folklore he had learned from his parents, published as *Ikolo the Wrestler and Other Ibo Tales* (1947), and short stories, five of which appeared in *African New Writing* (1947). In 1947 he became a teacher of English and science at Igbobi College, Yaba, while studying pharmacy, and telling a weekly story on Radio Nigeria, a spin-off from which was a commission to produce a romantic novella. *When Love Whispers* (1948), published in Onitsha, is one of the first Nigerian works of fiction in English, and is regarded as a forerunner of the Onitsha market literature. He taught at the School of Pharmacy, Lagos, from 1949 to 1951, when he went to do five years' training at Chelsea School of Pharmacy, London University. On the voyage out he wrote *People of the City* (1954; rev. edn 1963), a novel of the pressures of modern Lagos. In England, when not dispensing drugs, he wrote and broadcast for the BBC. Back in Nigeria, after a year as a government superintendent pharmacist, he switched careers to be Head of Features, Nigerian Broadcasting Corporation, and then in 1961 Director of Information, Federal Ministry of Information, in which capacity he controlled the national media. *Jagua Nana* (1961) is a character study of an ageing prostitute who first emerged in 'Fashion Girl'—see in *Lokotown and Other Stories* (1966). A sequel, *Jagua Nana's Daughter*, appeared in 1986. In *Iska* (1966) he projected civil war between Hausa and Ibo. When it actually materialized, he returned to his homeland of the breakaway state of Biafra; until its defeat in 1970 he served as Controller of Broadcasting. He fictionalized the conflict in *Survive the Peace* (1976). Subsequently he exercised in Eastern Nigeria all his professional interests: as proprietor of a pharmaceutical trading company, managing director of a newspaper group, a state commissioner for information, and chairman of a state library board and a state hospitals' board. A thoughtful storyteller/social commentator with few pretensions as a literary stylist, he acknowledges the influence of SIMENON and WALLACE on his working methods. He has also written fiction for children. See Ernest Emenyonu, *Cyprian Ekwensi*, 1974 (critical study).

ELDERSHAW, M. BARNARD see BARNARD.

ELIOT, GEORGE, pseudonym of Mary Ann Evans (1819–80) British novelist, was born in Astley, Warwickshire, the youngest surviving child of an estate manager and his second wife, who soon after the birth moved to Griff House, Chilvers Coton. She went to boarding school at five, and left Nantglyn School, Coventry, in 1835, shortly before her mother's death. On her brother Isaac's marriage in 1841, she and her father moved to Foleshill, on the edge of Coventry, where she became closely associated with the family of the freethinker and philosopher, Charles Bray (1811–84). In 1842 she shocked her own family by refusing to attend church, and though she resumed going, she was now an agnostic in that her faith was in humanity rather than in God. Through the Brays she got the job of translating *The Life of Jesus Critically Examined by Dr David Friedrich Strauss*, which was published without her name by John Chapman (1821–94) in 1846. This study of the Gospels in the light of both orthodox and rationalist views was well received by radical thinkers. After the death of her father in 1849, she went to the Continent and then lodged in London in an uneasy relationship with Chapman, his wife, and his mistress, while working as assistant editor of the *Westminster Review*. In July 1854 Chapman published Ludwig Feuerbach's *The Essence of Christianity*, 'translated by Marian Evans'. On 20 July she and George Henry Lewes (1817–78), the writer on science and philosophy, left together for Germany. On their return they lived as man and wife; Lewes, having condoned his wife's adultery by registering in his name several of her children by her lover, Thornton Hunt (1810–1873), son of HUNT, was prevented from obtaining a divorce—see Rosemary Ashton, *G. H. Lewes: a Life* (1991).

It was Lewes who suggested, for economic motives, that Marian should try writing fiction. In 1856 she began a story, 'The Sad Fortunes of Reverend Amos Barton', which Lewes submitted to Blackwood's of Edinburgh, who printed it and two further stories in *Blackwood's Edinburgh Magazine*, and published them in volume form as *Scenes of Clerical Life* by 'George Eliot' (1858). This was followed by *Adam Bede* (1859), which received excellent notices. Speculation was now rife about the identity, and sex, of the author, whose alarm that her irregular domestic arrangements would harm her literary reputation was justified in that the reception of *The Mill on the Floss* (1860), published after the

truth broke, was mixed. *Silas Marner: the Weaver of Raveloe* (1861) restored her standing as the leading novelist of the day, without making her socially acceptable. *Romola* (1863), published by Smith, Elder, was a financial failure. When *Felix Holt, the Radical* (1866) was rejected by Smith, Elder, she returned to Blackwood's, who were subsequently persuaded by Lewes to publish *Middlemarch: a Study of Provincial Life* (1871–72) initially in eight volumes in instalments over a year. It was hailed as a masterpiece and made her £8000 between then and 1879. In the meantime she had been struggling with poetry, which was published as *The Spanish Gypsy* (1868) and *The Legend of Jubal, and Other Poems* (1874)—see in *Selected Essays, Poems and Other Writings*, ed. A. S. Byatt and Nicholas Warren (1990). Her final novel was *Daniel Deronda* (1876). In 1880, two years after Lewes's death, Marian married, which led her brother to communicate with her after 23 years. Her husband was her accountant, John Cross (1840–1924), who on their honeymoon in Venice tried to commit suicide by jumping from the balcony into the canal. She died only a few months later and, interment in Westminster Abbey having been refused, was buried in unconsecrated ground in Highgate Cemetery.

DAICHES in *A Critical History of English Literature* (new edn 1969) begins his assessment of George Eliot, 'Before [her] the English novel had been almost entirely the work of those whose primary purpose was to entertain' and concludes: 'A sage whose moral vision is most effectively communicated through realistic fiction [was] an unusual phenomenon . . . when George Eliot began to write. If it has been less unusual since, that is because George Eliot by her achievement in fiction permanently enlarged the scope of the novel.' She was different in that the logical development of a situation transcends mere considerations of dramatic plot. Her intellect enabled her to investigate shades of morality and to present characters which are psychologically consistent—only when dealing with children, and then not after *Silas Marner*, the last novel in which she re-explored her own childhood, does her perception falter. The dilemmas of her characters are always expounded in the context of their environment and often reflect actual experiences. The breadth and depth of her interests, and the understanding and making of her art, are demonstrated in *Selected Critical Writings*, ed. Rosemary Ashton (1992). See Gordon S. Haight, *George Eliot: a Biography*, new edn 1994; Frederick Karl, *George Eliot: a Biography*, new edn 1996; Rosemary Ashton, *George Eliot: a Life*, 1996; Rosemarie Bodenheimer, *The Real Life of Mary Ann Evans: George Eliot, Her Letters and Fiction*, new edn 1996 (critical biography); Joan Bennett, *George Eliot: Her Mind and Art*, rev. edn 1962; Rosemary Ashton, *George Eliot*, 1983 (introduction to her thought).

ELIOT, T(HOMAS) S(TEARNS)

(1888–1965) poet, dramatist, and critic, was born in St Louis, Missouri, and educated at Smith Academy, St Louis, and Harvard University. After graduating in philosophy and logic, and then spending a year at the Sorbonne in Paris, where he read French literature, he returned to Harvard to study epistemological theory, ancient Indian languages, and metaphysics. During this time he wrote 'The Love Song of J. Alfred Prufrock', 'Preludes', 'Portrait of a Lady', and 'Rhapsody on a Windy Night', all poems of considerable significance. The outbreak of war in 1914 interrupted his further studies at Marburg University, and he transferred to Merton College, Oxford, to read Greek philosophy. After two years teaching at boys' schools, he joined the Colonial and Foreign Department of Lloyds Bank, for which he worked until 1925. His first volume of poetry, *Prufrock and Other Observations*, was published in 1917, followed by *Poems* (1919) and *Ara Vos Prec* (1920). He was now not only giving a new direction to English and American poetry, but in *The Sacred Wood: Essays on Poetry and Criticism* (1920) he offered *inter alia* a new assessment of parts of the accepted canon of English literature itself, and argued that a poet should write from a 'historical sense' of European literature from HOMER onwards as well as from his own national literary tradition. His wife's illness (he had married in 1915) and other worries contributed to a temporary bout of writer's block; the sudden release from it on a Swiss holiday resulted in the creation of 'The Waste Land'. This long, beautiful, symbolic poem of disillusionment, in a form incorporating suggestions by his friend POUND, he himself published in 1922 in the first issue of a new literary magazine, *The Criterion*, which he founded and edited until 1939.

In 1925 he became a director and an editor of the London publisher Faber & Faber, for whom he worked for the rest of his life and built up an enviable list of modern poets. *Poems, 1909–25* (1925) brought together what had already been published, with the addition of 'The Hollow Men', and represented the end of one poetic phase and the beginning of another, more questioning one, epitomized in the stylized, Dante-esque world of *Ash-Wednesday* (1930). In 1927 he took British nationality and also became a member of the Church of England. The ultimate expression of his spiritual redemption in terms of time and eternity is in the poems 'Burnt Norton' (1936), 'East Coker' (1940), 'The Dry Salvages' (1941), and 'Little Gidding' (1942), published together as *Four Quartets* (1944).

With *Sweeney Agonistes: Fragments of an Aristophanic Melodrama* (1932) he explored the potential of the modern poetic drama, about which he had written in *The Sacred Wood*. *Murder in the Cathedral* (1935), for its religious associations in particular, is often performed. Though the comedy, *The Cocktail Party* (1950), and the more farcical *The Confidential Clerk* (1954) were admired in their time as stage plays, he is, in contrast to FRY, more a poet than a dramatist. A musical adaptation of his juvenile-orientated but sophisticated rhymes, *Old Possum's Book of Practical Cats* (1939), has been produced under the title of *Cats* (1981).

As a poet, Eliot makes considerable demands on his readers, and it is up to them to respond. He is regarded as the founder of modernism in poetry, of whom as early as 1932 LEAVIS could write in *New Bearings in English Poetry*, 'We have here . . . poetry that expresses freely a modern sensibility, the ways of feeling, the modes of experience, of one fully alive in his own age.' As a poet-critic in the tradition of DRYDEN, COLERIDGE, and ARNOLD, his influence on the understanding and appreciation of literature has been profound. He pointed the way to a more incisive interest in Elizabethan and Jacobean drama, particularly MASSINGER and WEBSTER, and in DONNE and other Metaphysical poets. In *The Idea of a Christian Society* (1939) and *Notes Towards the Definition of Culture* (1948) he turned his attention to the criticism of modern society. His Clark Lectures at Cambridge (1926), followed by the Turnbull Lectures at Johns Hopkins University (1933), were eventually published as *The Varieties of Metaphysical Poetry*, ed. Ronald Schuchard (1994). He was awarded the Nobel Prize for Literature, and also the OM, in 1948.

Eliot's wife, from whom he had been permanently separated since the early 1930s, died in 1947. He married Valerie Fletcher in 1957. Questions of his anti-Semitism resurfaced publicly in 1996 with an adversarial study by Anthony Julius, *T. S. Eliot, Anti-Semitism and Literary Form*, and her brave decision to allow the publication, under the title of *Inventions of the March Hare: Poems 1909–1917*, ed. Christopher Ricks (with voluminous annotations revealing the poet's sources), of a notebook of early verses which Eliot had expressly stated should never be published. See *The Complete Poems and Plays of T. S. Eliot*, 1969; *Selected Prose of T. S. Eliot*, ed. Frank Kermode, 1975; Lyndall Gordon, *Eliot's Early Years*, new edn 1988, and *Eliot's New Life*, new edn 1989 (biography); Tony Sharpe, *T. S. Eliot: a Literary Life*, 1991; Helen Gardner, *The Art of T. S. Eliot*, new edn 1968; A. David Moody, *Thomas Stearns Eliot: Poet*, 2nd edn 1995 (critical study); David E. Jones, *The Plays of T. S. Eliot*, new edn 1963.

ELLIOT, JEAN

(1727–1805) Scottish poet, was born at the family seat, Minto House, Roxburghshire, the third daughter of Sir Gilbert Elliot of Minto (1693–1766), a judge of the Court of Session. It is said that one night in 1756, while they were being driven home in the family coach, her brother Gilbert (1722–77), man of letters and future eminent politician, bet her 'a pair of gloves or a set of ribbons' that she could not write a successful song about the battle of Flodden (1513). 'The Flowers of the Forest', written in Scots, and arguably the most popular and certainly the most moving of ballads on the subject, was published anonymously and was initially believed to be a genuine relic. On the death of her father, she and her mother and sisters moved to a house in Brown Square, Edinburgh, where she lived on alone after they died. She was said to be the last woman in the city regularly to go out in her own sedan chair. The identity of the author of the ballad was discovered, long after it was known to be a modern composition, by a trio of folklorists, one of whom was WALTER SCOTT, who printed it in *Minstrelsy of the Scottish Border* (1802–03) as 'by a lady of family in Roxburghshire'. HENRY MACKENZIE, who was her neighbour in Edinburgh, described her as 'one of the most sensible women of her time, tho' she wrote poetry'. No other poem known to be by her has survived.

ELLIS, HAVELOCK see SCHREINER.

ELLISON, RALPH (WALDO) (1914–94) American novelist and critic, was born in Oklahoma City, and educated at a local high school and Tuskegee Institute, Alabama, where he majored in music, his instrument being the trumpet. He has said: 'In 1935 I discovered Eliot's *The Waste Land* which moved and intrigued me but defied my powers of analysis—such as they were—and I wondered why I had never read anything of equal intensity and sensibility by an American Negro writer.' In 1945 he returned from serving at sea in the US Merchant Navy, having been unable to start the novel which he had been awarded a Rosenwald Fellowship to write. He struggled for several years with *Invisible Man* (1952), which won the National Book Award. A first-person odyssey of a nameless black from the South to New York, it was criticized, as was the work of BALDWIN, for not reflecting the 'protest' philosophy of RICHARD WRIGHT, who had been one of Ellison's early patrons. In an essay included in his collection, *Shadow and Act* (1964), he replied to the charge by postulating that human experience is both more complex and richer than mere protest. A later volume of essays is *Going to the Territory* (1986). From 1958 he taught folklore, black studies, creative writing, and Russian and American literature at several colleges and universities, being Albert Schweitzer Professor in the Humanities at New York University 1970–79. Among his retirement pastimes were birdwatching and growing African violets. Fragments of an uncompleted second novel appeared in literary journals, most notably 'And Hickman Arrives' (*Noble Savage*, March 1960). See *The Collected Essays*, ed. John F. Callahan, 1995; Amritjit Singh (ed.), *Conversations with Ralph Ellison*, 1995; Robert G. O'Mealley, *The Craft of Ralph Ellison*, 1980 (critical study).

ÉLUARD, PAUL see DEVLIN; ELYTIS.

ELYOT, (Sir) **THOMAS** (*c*.1490–1546) English prose writer, was probably born in Wiltshire, where there were family estates. He was educated at home and at the Middle Temple, finally taking a degree in civil law at Oxford in 1524. In 1511, at the instigation of his father, Sir Richard Elyot (*d*. 1522), a judge of the King's Bench, he was appointed Clerk of Assize on the Western Circuit. In about 1525, through the influence of Cardinal Wolsey (*c*.1475–1530), he became Chief Clerk of the King's Council; he was forcibly retired after Wolsey's fall in 1530, but was rewarded with a knighthood. At his manor near Cambridge he now wrote *The Boke Named the Governour* (1531), in which he brought the principles of the New Learning to bear on the education of young men for leadership. While he advocated a thorough knowledge of classics (such as survived in British independent schools until the middle of the 20th century), and, for recreation, artistic pursuits and sport (except football, 'wherein is nothing but beastly fury and extreme violence'), he wrote in English, in a deliberate attempt to encourage others to use and 'augment' the language and to improve standards of translation. He was rewarded by Henry VIII with a diplomatic post in Europe, but after 1532 he concentrated on literary works. The most significant of these are a series of Platonic dialogues including *Of the Knowledge Whiche Maketh a Wise Man* (1533) and *The Defence of Good Women* (1545), the first Latin–English dictionary (1538), and *The Castel of Helth* (1539), a layman's guide to medicine and hygiene, which was attacked by doctors because he was not qualified and by members of his circle because it was not a suitable subject for a knight.

ELYTIS, ODYSSEUS, pseudonym of Odysseus Alepoudelis (1911–96) Greek poet, was born in Heraklion, Crete, the sixth child of a wealthy soap manufacturer. The family moved to Athens when he was three. He read law at Athens University, but did not take his degree. He published his first book of verse in 1939, and served as a lieutenant in Albania during World War II. After the war he worked for the National Broadcasting Institution, with a break for further study in Paris at the Sorbonne. He was subsequently President of the Governing Board of Greek Ballet 1956–58, and Adviser to the Greek National Theatre 1965–68. He adopted a pseudonym to avoid the link with the brand of soap made by his family, the choice being ascribed to various linguistic connections with the name: *Hellas* [Greece]; *elpida* [hope]; *eleftheria* [freedom]; *Eleni* [Helen]; *alytis* [wanderer], which in its classical Greek form is used by HOMER to describe Odysseus (the sea is a recurrent motif in Elytis's verse and other writings); and Paul Éluard (1895–1952), the French Surrealist poet whose work, with that of similar writers of his time, was one of the early influences on Elytis—see Paul Éluard, *Ombres et Soleil/Shadows and Sun: Selected Writings of 1913–1952*, tr. Lloyd Alexander and Cicely Buckley (bilingual edn 1995). In [*The Axion Esti*] (1959; tr. Edmund Keeley and George Savidis, 1980), a long, complex poem in densely allusive language which was 14 years in the writing, life and the creative power of Nature and the poet himself are ranged against the destructive force of his country's enemies. He was a reclusive person; though many of his poems were inspired by women, he was apparently too devoted to his work ever to marry. He was awarded the Nobel Prize for Literature in 1979. See *The Collected Poems*, tr. Jeffrey Carson and Nikos Saris, 1997; *The Sovereign Sun: Selected Poems*, tr. Kimon Friar, 1990.

EMECHETA, (FLORENCE) BUCHI

(*b.* 1944) Nigerian novelist, was born in Lagos, the daughter of a railway porter, on whose early death her mother, who as a child had been sold as a family slave, returned to her native village in Ibusa, Eastern Nigeria. Emecheta, who would otherwise have been forced to marry at 12, secretly sat for a scholarship at the Methodist Girls' High School, Lagos, where she went as a boarder. She left at 16, and bowed to family pressure to marry (but to the man of her choice). Still only 17, and now a mother of two, she earned enough in a job at the American Embassy in Lagos to join her student husband in London. She left him finally in 1964, 'a little over twenty, dragging four cold and dripping babies with me, and pregnant with a fifth'. She got work as a librarian in the British Museum, took an A level in Latin, and embarked on a course of study which led to a degree in sociology at London University in 1972. She browbeat Richard Crossman (1907–74), then Editor of the *New Statesman*, into publishing a series of articles on her experiences in London, 'Life in the Ditch', which became her novel, *In the Ditch* (1972), with a sequel *Second Class Citizen* (1974)—published together as *Adah's Story* (1983). There followed three novels exploring the traditional position of women in Nigeria: *The Bride Price* (1976), the original manuscript of which, written in her early London days, her husband had burned; *The Slave Girl* (1977); and *The Joys of Motherhood* (1979). Now also a community worker and adviser on race relations, she lectured in the USA in 1979. *Destination Biafra* (1982) is an

only marginally fictionalized account of the sufferings in her home region during the civil war. She had returned there in 1980, as a visiting professor at Calabar University, the experience of which is the basis of *Double Yoke* (1982). In *Gwendolen* (1989), the effects of child abuse and the growing apart of Afro-Caribbean and African cultural traditions extend her range beyond immediate, or vicarious, experience. See *Head Above Water*, new edn 1994 (autobiography to 1977).

EMERSON, RALPH WALDO

(1803–97) American philosopher and poet, was born in Boston, Massachusetts, the fourth of eight children of a Unitarian minister who died when the boy was seven. His mother kept a series of boarding houses in order to educate her sons, and Emerson went to the Boston Public Latin School and Harvard College, from which he graduated 30th in a class of 59 in 1821. In 1825, after teaching at his brother's school for young ladies, and writing poetry, drama criticism, essays, and fiction in his spare time, he enrolled at Harvard Divinity School, only to have to go back to teaching because of eye trouble. He returned to Harvard in 1827. In 1829 he was ordained a junior pastor of Boston's Second Church, and married Ellen Tucker. She was 19, and died of tuberculosis 16 months later. In 1832, having delivered a sermon in which he questioned the orthodox view of the Lord's Supper, he resigned from the ministry, and sailed for Europe. He saw LANDOR in Italy, and attended a Fourth of July dinner with 98 of his countrymen in Paris. In London he met MILL and sat for an hour with COLERIDGE, who monopolized the conversation. He travelled into the desolation round Craigenputtock Farm, which was the beginning of a lifelong and fruitful friendship with CARLYLE, and visited Rydal Mount to see WORDSWORTH, 'the hard limits' of whose thought disturbed him.

On his return he settled in Concord, able to subsist as a lecturer on a legacy from Ellen. In 1835 he married Lydia Jackson (1802–92), whom he renamed Lidian but preferred to call 'Queenie', and who stressfully bore the burden of running a household often peopled by visiting eccentrics. He helped to found the Transcendental Club, for the informal exchange of modern views on philosophy, theology, and literature. The essence of transcendentalism is expressed in his first book, *Nature* (1836), in which he argues that man can stretch beyond his known capabilities by transcending reason, through faith in himself and in the benevolent power of the universe. THOREAU and MARGARET FULLER, who for two years edited the movement's journal, the *Dial*, were notable literary disciples of his thought at this time. In 1837 he delivered before the Phi Beta Kappa Society, Harvard, in the presence of Thoreau's graduating class, his celebrated oration on 'The

American Scholar', which HOLMES hailed as 'our intellectual Declaration of Independence'.

In 1838 he delivered the Divinity School Address at Harvard, on the state of Christianity, which caused him to be banned from speaking there for over three decades. *Essays* (1841) and *Essays: Second Series* (1844), drawn from his journals and lectures, earned him the status of prophet; *Poems* (1846) confused the public with its philosophical implications but pleased refined critics. *Representative Men* (1850), studies of great figures in terms of their times, and *English Traits* (1856), sketches developed from his two visits (the second in 1847–48), were more to popular taste, and he now, to emphasize his clubbable nature, took to smoking cigars. He espoused the cause of the abolitionists, and spoke out publicly against the Fugitive Slave Act of 1850. In 1872 his memory began to be erratic, and after a severe fire at his home (ALCOTT was among those who came to the scene, and made herself responsible for saving manuscripts), another European trip was felt to be the right thing for his health. With his daughter Ellen (1839–1909) he visited France, Italy, Egypt, and Greece, as well as Britain, and returned to Concord to the playing of bands and the cheering of crowds. He continued to go to meetings of his clubs, but recognized little, not even the face of the corpse at the funeral of LONGFELLOW. Special trains were laid on for his own funeral, to which over a thousand mourners came from outside Concord. No single person has had such an influence on the course of American literature. See *Ralph Waldo Emerson*, ed. Richard Poirier, 1990 (selection from lectures, essays, and poetry); *Essays and Poems*, ed. Tony Tanner, 1992; *Collected Poems and Translations*, ed. Harold Bloom and Paul Kane, 1994; *Emerson's Literary Criticism*, ed. Eric W. Carlson, new edn 1996; Ralph L. Rusk, *The Life of Ralph Waldo Emerson*, 1949; Robert D. Richardson, Jr, *Emerson: the Mind on Fire*, 1995 (critical biography); Carlos Baker, *Emerson Among the Eccentrics: a Group Portrait*, introduction and epilogue by James R. Mellow, 1996 (his family, his friends, and their attitudes); Donald Yanella, *Ralph Waldo Emerson*, 1982 (critical study).

EMPSON, (Sir) **WILLIAM** (1906–84) British poet and critic, was born at Yokefleet Hall, Howden, Yorkshire. His father died when he was ten. He was educated at Winchester College and Magdalene College, Cambridge, where he had poems published in the *Cambridge Review* and *Cambridge Poetry 1929*, and submitted to his tutor, in place of a weekly essay, the basis of the first of his major critical works, *Seven Types of Ambiguity* (1930). An alleged breach of chastity caused the removal of the fellowship at his college to which he had been elected. Instead he became Professor of English at Tokyo University of Literature and Science from 1931 to 1934. While he was there he wrote *Some Versions of Pastoral* (1935), in which, from a starting point of a discussion on proletarian literature, he provocatively treats the pastoral element in CARROLL's *Alice in Wonderland*, as well as in SHAKESPEARE, MILTON, and GAY. He was Professor of English at Peking National University 1937–39 and 1947–52, after which he was Professor of English at Sheffield University until his retirement in 1971. In the postwar period he published *The Structure of Complex Words* (1951) and *Milton's God* (1961). He believed that criticism should embrace many relevant experiences, and he wrote with humour as well as with wide-ranging insight. His verse makes up in impressiveness and some brilliant individual lines for what it lacks in general accessibility. Several volumes of critical essays have been published posthumously, of which *The Strength of Shakespeare's Shrew: Essays, Memoirs and Reviews*, ed. John Haffenden (1996) also contains autobiographical material. He was knighted in 1979. See *Collected Poems*, new edn 1984.

ENGELS, FRIEDRICH see MARX.

ENRIGHT, D(ENNIS) J(OSEPH) (*b*. 1920) British poet, novelist, and critic, was born in Leamington Spa, Warwickshire, and describes his working-class upbringing in the poems in *The Terrible Shears: Scenes from a Twenties Childhood* (1973). He won scholarships to Leamington College and Downing College, Cambridge, where he was a pupil of LEAVIS. He was subsequently awarded a DLitt degree by Alexandria University for his thesis *A Commentary on Goethe's 'Faust'* (1949), after a public viva conducted in French before an Egyptian academic board. His peripatetic, often unconventional and occasionally controversial academic career—see his caustic *Memoirs of a Mendicant Professor* (1969)—took him in turn to Egypt, Japan, West Germany, Thailand, and Singapore, where he was Professor of English at the university 1960–70. Much of his poetry, from that published in *The Laughing Hyena and Other Poems* (1953) to that in *Instant Chronicles: a Life* (1985) has been inspired by foreign parts, particularly the East, and is often ironic while also responding to the misery he has witnessed there; *Under the Circumstances: Poems and Proses* (1991) deals in quirks and oddities. The East features, too, in his novels, of which the first, *Academic Year* (1955), was reissued in 1985 with an introduction by THWAITE. *Interplay: a Kind of Commonplace Book* (1995) comprises philosophical, literary, and nostalgic recollections. His critical works include *Man is an Onion: Essays and Reviews* (1972) and *Fields of Vision: Essays on Literature, Language, and Television* (1988). *The World of Dew: Aspects* *of Living Japan* (1955) is both accurately realized and amusing. He has edited *The Oxford Book of Contemporary Verse 1945–1980* (1980). He was made OBE in 1991. See *Collected Poems*, rev. edn 1987; *Selected Poems 1990*, 1990; *Old Men and Comets*, 1993 (subsequent collection).

ERASMUS, DESIDERIUS (1466–1536) Dutch humanist scholar and prose writer in Latin, was born in Rotterdam, the second of two illegitimate sons of a widow and of a scholarly scribe who at some point became a priest. He was educated at chapter schools at Gouda, Deventer, and, after the death of his parents in about 1484, at Bois-le-Duc ('s-Hertogenbosch), from which in 1487, reluctantly acceding to his guardians' wishes, he entered the Augustinian Order at Steyn. He was ordained priest in 1492. After serving as Latin secretary to the Bishop of Cambria, he studied theology at Collège Montaigu, Paris University, supporting himself by taking in private pupils from England. One of these was William Blount (*d.* 1534), Lord Mountjoy, at whose invitation he visited England in 1499, meeting THOMAS MORE and the royal children of Henry VII. Back in Paris, he published *Adagiorum Collectanea* (1500), a collection of 818 Greek and Latin adages, which he expanded over the years and which became a source of inspiration for many European writers. In between Continental travel (he was awarded a doctorate in theology at Turin in 1506), private teaching, research, and study, he made three further visits to England. During the second of these (1509–14), he lectured in Greek studies at Cambridge, and wrote, while ill at More's house, the playful satire *Encomium Moriae* (authorized edn 1512; tr. Betty Radice as *Praise of Folly*, 1971), whose Latin title is a pun on the name of his host.

From 1517 to 1521 Erasmus lived mainly in Louvain, where he prepared the first authorized edition of *Colloquia* [Colloquies] (1522), a series of witty, irreverent dialogues and essays, which had begun as exercises in conversational Latin and became an instrument of religious reform. After settling in 1521 in Basel, where he acted as general editor for the printer John Froben (*d.* 1549), he continued his campaign with *De Libero Arbitrio* [On Free Will] (1524), a protest against the extremism of LUTHER which had been suggested by Henry VIII, to whom he sent an advance copy of the text. Now aligned neither with orthodox Catholics nor with the Lutherans, he moved in 1529 to Freiburg, from which he returned to Basel in 1535 to supervise the publication of *Ecclesiastes* (1535), his treatise on the art of preaching. He refused Pope Paul III's offer of a cardinal's hat, and died in seclusion, maintaining the motto on his personal seal, '*Cedo nulli*' [I yield to no one]. Prolific writer, over three thousand of

whose letters survive, and editor of the Greek New Testament and the writings of ST JEROME, he is the embodiment of humanism. See *The Erasmus Reader*, ed. Erika Rummel, 1990; Léon E. Halkin, *Erasmus: a Critical Biography*, tr. John Tonkin, new edn 1994; James McConica, *Erasmus*, 1991 (introduction to his life and works).

ERDRICH, (KAREN) LOUISE (*b.* 1954) American novelist and poet, was born in Wahpeton, North Dakota, the eldest of seven children of German-American and French-Chippewa descent. At Dartmouth College, which she entered in 1972, her tutor in Native American Studies was Michael Dorris (*b.* 1946), Native American writer, whom she later married and who has influenced the development of her work—the novel *The Crown of Columbus* (1991) was published under their joint names. After experience in several different jobs, including editor for the Circle-Boston Indian Council and a textbook writer for Charles Merrill Inc., she determined to be a professional author. For part of a further degree at Johns Hopkins University she submitted poems which were subsequently published in her first collection, *Jacklight* (1984). *Love Medicine* (1984; rev. edn, with five new sections, 1993), *The Beet Queen* (1986), *Tracks* (1988), and *The Bingo Palace* (1994) comprise a tetralogy of novels in which the Chippewa culture and experience are the background to a series of linked character studies spanning the years 1912 to the present. *Tales of Burning Love* (1996) is an emotion-packed study of a man's five marriages. *The Blue Jay's Dance: a Birth Year* (1995) is a lush prose account of Erdrich's experience of the birth of her third daughter, from conception to babyhood.

ERVINE, ST JOHN (1883–1971) Irish dramatist and critic, was born in Belfast, went to London as an insurance clerk when he was 17, got to know G. B. SHAW, and became hooked on the stage. *The Magnanimous Lover*, a one-act play written in 1907, was one of four realistic, unsparing Ulster dramas which were produced at the Abbey Theatre, Dublin, between 1911 and 1915—see *Four Irish Plays* (1914). He was also writing novels, of which *Mrs Martin's Man* (1914), which deals with the 1798 Rebellion in Ireland, is best regarded. He became Manager of the Abbey in 1915, but was replaced after a brief regime during which the actors could accept neither his policy nor his views. He then joined the Army as a trooper, and lost a leg in 1918 while serving in France as a lieutenant in the Royal Dublin Fusiliers. After World War I he became Drama Critic of the *Observer*, while continuing himself to write plays. The most successful of these, *Mary, Mary Quite Contrary* (1923), *Anthony and Anna* (1925), and *The First Mrs Fraser* (1929), were light pieces far removed in tone and milieu from his Irish dramas. He returned to Ulster settings with *Boyd's Shop* (1936) and *Friends and Relations* (1941, published 1947), in which the bitter realism has given way to a more genial approach to quite different forms of intolerance. He was Professor of Dramatic Literature of the Royal Society 1933–36. He also wrote a number of biographical studies, of which the best is *Bernard Shaw, His Life, Work and Friends* (1956), the longest *God's Soldier: General William Booth* (1934), and the most unbalanced *Oscar Wilde: a Present Time Appraisal* (1951). See *Selected Plays*, ed. John Cronin, 1988.

ESCHENBACH, WOLFRAM VON see WOLFRAM VON ESCHENBACH.

ESSON, (THOMAS) LOUIS (BU-VELOT) (1879–1943) Australian dramatist, was born in Edinburgh and was at the age of four brought by his widowed mother to Melbourne, where he grew up in the house of his uncle, who was an artist. He was educated at Carlton Grammar School and attended lectures at Melbourne University. He became a freelance journalist and critic, and embarked on a world tour, which took in a visit to the Abbey Theatre, Dublin, in 1905. YEATS advised him 'to keep within your own borders' as a writer, to which SYNGE added that there must be plenty of material for folk drama in the outback, 'with shepherds going mad in lonely huts'. *The Time is Not Yet Ripe* was first performed by the Melbourne Repertory Company in 1912, and published the same year. This topical, and still topical, Australian political comedy, which sparkles with wit, was not produced again until 1972, and was republished in 1973 (ed. Philip Parsons). *Three Short Plays* (1911) was reissued in London as *Dead Timber and Other Plays* (1920), and included *The Drovers*. This study of the situation of an injured drover left behind when the herd has to move on has been compared in impact with Synge's *Riders to the Sea*. After another extended overseas trip, Esson founded with PALMER in 1921–22 the Pioneer Players, a predominantly amateur company. The first production was his comedy, *The Battler*: the last, in 1926, was his Melbourne underworld drama, *The Bride of Gospel Place*. See Vance Palmer, *Louis Esson and the Australian Theatre*, 1948; Peter Fitzpatrick, *Pioneer Players: the Lives of Louis and Hilda Esson*, 1996; and in Leslie Rees, *The Making of Australian Drama*, 1973.

ETHEREGE, (Sir) **GEORGE** (1634/5–91) English dramatist, came of a well-to-do Oxfordshire or Berkshire family, travelled abroad, studied law in London, and became a man about town. The first of his three comedies, *The Comical Revenge: or, Love in a Tub* (1664), was well received. *She Wou'd if She Cou'd* (1668), which SHADWELL called 'the best Comedy that has been written since the Restauration of the Stage', failed initially because of poor acting. His friend and drinking companion ROCHESTER, in his critical essay 'A Session of Poets' (1675), complained that one who had such 'fancy, sense, judgment, and wit' should be so idle. Whatever the effect, Etherege now produced in *The Man of Mode: or, Sr Fopling Flutter* (1676) a consistently witty, well-characterized, and well-controlled play, and in the lover Dorimant, 'a Devil, but he has something of the Angel yet undefac'd in him', a character whose traits were identified with those of Rochester by the critic John Dennis (1657–1734) in *A Defence of Sir Fopling Flutter* (1722). The play was first performed before the King in March 1676, in the cast being Elizabeth Barry (1658–1713), mistress of Rochester and probably also of Etherege, by whom she is said to have had a child. In June of that year, there was an incident in Epsom which began as a drunken frolic and ended with a death, after which Rochester and Etherege lay low to avoid committal proceedings. In about 1680 Etherege received a knighthood, which people said he had purchased in order to impress a rich widow, whom he then married. He was ambassador to the German assembly at Ratisbon 1685–89, from where he wrote entertaining letters—see *Letters of Sir George Etherege*, ed. Frederick Bracher (1974). After the abdication of James II he lived in Paris, where he died.

EUCLID see PASCAL.

EURIPIDES (480–406 BC) classical Greek dramatist, was born in Salamis, traditionally on the day of the Greek naval victory there over the Persians. His family were middle-class landowners. He wrote about ninety plays, of which 18 complete tragedies and one satyric drama survive. He first competed at the Dionysia in 455, and won the prize in 441. He had three more victories, the last with *Orestes* in 408. He then went to the court of the King of Macedonia, whose hounds, it is said, accidentally tore him to pieces. He was a master of theatrical surprises. By representing gods, monarchs, and heroes as real people, he effectively invented domestic drama. He introduced from forensic oratory the device of argument upon the stage, and made a feature of the prologue. He detached the choruses from the action and presented them as lyrical interludes of poetic beauty. Especially notable works are *Medea* (431), *Hippolytus* (428), *Trojan Women* (415), and *Bacchae* (405). His satyric play, *Cyclops*, was translated in 1819 by P. B. SHELLEY, who wrote to HUNT that the Greek plays were tempting him 'to throw over their perfect and glowing forms the grey veil of my own words'. See *After the Trojan War: The Women of Troy, Hecuba, Orestes* tr. Kenneth McLeish,

1994; *Alcestis and Other Plays*, tr. John Davie, ed. Richard Rutherford, new edn 1996.

EVANS, MARY ANN see ELIOT, GEORGE.

EVELYN, JOHN (1620–1706) English prose writer and diarist, was born on the family estate of Wotton in Surrey, but was boarded out with his grandparents in Sussex, whose home he refused to leave to go to Eton. So he was educated locally, then at Balliol College, Oxford (without taking a degree), and subsequently studied law in London. He joined the army of Charles I too late to participate in the defeat at Brentford in 1642, and then, perhaps prudently, returned home before he could be associated with the cause. This kind of discretion governed his life, which he dedicated to learning and public service, without ever seeking, or accepting, the outward trappings of success—he even refused a knighthood. His famous diary, which he kept from 1641 until his death, was first published as his *Memoirs* in 1818, having apparently been found the year before in a clothes basket at Wotton. It is a record of an age rather than the revelations of an individual. Events and places (he was an inveterate traveller and guide) are often described with the help of newspaper and other records. There are, however, graphic first-hand accounts of the Great Fire of London in 1666 and of the freeze of 1683–84, and penetrating observations on unusual aspects of life, and on the impact of religion upon daily existence at different levels. Among the books published during his lifetime were *Fumifugium* (1661), a plea for a smokeless London; and *Sylva: or a Discourse on Forest Trees* (1664), on which he was an authority. See *The Diary*, ed. John Bowle, 1985; *The Diary of John Evelyn*, ed. Guy de la Bédoyère, new edn 1995; *The Writings of John Evelyn* ed. Guy de la Bédoyère, 1995; John Bowle, *John Evelyn and His World: a Biography*, 1981.

EWART, GAVIN (1914–95) poet, was born in London and educated at Wellington College, whose headmaster he offended with an otherwise celebratory lyric inspired by a rugby football victory and with 'The Fourth of May', published in 1934, after he had left, in *Out of Bounds*, an anti-public school magazine. At 17 he had also contributed poems to GRIGSON's *New Verse*. He went to Christ's College, Cambridge, and was later commissioned in the Royal Artillery in World War II, serving in North Africa and Italy, and finding himself incapable of 'rushing about in a tank like Keith Douglas [see KEITH DOUGLAS] writing poems between battles'. He worked for the British Council from 1946 to 1952, after which he was an advertising copywriter until 1971, when he lost his job and became a freelance writer. Twenty-five years separated the publication of his first book, *Poems and Songs* (1939), from his second, *Londoners* (1964), a series of mainly topographical poems which ALAN ROSS had commissioned in 1959, but his favoured topics remained unchanged, the lightness of touch and technical ingenuity survived, and both remained features of subsequent collections. *Pleasures of the Flesh* (1966) contains some of his more erotic verse: a tenderness, born no doubt of age, infuses some of his later work. A quality of compassion as well as of graphic description distinguish horrific poems of contemporary brutality, such as 'Thriller' and 'The Gentle Sex'. Ewart was a master of the epigram in many forms—see *All My Little Ones: the Short Poems of Gavin Ewart* (1978). He edited and contributed to *Other People's Clerihews* (1983). Latterly he found success, and rewards, on the poetry-reading circuit, regularly appearing on American campuses in the spring. See *The Collected Ewart 1933–1980*, 1980; *Collected Poems 1980–1990*, 1991; *85 Poems*, 1993; *Selected Poems 1933–1993*, 1996 (his own final choice).

EZEKIEL, NISSIM (*b.* 1924) Indian poet, was born in Bombay of a Jewish family long established there, and was educated at Antonio D'Souza High School and Bombay University. He spent the years 1948–52 in London, after which he combined the teaching of English with editing literary journals, and was Art Critic of *The Times of India* from 1964 to 1967. He was Visiting Professor at Leeds University in 1964, and at Chicago University in 1967, and was Reader in American Literature at Bombay University 1972–81, and Professor 1981–85. An Indian who writes poetry in English 'because one cannot write it in any other language' (for that was what was spoken at home), he has described his main themes as 'love, personal integration, the Indian contemporary scene, modern urban life, spiritual values'. His first collection was *A Time to Change and Other Poems* (1952). His unusual blend of cultural backgrounds enables him to interpret the Indian scene as a close observer who also has an inherent understanding of it, which he often does with sharp wit or gentle humour, factors not normally associated with Indian verse. See *Collected Poems 1952–1988*, new edn 1992; *Selected Prose*, introduction by Adil Jussawalla, 1993.

F

FAIR, A. A. see GARDNER.

FAIRBURN, A(RTHUR) R(EX) D(UGARD) (1904–57) New Zealand poet, was born in Auckland and educated at Auckland Grammar School, which he left at 16 and became a clerk in an insurance company. He was a labourer and freelance writer between 1926 and 1930, when he went to England. 'The Rhyme of the Dead Self' ('Tonight I have taken all that I was / and strangled him that pale lily-white lad . . .'), the final poem in *He Shall Not Rise* (1930), suggested a disavowal of its contents. On his return to New Zealand he repudiated most contemporary English literary influences and became a leading member of the radical Phoenix group in Auckland. He was a relief worker during the Depression, after which he edited the Auckland Farmers' Union journal, *Farming First. Dominion* (1938) is a part-satirical, part-lyrical nationalist epic poem. He was a radio scriptwriter from 1943 to 1946, after which he tutored in English and later taught history and theory of fine arts at Elam School of Fine Arts. *The Rakehelly Man and Other Verses* (1946) includes possibly his best comic verse. See *Collected Verse*, ed. Denis Glover, 1966; Denys Trussell, *Fairburn*, 1985 (critical biography).

FALCONER, WILLIAM (1732–70) Scottish poet, was born in Edinburgh, the son of a wig-maker. He was second mate of a merchant ship, *Britannia*, when it was wrecked off the Greek coast in 1750. He had poems published in the *Gentleman's Magazine* from 1751. His major work, *The Shipwreck*, 'a Poem in Three Cantos, by a Sailor', was 'printed for the author' in 1762. There is the statutory love interest and some expendable classical allusions, but the nautical sequences and descriptions are splendid. He then joined the Royal Navy as a midshipman, transferring to the supplies branch as a purser, while continuing to write. In 1768 he turned down the offer of a partnership from John Murray (1745–93), founder of the publishing company. The next year he sailed in the frigate *Aurora*, bound for India. After calling in at the Cape, she was never seen again. His widow, Jane (née Hicks), whom in his verse he addressed more poetically as Miranda, lived comfortably until 1796 on the proceeds from his reference work, *The Universal Marine Dictionary* (1769).

FALKNER, J(OHN) MEADE (1858–1932) British novelist, was born in Manningford Bruce, Wiltshire, the eldest son of the curate, and was educated at Marlborough College and Hertford College, Oxford. He then became tutor to the sons of (Sir) Andrew Noble (1831–1915), the arms manufacturer, who appointed him his private secretary when the boys grew up. When Noble's business became a limited company in 1897, Falkner was appointed company secretary, becoming a member of the board in 1901 and ultimately its Chairman, in which capacities he negotiated many contracts with European governments, from whom he received appropriate decorations. His real interests, however, lay elsewhere. Walking and bicycling holidays provided the background and inspiration for guide books on Oxfordshire (1894) and Berkshire (1902); his knowledge of antiquities led to the honorary appointments of Librarian to Durham Cathedral and Reader in Palaeography at Durham University. He wrote three novels. *The Lost Stradivarius* (1895) has supernatural as well as antiquarian elements, while the *Nebuly Coat* (1903) centres on the imminent collapse of the tower of an ancient church. *Moonfleet* (1898), a novel of smugglers in the mid-18th century whose setting is a real Dorset village, though not regarded at the time as his best, has effortlessly survived as an adventure story for children in the tradition of STEVENSON. Falkner was a generous benefactor of libraries and of the Cotswolds' town of Burford, in whose churchyard he is buried. He also wrote poetry of a descriptive nature which has pleasing rhythms.

FARQUHAR, GEORGE (1678–1707) Irish dramatist, was born in Londonderry, one of seven children of a poor Church of England cleric, and was educated at Trinity College, Dublin, initially as a sizar (a student with a maintenance grant in return for certain domestic duties). He became an actor with Dublin's Smock Theatre, but left (to go to London), having inadvertently wounded a colleague in a stage duel through not using a blunted sword. His first comedy, *Love and a*

Bottle (1698), was moderately successful: *The Constant Couple; or a Trip to the Jubilee* (1699) did better. Several flops followed, and Farquhar's financial position was not advanced when he discovered that the widow with two children whom he had married was penniless. He was commissioned in Lord Orrery's regiment and sent to Lichfield and Shrewsbury to drum up recruits. He drew on this experience to write *The Recruiting Officer* (1706), which was so highly thought of by a London impresario that he advanced him £16 2s.6d. Having resigned his commission, Farquhar fell ill and into financial straits again. His actor friend Robert Wilks (1665–1732) gave him 20 guineas as an encouragement to write *The Beaux' Stratagem* (1707), whose first performance he only just lived to see. Stock situations and characters abound (though the name of Lady Bountiful has since entered the language), but the dialogue has a splendid vitality, and the ultimate denouement is not the conjoining of the lovers, Aimwell and Dorinda, but the divorce by consent (after an exchange which draws heavily on MILTON's pamphlet on divorce) of the Sullens so that the wife may marry Aimwell's companion. In both plays the action is moved out of London and the treatment is more humane than it is in earlier comedy. See *Works*, ed. Shirley Strum Kenny, 2 vols 1988; *The Recruiting Officer and Other Plays*, ed. William Myers, 1995.

FARRELL,   JAMES   T(HOMAS) (1904–79) American novelist, short-story writer, and critic, was born in Chicago of Irish descent, and was brought up by his maternal grandparents, his teamster father being unable to support a growing family. He studied classics at St Cyril High School, after which he took night classes at De Paul University while working as a telephone clerk. After four years at Chicago University he dropped out, to be a writer. *Young Lonigan: a Boyhood in Chicago Streets* (1932), which grew into *Studs Lonigan: a Trilogy* (1935), represented a reversion to the naturalism of a previous generation of writers, exposing the Irish-Catholic 'apartment culture' of Chicago's South Side, in which the pursuit of material wealth leads to spiritual destitution and, in the case of Lonigan, to a violent death. Chicago is also the environment or starting point of three further novel sequences: featuring Danny O'Neill, beginning with *A World I Never Made* (1936); Bernard Carr, with *Bernard Clare* (1946); and the writer Eddie Ryan, whose background has parallels with Farrell's, with *The Silence of History* (1963). Many of his short stories interact with or complement the novels—see *The Short Stories of James T. Farrell* (1937), *An Omnibus of Short Stories* (1957), *Judith and Other Stories* (1973). In response to counterattacks by Marxist critics whom he had accused of subjecting literature to political expediency, he published *A Note on Literary Criticism* (1936), the first of several critical studies and collections of essays. *The Collected Poems of James T. Farrell* (1965) contains just 42 short reflections, mainly written in the 1930s and 1960s.

FARRELL, MICHAEL (1899–1962) Irish novelist, was born in Carlow and read medicine at the National University; during his time there he was involved in the 'Troubles' and briefly imprisoned. He then worked as a marine superintendent in the Belgian Congo, after which he returned to Ireland and married the proprietor of a handweaving business. He now resumed his medical studies at Trinity College, Dublin, but gave them up for journalism and for work with Radio Éireann. He wrote regularly for *The Bell* under O'FAOLAIN's editorship during World War II, after which he successfully managed his wife's business. In the early 1930s he had begun to write a novel in which an orphan Catholic boy grows up in comfortable surroundings, but whose life, beliefs, and character are radically altered by the 1916 Rising. In 1937 O'Faolain was reluctantly allowed, or surreptitiously managed, to take the vast manuscript in a suitcase to London, where a publisher readily agreed to bring it out when it had finally been revised. Farrell, unable to let it go, worked on the book for the rest of his life. It was published after his death as *Thy Tears Might Cease* (1963), edited and shortened by some hundred thousand words by the Irish poet and critic Monk Gibbon (1896–1987). In this form defects are apparent which might not be so obvious in a longer version, but it is convincing in its portrayal of various people's lives at the time and of the effects of the events on the community.

FAST, HOWARD (MELVIN) (*b.* 1914) American novelist, was born in New York City of Jewish parents, and with his two older brothers was brought up by their father, a factory worker, after their mother's early death. He was educated at George Washington High School, New York, which he left at 16 to join the navy. Rejected as too young, he did various jobs, and while a messenger boy in the New York Public Library was introduced to G. B. SHAW's *The Intelligent Woman's Guide to Socialism and Capitalism*, which 'took the senseless hate and resentment [against class oppression and class injustice] and directed it to paths of understanding, reason and creation'. He published his first novel, *Two Valleys*, in 1933. In *Conceived in Liberty: a Novel of Valley Forge* (1939), *The Last Frontier* (1941), *The Unvanquished* (1942), *Citizen Tom Paine* (1946), and *Freedom Road* (1944) he explores radical themes through incidents and figures in American history. He found them too in ancient history for *My Glorious Brothers* (1948), about Judas Maccabeus, and *Spartacus* (1951), which was privately printed in the USA after he had served three months in jail and been blacklisted for refusing to cooperate with the Committee on Un-American Activities. He describes his break with Communism in *The Naked God: the Writer and the Communist Party* (1957), and includes an account of the American Communist Party in *Being Red: a Memoir* (1990). A San Francisco family saga begins at the time of the 1906 earthquake with *The Immigrants* (1977); subsequent volumes sweep through American and world history, culminating in *The Immigrant's Daughter* (1985). *The Bridge Builder's Story* (1995) begins with a European honeymoon in 1939 and covers the central crises of the times. As E. V. Cunningham he has written 'entertainments', including a range of thrillers each named after its female protagonist, from *Sylvia* (1960) to *Cynthia* (1968). See Andrew MacDonald, *Howard Fast: a Critical Companion*, 1996.

FAULKNER, WILLIAM (1897–1962) American novelist and short-story writer, was born William Cuthbert Falkner in New Albany, Mississippi, the eldest of four sons of a hard-drinking railroad operator (who later diversified his interests), and a great-grandson of Colonel William Clark Falkner (1825–1889), railroad pioneer and novelist. In 1902 the family moved to Oxford, Mississippi, where he lived for most of his life. As avid a reader as he was a horse rider, he was bored by school, which he left in 1915 to work as a book-keeper. In 1918 Estelle Oldham (1896–1972), whom he had been dating for several years, married someone else. He enlisted in the Royal Canadian Air Force and spent five months in Toronto, training as a pilot cadet, an experience which he later romanticized. He was a special student at the University of Mississippi from 1919 to 1921, when he finished a sequence of love poems, 'Vision in Spring', which he bound up and presented to Estelle. In 1924, having resigned as a postmaster at the university under threat of legal proceedings, and been dismissed as a scoutmaster for drinking, he went to New Orleans, having at last had a book of pastoral verse, *The Marble Faun* (1924), accepted for publication. Here he wrote his first novel, *Soldiers' Pay* (1926), a study of postwar disillusionment, which ANDERSON recommended to his publisher. On the advance he travelled in Europe, from which he returned to Oxford and wrote *Mosquitoes* (1927), a satirical novel based on the New Orleans artistic set. *Sartoris* (1929), cut and edited by a friend from a rejected novel, 'Flags in the Dust', established the Southern territory of Yoknapatawpha County and the Sartoris family, based on his own, which were to recur in many novels and stories. In 1929 he married Estelle, now divorced and with two children (born 1919 and 1923): on their honeymoon she tried to commit suicide by walking into the sea. They had two daughters, Alabama (born in 1931), who lived for only nine days, and Jill (*b.* 1933).

The Sound and the Fury (1929) is an analysis of a tragic family situation from four different points of view, using stream-of-consciousness techniques. *As I Lay Dying* (1930), with its unusual milieu, the journey of a poor Southern white family to town with the mother's body, its narrative form of 59 monologues by 15 characters, and its blend of the comic, grotesque, and poignant, was a critical *tour de force*. The story, put out by himself in the introduction to a separate edition of *Sanctuary* (1931), that to gain a popular following at last, 'I invented the most horrific tale I could imagine and wrote it in about three weeks', has been shown to be false. It certainly has horrific elements, and its judicious mixture of sex (including the rape of a college student with a corn cob), violence, corruption, perjury, and rough justice, made its popular appeal inevitable, but it was conceived and written over several months in 1929, and subsequently revised. *Light in August* (1932) is a searching analysis of Southern society and its racial bigotry.

In 1932 Faulkner made the first of several turbulent visits to Hollywood (the last was in 1951), where he was the principal screenwriter of HEMINGWAY's *To Have and Have Not* (1945) and CHANDLER's *The Big Sleep* (1946). In *Absalom, Absalom!* (1936), for some his most difficult book because of its elusive meanings, for others his most brilliant, elements of the history underlying his fictional county are introduced by four narrators, each offering a different interpretation of the facts. *The Hamlet* (1940) features the Snopes family, counterpoint to that of Sartoris; their rapacities and other interventions into the life of the community are further observed in *The Town* (1957) and *The Mansion* (1960). His overtly anti-racist novel of the modern South, *Intruder in the Dust* (1948), came out just before his nomination for the Nobel Prize for Literature, for which he failed by three votes to gain the necessary unanimity. The award was confirmed in 1950, and with his reputation further enhanced by the publication of *Collected Stories* (1950), he went to Stockholm to accept it, with a speech which because of his nervousness (on this occasion he was sober) and thick Southern accent was largely unintelligible, but which in print made memorable reading. He had been working since 1943 on *A Fable* (1954), which won both the National Book Award and the Pulitzer Prize, and for which he departed from his usual environment to re-enact the Crucifixion and Resurrection of Jesus Christ through the persona of the Unknown Soldier of World War I. The last decade of his life was one of continuing honours, a succession of affairs, and self-demolition by drinking and being thrown off his horse. Three weeks after one such fall he was taken to hospital, where he died that night of a heart attack. See Joseph L. Blotner, *Faulkner*, condensed and rev. edn 1984 of *Faulkner: a Biography*, 2 vols 1974; Frederick R. Karl, *William Faulkner: American Writer*, 1989 (critical biography); Richard Gray, *The Life of William Faulkner: a Critical Biography*, new edn 1996; Joel Williamson, *William Faulkner and Southern History*, 1993 (critical biography); David Dowling, *William Faulkner*, 1989 (critical study); Olga W. Vickery, *The Novels of William Faulkner: a Critical Interpretation*, rev. edn 1993.

FEINSTEIN, ELAINE (*b.* 1930), née Coolin, British poet, novelist, and translator, was born in Bootle, Lancashire, of Jewish origin from Odessa, and was educated at the Wyggeston Girls' School, Leicester, and Newnham College, Cambridge. She married an immunologist, and after working for Cambridge University Press from 1960 to 1962, was Lecturer in English, Bishop's Stortford College 1963–66, and Assistant Lecturer in English, Essex University 1967–70. Her initial poetic inspiration came from the west, the Black Mountain poet OLSON, with whom she corrresponded, as well as from EMILY DICKINSON and other American writers, and then from the east, in the form of TSVETAEVA, whose selected poems she translated (1971; rev. edns 1981 and 1993) and whose biography she has written (1987). Her own poetry, from *In a Green Eye* (1966) to *City Music* (1990), celebrates and reflects upon emotions and the comparative freedoms of different styles of life in a variety of settings, metropolitan, East Anglian, European—see also *Selected Poems* (1994). Her novels (and short stories), initally an extension of her poetry, have enabled her to broaden and at the same time intensify her view of a range of family relationships. Her first, *The Circle* (1970), is a study of marriage. *The Survivors* (1982) and *The Border* (1984) have Jewish themes which in traditional fashion span generations and geographical locations. *Loving Brecht* (1992) follows, through the persona of a fictitious lover, the experiences of the real women in the life of BRECHT, against the traumatic background of the events of the time. *Dreamers* (1994) imbues the Jewish situation in mid-19th-century Vienna with the trappings of a romance. *Lawrence and the Women: a Life of D. H. Lawrence* (1992) is a biographical study from the angle of the women who knew him.

FERBER, EDNA (1887–1968) American novelist, was born in Kalamazoo, Michigan, of Jewish parents, and was brought up in Appleton, Wisconsin, where she went to Ryan High School. She gave up the idea of the stage when her father, a storekeeper, went blind. She became a reporter on the *Appleton Daily Crescent*, and then the Milwaukee *Journal* and Chicago *Tribune*, which she left in 1910 to write fiction full time. She published a story in *Everybody's Magazine* in 1910. After she had thrown away her first novel, *Dawn O'Hara: the Girl Who Laughed* (1911), her mother rescued it and sent it to a publisher. *Roast Beef Medium: the Business Adventures of Emma McChesney* (1913), and two sequels, were unusual for their time as cheerful revelations of an emancipated divorcée, and Ferber's journalistic instinct and ability to create romance enabled her to find big stories and present them in a popular way. Such were *So Big* (1924), the struggles of a woman farmer, which won the Pulitzer Prize, *Cimarron* (1930), about the Oklahoma oil boom, and *Giant* (1952), an exposé of the Texan nouveau riche culture. *Show Boat* (1926) became, in the hands of Jerome Kern (1885–1945) and Oscar Hammerstein (1895–1960), the first musical seriously to tackle adult themes. *Fanny Herself* (1917) is a semi-autobiographical study of a Jewish family in a Midwest town; a subject she treated autobiographically in *A Peculiar Treasure* (1939), to which *A Kind of Magic* (1963) is the sequel. With George S. Kaufman (1889–1961) she wrote several stage comedies, of which *Dinner at Eight* (1932) was especially successful.

FERGUSON, (Sir) SAMUEL (1810–86) Irish poet and antiquary, was born in Belfast and educated at the Academical Institution, Belfast, and Trinity College, Dublin, after which he studied law, being called to the Irish Bar in 1838 and appointed Queen's Counsel in 1859. In 1867 he became Ireland's first Deputy-Keeper of Public Records, and was knighted for his services in 1878. He contributed to the *Dublin University Magazine* on its inception in 1833, and before that had work accepted by *Blackwood's Edinburgh Magazine*. He disliked nationalistic notions and argued instead for a better understanding by the Anglo-Irish of their Catholic countrymen; to which end he set about translating and recasting in effective verse versions of Gaelic legends and sagas, which began to appear in print in 1834. His most substantial works in this field are *Lays of the Western Gael, and Other Poems* (1865) and *Congal: a Poem in Five Books* (1872), but he was also an original poet in his own right (see especially 'The Fairy Thorn', 'The Fair Hills of Ireland', 'Lament for Thomas Davis'), to whose influence YEATS testified in an article in the *Dublin University Review* in 1886. Ferguson was elected President of the Royal Irish Academy in 1882. See *Poems*, ed. Padraic Colum, 1963; Peter Denman, *Samuel Ferguson: the Literary Achievement*, 1990.

FERGUSSON, ROBERT (1750–74) Scottish poet, was born in Edinburgh of parents from Aberdeenshire. He was educated at the High School of Edinburgh and then, on a bursary provided by a Rev. David Fergusson of Strathmartine for 'two poor male children' of his own surname, at Dundee Grammar School and St Andrews University, where he began to read for the Church. He abandoned his studies in 1768 after his father's death, having already, at the age of 14, demonstrated his precocious talent with a witty elegy on the death of the Professor of Mathematics, written in Scots in the 'standard habbie' stanza form popularized by RAMSAY. To support his mother and himself, he took a job as a copier of legal documents, and out of office hours mixed with theatrical people—his first published works were three songs in English for 'Favourite Scottish Airs' incongruously added to a performance in 1769 of an opera by Metastasio (1698–1782) with music by Thomas Arne (1710–78). During 1771 he regularly contributed to the *Weekly Magazine or Edinburgh Amusement*, founded in 1768 by Walter Ruddiman (1719–81), occasional poems, mock-heroics, and pastorals, all in English, which were amusing enough as Augustan imitations, and hugely popular. His true métier surfaced on 2 January 1772, with the appearance of 'The Daft Days', written in Scots and celebrating the Christmas and New Year holidays. There followed over the next two years some thirty poems in a literary form of Scots for which he laced the language spoken in Edinburgh with terms and usages from Aberdeenshire. These included satires on city pretentious and low life and on local and national political issues; acutely observed nature poems ('On Seeing a Butterfly in the Street', 'Ode to the Gowdspink'); a rural evocation ('The Farmer's Ingle'); and various topical and occasional verses ranging from his tribute to St Andrews University for its gastronomic hospitality to JOHNSON in 1773, to 'To My Auld Breeks', and to the unfinished 'Auld Reekie', a colourful panegyric of Edinburgh in which one can practically smell the streets of the teeming city.

In 1773 Ruddiman published *Poems by R. Fergusson*, but later that year the poet lapsed into religious mania, gave up his job, destroyed his unpublished manuscripts, and became a recluse. In July 1774 he was well enough to visit friends and to share in an election celebration, but shortly afterwards he caught his foot in a stair-rod at home and crashed downstairs on to his head. When he recovered consciousness he was raving so violently that his mother prevailed on two friends to take him in a sedan chair to the Edinburgh lunatic asylum, where he died on 16 October. He was only just 24, but he had confirmed the use of Scots as a vital and vigorous medium of poetry, in which he was followed by BURNS. See David Daiches, *Robert Fergusson*, 1982 (critical study); also RAMSAY.

FERLINGHETTI,   LAWRENCE (MENDES-MONSANTO) (*b.* 1919) American poet and publisher, was born in Yonkers, New York, and spent his infancy in France. He was educated at Mount Hermon School, Greenfield, Massachusetts, and the University of North Carolina, where he graduated in journalism. After serving as a lieutenant commander in the US Naval Reserve in World War II, he went on to Columbia University, New York, and the Sorbonne, Paris, where he received his doctorate in 1949. He taught French in San Francisco, and then in 1952 co-founded City Lights Books, the first all-paperback store in the country, of which he became owner in 1955. It was the first venue and the prime focus of the San Francisco Renaissance, and as publisher brought out GINSBERG's *Howl*—reissued in *Howl and Other Poems* (1996)—, and subsequently works by authors including BOWLES, BURROUGHS, LEVERTOV, KEROUAC, FRANK O'HARA, and OLSON. He edited *City Lights Journal* (4 vols 1963–78) and (with Nancy Peters) *City Lights Review* (1987–). As poet as well as impresario, Ferlinghetti was an instigator of the Beat movement, and has published many volumes of mainly experimental verse since *Pictures of the Gone World* (1955)—see also *Endless Life: the Selected Poems* (1981) and *These Are My Rivers: New and Selected Poems 1955–1993* (1994). *Her* (1960) is a novel set in Paris, 'a surreal semi-autobiographical blackbook record of a semi-mad period of my life'. He had a one-man exhibition of his paintings in San Francisco in 1985. See Neeli Cherkovsky, *Ferlinghetti: a Biography*, 1979.

FERRIER, SUSAN (1782–1854) Scottish novelist, was born in Edinburgh, the youngest of ten children of James Ferrier (1744–1829), Writer to the Signet and legal adviser to the 5th Duke of Argyll (1723–1806), through whose influence he became a clerk of session and thus a colleague of WALTER SCOTT. In 1804, after the death of her mother and the marriage of her sister, she took over the running of her father's house. In about 1810 she began, initially in collaboration with Charlotte Clavering, the 22-year-old niece of the Duke of Argyll, a novel of contemporary manners, published anonymously as *Marriage* (1818). Its didacticism, which she strengthened in a later edition of 1841, is quite submerged in the wit, shrewd observation, and social comment. Scott, in his rather precipitate announcement at the end of *A Legend of Montrose* (1819) of his withdrawal from the Scottish novel, nominates as a successor 'the author of the very lively work entitled *Marriage*'. In *The Inheritance* (1824) and *Destiny* (1831), for which Scott negotiated on her behalf a payment of £1700 for the publishing rights, the characterization and humour are more crudely done. Scott records inviting her to dinner in 1830 to charm an awkward American guest. Her eyesight was now failing, and after a final visit to London that year to consult an oculist, she lived in a darkened room, though she visited Scott at

Abbotsford shortly before his death and was much comfort to him with her tact and conversation. Only in 1850 did she allow her authorship to be acknowledged, which has been attributed to her reluctance to be associated with a new form of writing which had an appeal to a broader public than had hitherto read fiction. See Mary Cullinan, *Susan Ferrier*, 1984 (biographical/critical study).

FIELD, BARRON (1786–1846) British editor and poetaster, was the second son of the apothecary to Christ's Hospital, where he may have been educated. While studying law at the Inner Temple, he supported himself by writing reviews and drama criticism and was a member of the circle of COLERIDGE and LAMB. He was called to the Bar in 1814, but, finding work hard to get, accepted a post as a judge of the Supreme Court of New South Wales, where he arrived in 1817. During his seven-year stint he wrote, and had printed by the government printer for private circulation to his friends, *First Fruits of Australian Poetry* (1819), the first volume of verse to be produced in Australia. It consisted of 'Botany Bay Flowers' and 'The Kangaroo', of which Lamb, entering into the spirit of the publication, wrote in the *Examiner*: 'We can conceive it to have been written by Andrew Marvell, supposing him to have been banished to Botany Bay.' Field edited and had published in London *Memoirs of the First Thirty-Two Years of the Life of James Hardy Vaux* (1819), the first full-length autobiography written in Australia. Vaux (1782–after 1841) was three times transported for theft and forgery, and the volume incorporated his 'Vocabulary of the Flash Language', the first dictionary to be compiled in Australia. On his return to England, Field edited *Geographical Memoirs on New South Wales* (1825). His last official post was that of Chief Justice in Gibraltar.

FIELDING, HENRY (1707–54) British novelist, dramatist, and journalist, was born at Sharpham Park, Somerset, the eldest son of an army officer, who became a lieutenant general in 1739. He was educated at Eton, which he had barely left when he fell violently in love with an orphan heiress, whose guardian was so frightened of her suitor that he had her sent away. Fielding now threw his considerable and athletic bulk into the pleasures of London, to pay for which he started to write plays, the first being a comedy of manners, *Love in Several Masques* (1728). After a period abroad, studying law at Leyden, he resumed a dramatic career, completing in all over thirty plays. Of these, *Tom Thumb* (1730), subsequently reworked and presented as *The Tragedy of Tragedies* (1731), and *Pasquin* (1736), both burlesques of stage conventions, playwrights, and politicians of the time, are notable for their wit. He married in 1734 and in

1736 took a lease on the Haymarket Theatre, only to be forced out of business by the censorship and theatre Licensing Act of 1737, to the framing of which his own plays and productions had contributed—see Robert D. Hume, *Henry Fielding and the London Theatre 1728–1737* (1988). He was admitted to the Bar, and practised on the Western Circuit. The success of SAMUEL RICHARDSON's *Pamela* (1740), which he felt exhibited dubious morality, nettled him into producing a burlesque novel, *An Apology for the Life of Mrs Shamela Andrews* (1741). He followed this, in a less boisterous and more comic vein, with *The History of the Adventures of Joseph Andrews, and of His Friend Mr Abraham Adams, Written in Imitation of the Manner of Cervantes* (1742), which as it develops ceases to be a parody and becomes, beneath the picaresque plot, an attack on affectation and hypocrisy in general. The writer of burlesque surfaces again in *The Life of Mr Jonathan Wild the Great* (1743), a skilfully presented novel, based on the exploits of a criminal who was hanged in 1725, in which normal standards are upturned: greatness is deliberately confused with goodness, and kindness with weakness.

After his wife's death, probably in 1743, Fielding returned to political journalism, which he had practised briefly before. He edited the pro-government *The True Patriot* during the Rebellion of 1745, and *The Jacobite's Journal* from 1747 to 1748—see *The Jacobite's Journal and Related Writings* (1974) and *The True Patriot and Related Writings* (1987), both ed. W. B. Coley. He married his late wife's maid in 1747 (their first child was christened three months later), and from 1749 to 1753 served energetically and with distinction as a magistrate for Westminster and Middlesex—his legal and social pamphlets of this period are in *An Enquiry into the Causes of the Late Increase of Robbers, and Related Writings*, ed. Malvin R. Zirker (1987). In *The History of Tom Jones, a Foundling* (1749) he succeeded in putting together and sustaining through one mock-heroic masterpiece all the aims he had previously expressed about structure and narrative, morals, and artistic standards. *Amelia* (1752), Fielding's own favourite, is by contrast a novel of harsh domestic incident and social comment, modelled on classical epic lines. Its lack of spark has been regarded by some critics as a reflection of the author's ill-health—he suffered badly from gout. In 1754, with his wife and daughter, he sailed for the warmer weather of Portugal, as he describes with good humour and realism in *The Journey of a Voyage to Lisbon* (1755). It was his last book, and his last journey, for he died in Lisbon two months after their arrival.

In the preface to *Joseph Andrews*, Fielding describes his novel as a 'comic epic poem in prose'. In Book IX. i. of *Tom Jones* he sets out the qualifications which are 'in a pretty high degree necessary to this order of historians' (i.e. novelists). They are 1) 'genius', which he defines as 'invention and judgment'; 2) a 'good sense of learning'; 3) 'conversation' (i.e. being fully conversant) with 'the characters of men' of 'all ranks and degrees'; 4) 'Nor will all the qualities I have hitherto given my historian avail him, unless he have what is generally meant by a good heart, and he capable of feeling.' While in some ways his brand of morality, whereby goodness of heart and generosity outweigh the natural proclivities of youth, may be no more admirable than that of Richardson, subsequent generations of readers have responded enthusiastically to the ingenuity of the three-fold plot of *Tom Jones*, its satire as well as its mock-heroic banter, the attention to descriptive detail, the clever drawing and contrasting of characters, and the gusto of the writing. See Martin C. Battestin, *Henry Fielding: a Life*, new edn 1993; Donald Thomas, *Henry Fielding*, 1988 (biography); Jennifer Uglow, *Henry Fielding*, 1995 (critical introduction).

FIELDING, SARAH (1710–68) British novelist, younger sister of FIELDING, was born in East Stour, Dorset. Family conflicts followed her mother's death, when she was seven, and her father's remarriage to a Catholic widow; at one point he attempted to kidnap all six children from their grandmother's home. She was for a time at a boarding school in Salisbury. After her grandmother's death in 1733 she and her three unmarried sisters shared a house in Hammersmith. In May 1744 she published *The Adventures of David Simple*, a moral fable in the form of a picaresque romance, the second edition of which, that autumn, was revised by Henry Fielding, with whom she went to live after his wife's death in November until he remarried in 1747. *The Governess: or, Little Female Academy* (1749), moral stories and fairy tales within a framework of a series of boarding school days, makes her the first writer of fiction to use such a setting. It was printed by SAMUEL RICHARDSON, who became, in spite of his aversion to her brother, a firm friend and a fervent admirer of her work. *The Adventures of David Simple, Volume the Last* (1753) continues her first novel, and contains her most tragic writing, as well as skilful analysis of enigmatic characters. In *The Countess of Dellwyn* (1759) she delved deeper into character contrasts, in this case a wife with a much older husband, while in *The History of Ophelia* (1760) she tartly observed and overturned society customs. She never married, and after Henry's death in 1754 was supported financially by her half-brother, Sir John Fielding (d. 1760), magistrate and social reformer, who had been blinded in an accident when he was 19. She died in Bath, where she was then living. See *The Adventures of David Simple: and Volume the Last*, ed. Malcolm Kelsall, 1987.

FIELDS, ANNIE ADAMS see JEWETT.

FIELDS, JAMES T. see JEWETT.

FIGES, EVA (b. 1932), née Unger, British novelist and critic, was born in Berlin and escaped with her family to Britain in 1939—see her autobiographical *Little Eden: a Child at War* (1978). She was educated at Kingsbury Grammar School and Queen Mary College, London University, after which she held editorial posts in publishing until 1967. She married in 1954, and was divorced nine years later. Her first novel, *Equinox* (1966), is about the reshaping of life after a broken marriage. *Konek Landing* (1969) features the Holocaust, images of which recur in other novels, most of them being modernist in technique and reflecting the characters' inner consciousness. *Waking* (1981) describes the experience of awakening at several points in the life of the female narrator: in *The Seven Ages* (1986), the responses are by women at different points in historical time. In *The Tree of Knowledge* (1990) she uses reminiscences of MILTON's youngest daughter as a basis for addressing some universal issues, including the rights of women and the purpose of education. *The Knot* (1996) is a working demonstration, in fictional form, of linguistic theory and the development of a person's language. The influential *Patriarchal Attitudes: Women in Society* (1970) is an early contemporary feminist study. In *Sex and Subterfuge: Women Writers to 1850* (1982) she examines the way in which women from BURNEY onwards reshaped the English novel. She has also written children's books and translated novels from French and German.

FINCH, ANNE see POPE.

FINDLEY, TIMOTHY (b. 1930) Canadian novelist, dramatist, and actor, was born in Toronto and educated at St Andrews College, Aurora, Jarvis Collegiate, Toronto, and the Royal Conservatory of Music. He appeared at the inaugural season in 1953 of the Stratford Shakespearean Festival, and then studied at the Central School of Speech and Drama in London. He toured with the H. M. Tennent company for three years, and acted in WILDER's *The Matchmaker* in London and the USA, after which he spent a year as a studio writer in Hollywood. He then returned to Canada, where he was a stage, television, and radio actor until 1962, when he became a full-time writer. As an adolescent he had occupied himself during a year in bed with a blood disorder by writing long romantic novels, later accidentally destroyed. Now he embarked on a series of novels which draw on past events to highlight present preoccupations, often through bizarre confrontations and paradoxes. In his first, *The Last of the Crazy People* (1967), these build up during a hot summer in southern Ontario; in *The Wars* (1977), which won the Governor General's Award, they illuminate the perpetual futility of war. The narrator of *Famous Last Words* (1981) is a character in a poem by POUND, who has a role in a novel which explores the relationship between aestheticism and Fascism. He has also published a volume of short stories, *Dinner Along the Amazon* (1984). The play, *Can You See Me Yet?* (1977), set in 1938, is a study of the borderline between despair and insanity. As scriptwriter he was responsible for seven episodes of the television presentation in 1971–72 from DE LA ROCHE's 'Whiteoaks' saga. See Carol Roberts, *Timothy Findley: Stories from a Life*, new edn 1994 (biographical/critical study).

FINLAY, IAN HAMILTON (b. 1925) Scottish poet, was born in Nassau, Bahamas, and was brought up in Scotland, where he left school at 13. He published a book of short stories in 1958, and a slim volume of short, epigrammatical poems and Orkney lyrics, *The Dancers Inherit the Party*, in 1960— reissued with *Glasgow Beasts, an a Burd* (1995). In 1961 he and his wife established the Wild Hawthorn Press, which has published most of his subsequent printed work in a variety of media: books, booklets, cards, prints, and ceramic tiles. In 1963 he explained his conversion to a more concrete form of expression as beginning 'with the extraordinary (since wholly unexpected) sense that the syntax I had been using, *the movement* of language in me, at a physical level, was no longer there—so it had to be replaced with something else, with a syntax and movement that would be true of the new feeling (which existed in only the vaguest way, since I had, then, no form for it . . .)'. His first book in his new mode was *Rapel* (1963); the first poem in the revolutionary style of sandblasting on to glass, 'Wave Rock', was created in 1966. The garden of his home at Stonypath, near Dunsyre, Lanarkshire, to which he moved in 1967, is both a philosophical exposition of his craft and a display of his work in the context of landscape with water, in which even images of war find expression. The associations with which he aims to invest his language are aural, as well as visual and tangible.

FINLAYSON, RODERICK (1904–92) New Zealand short-story writer and novelist, was born in Auckland and educated at Seddon Memorial Technical College and Auckland University School of Architecture. His apprenticeship as an architectural draughtsman was cut short by the slump in 1928. As a somewhat rebellious youth he had 'turned away from the Pakeha and turned to the

Maori', by whom in the Bay of Plenty he had been 'welcomed into a Maori home, accepted as one of the family, and soon admitted to and even consulted in their family discussions'. The discovery in a library of *Cavalleria Rusticana*, stories about the Sicilian peasantry by VERGA (translated by D. H. LAWRENCE) gave him the model and the inspiration to write of the Maori, in which he was encouraged by the poet and essayist D'Arcy Cresswell (1896–1960). In due course the innate dubiousness of 'bluff New Zealand editors' was dispelled, and with the collections *Brown Man's Burden* (1938) and *Sweet Beulah Land* (1942) he was confirmed as the first writer to invest Maoris with their true identity. During the 1950s he was a writer for the Department of Education School Publications Branch, and he also worked as a print-room assistant for the Auckland City Council. Of his two novels, *Tidal Creek* (1948) is a series of linked, humorous sketches, and *The Schooner Came to Atia* (1952) a melodramatic missionary tale. *Brown Man's Burden and Later Stories*, ed. Bill Pearson (1973) demonstrated that he had not lost touch with the changing needs of the Maori community, and the three novellas in *Other Lovers* (1976) that he had a wider awareness of traditions and social issues.

FIRBANK, (ARTHUR ANNESLEY) RONALD (1886–1926) British novelist, was born in London, the son of a Member of Parliament and grandson of a self-made railway tycoon. Nervous, shy, and suffering already from the throat condition that ultimately killed him, he went to school for the first time at 14, to Uppingham, where he lasted two terms. He had private tuition, and spent a summer in Tours and one in Madrid, before going to Cambridge, having already privately published two stories, *Odette d'Antrevernes and A Study in Temperament* (1905), and written others—see *The Early Firbank*, ed. Steven Moore (1991). He was at Trinity Hall for only five terms, sat no examination, and was received into the Catholic faith. Though on his father's death in 1910 the family fortune was found to have evaporated, he continued to travel and to haunt the meeting places of the London literary set. In 1914 he announced that he was now to be called Ronald, not Arthur, and went virtually into retreat in Oxford. He persuaded a publisher to let him pay for the production of his first novel, *Vainglory* (1915). *Inclinations* (1916), *Caprice* (1917), and *Valmouth* (1919), proceeding mainly by means of allusive dialogue, are his most distinctive, witty, and least bizarre books, of which he said in self-parody, 'His work calls to mind a frieze with figures of varying heights all trotting the same way.' *Prancing Nigger* (1924), published in the USA as *Sorrow in Sunlight*, was the last to appear before his death in Rome. So little was known about him locally that he was buried in the

Protestant cemetery (in the company of KEATS and the ashes of P. B. SHELLEY), from which his body was later transferred to a Catholic burial place. See Brigid Brophy, *Prancing Novelist*, 1973 (biography); Mervyn Horder (ed.), *Ronald Firbank: Memoirs and Critiques*, 1977.

FITCH, CLARKE see SINCLAIR, UPTON.

FITZGERALD, EDWARD (1808–83) British poet and translator, was born near Woodbridge, Suffolk, and educated at King Edward VI's Grammar School, Bury St Edmunds, and Trinity College, Cambridge. With a brief interval for a disastrous marriage in 1856 to the daughter of his late friend, the Quaker poet Bernard Barton (1784–1849), he lived quietly with or near his parents until their deaths, and then in various parts of East Anglia, where he could indulge in his outdoor pursuit of sailing. From his self-imposed seclusion he cultivated literary friendships by means of a voluminous, elegant, and witty correspondence—see *Letters*, ed. J. M. Cohen, 1960. His first literary work was a free translation of six dramas of CALDÉRON, published in 1853. In 1857 he was sent a manuscript of epigrams by OMAR KHAYYÁM. The verse form of rhyming quatrains and the poet's philosophy appealed to FitzGerald enough to attempt a poetic translation, first published anonymously in 1859 at his own expense as *The Rubáiyát of Omar Khayyám*. He issued an enlarged edition in 1868, which was reviewed in the *North American Review* in 1869, and in Britain in *Fraser's Magazine* in 1870, but it was not until 1872 that even his friends knew the identity of the translator. Further editions, with variations, followed. His aim was to reproduce the spirit and form of the work, rather than the precise meaning—the famous 'Book of Verses underneath the Bough' is in the original Persian a leg of mutton, but that would have offended his readers' poetic sensibilities. The result, in whatever edition it is read, is a finely polished, rhythmical expression of Victorian hedonism, whose nostalgic melancholy appealed, and still appeals, to generations whose existence is haunted by perplexity. See Robert Bernard Martin, *With Friends Possessed: a Life of Edward FitzGerald*, 1985.

FITZGERALD, F(RANCIS) SCOTT (KEY) (1896–1940) American novelist and short-story writer, was born in St Paul, Minnesota, the only survivor of four children of upper-middle-class parents who married in their thirties. He was educated at St Paul Academy, Newman School, New Jersey (a Catholic boarding school), and Princeton, from which he withdrew in 1917 and joined the army as a provisional 2nd lieutenant. In Montgomery, Alabama, near where he was stationed, he met and fell for Zelda Sayre

(1900–48), a flighty Southern belle. She broke off their engagement after he had been discharged from the army at the end of hostilities, his job with a New York advertising agency had come to nothing, and his novel about college life had been rejected. He 'crept home to St Paul', and rewrote it. It was accepted (as were nine short stories by magazines), and a week after its publication as *This Side of Paradise* (1920) Zelda married him in New York—they had a daughter, Frances (Scottie) (1921–88). Fitzgerald consolidated his reputation as the representative of the younger generation with two books of short stories, *Flappers and Philosophers* (1920), in which was 'Bernice Bobs Her Hair', and *Tales of the Jazz Age* (1922), which included 'The Diamond as Big as the Ritz' among some earlier, less good pieces. His second novel, *The Beautiful and Damned* (1922), which he conceived as the account of how a 25-year-old 'and his beautiful young wife are wrecked on the shoals of dissipation' was only too prophetic. He and his even more erratic wife managed by wild living to go through his earnings at a rate that even two years of comparatively economic living in Europe could not assuage. Yet he was maturing as a writer, and in *The Great Gatsby* (1925) he produced a structured, stylish novel about the corrupting influence of his age which stands as a memorial to it. There followed a barren period, after a summer which he described as '1000 parties and no work'.

When in 1930 Zelda had the first of several schizophrenic breakdowns, Fitzgerald concentrated on writing stories for magazines to pay the bills. *Tender is the Night* (1934) is in part a complement to Zelda's autobiographical novel, *Save Me the Waltz* (1932). Written, and several times rewritten, under various titles, over the years which followed *The Great Gatsby*, it charts the decline of a psychiatrist who marries his desirable patient. In 1937, with Zelda almost a permanent resident in Highland Hospital, Asheville, North Carolina, and Fitzgerald suffering from cirrhosis, tuberculosis, and continued alcoholism, he went to Hollywood for the third time to try and earn a living by writing for the screen. There he met Sheilah Graham (1905–88), an English-born gossip-columnist, whose life with him she recounted in *Beloved Infidel* (1958), written with Gerold Frank—there is a less fantasized account of the affair by her son, Robert Westbrook, *Intimate Lies: F. Scott Fitzgerald and Sheilah Graham* (1995). When Fitzgerald died of a heart attack at 44, he left an unfinished melodramatic Hollywood romance, *The Last Tycoon* (1941), based on the career of the creative movie mogul, Irving Thalberg (1898–1936), and prepared for publication by EDMUND WILSON; a different version, ed. Matthew J. Bruccoli as *The Love of the Last Tycoon: a Western*, was published in 1995. Wilson also edited *The Crack-Up* (1945), a collection of essays and other autobiographical items. Zelda was one of nine patients who died in a fire at Highfield in 1948—her story is in Nancy Milford, *Zelda Fitzgerald: a Biography* (1970), and her works in *The Collected Writings*, ed. Matthew J. Bruccoli (1992). See *The Short Stories of F. Scott Fitzgerald*, ed. Matthew J. Bruccoli, new edn 1995; *F. Scott Fitzgerald on Authorship*, ed. Matthew J. Bruccoli and Judith S. Baughman, 1996; Matthew J. Bruccoli, *Some Sort of Epic Grandeur: the Life of F. Scott Fitzgerald*, new edn 1993; Jeffrey Meyers, *Scott Fitzgerald: a Biography*, new edn 1995; John B. Chambers, *The Novels of F. Scott Fitzgerald*, 1989 (critical study); Andrew Hook, *F. Scott Fitzgerald*, 1992 (critical study).

FITZGERALD, PENELOPE (*b.* 1916), née Knox, British novelist and biographer, was born in Lincoln (of which her maternal grandfather was Bishop), the only daughter of E. V. Knox (1881–1971), writer and Editor of *Punch*, whose joint biography (with his three brothers) she wrote (1977). She was educated at Wycombe Abbey School, Buckinghamshire, and Somerville College, Oxford, and married Desmond Fitzgerald (*d.* 1976) in 1941. Each of her novels, of which the first was *The Golden Child* (1977), a comic murder mystery with a spy element, has a distinctive setting in which the characters glow and situations develop naturally. *The Bookshop* (1978), run by an intelligent middle-aged widow, is in a small Suffolk town. The families in *Offshore* (1979), which won the Booker prize for fiction, inhabit one of those fascinating conglomerates of houseboats on the Thames, as did her own family at one time (the boat sank). *Human Voices* (1980) recalls, with much humour, her own experiences in the BBC during World War II. In *At Freddie's* (1982) the children at a run-down London drama school almost steal the show from the monstrous proprietor. *Innocence* (1986) is set in Italy, *The Beginning of Spring* (1988) in Moscow before the Revolution of 1917, and *The Gate of Angels* (1990) in a Cambridge college in Edwardian times. *The Blue Flower* (1995) centres on the tragic engagement of HARDENBERG to 12-year-old Sophie von Kuhn. Her other biographies are of the painter Edward Byrne-Jones (1975) and of MEW and her circle (1984).

FITZGERALD, ROBERT D(AVID) (1902–87) Australian poet, was born in Hunters Hill, New South Wales, and educated at Sydney Grammar School. In 1921 he gave up his science course at Sydney University to train as a surveyor. *To Meet the Sun* (1929) incorporated *The Greater Apollo: Seven Metaphysical Songs*, which had been privately printed in 1927. After spending the years 1931–36 surveying tribal boundaries for the Native Lands Commission in Fiji, he became a municipal surveyor, and then worked for

the Department of the Interior from 1939 until his retirement. *Moonlight Acre* (1938), in which were the two longer philosophical poems, 'The Hidden Bole' and 'Essay on Memory', established him (with SLESSOR) as the most significant Australian poet of the 1930s. *Heemskerck Shoals* (1949) and *Between Two Tides* (1952) recall incidents in the history respectively of Fiji and Tonga. Other notable poems are 'The Face of the Waters' (1944), and two from history, 'Fifth Day' (1953) and 'The Wind at Your Door' (1958). His critical prose is collected in *Of Places and Poetry* (1976). He was made OBE in 1951 and AM in 1982. See *Forty Years' Poems*, 1965; *Product: Later Verses*, 1977; A. Grove Day, *Robert D. Fitzgerald*, 1973 (critical study).

FITZMAURICE, GEORGE (1878–1963) Irish dramatist, was born in Co. Kerry, the tenth of 12 children of a Church of Ireland minister and his Catholic wife. He became a clerk in the civil service in Dublin, which he was for the rest of his working life, apart from two years' British army service in World War I. His sentimental comedy of shattered illusions, *The Country Dressmaker*, was produced at the Abbey Theatre in 1907, and was revived several times. Of the other plays published in *Five Plays* (1914), *The Pie-Dish* (1908) and *The Magic Glasses* (1913), two one-act dramas in which the fantasy verges on the grotesque, were performed at the Abbey, while *The Dandy Dolls*, which has an even more bizarre quality about its theme and language, and *The Moonlighter*, a tragedy of the Land Wars, were rejected. After his peasant comedy, *'Twixt the Giltinans and the Carmodys*, had been performed in 1923, but to critical notices, Fitzmaurice became a literary recluse, only occasionally allowing one of his plays to be performed or printed, though he continued to write them. The extent and quality of his activity could only be appreciated after his death, with the posthumous publication of his complete oeuvre. See *The Plays of George Fitzmaurice, Vol. 1 Dramatic Fantasies*, introduction by Austin Clarke, 1967, *Vol. 2 Folk Plays* and *Vol. 3 Realistic Plays*, introductions by Howard K. Slaughter, 1970; Carol W. Gelderman, *George Fitzmaurice*, 1979 (critical study).

FLAUBERT, GUSTAVE (1821–80) French novelist, was born in Rouen, the son of a prosperous doctor, and was educated there as a weekly boarder at Collège Royal, from which he was expelled in his final year for leading a revolt against a class punishment. He passed his baccalaureate from home and then spent the years 1841–45 unenthusiastically studying law in Paris. After suffering the first of a series of epileptoid attacks in 1844, he established the outward pattern of his career: to spend the winter at the family home in Rouen and the summer at their holiday chalet in Croisset, reading, contemplating, writing, and smoking. There were trips to Paris, where in 1846 he began an affair with the poet Louise Colet (1810–76) which lasted until 1854—see Francine du Plessix Gray, *Rage and Fire: a Life of Louise Colet—Pioneer Feminist, Literary Star, Flaubert's Muse* (1994). In 1855 he became attracted to his niece's English governess, 26-year-old Juliet Herbert, whom he was still meeting for amorous purposes in England or France over twenty years later. He worked on his first novel, *Madame Bovary*, for five years, and was engaged in cutting it shortly before sending it to *La Revue de Paris*, in which it was serialized in 1856. Its author, publisher, and printer were prosecuted for an 'outrage to public and religious morals and to morality', and were acquitted only after Flaubert's counsel had argued for four hours. Published, with a dedication to his lawyer, in volume form in 1857 (tr. Eleanor Marx-Aveling, 1891; tr. Gerard Hopkins, 1949; tr. Francis Steegmuller, 1957, reissued 1993; tr. Germain Bree, 1990; tr. Geoffrey Wall, 1993), this painful, realistic tragedy of middle-class provincial life and morals was a *succès de scandale* which became recognized as a landmark in European fiction. He did a field trip to north Africa for *Salammbô* (1862; tr. M. French Sheldon, 1886; tr. A. J. Krailsheimer, 1977), a rather overwrought historical romance of the revolt of the Roman mercenaries after the defeat of Carthage, which was enthusiastically reviewed by SAND. A warm literary friendship ensued—see *Flaubert–Sand: the Correspondence*, ed. Alphonse Jacob, tr. Francis Steegmuller and Barbara Bray (1993). *L'Education Sentimentale* (1869; as *A Sentimental Education* tr. D. F. Hannigan, 1898; tr. Douglas Parmée, 1989) is his ultimate expression of the pessimism which invests his work. The strange philosophical allegory, *La Tentation de Sainte Antoine* (1874; as *The Temptation of St Antony* tr. Hannigan, 1895; tr. Kitty Mrosovsky, 1983) had first been conceived in 1848 and was reworked several times. *Trois Contes* (1877; tr. George Burnham Ives as *Stories*, 1903; tr. A. J. Krailsheimer as *Three Tales*, 1991), new pieces written in 1875–76, illustrates his expertise as a short-story writer.

FLECKER, JAMES ELROY (1884–1915) British poet, was born in Lewisham, London, and educated at Dean Close School, Cheltenham (of which his father was Headmaster), Uppingham School, and Trinity College, Oxford, where a contemporary remembered him as an immature youth, with a penchant for conversation and a facility for verse. In 1908 he decided to enter the Consular Service, and took a course in oriental languages at Caius College, Cambridge. He was taken ill with tuberculosis during his first assignment in Constantinople and, having served in various places in the East, gave

up his career in 1913. He spent the last eighteen months of his life in Switzerland on his doctor's advice. His first book of poems, *The Bridge of Fire*, was published in 1907, and was followed by three more, including *The Golden Journey to Samarkand* (1913). Initially he tended towards the classical and romantic, and practised his craft by translating classical and European models. Latterly he was attracted to the French literary movement, the Parnassians, in whose work he saw a reaction against the 'perfervid sentimentality and extravagance of some French Romantics', and whose aim was to create a statuesque and objective beauty. His best-known work is *Hassan*, published posthumously in 1922, an oriental play in verse in which the spareness of the approach serves to heighten the lushness of the setting and the drama of the situation. It was first produced in 1923, with incidental music by Frederick Delius (1862–1934). See *Poems: a New Selection*, ed. Stephen Parry, 1980.

FLEMING, IAN (1908–64) British novelist, was born in London, a younger brother of the traveller and writer Peter Fleming (1907–71), their father being killed in the war in 1917. He was educated at Eton and, at his mother's wish, at the Royal Military Academy, Sandhurst, from which he withdrew after a year and studied languages at the universities of Munich and Geneva. He was Reuter's Moscow Correspondent from 1929 to 1933, during which he covered the trial of some Britons for spying and sabotage. He worked in the city until World War II, which he spent as personal assistant to the Director of Naval Intelligence. After the war he was for a time Foreign Manager of the Kemsley (later Thomson) newspaper group. He had built a house in Jamaica in 1946, where after his marriage in 1952 he used to spend the winter months writing the next instalment of the exploits of his secret agent hero, James Bond, alias '007', a man with several traits in common with his creator. *Casino Royale* (1953) was a first novel of an unusual nature and of unusual promise. Such was the response to the judicious blend of sex, violence, intrigue, and healthy adventure, and to the meticulously-sketched background of sophisticated high living, that, Sherlock Holmes-like, Bond had to be resuscitated after being ingeniously kicked to death at the end of *From Russia, with Love* (1957). In subsequent books, while the enormity increases of the crimes Bond is called upon to frustrate, the author's essential hold on reality is maintained by some fine golf, card-playing, and skiing sequences. Fleming was also a knowledgeable and enthusiastic book collector, and was publisher of the *Book Collector* from 1949 until his death. See *A James Bond Quartet: Casino Royale; Live and Let Die; Moonraker; From Russia, with Love*, 1992; *A James Bond Quintet*, 1993; John Pearson, *The Life of Ian Fleming*, new edn 1989; Andrew Lycett, *Ian Fleming*, new edn 1996 (biography); Kingsley Amis, *The James Bond Dossier*, 1965.

FLEMING, MARJORY (15 Jan. 1803—19 Dec. 1811) Scottish author and the youngest subject in the *Dictionary of National Biography*, was born in Kirkcaldy, Fife. Her father was an accountant and her mother was of a professional, cultured Edinburgh family among whose acquaintances was WALTER SCOTT. A visit from her mother's niece, Isabella Keith (*c*.1790–1837), who later married a brother of JOHN WILSON, led to Marjory spending a great deal of time from the age of five staying with her aunt and being taught by Isabella, for whose scrutiny and correction she wrote in 1810 and 1811 three journals, comprising some nine thousand words of prose and 560 lines of verse. These, with eight letters and a poem written four days before her death at home from complications after an attack of measles, comprise her literary canon. Her undoubted precocity and the charming eccentricity of her spelling should not be allowed to obscure her genuine powers of observation and expression and her cheerfully critical judgments and philosophical comments on people, literature, history, religion, and life in general. TWAIN wrote of her in an article in *Harper's Bazaar* (1909): 'She was made out of thunder-storms and sunshine, and not even her little perfunctory pieties and shop-made holinesses could squelch her spirits or put out her fires for long.' See *The Complete Marjory Fleming, her Journals, Letters, and Verses*, ed. Frank Sidgwick, 1934.

FLETCHER, ANDREW, OF SAL-TOUN (1653–1716) Scottish political philosopher, was the son of Sir Robert Fletcher of Saltoun and Innerpeffer (*d*. 1665), who entrusted the boy's education to Gilbert Burnet (1643–1715), later Bishop of Salisbury, to whom he had presented the Episcopalian living of Saltoun. Fletcher finished his education abroad. In the Scottish Parliament in 1681, he opposed and then proposed amendments to the Test Act, and then caused sufficient embarrassment to have to retire to the Continent. He returned as joint commander of the cavalry of the Duke of Monmouth (1649–85) in the rebellion against the Crown. He was fortuitously dismissed for a military misdemeanour just before the crucial defeat at Sedgemoor, and fled to the Continent, where he was put in prison but extricated by a mysterious stranger. In his absence he was sentenced to death and to forfeiture of his possessions. He sailed for England with the new King, William, in 1688, and returned to Scotland, being restored to his estates in 1690. Initially he favoured union of the Scottish and English parliaments as a means towards economic prosperity, in the interests of

which he wrote *A Discourse Concerning Militias and Standing Armies* (1697) and *Two Discourses Concerning the Affairs of Scotland* (1698). He was elected to Parliament again in 1703; *Speeches by a Member of Parliament which Began at Edinburgh the 6th of May, 1703* (1703) reflects his concern at the way things were turning out. *An Account of a Conversation Concerning the Right Regulation of Governments For the Common Good of Mankind* (1704), in the form of a Platonic exposition, argues not for union as such, but for a kind of devolution, with the continuance of a separate Scottish parliament. After the Act of Union in 1707 he was imprisoned on suspicion of being a Jacobite. On his release, this courageous, hot-tempered nationalist became a farmer, and revolutionized the processing of barley in his district. See *Selected Political Writings and Speeches*, ed. David Daiches, 1979.

FLETCHER, JOHN (1579–1625) English poet and dramatist, was born in Rye, Sussex, the younger son of the future Dean of Peterborough who insensitively delayed the execution of Mary, Queen of Scots, with his prepared sermon. He was educated at Benet College, Cambridge. His association with BEAUMONT began in about 1606, and he is credited with having a hand in over fifty plays, including SHAKESPEARE's *Henry VIII* and *The Two Noble Kinsmen*. The earliest play known to be by Fletcher alone is *The Faithfull Shepheardesse* (*c*.1609), a tragicomedy, which he defines as a play of familiar people in situations which could result in death but do not do so. This particular play is a complex exposition of pastoral love both spiritual and physical, with a dash of the supernatural. Other tragicomedies include *The Humorous Lieutenant* (*c*.1619), in which an aphrodisiac taken by the wrong victim causes much farce, and *The Island Princess* (*c*.1621), a more romantic drama. Sheer comedy is best represented by *The Wild Goose Chase* (*c*.1621), whose infighting between the sexes and witty dialogue look forward to Restoration comedy. He also wrote two tragedies of Imperial Rome, *Bonduca* (*c*.1612) and *Valentinian* (*c*.1614). Fletcher became chief playwright of the King's Men. Among his songs which have passed into literary heritage are 'Melancholy' ('Hence all you vain delights . . .') and 'Hear, ye Ladies'. He died of the plague, having stayed in London to have a suit made up before going into the country. See Clifford Leech, *The John Fletcher Plays*, 1962.

FLORIO, JOHN see BOCCACCIO; MONTAIGNE.

FONTANE, THEODOR (1819–98) German novelist and poet, was born in Neuruppin, the eldest child of a pharmacist with a weakness for gambling, and was brought up in Swinemunde, where he was educated mainly by his father. After four years at Klo-densche Gewerbeschule, a technical college in Berlin, he trained as a pharmacist, and practised in Leipzig, Dresden, and (after a year's military service) Berlin. In 1850 he gave up dispensing medicines for writing verse, of which he published a book. He was on his way to join the forces of Schleswig-Holstein in their revolt against Denmark when he received the offer of a position in the literary bureau of the Prussian Ministry of the Interior. He married on the strength of it, and though the bureau was soon made redundant, he managed to scrape a living from part-time journalism. In 1855 he went to England as a journalist and press agent for the Prussian Government. He returned in 1859, and published *Jenseit des Tweed* (1859; tr. Brian Battershaw as *Across the Tweed*, 1965), a relaxed account of two weeks in Scotland as a tourist, during which he intensified his interest in the tradition which had led him to Germanize Scottish ballad themes in 'Archibald Douglas' (1853) and 'Lied des James Monmouth' (1854). In 1870 he gave up his position as editor of the London column of the *Kreuzzeitung* and became Theatre Critic of the *Vossische Zeitung*. At this time he was known primarily as a historian and balladist—an enlarged edition of *Balladen* (1860) was published in 1875. His first novel, *Vor dem Sturm* (1878; tr. R. J. Hollingdale as *Before the Storm*, 1985), explores the mood in Prussia during the winter of 1812–13, before the War of Liberation against Napoleon. Subsequently he became a significant exponent of the novel of class hypocrisy—*Irrungen, Wirrungen* (1888; tr. Sandra Morris as *A Suitable Match*, 1968)—and of adultery—*Effi Briest* (1895; tr. Douglas Parmée, 1967; tr. Helen Chambers and Hugh Rorrison, 1995): see also *Two Novellas: The Woman Taken in Adultery; The Poggenpuhl Family*, tr. Gabriele Annan (1979). His last novel, *Der Stechlin* (1899; tr. William L. Zwiebel as *The Stechlin*, 1995), its action confined to one wedding and a funeral and its narrative largely to humorous dialogue, presents an analysis of current cultural and political themes.

FORD, FORD MADOX (1873–1939) British novelist, essayist, poet, and critic, was born Ford Hermann Hueffer in Merton, Surrey, changing his name in 1919. He was the son of the German-born music critic Francis Hueffer (1845–89) and a grandson of the artist Ford Madox Brown (1821–93). His mother's sister married D. G. ROSSETTI's younger brother William. He was educated at University College School. Early publications were *The Brown Owl: a Fairy Story* (1892)—with a feminist princess, animal guardian, wicked chancellor, and adult asides—and studies of Ford Madox Brown (1896) and Rossetti (1902). In 1894 he eloped with the 17-year-old Elsie Martindale (d. 1949), who in 1910

successfully sued him for restitution of conjugal rights; she subsequently obtained damages from a newspaper for describing the novelist Violet Hunt (1866–1942), with whom he had a stormy affair, as 'Mrs Ford Madox Hueffer'. With CONRAD, he wrote the novels *The Inheritors* (1901) and *Romance* (1903). In *The Fifth Queen* (1906), *Privy Seal* (1907), and *The Fifth Queen Crowned* (1908), about Henry VIII's fifth wife, Katharine Howard, the main characters are the historical protagonists in the conflicts of the times. *The Good Soldier: a Tale of Passion* (1915) is a novel of complex relationships.

In spite of his age, Ford served as an officer in France during World War I, and was severely wounded and gassed. The four novels called 'Tietjen's Saga' after their principal character—*Some Do Not . . .* (1924), *No More Parades* (1925), *A Man Could Stand Up . . .* (1926), and *Last Post* (1928), which he wrote as an afterthought and then regretted—span the war years. Impressive and ahead of their time in their portrayal of the miseries of the conflict, they were later published together as *Parade's End* (1950). After 1923 Ford divided his time between France and the USA, where he was appointed Lecturer in Comparative Literature at Olivet College, Michigan, in 1937. He was an early advocate of impressionism in fiction and poetry, and an inspirational editor. He edited *The English Review* from 1908 to 1910, and founded the *transatlantic review* in 1924. His critical works include *Portraits from Life* (1937; 1938 as *Mightier Than the Sword*), and studies of HENRY JAMES (1913) and CONRAD (1924). See *The Bodley Head Ford Madox Ford*, Vols 1–4 (introduction by Graham Greene) 1962–63, Vol. 5 (ed. Michael Killigrew) 1971; Alan Judd, *Ford Madox Ford*, new edn 1993 (biography); Max Saunders, *Ford Madox Ford: a Dual Life—Vol. 1, The World Before the War, Vol. 2, The After-War World*, 1996.

FORD, JOHN (1586–?c.1655) English dramatist, was born in Devon of a landowning family. He may have been to Oxford; he certainly studied law at the Middle Temple from 1602. A few poems and pamphlets are attributed to him between 1606 and 1620, after which he probably collaborated with DEKKER and others on a number of plays, including *The Witch of Edmonton* (performed 1621) and *The Faire Maide of the Inne* (1626). The first known play by him alone is *The Lover's Melancholy* (published 1629), which draws on ROBERT BURTON for terminology and symptoms. Burton is also the source of the reactions of jealousy against his wife displayed by Bassanes at the discovery of his sterility in *The Broken Heart* (1633), a tragedy of frustrated sexual passions. In *Love's Sacrifice* (1633) Ford asks himself what might happen not if a husband suspects his wife of adultery with a close friend (as in SHAKESPEARE'S

Othello), or if she has actually done so (as in HEYWOOD's *A Woman Killed with Kindness*); but if she has professed love for the friend but refuses to consummate it. *'T is Pitty Shees a Whore* (performed *c.*1624, published 1633) has affinities with *Romeo and Juliet* except that the lovers are brother and sister. While the quiet, pervasive quality of the poetry is widely acknowledged, there is some disagreement about the play itself. T. S. ELIOT in *Elizabethan Dramatists* (1963) is critical of 'the passion of Giovanni and Annabella [which] is not shown as an affinity of temperament due to identity of blood; it hardly rises above the purely carnal infatuation'. To H. J. Oliver in *The Problem of John Ford* (1955) it 'is, I believe, one of the finest tragedies outside Shakespeare'. (PEPYS, who saw it in 1661, calls it 'a simple play, and ill acted, only it was my fortune to sit by a most pretty and most ingenious lady, which pleased me much'.) *The Chronicle Historie of Perkin Warbeck* (published 1634) has earned similarly conflicting judgments, but it was an unusual play for its time, and the motivation is cleverly handled and the characterization convincing. See *'Tis Pity She's a Whore and Other Plays*, ed. Marion Lomax, 1995; Clifford Leech, *John Ford and the Drama of His Time*, 1957.

FORESTER, C(ECIL) S(COTT)

(1899–1966) British novelist, was born Cecil Lewis Troughton Smith in Cairo, the son of a schoolmaster, and took the name of Forester in 1923. He grew up in London's suburbs, where he haunted the public library and started the habit, which he maintained all his life, of reading a book a day. From Alleyn's School he went to the science sixth form of Dulwich College. He followed a brother to Guy's Hospital, but withdrew without qualifying in order to be a writer. The thriller, *Payment Deferred* (1926), was his fifth novel but the first to gain him international recognition. He now established a new formula, with five novels of suspense and high adventure which offer unusual angles on the Peninsular War, the South African War, and World War I: *Death to the French* (1932) and *The Gun* (1933); *Brown on Resolution* (1929); and *The African Queen* (1935) and *The General* (1936). He began writing Hollywood film scripts in 1932, was war correspondent for *The Times* in Spain 1936–37, and was in Czechoslovakia in 1939 when the Nazis invaded. On the outbreak of war he joined the Ministry of Information, and wrote stories and articles about Britain at war for publication in the USA. He sailed in a warship to gain first-hand experience and detail for *The Ship* (1943), but on a similar mission to the Bering Sea with the US Navy he contracted arteriosclerosis, which ultimately crippled him. His indomitable, sensitive, often seasick, but always resourceful seaman at the time of the Napoleonic

Wars, Horatio Hornblower, first appeared in *The Happy Return* (1937). Written out of chronological order, the 12 novels span his career from midshipman to admiral (and peer of the realm). See *Long Before Forty*, 1967 (autobiography); *The Hornblower Companion*, new edn 1991.

FORSTER, E(DWARD) M(ORGAN)

(1879–1970) British novelist, short-story writer, and critic, was born in Dorset Square, London, the only surviving child of an architect, who died of consumption a year later. The boy's creative talents were inspired and his psychological development affected by three women: his mother, who died in 1945; his maternal grandmother; and his father's aunt, Marianne Thornton, who died in 1887, leaving him £8000 in trust and the capital when he was 25, which enabled him to travel and to write. His early childhood in a Hertfordshire country house was happy and idyllic, and here he had an emotional relationship with a member of his own sex, symbolically recalled in his story 'Ansell', written in about 1903. He attended Tonbridge School as a day boy, which was the source of his lifelong antipathy towards the middle-class values he found there. At King's College, Cambridge, he had a moderate academic career, and abandoned religion, but discovered comradeship and freedom of thought and expression. His subsequent Continental travels, partly with his mother, confirmed his attitude to the English middle class but also fostered his first story, 'The Story of a Panic'—see *Collected Short Stories* (1947)—which was inspired by and set in and around Ravello. It was printed in 1904 in the *Independent Review*, founded by some of his Cambridge contemporaries. Of the four novels he then published, *Where Angels Fear to Tread* (1905) and *A Room with a View* (1908) involve differences between the English and Italian temperaments. In *The Longest Journey* (1907), the contrast is between conventional and personal values, and in *Howards End* (1910) between the creative imagination and commercial gain. All these works are distinguished by his manipulation of his characters in their search for harmony and by his quiet, pervasive humour.

In 1913–14 he wrote a homosexual novel, *Maurice*, which was posthumously published in 1971, as were a number of stories written between 1903 and 1958 which were collected into *The Life to Come* (1972). Between visits to India in 1913 and 1921, Forster served with the Red Cross in Egypt in World War I, where he wrote *Alexandria: a History and a Guide* (1922), the stock of which, according to the publishers, was burnt in a fire shortly after publication. They enclosed a check as compensation out of the insurance money. A few weeks later they reported that the books had been found safe, but in view of the insurance situation they had decided to burn them! Out of Forster's eastern experiences came what proved to be his last novel and final fictional statement on universal harmony and diversity, *A Passage to India* (1924); its three parts, Mosque, Caves, Temple, symbolize respectively the Muslim, Western, and Hindu approaches to truth, rationality, and spirituality. His Clark Lectures at Cambridge in 1927 on elements of fiction from DEFOE to D. H. LAWRENCE were published as *Aspects of the Novel*—new edn, ed. Oliver Stallybrass (1976). Collections of his critical essays and reviews are *Abinger Harvest* (1936) and *Two Cheers for Democracy* (1951). In 1946 he was appointed an Honorary Fellow of King's College, where he lived until his death, being made CH in 1953, and awarded the OM in 1969. See P. N. Furbank, *E. M. Forster: a Life*, 2 vols new edn 1994; Nicola Beauman, *Morgan: a Life of E. M. Forster*, new edn 1994; John Colmer, *E. M. Forster: the Personal Voice*, new edn 1983 (critical study).

FOULIS, HUGH see MUNRO, NEIL.

FOURNIER, ALAIN HENRI see ALAIN-FOURNIER.

FOWLER, WILLIAM (1560–1612) Scottish poet, was born in Edinburgh, the son of a burgess of the town, and was probably educated at St Andrews University before going to France, like many Scottish students, to complete his studies. Here open commitment to Protestantism led him into an argument with John Hamilton (*fl.* 1568–1609), Professor of Philosophy at the Royal College of Navarre, and to his being attacked in the street. He returned hastily to Scotland, where he continued the disputation with *An Answer to the Calumnious Letter and Erroneous Propositions of an Apostate named M. Io. Hammiltoun* (1581). A visit to the French Ambassador in London in 1582 was misconstrued by the authorities and he was imprisoned. On his release he continued the visits, but as a spy for Sir Francis Walsingham (*c.*1530–90), secretary of state to Elizabeth I. In 1584 his literary qualifications gained him an entrée to the court of JAMES VI, and he was in 1585 appointed lay parson of Hawick. He was involved in the negotiations in 1589 for James's marriage to Anne of Denmark, and became the Queen's Master of Requests and Deputy Secretary. His *A True Reportarie . . .* of the baptism of Prince Henry in 1594 is of much historical interest. On the death of Elizabeth in 1603 he accompanied the royal couple to London, though his effectiveness as a courtier was undermined by poor health and frequent visits to Scotland to supervise his affairs. He died a rich man, leaving his property, which included the Dean's House, Restalrig, to his eldest son, and his manuscripts to his nephew, DRUMMOND. He was,

with MONTGOMERIE and John Stewart of Baldynneis (*c.*1539–*c.*1606), a prominent Scottish court poet and writer of sonnets, of which his 'Tarantula of Love' comprises 75. He translated PETRARCH's *Triumphs* and MACHIAVELLI's *The Prince*. See *The Works of William Fowler*, ed. Henry W. Meikle, James Craigie, and John Purves, 3 vols 1914–40.

FOWLES, JOHN (*b.* 1926) British novelist, was born in Leigh-on-Sea, Essex, and educated at Bedford School, Edinburgh University, and, with a gap for National Service in the Royal Marines, New College, Oxford, where he read French. He lectured in English at Poitiers University in 1950–51, at Anargyrios College, Greece 1951–52, and then taught in London until 1963 . *The Collector* (1963), in the form of a psychological thriller, was the first and is the most direct of his novels. *The Magus* (1965), long (617 pages), complex, mysterious, and ambiguous, even in its revised version (1977), is a critic's rather than a general reader's cornucopia. The same narrative impulse, in this case deriving from Victorian models, is a feature of *The French Lieutenant's Woman* (1969), which has three endings, and in which the 19th-century characters inhabit both the historical and the subconscious worlds. In *Daniel Martin* (1977), the self-seeking hero is conducted through history and between several geographical settings. With *A Maggot* (1985) the focus of the relationship between the sexes shifts to the female. In *The Aristos: a Self-Portrait in Ideas*, begun at Oxford and published in 1965 (rev. edn 1968)—*aristos* is the Greek word meaning 'best'—Fowles expresses his aim as being 'to preserve the freedom of the individual against all those pressures-to-conform that threaten our century'. MALCOLM BRADBURY has concluded: 'The modern novelist can be both the god of freedom and the tricky impresario, and Fowles, aided by his enigmatic muses, has found extraordinary ways to do both.' His poetry was first published in book form in *Poems* (1973). See Simon Loveday, *The Romances of John Fowles*, new edn 1988.

FRAME, JANET (*b.* 1924) New Zealand novelist, short-story writer, and poet, was born in Dunedin, the third child of an engine driver of Scottish parentage, and inherited from her mother the 'habit of writing poems'. Her prize as dux of her primary school was a year's subscription to the Oamaru Public Library, from which the whole family benefited. She went on to Waitiki Girls' High School, and then to Otago University Teachers' Training College. In 1945, shortly after having had her first story, 'University Entrance', published in the *Listener*, she walked out of her classroom during teaching practice, 'knowing I would never return'. After attempting suicide and spending six weeks in hospital, she was diagnosed as schizophrenic. She was 'declared sane' the following year, but the death of her younger sister while swimming, mirroring exactly the tragedy of her elder sister ten years earlier, was a terrible setback. From then until 1954, when she was finally discharged, she spent most of her time in hospital, being subjected to electrical shock therapy. In between times she worked as a hotel waitress or housemaid, and managed to write *The Lagoon: Stories* (1952). SARGESON befriended her, giving her accommodation and a place to work in the form of an army hut in his garden. In *Owls Do Cry* (New Zealand 1957, UK 1961), her first novel, many of the circumstances of her own upbringing are reflected in the experiences of the Withers family. A grant from the New Zealand Literary Fund enabled her to travel overseas. She stayed in Andorra, Ibiza, and London, where psychiatrists at the Maudsley Hospital pronounced that she had never suffered from schizophrenia and prescribed writing as a cure, backed by outpatient treatment. During the next four years, during most of which she subsisted on National Assistance, she completed her Withers family trilogy with *Faces in the Water* (1961), a nightmare descent into the atmosphere of a mental hospital, and *The Edge of the Alphabet* (1962), in which an unsuccessful quest by an epileptic (such as was her own brother) has a symbolic resolution. She also wrote the disturbing allegory, *Scented Gardens for the Blind* (1963), and 'two volumes of stories from which the *New Yorker* and other magazines that I learned were known as "glossies" chose stories'.

Her father's death precipitated her return to New Zealand after being away for seven years. The award of the Scholarship in Letters for 1964 and the Robert Burns Fellowship at Otago University in 1965 gave her some immediate security. The mirror image in *The Adaptable Man* (1965), her only novel set entirely in England, is an extension of the 'Mirror City' which is her own world and without which she cannot rationally exist in the real world: the impressions which contributed to the novel were garnered during an otherwise unproductive sojourn in an isolated cottage in East Suffolk. In *The Rainbirds* (1968) the protagonist's voyage is into death, after he has been declared dead and come to life in hospital. *Daughter Buffalo* (1972) also explores death, through the obsession with it that Frame had observed in New Zealand and in the USA, where the book was written. Also written in the USA was *Intensive Care* (1970), in which New Zealand becomes a symbolic Vietnam and destruction threatens any living thing, animal or vegetable. C. K. STEAD, reviewing *Living in the Maniototo* (1979), picked out the proposition, 'I feel that language in its widest sense is the hawk suspended above eternity', and suggested that her fiction also leaves the reader with the sense that it is 'a

vast illusory palace erected over the chasm of death'—the image of the hawk has persisted with Frame since its appearance ('A hawk came out of the sky') in her first story, composed when she was three. In *The Carpathians* (1988) the inhabitants of a street in a New Zealand provincial town suffer a collapse of language under the influence of the Gravity Star and of the Memory Flower which 'grows always from the dead'. Her poetry has been published as *The Pocket Mirror* (1967). In three autobiographies, *To the Is-land* (1982), *An Angel at My Table* (1984), and *The Envoy from the Mirror City* (1985), she recounts in a spare and dignified manner aspects of her life up to her return home in 1964, without dwelling on the fears, real and unreal, such as she explores in her fiction—in one volume as *An Autobiography* (1989). She was made CBE in 1983. See *The Janet Frame Reader*, ed. Carole Ferrier, 1995 (feminist collection); Margaret Dalziel, *Janet Frame*, 1982 (critical study).

FRANCE, ANATOLE, pseudonym of Jacques-Anatole-François Thibault (1844–1924) French novelist and critic, was born in Paris, the only child of an antiquarian bookseller who used the pen name France Libraire for bibliographical articles. He was educated at Collège Stanislaus, a Jesuit school, which he hated, and having been given up by his father as useless, heeded his Flemish mother's urging to become a writer. A publisher's reader and for many years, until in 1891 he fell out with his superior, a librarian at the Senate, he published poetry, criticism, short fiction, and a poetic drama in the 1870s, and then a novel, *Le Crime de Sylvestre Bonnard* (1881; tr. Lafcadio Hearn as *The Crime of Sylvestre Bonnard*, 1891), a character study of a gentle bibliophile. He was Literary Editor of *Le Temps* 1888–91. His election in 1896 to the Académie Française confirmed his credentials as an influential literary figure: his support of ZOLA in the case of Alfred Dreyfus in 1898 established him as a political notability. *Les Dieux Ont Soif* (1912; tr. Alfred Allinson as *The Gods Are Athirst*, 1913; tr. Frederick Davies as *The Gods Will Have Blood*, 1979), a graphic portrayal, beginning in 1793, of the conflict between ideals and actions during the French Revolution, is his most satisfying work and most lasting novel. His divorce in 1892 was precipitated by his liaison with the Parisian literary hostess, Mme Arman de Caillavet, after whose death in 1910 he installed in his house, and ultimately married, her maid. A banquet given in his honour in London in 1913 was attended by KIPLING, WELLS, BARRIE, G. B. SHAW, ARNOLD BENNETT, MASEFIELD, and GALSWORTHY. He was awarded the Nobel Prize for Literature in 1921.

FRANCIS, DICK (*b.* 1920) British novelist, was born in Tenby, Pembrokeshire, and educated at Maidenhead County Boys' School,

Berkshire. He served in the Royal Air Force as a flying officer in World War II. He rode as an amateur National Hunt jockey from 1946 to 1948, when he went professional, being champion jockey in 1953–54. He retired after his horse, owned by the Queen Mother, mysteriously sank to the ground thirty yards from the winning post when leading the Grand National by 10 lengths. He was racing correspondent of the *Sunday Express* from 1957 to 1973. With *Dead Cert* (1962) he established a literary milieu (the world of horse racing), a stock hero-type (tough, he needs to be, and only marginally involved romantically during the course of the story), and a formula (a mystery, criminal skulduggery, often murder) on which by *To the Hilt* (1996) he had worked 35 tersely-titled and ingenious variations. The books score because of the compelling nature of the detail, the variety of the settings, and the overriding soundness of their values. *The Sport of Kings: the Autobiography of Dick Francis* (1957) has been, and has had to be, several times updated—a new edition, *Sport of Queens*, was published in 1995. He was made OBE in 1984.

FRANK, ANNE(LIESE MARIE) (1929–45) Dutch diarist, was born in Germany in Frankfurt-am-Main of Jewish parents, who in 1933 emigrated to Amsterdam, where the family became members of the Liberal Jewish congregation and assimilated into the community. In 1941 she and her elder sister were forced to transfer from the Montessori school to the secondary school for Jews only. On 14 June 1942 she began a diary in a manuscript book given to her for her birthday two days before. On 9 July, the Franks, with another family and a dentist, went into hiding in a secret annexe which her father had constructed in the office building in which he worked. On 4 August 1944, three days after the last entry in the diary, the Gestapo raided the building and arrested the occupants; the eight Jews were sent to concentration camps. Seven months later, and a few days after her sister, Anne died of typhoid in Bergen-Belsen, to which they had been transferred from Auschwitz. The diary, in a series of notebooks and loose sheets (the latter containing rewritten versions of the entries, which she hoped to publish 'after the war'), was discovered in the annexe, and preserved. In a form transcribed by her father, Otto Frank (1889–1980), the only one of the eight who survived, it was published in Holland as *Het Achterhuis* (1947; tr. B. M. Mooyart-Doubleday, incorporating additional passages, as *The Diary of a Young Girl*, introduction by Eleanor Roosevelt (in UK by Storm Jameson), 1952; as *The Diary of Anne Frank*, 1954). As well as being a lucid account of the inner experiences of an articulate teenager, of her relations with others, and of her understanding of what was happening to her world and her people, it has become a symbol of Jewish suffering during World War II. By the mid-1980s it had sold 16 million copies world wide; in 1993–94, it was the third most-borrowed non-fiction work in libraries in the UK.

Further insight and background are in *The Diary of Anne Frank, Critical Edition*, ed. David Barnouw and Gerrold van der Stroom (1989)—see also *The Diary of a Young Girl: the Definitive Edition*, ed. Otto H. Frank and Mirjam Presslet, tr. Susan Massotty (1995). Other writings are in *Verhaaltjes en Gebeurtenissen uit het Achterhuis* (1982; tr. Ralph Manheim and Michel Mok as *Anne Frank's Tales from the Secret Annex*, 1983). There is an excellent, objective critical essay by BERRYMAN in his *The Freedom of the Poet* (1976). Lawrence Graver, *An Obsession with Anne Frank: Meyer Levin and the 'Diary'* (1995) is an account of the traumas that attended the dramatization of the book and of the bitter thirty-year campaign by the writer Meyer Levin (1905–81) to achieve what he believed to be his rights in the matter. (An obsession with Frank of a different kind is posited by the fictional narrator of PHILIP ROTH's *The Ghost Writer*.)

FRANK, WALDO see TOOMER.

FRANKLIN, BENJAMIN (1706–90) American philosopher, political critic, scientist, statesman, prose writer, and printer, was born in Boston, the eighth of ten children by his second wife of a Northamptonshire tallow chandler and soap boiler who had immigrated in 1683. 'Put to the Grammar School at Eight Years of Age, my Father intending to devote me as the Tithe of his Sons to the Service of the Church', he was removed (his father having reconsidered the cost) and put into the family business. At 12, he rebelled, and to stop him going to sea he was apprenticed to his half-brother, James Franklin (1697–1735), a local printer. In 1721 James established the *New England Courant*, the fourth American newspaper, and the most outspoken, which soon embroiled itself, albeit on the wrong side, in the controversy over smallpox inoculation. In 1722 Franklin got himself into print by shoving a satirical article, signed 'Silence Dogood', under the printing house door; it became the first of 14 such contributions. The following year, having been publisher of the paper for three months (James being disbarred after serving a month in jail on the order of the Speaker of the Assembly), he broke his indentures and went to Philadelphia. In 1728, after a disastrous time in London, he established his own business, and in 1729 bought the bankrupt *Universal Instructor*, which he renamed the *Pennsylvania Gazette* and spiced with humour and satire, enlivened by his own stylish contributions. *Poor Richard's Almanack* for 1733, a compilation of tags and homespun philosophy, was the first of 25 such annual publications. The final one (1757) was prefaced with 'a connected Discourse', known as *The Way to Wealth*, promoting industry, frugality, and prudence, which was reprinted many times and translated into seven languages before the end of the century.

In 1730 he married Deborah Read Rogers (1708–74); it was a tangled arrangement, for her husband was probably still alive, and the Franklin elder son, William (*c*.1731–1813), was probably not hers. Nevertheless 'she prov'd a good and faithful Helpmate, assisted me much by attending the shop, [and] we throve together'. He founded the Philadelphia Library Company in 1731, and the Union Fire Company in 1736, when he also became Clerk to the Pennsylvania Assembly. The next year he became Postmaster of Philadelphia, which led to his being appointed joint Deputy Postmaster General of North America in 1753 and Postmaster General in 1775. *A Proposal for Promoting Useful Knowledge* (1743) initiated the formation of the American Philosophical Society, of which he was the first secretary. In 1748 he retired from active participation in the printing business (he remained a partner until 1766) and, having already invented the 'Franklin stove', busied himself with electrical experiments. These he described in letters to England to Peter Collinson (1694–1768), a Fellow of the Royal Society, who published them as *Experiments and Observations on Electricity, Made at Philadelphia* (3 parts 1751–54; expanded 4th edn 1769), a landmark in scientific literature. By the middle of 1752 he had effectively invented the lightning conductor. The Royal Society awarded him a medal, and elected him a Fellow in 1756.

Franklin now came into his own as a statesman. In England between 1757 and 1762 he was agent for Pennsylvania in negotiations with the proprietors of the state, Thomas Penn (1702–75) and his younger brother Richard (*d*. 1771), and published *The Interest of Great Britain Considered with Regard to Her Colonies* (1760), arguing for the retention of Canada after the war with France. He was back in England in 1764, where he represented also Georgia, Massachusetts, and New Jersey in discussions on the colonies—see David T. Morgan, *The Devious Dr Franklin, Colonial Agent: Benjamin Franklin's Years in London* (1996). In 1775, having given up hope of a peaceful settlement, he returned home, where his wife, whom he had not seen for ten years, had died only a few months before. He helped prepare the Declaration of Independence, and when the war began was sent by Congress as one of three commissioners in France. He was accompanied by two grandsons (aged seven and 16), and in the comfortable residence in the Paris suburb of Passy which had been assigned to him he installed a press, on which he printed official papers

and, for private circulation, a series of humorous essays which he called '*bagatelles*', including *The Dialogue between Franklin and the Gout*—see *Franklin's Wit and Folly: the Bagatelles*, ed. Richard E. Amacher (1953). Officially appointed Minister Plenipotentiary in 1779, he was a power in the peace negotiations with Britain which concluded with the Treaty of Paris (1783). He was allowed to return home in 1785, having first asked to be relieved of his post in 1781. He finally retired from public life at the age of 82, when he resigned as President of the Supreme Executive Council of Pennsylvania. At his death he was still working on his *Autobiography*, which he had begun in England in 1771 and which, though it breaks off in 1757, is for its style and eternal optimism as much an ornament to American literature as the man himself was to his age. See *The Autobiography of Benjamin Franklin*, ed. Leonard W. Labaree and others, 1964; *Autobiography and Other Writings*, ed. Ormond Seavey, 1993; Ronald W. Clark, *Benjamin Franklin: a Biography*, rev. edn 1989.

FRANKLIN, (STELLA MARIA SARAH) MILES (1879–1954) Australian novelist, was born, a fifth-generation Australian, on the family property of Talbingo, New South Wales, and was brought up on her father's cattle station—see the posthumously published *Childhood at Brindabella* (1963)—and, from 1889, at Bangalore, near Goulburn. At 16 she wrote a novel which was sent to LAWSON. He recommended it to his publisher, Blackwood's of Edinburgh. They published it as *My Brilliant Career* (1901), with a foreword by him, in which he revealed that it was written by 'just a little bush girl'. Ebullient and outspoken, and described by the critic A. G. Stephens (1865–1933) as 'the very first Australian novel. . . . There is not one of the others that might not have been written by a stranger or sojourner', it caused offence locally, where it was taken to be autobiography. An even more emphatically feminist sequel, *My Career Goes Bung*, 'planned as a corrective' and written in 1902, was not published until 1946 because of libel fears. After being a housemaid, while writing for the *Bulletin* as Mary Anne and mixing with the Melbourne literary set, Franklin went to the USA, where she worked for the Women's Trade Union League with the Australian feminist, Alice Henry (1857–1943). She served in the Balkans with the Scottish Women's Hospital Unit in World War I, after which she became political secretary of the National Housing and Town Planning Council in London. Here she wrote *Up the Country* (1928) and two more novels in the sequence of six covering the pioneering days, published as by Brent of Bin Bin, an identity she refused to acknowledge until just before her death. She finally returned to Australia in 1933, and published under her own name *All That Swagger* (1936), a family saga covering the 1830s to 1930s. She left £9800 in her will for an annual award for a novel of Australian life of 'the highest literary quality'. The first winner was PATRICK WHITE (1957). See the complementary biographical studies: Marjorie Barnard, *Miles Franklin*, new edn 1989; Verna Coleman, *Miles Franklin in America*, 1981; and Colin Roderick, *Miles Franklin: Her Brilliant Career*, 1982.

FRASER, G(EORGE) S(UTHER-LAND) (1915–80) Scottish poet and critic, was born in Glasgow and brought up in Aberdeen, where his father was Town Clerk. He was educated at Aberdeen Grammar School and St Andrews University, after which he worked as a journalist on the *Aberdeen Press and Journal*. He was at this time associated with the New Apocalypse (see TREECE), to whose anthology, *The White Horseman* (1941), he contributed an introduction. His *The Fatal Landscape and Other Poems* was published in 1941. He served in the Middle East in World War II, during which he wrote some of his best reflective verse, exemplified by the title poems of *Home Town Elegy* (1944) and *The Traveller Has Regrets and Other Poems* (1948). After the war he married and settled in London, where he wrote reviews and leading articles for *The Times Literary Supplement* and other critical journals, with a break in Japan in 1950–51 as Cultural Adviser in succession to BLUNDEN. He was Lecturer in English at Leicester University 1958–63, and then Reader in Modern English Literature until his death. His critical works include *Lawrence Durrell: a Study* (1968) and the formative *The Modern Writer and His World* (1953; 2nd rev. edn 1970). See *Poems of G. S. Fraser*, ed. Ian Fletcher and John Lucas, 1981; *A Stranger and Afraid: the Autobiography of an Intellectual*, 1983.

FRAYN, MICHAEL (*b.* 1933) British dramatist, novelist, and journalist, was born in Mill Hill, London, and educated at Kingston Grammar School and Emmanuel College, Cambridge, where he had a musical play produced in 1957. He was a columnist on the *Guardian* (1959–62) and the *Observer* (1962–68). His first West End play was *The Two of Us* (1970), four amusing sketches. Subsequent plays include *Alphabetical Order* (1975; in *Alphabetical Order and Donkeys' Years*, 1977), a comic situation piece set in the cuttings' library of a provincial newspaper, which won him the first of four *Evening Standard* drama awards, and *Noises Off* (1981), about theatre life. He has also adapted plays of CHEKHOV, TOLSTOY, and ANOUILH. From his first novel, *The Tin Men* (1965), through to *A Landing on the Sun* (1991) and *Now You Know* (1992), he has found in the world of bureaucracy fantastical, farcical, sometimes poignant, situations to embellish with his particular brand of wit and satire. He married Claire Tomalin (*b.*

1933), biographer of WOLLSTONECRAFT and of DICKENS's mistress Nelly Ternan, in 1993. See *Plays 1*, 1985, *Plays 2*, 1992.

FRAZER, (Sir) J(AMES) G(EORGE) (1854–1941) British anthropologist and classicist, was born in Glasgow and educated at Larchfield Academy, Helensburgh, Glasgow Academy, and Trinity College, Cambridge, where he read classics and was in 1879 elected to a fellowship for life. He was called to the Bar in 1882, but never practised. His activities in the field of classical scholarship resulted in an annotated Sallust (1884) and a monumental edition of Pausanias (1898), while inspiring what was to become the preoccupation of a lifetime. For in attempting to unravel a crux in VIRGIL's *Aeneid* about the succession to the priesthood of Diana at Aricia, he found himself exploring mysteries of religion, magic, superstition, mythology, and primitive customs in all parts of the globe. *The Golden Bough: a Study in Comparative Religion* was published in two volumes in 1890, with a revised version in three volumes in 1900. Frazer was already contemplating and preparing an enlarged edition, which was finally complete in 1915 in 12 volumes. He now began work on the one-volume abridged edition, with the subtitle *A Study in Magic and Religion* (1922), to which he added an 'Aftermath' in 1936. This was by no means all that he contributed to the exegesis of these and other aspects of social anthropology, and while his effect on succeeding anthropologists has been slender, there are many novelists and poets in whose writings his influence can readily be traced, including BELLOW, BUCHAN, CONRAD, T. S. ELIOT, D. H. LAWRENCE, MAILER, MURDOCH, POWELL, SPARK, SYNGE, and YEATS. He was knighted in 1914 and awarded the OM in 1925. His death in Cambridge was followed only a few hours later by that of his wife. See *The Golden Bough*, abridged and ed. Robert Fraser, 1994; Robert Ackerman, *J. G. Frazer: His Life and Work*, new edn 1990; Robert Fraser, *The Making of the Golden Bough: the Origins and Growth of an Argument*, 1990; Robert Fraser (ed.), *Sir James Frazer and the Literary Imagination*, 1990.

FREELING, NICOLAS (*b.* 1927) British novelist, was born in London's Gray's Inn Road, and educated at schools in England and France, and also at Dublin University. Since then he has lived on the Continent, first as a chef in many countries, and latterly as a novelist in Strasbourg: *The Kitchen* (1970) is a quirky memoir of his former existence and *Cook Book* (1971) of his metamorphosis into the latter. His first two detective novels, *Love in Amsterdam* (1962) and *Because of the Cats* (1963), set in Holland, where his wife comes from, were immediately distinctive not just for their setting, but also for the depth of characterization and motives, and for the style, with its swift and often staccato dialogue and wide-ranging literary allusions. Though there was no resurrection for his detective, Van der Valk, who met a violent death after ten novels, his widow Arlette, remarried to an English academic, reappears as a private detective in her own right in *The Widow* (1979). In *Lady Macbeth* (1988) she interacts with Freeling's second major creation, Inspector Henri Castang of the Police Judiciaire in a French provincial city, who first appears in *The Night Lords* (1978). With the advent of Castang, Freeling's novels have become even more refreshingly cosmopolitan, and German, English and Belgian locations and habits have come under his scrutiny. Though he is claimed as a genre novelist, there is no formula about his composition. 'When I started, crime fiction was stuck with the old whodunnit and everyone got bored with that. Then, in the 1960s, the form got more ambitious, the whydunnit came in and I played my part in that. Now I think I'm bored with that, too. So I'm trying to make the crime novel rejoin the mainstream of literature.' *A City Solitary* (1985) is a psychological thriller in which the minds and motivation of all the main characters are explored. *The Seacoast of Bohemia* (1994), his 33rd novel, vastly extends our knowledge of the character, and elliptical thinking, of Castang, and of his wife. *This Is the Castle* (1968), though it contains a violent death, is a study of relationships and of the imagination of Duthiel, a novelist in whom those that look may find some of the characteristics and youthful exploits of his creator. *Crime and Fiction* (1993) is a critical study—see also *Criminal Convictions* (1994), essays.

FREEMAN, MARY E(LEANOR) WILKINS (1852–1930) American novelist and short-story writer, was born Mary Ella Wilkins in Randolph, Massachusetts, the daughter of a carpenter. In 1867 he bought a half-share in a store in Brattleboro, Vermont, where she went to the high school, after which she spent a year at Mount Holyoke Female Seminary. Her father's business failed, he returned to carpentry, and in 1877 they moved into the home of a clergyman, to whom Mrs Wilkins was housekeeper; it was a blow for a family whose Puritan belief was that poverty is a punishment for sin. Left alone in 1883 after the deaths of her parents and sister, she turned to her writing, of which she had had some children's poems and an adult story published. In 1884 she returned to Randolph after *Harper's New Monthly* had accepted 'A Humble Romance', which was to be the title story of her first collection (1887). *A New England Nun, and Other Stories* (1891), like the earlier book 'studies of the descendants of the Massachusetts Bay colonists', is expressive of the Puritan will at a time when women were beginning to assert

themselves against the old pressures—see especially 'The Revolt of "Mother" '. Though she continued to write for thirty years, and the New England novels *Jane Field* (1892) and *Pembroke* (1894) have powerful moments, and *The Shoulders of Atlas* (1908) won the New York *Herald* transatlantic contest, nothing quite matches up to the insight of the early stories. In 1902 she married Dr Charles Freeman of Metuchen, New Jersey, a qualified physician who preferred to run a coal and lumber business. She was legally separated from him in 1922 after his confirmed alcoholism had caused him to be committed to an asylum. He died the next year, having disinherited her. She successfully contested the will. See *Selected Stories of Mary E. Wilkins Freeman*, ed. Marjorie Pryse, new edn 1984; Perry D. Westbrook, *Mary Wilkins Freeman*, 1988 (biographical/critical study); Leah Blatt Glasser, *In a Closet Hidden: the Life and Works of Mary E. Wilkins Freeman*, 1996.

FRENEAU, PHILIP (1752–1832) American poet and journalist, was born in New York of Huguenot ancestry, and was educated at the Latin school at Penelopen and at the College of New Jersey in Princeton, where at his graduation in 1771 BRACKEN-RIDGE recited their joint poem, 'The Rising Glory of America'. In 1775, having taught in Maryland, and published in New York *The American Village* (1772), incorporating 'several other original Pieces in Verse', and some individual poems on topical subjects, he sailed for the island of Santa Cruz. When the mate died at sea, he was invited by the master, who was also his host, to take the man's place, thus initiating his second career. He stayed in the West Indies for three years, and wrote more poetry, including 'The Island Field Hand' (also known as 'To Sir Toby'), expressing horror at slave conditions on a Jamaican sugar plantation. In 1780, on a return trip to the West Indies as a passenger, his ship was attacked and captured by a British frigate and taken to New York. He described his subsequent privations in the four cantos of *The British Prison-Ship* (1781). From 1781 to 1784 he edited in Philadelphia the *Freeman's Journal or North American Intelligencer*, in which he published the anti-British poems which earned him the title of 'Poet of the American Revolution'. Between 1784 and 1790, and again from 1803 to 1807, he was master of ships plying between American ports, and latterly between Charleston and the Azores, which he did for the money. He was founder-Editor of the *National Gazette* 1791–93, whose columns he filled with poems on the Rights of Man, the Age of Reason, and Republicanism for France and America. When the paper folded, he retired to Mount Pleasant, Monmouth, where he founded the *Jersey Chronicle*. Further collections of his verse appeared in 1786, 1788,

1795, and 1815. He died in a blizzard, having determined to walk the two miles home, and 'got lost and mired in a bog'. See *The Poems of Philip Freneau*, ed. Fred Lewis Pattee, 3 vols, new edn 1963.

FREUD, SIGMUND (1856–1939) Austrian psychoanalyst, was born in Freiburg, the eldest of eight children by his second marriage of a Jewish wool merchant. He was educated at the gymnasium in Vienna and at Vienna University, where he qualified as MD in 1881, having felt 'an overpowering need to understand something of the riddles of the world in which we live'. Committed to a career in neuropathology, and needing to establish a home, he took a post at the Vienna General Hospital while being attached to the university as *privat dozent*, which gave him an opening to study for a year in Paris under Jean Martin Charcot (1825–93). He returned in 1886, married (after a four-year engagement), and while working in the Institute for Children's Diseases set up in private practice as a psychopathologist, in which field his first work, with Josef Breuer (1842–1925), was *Studien über Hysterie* [*Studies in Hysteria*] (1895). In *Die Traumdeutung* [*The Interpretation of Dreams*] (1900) and *Drei Abhandlungen zur Sexualtheorie* [*Three Essays on the Theory of Sexuality*] (1905) he elucidated his theories of the infantile libido as a driving force in the development of personality. In 1902 he was appointed to an 'extraordinary' professorship at Vienna University, and though he collected opponents as well as disciples, psychoanalysis became accepted as a branch of science.

In 1938 international pressure secured his extrication from Nazi-controlled Austria to England, where he died of cancer, for which he had had 33 operations over sixteen years, including the excision of his lower jaw. His interests extended to cultural, social, and literary as well as scientific and medical concerns, demonstrated in such works as *The Psychopathology of Everyday Life* (tr. 1914) and *Totem and Taboo* (tr. 1919); from the 1920s he obstinately adhered to his conviction that the works of SHAKESPEARE were written by Edward de Vere (1550–1604), Earl of Oxford. *An Autobiographical Study* was published in Britain in 1935. His theories encouraged critics, and readers, to search beneath the surface of a text for hidden motives and connections, and largely put paid to the one-dimensional biography. They have influenced writers as widely diverse as D. H. LAWRENCE and STRACHEY, whose *Elizabeth and Essex* was written with them in mind and then subjected to critical analysis by Freud. Strachey's younger brother, James Strachey (1886–1967), translated and edited Freud's works. See Peter Gay, *Freud: a Life for our Time*, new edn 1995; Ernest Jones, *The Life and Work of Sigmund Freud*, new edn 1993; Anthony Storr, *Freud*, 1989 (introductory study).

FRIEL, BRIAN (*b.* 1929) Irish dramatist and short-story writer, was born in Omagh, Co. Tyrone, and educated at St Columba's College, Derry, St Patrick's College, Maynooth, and St Joseph's Training College, Belfast. He then taught in schools in Derry until 1960, when he became a full-time writer, having had two radio plays produced by the BBC and several stories published in the *New Yorker*. In 1963, having now had three plays produced, including *The Enemy Within* (published 1975), which is about St Columba's band of exiles, he spent five months in Minneapolis watching Sir Tyrone Guthrie (1900–71) direct. The play which immediately came out of this, *Philadelphia, Here I Come!* (1965), played in Dublin, New York, and London. It explores the very Irish theme of emigration, using two actors to represent the complementary but changeful moods of the principal character. In *The Loves of Cass McGuire* (1967), an old woman returns from her American exile to disillusionment, while in *Lovers* (1968), it is hopes of young love which are shattered. Contemporary violence is the background to *The Freedom of the City* (1974), in which private confusions cannot under such circumstances be maintained with any illusion of hope. In 1980 Friel co-founded and became a working director of the Field Day theatre company, Derry, which performed his *Translations* (1980) and *Communication Cord* (1982) and for which in 1990 HEANEY, also a director, contributed a version of SOPHOCLES's *Philoctetes* as *Cure at Troy*. *Dancing at Lughnasa* (1990), set in the Donegal countryside in 1936, has a static scenario, within which time flickers back and forth, and the varied characters which make up the eccentric family recall or play out aspects of their lives. Friel's short stories—see *Selected Stories* (1979)—also tend to have rural Irish settings, and are humorous and nostalgic. He was appointed to the Irish Senate in 1987. See *Plays, One*, new edn 1996 of *Selected Plays*, 1984; George O'Brien, *Brian Friel*, new edn 1990 (critical study); Richard Pine, *Brian Friel and Ireland's Drama*, 1990; Elmer Andrews, *The Art of Brian Friel: Neither Dreams nor Reality*, 1995; George O'Brien, *Brian Friel: a Reference Guide*, 1995.

FRISCH, MAX (1911–91) Swiss dramatist and novelist, was born in Zurich and became a freelance foreign correspondent in 1933 after studying German literature and philosophy at Zurich University, which he left without a doctorate owing to shortage of money. He subsequently took a diploma in architecture, which he practised in Zurich from 1945 to 1954, having remained in neutral Switzerland during World War II. After writing the *bildungsroman* type of fiction out of his system during the prewar years, he turned in the 1950s to novels such as *Stiller* (1954; tr. Michael Bullock as *I'm Not Stiller*,

1958) and *Homo Faber* (1957; tr. Bullock, 1974), in which identity is explored and man's ability to control his life in the technological age is challenged. He became a full-time writer in 1955; after extensive travels in North and South America, he settled in Rome, returning to Zurich early in the 1980s. His first play, *Nun singen sie wieder* [Now they Are Singing Again] (1946) was also the first significant German drama to try to deal with World War II. *Biedermann und die Brandstifter* (1958; tr. as *The Fire Raisers*, 1961), 'a didactic play without a message' originally written for radio, is a satirical, at times farcical, attack on middle-class complacency, which was appreciated by British audiences for its affinity to the Theatre of the Absurd. More disturbing is *Andorra* (1961; tr. 1964), in which a wrongful assumption that a man is Jewish is the basis of an exploration of image-making. See *Three Plays: Fire Raisers, Andorra, Triptych*, tr. Michael Bullock and Geoffrey Skelton, 1992; *Novels, Plays, Essays*, ed. Rolf Kieser, 1989.

FROISSART, JEAN (*c*.1337–*c*.1410) French chronicler and poet, was born in Valenciennes and in 1361 went to England, where he attached himself to the court of the Queen, Philippa of Hainault (the territory in which he was born), as a household clerk and poet. He also travelled to Scotland and into Wales. In 1368 he was a member of the sparkling retinue which accompanied Lionel (1338–68), Duke of Clarence, the King's third son, to Milan for his short-lived second marriage. On the way back he learned of the Queen's death, and decided to stay where he was, in the Netherlands. For Robert of Namur, the first of three noble lords who were his patrons, he began his 'Chronicles', which effectively cover the preliminaries to and the first sixty years of the Hundred Years' War between England and France, which technically began in 1337. In 1373, about the time he finished the first of three versions of Book I, the earlier part of which is based on the chronicle of Jean Le Bel (*c*.1290–*c*.1370), he took holy orders and became parish priest of Estinnes-au-Mont, Brabant. In 1383 he was appointed a canon of Chimay, near Liège, from where he did a field trip to Foix in the Pyrenees in 1388. In 1395 he returned to England, where he presented a specially copied, illuminated, and bound collected edition of his 'writings on love and morality' to Richard II, with whose downfall and death five years later he concluded the fourth and final book of his great work. Vividly told, with touches of detail that add verisimilitude, it is a contemporary's record of the tempo as well as the temper of the times, and a rich source of social history. An English translation by Sir John Bourchier (1467–1533), Lord Berners, was published 1523–25. CHAUCER draws on four of Froissart's poems in the space of 25 lines of the Prologue to *The Legend*

of Good Women. See *Chronicles*, ed. and tr. Geoffrey Brereton, new edn 1978.

FROST, ROBERT (1874–1963) American poet, was born in San Francisco and taken by his mother to Lawrence, Massachusetts, on the death of his wastrel father at 34. He was educated at Lawrence High School, but dropped out of Dartmouth College in his first term (he subsequently spent the years 1897–99 at Harvard as a special student). 'My Butterfly', littered with poetic diction, was commercially published in a magazine in 1892. He reprinted it privately with four other poems in *Twilight*, in an edition of two copies, one of which he presented to Elinor White, his fiancée, with whom he had been at school. When she did not seem suitably impressed, he tore up the other copy and considered suicide. They were married in 1895, and in 1900, after the death of their first son, they moved into a farm near Derry, New Hampshire. There, he farmed unsuccessfully while more children were born (and died); earned some money by teaching part time at Pinkerton Academy; and wrote poetry, most of it inspired by the countryside, the seasons, and the daily doings and recurrent tragedies of rural life. In 1912, having sold the farm and taught for a year at New Hampshire State Normal School, Plymouth, he packed up their belongings and his manuscripts, and sailed with his wife and four children to England, where he established himself in Beaconsfield, Buckinghamshire, and, now 38, looked for a publisher. The first one he tried accepted *A Boy's Will* (1913) in three days. POUND sent an appreciative review to *Poetry: a Magazine of Verse*, Chicago, and after the publication of *North of Boston* (1914), Frost was able to return to the USA with something of a reputation. He bought a farm in New Hampshire, with which region and Vermont, where he moved in 1920, he would now always be identified. *Selected Poems* (1923) illustrates his own judgment of his work at that time and his method of grouping it. *New Hampshire* (1923), which won the first of his four Pulitzer prizes, contained the extensive 'New Hampshire' ('I met a lady from the South who said . . .'), as well as 'The Axe-Helve', 'Fire and Ice', and 'Stopping by Woods on a Snowy Evening'.

Academia now welcomed him as a teacher: Amherst College and University of Michigan between 1917 and 1938; Harvard (1939–42); Dartmouth College (1943–49); and then Amherst again. Yale awarded him his first honorary doctorate in 1924: 33 years and many doctorates later, he went to England at the age of 83, to receive similar distinctions from both Oxford and Cambridge. As a national institution he was honoured (a year late, as it transpired) by a resolution of the US Senate celebrating his 75th birthday; in 1961, at the inauguration of President Kennedy (1917–

63), he recited from memory 'The Gift Outright', being unable, because of the weather, to see to read the poem he had composed for the occasion. *Complete Poems of Robert Frost* (1949) proved a misnomer, as *In the Clearing* (1962) followed. Frost's rhythmical lyrics and narrative poems, and his dialogues and dramatic monologues in which ordinary speech is so uncannily reflected, are distinguished by unusual powers of observation and by moral and psychological insights. The underlying darkness is a reflection of his own troubled emotional state, and of personal tragedy. His younger sister was committed to a mental institution, where she died in 1929. The death of his daughter Marjorie from puerperal fever in 1934 was followed suddenly by that of his wife in 1938, and by the suicide of his only surviving son, Carol, in 1940. See *Collected Poems, Prose, and Plays*, ed. Richard Poirier and Mark Richardson, 1995; *The Poetry of Robert Frost*, ed. Edward C. Lathem, new edn 1990; *Selected Poems*, ed. Ian Hamilton, 1973; Lawrence Thompson and Richard Winnick, *Robert Frost*, 3 vols 1966–76, abridged edn as *Robert Frost: a Biography*, ed. Edward C. Lathem, new edn 1990; Jeffrey Meyers, *Robert Frost: a Biography*, 1996; Jeffrey S. Cramer, *Robert Frost among His Poems: a Literary Companion to the Poet's Own Biographical Contexts and Associations*, 1996; Richard Poirier, *Robert Frost: the Work of Knowing*, rev. edn 1990 (critical study); Philip L. Gerber, *Robert Frost*, rev. edn 1982 (critical study).

FRY, CHRISTOPHER (*b.* 1907) British dramatist, was born in Bristol, had a Christian upbringing, and was educated at Bedford Modern School. He worked as a schoolmaster, and as an actor and producer in local 'rep', before writing *The Boy with a Cart* (1939), about St Cuthman of Sussex, as an experiment for a local cast of amateurs. *The Firstborn*, written in 1945 but not produced in London until 1952 in a revised version, has the plagues of Egypt as its theme and Moses as its chief character; *Thor with Angels* (1949) was written to be performed in the Chapter House of Canterbury Cathedral, and *A Sleep of Prisoners* (1951) is set in a church. In the meantime he had shown in *A Phoenix Too Frequent* (1946), a one-act play loosely based on an incident in PETRONIUS, that his verse form could be adapted to broad comedy, and in *Venus Observed* (1950) to the modern romance of manners. *The Lady's Not for Burning* (1949), set in a stylized segment of the Middle Ages, has as its chief characters a world-weary vagabond who wishes to be hanged and a suspected witch who has no desire to be burned. *The Dark is Light Enough: a Winter Comedy* (1954), set in 1848, the year of revolutions in Europe, explores the workings of providence. Fry has also successfully translated and adapted plays by ANOUILH and GIRAUDOUX. See *Selected Plays*, 1985; Glenda Leeming,

Christopher Fry, 1990 (biographical/critical study).

FRYE, NORTHROP (1912–91) Canadian critic, was born in Sherbrooke, Quebec. The son of a hardware salesman, he was taught by his mother to read and play the piano when he was three. He was educated at high schools in Moncton, New Brunswick, and then took a course in business studies, which involved participating in a typing competition in Toronto. He came second, and liked the place so much that he enrolled at Victoria College, Toronto University, where he read English and philosophy. He went on to study theology at Emmanuel College, and was ordained a minister of the United Church in 1936. After preaching in the prairies of Saskatchewan for a short time, he decided to become an academic and writer, in preparation for which he did further studies in English at Merton College, Oxford. He returned to Victoria College as a lecturer in English, becoming Chairman of the English Department in 1952, and Principal of the College in 1959. In 1967 he became Toronto University's first Professor of English, and in 1978 he was appointed Chancellor of Victoria University, Toronto. He contributed not only to the development and wider appreciation of Canadian literature, on which he published *The Bush Garden: Essays on the Canadian Imagination* (1971) and *Divisions on a Ground: Essays on Canadian Culture* (1982), but also to the greater understanding of English literature itself. *Fearful Symmetry: a Study of William Blake* (1947) threw brilliant light on a writer who had up till then been regarded as hardly in the mainstream of English poetry. In *Anatomy of Criticism* (1957) he argued for 'a coordinating principle, a central hypothesis which, like the theory of evolution in biology, will see the phenomena it deals with as parts of a whole'. Other significant works include *A Natural Perspective: the Development of Shakespearean Comedy and Romance* (1965) and *The Great Code* (1982), a study of the Bible in terms of its literary form and as a literary archetype. His collection of lectures, *Northrop Frye on Shakespeare* (1986), won the Governor General's Award—see also *Myth and Metaphor: Selected Essays 1974–1988* (1992) and *The Eternal Act of Creation: Essays 1979–1990* (1993), both ed. Robert C. Denham. He was made Companion, Order of Canada, in 1972. See *The Legacy of Northrop Frye*, ed. Alvin A. Lee and Robert D. Denham, 1994; Joseph Adamson, *Northrop Frye: a Visionary Life*, 1993; A. C. Hamilton, *Northrop Frye: Anatomy of His Criticism*, new edn 1991.

FUENTES, CARLOS (*b.* 1928) Mexican novelist and short-story writer, was born in Mexico City, the son of a career diplomat. He went to school in Washington, D.C., to an English-type prep school in Chile, and to Colegio Frances Morelos, Mexico City, after which he studied at the Catholic University, Washington, and the National University of Mexico, where he read law. He was a member of the Mexican delegation to the International Labor Organization, Geneva (1950–52), and then rebelled against his family background and joined the Communist Party. After posts in press and cultural relations, he was Head of the Department of Cultural Relations, Ministry of Foreign Affairs 1957–59. His first novel, *La Región Más Transparente* (1958; tr. Sam Hileman as *Where the Air Is Clear*, 1960), a study of the death of Mexico City, was written in an experimental style new to Mexican literature. His third, *La Muerte de Artemio Cruz* (1962; tr. Hileman as *The Death of Artemio Cruz*, 1964), employs several narrative techniques to follow in deathbed flashbacks the rise of a peasant at the time of the Mexican Revolution of 1910 to industrial tycoon. *Terra Nostra* (1975; tr. Margaret Sayers Peden, 1977) is a fanciful exploration of Mexican and Spanish history. He was Mexican Ambassador to France from 1974 to 1977, during which time he wrote nothing ('Diplomacy in a sense is the opposite of writing'); immediately afterwards he rented a house outside Paris where he wrote *Una Familia Lejana* (1980; tr. Peden as *Distant Relations*, 1982). *El Naranjo, o los Circulos del Tiempo* (1988; tr. Alfred MacAdam as *The Orange Tree*, 1994) comprises five linked novellas reflecting the quest for a Mexican identity. The real-life protagonist of *Diana o la Cazadora Solitaria* (1995; tr. MacAdam as *Diana: the Goddess Who Hunts Alone*, 1995) is Jean Seberg, the American film actress who committed suicide in Paris in 1979 at the age of 41, and with whom Fuentes had had a brief affair in 1970 in Mexico while she was filming there. Collections of short fiction include *Burnt Water: Stories*, tr. Peden (1980), and *Constancia and Other Stories for Virgins*, tr. Thomas Christianssen (1990) See Raymond Leslie Williams, *The Writings of Carlos Fuentes*, 1996.

FUGARD, ATHOL (*b.* 1932) South African dramatist, was born in Middleburg, Cape Province, of mixed Afrikaner and English parentage ('My mother was an Afrikaner, a peasant soul with an incredible sense of justice'), and was educated at Port Elizabeth Technical College and Cape Town University. His 'traumatic' experience as a clerk in the Native Commissioner's Court in Johannesburg dealing with pass violations directly inspired his first two plays, *No-Good Friday* and *Nongogo*, written for and performed in 1958 by his multiracial theatre group—published in *Dimetos and Two Early Plays* (1977). What he later termed 'The Family Trilogy' powerfully and movingly, and with the use of only two or three actors, explores a series of relationships. In *The Blood Knot* (1963) two half-

brothers play out the realities and fantasies of interracial tension; *Hello and Goodbye* (1966) centres on the desperation of a poor white brother and sister as they await their father's death and a non-existent inheritance; the couple in *Boesman and Lena* (1969) represent coloured man and woman, and parent and parent. Fugard was associated with the establishment in 1963 of an African drama group in Port Elizabeth, the Serpent Players, of which he became a director in 1965; in 1972 he co-founded The Space theatre in Cape Town. In 1967 he began to experiment with improvised drama, an outcome of which was *Sizwe Bansi is Dead* (performed 1972), about the pass laws, *The Island* (1973), set in Robben Island prison, and *Statements after an Arrest under the Immorality Act* (1974 at the Royal Court, London)—published as *Statements: Three Plays* (1974).

Fugard's plays are in the mainstream of modern dramatic technique, and while offering a protest, explore human nature and human identity. One of his best-known works, *Master Harold . . . and the Boys* (1982), comes from a period of disillusionment, of which Fugard says, 'I really began to despair of seeing the end of apartheid in my own life.' The 1990s brought the announcement of its demise, and he responded with *Playland* (1992), a two-hander between a black nightwatchman and a white veteran of the conflict on the Namibian border. Set in a travelling funfair on New Year's Eve 1989, this anguished study of guilt and, ultimately, reconciliation has an underlying and courageous optimism. Of the end of apartheid, he said: 'My writing career has coincided with those 40 years of official apartheid. I was telling stories people didn't want to hear, trying to make people aware of that other world which apartheid had sealed them from. I was the first playwright to put blacks and whites on the stage together in South Africa.' His response as a dramatist was *Valley Song*, a two-hander about the real meaning of changes and the unease caused by sudden freedom, which he directed and in which he played the dual part of the author and an old colored man at its world première in London (1996). His only novel, *Tsotsi* (1980), a stark tale of a Sophia Town thug who finds ultimate but fleeting redemption, was written in 1959–60. See *Selected Plays*, 1987; *The Township Plays*, ed. Dennis Walder, 1993; *Cousins: a Memoir*, 1994 (autobiographical study).

FULLER, (SARAH) MARGARET (1810–50) American critic and journalist, was born in Cambridgeport, Massachusetts, the eldest by five years of nine children of a prominent lawyer, who taught her until at 13 she went for two years to the Misses Prescotts' school in Groton. On his death in 1835 she became the family breadwinner, and taught in Boston and then Providence, while translating from German. In 1839 she moved the family to Boston, where she established her regular winter 'Conversations' for women. Having become friends, and intellectually if not physically in love, with EMERSON, she edited for its first two years (1840–42) the Transcendentalist journal, the *Dial*, in which appeared in 1843 her 'The Great Lawsuit: Man *versus* Men, Woman *versus* Women', a seminal feminist text which was published in an extended form as *Woman in the Nineteenth Century* (1845). *Summer on the Lakes, in 1843* (1844), discursive reflections on a Western trip, so impressed Horace Greeley (1811–72), founder of the New York *Daily-Tribune*, that he appointed her its literary critic, and raised no objection to her going abroad in 1846. She saw CARLYLE in London, MARTINEAU and WORDSWORTH in the Lake District, and SAND and MICKIEWICZ in Paris, before settling in Rome, where she began research for an Italian history. She also met the Marchese d'Ossoli, ten years her junior, by whom she became pregnant. They married secretly in 1848. After the fall of Republican Rome in 1849, they went to Florence with the baby to get a passage to the USA. The ship was wrecked off Fire Island, New Jersey, and all three of them were drowned. E. B. BROWNING, who had befriended them in Florence, wrote to M. R. MITFORD that the 'socialist' book the Marchesa d'Ossoli was writing on Italy would have drawn such fierce criticism that 'it was better for her to go', and went on: 'Was she happy in anything, I wonder? She told me that she never was.' See *The Essential Margaret Fuller*, ed. Jeffrey Steele, 1992; *The Portable Margaret Fuller*, ed. Mary Kelley, 1995; *Woman in the Nineteenth Century and Other Writings*, ed. Donna Dickenson, 1994; Charles Capper, *Margaret Fuller: an American Romantic Life, the Private Years*, new edn 1995 (first of 2 vols); Donna Dickenson, *Margaret Fuller: Writing a Woman's Life*, 1993; Joan von Mehren, *Minerva and the Muse: a Life of Margaret Fuller*, new edn 1996.

FULLER, ROY (1912–91) British poet, novelist, and lawyer, was born in Failsworth, Lancashire, and educated at Blackpool High School, which he left at 16 to become an articled clerk to a local solicitor and support his widowed mother. He qualified as a solicitor in 1934, and in 1936 joined the staff of the Woolwich Equitable Building Society in London, with whom he was (with an interval for war service as a radio mechanic in the Royal Naval Volunteer Reserve) for the rest of his working life, becoming a director in 1969. He was Chairman of the Legal Advisory Panel of the Building Societies Association 1958–69. In contrast to this settled business life, his early poetry, first published in book form in *Poems* (1940), was, like that of other poets of the 1930s, of a political or social nature. Subsequently he demonstrated a preoccupation

with the frailty of natural existence and the imminence of catastrophe, while also reflecting on the creative process, in particular art, in a controlled and careful style—see *New and Collected Poems 1934–1984* (1985). He began writing novels in the 1950s, developing his technique in this alternative form of expression, in which he is particularly concerned with inner struggles and ambiguous relationships. After *The Carnal Island* (1970) he wrote no new novel until *Stares* (1991), set in the claustrophobic community of a private mental home. In his creative persona, Fuller won the Queen's Gold Medal for Poetry in 1970, and was Professor of Poetry at Oxford 1968–73, while still working full time at his London office—volumes of his Oxford lectures were published in 1971 and 1973. His influence as a governor of the BBC from 1972 to 1979 drew on the experience gained in both his professional lives. His only son John Fuller (*b.* 1937), also a poet and novelist, edited his father's *Last Poems* (1993). See *The Strange and the Good: Collected Memoirs*, 1989; *Spanner and Pen*, 1991 (later autobiography); Neil Powell, *Roy Fuller: Writer and Society*, 1995 (critical biography).

FURPHY, JOSEPH (1843–1912) Australian novelist, was born at Yering in the Upper Yarra Valley, the second son of Protestant Irish immigrants who had arrived in 1841. He went to school in Kangaroo Ground and Kyneton, and was gold digger, labourer, tenant of the farm-vineyard belonging to the mother of his 16-year-old French wife, and smallholder, before moving to Hay in the Riverina as a bullock driver. For all the hardships, he wrote in *Such is Life*, 'the Australian attains full consciousness of his own identity . . . in places like this. . . . To me the monotonous variety of this interminable scrub has a charm of its own.' Ruined by the drought of 1883, he went to work in his elder brother's foundry in Shepparton, Victoria, where for relaxation and mental stimulation he wrote a novel. In 1897, with a brief note in which he described its 'bias' as 'offensively Australian', he sent it to the *Bulletin*, to which he had contributed short pieces since 1889 as Warrigal Jack and Tom Collins. *Such is Life: Being Certain Extracts from the Diary of Tom Collins* was finally published by the *Bulletin* itself in 1903 in a much revised and shorter version, and sold only 1100 copies in his lifetime. While outwardly a realistic re-creation of bush life and exploits without romantic trimmings, it is also, in the intriguing relationship between author and mouthpiece, in its philosophy of the pattern of human existence, and in its variety of modes of expression (Furphy was extremely well read), a most significant development in Australian fiction. It might have sunk without trace but for Kate Baker (1861–1953), who first met Furphy when she was a young teacher, and who encouraged him while he was alive and promoted his work thereafter. Her efforts resulted ultimately in the publication of *Rigby's Romance* (1921) and *The Buln-Buln and the Brolga* (1948), which he had fashioned out of abandoned chapters of *Such is Life*. She also edited, and paid for the publication of, *The Poems of Joseph Furphy* (1916), and with MILES FRANKLIN wrote *Joseph Furphy: the Legend of a Man and His Book* (1944). She was made OBE in 1937 for her services to literature. See John Barnes, *The Order of Things: a Life of Joseph Furphy*, 1991.

FUSELI, HENRY see WOLLSTONECRAFT.

G

GADDIS, WILLIAM (*b.* 1922) American novelist, was born in New York City. At Harvard 1941–45, he was President of the *Lampoon*, which published some of his work, but did not take his degree. After being a checker for the *New Yorker* (1946–47), he lived and travelled in South America, North Africa, and Europe for eight years. *The Recognitions* (1955), his massive first novel, a cosmopolitan study of deception and artistic forgery, reflects the postmodernist preoccupation with disentangling strands of truth from a wealth of erudition. Twenty years later came *JR* (1975), written entirely in speech, and suggesting an American life in which wealth and conspiracy, love and betrayal, and power and decadence go hand in hand. In accepting the National Book Award for it, Gaddis made a public plea for the identity and character of a writer, and their views on writing, to be subordinate to the text—he has defined his literary technique as 'authorial absence'. A further decade passed before *Carpenter's Gothic* (1985), in which the spread of a particular piece of disinformation is the point of departure for an exploration of disorder on a global scale. *A Frolic of His Own* (1994; National Book Award)—the title is a legal term—opens with an echo of HOLMES: 'Justice?—You get justice in the next world, in this world you have the law.' About the American legal system in the same way as Gaddis's first novel was about forgery and his second business, it develops, through his distinctive style, into a comic exposé of a demented society. See Steven Moore, *William Gaddis*, 1989 (biographical/critical study).

GALDÓS, BENITO PÉREZ see PÉREZ GALDÓS.

GALLANT, MAVIS (MAVIS DE TRAFFORD YOUNG) (*b.* 1922) Canadian short-story writer and novelist, was born in Montreal, and was brought up bilingual. After her father's early death she went to 17 schools in Canada and the USA, from which she returned in 1941 to work in Montreal. She had a brief marriage to pianist Johnny Gallant. She was a features writer for the *Standard* from 1944 to 1950, then travelled to Spain. After selling stories to the *New Yorker*, she went to live in Paris. A writer al-most exclusively of short fiction, she has since the publication of her first collection, *The Other Paris* (1956), offered within each a series of stories which are also comments on a central theme. She has expressed her ties with her native country in the Introduction to *Home Truths: Selected Canadian Stories* (1981), which won the Governor General's Award: 'I suppose that a Canadian is someone who has a logical reason to think he is one. My logical reason is that I have never been anything else.' Herself an expatriate, she is particularly concerned with cultural frontiers, as in *Overhead in a Balloon: Stories of Paris* (1985) and *In Transit* (1988), while in *The Pegnitz Junction* (1973) the alienation is that of a whole people, the post-World War II Germans, from their past. Her skilfully etched characters are often innocents in an anxious alliance with experience, or people for whom experience has not entirely eradicated earlier uncertainties. Most of the stories in *Across the Bridge* (1994) are set either in Montreal or in Paris and are concerned with survival in the face of changing attitudes and values. *Paris Notebooks: Essays and Reviews* (1988) is a collection of incisive critical essays and social and political commentaries. She was made Officer, Order of Canada, in 1981. See *Collected Stories*, 1996; Janice Kulyk Keefer, *Reading Mavis Gallant*, 1989; Judith Skelton Grant, *Mavis Gallant and Her Works*, 1994.

GALSWORTHY, JOHN (1867–1933) British dramatist, novelist, short-story writer, and poet, was born at Kingston Hill, Surrey, and educated at Harrow and New College, Oxford. On a sea voyage to complement his study of marine law, he met CONRAD, who influenced his ultimate choice of career and became a lifelong friend. After publishing a volume of stories and several novels under the pseudonym of John Sinjohn, Galsworthy achieved a remarkable 'double' in 1906 with his first play, *The Silver Box*, a study of the comparative justice meted out to rich and poor, and with the novel, *The Man of Property*, which by the addition of two sequels, *In Chancery* (1920) and *To Let* (1921), and two linking passages, grew into *The Forsyte Saga* (1922). Only a very good novelist could have sustained the reader's interest in so many characters from a single strand of society and in the process evoke sympathy for the soul-less Soames, but attempts to expand the saga further were not so effective: better fiction is to be found in his shorter stories, especially those about love. (There is a parallel between the predicament of Irene, Soames's unhappy wife, and that of Ada, née Cooper, who became Galsworthy's wife in 1905, after being married to his first cousin.) Galsworthy's preoccupation with the iniquities of the class system is displayed with scrupulous fairness in his plays, notably *Strife* (1909), about industrial relations, and *The Skin Game* (1920), in which landed rich confronts nouveau riche. Galsworthy refused a knighthood in 1918. He was awarded the OM in 1929, and the Nobel Prize for Literature in 1932. See *Five Plays*, 1984; Catherine Dupré, *John Galsworthy: a Biography*, 1976; James Gindin, *John Galsworthy's Life and Art: an Alien's Fortress*, 1987.

GALT, JOHN (1779–1839) Scottish novelist, biographer, and poet, was born in Irvine, Ayrshire, the son of the captain of a West Indies merchant ship, and was educated at the grammar school in Greenock, to which the family had moved. He worked in the Customs House and then as a clerk with a local merchant, while contributing articles and verses to local and Scottish newspapers and journals. In 1804 he went to London, studied law, and got a job which entailed Continental trips to assess export potentials. On one of these he met BYRON, of whom he later wrote a biography (1830). During the ensuing decade his literary bent asserted itself, and an account of his travels (1812) and a biography of Cardinal Wolsey (1812) were followed by a volume of five tragedies with female heroines (1812), and by some early attempts at fiction and other minor works. He also wrote for literary periodicals and latterly acted as a parliamentary lobbyist for commercial concerns. It had been his ambition to write what 'would be for Scotland what the Vicar of Wakefield is for England', but when he offered such a book to WALTER SCOTT's publisher, Archibald Constable (1774–1827), it was turned down. *The Ayrshire Legatees: or, The Pringle Family*, in which a family describes in letters a trip to London, was published in 1821, after being serialized in *Blackwood's Edinburgh Magazine*. Its popularity encouraged William Blackwood (1776–1834) to ask for something similar. *Annals of the Parish: or, The Chronicle of Dalmailing During the Ministry of the Reverend Micah Balwhidder* (1821), the book which Constable had rejected, charts in the form of delightful sketches of rural life the social changes of the preceding half-century, which are re-examined from a small-town angle in *The Provost* (1822). *The Entail: or, The Lairds of Grippy* (1823) is an early saga novel, in which an ob-session with recovering family property affects three generations.

In 1826 Galt went to Canada to supervise the land-settlement operations of the Canada Company, and founded the town of Guelph. Ill-health and personality clashes led to his return in 1829, whereupon he was imprisoned for debt, and had on his eventual release once more to support his family with his pen. To this period belong *The Member* (1832), a forerunner of the English political novel, and *The Radical* (1832), another of his imaginary autobiographies. In 1834, paralysed by several strokes, and with his wife dead and his three sons having emigrated to Canada, he went to live with a sister in Greenock, where he bravely dictated to the last. Galt wrote too rapidly (he often had to) to be consistent, and his direction suffered from the failure of his particular gifts to be fully recognized during his life. Yet he was not only a most effective interpreter of Scottish lowland life and thus a significant contributor to the development of the Scottish novel, but also an instigator of the novel of political, economic, and social reality. Of his sons, Sir Thomas Galt (1815–1901) became a chief justice, and Sir Alexander Tilloch Galt (1817–1893) Finance Minister of Canada. See *Selected Short Stories*, ed. Ian A. Gordon, 1996; *An Autobiography*, ed. Ian A. Gordon, 1985; Ian A. Gordon, *John Galt: the Life of a Writer*, 1972; P. H. Scott, *John Galt*, 1985 (critical study).

GARCÍA LORCA, FEDERICO (1898–1936) Spanish poet and dramatist, was born in Fuentevaqueros, near Granada, the son of a landowner and his second wife, who had been a local teacher. He was educated at the College of the Sacred Heart, Granada, and Granada University, where he failed three courses while also pursuing elsewhere his main interest of music. In 1919 he transferred to Madrid University, where he established himself for the next ten years in the Residencia de Estudiantes, and managed in 1923 to complete the requirements for a law degree. He published a volume of early lyrics in 1921, and came under the influence of, and influenced, the young Surrealist painter Salvador Dali (1904–89), who contributed a subversive article to Lorca's arts journal, *El Gallo*, which lasted for two issues in 1928. For *Primer Romancero Gitano* (1928; tr. Rolfe Humphries as *The Gypsy Ballads*, 1953) he invented a gypsy mythology as a medium through which to express his own concerns and frustrations.

A trip to New York in 1929 opened his eyes to what was to him an alien world, reflected in the posthumous collection, *Poeta en Nueva York* (1940; tr. Ben Belitt as *Poet in New York*, 1955). *La Zapatera Prodigiosa* (produced 1930; tr. James Graham-Luján and Richard L. O'Connell as *The Shoemaker's Prodigious Wife* in *Five Plays*, 1964), a farce in which he overlaid new ideas on traditional materials, was his first play to make an international impact. His experience in the early 1930s as director of a travelling theatre, which brought Spanish classical drama to peasant audiences who were seeing a play for the first time, influenced the choice of themes as well as forms in his own development as a playwright. *Bodas de Sangre* [*Blood Wedding*] (1933), *Yerma* (1934), and *La Casa de Bernarda Alba* [*The House of Bernarda Alba*] (written in 1934; first performed in 1945)—tr. Graham Luján and O'Connell as *Three Tragedies* (1959)—between them constitute his dramatic statements on passion, reality, and fate, with individual excursions into the forces of authority and the maternal instinct—see also *Blood Wedding*, tr. Brendan Kennelly (1996), tr. Ted Hughes (1996). In 1936 he returned home to Granada from Madrid to wait for the end of the political crisis which was the cause of the Spanish Civil War, but arrived as the Nationalist forces were conducting a purge of intellectuals. He was captured and shot by firing squad. See *Four Major Plays*, tr. John Edmunds, ed. Nicholas G. Round, 1997; *Selected Verse*, ed. Christopher Maurer, new edn 1996; *Selected Poems*, tr. Merryn Williams, 1992 (bilingual edn); Ian Gibson, *Federico García Lorca: a Life*, new edn 1990.

GARCÍA MÁRQUEZ, GABRIEL (*b.* 1928) Colombian novelist and short-story writer, was born in Aracataca, where he lived with his grandparents for his first eight years. He was educated at a Jesuit high school and the National University of Colombia, Bogota, and then became a journalist, which he insists is his 'true profession'. His first writings appeared in *El Spectador*, whose correspondent he was in Paris in 1954–55 until it was suppressed. He became Director of the Cuban press agency in Bogota in 1959, and retired from full-time journalism in 1965. His first novel, *La Hojarasca* (1955; tr. Gregory Rabassa as the title story of *Leafstorm and Other Stories*, 1972), was inspired by a trip back to Aracataca, which he had not seen since he was a child. His first major work to appear in English was *Cien Años de Soledad* (1967; tr. Rabassa as *One Hundred Years of Solitude*, 1970), in which he combines journalistic techniques with the storytelling tone of his grandmother to recount seven generations of disaster in the mythical town of Macondo. In *El Otoño del Patriarca* (1975; tr. Rabassa as *The Autumn of the Patriarch*, 1976), 'magic realism' illuminates the characteristics of dictatorship displayed by a monstrous imaginary archetype. By contrast, *El General en Su Laberinto* (1989; tr. Edith Grossman as *The General in His Labyrinth*, 1990) uses imaginative realism to re-create the last journey of Simon Bolívar (1783–1830), liberator of South America from Spain.
The 12 stories in *Doce Cuentos Peregrinos*

(1992; tr. Grossman as *Strange Pilgrims*, 1993), which had been gestating for 18 years and which together constitute a book 'closest to the one I had always wanted to write', are about 'the strange things that happen to Latin Americans in Europe'. With *Del Amor y Otros Demoinios* (1993; tr. Grossman as *Of Love and Other Demons*, 1995), which sprang from an experience when the author was a young newspaper reporter in 1949, he returns to his hyperbolic vein and to the identity of Latin America through a tragic love story about crossing divides. See also *Collected Stories*, tr. Rabassa and J. S. Bernstein (1991). García Márquez was awarded the Nobel Prize for Literature in 1982. See Michael Bell, *Gabriel Garcia Marquez: Solitude and Solidarity*, 1993 (critical study).

GARDNER, ERLE STANLEY (1889–1970) American novelist, was born in Malden, Massachusetts, and as a child followed his father, a mining engineer, through California, Oregon, and the Klondike. He was educated at Palo Alto High School, California, and claims to have been expelled from college for slugging a teacher, a skill he put to more profitable use in the ring in his teens. He studied law in local firms, and was admitted to the California Bar in 1911. He practised first in Oxnard, where he successfully defended a client by getting several Chinamen to exchange identities and thus confuse a key prosecution witness, and then in Ventura. In the 1920s he began to write western and mystery stories for magazines, and on the publication of his first novel, *The Case of the Velvet Claws* (1933), written in three days, which was his usual rate of output, he gave up the law for the dictating machine. Perry Mason, who features in that book and in 81 subsequent ones, changed his demeanour, his ethics, and his tactics over the years under the influence of the television presentations and changes in the law, but the dialogue and the courtroom drama largely continue to sparkle. The reader experiences the opposite side of the forensic coin in the series about Douglas Selby, beginning with *The D. A. Calls it Murder* (1937). As A. A. Fair, one of three pen names, he wrote a further extensive series of thrillers, about a private eye and his large, female associate.

GARIOCH, ROBERT, pen name of Robert Garioch Sutherland (1909–81) Scottish poet and translator, was born in Edinburgh and educated at the High School of Edinburgh and Edinburgh University, after which he became a teacher. He served in the Royal Corps of Signals in World War II and was taken prisoner near Tobruk in June 1942, spending the rest of the war in Italian and German prisoner-of-war camps. His experiences, written down shortly afterwards and published as *Two Men and a Blanket* (1975), are described with sound sense and considerable good humour. His satirical bent and his easy familiarity with Scots, a legacy of his childhood, were publicly demonstrated in 1933 in *The Masque of Edinburgh* (published in an enlarged version in 1954), but his first two books of verse were privately printed. *Selected Poems* was published in 1966, shortly after which he returned from London to Edinburgh, where he researched for the *Dictionary of the Older Scottish Tongue* and continued to cast his poetic eye over the quirks and hypocrisies of daily and public life. His sonnet 'At Robert Fergusson's Grave' is a mark of his affinity with FERGUSSON, whose metres he sometimes imitated and whose attitude of quiet rebellion and powers of incisive observation he shared. He could be as devastating and amusing about the Edinburgh Festival ('Embro to the Ploy'), the profession of teaching ('Sisyphus'), and the local council ('In Princes Street Gardens'), as about the emotions of dog-lovers ('Nemo Canem Impune Lacessit'). He translated into Scots *Jephthah and The Baptist* (1959) from the Latin of BUCHANAN, French poems of APOLLINAIRE, and Italian sonnets of Giuseppe Belli (1791–1863). See *Complete Poetical Works*, ed. Robin Fulton, 1983.

GARLAND, (HANNIBAL) HAMLIN (1860–1940) American short-story writer and novelist, was born near West Salem, Wisconsin, into a struggling rural family, and grew up as his father's labourer on farms in the Midwest. He graduated from Cedar Valley Seminary, Iowa, in 1881, and was a homesteader in the Dakotas until 1884, when he went to Boston. He was befriended by HOWELLS, and taken on as a teacher at the Boston School of Oratory. Shattered after a visit to his family in 1887, when he saw afresh the conditions of the rural poor, and encouraged by another realist writer, Joseph Kirkland (1830–94), to use his farm background as a basis for fiction, he wrote the tales that appeared in *Main-Travelled Roads: Six Mississippi Valley Stories* (1891) and *Prairie Folks* (1892). *Jason Edwards: an Average Man* (1892) and *A Spoil of Office* (1892) are propagandist novels; in *Rose of Dutcher's Coolly* (1895) he produced a feminist study of some merit, which follows a farm girl's escape from manual labour and spiritual barrenness to college and then a career as a writer. Subsequently he turned to writing popular romantic fiction, from which he firmly verged in 1917 with *A Son of the Middle Border*, a distinguished autobiography, whose sequel, *A Daughter of the Middle Border* (1921), won the Pulitzer Prize. In a critical work, *Crumbling Idols* (1904), he describes as 'veritism' the kind of realism to which he had earlier subscribed. See Joseph B. McCullough, *Hamlin Garland*, 1978 (biographical/critical study).

GARNEAU, HECTOR DE SAINT-DENYS see HÉBERT.

GARNETT, DAVID (1892–1981) British novelist, was born in Brighton, the only child of Edward Garnett (1868–1936), the distinguished publishers' reader, and Constance Garnett (1861–1946), the Russian translator, and was educated at University College School and the Royal College of Science, where he studied botany. He was a conscientious objector during World War I, but served in France with the Friends' War Victims' Relief Mission. He was a member of the Bloomsbury Group, and later married as his second wife the daughter of Vanessa Bell (1879–1961), sister of VIRGINIA WOOLF. It was in Bloomsbury that after the war he opened with Francis Birrell (1889–1935) the bookshop in whose cellar (Sir) Francis Meynell (1891–1975) set up in 1923 the Nonesuch Press, with which Garnett became closely associated. He had by now begun his career as a novelist. In *Lady into Fox* (1922) and *A Man in the Zoo* (1924), he extended the natural circumstances of life in an allegorical manner into a realization of where they might lead. Animal nature is a driving force in subsequent novels, notably *The Sailor's Return* (1925), *Go She Must!* (1927), and *No Love* (1929), in which resignation and despair may ironically still be found to bring their compensations. He was Literary Editor of the *New Statesman and Nation* before World War II, at the begining of which he joined the Air Ministry with the rank of flight lieutenant—he had earlier learned to fly, as he describes in *A Rabbit in the Air* (1932). He then became a member of the Political Warfare Executive. He was a director of the publishing house of Rupert Hart-Davis from 1946 to 1952, after which he returned to writing novels. He was made CBE in 1952. See *The Golden Echo*, 1953, *Flowers of the Forest*, 1955, *The Familiar Faces*, 1962 (autobiography).

GARRICK, DAVID see BROOKE, FRANCES; HOME; JOHNSON; MACKLIN; MORE, HANNAH.

GARRISON, FREDERICK see SINCLAIR, UPTON.

GASKELL, ELIZABETH (1810–65), née Stevenson, British novelist and biographer, was born in Chelsea, London, the daughter of a civil servant. Her mother died the following year, and she was brought up by her aunt in Knutsford, Cheshire (the Cranford of her writings). After lessons at home, she spent several useful years at a girls' boarding school at Stratford-upon-Avon. When she was 21 she married William Gaskell (1805–84), a Unitarian minister and classical scholar. They lived in Manchester, and had four daughters, and a son, after whose death in infancy on a family holiday in 1845 Mr

Gaskell encouraged his wife to write a novel. *Mary Barton* (1848) was unusual for its time in that its background is working class and its theme industrial relations. It impressed DICKENS, in whose journals much of her subsequent work first appeared. *Cranford* (1853), her best-known novel, is a series of linked sketches of provincial life in which the characters are beautifully drawn. In *North and South* (1855) she returns to the industrial north, contrasting it with the manners of the rural south. She had in 1850 been introduced to CHARLOTTE BRONTË, whose confidante she became and on whose death Mr Brontë invited her to write an authorized biography. *The Life of Charlotte Brontë* (1857) is one of the finest English literary biographies. Gaskell died suddenly at a family gathering in the country house she had bought for her husband's retirement. She left an unfinished novel, *Wives and Daughters* (1866), a perceptive, witty study of family relationships. Shorter fiction is in *The Moorland Cottages and Other Stories*, ed. Suzanne Lewis (1995). See Winifred Gérin, *Elizabeth Gaskell*, new edn 1980 (biography); Jenny Uglow, *Elizabeth Gaskell: a Habit of Stories*, new edn 1994 (biography); Terence Wright, *Elizabeth Gaskell: 'We Are Not Angels'—Realism, Gender, Values*, 1995 (critical study); W. A. Craik, *Elizabeth Gaskell and the English Provincial Novel*, 1975.

GAUTIER, THÉOPHILE (1811–72) French novelist, poet, and critic, was born in Tarbes and in 1814 taken by his parents to Paris, where he entered Collège Louis-le-Grand as a boarder in 1822. After three months he was removed in a state of shock, and went to Collège Charlemagne as a day boy. Closely associated with NERVAL and HUGO, at the first performance of whose *Hernani* he led the Romantic claque, he published a book of verse when he was 18, and a collection of satirical stories two years later. *Mademoiselle de Maupin* (1835–36; tr. 1887; tr. Joanna Richardson, 1981), a historical romance about the 17th-century bisexual adventuress, is more significant for its preface. Written in response to pressures of state censorship, and probably added to fill out the two volumes, it expounds the doctrine of 'art for art's sake', which he later redefined as 'form for beauty's sake'. This is especially reflected in his final volume of poetry, *Emaux et Camées* [Enamels and Cameos] (1852; expanded edn 1872)—see also *The Gentle Enchanter: Thirty-Four Poems*, tr. Brian Hill (1960). He wrote the story lines of several ballets, most notably *Giselle* (1841), music by Adolphe Adam (1803–56), which he composed for his idol, Carlotta Grisi (1819–99). Rejected by her as a lover, he took up instead with her sister, Ernesta, with whom he lived for twenty years (with an interval from 1849 to 1852 for a more passionate and more poetically inspiring attachment elsewhere) and

who was the mother of Judith Gautier (1845–1917), the author and translator.

GAY, JOHN (1685–1732) British poet and dramatist, was born in Barnstaple, Devon, and cared for by an uncle after being orphaned at the age of ten. He was educated at Barnstaple Grammar School and then apprenticed to a London silk dealer, whom he left to join the literary circle of the time. He published an anonymous burlesque in blank verse, *Wine* (1708), and then several plays and volumes of minor poetry, including a mock-pastoral, *The Shepherd's Week* (1714), and *Trivia: or the Art of Walking in the Streets of London* (1716), regarded as the prototype of the 'urban eclogue'. Such were the influence of his friends and the attention of his various patrons that *Poems on Several Occasions* (1720) earned him a large sum which he invested, and lost, in the South Sea Company (after which he was, perhaps appropriately, appointed Lottery Commissioner). *Fables* (1727) comprises moral tales in verse in which the acerbic and often topical moral usually outweighs the tale. All his previous writing experience crystallized in *The Beggar's Opera* (1728), a musical comedy of London low life, incorporating parallels with the current political situation, and songs set to popular tunes of the day, some of which echoed contemporary classical composers. Its success was also due to the situations, characters, and lyrics—the source of the lines 'If with me you'd fondly stray / Over the hills and far away' and 'How happy could I be with either / Were t'other dear charmer away'. JOHNSON in *Lives of the Poets* records that *The Beggar's Opera* 'had the effect, as was ludicrously said, of making Gay rich and Rich gay'—John Rich (c.1692–1761) put it on after CIBBER had turned it down. A sequel, *Polly* (1729), was banned from the stage for political reasons but published to acclaim. A pastoral opera, *Acis and Galatea*, set to music by George Frederick Handel (1685–1759), was performed in 1731. Gay's last years were spent as the permanent guest of the Duke and Duchess of Queensberry. See *Dramatic Works*, ed. John Fuller, 2 vols 1983; David Nokes, *John Gay: a Profession of Friendship*, 1995 (biography).

GEE, MAURICE (b. 1931) New Zealand novelist and children's writer, was born in Whakatane, Bay of Plenty, and educated at Avondale College, Auckland, and Auckland University, after which he did a year at Auckland Teachers College. He worked as a teacher, casual labourer, and librarian (he was City Librarian, Napier 1970–72), before becoming a full-time writer in 1976. He began to have stories published in *Landfall* in the late 1950s, of which 'The Loser' (1959), whose setting is the murkier side of horse racing, was especially admired—see his collection *A Glorious Morning, Comrade* (1975).

After a first novel of youth, *The Big Season* (1962), he embarked on a range in which family relationships and tense situations are explored in small town settings. Especially notable is the trilogy, *Plumb* (1978), *Meg* (1981), and *Sole Survivor* (1983), which encapsulates a hundred years of New Zealand life and political history while playing out the saga of a family. In *Prowlers* (1987) and *The Burning Boy* (1990) he further illuminates the New Zealand mind. *Going West* (1992), an ingenious investigation into the life, and death, of an anti-social poet, incorporates satirical sketches of New Zealand literary society in the 1950s. *Crime Story* (1995) encompasses a society inflicted with personal violence and tensions. By contrast, his best children's novels, which include *Under the Mountain* (1979) and *The Halfmen of O* (1982), have an alternative world underlying the real one. See Bill Manhire, *Maurice Gee*, 1987 (critical study).

GENET, JEAN (1910–86) French novelist and dramatist, was born in Paris and brought up by a peasant family in the Morvan region under the auspices of the National Foundling Society. At ten he began to steal, and at 16 he was consigned to the Mettray Reformatory, from which, now homosexual as well as criminal, he escaped in 1926 and joined the Foreign Legion. He deserted after a few days with some officers' suitcases. From 1932 to 1940 he bummed around Europe, sampling the jails as he went. In Fresnes prison in 1942, he wrote *Notre-Dame-des-Fleurs* (1944; tr. as *Our Lady of the Flowers*, 1949), a dark, symbolic novel of homosexual criminal life in Montmartre. After a further novel, the production in 1947 of his first play, *Les Bonnes* (tr. as *The Maids*, 1957), and the publication of an autobiography, *Journal du Voleur* (1948; tr. as *The Thief's Journal*, 1965), he was in 1948, having served ten terms in jail, sentenced automatically to life imprisonment. A petition organized by literary figures, including COCTEAU, GIDE, MAURIAC, and SARTRE, secured his release and a presidential pardon. His work (translated by Bernard Frechtman) usually features conflicts between authority and servitude in a variety of forms, and between illusion and reality, such as are given dramatic expression in *Le Balcon* (1956; tr. as *The Balcony*, 1958). See Edmund White, *Genet*, new edn 1994 (biography).

GEOFFREY OF MONMOUTH (*c*.1100–55) chronicler, was probably born in Monmouth, and between 1129 and 1151 lived in Oxford, possibly as a canon of the secular college of St George. Here he wrote, in Latin, *Historia Regum Britanniae* [History of the Kings of Britain], which he claims to have translated from 'a certain very ancient book written in the British [i.e. Welsh] language', given to him by Walter (*d*. *c*.1151), Archdeacon of Oxford. It is more likely that he used a wide range of written and oral sources to create his imaginative history with a basis of fact, covering nineteen hundred years from the birth of a mythical Brutus, great-grandson of Aeneas of Troy, to the death of the historical Cadwallader in AD 689. A considerable part is devoted to a King Arthur who is the prototype of the Arthur of later legend. Geoffrey also wrote, in Latin verse, a life of Merlin, which he dedicated to Robert de Chesney (*d*. 1166), Bishop of Lincoln from 1148. In 1151 he was appointed Bishop Elect of St Asaph, Flintshire, for which he was ordained a priest at Westminster, before he could be consecrated. His 'History', which he finished in 1136, quickly became popular, to judge from the fact that over two hundred 12th-century manuscripts survive. It was translated into French verse by the Norman poet Robert Wace (*c*.1100–*c*.1175) as *Roman de Brut* (1155), which is the basis of LAYAMON's version. See *The History of the Kings of Britain*, tr. Lewis Thorpe, new edn 1968.

GEOGHEGAN, EDWARD (1812–after 1852) Australian dramatist, arrived in Sydney on a convict ship in 1840, having been sentenced in Dublin, where he was a medical student, to seven years' deportation for obtaining 'goods' by false pretences. For participating in illegal trade in shoes and curios, he served his full term on Cockatoo Island, as a medical dispenser. He also wrote several plays—anonymously, because as it was an offence for a convict to appear on the stage, managers were concerned that the law might also apply to a dramatist. *The Hibernian Father*, described by him as 'Original 5 Act Tragedy', and *The Currency Lass*, 'Original 2 Act Opera', the first play with an Australian theme to be performed in Australia, were produced at the Royal Victoria Theatre, Sydney, in 1844; as were his adaptations of BULWER-LYTTON's *The Last Days of Pompeii* and DICKENS's *A Christmas Carol*. The last record of him is a letter to the Colonial Secretary, written from Victoria in 1852. See *The Currency Lass*, ed. Roger Covell, 1976.

GERALD OF WALES see GIRALDUS CAMBRENSIS.

GERHARDIE, WILLIAM (1895–1977) British novelist and prose writer, was born Gerhardi in St Petersburg, Russia, the son of a British industrialist, and added the final 'e' late in life. He was educated at the Reformierte Schule, and was sent to London in 1913 to train for a career or find a rich wife. The war interrupted the career, and he enlisted in the Army as a trooper, was commissioned, served in the British Embassy in Petrograd and then with the Military Mission in Vladivostok, and was made OBE in 1920. He then went to Worcester College, Oxford, and wrote *Anton Chekhov: a Critical Study* (1923) and *Futility: a Novel on Russian Themes* (1922), a witty dissection of Russian manners. His own experiences were also the basis of *The Polyglots* (1925), which earned him critical acclaim, especially for its fusion of comic and tragic elements in the evolution of the characters. He travelled widely, and wrote (wherever he happened to be) several volumes of stories and a further novel, *Pending Heaven* (1930), before finally settling in London and publishing his autobiography, *Memoirs of a Polyglot* (1931). His last novel, *My Wife's the Least of It*, appeared in 1938, and an extensive history of the Romanovs in 1940; whereupon he signed a contract for *God's Fifth Column*, a historical study of the previous fifty years. It was announced for publication in 1942, but he withdrew it for revision on being appointed to the staff of the BBC, for whom he went on to devise and edit the 'English by Radio' series. He resigned in 1945 'to concentrate more fully on literary work', effectively becoming a recluse in his flat. For the next 32 years he was said to be writing a monumental four-part novel called 'The Present Breath', of which the final two chapters were printed in a literary compilation in 1962. On his death there was no trace of any other part of the narrative, only a complex filing system in a massive array of cardboard boxes. There were also manuscripts of what seemed to be several lengthy non-fiction works, which turned out to be different drafts of the still unfinished *God's Fifth Column*; a version of it, edited by Michael Holroyd and Robert Skidelsky, finally appeared in 1981. See Dido Davies, *William Gerhardie: a Biography*, new edn 1991.

GHOSE, MANMOHAN (1869–1924) Indian poet, was born in Bhagalpore, the son of a surgeon who took his family to England when the boy was ten, and left him and his two brothers there to be educated. He went to Manchester Grammar School and St Paul's School, where he struck up a friendship with BINYON, and then on a scholarship to Christ Church, Oxford, where with Binyon and two others he published a book of verse, *Primavera* (1890). After eight terms he left, pleading financial reasons. Having failed to find a job in London, he returned to Oxford and took a pass degree. In 1904 he went back to India, where he taught English literature, being appointed to Presidency College, Calcutta, in 1902. In 1898 he had made an arranged marriage with a 16-year-old Bengali, who disintegrated physically and mentally after a fall in 1905. His career suffered because of his brothers' revolutionary activities; this was probably the cause also of his abandoning work on his epic poem, 'Perseus', which was wrongly suspected of being subversive. His wife died in the flu epidemic of 1918, to be remembered in 'The Dewdrop', 'The Rider on the White Horse', and other mystical lyrics. In 1921 his sight failed and he retired from teaching. He received stoically in 1923 the news that the bank which held his savings had collapsed. He died only minutes after asking his daughter to stop reading aloud WALTER SCOTT's *Quentin Durward*, which she had been doing at his request for several hours. He was a poet in the English, not Indian, or even Anglo-Indian tradition, whose only collection in his lifetime was *Love-Songs and Elegies* (1898). Possibly on the advice of his lawyer, he wrote 'Nollo and Damayanti: an Indian Mystery Play' at a time when his political loyalties were under scrutiny. See *Selected Poems*, ed. Lotika Ghose, 1974.

GHOSE, ZULFIKAR (*b.* 1935) British poet, novelist, and critic, was born in Sialkot (now in Pakistan), and went with his family to what is now India, and from there to England, where he read English and philosophy at Keele University. He married a Brazilian in 1964. He was cricket correspondent of the *Observer* from 1960 to 1965, and taught in London schools until 1969, when he went to Austin to lecture in English at the University of Texas. He has explained that 'even when returning to Pakistan for a visit, I have remained an alien whose unconscious desire is to attach himself to a land with which he can claim an identity'. His first book of verse, *The Loss of India* (1964), recalls the history and landscapes of the country he knew as a child. *Jets from Orange* (1967) evokes the sights and sounds of England and Provence as well, and *The Violent West* (1972) those of the USA. The same preoccupations with landscapes and with the quest for a 'home' inform his novels, of which the first, *The Contradictions* (1966), has an East/West theme; *The Murder of Aziz Khan* (1967) is a naturalistic story of a peasant farmer's pointless struggle against modern development and contemporary skulduggery. In his historical trilogy, 'The Incredible Brazilian' (1972, 1975, 1978), he is in effect delineating new potential roots; while in *A New History of Torments* (1982) a South American finds an alternative but ultimately destructive rural Eden. *The Triple Mirror of the Self* (1992) is a part-philosophical novel of a search for the identity of an expatriate South Asian poet, which begins in the Brazilian rainforest and in its concluding section returns to the pre-Partition India in which Ghose grew up. His critical works include *The Fiction of Reality* (1983), *The Art of Creating Fiction* (1991), and *Shakespeare's Mortal Knowledge: a Reading of the Tragedies* (1992). See *Selected Poems*, 1991; *Confessions of a Native-Alien*, 1965 (autobiography).

GIBBON, EDWARD (1737–94) British historian, was born in Putney, London. A bookish but sickly child, he was educated at Westminster School (where his aunt had set up a boarding house, it is said for his benefit) and for 14 profligate months at Magdalen College, Oxford, where he became a Catholic. In Lausanne, to which he was sent by his father for four years, he accepted Protestantism again, learned French, studied Latin, and became engaged (and at his father's insistence then broke off the engagement) to Suzanne Curchod (1737–94), who later became the mother of STAËL. Gibbon's *Essai sur l'Étude de la Littérature* (1761) was translated into English in 1764, though he was never much interested in the English edition. Sitting on the Capitol Hill in Rome in 1764, he had the idea of writing a history of the decay of the ancient city, later elaborated into *The History of the Decline and Fall of the Roman Empire* (7 vols 1776–88). He entered Parliament in 1774 and served in a minor government post from 1779 to 1782. His treatment of the rise of Christianity in the first volume of his great work caused controversy, and after the appearance of Vols II and III he returned to Lausanne, where he lived quietly for the rest of his life, corpulent from his sedentary occupation, and a dandy. His grasp of history is excellent, the arrangement and flow of his material masterly, and his prose, enlivened by touches of humour and apocalyptic detail, superb. He wrote from a standpoint within the Roman world, and his religious views are anticlerical but not necessarily anti-Christian. See Roy Porter, *Edward Gibbon*, new edn 1995 (biography); J. W. Burrow, *Gibbon*, 1985 (introduction to his work).

GIBBON, LEWIS GRASSIC, pseudonym of James Leslie Mitchell (1901–35) Scottish novelist, was born in a croft in Auchterless, Aberdeenshire, and was educated at Arbuthnott Village School and Mackie Academy, Stonehaven, which he left after a year to try journalism. From 1919 to 1923 he served in the Middle East in the Royal Army Service Corps. Having on his release failed for five months to earn a living as a writer, he enlisted as a clerk in the Royal Air Force for six years. After his discharge he lived in Welwyn Garden City until his early death from a perforated ulcer. As J. Leslie Mitchell he wrote several anthropological works, including *Hanno, or the Future of Exploration* (1928) and *The Conquest of the Maya* (1934), and seven novels. He used the pseudonym Lewis Grassic Gibbon for a life of the Scottish explorer Mungo Park (1934) and for his Scottish novels, in which he employs a stylized form of dialogue to represent the speech of the North East, the setting of *Sunset Song* (1932), *Cloud Howe* (1933), and *Grey Granite* (1934). Reissued in 1946 as a trilogy entitled *A Scots Quair*, they reflect, through the experiences of twice-married Chris Guthrie, the contrasts and clashes of culture, language, and living conditions inherent in Scottish life, and the hypnotic intensity of the land. Rural life features strongly in two of his short stories, 'Clay' and 'Smeddum', which are as good as anything he wrote after *Sunset Song*. See Ian Campbell, *Lewis Grassic Gibbon*, 1985 (critical study).

GIBBONS, STELLA see WEBB, MARY.

GIDE, ANDRÉ (1869–1951) French novelist, dramatist, prose writer, and critic, was born in Paris, the son of an academic lawyer who died in 1880, and of a wealthy industrialist's daughter, who brought him up according to strict Protestant principles and sent him to a number of different schools in the hope of straightening out his psychological make-up. She opposed his determination to become a writer, but when she died in 1894 she left him more than enough to continue his literary career, which had begun with an anonymous novel of the spiritual quest of an adolescent, *Les Cahiers d'André Walter* (1891; tr. Wade Baskin as the *The Notebook of Andre Walter*, 1968). His literary talent manifested itself in a variety of forms, including drama, as well as in further philosophical novels such as *Les Nourritures Terrestres* (1897; tr. Dorothy Bussy as *Fruits of the Earth*, 1949) and *Les Caves du Vatican* (1914; tr. Bussy as *The Vatican Cellars*, 1952). He travelled restlessly in Europe and Africa, and worked for refugees of World War I and the Spanish Civil War. His documentary account, *Voyage au Congo* (1927), led to the establishment of an enquiry into cruelty and other malpractices on the part of franchise holders. A puritan as well as a homosexual with pederastic tendencies, he married his cousin Madelaine Rondeaux (*d.* 1935) in 1895, and had a daughter in 1923 by Elisabeth van Rysselberghe. The two key texts in the exposition and justification of his sexual inclinations are the quasi-Platonic dialogue, *Corydon* (1924; tr. Hugh Gibb, 1950), and the autobiographical study, *Si le Grain ne Meurt* (1920–21; tr. Bussy as *If It Die . . .*, 1950). An admirer of English literature, he translated CONRAD's *Typhoon* (1918) shortly after beginning to study the language through a Berlitz course and by reading DEFOE's *Robinson Crusoe*, and followed it with his version of SHAKESPEARE's *Antony and Cleopatra* (performed 1920). He was awarded the Nobel Prize for Literature in 1947.

GILBERT, (Sir) W(ILLIAM) S(CHWENK) (1836–1911) British dramatist and poet, was born in London, the son of William Gilbert (1804–90), naval surgeon turned novelist. 'Bab', as he was known, was a much-travelled infant who was kidnapped by brigands in Naples when he was two, and ransomed for £25. He was educated at Great Ealing School and King's College, London, and spent four unhappy years as a civil service clerk, resigning to study law on the proceeds from a legacy. He was called to the Bar in 1863, and practised on the Northern Circuit without financial success. He was at the same time earning from verses and articles with his own illustrations, signed 'Bab', in the periodicals *Fun* and *Punch*, which in 1866 rejected his skit on COLERIDGE, 'The Yarn of the Nancy Bell', as being 'too cannibalistic' for its readers. It was subsequently one of the witty, often satirical, and technically inventive poems in *The Bab Ballads* (1869). Initially on the recommendation of the dramatist T. W. Robertson (1829–71), he wrote several burlesques for the stage, followed by a series of comedies, of which the brilliant *Engaged* (1877) was criticized for its cynicism. The collaboration with the composer (Sir) Arthur Sullivan (1842–1900) began with a burlesque, *Thespis, or the Gods Grown Old* (1871). The first of the famous Savoy Operas, which from 1881 played at the Savoy Theatre, built for the purpose by Richard D'Oyly Carte (1844–1901), was *Trial by Jury* (1875). The partnership lasted for twenty years, continuously threatened and sometimes interrupted by Gilbert's ill-temper and pedantic demands, and generated such lasting productions as *The Pirates of Penzance* (1880), *Iolanthe* (1882), *The Mikado* (1885), and *The Gondoliers* (1889), in which the music often extracts pathos from what otherwise might seem cynicism or mere whimsy, and enhances the intricate texture and satire of the libretti. Gilbert built the Garrick Theatre from his proceeds, and was knighted in 1907 for his contribution to the stage. He died of a heart attack after trying to save a young lady whom he believed to be drowning in the private swimming pool on his Harrow estate. See *The Complete Annotated Gilbert and Sullivan*, ed. Ian Bradley, new edn 1996; Hesketh Pearson, *Gilbert: His Life and Strife*, new edn 1978 (biography); Jane W. Stedman, *W. S. Gilbert: a Classic Victorian and His Theatre*, 1996 (biography).

GILMAN, CHARLOTTE PERKINS

(1860–1935) American novelist and social critic, was born Charlotte Perkins in Hartford, Connecticut, a great-niece of STOWE through her father, who left home permanently when his wife, after the death of a fourth child in infancy, was advised not to have another. She moved home with her mother 18 times in 14 years, during which she had only four years' formal education. In 1878–79 she attended the Rhode Island School of Design, with a view to earning a living as an artist and teacher. Her first published poem, 'In Duty Bound' (*Women's Journal*, 1884), an indictment of the married state, appeared four months before she succumbed to convention and married Walter Stetson, an artist. A daughter was born in 1885; they separated in 1888 (divorced 1894) after the conflicting demands of marriage and a creative and public life had given Gilman a nervous breakdown, such as she graphically describes

in her story, 'The Yellow Wall-Paper' (1892). During the 1890s she was active in the Nationalist cause (see BELLAMY) in California. Her first book was a collection of verse, *In This Our World* (1893)—see also *Later Poetry of Charlotte Perkins Gilman*, ed. Denise D. Knight (1996). A reception was given for her by Lester Ward (1841–1913), the sociologist and reformer, at the Women's Suffrage Convention, Washington, D.C., in 1896, after which she increased her public appearances and visited England to speak. In *Women and Economics* (1898), drafted in five weeks, she set out her views on 'the economic factor between men and women as a factor in social evolution'. In 1900, having passed what she reckoned was the age of child-bearing, she married her cousin, Houghton Gilman (*d.* 1934), a New York patent attorney. *Concerning Children* (1900), *The Home: Its Work and Influence* (1903), and *Human Work* (1904), a sequel to *Women and Economics*, are studies mainly of family and domestic issues; *The Man-Made World* (1911) is concerned with sexual discrimination in its wider forms. She personally wrote, edited, and published the 86 issues of the *Forerunner* (each of 28 pages) that appeared between 1909 and 1916, in which she serialized her feminist novels, *What Diantha Did* (1910) and *The Crux* (1911), and three Utopian romances satirizing the male state, *Moving the Mountain* (1911), 'Herland' (1915), and 'With Her in Ourland' (1916). Diagnosed in 1932 as suffering from inoperable breast cancer, she 'promptly bought sufficient chloroform as a substitute', with which in due course she ended her own life, in bed, after her bath. See *The Yellow Wall-Paper and Other Stories*, ed. Robert Shulman, 1995; Carol Farley Kessler, *Charlotte Perkins Gilman: Her Progress towards Utopia, with Selected Writings*, new edn 1995; *The Living of Charlotte Perkins Gilman: an Autobiography*, new edn 1991; Ann J. Lane, *To 'Herland' and Beyond: the Life and Work of Charlotte Perkins Gilman*, new edn 1997; Gary Scharnhorst, *Charlotte Perkins Gilman*, 1985 (biographical/critical study).

GILMORE, MARY

(1865–1962), née Cameron, Australian poet and journalist, was born at Cottawalla, near Goulburn, New South Wales, and was a pupil teacher when she was 12. While teaching in the mining town of Silverton and then in Sydney, she became associated with the labour and radical movements. In 1896 she joined the New Australia scheme of William Lane (1861–1917) in Paraguay, where she married Alexander Gilmore, a shearer from Victoria. They returned in 1902 to a remote farm in Victoria. In 1908 she became the first editor of the Women's Page of the Sydney *Worker*, which she remained until 1931, campaigning vigorously there and elsewhere for fair treatment for the disadvantaged of all kinds. In 1911 she separated from her husband and took her son to

Sydney. *Marri'd and Other Verses* (1910) was the first of a dozen collections, of which the last was published when she was 89. Her poems, short, rhythmical, and to the point, embrace many themes pertinent to the Australian identity, none being more effective than the patriotic verses written during World War II, notably 'No Foe Shall Gather Our Harvest' (1941). Two prose studies, *Old Days, Old Ways* (1934) and *More Recollections* (1935), are lyrical evocations of the old pioneer life and its values. She was made DBE in 1937. See *Selected Poems*, ed. Robert D. Fitzgerald, 1963; W. H. Wilde, *Courage a Grace: a Biography of Dame Mary Gilmore*, 1989; and in Douglas Stewart, *The Broad Stream: Aspects of Australian Literature*, 1975.

GINSBERG, ALLEN (1926–97) American poet, was born in Newark, New Jersey, of Jewish parents. His conventional father, Louis Ginsberg (1896–1976), was a high school teacher and poet. His mother, a Russian emigrée, had political obsessions and died in a mental asylum in 1956, her life and living death being immortalized in her son's moving 'Kaddish' (the Jewish prayer of mourning) in *Kaddish and Other Poems 1958–1960* (1961). He was educated at Paterson High School, New Jersey, and at 17 entered Columbia University, New York, from which he was expelled after two years for a variety of offences. He returned in 1946 after training at the Merchant Marine Academy, and graduated two eventful years later. In a Harlem apartment he had the first of a series of mystical visions of BLAKE, which gave direction to his early poetry—see *Empty Mirror* (1961) and *The Gates of Wrath: Rhymed Poems 1948–1952* (1972). He also got himself involved with some stolen goods, and instead of jail spent eight months in a psychiatric hospital. He worked as a book reviewer and market researcher, and then went via Cuba to Mexico, where he explored Maya ruins and wrote 'Siesta in Xbalba', before settling in San Francisco. W. C. WILLIAMS, his friend and literary consultant, wrote in an introduction to his first collection, *Howl and Other Poems* (1956), 'Hold back the edges of your gowns, Ladies, we are going through hell.' The cultural apocalypse projected by the title poem, and unsuccessful litigation to brand the book as obscene, ensured its continuing status as the poetic bible of the Beat Generation—see also KEROUAC. He now travelled widely; experimented with hallucinogenic drugs; and adopted Buddhist beliefs, to which he formally committed himself in 1972—the original experience is described in 'The Change: Kyoto–Tokyo Express' (1963).

During the 1960s Ginsberg became a peaceful public protester whose chanting influenced crowds and the police, and a persuasive presence at hearings for reform. In his creative persona he became a public poet, de-

claiming to vast audiences and performing spontaneously-composed blues songs to musical accompaniment. He regularly published collections of verse, of which *The Fall of America: Poems of These States 1965–1971* (1972) won the National Book Award. His spiritual interests further manifested themselves in 1974 when he helped to found the Jack Kerouac School of Disembodied Poetics, of the Naropa Institute, Colorado. In a journal entry in 1984, he described himself as: 'Poet, but sick of writing about myself / Homosexual role model, noted for stable relationship . . . / Buddhist agitator . . . / Scholar . . . / Peacenik Protester . . .'. See *Collected Poems 1947–1985*, 1995; *Cosmopolitan Greetings: Poems 1986–1992*, new edn 1995; *Journals: Early Fifties, Early Sixties*, new edn 1993; *Journals: Mid Fifties 1954–1958*, ed. Gordon Ball, new edn 1996; Barry Miles, *Ginsberg: a Biography*, 1989; Michael Schumacher, *Dharma Lion: a Critical Biography of Allen Ginsberg*, new edn 1994; Thomas F. Merrill, *Allen Ginsberg*, rev. edn 1988 (critical study).

GINZBURG, NATALIA (1916–91), née Levi, Italian novelist and dramatist, was born in Palermo of a Jewish father, who was a professor of biology, and a Catholic mother, and was brought up in Turin, where she was educated at home by a governess. Her first story, published in 1934, about a bored and repressed child, reflected the subject matter of much of her future fiction, in which the characters react to or against boredom. In 1938 she married Leone Ginzburg, a Russian scholar (he became a leading member of the Italian Resistance and died in prison in 1944 after being handed over to the Germans). Exiled with him by the Fascists to the Abruzzi mountains, she wrote there her first novel, *La Strada che va in Città* [*The Road to the City*] (1942), under the name of Alessandra Tornimparte because of the legislation against Jews. *È Stato Così* (1947; tr. Frances Frenaye as 'The Dry Heart' in *The Road to the City*, 1949) is a study of a woman who kills her husband simply out of a conviction that she was fated to do so. Ginzburg worked for the publisher Einaudi from 1944 to 1949, and in 1950 married Gabriele Baldini (d. 1969), translator into Italian of the whole of SHAKESPEARE; they lived in London from 1959 to 1962 when he was Director of the Italian Institute. Other notable novels include *Le Voci della Sera* (1961; tr. D. M. Low as *Voices in the Evening*, 1963), which especially demonstrates her attraction to the work of COMPTON-BURNETT (whom she called 'la grande signorina'), and *Lessico Famigliare* (1963; tr. Low as *Family Sayings*, rev. edn 1984), based on recollections of her own upbringing. Having in 1964 denied that she had any intention of writing for the stage, she began the following year to do so, with a series of marital farces in experimental style, of which *L'Inser-*

zione (1968; tr. Henry Reed as *The Advertisement*, 1969) was performed at the National Theatre, London, in 1968. She was elected a parliamentary deputy for the independent left in 1983.

GIRALDUS CAMBRENSIS (GERALD OF WALES), also known as Girald de Barri (1146–1223) Welsh cleric and prose writer, was born at Manorbier Castle, Pembrokeshire, and studied in Paris. He was ordained in 1772, and became Archdeacon of St David's; he was elected Bishop in 1176, but Henry II blocked the appointment. He was elected again in 1198, but this time it was Archbishop Hubert of Canterbury (*d.* 1205) who was the principal objector to the post being held by a Welshman. Giraldus made three trips to Rome in pursuit of his claim, tried litigation, and even attempted to raise the Welsh nation in his support, but after four years he gave up and retired to his books. His extensive works in Latin are notable for their historical, topographical, and sociological interest, as well as for their colourful descriptions of characters, shrewd observations, and scurrilous stories, even about Henry II. *Gemma Ecclesiastica* is a satirical survey of the life and manners of the clergy of his time, the homes of many of whom, he alleges, are cluttered up with infants and their gear. He wrote [*The History and Topography of Ireland*], tr. John J. O'Meara, (rev. edn 1982), which in about 1187 he declaimed for three days to the assembled academics and scholars of Oxford, and an itinerary of Wales, in which he expounds the very tactics which Edward I used to subdue its people almost a century later. *De Rebus a Se Gestis* [About His Own Doings] and the substantial autobiographical parts of *De Jure et Statu Meneuensis Ecclesiae* [About the Rights and Position of the Church of St David] have been translated by H. E. Butler as *The Autobiography of Giraldus Cambrensis* (1937). See Robert Bartlett, *Gerald of Wales 1146–1223*, 1982.

GIRAUDOUX, JEAN (1882–1944) French dramatist and novelist, was born in Bellac, Limousin, and educated at the lycée in Chateauroux, the Lycée Lakanal, Paris, and the École Normale Supérieure, where he studied German literature. He failed his *agrégation*, spent a year as an exchange student at Harvard, and then became a journalist and a writer of short stories, a collection of which was published in 1909. Having passed into the Foreign Service in 1910, he served as a sergeant in World War I, being wounded both at the battle of the Marne and during the Dardanelles campaign. He married in 1921 and resumed his career, being appointed Inspector General of Diplomatic and Consular Posts Abroad in 1934, while also developing his literary talents. With the help of the actor/director Louis Jouvet (1887–1951) he turned his novel *Siegfried et le Limousin* (1922) into a play about French–German relationships, *Siegfried* (1928; tr. Philip Carr, 1930), which was notable for its verbal inventiveness. During the 1930s, and until GENET, IONESCO, and BECKETT introduced new forms of theatrical expression, his dramas of dialogue dominated the French stage. British and American audiences responded particularly to *Amphitryon 38* (1929; tr. S. N. Behrman, 1938), a witty version of the legend of the seduction of Alcmene by Jupiter; *La Guerre de Troie n'Aura pas Lieu* (1935; tr. Christopher Fry as *Tiger at the Gates*, 1955), an examination of aspects of the Trojan War; and the posthumously performed *La Folle de Chaillot* (1945; tr. Maurice Valency as *The Madwoman of Chaillot*, 1949), a whimsical but philosophical approach to the conflict between the forces of good and evil.

GISSING, GEORGE (1857–1903) British novelist, was born in Wakefield and educated at a Quaker boarding school and Owens College, Manchester. A brilliant academic career was cut short when he was expelled, having been sentenced to prison for stealing in order to 'rescue' a girl of the streets, whom he later unwisely married. After suffering great hardship in England and America in search of a job, he managed to study philosophy briefly at the university in Jena and, with the help of a legacy, wrote and paid for the publication of *Workers in the Dawn* (1880), the first of a number of novels intended to reveal the 'hideous injustice of our whole system of society'. It failed to impress the public, but through it he found employment as a tutor. He wrote 22 novels in all, which in many cases chart the unhappy progress of his life, while graphically mirroring the conditions and feelings of the lower middle class. *New Grub Street* (1891), the most profound and perceptive of them, explores the seamier aspects of the literary world of his time. Long saved-up-for trips to Greece and Italy resulted in a travel book, *By the Ionian Sea* (1901), and a scholarly, blockbusting novel of later Rome, *Veranilda* (1904). *The Private Papers of Henry Ryecroft* (1903), a fictitious author's journal, represents his aspirations rather than his experience. Gissing brought an academic rather than simply an imaginative approach to the novel of contemporary reality. See John Halperin, *Gissing: a Life in Books*, new edn 1987 (biography); John Sloane, *George Gissing: the Cultural Challenge*, 1989 (critical study); Robert L. Selig, *George Gissing*, rev. edn 1995 (critical study).

GLASGOW, ELLEN (1874–1945) American novelist, was born in Richmond, Virginia, where she lived all her life. The ninth of ten children of a manufacturer of Scottish–Irish Calvinist descent and of a Virginia aristocrat, she attended local private schools and read in her father's library. At 16 she began to lose her hearing, an affliction which increased her instinctive desire for privacy. Though she travelled extensively in Europe, and several times visited England, where she met on friendly terms HARDY (who was an early influence on her writing), BENNETT, and GALSWORTHY, her novels are rooted in the South, whose history and manners she explored from several angles. *The Descendant* (1897), partly set in New York, which she did not know, was published anonymously. Her third, *The Voice of the People* (1900), began a range of novels whose background effectively represents a social history of Virginia from before the Civil War to the 1914–18 war. In *Virginia* (1913) and *Life and Gabriella* (1916), whose target is Southern aristocratic womanhood, the analysis becomes more ironic. The lower-middle-class protagonist of *Barren Ground* (1925) triumphs over rural hardships and private despair through fortitude. There followed the three 'Queenborough' comedies of manners, *The Romantic Comedians* (1926), *They Stooped to Folly* (1929), and *The Sheltered Life* (1932). Her last two novels, *Vein of Iron* (1935) and *In This Our Life* (1941), which won the Pulitzer Prize, are darker portraits of modern life. If there was a Southern literary renaissance, it began with her. *A Certain Measure: an Interpretation of Prose Fiction* (1943) comprises the prefaces she wrote for a collected edition of her novels. In her posthumously-published autobiography, *The Woman Within* (1954), she refers to her love for Gerald B——, who died in 1905 but who has not been identified, and to her tormented engagement in 1917–19 to Harold S—— (Henry W. Anderson, a prominent lawyer, who ran unsuccessfully for the governorship of Virginia). See Julius Rowan Raper, *From the Sunken Garden: the Fiction of Ellen Glasgow*, 1980.

GLASPELL, SUSAN (1876–1948) American dramatist, novelist, and short-story writer, was born in Davenport, Iowa, where her father's family had settled from England in 1835; her mother's parents were Irish. She was educated at local public schools and at Drake University, which she entered in 1897 when she was, according to the records, 21. After working as a reporter on the Des Moines *Daily News* for two years, during which she graduated to writing her own pseudonymous column, she returned to Davenport to write full time to earn a living. She began with local-colour, small-town short stories largely aimed at readers of women's magazines—*Lifted Masks* (1912) contained seven original stories and six published between 1903 and 1909. *The Glory of the Conquered* (1909) and *The Visionary* (1911) are novels of romantic idealism, but her third, *Fidelity* (1915), about a woman who runs away with a married man, reflected her own situation. In 1913 she married George Cram Cook

(1873–1924), novelist, dramatist, and actor, after he had had to wait for a divorce from his second wife. With him she wrote in 1914 her first one-act play, *Suppressed Desires*, which was performed in 1915 by the Provincetown Players, a group they founded particularly to enable American dramatists to participate in the production of their works—see also O'NEILL. In 1916–17 the group transferred to Greenwich Village, New York, and performed in the Playwrights' Theatre, where Glaspell's first full-length play, *Bernice* (1917), a blend of American realism and European expressionism, was produced in 1919. So too were *Inheritors* (1921), primarily an exploration of the American situation after World War I, and *The Verge* (1921), an innovative study of a monstrous woman in search of self-fulfilment.

When in 1922 the success of the amateur company was, under Cook's direction, such that it seemed to him to be defeating its own ends, he retired with his wife to Greece, where until his death in Delphi he worked to re-establish the ancient classical culture—Glaspell's *The Road to the Temple* (1927) is a biography of him. Travelling in Europe, she met Norman Matson, whom she married in 1925 (divorced 1931); together they wrote *The Comic Artist*, first produced in London in 1928. *Alison's House* (1930), her last play, won the Pulitzer Prize for its portrayal of the conflict between the artist and the real world, recaptured 18 years after the death of a thinly-disguised EMILY DICKINSON. Latterly she lived in Cape Cod and returned to fiction, of which the Midwest regional novels *The Morning Is Near Us* (1939) and *Judd Rankin's Daughter* (1945) are regarded as the most notable. See *Plays*, ed. C. W. E. Bigsby, 1987; Arthur E. Waterman, *Susan Glaspell*, 1966 (biographical/critical study); Linda Ben-Zvi (ed.), *Susan Glaspell: Essays on Her Theater and Fiction*, 1995.

GLASSCO, JOHN (1909–81) Canadian poet and novelist, was born in Montreal and educated at Bishop's College School, Lennoxville, Lower Canada College, Montreal, and McGill University, which he left in 1928 without a degree to make an alternative life in Paris. His lively account of his three years there, which were terminated by his having to return home with tuberculosis, was published much later as *Memoirs of Montparnasse* (1970; ed. Michael Gnarowski, 2nd edn 1996); it includes classic character sketches of CALLAGHAN, HEMINGWAY, JOYCE, GEORGE MOORE, and STEIN, among others. During this time his surrealist poem, 'Conan's Fig', was printed in *transition*. In 1935, after a major lung operation, he settled in Foster, Quebec, of which he was Mayor from 1952 to 1954, and where in 1951 he founded the Foster Horse Show. His poetry, the first collection of which was *The Deficit Made Flesh* (1958), embraces rural elegiac, literary, and philosophical modes. *Selected Poems* (1971) won the Governor General's Award. His fiction, of which he was inordinately proud and which he wrote under various names, is by his own admission 'pure pornography'. It includes *The English Governess* (1960; under his own name as *Harriet Marwood, Governess*, 1976), *Fetish Girl* (1972), and his completion of the unfinished novel by Aubrey Beardsley (1872–98), *Under the Hill* (1959).

GLOVER, DENIS (1912–80) New Zealand poet, typographer, and publisher, was born in Dunedin and educated at Auckland Grammar School, Christ's College, and Canterbury University College, of whose English department he was a member from 1936 to 1938 and from 1946 to 1948. In 1936 he founded the Caxton Press, Christchurch, to print and publish fine books, among which were some of his earlier volumes of verse, including *Six Easy Ways of Dodging Debt Collectors* (1936). During World War II he served as an officer in the Royal Navy, winning the Distinguished Service Cross. In 1947, in response to the initiative of BRASCH, he undertook the publication of the literary journal, *Landfall*, which is still published by Caxton. Subsequently he taught typography. He was from the start a satirical as well as a fine lyrical poet, with an appreciation of the landscape ('Holiday Piece') and even of some modern developments ('The Road Builders'), and a wry tone ('The Magpies'). After the war he developed the device of a persona, most successfully in *Sings Harry and Other Poems* (1951), less so in *Arawata Bill: a Sequence of Poems* (1953), through whom he evokes traditional themes. *Diary to a Woman* (1971), incorporating *To a Particular Woman* (1970), expressing romantic love between older people, gave his oeuvre an unexpected extra dimension. See *Selected Poems*, 1980; *Hot Water Sailor 1912–1962 and Landlubber Ho! 1963–1980*, 1981 (autobiography).

GODDEN, RUMER (*b.* 1907) British novelist and children's writer, was born in Eastbourne, Sussex, the daughter of an agent for India's Inland Navigation, and spent her childhood in India—see (with Jan Godden) *Two Under the Indian Sun* (1966). She was educated at home by a maiden aunt and then in England at Moira House, Eastbourne, after which she used a small legacy to train as a dancing teacher. She returned to India, where she opened a dancing school in Calcutta in 1929, and married in 1934. After publishing a fanciful novel and a poignant Indian romance, she drafted, on board ship between Bombay and Tilbury, *Black Narcissus* (1939), the enormously successful story of nuns in a mission in the Himalayas. *Rungli-Rungliot (Thus Far and No Further)* (1943) is a recapitulation of the diary she kept on a tea estate

after the break-up of her marriage in 1941. India is the setting of a number of the novels she has written subsequently, from *Breakfast with the Nikolides* (1942) to the chaos that reigns in *Coromandel Sea Change* (1991). Another theme (following her conversion to Roman Catholicism) is the religious life, as in *In This House of Brede* (1969) and *Five for Sorrow, Ten for Joy* (1979). In addition to two distinguished novels *about* childhood, *An Episode of Sparrows* (1955) and *The Greengage Summer* (1958), she has written most effectively *for* children, who, through *The Dolls' House* (1947) and her other doll-based stories in particular, are able vicariously to experience the drama (and traumas) of adult life. Having returned to England after World War II, she remarried in 1949, and for a time lived in HENRY JAMES's house in Rye. She was made OBE in 1993. See *A Time to Dance, No Time to Weep*, new edn 1989, and *A House with Four Rooms*, new edn 1991 (autobiography).

GODWIN, WILLIAM (1756–1836) British philosopher and novelist, was born in Wisbech, Cambridgeshire, the son of a Presbyterian minister. He was educated for the ministry at Hoxton Academy, but finding that his views were at variance with the movement and even with a belief in God, he became a writer. *An Enquiry concerning Political Justice* (1793) was subversive in that it decried marriage as an institution, anarchic in its rejection of laws and government, and radical in its reconciliation of private interest with public good. *Things as They Are: or, The Adventures of Caleb Williams* (1794) is a novel of retribution. In 1796, having flirted with INCHBALD and been turned down by OPIE, he began an affair with WOLLSTONECRAFT. They were married by mutual consent when she became pregnant with MARY SHELLEY, after whose birth she died. He married Mary Jane Clairmont (*d.* 1841) in 1801, and established her in a small publishing business, which brought out the LAMBS' tales from Shakespeare, but collapsed in the recession of the 1820s. He wrote more novels; histories; lives of CHAUCER (1803) and of his first wife, *Memoirs of the Author of a Vindication of the Rights of Women* (1798); two tragedies; and further philosophical works, including *Essay on Sepulchres* (1809) and *Thoughts on Man, His Nature, Productions, and Discoveries* (1831). His chief claim to posterity is as the guru of the Romantic poets, especially COLERIDGE, SHELLEY, and WORDSWORTH. See Peter H. Marshall, *William Godwin*, 1984; William St Clair, *The Godwins and the Shelleys: the Biography of a Family*, new edn 1991.

GOETHE, JOHANN WOLFGANG (von) (1749–1832) German poet, dramatist, novelist, and critic, was born in Frankfurt-am-Main and educated by his father, a lawyer, until he went to Leipzig University to read law in 1765. He studied art on the side, had his first romance, and wrote some lyrics and two light plays, before having a severe haemorrhage in 1768 and returning home. Two years later he was able to continue his studies in Strasbourg, where under the influence of the critic Johann Gottfried Herder (1744–1803) he became interested in folk song and ballad. He also began his lifelong admiration of SHAKESPEARE, the first manifestation of which was a historical drama, *Götz von Berlichingen mit der eisernen Hand* (1773), which in an enthusiastic if not entirely accurate translation as *Goetz of Berlichingen with the Iron Hand* (1799) was the first book to carry the name of WALTER SCOTT. The inspiration for *Die Leiden des jungen Werthers* (1774; tr. Richard Graves as *The Sorrows of Werter*, 1779), an epistolary novel of melodramatic melancholy which gave the name of Wertherism to a state of morbid sentimentalism and sparked off several suicides, was his own thwarted love for Lotte Buff, the fiancée of a close friend. Now the national literary trendsetter, and already at work on early versions of his *Faust*, he was in 1775 invited by the 18-year-old Carl August, ruler of the Duchy of Saxe-Weimar-Eisenach, to join his court. He was appointed a member of the administration, with responsibilities for finance, agriculture, and mines. He also entered into an intense relationship with Charlotte von Stein (1742–1827), the intellectual wife of the Master of Horse and the 'Lida' of his poems. In 1782 he was made Acting President of the Chamber, and granted a patent of nobility. In 1786 he took leave of absence in Italy for two years. He returned refreshed by his encounter with classical antiquities; obtained permission to be relieved of all but cultural duties (he was made director of the state theatre) and those appertaining to scientific study and development; and met and set up house with Christiana Vulpius (*d.* 1816), a maker of artificial flowers—they married in 1806, having had several children, of whom only one, August (1789–1830), survived infancy.

A new-found sensuality, as well as his cultural self-discovery, inform the poems in *Romische Elegien* (1788; tr. Michael Hamburger as *Roman Elegies*, 1996), and classical themes and structures were now reflected in his plays. In the late 1770s he had begun a novel about a young man and the stage; a manuscript was discovered in 1909 and published as *Wilhelm Meisters Theatralische Sendung* (ed. Harry Maync, 1911; tr. Gregory A. Page as *Wilhelm Meister's Theatrical Mission*, 1913; tr. John R. Russell as *Wilhelm Meister's Theatrical Calling*, 1995). He later used it as the basis of about half of *Wilhelm Meisters Lehrjahre* (1795), which, with its sequel, the prototype of the *Bildungsroman*, were translated as *Wilhelm Meister's Apprenticeship* (1824) and *Wilhelm Meister's Travels* (in Ger-

man Romance, 1827) by CARLYLE, who refers to Goethe in 'The Hero as Man of Letters' (1840) as 'for the last hundred years, by far the notablest of all Literary Men', and commends him in *Sartor Resartus* for his 'inspired melody'. (Goethe wrote a testimonial in support of Carlyle's application for the chair of Moral Philosophy at St Andrews in 1828: it arrived late, and he did not get the job.)

In 1794 Goethe began a friendship, which amounted also to a literary partnership, with SCHILLER, with whose encouragement he resumed work on and completed the first part of his great poetic drama, *Faust* (1808; tr. A. Hayward, 1833 (prose); tr. John Anster, 1835 (verse); tr. F. D. Luke, 1987). BYRON, who had heard extracts translated in 1816, dedicated *Sardanapalus* (1821) to 'the illustrious Goethe . . . the first of existing writers who has created the literature of his own country'. P. B. SHELLEY translated Scenes I and II into elegant verse, appending a literal translation of what he calls the 'astonishing' opening chorus, of which 'it is impossible to represent in another language the melody of the versification'. The second (more symbolic and less dramatic) part was finished in 1831 and published posthumously (tr. David Luke, 1994). See also *Faust 1 and 2*, ed. and tr. Stuart Atkins (1994); tr. Christa Weisman and Howard Brenton (1995); tr. Louis MacNeice (1951, abridged). The first study of Goethe in any language based on primary sources was G. H. Lewes, *The Life and Works of Goethe* (1855), for which GEORGE ELIOT translated prose passages. See *The Collected Works*, ed. Victor Lange, Eric A. Blackall, and Cyrus Hamlin, tr. Michael Hamburger and others, 12 vols new edns 1994–95; *Selected Poems*, ed. Christopher Middleton, 1983 (bilingual edition); Nicholas Boyle, *Goethe: the Poet and the Age, Vol. I The Poetry of Desire 1749–1790*, new edn 1992 (biography).

GOGARTY, OLIVER ST JOHN (1878–1957) Irish poet, dramatist, politician, and surgeon, was born in Dublin and educated at Stonyhurst College and Clongowes Wood, Kildare, and at the Royal University and Trinity College, Dublin, where he read medicine and won the Vice-Chancellor's prize for poetry three times. In 1904 he spent two terms at Oxford, hoping to win the Newdigate Prize (he came second), after which he rented the Martello tower which appears, with a portrait of himself, in JOYCE's *Ulysses*. Sport also affected his studies (he played professional soccer and was a champion cyclist), but he qualified in 1907, and specialized in ear-nose-and-throat surgery, which he practised in Dublin. A play of slum life, *Blight, the Tragedy of Dublin* (1917), under the pseudonym of Alpha and Omega, was followed by two more at the Abbey Theatre. *The Ship and Other Poems* appeared in 1918. The title of his next collection, *An Offering of Swans* (1923), refers to his vow, while swimming to freedom from a gang of Republican gunmen during the Civil War (1922–23), to present two birds to the River Liffey. He was a member of the first Irish Senate, but the burning-down of his house in Galway and an attempt on his life led to a year in London. A successful libel action against his reminiscent *As I Was Going Down Sackville Street* (1937) was one reason for his leaving Ireland for the USA. Its successors, *Follow St Patrick* (1938) and *Tumbling in the Hay* (1939), are more readable and amusing than the novels he subsequently published. His wit, in and out of the Senate, is legendary, and he wrote some excellent lyrics and an expressive range of poems on classical and topographical themes. See *Collected Poems*, 1951; J. B. Lyons, *Oliver St John Gogarty: a Biography*, 1980.

GOGOL, NIKOLAI (VASILIEVICH) (1809–52) Russian dramatist and novelist, was born in Sorochintsy, Ukraine, the son of a landowner, and left school in 1828 to go to St Petersburg. After two years as a civil service clerk (14th grade), he got a job teaching history at an institute for young ladies. After publishing two volumes of stories, [*Evenings on a Farm near Dikanka*] (1831–32), in which he made imaginative use of Ukrainian folklore, he was in 1834, at the instigation of literary friends, appointed a lecturer in world history at St Petersburg University. Neither his knowledge nor his technique proved up to the task, but when he resigned after 16 months he had in the meantime become established as a writer of fiction and had written two plays. *Mirgorod* (1835) comprised four Ukrainian tales, each parodying a different literary genre: [*Arabesques*] included the earlier of his notable stories set in a nightmarish St Petersburg—see *The Diary of a Madman and Other Stories*, tr. Ronald Wilks (1972). His first play, [*Marriage*], not produced until 1842, is an out-and-out domestic farce. [*The Government Inspector*] (1836) contained farcical elements which were overemphasized in the production, though it was probably these which appealed most to Tsar Nicholas I, who commanded his family and ministers to see it. Mortified by what he regarded as misinterpretation of his aims, Gogol left the country. Though he published in 1842 a revised version of this splendidly constructed satire on provincial life and government, it did not replace the existing one until 1888—see *The Government Inspector*, tr. Edward O. Marsh and Jeremy Brooks (1968).
He returned to Russia only twice during the next six years. The second time was in 1842, when he published [*Dead Souls*] (tr. George Reavey, 1971; tr. Bernard Guilbert Guerney, rev. edn ed. Susanne Fusso, 1996), a tale with hilarious elements (which has become an international classic) involving the purchase of deceased serfs who are still on government records and thus subject to tax; it was intended as the first part of a projected three-volume picaresque satire. He then embarked on an even more unsettled period of travel, during which he made a pilgrimage to Jerusalem and conceived as his divine destiny the reformation of Russia through literature. In this evangelistic state he tried to transform his novel into a Utopian vision, which he never completed and ultimately destroyed. He returned to Russia in 1848 and died in Moscow of self-imposed starvation and inadequate medical treatment, a religious fanatic whose mind had become unhinged. See *Plays and Petersburg Tales*, tr. Christopher English, introduction by Richard Peace, 1996.

GOLDING, (Sir) WILLIAM (1911–93) British novelist, was born in St Columb Minor, Cornwall, and educated at Marlborough Grammar School (at which his father taught science) and Brasenose College, Oxford. Before World War II, in which he served in the Royal Navy and commanded a rocket ship, he was an actor and stage producer, and for a year a teacher. He also published a book of verse, *Poems* (1934). His first novel, *Lord of the Flies* (1954)—the title is the meaning of the Hebrew term for Beelzebub—illustrates how internal and external pressures can cause a society to disintegrate, exemplified in this case by a group of marooned children. Though some of his novels may at first sight appear to reflect different treatments of similar themes—*The Inheritors* (1955) investigates the destruction of a primitive culture, and *Pincher Martin* (1956) is also set on a desert island, while *Free Fall* (1960) and *The Pyramid* (1967) both recall a young man's experiences on the road towards maturity—in effect each has a fresh starting point and develops along distinctive lines. His leitmotifs are broadly creation, temptation, destruction, and preservation, all of which are present in *The Spire* (1964). His distinguished maritime trilogy, *Rites of Passage* (1980), which won the Booker prize for fiction, *Close Quarters* (1987), and *Fire Down Below* (1989), uses a sea voyage to Australia in Napoleonic times as the medium through which emotions and drama are fomented. It was reissued in one volume as *To the Ends of the Earth: a Sea Trilogy* (1992), in an introduction to which he confessed that only after finishing the first book did he think of adding more. *The Double Tongue* (1995) is a posthumously-published second draft of the fictional memoirs of a 1st-century BC priestess of Delphi. He published two volumes of essays, *The Hot Gates* (1965) and *A Moving Target* (1982). He was made CBE in 1966, awarded the Nobel Prize for Literature in 1983, and knighted in 1988. See James Gindin, *William Golding*, 1988 (critical study); Kevin McCarron, *William Golding*, 1994 (critical introduction).

GOLDONI, CARLO (1707–93) Italian dramatist, was born in Venice and educated at schools in Perugia and Rimini. He went on to the ecclesiastical college at Paria, from which he was expelled in his first year for writing a satirical drama about the college. He managed to pass his law examinations when he was 25, but debts and lack of business forced him into the role of provider of scenarios for a travelling *commedia dell'arte* company. In 1736, seeing a pretty girl, Nicoletta Conio, on a balcony in Genoa, he invited her father to the theatre and arranged to marry her—he developed smallpox on their wedding night but 'luckily . . . I did not become uglier than I was before'. He practised law for seven years in Venice, writing scenarios in his spare time, and then moved to Pisa. In 1747 he was approached by the Pantaloon of the Medebac company to return to Venice as full-time comic dramatist, on the strength of the successful performance of a play of his in which the dialogue was written, not improvised. During the next 15 years he wrote about two hundred plays and transformed the *commedia dell'arte* into an Italian theatre in which masks and the stock characters were things of the past; the play which finally did the trick was *I Due Gemelli Veneziani* [*The Venetian Twins*] (1748), in which the former Pantaloon played both twins. Other realistic comedies of this period include *La Vedova Scaltra* [*The Artful Widow*] (1748), *La Locandiera* [tr. as *The Mistress of the Inn*, also as *Mirandolina*] (1753), and *La Casa Nova* [*The Superior Residence*] (1760). *Il Servitore di Due Padrone* [*The Servant of Two Masters*] (1745) has proved especially popular with British and American audiences, and has been adapted and given an antipodean flavour by the Australian dramatists Ron Blair (*b.* 1942) and Nick Enright (*b.* 1950).

In 1762 the attacks of jealous rivals and critics finally drove Goldoni into exile in Paris, where from writing plays for the King's company of Italian players he graduated to comedies in French, including *Le Bourru Bienfaisant* [*The Beneficent Bear*] (1771). Virtually blind from 1765, he was for a time tutor at Versailles to the French princesses. When the Bastille fell to the mob in 1789 his royal pension was suspended. Nineteen days after the execution of Louis XVI it was restored by the National Convention, which did not know that Goldoni had died a few hours earlier. An annuity was paid to his widow and a performance of *Le Bourru Bienfaisant* laid on for the benefit of his family at the newly named Théâtre de la Nation. See *Four Comedies*, tr. Frederick Davies, 1968.

GOLDSMITH, OLIVER (1728–74) Irish dramatist, novelist, poet, and journalist, was born in Pallasmore, Co. Longford, the fifth child of a curate who became Rector of Kilkenny West. He suffered an attack of smallpox in childhood which permanently disfigured him. His father having overstretched himself in the matter of a dowry for an elder daughter, Goldsmith went to Trinity College, Dublin, as a sizar. After failing to settle to anything but riotous living, he was paid for by members of his family to read medicine at Edinburgh University, which he abandoned after two years to wander through Europe on foot. He arrived in London in 1756, penniless but claiming to have acquired a medical degree on his travels. He became a journalist and in 1759 published anonymously *An Enquiry into the Present State of Polite Learning in Europe*, while writing for several journals including his own, *The Bee*, which folded after eight issues. A series of observations of the London scene in the *Public Ledger*, written as though by a Chinese and bearing the unmistakable Irish stamp of polite irony towards the English, were collected as *The Citizen of the World* (1762). He had now become a member of the circle of JOHNSON, who encouraged him to finish his philosophical poem, *The Traveller: or a Prospect of Society* (1765), the first work to carry his name, and found a publisher for *The Vicar of Wakefield: a Tale* (1766). This gentle, human story of multiple misfortunes with a mercifully happy conclusion has in the course of it the poems 'When lovely woman stoops to folly' and 'An Elegy on the Death of a Mad Dog', with its famous closing line, 'The dog it was that died'. His major long poem, *The Deserted Village* (1770), reflects in flowing couplets nostalgia for the homeliness and innocence of rural life.

In the meantime he had turned to the stage, about which he had often expressed his views in print. *The Good Natur'd Man: a Comedy* (1768) is amusing enough but structurally uneven. The extended joke upon which the action of *She Stoops to Conquer: or, The Mistakes of a Night* (1773) is founded is timeless, and the absurdity of many of the resulting situations goes unnoticed in a continuous flow of economically-presented comic set pieces and exchanges between likeable characters. Overgenerous and improvident, Goldsmith spent or gave away his earnings as he received them, and at the height of his fame was forced to indulge in hackwork, albeit in his natural literary style. He produced histories of Rome (1769; abridged by himself 'for the use of schools' 1772), England (1771), and Greece (1774), as well as *An History of the Earth and Animated Nature* in eight volumes (1774). It is said that his death from a fever was hastened by overwork, debts, and his insistence on doctoring himself, and that BURKE burst into tears when he heard the news, and Sir Joshua Reynolds (1723–92) laid down his brush and painted no more that day. See *Collected Works*, ed. Arthur Friedman, 5 vols 1966; *Poems and Plays*, ed. Tom Davis, new edn 1993; Andrew Swarbrick (ed.), *The Art of Oliver Goldsmith*, 1984.

GONCHAROV, IVAN (ALEKSAN-DROVICH) (1812–91) Russian novelist, was born in Simbirsk, the son of a grain merchant who died when he was seven. His education was taken on by a family friend, who sent him to boarding school and then, at ten, to Moscow Commercial School, after which he studied philology at Moscow University. After a few months as secretary to the Governor of the province of Simbirsk, he went in 1834 to St Petersburg, where he remained a civil servant for over thirty years. In 1844 he began his first novel, [A Common Story] (1847; tr. Constance Garnett, 1894), a study of the conflict between decayed landed aristocracy and emerging bourgeoisie. In 1849 he published in a journal ['Oblomov's Dream'], a crucial section of his major novel, which he now set aside. In 1852–55 he was on a voyage round the world in the frigate Pallas, as secretary to the admiral commanding the expedition. After his return to St Petersburg via Siberia, he published an account which includes observations on London and on aspects of British life. He was appointed a literary censor in 1856. Oblomov (tr. C. J. Hogarth, 1915; tr. David Magarshack, 1954) was finished in 1857 and finally published in a St Petersburg periodical in 1859. This study of an indolent romantic has universal psychological intimations that transcend a setting which was soon to disappear. He resigned from the civil service in 1867, published a third novel, [The Precipice] (1869), and subsequently lived out his life in his flat in St Petersburg, a recluse who suffered from delusions.

GONCOURT, EDMOND DE (1822–96) and **JULES DE** (1830–70) French novelists, dramatists, and prose writers, were born respectively in Nancy and Paris, where Edmond went to Collège Henri IV and Jules to Collège Bourbon. The death of their mother left them financially secure, and after travelling with sketchbooks through Burgundy, Dauphiné, Provence, and Algeria, they settled in Paris in the Rue Saint-Georges, which was their home for the next twenty years. Hypochondriac, mistrustful of women, hardly ever away from each other for more than a few hours, they were driven by vanity to produce, in the course of an extraordinarily close literary collaboration, numerous plays and a whole range of books, including novels of the realistic school, art criticism, and social history. After the death of Jules from syphilis, contracted when he was 19, Edmond decided to give up writing the journal which they had kept since 2 December 1851. He resumed it as a tribute to his brother, intending that it should not be made public until 20 years after his own death. After revealing its existence to DAUDET, he was persuaded to publish it serially, the first volume in 1887. Witty, wicked (especially about the great and their

lovers), and colourfully descriptive, it is a revealing eye-witness record of events, people, and places, and a first-hand account of conversations with literary and other luminaries of the times. In his will, Edmond endowed the Académie Goncourt for the encouragement of young writers and an annual literary prize (Prix Goncourt). See Pages from the Goncourt Journal, ed. and tr. Robert Baldick, new edn 1988.

GONGORA (Y ARGOTE), LUIS DE (1561–1627) Spanish poet, was born in Cordoba, and left Salamanca University in 1580 having taken minor orders but without a degree. He was ordained deacon in 1585 and appointed prebendary of Cordoba Cathedral in succession to his uncle; he held the post until 1611, when he resigned in favour of his nephew and retired to his country home to write. His verse, in the form mainly of ballads and sonnets, had already caused contention for its poetics, his chief and most virulent opponents being VEGA and the prolific poet, novelist, and satirist, Francisco de Quevedo (1580–1645). The publication in 1613–14 of La Fábula de Polifemo y Galatea [The Fable of Polyphemus and Galatea], a retelling of a story from OVID's Metamorphoses, and of the first and (unfinished) second part of Las Soledas (tr. Edward M. Wilson as The Solitudes, rev. edn 1965), a metaphorical narrative poem in a bucolic setting, intensified the argument between culteranismo, or Gongorism (complex poetic thought and ornate language), and conceptismo (affected poetic language and intricate style). In 1617 he settled in Madrid, became a priest, and was made a chaplain of honour to Philip III. In the chaos following the accession of Philip IV in 1621, he attempted unsuccessfully to arrange for the publication of an edition of his poetry to pay his bills. In 1625 he was evicted from his home by the new owner, who was Quevedo, and had to sell his furniture to buy food. A complete edition of his works was published posthumously by his friend, Juan López de Vicuña, as Obras en Verso del Homero Español [The Poetical Works of the Spanish Homer] (1627), and was promptly banned by the Inquisition. See Selected Shorter Poems, tr. Michael Smith, 1995 (bilingual edn).

GORDIMER, NADINE (b. 1923) South African novelist and short-story writer, was born in Springs, Transvaal, the daughter of a Jewish watchmaker who had emigrated from Lithuania at 13, and who later saved up to bring out nine sisters, one by one. A hyperactive child who wanted to be a dancer, she was found at ten to have a rapid heartbeat. Her mother removed her from the local convent school and forbade all exercise. She went to a private tutor until she was 16, having spent the intervening years in the company of adults, and having had a short story published in *Forum*, a current affairs magazine. Unable to do a degree course for lack of educational qualifications, at 21 she took general studies for a year at Witwatersrand University. 'This was the first time in my life I'd mixed with blacks, and was more or less the beginning of my political awareness.' *Face to Face: Short Stories* was published in South Africa in 1949; *The Soft Voice of the Serpent and Other Stories* appeared in the USA in 1952 (in UK 1953), following the publication of a story by her in the *New Yorker*.

In an interview with ALAN ROSS (*London Magazine*, May 1965) she stated: 'I have no religion, no political dogma—only plenty of doubts about everything except my conviction that the colour-bar is wrong and utterly indefensible.' And in a *Paris Review* interview in 1979—in *Writers at Work: Sixth Series* (1985): 'The real influence . . . on my writing is the influence of politics on people. . . . I am dealing with people; here are people who are shaped and changed by politics.' Underlying her work, in which she has faithfully reflected shifts and alterations in the system, is the belief in a collective conscience to bring about change.

The end of the journey of Helen, in *The Lying Days* (1953), from youth to a confused maturity, hedged by family conventional moralities and the moral dilemma of the society around her, is escape to Europe. *A World of Strangers* (1958) begins with the arrival of a Briton in Johannesburg, and explores his romance with an upper-class white woman and his relationship with Steve, a charming African. For the depiction of a friendship across the colour line, the paperback edition was banned. So was *The Late Bourgeois World* (1966), in which the former wife of a liberal activist gets drawn into revolutionary activism, and which, Gordimer has explained, 'came up with conclusions that did not fit in with the official view of events'. In *A Guest of Honour* (1970) an Englishman's love affair with the new African state he had served in colonial days, and with the white woman he meets, are the main strands of a novel which examines the European political role in Africa. *Burger's Daughter* (1979), for reproducing a student document distributed during the 1976 riots in Soweto, was banned in South Africa shortly after its publication in the UK and USA; it was then unbanned in the light of the critical attention it attracted abroad see Gordimer and others, *What Happened to Burger's Daughter: or, How South African Censorship Works* (1980). It was also, as she publicly revealed 15 years later, an extrapolation of the experiences of a family she knew, a 'coded homage paid to a [revolutionary hero], an anti-apartheid activist, who had died serving a life sentence, his ashes withheld from his daughters by the prison authorities of the day', whose accuracy was confirmed by one of the daughters. The

Conservationist (1974), which won the Booker prize for fiction, offers a psychological, and *July's People* (1981) an economic interpretation of the end of white rule in South Africa; the central female character of *A Sport of Nature* (1987) is the means through which a united Africa is envisaged. *My Son's Story* (1990) returns to contemporary Johannesburg, and deals with the specific predicament of a coloured family in which the father is a political activist. *None to Accompany Me* (1994) is a study of two activist families, one white, one black, and of the uneasy post-apartheid period leading up to free elections.

Selected Stories (1975) draws from five previous collections, in which she brings to bear the special art of the short-story writer on themes reflecting her basic belief—see also *Jump and Other Stories* (1991). *Writing and Being* (Charles Eliot Norton Lectures, 1995) includes statements about her own position as a committed novelist in solidarity with suffering blacks, and essays on ACHEBE and MAHFOUZ. She married in 1954, as her second husband, Reinhold Cassirer. She was awarded the Nobel Prize for Literature in 1991. See Judie Newman, *Nadine Gordimer*, 1988 (critical study); Stephen Clingman, *The Novels of Nadine Gordimer: History from the Inside*, 1992; Dominic Head, *Nadine Gordimer*, 1994 (critical study).

GORDON, ADAM LINDSAY (1833–70) Australian poet, was born in the Azores, the son of a former officer in the Bengal Cavalry and of the daughter of the Governor of Berbice, British Guiana. He was educated at Cheltenham College and the Royal Military Academy, Woolwich, which he left possibly because of poor eyesight. An escapade connected with a racehorse caused his departure in 1853 for South Australia, where he was for two years in the ranks of the Mounted Police. He then drifted, doing some horse breaking, unable to raise the money to return home. By the time his mother's legacy arrived in 1864, he was married to a Scottish immigrant and had settled in the Mount Gambier district. When a local printer wanted to reproduce the engravings by the Scottish painter, (Sir) Joseph Noël Paton (1821–1901), for the Border ballad, 'The Dowie Dens of Yarrow', but could not lay hands on a copy of the verses, Gordon supplied six ballads of his own, based on the story, which were published as *The Feud* (1864). He sat for a year in the South Australian Parliament. When his investments failed, he rode in steeplechases, winning the Adelaide Grand National in 1865. *Sea Spray and Smoke Drift* (1867) comprised horsey poems in ballad metre, originally written for journals, and some more thoughtful pieces, including the 'Ye Wearie Wayfarer' sequence. In 1867 he moved to Ballarat, where he invested in a livery stable. It collapsed, and he returned to the racing saddle, suffering several accidents. In June 1870 he learned that his claim to the property of the Gordons of Esslemont, Aberdeenshire, was invalid in Scottish law. A few days later, with copies of his next collection ready for release, but having no money to pay the printer's bill, he shot himself. *Bush Ballads and Galloping Rhymes* (1870) is the work of an accomplished balladist whose name flourished for some fifty years and whose bust has stood in Poet's Corner, Westminster Abbey, since 1934. His significance as a genuine Australian poet rests now on only a few poems, notably 'A Dedication', 'The Sick Stockrider', 'The Song of the Surf', 'The Swimmer', and 'The Wreck'. See Geoffrey Hutton, *Adam Lindsay Gordon: the Man and the Myth*, 1978; Brian Elliot, *Adam Lindsay Gordon*, 1973 (critical study with examples); Geoffrey Hutton, *Adam Lindsay Gordon*, 1996 (critical study).

GORDON, CAROLINE see TATE, ALLEN.

GORE, CATHERINE (1799–1861), née Moody, British novelist and dramatist, was born in East Retford, Nottinghamshire, the daughter of a wine merchant, and was regarded as a literary prodigy in her youth. In 1823 she was married in a fashionable London church to an army captain, who retired from the service that same year. After two books of verse, she published several novels, but it was with *Women as They Are: or, The Manners of the Day* (1830) that she joined the newly popularized 'silver-fork' school, which aimed to portray fashionable life realistically. *Pin-Money* (1831), the outcome of which turns on the arrangements whereby a wife pays her own bills, was, she claims, an attempt 'to transfer the familiar narrative of Miss Austen to a higher society' and was 'addressed by a woman to readers of her own sex'. The family lived in France for some years from 1832, but she kept up her prolific output, to the extent that *Cecil: or, The Adventures of a Coxcomb* (1841), regarded as her best novel, was published anonymously in case she was thought to be overwriting, and because *Greville: or, A Season in Paris* (1841) appeared the same week. *The Banker's Wife: or, Court and City* (1843), featuring a corrupt financier, was sadly prophetic, as in 1855 the bank of which her guardian was a partner crashed, and she lost £20,000. Her first play, *The School for Coquettes*, ran successfully in 1831. Her last, *Quid pro Quo: or, The Day of the Dupes* (1844), won a prize of £500 for an original English comedy. Latterly she lost her sight and lived in seclusion, having written some sixty novels and 12 plays. She died in Hampshire, survived by only two of her ten children.

GORKY, MAXIM, pen name of Alexei Maximovich Peshkov (1868–1936) Russian novelist, dramatist, and social and political agitator, was born in Nizhny Novgorod (now

Gorky). After the death of his father, a carpenter, from cholera in 1871, he lived with his mother in his grandparents' home. When she too died, he was at the age of 11, after just a year's elementary education, sent out to work. After brief spells with a bootmaker and a draughtsman, he ran away to the river boats. He returned for a time, and then roamed the country on foot, absorbing the prevailing atmosphere of suffering, barbarity, stoical patience, and jocularity, and, after an attempt at suicide, finally came to terms with himself. His experiences and observations, fired by his voracious reading, resurfaced in literary forms: as stories, many of which first appeared in the Nizhny Novgorod newspaper for which he worked for a time; as plays, of which the second, [*The Lower Depths*] (1902), was successfully performed at the Moscow Art Theatre; and as novels, including *Foma Gordeyev* (1899), in which the protagonist of the title rejects the bourgeois society of his birth. Such works appeared in English even before his revolutionary activities resulted in his arrest in 1905 and his subsequent release as the result of a petition by politicians and writers. He travelled to the USA, where he had a mixed reception, attacked the prevalence of capitalism, and wrote [*Mother*] (1906; tr. 1907; in Britain tr. as *Comrades*, 1907), a novel of social realism which came to typify the doctrine of Socialist Realism. He went on to Capri, and after the general amnesty in 1913 returned to Russia, where he engaged in political and literary journalism until ill-health forced him into semi-retirement in Italy in 1921. He returned again in 1928, to play an enigmatic part in the development of literature under Communism and of Communism itself. He is said to have been poisoned by political adversaries. His most lasting work in English is his three-volume autobiography (1913–22; tr. Ronald Wilks as *My Childhood*, 1966, *My Apprenticeship*, 1974, and *My Universities*, 1979). See Henri Troyat, *Gorky*, tr. Lowell Bair, 1994 (biography).

GOSSE, (Sir) EDMUND (1849–1928) British critic, was born in Hackney, London, the only child of Philip Gosse (1810–88), the fundamentalist writer on zoology. After his mother's death in 1857, he went with his father to Devon, where he was educated at local schools. The conflict between the generations inflicted by his restricted upbringing is explored in *Father and Son: a Study of Two Temperaments* (1907). He became a library assistant in the British Museum in 1865, and responded to his new intellectual freedom by studying languages as well as literature, and by engineering meetings with notable writers. He was also writing verse, of an accomplished but unoriginal kind—see *The Collected Poems* (1911). In 1871 he returned from a Norwegian trip with a copy of a new play by IBSEN, a study of which (with the aid of a dictionary) led to a number of articles which brought the dramatist to the notice of British critics and the public. In 1875 he became a translator to the Board of Trade. After the publication of *Seventeenth Century Studies* (1883) he embarked on an extensive range of critical and biographical studies of THOMAS GRAY (1884), CONGREVE (1888), PATMORE (1905), THOMAS BROWNE (1905), and SWINBURNE (1917), among others, of which *The Life and Letters of Dr John Donne* (1899) was a particularly significant development in criticism. After an American lecture tour in 1855 he became Clark Lecturer in English Literature at Trinity College, Cambridge, where he repeated his American lectures and published them as *From Shakespeare to Pope* (1885), the accuracy of which was, quite correctly, questioned in the critical press. He was Librarian to the House of Lords 1904–14, and in 1918 began a regular column in the *Sunday Times*. He was knighted in 1925, and was awarded public honours also by Norway, Sweden, Denmark, and France for his services to literature. See Ann Thwaite, *Edmund Gosse: a Literary Landscape*, new edn 1985 (biography).

GOTTFRIED VON STRASSBURG (*fl. c.*1200) German poet, the author of *Tristan*, was probably a member of the urban upper class and may have served in the local town or episcopal secretariat. He was certainly educated in theology, rhetoric, and law, and was well versed in classical as well as French and German literature. His unfinished narrative poem in rhyming couplets is the ultimate account of the love story of Tristan and Isolde, which resurfaces in MALORY, and an exploration of philosophical, social, and religious issues of the time, as well as an intricately wrought work of poetry. His principal source was the Anglo-Norman Tristan poem (*c.*1170) of Thomas of Britain, of which the discovery of a further fragment was announced in 1995. See *Tristan, with the Surviving Fragments of the 'Tristan' of Thomas*, tr. A. T. Hatto, 1960.

GOWER, JOHN (*c.* 1330–1408) English poet, was of a landed family and probably spent much of his early life in Kent, where he later invested in real estate. He was closely associated with the royal court, but from 1377 until his death lived in lodgings in the Priory of St Mary Overey in Southwark. He was a friend of CHAUCER (who saddled him with the title 'moral Gower'), but latterly they appear to have fallen out. *Mirour de l'omme* [Mirror of Man]—its Latin title is *Speculum Meditantis*—is a long exhortation about sin, written in the late 1370s in Anglo-French, the upper-class and court language of the time. He then began *Vox Clamantis* [The Voice of One Crying . . .], a critique of corruption at all levels of society, including the clergy,

written in Latin elegiacs, to which he added an introductory book citing the Peasants' Revolt of 1381 as justification of his arguments. In *Confessio Amantis* [The Lover's Confession], written between 1386 and 1390 in English octosyllabic couplets, he takes a more relaxed tone. Too much moralizing, he says, often dulls a man's wits, so 'I wolde go the middel weie / And wryte a bok between the tweie, / Somwhat of lust, somewhat of love . . .'. The 'love' involves analysing each of the Seven Deadly Sins in five ways, while the 'lust' (or pleasure) is in the wry dialogue between the lover and his confessor, and in the stories which the poet retells from many sources. See J. H. Fisher, *John Gower: Moral Philosopher and Friend of Chaucer*, 1964; and in C. S. Lewis, *The Allegory of Love*, new edn 1977.

GRAFTON, RICHARD see HOLINSHED.

GRAHAM, ENNIS see MOLESWORTH.

GRAHAM, JAMES see MONTROSE.

GRAHAM, R(OBERT) B(ONTINE) CUNNINGHAME (1852–1936) Scottish prose writer and traveller, was born in London, of the ancient lines of the Cunninghams, earls of Glencairn, and the Grahams, earls of Menteith. His grandfather was the songwriter Robert Graham (*c.*1735–97), and his father was a Scottish landowner, to whose estates he succeeded in 1883. After two years at Harrow and a year at a private school in Brussels, he made the first of several trips to South America, where he rode with gauchos and was known as 'Don Roberto', the name given in his honour after his death to a new city in Argentina. He was Liberal MP for North-West Lanarkshire 1886–92; in 1888 he founded with Keir Hardie (1856–1915) the Scottish Labour Party, of which he was the first President. *Mogreb-el-Acksa: a Journey in Morocco* (1898) is an account of a hazardous expedition, and he also wrote Latin-American historical and biographical studies. His first collection of stories and sketches was *The Ipané* (1899). Further volumes, notably *Success* (1902), in which the much-anthologized 'Beattock for Moffat' first appeared, *Faith* (1909), *Hope* (1910), and *Charity* (1912), reflected the breadth of his travels and the depth of his insight into the human condition, as well as his understanding of the Scottish character. He was a founder member and in 1928 the first President of the Scottish National Party, which with his literary talent and associations qualify him to be an instigator of the Scottish Renaissance. He married the Chilean poet, Gabriela de la Balmondière (*d.* 1906) and is buried beside her in the ruins of Inchmahome Priory in the Lake of Menteith. See Cedric Watts and Lawrence Davies,

Cunninghame Graham: a Critical Biography, 1979.

GRAHAM, W(ILLIAM) S(YDNEY)

(1918–86) Scottish poet, was born in Greenock and educated at Greenock High School, which he left early to train as an engineer. Thereafter, apart from a year at Newbattle Abbey College, he spent most of his life in Cornwall. A Scottish poet writing in English, whose early work, first published in *Cage Without Grievance* (1942), was good enough to be compared in some respects to, and thus suffer from any affinities with, that of HOP-KINS, JOYCE, and DYLAN THOMAS, he developed, through his preoccupation with the poem as a one-way medium of communication, a clarity of language and intensity of voice which are consistently musical. These qualities were readily apparent in *The White Threshold* (1949) and *The Nightfishing* (1955). His main themes are the sea in all its aspects and moods, his childhood (as 'Loch Thom' and 'To Alexander Graham'), the process of making poetry itself (as 'What Is Language Using Us For?'), and love, both youthful and mature (as 'Alice Where Art Thou' and 'I Leave This at Your Ear'). See *Collected Poems 1942–1977,* 1979; *Uncollected Poems,* 1990; *Selected Poems,* 1996; Tony Lopez, *The Poetry of W. S. Graham,* 1990.

GRAHAME, KENNETH (1859–1932)

British essayist and children's novelist, was born in Edinburgh of a family with an ancient Scottish heritage, the son of a barrister. When his mother died of scarlet fever in 1863, his father, unable to cope with four children, packed them off to live with their grandmother at Cookham Dean, Berkshire, and then Cranbourne. He was educated at St Edward's School, Oxford, but instead of going on to Oxford University, relatives insisted he became a clerk in the Bank of England. (To compensate for his disappointment, on his death he left the residue of his estate, including all his royalties, to the Bodleian Library, which still uses the income to buy rare books and manuscripts, and to finance its own publications.) He remained at the Bank of England until his retirement from ill-health in 1908, having become Secretary in 1898, and survived a lethal bout of pneumonia in 1899 and a shot from a madman's gun in 1903. His literary aspirations were encouraged by HEN-LEY, who first published his essays and sketches. *Pagan Papers* (1894) reprinted some of these and was well received. *The Golden Age* (1895) and *Dream Days* (1898), in which is the hilarious fairy tale 'The Reluctant Dragon', are collections of stories and impressions of childhood, largely based on idyllic recollections of Cookham and Cranbourne. They were much admired by a readership as widely spread as SWINBURNE and Theodore Roosevelt (1858–1919).

In 1899, hitherto a confirmed bachelor, Grahame married; a son, Alastair, was born the following year. *The Wind in the Willows* (1908), inspired by the river and wood by Cookham Dean, to which they had moved, was written for Alastair. By contrast with the earlier books, the protagonists are animals, but they are so precisely, sympathetically, and consistently drawn, without any loss of their essential animal characteristics, that the story can be enjoyed at several levels. Certainly Roosevelt, now President of the USA, thought so, and wrote to Grahame from the White House to tell him this. Whether 'Toad, the motor-car snatcher, the prison-breaker, the Toad who always escapes' was specifically created to make his over-bumptious son aware of his fault, or whether he is an imaginative extension of the outwardly quiet, respectable public servant, the incorrigible Toad ends the book only moderately deflated. Alastair died on a railway line while an undergraduate at Oxford. His parents moved to Pangbourne, where they lived in seclusion, from which they emerged to see MILNE's stage adaptation of the book, *Toad of Toad Hall,* in 1929. See Peter Green, *Kenneth Grahame: a Study of His Life, Work and Times,* 1959; Alison Prince, *Kenneth Grahame: an Innocent in the Wild Wood,* new edn 1996 (biography).

GRANT, ANN (of Laggan) (1755–1838),

née MacVicar, Scottish prose writer, was born in Glasgow, the daughter of a farmer who joined the Army and was posted to North America. In 1773 he was appointed barrack-master at Fort Augustus, Inverness-shire, where in 1779 Ann married the garrison chaplain, who was Minister of the parish of Laggan nearby. He died suddenly in 1801, leaving her with eight children to support. *Poems on Various Subjects* (1803) elicited three thousand subscribers. *Letters from the Mountains* (1803), a selection from her correspondence of some thirty years, was influential in that it provided authentic backing and detail to complement the romantic image of the Highlands which MACPHERSON had instigated and WALTER SCOTT would shortly offer. In 1810 she moved to Edinburgh, where she took in lodgers, mixed with the literary set, and wrote *Essays on the Superstitions of the Highlands of Scotland* (1811). In 1825 Scott was instrumental in getting her a pension, half of which was then assigned to someone else. Mrs Grant, 'proud as a Highland-woman, vain as a poetess, and absurd as a bluestocking', objected to the division, but was prevailed upon to 'take her pudding', as Scott recalls. She was a lively critic of contemporary literature as well as of manners. In an unpublished letter to a friend in 1812, she comments: 'These Lake Poets who "worship under every green tree", and burn incense on the high places of Skiddaw worship nature in an idolatrous and most unnatural manner. . . . I have been told that Southey who now goes to Church, used formerly to go near the top of Skiddaw in summertime and there skip and dance about under the idea that then the Deity is honoured and gives as a reason that the inferior animals in this manner express their joy.'

GRANVILLE-BARKER, HARLEY see
IBSEN; SHAW, GEORGE BERNARD.

GRASS, GÜNTER (b. 1927) German novelist, poet, and dramatist, was born in Danzig (now Gdansk, Poland), the son of a grocer, and was still at the local gymnasium when he served as an anti-aircraft gunner in World War II. Conscripted into the army, he was wounded during the Russian advance and ended the war in an American prisoner-of-war camp. After a brief apprenticeship to a stone carver, he took sculpture and painting at Dusseldorf Art Academy, resuming his studies in Berlin after two years of travel in France and Italy—his work was exhibited in Stuttgart and Berlin in 1956–57. A poem submitted by his wife to a broadcasting competition in 1955 won third prize and led to a modest collection of verse and prose (1956). From poetry based on dialogue to writing drama was a natural transition. Between 1954 and 1957 he composed several plays in the tradition of the Theatre of the Absurd—see Four Plays, tr. Ralph Manheim, introduction by Martin Esslin, 1967. A similar view of the contemporary world as having no meaning, purpose, or coordinating principles informs the sequence of picaresque novels which begins in Langfuhr (Danzig) three years before he was born—Die Blechtrommel (1959; as The Tin Drum, 1962), Katz und Maus (1961; as Cat and Mouse, 1963), and Hundejahre (1963; as Dog Years, 1965), all tr. Manheim. A committed socialist, he campaigned vigorously during the 1960s for the Social Democratic Party, for whose leader, Willy Brandt (1913–92), he wrote speeches. In Der Butt (1977; tr. Manheim as The Flounder, 1978) he extended the canvas of the Danzig trilogy to make the whole of German history the background to his imaginative comment. Der Unkenrufe (1992; tr. Manheim as The Call of the Toad, 1992) begins a few days before the crumbling of the Berlin Wall in 1989, and presents, against a documentary background of topical events, a symbolic study of the failings of modern political entrepreneurship which are mirrored in the story of a middle-age romance. His verse is in Selected Poems, tr. Michael Hamburger and Christopher Middleton (1980).

GRAVES, ROBERT (VON RANKE)
(1895–1985) British poet, novelist, translator, classicist, critic, and unorthodox mythologist and biblical scholar, was born in Wimbledon,

London. His father, Alfred Perceval Graves (1846–1931), was an Anglo-Irish poet and songwriter; on his mother's side he was a great-nephew of Leopold von Ranke (1795–1886), the German historian. He was educated at Charterhouse, enlisted in the Royal Welch Fusiliers at the outbreak of World War I, and was badly wounded on the Somme. After the war he went up to St John's College, Oxford, and though illness prevented his taking his degree, he was awarded that of BLitt for his thesis, Poetic Unreason and Other Studies (1925). In Goodbye to All That (1929), one of the best of all autobiographical studies, he records his life at school, at the front, and as a struggling writer—his father's To Return to All That (1930) is in part an autobiographical reply. His other most seminal prose work is The White Goddess: a Historical Grammar of Poetic Myth (1948; rev. edn 1966), a treatment of mythology in which he ascribes the poet's impulse to an ancient matriarchal presence, who recurs figuratively as the opponent of Christ in his novel King Jesus (1946). The impetus for his mythological thinking came from W. H. R. Rivers (1864–1922), author of Medicine, Magic, and Religion (1924), who was the psychologist who treated SASSOON for his wartime breakdown. Graves's I, Claudius (1934) and Claudius the God and His Wife Messalina (1934) rank as the best historical novels of the Roman period—their timely appearance as a television drama series in 1975 saved the author from financial embarrassment.

Graves largely rejected the poetry of his experiences in the war and immediately after it, to come to stand pre-eminent as a poet of romantic and sexual love, whose skilfully honed work has an underlying tension, often heightened by supernatural elements. Among his criticism is On Poetry: Collected Talks and Essays (1969). He separated from his first wife in 1929 (they were divorced in 1949), and maintained a ménage in Majorca with the American poet, Laura Riding (1901–91), after she had thrown herself out of the window of their 4th-floor London flat in pique at being rejected by another man. The relationship proved creatively beneficial to them both, and lasted until she left him in 1939 for an American critic. Of her, Graves said: 'She is like a great natural fact like fire or trees or snow and either one appreciates her or one doesn't'—see Deborah Baker, In Extremis: the Life of Laura Riding (1993). He then went to live with Beryl Pritchard (they married in 1950). They returned after World War II to settle permanently in Majorca, where Beryl was expected to welcome the sequence of regenerative young muses who attended to his psychological and creative well-being. He was Professor of Poetry at Oxford 1961–66. See Complete Poems Vol. 1, ed. Beryl Graves and Dunstan Ward, 1995; The Centenary Selected Poems, ed. Patrick Quinn, 1995;

Complete Short Stories, ed. Lucia Graves, 1996; *Collected Writings on Poetry*, ed. Paul O'Prey, 1995; Richard Perceval Graves, *Robert Graves: Vol. 1 The Assault Heroic 1895–1926*, new edn 1995, *Vol. 2 The Years with Laura 1926–1940*, new edn 1995, *Vol. 3 And the White Goddess 1940–1985*, new edn 1996; Miranda Seymour, *Robert Graves: Life on the Edge*, new edn 1997 (biography); Martin Seymour-Smith, *Robert Graves: His Life and Work*, 2nd edn 1995.

GRAY, ALASDAIR (*b.* 1934) Scottish novelist, was born in Glasgow, the son of 'a working-class bloke, a journeyman blacksmith. He was a Fabian-style socialist who read the complete works of Lenin, and also the complete works of Shaw, which I came to like.' He was educated at Whitehill Senior Secondary School, where he was encouraged to write, and at Glasgow School of Art, from which he won a travelling scholarship. He taught art for three years, and then became a scene painter, before going freelance in 1963. His murals decorate Glasgow restaurants, and in 1976–77 he was the official painter of local dignitaries for the People's Palace Museum. At the same time he was writing plays for the local stage, and for radio and television, while continuing to work on a novel which he had begun when he was 18. *Lanark: a Life in Four Books* was finally published in 1981. This strange intermingling of fantasy and naturalism, high and low comedy, and literary jokes is at the very least an outstanding original work. It also reflects the traditional Scottish literary dichotomy of concern for and also intolerance at so much of what the Scots stand for. In *1982, Janine* (1984) and *Something Leather* (1990) the inventiveness is more bizarre, though the latter introduces the admirable tactic of representing phonetically not the dialect of Glasgow, as would be the usual practice, but the standard speech of its English characters. *Poor Things: Episodes from the Early Life of Archibald McCandless MD, Scottish Public Health Officer* (1992), lavishly illustrated by the author, manages to be literary pastiche, sexual satire, Glasgow social history, and feminist parable. In *A History Maker* (1994) the fantastic is set against a background of 23rd-century Scotland in which war has become a stylized television sport. See Robert Crawford and Thom Nairn (eds), *The Arts of Alasdair Gray*, 1991.

GRAY, THOMAS (1716–71) British poet, was born in London, the son of a bad-tempered scrivener, and educated, thanks to his mother, at Eton and Peterhouse, Cambridge, though he did not take his degree in law until some years later, having in the meantime travelled in Europe with his schoolfriend, HORACE WALPOLE. He preferred to study rather than practise law and for most of his life lived in Cambridge, being appointed Professor of Modern History in 1768, though he

never gave a lecture. He removed his lodgings from Peterhouse to Pembroke Hall in 1756 after undergraduates had placed a tub of water under his window and raised the fire alarm. Gray, who had a pathological fear of fire, shinned down his personal rope ladder, and into the tub! Reserved and shy, he emphatically refused the Poet Laureateship in 1757, and his output reflects his contemplative and fastidious nature. *Ode on a Distant Prospect of Eton College* was published anonymously in 1747. He worked on *An Elegy Wrote in a Country Churchyard* (1751) for nine years and it too was first published anonymously, as a pamphlet, after the poet had refused permission for it to be printed in a magazine. Its outstanding place in 18th-century poetry has been magnified by its down-to-earth appeal, and its lasting popularity ensured by the familiar quotations enshrined in it. *Poems by Mr Gray* (1768) included these and the mock-heroic 'Ode, on the Death of a Favourite Cat', with seven poems which illustrate his absorption with Greek, Celtic, and Norse studies. See Roger Lonsdale (ed.), *The Poems of Thomas Gray, William Collins, Oliver Goldsmith*, new edn 1976; and in David Cecil, *Two Quiet Lives*, new edn 1989 (with DOROTHY OSBORNE).

GREEN, HENRY, pseudonym of Henry Vincent Yorke (1905–73) British novelist, was born at Forthampton Court, Gloucestershire. While he was at Eton he began a novel, *Blindness* (1926), which apart from its maturity as an original piece of work was unusual for a first novel in that its theme has no autobiographical basis. He did not complete his time at Magdalen College, Oxford, being persuaded by his parents to enter the family engineering firm in Birmingham, H. Pontifex and Sons—he used his apprenticeship on the shop floor in *Living* (1929). In his next novel, *Party Going* (1939), his style became more idiosyncratic and symbolic. During World War II he served in the London Fire Service, using his experiences in *Caught* (1943). By 1950, the year in which *Nothing*, his eighth novel, was published, he had become acclaimed in the USA as well as by critics in Britain as an experimental, comic novelist, but in dispensing largely with narrative and comment, as well as with definite and indefinite articles, he had also become increasingly abstract. *Doting* (1952) was his last work. In 1959 he resigned from managing the affairs of the firm, which he had done from its London office, and deteriorated into a pathetic, reclusive physical state, in which he spent his last twenty years. A man whose reticence and conventional appearance belied the adventurousness of his writing, he always refused to be photographed in public except from behind. See *Pack My Bag: a Self-Portrait*, new edn 1994 (autobiography to 1939); *Surviving: the Uncollected Writings*, ed. Matthew Yorke, new edn

1994; Rod Mengham, *The Idiom of the Time: the Writings of Henry Green*, 1983.

GREENE, GRAHAM (1904–91) British novelist, short-story writer, dramatist, and critic, was born in Berkhamsted, Hertfordshire, and educated at Berkhamsted School (of which his father became Headmaster in 1910) and Balliol College, Oxford. While he was at school he wrote poetry, stories (one of which was published in the *Star*), and a play, which was accepted by a dramatic society but never performed. Verses written at Oxford, by his own account mainly inspired by love for his sisters' governess, were published in various journals, in the *Oxford Outlook*, which he edited, and in book form as *Babbling April* (1925). When he became engaged to a Catholic, he decided to discover more about her beliefs and as a result was himself converted in 1926, the year before they married. After working unpaid for the *Nottingham Journal*, he joined *The Times* as a subeditor in 1926, which he regards as having been a formative experience for a novelist. After many false starts and the rejection of a detective story, he got the idea for a new novel while in hospital recovering from an appendectomy. He finished it and it was accepted. *The Man Within* (1929) is a historical romance with Gothic features, whose pursuit theme recurs in different forms in all his subsequent novels, whether the character is trying to run away from society, the police, his own conscience, or God. Emboldened by its success, he persuaded the publisher to advance him money against two further novels, and he threw up his job. He relates, 'I sometimes find myself wishing that, before starting my second novel . . . I had found an experienced mentor.' The two novels, in much the same vein as his first, were financial failures and he later suppressed them. In debt and in distress, having wasted time by writing a biography of ROCHESTER which his publisher rejected (it was finally published in 1974), he started a thriller. *Stamboul Train* (1932) was published only after changes were made to the printed copies under the threat of a libel action from PRIESTLEY, whom he had never met. It was a popular success, and his reputation, and way of living, were established.

In his early autobiography, *A Sort of Life* (1971), Greene writes: 'If I were to choose an epigraph for all the novels I have written, it would be from [ROBERT BROWNING'S] "Bishop Blougram's Apology": "Our interest's in the dangerous edge of things. / The honest thief, the tender murderer. . . . / We watch while these in equilibirium keep / The giddy line midway".' He was himself no stranger to personal danger, as witness *Journey Without Maps* (1936), an account of a trip through Liberia. The inveterate traveller in him (a reflection also of his solitary nature) is revealed in the foreign and often exotic settings of many of his novels: Mexico for *The Power and the Glory* (1940); Sierra Leone (where he was a secret agent for the Foreign Office in World War II) for *The Heart of the Matter* (1948); Vietnam for *The Quiet American* (1955); Cuba for *Our Man in Havana* (1958); a leper colony in the Congo for *A Burnt-Out Case* (1961); Haiti for *The Comedians* (1966); Argentina for *The Honorary Consul* (1973). The priest who is the subject of his engaging clerical comedy set along the byways of Spain, *Monsignor Quixote* (1982), bears a close resemblance to Greene's friend and confessor, Father Leopoldo Duran, author of a flattering memoir, *Graham Greene: Friend and Brother* (tr. Euan Cameron, 1994). Also significant is the journalistic instinct which enabled him to select situations of topical interest, a sense further affirmed by his controversial pamphlet, *J'Accuse: the Dark Side of Nice* (1982). Violence, suspense, or mere unease are always below the surface of his English novels, too, such as *England Made Me* (1935), *A Gun for Sale* (1936), and *The End of the Affair* (1951). The Catholic element in his novels, which was first evident in *Brighton Rock* (1938) and is a central concern in *The Heart of the Matter*, serves as a natural concomitant to the action rather than as an expression of a particular message. His spiritual convictions and personal loyalties are more manifest in the paradoxes of his private life and in his public image (latterly he advocated a reconciliation of Catholicism with Communism).

In the introduction to *Collected Stories* (1972) Greene relates his surprise at realizing 'that since the beginning I have really been all the time a writer of short stories', and these examples of a different approach to that which he employed as a novelist include some of his rare, and late, excursions into humour in what he calls 'comedies of the sexual life'. Of his plays, *The Living Room* (1953) treats of despair in Catholic terms, *The Potting Shed* (1957) is a drama with a spiritual solution, and *The Complaisant Lover* (1959), outwardly a comedy, has melancholic undertones—see *The Collected Plays of Graham Greene* (1985). *Reflections*, ed. Judith Adamson (1990), a collection of his journalism, includes studies of authors. Articles he wrote for the *Spectator* and elsewhere are in *Mornings in the Dark: the Graham Greene Film Reader*, ed. David Parkinson (1993); and public correspondence in *Yours etc: Letters to the Press 1945–1989*, ed. Christopher Hawtree (1991)—see also *Collected Essays* (1969). *A World of My Own: a Dream Diary*, edited by Yvonne Cloeta, the last and most faithful of his several mistresses, is an intriguing collection of accounts of his dreams. He was made CH in 1966 and awarded the OM in 1986. See *Fragments of Autobiography: A Sort of Life, Ways of Escape*, 1991; *Reflections 1923–1988*, 1990; Norman Sherry, *The Life of Graham Greene: Volume One, 1904–39*, new edn 1996, *Volume Two,*

1939–1955, new edn 1996; Michael Shelden, *Graham Greene: the Enemy Within*, 1995 (biography); Grahame Smith. *The Achievement of Graham Greene*, 1985; Paul O'Prey, *A Reader's Guide to Graham Greene*, new edn 1990; Peter Mudford, *Graham Greene*, 1996 (critical introduction).

GREENE, ROBERT (1558–92) English dramatist, prose fiction writer, and journalist, was born in Norwich and educated at St John's College, Cambridge, as a sizar, taking a second degree, in medicine, at Clare Hall in 1583, and being awarded a further degree at Oxford in 1588. NASHE wrote, 'Debt and deadly sinne, who is not subject to? with any notorious crime I never knew him tainted . . . his only care was to have a spel in his purse to conjure up a good cuppe of wine with at all times.' Greene wrote fast, and often carelessly, for the money. His precise position in time makes him an innovator once he had survived his Euphuistic phase, which began with *Mamillia* (1580), a romance in the style of LYLY; popular successes were *Pandosto, the Triumph of Time* (1588) and *Ciceronis Amor* (1589), also known as *Tully's Love*. In 1591 he published the first of his topical pamphlets, written in the forthright idiom of the day, about the growing menace of the petty criminal, *A Notable Discovery of Cozenage*. It was shortly followed by *The Second Part of Cony-catching* and *Third and last Part . . .* , by *A Disputation between a Hee Conycatcher and a Shee Conycatcher*, by *Quippe for an Upstart Courtier*, and by *The Blacke Bookes Messenger*. For these he employed a variety of forms: didactic fiction, debate by practitioners, fictional biography, and allegory, interspersed with in all about thirty-five individual tales or anecdotes.

Greene's Groats-worth of Witte Bought with a Million of Repentance (1592), a pointedly autobiographical prodigal son story, much of it written during his final illness, towards the end breaks into the warning to his literary contemporaries in which appears the first reference to SHAKESPEARE as a dramatist. His known contribution to the stage is a handful of comedies, of which the most notable are *The Honorable Historie of frier Bacon and frier Bongay* (printed 1594) and *The Scottish Historie of James the Fourth* (1598). In both of these, history, romance, and the supernatural are cleverly combined and presented with realism and humour in blank verse which is at times most felicitous. His lyrical poems, most of them inserted into his prose works, have a graceful and distinctive charm. Greene died in poverty a month after dining rather too enthusiastically on Rhenish wine and pickled herring, having begged his estranged wife by letter to give £10 to the shoemaker who had taken him in. See John Clark Jordan, *Robert Greene*, new edn 1965 (critical study).

GREER, GERMAINE (*b.* 1939) Australian critic, was born in Melbourne and educated at the Star of the Sea Convent and the universities of Melbourne, Sydney, and Cambridge. She lectured in English at Warwick University from 1967 to 1972. She became an international personality with the American publication in 1971 of *The Female Eunuch* (1970), an outspoken and rational analysis of female sexual stereotypes which became for many a textbook on the liberation of women. She subsequently divided her time between England and southern Tuscany, with an interlude in the USA (1979–82) as Founder-Director of the Tulsa Centre for the Study of Women's Literature. Subsequent predominantly feminist studies are *The Obstacle Race* (1979), about women and painting; *Sex and Destiny: the Politics of Human Fertility* (1984); *The Change* (1991), which argues for an acceptance of the enriching and liberating effect of the menopause; and *Slip Shod Sibyls: Recognition, Rejection and the Woman Poet* (1995), a study of the attitudes of and towards women poets which incorporates some original views on heterosexual love in Elizabethan poetry. Other works include *The Madwoman's Underclothes: Essays and Occasional Writing 1968–1985* (1986) and *Daddy, We Hardly Knew You* (1989), an investigation into the identity and fate of her father.

GREGORY, (ISABELLA AUGUSTA), LADY (1852–1932), née Persse, Irish dramatist, prose writer, and translator, was born in Roxborough, Co. Galway, and was privately educated. In 1880 she married Sir William Gregory (1817–92), of neighbouring Coole Park, former Governor of Ceylon, who encouraged her literary career, which opened with a series of political pamphlets. Another influence was BLUNT, with whom she was to have a passionate romance. She collected Galway folklore, which in due course she used as the basis of several books, beginning with *A Book of Saints and Wonders* (1906). She learned Irish, which enabled her to produce three significant works of Irish literature, *Cuchulain of Muirthemne* (1902), *Gods and Fighting Men* (1904), and *The Kiltartan Poetry Book: Translations from the Irish* (1919). Kiltartan was a neighbouring village, and she based the diction of her translations on the English of its inhabitants—she even did *The Kiltartan Molière* (1910).

A meeting with YEATS in 1894 began a lifelong friendship and a close working relationship. It also led to the creation of the Irish Literary Theatre and then of the Irish National Dramatic Society, and to the foundation in 1904 of the Abbey Theatre, of which she was a working director until her death. At the age of 50 she became an adept writer of one-act comedies, tragicomedies based on folklore, and tragedies, of which the most memorable is *Dervorgilla* (1907). She made

Coole Park a meeting place for Irish people of letters, discovered and encouraged the genius of O'CASEY, defended the work of SYNGE and other forward-looking writers, and fought for political and cultural causes in which she believed. One of her most tenacious campaigns was to try to secure for Ireland the collection of French Impressionist paintings which her nephew, the collector Sir Hugh Lane (1875–1915), had left to the nation by means of a codicil to his will transferring them from the National Gallery in London. The codicil was unwitnessed, he was drowned when the *Lusitania* was torpedoed, and the pictures remained where they were. See *Selected Writings*, ed. Lucy MacDiarmid and Maureen Waters, 1995; *Lady Gregory's Diaries 1892–1902*, ed. James Pethica, 1996; *The Coole Edition of Lady Gregory's Writings*, ed. Colin Smythe and T. R. Henn, 1970–82, which includes (Vol. XIII) the posthumous *Seventy Years*, 1974 (autobiography); Mary-Lou Kohfeldt, *Lady Gregory: the Woman Behind the Irish Renaissance*, 1985.

GREVILLE, (Sir) **FULKE** (1554–1625) English poet and prose writer, was born at the family seat of Beauchamp Court, Warwickshire, and was educated at Shrewsbury School, which he joined on the same day as SIDNEY, and at Jesus College, Cambridge. In 1577 he and Sidney, now firm friends with shared literary tastes, appeared at court, where Greville, as did everyone else, fell in and out of favour, but was occasionally allowed to go abroad. He sat as Member of Parliament for Warwickshire and towards the end of Elizabeth I's reign became Treasurer of the Navy, a post he retained on the accession of James I (VI of Scotland) in 1603, when he was knighted. In 1614, now elderly in terms of the times, he was appointed Chancellor of the Treasury, being made 1st Lord Brooke on his retirement in 1621. The only work published during his lifetime, and that without permission, was *Mustapha* (1609), a dark closet drama with some powerful lines. 'Caelica', a sequence of lyrics, appeared in 1633 in an edition of his early works, in which, and in *Remains* (1670), the most interesting poems are a series of treatises on philosophical subjects such as 'Monarchy' and 'Religion'. His most famous work is his study of Sidney, written after 1610 and published in 1652. It is not so much a biography as an appreciation, incorporating his considered views on the political and intellectual climate of the Elizabethan age and on Elizabeth herself. A servant, who had been passed over in his will, stabbed him to death, according to AUBREY while doing him up after he had been to the lavatory, and then killed himself. He composed his own epitaph for his tomb: 'Fulke Greville, servant to Queen Elizabeth, councillor to King James, and friend to Sir Philip Sidney.' See *The Prose Works of Fulke Greville, Lord Brooke*, ed. John Gouws, 1986.

GREY, ZANE (1872–1939) American novelist, was born Pearl Zane Gray in Zanesville, Ohio, and changed the spelling when he began to use his middle name in place of his first, because readers thought he was a woman. Destined for dentistry by his father, a doctor, he entered the University of Pennsylvania on a baseball scholarship and, after graduating in 1896, set up in dental practice in New York City. Having had *Betty Zane* (1904), a historical romance of the American War of Independence, rejected by numerous publishers, he borrowed money from a patient and published it himself. After two sequels had appeared commercially, he undertook a fact-finding exploration of the West under the guidance of the legendary C. J. 'Buffalo' Jones (1844–1918). *The Heritage of the Desert* (1910) was a major success, and established his recurrent motif of the West as a character builder. *Riders of the Purple Sage* (1912), in which he criticizes Mormonism and extols the perfection of love between man and woman, was the first to have a mountain background. The sixty westerns that he published during his lifetime have settings as wide apart as Texas, Arizona, Wyoming, and Washington. The income from them enabled him to extend his boyhood passion for angling to big-game fishing in the South Pacific; he wrote numerous fishing articles and stories, collected into such works as *Tales of Fishing Virgin Seas* (1919) and *Tales of Fresh-Water Fishing* (1928). See Carlton Jackson, *Zane Grey*, 1989 (biographical/critical study).

GRIEVE, CHRISTOPHER MURRAY see MACDIARMID.

GRIFFIN, GERALD (1803–40) Irish novelist, dramatist, and poet, was born in Limerick, the seventh son of a brewer, and was educated locally, having weathered a childish escapade in which his younger sister was shot through both thighs. In 1820 his parents emigrated to Pennsylvania and he went to live in Adare with an elder brother, a doctor. Having already written tragedies and verse, he went to London in 1823 to try and earn a living, in which he was encouraged and helped by JOHN BANIM. After supporting himself precariously by hackwork, he published *Holland-Tide: or, Munster Popular Tales* (1827) and *Tales of the Munster Festivals* (1827), which attempted to be 'illustrative of manners and scenery precisely as they stand in the South of Ireland'. A further series took the form of a complete novel, *The Collegians: or, The Colleen Bawn: a Tale of Garryowen* (1829), based on an actual murder. Written to satisfy his publisher's demand for speed (a messenger collected each day's stint after breakfast to take it to the printer), it is nevertheless a rich and successful embodiment of a whole spectrum of Irish provincial life in the 1770s, and the basis of BOUCICAULT's *The Colleen Bawn*. In *The Rivals* and *Tracy's Ambition*, two dramatic representations of conflicts and issues of the times, published together in 1830, a moralizing tone emerges. In the same year he contributed a series of tales 'illustrative of the five senses' to the *Christian Physiologist*. The only other works published during his lifetime were *Tales of My Neighbourhood* (1835) and two rather indigestible historical romances. He had already spent a term studying law as an alternative way of life. In 1838 he destroyed his manuscripts and joined the teaching order of the Christian Brothers in Dublin. He died of typhus at the monastery in Cork. Some of his unpublished work survived, of which *Gisippus*, a tragedy written in his teens, was produced in 1842. See John Cronin, *Gerald Griffin: a Critical Biography*, 1978.

GRIGSON, GEOFFREY (1905–85) British poet, critic, prose writer, and editor, was born in Cornwall, the youngest of the Vicar of Pelynt's seven sons, of whom three died in World War I and three in World War II. His unhappiness as a child (he was sent to boarding school when he was five) extended to his time at St Edmund Hall, Oxford, as he describes in *The Crest on the Silver: an Autobiography* (1950). Thereafter, things looked up. After working on the *Yorkshire Post*, he became Literary Editor of the *Morning Post*, and founded the influential poetry magazine, *New Verse*, which he edited from 1933 to 1939. He was also writing mainly short, often terse, poems of a marked visual and sometimes topical nature, some of which appeared in *Several Observations: Thirty-Five Poems* (1939). He worked for the BBC in the West Country during World War II, after which he settled in a Wiltshire farmhouse, where he wrote a wide range of critical studies on art as well as literature, and topographical works, and edited numerous anthologies and collections of individual poets. He was a sometimes abrasive but always readable critic, some of whose essays and reviews were collected in *The Contrary View: Glimpses of Fudge and Gold* (1974) and *Blessings, Kicks and Curses: a Critical Collection* (1982). His third wife, Jane Grigson (1928–90), was a notable writer on cookery, as also is their daughter, Sophie Grigson (*b.* 1959). See *The Collected Poems of Geoffrey Grigson 1924–1962*, 1963; *Collected Poems 1963–80*, 1982.

GRILE, DOD see BIERCE.

GRIMM, JACOB (1785–1863) and **WILHELM** (1786–1859) German philologists and folklorists, were born in Hanau, attended the public school in Kassel, and studied at Marburg University. Jacob's investigations into Teutonic languages, furthered while librarian to the King of Westphalia from 1807 to 1813 and then at Kassel, resulted in *Deutsche Grammatik* (1819–37), in the course of which he propounded Grimm's Law of phonetic change. The brothers forgathered at Gottingen University in 1830, but were dismissed and banished in 1837 for their part in the protest against the new King of Hanover's abrogation of the constitution. They resurfaced in Berlin in 1841, where they were appointed professors and elected to the Academy of Sciences. Their individual researches and academic literary endeavours were most formatively combined in *Kinder- und Hausmärchen* (1812–22), their collection of Germanic folk tales. It was first translated into English by Edgar Taylor (1793–1839) as *German Popular Stories* (1823–26), with engravings by George Cruikshank (1792–1878), illustrator of WALTER SCOTT and DICKENS. See Jack Zipes, *The Brothers Grimm: From Enchanted Forests to the Modern World*, new edn 1989 (critical study).

GROSSMAN, EDITH (1863–1931), née Searle, New Zealand novelist, was born in Australia in Beechworth, Victoria, and came with her parents to New Zealand in 1878. She was educated at Invercargill Grammar School, Christchurch Girls' High School, and Canterbury College, graduating as MA (one of the first women to do so) in 1885. She gave up being Headmistress of Wellington Girls' High School in 1890, when she married Professor Joseph Penfound Grossman, a teacher whose subsequent peculations make him a character as marked as any in his wife's fiction. *Angela: a Messenger* (1890), set in Wairarapa, is essentially a temperance tract. The terrors of drink recur in *In Revolt* (1893) and its sequel, *A Knight of the Holy Ghost* (1907), in which feminist ideals are brutally and ultimately tragically put to the test in an Australian setting. *The Heart of the Bush* (1910) is a significant colonial novel in that it is a genuine attempt, which largely succeeds, to face the issues of an identity divided between New Zealand and 'Home', and the adjustments which may be needed, on both sides, if a marriage is to succeed.

GROSSMITH, GEORGE (1847–1912) British entertainer, was born in London, the son of a police-court reporter for *The Times*, and was educated at North London Collegiate School for Boys. From 1866 to 1869 he assisted his father at Bow Street Court, after which his talent for composing and singing his own comic songs asserted itself. From 1877 to 1889 he was a lead singer with the D'Oyly Carte company in the GILBERT and Sullivan operas, creating the characters of Major General Stanley (*The Pirates of Penzance*), Bunthorne (*Patience*), and the Lord Chancellor (*Iolanthe*). Then, until 1906, he was occupied with his own 'recitals', which he took round Britain and Ireland, and to Canada and the USA. *The Diary of a Nobody* (1892), written with his brother Weedon (1854–1919), the actor, artist, and dramatist, was first serialized in *Punch*. A classic of understated social humour, it illustrates painlessly and with the deftest of characterization the class structure and inhibitions on which the Victorians subsisted. He wrote two volumes of memoirs, *A Society Clown: Reminiscences* (1884) and *Piano and I: Further Remembrances* (1910).

GROVE, FREDERICK PHILIP (1879–1948) Canadian novelist, was born Felix Paul Greve, the son of a tram driver, in Radomno, East Prussia, and attended the Gymnasium des Johanneums in Hamburg. He left Friedrich-Wilhelms University, Bonn, after two years, resuming his studies a year later at Maxmiliens University, Munich, which he left in 1902 without taking a degree. He published in German a book of poems and a verse drama (1902), and two studies of WILDE (1903), and embarked on a concentrated stint of translation into German of authors who included the BROWNINGS, MEREDITH, PATER, SWINBURNE, and WELLS. In 1902 he began an affair with Elsa Endell (1874–1927), née Ploetz, recently married to an architect. They married in 1904, the year in which she was divorced and he was released from prison after serving a sentence for fraud. In the course of a period of frenzied literary activity, he wrote two novels, of which *Fanny Essler* (1905; tr. Christine Helmers, A. W. Riley, and Douglas O. Spettigue, 1984) is a study of the restraints of society on the activities of a woman closely resembling Elsa. In 1909, in financial straits, he faked suicide and disappeared to North America, where he resurfaced in Manitoba in 1913 as a teacher called Fred Grove, and the following year married Catherine Wiens (1892–1972), also a teacher. (Elsa became Baroness Freytag-Loringhoven by her marriage in 1913 in New York, where she later achieved notoriety as a Dada poet and eccentric poseur, who decorated her cheeks with postage stamps and her breasts with metal tea balls.)

Grove became a Canadian citizen in 1920. *Over Prairie Trails* (1922) and *The Turn of the Year* (1923), his first books in English, are sketches evocative of his own experiences and observations. *Settlers of the Marsh* (1925), begun in German and rewritten in English, was the first of several novels in which the settlement of western Canada is the background to a study of personal conflicts and disillusionment. National lecture tours in 1928–29 brought him some public recognition. In 1929 he became President of Ariston Press, Ottawa, from which he resigned (in disillusionment) in 1931 and became a dairy farmer near Simcoe, Ontario; he used the lat-

ter experience as background in *Two Generations: a Story of Present-Day Ontario* (1939). *The Master of the Mill* (1944) is a saga of an Ontario industrial family; in *Consider Her Ways* (1947) he abandoned realism for allegorical satire, in which a colony of ants study human behaviour. *In Search of Myself* (1946), an elaborate construction of disguises presented as autobiography, was ironically given the Governor General's Award for non-fiction. See Douglas O. Spettigue, *Frederick Philip Grove*, 1969, and *FPG: the European Years*, 1973 (biography); W. J. Keith, *Frederick Philip Grove and His Works*, 1994.

GUNN, NEIL M(ILLER) (1891–1973) Scottish novelist, was born in Dunbeath, Caithness, the son of a fishing skipper, and was educated at the village school until he was 12. Then, because times were bad, he was sent to live with a married sister in Galloway. He prepared for entry into the civil service and in 1911 was appointed an officer in the Customs and Excise, being stationed in Argyll during World War I. After marrying and spending a year in Wigan, he became Excise Officer at the Glen Mhor distillery in Inverness. With the encouragement of MACDIARMID, he placed short stories—see *Hidden Doors* (1929)—and wrote *The Grey Coast* (1926) and *Morning Tide* (1931), in which he realistically depicts the break-up of Highland life. For his next book he persuaded his publisher to bring out *The Lost Glen* (1932), his angriest and bleakest assessment of the clash of cultures destroying his native land, which had been serialized in the *Scots Magazine* in 1929. Immediately after the publication of *Highland River* (1937), one of several novels in which he explores the maturing of a boy's mind, he resigned from the Customs to write full time. *The Silver Darlings* (1941), also concerned with growing up, is in addition an adventure story which spans two generations of changes to the fishing industry after the Highland Clearances. Latterly the exposition of his belief in the preservation of a continuity of life became more symbolic, as in *The Silver Bough* (1948), his images more violent, as in *Bloodhunt* (1952), and his vision more metaphysical, as in *The Other Landscape* (1954). He is a significant Scottish novelist in that he was the first to write about the Highlands from the inside, and he had considerable intellectual as well as descriptive and imaginative powers. See *The Atom of Delight*, new edn 1996 (autobiography); Margery McCulloch, *The Novels of Neil M. Gunn: a Critical Study*, 1987.

GUNN, THOM(SON) (b. 1929) British poet, was born in Gravesend, Kent, and educated at University College School, Trinity College, Cambridge, and Stanford University, California. A volume of his poems was published in 1953, and a second, *Fighting*

Terms, in 1954 (rev. edn 1958). He was a member of the English Department, University of California from 1958 to 1966, and was appointed Visiting Lecturer in 1975, having in the meantime become a full-time writer and settled in San Francisco. His early poetry is in conventional forms and often contains images from classical literature; whence comes the title of his collection, *Moly* (1971), the herb which Hermes supplied to Odysseus to protect him from being transformed by Circe into a pig. Gunn's translocation to America influenced not only the settings ('Metal Landscapes (and the Statue of Liberty)', 'Street Song', 'The Sand Man', and others) but also his poetic forms and themes, which became more free. These particular developments are illustrated by poems in *The Passages of Joy* (1982), in which homosexuality is frankly treated; there is also a nostalgic look at London ('Talbot Road'), and a neat, heterosexual story-poem, 'Adultery'. In an autobiographical fragment (1978), he stresses the continuities in his life 'between America and England, between free verse and metre, between vision and everyday consciousness'. AIDS is the theme of the final section of *The Man with Night Sweats* (1992), a collection which covers the ten years since his previous one, in terms especially of the scourge which in the meantime affected society and infected particular friends. See *Collected Poems*, new edn 1995; *The Occasions of Poetry: Essays in Criticism and Autobiography*, ed. Clive Wilmer, 1982; *Shelf Life: Essays, Memoirs and an Interview*, 1994.

GURNEY, IVOR (1890–1937) British poet and composer, was born in Gloucester and educated at King's School, Gloucester, after which he was articled to the cathedral organist as a pupil. In 1911 he won a scholarship to the Royal College of Music, where he began to set Elizabethan lyrics to music with masterly skill. He volunteered for war service in 1914, but was rejected because of his sight; in 1915 he was posted to the 2nd/5th Gloucester Regiment, with whom he trained and played in the band. He was in Flanders from May 1916 to September 1917, when he was gassed and returned to Britain. Throughout this time he sent poetry and music to a friend in England, and 46 of his poems were pub-

lished as *Severn and Somme* (1917). He was back in hospital in February 1918 with a stomach complaint, after which he began to show suicidal tendencies. He was discharged from the army and spent the next four years in a state of restlessness, unable to settle in any place or job (he tried cinema pianist, tax clerk, farm worker, and cold-storage operator), often sleeping rough or walking through the night. In 1922 he was committed to a local asylum and then moved to the City of London Mental Hospital, Dartford, where he spent the rest of his life, though between 1922 and 1926 he produced over a thousand manuscripts of poetry and music. A third volume of verse had been turned down in 1919, but song-cycles of HOUSMAN poems were published in 1923 and 1926, and *Lights Out*, settings of poems of EDWARD THOMAS, also in 1926. His war poems are distinctive for their detailed images, and these and his later works abound with reflections on his native Gloucestershire. See *Selected Poems*, ed. P. J. Kavanagh, 1990; *Collected Letters*, ed. R. K. R. Thornton, 1990; Michael Hurd, *The Ordeal of Ivor Gurney*, 1978 (biography).

GUSTAFSON, RALPH (*b.* 1909) Canadian poet, was born in Lime Ridge, Quebec. He took degrees at Bishop's University, Lennoxville, and at Oxford. From 1934 to 1938 he lived in England, where his first book of poetry, *The Golden Chalice* (1935), and a verse play, *Alfred the Great* (1937), were published. He then settled in New York, where he worked for the British Information Services from 1942 to 1946, and published *Flight into Darkness: Poems* (1944), in which he presented reflections on the enormities of war in a style which had now become more in keeping with modernist poetic techniques. Postwar journeying in Canada gave him the inspiration for *Rocky Mountain Poems* (1960) and *Rivers Among Rocks* (1960), and subsequent travels in Europe that for *Sift in an Hourglass* (1966) and *Ixion's Wheel* (1969). His interest in music, of which he became a critic for the Canadian Broadcasting Corporation in 1960, is also reflected in his poetry. *The Vivid Air: Collected Stories* was published in 1980. See *The Moment is All: Selected Poems 1944–1983*, 1983; Dermot McCarthy, *A Poetics of Place: the Poetry of Ralph Gustafson*, 1991.

H

HAFIZ, pen name ['one who can recite the Koran by heart'] of Shams ud-Din Muhammad (*c.*1325–89) Persian poet, was born, lived, and died in Shiraz, where he lectured in Koranic exegesis. Though, as his fame as an oral poet grew, he was invited to visit the courts of foreign rulers as far away as southern India, he refused to leave his native city. A Shiite Muslim whose poetry is infused with Sufism, he introduced a remarkably colloquial tone into his work. Some six hundred poems are attributed to him, most in the form of the *ghazal*: a short lyrical piece of between six and 15 couplets, the first one rhyming, with the rhyme repeated in the second line of each subsequent couplet; the last couplet usually incorporates a reference to the poet's name. A collection of his poems made during his lifetime was said to have been lost: another was assembled after his death by a friend, Muhammad Gulandam. Gertrude Bell (1868–1926), Middle Eastern traveller, scholar, and stateswoman, first translated a selection into English as *Poems from the Divan of Hafiz* (1897), which includes a study of his times. Subsequent translations include *Thirty Poems*, tr. Peter Avery and John Heath-Stubbs (1952) and *Poems of Hafez*, tr. Reza Saberi (1995).

HAGGARD, (Sir) **H(ENRY) RIDER** (1856–1925) novelist, was born at West Bradenham Hall, Norfolk, the sixth child of a squire who had made his money in trade and hankered after being regarded as a gentleman—see Victoria Manthorpe, *Children of the Empire: the Victorian Haggards* (1996). Because cash was now running out, he was sent to Ipswich Grammar School. In 1875 he became secretary to the Governor of Natal, transferring to the staff of the Special Commissioner of the Transvaal in 1877. He married a Norfolk heiress in England in 1879, and, after a brief return to South Africa, managed her estates. As an additional pursuit he studied law and was called to the Bar in 1884, but gave that up to write. He had published two romances when a laudatory review of STEVENSON's *Treasure Island* led him to buy and study it, and then to write, in about six weeks, *King Solomon's Mines* (1885), dedicated 'by the narrator Allan Quatermaine to all the big and little boys who read it'. That book, *She* (1887), which opens up the tribal mysteries of Africa, and *Allan Quatermaine* (1887), in which the magnificent Zulu, Umslopogaas (taken from life), first appears, are the three of many novels he wrote about Africa which have stood the test of time. He also investigated conditions of agriculture and the rural population of England, on which he reported in *Rural England* (2 vols 1902). In 1905 he visited the USA as a special commissioner to study Salvation Army settlements with a view to similar schemes being established in South Africa, which in *The Poor and the Land* (1905) he advocated should be adopted in Britain too. He was a member of the Dominions Royal Commission 1912–17, and was associated with national committees on unemployment and resettlement, soil erosion, and afforestation. He was knighted in 1912, and created KBE in 1919. See *The Days of My Life: an Autobiography*, ed. C. J. Longman, 2 vols 1926; Tom Pocock, *Rider Haggard and the Lost Empire: a Biography*, 1993; Morton N. Cohen, *Rider Haggard: His Life and Work*, 2nd edn 1968.

HAKLUYT, RICHARD (*c.* 1552–1616) English geographer, was born in Herefordshire and educated at Westminster School and Christ Church, Oxford, after which he took holy orders. His passion for exploration, on which he gave lectures, led to *Divers Voyages Touching the Discoverie of America* (1582), probably as a result of which he was appointed chaplain to the British Ambassador in Paris. Here he researched into the political implications of American trade, and was spurred by the availability of material on other nations' voyages to produce something on England's contribution. *The Principall Navigations, Voiages and Discoveries of the English Nation* (1589) was published after his return to England. In 1590 he was appointed Rector of Wetheringsett, Suffolk, from where he prepared the enlarged version of 1600, with the addition of the word '*Traffiques*' (trade) to the title. It comprises over a hundred mainly first-hand accounts: some, like those of RALEGH, were reprinted from contemporary or earlier books; some were translated by himself; others were written for the purpose and, even at their most pedestrian, are charged with the romance of the subject matter and with the enthusiasm of the editor. The historian J. A. Froude (1818–94) described it as 'the prose epic of the modern English nation'. It is also a milestone in the development of scientific exploration. Hakluyt was made a prebendary of Westminster in 1602, and an archdeacon in 1604. His editorial mantle was assumed by Samuel Purchas (1577–1626), whose *Purchas His Pilgrimage* (1613) inspired COLERIDGE's 'Kubla Khan', and who subsequently, using manuscripts he had inherited from Hakluyt and other sources, produced *Hakluytus Posthumus: or, Purchas His Pilgrimes* (1625), the longest English work printed in England up to that time. See *Voyages and Discoveries*, ed. Jack Beeching, 1972.

HALIBURTON, THOMAS CHANDLER (1796–1865) Canadian humorist, prose writer, and politician, was born in Windsor, Nova Scotia, the only child of a judge, and was educated there at King's College School and King's College, being called to the Nova Scotia Bar in 1820. He published anonymously *A General Description of Nova Scotia* (1823), which, reissued under his own name in a recast and extended form as *An Historical and Statistical Account of Nova Scotia* (1829) to publicize himself and the achievements of his native settlement, is a significant piece of Canadian historical writing. He was Member for Annapolis Royal in the Nova Scotia House of Assembly from 1826 to 1829, when he was appointed a judge of the Court of Common Pleas. He became a justice of the Supreme Court in 1841. He channelled his criticism of local society and public events into a series of satirically pointed sketches in the *Novascotian* in 1835–36, which became *The Clockmaker: or, The Sayings and Doings of Samuel Slick of Slickville* (3 vols 1837–40). Slick, a brash but philosophical American con man ('If a chap seems bent on cheatin' himself, I like to be neighbourly and help him do it'), is a character in the mainstream of American humour. He reappears as a diplomat in *The Attaché: or, Sam Slick in England* (4 vols 1843–46), and as a presidential envoy in Nova Scotia to study the fishing industry in *Sam Slick's Wise Saws and Modern Instances: or, What He Said, Did, or Invented* (1853). In between times Haliburton wrote, for the English Tory journal *Fraser's Magazine*, the sketches and stories which became *The Old Judge: or, Life in a Colony* (1849), a loosely-constructed miscellany in which Canadian folklore and tradition, and Canadian speech, first find literary expression. In 1856 he resigned his post and emigrated to England, where he was prevailed upon to stand as Conservative candidate for Launceston, Cornwall, which he represented in Parliament from 1859 to 1865. He died at his home in Isleworth, Middlesex. See Stan Mc-

Mullin, *Thomas Chandler Haliburton and His Works*, 1994.

HALL, EDWARD see HOLINSHED.

HALL, RADCLYFFE, pseudonym of Marguerite Radclyffe-Hall (1880–1943) British novelist, who preferred to be known as 'John', was born in Christchurch, Hampshire, to a couple whose marriage finally broke up a few weeks later. She had no regular schooling, and inherited her grandfather's fortune when she came of age in 1901. She then travelled, published (between 1906 and 1915) five books of verse, and in 1907 met in Homburg the first of her serious loves, Mabel ('Ladye') Batten (1857–1916), patron of the arts. In 1915 Ladye sent a batch of Hall's short stories to the publisher William Heinemann (1863–1920), who took the couple out to lunch and urged Hall to write a novel. That same year Hall met Una (Lady) Troubridge (1887–1963). They became lovers, and lived together from 1920. *The Forge* (1924) and *A Saturday Life* (1925), two light novels about artistic aspirations, readily found a publisher. *The Unlit Lamp* (1924), a rather grimmer tale of over-possessive motherhood, was taken on by the eleventh publisher to whom it had been offered by Hall's agent. *Adam's Breed* (1926), originally called *Food*, the gastronomic but ultimately spiritual quest of a sensitive Italian waiter, won several prizes. *The Well of Loneliness* (1928), a study of a lesbian novelist, was put out in a small edition at a high price, with a plain cover. It was suppressed in Britain under the Obscene Libel Act. A similar decision in the USA was overturned on appeal, and a Victory Edition issued there. It was not reissued in Britain until 1949; shortly before that it had been selling 100,000 copies a year elsewhere in the world. Hall published two more, less controversial, novels, and a book of short stories, *Miss Ogilvy Finds Herself* (1934). In 1934 she fell in love with Evguenia Souline (1903–c.1960), an unprepossessing Russian nurse who had been engaged in Paris to tend to Una's enteritis. The three set up an unusual *ménage à trois* in Florence, before returning to Britain at the outbreak of World War II. Una wrote *The Life and Death of Radclyffe Hall* in 1945, but withheld publication until 1961. See Michael Baker, *Our Three Selves: the Life of Radclyffe Hall*, 1985; Claudia Stillman Franks, *Beyond the Well of Loneliness: the Fiction of Radclyffe Hall*, 1983.

HALL, RODNEY (*b.* 1935) Australian poet and novelist, was born in Solihull, Warwickshire, of an English father, who died six months later, and a mother whose family had returned to England after being ruined by the fires in New South Wales in 1923. After World War II he was brought to Australia, and was educated until he was 16 at Brisbane

Boys' College. He has lived 'as a writer, actor and musician, just occasionally lapsing into respectable employment'. He has been Lecturer in Recorder, Canberra School of Music, and was Poetry Editor of the *Australian* 1967–78. His first book of verse, published in London, was *Penniless till Doomsday* (1962), and through subsequent collections, notably *The Autobiography of a Gorgon* (1968), *The Law of Karma* (1968), and *The Most Beautiful World: Fiction and Sermons* (1981), he has developed a free style, a witty outlook, and a technique whereby his poems form a progression of theme and thought—see also *Selected Poems* (1975). His novels, each representing a different fictional form, illustrate aspects of Australian life and include *Just Relations* (1982), winner of the MILES FRANKLIN Award. *Captivity Captive* (1988), *The Second Bridegroom* (1991), and *The Grisly Wife* (1993) comprise a trilogy of historical novels set largely in 1898, 1838, and 1868 respectively, in which the unsolved Gatton murders in 1898 are the focal point of a study of cultural restrictions, colonial attitudes, and religious fanaticism. He compiled *The Collins Book of Australian Poetry* (1981). He chaired the Australia Council 1991–94, having been made AO in 1990.

HAMBURGER, MICHAEL (*b.* 1924) British poet, critic, and translator, was born in Berlin, the son of a paediatrician, and emigrated with his family to Britain in 1933. He was educated at Westminster School and Christ Church, Oxford, and served in the Royal Army Education Corps from 1943 to 1947. After teaching at University College, London, he was Lecturer in German, then Reader, at Reading University 1955–64, after which he held visiting professorships at several American universities. His first book of verse was *Later Hogarth* (1945); significant subsequent collections are *Travelling: Poems 1963–1968* (1969) and *Real Estate* (1977). Nature is a recurring feature, either descriptively treated, as in 'April Day: Binsey', or as a filter through which other, often melancholy, images appear, as in 'Memory', or in 'The Search', in which he expresses the subconscious sensibility of Jews who survived or escaped the Holocaust. In the early 1960s he abandoned the restrictions of more traditional forms of verse in order to give fuller rein to his deeper feelings. *The Truth of Poetry: Tensions in Modern Poetry from Baudelaire to the 1960s* (1969) is a serious but accessible study. He has successfully translated into English the poetry of HÖLDERLIN, GOETHE, and RILKE, among other European works of literature, and was awarded the 1990 European Community prize for his translation of Paul Celan (1920–70). He was made OBE in 1992. See *Collected Poems 1941–1994*, 1995; *Testimonies: Selected Shorter Prose 1950–1987*, 1989; *String*

of Beginnings: Intermittent Memoirs 1924–1954, new edn 1996.

HAMILTON, CHARLES see RICHARDS.

HAMMETT, (SAMUEL) DASHIELL (1894–1961) American novelist, was born on a run-down farm in Maryland, and was educated at Public School No 72, Baltimore, and Baltimore Polytechnic Institute, which he left at 15 to support his family when his father fell ill. He had numerous jobs before joining Pinkerton's National Detective Agency in 1915. He enlisted in the Army in 1918, served in Maryland, and was discharged the following year with tuberculosis and a disability pension. In 1922, married, with a child, and ill, he had a one-hundred-word story published in MENCKEN's *Smart Set*. In 1928 he submitted to the house of Knopf 'an action-detective story', describing himself as a former Pinkerton operative who had 'more recently published fiction, book reviews, verse, sketches and so on, in twenty to twenty-five magazines'. It was published as *Red Harvest* (1929), followed immediately by *The Dain Curse* (1929), which has an extra background of religious cults in California. In the fall of 1929 he left his family in San Francisco and went with a girlfriend to New York. After the publication of *The Maltese Falcon* (1930), a thriller of deception and self-deception featuring the private eye Sam Spade which by 1941 had been filmed three times, he finished *The Glass Key* (1931) and went to Hollywood. He returned accompanied by HELLMAN, with whom he lived on and off for the rest of his life.

Though he published collections of stories, Hammett only wrote one more novel, *The Thin Man* (1934), in which sophistication and wit enhance the portrayal of the married life of the hard-drinking sleuth. In 1942, having been several times fired as a screenwriter and been hospitalized for alcoholism, he enlisted in the Army as a private, served on home stations, and was discharged in 1945 with the rank of master sergeant. In 1951 he was sentenced to six months' jail for contempt of court, for refusing to answer questions as trustee of the bail fund of the Civil Rights Congress. His problems were compounded by his Communist affiliations and the depredations of the Internal Revenue, to whom he had paid no taxes for twenty years, and who sequestrated his income. *The Big Knockover: Selected Stories and Short Novels*, ed. Lillian Hellman (1966; reissued as *The Big Knockover and Other Stories*, 1993) includes 'Tulip', an unfinished novel which is in tone different from his usual published writing. See William Marling, *Dashiell Hammett*, 1983 (critical study); Julian Symons, *Dashiell Hammett*, 1985 (critical study); Robert E. Skinner, *The Hard-Boiled Explicator: a Guide to the Study of Das-*

hiell Hammett, Raymond Chandler and Ross Macdonald, 1985.

HAMSUN, KNUT (1859–1952) Norwegian novelist, was born of peasant aristocratic stock in Lom, the son of Peder Pedersen, and took his name from that of the ancestral farm. He was brought up by an uncle in the Lofoten Islands, and was then apprenticed to a shoemaker, whom he left to try and earn enough to see him through university. He never apparently achieved this. Instead he had a number of jobs, went to the USA, where he lectured in French literature in Minneapolis and was a streetcar conductor in Chicago, returned to Norway, and then went back to North America for two more years, during which he was a fisherman off the Newfoundland coast. In 1890 he publicly attacked writers of realism, including IBSEN, and published [*Hunger*], a psychological novel expressing the agonies and inner conflicts of a starving artist; it was followed by further experiments in modernism which included *Pan* (1894) and *Victoria* (1898). Though [*Hunger*] was published in Britain (1899) in a translation by 'George Egerton', Mary Bright (1859–1945), née Dunne, the Australian-born Irish novelist, who had met (and reputedly fallen in love with) Hamsun in Norway in 1887, subsequent novels were not translated into English until the 1920s, by which time he had entered his period of writing about social issues. [*The Growth of the Soil*] (1917; tr. W. Worster, 1921), a paean to the nobility of peasant ways, was instrumental in his being awarded the Nobel Prize for Literature in 1920. He openly supported the Nazi invasion of Norway in World War II, after which he was arrested for collaboration and for a time confined in a mental asylum.

HARDENBERG, FRIEDRICH see THOMSON, JAMES (1834–82).

HARDWICK, ELIZABETH see LOWELL, ROBERT.

HARDY, THOMAS (1840–1928) British novelist, short-story writer, and poet, was born in Higher Bockhampton, near Stinsford, Dorset, the eldest child of a master stonemason. He was educated at a local private school until he was 16, when he was apprenticed to a church architect in Dorchester. In 1862 he went to London to further his studies and his career, which he did while continuing to educate himself in classics and poetry. A bout of illness led him to return home in 1867 and to work for his former employer. Writing interested him passionately. Having had many poems rejected by London literary journals, he decided to try his hand at fiction. His first attempt, a combination of socialist satire and rusticity, was accepted, but the publisher's reader, who was MEREDITH, advised him to withdraw it and write something with a bit more plot. The result was *Desperate Remedies* (1871), a story of murder and intrigue, whose anonymous appearance with a different publisher Hardy himself subsidized, though he got most of his money back from sales. He used some of the country scenes from his first novel as a basis for *Under the Greenwood Tree* (1872), a rustic comedy. Yokels reappear as minor characters in *A Pair of Blue Eyes* (1873), in which he exercised his penchant for heavy romance and high drama, using as a starting point his own experience of conducting a survey of a remote Cornish church, at which he met his future wife.

In the meantime he had been invited to write a serial for *Cornhill Magazine*. The impact of his anonymous contribution, *Far from the Madding Crowd* (1874), was such that some critics attributed it to GEORGE ELIOT, which Hardy resented, though its success meant that he was now able to give up his job and to marry. *Far from the Madding Crowd* is firmly and recognizably set in what he calls by its ancient name of Wessex, and he gets exactly right the balance between the steady, ritual progress of the country year, the eruptions of passion and violence, and the courting of the magnetic and erratic Bathsheba Everdene by her patient shepherd, Gabriel Oak, who wins her on the very last page. There is even more passion, and more tragedy, in *The Return of the Native* (1878), for which, at the request of the journal which first accepted it, the subplot was changed so as to have a happy ending; its main theme, though simple and controlled, depends overmuch on chance. The subtitle of *The Mayor of Casterbridge: the Life and Death of a Man of Character* (1886) only partly sums up this powerful study of a tragic hero in the Shakespearian mould. These are the most readable of his 17 novels and volumes of short stories, but the greatest fame, and controversy, were reserved for *Tess of the d'Urbervilles: a Pure Woman* (1891), even in its bowdlerized form. When *Jude the Obscure* (dated 1896), written with rather less attention to art, got a still more critical press, he gave up fiction for good.

Hardy had continued all this time to write poetry. Now, with *Wessex Poems, and Other Verses* (1898), a third of which he had composed in the 1860s, he began to publish it. He is not a great poet, but he wrote some very good short poems and ballads among the nine hundred in *Collected Poems* (1930). His style is rugged, his tone often melancholic, and his humour grim, but his choice of words is magical and his meaning is always clear. Particularly poignant is the group, 'Poems of 1912–13', which he wrote after his wife's death, having discovered among her papers notes about their marriage. His most ambitious work of all, *The Dynasts: a Drama of the Napoleonic Wars*, 'intended simply for mental performance and not for the stage', was first conceived in 1875 and published in three parts (1904–08), but he continued to tinker with it for much of the rest of his life. The scope is vast and the stage directions are often on a cosmic scale, but the mixture of blank verse and prose, fact and historical imagination, and humble as well as noble characters, gives a total effect of grandeur. His second marriage in 1914 proved so agreeable that he felt able to dictate to his wife large chunks of the two biographies of him that were published under her name in 1928 and 1930. His final rites were typical of his creative duality. While his ashes were being carried for interment in Westminster Abbey by a squad of literary pallbearers, his heart, having been cut from the corpse, was being buried in Stinsford churchyard, where he had wished to lie. He was awarded the OM in 1910. See *The Complete Stories*, ed. Norman Page, 1996; *Complete Poems*, ed. James Gibson, new edn 1988; *Selected Poems*, ed. Harry Thomas, new edn 1993; *Selected Poems*, ed. Andrew Motion, new edn 1994; *Selected Poetry*, ed. Samuel Hynes, 1996; Martin Seymour-Smith, *Hardy*, new edn 1995 (critical biography); Michael Millgate, *Thomas Hardy: His Career as a Novelist*, 2nd edn 1994; J. I. M. Stewart, *Thomas Hardy*, 1971 (critical biography); Trevor Johnson, *A Critical Introduction to the Poems of Thomas Hardy*, 1991; Merryn Williams, *A Preface to Hardy*, 2nd edn 1993.

HARPUR, CHARLES (1813–68) Australian poet, was born in Windsor, in the Hawkesbury River district of New South Wales, and sometimes signed his verses 'A Hawkesbury Lad'. His parents, who married in 1814, were convicts, his father being an Irish highwayman who was transported for life in 1800 but was later pardoned and became the local schoolmaster. Harpur worked as a bush-labourer, and a letter-sorter in Sydney, and then retired to the Hunter River district, where he read, wrote articles and poems for newspapers, and sporadically looked after his brother's post office. His *Thoughts: a Series of Sonnets* (1845) was the first sonnet sequence to be published in Australia. In 1850 he married Mary Doyle, whom for seven years he had bombarded with love sonnets, addressed to 'Rosa'. 'The Bushrangers', published in *The Bushrangers: a Play in Five Acts, and Other Poems* (1853), was the first play with an Australian setting to appear in book form in Australia, though he had been working on this verse drama of the bushranger Jack Donohoe (died in a shoot-out 1830) for 18 years. Harpur was now reluctantly farming sheep, but matters improved on his appointment in 1859 as an assistant gold commissioner. His death, of hardening of the lungs, followed a series of misfortunes. He was made redundant, his farm was destroyed by floods, and his favourite son accidentally shot himself. A prickly character,

who was convinced of his destiny as Australia's first genuine national poet, Harpur brought Wordsworthian romanticism and religious mysticism to Australian landscapes and themes. See *The Poetical Works of Charles Harpur*, ed. Elizabeth Perkins, 1984; Judith Wright, *Charles Harpur*, rev. edn 1977 (critical study).

HARRIS, 'FRANK' [JAMES THOMAS] (1856–1931) writer of fiction, claimed to have been born in Galway. He was the third son of a Welsh seaman and the daughter of a Baptist minister. At 14 he took himself to the USA, and after doing a series of menial jobs reached Kansas, where he attended the State University in about 1872. Having studied further in Europe, he materialized in London in 1883. Largely by force of personality he achieved the editorship of the *Evening News*, and then the *Fortnightly Review*, which he revitalized to his own ends. A marriage to a wealthy Park Lane widow was as short-lived as were his political ambitions. In 1894 he eloped (with a woman whom he later married), published *Elder Conklin and Other Stories*, largely derived from his American experiences, and bought the *Saturday Review*. He sold it in 1898, having through his editorial flair made it the most influential political and literary review in the country. He now published a further volume of stories, *Montes the Matador* (1900), and wrote two plays, *Mr and Mrs Daventry* (1910), the idea for which he claimed to have bought from WILDE, and *Shakespeare and His Love* (1910), a product of a phase in which he also produced two fanciful studies of SHAKESPEARE (1909 and 1910). His continuing interest in the affairs of various journals finally landed him in prison for contempt of court. He returned to the USA, where he published at his own expense his biography of Wilde (1916), and until it was suspended ran *Pearson's Magazine* as a vehicle for scurrilous anti-British sentiments. In *My Life and Loves* (1922–27), his notorious autobiography, the 'loves' are even more preposterous, and much more tedious, than the 'life'. He died in Nice. See Hugh Kingsmill, *Frank Harris*, new edn 1987 (biography).

HARRIS, GEORGE WASHINGTON (1814–69) American humorist, was born in Allegheny City, Pennsylvania. At the age of five he was brought to Knoxville, Tennessee, by his 21-year-old half-brother, Samuel Bell, who in due course took him on as an apprentice metalworker. In 1835, now captain of the river steamboat *Knoxville*, Harris married Mary Emeline Nance. In 1839 he bought 375 acres of land in Blount County, where they lived among fine furniture, including a bookcase with 75 books, and he wrote anonymous political articles for the Democratic Knoxville *Argus*. Failing as a gentleman landowner, he opened a metalwork shop in Knoxville in 1843, and began contributing 'sporting epistles' to the New York *Spirit of the Times*, which in 1845 published his dialect tale, 'The Knob Dance—a Tennessee Frolic'. In 1849 he was superintendent of the Holston Glass Works, while also practising as a silversmith. Local people he met on a business trip to the copper mines of Ducktown in 1854 provided the inspiration for 'Sut Lovengood's Daddy "Acting Horse" ' (*Spirit*, 1854), the first vivid, ribald sketch of his uniquely awful creation, Sut Lovingood (as the spelling became). A confirmed secessionist, and in 1859 elected to the Democratic State Central Committee, he wrote political analysis as well as Lovingood sketches for the Nashville *Union and America*, to which in 1861 he also contributed three Lovingood lampoons of the newly elected President, Abraham Lincoln. The Harris family probably left Nashville before it fell to the Unionists in 1862; during the Civil War they lived in Chattanooga, Decatur, and Trenton. After the war Harris bought the right-of-way for the Wills Valley Railroad and resumed his political sketch-writing.

Sut Lovingood. Yarns Spun by a 'Nat'ral Born Durn'd Fool[']. *Warped and Wove for Public Wear* (1867), his only book, contained eight of his thirty or so published stories, with 16 new ones. That same year his wife died and his housekeeper, fearing scandal, left. In October 1869 he married in Decatur a striking blonde widow, Jane E. Pride. In December he took with him on a business trip to Lynchburg, Virginia, the manuscript of a second book, *High Times and Hard Times*, to see if he could arrange for it to be printed. On the return journey he was taken ill on the train, and died in Knoxville, having in answer to a doctor's question said, 'Poisoned!'—the cause was probably apoplexy. The manuscript was never traced. The Lovingood stories, written mainly in phonetic dialect, are regarded as triumphs of composition, characterization, and broad humour. See Milton Rickels, *George Washington Harris*, 1965 (biographical/critical study).

HARRIS, JOEL CHANDLER (1848–1908) American humorist, novelist, and journalist, was born near Eatonton, Georgia, the son of an Irish labourer who deserted his wife, a seamstress, shortly afterwards. The townspeople rallied round and paid the boy's school fees. At 14 he became a printer's apprentice on a new weekly, the *Countryman*, published at the owner's estate of Turnwold, where he went to live. He was soon writing humorous pieces, and in 1870, after working on other papers, he became an associate editor of the Savannah *Morning News*, for which he wrote a daily column on local affairs as well as witty sketches. He married in 1873, and three years later, to avoid an epidemic of yellow fever, took his family to Atlanta,

where for 24 years he was an editor and staff writer on the *Atlanta Constitution*, in which appeared the first Uncle Remus story in October 1876. *Uncle Remus: His Songs and His Sayings: the Folklore of the Old Plantation* (1880) was the first of several collections of Negro folklore, which he had first come across at Turnwold, inventively reworked into series of pointed, witty tales. Among many other works, which include adult novels and stories specifically written for children, are two particularly notable books of short pieces, *Mingo and Other Sketches in Black and White* (1884), studies of the breaking down of race and class contrasts, and *Free Joe and Other Georgian Sketches* (1887), which illustrates the tragic predicament of the displaced freedman. In 1907 he founded with his son Julian *Uncle Remus' Magazine*, with MARQUIS as associate editor. See *The Complete Tales of Uncle Remus*, ed. Richard Chase, 1955; Bruce R. Bickley, *Joel Chandler Harris*, 1987 (biographical/critical study).

HARRIS, JOHN BEYNON see WYNDHAM.

HARRIS, MAX see MCAULEY.

HARRIS, WILSON (*b.* 1921) Guyanese novelist, poet, and critic, was born in New Amsterdam of European, African, and Amerindian ancestry, and was educated at Queen's College, Georgetown. He was a government land surveyor during the 1940s and 1950s, and had poems, stories, and essays published in the literary magazine, *Kyk-over-al*. He also had three volumes of poetry printed, of which *Eternity to Season*, a heroic allegory of the labouring population, was reissued in the UK in a revised edition in 1979. He emigrated to England in 1959. In his lecture, 'Tradition and the West Indian Novel' (1964), in *Tradition, the Writer, and Society: Critical Essays* (1967), he said: 'Political radicalism is merely a fashionable attitude unless it is accompanied by profound insights into the experimental nature of the arts and the sciences.' His novels are experimental particularly in their form of narrative and the depths inherent in the dialogue. *Palace of the Peacock* (1960) is the first in *The Guyana Quartet* (1985), in which fragments of the country's past become a composite picture of its land and peoples. He continued with a second sequence, *The Eye of the Scarecrow* (1965) to *Ascent to Omai* (1970), in each of which a family's loss or void in the past is reflected in its present circumstances. He has subsequently extended his geographical canvas and included in his vision the art of the painter, such as is the protagonist of *Da Silva da Silva's Cultivated Wilderness* (published with *Genesis of the Clowns*, 1977) and *The Tree of the Sun* (1978). *Carnival* (1985), *The Infinite Rehearsal* (1987), and *The Four Banks of the*

River of Space (1990)—reissued together as *The Carnival Trilogy* (1993), with an introduction by the author—represent a return to Guyanese material and a debate, conducted with reference to myth and literature, about the responsibility of the individual in 'the waste land'. They look forward to *Resurrection at Sorrow Hill* (1993), in which, through metaphor, parable, and narrative, hope is seen to triumph over death. In *Jonestown* (1996), the mass suicide in 1978 in Jonestown of several hundred American followers of a 'messianic' pastor is at the heart of a wider vision of the problems which beset post-colonial territories. See Hena Maes-Jelinek, *Wilson Harris*, 1982 (critical study); Hena Maes-Jelinek (ed.), *Wilson Harris: the Uncompromising Imagination*, 1991; and in Bruce King (ed.) *West Indian Literature*, 2nd edn 1995.

HARRISON, WILLIAM see HOLINSHED.

HARTE, (FRANCIS) BRET(T) (1836–1902) American short-story writer, novelist, and poet, was born in Albany, New York, of English, Dutch, and Jewish descent. After the death in 1845 of his father, an unworldly teacher and scholar, the family stopped travelling, and settled in Brooklyn. He left school at 13, did office work, and then in 1854 followed his mother to Oakland, California, where she had married a local dignitary. After a few years he joined his married sister in Aracta, a base for the mining country, where he wrote for the *Northern Californian*. In 1860 he was in San Francisco, where he set type for and contributed poems and sketches to the *Golden Era*. He moved on to a clerkship in the Surveyor General's office and, after his marriage in 1862, to the post of Secretary of the Branch Mint. *The Lost Galleon and Other Tales* (1867) was a collection of verse; *Condensed Novels and Other Papers* (1867) included some clever parodies. In 1868 he became the first Editor of *Overland Monthly*, in which appeared the two sentimental but wittily written stories for which he is best remembered, 'The Luck of Roaring Camp' (August 1868) and 'The Outcasts of Poker Flat' (January 1869), and his humorous narrative poem, 'Plain Language from Truthful James' (September 1870), also known as 'The Heathen Chinee'. In 1871 he visited the American East, where his reputation was such that *Atlantic Monthly* offered him the unprecedented sum of $10,000 for 12 poems or sketches over the next year. He moved to Boston, but either because of the poor quality of his work or its late delivery, his contract was not renewed. The success of a novel of the gold rush, *Gabriel Conroy* (1876), filled the coffers for a while, but though he continued to write prolifically and desperately, and enlarged editions of *The Poetical Works* (1872) appeared in 1896 and 1902, the basis of his reputation continued to be the vision of the Wild West

which he offered in his San Francisco years. In 1878 he gladly accepted the post of Consul in Krefeld, Prussia, and firmly left his wife at home. In 1880 he transferred to Glasgow, where he remained until the change of administration in 1885. Latterly he appears to have lived in England in a *ménage à trois* with a Belgian couple. See *Selected Stories and Sketches*, ed. David Wyatt, 1995.

HARTLEY, L(ESLIE) P(OLES) (1895–1972) British novelist and short-story writer, the only son of a retired solicitor who managed a prosperous brick factory, was brought up in the family home of Fletton Tower, near Peterborough. He was educated at Harrow and Balliol College, Oxford, with a two-year gap for war service on the home front. From 1922 to 1939 he spent half of each year in Venice, which features in many of his stories and 17 novels, and wrote book reviews for several journals. Apart from a short novel in the manner of HENRY JAMES, *Simonetta Perkins* (1925), his early published works are stories of the macabre—*Night Fears and Other Stories* (1924) and *The Killing Bottle* (1932). His first major novel, *The Shrimp and the Anemone*, was begun in the 1920s, but he did not publish it until 1944, feeling that it might be unfairly regarded as overtly autobiographical. It reveals, with great psychological insight, the intellectual relationship between a boy and his elder sister, which is continued in *The Sixth Heaven* (1946) and *Eustace and Hilda* (1947), the title by which the trilogy is known. In *The Go-Between* (1953), the position and tribulations of a child in an adult world are further explored in an Edwardian country-house setting. In this book, too, and in *The Hireling* (1957), the apparent dangers of sexual relationships between different classes loom large. After World War II he divided his time between London and his house on the Avon near Bath, where he was tended latterly by a succession of sinister male servants. He was made CBE in 1956. His two sisters lived on at Fletton; the younger died in 1994 having given instructions that all family papers were to be destroyed. See *The Complete Short Stories of L. P. Hartley*, 1973; Adrian Wright, *Foreign Country: the Life of L. P. Hartley*, 1996; Anne Mulkeen, *Wild Thyme, Winter Lightning: the Symbolic Novels of L. P. Hartley*, 1974.

HARVEY, GABRIEL see NASHE; SPENSER.

HARWOOD, GWEN (b. 1920), née Foster, Australian poet, was born in Taringa, Queensland, and educated at Brisbane Girls' Grammar School. She studied and taught music, and was organist at All Saints' Church, Brisbane. In 1945 she married William Harwood, a lecturer in linguistics, and moved to Tasmania, where they had four children and ultimately retired to Oyster

Cove. She began writing poetry in her late thirties, in hospital. Among the satirical excursions and conventionally crafted, vividly presented expressions of mental and physical pain and feminine frustration in *Poems* (1963) and *Poems: Volume Two* (1968) are ironic projections of persona which emerge through the characters of two restless professors, the unfulfilled Eisenbart and the alcoholic Kröte. *The Lion's Bride* (1981) opens with an allegory (or is it an allegory?) of life and death, and contains poems inspired by the Tasmanian landscape. Francis Geyer, T. F. Kline, Walter Lehmann, and Miriam Stone are pen names which Harwood has employed from time to time. See *Collected Poems*, 1991; Stephanie Trigg, *Gwen Harwood*, 1994 (critical study).

HAŠEK, JAROSLAV (1883–1923) Czech novelist and journalist, was born in Prague, the son of a schoolmaster who died of drink in 1886. He was expelled from school in 1897 for participating too boisterously in the anti-German riots. His bohemian proclivities, which he sublimated during three years at the Commercial College, subsequently returned. After being dismissed from the Slavia Bank he took up freelance journalism and joined the anarchist movement, being jailed in 1907 for assaulting a policeman. To impress the parents of Jarmila Mayerová, with whom he was in love, he published some stories and got a job as editor of a natural history magazine, only to be dismissed for writing about fictitious animals. The marriage took place in 1910, but soon after they had had a son in 1912, Jarmila returned to her parents and Hašek to his former lifestyle. A prototype of 'good soldier Švejk' emerged in his stories in 1911, to be completely realized and rationalized once Hašek had been, as Švejk was to be, drafted into the 91st Infantry Regiment in 1915. Soon captured by the Russians, he spent five years in Russia, during which he graduated from prisoner to *apparatchik*. Invited by the Social Democratic Party to return to Czechoslovakia in 1920, he brought with him a Russian woman whom he had bigamously married. Having published a book of Švejk stories in Kiev in 1917, he now embarked on a four-volume account of his creation's exploits. When no publisher dared take it on, he published the first volume privately in 1921. The response from the public was sufficient for him to find a commercial publisher for the whole work, and to buy a cottage in Lipnice. He died without finishing the fourth volume, and it was not until the necessary time had elapsed between the end of World War I and its acceptance as a serious subject for literature (see also ALDINGTON, BLUNDEN, FREDERIC MANNING, REMARQUE, and SHERRIFF) that his broad humour and inventive characterization were universally accepted. See *The Good Soldier Švejk: and His For-*

tunes in the World War, tr. Cecil Parrott, new edn 1993.

HAUPTMANN, GERHART (1862–1946) German dramatist and novelist, was born in Ober-Salzbrunn and educated at the Realschule am Zwinger, Breslau. He then trained on an uncle's farm, took sculpture at the Königliche Kunstund Gewerbeschule, Breslau, and drawing at the Königliche Akademie, Dresden, and studied at Berlin University, while also having acting lessons. He married Marie Thienemann (1860–1914) in 1885 (they had three sons), and began the life of a writer. The naturalism of the novella *Bahnwärter Thiel* [Flagman Thiel] (1888) was more than matched in his first play, *Vor Sonnenaufgang* (1889; tr. Leonard Bloomfield as *Before Dawn*, 1909), which, though it was admired by FONTANE, earned for its author from another critic the title of the 'most immoral playwright of the century'. *Die Weber* (1893; as *The Weavers* tr. Mary Morison, 1899; tr. Horst Frenz and Miles Waggoner, with *Hannele* and *The Beaver Coat*, 1951) is significant in its application of Naturalistic techniques and 'open' dramatic form to documented history. *Michael Kramer* (1900) so impressed JOYCE that he employed his rudimentary German to translate it into English. Mythological material and symbolism are features of later plays such as *Und Pippa tanzt* (1906; tr. Mary Harned as *And Pippa Dances*, 1907), and of novels such as *Der Narr in Christo, Emanuel Quint* (1910; tr. Thomas Seltzer as *The Fool in Christ: Emanuel Quint*, 1911) and *Die Insel der grossen Mutter* (1924; tr. Willa and Edwin Muir as *The Island of the Great Mother*, 1925). After being divorced in 1904 Hauptmann married Margarete Marschalk (1875–1957), whom he had first met when she was 14 and by whom he had had a son in 1900. In 1906 he was briefly but totally infatuated with Ida Orloff (1889–1945), a teenage temptress who acted as herself in *Pippa*. He was awarded the Nobel Prize for Literature in 1912. See *Plays: Before Daybreak, The Weavers, The Beaver Coat*, ed. Reinhold Grimm and Caroline Monlina y Vedia, 1994.

HAVEL, VÁCLAV (*b.* 1936) Czech dramatist, essayist, and statesman, was born in Prague of a wealthy family of land developers, and was barred by his bourgeois upbringing from having a university education. After two years at technical college, followed by another two of military service, he attached himself to the theatre in a variety of working capacities, and became a playwright. Two of his first cycle of full-length plays were published in the UK (tr. Vera Blackwell) as *The Memorandum* (1967) and *The Garden Party* (1969), each partly a vehicle for his political ideas and partly an analysis of the phenomenon of language as an instrument of power. After the Soviet invasion of his country in 1968 his works were banned, but still circulated surreptitiously. He became the leading spokesman for the rights organization, Charter 77, and was three times imprisoned, on the last occasion, in 1979, for $4^1/2$ years. During the 1989 political revolution he became leader of Civic Forum, the anti-Communist alliance, and was subsequently elected President of Czechoslovakia; he resigned in 1992 after failing to get the support of the Slovak nationalists. He was elected President of the Czech Republic in 1993. *Letters to Olga*, tr. Paul Wilson (1989), written from prison to his wife, née Splíchalová (1933–96), whom he married in 1964, and *Summer Meditations: on Politics, Morality and Civility in a Time of Transition*, tr. Wilson (1992) are enlightening on his political views. *Disturbing the Peace: a Conversation with Karel Hvížďala*, tr. Wilson (1990) offers a double perspective in that he discusses his relationship with the theatre as well as his civic views. See *Open Letters: Selected Prose 1965–1990*, ed. and tr. Paul Wilson, new edn 1992; *Selected Plays 1963–1983*, tr. Vera Blackwell, 1992; *Selected Plays 1984-1987*, tr. Tom Stoppard and others, 1994.

HAWKINS, ANTHONY HOPE see HOPE.

HAWTHORNE, NATHANIEL (1804–64) American novelist, and short-story and children's writer, was born in Salem, Massachusetts, the only son of Nathaniel Hawthorne (or Hathorne), a sea captain whose family had been Puritan immigrants four generations earlier, and who died in Surinam, Dutch Guiana, in 1808. He was brought up in the home of his mother's parents, the Mannings; his uncles took responsibility for his education. A foot injury incurred while playing ball in 1813 left him on crutches for some time. In 1818 the family moved for two years to Raymond, Maine, on the wild shore of Lake Sebago, where he went 'savagizing' in the woods and thoroughly enjoyed the solitude. In 1819 he spent a term at Rev. Caleb Bradley's boarding school, near Portland, from which he went to Samuel L. Archer's School, Salem, before being prepared for college by a tutor at home. Horatio Bridge (1806–93), Franklin Pierce (1804–69), LONGFELLOW were contemporaries at Bowdoin College, Maine, from which he graduated in 1825 convinced that he would be a writer but without any clear idea of how to go about it. For the next twelve years he lived mainly at home in Salem, reading, studying (especially colonial history), and writing. He published *Fanshawe* (1828), a Gothic romance in a realistic college setting, at his own expense, and then suppressed it, burning every copy he could lay hands on—he never told his wife of its existence. When the publisher to whom he had offered 'Seven Tales of My

Native Land' delayed a decision, he withdrew the manuscript and destroyed it, in frustration. Stories written for two further books, 'Provincial Tales' and 'The Story Teller', were dismantled from their frameworks by the editors of the annual *Token* and of the *New England Magazine*, who printed them anonymously, so that 'no objection arises from having so many pages by one author'. Among them were 'The Gentle Boy' (1832), 'Roger Malvin's Burial' (1832), 'Young Goodman Brown' (1835), 'Wakefield' (1835), 'The Maypole of Merry Mount' (1936), and 'The Minister's Black Veil' (1836). In 1836 he was reduced to editing, for several months in Boston, the *American Magazine of Useful and Entertaining Knowledge*, and to compiling for children, with his sister Elizabeth (1802–83), *Peter Parley's Universal History on the Basis of Geography* (1837). The breakthrough, when it came, was initiated by Bridge, who, unknown to Hawthorne until much later, subsidized the publication of *Twice-Told Tales* (1837).

Through Elizabeth Peabody (1804–94), the educationist and promoter of causes, of which she regarded Hawthorne as one, he met her sister Sophia (1809–71), a semi-invalid whose symptoms have been likened to those of E. B. BROWNING. In 1838 they became engaged. To earn some money on which to marry, he took a post as an inspector at the Boston Custom House, which seems to have involved counting tubs of coal and salt. During this time he wrote little except eloquent love letters to Sophia and *Grandfather's Chair* (1841), New England historical stories for children, published by Elizabeth Peabody from her bookshop in Boston. He and Sophia were married in 1842, and for several years lived at the Old Manse, Concord, where he wrote the new tales that appeared in *Mosses From an Old Manse* (1846). Now also with two children to support, in 1846 he accepted the politically-controlled post of Surveyor at the Salem Custom House, from which he was removed in 1849 when the Whigs came to power. The controversy nettled him into a feverish bout of creativity, in which he wrote *The Scarlet Letter: a Romance* (1850), originally intended as one of a collection of tales, but published on its own, with an autobiographical introduction, 'The Custom-House', in which he gave his version of the affair. Set in 17th-century New England, and evoking 'a people amongst whom religion and law were almost identical', the story was quickly recognized on both sides of the Atlantic as an outstanding study of attitudes to sin and guilt, and of human psychology.

Mere fame, however, did not pay the bills. Though he published two contemporary novels, *The House of the Seven Gables* (1851), with echoes of the past, and *The Blithedale Romance* (1852), about a Utopian community, *The Snow-Image and Other Twice-Told Tales* (1851), and some children's books, including *Tanglewood Tales for Girls and Boys* (1853), he was glad to accept in 1853 the invitation of Pierce, now President of the United States, to be Consul in Liverpool. He served until 1857, after which he and his family spent two years in Rome and Florence, where he began *The Marble Faun* (1860; in Britain as *Transformation*, 1860), an Italian romance of innocence, experience, and guilt, with historical and mythological symbolism. When he died, probably of a brain tumour, he left four unfinished novels. EMERSON wrote in his journal: 'Yesterday we buried Hawthorne in Sleepy Hollow, in a pomp of sunshine and verdure, and gentle winds. . . . I thought him a greater man than any of his works betray, that there was still a great deal of work in him, and that he might one day show a purer power.' There were three children in all. The eldest, Una, caught a fever while sketching in the Colosseum in Rome in 1858, resulting in spells of insanity, and died unmarried at 32. Julian Hawthorne (1846–1934), author of popular novels and family biographies, served a prison sentence for fraud. Rose, the youngest, became a Dominican sister caring for terminal cancer patients. See Edwin Haviland Miller, *Salem Is My Dwelling Place: a Life of Nathaniel Hawthorne*, new edn 1993; T. Walter Herbert, *Dearest Beloved: the Hawthornes and the Making of the Middle-Class Family*, new edn 1995 (history of their marriage); Edward Wagenknecht, *Nathaniel Hawthorne: the Man, His Tales, and Romances*, 1989; Terence Martin, *Nathaniel Hawthorne*, rev. edn 1984 (critical study).

HAY, GEORGE CAMPBELL see HAY, JOHN MACDOUGALL.

HAY, IAN, pseudonym of John Hay Beith (1876–1952) Scottish novelist and dramatist, the grandson of a founder of the Free Church of Scotland, was born in Manchester and educated at Fettes College and St John's College, Cambridge. After writing *Pip: a Romance of Youth* (1907), still one of the best novels featuring cricket, and other novels in a similar buoyant vein, he gave up teaching for authorship. In 1914 he was commissioned in the Argyll and Sutherland Highlanders, serving with them and the Machine Gun Corps in France until 1916, and winning the Military Cross. During this time he wrote *The First Hundred Thousand* (1915) and *Carrying On* (1917). Their crisp, nonchalant style reflects the optimistic mood in which the war was then being conducted and the public school ethos which dominated its command, but they contain enough pathos and stark observation not to be dismissed as insensitive reportage. He was then posted to the British War Mission in the USA, and was made CBE in 1918. After the war he deftly adapted for the stage some of his novels, including

Happy-go-Lucky (1913), *A Safety Match* (1921), and *Housemaster* (1936), and collaborated with others, including WODEHOUSE, in dramatizing their works. He was Director of Public Relations at the War Office 1938–41, with the rank of major general. He was an unusual member of the monarch's body guard in Scotland, the Royal Company of Archers, in that he was an excellent shot with the bow.

HAY, JOHN MACDOUGALL (1881–1919) Scottish novelist, was born in Tarbert, Argyllshire, and educated at the local school and at Glasgow University. He taught in the West Highlands, but during or as a result of a severe attack of rheumatic fever, he decided to become a Church of Scotland minister. He returned to Glasgow University in 1905, keeping himself by freelance journalism, at which he had had some success in his undergraduate days. In 1909 he was appointed Minister of Elderslie, an urban parish, where he continued to work at a novel, *Gillespie* (1914), whose main character's driving ambition and demonic single-mindedness brings suffering to his family and destruction to the community and, ultimately, to himself. But for being published at the beginning of World War I, it might have had a similar impact to that of GEORGE DOUGLAS's *The House with the Green Shutters*, with which it has affinities and shares an intensity of vision and language. A second novel, *Barnacles* (1916), and a volume of free verse, *Their Dead Sons* (1918), were his only other published books. He died of tuberculosis. His son, George Campbell Hay (1915–84), taught himself Gaelic, in which he became a notable poet, as well as writing verse in English and Scots.

HAYDEN, ROBERT (1913–80) American poet, was born Asa Bundy Sheffy in the black ghetto of 'Paradise Valley', Detroit, and was shortly afterwards left with neighbours, who brought him up and gave him new names. His education was handicapped by myopia, but while going through the local school system he also took violin lessons at the Institute of Musical Art, and he had a poem, 'Africa', published in *Abbot's Weekly* in 1931. He went on to Detroit City College, where he majored in Spanish. He was then assigned by the Federal Writers' Project to research local history, negro folklore, and the anti-slavery movement during the years before the Civil War, which he later combined with the experience of his own upbringing as the essence of his most notable verse. As a part-time student, he won an award at the University of Michigan for a manuscript of poems, which was published in an enlarged form as *Heart-Shape in the Dust* (1940). As a full-time student from 1941 to 1944 he was taught by AUDEN. He was a professor of English at Fisk University from 1946 to 1969, and at the University of Michigan from 1969 until his death. His best-known poem is 'Middle Passage', a collage of vivid impressions of the Atlantic slave ships, which he first wrote in 1945 and revised for inclusion in *A Ballad of Remembrance* (1962). In 1976 he became the first black poet to be Consultant to the Library of Congress. See *Collected Poems*, ed. Frederick Glaysher, 2nd edn 1996; *The Collected Prose*, 1984; Fred M. Fetrow, *Robert Hayden*, 1984 (critical study).

HAYLEY, WILLIAM see BLAKE; SMITH, CHARLOTTE.

HAYWOOD, ELIZA (*c*.1693–1756), née Fowler, English novelist and dramatist, was born in London, the daughter of a shop-keeper. She married a Norfolk clergyman, Valentine Haywood, had a son who was baptized in London in 1711, and made her acting debut in Dublin in 1715. Her first novel, *Love in Excess: or, The Fatal Enquiry*, was published in three volumes in 1719–20. In 1721 her husband announced in a press advertisement that she had left him. She now began to turn out further steamy novels and somewhat scandalous 'secret histories' at such a pace that a collected *Works* was called for in 1724. She was also writing plays (including a comedy, *A Wife to be Lett*, in which she herself appeared in 1724), and publishing translations from the French. She seems during this time to have had two illegitimate children and several lovers, and she appears in Book II of POPE's *The Dunciad* (1728) as the indelicately-attired prize for a rather disgusting contest between two booksellers. During the 1730s she wrote little but did more acting, until the Licensing Act of 1737. She set up briefly as a publisher in Covent Garden in about 1740, and edited the monthly *Female Spectator* (the first magazine for women edited by a woman) from 1744 to 1746, and the weekly *Parrot* in 1746. By now the demand for popular fiction which she herself had helped to create was being very properly and differently met by SAMUEL RICHARDSON, HENRY FIELDING, and SMOLLETT in particular, but with true professional aplomb she produced *The History of Miss Betsy Thoughtless* (1751). The heroine, after losing her lover through her own vanity, seeks to become an independent woman, marries an unsuitable husband, leaves him, and is finally reunited with her lost lover, but in marriage, and only after the deaths of her husband and his wife. See *Three Novellas: The Distress'd Orphan, The Double Marriage, The City Jilt*, ed. Earla A. Wilputte, 1995.

HAZLITT, WILLIAM (1778–1830) British essayist and critic, was born in Maidstone, Kent, the son of a Unitarian minister who then moved to Ireland and America, before settling in Wem, Shropshire. At 14, Hazlitt was entered for the ministry at New College, Hackney, but abandoned his faith three years

later. In 1798 he met COLERIDGE, under whose influence he determined to be a writer, though in the meantime he studied painting, for which he had some talent. In 1804 he joined Coleridge and WORDSWORTH in the Lake District, but had to leave after attempting sexual assaults on local girls, one of whom he spanked when she resisted his advances. After some time in the wilderness he ventured to London, was taken up by LAMB, and became a reporter for the *Morning Chronicle*. He was soon promoted to writing dramatic and literary reviews, and moved on to other journals, including *The Times*. Within a few years he had enough material to publish *Characters of Shakespeare's Plays* (1817), *A View of the English Stage: or a Series of Dramatic Criticisms* (1818), and *Lectures on the English Poets* (1818). His attacks on the Romantic poets caused some offence, though he later reconsidered his judgments in *The Spirit of the Age: or Contemporary Portraits* (1825), where he developed his belief that to a critic the personality of the writer is as relevant as what he writes. A stimulating essayist with a wide range of literary styles, Hazlitt wrote perceptively and equally well about English poetry, prose, and drama from their beginnings and extended the field of literary historiography into his own times. He had two broken marriages and an unfortunate love-affair, details of which he paraded in *Liber Amoris: or, The New Pygmalion* (1823). See *Selected Writings*, ed. Jon Cook, 1991; Stanley Jones, *Hazlitt: a Life, from Winterslow to Frith Street*, new edn 1991; J. B. Priestley and R. L. Brett, *William Hazlitt*, 1994 (critical introduction).

HEAD, BESSIE (1937–86) novelist, was born in Pietermaritzburg, South Africa, in the mental asylum in which her mother, the daughter of a wealthy racehorse owner, had been confined (and where she died) for being pregnant by a black stable-hand. She was brought up by black foster parents, and was educated at a mission school for orphans. After four years' teaching in primary schools, she became a journalist with Drum Publications, Johannesburg. She married Harold Head in 1961, but in 1964, having been involved in the trial of a friend for African nationalist activities, she left him and went into exile in Botswana, of which she was granted citizenship in 1979. Her first novel, *When Rain Clouds Gather* (1969), reflects her own experience as a refugee from apartheid living at the Bamagwato Development Farm. *Maru* (1971) is a penetrating reminder that there can be questions of colour, and even racism, where there are no whites. In *A Question of Power* (1973) she re-creates the hallucinations of a disturbed mind, such as she herself had suffered, in the context of exile and rejection on the grounds of colour. *A Bewitched Crossroad: an African Saga* (1984) draws on and uses oral sources to present a slice of Bamagwato history. She died of hepatitis. *Tales of Tenderness and Power* (1990) takes stories from all her writing life. See *A Woman Alone: Autobiographical Writings*, ed. Craig MacKenzie, 1992; Gillian Stead Eilersen, *Bessie Head, 'Thunder Behind Her Ears': a Biography*, 1996.

HEANEY, SEAMUS (*b.* 1939) Irish poet and critic, was born in Mossbawm, Co. Derry, the eldest of nine children of a Catholic cattle dealer and farmer, and was educated at St Columb's College, Derry, and Queen's University, Belfast. He has lectured on poetry at Queen's University and at Harvard. The twin preoccupations of his youth, the land which gave his family their living and the sectarian hatred against Catholics in Northern Ireland (he has lived in the Irish Republic since 1972), have influenced his choice of themes, which he has presented with effective rhythm and without obscurity, a reflection also of his loyalty to his unbookish ancestry. He feels deeply, too, about the peat-bog caches of Ireland's ancient heritage (mud is a recurrent image in his verse), and has compared the sacrificial and penitential victims whose bodies have been unearthed (described in 'The Grauballe Man', 'Punishment', and 'Bog Queen') with those who have lost their lives in the conflicts in modern Ireland. Memories of childhood abound, as in the title poem of *Death of a Naturalist* (1966), while *The Haw Lantern* (1987) contains a sonnet sequence to the memory of his mother, who died in 1984. *Seeing Things* (1991) marks a change, in that he is ready to relate classical literature to today, rather than avoid literary allusions which the ordinary reader might miss. It also introduces a new form, which he calls 'Squarings', a sequence of 12-line poems in unrhymed tercets. A critical work, *The Government of the Tongue* (1988), explores the place of poetry in the contemporary environment, while expressing his own ambivalent attitude to poetry as his chosen career.

Heaney was appointed Boylston Professor of Rhetoric and Oratory at Harvard in 1985, and was Professor of Poetry at Oxford 1989–94. He was awarded the Nobel Prize for Literature in 1995—see *Crediting Poetry: the Nobel Lecture* (1996). The citation referred to his analysis of the violence in Northern Ireland but 'with the express reservation that he wants to avoid the conventional terms'. In his Oxford lecture, 'Frontiers of Writing'—in *The Redress of Poetry* (1995)—he answers critics who suggest he should in his work have taken sides in the conflict. His collection *The Spirit Level* (1996) reflects what he calls the 'fluid and restorative relationship between the mind's centre and its circumference', while at the same time bringing home the raw pain inherent in recent Irish history. See *New Selected Poems 1966–1987*, new edn 1991; *Preoccupations: Selected Prose 1968–1978*, new edn 1981; Ronald Tamplin, *Seamus Heaney*,

1989 (critical study); Michael Parker, *Seamus Heaney: the Making of a Poet*, new edn 1994 (critical study); Bernard O'Donoghue, *Seamus Heaney and the Language of Poetry*, 1994; Anthony Curtis, *The Art of Seamus Heaney*, 1995; Andrew Murphy, *Seamus Heaney*, 1996 (critical introduction).

HEARN, (PATRICK) LAFCADIO (1850–1904) novelist, journalist, and translator, was born in the island of Lafcadio, Greece, of a British army surgeon and a member of an ancient Ionian family. His mother went mad, and he was brought up in Dublin by a widowed Roman Catholic great-aunt, by whom he was left to fend for himself after education in England at St Cuthbert's College, Ushaw, where he lost an eye, and for a year in France at a seminary near Rouen. In 1869 he arrived in Cincinnati, Ohio, and there, and in New Orleans from 1881 to 1887, he scraped what living he could from journalism, his progress being hampered by his association (and possibly marriage) with a black woman. He wrote effective 'Creole Sketches', and published two volumes of curious tales, *Stray Leaves from Strange Literature* (1884) and *Some Chinese Ghosts* (1887). *Chita: a Memory of the Last Island* (1889), is a Symbolist novel. In Martinique, about which he wrote *Two Years in the French West Indies* (1890), he discovered the ready-made plot of *Youma: the Story of a West Indian Slave* (1890). In 1890 he went to Japan to write some articles for *Harper's New Monthly Magazine*, and stayed for the rest of his life. He married the daughter of an old samurai family, which adopted him, with the name of Yakumo Koizumi, when in 1895 he became a citizen of Japan. He was Professor of English Literature at the Imperial University, Tokyo, from 1896 until forced to resign in 1903. He wrote some interesting works on Japanese culture, including *Glimpses of Unfamiliar Japan* (1894) and *Japan: an Attempt at Interpretation* (1904). His translations include *Gombo Zhèbes: Little Dictionary of Creole Proverbs* (1885), and works of DAUDET, FRANCE, GAUTIER, MAUPASSANT, and ZOLA. See *Lafcadio Hearn: Japan's Great Interpreter, a New Anthology of His Writings 1894–1904*, ed. Louis Allen and Jean Wilson, 1992.

HEATH-STUBBS, JOHN (*b.* 1918) British poet, critic, dramatist, and translator, was born in London, but lived in Hampshire from the ages of six to 24. He was educated in the Isle of Wight, at Worcester College for the Blind, and at The Queen's College, Oxford, where he was influenced by the teaching of C. S. LEWIS and CHARLES WILLIAMS, and was a considerable influence on KEYES. His first book of verse, *Wounded Thammuz*, was published in 1942. He was Gregory Fellow in Poetry, Leeds University 1952–55, Visiting Professor of English, Alexandria University 1955–58, and Lecturer in English, College of

St Mark and St John, Chelsea 1963–73. HAM-
BURGER has cited the 'courage and dignity'
with which Heath-Stubbs 'has borne the affliction . . . of not [being] preferred because
the Establishment to which he has always
been committed was shifting all the time, and
he was not'; the poet and critic C. H. Sisson
(b. 1914) has described him as 'a Johnsonian
presence with a Miltonic disability', a reference to his blindness. Neverthless he is an essentially human as well as a humorous poet,
much of whose work brings the past to bear
on the present, and the present on the future,
as for example in 'Saint Francis Preaches to
the Computers', 'Apologia of a Plastic
Gnome', 'Further Adventures of Dr Faustus',
and 'To a Poet a Thousand Years Hence',
which also demonstrate his ironic wit. His
verse dramas have been published in *Helen
in Egypt and Other Plays* (1958), and he has
translated into English the poetry of LEOP-
ARDI (1946), and, with Peter Avery, HAFIZ
(1952) and OMAR KHAYYÁM (1979). He was
awarded the Queen's Gold Medal for Poetry
in 1973, and made OBE in 1989. See *Collected
Poems 1943–1987*, 1988; *Selected Poems*, 1990;
Sweetapple Earth, 1993 (subsequent collection); *Hindsights: an Autobiography*, new edn
1994.

HÉBERT, ANNE (b. 1916) French-Canadian novelist and poet, was born in Sainte-
Catherine-de-Fossambault, Quebec, the
daughter of a literary critic, and was educated in Quebec at Collège Saint-Coeur de
Marie and Collège Notre Dame. She was influenced by her cousin, the poet of cultural
liberation for Quebec, Hector de Saint-Denys
Garneau (1912–43), whose early death
deeply affected her and the course of her
writing. She published a book of verse in
1942, and then in 1950, at her own expense,
Le Torrent (tr. Gwendolyn Moore as *The Torrent: Novellas and Short Stories*, 1973), whose
title story in particular reflects her attitude of
revolt against the prevailing order of things.
The poems in *Tombeau des Rois* (1953; tr. Peter
Miller as *The Tomb of the Kings*, 1967; tr. Joanne Collier, ed. Timothy Mathews and Michael Worton, as *Tomb of the Kings*, bilingual
edn 1996) present an exploration of self in the
face of death. It was reissued with a second
cycle, 'Mystère de la Parole', as *Poèmes* (1960,
winner of the Governor General's Award; tr.
Alan Brown as *Poems by Anne Hébert*, 1975)—
see also *Selected Poems*, tr. A. Poulin (1987).
During the 1950s she worked for Radio Canada and the National Film Board, and with a
government grant spent three years in Paris,
where she wrote her first novel, *Les Chambres
de Bois* (1958; tr. Kathy Mezei as *The Silent
Rooms*, 1974), whose theme of liberation is
similar to that embodied in her verse. *Ka-
mouraska* (1970; tr. Norman Shapiro, 1973),
which explores in a 19th-century setting a
woman's anguish at her past, is the first of

four novels of strange happenings, breathless
suspense, witchcraft, and the murder of innocent victims, which in *Héloïse* (1980; tr. Sheila
Fischman, 1982) is the work of a female vampire who haunts the Paris Metro.

HECHT, ANTHONY (b. 1923) American
poet and critic, was born in New York City,
and was educated at Bard College, Annan-
dale-on-Hudson. After serving in the US
Navy in World War II, he became a university
professor, in which capacity he has taught
principally at New York University, Smith
College, Bard College, and Rochester University, becoming University Professor, Graduate School, Georgetown University, in 1985.
His first book of verse, *A Summoning of
Stones*, was published in 1954; *The Hard Hours*
(1967; Pulitzer Prize) contained 15 poems
from that book, together with *The Seven
Deadly Sins* (1958) and other poems. *The Venetian Vespers* (expanded edn 1979) includes
some longer poems reflecting especially on
ecological, architectural, and social contrasts.
Recent volumes are *The Transparent Man*
(1990) and *Flight among the Tombs* (1996), a
witty, elegant collection comprising the sequences 'Presumptions of Death', and
'Proust on Skates'. *Collected Earlier Poems* was
published in 1990. He is a poet-critic in the
tradition of AUDEN and RANSOM, whose carefully crafted verse displays erudition, humour, and a concern for human relationships
as well as for such international catastrophes
as the Black Death and the Holocaust. His
critical works include *Obbligati: Essays in Criticism* (1986), a study of Auden (1993), and *On
the Laws of the Poetic Art* (A W Mellon Lectures, 1995).

HEINE, HEINRICH (1797–1856) German
poet and critic, was born Harry Heinrich, of
Jewish parentage and upbringing, in Dusseldorf, and was trained there and in Frankfurt and Hamburg for a business career. In
1819 his rich uncle Solomon, a Hamburg
banker, with whose daughter Heine had
fallen in love, sent him to study law at Bonn
University. He transferred to Gottingen,
which he left for Berlin after being involved
in a duel. He later returned to Berlin to become LLD in 1825, having already published
a book of verse (1822) and two tragedies
(1823). He now (for the sake of convenience)
had himself baptized, and embarked on a period of travel (including England and Italy),
on which he based the quirkish prose reminiscences, *Reisebilder* (4 vols 1826–31; tr.
Charles Godfrey Leland as *Pictures of Travel*,
1855). *Buch der Lieder* (1826; tr. J. E. Wallis as
Book of Songs, 1856) established his claim to
be the poetic successor of GOETHE. The political situation in Germany and his interest in
the social philosophy of Comte de Saint-
Simon (1760–1825) moved him in 1831 to
seek voluntary exile in Paris (he accepted a

subsidy, which he did not really need, from the reactionary French government in 1840), where he set about explaining the German character to the French in essays among the miscellaneous prose and verse in *Der Salon* (4 vols 1834–40). Similar sentiments, and the polarities of his vision, are reflected in two mock-heroic poems: *Deutschland: Ein Wintermärchen* [Germany: a Winter's Tale] (1844), a political satire, and *Atta Troll: Ein Sommernachtstraum* [Atta Troll: a Summer Night's Dream] (1847), which he described as 'the last free forest-song of Romanticism'.

In 1834 he began living with a 19-year-old semi-literate grisette, Crescentia Mirat (*d.* 1883), whom he called 'Mathilde'. They married in 1841. From about 1848 he was confined to his 'mattress-grave' (a pile of mattresses on the floor) with an excruciating form of tertiary syphilis which affected his spine. He still managed calmly to compose in his head, and to dictate, the two cycles of *Lazarus Poems* (tr. Alistair Eliot, 1992). His secretary during his final years, to whom as Mouche he wrote several poems, was Elise Krinitz, who after his death became the mistress of the French philosopher and historian Hippolyte Taine (1828–93), and was subsequently a schoolteacher in Rouen. Regarded by Jews as a renegade, by Christians as a Jew, by the French as a German, and by many Germans as a turncoat, he was the first considerable writer of Jewish birth in modern times to have felt free to indulge in humour. GEORGE ELIOT's article, 'German Wit: Heinrich Heine', appeared in the *Westminster Review* a month before his death. *Poems of Heine Complete: translated* [by Edgar Alfred Bowring] *in the Original Metres* was published in 1858. ARNOLD's significant critical essay was printed in *Cornhill Magazine* in 1863. See *The Complete Poems*, tr. Hal Draper, new edn 1984; *Songs of Love and Grief*, tr. Walter W. Arndt, foreword by Jeffrey L. Sammons, 1996 (bilingual edn); *Selected Prose*, ed. and tr. Ritchie Robertson, 1993; Ernst Pawel, *The Poet Dying: Heinrich Heine's Last Years in Paris*, 1995; Ritchie Robertson, *Heine*, 1988 (study of his thought).

HEINLEIN, ROBERT A(NSON) (1907–88) American novelist, short-story writer, and children's novelist, was born in Butler, Missouri, the third of seven children of poor parents. After Kansas City Central High School, he worked his way through a year at Kansas City Junior College, and then obtained a place at the US Navy Academy, Annapolis, from which he passed 20th out of 243 in 1929. He served as a gunnery officer, but was discharged in 1934 with tuberculosis. After postgraduate study in physics at the University of California, he tried real estate, silver mining, and politics, without success. In 1939 he responded to the challenge of a $50 prize contest by writing a story, 'Life-

Line', which he sent instead to *Astounding Science Fiction*, reckoning that he would earn more. By 1941 he was supplying, under his own name and that of Anson MacDonald, a fifth of the magazine's copy. He spent the years 1942–45 as a civil research engineer at the Naval Air Experimental Station in Philadelphia. An innovator in that he employed his knowledge of technology as a starting point from which seriously to explore new situations, he became with *Stranger in a Strange Land* (1961), his eighth adult novel, the first science fiction writer to feature in the *New York Times* bestseller list. It also confounded both him and critics by becoming a hippie text. In much the same way, *The Moon is a Harsh Mistress* (1966) was a cult book for libertarians. His range of forms within the genre is wide, embracing also the fantasy world of *The Number of the Beast* (1980) and the irony of *The Cat Who Walks Through Walls: a Comedy of Manners* (1985). Other pen names of his magazine days are Simon Yorke, Lyle Monroe, John Riverside, and Caleb Saunders. See Leon Stover, *Robert Heinlein*, 1987 (critical study).

HELLER, JOSEPH (*b.* 1923) American novelist, was born in the Coney Island section of Brooklyn, New York, of Jewish immigrant descent, and after Abraham Lincoln High School worked for a year as a filing clerk before enlisting in the US Army Air Force in 1942. In 1944–45 he flew sixty combat missions from Corsica as a wing bombardier. After graduating from Columbia University, New York, he did further study at Oxford as a Fulbright scholar, and then taught composition for two years at Pennsylvania State University. He then went into advertising, rising from copywriter on *Time* magazine to promotion manager for *McCall's*, while working at night on the design of his first novel, *Catch-22* (1961). Set in the wartime milieu in which he served, this black, philosophical comedy of modern existence became what has been called the most popular serious novel of the decade, and donated its title as a coinage to the language. Heller spent some seven of the next 12 years writing *Something Happened* (1974), a penetrating study of a tormented business executive and his relations in the office and at home, especially with his children. *Good as Gold* (1979) and *God Knows* (1984) are Jewish novels not just because the protagonist of the first is a Jewish academic, comically caught between two polarities of assimilation, and of the second is King David himself, with a splendid line in anachronistic wisecracks, but because they reflect Jewish tradition. Several of the characters in *Catch-22* reappear, fifty years on, in *Closing Time* (1994), an even more surreal romp through the madness which Heller sees afflicting modern America. He made a stage dramatization of *Catch-22*

(1973) and also wrote an Absurdist drama, *We Bombed in New Haven* (1968). *No Laughing Matter* (1986), written with Speed Vogel, is largely an account of how he coped with the onset of and recovery from the dangerously crippling neurological condition, Guillain-Barré syndrome. See Adam J. Sorkin (ed.), *Conversations with Joseph Heller*, 1993; Judith Ruderman, *Joseph Heller*, 1992 (critical study).

HELLMAN, LILLIAN (1905–84) American dramatist, was born of Jewish descent in New Orleans, to which her father's parents had emigrated from Germany in the 1840s. She resented her mother's rich middle-class family, who were from Demopolis, Alabama, but after she had written them out of her system in *The Little Foxes* (1939), 'this conflict was to grow less important'. When her father, having 'lost my mother's large dowry', became a travelling salesman, she spent half her time in New Orleans and half in New York, making 'my New Orleans teachers uncomfortable because I was too far ahead of my schoolmates, and my New York teachers irritable because I was too far behind'. After two years at New York University, she got a job with a publishing firm, which she left after a year to marry Arthur Kober; in 1930 they went to Hollywood, where she read manuscripts and he wrote scenarios. One evening she met HAMMETT, who was 'getting over a five day drunk. . . . We talked of T. S. Eliot . . . and then went and sat in his car and talked at each other until it was daylight.' When he returned to New York, she went with him (she was divorced in 1932).

Hammett, with whom she lived on and off for the rest of his life, was a stern critic of her plays. The first was *The Children's Hour* (1934), a study of good and evil in a girls' school, where two teachers are maliciously accused of having a lesbian relationship; with hindsight it presages the anti-Communist witch hunts of the 1950s during which Hellman was to be blacklisted. *Days to Come* (1936) failed: not so *The Little Foxes*. Having seen at first hand Fascist inhumanity in Spain in 1937, she demonstrated her convictions in an anti-Nazi drama, *Watch on the Rhine* (1941). She returned to her 'Little Foxes' family, twenty years earlier, in *Another Part of the Forest* (1947), and created a New Orleans family, based on the other side of hers, for *The Autumn Garden* (1951) and *Toys in the Attic* (1960). Sharp dialogue backs a destructive, often self-destructive, power at work in her characters and situations. She visited the USSR in 1944 in connection with productions there of her plays. In 1952 she was called before the House of Representatives Committee on Un-American Activities. In refusing to testify, she said: 'To hurt innocent people whom I knew many years ago in order to save myself is, to me, inhuman and indecent and dishonorable. I cannot and will not cut my con-

science to fit this year's fashions . . .'. *An Unfinished Woman* (1969) is an impressionistic autobiographical study; it was reissued, with *'Pentimento': a Book of Portraits* (1973), which includes her relationship with HAMMETT, and *Scoundrel Time* (1976), an account of the investigations into Communist activities, as *Three* (1979). *Maybe* (1980) is a final volume of reminiscences. See *The Collected Plays of Lillian Hellman*, 1972; Carl Rollyson, *Lillian Hellman: Her Legend and Her Legacy*, new edn 1989.

HEMANS, FELICIA (1793–1835), née Browne, British poet and translator, was born in Liverpool of a talented family, and brought up in Wales, where, her father having abandoned his family and gone to Canada, she was taught French, Italian, Spanish, and Portuguese by her mother, and Latin by the local vicar. *Poems* (1808), the contents of which was written between the ages of eight and 13, created a stir both before and after publication. P. B. SHELLEY was sufficiently impressed by it, and by an account of its author's looks, to try and enter into a correspondence with her, but was put in his place by her mother. She had published two more volumes of verse by 1818, when she married Captain Alfred Hemans, a former army officer, wounded in the Peninsular war and retired without pay, in 1812. He walked out on her and went to Italy six years later, leaving her with five sons—evidence suggests that he was humiliated not only by her versifying but by her ability to earn from it. *Translations from Camoens and Other Poets* appeared in 1818, followed regularly by further competent efforts in a variety of forms. She lived variously in Dublin, Wales, and Lancashire, and in 1829 visited Scotland, where WALTER SCOTT took her for a walk: 'She is young and pretty. . . . There is taste and spirit in her conversation. My daughters are critical, and call her blue, but I think they are hypercritical.' Her popularity was considerable, and a collected edition of her poems was published in the USA in 1825. Her best-remembered lines, 'The boy stood on the burning deck . . .' (from 'Casabianca') and 'The stately homes of England, / How beautiful they stand' ('The Homes of England'), belie her true ability, though her contribution is perhaps best summed up by Professor Ian Jack in *English Literature 1815–1832* (1963): 'For her, we feel, poetry was a feminine accomplishment more difficult than piano-playing and embroidery but no less respectable.' See JEWSBURY.

HEMINGWAY, ERNEST (MILLER) (1899–1961) American novelist and short-story writer, was born in Oak Park, Illinois, the second of six children of a general practitioner, who in 1928 shot himself. He was educated at Oak Park High School, where he wrote stories for the two student journals and played a lot of sport. Not regarding himself as university material, he obtained through an uncle a job as cub reporter on the *Kansas City Star*, which he gave up in 1918 after a few months to volunteer for ambulance duties in World War I. He was posted to Italy, infiltrated himself into the front line at Fossalta di Piave, and was blown up by a mortar shell. He returned home with a medal for bravery and 227 scars on his legs. In 1921 he married Hadley Richardson, eight years his senior. On the money from her trust fund and with a commission as foreign correspondent of the Toronto *Star*, they went to Paris, where ANDERSON had provided introductions to STEIN and other expatriate members of the literary set. *A Moveable Feast*, written with hindsight in the late 1950s and published posthumously (1964), comprises sketches of people he knew during those years—see also Peter Griffin, *Less than a Treason: Hemingway in Paris* (1992). He travelled in Europe and spent much time in Spain. He published in Paris *Three Stories and Ten Poems* (1923) and *In Our Time* (1924), reissued in the USA (1925) with the sketches of violence interspersed with stories of an adolescent growing up. Further books now followed: *The Torrents of Spring* (1926), a parody of Anderson; *Men Without Women* (1927), a significant short-story collection; and *The Sun Also Rises* (1926; in UK as *Fiesta*, 1927), his first major novel, which reflects in theme and structure the rootless existence of postwar expatriates in Europe. Hadley divorced him and in 1927 he married her friend—see Gioia Diliberto, *Hadley: a Life of Hadley Richardson Hemingway* (1992). In 1928 he set up a permanent base in the USA, in Key West, Florida, which he used as a winter home.

In *A Farewell to Arms* (1929) an American officer in the Italian ambulance service in World War I falls in love with a nurse, as Hemingway himself had done, and is then wounded. The rest is imaginative reconstruction, a bleak vision of useless waste of life, vividly presented in the economic style and with the telling, spare dialogue that are his hallmarks. Always accident-prone, he badly broke his right arm in 1930 when his car turned over, which held up progress on his scholarly, often philosophical study of bull-fighting as an art, *Death in the Afternoon* (1932). *Green Hills of Africa* (1935) is his account of big-game hunting in Kenya and Tanganyika. As a correspondent again, he made four visits to Spain during the Civil War of 1936–39, during which he became firmly associated with the Loyalist cause, but refused a fighting role because of 'the carnival of treachery and rottenness on both sides'. Another war correspondent was Martha Gellhorn (*b.* 1908), later a novelist in her own right, whom he had met in Key West in 1935; they married in 1940 after his second divorce. Betrayal on both sides in the Spanish war is a feature of *For Whom the Bell Tolls* (1940)—the title is from DONNE's *Devotions*—in which the blowing up of a bridge behind the enemy lines is the mainspring of the plot and a symbol of the futility of politicization.

In 1942 he established a private watch for Nazi submarines off Cuba, where he was then living, by equipping his yacht as an armed Q-boat; the posthumously published *Islands in the Stream* (1970) is a fictionalized account of the operation. In 1944 he flew to London to write articles about the Royal Air Force at war, and managed to get himself into Normandy shortly after the Allied landings, and then to attach himself to the 4th Infantry Division. He saw plenty of action during the advance, at one point mobilizing his own band of partisans, and was a member of a private army of irregulars which played a part in the liberation of Paris.

Martha divorced him in 1945, and the following March he formalized his marriage to Mary Welsh, whom he had met in London in 1944, and with whom he set up home in Ketchum, Idaho. *The Old Man and the Sea* (1952), a basically simple story of fortitude in the face of disaster, which lends itself to allegorical interpretation, was instrumental in his winning the Nobel Prize for Literature in 1954 'for his powerful and style-forming mastery of the art of modern narration . . .'. In some respects the award was posthumous, as after the first of two plane crashes in Uganda in January he and Mary were reported dead, and obituaries had appeared in the world press. In the second he suffered injuries from which he did not recover mentally. In June 1961 he was discharged from a psychiatric clinic, although he had twice threatened suicide. Two days after getting home he emptied a double-barrelled shotgun into his head. See *Complete Short Stories of Ernest Hemingway*, ed. John Patrick and Gregory Hemingway, new edn 1991; Michael S. Reynolds, *The Young Hemingway*, new edn 1987, *Hemingway's First War: the Making of 'A Farewell to Arms'*, new edn 1987, and *Hemingway: the American Homecoming*, 1992; Kenneth Schuyler Lynn, *Hemingway: His Life and Work*, new edn 1995; Carlos Baker, *Hemingway, the Writer as Artist*, 4th edn 1992 (critical study); Miriam B. Mandel, *Reading Hemingway: the Facts in the Fictions*, 1995 (critical study); Marie Rose Burwell, *Hemingway: the Postwar Years and the Posthumous Novels*, 1996 (critical study).

HENDRY, J. F. see TREECE.

HENLEY, W(ILLIAM) E(RNEST) (1849–1903) poet and critic, was born in Gloucester, the eldest son of a local bookseller, and was educated at the Crypt Grammar School, Gloucester. At 12, he was crippled with tubercular arthritis, which early on necessitated the amputation of a foot. To save the other one, he went to Edinburgh in 1873, where for 20 months he was the patient of Professor Joseph (later Lord) Lister (1827–1912), the founder of antiseptic surgery. During this time he was introduced to STEVENSON, with whom he later collaborated in writing four plays, none of which had much popular success. He also wrote a sequence of 'Hospital Verses', part of which, including the much-quoted 'Invictus' ('Out of the night that covers me, / Black as the pit from pole to pole . . .'), was first published in 1875 in *Cornhill Magazine*, and the whole in *A Book of Verses* (1888). He was Editor of the *Scots Observer* (later *National Observer*) from 1889 to 1894; the contributors included BARRIE, HARDY, KIPLING, and YEATS. *The Song of the Sword and Other Verses* (1892), which contained a collection of 'London Voluntaries', was reprinted with additions in 1893 as *London Voluntaries*, and reissued as *Poems* in 1898. *For England's Sake: Verses and Songs in Time of War* (1900) mirrors the patriotic spirit at the beginning of the Boer War, and offers an extraordinary contrast to his more personal and reflective poems, often written in experimental rhythms.

HENRI, ADRIAN see MCGOUGH.

HENRY, O., pseudonym of William Sidney (or Sydney) Porter (1862–1910) American short-story writer and journalist, was born in Greensboro, North Carolina, where he was educated at a private school. He left at 15 to be apprenticed to a pharmacist, and in 1881 obtained a state licence to practise. He then went to Texas, where he worked on a ranch, as a book-keeper, and as a draughtsman in the state land office. He was a teller in the National Bank, Austin, from 1891 to 1894, when he bought the magazine, the *Iconoclast*, which he renamed the *Rolling Stone* and sold back to the original owner after a year. In 1896 he was charged with embezzlement from the National Bank, and fled to Honduras. He returned home because of his wife's illness, and gave himself up when she died. He was sentenced to five years in the Federal Penitentiary, Columbus, Ohio. He worked in the prison pharmacy, and to suppport his daughter wrote stories as O. Henry (also Oliver Henry and S. H. Peters), the first of which appeared in *McClure's Magazine* in 1899. On his release after just over three years, he went to New York, where he became during his lifetime America's most highly regarded and also most prolific writer of short stories, many of which were published in *Sunday World*. Those in his first collection, *Cabbages and Kings* (1904), are set in Central America and reflect characters he met during his exile. With *The Four Million* (1906), a reference to the population of New York City, and other volumes, he became the champion of the ordinary people of the city, evoking their trage-

dies and aspirations with humour and artistry, usually with an arresting opening to the story and a surprising twist at the end. There were enough stories for several collections to be published posthumously. See *Collected Stories*, 1994; *Selected Stories*, ed. Guy Davenport, 1993.

HENRYSON, ROBERT (*c*.1425–*c*.1500) Scottish poet, is named in DUNBAR's 'Lament for the Makaris' (printed in 1508): 'In Dunfermelyne he [Death] hes done roune [talked] / With Maister Robert Henrisoun'. 'Maister' usually means Master of Arts, and though there is no firm evidence of his having attended St Andrews or Glasgow University, he may have studied abroad, and he displays enough knowledge of law to have done so. Or the title may refer simply to the calling of schoolmaster, in which case he probably taught at the grammar school of Dunfermline Abbey. He, Dunbar, and GAVIN DOUGLAS in particular are sometimes called 'Scottish Chaucerians', and though Henryson, more than the others, owes and ackowledges a debt to CHAUCER, the term is misleading if it is meant to imply that they were merely imitators.

In *Testament of Cresseid*, Henryson employs as a starting point Chaucer's *Troilus and Criseyde* and its metre (but with the telling, and very Scottish, addition of alliteration), and develops from the situation an original, tragic, and moving end to the story. Cresseid, used and then abandoned by Diomeid, descends to prostitution in the Greek camp, reproaches the gods for her state, and is struck with leprosy as punishment. As she sits by the roadside with her leper's cup and clapper, her former lover Troilus passes by. Something reminds him of the young woman he once knew, and he throws her alms, but they do not recognize each other. Henryson's wit flows in his 'Fables', 14 morality tales, again in rhyme royal, lightly based on the legendary Aesop but set in the contemporary social climate of Scotland, in which the attributes of his animals are described with a refreshing pre-Romantic realism and the same attention to detail that POTTER gave to her characters five hundred years later. The dialogue with which he invests them is appropriate, colloquial, and pithy. His third sustained work is *Orpheus and Eurydice*, a reworking of the classical legend as a Christian allegory. Two of his shorter poems are especially noteworthy, and enjoyable. 'The Bludy Serk' ('The Bloodstained Shirt') suggests the existence already of a ballad tradition and of the traditional ballad metre. 'Robene and Makyne', probably the earliest pastoral dialogue in post-classical European poetry, has a secular, and pointed, moral. Robene is more concerned with counting his sheep than making love to Makyne. When he gets round to responding, she has had second thoughts.

Henryson's achievement was remarkable. He brought to his poetic talent a profoundly religious but compassionate nature, a ready wit, and the ability to illuminate precisely and graphically the cosmic knowledge and social background of his times. *The Morall Fabillis of Esope, Compylit in Eloquent and Ornate Scottis Meter* was first published in Edinburgh in 1570. *Testament of Cresseid* was first printed by William Thynne in his edition of *The Workes of Chaucer* (1532). See *The Poems*, ed. Denton Fox, 1987; Matthew P. MacDiarmid, *Robert Henryson*, 1981 (critical study).

HENTY, G(EORGE) A(LFRED)

(1832–1902) British novelist, was born in Trumpington, Cambridge, the eldest son of a stockbroker, and was educated at Westminster School and Gonville and Caius College, Cambridge, which he soon left without taking a degree. He served in the Hospital Commissariat in the Crimean War (1854–56); his letters describing the siege of Sebastopol were published in the *Morning Advertiser*. After being invalided home with fever, he held senior posts in the Commissariat Department, but then preferred to seek a career as a roving journalist and war correspondent; between 1866 and 1876 he witnessed actions on land and sea in Europe, Abyssinia, and West Africa. He then settled down to write fiction, mainly stories for boys; when he ran out of settings and heroic situations of which he had personal experience, he transposed his formula to historical times and events. Thus in 1883, for instance, he produced *With Clive in India*; *By Sheer Pluck: a Tale of the Ashanti Wars*; *Jack Archer: a Tale of the Crimea*; and *Friends, Though Divided: a Tale of the Civil War*. He was a storyteller who took trouble with his background detail, not an interpretive historian. His main intent, described in a posthumous article in the *Boys' Own Paper*, was 'to endeavour to inculcate patriotism', and he claimed 'that very many boys have joined the cadets and afterwards gone into the Army through reading my stories'. Mention should also be made of his last published book, *A Soldier's Daughter* (1906), in which Nita Acworth, a crack shot and a fair boxer and cricketer, saves the day and the reputation of her father's regiment in India. Henty was a keen sailor, who took part in races across the North Sea in his own yacht, in which he died in Weymouth Harbour.

HERBERT OF CHERBURY, (EDWARD), 1ST LORD

(1582–1648) English prose writer and poet, the eldest brother of GEORGE HERBERT, was born at Eyton-on-Severn, Shropshire, of a prominent landed family, and was educated at University College, Oxford. During his time at Oxford he was married, at 16, to a cousin five years older than he was, and his mother came to live with them. He was ambassador to France from 1619 to 1624, when he was recalled and rewarded with a token Irish peerage. Though he was created Baron Herbert of Cherbury in 1629, was assiduous in serving and petitioning the royal house, and began a definitive biography of Henry VIII (published posthumously in 1649), the lukewarm response of Charles I and his own ill-health prevented him from giving whole-hearted support to the royalist cause during the Civil War. In 1644 he surrendered his castle at Montgomery to the Parliamentary forces rather than lose his library, and retired to his London house, where he devoted himself to literature. He was an adept philosopher in verse rather than a true poet, and it was largely as a philosopher that he made his mark in prose. *De Veritate*, a treatise in Latin, had been published in Paris in 1624; he enlarged on its deistic principles in *De Religione Laici* (1645) and *De Religione Gentilium* (1663). His most lasting contribution to English literature is his autobiography to 1624, first published by HORACE WALPOLE in 1764. Vivid, racy, and often amusing, it presents the philosopher poet as a man of action, court and diplomatic intriguer, and amorist, but always as a gentleman. See *The Poems English and Latin*, ed. G. C. Moore Smith, new edn 1968; *The Life of Edward, First Lord Herbert of Cherbury: Written by Himself*, ed. J. M. Shuttleworth, 1976.

HERBERT, GEORGE

(1593–1633) English poet, was born in Montgomery, Wales, a younger brother of LORD HERBERT, and was educated at Westminster School and Trinity College, Cambridge, where he became a Fellow, and was later appointed Public Orator of the University. Though taking orders within seven years was a condition of his college post, and he was a devout Anglican, he first settled for politics and was elected Member of Parliament for Montgomery in 1624 and again in 1625. Only in 1630 did he decide on ordination, in which he may have been influenced by his mother's friend DONNE. For the rest of his life he was Rector of Bemerton, Wiltshire. *A Priest to the Temple; or the Country Parson; His Character, and Rule of Holy Life*, first published in full in 1671, is a prose treatise on the duties and responsibilities of such a position. From Cambridge he had addressed two sonnets to his mother in which he dedicated his poetic inspiration totally to religious themes. Much of his poetry was written in his thirties and reflects primarily the spiritual struggles which haunted his earlier years. Particularly effective are 'The Collar' and 'The Pulley'. His often original and ingenious metrical forms include two early examples of concrete verse, 'The Altar' and 'Easter Wings', and his poetry is particularly distinguished by his frequent use of homely images. His poems were published in 1633, after his death from consumption, as *The Temple: Sacred Poems and Private Ejaculations*. See *Complete English Poems*, ed. John Tobin, 1992; *The English Works, with Walton's 'Life'*, ed. Ann Pasternak Slater, 1995; [*Selected Verse*] ed. Louis L. Martz, 1994; James Boyd White, *'This Book of Starres': Learning to Read George Herbert*, new edn 1995; T. S. Eliot, *George Herbert*, rev edn ed. Peter Porter 1994 (critical introduction).

HERBERT, (ALFRED FRANCIS) XAVIER (1901–84) Australian novelist, was born in Port Hedland, Western Australia, and grew up among Aboriginal children. He was educated at the Christian Brothers College, Fremantle, and the Technical College, Perth. After qualifying as a pharmacist, he studied medicine for a year at Melbourne University, which he left to be a writer—his first story, as Herbert Astor, was published in the *Australian Journal* in 1926. After working in northern Australia as a railway labourer, pearl diver, and prison warder, he sailed from Darwin for London in 1930. On board he met Sadie Nordern, a Jewish woman whose marriage had failed and who later became his wife. When he returned to Australia in 1932 he had with her encouragement written the vast manuscript of *Capricornia*, which was accepted for publication subject to revisions, but abandoned after being set in type when the firm went into liquidation. One copy was finally 'issued' in 1937 to meet the conditions of the Sesquicentennial Commonwealth Prize, which it won: formal publication was in 1938. While social protest, especially about the treatment of Aborigines, predominates, it is also a novel about the land and the effect of the seasons, with a human cast of hundreds. Having falsified his age, Herbert served in the ranks in the Pacific during World War II, after which he settled in northern Queensland. Criticism of the style and eccentric punctuation of his next work, the novella *Seven Emus* (1959), caused him to rewrite *Soldiers' Women* (1961), a wartime novel of female sexuality, on which subject his views were fairly hidebound. *Poor Fellow My Country* (1975), on which he worked, often in complete isolation, for nine years, is said to be the longest novel ever published in Australia. Regarded by most critics more as an immense poem than a story, it embodies his ultimate statements about colonialism, while evoking the culture and people which it destroyed. *Larger than Life* (1963) is a collection of short stories. *Disturbing Element* (1963) is a somewhat imaginative autobiography to 1925. See Laurie Clancy, *Xavier Herbert*, 1981 (biographical/critical study).

HERODOTUS (484–420 BC) classical Greek historian, was born of a noble family in Halicarnassus, on the coast of Asia Minor, which he left when young to escape an oppressive rule. During his life he travelled through Asia Minor, the Near East, Egypt, Thrace, Scythia, and Greece in search of material, finally settling in the new Athenian colony of Thurii, in southern Italy. There is a tradition that in 446 he gave a public reading from his history in Athens, and was rewarded with ten talents of silver, the equivalent of about 250 kg in weight. The nine books of his great work were written, he tells us, to preserve from decay the wonderful deeds of the Greeks and the Barbarians (Persians), and to put on record the grounds of their conflict, culminating in the final defeat of Xerxes in 479. The original meaning of the Greek word 'history' is research, and in the investigation and verification of sources, as well as the arrangement and presentation of a unified theme, the realistic treatment of battle scenes and of human behaviour, and the understanding of the points of view of both sides, he is justly known as the 'Father of History'. See *The Histories*, tr. Aubrey de Sélincourt, new edn 1996.

HERRICK, ROBERT (1591–1674) English poet, was born in Cheapside, London, the seventh child of a goldsmith who, a year later, fell, or jumped, to his death from the upper floor of the house. He may have been educated at Westminster School. At 16 he was apprenticed to his uncle, another goldsmith, from whom he got his release in 1613 to go to St John's College, Cambridge, though he took his BA and MA degrees from Trinity Hall. He was ordained in 1623, but preferred the literary life of London and the frequent company of JONSON, before being given the living of Dean Prior in distant Devonshire by Charles I in 1629. Here he remained for the rest of his long life except for the years 1647–62, during most of which he was suspended by Parliament for his royalist affiliations. *Hesperides: or Works both Humane and Divine* (1648)—with a separate section and title page for 'Noble Numbers: or his Pious Pieces'—included most of his lyrics. Delicately constructed and infused with wit, they reflect some discontent with country routine, but still represent a joyous return to classical forms and themes, and a celebration of romantic love and rustic life (especially fruit, cream, flowers, and revels). 'To the Virgins, to Make Much of Time' ('Gather ye rosebuds while ye may . . . '), said to be perhaps the most popular lyric of the 17th century, typifies his constant refrain and accurately evokes the hedonism and transience of HORACE's *'carpe diem . . .'* [reap today's harvest . . .]. Much of his religious poetry is characterized by a childishness which some critics have regarded as naivety or complacency and others as a conscious attempt to counter the Puritan preoccupation with original sin. See *Selected Poems*, ed. David Jesson-Dibley, 1980.

HESIOD (*fl. c.*700 BC) early Greek didactic poet, was by his own account a native of Ascra, Boeotia, to which his father had emigrated from Cyme, on the coast of Asia Minor, because of poverty. Inspired by the muses of Mount Helicon, he won a prize at a poetry recital at a funeral in Chalcis. *Theogony* describes the beginning of the world and then of the gods. Man existed before woman, whose creation is seen as Zeus's revenge for being hoodwinked by Prometheus. *Works and Days* begins as a protest against the poet's brother for unfraternal conduct over their inheritance, and develops into a mythological history of man's tough lot, to which is appended a farmer's calendar, with digressions. Hesiod is said to have been murdered by the brothers of a woman he had seduced. See *Poems*, tr. R. M. Frazer, 1983.

HESSE, HERMANN (1877–1962) German novelist, poet, and critic, was born in Calw, Wurttemberg, into a family of Protestant missionaries. He ran away from Maulbronn Preparatory Seminary in 1892 after six months, attended the gymnasium in Bad Canstatt for a year, and was then allowed by his parents to work in the local tower clock factory. In 1895 he became instead a bookseller's apprentice in Tubingen, and went to Basel when he qualified in 1899. The success of *Peter Camenzind* (1904; tr. W. J. Strachan, 1961), a novel which has robust humour as well as Romantic sentimentality, enabled him to give up bookselling and to marry. In 1912 he moved to Switzerland, where he lived first in Berne, and then in Montagnola, becoming a Swiss citizen in 1923. *Demian* (1919; tr. Michael Roloff and Michael Lebeck, 1965), his 15th and first major novel, a *Bildungsroman* written while undergoing psychoanalysis, was published as by Emil Sinclair. An embarrassed Hesse had to reveal his identity when it won the FONTANE prize for new writers, which he had to refuse. *Siddhartha* (1922; tr. Hilda Rosner, 1951), subtitled 'An Indian Poetic Work', combines both Eastern and Western symbolism. *Der Steppenwolf* (1927; tr. Basil Creighton as *Steppenwolf*, 1929, rev. edn 1963) shocked for its pseudo-realistic depiction of anti-heroism. During the 1930s in Germany his books were 'undesirable' rather than 'forbidden', which did little to enhance his reputation or sales elsewhere. The Nazi response to his articles in a Swedish journal about the German literary scene caused him to cease critical writing from 1937 until after World War II. His final novel, *Das Glasperlenspiel* (1943; tr. Richard and Clara Winston as *The Glass Bead Game*, 1970), which he began in 1931 and in which an amalgam of literary forms support an enigmatic Utopian philosophy, was mainly instrumental in his being awarded the Nobel Prize for Literature in 1946.

HEWETT, DOROTHY (*b.* 1923) Australian dramatist and poet, was born in Perth, and claims, 'From an early age I wanted to be a bohemian.' She was educated by correspondence on her father's wheat farm at Wickepin until she was 12, when she went to Perth College. At 19 she had poetry published in *Meanjin*, joined the Communist Party, and failed after her first year at the University of Western Australia (she returned later to graduate as MA in 1963). At 20 she attempted suicide; at 21 she married a law student; and at 22 she won a national poetry competition. During the 1950s she lived in Sydney with a boilermaker, by whom she had three sons. *Bobbin Up* (1959), an inventive novel, reflects her experiences in an inner-city environment. In 1960 she married Merv Lilley (*b.* 1919), a former seaman, with whom she published a book of verse, *What About the People* (1962). She was Senior Tutor in English, University of Western Australia 1964–73. Her own first volume, *Windmill Country*, was published in 1968, the year her naturalistic working-class drama, *This Old Man Comes Rolling Home*, was performed. Subsequent plays are expressionistic, matching the direction of her verse; in both media she is regarded as a romantic who is concerned particularly with exploring questions of sexuality and of self, and who happily courts controversy. A poem, subsequently replaced, in her fourth collection, *Rapunzel in Suburbia* (1975), was the subject of legal action by her first husband; public disturbance greeted her depiction on stage of menstruation in *Bon-Bons and Roses for Dolly* (1972). She was made AO in 1986. See *Alice in Wormland: Selected Poems*, ed. Edna Longley, 1990; *Collected Plays*, 1992; *Selected Critical Essays*, ed. Bruce Bennett, 1995; *Wild Card: an Autobiography 1923–1958*, 1990; and in Mary Chamberlain (ed.), *Writing Lives: Conversations Between Women*, 1988.

HEWITT, JOHN (1907–87) Irish poet, was born in Belfast of Nonconformist parents, and was educated at the Methodist College, Belfast, and Queen's University—see his collection of sonnets, *Kites in Spring: a Belfast Boyhood* (1980). From Art Assistant he rose to Deputy Director of the Belfast Museum and Art Gallery, and was then Director of the Herbert Art Gallery and Museum, Coventry, from 1957 to his retirement in 1972. He then returned to Belfast, to continue to foster the development of the arts there, as he had done particularly in the 1940s. He was Poetry Editor of the Lyric Theatre journal, *Threshold*, from 1957 to 1963, and was made a freeman of the city in 1983. He expressed his commitment to an Ulster tradition of rural verse with *Rhyming Weavers and Other Country Poets of Antrim and Down* (1974) and in his own poetry of the countryside. He was equally affected by the political issues which have torn the region apart, and wrote of them with a sober realism. See *The Collected Poems of John Hewitt*, ed. Frank Ormsby, new edn 1993.

HEYER, GEORGETTE (1902–74) British novelist, was born in Wimbledon, London, the eldest child of a teacher, and was educated at 'numerous high-class seminaries'. Her first historical novel, which began as a story told to a sick brother, was written when she was 17 and published as *The Black Moth* in 1921. Several novels later, with *These Old Shades* (1926), she effectively established the genre of the Regency romance, in which the historical background is meticulously researched and the romance decorously handled. It is primarily with these that she earned a vast and faithful following of both sexes, but she also delved into other eras for her backgrounds, and into the military history of her favourite period for *An Infamous Army* (1937) and *The Spanish Bride* (1940). In 1925 she married G. Ronald Rougier (d. 1976), a mining engineer, whom she accompanied to East Africa and Yugoslavia. On their return to England she encouraged him to read for the Bar, to which he was called in 1939, becoming QC in 1959. It was he who suggested plots and legal niceties from which she created a number of detective stories. She also wrote several contemporary novels, beginning with *Helen* (1928), all of which she later suppressed. See Jane Aiken Hodge, *The Private World of Georgette Heyer*, 1984.

HEYWOOD, THOMAS (c.1570–1641) English dramatist, poet, translator, and miscellaneous writer, was born and brought up probably in Lincolnshire and studied at Cambridge. By 1598 he was a playwright for the Lord Admiral's Men. In the preface to *The English Traveller* (1633) he refers to having had 'an entire hand, or at least a main finger' in 220 plays, and the bookseller Francis Kirkman (*fl.* 1674) describes him as acting regularly but still writing 'a sheet every day', even if many of them were the backs of tavern bills. His verse is rugged (LAMB called him a 'prose Shakespeare'), but his distinction is in exploiting the possibilities of the drama of domestic life. Thus the interest in the two parts of *Edward the Fourth* (1600) is the relationship between Jane Shore, the King's mistress, and her husband. The theme of *A Woman Killed with Kindness* (1607) is the seduction of a happily-married woman by her husband's best friend; its development, though melodramatic, is sympathetic and catches the situation's underlying horror and confusion. *The English Traveller* is also convincing once the more complex circumstances are accepted. Other plays have classical or more romantic plots. *An Apology for Actors* (1612) is a thesis on the contemporary stage. *Gynaikeion: Nine Books of Various History Concerning Women* (1624) is an early feminist historical study. See Frederick S. Boas, *Thomas Heywood*, 1950 (critical study); Arthur M. Clark, *Thomas Heywood: Playwright and Miscellanist*, 1931, a critique of which is in T. S. Eliot, *Elizabethan Dramatists*, new edn 1982.

HIGGINS, F(REDERICK) R(OBERT) (1896–1941) Irish poet, was born in Foxford, Co. Mayo, in the Irish-speaking Catholic west, but was brought up and went locally to school in Co. Meath, in the Protestant east, going to work in a Dublin office when he was 14. An early supporter of the labour movement, he instigated a clerical workers' union, and edited a number of trade and specialist journals, as well as the first Irish women's magazine, which folded after two issues (entitled *Welfare* and *Farewell*). The poems in *Salt Air* (1923), and in the rather more substantial *Island Blood* (1925) and *The Dark Breed* (1927), are exuberant and melodious, most of them being rooted in Irish folk tradition, which he regarded as the essential starting point for an Irish poet. With *Arable Holdings* (1933), theme and meaning had become secondary to the melodic effect, and in *The Gap of Brightness* (1940) to symbolism, too. He was a close friend of YEATS, and a director of the Abbey Theatre, where his verse play, *The Deuce of Jacks*, about the blind ballad singer 'Zozimus', was produced in 1935.

HIGGINS, GEORGE V(INCENT) (b. 1939) American novelist, was born in Brockton, Massachusetts, and educated at Rockland High School, Boston College (where he studied English), Stanford University, and Boston Law School, being admitted to the Massachusetts Bar in 1967. Between times he had been a newspaper reporter, attorney's researcher, and legal assistant. He was Deputy Assistant and then Assistant Attorney General for Massachusetts 1967–70, and Assistant US Attorney 1970–73. Subsequently he ran his own law firm. *The Friends of Eddie Coyle* (1972) was the first to be published of his fictional studies of criminal, or merely antisocial, behaviour and political skulduggery. He builds up his plot, in the same way as a trial lawyer his case, almost entirely through dialogue that is often laconic, relying on authenticity of language for the delineation of character. *A City on the Hill* (1975) and *A Choice of Enemies* (1984) are primarily political novels; *Kennedy for the Defense* (1980), *Penance for Jerry Kennedy* (1985), and *Sandra Nichols Found Dead* (1996) feature a criminal lawyer, and *Impostors* (1986), about business interests, an emancipated female investigator. In *Swan Boats at Four* (1995), he leaves his normal New England settings for a web of maritime confidence tricks and betrayals.

HIGGINSON, THOMAS WENTWORTH see DICKINSON, EMILY; JACKSON.

HIGHSMITH, PATRICIA (1921–95) American novelist and short-story writer, was born Patricia Plangman in Fort Worth, Texas, but took her stepfather's name. She was brought up in New York, where she reckoned that the books on psychiatry on the family shelves caused her to start 'writing these weirdo stories when I was 15 or 16'— they included one about a pyrotechnic nanny, which was rejected by her school magazine as too unpleasant. She graduated from Barnard College in 1942, undecided whether to be a writer or a painter, and began by writing scripts for comic books. Her first novel, *Strangers on a Train* (1950), an ingenious crime story in which two potential murderers exchange victims, became one of the most famous films of Alfred Hitchcock (1899–1980). Irritated by being immediately classified as a 'suspense' writer, which always riled her, she next wrote, as Claire Morgan, a story of lesbian love which has been referred to as the first homosexual novel not to end in tragedy, *The Price of Salt* (1952; reissued under her own name as *Carol*, 1990). In subsequent works she used as her main theme the exploration and consequences of criminal or psychopathic behaviour. Her most notable creation is Tom Ripley, who murders because it is the most convenient way of maintaining his easy existence in his chateau near Fontainebleau; she regaled readers with his exploits in five novels from *The Talented Mr Ripley* (1955) to *Ripley Under Water* (1991). *This Sweet Sickness* (1960) is a memorable study of obsessive love. *Small g: a Summer Idyll* (1995), a merry-go-round of bisexual, gay, and lesbian love and violence, whose focus is a bar in Zurich, was printed a few days before her death, and published posthumously. A recent volume of short stories is *Tales of Natural and Unnatural Catastrophes* (1988). *Plotting and Writing Suspense Fiction* (rev. edn 1981) is illustrated with examples of her own methods and sources. She came to England in 1962, but after five years in Suffolk she moved to France, and then to a small village outside Lugano in Switzerland, where her preferred companions were her cats and journalists were treated with the message: 'My idea of a good time is to buy enough food and milk and catfood and beer to last for ten days without needing to go out again.'

HILL, GEOFFREY (b. 1932) British poet, was born in Bromsgrove, Worcestershire, and educated at the County High School, Bromsgrove, and Keble College, Oxford. He taught English at Leeds University from 1954, being appointed Professor of English Literature in 1976. In 1981 he became a Fellow of Emmanuel College, Cambridge, and a lecturer in English of the university. The chronologically-arranged *For the Unfallen: Poems 1952–1958* (1959), hailed as one of the most significant first books of verse published in the 1950s, contained such feats of evocative compression as 'Genesis', and the sequence 'Of Commerce and Society', on the general theme of death. Victims of war are remembered in *King Log* (1968), notably in the sonnet sequence, 'Funeral Music', recalling the 15th-century Wars of the Roses. The legends which have grown up around Offa, the 8th-century King of Mercia, are springboards for the prose poems in *Mercian Hymns* (1971). Hill's scholarship and instinct to penetrate the intricacies of human motivation are further demonstrated in *The Mystery of the Charity of Charles Péguy* (1983), a verse reflection on the life, work, and death of the reforming French poet and polemicist (1873–1914), who was killed in the battle of the Marne. Aspects of European history are woven into *Canaan* (1996), his first new collection for over ten years. Works of criticism are *The Lords of Limit: Essays on Literature and Ideas* (1984) and *The Enemy's Country: Words, Contexture, and Other Circumstances of Language* (1991). See *New and Collected Poems 1952–1992*, 1994.

HILL, JAMES see JAMESON, STORM.

HILLYER, ROBERT see ROETHKE.

HIPPOCRATES see RABELAIS.

HOBBES, THOMAS (1588–1679) English philosopher, was born prematurely (owing to his mother's alarm at the mobilization of the Spanish Armada) at Westpool, Wiltshire. His father, the vicar, disappeared after assaulting a neighbouring parson, and Thomas and his two siblings were brought up by an uncle, a Malmesbury glover. He was educated at local schools, where he was learning Latin and Greek at six, and at Magdalen Hall, Oxford. He then became (and remained for much of the rest of his life) tutor or companion to the Cavendish family, earls of Devonshire, in which capacity he made several Continental tours and met leading European thinkers. In the early 1620s he also worked for BACON. In 1640 he was an early escaper to France from the authoritarian attitude of the Long Parliament, where he published *De Cive* (1642), a treatise on government, and in 1646 became mathematical tutor to the future Charles II. The work in which he discussed his absolutionist theory of sovereignty, *The Elements of Law, Natural and Politic*, which had been circulating in manuscript since 1640, was published in two parts, *Humane Nature* and *De Corpore Politico*, in 1650. When *Leviathan* (1651), the ultimate statement of his political philosophy, offended the clerical hierarchy in France, he returned to England. After the Restoration of the Monarchy in 1660 he enjoyed favour at court, which he needed on more than one occasion in the light of the opposition to his supposedly anticlerical views. He was also involved in scientific controversies, notably with the mathematician John Wallis (1616–1703), who refuted some of his geometry in *De Corpore* [About Body] (1655). In his eighties he translated the whole of HOMER into English verse and wrote an autobiography in Latin verse. He was both empiricist (and empirical psychologist) and rationalist, of whom, in his fullest biographical sketch, AUBREY writes: 'He had read much, if one considers his long life, but his contemplation was much more than his reading. He was wont to say that if he had read as much as other men, he should have known no more than other men.' See Richard Tuck, *Hobbes*, 1989 (introduction to his philosophies); Tom Sorell (ed.), *The Cambridge Companion to Hobbes*, 1996 (critical essays).

HOBSBAUM, PHILIP see LUCIE-SMITH.

HOCCLEVE, THOMAS (*c*.1369–*c*.1450) English poet, began to work as a clerk/copyist in the Privy Seal in about 1378, and had his salary raised to £10 a year in 1399, and to £13 6s. 8d in 1408. This, with his private means of £4 a year, should have been adequate, but his pay was often late and he lived a gay bachelor life—dressing fashionably, travelling to the office by boat, eating and dining in taverns, and entertaining pretty girls. All this we know from 'La Mâle Règle', a poem which includes a plea to the Treasurer, asking for his back pay. A few years later, his long-awaited benefice having failed to materialize, he married, for love. Money problems increased, and he had a mental breakdown, from which he recovered sufficiently to go back to his tedious job but not enough to persuade his friends that he was not becoming insane. He was finally retired to a Hampshire priory in about 1425. His longest work, 'The Regiment of Princes' (1412), written to educate the future Henry V, was mainly composed from the Latin *De Regimine Principium* of the Italian philosopher Aegidius Romanus (*d*. 1316). There were other translations, some occasional verses, religious lyrics, and miscellaneous pieces. He was a fervent admirer of CHAUCER, who, he says, 'fayn wolde han me taght, / But I was dul, and lerned lite or naught', which largely sums up his poetic ability. The personal observations and autobiographical references in his works, however, and the mere fact that we have a name and identity for him, make him of interest to the social as well as the literary historian. See *Selections*, ed. M. C. Seymour, 1981.

HOCHWÄLDER, FRITZ (1911–86) Austrian dramatist, was born and educated in Vienna, where he attended gymnasium and took evening classes at the Volkshochschule. After being apprenticed to an upholsterer, he fled to Switzerland in 1938 when the Nazis

took over. His first significant play, *Das heilige Experiment* (produced 1943; tr. Eva Le Gallienne as *The Strong Are Lonely*, published 1954), a study of inner conflict with a 'moment of truth' motif which is the basis of his drama, was written while he was on leave from the labour camp to which he and other political refugees were assigned during World War II. In subsequent plays, notably *Der öffentliche Ankläger* (1948; tr. Kitty Black as *The Public Prosecutor*, 1958), set during the French Revolution, and *Der Himbeerpflücker* (1965; tr. as *The Raspberry Picker*, in *The Public Prosecutor and Other Plays*, 1979), a disturbing representation of post-World War II morality, he was, like other writers who survived the Nazi regime, deeply concerned with questions of responsibility and guilt.

HODGSON, RALPH (1871–1962) British poet, was born in Darlington, Co. Durham, the sixth of seven sons (there were also three daughters) of a coal merchant, on whose death when the boy was young the family was split up. He was brought up at Gatton in Surrey, where he acquired a taste for the countryside. He spent some time in the USA, and worked as a scene-painter in a New York theatre. In the 1890s he contributed line drawings to London newspapers and magazines, some of which he signed 'Yorick'. In 1912 he edited *Fry's Magazine of Outdoor Life* for the sporting idol and journalist C. B. Fry (1872–1956). The following year he founded, with the artist and designer, Claud Lovat Fraser (1890–1921), and the literary historian and critic, Holbrook Jackson (1874–1948), 'The Sign of the Flying Fame', a press which issued chapbooks and broadsides (including some of his own poems). His first book of verse, *The Last Blackbird, and Other Lines*, was published in 1907. He wrote nothing during World War I, in which he served, and little of significance afterwards, but *Poems* (1917), which made some impact, contained the joyous 'A Song of Honour'; his best nature poem, 'The Bull', which is all animal and nothing anthropomorphic; and the neat 'Time, You Old Gipsy Man'. He was Lecturer in English, Sendai University, Japan 1924–38, after which he lived in the USA. His interests included book collecting and the breeding of bull terriers, of which he was a judge at Crufts Dog Show. He was awarded the Queen's Gold Medal for Poetry in 1954. See *Collected Poems*, 1961.

HOFF, H. S. see COOPER, WILLIAM.

HOFFMANN, ERNST THEODORE WILHELM (1776–1822) German novelist and musician, was born in Konigsberg and studied law there at the university. He held official posts in the legal service in Glogau, Berlin, Posen (which he left after overdoing the satire in his writing), Plozk, and Warsaw, where he was when it was occupied by the French in 1808. Without a full-time job, he pursued his musical interests—sufficiently strong for him to substitute Amadeus for Wilhelm in deference to Wolfgang Amadeus Mozart (1756–91)—by teaching, composing, and conducting, while also being associated with the new theatre at Bamberg from 1808. He resumed his legal career in Berlin in 1814, when he also published the first volume of his extravagantly conceived, often grotesque, stories, which gave a new twist to the Romantic tradition, while anticipating the later preoccupation with the scientific psychology of the individual. *Tales of Hoffmann* (1881), the opera by Jacques Offenbach (1819–80), is based on his stories, with excursions into the complexities of his emotional life. See *Tales of Hoffmann*, tr. R. J. Hollingdale, 1982.

HOGG, JAMES (1770–1835) Scottish poet, novelist, and journalist, the 'Ettrick Shepherd', was born in Selkirkshire and had little education beyond an inheritance of Border ballads and folklore. First a cowherd and then a shepherd, he had some poems printed in Edinburgh as *Scottish Pastorals* (1801). A meeting with WALTER SCOTT led to their collaborating in collecting Volume II of *Border Minstrelsy* (1803), and a second book of Hogg's verse, *The Mountain Bard* (1807), written in imitation of the traditional ballads, did better than the first. He also earned £300 for a treatise on the diseases of sheep, and with his literary profits set up as a farmer, only to go bankrupt. In 1810 he sampled the literary life of Edinburgh, and for a year published a critical journal, the *Spy*. *The Queen's Wake* (1813), a poetic sequence in honour of Mary, Queen of Scots, which includes the charming fairy kidnap poem 'Kilmeny', made his reputation and earned him a rent-free farm in Yarrow from the Duke of Buccleuch. His dedication to his country life led him in 1821 to refuse an invitation to accompany Scott to the coronation of George IV (with the best seats, free accommodation, and the possibility of royal patronage in return for a coronation ode), on the grounds that the date clashed with the annual Borders fair. From 1817 to 1830 he was chief contributor with JOHN WILSON and John Gibson Lockhart (1794–1854) to *Blackwood's Edinburgh Magazine*—see *The Shepherd's Calendar*, ed. Douglas S. Mack (1995). His first novel, *The Brownie of Bodsbeck* (1818), incurred the displeasure of Scott for its sympathetic treatment of the Covenanters, and was, like GALT's *Ringan Gilhaize* (1823), seen as a reply to Scott's *Old Mortality* (1816), though in fact it had been written some years earlier. Three other novels, *The Three Perils of Man* (1822), a folk-fantasy, *The Three Perils of Woman* (1823), an attempt at the fiction of manners, and *The Private Memoirs and Confessions of a Justified Sinner* (1824), were all condemned or ignored

in his lifetime; but the last, a powerful psychological account of possession, is one of the finest novels in the Scottish tradition. See *Selected Poems and Songs*, ed. David Groves, 1986; *Selected Stories and Sketches*, ed. Douglas S. Mack, 1983; David Groves, *James Hogg: the Growth of a Writer*, 1988.

HÖLDERLIN, FRIEDRICH (1770–1843) German poet, was born in Lauffen and educated at the monastic school at Maulbronn and at Tubingen University, where he read theology, wrote poetry, conceived his novel, *Hyperion*, and broke off his engagement to the cousin of a friend on the grounds of his instability. Through SCHILLER he obtained a post as resident tutor in Walterhausen in 1793. In 1795 he took up a similar position in the home of a Frankfurt banker, with whose wife, Susette Gontard (d. 1802), he fell violently in love. He addressed her in his verse as Diotima, under which name she reappears as the heroine of *Hyperion* (2 vols 1797–99; tr. Karl W. Maurer, 1965), in which the Greek struggle for independence in 1770 is the starting point for philosophical contemplation of nature and society. In 1798 he walked out on his employer after an argument and went to Homberg, where he translated PINDAR and corresponded with Susette, whom he visited on the first Thursday of each month. Symptoms of schizophrenia appeared in 1802, after he had had further tutorial jobs in Switzerland and in Bordeaux. It is to the ensuing three years that much of his most mature poetry belongs, innovative and marked by purity of language and clarity of vision. In 1805 he became permanently insane. After a year in a clinic, he was taken in by a carpenter in Tubingen, in a room in an old tower of whose house he lived for 36 years. A selection of his work was published in 1826, with a second edition in 1843, by which time he could recognize the poems, but not his name. See *Poems and Fragments*, tr. Michael Hamburger, new edn 1994 of rev. edn 1980 (bilingual edn); *Selected Poems*, tr. David Constantine, 1996; David Constantine, *Hölderlin*, new edn 1990 (critical biography).

HOLINSHED, RAPHAEL (d. 1580) English historian, was born in Cheshire and probably educated at Cambridge, after which he is said to have taken holy orders. Early in the reign of Elizabeth I he was working in London as a translator in the printing office of Reginald Wolfe (d. 1573), under whose direction he helped to compile the British sections of a history and geography of the world, from various sources: FROISSART, BOECE, John Major (1469–1550), Edward Hall (c.1500–47), and Richard Grafton (d. c.1572); a manuscript on Ireland by the saint Edmund Campion (1540–81); and voluminous notes left by John Leland (c.1505–52). A more modest work, comprising just the history and topography of England, Scotland, and Ireland, was finally published in 1577, and known as 'Raphael Hollingeshed's Cronycle', though there was considerable input from STANY-HURST on Ireland 1509–47, William Harrison (1534–93) on the description of England, John Hooker alias Vowell (c.1525–1601), and Francis Thynne (c.1545–1608). It was, however, much censored in obedience to the Government, as was a further edition of 1586–87. The expurgated passages were not printed until 1722; the full text, in six volumes, first appeared in 1807–08. The chief interest in the work today is the use SHAKESPEARE made of it as a source for his historical plays, and also for *Macbeth*, *King Lear*, and part of *Cymbeline*. See Allardyce and J. Nicoll, *Holinshed's Chronicle as Used in Shakespeare's Plays*, 1927; Annabel Patterson, *Reading Holinshed's 'Chronicles'*, 1994 (critical study).

HOLMES, OLIVER WENDELL (1809–94) American novelist, poet, prose writer, and physician, was born in Cambridge, Massachusetts, the eldest son of Rev. Abiel Holmes (1763–1837), the historical writer, by his second wife and, through her, great-grandson of a great-granddaughter of BRADSTREET. He was educated at a private school in Cambridgeport, for a year at Phillips Academy, at Harvard, where he was Class Poet of 1829, and at Dane Law School, Cambridge, after which he studied at Trenant Medical School. His poem, 'Old Ironsides' (Boston *Daily Advertiser*, 1830) was instrumental in the preservation of the frigate, *Constitution*, which had a famous victory in the War of 1812; 'The Last Leaf' was published in the *Amateur* in 1831; and *New-England Magazine* printed two lively and discursive essays under the general title of 'The Autocrat of the Breakfast-Table' in 1831–32. After further medical study in Paris, and travel in Europe, he qualified as MD at Harvard Medical School in 1836, when he also published *Poems* (rev. edns 1846, 1848, 1849). He was Professor of Anatomy at Dartmouth Medical College 1838–40, and at Harvard Medical School 1847–82. His paper to the Boston Society for Medical Improvement, 'The Contagiousness of Puerpural Fever' (1842), was a milestone in the discovery of the causes of infection. In 1846 he coined the term 'anaesthesia' (adjective 'anaesthetic'), to signify the rendering of a patient insensible. He resuscitated his 'Autocrat' formula in *Atlantic Monthly* in 1857 with a piece beginning, 'I was just going to say, when I was interrupted . . .'. *The Autocrat of the Breakfast-Table: Every Man His Own Boswell* (1858) was followed by *The Professor at the Breakfast-Table* (1860) and *The Poet at the Breakfast-Table* (1872). He also wrote three books for which he accepted the description 'medicated novels', applied to them by 'a dear old lady': *Elsie Venner: a Romance of Destiny* (1861), *The*

Guardian Angel (1867), and *A Mortal Antipathy: First Opening of the New Portfolio* (1885), in which he explored the effect of genetic and psychological factors on human behaviour. In 1886 he visited Britain, where he received honorary doctorates at Oxford, Cambridge, and Edinburgh. His son, Oliver Wendell Holmes, Jr (1841–1935), was an eminent jurist and the author of *The Common Law* (1881)—see David H. Burton, *Oliver Wendell Holmes, Jr*, 1980. See Mirian Rossiter Small, *Oliver Wendell Holmes*, 1962 (biographical/critical study).

HOLTBY, WINIFRED (1898–1935) English novelist, was born at Rudston House, an estate in Yorkshire of 940 acres. Her mother became the first woman alderman on the East Riding County Council. She boarded at Queen Margaret's School, Scarborough, and on an outing in 1911 was bemused to find in a shop a book of her own poetry, which her mother had had privately printed. She went on to Somerville College, Oxford, with a year out to serve in France with the Women's Army Auxiliary Corps. A second-class degree seemed to justify her earlier decision to turn down the college's offer of a history tutorship. With her close friend Vera Brittain (1893–1970), author of *Testament of Youth* (1933), she began the hazardous but, for both, successful pursuit of a journalistic career in London, during which she wrote articles, reviews, and poems, and when Brittain married (Sir) George Catlin (d. 1979), political economist, set up a periodic *ménage à trois* with them—see Paul Berry and Mark Bostridge, *Vera Brittain: a Life* (1995). In 1926 she was appointed a director of *Time and Tide*. Her first novel, *Anderby Wold*, was published in 1923. During the next 12 years she wrote five more novels, two volumes of short stories, a critical study of VIRGINIA WOOLF (1932), and other works, while travelling widely, notably to South Africa, to speak on international issues, in addition to her day-to-day work. She died of kidney cancer, diagnosed in 1932, having finished *South Riding: an English Landscape* (1936), a regional novel in which the complexities of local government are laid bare and the characters of some of those involved in and with it are revealingly explored. Tall, blonde, and statuesque, she was a confirmed feminist, with a lifelong male admirer who simply could not make up his mind, until it was too late. See Vera Brittain, *Testament of Friendship*, new edn 1980 (biography); and in Carolyn G. Heilbrun, *Hamlet's Mother and Other Women: Feminist Essays in Literature*, 1990.

HOLUB, MIROSLAV (b. 1923) Czech poet and medical scientist, was born in Plzen, and with his generation of writers 'began to write poetry in war-time, hiding somewhere and somehow from the German *Arbeitsumt* (labour administration) and *Totaleinsatz* (forced labour) and from the Allied bombs'. After the war he studied at Charles University School of Medicine, Prague, qualifying as MD in 1953, and the Academy of Sciences, where he became PhD in immunology in 1958, the year in which he published his first book of verse. Subsequently his two careers have gone hand in hand: Holub the immunologist becoming a senior scientist at the Institute of Clinical and Experimental Medicine, Prague, in 1972; Holub the author writing and lecturing internationally, though his works were banned from appearing in his own country during the 1970s and he was forbidden to publish a collected edition in the UK in 1984; and Holub the scientist/poet injecting into his verse a clarity of vision which is akin to that of the microscope. This symbiosis of science (including natural history) and poetry is the main theme of *The Dimension of the Present Moment and Other Essays*, tr. David Young and Dana Háborá (1990). In *Poems Before and After: Collected English Translations*, tr. Ian and Jarmila Milner, Ewald Osers and George Theiner (1990), the poems are divided into those written 'before' and 'after' the Soviet invasion of 1968. The poems in *Vanishing Lung Syndrome*, tr. Young and Háborá (1990), organized into sections each denoting a medical state, and containing some of his bitterest criticism of his society, were written betwen 1985 and 1989, before the astonishing events which brought HAVEL to the presidency. A subsequent volume is *Supposed to Fly: a Sequence from Pilsen, Czechoslovakia*, tr. Osers (1996).

HOME, JOHN (1722–1808) Scottish dramatist, was born in Leith, the son of the Town Clerk, and was educated at the local grammar school and for the Church at Edinburgh University. In the '45 Rebellion he fought as a volunteer on the government side at Prestonpans and Falkirk, after which he was imprisoned in Doune Castle, from which he led an escape. He was appointed Minister of Athelstaneford in 1747, and later that year took down to London his verse drama, *Agis*, only to have it rejected by the actor-manager David Garrick (1717–79). The same happened to *Douglas*, a romantic tragedy based on an old ballad, but it was put on at the Canongate Theatre, Edinburgh, in 1756. The first-night audience responded enthusiastically to a genuine Scottish play, the cry of 'Whaur's your Wullie Shakespeare noo?' went up, and *Douglas* played to packed houses in Edinburgh, and was performed at Covent Garden, London, three months later. The Church of Scotland was less than enthusiastic that a minister should have written a play for public performance, and Home had to resign his parish, while local presbyteries even took punitive action against ministers who had been to see it. He became private secretary to the

statesman, the 3rd Earl of Bute (1713–92), a post he combined with that of tutor to the Prince of Wales, on whose accession as George II in 1760 he received a pension of £300 a year; he later acquired the sinecure of Conservator of Scots Privileges in Campvere, Holland. He now had little difficulty in getting Garrick to stage his plays, even *Agis*, but none, after *Douglas*, achieved any success. In 1776 he travelled to Bath and back to Edinburgh with the dying DAVID HUME, who left him in his will ten dozen bottles of claret and one of port, with a further six dozen of port if he finished the original one in two sittings. He settled in Edinburgh in 1779, and in his old age published *The History of the Rebellion in the Year 1745* (1802), which is interesting as a personal record but is defective in that the severities meted out to the Highlanders by the Duke of Cumberland (1721–65) were bowdlerized in deference to the King, Cumberland's nephew.

HOMER Greek epic poet, may have lived in the 8th century BC, may have come from the island of Chios, off the coast of Asia Minor, and may have been blind. He was certainly a bard, and it is likely that he composed both the *Iliad* and the *Odyssey*, which he may have written down in some form for his own convenience—the division of each into 24 books was the work of later Alexandrian scholars. The *Iliad* is the story of the siege of Troy largely in terms of the wrath of Achilles, first against King Agamemnon, who has deprived him of his slave-girl, Briseis, and then against the Trojan prince, Hector, who, while Achilles was sulking in his tent, slew his bosom friend, Patroclus. The *Odyssey* takes up, ten years after the fall of Troy, the mythological wanderings of the Greek hero, Odysseus, until his reunion with his patient wife, Penelope, in his home in the island of Ithaca, and his terrible revenge on her persistent suitors. They are the earliest, the most influential, and the most read epic poems in any language. They were translated into Latin verse in the 1st century AD, and into English verse by CHAPMAN, POPE, and COWPER. See *Iliad*, tr. Martin Hammond, 1987 (prose), tr. Robert Fagles, new edn 1992 (verse); *Odyssey*, tr. E. V. Rieu, rev. by D. C. H. Rieu, 1991 (prose), tr. T. E. Lawrence, new edn 1991 (prose), tr. Allen Mandelbaum, new edn 1994 (verse), tr. Robert Fagles, introduction and notes by Bernard Knox, 1996 (verse); *Homer in English*, ed. George Steiner, assisted by Aminadava Dykman, 1996; M. I. Finley, *The World of Odysseus*, new edn 1991 (historical study); W. A. Camps, *An Introduction to Homer*, 1980; Jasper Griffin, *Homer*, 1980 (introduction to the poet's thought and imagination).

HOOD, HUGH (b. 1928) Canadian novelist and short-story writer, was born in Toronto of an English-Canadian father and a French-

Canadian mother, and was educated at De La Salle College and St Michael's College, Toronto University. He taught English at Toronto University, St Joseph College, West Hartford, USA, and from 1961 at the Université de Montréal. His first book, the collection of short stories, *Flying a Red Kite* (1962), is of transitional significance in its reflection of the urge for freedom and change which was abroad in Canada at that time. *Selected Stories* (1978), his fifth collection, has been succeeded by others, including *August Nights* (1985). As what he has called a 'moral realist', he is concerned also with merging real characters in real situations with the world of their imagination, and thus exploring the fabric of society. His first two novels, *White Figure, White Ground* (1964) and *The Camera Always Lies* (1967), are studies respectively of an artist and an actress. With *The Swing in the Garden* (1975) he embarked on a 12-novel cycle called 'The New Age', in which a man's reminiscences of his family in south Ontario link a series of interpretations of national and international events from 1880 into the 21st century.

HOOD, THOMAS (1799–1845) British poet, was born in London, the son of a bookseller from Scotland, and was a clerk when he was 13. His health broke down, he went to relations in Dundee, and on his return was apprenticed to his uncle, an engraver. In 1721 he became more congenially (to him) employed as a subeditor on the *London Magazine*. In 1825 he married a sister of the poet J. H. Reynolds (1796–1852), with whom he published anonymously the mildly satirical *Odes and Addresses to Great People* (1825), after which he became a full-time writer. *The Plea of the Midsummer Fairies, Hero and Leander, Lycus the Centaur, and Other Poems* appeared in 1827, and the grim but impressive *The Dream of Eugene Aram, the Murderer* in 1831, having first been published in 1829 in the *Gem*, which he was editing at the time. Among other books, he also wrote a novel, *Tylney Hall* (1834). In 1834, having lost a lot of money, possibly through a publisher's failure, he gave up his property to his creditors and went abroad. On his return in 1840 he edited the *New Monthly Magazine* for a time, and, just before his death, was awarded a Civil List pension. His metrical ability can be seen in 'The Bridge of Sighs', like 'The Song of the Shirt' one of the poems in which he brought to public notice social problems and injustices. He is also the author of 'Ruth' ('She stood breast-high amid the corn . . .') and 'Past and Present' ('I remember, I remember / The house where I was born'), and the perpetrator of many puns, including 'They went and told the sexton, and / The sexton toll'd the bell' ('Faithless Sally Browne'). Tom Hood (1835–74), poet and artist, was his son, and with his sister, Frances

Freeling Broderip (1830–78), also an author, produced *Memorials of Thomas Hood* (1860). See *Selected Poems*, ed. Joy Flint, 1992.

HOOKER, JOHN see HOLINSHED.

HOOKER, RICHARD (1554–1600) English theologian, was born in Heavitree, Exeter, of poor parents, and was educated at Exeter Grammar School and, initially with the sponsorship of John Jewel (1522–71), Bishop of Salisbury, at Corpus Christi College, Oxford, of which he then became a Fellow. He took holy orders in 1581, and was then apparently tricked into marriage with the daughter of a woman who had nursed him through a 'distemper and cold'. In 1585 he was appointed Master of the Temple in London, where he preached every Sunday morning to the legal establishment. A long-running theological altercation with the afternoon preacher, the Puritan Walter Travers (c.1548–1635), ended with Archbishop Whitgift of Canterbury (c.1530–1604) suspending Travers, while Hooker at his own request retired to the living of Boscombe in Dorset. He was translated to Bishopsbourne, Kent, by Elizabeth I after the publication in 1593 of the first four books of *Of the Laws of Ecclesiastical Polity*. The seminal fifth book, containing the justification of the Church of England, was published in 1597; the final three were finished just before he died. His distinction is that he elucidates the confused Church history of his time, explains the philosophy of the settlement forged by the Queen and Whitgift to establish a national religion, and propounds the background to the religious thought of writers such as DONNE, MILTON, SHAKESPEARE, and SPENSER. His use of English rather than Latin in which to write a work of scholarship was itself a landmark, were it not also that a writer of English prose could now fairly be compared with CICERO for style and effective argument. See Peter Munz, *The Place of Hooker in the History of Thought*, 1952.

HOPE, A(LEC) D(ERWENT) (b. 1907) Australian poet and critic, was born in Cooma, New South Wales, and spent his childhood in Tasmania, where he went to school for one month in the year with the shearers' children. The rest of the time he was taught Latin by his father, a Presbyterian minister, and other subjects by his mother, a former teacher. He graduated from Sydney University in 1928 and from Oxford in 1931. After various posts in education and in industrial psychology, and teaching at Sydney Teachers' College, he joined the English department of Melbourne University in 1945 as Senior Lecturer. In 1951 he was appointed to the chair of English at Canberra University College, later part of the Australian National University, of which he was appointed Professor Emeritus on his retirement in 1968. An early poem, 'Australia' (1939), looks to 'the last of lands, the emptiest . . . the Arabian desert of the human mind' to provide inspiration to combat 'the chatter of cultured apes / Which is called civilization over there'. His first book of poetry, *The Wandering Islands* (1955), startled because of its largely un-Australian themes and its combination of erudition and eroticism. There followed a phase in which his attention to mythology, and sometimes to scientific thought, combined with scholarly reflection, has been compared to the poetic philosophy of KEATS, and which produced such fine long poems as 'The Double Looking Glass' and 'Vivaldi, Bird and Angel'. His work also looks back via AUDEN to the Augustan poets, especially SWIFT and POPE, and to DONNE, with insight and with a wit which can be tender or, as in *Dunciad Minor: an Heroick Poem* (1970), a satire on modern literary criticism, downright wicked. He is, with JUDITH WRIGHT, the foremost Australian poet of that generation. As a reviewer from 1941, when he labelled the Jindyworobaks (see INGAMELLS) 'the Boy Scout School of Poetry', he could be devastating when dealing with what he regarded as second rate, while always upholding and sometimes formulating critical standards. His critical works include *The Cave and the Spring: Essays on Poetry* (1965) and *The New Cratylus: Notes on the Craft of Poetry* (1979). He was made OBE in 1972 and AC in 1981. See *Collected Poems 1930–1970*, 1972; *A Late Picking: Poems 1965–1974*, 1975; *Antechinus: Poems 1975–1980*, 1981; *Selected Poems*, ed. David Brooks, 1992; Kevin Hart, *A. D. Hope*, 1993 (critical study).

HOPE, ANTHONY, pseudonym of Anthony Hope Hawkins (1863–1933) British novelist, was born in Clapton, London, and educated at Marlborough College and Balliol College, Oxford, where he got a first in Greats and was President of the Oxford Union. Until he married an American much younger than himself in 1903 he lived with his widower father, the Vicar of St Bride's in the City of London. He was called to the Bar in 1887, and by 1893 had stood unsuccessfully for Parliament, held legal briefs for various organizations including the Great Western Railway, and published five novels. The outline of the novel which then changed his career, and his life, unfolded itself as he walked home after winning a case. *The Prisoner of Zenda* was written in a month and published in 1894. He had devised a fresh approach to the modern adventure story, with a dashing hero and tender love interest, set with royal trappings in a country in southeastern Europe named Ruritania, which has passed into the English language as a term for a fictitious land of romance. Having in the same year published *The Dolly Dialogues*, a

sophisticated and witty novel of contemporary social manners, he sent apologetic letters to his legal clients and retired from practice. He wrote further romances, and also novels of character and situation, but apart from *Rupert of Hentzau* (1898), a sequel to *The Prisoner of Zenda*, none has survived his own times. During World War I he worked for the Ministry of Information, and was knighted in 1918 for his services. He never felt he had lived up to his own expectations. He wrote (1925): 'I have had a day beyond the average dog's— not what I dreamed, not the championship bench, but beyond the Average Dog!' See in Margery Fisher, *The Bright Face of Danger*, 1986.

HOPKINS, GERARD MANLEY (1844–89) British poet, was born in Stratford, Essex, the eldest of nine children of a marine insurance expert with literary ability, and was educated at Highgate School and Balliol College, Oxford, where he got a first in Greats. He suppressed his ambition to be a painter-poet, such as was D. G. ROSSETTI, because painting would 'put a strain on the passions which I should think it unsafe to encounter', and in 1866 he was received by NEWMAN into the Catholic Church, to his family's disapproval. In 1868, when he began training for priesthood in the Society of Jesus, he burned the finished copies of all his poems, resolving to write no more 'unless it were the wish of my superiors'. In 1874 he began a theology course at St Beuno's College in Wales, where he learned Welsh in order to study classical Welsh poetry. In 1875, with the encouragement of the Rector, he gave vent to his exciting poetic talent by writing 'The Wreck of the Deutschland', in memory of five Franciscan nuns, exiled for their faith, who went down with the ship—see Sean Street, *The Wreck of the Deutschland* (1992). It was rejected by the Jesuit journal, *The Month*, for its metrical 'oddities', but at least he now felt free to write poetry again. In 1877 he composed ten nature sonnets of extraordinary originality, including 'The Windhover', and 'Pied Beauty' ('Glory be to God for dappled things . . .'), which he describes as 'curtal'. After being ordained in 1877 he served the society in various capacities but with only moderate distinction in several cities, the conditions in some of which deeply affected him. In 1884 he was appointed Professor of Greek Literature at University College, Dublin. The spiritual and physical distance from home, expressed in the sonnet, 'To seem the stranger lies my lot . . .', and doubts about his work moved him to frustration and despair, in which state he wrote several further sonnets of tragic intensity. He died of typhoid and was buried in Dublin.

None of Hopkins's poetry was published in his lifetime, but his friend BRIDGES introduced some of it later into anthologies and then himself edited and published the first collected edition in 1918. Hopkins employed verbal and metrical innovations to illuminate what he called 'inscape', which is broadly his perception of the total spiritual and physical design of individual and collective manifestations of nature. He wrote in what he termed 'sprung rhythm', derived from Anglo-Saxon poetry, in which the stresses correspond to the beats in a musical measure rather than to syllabic weight, building up a total and sometimes startling harmony by alliteration and other devices, linguistic coinages, and composite words. He stands quite outside the normal conventions of Victorian poetry, and though all critics do not agree on his ultimate poetic status, he provided much inspiration to AUDEN and other poets of the 1930s, and in 'Spring and Fall' ('Margarét, áre you grieving / Over Goldengrove unleaving? . . .') wrote one of the finest lyrics in the English language. See *The Poems of Gerard Manley Hopkins*, ed. W. H. Gardner and N. H. Mackenzie, new edn 1970 of 4th edn 1967; *Selected Poetry*, ed. Catherine Phillips, 1996; Robert Bernard Martin, *Gerard Manley Hopkins: a Very Private Life*, new edn 1992; Norman White, *Hopkins: a Literary Biography*, new edn 1995; Graham Storey, *A Preface to Hopkins*, 2nd edn 1992; and in F. R. Leavis, *New Bearings in English Poetry*, new edn 1972.

HORACE (QUINTUS HORATIUS FLACCUS) (65–8 BC) Roman lyric poet, was born in Venusia, Apulia, the son of a freedman, who took him to Rome to be educated. At 18 he went to Athens to continue his studies, was caught up in the civil war which followed the death of CAESAR, and fought as a legionary commander at Philippi, unfortunately for the wrong side. He was pardoned, but on his return to Rome found that his father's estate had been confiscated. He became a civil service clerk and in his spare time wrote verses, which caught the eye of VIRGIL, and led to his being set up by Virgil's patron, Maecenas, in a farm near Tibur. Between this, a country cottage, and a house in Rome, he lived a comfortable bachelor existence, exercising Epicurean tendencies when it suited him. His main works comprise 17 'Epodes' on a variety of political and satirical themes, with some love poems; 103 'Odes' reflecting events of the time and of his personal life, written in a variety of Greek metres whose rules he followed strictly; three books of 'Epistles', of which the third is the literary essay, *Ars Poetica*; and two books of satires. His influence on English lyrical and satirical poetry, and on literary criticism, has been profound, and on none more than POPE, who wrote the Horatian 'Ode to Solitude' at the age of 12, and published his collected *Imitations of Horace* in 1738. See *Horace in English*, ed. D. S. Carne-Ross and Kenneth Haynes, 1996; Peter Levi, *Horace: a Life*, 1997.

HORNE, RICHARD HENRY (or **HENGIST**) (1802–84) British poet, dramatist, critic, and children's writer, was born in London and educated at the Royal Military College. When no army appointment materialized, he joined the Mexican navy, saw action in the war against the Spanish, escaped being eaten by a shark, travelled in the USA, was shipwrecked, and survived a mutiny and a fire on board ship on his way back to England. He began to write poetry; publicly advocated the establishment of a Society of English Literature and Art; and in 1837 published two poetic dramas, *Cosmo de Medici* and *The Death of Marlowe*. In 1839 he started a correspondence with E. B. BROWNING. Two years later he proposed that they should write a play together. It was never finished, and they did not meet until 1851, but in the meantime she provided advice and material for his *A New Spirit of the Age* (1844), a survey of contemporary literature, though she was unhappy with the entry relating to herself. (Her poem 'Cry of the Children' was inspired by his official report on child labour.) *Orion* (1843), an epic poem which has more allegory than action but contains some good passages, was priced at one farthing, 'to mark the public contempt into which epic poetry has fallen'—he further stipulated that no copy should be sold to anyone who pronounced its title 'Oríon'. *Memoirs of a London Doll, Written by Herself* 'Edited by Mrs Fairstar' (1846) confirmed his versatility and gives him an honourable place in the history of children's literature. In 1852 he went to Australia, where he served in various paramilitary and judicial capacities. He returned to England in 1869, having assumed the 'Hengist' in place of 'Henry'; he was still writing verse and prose for magazines in 1883. See Ann Blainey, *The Farthing Poet: a Biography of Richard Hengist Horne 1802–1884, a Lesser Literary Lion*, 1968.

HOUSMAN, A(LFRED) E(DWARD) (1859–1936) British classicist and poet, was born in Bromsgrove, Worcestershire, one of seven children; his mother died on his 12th birthday. He was educated at Bromsgrove School and St John's College, Oxford, where after one lecture by the legendary classical scholar, Professor Benjamin Jowett (1817–93), he was disgusted by the emphasis on a broad education rather than on the niceties of scholarship. Early on he followed his own interests into the textual study of PROPERTIUS. He took first class honours in his preliminary classical examinations, but failed his finals completely. He was passionately attached to another undergraduate, Moses Jackson, with whom he shared lodgings in London from 1882 to 1887, when Jackson married and went to India. While a clerk in the Patent Office, Housman exercised his brilliant mind by publishing learned articles on classical authors and texts. He became Professor of Latin at London University in 1892, and began his monumental edition of the five books on astrology of the Latin poet Manilius (published 1912–30). He was elected Professor of Latin at Cambridge in 1910. The leading classicist of his time, his intricate attention to textual criticism was leavened by a sarcastic wit, especially when discussing previous editors. In 1896 he had startled the academic world by publishing a volume of lyrics, *A Shropshire Lad*. Clearly written during or immediately after his emotional entanglement with Jackson, heartfelt in their preoccupation with death and unrequited love, and deeply expressive in their topographical, patriotic, nostalgic, and classical allusions, they have a resounding appeal to the young and the romantic. *Last Poems* came out in 1922, and *More Poems*, edited by his brother LAURENCE HOUSMAN, in 1936. One of the first to travel regularly by air, Housman paid an annual visit to Paris, where a fish dish was created in his name at the Tour d'Argent. See *Collected Poems and Selected Prose*, ed. Christopher Ricks, new edn 1989; Norman Page, *A. E. Housman: a Critical Biography*, 1996; Keith Jebb, *A. E. Housman*, ed. John Powell Ward, 1992 (biographical/critical study); John Bayley, *Housman's Poems*, 1992 (critical study).

HOUSMAN, LAURENCE (1865–1959) British dramatist, novelist, and poet, a younger brother of A. E. HOUSMAN, was born in Bromsgrove and educated at Bromsgrove School, subsequently studying art in London. He became Art Critic of the *Manchester Guardian* in 1895. He also published two books of verse and then (anonymously) *An Englishwoman's Love-Letters* (1900), which caused a mild sensation. His early work for the stage ran into problems of censorship, but *Little Plays of St Francis* (1922), in the form of a series of mini-plays, became a stand-by for amateur companies. *Angels and Ministers*, a first offering of fairly cynical but witty scenes about Queen Victoria and her court, was published in 1921, but was not publicly performed until 1937, in an extended version entitled *Victoria Regina*. He wrote two satirical novels of topical interest, *Trimblerigg* (1924) and *The Life of H.R.H. the Duke of Flamborough* (1928). He was a staunch supporter of women's suffrage and a pacifist. See *The Unexpected Years*, 1937 (autobiography).

HOWELLS, WILLIAM DEAN (1837–1920) American novelist, dramatist, poet, critic, journalist, and editor, was born in Martin's Ferry, Ohio, the second son of an unsuccessful printer and publisher, for whose paper the boy was setting type when he was nine. The family moved several times before settling in Jefferson in 1852, as Howells recounts in *My Year in a Log Cabin* (1893)—later

included in *Years of My Youth* (1916). He was soon contributing to newspapers and magazines, and in 1858 became a reporter on, and in 1860 News Editor of, the *Ohio State Journal*. After his poetry had appeared in *Atlantic Monthly*, he made a trip in 1860 to Boston, where he was fêted by HOLMES and J. R. LOWELL. *Lives and Speeches of Abraham Lincoln and Hannibal Hamlin* (1860), written as a campaign document, earned him the appointment as Consul in Venice (1861–65); his 'Letters from Venice' in the Boston *Advertiser* were collected as *Venetian Life* (1866). In 1866 he became Assistant Editor of *Atlantic Monthly*, and as Editor-in-Chief (1871–81) he encouraged younger writers such as HENRY JAMES and TWAIN, while publishing the older guard of EMERSON, LONGFELLOW, and WHITTIER. From 1886 to 1892 he conducted the 'Editor's Study' column of *Harper's Monthly*. An occasional teacher, he refused more professorships than he ever held. His first volume of verse, *Poems of Two Friends* (1860), was written with John J. Piatt (1835–1917), a colleague on the *Ohio State Journal*. His narrative poems in that book and in *Poems* (1873) and *Stops of Various Quills* (1895) were the most highly regarded of his verses.

As a dramatist whose first play, *The Parlor Car*, was published in 1876, and his last, *Parting Friends*, in 1911, both subtitled 'a farce', he was more concerned with giving innocent amusement than with making profound statements. He wrote over forty novels, most of which reflect his definition of fiction, that it should be 'true to the motives, the impulses, the principles that shape the life of actual men and women'. From the 'poor real life' of *Their Wedding Journey* (1872), he turned to social issues such as inform *A Modern Instance* (1882) and *The Rise of Silas Lapham* (1885), and to the more radical expressions of unease in *A Hazard of New Fortunes* (1889) and *The World of Chance* (1893). He abandoned realism for Utopianism in *A Traveler from Altruria* (1894). See Kenneth S. Lynn, *William Dean Howells: an American Life*, 1971; Kenneth E. Eble, *William Dean Howells*, 2nd edn 1982 (biographical/critical study).

HUDSON, W(ILLIAM) H(ENRY) (1841–1922) naturalist and novelist, was born of American parents near Buenos Aires, in a house 'quaintly named *Los Veinte-cinco Ombues*, which means "The Twenty-five Ombú Trees" '. He vividly records his South American boyhood in *Far Away and Long Ago: a History of My Early Life* (1918), up to the time when an attack of typhus at 15, followed by rheumatic fever caught while droving cattle in a storm, left him with a permanently weak heart and in continuous danger of a sudden death. He took to reading, and to wandering from place to place, finally coming to England in 1869 (he became a British subject in 1900). In 1877 he married a singer some years older than he was. After trying to run a London boarding house, they settled for bleak lodgings and near poverty. He now wrote a novel of revolution in Uruguay, *The Purple Land That England Lost* (1885). He was a plain, direct writer, as befitted his chosen calling of naturalist, but this and, of his other novels, *El Ombú* (1902), more in the form of a series of sketches, and *Green Mansions: a Romance of the Tropical Forest* (1904) have some quality. *The Naturalist in La Plata* (1892) and a book of essays on English natural history, *Birds in a Village* (1893), brought him a more discerning clientele, and a Civil List pension in 1901 enabled him to get out of London to explore. The result was a number of studies not only of bird life but also of the countryside itself and its lore, notably *Hampshire Days* (1903) and *A Shepherd's Life: Impressions of the South Wiltshire Downs* (1910), which still appeal for their freshness and evocative flavour. See Ruth Tomalin, *W. H. Hudson: a Biography*, new edn 1984; David Miller, *W. H. Hudson and the Elusive Paradise*, 1990 (study of the novels).

HUEFFER, FRANCIS see FORD, FORD MADOX.

HUGHES, LANGSTON (1902–67) American poet, dramatist, short-story writer, and journalist, was born in Joplin, Missouri, of a divided family; he lived mainly with his maternal grandmother until he was 12, and then with his mother, a former grammar school teacher. He went to Central High School, Cleveland, where he had poems published in the school magazine. After a year with his father in Mexico, he did a year at Columbia University, from which he dropped out and worked as a seaman on Atlantic trips, as a cook in a Montmartre nightclub, and as an assistant waiter at a Washington hotel; he got VACHEL LINDSAY to read three of his poems at a recital by leaving them beside his plate. A poetry award from the black journal, *Opportunity*, drew him to the attention of Carl van Vechten (1880–1964), the novelist and music critic. He introduced Hughes's poems to the publisher Alfred A. Knopf (1892–1984), who brought out *The Weary Blues* (1926) and *Fine Clothes to the Jew* (1927). Further supporters financed his attendance at Lincoln University, where he graduated as BA in 1929, and, until he could subsist on his writing (he published a novel, *Not Without Laughter*, in 1930), covered his living expenses in New York City, where he became accepted as the leading poet of the Harlem Renaissance. In the period of activism during the 1930s he visited Haiti, Cuba, Mexico, and the USSR, wrote radical verse, founded black theatres in Harlem, Chicago, and Los Angeles, and wrote plays, of which *Mulatto* (1935) played also on Broadway. During World War II he was a member of the Music War Board and the Writers War Board. In 1943 he began contrib-

uting to a Chicago newspaper sketches about Jesse B. Semple (= Simple), a folk creation whose innocence enables him to expose sham; five collections of these appeared in volume form. Besides further books of verse, three collections of short stories (1934, 1952, 1963), another novel (1958), more plays, and libretti, he published two volumes of autobiography, *The Big Sea* (1940) and *I Wonder as I Wander* (1956). His verse is predominantly of two kinds: poetry of protest, and lyrics of black life, for which he often employed musical rhythms drawn from blues and jazz. See *The Collected Poems*, ed. Arnold Rampersad and David Roessel, new edn 1995; Arnold Rampersad, *The Life of Langston Hughes, Volume 1: 1902–1941, I, Too, Sing America*, new edn 1988, *Volume 2: 1941–1967, I Dream a World*, new edn 1989; Faith Berry, *Langston Hughes: Before and Beyond Harlem*, new edn 1995 (biography); James A. Emmanuel, *Langston Hughes*, 1967 (critical study).

HUGHES, RICHARD (1900–76) British novelist of Welsh descent, was born in Weybridge, Surrey; his elder brother died eight days later, his sister in 1902, and his father, a civil servant, in 1905. His mother wrote articles and short stories. He won a scholarship to Charterhouse and then, after a year in the army, went on a classical scholarship to Oriel College, Oxford. His results in both university examinations were appalling, but he was joint Editor, with GRAVES, of *Oxford Poetry 1921* and had a volume of his own, *Gipsy Night, and Other Poems*, published in 1922, followed by *Confessio Juvenis: Collected Poems* (1926). *The Sister's Tragedy, and Three Other Plays* (1924) included *Danger*, the first play written for radio. He also edited a selection of SKELTON (1924). This literary activity, however, gave no intimation of the immortality which was to attend his first novel, *A High Wind in Jamaica* (1929; in USA as *The Innocent Voyage*, 1929), inspired by a real-life situation in 1822, in a manuscript passed on to his mother by a family friend. This deceptively simple and unlikely tale of the unintentional hijacking of seven amoral children by a band of incompetent pirates in the 1860s has achieved its status through its irony, wit, and suspense. The sea also features in *In Hazard* (1938), in which the responses of a steamer's crew to a hurricane and internal disruptions are vividly explored—the research was based on the actual experience of a commercial liner in 1932. Hughes worked in the Admiralty during World War II, at the end of which he was made OBE and turned down the offer of the governorship of South Georgia and the Falkland Islands in order to write. It was not until 1961 that his next novel, *The Fox in the Attic*, appeared. It is the first of three volumes of a projected 'historical novel of my own time' (to be called *The Human Predicament*), beginning in Germany in 1923 and invoking real as well as fictional characters. It was never completed, but *The Wooden Shepherdess*, taking the action up to the Night of the Long Knives in 1934, was published in 1973. See Richard Perceval Graves, *Richard Hughes: a Biography*, 1994; Richard Poole, *Richard Hughes: Novelist*, 1986; Paul Morgan, *The Art of Richard Hughes: a Study of the Novels*, 1993.

HUGHES, TED (*b*. 1930) British poet, children's writer, dramatist, and critic, was born in Mytholmroyd, Yorkshire, and educated at Mexborough Grammar School and Pembroke College, Cambridge. He had a variety of jobs, including rose gardener and zoo attendant, before marrying PLATH in 1956; they then lived in the USA for two years. His first books, *The Hawk in the Rain* (1957) and *Lupercal* (1960), established him correctly as a poet of stature but incorrectly as primarily a poet of nature. The predatory personae of many of these early poems and the protagonist of *Crow: From the Life and Songs of the Crow* (1970) represent the sharp extremes that punctuate the struggles accompanying birth, life, and death. *Gaudete* (1977) is a story of the supernatural, in which a wooden changeling is substituted for an Anglican clergyman, and reflects the man's consciousness during his absence from the earth. The influence of Hughes's observation of nature and the countryside recurs in *Remains of Elmet* (1979) and *River* (1983), both with complementary photographs—see also *Three Books: Remains of Elmet, Cave Birds and River* (rev. edns, in one volume, 1993)—and *Moortown* (1979), in which there are two mythological sequences, 'Prometheus on His Crag' and 'Adam and the Sacred Nine'. He is a thoroughly modern poet in that he is concerned with realities, and if the starkness of some of his images offends the sensitivity, then so also do the violence and brutality which appear to have become part of our normal existence. He published a new volume of poetry, *Wolfwatching*, in 1989. *Meet My Folks* (1961) was a refreshing change from the somewhat saccharine nature of children's poetry of earlier generations.

Difficulties of a Bridegroom: Collected Short Stories (1995) comprises six tales of the effects of the persecution or slaughter of animals which accompanied verses in *Wodwo* (1967), with three uncollected pieces (1954, 1978, 1993). In *Shakespeare and the Goddess of Complete Being* (1992), the ideas for which came to him in a dream, he finds a mythological formula which links the plots of most of the plays. He was awarded the Queen's Gold Medal for Poetry in 1974, made OBE in 1977, and appointed Poet Laureate in 1984. In a rare interview in 1996 he revealed that his notorious reticence in public is primarily due to the instinctive fear that if he speaks about his work, it will vanish: 'All the steam goes out of it. If I talk about anything I'm writing, that's the end. I can't write any more. If you give it away by talk, you don't give it away through writing.' See *New Selected Poems 1957–1994*, 1995; *Collected Animal Poems: Vol. 1 The Iron Wolf, Vol. 2 What is the Truth?, Vol. 3 A March Calf, Vol. 4 The Thought-Fox*, 1995 (the first two are also for younger readers); *Winter Pollen: Occasional Prose*, ed. William Scammell, new edn 1995; Craig Robinson, *Ted Hughes as Shepherd of Being*, 1989 (critical study).

HUGHES, THOMAS (1822–96) British novelist, was born in Uffington, Berkshire, the son of a cleric, and was educated at Rugby School under Dr Thomas Arnold (1795–1842), and at Oriel College, Oxford. He was called to the Bar in 1848, becoming QC in 1869. An active Christian socialist, he contributed to the movement's journals and promoted its causes, making the proposal in 1854 which instigated the Working Men's College, Great Ormond Street, of which he was Principal 1872–83. The literary quality of the manuscript of a story about Rugby surprised even the close friend to whom it was shown. It was published anonymously as *Tom Brown's School Days* 'By an Old Boy' (1857). Its success and its standing as the prototype of the school story for boys have given Hughes the status of a 'one book' author, which he was. *The Scouring of the White Horse: or, The Long Vacation Ramble of a London Clerk* (1859) is little more than a countryside social sketch. Even a contemporary critic found *Tom Brown at Oxford* (1861) 'purposeless and depressing', though there is some interest for social historians in its reflection of the shame of being poor and in the 'perplexities and doubts, and dreams, and struggles' which afflicted the minds of believers (such also as CLOUGH) at Oxford in the 1840s. He also wrote several biographical studies. He was a Liberal Member of Parliament 1865–74, and in 1879 set up a model community (needless to say named Rugby) in Tennessee, USA, from the operation of which he withdrew, having gained no profit and little satisfaction, though his elderly mother lived there until her death. He was appointed a county court judge in 1882. See E. C. Mack and W. H. G. Armytage, *Thomas Hughes: the Life of the Author of Tom Brown's School Days*, 1953.

HUGO, VICTOR (1802–85) French novelist, poet, and dramatist, was born in Besançon, the son of a Napoleonic general whose marriage was shaky. He was brought up in Italy, Spain, and France, where he attended the École Polytechnique and in 1817 had a poem recognized by the Académie Française. In 1819 he founded the journal *Conservateur Littéraire* with his two older brothers, the second of whom went mad at the wedding of Hugo to Adèle Foucher in 1822. Also in 1822, he published his first book of romantic poetry and was granted by Louis XVIII the first of two pensions. *Cromwell* (1828), a verse play which was never performed, is more significant for its preface, in which he delineated three stages of literature—lyric poetry, epic poetry, and drama with pronouncements also on 'the grotesque'. *Hernani* (1830; tr. Lord F. Leveson Gower, 1830), a play whose poetry transcends a convoluted plot, enjoyed a sensational opening night, thanks largely to GAUTIER and his claque. His fourth romantic novel, *Notre-Dame de Paris* (1831; tr. Frederic Shobel as *The Hunchback of Notre-Dame*, 1834; tr. A. J. Krailsheimer, 1993), an improbable tale in which wild passions are played out in a richly evoked medieval setting, is admired also for its finished literary style. He turned to prose for the play *Lucrèce Borgia* (1833; tr. and adapted by W. Young as *Lucretia Borgia*, 1847), produced in the year in which he began his long-term affair with Juliette Drouet (*d.* 1883), for whose closeted existence until the death of his wife in 1868 he tried to make up with poetic tributes.

A politician whose affiliations changed with the times, he spoke out in the Legislative Assembly in 1849–50 on privacy, papacy, and Church domination of education, and for universal suffrage and press freedom—he was expelled in 1852 for his opposition to the coup of Napoleon III. He returned to France in 1870, having spent many of the ensuing years, during which he twice refused an amnesty, in the Channel Islands. He also published, in addition to political and polemical works, two massive volumes of poetry; the novel *Les Misérables* (1862; tr. Charles E. Wilbour, 1862), his fictional statement on contemporary morals and social redemption; and *William Shakespeare* (1864), a curious justification of his own position in the literary genealogy of the world. He was elected to the Senate in 1876, and ceased writing in 1878 after a stroke, though works written long before continued to be published up to and after his death. As a poet he is regarded as being of European, rather than just national, standing—see *The Distance, the Shadows: Selected Poems*, tr. Harry Guest (1981). He was made Vicomte in 1845.

HULME, KERI (*b.* 1947) New Zealand novelist, short-story writer, and poet, was born in Christchurch of Maori, Scottish (Orkney), and English (Lancashire) descent, and was educated at Aranui High School and for four terms at Canterbury University. She worked as a tobacco picker, fish and chips cook, woollen mill worker, senior postwoman, and television director, and studied law, before becoming a full-time writer in 1972. *The Silences Between: Moeraki Conversations* (1982) is a sequence in verse. She worked on *The Bone People*, which was originally a short story, 'Simon Peter's Shell', for

12 years. It was finally published in 1984 by Spiral, a collective in Wellington three hundred miles from the remote Westland coast settlement to which she had retired. Impressionistic, partly symbolic, and deeply redolent of the ancient traditions of New Zealand and the English spoken there, it won the Book of the Year Award for fiction and the Mobil Pegasus Award for Maori Literature in its country of origin, and then the Booker prize for fiction when published in the UK in 1985. Subsequent publications include *Lost Possessions* (1985), a novella, *Te Kaihu: The Windeater* (1986), short stories, and *Strands* (1992), a collection of verse.

HUME, DAVID (1711–76) Scottish philosopher, was born in Edinburgh, the son of a minor Berwickshire landowner who died soon afterwards, leaving his widow to rear and educate three children. He studied law for a time at Edinburgh University, but gave that up to pursue philosophy. He had a nervous breakdown in 1729, after which he briefly tried commerce in Bristol, for which he realized he had no aptitude. He went into frugal seclusion in France, where between 1734 and 1737 he wrote the astonishing *A Treatise of Human Nature* (1739), which develops and consolidates the empirical theories of LOCKE and BERKELEY. *Essays Moral and Political* (1741–42) was written on the family estate. His dismissal of religion in his works cost him the chances of professorial posts at both Edinburgh and Glasgow University. He was for a year tutor to the mad Marquis of Annandale, and then served in a staff capacity on various military missions. He was Keeper of the Advocates' Library, Edinburgh 1752–57, Secretary to the British Ambassador in Paris 1763–65, and an under-secretary of state in the Home Department 1767–68, after which he retired to Edinburgh. *Philosophical Essays Concerning Human Understanding* was first published in 1748, and *Political Discourses*, which anticipated ADAM SMITH, in 1752. *The History of England from Julius Caesar to 1688*, which treats the subject retrogressively, was finally completed in 1762, and brought him fame in France as well as in Britain. *Dialogues Concerning Natural Religion* (1779) was written in about 1750, but at his own request was not published in his lifetime. He died of bowel cancer, having cheerfully anticipated a 'speedy dissolution'. See A. J. Ayer, *Hume*, 1980 (introduction to his philosophy).

HUNT, (JAMES HENRY) LEIGH (1784–1859) British essayist, poet, journalist, and editor, was born in Southgate, London, and educated at Christ's Hospital. A selection of his verses, with the title of *Juvenilia*, was printed in 1801 on the initiative of his father, an improvident and usually impoverished preacher. With his brother John (1775–

1848) he established in 1808 a radical journal, the *Examiner*, but both were imprisoned for two years in 1813 for libelling the Prince Regent as a liar and 'a fat Adonis'. In prison, Hunt lived with his family and received his friends, who included BYRON and LAMB. In 1822 he took his wife and seven children to Italy, where he was to edit the *Liberal* with Byron and P. B. SHELLEY. Shelley's death, the closure of the journal after four issues, and the understandable problems of staying with Byron, after whose death they were left without support, caused their return in 1825. A series of articles, which he turned into *Lord Byron and Some of His Contemporaries* (1828), did not embellish the truth, and caused offence. Hunt was only a moderate poet, whose most ambitious work, *The Story of Rimini* (1816), reveals an unhappy conflict between looseness of style and loftiness of theme, and whose only memorable poems are 'Abou ben Adhem' and the rondeau 'Jenny Kissed Me', addressed to the wife of CARLYLE. Much of his prose suffers in comparison with that of contemporaries such as Lamb, HAZLITT, and DE QUINCEY because, more than theirs, it was written purely as journalism, but he was a sound critic, whose essay 'An Answer to the Question What is Poetry' (1844) bears rereading. His influence in encouraging, and publishing, the young KEATS and Shelley was incalculable. See *Autobiography*, ed. J. E. Morpurgo, 1949; Edmund Blunden, *Hunt: a Biography*, 1930.

HUNTER, EVAN (*b.* 1926) American novelist, was born Salvatore A. Lombino in New York City, and was educated at Evander Childs High School, Cooper Union, and Hunter College. After service in the US Navy, he taught in two vocational high schools, and worked for six months for a literary agency, where he handled the work of WODEHOUSE, who became a lifelong friend. He began to write in the early 1950s under a variety of names, including Richard Marsten and Hunt Collins. *The Blackboard Jungle* (1954), a searing novel of a teacher's problems, established the Evan Hunter name and also his motif as a writer who confronts social issues through the need of a protagonist to establish an identity within a particular environment or situation. *Sons* (1969) reflected public concern about the Vietnam War, *Love, Dad* (1981) the hippie culture. As Ed McBain he began with *Cop Hater* (1956) an extensive sequence of novels (he regards each book as a chapter of a single work), whose theme is 'crime and punishment', whose milieu is the 87th Precinct of an American city, and whose protagonists are the detectives and criminals who carry on their grim business there. Other crime novels involve the investigator Matthew Hope, who gets shot in the opening paragraph of *There Was a Little Girl* (1994).

HURSTON, ZORA NEALE (?1901–60) American novelist and folklorist, was born in Eatonville, Florida, the first black incorporated community in America. Her early schooling was sporadic, and in 1915 she worked as a wardrobe girl with a GILBERT and Sullivan touring company. She registered at Morgan Academy in 1916, and Howard University in 1918, where she had a story, 'John Redding Goes to Sea', published in the student journal in 1921. After having two further stories and a play, 'Color Struck', published in the new *Opportunity: a Journal of Negro Life*, she arrived in New York in 1925, and was enabled to go on a scholarship to Barnard College, from which she graduated in 1928. The anthropologist, Franz Boas (1858–1942), saw a paper of hers, took her on as an assistant at Columbia University, and arranged a fellowship for her to collect folklore in the South. Several expeditions later she produced *Mules and Men* (1935), the second part of which is a study of voodoo, and *Tell My Horse* (1938), on Haiti and the West Indies. Closely identified with the Harlem Renaissance, she wrote four novels, of which *Jonah's Gourd Vine* (1934), whose chief character, a preacher, is based on her father, *Their Eyes Were Watching God* (1937), which has a genuine feminist message, and *Moses, Man of the Mountain* (1939) draw on elements of folklore. *Seraph on the Suwanee* (1948), whose protagonists are white, was criticized as being assimilationist. In 1948 she was wrongly accused of the sexual abuse of a ten-year-old boy. The charges were dropped, but information had been leaked to the press. She disappeared, and was found two years later working as a maid to a white family in Florida. Much of her last ten years was spent researching and writing a massive biography of Herod the Great, which no one would publish. Two brief marriages, to Herbert Sheen, a jazz player, in 1927, and to Albert Price III, 15 years her junior, in 1939, ended in divorce. *Dust Tracks on a Road* (1942) is a selective autobiography. See *A Zora Neale Hurston Reader*, ed. Dorothy Abbot, 1992; *Novels and Stories* and *Folklore, Memoirs, and Other Writings*, ed. Cheryl A. Wall, 1995; Robert Hemenway, *Zora Neale Hurston: a Literary Biography*, new edn 1986.

HUXLEY, ALDOUS (1894–1963) British novelist, short-story writer, essayist, poet, critic, and dramatist, a grandson of T. H. HUXLEY, was born in Godalming, Surrey, of an illustrious literary and scientific family, and was educated at Eton and Balliol College, Oxford. An eye disease contracted at school made the pursuit of science impossible, so he turned to literature. His first book, *The Burning Wheel* (1916), was followed by three further volumes of verse, before he published *Limbo* (1920), a volume of short stories. He began his career as a novelist, and also his

satirical phase, with *Crome Yellow* (1921) and
another biting story of postwar Britain, *Antic
Hay* (1923). *Those Barren Leaves* (1925) and
Point Counter Point (1928), in which D. H. LAW-
RENCE appears in the sympathetic form of
Mark Rampson, were written in Italy, and reflect Huxley's early preoccupation with form
rather than content. This changed, and his
entry into a more sociological phase was confirmed, with *Brave New World* (1932), in which
the Utopian image is turned upside down
and the future is seen in terms of a dehuman-
ized society—his essay *Brave New World Revisited* (1959) chillingly reconsiders his 1932
fictional prognosis. *Eyeless in Gaza* (1936), in
form as well as content, heralds a final, philosophical phase, in which pacifism and mysticism are predominant influences. *Grey Eminence: a Study in Religion and Politics* (1941) is
a distinguished biography of Cardinal Richlieu's adviser, Father Joseph.

Huxley travelled and lived abroad from
1923, though during the 1930s he and his
wife made periodic trips to England to do
fieldwork for articles on the industrial situation—see *The Hidden Huxley: Contempt and
Compassion for the Masses*, ed. David Bradshaw (1994). In 1938 they settled in California,
where he sublimated his aversion to the cinema and wrote some Hollywood film scripts,
including (with Jane Murfin) that of AUSTEN's
Pride and Prejudice (1940). His search for a
transcendental philosophy led him to develop a form of mysticism based on oriental
models, which he expounded in such works
as *The Perennial Philosophy* (1946) and *Themes
and Variations* (1950). He explored further
ways of releasing the mind from the con-
straints of the body by taking psychedelic
drugs (mescalin and LSD)—see *The Doors of
Perception* (1954) and *Heaven and Hell* (1956).
See *Collected Short Stories*, 1957, as *The Gioconda Smile: and Other Stories*, 1984; *Collected
Essays*, 1960; Sybille Bedford, *Aldous Huxley:
the Apparent Stability 1894–1939* and *The Turning Points 1939–1963*, new edns, in one volume, 1993 (biography); Christopher S. Ferns,
Aldous Huxley: Novelist, 1980 (critical study).

HUXLEY, T(HOMAS) H(ENRY)
(1825–95) British biologist and prose writer,
was born in Ealing, Middlesex, the son of a
schoolmaster, but after the family's move to
Coventry appears largely to have educated
himself by reading. He entered London University in 1842 and was awarded a scholarship to study at Charing Cross Hospital,
graduating in 1845 with gold medals for
anatomy and physiology. He joined the
Royal Navy, and was posted as assistant surgeon in HMS *Rattlesnake*, on survey duties between Australia and the Barrier Reef. In Sydney he fell in love with a local girl. His
research into marine life brought him a Fellowship of the Royal Society, and in 1854 a
lectureship in natural history at the Royal

School of Mines. He now wrote to the young
woman he had met, who sailed for England
with her parents and married him. While he
did not fully subscribe to the theory of evolution which DARWIN publicly propounded in
1859, he was a fervent supporter of the man.
At the meeting of the British Association for
the Advancement of Science in Oxford in
1860 he rounded on Bishop Samuel Wilberforce (1805–73), who had asked whether
Huxley was descended from an ape on his
grandfather's or grandmother's side, and observed that he would rather have an ape for
an ancestor than a bishop. In *Evidence as to
Man's Place in Nature* (1863) he offered conclusive proof of man's animal origins, expressed with flowing rhetoric and an appreciation of social and religious implications
to which Darwin could not have aspired. *Lay
Sermons* (1870) included his famous lecture
'On the Physical Basis of Life', and in *Evolution and Ethics* (1893) he set out plainly that
man's moral nature could not compete with
the natural cosmic process. He coined the
term 'agnosticism' to describe his attitude to
religion. As one of the original members of
the London School Board, he firmly influenced the composition of the curriculum in
schools. See Charles Darwin and T. H. Huxley, *Autobiographies*, ed. Sir Gavin de Beer,
new edn 1997; Adrian Desmond, *Huxley: the
Devil's Disciple*, new edn 1997 (biography to
1870) and *Huxley: Evolution's High Priest*,
1997.

HUYSMANS, J(ORIS)-K(ARL) (1848–
1907) French novelist, was born Georges-
Marie-Charles in Paris, of a Dutch father and
a French mother, who after her husband's
death in 1856 married a bookbinder called
Og. He was educated at the Lycée Saint-
Louis, passing his baccalaureate in 1866.
After a year studying law, he entered the
Ministry of the Interior, where he worked for
thirty years, latterly in the Sûreté Générale,
the equivalent of the British Criminal Investigation Department. A series of prose poems,
published at his own expense in 1874,
launched him on the literary path, and he
now adopted what he believed to be the
Dutch form of the name Georges-Charles. Because of its subject, he was advised to publish
Marthe (1876; tr. Samuel Putnam, 1948), a
blameless study of a prostitute which belongs to the Naturalistic school of novels, in
Belgium. Coming back through the customs
with four hundred copies stowed in his baggage, he had most of them confiscated. *À Rebours* (1884; tr. Robert Baldick as *Against Nature*, 1959), which he once called 'vaguely
clerical and mildly "queer" ', and with which
ZOLA reckoned he 'delivered a terrible blow
to Naturalism', is regarded as significant in
the recognition of the Decadent movement in
Europe. It also led to a long process of conversion to Catholicism, culminating in 1892.

After his retirement from the civil service in 1898 as *sous-chef de bureau*, he lived for two years as a Benedictine oblate at Ligugé, near Poitiers, from which he returned to Paris to lead a vagrant existence after the monks of his calling went into exile in 1901 in the wake of the law against religious associations. EDMOND DE GONCOURT nominated him as one of the original ten members of the Académie Goncourt.

HYDE, DOUGLAS (1860–1949) Irish scholar, poet, dramatist, translator, and statesman, was born in Frenchpark, Co. Roscommon, the third son of a Protestant rector. In 1873 he came home with measles after a few weeks at his Dublin boarding school, and did not return. Instead he received an excellent education at home, where he developed a passion for the Irish language and its oral and literary traditions. He had a glittering career at Trinity College, Dublin, from 1880 to 1888, finishing with a doctorate in law while having twice won the Vice-Chancellor's prizes for both prose and verse. He was also writing in Irish, in which he published his first book, a collection of folk tales and rhymes (1889). *Beside the Fire: a Collection of Irish Gaelic Folk Stories* (1890), some of which he presented in both languages, was the first truly scholarly work on the subject; in *Love Songs of Connacht* (1893) he offered most of the original poems in both an English verse and a literal prose rendering. He wrote *The Story of Early Gaelic Literature* (1895) and *A Literary History of Ireland* (1899), and several plays, *Casadh an tSugáin* (later translated by GREGORY as *Twisting the Rope*) being put on in Dublin in 1901 with himself in the cast—see *Selected Plays: in English and Irish*, ed. G. W. and J. E. Dunleavy, Irish plays tr. Isabella A. Gregory (1991). He was elected President of the National Literary Society in 1892, and was President of the Gaelic League from its inception in 1893 to his resignation in 1915, when its aims were extended to promote 'a free, Gaelic-speaking Ireland'. He was Professor of Modern Irish at Trinity College, Dublin 1903–32, and was the first President of Ireland from 1939 to 1944.

HYDE, ROBIN, pen name of Iris Guiver Wilkinson (1906–39) New Zealand novelist, poet, and journalist, was born in Cape Town, South Africa, and brought to Wellington a few months later. She was educated at Wellington Girls' College, and then became a journalist on the *Dominion*, returning to her work as a parliamentary reporter on crutches after a knee infection left her permanently lame when she was 19. Pregnant after a brief affair, she had a stillborn child (Robin Hyde) in Sydney in 1926. She returned to New Zealand and journalism, and also, as a memorial to her dead child, to poetry (at which she had shown precocity at school), with *The Desolate Star and Other Poems* (1929). After the birth in 1930 of a son, who lived, she became a staff editor on the *New Zealand Observer*, Auckland, to which she contributed indefatigably under a variety of by-lines. In 1933, having attempted suicide, she was admitted voluntarily to Auckland Mental Hospital. During her four years there she published two more volumes of poetry, and wrote several further books: *Journalese* (1934), reminiscences of her trade; *Check to Your King: the Life History of Charles, Baron de Thierry* (1936), a fictional biography; *Passport to Hell: the Story of James Douglas Stark* (1936), a factional reconstruction of the exploits of a World War I anti-hero, and its sequel, *Nor the Years Condemn* (1938); *Wednesday's Children* (1937), a fantasy novel; and the first draft of *The Godwits Fly* (1938), an autobiographical novel based on her childhood, youth, and an early unfulfilled romance. In 1938 she succumbed to the pull of the cultural links she felt with England, and set out via China, where she made a dangerous sortie into the war zone—see her *Dragon Rampant: Reminiscences of the Sino-Japanese War* (1939). Her death in England of a drug overdose was recorded as suicide. The title sequence of *Houses by the Sea and Other Poems* (1952), begun in Auckland and finished overseas, and other verses from the final period of her life, are regarded as notable evocations of the New Zealand experience—see also *Selected Poems*, ed. Lydia Wevers (1984).

I

IBSEN, HENRIK (1828–1906) Norwegian dramatist, was born in Skien, the son of a general merchant, who went bankrupt in 1835 and moved his family out of town. He left school at 15 and was apprenticed to an apothecary in Grimstad, where he studied for university entrance, read widely in European literature, and in 1846 had a son by a maid of the house who was ten years his senior. He also began to write plays, of which he privately published *Catalina* (1850) after it had been rejected by the Christiania Theatre. Two weeks later he moved to Christiania (Oslo), and failed the arithmetic and Greek papers for his entrance examination. A second play, [*The Burial Mound*], was put on at the Christiania Theatre in September 1850, and he then accepted the post of 'dramatic author' at the newly-established Norwegian Theatre in Bergen. In 1857, having had four verse dramas of the heroic ages produced there, only one of which had any success, he moved to the Norwegian Theatre in Christiania, which had been founded to counter the Danish influence of the Christiania Theatre. [*The Vikings at Helgeland*] was produced in 1858, the year in which he married Suzanne Thoresen, a pastor's daughter: they had a son in 1859. In 1862, after public attacks on his personal efficiency, the company went bankrupt. He was taken on at a low salary by the Christiania Theatre, which staged [*The Pretenders*] (1864), a further historical play. He now accepted a travel grant to go abroad. It was 27 years before he returned permanently to Norway.

From Rome, where he wrote the dramatic poems *Brand* (1866) and *Peer Gynt* (1867), the family moved to Dresden. [*The League of Youth*], a modern political comedy in prose, was performed in Christiania in 1869, when he also represented Norway at the opening of the Suez Canal. His collected verse was published in 1871—see *Poems*, ed. and tr. John Northam (1986). In 1875 he moved to Munich for his son's education, and began his first great sequence of works: [*The Pillars of Society*] (1877), [*A Doll's House*] (1879), [*Ghosts*] (1881), and [*An Enemy of the People*] (1882), realistic plays of contemporary issues, some aspects of which caused considerable public controversy. In a second cycle, [*The Wild Duck*] (1884), *Rosmersholm* (1887), [*The Lady*

from the Sea] (1888), *Hedda Gabler* (1890), and [*The Master Builder*] (1892), the concern is more with the individual in the modern world, with the use of symbolism to highlight the message. Ibsen returned to Norway for a holiday in 1891, and decided to stay. He settled in Christiania, where a stroke in 1900 put paid to further work; his last play, [*When We Dead Awaken*], which he described as a 'dramatic epilogue', was finished in 1899.

Ibsen's Norwegian upbringing and character imbued him with an insight into conflicts of the mind and hypocrisies in social attitudes, his self-imposed exile with the freedom 'to write freely, frankly, and without reservation', and his instinctive theatrical sense with the ability to use a variety of forms in such a way as to provide a firm base for the development of drama in the 20th century. His first play to be produced in London was *The Pillars of Society* (tr. William Archer, 1880). It was followed by *A Doll's House* (1889), nominated by the theatre scholar Harley Granville-Barker (1877–1946) as 'the most dramatic event of the decade', *Rosmersholm* (1891), *Hedda Gabler* (1891), and *The Lady from the Sea* (1891). Writing about *Ghosts*, with which the Independent Theatre Club was inaugurated in 1891, Clement Scott (1841–1904) likened its author to 'one of his own Norwegian ravens emerging from the rocks with an insatiable appetite for decayed flesh'. Other critics were more outspoken. By this time, however, Ibsen had become an author of European stature on his way to achieving international eminence. There are fine modern translations by Michael Meyer and James McFarlane. See Michael Meyer, *Ibsen*, new edn 1992 (biography); David Thomas, *Henrik Ibsen*, 1993 (critical study).

IHIMAERA, WITI (*b.* 1944) New Zealand novelist and short-story writer, was born in Gisborne of Maori descent. He was educated at Te Karaka Maori District High School, and later at the universities of Auckland and Victoria. After being a journalist, he became a career diplomat, serving with the New Zealand Ministry of Foreign Affairs as second secretary in Canberra, consul in New York, and Counsellor on Public Affairs, Washington. *Pounamu Pounamu* (1972), the first collection of short stories by a Maori, formed a trio with two novels, *Tangi* (1973) and *Whanau* (1974), in which the dual cultural heritage of Maori and Pakeha is explored in terms of the disappearance of traditional rural life. A second book of stories, *The New Net Goes Fishing* (1977) embraces urban themes. *The Matriarch* (1986) is an imaginative reconstruction of the struggle for identity by the Maori who once possessed the Gisborne Flats. Three characters dominate the story: Te Kooti, the prophet, Wi Here, the Parliamentarian, and his protégée, Artemis Riripeti Mahana, the chieftainess, grandmother of the young academic whose meeting with his blind uncle is the start of a quest for his spiritual and cultural roots. Subsequent books include *The Whale Rider* (1987), a novella, and *Dear Miss Mansfield: a Tribute to Kathleen Mansfield Beauchamp* (1989), stories. In 1991 he took up a teaching post at Auckland University.

INCHBALD, ELIZABETH (1753–1821), née Simpson, British novelist and dramatist, was born in Stanningfield, near Bury St Edmunds, the eighth of nine children of a Catholic farmer, who died in 1761. She was beautiful, but she had a stammer, and when she applied for a job with the Norwich theatrical company which her elder brother had joined, she was turned down. In 1772 she ran away to London to be an actress, but after being molested by a manager who had offered to help her, she agreed to marry Joseph Inchbald, a 36-year-old actor and painter. She made her stage debut in Bristol as Cordelia to his Lear. They joined the Scottish touring company of West Digges (1720–86), from whom they parted in 1776 after a dispute between Mr Inchbald and an Edinburgh audience. When they returned to England later that year after two months in Paris, they were in such financial straits that they had to eat turnips from a field. They found work in Liverpool, where Elizabeth began a lifelong friendship with the actress Sarah Siddons (1755–1831), with whose brother, the tragic actor John Philip Kemble (1757–1823), she fell in love—even after the sudden death of her husband from a heart attack in 1779 Kemble never proposed marriage to her, nor did they ever have an affair. Kemble, who was co-manager with SHERIDAN of Drury Lane Theatre 1788–1796, married Priscilla Brereton (1756–1845), the widow of an actor and herself an actress, in 1787.

Inchbald continued to act until 1789, by which time she had had ten of her own plays produced, including the topical *The Mogul Tale: or, The Descent of the Balloon* (1788), and by shrewdly investing her earnings had an income of £58 a year. In 1790 the Second Catholic Relief Act ensured new openings for Catholics in the community. She resuscitated a novel of Catholic life which had been rejected in 1779, and grafted on a second half. It was now accepted for publication as *A Simple Story* (1791), and is the first Catholic novel in English. In a second novel, *Nature and Art* (1796), her stance on moral education and social injustice owes something to the personal influence of GODWIN. She continued to write plays with a moral content, contributed individual prefaces to the 25-volume *The British Theatre* (1806–19), and edited two selections of plays. She died in a genteel Catholic retirement home in Kensington, having burnt her memoirs, for which she had been offered £1000.

INGAMELLS, 'REX' [REGINALD CHARLES] (1913–55) Australian poet and critic, was born in Ororoo, South Australia, and educated at Port Lincoln High School, Prince Alfred College, and Adelaide University. After a spell as a teacher he became a freelance journalist, and published *Gumtops* (1935), the first of several books of verse. In a prose study, *Conditional Culture* (1938), he postulated that 'the real test of a people's culture is the way in which they can express themselves in relation to their environment', and argued for the use of terms derived from the Aboriginal language. Jindyworobak, which he used to denote 'distinctive quality in Australian literature', was the name by which the literary movement became known. *The Jindyworobak Anthology*, which he edited, appeared annually from 1938 to 1953, except for some of the war years. His *The Great South Land* (1951) is a vast historical survey in verse in which he attempted to view his subject also from an Aboriginal point of view. He died in a car crash.

INNES, MICHAEL see STEWART, J. I. M.

IONESCO, EUGÈNE (1912–94) French dramatist, was born in Slatina, Romania, his mother being French. The family spent the years 1913–25 in France, where he went to a local *école communale* in Paris and to a village school in La Chapelle-Anthenaise. After returning to Romania he studied French at Bucharest University, published literary criticism, and taught in a Bucharest school until 1939, when he went back to Paris on a government grant to research for a thesis on 'themes of sin and death in French literature since Baudelaire', of which it appears he wrote nothing. He worked in a publishing house and did some journalism. While learning English from a course book in 1948, he was struck with the idea for a play. *La Cantatrice Chauve* (1950; tr. Donald Watson as *The Bald Soprano* in *Four Plays*, 1958), an 'anti-play' attacking 'universal petty-bourgeoisie' which is a frontrunner of the Theatre of the Absurd, opened in Paris in 1950 to an audience of three. *La Leçon* (1951; tr. as *The Lesson* in *Four Plays*), about communication and the employment of language as an instrument of power, has a brutal climax which is a prelude to a reprise of an identical situation. When it was revived in London in 1958 with *Les Cha-*

ises (1952; tr. as *The Chairs* in *Four Plays*), KEN-
NETH TYNAN (*Observer*, 27 June) concluded
that 'Ionesco's theatre is pungent and exciting, but it remains a diversion. It is not on the
main road: and we do him no good, nor the
drama at large, to pretend that it is.' To which
Ionesco replied: 'A work of art has nothing to
do with doctrine. . . . Any work of art which
[is] idealogical and nothing else would be
pointless, tautological, inferior to the doctrine it claims to illustrate . . .'. Among his
many subsequent plays are three surrealist
fantasies in which the triple incarnation of a
publisher's production assistant engages in
conflict with illusion, with levitation and a
vision of hell, and ultimately with death: *Rhi-
nocéros* (1959; tr. Derek Prouse in *Plays IV*,
1960); *Le Piéton de l'Air* (1962; tr. Watson as *A
Stroll in the Air* in *Plays VI*, 1968); and *Le Roi
Se Meurt* (1962; tr. Watson as *Exit the King* in
Plays V, 1963). His main themes were the pain
of living and the fear of death: he told an interviewer in 1988, 'The world is a joke that
God has played on man.' After more than
thirty plays, two novels, and a number of critical works, he gave up writing for painting.

IRELAND, DAVID (*b.* 1927) Australian
novelist, was born in Lakemba, New South
Wales, and had a number of different jobs,
including working in an oil refinery, before
becoming a full-time writer in 1973. *Image in
the Clay*, a violent play about an Aboriginal
settlement on the fringe of a town, was performed at the Pocket Theatre, Sydney, in
1962, and published in 1964: it later became
his single realistic novel, *Burn* (1974). His
usual method is to build up a surrealist
image of Australian society by means of fragmented scenes, and to satirize, and often savage, the systems which he finds inherent in
it. *The Chantic Bird* (1968) concerns a teenage
delinquent; in *The Unknown Industrial Prisoner* (1971) the victims are the staff of an oil
refinery. The milieu of *The Flesheaters* (1972)
is a 'home' for down-and-outs, incurables,
and the aged. *A Woman of the Future* (1979) is
an allegory of successful womanhood. In *City
of Women* (1981), women have taken over
completely. *Archimedes and the Seagle* (1984) is
an animal fable which conversely offers redemption and joy even in the context of modern urban and social dehumanization. *Blood-
father* (1987) is a spiritual *Bildungsroman*. He
won the MILES FRANKLIN Award in 1972,
1977, and 1980, and was made AO in 1981.
See Helen Daniel, *Double Agent: David Ireland
and His Work*, 1982.

IRON, RALPH see SCHREINER.

IRVING, WASHINGTON (1783–1859)
American essayist and historical writer, was
born in New York City, the youngest of 11
children of a Scottish-born father and an English-born mother, and was educated at Jos-
iah Henderson's seminary. He studied under

lawyers, to the daughter of one of whom he
became engaged, but she died in 1808. He
also contributed a column of theatrical criticism, 'Letters of Jonathan Oldstyle', to the
Morning Chronicle, founded by his brother
Peter (1771–1838), and through 1807 wrote
and published, with his oldest brother William (1766–1821) and James Paulding (1778–
1860), a satirical magazine, *Salmagundi*. A
similar sense of fun informed his *A History of
New York, from the Beginning of the World to the
End of the Dutch Dynasty* 'By Diedrich Knick-
erbocker' (1809). In 1815, after serving as a
colonel in the New York Militia in the War of
1812, he sailed for Europe. He was away for
17 years, initially out of pride, in that the Liverpool end of the family hardware business
(managed by Peter), for which he was working, went bankrupt. A memorable visit in
1817 to Abbotsford to call on WALTER SCOTT,
who had been much amused by *A History of
New York* and invited him to stay several
days, inspired him to press on with *The Sketch
Book of Geoffrey Crayon, Gent*, published in
parts in America in 1819, and in Britain in
two volumes in 1820. Among the elegant essays on English themes were the stories of
rural New York, 'Rip Van Winkle', translated
from its original German setting, and 'The
Legend of Sleepy Hollow', which were immediately recognized as stylistic treasures.
In 1826, at the invitation of the American
Minister to Spain, he went to Madrid, where
he worked on *A History of the Life and Voyages
of Christopher Columbus* (1828), and gained
material for several other works, including
*The Alhambra: a Series of Tales and Sketches of
the Moors and Spaniards* (1832). In 1832, having spent two years conscientiously performing the duties of secretary of the American
legation in London, he returned home, satisfied at last that he had rehabilitated himself
by his literary reputation and public service.
Conscious, however, that he needed to belie
his image as a European writer, he included
'A Tour on the Prairies', narratives of an expedition on horseback in the West, as one of
four studies in *The Crayon Miscellany* (1835)—
another is an enthusiastic account of his stay
with Scott—and published two historical
works on American themes. He was Minister
to Spain from 1842 to 1846, after which he
returned to his home and extended household (at times including five nieces) at Sunnyside, near Tarrytown, on the Hudson river.
He now put together a biography of GOLD-
SMITH (1849), and worked heroically on his
Life of Washington (1855–59), the final volume
of which he completed shortly before his
death. See Mary Weatherspoon Bowden,
Washington Irving, 1981 (critical study).

ISHERWOOD, CHRISTOPHER (1904–
86) British novelist and dramatist, was born
in High Lane, Cheshire, the son of an army
officer who died in action in World War I. He
was educated at St Edmund's School, Hind-

head, where he first encountered AUDEN, and Repton School, where he met Edward Upward (*b*. 1903), with whom at Corpus Christi College, Cambridge, he wrote stories of a fantasy world called Mortmere in which contemporary society was mirrored and satirized—see *The Mortmere Stories* (1995). He was expelled for deliberately failing his second year examinations. *All the Conspirators* (1928) and *The Memorial: Portrait of a Family* (1932) are angry novels about the conflict between the generations. He taught English in Berlin from 1930 to 1933. Out of this experience came *Mr Norris Changes Trains* (1935) and *Goodbye to Berlin* (1939), in which the narrator/observer is himself, in the first as 'William Bradshaw', his second and third names, and in the second as Christopher Isherwood. Elements from *Goodbye to Berlin*, featuring the promiscuous cabaret performer, Sally Bowles, were made into a play, *I Am a Camera* (1951) by John van Druten (1901–57), from which the musical *Cabaret* (1966) was adapted. The two novels were published together as *The Berlin Stories* (1946) and represent all that exists of a much longer work about the end of the Weimar Republic, to be called 'The Lost'.

In the 1930s he wrote three ideological plays with Auden, with whom he left the UK in 1939 to live permanently in the USA, of which he became a citizen in 1946—see *Diaries 1939–1960*, ed. Katherine Bucknell (1996). He worked for film companies in Hollywood, where he developed an interest in Hindu philosophy, and wrote, co-translated, and edited several works relating to Vedanta. Of his postwar novels, *Prater Violet* (1945) reflects his experience as a screenwriter, and in his last, *A Meeting by the River* (1967), the lives and characters of two brothers are contrasted. See *Where Joy Resides: an Isherwood Reader*, ed. Don Bachardy and James White, 1991; *Lions and Shadows: an Education in the Twenties*, new edn 1979, *Kathleen and Frank*, new edn 1992, *Christopher and His Kind 1929–1939*, new edn 1987, *My Guru and His Disciple*, new edn 1988 (autobiographical studies); Jonathan Fryer, *Eye of the Camera: a Life of Christopher Isherwood*, rev. edn 1993; Stephen Wade, *Christopher Isherwood*, 1991 (critical study).

J

JACKSON, HELEN HUNT (1830–85), née Fiske, American poet and novelist, was born in Amherst, Massachusetts, where she was a childhood friend of EMILY DICKINSON. She attended Amherst Academy, for which she proved too lively, and then boarding schools at Hadley, Charleston, Pittsfield, and Falmouth, followed by Ipswich Female Seminary, from which, after being orphaned by her father's death in 1847, she went to the progressive Abbott Institute, New York City. In 1852 she married Edward Hunt, an army officer, whose death from an accident in the Brooklyn Naval Yard in 1863 was followed two years later by that of their surviving son, aged nine. During a period of recovery she contributed poems to the New York *Evening Post* under the name of Marah. In 1866 she moved into Mrs Hannah Dame's literary boarding house in Newport, Rhode Island, where the critic, and mentor of Dickinson, Thomas Higginson (1823–1911), lived; a thriving friendship ensued. She contributed stories, essays, and reviews, signed 'Saxe Holm', 'Rip Van Winkle', or with initials, to literary journals. *Verses by H. H.* (1870; enlarged cdn 1874) was highly praised by EMERSON, who included five of her poems in his anthology, *Parnassus* (1874). She is, however, best remembered for two prose works exposing the American government's treatment of the Indians: *A Century of Dishonor* (1881), a copy of which she presented to each congressman, and *Ramona* (1884), a fictional restatement of her convictions. Both were written after her marriage in 1875 to William S. Jackson of Colorado Springs, where she came face to face with the conditions which stimulated her crusading nature. After her death, Dickinson wrote: 'Helen of Troy will die, but not Helen of Colorado.'

JACOB, VIOLET (1863–1946), née Kennedy-Erskine, Scottish poet and novelist, was born in Montrose, the daughter of the 18th Laird of Dun. She married an army officer, with whom she spent some years in India—see *Diaries and Letters from India 1895–1900*, ed. Carol Anderson (1990), in which the grandeur is shrewdly and humorously observed and which includes examples of her own paintings. Her first two books after her return to northeast Scotland were historical novels, of which *The Times Literary Supplement* reviewer said that *The Interloper* (1904) merited 'superlatives of criticism'. She is better known for her poetry in the local dialect of Scots, of which her most notable collections are *Songs of Angus* (1915) and *The Northern Lights and Other Poems* (1921). She was contributing to MACDIARMID's anthologies, *Northern Numbers* (1920–24), at a time when he himself was still writing in English. Her work is usually concerned with the individual in a rural setting, and his or her fears, frustrations, and pangs of love, and she is capable of representing considerable depth of feeling. A recent collection of her short stories is *The Lum Hat and Other Stories: Last Tales of Violet Jacob*, ed. Ronald Garden (1982).

JACOBS, W(ILLIAM) W(YMARK) (1863–1943) British short-story writer and novelist, was born in Wapping, the eldest son of a Thames wharf manager, who gave him a private schooling in spite of restricted finances. He then studied at Birkbeck College and entered the civil service in 1879 as an apprentice clerk, becoming fully fledged in the Savings Bank Department in 1883. The comings and goings of ships and those who manned and serviced them, and the totally contrasting atmosphere of occasional holidays in the country, fired his imagination. In about 1890 J. K. JEROME accepted some stories and sketches for the *Idler* and *To-day*, and by 1895 his work was also appearing in *Strand Magazine*. His first collection, *Many Cargoes*, was published in 1896, and in 1899 he felt able to retire from being a clerk to become a full-time writer. *Light Freights* (1901) established his hallmarks even more firmly. His comic stories tend to centre either on the river and the domestic lives of those who earn their living from it, or on the inhabitants of the country village of Claybury. His other genre was the horror story which borders on the supernatural, of which 'The Monkey's Paw' is the supreme example. His novels are light, and episodic. He also wrote, on his own account or in collaboration, a number of plays, of which *The Boatswain's Mate* (1907) became an opera, produced in 1916 with music by (Dame) Ethel Smyth (1858–1944). See *Selected Stories*, ed. Hugh Greene, 1975; *The Monkey's Paw and Other Stories*, 1994.

JACOBSON, DAN (b. 1929) British novelist, short-story writer, and critic, was born in Johannesburg, South Africa, of Jewish parents who had emigrated from Lithuania when young, and was brought up in Kimberley. He graduated from Witwatersrand University in 1949. He taught for a year at a Jewish school in London, and on his return was a journalist for the South African Jewish Board of Deputies and then for an industrial company. He settled permanently in Britain in 1958. He was appointed a lecturer at University College, London, in 1976, Reader in English in 1980, Professor in 1988, and Professor Emeritus in 1994. His first five novels and many of his short stories—see especially the collection *Beggar My Neighbour* (1964)—have South African themes. *The Trap* (1955) and *A Dance in the Sun* (1956), published together with a new preface (1988), each centre on a single episode in the bleak northern veldt. *The Evidence of Love* (1960), while treating naturalistically the theme of interracial sex, has a most unusual outcome for a South African novel. *The Beginners* (1966) is a family saga which explores the place of the South African of European parentage in the country of his birth, and of the Jew in the wider context of the modern world. *The Rape of Tamar* (1970) has a biblical theme, and marks the beginning of a phase of more inventive narrative techniques, which give a nightmare quality to *The Confessions of Josef Baisz* (1977). *Hidden in the Heart* (1991) offers a new angle on living in the past. In *Her Story* (1987) he explores in a biblical setting 'the secret entanglements of pleasure and shame, of display and denial'; in *The God-Fearer* (1992) he invents an alternative history, in which medieval Europe is governed by Old Testament devotees, and the 'Christer' people are the oppressed minority, a theme which has affinities with those he investigates in his study, *The Story of the Stories: the Chosen People and Its God* (1982). *Adult Pleasures* (1988) is a work of literary criticism. *The Electronic Elephant: a South African Journey* (1994) is a vivid account of a journey by car along southern Africa's Great North Road. See *Time and Time Again: Autobiographies*, 1985.

JAMES I (1394–1437) King of Scotland, poet, was born in Dunfermline. When he was 11, he was sent for safety to France by his father, Robert III, but was captured en route by the English. Robert died on hearing the news, and the new King spent the next 18 years in England, where he was well educated and looked after. He was finally freed in exchange for hostages from the Scottish nobility, and sent back to his own people with a bill for £40,000 for his board and lodging. In the meantime he had married Joan Beaufort (d. 1445), daughter of the Earl of Somerset. Firm but ruthless in the pursuit of necessary reforms, and merciless in dealing with his turbulent nobility and recalcitrant Highland chiefs, he was assassinated by members of an aristocratic conspiracy while taking an extended Christmas break at the monastery of Blackfriars in Perth. While he was in England, as a gift to his new bride or in celebration of their first meeting, he wrote *The Kingis Quair* [The King's Book], 197 stanzas in what is appropriately known as rhyme royal (though it had been used by CHAUCER for *Troilus and Criseyde*). Reminiscent of LYDGATE, however, rather than Chaucer, it is the earliest-known Scottish poem in the courtly love vein, while endorsing the married state and reflecting an acute observation of nature and a Christian outlook. The language is significant in that it incorporates usages, words, and rhymes from the northern English dialect from which Middle Scots developed. See *The Kingis Quair*, ed. J. Norton-Smith, 1971.

JAMES VI (I OF ENGLAND) (1566–1625) King of Scotland (from 1603 also of England), poet and prose writer, the only child of Lord Darnley (1545–67) and Mary, Queen of Scots, was born in Edinburgh Castle and became King when his mother was forced to abdicate and flee to England in 1567. He was educated at Stirling Castle under the supervision of BUCHANAN, spoke Latin before he had learned Scots, and at 12 (when he was dubbed 'The wisest fool in Christendom' by a French statesman who had been told he was a fool) he was widely read in many fields of study. In 1582 he was kidnapped by a conspiracy of nobles and held for a year, after which he reorganized his court and formed the Castalian Band, a group of poets among whom were MONTGOMERIE and FOWLER. He was himself writing quite tolerable verse at this time, some of which was published in 1585 with a preface in which he discusses poetic forms. More poems, *His Majesties Poeticall Exercises at Variant Houres*, appeared in 1585. *Daemonologie* (1597), a prose work on witchcraft, reflects the hysteria of the time and his own misguided preoccupation with the subject. *Basilicon Doron* (1599), his rules of kingship, which included not being dictated to by the Protestant Church, was originally written for the young Prince Henry (1593–1612). When James succeeded to the English throne of Elizabeth (his first cousin twice-removed), he had, in spite of his ungainly appearance and disgusting table manners, improved his country's trade and industry, finally ended feudalism, strengthened the power of Parliament, and (largely by cunning) established himself as Head of the Church as well as of State. He was also to become the first Scottish monarch for over two hundred years to die in his or her bed, apart from his grandfather, James V, who succumbed to depression at the age of 30. James greeted his new subjects with *A Counterblaste to Tobacco* (1604): 'Have you not reason then to bee ashamed, and to forbeare this filthie noveltie, so basely grounded, so foolishly received and so grossly mistaken in the right use thereof? . . . A custome lothsome to the eye, hatefull to the Nose, harmefull to the braine, dangerous to the lungs, and in the black stinking fume thereof, neerest resembling the horrible Stigian smoke of the pit that is bottomlesse.' This treatise was diplomatically written in English, rather than his native Scots, and for the publication of his *Workes* (1616), he substituted wherever possible English equivalents of Scots words. It was at his instigation that the Hampton Court Conference was held in 1604, at which he proposed a revision of the English Bible, resulting in the Authorized Version of 1611.

JAMES, C(YRIL) L(IONEL) R(OBERT) (1901–89) Trinidadian novelist, historian, and critic, was educated at Queen's Royal College, Port-of-Spain, and became a teacher and journalist. In 1929–30 he jointly edited the two issues of *Trinidad*, the island's first literary magazine. In 1932 he emigrated to England, taking with him the manuscript of a novel, though 'the real magnum opus was to be my second novel'. The second novel never materialized, but *Minty Alley* (1936; new edn, with introduction by Kenneth Ramchand, 1971), set in a barrack-yard, is a forerunner of the West Indian novel of social realism. His historical study, *The Black Jacobins: Toussaint L'Ouverture and the San Domingo Revolution* (1938; rev edn 1963 in USA, 1980 in UK), is regarded as having influenced the emergence of the West Indian historical novel. He was at this time also writing about cricket, in which field he became a journalist in the class of CARDUS. He spent the years 1938–53 in the USA, where he lectured on politics and literature. He was Secretary of the West Indian Federal Labour Party 1958–60. A Marxist philosopher, he published his selected writings in three volumes 1977–85. See *The C. L. R. James Reader*, ed. Anna Grimshaw, 1992; *C. L. R. James: His Intellectual Legacies*, ed. Selwyn R. Cudjoe and William E. Cain, 1995; *Beyond a Boundary*, new edn 1996 (autobiography); Farrukh Dhondy, *C. L. R. James: a Life*, 1996; Kent Worcester, *C. L. R. James: a Political Biography*, 1996.

JAMES, HENRY (1843–1916) novelist, short-story writer, dramatist, and critic, was born in New York, the second son of Henry James (1811–82), a philosophical and theological writer of Irish parentage—see Alfred Habegger *The Father: a Life of Henry James, Sr* (1995). He was the brother of the philosopher and psychologist, William James (1842–1910), who in his *Principles of Psychology* (1890) coined the term 'stream of consciousness', and of Alice James (1848–92), diarist and letter writer—see Jean Strouse, *Alice James* (1980). For a portrait of the whole family see

R. W. B. Lewis, *The Jameses: a Family Narrative* (1991). Henry was taken to Europe at six months and then educated at various private schools in New York, while being allowed a great deal of freedom to roam around the city and to formulate and express his thoughts. He describes his earlier years in *A Small Boy and Others* (1913) and *Notes of a Son and Brother* (1914)—see also *The Middle Years* (1917). In 1855 the family went abroad for several years, during which he acquired a lifelong taste for Europe. In 1862, shortly after suffering a mysterious back injury, he entered Harvard to read law, but soon gave that up in favour of a less conventional career, which he heralded by getting published in 1864 what has been identified as his first story, 'A Tragedy of Errors'. During the next ten years he revisited Europe twice and wrote many stories, reviews, and articles for English and American journals—see especially *Travelling in Italy with Henry James: Essays*, ed. Fred Kaplan (1994). His first novel, *Watch and Ward*, appeared as a serial in 1871 (in volume form in 1878). His first book of short stories, *A Passionate Pilgrim and Other Tales*, was published in 1875, the year he returned to Europe, determined to settle there for good. After trying Paris, he decided on London, where he lived first in lodgings off Piccadilly and then in a flat in Kensington. He acted as a dispassionate observer, rather than a participant in, or even a critic of, the social, political, and economic changes of the times, and made a subsidiary art of the pleasure of dining out. He never married.

James's particular distinction as a novelist is that, born and bred in what was then the New World and living in and fully appreciating the social and cultural traditions of the Old, he created a new (if not always a welcome) bridge of understanding. Further, by a judicious mixture of what he called 'drama', the presentation of a scene without any intervening interpretation, and 'picture', the reflection of the action through the consciousness of a character, he developed a new approach to his craft. For the sake of critical convenience his career is often divided into three phases. The theme of the innocent American abroad dominates the first phase, which begins with *Roderick Hudson* (1876) and culminates triumphantly with *The Portrait of a Lady* (1881). The next phase comprises novels with American settings, such as *Washington Square* (1881) and *The Bostonians* (1886), and studies of clashes between the classes, such as *The Princess Casamassima* (1886) and *The Tragic Muse* (1890). At this point in his literary development he appears to have abandoned hope of popular acclaim; in his subsequent novels he is more concerned with the perfection of his art form, in reworking earlier themes with increased depth, as in *The Ambassadors* (1903), and in varying the patterns of sexual relationships, as in *The Wings of the Dove* (1902) and *The Golden Bowl* (1904). His two most famous pieces of shorter fiction are *The Aspern Papers* (1888), based on his knowledge of BYRON, SHELLEY, and Claire Clairmont (1798–1879), whose theme is the morality of disturbing the past, and the tale of supernatural possession, *The Turn of the Screw* (1898), each of which responds to various interpretations. The moderate reception given to his novels in his middle phase led him to experiment with drama. Only a handful of his plays were performed, and he was jeered when in 1895 he took a bow on the first night of *Guy Domville*; the occasion also marked the first meeting of SHAW and WELLS. His literary criticism is another thing altogether, and is seen at its best in the prefaces to the revised editions of his novels, first published in New York 1907–09—see also *Literary Criticism* (2 vols 1985).

In 1898 he bought Lamb House in Rye, Sussex, though he had a room permanently kept for him at the Reform Club for his frequent visits to London; in 1913 he acquired in addition a flat in Cheyne Walk, Chelsea. The outbreak of World War I came as a profound shock to him, and he demonstrated his patriotism for his adoptive country by becoming a British citizen in 1915. He was awarded the OM in the New Year Honours List in 1916, and died two months later in London. See Leon Edel, *Henry James: a Life*, new edn 1996 (single-volume edn of *The Life of Henry James*, 5 vols 1953–72); Fred Kaplan, *Henry James: the Imagination of Genius*, new edn 1994 (biography); Sheldon M. Novick, *Henry James: the Young Master*, 1996 (biography to the 1880s); S. Gorley Putt, *A Preface to Henry James*, 1987; Judith Wood, *Henry James: the Major Novels*, 1991; Barbara Hardy, *Henry James: the Later Writing*, 1996 (critical introduction); Tony Tanner, *Henry James and the Art of Non-Fiction*, 1995.

JAMES, M(ONTAGUE) R(HODES) (1862–1936) British scholar and short-story writer, was born in Goodnestone, Kent, the son of a cleric, and was educated at Eton and King's College, Cambridge, where he got a first in classics and won prizes for divinity. His professional career was a tribute to both his academic and his administrative abilities. He became a Fellow of King's in 1887, and was Provost 1905–18, while also being Director of the Fitzwilliam Museum 1893–1908. He was Provost of Eton 1918–36. His particular fields of scholarship were the apochryphal literature of the Bible—*The Apochryphal New Testament* (1924), which he edited and translated, is still the standard edition—and medieval manuscripts. Between 1895 and 1932 he catalogued the manuscript holdings of every Cambridge college, as well as those of the Fitzwilliam Museum, Westminster Abbey, Lambeth Palace, Aberdeen University, and the John Rylands Library, Manches-

ter. There is little doubt that these interests, and the historic surroundings in which he carried on his bachelor existence, contributed to his mastery of the story of the macabre, a talent which receives no mention in the *Dictionary of National Biography*. *Ghost-Stories of an Antiquary* (1904), and subsequent volumes in a similar vein, are all the more believable, and thus horrific, for being written by a man who had steeped himself in myth and folklore and the conditions and intellectual processes by which they are generated, and who was also a sincere Christian. He was awarded the OM in 1930. See *Casting the Runes and Other Ghost Stories*, ed. Michael Cox, 1987; Michael Cox, *M. R. James: an Informal Portrait*, new edn 1986.

JAMES, P(HYLLIS) D(OROTHY) (*b.* 1920) British novelist, was born in Oxford, the daughter of a tax official, and was educated at Cambridge Girls' High School. As her parents were unable to afford university, she went to work in the tax office in Ely, where she met a medical student, Connor White (*d.* 1964). They married in 1941 and moved to London, where she worked as a Red Cross nurse and at the Ministry of Food, and thought about a novel, 'but there was so much bombing I didn't think it was worth beginning since I probably wouldn't be around to finish it'. Her husband's war experience left him with a mental illness from which he did not recover. To support themselves and their two daughters she became a civil servant, working in hospital administration from 1949 to 1968, when she joined the Home Office as Principal in the Police Department, later transferring to the Criminal Policy Department, with which she was from 1972 to 1979. *Cover Her Face* (1962), written early in the morning and at weekends, introduced to the crime novel a new brand of detective, Commander Adam Dalgliesh, sensitive, lonely, and a published poet, who in *An Unsuitable Job for a Woman* (1972) is viewed through the eyes of another unusual creation, Cordelia Gray, tyro private detective. James's books begin with a situation or setting, and depend on ingenious motives and interesting relationships for their exposition. *Innocent Blood* (1980), not a detective story but a psychological thriller, delves deepest in character study and suspense. With its publication in the USA she became a best-selling author. *The Children of Men* (1992) by complete contrast a dystopian novel in which she projects an England in 2021 in which, as on the whole planet, no child has been born for 25 years. She returned to her more normal vein, and to Dalgliesh, in *Original Sin* (1994), set in a traditional London publishing house. She was a governor of the BBC 1988–93, and a member of the British Council 1988–93 and of the Arts Council 1988–92. She received a life peerage in 1991, becoming Baroness James.

JAMES, WILLIAM see JAMES, HENRY; SINCLAIR; STEIN.

JAMESON, ANNA BROWNELL (1794–1860), née Murphy, British critic and novelist, was born in Dublin, the eldest daughter of the miniature-painter, Denis Brownell Murphy (d. 1842). The family came to England in 1798; when she was 16 she became a governess. After a broken engagement she took a post which involved accompanying her charge on a Continental tour—her fictional account (1825), much in the style of STAËL's *Corinne*, was reissued as *Diary of an Ennuyée* (1826) and made an impression for its emphasis on female independence. She now married her former fiancé, Robert Jameson (d. 1854), who after a few years departed for Dominica. In the meantime she became a notable critic with books such as *The Loves of the Poets* (1829) and *Characteristics of Women* (1832), a study of SHAKESPEARE's heroines. In 1836 her husband persuaded her to join him in Canada, where he had become Attorney General, but she returned after two years. An inveterate traveller, she organized the BROWNINGS when they arrived in Paris in 1846 after their clandestine marriage. Her husband's death, without any provision for her, affected her security but increased her energy. She died of a cold caught while returning to her lodgings from the British Museum, where she had been researching her unfinished 'History of Our Lord', the fourth part of *Sacred and Legendary Art*, which had begun with legends of the angels and stories of the saints (1848). E. B. BROWNING described her as having 'the lightest of eyes, the lightest of complexions, no eyebrows, and what looks to me like very pale red hair, and thin lips of no colour at all'. CARLYLE, who did not like her at all, called her 'a little hard, brown, red-haired, freckled, fierce-eyed, square-mouthed woman'. See Clara Thomas, *Love and Work Enough: the Life of Anna Jameson*, 1967.

JAMESON, (MARGARET) STORM (1891–1986) British novelist and critic, was born in Whitby, Yorkshire, of a family of shipbuilders (her father was a ship's captain), and had a Nonconformist upbringing. She was educated at Scarborough Municipal School and Leeds University, where she was not only the first woman BA in English, but also got a first. During the 1920s she worked in London as an advertising copywriter, as Editor of *New Commonwealth*, and as English representative of the American publishing firm of Alfred A. Knopf. Her first novel, *The Pot Boils*, was published in 1919. She was a prolific writer, the more notable of whose subsequent novels include the 'Triumph of

Time' trilogy (1927–31), about a Whitby ship-building dynasty; another trilogy (or by her own account 'an unfinished series'), 'The Mirror in Darkness' (1934–36), in which the 'new woman' is a projection of her own personality; and *Cousin Honoré* (1940), a study of character and also of the French/German political and behavioural divide in Alsace between the two world wars. In 1937–38 she wrote three novels under the pseudonyms of James Hill or William Lamb. She also translated novels and stories of MAUPASSANT. As an eloquent anti-Nazi and a tireless worker for refugee writers and intellectuals, she was an ideal President of the English Centre of PEN 1938–45, and it is of note that the original UK edition of FRANK's *Diary* carried a substantial foreword by her. She recorded in 1981 that *Parthian Words* (1970), an outspoken study of modern fiction, 'contains my declaration of faith as a writer'. See *Journey from the North*, 2 vols, new edn 1984 (autobiography).

JANSSON, TOVE (b. 1914) Finnish children's writer (in Swedish), was born and brought up in Helsinki, the daughter of a sculptor—see her childhood impressions, [*Sculptor's Daughter*] (1968; tr. Kingsley Hart, 1969)—and studied art in Stockholm, Helsinki, and Paris. Of school, she has said: 'I didn't understand what it was all about . . . I just waited for it to stop. All I enjoyed was the writing.' An artist and illustrator, she originally devised the Moomins, curious, affable, endearingly rotund, troll-like creatures who solve their domestic and environmental problems through art and deep thought, for a strip cartoon; the first story book, [*Comet in Moominland*] (1946; tr. Elizabeth Portch, 1951), was followed by seven further miniature sagas, all illustrated by herself—the first to be published in English was [*Finn Family Moomintroll*] (1949; tr. Portch, 1950). [*The Summer Book*] (1972; tr. Thomas Teal, 1974) is a series of situations, rather than stories, featuring a small girl and her grandmother, which are evocative equally of childhood and old age. She spent several weeks in London in 1954 composing a Moomins' strip for the *Evening News* and trying 'to learn English from the novels of P. G. Wodehouse'. She was awarded the Hans Christian ANDERSEN Medal in 1966.

JARRELL, RANDALL (1914–65) American poet, critic, and translator, was born in Nashville, Tennessee, where at the age of eight he posed for the figure of Ganymede on the Pantheon in the Centennial Park. His divided childhood is reflected in many poems, notably '90 North' and 'The Prince'. He was educated at Hume-Fogg High School, Nashville, and Vanderbilt University, where he studied creative writing under RANSOM, and wrote a postgraduate dissertation on A. E. HOUSMAN. His first book of verse, *Blood for* *a Stranger* (1942), was published while he was teaching at the University of Texas. His second, *Little Friend, Little Friend* (1945), came out while he was doing war service as an air force instructor near Tucson, Arizona, which supplied him with the background for some unusual, vicarious war poems, such as 'The Death of the Ball Turret Gunner' and 'Siegfried'. He then returned to teaching, at the Women's College, University of North Carolina, Greensboro, of which he became a full professor in 1958. He continued to write poetry of everyday happenings and heartbreaks, adopting a female persona for the title poem of *The Woman at the Washington Zoo* (1960), and reliving childhood experiences in *The Lost World* (1965). He was equally respected as a critic—*The Third Book of Criticism* (1969) and *Kipling, Auden & Co: Essays and Reviews 1935–1964* (1980) were published posthumously—and as a translator, especially of GOETHE, the GRIMMS, and RILKE. His only novel, *Pictures from an Institution* (1954), is a rollicking skit on the creative writing department of a women's college. He suffered a nervous breakdown in 1964, and died when struck by a car on a highway. See *The Complete Poems*, new edn 1996; *Selected Poems*, ed. William H. Pritchard, new edn 1991; William H. Pritchard, *Randall Jarrell: a Literary Life*, new edn 1991; Mary Jarrell, *Remembering Randall, Poet-Critic*, 1996; Suzanne Ferguson, *The Poetry of Randall Jarrell*, 1971.

JEFFERIES, (JOHN) RICHARD (1848–87) British naturalist, novelist, and prose writer, was born near Swindon, the son of a small farmer, and was educated locally and in Kent. At 16 he and a friend ran away to France, intending to walk to Moscow, but changed their destination to America, turned back, and reached Liverpool. Finding that they had not enough money for the voyage, they returned to Swindon. He was encouraged to write by the Editor of the *North Wilts Herald*, for which he became a reporter. Unemployed after a visit to Belgium in 1870, he came to public notice in 1872 with a letter to *The Times* on the plight of farm workers. With what he earned from a family history, *A Memoir of the Goddards of North Wilts* (1873), and other sources, he got married and subsidized the publication of a society novel, *The Scarlet Shawl* (1874), which failed, as did its successor. He finally established himself and the source of his particular genius with *The Gamekeeper at Home: Sketches of Natural History and Rural Life* (1878). Between his country novels, *Greene Ferne Farm* (1880) and *The Dewy Morn* (1884), came *Bevis: the Story of a Boy* (1882), in which his lyrical observation of nature is heightened by the fire of youth. *After London: or, Wild England* (1885) is an excursion into imaginative science fiction. There is strong characterization and family conflict in *Amaryllis at the Fair* (1887), written

while he was painfully dying from a long illness, too proud to seek help from the Royal Literary Fund. He expressed his spiritual yearnings and pantheistic beliefs in *The Story of My Heart: My Autobiography* (1883). His most famous collection of essays is *The Open Air* (1885). See Samuel J. Looker, *Richard Jefferies, Man of the Fields: a Biography and Letters*, 1965.

JEFFERS, (JOHN) ROBINSON (1887–1962) American poet, was born in Pittsburgh, Pennsylvania, the elder son of a 49-year-old professor of Old Testament literature and his 27-year-old wife. He was learning Greek from his father at five, and attended boarding schools in Switzerland and Germany while his parents went on their travels. When they moved to Pasadena, California, in 1903, he went to Occidental College, and studied literature and then medicine at the University of California, of which he was heavyweight wrestling champion. He fell in love with a fellow student, Una Kuster (1885–1950), the wife of a lawyer, and in spite of efforts to part them, they married in 1913 after her divorce. A legacy from his grandfather financed the publication of a book of verse, *Flagons and Apples* (1912), an early manuscript of which he had mislaid during a saloon drinking session. The couple moved to Carmel, on the coast south of San Francisco, in 1914. Here he built a tower house of stone, facing 'the final Pacific', and, happily married and the father of twin boys, settled down to reflect the wildness of his surroundings in verse. *Californians* (1916) was published, and forgotten. After several rejections, he privately published *Tamar and Other Poems* (1924), whose reception by the critics encouraged a publisher to bring out an expanded edition, *Roan Stallion, Tamar and Other Poems* (1925). *The Selected Poetry of Robinson Jeffers* (1938) was drawn from 11 previous volumes. Strongly conservative, and popular only as long as readers could find little form or meaning in the modernists, he wrote lyrics in free verse and grim narrative poems in blank verse. His adaptation of *Medea* of EURIPIDES (1946) ran successfully as a play. See *The Collected Poetry of Robinson Jeffers*, ed. Tim Hunt, 3 vols 1988–91; Robert J. Brophy, *Robinson Jeffers: the Dimensions of a Poet*, 1994.

JENNINGS, ELIZABETH (*b.* 1926) British poet, was born in Boston, Lincolnshire, of a Catholic family, and was educated at Oxford High School and St Anne's College, Oxford, after which she was a library assistant in Oxford City Library until 1958. Since 1961 she has been a freelance writer. *Poems* was published in 1953, with *A Way of Looking* in 1955; she was the only woman contributor to CONQUEST's anthology, *New Lines* (1956). Images of childhood, people, and places (especially Italy) gave way in *Recoveries* (1964) and

The Mind Has Mountains (1966) to visions of hospital and to explorations of a disturbed mind (caused by a mental breakdown), which are set at rest in *Growing-Points: New Poems* (1975) and *Consequently I Rejoice* (1977). Her interest in craftsmen is reflected by her translations of *The Sonnets of Michelangelo* (rev. edn 1969), and in painting by poems on Van Gogh; while her religious conviction is seen particularly in such poems as 'The Annunciation', 'The Visitation', 'A Requiem', and her imaginative projections into the personalities of saints. She has written several critical studies, and compiled *The Batsford Book of Religious Verse* (1981). A committed Roman Catholic, she lives on her own in a bedsitter given to her by the Oxford city council, spending most of the day in a local coffee shop, where she writes reviews and letters; at night she reads and composes poetry. She was made CBE in 1992. See *Collected Poems 1953–1986*, new edn 1987; *Times and Seasons*, 1992, and *Familiar Spirits*, 1994 (subsequent collections).

JEROME, ST (HIERONYMUS) (*c.*340–420) was born near Aquileia, Dalmatia, of a wealthy Christian family, and was educated in Rome, after which he returned home and entered into a regimen of asceticism, as a reaction to what he had experienced and seen. After a period spent in the desert of Chalcis, he was ordained priest in Antioch. In 382 he came to Rome, where he became secretary to Pope Damasus and spiritual consultant to several high-born ladies, of whom Paula and her daughter accompanied him to Bethlehem, where he settled in 386, and where Paula founded a monastery and three convents. His numerous works in Latin include biographical studies, polemical treatises, and commentaries. He translated the Old Testament into Latin from the Hebrew, and made a fresh translation of the New Testament from the Greek. The resulting 'Vulgate' Bible, revised under Pope Clement VIII (1592–1605), is the authorized text of the Roman Catholic Church. ERASMUS published an edition of his works in 1519.

JEROME, JEROME K(LAPKA) (1859–1927) British novelist, dramatist, and journalist, was born in Walsall, the son of a Nonconformist preacher and colliery owner who, when the mine failed, set up as a wholesale ironmonger in east London. He was educated at Marylebone Grammar School, which he left at 14. He worked as a railway clerk, teacher, actor, and journalist, before having a play, *Barbara*, produced in 1886. He also published two books of sketches, *On the Stage and Off: the Brief Career of a Would-be Actor* (1888) and *The Idle Thoughts of an Idle Fellow: a Book for an Idle Holiday* (1889). *Three Men in a Boat (To Say Nothing of the Dog)* (1889) began as a study of the Thames ('The Story of the Thames'), with linking passages recording a trip by rowing boat. The editor wisely cut out the history and topography, leaving what its author termed 'hopeless and incurable veracity', which is the chief joy of this classic humorous tale; anyone who has gone boating or camping, or prefers not to, will recognize the essence of truth. A less famous sequel is *Three Men on the Bummel* (1900), in which the trio holiday in Germany. Jerome was a founder of the *Idler* literary magazine, which he edited from 1892 to 1897. The twopenny weekly paper, *To-day*, which he established in 1893, folded in 1897 after a lawsuit. He wrote other novels and books of essays and sketches, and many more plays, of which *The Passing of the Third Floor Back* (1908), from his own story, a sentimental tale of the moral regeneration of the occupants of a lodging house, is remembered. In his late fifties, he drove a French ambulance on the Western front. He died while on a motoring tour of Britain. See *My Life and Times*, new edn 1983; Joseph Connolly, *Jerome K. Jerome: a Critical Biography*, 1982.

JEWETT, SARAH ORNE (1849–1909) American novelist and short-story writer, was born in South Berwick, Maine, granddaughter, on one side, of a sea captain and shipowner and, on the other, of a literary-minded medical man; she was the daughter of a country doctor, whom she accompanied on his rounds when sickness kept her from school, as it often did. She attended Berwick Academy in a desultory fashion from 1861 to 1865, by which time she had been inspired by STOWE's *The Pearl of Orr's Island* to record and reflect, for the edification of the rest of the nation, the New England environment, to which she always remained intensely loyal. Her earliest efforts, signed 'Alice Eliot', 'A. C. Eliot', or 'Sarah O. Sweet', were mainly published in children's magazines. Her career properly began with the acceptance by HOWELLS of her story, 'Mr Bruce' (1869), for *Atlantic Monthly*. He encouraged her to fit a number of sketches into a fictional framework, which became her first book, *Deephaven* (1877). In *A Country Doctor* (1884), she 'tried to give some idea of my father's character'. *A White Heron and Other Stories* (1886) represents her short writing at its most mature: *The Country of the Pointed Firs* (1896), an episodic novel, has proved her most lasting single work. She struck up an enduring friendship with Annie Adams Fields (1834–1915), miscellaneous writer and literary biographer, the wife of Howells's predecessor, James T. Fields (1817–81). On four trips together to Europe (1882, 1892, 1898, 1900) they hobnobbed with writers such as HENRY JAMES, KIPLING, READE, TENNYSON, and even CHRISTINA ROSSETTI. Her attitude to her craft may be summed up by her advice to CATHER: 'One must know the world *so well* before one can know the parish.' In 1901 she was the first woman to be awarded an honorary doctorate by Bowdoin College. In 1902, on her 53rd birthday, she was thrown from her carriage and suffered injuries which ended her writing career. See *Novels and Stories*, ed. Michael Davitt Bell, 1994; *The Best Stories of Sarah Orne Jewett*, ed. Charles G. Waugh and others, 1988; *The Country of the Pointed Firs and Other Stories*, ed. Marjorie Pryse, 1994; *The Country of the Pointed Firs and Other Fiction*, ed. Terry Heller, 1996; Paula Blanchard, *Sarah Orne Jewett: Her World and Her Work*, 1994; Richard Cary, *Sarah Orne Jewett*, 1962 (critical study).

JEWSBURY, GERALDINE (1812–80) British novelist, was born in Measham, Derbyshire. The family moved to Manchester in about 1818. After the death of her mother, she was brought up by her sister Maria (1800–33), a poet and prose writer, after whose marriage in 1832 she kept house for her father until his death in 1840, and then for a brother until his marriage in 1853. In 1841 she met CARLYLE and his wife, with whom she struck up a firm rapport, though it was against Jane Carlyle's better judgment that, at her husband's suggestion, she invited Geraldine to stay 'for two or three weeks' at Cheyne Row in 1843. The visit lasted six weeks and was not a success, though the friendship was maintained until Mrs Carlyle's death. Mrs Alexander Ireland in *Life of Jane Welsh Carlyle* (1891) writes, of 1845: 'Perhaps a quiet cigarette with Miss Jewsbury, who really loved her, was her greatest solace at this time.' The love was sincere, but Mrs Carlyle was exasperated by the attendant 'tiger-jealousy'. Jewsbury's first novel, *Zoë, the History of Two Lives* (1845), was a sensation for its theme of the love of a Catholic priest for a beautiful woman. It almost got her a husband, for a journalist friend of the Carlyles entered into a correspondence with her about it, and then found himself having to propose. She was an arch flirt, but she never married, though she wrote: 'I wish I had a good husband and a dozen children! Only the difficulty is that "women of genius" require very special husbands.' She wrote five more novels, including *The Half Sisters* (1848) and *Marian Withers* (1851), a Lancashire regional story. After moving to London in 1854 she became a reviewer for the *Athenaeum*. See Norma Clarke, *Ambitious Heights: Writing, Friendship, Love (the Jewsbury Sisters, Felicia Hemans and Jane Carlyle)*, 1990.

JHABVALA, RUTH PRAWER (*b.* 1927), née Ruth Prawer, novelist and short-story writer, was born in Cologne of Polish Jewish parents, with whom she fled to England in 1939. She was educated at Hendon County School and London University, graduating in English literature in 1951, in which year she married an Indian architect and went with him to India, where they had three daughters. She has lived in New York since 1975, and is now a US citizen. In 1972 she commented that 'the central fact' of her fiction was that she was 'a European living permanently in India, [with] an Indian family', and 'this makes me not quite an insider but it does not leave me entirely an outsider either'. Her eight Indian novels, which began with *To Whom She Will* (1955), are primarily concerned with the conflicts between Western, or Westernized, cultural and social conventions and the traditions and tribulations of the Indian experience. In the last of these, *Heat and Dust* (1975), which won the Booker prize for fiction, the present and the past are used to illuminate a scandalous romantic escapade. Her European roots and the experience of the USA provide the structure and essence of *In Search of Love and Beauty* (1983); in *Three Continents* (1987) an additional disturbing element is introduced in the form of Eastern fraudulence. *Shards of Memory* (1995) is even more cosmopolitan, the connection between the characters, who span five generations of a family, being the Master, a one-man spiritual sect, based in a cave in the Himalayas, whose watchword is 'One step higher'. Similar themes and conflicts inform the sharply delineated situations in her short stories, of which the contents of several volumes, beginning with *Like Birds, Like Fishes and Other Stories* (1963), are distilled into *Out of India: Selected Stories* (1986). She is also the principal author of several notable screenplays, including *Shakespeare Wallah* (1973).

JIMÉNEZ, JUAN RAMÓN (1881–1958) Spanish poet, was born in Moguer, the youngest child of a prosperous wine grower. After completing his secondary education at San Luis Gonzaga, a Jesuit school near Cadiz, he studied painting in Seville, began but abandoned a law course at the university, and returned home, having chosen poetry as his career. He published two books of verse in 1900, and went on writing, in spite of the fact that a nervous breakdown (partly precipitated by the death of his father) caused him to spend the next five years in sanatoriums in Bordeaux and Madrid. After several years at home, during which he published nine further volumes, he settled in Madrid in 1912. *Platero y Yo* (1914; as *Platero and I*, tr. Eloïse Roach, 1957; tr. Antonio Frasconi, bilingual edn 1994), a pastoral/philosophical prose poem of the narrator and his amiable donkey, is a further product of these years. In 1916 he travelled to New York, where he married Zenobia Camprubí Aymar, crystallizing the total experience in *Diaro di un Poeta Recién Casado* [The Diary of a Newly Married Poet] (1917), comprising six groups of poems. In 1936, at the outbreak of the Spanish Civil War, they returned to the USA, he as a cultural emissary of the Spanish Republic. They lived in Puerto Rico, Cuba, Miami (where he lectured at the University of Miami and Duke University), Washington, D.C., Maryland, and finally Puerto Rico again in 1951. Zenobia died in 1956 two days after the announcement of his award of the Nobel Prize for Literature. See *Three Hundred Poems 1903–1953*, tr. Eloïse Roach, 1962.

JOHN OF THE CROSS, ST (SAN JUAN DE LA CRUZ) (1542–91) Spanish poet and religious reformer, was born Juan de Yepes in Fontiveros. He was the youngest of three sons of a member of the local nobility who had been disowned by his family for marrying a peasant girl, became a weaver, and died in 1548. In 1552 his mother settled in Medina del Campo, where he attended the free Jesuit school and worked in the Hospital de las Bubas. He entered the Carmelite Order in 1563 as Fray Juan de Santo Matía, and then studied at Salamanca University. After being ordained priest in 1567, he was prevailed upon by TERESA OF AVILA to join the Order of Discalced (or Reformed) Carmelites, and became Fray Juan de la Cruz. In 1570 he was named director of the Order's college in Alcala de Henares; in 1572 he was appointed confessor and spiritual director to the 130 nuns in the Convent of the Incarnation in Avila, whose scandalous behaviour had brought the establishment into disrepute. The traditional Carmelites incarcerated him in solitary confinement in 1577 in their convent in Toledo, from which he escaped after nine months. He was given asylum in Andulasia, where he wrote out the poems he had composed in his head while in prison, to some of which he added detailed commentaries. In 1579 he was appointed Rector of the Carmelite college at Baeza; in 1581 he became Prior of the convent at Los Matires, and in 1588 of that at Segovia. In 1591 he was voted out of all offices by the governing body of the Order, and in the face of impending false accusations chose to go to the monastery in Ubeda, where he was treated by the Prior as a mere friar. He died shortly afterwards, having called on his deathbed for a recitation of his poems. Some of them were printed in Alacala in 1618 in a collection of spiritual works; *Cántico Espiritual: Canciones entre el Alma y el Esposo* [Spiritual Canticle: Songs between the Soul and the Bridegroom] appeared in Brussels in 1627. He was canonized in 1726. See *Poems*, tr. Roy Campbell, new edn 1979 (bilingual edn); *The Poems of St John of the Cross*, tr. J. F. Nims, 3rd edn 1995 (bilingual edn).

JOHNSON, PAMELA HANSFORD see SNOW.

JOHNSON, SAMUEL (1709–84) British essayist, critic, poet, novelist, and lexicographer, was born in Lichfield, Staffordshire, the eldest son of a bookseller, and was educated at Lichfield Grammar School, King Edward VI School, Stourbridge, and Pembroke College, Oxford, which he left after a year for lack of funds. As a child he suffered from scrofula and smallpox, and all his adult life from defective eyesight, a convulsive tic, melancholia, and general ill health. After teaching for a few years, he married in 1736 a widow 20 years older than he was (she died in 1752), but with money she brought him he opened a school at Edial, Staffordshire, which attracted only three pupils, one of them being David Garrick (1717–79), the actor-manager and dramatist. In 1737 he went to London to earn a living by writing. He worked for the *Gentleman's Magazine*, published *London* (1738), a poem in imitation of JUVENAL, and in 1744 a biography of the poet Richard Savage (*c*.1697–1743), a literary genre at which he came to excel—for an account of their friendship see Richard Holmes, *Dr Johnson and Mr Savage* (1993).

In 1747 he began work on his monumental *Dictionary of the English Language*. Its publication in 1755 was the occasion of Johnson's celebrated letter to CHESTERFIELD, who had slighted him when he originally came seeking support for the venture, and now wanted his name to be associated with it: '. . . The notice which you have been pleased to take of my labours, had it been early, had been kind; but it has been delayed till I am indifferent, and cannot enjoy it; till I am solitary, and cannot impart it; till I am known, and do not want it.' Another satirical poem, *The Vanity of Human Wishes*, had appeared in 1749, the year in which Garrick staged his tragedy, *Irene*. Between 1750 and 1752 he edited and largely wrote a twice-weekly journal, the *Rambler*. In 1756 he published proposals for an edition of SHAKESPEARE with a critical preface by himself: it finally came out in 1765. Between 1758 and 1760 he contributed to the *Universal Chronicle* a series of essays which were later collected as *The Idler* (1761). To pay off his mother's funeral expenses, he wrote in a week *The Prince of Abissinia* (1759), an eastern romance in the form of a didactic fable—it subsequently became known as *The History of Rasselas*, after its hero.

The grant in 1762 of a permanent pension from the Crown eased his financial problems and enabled him to enjoy his position as what SMOLLETT called 'the great Cham of literature', which was cultivated by his biographer, BOSWELL, whom he first met in 1763. In 1764 he made the acquaintance of a wealthy brewer, Henry Thrale (*c*.1728–81), at whose house, Streatham Park, he became an almost permanent house guest, and with whose 23-year-old wife he established a relationship so close that when she remarried after her husband's death (of apoplexy, after overeating), he never forgave her—see James L. Clifford,

Hester Lynch Piozzi (Mrs Thrale), introduction by Margaret Anne Doody (2nd edn rev. 1987). In 1773, at the age of 64, he courageously accepted Boswell's invitation to undertake the exhausting Scottish trip which he wrote up as *A Journey to the Western Isles of Scotland* (1775)—see also Pat Rogers, *Johnson and Boswell: the Transit of Caledonia* (1995). His last work was *Prefaces Biographical and Critical to the Works of the English Poets* (1779–81), reissued in 1781 as *Lives of the English Poets*. He died in London and was buried in Westminster Abbey. He was awarded the degree of LLD by Dublin University in 1765, and by Oxford in 1775. His fame as a conversationalist has tended to obscure his excellence as a prose writer, and though as a critic he had serious blind spots, these are so obvious to the modern reader that his general insight and directness are still valid. See *Samuel Johnson: Selected Works*, ed. Donald Greene, 1984; *Complete Poems*, ed. J. D. Fleman, 1982; James Boswell, *Life of Johnson*, ed. R. W. Chapman, introduction by Pat Rogers, 1980; Robert De-Maria, Jr, *The Life of Samuel Johnson: a Critical Biography*, new edn 1994; Nicholas Hudson, *Samuel Johnson and Eighteenth-Century Thought*, 1988; Pat Rogers, *Johnson*, 1993 (critical introduction); Allen Reddick, *The Making of Johnson's Dictionary 1746–1773*, new edn 1996.

JOHNSTON, (WILLIAM) DENIS

(1901–85) Irish dramatist, was born in Dublin and educated at St Andrew's College, Dublin, Merchiston Castle School, Edinburgh, Christ's College, Cambridge, and Harvard Law School, afterwards practising as a barrister in England and Ireland. He produced plays for the Abbey Theatre and the Dublin Gate Theatre, of which he was a director from 1931 to 1936; he was then until 1939 a radio and television writer and producer for the BBC. In his first play, *The Old Lady Says 'No!'* (1929), the romantic and the more realistic view of the rebel Robert Emmet (1778–1803) are contrasted—a first version, called 'Shadowdance', was returned by the Abbey Theatre (see GREGORY) with a cryptic note attached, 'The old lady says "no" ', which became the title. The intellectual depths of *The Moon in the Yellow River* (1931) may have caused it to be partly misunderstood as the kind of serious play he was parodying. *Storm Song* (1934) satirizes the film-making industry; *Blind Man's Buff* (1936) is a treatment of justice through a murder trial. Johnston was a BBC war correspondent in World War II, being mentioned in dispatches and appointed OBE—see his account, *Nine Rivers from Jordan: the Chronicle of a Journey and a Search* (1953). He went to the USA in 1950, and was a professor of English, Mount Holyoke College, Massachusetts, until 1960, and Chairman of the Department of Theatre and Speech, Smith College 1960–66. Of his post-

war plays, *The Scythe and the Sunset* (1958) achieved critical acclaim and (in Ireland) critical understanding. His literary study, *In Search of Swift* (1959), has its parallels in his play, *The Dreaming Dust* (performed in New York 1954, London 1962). *Orders and Desecrations: the Life of the Playwright*, ed. Rory Johnston (1992) is a collection of broadcasts and journalism with linking head-notes. The novelist Jennifer Johnston (*b.* 1930) is his daughter. See *The Dramatic Works*, ed. Joseph Ronsley, 1992; *The Brazen Horn*, rev. edn 1976 (autobiographical study); Gene A. Barnett, *Denis Johnston*, 1978 (critical study).

JOHNSTON, GEORGE

(1912–70) Australian novelist, was born in Malvern, Melbourne, the son of a tramway sheds foreman, and was educated at state schools. After training in a studio as a lithographer and studying art at the National Gallery School, he became a journalist, and served in many sectors of the action as a war correspondent during World War II. In 1947 he married, as his second wife, Charmian Clift (1923–69), with whom he wrote *High Valley* (1949), winner of the 1948 *Sydney Morning Herald* literary competition, and two other novels—*Strong Man from Piraeus*, ed. Garry Kinnane (1983) is a collection of their short stories. In 1954 he gave up his job as European Editor of the Sydney *Sun* to live with his family on the Greek island of Hydra. Here he wrote prolifically: radio and television plays as well as fiction, which included a series of thrillers as Shane Martin. His major work is the semi-autobiographical trilogy about David Meredith, who had appeared in *Closer to the Sun* (1960) and *The Far Road* (1962). Meredith's life, tribulations, wanderlust, and psychological quest for self-understanding and self-fulfilment occupy *My Brother Jack* (1964) and *Clean Straw for Nothing* (1969), both of which won the MILES FRANKLIN Award, and the unfinished *A Cartload of Clay* (1971). In 1964, knowing that his tuberculosis was incurable, he returned to Sydney, where Charmian, despite her own literary and journalistic achievements, committed suicide in 1969. Their son Martin Johnston (1947–90) was a novelist and poet—see Martin Johnston, *Selected Poems and Prose*, ed. John Tranter (1993). See Garry Kinnane, *George Johnston: a Biography*, new edn 1996.

JONES, DAVID (MICHAEL)

(1895–1974) painter, engraver, poet, and critic, was born in Brockley, Kent. His father, a printer and a staunch Protestant, was Welsh, but had been discouraged by his parents from speaking the language at home. The boy began to show talent for drawing at a very early age, and went to Camberwell School of Art in 1910, by which time he had absorbed, in English translation, much of the heritage of Welsh literature and 'felt' Welsh. He enlisted in the Royal Welch Fusiliers as a private in 1915, was wounded in 1916, and returned to England with trench fever in February 1918—see *A Fusilier at the Front: His Record of the Great War in Word and Image*, ed. Anthony Hyne (1996). He then studied at Westminster School of Art until 1921, in which year he became a Catholic and began work under the sculptor and typographer Eric Gill (1882–1940), to whose daughter he became engaged, though after three years she broke off the relationship. An edition of COLERIDGE's *The Rime of the Ancient Mariner*, with copper engravings by Jones, was published in 1929, shortly after he had begun an intricate literary work, *In Parenthesis* (1937), in which art is related to war, with a focus on the situation in Flanders in 1916. Of *The Anathemata* (1952), a sympathetic critic propounded: 'While this is a fluid epic, an epic without narrative in any sense permissible to literary criticsm, it may be hazarded that the central narrative of the Christian religion is everywhere present by implication . . .'. Latterly Jones lived in Harrow, Middlesex. His occasional writings were collected in *Epoch and Artist* (1959) and *The Dying Gaul and Other Essays* (1978), both edited by Harman Grisewood. He was made CBE in 1955 and CH in 1974. See *Selected Works of David Jones: from In Parenthesis, The Anathemata, The Sleeping Lord*, ed. John Matthias, new edn 1993; *Dai Greatcoat: a Self-Portrait of David Jones in His Letters*, ed. René Hague, 1980; William Blissett, *The Long Conversation: a Memoir of David Jones*, 1981.

JONES, EVERETT LEROY see BARAKA.

JONES, GWYN (b. 1907) Welsh scholar, novelist, and translator, was born in Blackwood, Monmouthshire, and educated at Tredegar Grammar School and University College, Cardiff. He was Professor of English Language and Literature, University College of Wales 1940–65, and of University College, Cardiff 1965–75. In his novel *Richard Savage* (1935), the life of the 18th-century poet of whom JOHNSON wrote a biography is set in the colourful background of his times; *Garland of Bays* (1938) uses ROBERT GREENE as the focus for scenes from the Elizabethan age. Thereafter, as in *Times Like These* (1936), a novel of South Wales miners during the 1926 General Strike, his fiction has largely Welsh settings, while concentrating on wider as well as Welsh issues, exemplified by *The Flowers Beneath the Scythe* (1952) and many of his short stories—see *Selected Short Stories* (1974). His translations include the 11 tales of the Celtic epic, *The Mabinogion* (with Thomas Jones, rev. edn 1975), and *Eirik the Red and Other Icelandic Sagas* (1961). Among his historical works are *A History of the Vikings* (rev. edn 1984) and *The Norse Atlantic Saga* (rev.

edn 1986). He was made CBE in 1965. See Cecil Price, *Gwyn Jones*, 1976 (critical study).

JONES, JAMES (1921–77) American novelist, was born in Robinson, Illinois. After graduating from Robinson High School in 1939, he enlisted in the US Air Force. He transferred to the infantry while serving in Hawaii, where he was when the Japanese bombed Pearl Harbor in 1941, and where he found in the barracks' library THOMAS WOLFE's *Look Homeward, Angel*, which convinced him 'that I had been a writer without knowing it or without having written'. Twice promoted, and twice reduced to private, he fought at Guadalcanal, where he killed a Japanese soldier with a knife in hand-to-hand combat, and was wounded in the head by a mortar fragment. Having had a novel rejected by Wolfe's editor, he took writing courses at New York University, had a war story, 'Temper of Steel', published in *Atlantic Monthly* (1948), and wrote *From Here to Eternity* (1951), which won the National Book Award. Set in and around the barracks in Hawaii in which he served, it caused a sensation for its exposé of army brutality and its outspokenness about sex. With his earnings he built a home in Marshall, Illinois, and helped set up a writers' colony. The *New Yorker* described *Some Came Running* (1958), a novel of a small Illinois town, as 'twelve hundred and sixty pages of flawlessly sustained tedium'. He and his wife were now living in Paris, where he planned to write a book about American expatriates. Instead he became a central figure of the literary and artistic set, and returned to the milieu of war with *The Thin Red Line* (1962). In 1974 they settled in Long Island, New York, where he embarked on the third volume of his war trilogy, *Whistle* (1978), which he had not quite finished when he died. It was completed by Willie Morris from his notes. See Frank MacShane, *Into Eternity: James Jones, the Life of an American Writer*, 1985; James R. Giles, *James Jones*, 1981 (critical study).

JONG, ERICA (b. 1942), née Mann, American novelist and poet, was born and brought up in Manhattan, New York, of an artistic family, and was educated at the High School of Music and Art and at Barnard College, where she switched from medicine to English. She then took a postgraduate degree at Columbia University with a thesis on POPE, and has taught English at university level since 1964. After marrying at 19, with a divorce three years later, she married Allan Jong, a Freudian psychiatrist. After their divorce in 1975 she married Jonathan Fast, only son of FAST; the marriage lasted six years. In 1989 she married Ken Burrows, a lawyer, who in 1996 represented the actress Joan Collins in her successful lawsuit against the publisher Random House. Jong is regarded as a poet of the confessional school, who (by her own account) writes 'out of a naked female consciousness'; her first book of verse was *Fruits and Vegetables* (1971), and she has regularly published collections since—see also *Becoming Light: Poems New and Selected* (1992). In four novels, beginning with *Fear of Flying* (1973), heavily autobiographical and written out of the experience of two disastrous marriages, she deals frankly and wittily with the sexuality of her protagonist, Isadora Wing, whose unfinished novel, with appropriate apparatus, appears posthumously as *Any Woman's Blues* (1990). Jong's acquaintance and affinity with literature of the classical, French, and English traditions are enthusiastically demonstrated in *Fanny, Being the True History of the Adventures of Fanny Hackabout-Jones* (1980), an 18th-century romp with a 20th-century application. The heroine of *Serenissima* (1987) is in this life a film star playing in an adaptation of *The Merchant of Venice*, and in an earlier existence the daughter of a Jewish moneylender in Venice, where she meets, and is bedded by, a young SHAKESPEARE. *Of Blessed Memory* (1997) is a Jewish modern saga. *Fear of Fifty: a Midlife Memoir* (1994) is less an autobiography than a vehicle for her thoughts on the female experience.

JONSON, BEN(JAMIN) (1572–1637) English poet and dramatist, was probably born in London. His own account of his early life was recorded by DRUMMOND, whom Jonson visited in 1618 on a trip to Scotland and back, on foot. His grandfather came from the Borders, 'served Henry VIII, and was a gentleman'. His father, having been imprisoned under Mary Tudor and forfeited his estate, subsequently became a minister, and died a month before the poet's birth. His mother then married a bricklayer, and Jonson was 'brought up poorly, put to [Westminster] school by a friend'; became an apprentice bricklayer, 'which he could not endure'; and joined the forces in Flanders, where he killed an opponent in single combat 'in the face of both the camps', before returning 'to his wonted studies' in England. In 1594 he married Anne Lewis, 'a shrew yet honest'. His poem 'On My First Daughter' commemorates the death of their eldest child at the age of six months. He became an actor with a strolling company, graduating to actor-writer, and was in 1597 imprisoned for his part in a lost play, *The Isle of Dogs*. His comedy *Every Man in His Humour* was performed in 1598 by the Lord Chamberlain's Men, with SHAKESPEARE in the cast. In the same year he killed another actor in a duel and served a prison sentence, during which he was converted to the Catholic faith, which he upheld for 'twelve years'.

Every Man out of His Humour, with less plot but more satire, was performed in 1599. In *Cynthia's Revels* (1600), ostensibly a masque in honour of the aged Elizabeth I, he satirized not only the court but also some of his fellow dramatists, thus initiating the 'War of the Theatres' (1600–01); his contribution to the proceedings was *Poetaster* (1601), to which DEKKER (possibly with the help of MARSTON) retorted with *Satiro-Mastix, or the Untrussing of the Humorous Poet* (1602). *Sejanus* (1603), a Roman tragedy, failed, perhaps because the excellent classicist in him demanded too much realism; but in this it looked forward to *Volpone, or the Fox* (1607), a comedy in which the excesses of ancient Rome are transplanted to modern Venice and represented in terms of the characters' animal-symbolism as well as of their 'humours', that is their psychological temperaments. In the meantime he had become writer of masques to the court of James I (VI of Scotland), and gone to prison again, for anti-Scottish observations in *Eastward Hoe* (1605), written jointly with CHAPMAN and Marston. All the characters in *The Alchemist* (1610, published 1612), one of the finest of social comedies, are middle-class knaves, dupes, or potentially either, and the satire is harsh and uncompromising. In *Bartholomew Fair* (performed 1614), Jonson found similar vices and failings to ridicule among the working classes.

In 1616 he did what had before only been done for the dead, and published his *Workes*, comprising plays, masques, and poems (the latter divided into 'Epigrammes' and 'The Forest'). This act of self-publicity brought him some derision, but it was significant in giving literary respectability to plays, and its success heralded the great Shakespeare folio of 1623. He wrote no further plays until *The Staple of News* (1626, published 1631), a glance at the new business of journalism. He received the honorary degree of MA from Oxford in 1619. His life was severely ruptured by a fire in 1623, which destroyed books, notes, and manuscripts, and by a stroke in 1628. He continued cheerfully to write and study, and friends responded to pleas, often in verse, for relief from poverty, though he fell out with the architect Inigo Jones (1573–1652) over the relative importance in royal masques of spectacle and speech, and his later plays met with poor response.

This veritable heavyweight, who scaled 'Full twentie stone; of which I lack two pound' ('Epistle to Mr Arthur Squib'), and whose appearance was dominated by 'My mountain belly, and my rockie face' ('My Picture Left in Scotland'), was not the greatest poet of his age, though some of his occasional poems and lyrics ('Come my Celia, let us prove . . .', 'Drink to me, only, with thine eyes . . .', 'Queen and huntress, chaste, and fair . . .') would be others' masterpieces. But he was a founder of the satirical drama, the acknowledged leader of the literary coterie of his time, and the sage of younger writers, who dubbed themselves the 'Sons of Ben'.

See *Complete Critical Edition*, ed. C. H. Herford, and Percy and Evelyn M. Simpson, 11 vols 1925–52 (includes biography); *The Complete Poems*, ed. George Parfitt, 1981; *Selected Poetry*, ed. George Parfitt, 1992; *The Alchemist and Other Plays*, ed. Gordon Campbell, 1995; Rosalind Miles, *Ben Jonson: His Craft and Art*, 1991; Richard Allen Cave, *Ben Jonson*, 1991 (critical study).

JOWETT, BENJAMIN see HOUSMAN.

JOYCE, JAMES (AUGUSTINE ALOYSIUS) (1882–1941) Irish novelist, poet, and dramatist, was born in Dublin, the eldest of ten children of an artistic mother and a father whose conviviality and fecklessness led to the decline of the family fortunes. He was educated at the Jesuit Belvedere College; having decided against the priesthood, he read languages at University College, Dublin, where he caused an academic stir in 1900 by having a critical article, 'Ibsen's New Drama', published in the European literary periodical, *Fortnightly Review*. After graduating in 1902 he went to Paris, ostensibly as a medical student but in reality a near-destitute writer. The death of his mother in 1904 caused his return to Dublin, where for a time he shared with GOGARTY the Martello tower which features in the opening section of *Ulysses*. A casual meeting with Nora Barnacle (1884–1951), a barmaid, led to a formal date on 16 June 1904. In October they eloped to Zurich, and then lived in Pola and Trieste, where he worked as a teacher of English. They were married in 1931, after they had had two children: Giorgio (1905–76), and Lucia (1907–82), who developed schizophrenia. Joyce returned to Dublin only once, in 1912, by which time he had undergone virtually all the physical and emotional experiences which inspired his published works. The first was *Chamber Music* (1907), a collection of 36 short lyrical poems of extraordinarily, considering the man, conventional language and metre. A second, even slimmer volume, *Pomes Penyeach* (1927), priced at a shilling (twelve pence) and containing 13 pieces, shows some advance towards the then prevailing mode, but it was his prose which had the greater influence on modern poetry.

The couple spent World War I in straitened circumstances in Zurich. Joyce chose Dublin to represent 'the centre of paralysis' of his native country for the 15 stories in *Dubliners* (1914), which reveals, often sardonically, the squalor and frustration of the lower middle class and culminates in 'The Dead', in which a particular human predicament reflects the complexity of life itself. Like his play, *The Exiles* (1918), written in about 1914, 'The Dead' records an incident (symbolic of the gulf between the east and west of Ireland) in his relationship with Nora. He had in his teens begun a vast autobiographical novel, *Stephen Hero*, a fragment of which was published posthumously in 1944. From it he extracted and recast *A Portrait of the Artist as a Young Man* (1916), in which Stephen Dedalus, who reappears in *Ulysses*, is not Joyce, but his consciousness is the means through which the author filters the relationship between the imagination and reality. *Ulysses* is in time a continuation of *A Portrait of the Artist as a Young Man*, the whole action taking place, significantly, on 16 June 1904, and symbolically paralleling incidents and characters in the wanderings of HOMER's Odysseus. It was begun in 1914, originally as a short story, and some chapters were published in 1919 in London in the *Egoist*. In the meantime serialization had started in the USA in the *Little Review*, but subsequent chapters were intercepted by the postal authorities and burned. In 1921 three judges upheld a complaint, and banned further publication. Joyce kept on writing, and the book was published in 1922 by a small press in Paris, where he had moved with his family in 1920. An English and American edition was printed in Dijon and distributed from Paris, but many copies were identified en route to their purchasers and destroyed. By 1930 eight reprints of the original edition had been sold, and the book had been translated into French, German, Czech, and Japanese. It was finally cleared for publication in the USA in December 1933 and published in January 1934, and appeared in Britain in 1936 without legal opposition.

Joyce received virtually no money in his lifetime from his writing, and subsisted largely on the financial assistance of patrons. His eyesight deteriorated rapidly, to the extent that for his last and, to him, most significant book, he had to commit to memory whole sections and to rely on amanuenses to decipher and transcribe his notes. He worked on it for 17 years, too superstitious to reveal its title until it was finished—sections of it were published in New York between 1927 and 1930 as 'Work in Progress'. Where *Ulysses* had been concerned with a single day, *Finnegans Wake* (1939) is a record of a night, in which the mind of the sleeping H. C. Earwicker is interpreted with astonishing virtuosity and invention of language. See *A James Joyce Reader*, ed. Harry Levin, rev. edn 1993; Richard Ellmann, *James Joyce*, 2nd edn 1984 (biography); Brenda Maddox, *Nora: a Biography of Nora Joyce*, new edn 1989; Nicholas Fargnoli and Michael Patrick Gillespie (eds), *James Joyce A to Z: an Encyclopedic Guide to his Life and Work*, 1995; Derek Attridge (ed.), *The Cambridge Companion to James Joyce*, 1990; Sydney Bolt, *A Preface to James Joyce*, 2nd edn 1992; Samuel L. Goldberg, *The Classical Temper: a Study of Joyce's Ulysses*, 1961; Harry Blamires, *The New Bloomsday Book: a Guide through 'Ulysses'*, 3rd edn 1996.

JULIAN OF NORWICH see KEMPE.

JUVENAL (DECIMUS JUNIUS JU-VENALIS) (*c*.55–*c*.140) Roman satirical poet, was born in Aquinum, the son of a wealthy Spanish freedman, and may have commanded an auxiliary cohort in Britain and held civil offices in his home town before trying to earn a living in Rome by public speaking. During the reign of Domitian, he seems to have been exiled for a time to Egypt, undoubtedly for saying or writing something offensive to the emperor, but not offensive enough to merit execution. His 16 surviving 'Satires' were published between 110 and 130, in the reigns of Trajan and Hadrian. He employs a mixture of sarcasm, invective, and broad humour to attack various social targets, including homosexuals, women, conditions in Rome, extravagance, human parasites, and vanity, while moralizing on such topics as learning, guilty consciences, parental example, and the treatment of civilians by the military. See *The Sixteen Satires*, tr. Peter Green, rev. edn 1974.

K

KAFKA, FRANZ (1883–1924) Austrian novelist and short-story writer, was born in Prague, the eldest child of German-speaking Czech Jewish parents. His childhood was lonely, as his two brothers died in infancy and the next child, a sister, was six years younger than he was. His father, a haberdashery wholesaler, required his wife's attention day and night, and appears to have dominated his son—see 'To My Father', a long diatribe written in 1919, which he intended should be personally delivered by his mother, who sensibly did nothing of the sort. He went to the German grammar school and the Imperial and Royal Karl-Ferdinand German University, from which he received a doctorate in jurisprudence in 1906. After two years in a commercial insurance office, he found what he was looking for: a job with the Workers Accident Insurance Institute, which, as a semi-governmental organization, closed at 2 pm, giving him the rest of the day in which to write. Kafka was fraught with neuroses and afflicted with long-standing tuberculosis, yet was able to express himself in writing; his allegories of his own condition are, by extension, reflections of the experiences of others too. Though he worked intensively on three novels, the only publications during his lifetime were six volumes of short pieces, beginning with *Betrachtung* [Observations] (1913) and *Der Heizer, Ein Fragment* [The Stoker] (1913), the initial chapter of his novel, *Amerika*.

His personal inhibitions extended to his love life. He was engaged to Felice Bauer for five years, and carried on an extensive correspondence with her in Berlin. When the relationship ended in 1919, she married another man. At 38, while engaged to someone else, he carried on an unconsummated affair with a married Czech woman, Milena Jesenská (1896–1944)—see Mary Hockaday, *Kafka, Love and Courage: the Life of Milena Jesenská* (1995). In 1923, while holidaying with his sister at the Baltic resort of Muritz, he met Dora Diamant, a 19-year-old Polish Orthodox Jewess, with whom he lived in Berlin until he had to be brought back to Prague in March 1924 in the throes of his final illness. He died six months later in a sanatorium in Kierling. The novels, *Der Prozess* (1925; tr. as *The Trial*, 1937), *Das Schloss* (1926; tr. as *The Castle*, 1930), and *Amerika* (1927; tr. as *America*, 1940), all of them fragmentary and without ends if not unfinished, were published at the instigation of his friend and biographer, Max Brod (1884–1968), and translated by Willa and Edwin MUIR. Heavily symbolic and of a nightmare quality (hence the term 'Kafkaesque'), they are expressions of an individual's struggle in the face of a variety of inimical situations. See *The Complete Novels*, tr. Willa and Edwin Muir, new edn 1992; *The Complete Stories*, ed. Arthur Samuelson and Nahum N. Glatzer, new edn 1995; *Collected Stories*, tr. Edwin Muir, introd. Gabriel Josipovici, 1993; Max Brod, *Franz Kafka: a Biography*, new edn 1995; Ronald Hayman, *K: a Biography of Kafka*, new edn 1996.

KANT, IMMANUEL (1724–1804) German philosopher, was born in Konigsberg, the fourth of nine children of a pious harnessmaker, and was educated at the local Pietist school and at Konigsberg University. Despite his humble background, and stunted and deformed body, he worked to be accepted socially, was tutor in various households, and published some startling essays on dynamics and on NEWTON's theories of the universe. He obtained an unpaid teaching post at the university in 1755, and a professorship finally in 1779. Rejecting both the rationalism of G. W. Leibniz (1646–1716) and the empiricism of DAVID HUME, he developed in *Kritik der reinen Vernunft* (1781; tr. Norman Kemp-Smith as *Critique of Pure Reason*, 1929) his theory of 'transcendental idealism'; he filled out his arguments in *Grundlegung zur Metaphysik der Sitten* (1785; tr. H. J. Paton as *The Moral Law: or, Kant's Groundwork of the Metaphysic of Morals*, 1948) and *Kritik der Urtheilskraft* (1790; tr. James Creed Meredith as *The Critique of Judgement*, 1952). COLERIDGE, who probably began to read Kant in Germany in 1798–99, cites these works in *Biographia Literaria* (Chapter IX) as among those of his which 'I still read . . . with undiminished delight and increasing admiration'. CARLYLE frequently used his ideas as starting points for his own deductions. See Roger Scruton, *Kant*, 1982 (introduction to his thought).

KÄSTNER, ERICH (1899–1974) German novelist, journalist, and children's writer, was born in Dresden, the son of a master saddler who had come down in the world. He went to the local *Lehrerseminar* for training teachers, but after service in the infantry in World War I was able, as a war veteran, to go to König-Georg-Gymnasium and from there on a scholarship to Leipzig University. He became a journalist and theatre critic, moving to Berlin in 1927 after losing his main job for casting an erotic slur in a poem celebrating the centenary of the composer Ludwig van Beethoven (1770–1827). In 1928 he published the first of a number of collections of verse, and also *Emil und die Detektive* (tr. Eileen Hall as *Emil and the Detectives*, 1931), the prototype of the modern children-versus-crooks story, in which the protagonists on both sides are realistically portrayed and the values utterly sound. *Fabian: die Gesichte eines Moralisten* (1931; tr. Cyrus Brooks as *Fabian: the Story of a Moralist*, 1932) was the first of several adult novels in which geographical and psychological journeys illustrate contemporary paradoxes. When Hitler came to power in 1933 he returned from Zurich to Germany, where, although his books were banned and publicly burned, he remained throughout the Nazi period and World War II, after which he settled in Munich. Other notable children's novels which contributed to his being awarded the Hans Christian ANDERSEN Medal in 1960 are *Emil und die drei Zwillinge* (1934; tr. Brooks as *Emil and the Three Twins*, 1935), originally published in Switzerland, and *Das doppelte Lottchen* (1949; tr. Brooks as *Lisa and Lottie*, 1951), the first story for children properly to confront the problems of a family divided by divorce.

KAVANAGH, DAN see BARNES, JULIAN.

KAVANAGH, PATRICK (1904–67) Irish poet, novelist, critic, and journalist, was born in Iniskeen, Co. Monaghan, the son of a part-time cobbler and small farmer, whose trades he followed after leaving school at 12 until he moved to Dublin in 1939, where for the rest of his life he supported himself largely by journalism. In the meantime he had educated himself and written some fine lyric verse which depicted the realities of rural life (*Ploughman and Other Poems* was published in 1936), and an often hilarious early autobiography, *The Green Fool* (1938). His concern about the nature and function of literature and the responsibility of the author is demonstrated in much of his critical writing. It is further reflected in *The Great Hunger* (1942), a strong, despairing poem of the land, and *Tarry Flynn* (1948), a semi-autobiographical if in some respects fanciful novel. For three months in 1952 he published his own weekly newspaper. A lost libel action against the *Leader* in 1952, for allegedly impugning his professional reputation, was immediately followed by his going into hospital with lung

cancer. He referred to his recovery from both disasters as his 'rebirth', which he celebrated by changing his tune from savagery and attempted satire on modern issues, government, art, and Irish life, to more personal themes in which innocence and comedy predominate, as in his impressive 'Canal Poems'. This return to simplicity is well illustrated in *Come Dance with Kitty Stobling, and Other Poems* (1960). See *Collected Poems*, rev. edn 1973; *Selected Poems*, ed. Antoinette Quinn, 1996; *Collected Pruse*, 1967; Antoinette Quinn, *Patrick Kavanagh: Born Again Romantic*, new edn 1993 (critical study).

KAVANAGH, P(ATRICK) J(OSEPH GREGORY) (*b*. 1931) British poet, novelist, and journalist, was born in Worthing, Sussex, the younger son (by 11 years) of Ted Kavanagh (1892–1958), who wrote the scripts for the wartime radio comedy show, *Itma* (*It's That Man Again*), starring Tommy Handley (1892–1949). He was educated at Douai School and (having volunteered for active service in Korea while doing National Service 'in an Irish regiment, of course') at Merton College, Oxford. In 1953 he met Sally Philipps, daughter of ROSAMOND LEHMANN. They married in 1957, when he began a two-year stint as a British Council lecturer in Indonesia, where she died of polio the following year. *One and One* (1959) was the first of several collections of verse published in the succeeding thirty years of a formal poet who aims to be accessible and entertaining, and who has a knack for the apposite, but unusual, descriptive phrase. *A Song and Dance* (1968), the first of six novels between then and 1986, won the *Guardian* award for fiction. *The Perfect Stranger* (1966), an introspective autobiographical study, was written 'because I wanted to try and make sense of the sudden death of my wife'. *Finding Connections* (1990) is a record of an investigation into his family and its roots, in the course of which he travelled to Ireland, Tasmania, and New Zealand. *Voices in Ireland: a Traveller's Literary Companion* (1994) is a meditation on landscape and literature, divided into geographical sections. See *Collected Poems*, new edn 1995.

KAWABATA YASUNARI (1899–1972) Japanese novelist, was born and grew up in Osaka, where the loss of most of his family by the time he was 14 established the tragic view of life which imbues his fiction. In 1918 he went to Tokyo, where he read Japanese literature at the Imperial University, after which he became a journalist and freelance writer. A novelist whose effect is achieved principally through the juxtaposition of images and the arrangement of open-ended incidents and fantasies, he established his name in the West with [*Snow Country*] (1937; rev. edn 1948; tr. Edward G. Seidensticker, 1957), the love story of a geisha from the mountains for a Tokyo man, and was awarded the Nobel Prize for Literature in 1968. Subsequent publications in English include *The House of the Sleeping Beauties and Other Stories*, tr. Seidensticker (1969) and [*The Lake*] (1955; tr. Reiko Tsukimura, 1974), an enigmatic study of a lonely teacher's obsession for beautiful women whom he can never attain. Kawabata played no role in the militaristic policies of World War II, after which he remained attached to the traditional cultural elements of his country. It is said that the suicide of MISHIMA, his protégé, was instrumental in his killing himself too, which he did just over a year later in his apartment by the sea.

KAZANTZAKIS, NIKOS (1885–1957) Greek novelist and poet, was born in Heraklion, Crete, and obtained a degree in law at Athens University in 1906, after which he studied philosophy, literature, and art in Paris, Germany, and Italy. He was an inveterate traveller and spiritual explorer, whose principal literary works in the 1920s were heavy plays, light travelogues, and a 30,000-line philosophical epic poem (1928) taking up where HOMER's *Odyssey* ends (tr. Kimon Friar as *The Odyssey: a Modern Sequel*, 1958). While on the island of Aegina during the German occupation of Greece in World War II, he wrote [*Zorba the Greek*] (1946; tr. Carl Wildman, 1952), a novel of the 'magic realism' school. Once in a fictional vein, he followed with several modern parables, of which [*Christ Recrucified*]—in USA *The Greek Passion*—(1954; tr. Jonathan Griffin, 1954), in a timeless rural setting, and [*The Last Temptation of Christ*] (1955; tr. P. A. Bien, 1960) are particularly notable examples of the genre. He served as a cabinet minister in 1945, and directed Unesco's programme of translations of the classics in 1947–48.

KEATS, JOHN (1795–1821) British poet, was born in Finsbury, the eldest of four children of the groom at the stables of the Swan and Hoop Inn in the City of London, who had married the proprietor's daughter and in 1802 inherited the business. In 1803 the poet entered John Clarke's School, Enfield, and in 1804 his father was killed in a riding accident; whereupon his mother remarried and boarded the children out with her parents. She left her new husband in 1806, and returned to the children in 1809, but died the following year. Guardians were now appointed, at the instigation of one of whom Keats was apprenticed to a surgeon. He wrote his first poems in 1814, and in February 1815 celebrated with a sonnet the release from prison of HUNT, whom he later met and who published 'O Solitude, if I must with thee dwell . . .' in the *Examiner* in 1816. Keats had continued his medical studies at Guy's Hospital and was now a member of the Society of Apothecaries. He had also written 'On

First Looking into Chapman's Homer' (see CHAPMAN), been cited (with P. B. SHELLEY) in an *Examiner* article on 'Young Poets', and met Hunt's literary friends. Shortly after his 21st birthday, now legally free, he was advised to set up in practice. He replied: 'I mean to rely on my Abilities as a Poet. My mind is made up. I know that I possess these Abilities greater than most Men and therefore am determined to gain my Living by exercising them.' His guardian was so taken aback that he could only mutter, 'Silly boy!' Less than 4¹/₂ years later, Keats was dead.

In March 1817 he published *Poems*, a collection of his poetry up to that time. It began and ended with two longer poems in rhyming couplets: 'I stood tip-toe upon a little hill . . .', which looks forward to *Endymion*; and 'Sleep and Poetry', written after a night on Hunt's sofa, in which he expresses his ambition, 'O for ten years, that I may overwhelm / Myself in poesy; so I may do the deed / That my own soul has to itself decreed.' From April until the end of November he stayed in various places in the south of England and wrote the more than four thousand lines of his allegorical romance, *Endymion*, which was published, with its abrupt ending, in April 1818. He reacted philosophically to an attack in *Blackwood's Edinburgh Magazine* on him and other members of the 'Cockney School' of Hunt's followers. In June he and Charles Brown (1786–1842) set off on a walking tour of the Lakes and Scotland—see Carol Kyros Walker, *Walking North with Keats* (1992). At Oban he developed a sore throat, which got so bad that Brown sent him back to London by boat from Inverness. On his return he found his brother Tom ill with tuberculosis, and nursed him until he died in December. In the meantime he had met and fallen in love with the 18-year-old Fanny Brawne, who shortly afterwards moved with her mother into a house in Hampstead, the other half of which was occupied by Brown and was where Keats was living too.

From January to October 1819, between bouts of depression and recurrences of throat trouble, and while tinkering with 'Hyperion', Keats composed in various places a succession of masterpieces: 'The Eve of St Agnes', 'La Belle Dame Sans Merci', his six great odes (including 'Ode on a Grecian Urn' and 'To Autumn'), and the two parts of 'Lamia'. He also wrote sonnets (including 'To Sleep') which for quality and feeling matched those of WORDSWORTH, as well as (with Brown) the blank-verse drama, 'Otho the Great'. Back in Hampstead at the end of the year, he became engaged to Fanny, but his health worsened; so did his finances with the appearance from America of his brother George (*d.* 1842), with whom he made a settlement which left him virtually destitute. *Lamia, Isabella, The Eve of St Agnes, and Other Poems* was published in July 1820 and was very well received. By now he had suffered two lung haemorrhages, and after being looked after by the Hunts when Brown vacated his half of the house, he was taken in by the Brawnes and nursed by Fanny. On medical advice, he sailed to Italy for the winter with the painter Joseph Severn (1793–1879). On 30 November he wrote from Rome his last known letter, to Brown. He died on 23 February 1821 and was buried in the Protestant cemetery. He was a little over 25. Fanny put on widow's weeds when she heard the news. (She married Louis Lindon, 12 years younger than herself, in 1833, and died in 1865.) The feverish restlessness that drove Keats to poetry and, when he could no longer harness his faculties, to despair, is illustrated in his letters, as is his genius for friendship and his care for ordinary people and ordinary things. See *The Poems of John Keats*, ed. Miriam Allott, new edn 1972; *Selected Poetry*, ed. Elizabeth Cook, new edn 1996; *Letters*, ed. Robert Gittings, 1970; W. J. Bate, *John Keats*, new edn 1992 (biography); Stephen Coote, *John Keats: a Life*, new edn 1996; Aileen Ward, *John Keats: the Making of a Poet*, rev. edn 1986.

KEESE, OLIVE see LEAKEY.

KELL, JOSEPH see BURGESS.

KELLY, JAMES PLUNKETT see PLUNKETT.

KEMPE, MARGERY (*c*.1373–*c*.1438) English mystic, was the daughter of an alderman of Lynne, Norfolk, and married John Kempe, a burgess of the town, in 1393. After the birth of her first child she suffered from acute depression, out of which she was lifted by a vision of Christ. She resumed her extravagant ways, set up a brewery, which lost money, and then a mill, which failed. A further vision, of Paradise, induced her to become a flamboyant and somewhat boisterous mystic, given to visitations of ululation. Encouraged by Philip Repington (*d*. 1424), Bishop of Lincoln, and Thomas Arundel (1353–1414), Archbishop of Canterbury, both of whom she soundly lectured on their ways, she set out from Yarmouth in 1414 for the Holy Land, taking in Bologna, Venice, Assisi, Rome, and Middelburg. In 1417 she visited Spain; on her return she was examined on a charge of Lollardry, but acquitted. Her long-suffering husband and her son died in about 1432, and two years later she visited Danzig with her German daughter-in-law. In 1432 she had finished a rough, and largely unintelligible, draft of her spiritual autobiography, which in 1436 she began revising and dictating to a priest. An early copy of *The Book of Margery Kempe* was identified as such in 1934. It is significant as a social document and as the first biography to be written in English. As mysticism, as one might expect from an

enthusiastic, extrovert, married woman, it lacks the reflective nature of the revelations of the recluse, Dame Julian of Norwich (?1343–*c*.1429), whom Margery Kempe visited in 1413, and the spiritual quality of *The Cloud of Unknowing*, written by an unknown hand in about 1350. See *The Book of Margery Kempe*, tr. B. E. Windeatt into modern English, new edn 1985; *The Book of Margery Kempe*, ed. Tony Triggs in modern English, 1995; Clarissa W. Atkinson, *Mystic and Pilgrim: the Book and the World of Margery Kempe*, 1985.

KEMPIS, THOMAS À see THOMAS À KEMPIS.

KENDALL, HENRY (1839–82) Australian poet, was born on a run-down farm near Ulladulla, New South Wales, and was brought up on the Clarence River and, after his father's death, on his grandfather's farm near Wollongong, where he went to a school run by his mother. After two uncomfortable years as a cabin boy in an uncle's whaler, he found employment in Sydney, and in 1859 began to have verses published in local journals. In 1862 he sent some to *Cornhill Magazine* in London, whose editor, THACKERAY, did not reply, and to the *Athenaeum*, which printed them. *Poems and Songs*, by 'the boy-poet of Australia', was published in 1862. In spite of clerical jobs, journalism, and literary encouragement, he suffered poverty and debt, which after his marriage in 1868 were intensified by the rapacity of his sisters, his mother's drinking, and the activities of his twin brother, who forged a cheque in his name which he had to honour. A move to Melbourne did not help. *Leaves from Australian Forests* (1869) failed financially; his first child died; he lapsed into chronic depression and alcoholism; and his wife left him. He was rehabilitated by a family of timber merchants, who gave him a job and built him a house at Camden Haven, where his wife rejoined him in 1876. He won the *Sydney Morning Herald* prize for a poem on the International Exhibition of 1879. *Songs from the Mountains* (1880), withdrawn because of libel fears over a satirical poem and reissued the following year without it, did well. He was appointed an inspector of forests, but the travelling proved too much, and he died of consumption at the age of 43. He was a versatile but not a great poet, much of whose work vividly reflects the varying landscapes he knew and the vicissitudes of his life. See *The Poetical Works of Henry Kendall*, ed. T. T. Reed, 1966; W. H. Wilde, *Henry Kendall*, 1976 (critical biography).

KENEALLY, THOMAS (*b*. 1935) Australian novelist, was born of Irish Catholic descent in Sydney, and was brought up in the suburb of Homebush, where he was known as Mick and went around with the poems of HOPKINS permanently in his pocket. He was educated at a Christian Brothers' school and at St Patrick's College, Strathfield. Having given up studying for the priesthood shortly before he was due to be ordained, he taught in high school for four years. He has said, 'I would like to disown my first two novels' (published in 1964 and 1965). He was then commissioned by the University of New South Wales Drama Foundation to write a play. *Halloran's Little Boat*, produced in 1966, was based on his as yet unpublished third novel, *Bring Larks and Heroes* (1967), a study of Irish convicts in a colony at the end of the 18th century, which won the MILES FRANKLIN Award. Here, as in subsequent works, he does not flinch from describing violence. *The Chant of Jimmie Blacksmith* (1972), based on the life of the half-Aboriginal Jimmy Governor (1875–1901), is a story of hatred and injustice. Oppression, which features so strongly in these two novels, is the theme, on a national, racial, or personal level, of much of his fiction, for which he evokes a variety of meticulously dramatized settings: the France of Joan of Arc in *Blood Red, Sister Rose* (1974); America during the Civil War in *Confederates* (1979); the signing of the Armistice in 1918 in *Gossip from the Forest* (1975); and Yugoslavia during World War II in *Season in Purgatory* (1976). The Holocaust experiences, described in *Schindler's Ark* (1982), which won the Booker prize for fiction, cast their grim shadow as far as Sydney in *A Family Madness* (1985); the dispossession both of Palestinians and of Aboriginals motivates the topically-inspired *Flying Hero Class* (1991). *A River Town* (1995) describes tensions and prejudices in a remote Australian town in 1900. *Memoirs from a Young Republic* (1993) is part autobiography, part republican polemic. *Act of Grace* (1988) and *Chief of Staff* (1992) are novels chronicling the impact on Australia of World War II, written as William Coyle. He was made AO in 1983. See *Homebush Boy*, new edn 1996 (early autobiography); Peter Quartermaine, *Thomas Keneally*, 1991 (critical study).

KENNELLY, BRENDAN (*b.* 1936) Irish poet, was born in Ballylongford, Co. Kerry, into a large family which ran a pub, and was educated at St Ita's College, Tarbert, Trinity College, Dublin, and Leeds University—for images of his early life see especially *Love-Cry* (1972). He began as a junior lecturer at Trinity College in 1963, and became Professor of Modern Literature in 1973. Of his poetry, he has said: '. . . I select appropriate images from aspects of my experience and try to use them in such a way that they express what goes on within.' He began publishing his work in 1959, since when his output has been as prolific as the range of his relevant experience is wide, and includes the highly-praised sequence, *Cromwell* (1983). His diction at its best is stark, austere, and penetrating. His conviction that 'this [Irish] culture is now in an advanced state of self-parody' is worked out in *The Book of Judas* (1991), intended for entertainment, a 'poem' (comprising actually 587 individual poems) in which his Judas recurs as the archetypal fall guy in historical and contemporary contexts. *Poetry My Arse* (1995) is a bawdy, unheroic, epic poem of modern Dublin life and society. He has also written two youthful novels, *The Crooked Cross* (1963), about life at university, and *The Florentines* (1967), a rural study; composed stage versions of *Medea* (1991) and *The Trojan Women* (1993) of EURIPIDES; and edited *The Penguin Book of Irish Verse* (rev. edn 1981). See *A Time for Voices: Selected Poems 1960–1990*, 1990; *Breathing Spaces: Early Poems*, new edn 1993; *Journey into Joy: Selected Prose*, ed. Ake Persson, new edn 1995.

KEROUAC, JACK [JEAN-LOUIS] (1922–69) American novelist, was born in Lowell, Massachusetts, of French-Canadian parents, and won football scholarships to Horace Mann High School, New York, and Columbia University, New York, where he became associated with BURROUGHS and GINSBERG. He served in the US Merchant Marine in World War II, after which he spent two years writing *The Town and the City* (1950), a semi-autobiographical novel of youth which is his most conventional work. Several wild trips across the country with Neal Cassady (1926–68) were the basis of *On the Road*, in which he used the term 'beat generation . . . to describe guys who run around the country in cars looking for odd jobs, girlfriends, and kicks'. Typed straight on to a teleprinter roll in 1951, it was not published until 1957, when it became the prose manifesto of the culture it evokes. Meanwhile he was 'hopping freights, hitch-hiking, and working as a railroad brakeman, deckhand and scullion on merchant ships, government fire lookout, and hundreds of assorted jobs'. Some of the time he lived in a *ménage à trois* with Cassady and his wife, which became *à quatre* when Ginsberg joined in—see Carolyn Cassady, *Off the Road: Twenty Years with Cassady, Kerouac and Ginsberg* (1990). He was also writing further books towards a consciously organized canon of prose and verse, in which the exploration of oriental mysticism of *The Dharma Bums* (1958) is an extension of the romantic anarchy and drug experimentation which run through *On the Road* and *Visions of Cody* (1959; complete version 1972). When he died, of an abdominal haemorrhage, he was living in St Petersburg, Florida, with his third wife and his invalid mother. See *Selected Letters 1940-1956*, ed. Ann Charters, new edn 1996; Gerald Nicosia, *Memory Babe: a Critical Biography of Jack Kerouac*, new edn 1994; Ann Charters, *Kerouac: a Biography*, new edn 1996; Warren French, *Jack Kerouac*, 1987 (critical study); Tim Hunt, *Kerouac's Crooked Road: Development of a Fiction*, new edn 1997.

KEYES, SIDNEY (1922–43) British poet, was born in Dartford, Kent, the son of an army officer. His mother died of peritonitis a few weeks after his birth. He was brought up in Dartford in the home of his paternal grandfather, a self-made tycoon in the flour-milling industry, who had a dominant nature and great physical energy and strength, which he would demonstrate by hurling the furniture about. He was educated at Dartford Grammar School, Tonbridge School, and The Queen's College, Oxford, where he got a first in his preliminary history examinations, edited *Cherwell*, and met HEATH-STUBBS, who became his literary mentor. Keyes's volume of poems, *The Iron Laurel*, was ready for printing in 1941, but he delayed it until 1942 so that he could add 'The Foreign Gate', a poet-soldier's vision of the presence of Death, finished just before he joined the Army in Northern Ireland in April. He was commissioned in the Queen's Own Royal West Kent Regiment, and arrived in North Africa on 10 March 1943. At dawn on 29 April he led out a patrol. Neither he nor any of its members returned. He was not yet 21, but even without the poems which are believed to have been lost with him in the Tunisian desert, he had achieved an impressive corpus of pastoral and symbolic verse, in which from a starting point of the Romantics, and of poets such as RILKE and YEATS, he explores the imagination, and enquires into attitudes to death and destiny. See *Collected Poems of Sidney Keyes*, ed. Michael Meyer, 2nd rev. edn 1988.

KHAN, ISMITH (*b.* 1925) novelist, was born in Port-of-Spain, Trinidad, and educated at Queen's Royal College, Michigan State University, and the New School for Social Research, New York, at which he later taught creative writing. He worked in the New York Public Library from 1956 to 1961, and was an assistant professor of Caribbean and Comparative Literature at the University of California from 1971 to 1974. He became a US citizen in 1958. His novels, *The Jumbie Bird* (1963) and *The Obeah Man* (1964), set in the Caribbean and intended originally to help Caribbean readers to 'come to grips with their identity', explore superstition and isolation in the context of the Indian community of Trinidad.

KIELY, BENEDICT (*b.* 1919) Irish novelist and short-story writer, was born in Dromore, Co. Tyrone, and educated by the Christian Brothers, becoming a Jesuit novice in 1937. While convalescing from a severe tubercular spinal condition he decided to change his vocation, and became a journalist while studying at the National University of Ireland, from which he graduated in 1943.

Between 1945 and 1964 he was on the staff successively of the Dublin *Standard*, the *Irish Independent*, and the *Irish Press*, after which he taught creative writing at various American universities. He returned to Dublin in 1970 and was a visiting lecturer at University College. His earlier novels, beginning with *Land Without Stars* (1946), while taking various themes as a starting point, are explorations of sin, clerical life, and the transition from youth to maturity. It is with his short stories, of which the first volume was *A Journey to the Seven Streams: Seventeen Stories* (1963), that he is best able to bring out the essential Irishness in his creative make-up: satire, mock-heroic, and sheer comedy invest anecdotes and individuals in an Ireland of the present and immediate past—see also *A Letter to Peachtree and Nine Other Stories* (1987). In this he has a forerunner in CARLETON, another man of Tyrone, of whom he has written a biographical and critical study (1947). *Proxopera* (1977) and *Nothing Happens in Carmincross* (1985) are, by contrast, savage novels, in which he expresses his own and reflects others' anger and frustration at the violence which has overtaken his country. *Drink to the Bird: an Omagh Childhood Recalled* (1992) is a discursive memoir. He has also written *Modern Irish Fiction: a Critique* (1950) and edited *The Penguin Book of Irish Short Stories* (1981).

KIERKEGAARD, SÖREN (1813–55) Danish philosopher, was born in Copenhagen, the seventh child of a retired hosier and former serf who had become a wealthy man, and of his second wife, the illiterate maid of his first wife. He went to private school and then in 1830 to Copenhagen University, where after doing brilliantly in his foundation course he read theology in a rather haphazard fashion. His father's death in 1838 strengthened his resolve. He published a study of ANDERSEN's novels, finally took his degree in 1840, and got engaged to the daughter of a prominent civil servant. He broke off the engagement a year later, and went to Berlin to hear a course of lectures by the philosopher Friedrich Schelling (1775–1854). Having commented in a letter to his brother, 'Schelling drivels on quite intolerably', he returned to Copenhagen and embarked on a bout of furious literary activity which included [*Either/Or*] (1843), [*The Concept of Anxiety*] (1844), [*Stages on Life's Way*] (1845), and [*Concluding Scientific Postscript*] (1846), all published anonymously. In [*The Sickness unto Death*] (1849) and [*Training in Christianity*] (1850), also anonymous, he pursued his investigation of spirituality and of the role of the official Church in the exercise of Christian belief. He intensified his campaign against the secularity of the Church in nine issues of a broadsheet printed at his own expense in 1855. He died later that year after collapsing in the street. An original thinker who wrote idiosyncratically on literary, psychological, and religious themes, he anticipated the Existentialist movement and provided SARTRE and other modern philosophers with a base from which to explore the concept of anxiety (*Angst*). See *Papers and Journals: a Selection*, ed. and tr. Alistair Hannay, 1996; Bruce H. Kirmmse (ed.), *Encounters with Kierkegaard: a Life as Seen by His Contemporaries*, tr. Kirmmse and Virginia R. Laursen, 1996 (eyewitness accounts); Patrick Gardiner, *Kierkegaard*, 1988 (introduction to his thought and works).

KILVERT, FRANCIS (1840–1879) British diarist, was born in Hardenhuish, Wiltshire, of which his father was Rector, and was educated at Claverton Lodge, near Bath, and Wadham College, Oxford. He was ordained in 1863, and, in between serving in his father's parish, was curate at Clyro, before being appointed Vicar of St Harmon's, Rhyader, in 1876, and of Bredwardine in 1877, all three being in the Wye valley. He died of peritonitis a month after marrying Elizabeth Rowland (*d.* 1911). Portions of his diary from 1870 to 1879, in 22 notebooks, were discovered and edited by PLOMER, and published 1938–40 (rev. edn 1960). Only three of the original notebooks, covering part of 1870, survive today; they were published individually in 1982, 1989, and 1990. Kilvert was a highly literate man with a discerning eye for the rolling countryside of Herefordshire and the ruggedness of Wales, a sensual preoccupation with feminine beauty in girls of ten upward, and a descriptive turn of phrase He manages to be as interesting about croquet parties on the lawns of the gentry as he is about the trials and homes of the poorest of his parishioners, with whom he mixed with equal ease. See *Kilvert, the Victorian: a New Selection from the Diaries*, ed. David Lockwood, 1993; Frederick Grice, *Francis Kilvert and His World*, 1980.

KING, KENNEDY see DOUGLAS, GEORGE.

KING, STEPHEN (*b.* 1947) American novelist, was born in Portland, Maine; his father, a merchant mariner during World War II, walked out on his wife and family in 1949, and was never heard of again. Even before he attended high school in Lisbon Falls, Maine, King was writing science fiction stories, which he submitted to specialist magazines. His first story to be published professionally was 'The Glass Floor' in *Startling Mystery Stories* in 1967, when he was at the University of Maine. He graduated in English in 1970; unable to get a high school teaching post, he worked in an industrial laundry. He married in 1972, and found a job as a teacher at Hampton Academy, Maine, while continuing to write stories that were published and novels that were not. Inspired by the example of three successful horror novels, Ira Levin, *Rosemary's Baby* (1968), Thomas Tryon, *The Other* (1971), and William Blatty, *The Exorcist* (1971), he began in 1971 to turn a short story into a novel. It was accepted after further rewriting of the latter part, and published as *Carrie* (1974), about a 16-year-old with inherited telekinetic powers who in justifiable anger uses them in an orgy of destruction. Here he already displayed factors which have subsequently established him as an author many of whose works are at one end of the scale hugely enjoyed by young adults (though often banned from school libraries) and are at the other a proper subject of academic criticism—see, for example, Edward Ingebretsen SJ, *Maps of Heaven, Maps of Hell: Religious Terror as Memory from the Puritans to Stephen King* (1995) and Sharon A. Russell, *Stephen King: a Critical Companion* (1996). His protagonists are often young people themselves; the horror usually lurks in the routines of everyday life, as in *The Dead Zone* (1979), *Cujo* (1981), *Christine* (1983), and *It* (1986); as a skilful exponent of a particular genre (and also a good writer) he plays on reader expectations of that genre. At the same time, on a critical level, his modern mythology often reflects traditional fairy tales, Christian symbolism, or, as in *Rose Madder* (1995), classical legend, while his horror, as in '*Salem's Lot* (1975), *Dolores Claiborne* (1992), and elsewhere, tends to be psychological rather than supernatural.

Different Seasons (1982) contains four novellas, including 'Apt Pupil', in which a Nazi war criminal insinuates himself, quite openly, into an American family. Shorter fiction is in *Night Shift* (1978) and *Four Past Midnight* (1990). King broke new ground when *The Green Mile* (1996), in much the same way as GEORGE ELIOT's *Middlemarch* 125 years earlier, was published serially in mass-market paperback form in six monthly instalments. A full-time writer, he also owns a publishing firm and a rock 'n' roll radio station in his hometown of Bangor, Maine. As he first revealed in an interview in a local paper in 1985, he has also published several novels as Richard Bachman—see Michael R. Collings, *Stephen King as Richard Bachman* (1986). *Danse Macabre* (1981) is a collection of autobiographical and critical essays. See Joseph Reino, *Stephen King: the First Decade, 'Carrie' to 'Pet Sematary'*, 1988 (critical study).

KINGLAKE, A(LEXANDER) W(ILLIAM) (1809–91) British historian and traveller, was born in Taunton, Somerset, and gained through his mother an enthusiasm for riding and for HOMER (in POPE's translation). He was educated at Eton and Trinity College, Cambridge, where TENNYSON and THACKERAY were his friends, and then read for the Bar, to which he was admitted in 1837. In about 1835 he undertook a hazardous excursion through the Middle East, an account of which, after agonizing over several drafts, he finally published in 1844 as *Eothen: or, Traces of Travel brought home from the East. Eothen* (the word is Homeric Greek for 'from the East') is a delightfully-written personal record in the tradition and spirit of English (and in the case of LITHGOW, Scottish) travellers who have found that part of the world a source of amusement as well as of wonder. In 1854 he went to the Crimea as an observer of the campaign, and fell off his horse while watching the battle of Alma. Field Marshal Lord Raglan (1788–1855) saw the mishap and invited him to dinner that night. After Raglan's death, his widow gave Kinglake all Raglan's papers and encouraged him to write a history of the war. *The Invasion of the Crimea* (8 vols 1863–87), deeply researched and written with style and wit, is all the more vivid for its author having witnessed some of the events he describes. Kinglake was Liberal Member of Parliament for Bridgwater from 1857 to 1868, when he lost his seat, and the town the franchise, because of alleged corruption, of which he himself probably knew nothing. On his death he instructed that any unpublished manuscripts should be destroyed. See Gerald de Gaury, *Travelling Gent: the Life of Alexander Kinglake,* 1972.

KINGSLEY, CHARLES (1819–1875) British novelist, academic, and poet, was born at Holne Vicarage, near Dartmoor, and educated at King's College, London, and Magdalene College, Cambridge, where he got a first in classics. He entered the Church and in 1844 became Rector of Eversley, Hampshire, where he spent most of the rest of his life. *The Saint's Tragedy,* a drama, about St Elizabeth of Hungary, in a mixture of blank verse and prose, was published in 1848. *Yeast* (1851) and *Alton Locke* (1850) are novels dealing with the issues of the rural and urban working class respectively. *Westward Ho!* (1855) is social propaganda of a different kind, in the form of a stirring attempt to stiffen patriotic sinews through an account of Elizabethan naval heroism. Kingsley was Professor of Modern History at Cambridge 1860–69, and in 1864 attacked NEWMAN in an anonymous review in *Macmillan's Magazine,* which precipitated the writing of Newman's *Apologia pro Vita Sua. The Water Babies* (1863), with *The Heroes, or Greek Fairy Tales* (1856) his lasting work for children, is a didactic fantasy with a social purpose. *Hereward the Wake* (1866) records in fictional form the exploits of that legendary hero. Kingsley was appointed a canon of Westminster and a chaplain to Queen Victoria in 1873. His enthusiasm for health and strength of body and mind led to his being regarded as a chief exponent of 'muscular Christianity', though he was also a considerable scholar and a fine prose writer,

if not much of a poet. See Robert Bernard Martin, *The Dust of Combat: a Life of Kingsley,* 1959.

KINGSLEY, HENRY (1830–76) British novelist, a younger brother of CHARLES KINGSLEY, was born in Barnack, Northamptonshire, and educated at King's College, London, and Worcester College, Oxford, which he left in 1853 without a degree, and went to Australia. He looked for gold in Bendigo and Beechworth, worked sheep at Langi Willi, and made two epic treks, from western Victoria to Sydney, and from Sydney, by another route via Gippsland, to Melbourne. He returned to England in 1858 with parts of the manuscript of *The Recollections of Geoffry Hamlyn* (1859). The final version of this saga of three emigrant families was supervised by his brother and romanticized at the request of his publisher and his dying father, who begged him to eliminate 'everything in the book which might prevent it lying on a drawing room table'. Even so, it remains a vivid, and significant, re-creation of colonial life in the 1830s and 1840s. *Ravenshoe* (1862) is a tangled novel of an English landed family and its inheritance. *The Hillyars and the Burtons* (1865) is a further Australian novel, in which the interweaved and divergent fortunes of two families from different backgrounds are played out. Thereafter, though he wrote a dozen more novels, his reputation receded, and in 1869 he took the post in Edinburgh of Editor of the *Daily Review,* doubling as correspondent during the Franco-Prussian war in 1870. He returned to London in 1871, and died of throat cancer in Sussex, to which he had moved in 1875, having latterly fallen out with his brother, from whom he frequently requested loans of money. See J. S. D. Mellick, *The Passing Guest: a Life of Henry Kingsley,* 1983.

KINNELL, GALWAY (*b.* 1927) American poet, was born and brought up in Providence, Rhode Island. After serving in the US Navy (1945–46), he went to Princeton, where he and his classmate MERWIN used to read their poetry to each other, and then took a further degree at Rochester University. After living in France on a Fulbright scholarship, he was subsequently a journalist in Iran, and a field worker in Louisiana for the Congress of Racial Equality. He has taught at a number of colleges and universities, most recently New York University. His earlier verse, in *What a Kingdom It Was* (1960) and in the two collections *First Poems 1946–1954* (1970) and *The Avenue Bearing the Initial of Christ into the New World: Poems 1946–1964* (1974), tended towards the traditional and intricate, but gave way to freer forms in *Body Rags* (1968). *The Book of Nightmares* (1971) is a long sequence of reflections on the mortality of all things, a recurring theme in his work which he treats in many different ways. In 'The Bear' (1968) and 'The Porcupine' (1969) the narrator takes on the persona of the dying animal; in 'The Fundamental Project of Technology' (1985) he meditates on the moment when the atom bomb exploded over Nagasaki in 1945. *Selected Poems* (1982) won the Pulitzer Prize. Significant later collections include *The Past* (1985) and *When One Has Lived a Long Time Alone* (1990), which are partly autobiographical. He has published several editions of translations of VILLON and a critical work, *The Poetics of the Physical World* (1969). See *Walking Down the Stairs: Selections from Interviews*, ed. Donald Hall, 1978.

KINSELLA, THOMAS (*b.* 1928) Irish poet and translator, was born in Dublin and educated at O'Connells and at University College, Dublin, from which he joined the Irish civil service. After being elected to the Irish Academy of Letters in 1965, he resigned his post as Assistant Principal Officer, Department of Finance, to be a writer-in-residence at Southern Illinois University, subsequently becoming a professor of English there and at Temple University, Philadelphia. MONTAGUE has described Kinsella's early poems as the work of 'an intellectual troubadour, his desire to sing increasingly crossed by a need to explain'. Another critic has pointed out that when he began writing in the 1950s, the dominance of Irish prose led to his seeking models overseas. Increasingly he achieved, along with several literary awards, an individual voice in which to meditate on love, marriage, death, the ordeal of life itself, and what he calls 'the artistic act'. *Notes from the Land of the Dead and Other Poems* (1972) heralded a new phase, in which his poetry, by his own definition, 'turned downward into the psyche toward origin and myth'. In 1972 he founded a private press in Dublin, which published under the imprint of Peppercanister a number of his topical broadsides, including *Butcher's Dozen* (1972) and *The Good Fight* (1973), and his pamphlets reflecting personal attitudes and issues in family and social history, five of which were subsequently reissued in one volume as *Blood and Family* (1988). *Poems from Centre City* (1994) centres on his exile from Dublin. In *The Dual Tradition: an Essay on Poetry and Politics in Ireland* (1995) he develops the theme he expressed in his introduction to *The New Oxford Book of Irish Verse* (1986): 'The Irish tradition is a matter of two linguistic entities in dynamic interaction, of two major bodies of poetry asking to be understood together as functions of a shared and painful history.' The Irish literary tradition comes through also in his translations, notably *The Táin* (2nd edn 1970). See *The Collected Poems*, 1996; Maurice Harmon, *The Poetry of Thomas Kinsella*, 1974; Thomas H. Jackson, *The Whole Matter: the Poetic Evolution of Thomas Kinsella*, 1995.

KIPLING, (JOSEPH) RUDYARD (1865–1936) British short-story writer, poet, novelist, and children's writer, was born in Bombay, the only son of John Lockwood Kipling (1837–1911), a sculptor and writer, who was teaching at the Bombay School of Art. He and his younger sister were brought to England and boarded with foster parents in Southsea from 1871 to 1877, when he went to the United Services College, Westward Ho!, Devon. He returned to India in 1882 and became a reporter on the *Civil and Military Gazette* in Lahore, where his father was now principal of the art college. He graduated to contributing sketches, stories, and verses, and in 1887 was transferred to the staff of the Allahabad *Pioneer. Departmental Ditties and Other Verses* and *Plain Tales from the Hills* were published in 1886 and 1888 respectively in India, and in 1889 and 1890 in Britain, where the initial reception was muted, though he was becoming known through paperbacks issued by the Indian railways, many of which were brought 'home'. He returned to England via America in 1889. His first novel, *The Light that Failed* (1890), was followed by a further volume of stories, *Life's Handicap* (1891), by *Barrack-Room Ballads and Other Verses* (1892), and by *The Naulahka* (1892), a novel written with his American agent, Wolcott Balestier (1861–91), whose sister Caroline (*d.* 1939) he married in 1892. The couple lived in her home town of Brattleboro, Vermont, until 1896, when they returned to England as the result of a bitter feud with her brother Beatty Balestier (*d.* 1936) over a piece of land opposite their new house. In the meantime Kipling had written his classic children's stories, *The Jungle Book* (1894) and *The Second Jungle Book* (1895), and some of his finest tales, published in *Many Inventions* (1893) and *The Day's Work* (1898), and had become famous.

More children's stories followed, including *Stalky & Co.* (1899) and *Kim* (1901), which is also a fine novel by any standards—see Peter Hopkirk, *Quest for Kim: In Search of Kipling's Great Game* (1996) for a background study. *Puck of Pook's Hill* (1906) and *Rewards and Fairies* (1910) are interspersed with verses illustrating his feeling for the immutability of the English landscape, which contrast sharply with his thumpingly rhythmical military ballads and patriotic songs. By 1902, when he settled in Sussex, his major literary work was done, but his activities as a public figure fiercely concerned with controversial issues and the growing threat, and then the actuality, of war were just beginning; though from 1915 he was hard hit by an undiagnosed ulcer and by the death in action in that year of his only son. He was a master in the craft of prose fiction, and ordinary readers who respond enthusiastically to the poems which accurately but sympathetically reflect the imperialistic attitude of the age, care little for the long-running critical argument as to whether he wrote good verse or bad poetry. In 1907 he was the first British author to receive the Nobel Prize for Literature. Though regarded as the national poet of his time, he made himself unavailable for selection as Poet Laureate and three times refused the OM, on the grounds that he could serve his King and country better from the sidelines. See *Short Stories*, ed. Andrew Rutherford, 2 vols 1993–94; *Selected Poems*, ed. Craig Raine, 1993; *Something of Myself: and Other Autobiographical Writings*, ed. Thomas Pinney, new edn 1991; Charles Carrington, *Rudyard Kipling: His Life and Work*, new edn 1986; Angus Wilson, *The Strange Ride of Rudyard Kipling: His Life and Works*, new edn 1994; J. M. S. Tompkins, *The Art of Rudyard Kipling*, rev. edn 1965; Peter Keating, *Kipling the Poet*, 1994 (critical study).

KIRBY, WILLIAM (1817–1906) Canadian novelist, was born in England in Kingston-upon-Hull, Yorkshire, the son of a tanner who emigrated to America in 1832. Kirby went in 1839 to Upper Canada, where he settled in Niagara-on-the-Lake and married into a staunch United Empire Loyalist family. He became a leading light in that movement, in support of which he wrote (as Britannicus) *Counter Manifesto to the Canadian Annexationists* (1849) and (under his own name) an epic poem, *The U. E. : a Tale of Upper Canada* (1859). He edited the *Niagara Mail*, and was a collector of customs from 1871 to 1895. He also wrote *The Golden Dog (Le Chien d'Or): a Romance of the Days of Louis Quinze in Quebec* (1896). The background of this long, thoroughly researched historical novel with Gothic elements is the power struggles which preceded the unity between the two Canadas. First published in the USA in 1877, its subsequent chequered bibliographical history highlighted holes in existing copyright laws. There is a modern edition, ed. Derek Crawley (1969). See Margot Northey, *William Kirby and His Works*, 1994.

KIRK, ROBERT (1644–?1692) Scottish prose writer, translator, and antiquary, was (significantly) the seventh son of Rev. James Kirk (1609–58), Minister of Aberfoyle. He was educated at the universities of St Andrews and Edinburgh, becoming Minister of Balquhidder in 1664, and of Aberfoyle in 1685. He made the first translation into Gaelic of metrical versions of the complete Psalter (1684). In 1688–89 he transliterated from Irish script into Roman characters the Gaelic Bible which had been initiated by William Bedell (1571–1642), and then spent almost a year in London seeing it through the press, while also attending services of all denominations and observing city life. He died, if he did die, while taking the air in his nightshirt on a fairy mound near the manse. Though an inscribed tombstone marks his grave in Aber-

foyle kirkyard, it is believed that his spirit was removed and held captive by the fairies, who were fearful that he would reveal the secrets of their way of life. WALTER SCOTT records a further tradition that Kirk reappeared to a cousin with explicit instructions as to how he might be restored to his body, which the man was too astonished to carry out when the time came. His manuscript was first published in 1893 as *The Secret Commonwealth of Elves, Fauns, & Fairies*, with a commentary by LANG. Kirk was a scholar with a charming literary style, who set out in scientific terms the findings of his research into an aspect of the supernatural in whose existence he had reasons to believe. He also argued that belief in fairies was not inconsistent with Christian belief. See *The Secret Commonwealth & A Short Treatise of Charms and Spels*, ed. Stewart Sanderson, 1976.

KIRKUP, JAMES (*b.* 1923) British poet, dramatist, and translator, was born in South Shields, and educated at South Shields High School and Durham University, being Gregory Fellow in Poetry, Leeds University 1950–52. He has held many academic posts, most prominently in Japan (about which he has written perceptive travel books) as Professor of English Literature at Japan Women's University and at Kyoto University. Of his poetry he says: 'I have attempted always to express an essence both of myself and of experience, a crystallization of my personal awareness of this world and worlds beyond.' A distinctive voice emerged in his second collection, *The Submerged Village and Other Poems* (1951). The title poem of *A Correct Compassion and Other Poems* (1952) evokes the surgeon's skill and the atmosphere of an open-heart operation which he witnessed. He returns to that theme in the ironical 'The Cure of the Matter' in *White Shadows, Black Shadows: Poems of Peace and War* (1970), which features racial contrasts. In 1977 his poem about a homosexual act performed on the body of Christ, 'The love that dares to speak its name', was the subject of the first prosecution for blasphemous libel since 1922: the Editor of *Gay News*, which printed it, was convicted. As dramatist he has adapted a French medieval mystery cycle, as well as plays by DÜRRENMATT and other European writers. His translations from French, German, Japanese, Italian, and Norwegian include works by BEAUVOIR, SCHILLER, IBSEN, LAYE, and KAWABATA—see also *A Certain State of Mind: an Anthology of modern, classic, and contemporary Japanese Haiku in Translation with Essays and Reviews* (1995). See *Collected Shorter Poems: Vol. 1 Omens of Disaster, Vol. 2 Once and for All*, 1996; *Throwback: Poems towards an Autobiography*, 1992; *The Only Child: an Autobiography of Infancy*, new edn 1970; *Sorrows, Passions, and Alarms: an Autobiography of Childhood*, 1959; *I, of All People: an Autobiography of Youth*, new edn 1990; *Me All Over: Memoirs of a Misfit*, 1994.

KLEIN, A(BRAHAM) M(OSES)

(1909–72) Canadian poet, was born in Ratno, Ukraine, of a Jewish family who emigrated to Montreal in 1910. His poem 'Autobiographical' (1951) evokes memories of his childhood, during which he received, and imbibed, a sound background in Hebrew and Talmudic scholarship. He was further educated at Baron Byng High School, Montreal, McGill University, and the Université de Montréal, where he studied law. He was called to the Quebec Bar in 1933, but practised only intermittently. He took up the cause of Zionism, became a speechwriter and public-relations adviser to the President of the Canadian Jewish Congress in 1939, and edited the *Canadian Jewish Chronicle* from 1938 to 1955. He began to publish his verse in US and Canadian journals in the 1920s, and during the late 1930s and early 1940s was writing poems reflecting the world crisis, in which he expressed grief ('Psalm XXXVI: a Psalm Touching Genealogy', 'Heirloom'), despair ('Sonnet in Time of Affliction'), and outrage ('Psalm VI: a Psalm of Abraham . . .'). In his first published collection, *Hath Not a Jew. . .* (1940), comprising his early work, and in *Poems* (1944), he explores his Jewish heritage and the isolation imposed by his Jewishness, basing his images and reflections on a wide and varied spectrum of experience. His satirical bent surfaced in *The Hitleriad* (1944)—'Heil heavenly muse, since also thou must be / Like my song's theme, a sieg-heiled deity . . .'—, in imitation of POPE, but the medium was basically unsuited to a theme of such enormity. With *The Rocking Chair, and Other Poems* (1948), which won the Governor General's Award, he set aside overtly Jewish themes for those which express the landscapes, situations, and culture of Quebec, as in the title poem, 'Grain Elevator', 'Indian Reservation: Caughnawaga', and the sharply ironic 'Portrait of the Poet as Landscape', in which the author-figure, a modern Lycidas, is ignored.

In 1949 he stood for Parliament as a Cooperative Commonwealth Federation candidate, but was heavily defeated. Shortly afterwards he went on behalf of the Canadian Jewish Congress to Europe, North Africa, and Israel to study conditions in refugee camps. Out of this experience grew his single sustained work of prose fiction, *The Second Scroll* (1951), a short but elaborate work whose structure and theme have parallels in the five books of the Hebrew Bible collectively known as the Torah. The search by a Canadian journalist for his uncle symbolizes the fateful progress of the Jews of eastern Europe between 1917 and 1949, and the whole is rounded off with a series of five 'glosses' in verse, prose, and dramatic form, in which the essential oneness of Judaism, Christian-

ity, and Islam is further emphasized. Soon after its publication Klein suffered a psychological breakdown, which led to his withdrawal from normal life and ultimately to his death. He is arguably the finest Jewish poet to write in English. His monumental commentary on JOYCE's *Ulysses*, which he first read in about 1929 and which influenced his writing, was never finished. See *The Complete Poems*, ed. Zailig Pollock, 2 vols 1991; *A. M. Klein: Short Stories*, ed. M. W. Steinberg, 1983; Usher Caplan, *Like One That Dreamed: a Portrait of A. M. Klein*, 1975; Zailig Pollock, *A. M. Klein: the Story of the Poet*, 1994; Noreen Goffman, *A. M. Klein and His Works*, 1994.

KLEIST, HEINRICH VON (1777–1811)

German dramatist and novelist, was born in Frankfurt-an-der-Oder, the fifth child and eldest son of a Prussian army officer. He fell out with his family when, in 1799, after seven years in the army, he resigned his commission to go to Frankfurt University. His creative life was dogged by international and political upheavals, by emotional crises (one of them sparked off by the revelation, from a study of KANT, that absolute knowledge obtained by the application of reason was unattainable, thus ruining his life plan), and by lack of money, to which his journalistic publishing ventures in Dresden and Berlin contributed. He was also unlucky. A potential patron withdrew his support when his daughter fell in love with Kleist; the premiere of *Der zerbrochene Krug* [*The Broken Pitcher*], put on by GOETHE in Weimar in 1808, was disastrously produced; hopes of court patronage after ceremonially presenting a birthday sonnet to the Queen were dashed when she died suddenly four months later. His seven plays hover between tragedy and tragicomedy. His eight stories, published as *Erzählungen* (2 vols 1810–11), are powerful evocations of situation and paradox—see *The Marquise of O. and Other Stories*, tr. David Luke and Michael Reeves (1978). He corresponded regularly with a long-suffering fiancée, and died in a meticulously planned and spectacular suicide pact with a terminally-ill married woman, who first helped him to burn his manuscripts. See Seán Allen, *The Plays of Heinrich von Kleist*, 1996 (critical study).

KNICKERBOCKER, DIEDRICH see IRVING.

KNOX, E. V. see FITZGERALD, PENELOPE.

KNOX, JOHN (1505–72) Scottish religious

reformer and prose writer, was born in Gifford, East Lothian, and educated at the universities of Glasgow and St Andrews, taking priest's orders in about 1530. In 1545, now allied to the Protestant cause, he acted as bodyguard to the reformer George Wishart (*c*.1513–46) until his trial and execution for heresy. When Wishart's supporters took revenge by murdering Cardinal Beaton (1494–1546) and holed themselves up in St Andrews Castle, Knox acted as their chaplain, and on their surrender was turned over to the French as a galley slave. He was released in 1549 and spent the next ten years in England and on the Continent, where he steeped himself in the teachings of CALVIN. He also preached the doctrines of reform and wrote copiously, notably *The First Blast of the Trumpet against the Monstrous Regiment* [i.e. rule] *of Women* (1558), a very early example of a privately-sponsored pamphlet, aimed especially at Mary Tudor. He was appointed Minister of the High Kirk in Edinburgh in 1559, his appearance in the pulpit in Perth sparking off two days of riots. The return from France of the young, Catholic, Mary, Queen of Scots, in 1561 began six years of mutual antagonism. *The Historie of the Reformation of Religioun within the Realm of Scotland*, completed in about 1567, is a valuable if biased source of information, in which he makes the most of juicy court scandals. While he uses Scots words, the forceful, colloquial style is more English than that spoken or written in 16th-century Scotland. In spite of his professed misogyny, he was twice married, the second time to a 17-year-old who was 42 years his junior, by whom he had two daughters. See Jasper Ridley, *John Knox*, 1968 (biography); Stewart Lamont, *John Knox and the European Reformation*, 1991.

KOCH, KENNETH see O'HARA, FRANK.

KOESTLER, ARTHUR (1905–83) novelist and prose writer, was born in Budapest of Jewish parents who moved to Vienna at the outbreak of World War I. He was educated there at the Polytechnic High School and Vienna University, where he read engineering. He was a journalist in the Middle East, Paris, and Berlin, but lost his editorial post in 1932 when he joined the Communist Party, in which he saw the only answer to Nazism. He went freelance, and while reporting the Spanish Civil War from the Republican side was captured and imprisoned; he expected execution, but was released in 1937 through the intervention of the British Government. He now resigned from the party. In Paris he wrote two novels in German, published as *The Gladiators* (tr. Edith Simon 1939), in which the dissident is Spartacus, and *Darkness at Noon* (tr. Daphne Hardy 1940), whose similar theme is the doom of an elderly Bolshevik. He was interned in 1939, but engineered an escape to Britain, of which he became a citizen in 1948. Subsequent novels, written in English and including *Arrival and Departure* (1943) and *The Call-Girls: a Tragi-Comedy with Prologue and Epilogue* (1972), are also polemical. Two strands dominate his non-fiction: the quest for social and political reform, notably the abolition of capital punishment, and his belief in a scientific basis for telepathy, such as he expresses in *The Case of the Midwife Toad* (1971) and *The Roots of Coincidence* (1972)—he endowed in his will a chair in parapsychology, which was established at Edinburgh University. He committed suicide with his third wife, after seven years of crippling illness. He was made CBE in 1972. See *Spanish Testament*, rev. edn 1954, *Scum of the Earth*, new edn 1992, *Arrow in the Blue*, new edn 1983, *The Invisible Writing*, new edn 1969 (autobiography).

KROETSCH, ROBERT (*b*. 1927) Canadian novelist, poet, and critic, was born in Heisler, Alberta, and went to school there and in Red Deer, and then to the University of Alberta. He worked as a labourer and a riverboat purser for a transportation company in the Northwest Territories, and as an information officer at Goose Bay Air Force Base. In 1954–55 he studied under MACLENNAN at McGill University, and subsequently at Iowa University. He taught English at the State University of New York until 1978, when he returned to Canada to the University of Manitoba, of which he was appointed Distinguished Professor in 1985. His first novel, *But We Are Exiles* (1965), established his distinctive motif of devising parallels in Canadian reality with various aspects of mythology. *The Words of My Roaring* (1966), *The Studhorse Man* (1969), which won the Governor General's Award, and *Gone Indian* (1973) are linked, comic, quest novels of an Alberta small town community, whose counterparts are in the rape of Persephone, the wanderings of Odysseus, and American Indian legend respectively. The sensuous seduction of Vera Lang by a swarm of bees begets the disasters which by surreal means afflict the male protagonists of *What the Crow Said* (1978). *The Stone Hammer: Poems 1960–1975* was published in 1975, since when he has assembled his poetry and prose poems into an ongoing sequence, of which *Field Notes: Collected Poems* (1981) and *Advice to My Friends: a Continuing Poem* (1985) are the first two volumes—see also *Complete Field Notes: the Long Poems of Robert Kroetsch* (1989). *The Lovely Treachery of Words: Essays Selected and New* (1989) contains significant studies of Canadian literature. See Ann Munton, *Robert Kroetsch and His Works: Poetry*, 1992; Peter Thomas, *Robert Kroetsch and His Works: Fiction*, 1992.

KUMAR, SHIV K(UMAR) (*b*. 1921) Indian poet, was born in Lahore, the son of a headmaster in whose home both English and Hindi were spoken. He was educated at Dayanand Anglo-Vedic High School and Foreman Christian College, Punjab University, later taking the degree of PhD at Fitzwilliam College, Cambridge. He was Professor of English at Osmania University, Hyderabad 1959–76, and of Hyderabad University 1976–79. He began writing poetry seriously when he was 49, and immediately went into print with *Articulate Silences* (1970), which he followed at discreet intervals with *Cobwebs in the Sun* (1974), *Subterfuges* (1976), *Woodpeckers* (1979), and *Trapfalls in the Sky* (1986). Whether he is writing about childhood ('My Mother's Lover'), growing up ('Broken Columns'), adulthood ('To a Prostitute', 'My Co-respondent'), India ('A Mango Vendor') or the USA ('A Letter from New York'), his work has a fresh and personal ring, and reveals in its ironic humour the influence of much travel as a visiting academic. He has written two novels, *The Bone's Prayer* (1979) and *Nude Before God* (1983), and a volume of short stories, and has edited a number of literary texts and compilations.

KUNDERA, MILAN (*b.* 1929) Czech novelist and critic, was born in Brno, attended Charles University, Prague, and taught film studies at the Academy of Music and Dramatic Arts from 1959 to 1969. His earlier novels, and a volume of short stories (tr. Suzanne Rappaport as *Laughable Loves*, 1974) are sardonic expressions of individualism in the face of Communism. He was officially censured in 1967 for publicly voicing his views, and after the Soviet invasion of Czechoslovakia in 1968 his works were banned. In 1975 he was allowed to emigrate to France, of which he became a citizen in 1981. He taught comparative literature at Rennes University from 1975 to 1980, when he was appointed to the École des Hautes Études, Paris. [*The Book of Laughter and Forgetting*] (1981, tr. Michael H. Heim, 1980), the first work of his exile, is an amalgam of personal and political comment, stories and reminiscences, in narrative form. In *Immortality*, tr. Peter Kussi (1991), which is similarly constructed and equally aphoristic, the setting is Western Europe and the enslavement is more subtle. [*The Joke*] (1967), his first novel, was reissued in 1992 in a revised translation (by Heim and others), authorized by Kundera, which is the fifth version in English. In *Slowness* (France, 1995; tr. Linda Asher, 1996), his first novel written

in French, two nights of seduction, two hundred years apart, are the springboard for some imaginings on the part of the author, or his persona, on bringing the past into the present, and on reality being a combination of the two. *The Art of the Novel*, tr. Asher (1988), is a collection of cross-cultural essays and dialogues. *Testaments Betrayed: an Essay in Nine Parts* (France, 1993; tr. Asher, 1995) is a series of reflections on the history of the novel from RABELAIS and CERVANTES to RUSHDIE.

KYD, THOMAS (1558–94) English dramatist, was born in the City of London, the son of a scrivener, and was educated at Merchant Taylors' School. From a letter of his to the Lord Keeper, it appears that in 1593 he had for six years been in service to a 'Lord', and that in 1591 he and MARLOWE shared a room. On 12 May 1593, while he was in prison on suspicion of inciting the populace against immigrant craftsmen, his lodgings were searched and copies found of an atheistical tract, which he claimed was Marlowe's. Kyd was later freed, having been tortured but not charged. The only play originally published as his is *Cornelia* (1594), a translation from the French of a Roman tragedy by Robert Garnier (*c.*1545–1600). HEYWOOD in *Apology for Actors* refers to 'M. Kid, in his Spanish Tragedy', and a play of that name was in print in 1592 and frequently reissued. Francis Meres (1565–1647) in *Palladis Tamia* (1598) calls Kyd 'our best for Tragedie'. *The Spanish Tragedy*, a drama of revenge and stark retribution, though lacking the poetic inspiration of Marlowe and SHAKESPEARE, is as significant in the development of Elizabethan tragedy as are *Tamburlaine* and *Titus Andronicus*. The plot is subtler than that of Shakespeare's *Richard III*, and the politics of dynastic marriage and the motivation of the unhappy Bel-imperia are presented with greater assurance than in *Romeo and Juliet*. From the appearance, as the play-within-a-play, of a version of *The Tragedye of Soliman and Perseda* (*c.*1592), it has been surmised that Kyd was its author too; a lost proto-Hamlet has also been attributed to him. See *The Spanish Tragedy*, ed. Philip Edwards, new edn 1977.

L

LACLOS, PIERRE CHODERLOS DE (1741–1803) French novelist, was born in Amiens, educated at the École d'Artillerie de la Fère, entered the army as a 2nd lieutenant in 1762, and saw no action until 1800, when he was a general of artillery at Naples. His single work of fiction, *Les Liaisons Dangereuses* (1782; tr. as *Dangerous Connections*, 1784; tr. Richard Aldington as *Dangerous Acquaintances*, 1924; tr. Douglas Parmée, 1995) is an epistolary novel, logically investigating personal and public morality and sexual relationships, in which two women fall under the spell of an utterly heartless libertine. A man of talent and energy (he offered to develop a new kind of bullet), Laclos was continually frustrated in his search for advancement. While serving in various garrisons, he wrote light verse and critical essays, including one on BURNEY's *Cecilia*. Waiting at a levee in London in the winter of 1789–90 for the Prince of Wales to finish his toilet, he confided to a countryman: 'I decided to write a work that should depart from the trodden path, make a stir, and reverberate on this earth after my demise.' He succeeded in all of these, but the scandal that attended its publication did not help his army career.

LA FAYETTE, MME DE (1634–93) French novelist, was born Marie-Madeleine Pioche de la Vergne in Paris, and married Comte de La Fayette (*d.* 1683) in 1655. After four years at his chateau in Nades, during which she had two sons, she settled without him in Paris, where she met LA ROCHEFOUCAULD at a literary salon. She was often in poor health, and he was plagued by gout, but their acquaintance grew into an affectionate friendship in which she offered solicitude and support, and he gave her literary advice and help with historical research. None of the three romances published during her lifetime carried her name, and only the last, *La Princesse de Clèves* (1678; tr. as *The Princess of Cleves*, 1679; tr. Terence Cave, with *La Princesse de Montpensier* and *La Comtesse de Tende*, 1992) is significant. Set in the French court in the 16th century, it is a psychological study of the course of a married woman's infatuation, which ultimately, when she is free to gratify

it, she resists. NATHANIEL LEE used the plot as the basis of a play of protest.

LA FONTAINE, JEAN DE (1621–95) French poet, was born in Chateau-Thierry, to which he returned from Paris in about 1642 after an unlikely spell of education for the priesthood by the Oratorians. He went back to Paris to study law, and in 1647 married the 14-year-old Marie Héricart. He published his first book, a version of *Eunuchus* [The Eunuch] of TERENCE in 1654. In 1658 he inherited his father's royal post of Maître des Eaux et Forêts (he later sold it), and divided his property with his wife, with whom he established a separate existence in the family home beside the ruins of the old castle. He now offered a narrative poem in rhyming couplets, 'Adonis', to Nicolas Foucquet (1615–80), the national Minister of Finance, who, on the recommendation of his secretary, a Paris acquaintance of La Fontaine, employed him as his personal laureate. After the fall and arrest of Foucquet, La Fontaine found a royal patron, the dowager Duchesse d'Orléans, the first of several aristocratic ladies to whom he played *cavalieri servente*. His *Contes et Nouvelles en Vers*, verse tales taken mainly from BOCCACCIO, MARGUERITE DE NAVARRE, and the 15th-century *Cent Nouvelles Nouvelles*, was published in four volumes 1665–75, the last of which was banned for its attribution of indecency to priests and nuns. In 1693, a sick La Fontaine repented of his *'livre abominable'* and renounced future royalties, an act which moved the ten-year-old Duc de Bourgogne, grandson of Louis XIV, to send him a purse of 50 golden louis as compensation. For the first collection of his verse *Fables* (1668), he drew mainly on Phaedrus, the 1st-century Roman writer who versified the beast-stories of the legendary Aesop; for the second (1678), on the equally legendary Indian philosopher, Bidpai, and other oriental traditions. His aptly, sometimes cynically, rounded-off tales, grave on occasions to the point of pessimism, as well as gay, are the work of a skilled versifier and storyteller in the tradition of OVID and HORACE, from whom he probably got ['The Town Rat and the Country Rat']. See *Selected Fables*, tr. James Michie, introduction by Geoffrey Grigson, new edn 1982; *Selected Fables*, tr. Christopher Wood, ed. Maya Slater, 1995 (bilingual edn).

LAFORGUE, JULES (1860–87) French poet, was born in Montevideo, Uruguay, of Breton parents who returned to Tarbes in 1866, and in 1876 moved to Paris, where he went to the Lycée Fontanes. After Mme Laforgue's death in childbirth in 1877, his father went back to Tarbes, leaving him in Paris, where he failed his baccalaureate three times. Through the good offices of friends, he was in 1881 appointed French reader to Empress Augusta of Germany, which involved being available twice a day to read to her from magazines as well as literature and works of general interest, and to travel around with her household. He held the post for five years, during which he also wrote seven critical articles for *Gazette de Beaux-Arts*; developed from his study of contemporary art the notion of new forms of verse, with which he first publicly experimented in *Les Complaintes* (1885), an innovative collection, published at his own expense, which took no notice of anything he had written before 1883; and made translations of WHITMAN, first published in *La Vogue*. In 1886 he married an English woman, with whom he lived in Paris until his death eight months later of tuberculosis. The 12 poems in *Dernier Vers* (1890; as *The Last Poems*, ed. Madeleine Betts, 1973) represent the first successful attempt to write free verse in French, and were a significant influence on the work of T. S. ELIOT and POUND.

LAGERKVIST, PÄR (1891–1974) Swedish novelist, dramatist, and poet, was born in Vaxjo and studied the humanities at Uppsala University in 1911 and 1912, when he published a novella. In Paris in 1913 he came under the influence of modernism in painting. This artistic trend is reflected in the poems in *Ångest* [Anguish] (1916), a reaction to the havoc and destruction of World War I; in his early plays; and in [*The Eternal Smile*] (1920; tr. Denys W. Harding and Erik Mesterton, 1934), a fictional exploration of idealistic spirituality. The protagonist of [*The Dwarf*] (1944; tr. Alexandra Dick, 1945), a novel in diary form set in Renaissance Italy, symbolizes the malevolent and destructive forces normally suppressed within human nature. *Barabbas* (1950; tr. Alan Blair, 1951), which evokes the predicament of man in the modern world through that of the biblical robber released from the condemned cell, was influential in his being awarded the Nobel Prize for Literature in 1951, and was staged in his own dramatization in 1953. A tragic playwright much influenced by STRINDBERG, he moved latterly towards a form of realism.

LAGERLÖF, SELMA (1858–1940) Swedish novelist and children's writer, was born at the family home of Marbacka, Varmland, fourth of five children. Lame from the age of three, probably from infantile paralysis, she was educated at home, and entered the Teachers' Seminary, Stockholm, when she was 23. In 1885, the year she accepted a position in a girls' school in Landskrona, her father died and Marbacka was sold. This was the impetus to continue and finish [*Gösta Berling's Saga*] (1891; tr. L. Tudeer, 1898), a remarkable blend of philosophy, romance, and Varmland folklore, written in a style inspired by CARLYLE's *On Heroes* . . ., with five chapters of which she had won a magazine story contest. After the publication of [*Invisible Links*] (1894; tr. Pauline Bancroft Flach, 1899), she gave up her teaching post, and moved to Dalecarlia. The inspiration for [*Jerusalem*] (1901; tr. Jessie Bröchner, 1903) and [*The Holy City*] (1902; tr. Velma Swanston Howard, 1918) was the migration to Jerusalem a few years earlier of a group of local families, under the influence of a revivalist from Chicago. The award of the Nobel Prize for Literature in 1909, when she was the first woman to receive it, enabled her to buy back Marbacka and develop the estate, on which she lived permanently from 1919. [*The Wonderful Adventures of Nils*] and [*The Further Adventures of Nils*] (1906–07; tr. Howard, 1908–11), originally written to meet the demands of the National Teachers' Association for a geography reader for schools, have become classics of children's tales of fantasy and adventure.

LA GUMA, ALEX (1925–85) South African novelist, was born and brought up in the Cape Coloured District Six of Cape Town, the setting, with its situations, of his first novel, *A Walk in the Night* (1962), published in Nigeria and reissued in the UK in *A Walk in the Night, and Other Stories* (1967). He was educated at Trafalgar High School and Cape Technical College. The son of a leader of the national non-white liberation movement, he joined the Communist Party, and was a member of its district committee until the party was banned in 1950. He was one of the 156 Africans charged in 1956 with contributing towards the Freedom Charter. He became a journalist on the radical newspaper, *New Age*, in 1960, when, as a member of the Coloured People's Congress, he was detained after the Sharpeville violence, and again in 1961 for organizing a strike. In 1962, he was without trial put under house arrest for five years, during which both he and his wife suffered periods of solitary confinement. The family then went into exile, first in Britain, and then from 1978 in Cuba, where he represented the African National Congress. *And a Threefold Cord* (1964), about life in a Cape Town ghetto, and *The Stone Country* (1967), which realistically re-creates the prison conditions that he had experienced (the prison symbolizes South Africa itself), were both written when he was under house arrest, and were first published in East Berlin. *In the Fog of a Season's End* (1972) features underground resistance to apartheid, and *Time of the Butcherbird* (1979) the forceful removal of people to the new Bantu homeland. La Guma is an artistic writer, whose personal experience of the situations he evokes, particularly in his earlier books and in the stories published between 1960 and 1964, make him a significant novelist of social realism and political reality.

LAMARCK, CHEVALIER DE see BUTLER, SAMUEL (*Erewhon*).

LAMB, CHARLES (1775–1834) British essayist and critic, was born in Crown Office Row in the Temple, London, the youngest of three children of a lawyer's clerk who survived infancy, and was educated at Christ's Hospital. After working in South Sea House, he obtained a clerkship in East India House in 1792, which provided a livelihood until he retired in 1825. A family streak of insanity affected him briefly when he was 20, and his sister Mary (1764–1847) more disastrously in 1796, when she killed their mother with a table knife. His guardianship of Mary was accepted, and he cared for her, renouncing marriage, for the rest of his life. His first literary efforts were unsuccessful, and comprised some verses (the quotability of 'The Old Familiar Faces' has ensured its survival), a novel, and a farce, *Mr H——* (1806), which he joined the first-night audience in hissing. Though his name alone was on the title page of *Tales from Shukespear* (1807), Mary wrote the 14 comedies, and he the six tragedies. His major critical work, *Specimens of English Dramatic Poets, who Lived about the Time of Shakespeare* (1808), contains extracts from and percipient comments on hitherto unappreciated writers; otherwise his best literary criticism is in his letters to friends, the most notable of whom was COLERIDGE. In 1820 he wrote 'The South-Sea House', the first of 67 essays in the *London Magazine* as Elia—he took a fellow-clerk's name for that essay to avoid embarrassing his brother John (1763–1821), who was still working there. A collected edition of these elegant, informal, often fanciful pieces was published in 1823, and *The Last Essays of Elia* (from various journals) in 1833. See *Selected Prose*, ed. Adam Phillips, 1986; *Elia and the Last Essays of Elia*, ed. Jonathan Bate, 1987; *Charles Lamb and Elia*, ed. J. E. Morpurgo, 1993 (selection); *The Letters of Charles and Mary Lamb* (1796–1817), ed. Edwin W. Marrs, 3 vols 1975–78; David Cecil, *A Portrait of Charles Lamb*, new edn 1986.

LAMB, WILLIAM see JAMESON, STORM.

LAMMING, GEORGE (*b.* 1927) Barbadian novelist, was born in Carrington Village and educated at Combermere School, after which he taught in Trinidad. His poetry at this time expressed his frustration at the cultural sterility of the West Indies. He emigrated to England in 1950, thus himself fuelling the myth to which he refers in his volume of critical essays, *The Pleasures of Exile* (1960), as 'one of the seeds which much later bear such strange fruit as the West Indian writers' departure from the very landscape which is the raw material of all their books'. In his first novel, *In the Castle of My Skin* (1953), the growth of a boy to maturity is seen against the modern developments which affect his village. The autobiographical element is continued in *The Emigrants* (1954), which reflects his own sense of alienation in England. *Of Age and Innocence* (1958) and *Season of Adventure* (1960), written after several years of travel in Europe, the USA, and the Caribbean, are set before and after the independence of a fictional island, San Cristobal. His next book, *Water with Berries* (1972), outwardly a realistic novel of the place of the artist, has an allegorical framework suggested by elements in SHAKESPEARE's *The Tempest*. *Natives of My Person* (1972) explores the tradition and mythology of the roots of West Indian society through the voyage of a 17th-century slave ship. See Sandra Pouchet Paquet, *The Novels of George Lamming*, 1982.

LAMPEDUSA, GIUSEPPE DI (Duke of Palma and Prince of Lampedusa) (1896–1957) Italian novelist, was born and brought up in the ancestral palace in Palermo. He was educated at home, being taught French by his domineering mother. In 1934, without telling his mother, he married Alessandra (Licy) von Wolff-Stomersee (*d.* 1982), a Freudian psychoanalyst and linguist, whom he had first met in London in 1925. It was she who in the early 1950s encouraged this shy, self-educated literary scholar, who spent his days mainly eating cakes in cafés and browsing in bookshops, to marshal his thoughts on English literature into a series of informal seminars for his young friends. In doing so he wrote over a thousand pages covering the period between *Beowulf* and GRAHAM GREENE, and discovered his vocation as a writer. The surprising (to him) success of a cousin's book of verse galvanized him into beginning a novel. He died of cancer a week after it had been firmly rejected by the firm of Mondadori. He left instructions for his family to pursue publication, and *Il Gattopardo* (1958; tr. Archibald Colquhoun as *The Leopard*, rev. edn 1961) appeared under the imprint of Feltrinelli, won the national Strega Prize, and was soon on its way to becoming the best selling and most widely translated 20th-century Italian novel. Plotless, but artfully organized into a series of situations and character studies, it recalls the passing of the old regime in Sicily in the 1860s. *The Siren and Selected Writings*, tr. Colquhoun and others

(1995) contains two stories, an autobiographical fragment ('Places of My Infancy'), and extracts from his writings on English literature. See David Gilmour, *The Last Leopard: a Life of Giuseppe di Lampedusa*, new edn 1991.

LAMPMAN, ARCHIBALD (1861–99) Canadian poet, was born in Morpeth, Canada West, the son of an Anglican clergyman, and suffered from rheumatic fever when he was six. He was educated at Trinity College School, Port Hope, and Trinity College, Toronto University, where he read classics, took inspiration from the publication of ROBERTS's *Orion*, and wrote poems and critical essays for *Rouge et Noir*, the college magazine. After a very brief spell as a teacher at Orangeville High School, he became in 1883 a clerk with the Post Office Department, Ottawa, where he worked for the rest of his life. He married in 1887 (there were three children, born in 1892, 1894, and 1898). He had poems published in American and British, as well as Canadian journals, and with money provided by his wife privately published *Among the Millet and Other Poems* (1888). In 1889 he fell in love with a fellow clerk, Katherine Waddell (1865–1926), with whom he may have lived for a time. The anguished relationship is discreetly reflected in a series of poems he wrote at the time—see *Lampman's Kate: Late Love Poems 1887–1897*, ed. Margaret Coulby Whitridge (1975). In 1892–93 he contributed a column, 'At the Mermaid Inn', to the Toronto *Globe* with D. C. SCOTT and the philosophical poet and miscellaneous writer, Wilfred Campbell (1858–1918). An edition of 550 copies of *Lyrics of Earth* (1895) was published in Boston, USA. He died soon after correcting the proofs of *Alcyone* (1899), of which 12 copies were then printed on the instructions of Scott, his literary executor, who edited *The Poems of Archibald Lampman* (1900). For his nature poetry, he is regarded as the best of the four poets of the Confederation Group, the others being CARMAN, Roberts, and Scott.

LANDOR, WALTER SAVAGE (1775–1864) British poet and prose writer, was born in Warwick, the eldest son of a doctor of considerable private means. He went to Rugby School, from which he was removed for impudence, and Trinity College, Oxford, from which he was suspended for firing off a shotgun in his rooms. He never returned. Instead, he had an affair with a young woman he met in Tenby (he calls her 'Ione' in his verse), quarrelled violently with his father, and found a publisher for *The Poems of Walter Savage Landor* (1795). On the beach at Swansea he met the Hon. Rose Aylmer (1779–1800), whose death in India inspired his elegy on her. During their brief friendship she lent him her library book, REEVE's *The Progress of Romance*, where he found the theme for his epic poem, *Gebir* (1798), which he later pub-

lished in Latin verse as *Gebirus* (1803). Shortly after the publication of *Poetry by the Author of Gebir* (1802) he met Sophia Jane Swift (*d.* 1851), who was about to marry her cousin. They became lovers nonetheless, and he addressed many poems to her as 'Ianthe'. In 1808 he fought as a volunteer against the French for the Spanish, whose war of liberation he also subsidized out of his own pocket. The same year he sold the family property in Staffordshire, which he had inherited in 1805, and bought Llanthony Abbey in Wales. Here, to a half-built house on the estate, he brought his 17-year-old bride, Julia Thuiller, in 1811. In 1814, having quarrelled with his creditors and his tenants, one of whom successfully sued him for libel, he went into voluntary exile, with his wife, in Italy. He was asked to leave Como for writing an 'insolent' poem in Latin, and he was threatened with expulsion from Florence for making derogatory remarks about the local police and for being critical of Italy in *Imaginary Conversations of Literary Men and Statesmen* (5 vols 1824–29). These dialogues, mainly between historical characters from many civilizations, often centre on dramatic situations or involve divergent personalities, though frequently he puts his own political and philosophical views into his speakers' mouths.

In 1835 he parted from his wife, leaving her and their four children in Fiesole, and returned to England with the manuscript of *Pericles and Aspasia* (1836), an evocation of classical Athens through a series of imaginary letters. From 1838 he lived in Bath, where he met his friends again, among the closest of whom were SOUTHEY, DICKENS, who portrayed him as Boythorn in *Bleak House*, and John Forster (1812–76), who was to write his biography (1869). He continued to write prolifically, the two most notable prose works of this period being *The Pentameron and Pentalogia* (1837), a dialogue between PETRARCH and BOCCACCIO with particular reference to DANTE, and *Imaginary Conversations of Greeks and Romans* (1853). In 1858, now 83, he hurriedly left for Italy rather than face a libel action, which in his absence he lost, arising from some satirical verses on a local woman, *Dry Sticks, Fagoted by Walter Savage Landor* (1858). After a year in Fiesole with his family, he fled to Florence, where the BROWNINGS cared for him until Elizabeth's death in 1861, and where he died. See Malcolm Elwin, *Landor: a Replevin*, 1958 (biography).

LANG, ANDREW (1844–1912) Scottish poet, novelist, translator, mythologist, and essayist, was born in Selkirk, the eldest son of the Sheriff-Clerk of Selkirkshire and an elder brother of T. W. Lang (1854–1902), who played cricket for Gloucestershire while still at school and to whom he later dedicated 'Ballade of Cricket'. He went to Edinburgh

Academy and St Andrews University, transferred to Glasgow University, and won an exhibition to Balliol College, Oxford, where he got a first in Greats. He was elected a Fellow of Merton College, but resigned after his marriage in 1875 to become a journalist in London, where he spent the rest of his life, latterly wintering in St Andrews. The range of his literary output, about 120 books of his own plus more than 150 to which he contributed, reflects his interests if not always his particular gifts. *Ballads and Lyrics of Old France, and Other Poems* (1872) contained the reflective 'Twilight on Tweed' and 'Sunset on Yarrow'. *XXII Ballades in Blue China* (1880) owed even more to the French, from which he also translated the medieval *chantefable*, *Aucassin and Nicolette* (1886). He made prose translations of HOMER's *Odyssey* (1879, with S. H. Butcher) and *Iliad* (1883, with Walter Leaf and Ernest Myers). Among many historical works is *Pickle the Spy* (1897), which conclusively revealed the identity of the traitor in the entourage of Charles Edward Stuart. In spite of his being an influential reviewer, his appreciation of contemporary literature was erratic, since he was unable to apply the test of time, but he wrote penetrating critical introductions to BURNS and STEVENSON, useful biographical studies of KNOX (1905) and WALTER SCOTT (1906), and amusing parodies in *Letters to Dead Authors* (1886). The collection of essays from the *Daily News*, *Lost Leaders* (ed. W. Pett Ridge, 1889) is still readable for its humour and breadth of subject matter, from golf to MONTAIGNE. His study of primitive beliefs, *Myth, Ritual and Religion* (1887; rev. edn 1899), was influential in his time; in *The Making of Religion* (1898) he propounded the existence of elements of religion in the consciousness of early man. Such studies were the inspiration of the 'Colour Fairy Books', of which he wrote in *The Lilac Fairy Book* (1910), 'I find out where the stories are, and advise, and, in short, superintend.' Largely unembellished and authentic, and often tough, these stories engineered a change of taste from the realistic story to the fairy tale which the public has never lost since. See Eleanor de Selms Langstaff, *Andrew Lang*, 1978 (critical study).

LANGLAND, WILLIAM (*c*.1330–*c*.1386) English poet, the author of *The Vision of William Concerning Piers the Plowman*, was a younger (or possibly illegitimate) son of an Oxfordshire gentleman farmer. From evidence in the poem, he was born in the parish of Colwall, near the Malvern Hills, was educated at the expense of his father and friends (probably at Malvern Priory), and took minor orders. At some point he moved to London, where he lived with his sensually-inclined wife, Kitty, and their daughter Calotte, and worked as an itinerant clerical hack, saying prayers for those who contributed to his up-

keep. *Piers Plowman* exists in three distinct versions: A-text (completed after 1362); B-text (a longer revision, written between 1377 and 1379); C-text (a further revision, probably finished just before the poet's death). (A possible fourth version, known as Z-text, was first published in 1983.) Brimming with stirring descriptions and powerful imaginative passages, and studded with colloquialisms and humour, it is the finest alliterative poem in Middle English and has been described by Professor Nevill Coghill in *Langland: Piers Plowman* (1964) as 'the greatest Christian poem in our language'. It opens with the poet being lulled to sleep in the Malvern countryside, and continues in a series of 'visions'. The whole represents an exhaustive pilgrimage after truth, reason, and the love of God, in the face of falsehood, temptation, ignorance, and the Seven Deadly Sins (graphically personified), and through disputation to the ultimate vision, and beyond to salvation. See *Will's Vision of Piers Plowman*, tr. E. Talbot Donaldson, ed. Elizabeth J. Kirk and Judith Anderson, 1990; *Piers Plowman*, ed. A. V. C. Schmidt, 2nd rev. edn 1995 (B-text); John Norton-Smith, *William Langland*, 1983 (critical study).

LARDNER, RING(OLD WILMER) (1885–1933) American short-story writer, humorist, and journalist, was born in Niles, Michigan, the youngest of nine children of wealthy, educated parents, and with two siblings was taught at home by a tutor until it was thought time for them to go to high school. All three failed the entrance examination, but were taken anyway. After graduating in 1901, and having been fired from two jobs as an office boy and one as a freight hustler, he was sent to the Armour Institute of Technology, from which he dropped out after a term. In 1905, while working for the local gas board, he proposed himself for a job as reporter on the South Bend *Times* in place of his brother, who was on vacation and could not accept it. In 1908 he became baseball correspondent of the Chicago *Examiner*. Several moves later, he was appointed 'In the Wake of the News' columnist on the sports page of the *Tribune*. From writing accounts as though by an unghosted player, he developed the technique in a series of six baseball stories in the *Saturday Evening Post* in 1914, which grew into *You Know Me Al* (1916). Of this book, VIRGINIA WOOLF wrote in 'American Fiction' (1925): '[He] does not waste a moment when he writes in thinking whether he is using American slang or Shakespeare's English; whether he is remembering Fielding or forgetting Fielding; whether he is proud of being American or ashamed of not being Japanese; all his mind is on the story. Hence all our minds are on the story. Hence, incidentally, he writes the best prose that has come our way.' Through his vernacular idiom, often in the form of a dramatic monologue, he revealed inner truths about ordinary, or typical, Americans, which he continued to do in *Gullible's Travels* (1917) and other volumes, including *The Big Town* (1921), the nearest he ever got to writing a novel. In 1919 he became a weekly columnist for the Bell Syndicate, and in 1921 moved with his family to Great Neck, Long Island. A neighbour was F. S. FITZGERALD, who encouraged him to publish, for the literary market, *How to Write Short Stories (With Samples)* (1924), unconnected pieces with burlesque critical trappings. Between 1926, when he was diagnosed as having tuberculosis, and his death, which was hastened by drink, he increased his involvement in the stage, without much success, and returned to journalism, for the money. See *The Best of Ring Lardner*, ed. David Lodge, new edn 1993; *The Ring Lardner Reader*, 1995.

LARKIN, PHILIP (1922–85) British poet and novelist, was born in Coventry and educated at King Henry VIII School and St John's College, Oxford. From 1955 until his death he was Librarian of the Brynmor Jones Library, Hull University. His first book of verse, *The North Ship* (1945), echoed AUDEN and YEATS, and it was not until *The Less Deceived* (1955) that a distinctive tone emerged, now that he had been encouraged by a study of HARDY to concentrate on projecting his own experiences and perception. In the meantime he had written two novels of youthful anguish, *Jill* (1946) and *A Girl in Winter* (1947). The appearance of his poems in CONQUEST's anthology, *New Lines*, suggested that he was a member, if not a leader, of the Movement, a group of writers who were offering a progressive but sardonic image, but Larkin's is a personal and private, not a public, voice. He is a poet of plain feeling and speaking, with shafts of humour. His technical control of rhyme, rhythm, metaphor, and adjectival phrases was painfully achieved by means of innumerable drafts: all come together in such poems as 'The Whitsun Weddings', 'Church Going', 'Toads', and 'Toads Revisited'. While the predominant themes in his last complete volume, *High Windows* (1974), are perhaps predictably the ebbing of life, disaster, and death, his mastery of form was as sure in 'The Old Fools' and 'The Building' as ever.

After the death of his mother in 1977 in her nineties, Larkin largely stopped writing poetry apart from occasional or protest verses; or else it was that he lost his expectancy of being able to write it. He was awarded the Queen's Gold Medal for Poetry in 1965. He edited *The Oxford Book of Twentieth-Century English Verse* (1973), and was jazz critic for the *Daily Telegraph* 1961–71. Essays are in *Required Writing: Miscellaneous Pieces 1955–1982* (1983). Controversy accompanied the publication of *Selected Letters of Philip Larkin 1940–1985*, ed. Anthony Thwaite (1992), Larkin ap-

parently having instructed that all unpublished writings should be destroyed; but there emerges a clear account of the making of a poet, alongside a portrait of a complex, retiring personality. He had avoided marriage; but for all his disclaimer, 'Sexual intercourse began / In nineteen sixty-three / (Which was rather late for me) . . .' ('Annus Mirabilis', 1967), it transpired that he had had a long-term relationship with one woman since his mid-twenties, and at 53 embarked also on affairs with a colleague and with his 'loaf-haired secretary'. See *Collected Poems*, ed. Anthony Thwaite, new edn 1993; Andrew Motion, *Philip Larkin: a Writer's Life*, new edn 1994 (biography); James Booth, *Philip Larkin: Writer*, 1992 (critical study); Andrew Swarbrick, *Out of Reach: the Poetry of Philip Larkin*, 1995.

LA ROCHEFOUCAULD, (MARILLAC, FRANÇOIS DE), DUC DE (1613–80) French prose writer, was born in Paris, and at 14 was married to the even younger Andrée de Vivonne (*d.* 1670), an heiress who bore him eight children but who otherwise played little part in his life. Soldier and courtier, he survived affairs, political intrigues, imprisonment, two years banishment to the family castle of Verteuil, and twice being wounded in action. He succeeded to the dukedom in 1650, but in 1653, having fought before Paris for the Prince de Condé (1621–86), whose sister had been his *grande passion*, he found himself financially ruined, and without Verteuil, which had been destroyed, or any prospect of a public career. He retired to the country and wrote his memoirs, which were first published abroad in an unauthorized edition in 1662. He returned to Paris in 1659, where he became a leading light of the literary salon of Mme de Sablé (1599–1678), and an intimate of LA FAYETTE and Mme de Sévigné (1626–96), the letter writer. His precisely worded 'Maxims', *Reflexions ou Sentences et Maximes Morales* (1665; tr. Leonard Tancock as *Maxims*, 1959), first published anonymously, went through five editions in his lifetime; the last comprised 504 aphorisms, to which later scholars have added 58 discovered among his papers and a further 79 which he had at various times withdrawn. There were several English editions during the 17th and 18th centuries, including BEHN's *Seneca Unmasqued, or Moral Reflections* (1685). CHESTERFIELD made great play of quoting La Rochefoucauld's maxims in letters to his son. See Richard G. Hodgson, *Falsehood Disguised: Unmasking the Truth in La Rochefoucauld*, 1995 (critical study).

LAURENCE, MARGARET (1926–87), née Wemyss, Canadian novelist and short-story writer, was born in Neepawa, Manitoba, the only child of a lawyer of Scottish descent. Two days after her fourth birthday, her mother died of a kidney infection, and after her father's death from pneumonia in 1935 she was brought up by her stepmother, who was also her mother's elder sister. Some of the situations in her childhood and adolescence are re-created in the 'semi-autobiographical' stories in *A Bird in the House* (1970). She attended the local high school, wrote her first story in 1940 (in which appeared 'Manawaka', the name she later used for her representative small prairie town), and had another printed that year in the *Winnipeg Free Press*. She then went to United College, Winnipeg, worked for a year as a reporter for the Winnipeg *Citizen*, and married Jack Laurence, a civil engineer, with whom she went to Somaliland in 1950 and the Gold Coast (shortly to be Ghana) in 1952. Her five years in Africa, during which she had two children, stimulated her literary creativity in several directions: short stories in which she explores, with uncanny understanding, attitudes to colonialism, independence, tradition, and the place of women, published together as *The Tomorrow-Tamer* (1963); a novel of the adjustment to independence, *This Side Jordan* (1960); an account of her East African experiences, *The Prophet's Camel Bell* (1963). She also found the interest which inspired her critical work, *Long Drums and Cannons: Nigerian Dramatists and Novelists 1952–1966* (1968)—the title is from OKIGBO.

In 1962, after she had drafted a second novel, the dichotomy between her vocation and her husband's caused their separation (they were divorced in 1969). She went with the children to England, where she settled in the village of Penn, Buckinghamshire, in a cottage rented from her London publisher. *The Stone Angel* (1964) became the first of four 'Manakawa' novels, which together cover the period from the Depression of the 1930s to the present, and examine small-town attitudes and the experiences of women who try to break away from the inhibitions of their environment. The death of Hagar in *The Stone Angel* at the age of 90 is the culmination of the cycle. *A Jest of God* (1966; reissued under its film title of *Rachel, Rachel*, 1968), is about the frustrations of a spinster schoolteacher, the disillusionment of whose married sister features in *The Fire-Dwellers* (1969). *The Diviners* (1974), which she called her 'spiritual autobiography', takes up the theme of dispossession, as a novelist searches for self-realization through two unconventional liaisons which reflect the experiences of the Métis and the 18th-century Scottish Highland immigrants. It won its author her second Governor General's Award, but for its outspokenness about sex was banned from use in schools, even with Grade 13 students, in Peterborough County, Ontario, where she had bought a house in Lakeford after her return to Canada in 1974. Regarded as Canada's finest novelist, she received honorary doctorates from ten Canadian universities, and was made Companion, Order of Canada, in 1977. She had just finished a preliminary draft of her memoirs when she was diagnosed as having terminal cancer. Before she died six months later, she managed to complete a further draft, which was edited by her daughter Jocelyn for publication as *Dance on the Earth: a Memoir* (1989). See George Woodcock (ed.), *A Place to Stand On: Essays by and about Margaret Laurence*, 1983.

LAVIN, MARY (1912–96) Irish novelist and short-story writer, was born of Irish parents in East Walpole, Massachusetts, where her father trained horses. In 1922 the family returned to Ireland, where she was educated at Loreto Convent, Dublin, and University College, Dublin. What sparked off her writing of fiction was a chance meeting with an elderly woman who remarked that she had recently had tea with VIRGINIA WOOLF. From this inspiration came her first volume of short stories, *Tales from Bective Bridge* (1942). Writing, and particularly the revelation of character through the short story, later became to her a 'passionate occupation', and the effectiveness of her control of this medium is enhanced by the way she selects and dramatically depicts the moment of truth when the protagonist becomes aware of the meaning or consequences inherent in a situation. 'The real short story is possibly an idea, buried deep in the writer's consciousness, which they, miraculously at times, see a chance of embodying in a story.' She also wrote two novels, *The House in Clewe Street* (1945), a study of lost adolescent innocence, and *Mary O'Grady* (1950), a family saga of the children of a Dublin suburb growing up into adulthood. She is an essentially Irish writer in that she has always remained in that country and her settings are exclusively Irish. She is in no particular Irish tradition, however, being rather one who wrote out of her personal feeling and perceptive experience, investing her characters with Irishness and making them all the more convincing for being so imbued. She married William Walsh in 1942; he died in 1954, leaving her with three young daughters to bring up. In 1969 she married Michael MacDonald Scott (*d.* 1990), a laicized Jesuit priest, and an authority on religious art, with whom she had fallen in love as a student, but had not seen since. See *The Stories of Mary Lavin*, 1987; Angeline A. Kelly, *Mary Lavin: Quiet Rebel—a Study of Her Short Stories*, new edn 1987.

LAWLER, RAY (*b.* 1921) Australian dramatist, was born in Footscray, Melbourne, the son of a labouring man who felt that each of his eight children should cultivate a sensible trade. Lawler left school at 13 to work in an engineering plant, but refused to sign as an apprentice. After ten years of factory work in the daytime, and acting lessons, amateur theatricals, and writing at night, he set up on his own, and in time became manager and producer of the Union Theatre, Melbourne University. Of his nine plays, only one, *Cradle of Thunder* (1949), had been produced when he was joint winner of a Playwrights Advisory Board prize. *Summer of the Seventeenth Doll* (1955, published 1957) was only staged, at his own theatre, after the Australian Elizabeth Theatre Trust had guaranteed the university against loss and appointed an independent producer. Reshaped, with Lawler in a leading role, it fulfilled the Australian need for an indigenous play of quality while also, in its unconventional situation, providing something peculiarly Australian. After touring Australia, it was put on in London in 1957, where it won the *Evening Standard* Award, and KENNETH TYNAN wrote: 'We have found ourselves a playwright, and it is time to rejoice.' American critics were less enthusiastic. After living abroad, and writing two further Australian plays, *The Piccadilly Bushman* (1959) and *The Man Who Shot the Albatross* (1972), Lawler returned to Australia in 1975 to work for the Melbourne Theatre Company, and wrote, within months, *Kid Stakes* (1975) and *Other Times* (1976), about the earlier lives of the characters in 'The Doll'. The three were first produced together in 1977 (published 1978; rev. edn 1985) as *The Doll Trilogy* in an all-day programme. He was awarded the OBE in 1980.

LAWLESS, HON. EMILY (1845–1913) Irish novelist and poet, was the eldest of eight children of the 3rd Baron Cloncurry, of Lyons House, Co. Kildare, who committed suicide when she was 14. She was educated at home, where the seeds were sown of her eccentricity and of her interest in science, which she put to good use by writing for natural history periodicals. She was an energetic sportswoman, to whom OLIPHANT, a close friend of her mother, constantly recommended 'a kind of benignant gentle dulness . . . as so good a relief from the intellectualism she loves'. After *A Chelsea Householder* (1882) and a second anonymous novel, she published under her own name *Hurrish* (1886), a sentimental but sensationalized and colourfully written novel of the violence which accompanied the recent Land League reforms in Ireland. She continued with Irish themes in *With Essex in Ireland* (1890), which was so convincing a representation of a 16th-century document that at first it was taken to be genuine, *Grania* (1892), a romantic Aran Islands' tale, and *Maelcho* (1894), in which a bard narrates the tale of the Desmond Rebellion (1579–82). Her ballads and lyrics, first published in volume form in *With the Wild Geese* (1902), are striking for their feeling for the harsh land of the west of Ireland and the people who tried,

many of them unsuccessfully, to earn a livelihood from it. Latterly she lived quietly in Surrey with a friend, having made the break from an Ireland for whose future she feared. See *The Poems of Emily Lawless*, ed. Padraic Fallon, 1965.

LAWRENCE, D(AVID) H(ERBERT) (1885–1930) British novelist, short-story writer, poet, travel writer, dramatist, and critic, was born in Eastwood, near Nottingham, the third son of a successful miner and of a former schoolteacher, who had higher aims for her often sick child than the colliery. At 13 he won a scholarship to Nottingham High School, where he spent three years, and after a spell as a clerk and then a pupil teacher, he went to Nottingham University College, qualifying as a teacher in 1908 and taking a post in Croydon. His first published work was a prize-winning story, printed anonymously in the *Nottingham Guardian* in 1907. Shortly afterwards his early poems were appearing in the *English Review*, whose Editor—FORD MADOX FORD—was especially encouraging about the manuscript of *The White Peacock*, on which he had been working for four years. After its publication in 1911, Lawrence gave up his job to concentrate on writing and to indulge his psychological and physical wanderlust. *The Trespasser* (1912) was followed by *Sons and Lovers* (1913), in which he re-creates the atmosphere and attitudes of the working-class home of his youth—an edition of 1992 (ed. Helen Baron and Carl Baron) has the cuts restored which were made by Edward Garnett (see GARNETT), Lawrence's friend and mentor, who edited it for the publisher. He extended his range with *Love Poems and Others* (1913), *The Widowing of Mrs Holroyd: a Drama* (1914, first performed 1920), and *The Prussian Officer, and Other Stories* (1914).

In 1914 he married Frieda Weekley (1879–1956), the German wife of his former university professor, with whom he had eloped two years earlier and who had three children—see Brenda Maddox, *The Married Man: a Life of D. H. Lawrence* (1994), in USA as *D. H. Lawrence: the Story of a Marriage*, and Rosie Jackson, *Frieda Lawrence* (1994), which includes Frieda's memoir *Not I, But the Wind* (1934) and other autobiographical writings. *The Rainbow* (1915) was successfully prosecuted for obscenity, as a result of which its successor, *Women in Love*, completed in 1916, was not published in Britain until 1921. This exacerbated his bitterness at the hounding the couple were getting for her German connections and for his opposition to World War I, in which he was unfit to serve. As soon as they could, they resumed their nomadic existence, fraught by continual financial worries, his chronic ill health, and a traumatic marital relationship. They went to places in Italy, reflected in *The Lost Girl* (1920) and *Aaron's Rod* (1922), and in the travel book, *Sea and Sardinia* (1921); to Ceylon; to Australia, where he wrote and set *Kangaroo* (1923), which shows a remarkable understanding of the country and people, considering that his stay was brief and his human contacts minimal; and Mexico, the setting of *The Plumed Serpent* (1926). He continued to write short stories, poems, and articles, even after terminal tuberculosis had been diagnosed. The couple next returned to Italy. Here he began to paint, only to have some of his pictures removed by the police from an exhibition in London. He also worked on three distinct versions of *Lady Chatterley's Lover*, which was privately printed in Italy in 1928, but not finally in full for public consumption until 1960, after a case for obscenity, brought by the Director of Public Prosecutions, failed at the Old Bailey. In 1930 his condition worsened, and he died in a clinic in Vence, in southern France. He was 44.

Lawrence's exceptional nervous energy, deep but circumscribed vision, powers of perception and description, and innate honesty of expression, were matched by his formidable all-round talent as a writer. In the preface to *Collected Poems* (1928) he wrote that 'many of the poems are so personal that, in their fragmentary fashion, they make up a biography of an emotional and inner life'. This is as true of the earlier poems about home and teaching as of the collection *Look! We Have Come Through!* (1917), which records his affair with Frieda and the early years of marriage. His disillusionment with humanity in the early 1920s is reflected in the attention given instead to the natural world in *Birds, Beasts and Flowers* (1923). To his short stories he applied a technique different from that of his novels, equally artistic (when he is at his best) and original, but more objective and less revealing of his own psyche. His novels, of which *Sons and Lovers*, *The Rainbow*, and *Women in Love* are justly praised, and *Lady Chatterley's Lover* often underestimated because it has been publicized for the wrong reasons, are about symbolic, intellectual, and environmental, as well as human, relationships. Some of his criticism is contained in *Selected Essays*, ed. Richard Aldington (1950), and his critical works include *Studies in Classic American Literature* (1923). See *Collected Stories*, introduction by Craig Raine, 1994; *Complete Poems*, ed. Vivian de Sola Pinto and F. Warren Roberts, new edn 1994; Keith Sagar, *Life of D. H. Lawrence*, new edn 1982; John Worthen, *D. H. Lawrence: the Early Years 1885–1912*, new edn 1992; Mark Kinkead-Weekes, *D. H. Lawrence: Triumph to Exile 1912–1922*, 1996; F. R. Leavis, *D. H. Lawrence: Novelist*, new edn 1994 (critical study); Graham Hough, *The Dark Sun: a Study of D. H.*

Lawrence, new edn 1983; John Worthen, *D. H. Lawrence*, 1991 (critical introduction).

LAWRENCE, T(HOMAS) E(D-WARD) (1885–1935) British soldier, prose writer, and translator, known as 'Lawrence of Arabia', was born in Tremadoc, Wales, the second of four illegitimate sons of a son of an Anglo-Irish landowning family and his Scottish housekeeper. The family moved to Oxford, and he went from Oxford High School to Jesus College, Oxford, where he wrote a thesis on the military architecture of crusader castles. In 1910 he went as an archaeologist to Syria, where he acquired the skills and contacts which enabled him during World War I, ostensibly as liaison officer with the rebel Arab forces, to organize them and lead them to victory against the Turks. In 1919 he was elected a Fellow of All Souls College, Oxford. In 1924 he resigned as an adviser on Arab affairs to the Colonial Office and retired into self-imposed obscurity in the ranks of the newly formed Royal Air Force, first as J. H. Ross and then as Aircraftsman T. E. Shaw, the name he took by deed poll in 1927. Having lost (on Reading station) the manuscript of his imaginative reconstruction of his Arabian exploits, he rewrote much of it from memory and published it in 1926 for private circulation as *The Seven Pillars of Wisdom: a Triumph*. (To ensure copyright in the USA, ten copies were printed in New York and offered for sale at a price which no one would want to pay.) He would not have it issued publicly during his lifetime, but agreed to a single printing only of an abridged version, *Revolt in the Desert* (1927). He also made a prose translation of HOMER's *Odyssey* (1932) and wrote an account of his RAF experiences, *The Mint*, first published in Britain in 1955. He left the service in February 1935 to live in the cottage he had bought nearby in Bovington, Dorset. On 13 May his powerful motorcycle left the road, and he died from his injuries. See *The Essential T. E. Lawrence*, ed. David Garnett, introduction by Malcolm Brown, new edn 1992; *Lawrence of Arabia, Strange Man of Letters: the Literary Criticism and Correspondence of T. E. Lawrence*, ed. Harold Orlans, 1993; Jeremy Wilson, *Lawrence of Arabia: the Authorised Biography of T. E. Lawrence*, new edn 1992; Paul Marriott and Yvonne Argent, *The Last Days of T. E. Lawrence: a Leaf in the Wind*, 1996.

LAWSON, HENRY (1867–1922) Australian short-story writer and poet, was born in a 'tent' in the Grenfell goldfields, New South Wales, the eldest child of Niels Larsen, a Norwegian ex-seaman, and his Australian wife, Louisa, née Albury. The boy, who was registered as Lawson, which then became the family name, began to go deaf at the age of nine. After some education at schools in Eurunderee and Mudgee, he helped his father on building work until 1883, when his parents separated and he went with his mother to Sydney. Here Louisa Lawson (1848–1920) established herself in radical and feminist circles, and as a journalist, editor, and poet—see Brian Matthews, *Louisa* (1987). Lawson worked as a carriage- and house-painter, studied for and twice failed university entrance, and in 1887 submitted a stirring poem, 'Song of the Republic', to the *Bulletin*, which printed it and other verses, including his first song, 'The Army of the Rear'. At this time, too, he wrote his early poems of social protest, 'The Watch on the Kerb', and 'Faces in the Street', which came to him on a station platform while seeing about a job. His first story, the poignant 'His Father's Mate', was published in the Christmas *Bulletin* 1888. On New Year's Eve, while painting a ceiling, he received a telegram from Mount Victoria saying that his father had died while building a row of cottages. He took the midnight train, and did what painting was still to be done on the cottages; then he went steerage to the town of Albany, Western Australia, to look for work. In 1892, after a few months on the Brisbane *Boomerang*, he was back in Sydney at the height of the Depression. He escaped by making a trip, sponsored by the *Bulletin*, into the bush, to Bourke, and then on foot to Hungerford and back. This provided copy for further stories and sketches, and also firsthand experience with which to turn his mock battle with PATERSON about the realistic and romantic schools of bush literature into a crusade, in the course of which he wrote several trenchant articles.

The quality of production of *Short Stories in Prose and Verse* (1894), published by his mother, led to bad blood between them: a better fate attended *While the Billy Boils* (stories) and *In the Days When the World Was Wide* (verse), both published by Angus and Robertson in 1896. In that year he married a nurse, Bertha Brendt (1876–1957), with whom he went to New Zealand in 1897 and, with their two children, to England in 1900. After their return to Sydney in 1903, they separated, and among Lawson's subsequent sojourns in jail for drunknnness were several for arrears of maintenance. That he survived for another twenty years was due to the charity of private and public figures. Though he continued sporadically, and when he did, profusely, to write verse (including new volumes in 1910, 1913, and 1915) and prose, his reputation rests on his earlier work, especially his short stories, for which he is rightly regarded as an innovator in technique and realism. He died in Abbotsford, New South Wales, and was the first Australian writer to have a state funeral. See *Henry Lawson: Collected Verse*, 3 vols 1967–69, *Short Stories and Sketches*, 1972, and *Autobiographical and Other Writings*, 1972, ed. Colin Roderick; Colin Roderick, *Henry Law-*

son: a Life, 1991; Brian Matthews, *The Receding Wave: Henry Lawson's Prose*, 1972 (critical study).

LAYAMON (*fl. c.*1200) poet, the son of Leovenath, was a priest at Arely Kings, Worcestershire, who decided that he would 'of Engle tha æthelæn tellen' [tell of the noble deeds of Englishmen]. He travelled widely to look for the best written sources, and found an English translation of BEDE's 'History', some books in Latin, and a copy of Wace's French *Brut* (see GEOFFREY OF MONMOUTH). Layamon's *Brut* is, at 16,000 lines, the longest English poem apart from SPENSER's *The Faerie Queen*, and Layamon is the first English poet to name himself clearly as the author of a work and to give some autobiographical details. He wrote in the Old English alliterative style, with the addition of assonance and rhyme, incorporating into his imaginative record (which is more about the British, who ended up in Wales, than the English, who pushed them there) the first references in English to King Lear and Cordelia, Cymbeline, King Coel, and Merlin (the Magician). He introduced into the King Arthur story the gifts he received when he was born, the description of his armour, the making of the Round Table, and the dream of Mordred's treachery. He is thus the English source of much of the Arthurian legend. See *Wace and Layamon: Arthurian Chronicles*, tr. Eugene Mason, introduction by Gwyn Jones, new edn 1962; *Layamon's Arthur: the Arthurian Section of Layamon's 'Brut'*, ed. and tr. W. R. J. Barron and S. C. Weinberg, new edn 1991.

LAYE, CAMARA (1928–80) Guinean novelist, was born in Karoussa, of a Malinke family of notable goldsmiths, and was educated at the technical college in Conakry. He then trained in France as an engineer, after which, while working by day as a mechanic in the Simca car factory, and continuing his education at evening classes, he relieved his sense of isolation from home by writing *L'Enfant Noir* (1953; tr. James Kirkup as *The African Child*, 1955), an imaginative re-creation of his childhood and youth, and the society in which he spent them, which is more autobiography than novel. *Le Regard du Roi* (1954; tr. Kirkup as *The Radiance of the King*, 1956) is a symbolic search for identification in an African setting. In 1956 he returned to Guinea, on whose independence he was appointed Director of Research and Studies at the Ministry of Information. *Dramouss* (1966; tr. Kirkup as *A Dream of Africa*, 1968) is a part-fictional, part-autobiographical continuation of *The African Child*, in which he exposed some of the nastier excesses of the current regime. Forced into exile in 1965, he settled in Senegal, where his research into Malinke oral tradition gave him the theme of *Le Maître de la Parole* (1978; tr. Kirkup as *The Guardian of* *the Word*, 1980). See Adele King, *The Writings of Camara Laye*, 1980.

LAYTON, IRVING (*b.* 1912) Canadian poet, was born Israel Lazarovitch in Neamtz, Romania, of Jewish parents, who brought him to Montreal when he was one. He was educated at Baron Byng High School and Macdonald College, where he studied agricultural science; after service in the Canadian Army he read economics at McGill University. He taught at Herziliah High School, Montreal, from 1945 to 1960, while also being a lecturer at the Jewish Public Library (1943–59) and at Sir George Williams University (1949–65). He was a professor of English literature at York University, Toronto, from 1970 to 1978. He was associated with the establishment in 1942 of the literary magazine *First Statement*, on whose editorial board he was before and after it became the *Northern Review* in 1945; it also published his first book of verse, *Here and Now* (1945). With DUDEK and SOUSTER he founded Contact Press in 1952. 'How to dominate reality? Love is one way; / imagination another' ('The Fertile Muck') is the keynote of much of his lyrical and reflective verse. Power by violent means and the outspoken expression of opposition to anything which, or anyone who, restricts the freedom of the artist are recurrent themes in many of his collections, of which *A Red Carpet for the Sun: Collected Poems* (1959) won the Governor General's Award, and *Fortunate Exile* (1987) particularly reflects his attitude to his Jewish background. *Waiting for the Messiah: a Memoir* (1986) is a literary autobiography of his early years. He was made Officer, Order of Canada, in 1976. Layton has been married five times, the last occasion in 1984. See *Fornalutx: Selected Poems 1928–1990*, 1992; Francis Mansbridge, *Irving Layton: God's Recording Angel*, 1995 (biographical study); Eli Mandel, *The Poetry of Irving Layton*, rev. edn 1981 (critical study).

LEACOCK, STEPHEN (1869–1944) Canadian humorist and prose writer, was born in England in the Isle of Wight, the third of 11 children of an asphalt contractor who, having tried to make a living as a farmer in southern Africa and Kansas, settled in Ontario, where his family, whom he later abandoned, joined him in 1876. Leacock was educated at Upper Canada College, where he then taught while studying modern languages at Toronto University. In 1899 he enrolled at Chicago University, where he obtained the degree of PhD in political economy in 1903. He was appointed to lecture in political science at McGill University, being William Dow Professor of Political Economy and Head of Department from 1908 until 'retired, much against my will, on grounds of senility, having passed the age of 65' in 1936. His first book was a textbook, *Elements of Political Science*

(1906; rev. edn 1921). In 1910 he privately printed, as *Literary Lapses: a Book of Sketches*, some of the humorous articles he had contributed over the years to North American journals, including the classic pieces 'My Financial Career' (on opening a bank account), 'Boarding House Geometry', and 'A, B, and C' (a skit on the conventional language of mathematical problems). It was seen by a publisher in Britain, who brought out an edition the same year. There followed *Nonsense Novels* (1911), the first of several volumes of literary parodies; *Sunshine Sketches of a Little Town* (1912), based on his observations of small-town life in Orillia, near which he had bought a country house on Lake Couchiching; *Arcadian Adventures with the Idle Rich* (1914), in which his sympathies are especially directed towards the victims of city materialists; and numerous other collections in which his innate kindliness often acts as a restraint on his satire.

Leacock recorded: 'I started giving public humorous lectures to help the Belgian refugees in [World War I], and went on after the war to help myself. My bread on the waters came back as cake. I lectured (1915–37) all over the United States from Kansas City to the sea, and through England and Scotland and in Canada from Halifax to Vancouver.' He never took money for himself when speaking in Canada, until his final tour in 1936, after which he wrote *My Discovery of the West: a Discussion of East and West in Canada* (1937), winner of the Governor General's Award for non-fiction. He also wrote historical and critical works, and studies of TWAIN (1932) and DICKENS (1933). See *The Bodley Head Leacock*, ed. J B Priestley, 1957; *Feast of Stephen: a Cornucopia of Delights*, new edn 1991; *The Boy I Left Behind Me*, 1946 (early autobiography); James Doyle, *Stephen Leacock: the Sage of Orillia*, 1994 (biographical/critical study).

LEAKEY, CAROLINE WOOLMER (1827–81) British novelist and poet, was born in Exeter, the sixth child of an artist. Though continuing illness restricted her education, she sailed for Hobart, Tasmania, in 1847 to help her sister there. Her health forced her to return in 1853, but not before she had written most of the poems in *Lyra Australia: or Attempts to Sing in a Strange Land* (1854), much of which is preoccupied with sickness and death and informed by her profound Christian spirit. She also absorbed the atmosphere of, and background to, the transportation of criminals to the colony, which she used in writing, as Olive Keese, *The Broad Arrow: Some Passages in the History of Maida Gwynnham, a Lifer* (1859). Published a decade before MARCUS CLARKE's *His Natural Life*, it is also the first Australian novel whose protagonist is a female convict.

LEAR, EDWARD (1812–88) British poet and painter, was born in Holloway, London, the 20th child of a stockbroker who went bankrupt in 1816. Asthmatic, depressive, and prone to epilepsy, he had to earn his living at 15, which he did by medical drawing. In 1831 he became a draughtsman for the Zoological Society, specializing particularly in birds, on which he published *Illustrations of the Family of the Psittacidae* (1832). He was then taken on as artist in residence at Knowsley Hall, near Liverpool, the home of Lord Stanley (1775–1851), who had established a menagerie there. For the children of the house Lear improvised comic verses, which, with his own line drawings, became *A Book of Nonsense* (1846), to all intents and purposes the birthplace of the limerick as we know it. From 1837 he lived mainly abroad, for his health, though he gave drawing lessons to Queen Victoria in 1845. He travelled widely, even as far as India, and produced sketch books and illustrated travel journals of Albania, Corsica, Greece, and Italy. He painted in both watercolour and oils, and exhibited at the Royal Academy in 1850. The romantic tone of *Nonsense Songs, Stories, Botany and Alphabets* (1871), in which were 'The Owl and the Pussy-Cat' and 'The Jumblies', gave way to musical melancholy in *Laughable Lyrics* (1877), especially 'The Dong with a Luminous Nose', 'The Courtship of the Yonghy-Bonghy-Bo', and 'The Pobble Who Has No Toes'. He died, unmarried, at his San Remo home. See *Complete Nonsense of Edward Lear*, ed. Holbrook Jackson, new edn 1993; *Selected Letters*, ed. Vivien Noakes, new edn 1990; Vivien Noakes, *Edward Lear 1812–1888*, 1988 (biography); Peter Levi, *Edward Lear: a Biography*, new edn 1996.

LEAVIS, F(RANK) R(AYMOND) (1895–1978) British critic, was born in Cambridge and educated at the Perse School, after which he served as a stretcher-bearer at the front in World War I. He read history and then English at Emmanuel College, Cambridge, where he wrote a thesis on the relationship between journalism and literature during the early development of the press in England. In 1929 he was appointed to a university probationary lectureship, which, with his fellowship at Emmanuel, was withdrawn in 1931. He was made Director of Studies in English at Downing College, and became a part-time university lecturer in 1936, a full-time lecturer in 1954, and was Reader in English 1959–62. His modest academic career was due to his prickly public exterior and his unfashionable (or prophetic) stance on such writers as HOPKINS, JOYCE, D. H. LAWRENCE, POUND, and T. S. ELIOT, and belies his influence as a critic and teacher. *New Bearings in English Poetry*, his first major publication, appeared in 1932, the year of the establishment

of the critical journal *Scrutiny*, of which he later wrote, 'my wife and I bore the major burden for two decades'—Q(ueenie) D. Leavis (1906–81), née Roth, author of *Fiction and the Reading Public* (1932) was one of his students, and together they wrote *Dickens the Novelist* (1970). Most of his subsequent critical works began with articles in *Scrutiny*, which they finally had to give up in 1953—see his *A Selection from Scrutiny* (2 vols 1968); they include *The Great Tradition* (1948) and *The Common Pursuit* (1952). In his Richmond lecture at Downing in 1962 he provocatively and publicly challenged SNOW's arguments about the two cultures. This single-minded man, whose professed aim was the 'pursuit of true judgment', was made CH in 1978. See *Valuation in Criticism and Other Essays*, ed. G. Singh, 1986; *Essays and Documents*, ed. Ian MacKillop and Richard Storer, 1995; Ian MacKillop, *F. R. Leavis: a Life in Criticism*, 1995 (biography); Michael Bell, *F. R. Leavis*, 1988 (biographical/critical study).

LE CARRÉ, JOHN, pseudonym of David Cornwell (*b*. 1931) British novelist, was born in Poole, Dorset. His mother left home when he was six; his roguish father, who has affinities with the father in *A Perfect Spy* (1986), was periodically in prison. At 16 he took himself away from Sherborne School and enrolled at Berne University, then did his National Service in the Intelligence Corps in Austria. He got a first in modern languages at Lincoln College, Oxford, and taught for two years at Eton, before joining the Foreign Service. From 1961 to 1964 he was Second Secretary at the British Embassy in Bonn, which features in *A Small Town in Germany* (1968). *Call for the Dead* (1961) and *A Murder of Quality* (1962) are more related to the thriller or the detective novel than to the spy story, but the enigmatic spy-master George Smiley appears in both. With *The Spy Who Came In from the Cold* (1963) and *The Looking-Glass War* (1965), he blew apart the murky environment in which the spy business operates. After an experimental novel, *The Naïve and Sentimental Lover* (1971), he gave Smiley a central role in a trio of novels spanning a complex, worldwide undertaking: *Tinker, Tailor, Soldier, Spy* (1974), *The Honourable Schoolboy* (1977), and *Smiley's People* (1980)—published together as *The Quest for Karla* (1982). The Arab/Israeli conflict is the theme of *The Little Drummer Girl* (1983). A retired Smiley is the linking thread of *The Secret Pilgrim* (1991). The rehabilitation of Eastern Europe resulted, with *The Night Manager* (1993), in a switch of attention to international skulduggery on the part of corporate millionaires in the West. In *Our Game* (1995), a fresh eastern-European element is explored in a tale of deception and several increments of bluff, involving spies who have served their time in the service. The use and future ownership of the gateway to world trade feature in *The Tailor of Panama* (1996). Le Carré's chilling sense of place, his characterization, dialogue, and attention to telling detail have added an artistic dimension to a modern genre which had reached its highest point with GRAHAM GREENE. In 1993 he succeeded in suppressing the outline of an unauthorized biography of himself. See Eric Homberger, *John Le Carré*, 1986 (critical study); Alan Bold, *The Quest for Le Carré*, 1988 (critical study).

LEDWIDGE, FRANCIS (1891–1917) Irish poet, was born in Slane, Co. Meath, the eighth child of an evicted tenant farmer who became a farm labourer. He was educated at the local school until he was 12. At 14 he was apprenticed to a Dublin grocer, whom he soon left to return home, where he worked in the fields, on the roads, in a copper mine, and then as a county council foreman. Happiest on the land and in contact with its creatures and flora, he had verses on such themes published in the *Drogheda Independent*. In 1912 he sent some to DUNSANY, who encouraged him, gave him the run of his library, introduced him to Dublin literary society, and selected and introduced *Songs of the Fields* (1915). In 1913, Ellie Vaughey, the landowner's daughter with whom Ledwidge was in love, broke off the relationship because of his family and financial circumstances, which deeply affected him and coloured his poetry. He took a post as a labour union official, organized the establishment of the local Irish Volunteers, and in 1914 enlisted in the Royal Inniskilling Fusiliers in World War I to fight 'an enemy common to our civilisation' and for 'the fields along the Boyne'. He served in the landings at Gallipoli and Salonika. This experience, added to the news of Ellie's death shortly after her marriage and to the shock of the fate of comrades and other poets in the Easter Rising of 1916, imbued his poetry with a sense of brooding and despair, but also with a heightened sense of his Irish national and literary heritage. His premonition of death was justified. He was killed outright near Ypres by a shell. See *The Complete Poems*, ed. Alice Curtayne, 4th edn 1974; *Selected Poems*, ed. Dermot Bolger, foreword by Seamus Heaney, 1992; Alice Curtayne, *Francis Ledwidge: a Life of the Poet*, 1972.

LEE, ANDREW see AUCHINCLOSS.

LEE, JOHN A(LEXANDER) (1891–1982) New Zealand novelist, was born in Dunedin of a Scottish father and a Romany mother. He was made a state ward in his teens, but escaped from industrial school and 'went on the swag', looking for casual labour, about which he later wrote two books of sketches and stories, *Shining with the Shiner* (1944) and *Shiner Slattery* (1964). During World War I he served as a sergeant with the New Zealand forces in France, winning the Distinguished Conduct Medal and losing an arm in combat. He was Labour Member of Parliament for Auckland East 1922–28, and for Grey Lynn 1931–43, being Under-Secretary to the Minister of Finance 1936–39, and Controller of the State Housing Department 1939–40. He was expelled from the party in 1940 after disputes over the leadership and monetary policy—see *Diaries 1936–1940* (1981). He subsequently went into business. His first novel, *Children of the Poor* (1934), narrated through the persona of Albany Porcello, begins, 'This is the story of how I became a thief . . . and the circumstances that made my sister a daughter of the streets.' Published anonymously, it created a sensation in both Labour and Conservative ranks when its authorship and autobiographical nature were revealed, and it had considerable impact overseas as a novel of social realism. A sequel, *The Hunted* (1936), is a better novel. An autobiography, *Delinquent Days* (1967), covers a similar period and similar circumstances in his own life.

LEE, LAURIE (1914–97) British poet and prose writer, was born in Stroud, Gloucestershire, and educated at Stroud Central School. His rural boyhood is sensuously recorded in *Cider with Rosie* (1959), Rosie being the girl of his innocent initiation into the potential excitements of sex. At 19, 'still soft at the edges', as he continues in *As I Walked Out One Summer Morning* (1969), he set out for London on foot, 'with a small rolled-up tent, a violin in a blanket, a change of clothes and a tin of treacle biscuits', going by way of Southampton, for he had never seen the sea. He played the violin in London streets, had a poem published, worked as a builder's labourer, was sacked, and decided to take a one-way ticket to Spain. He walked from Vigo to the Mediterranean, playing in cafés, came across and stayed with ROY CAMPBELL, and at the onset of the Civil War in 1936 was in Custillo, from which he was rescued by a British destroyer. He returned to Spain the following year, 'to make one grand gesture of personal sacrifice and faith', by fighting for the Republican cause. He describes the wintry horrors and skulduggery in *A Moment of War* (1991), the third part of his autobiographical trilogy—in one volume as *Red Sky at Sunrise* (1992). During World War II he was a film maker and scriptwriter, and he worked for the Ministry of Education from 1944 to 1946. The first of his modestly few books of verse, *The Sun My Monument*, was published in 1947, and is typical of his traditional and romantic, but not sentimental, poetic view. Many of the captions which adorned the Festival of Britain in 1950–51 were inspired and written by him.

He was made MBE in 1952. See *Selected Poems*, new edn 1985.

LEE, NATHANIEL (*c*.1649–92) English dramatist, the son of a clergyman, was educated at Westminster School and Trinity College, Cambridge, after which, having tried to earn a living on the stage, for which his nervousness made him unsuitable, he decided to write for it instead. *The Tragedy of Nero, Emperour of Rome* (1675) is the first of three tragedies in heroic couplets. It was dedicated to ROCHESTER, who was briefly his patron and whose death is mourned (in the character of Rosidore) in *The Princess of Cleve* (*c*.1681, published 1689), based on LA FAYETTE, a play which does not fit Lee's tragic-historical canon and may well have been written as some sort of protest. *Sophonisba: or, Hannibal's Overthrow* (1676) is said to have appealed particularly to the ladies, and three of his plays had dedications to royal mistresses. *Lucius Junius Brutus: Father of His Country* (1681), his best play, ran into censorship problems and was quickly taken off for its 'very scandalous expressions' of anti-monarchal feeling, notably in Brutus's great speech in Act V, with its hopes of a state 'Where there's no innovation of religion . . . / No desperate factions gaping for rebellion . . .'. He collaborated with DRYDEN on *Oedipus* (1679) and *The Duke of Guise* (1683). His dozen plays have flashes of brilliance, but many of the leading characters teeter on the verge of madness, into which he himself subsided in 1684. He was confined to Bedlam for several years, and on being discharged went back to the bottle. Returning home one night from an evening's drinking, he fell down in the snow and stifled. A collected edition of his works appeared in 1687.

LEE, WILLIAM see BURROUGHS.

LE FANU, (JOSEPH) SHERIDAN (1814–73) Irish novelist and short-story writer, was born in Dublin, the son of the Dean of Emly, whose mother was SHERIDAN's sister. A younger brother, William (1816–94), who became Commisssioner of Works, describes the young Le Fanu in *Seventy Years of Irish Life* (1893) as a practical joker and family poet. He was educated at home and at Trinity College, Dublin, where he contributed to the *Dublin University Magazine*, of which towards the end of his life he became proprietor and Editor (it was then no longer a university publication, but a leading European journal). He was called to the Bar in 1839, but preferred to become a newspaper baron, purchasing in turn the *Warder*, the *Evening Packet*, and the *Dublin Evening Mail*, which he amalgamated and made into the *Evening Mail*. His early political sympathies vacillated, but his devotion inspired two patriotic ballads, 'Shamus O'Brien' and 'Pauding Crohoore', written in about 1837. Local

politics and strife, with Gothic overtones, feature in his first novel, *The Cock and the Anchor, being a Chronicle of Old Dublin City* (1845). Then came another historical novel, followed by *Ghost Stories and Tales of Mystery* (1851), the initial workings of an ingenious mind. After the death of his wife in 1858 he withdrew from Dublin society (he became known as the 'Invisible Prince') but continued to write. To this period belong *The House by the Churchyard* (1863), a murder mystery, and *Uncle Silas: a Tale of Bartram-Haugh* (1864), to many the finest novel of psychological suspense, narrated by a girl who foresees her coming destruction at the hands of her guardian. *In a Glass Darkly* (1872) comprises five stories of uncanny evil. See Michael Begnal, *Joseph Sheridan Le Fanu*, 1971 (critical study); W. J. McCormack, *Sheridan Le Fanu and Victorian Ireland*, 1980.

LÉGER, MARIE-RENÉ-ALEXIS see SAINT-JEAN PERSE.

LE GUIN, URSULA (*b.* 1929), née Kroeber, American novelist and children's writer, was born in Berkeley, California, the youngest child of distinguished academics, and graduated from Radcliffe College in 1951. While crossing the Atlantic in the *Queen Mary* in 1953, en route to France to research her PhD thesis, she met Charles Le Guin, a historian, whom she married in Paris that same year. The thesis was never finished, and having had, and raised, three children, and written much, her career began modestly with *Rocannon's World* (1966), the first of a science fiction trilogy. Problems of genre affected the initial critical reception of *The Left Hand of Darkness* (1969), an exploration of an androgynous culture, and *The Dispossessed: an Ambiguous Utopia* (1974), in which time slips enable a scientist to compare an idealistic anarchist society with a capitalist/communist world, which were also classified as science fiction; and of *A Wizard of Earthsea* (1968), *The Tombs of Atuan* (1971), and *The Farthest Shore* (1972)—in UK also as *The Earthsea Trilogy* (1979)—which were originally published for children. *Malafrena* (1979) is a fantasy, and *Always Coming Home* (1985) experimental fiction, in which the reader is invited to participate in plot building from elements in a variety of literary forms. *Searoad: Chronicles of Klatsand* (1992) uses both horizontal present and vertical past narrative patterns to define a new feminine identity. *Four Ways to Forgiveness* (1996) comprises four linked novellas set in Hainish universe of *The Left Hand of Darkness*. Collections of short stories include *The Compass Rose* (1983), and of verse, *Hard Words and Other Poems* (1981). Critical essays, including studies relevant to her own writing, are in *The Language of the Night: Essays on Fantasy and Science Fiction*, ed. Susan Woods (1979) and *Dancing at the Edge of the*

World (1989). *Earthsea Revisioned* (1993) is a lecture, given in Oxford, about the ideas explored in *The Earthsea Trilogy* and a subsequent novel, *Tehanu: the Last Book of Earthsea* (1990), and expressing her views on the traditional relations between the sexes in heroic fantasy.

LEHMANN, JOHN (1907–87) British poet, prose writer, and editor, the brother of ROSAMOND LEHMANN, was born in Bourne End, Buckinghamshire, son by his American wife of Rudolph Chambers Lehmann MP (1856–1929), Editor of the *Daily News* and distinguished oarsman, whose mother, Nina, was a daughter of CHAMBERS and a close friend of WILKIE COLLINS. He was educated at Eton and Trinity College, Cambridge. He was a partner in the Hogarth Press (see LEONARD WOOLF) from 1946 to 1952, when he established his own publishing firm, John Lehmann Ltd. He established *New Writing* in 1936 and edited it and its offshoots until 1950, and he was founder-Editor of the *London Magazine* 1954–61. His first book of verse was *A Garden Revisited, and Other Poems* (1931). *Forty Poems* (1942) included two sections of poems relating to World War II. Subsequently he experimented with the 'prose poem'. His prose works include studies of the SITWELLS (1968) and BROOKE (1980). He was made CBE in 1964. See *Collected Poems 1930–1963*, 1963; *New and Selected Poems*, 1985; *In My Own Time: Memoirs of a Literary Life*, 1969—*The Whispering Gallery*, 1955, *I Am My Brother*, 1960, *The Ample Proposition*, 1966.

LEHMANN, ROSAMOND (1901–90) British novelist, the sister of JOHN LEHMANN, was born in Bourne End and educated privately and at Girton College, Cambridge, where she met her first husband. Her first novel, *Dusty Answer* (1927), partly set in Cambridge, charts a girl's sexual awakening and disillusionment. After a divorce in 1928, she married again, but that marriage also broke up, in 1940, after she had had two children and written three more novels. *Invitation to the Waltz* (1932) and its sequel, *The Weather in the Streets* (1936), follow a young woman's development from naivety to an adulterous affair and an abortion, while the man's wife embarks on a pregnancy. During World War II she wrote some fine short stories for her brother's *New Writing*, of which 'The Red-Haired Miss Daintreys', in *The Gipsy's Baby, and Other Stories* (1946), includes a statement on the creative impulse of her novels. The crisis in her own life after the break-up of her nine-year affair with C. DAY LEWIS is reflected in the harrowing treatment of the love triangle in *The Echoing Grove* (1953), which, in her own words, brought 'some cycle to a close'. She only wrote one more novel, *The Sea-Grape Tree* (1977), a sequel to the romantic *The Ballad and the Source* (1944). *The Swan in the Evening:*

Fragments of an Inner Life (1967), written after the sudden death in Java of her daughter a year after her marriage to P. J. KAVANAGH, describes her subsequent discovery of the spirit world—she became a vice president of the College of Psychic Studies. She is regarded as a woman's writer because of her insight into women's emotions and her ability to record their inner voices. She was made CBE in 1982. See Judy Simons, *Rosamond Lehmann*, 1992 (critical study).

LELAND, JOHN see HOLINSHED.

LENNOX, CHARLOTTE (1729/30–1804), née Ramsay, British novelist and dramatist, was probably born in Gibraltar, the daughter of an army officer who died while serving in New York province in about 1743, when she returned to England. In 1747 she published *Poems on Several Occasions* and married an improvident Scot, Alexander Lennox (*d. c.*1797), by whom she had a daughter in 1765 and a son in 1771. In 1749–50 she made several appearances on the stage. She also met JOHNSON, who gave an all-night party at the Devil Tavern to celebrate the completion of her first novel, *The Life of Harriot Stuart* (1751), part of which is set in America, where its romantic heroine is besieged by admirers and captured by Indians. *The Female Quixote* (1752) went into a second edition after four months. Partly a burlesque on French romances and partly a serious love story, it successfully combines the two genres. *Shakespear Illustrated: or, The Novels and Histories on Which the Plays Are Founded, Collected and Translated* (1753–54) is the first such compilation of literary sources. When her comedy, *The Sister*, based on her novel *Henrietta* (1758), was performed in 1769 (it was taken off after one night), GOLDSMITH was advised by an acquaintance to 'go and hiss it' because she had 'attacked' SHAKESPEARE in her book. *Old City Manners* (1775), based on *Eastward Hoe* (see JONSON), was more successful. In 1792 she received a pension from the Royal Literary Fund, but she died penniless, having spent her working life supporting her husband. Johnson, when he was 75 and she 55, announced after dining with BURNEY, HANNAH MORE, and the essayist and poet Elizabeth Carter (1717–1806): 'Three such women are not to be found: I know not where I could find a fourth, except Mrs Lennox, who is superior to them all.'

LEOPARDI, GIACOMO (1798–1837) Italian poet, was born in Recanati, the son of an impoverished count, in whose vast library he spent most of his youth, teaching himself Greek and studying literature and philology; he took to philosophy when in 1819 he had to spend a year without reading because of damage to his sight. He began publishing articles and translations in 1816, and verse (odes on Italy and on the monument to DANTE being erected in Florence) in 1818. *Versi* (1824) was published in Bologna, where he had gone after two years in Rome. He went on to Pisa and Florence, returning home in 1828 in shocking health. *I Canti* (1831) represents Italian lyric poetry at its most imaginative, affective, and musical: his pessimistic philosophical bent emerges in the prose *Operette Morali* [Moral Essays] (1827), which include ironic dialogues between mythical, historical, spiritual, and cosmological entities, and in 'Pensieri' [Thoughts]. In 1833 friends removed him to Naples; in a country retreat nearby he survived the cholera epidemic of 1836–37, but died of dropsy. See *A Leopardi Reader*, ed. and tr. Ottavio M. Casale, 1981; *Poems*, tr. Arturo Vivanti, 1988; *Selected Poems*, tr. Eamon Grennan, 1995; *The Canti: with a Selection of His Prose*, tr. J. G. Nichols, 1994.

LePan, Douglas (*b.* 1914) Canadian poet and novelist, was born in Toronto and educated there, and at University College, Toronto University, and Merton College, Oxford. He taught at Toronto University and Harvard until World War II, during which he served with the First Canadian Field Regiment in Italy. He then entered the Diplomatic Service, in which he held appointments in London and Washington, where he was Minister Counsellor. He was Secretary and Director of Research, Royal Commission on Canadian Economic Prospects 1955–58, and Assistant Under-Secretary of State for External Affairs 1958–59. He then returned to the academic world, being a professor of English at Queen's University, Ontario, from 1959 to 1964, and Principal, University College (1964–70) and University Professor (1970–79) at Toronto University. In three collections of verse, of which the first was *The Wounded Prince and Other Poems* (1948), and *The Net and the Sword* (1953) won the Governor General's Award, he has explored the Canadian experience in terms of the land, and has also, in his World War II poems, interpreted the feelings of those who fought on a front a whole ocean away from home—he marked the 50th anniversary of the end of the war with *Macalister, or Dying in the Dark* (1995), a verse drama on the life and the death in Buchenwald concentration camp of a college friend. *Far Voyages* (1990) comprises poems of love addressed to a young man. His novel, *The Deserter* (1964), which also won the Governor General's Award, is a study of an army deserter on the run searching for a meaningful existence in the immediate postwar world. *Bright Glass of Memory: a Set of Four Memoirs* (1979) is a literary account of aspects of his government service. See *Weathering It: Complete Poems 1948–1987*, 1987.

LERMONTOV, MIKHAIL (YURE-VICH) (1814–41) Russian novelist and poet,

was born in Moscow, lost his mother, who had married beneath her, when he was three, and was brought up by his maternal grandmother on the family estate of Tarkhany, Penza. After two years at school in Moscow and a further two at the university, he entered the Cavalry Training School at St Petersburg, and was commissioned in a regiment of hussars in 1834. He began writing verse when he was 14. His earlier published efforts reveal a strong influence of BYRON, some of whose personal traits are traceable to the same kind of irregular upbringing that Lermontov had. The official response to his angry poem protesting at the circumstances of the death of PUSHKIN in 1837 was to remove him from his regiment and dispatch him to serve in the Caucasus region. On his return in 1840, he was exiled again, to an infantry regiment, after being involved in a duel with the son of the French ambassador in St Petersburg. He returned on leave in 1841, hoping to be allowed to stay and devote himself to writing, but was ordered back to his regiment. Shortly afterwards he quarrelled with a fellow officer over a trivial insult and was challenged to a duel near Pyatigorsk. He was killed outright. [*A Hero of Our Time*] (1840; tr. 1854; tr. Vladimir and Dmitri Nabokov, 1958, reissued 1992), regarded as the first Russian psychological novel, builds up, by means of five linked first-person narratives, a portrait of the 'superfluous man', set apart by his talents but fated never to fulfil expectations. See also *Major Poetical Works*, tr. Anatoly Liberman (1984).

LESSING, DORIS (*b.* 1919), née Tayler, British novelist, short-story writer, and dramatist, was born in Kermanshah, Iran. Her father, who was a bank manager there for a while, had lost a leg in World War I; her mother had nursed him back to health. When Lessing was three, they moved, via Moscow and London, to Southern Rhodesia to seek a new life. For Mrs Tayler, 'I think her whole life came to an end when she landed on that farm and discovered what she was going to have to cope with.' A rebellious childhood culminated in her leaving the Girl's High School, Salisbury, at 14. She married a civil servant at 19, but left him and their two children three years later. In 1945, after a divorce, she married Gottfried Lessing, like her a Communist. They were divorced in 1949, when with her youngest child she went to London. The distinguished first volume of her autobiography, *Under My Skin* (1994), which won the James Tait Black Memorial Prize, finishes at this point.

Her first novel, *The Grass is Singing* (1950), is an extension of the experience of her rural African upbringing. She now embarked on the *bildungsroman* sequence of five novels, 'The Children of Violence', beginning with *Martha Quest* (1952). At the same time she was employing other themes derived from her early years in short stories—see *Collected African Stories* (1981). *The Golden Notebook* (1962) uses memories, experiences, and political activity in the search for identity of a 'free woman'. There followed three visionary novels, featuring psychological breakdown and the destruction of society, foreshadowing her science-fiction sequence 'Canopus in Argos: Archives'—five books from *Shikasta* (1979) to *The Sentimental Agents* (1983). In a reversion to realism and an attempt to subvert the reviewing system, Lessing then published, as Jane Somers, two novels featuring the plight of the elderly, *The Diary of a Good Neighbour* (1983) and *If the Old Could . . .* (1984). She reassumed her real name for two disturbing modern morality documents, *The Good Terrorist* (1985) and *The Fifth Child* (1988). *Love, Again* (1996), her first novel for eight years, is a love story within a love story, which has affinities with and contains meditations on aspects of its author's own life. *London Observed* (1992) is a collection of stories and sketches about her adopted city; *African Laughter* (1992), in USA as *The Real Thing*, is an account of returning to her roots. See *The Doris Lessing Reader*, 1989; Earl G. Ingersoll (ed.) *Putting the Questions Differently: Interviews with Doris Lessing 1964–1994*, 1996; Ruth Whittaker, *Doris Lessing*, 1988 (critical study); Elizabeth Maslen, *Doris Lessing*, 1994 (critical introduction).

LESSING, GOTTHOLD EPHRAIM (1729–81) German dramatist and critic, was born in Kamenz, the son of a pastor, and was educated at St Afra, Meissen, and Leipzig University, where he studied theology until his association with the local theatre, for which he wrote a play, led to family ructions and his switching to medicine. In 1748 he left Leipzig for Berlin, registering at Wittenberg University en route, and embarked on the life of a journalist and dramatist. His industry was such that after writing several comedies, of which *Die Juden* [The Jews] is significant for its attempt to combat anti-Semitism, he was able to spend a year in Wittenberg taking his degree and still publish six volumes of collected works in 1753–55. In addition to theatrical criticism, they included *Miss Sara Sampson* (performed 1755), a 'bourgeois tragedy' which was the first Continental play of its kind. He edited the drama journal, *Theatralische Bibliothek*, from 1754 to 1758, when he returned to Berlin after two years in Leipzig. In 1760 he disappeared, to surface in Breslau, where for five years he acted as secretary to the Prussian general in command, which gave him the leisure to read and to refresh himself socially and intellectually. One formative outcome was *Laokoon* (1766; tr. Edward Allen McCormick as *Laocoon: an Essay on the Limits of Painting and Poetry*, 1984), which GOETHE later described as 'transport-

ing us with a wrench from the region of a stilted perception into the broad, open fields of thought'. Another was *Minna von Barnhelm* (1767), regarded as the first modern German comedy, which became, in the form of James Johnstone's *The Disbanded Officer* (1786), the earliest German dramatic work to be adapted for the English stage. His employment as resident critic of the National Theatre in Hamburg (1767–68) lapsed because of the sensitivity of the actors, but produced, in *Hamburgische Dramaturgie* (1769), a vehicle for his projection of an indigenous drama. In 1770 he became court librarian in Brunswick. *Emilia Galotti* (1772; tr. Benjamin Thompson, 1800), a tragedy which is his most controversial play, has been interpreted as political protest, a psychological study of character, and a demonstration of social conflict. In 1776 he married the widow of a friend: she and their newborn child died a year later. Latterly he returned to theology in his writing.

LEVER, CHARLES (1806–72) Irish novelist, was born in Dublin, the son of an English architect, had a lively boyhood, and was educated at private schools (including Mr Wright's) and at Trinity College, Dublin, where he read medicine, continuing his studies in Gottingen. After accompanying an emigrant ship to Canada, he finally qualified in 1831, in time to be a Board of Health doctor during the cholera epidemic of 1832. Marriage did nothing to temper his lavish ways. In 1837 he began, anonymously in the *Dublin University Magazine*, a series of ebullient episodes of army life in Irish society as *The Confessions of Harry Lorrequer* (1839); he pursued a similar vein in *Charles O'Malley, the Irish Dragoon* (1841). In 1839 he set up practice in Brussels, where in 1841 he, LOVER, and the artist Hablot K. Browne (1815–82) drank 108 bottles of champagne between them in six days. He returned in 1842 to edit the *Dublin University Magazine*, and was attacked by nationalists for his apparent political affiliations, though in *Our Mess: Jack Hinton, the Guardsman* (1843) and other novels he criticized English rule. THACKERAY visited him in 1843, deplored his extravagance, and advised a move to London. Instead in 1845 he went to the Continent, where he spent the rest of his life, being made British Consul at Spezzia in 1857, and at Trieste in 1867, whose climate and society he detested. He had a talented literary imagination, but he wrote as he confessed he lived, 'from hand to mouth'. He wrote many novels, of which *A Day's Ride* (1863), so unsuccessful when serialized in *Household Words* that DICKENS took the unprecedented course of announcing when it would finish, features in G. B. SHAW's preface to *Major Barbara* as having made 'an enduring impression'. His last, *Lord Kilgobbin* (1872), written after the death of his wife, is regarded as a tragic masterpiece of Irish political and social despair.

LEVERSON, ADA (1862–1933), née Beddington, British novelist, was born in London of wealthy Jewish parents. She was well educated by tutors at home, and in 1881 married Ernest Leverson against her father's wishes. The marriage was not a success. She became friendly with BEERBOHM, GEORGE MOORE, and other literary figures. WILDE, whom she sheltered during his trial, called her 'The Sphinx', and she parodied him in a series of sketches in *Punch* in 1893. She wrote a regular women's column, as 'Elaine', in the *Sunday Referee* from 1903 to 1905. In 1905 financial problems caused her husband's flight to Canada. Left in reduced circumstances, she extended her literary range to the novel, of which she ultimately wrote six, all of them about marriages under stress. In the three featuring Bruce and Edith Ottley, *Love's Shadow* (1908), *Tenterhooks* (1912), and *Love at Second Sight* (1916)—published together as *The Little Ottleys* (1962)—Edith eventually achieves happiness when her awful husband walks out and goes to America. In *The Twelfth Hour* (1907) and *Bird of Paradise* (1914), the marriage is saved by the husband's realization of his love and responsibilities; in *The Limit* (1911) it is the wife who is brought back to her senses. Her books are amusing and well characterized, with excellent dialogue. See Violet Wyndham, *The Sphinx and Her Circle: a Biographical Sketch of Ada Leverson*, new edn 1988 (by her daughter); Julie Speedie, *Wonderful Sphinx: the Biography of Ada Leverson*, 1993.

LEVERTOV, DENISE (*b.* 1923) British-born American poet, was born in Ilford, Essex, descended on her father's side from the Russian Hasidic rabbi Shneur Zalman (1745–1813) and on her mother's from the Welsh mystic Angel Jones of Mold—see her poem 'Illustrious Ancestors' (1958). Her father, Paul Phillip Levertoff (1878–1954), having converted to Christianity while studying for the rabbinate, became an Anglican priest and wrote books in English, Russian, German, and Hebrew supporting the unification of Judaism and Christianity. She and her elder sister were educated at home by their mother, and by listening to BBC schools' broadcasts and to their parents reading aloud; she also had outside instruction in art, French, and music, and from the ages of 10 to 16 attended ballet school. The home was crammed with books, and European intellectuals were regular visitors. She published her first poem (in *Poetry Quarterly*) in 1940, and her first collection, *The Double Image*, in 1946. In between times she served as a nurse during World War II, and was then a tutor, nursemaid, and bookshop assistant on the Continent. In 1947 she married Mitchell Goodman, a 24-year-old Harvard student,

with whom she came to New York in 1948 and spent the years 1956–59 in Mexico (they were divorced in 1972). She became an American citizen in 1955. By the time her second volume, *Here and Now* (1956), had been published in the USA by FERLINGHETTI, she had discovered the poetry of W. C. WILLIAMS, and had begun the transition from 'a British Romantic with an almost Victorian background' to an American poet. Though she had no connection with Black Mountain College (see OLSON), she was a member of a group which included Black Mountain Poets such as CREELEY and DUNCAN. *With Eyes at the Back of Our Heads* (1960) contained poetic expressions of dissatisfaction with life in Mexico. In 1961 she published her fifth collection, *The Jacob's Ladder*, and was Poetry Editor of *The Nation*, a post to which she returned in 1963–65, by which time she was also teaching seminars and courses.

Levertov's active protests during the 1960s against US involvement in Vietnam are reflected in the political stance of several subsequent collections, though *The Sorrow Dance* (1967) also contained the 'Olga Poems' (first published in *Poetry*, 1965), a sequence in memory of her sister, who died in 1964 at the age of 49. In the same way, there are in *Life in the Forest* (1978) poems recording the final years of her mother, who had joined them in Mexico and stayed on after they left, dying 18 years later when she was over 90. Levertov was appointed a professor of English at Stanford University in 1982. A poet, then, with a private as well as a public voice, she evokes the family connections with mysticism in *Breathing the Water* (1987), which includes the sequence 'The Showings: Lady Julian of Norwich' (see also KEMPE), and a poem in the persona of CAEDMON. A more recent collection is *Sands of the Well* (1996). *Tesserae: Memories and Suppositions* (1996) comprises 27 poetic memoirs. Earlier verse is in *Collected Earlier Poems 1940–1960* (1979), *Poems 1960–1967* (1983), and *Poems 1968–1972* (1987). Essays on her own work are among those in *The Poet in the World* (1973) and *Light Up the Cave* (1981). See *Selected Poems*, 1986; *New and Selected Essays*, 1993; Harry Marten, *Understanding Denise Levertov*, 1989 (critical study).

LEVI, PETER (*b.* 1931) British poet, translator, and critic, was born of a Catholic family in Ruislip, Middlesex, the son and grandson of carpet importers. He was educated at Beaumont College from 1946 to 1948, when he left school and home to join the Society of Jesus. He later read classics and Byzantine and modern Greek at Campion Hall, Oxford. He was Lecturer in Classics at Campion Hall 1965–77, and at Christ Church 1979–82. In 1977, having resigned from the priesthood, he married CONNOLLY's widow. The poems in *The Gravel Ponds* (1960) are shot with striking visual images—'a holly tree dark and crimson', 'fox-coloured pheasant', 'yellow and green the ripening melons', 'black light streaming'. Classical and archaeological topics, Christianity, and nature particularly feature in subsequent collections, in which he is always conscious of the relationship between language and theme. Notable poetic sequences are *Pancakes for the Queen of Babylon: Ten Poems for Nikos Gatsos* (1968), 'Thirty Ways of Drowning in the Sea', and 'Rivers'. His translations include Pausanias, *Guide to Greece* (2 vols 1971), and George Pavlopoulos, *The Cellar* (1977). *The Life and Times of William Shakespeare* (1988) is an extensive and imaginative study; *Alfred Lord Tennyson* (1993), *Edward Lear* (1995), and *Eden Renewed: the Public and Private Life of John Milton* (1996) are critical biographies. *A Bottle in the Shade* (1996) is a Greek travel book flowing with zest, nostalgia, and literary allusions. The lectures he gave at Oxford, as Professor of Poetry 1984–1989, were published as *The Art of Poetry* (1991), which is useful also as an anthology of unusual items. See *Collected Poems 1955–1975*, 2nd rev. edn 1984.

LEVI, PRIMO (1919–87) Italian novelist, critic, and poet, was born in Turin of Jewish parents and was educated at the Liceo Massimo d'Azeglio and Turin University, where he graduated in chemistry. After two years of temporary work with firms prepared to ignore the regulations against Jews, he joined the Resistance, and was in 1943 betrayed to the Germans and transported to Auschwitz. He survived largely because of his scientific knowledge and qualifications, and at the end of the war returned to Turin, where from 1948 to 1974 he had a distinguished career as an industrial chemist. In *Se Questo e un Homo* (1947; tr. Stuart Woolf as *If This is a Man*, 1959), *La Tregua* (1958; tr. Woolf as *The Truce*, in USA as *The Reawakening*, 1965), and *I Sommersi e i Salvati* (1988; tr. Raymond Rosenthal as *The Drowned and the Saved*, 1988) he chronicled the experiences of Auschwitz with dignity and even flashes of humour, while exploring the mental predicament of those few, such as himself, who 'felt innocent, yes, but enrolled among the saved and therefore in permanent search of a justification in my own eyes and those of others. The worst survived—that is, the fittest; the best all died.' The structure and inspiration of the stories in *Il Sistema Periodico* (1975; tr. Rosenthal as *The Periodic Table*, 1984) derive from chemistry. *Se Non Ora, Quando?* (1982; tr. William Weaver as *If Not Now, When?*, 1986) is a celebration of the Jewish contribution to the Resistance in World War II and a contribution to the debate about Jewish passivity and consciousness. He committed suicide by falling down the stairwell of the apartment block in which he was born (and where he had lived for most of his life), unable, it is claimed, to suffer any longer the guilt of having survived the Holo-

caust. *The Sixth Day and Other Tales*, tr. Rosenthal (1990), is a collection of science-fantasy stories, some of them originally published as by Damiana Malabaila. See also *Collected Poems*, tr. Ruth Feldman and Brian Swann (2nd rev. edn 1992). See Mirna Cicione, *Primo Levi: Bridges of Knowledge*, 1995 (critical study).

LEWES, GEORGE HENRY see ELIOT, GEORGE; GOETHE.

LEWIS, ALUN (1915–44) Welsh poet and short-story writer, was born in Aberdare, the son of a schoolmaster, and went to Cowbridge Grammar School. At the age of 17 he won a scholarship to University College of Wales, Aberystwyth, where he got a first in history. In 1938, having undertaken a research studentship at Manchester University, the work for which bored him (see his story 'Attitude'), he qualified as a teacher. In 1940, with his conscription imminent, he volunteered on impulse for the Royal Engineers, and was moved about England for two years. Most of the stories in his collection, *The Last Inspection* (1942), illustrate what he called 'the rootless life of soldiers having no enemy', as does his best-known poem, 'All Day It has Rained . . .', which appeared in *Raider's Dawn and Other Poems* (1942). In 1941 he married—secretly, for his wife was a teacher and the rule, upheld by Lewis's father, now Director of Education for Aberdare, forbade married women to teach. In October he was commissioned in the South Wales Borderers and subsequently posted to India. Several poems record the trip, by troopship via Brazil, and his early reactions to the Orient. In February 1944 his unit was ordered out of reserve in Burma to fight the Japanese at Arakan. As Intelligence Officer, he could have remained, but he insisted on going into action. Before ground contact was made with the enemy, he was, according to the official history of his regiment, 'accidentally wounded by a pistol shot', and died at the casualty clearing station. See *Selected Poetry and Prose*, ed. Ian Hamilton, 1966 (includes biographical introduction); *Collected Poems*, ed. Cary Archard, 1994; *Collected Stories*, ed. Cary Archard, 1991; John Pikoulis, *Alun Lewis: a Life*, new edn 1991.

LEWIS, C. DAY, pen name of Cecil Day-Lewis (1904–72) Irish poet, critic, and novelist, was born in Ballintubber, the son of a Church of Ireland minister. The family moved to England in 1905. After the death of his mother in 1908, he was looked after by her sister (see his poem 'My Mother's Sister'), and educated at Sherborne School and Wadham College, Oxford. Here he mixed with left-wing poets (notably AUDEN, with whom he edited *Oxford Poetry* in 1927) and expressed left-wing views (he was briefly a member of the Communist Party), which coloured much of the verse he wrote between about 1928 and 1934. His first book, *Beechen Vigil* (1925), and its successor, *Country Comets* (1928), reveal no such leanings, while love lyrics to his wife included in *Transitional Poem* (1929) almost cost him his job at Cheltenham Junior School. *Overtures to Death* (1938) marks the second of several changes of direction; it reflects more general concerns (vividly presented in 'The Nabara') and the beginning of his frequent use of images from his childhood (as in 'Cornet Solo', 'The Gate', and 'Last Words'). *The Georgics of Virgil* (1940) is the first of his verse translations of the complete works of VIRGIL, and by the end of World War II he had become an eminent pillar of the Establishment. He delivered the Clark Lectures at Cambridge in 1946, published as *The Poetic Image* (1947), was Professor of Poetry at Oxford 1951–56, and was appointed Poet Laureate in 1968. In 1935 he published the first of an extensive series of detective novels under the pseudonym of Nicholas Blake. See *The Complete Poems of C. Day Lewis*, introduction by Jill Balcon, new edn 1996; *The Buried Day*, 1960 (autobiography); Sean Day-Lewis, *C. Day-Lewis: an English Literary Life*, new edn 1982 (biography).

LEWIS, C(LIVE) S(TAPLES) (1898–1963) British critic, popular theologian, novelist, and children's writer, was born in Belfast, the son of a court solicitor, and was educated at Malvern College, and privately, before winning a scholarship to University College, Oxford. He served in France in World War I, being wounded at Arras, and returned to Oxford in 1919, where he got a double first, in Greats and then in English. He was a Fellow of Magdalen College, Oxford, from 1925 to 1954, when he became Professor of Medieval and Renaissance Literature at Cambridge, to which he commuted weekly from the Oxford home he shared with his elder brother, the mother of a friend who had died in World War I, and, from 1957 until her death in 1960, his wife and her two sons. Lewis's ultimate acceptance of Christianity in 1931, or his examination of allegory, and sometimes both together, are reflected in almost everything he wrote. *The Pilgrim's Regress: an Allegorical Apology for Christianity, Reason and Romanticism* (1933) was followed by his classic work of literary criticism, *The Allegory of Love: a Study in Medieval Tradition* (1936). His Clark Lectures at Cambridge in 1944 were reworked into *English Literature in the Sixteenth Century* (1954). He published a trilogy of extra-terrestrial novels, beginning with *Out of the Silent Planet* (1938), reissued as *The Cosmic Trilogy* (1990), and a series of Christian apologiae, of which *The Problem of Pain* (1940) and *The Screwtape Letters* (1942) are still widely admired. His 'Narnia' sequence of seven novels, beginning with *The Lion, the Witch and the Wardrobe* (1950) and ending

with *The Last Battle* (1956), upholds his dictum that he was 'almost inclined to set it up as a canon that a children's story which is enjoyed only by children is a bad children's book'. See *Selected Literary Essays*, ed. Walter Hooper, new edn 1979; *Surprised by Joy: the Shape of My Early Life*, new edn 1995; *All My Road Before Me: the Diary of C. S. Lewis 1922–1927*, ed. Walter Hooper, new edn 1992; A. N. Wilson, *C. S. Lewis: a Biography*, new edn 1991; Walter Hooper, *C. S. Lewis: a Companion and Guide*, 1996.

LEWIS, NORMAN (b. 1918) British novelist, travel writer, and journalist, was brought up in Wales and in Middlesex, and was educated at Enfield Grammar School. He then worked in a variety of capacities, including cherry picker, wedding photographer, and racing motorcyclist, before getting married and embarking on his travels, starting with Spain. 'Travel came before writing,' he has explained, and his first book, *Sand and Sea in Arabia* (1938), was a volume of magnificent photographs. During World War II he served in the Intelligence Corps in the Mediterranean sector—see his war diary, *Naples 44* (1978). He published his first novel, *Samara*, in 1949; of subsequent novels, *The Day of the Fox* (1955), set against a background of the Spanish Civil War, *The Volcanoes Above Us* (1957), based on his personal experiences in Central America in revolt, and *The Sicilian Specialist* (1964), in which he revealed new facts about the Kennedy assassination, are highly regarded. His first two travel books proper, *A Dragon Apparent: Travels in Indo-China* (1951) and *Golden Earth: Travels in Burma* (1952), were written when these regions were out of reach of the ordinary traveller. A quartet of Asian books was completed with *A Goddess in Stone: Travels in India* (1991) and *An Empire of the East: Travels in Indonesia* (1993).

What he calls 'the great divide in my writings' followed his visit to Brazil in 1968, after which he wrote the article 'Genocide in Brazil'—reprinted in *A View of the World: Selected Journalism* (1986)—which led to a change in Brazilian law. After a further visit in 1979, he campaigned for the survival of the rain forests. *The Honoured Society: the Mafia Conspiracy Observed* (rev. edn 1984) is a study of the Sicilian Mafia. See *I Came, I Saw: 'An Autobiography'*, new, enlarged edn 1994 of *Jackdaw Cake*, 1985; *The World, the World*, 1996 (further memoirs).

LEWIS, (HARRY) SINCLAIR (1885–1951) American novelist, was born in Sauk Centre, Minnesota, the third son of a country doctor, and went to the local high schoool. At 13 he left home to enlist as a drummer boy in the Spanish-American War, but was hauled back from the railway station by his father. After six months at Oberlin Academy, Ohio, he entered Yale in 1903. He graduated in 1908, having contributed to the student journals, worked part time for local newspapers, gone on two summer vacation trips by cattle boat to England, and dropped out for a year, during which he was a janitor at UPTON SINCLAIR's colony in New Jersey until it burned down, lived in New York as a struggling writer, and went steerage to Panama to seek work on the canal. For two years he roamed the country, doing odd newspaper jobs (from two of which he was fired for incompetence) and conceiving ideas for plots, 14 of which he sold to LONDON for $5 each. He ended up in New York, having by 1911 published 66 articles, stories, and poems; after several jobs in publishing he became an editor with the George H. Doran Company. *Hike and the Aeroplane* (1912), written as Tom Graham, was a boys' story. His first novel, *Our Mr Wrenn* (1914), gently satirized the American in Europe. In 1915 he became a full-time writer, but he only emerged as a significant, and successful, novelist with his sixth, *Main Street* (1920), a much more devastating satire on life in a small Midwestern town. All his most accomplished works appeared in the 1920s. *Babbitt* (1922), an examination of a small-town businessman struggling to break out of his mould, was written in Europe; so was *Arrowsmith* (1925), a study of the conflicting ideals of a medical scientist, some of the research for which was conducted in the West Indies under the direction of Paul de Kruif (1890–1971), the bacteriologist and author of *The Microbe Hunters* (1926). In 1920 the trustees of the Pulitzer prizes overruled the selectors' choice of *Main Street* and gave the award to WHARTON's *Age of Innocence*, which was less critical of America. When *Arrowsmith* was awarded the prize, Lewis publicly refused it, out of spite and a desire for publicity as much as out of conviction. *Elmer Gantry* (1927), his funniest and also his wickedest novel, is an attack not so much on the Protestant ministry as on a society which allows a monstrous clergyman to flourish as an evangelist. *Dodsworth* (1929), whose theme is the loneliness of being at the top, marked a change towards a more sympathetic view of Midwestern manhood.

In 1930 he became the first American writer to win the Nobel Prize for Literature, 'for his powerful and vivid art of description and his ability to use wit and humour in the creation of original characters'. In a typically controversial acceptance speech, he named, as equally deserving of the award, ANDERSON, CABELL, CATHER, O'NEILL, and also DREISER, whom he had once publicly accused of plagiarism. Though he wrote ten more novels, of which *World So Wide* (1951) was published posthumously, only in *It Can't Happen Here* (1935), a warning about Fascism, and *Gideon Planish* (1943), an attack on professional philanthropism, in which Elmer Gantry makes a brief appearance, is there much

evidence of the earlier control of his satirical medium. See James M. Hutchisson, *The Rise of Sinclair Lewis 1920–1930*, 1996; Sheldon Norman Grebstein, *Sinclair Lewis*, 1962 (critical study); Martin Light, *The Quixotic Vision of Sinclair Lewis*, 1975 (critical study).

LEWIS, (PERCY) WYNDHAM (1882–1957) described himself in his autobiography, *Blasting and Bombardiering* (1937), as 'novelist, painter, sculptor, philosopher, draughtsman, critic, politician, journalist, pamphleteer, all rolled into one, like one of those portmanteau men of the Italian Renaissance'. Some deliberate confusion surrounds the circumstances of his birth. He was born in Amherst, Nova Scotia, the only child of Charles Edward Lewis (1843–1918), an American who had served with distinction in the Union Army in the Civil War, and Annie Stewart Preckett (1860–1920), the daughter of a boarding-house keeper in London, whom he had met there and married in 1876. The couple moved to Canada, where Charles became a travelling salesman. In 1888 they moved to the Isle of Wight, off the south coast of England; five years later Charles ran off with the family maid, and Annie went with the child to her mother in London, and became a laundress. She was able to send Lewis briefly to Rugby School, where he failed every subject but art, and then to the Slade School of Art, where he distinguished himself, but was expelled in 1901 for poor attendance and insubordination. After some years on the Continent, he emerged as a leader of the Vorticist artistic and literary movement, which flourished briefly between 1914 and 1920. He served at the front in World War I, latterly as an official war artist. After his first novel, *Tarr* (1918; rev. edn 1928), a revealing and stylistically startling portrait of Parisian bohemian life, he embarked on an ambitious but unfinished philosophical fantasy, of which *The Childermass* (1928) was published with two further parts in 1955–56 as *The Human Age*. His Fascist sympathies and unprovoked attacks on his literary contemporaries did not improve his public image, but he was regarded in his time as an experimental novelist of some stature—see also *The Apes of God* (1930), *The Revenge for Love* (1937), and *Self Condemned* (1954) and a writer of incisive if uneven criticism. See *The Essential Wyndham Lewis*, ed. Julian Symons, new edn 1991; *Creatures of Habit and Creatures of Change: Essays on Art, Literature and Society 1914–1956*, ed. Paul Edwards, 1989; Jeffrey Meyers, *The Enemy: a Biography of Wyndham Lewis*, 1980.

LILLO, GEORGE (1693–1739) British dramatist, was born in London, the son of a Dutch jeweller and his English wife. It has been suggested that a Nonconformist upbringing contributed to his comparatively late connection with the stage, for he had been for several years a partner in his father's business when he wrote *The London Merchant: or, The History of George Barnwell* (1731). Based on an Elizabethan ballad, it deliberately eschews 'Princes Distrest and scenes of royal Woe', and instead offers a tragedy of middle-class society, in which an apprentice is seduced by a scheming courtesan into committing murder and robbery. Critics (including POPE) praised it, audiences flocked to it, and for the next century apprentices were taken to see it as 'improving' entertainment, but it was left to Continental writers, such as GOTTHOLD LESSING with *Miss Sara Sampson* (1755) and DIDEROT with *Le Fils Naturel* (1757), consciously to follow his lead. His other success was *Fatal Curiosity*, a short three-act domestic tragedy, originally put on by HENRY FIELDING in 1736 as the other half of the bill to his own farce, *Tumble-Down Dick*. It was translated into several languages and ultimately became the inspiration for RUPERT BROOKE's *Lithuania*. Among other plays Lillo wrote an adaptation of the Elizabethan drama, *Arden of Feversham*.

LINDSAY, JACK (1900–90) Australian novelist, poet, critic, and translator, was born in Melbourne, the eldest child of NORMAN LINDSAY by his first marriage, and was educated at the Boys' Grammar School, Brisbane, and Brisbane University, where he got a first in classics. With SLESSOR he founded the short-lived but influential critical journal, *Vision*. In 1926 he emigrated to England, where he extended the activities of the Fanfrolico Press, a publisher and printer of finely-produced volumes which he had helped to establish in Sydney the previous year. From his first book of verse, *Fauns and Ladies* (1923), his first novel, *Cressida's First Lover: a Tale of Ancient Greece* (1931), his first critical work, on BLAKE (1927), and his first translation, *Lysistrata* of ARISTOPHANES (1925), he continued to be prolifically active in all these fields, as well as in history and biography. During World War II he served as a signalman in the British Army, and then spent two years, as a private, in the War Office, writing scripts for the army theatre unit. His three autobiographical studies, *Life Rarely Tells* (1958), *The Roaring Twenties: Literary Life in Sydney, New South Wales, in the Years 1921–1926* (1960), and *Fanfrolico and After* (1962), are vividly written personal, social, and cultural histories. Literary criticism is in *Decay and Renewal: Critical Essays on Twentieth Century Writing* (1976). He was made AM in 1981.

LINDSAY, NORMAN (1879–1969) Australian artist, novelist, and critic, was born in Creswick, Victoria, the fourth son of the ten children of an Irish doctor, and a younger brother of (Sir) Lionel Lindsay (1874–1961), the painter. He was educated at Creswick

Grammar School, which he left at 16 to go to Melbourne to assist Lionel, initially by ghosting topical drawings in a weekly paper. In 1901 he became a staff artist on the *Bulletin*, with which he was associated, as critic, reviewer, and contributor of stories, until shortly before his death. An early aversion to New Testament stories told by his mother led him eventually to the philosophy of NIETZSCHE, which is the starting point of his study, *Creative Effort: an Essay in the Imagination* (1920), and informs much of his fiction. His first novel, *A Curate in Bohemia* (1913), relives his time as an art student in Melbourne. *Redheap* (1930) and *The Cautious Amorist* (1932) were banned in Australia until 1958. Small-town society features strongly in *Saturdee* (1933), based on his boyhood recollections, and *The Cousin from Fiji* (1945), a comedy of the 1890s. His distinctive style and imagination, in his drawings as well as his prose, are seen at their most ebullient in *The Magic Pudding* (1918), a classic children's fantasy in which the humour of the situation and the verbal wit are precisely mixed. See *My Mask*, 1970 (personal reminiscences); John Hetherington, *Norman Lindsay: the Embattled Olympian*, 1973 (biography).

LINDSAY, ROBERT, OF PITSCOTTIE (c.1532–c.90) Scottish historian, was born on the family estate near Cupar, Fife. In 1553 he was granted an escheat on 'all the goods movable and immovable of the late Andrew Lindsay, burgess in Edinburgh'. The Pitscottie farmhouse in which he lived was rented from the Scotts of Balwerie. His *Historie and Cronikles of Scotland* is a continuation in time of BOECE, his first chapter being a translation of the last chapter of that work. It covers the years 1436 to 1575, when James Douglas (c.1525–81), 'Regent Morton', held sway and was trying to restore episcopacy to a land in which KNOX had until recently preached the principles of Presbyterianism. Lindsay was a staunch Protestant, and for this reason in particular, though his history was intended for publication, he expressed the wish that it should not be 'sprong as yit'. In the end it was not published until 1728. Kurt Wittig in *The Scottish Tradition in Literature* (1958) calls it 'the high water-mark' of Scottish prose up to that time. The style is racy, the eye journalistic, the direct speech convincing. Particularly memorable passages include the blowing up of James II by his own gun, the murder of James III's favourite, and the battle of Flodden. There are also some splendid oddities, such as the birth of a baby 'raknit to be ane man chyle bot from the waist upe was two fair, fair persouns witht all memberis and protratouris perteinand to twa bodyis'.

LINDSAY, (NICHOLAS) VACHEL (1879–1931) American poet, was born in

Springfield, Illinois, 'the Mystic Springfield in which I always live, wherever I happen to be . . . where one walks alone, from childhood, among historic structures, a place of clear visions'. Destined to be a missionary, he dropped out of Hiram College in 1901, studied art in Chicago and New York, and then took to missionizing for poetry. He tramped through the countryside, on one occasion from Springfield to New Mexico, declaiming his works, and bartering for food and lodging with copies of a leaflet, *Rhymes to be Traded for Bread*; 'A Gospel of Beauty' (1908) was the poem he most frequently recited. During the winters he campaigned for the Anti-Saloon League. The title piece of *General William Booth Enters into Heaven, and Other Poems* (1913), complete with instructions for varied musical accompaniment, was first published in *Poetry: a Magazine of New Verse*, and he now began to build up a readership. *The Congo, and Other Poems* (1914) included 'Abraham Lincolm Walks at Midnight', about his native Springfield. The title poem of *The Chinese Nightingale, and Other Poems* (1917) reflects a preoccupation with Orientalism extending also to a study of Egyptian hieroglyphics, with adaptations of which he decorated his *Collected Poems* (1923). He married in 1925, but with two children to support and his powers waning, he committed suicide by taking poison. See Edgar Lee Masters, *Vachel Lindsay: a Poet in America*, new edn 1969 (biographical/critical study).

LINKLATER, ERIC (1899–1974) Scottish novelist, was born in Penarth, south Wales, the son of a master mariner from Orkney, with which family connections were strongly maintained. He went to Aberdeen Grammar School. After being rejected by the Gordon Highlanders in World War I because of his eyesight, he contrived to join the Black Watch, with whom he served in France as a private, and was wounded in the head by a bullet. At Aberdeen University afterwards, he switched from medicine to English, and got a first. He was an assistant editor on the *Times of India* in Bombay, and then became assistant to the Professor of English at Aberdeen. On a two-year Commonwealth fellowship in the USA, he became a confirmed writer. *White Maa's Saga* (1929), his first novel, is set in Orkney. His third, *Juan in America* (1931), takes as its comic starting point the nocturnal encounter between Don Juan and the Duchess of Fitz-Fulke (see BYRON): a naive and accident-prone descendant of its unintended issue discovers modern USA. *Magnus Merriman* (1934) draws on, but does not mirror, Linklater's unsuccessful attempt to win a Parliamentary seat as a Nationalist.

In World War II he served as a major commanding the Royal Engineers in Orkney, and then in public relations in the War Office and

in Italy—*Private Angelo* (1946) reflects his understanding of the lot of the ordinary soldier and of the effect on the populace of invading and occupying forces. He returned to uniform in 1951, when he visited Korea with the rank of lieutenant colonel. In his later novels he continued to perform the very Scottish act of balancing satirical comedy, and often farce, with high drama and serious, sometimes funereal, matters, as in *Position at Noon* (1958) and *The Merry Muse* (1959), both of which delve also into literary history. Other works include some fine short stories—see *The Goose Girl and Other Stories*, ed. Andro Linklater (1991); historical and topographical works; plays, of which *Brakespear in Gascony* (1958) had some success; and two children's fantasies—the first, *The Wind on the Moon* (1944), won the coveted Carnegie Medal—whose appeal stems from the same instinctive feeling for the ridiculous which distinguishes his adult fiction. He was Rector of Aberdeen University 1945–48, Deputy Lieutenant of Ross and Cromarty 1968–73, and was made CBE in 1954. See *The Man on My Back*, 1941, *A Year of Space*, 1953, *Fanfare for a Tin Hat*, 1970 (autobiography); Michael Parnell, *Eric Linklater: a Critical Biography*, 1984.

LI PO (701–62) Chinese poet, was brought up in Ch'ang-ming, Szechwan, and wrote his earliest datable poem when he was 15; at about this time he fell in with a hermit, with whom he went to live in the mountains. After a period as a knight errant, he seems to have become merely a wanderer. In about 726 he married the granddaughter of a former chief minister, and lived with her family. After her death in about 735 he resumed his peripatetic existence, with a break in 742–44, when he was among the poets stationed at the Han-lin Academy in the capital, Ch'ang-an, to celebrate court activities and functions. In 742 he met the poet Tu Fu (712–70), whose admiration for him is recorded in more than a dozen poems. In 757 he joined the Yangtze fleet of Prince Lin, the 16th son of the Emperor, who had designs on the throne but was abandoned by his generals (and probably by Li Po), captured, and executed. Li Po was arrested and imprisoned, but released by a passing censor, who took him on his staff for a time. On the fall of the government commissioner who had formally approved his release, he was in 758 banished to Yeh-lang, Yunnam, for his association with Lin, but was freed the following year under a general amnesty. He was married four times in all, the last occasion in 756. A writer of considerable technical skill and innovative imagination, 'he appears', according to WALEY in *The Poetry and Career of Li Po* (1950), 'in his works as boastful, callous, dissipated, irresponsible and untruthful'. He was also a drunkard, who at a time of rampant bureaucracy seems never to have had a proper job. His poems survive through two collections, one by his literary executor and friend, Wei Hao, and one by the calligrapher Li Yang-ping, in whose house at Tang-t'u he died. See *The Selected Poems of Li Po*, tr. David Hinton, 1996; *Li Po and Tu Fu, Poems*, tr. Arthur Cooper, 1973.

LITHGOW, WILLIAM (1582–c.1654) Scottish traveller, prose writer, and poet, was born in Lanark, the son of a burgess of the town, and was educated at Lanark Grammar School. It is said that four brothers of a local girl he was courting set upon him and cut off his ears (as a result of which he acquired the nickname 'Lugless Will'), and that he went abroad to avoid further indignities. By the time he was 27 he had conducted a 'thorough survey' of Germany, Switzerland, and the Netherlands. In 1609 he set out from Paris on the first of three 'peregrinations', during which he covered by sea and on foot 36,000 miles, and visited Mediterranean and Adriatic lands and islands, the Middle East, and North Africa, including the Sahara. *The Totall Discourse, of the Rare Adventures, and painefull Peregrinations . . .* (1632) reveals him to be an eccentric and accident-prone traveller, who took with him a portable coffin, and who had a cool and practical nature, and an eye for the interesting, and bizarre, detail. His last call was Spain, where he was imprisoned as a suspected spy and tortured by the Inquisition. On his return to Britain he displayed his 'martyred anatomy' to 'all the court of England, even from the king to the kitchen', and was sent at the royal expense to recuperate in Bath. Failing to get his promised compensation from Spain, he assaulted (or by another account was assaulted by) the Spanish ambassador in the King's ante-chamber, and was imprisoned in the Marshalsea. He witnessed and wrote accounts of the sieges of Breda (1637) and Newcastle (1645), and described in *Present Survey of London and the English State* (1643) London's fortifications against the Royalist army at the beginning of the Civil War. An edition of his verse was published in 1863.

LIVESAY, DOROTHY (*b.* 1909) Canadian poet, was born in Winnipeg, the daughter of two journalists. She was educated at Glen Mawr, Toronto, Trinity College, Toronto University, and then for a year at the Sorbonne, Paris. She published her first book of poetry, *Green Pitcher* (1928), when she was 18, and her second, *Signpost*, in 1932; both demonstrated a command of imagist techniques, a lyrical bent, and a feminist outlook. In 1932 she returned to Toronto University to take a course in social work, which she practised in New Jersey and Vancouver between 1934 and 1939. She also joined, and worked for, the Communist Party. To this period belong poems of social and political protest ('In

Green Solariums', 'Montreal: 1933', 'Depression Suite'), and on the Spanish Civil War ('Catalonia', 'Words Before Battle'). In 1937 she married Duncan Macnair (*d.* 1959): they had two children. The political voice was still active in *Day and Night* (1944), which won the Governor General's Award, as did *Poems for People* (1947), in which the wartime efforts of the workers are celebrated ('West Coast: 1943', 'The Outrider') and sufferings are reflected upon ('In Time of War', 'London Revisited: 1946'). After the war she worked as a journalist and a documentary scriptwriter before teaching for two years in high school. She then became a Unesco English specialist in Paris, followed by three years in pre-independence Zambia, an experience which inspired the sequences 'The Second Language (Suite)' and 'Zambia'. Subsequently she was until 1983 writer-in-residence, associate professor, or visiting lecturer at Canadian universities.

In *The Unquiet Bed* (1967) and *Plainsongs* (1969), which marked a change to a more colloquial, less formal tone, she gives full expression to matters of female sexuality. *Collected Poems: The Two Seasons* (1972), chosen from poems written between 1926 and 1971, she calls 'a psychic if not a literal autobiography'. She continued the process with reflections on ageing in *Ice Age* (1975), *The Woman I Am* (1977), and *Feeling the World: New Poems* (1984). As concerned with the development of Canadian poetry as a whole as with her own, she founded in 1975 the journal *CV/II*, which she edited until 1977. *Beginnings* (1988), a fictionalized autobiography of her early years, is a revised edition of *A Winnipeg Childhood* (1973). She was made Officer, Order of Canada, in 1987. See Peter Stevens, *Dorothy Livesay: a Writer's Life*, 1992 (biographical/critical study); Paul Denham, *Dorothy Livesay and Her Works*, 1994; Lee Briscoe Thompson, *Dorothy Livesay*, 1987 (critical study).

LIVY (TITUS LIVIUS) (59 BC–AD 17) was born and died in Padua, lived most of his life in Rome, had two children, and knew the emperors Augustus and Claudius, the latter of whom he encouraged to write history. That is about all we know about this great writer and moderately good historian, whose reputation was such that it is said a Spaniard came all the way from Cadiz to Rome to look at him, and, having done so, went back home satisfied. His full history of Rome up to 9 BC comprised 142 books, of which we have 35, plus synopses of the rest. He is a popular historian in that he concentrates on narrative and character, paying particular attention to the speech he attributes to his protagonists. He drew on a wide range of sources and traditions without being very concerned about their accuracy, though he makes up for his vagueness about geographical and military detail with his sense of drama. See *The Early History of Rome: Books I–V*, tr. Aubrey de Sélincourt, new edn 1971; *Rome and Italy: Books VI–X*, tr. Betty Radice, 1982; *The War with Hannibal: Books XXI–XXX*. tr. Aubrey de Sélincourt, ed. Betty Radice, new edn 1972; *Rome and the Mediterranean: Books XXXI–XLV*, tr. Henry Bettenson, 1976.

LLEWELLYN, RICHARD, pen name of Richard Dafydd Vivian Llewellyn Lloyd (1906–83) Welsh novelist, was born in St David's, Pembrokeshire, the son of a hotelier, and was educated at schools in south Wales. At 16 he started to train for the hotel trade, first as a dishwasher at Claridge's in London, then in Italy. He served in the Army in India and Hong Kong between 1926 and 1931, when he returned to London and became a film critic for *Cinema Express*. He gained some studio experience, which helped him in writing a play, *Poison Pen*, performed in London in 1937. He also started a novel, the first few handwritten pages of which were shown by a portrait photographer of his acquaintance to Michael Joseph (1897–1958), who had just set up his own publishing firm. On the strength of these, the book was commissioned, an advance of £150 paid, and the author disappeared to write. Delivery dates went by, and nothing more was heard of him for two years, when he reappeared with a finished manuscript. *How Green Was My Valley* (1939), a first-person narrative of a Welsh mining community, written in a vibrant style whose rhythm and structures corresponded to the English spoken in Wales, was published a month after the declaration of war. It was immediately acclaimed and was subsequently translated into over twenty languages. During the war Llewellyn served in Italy as a captain in the Welsh Guards, and wrote *None But the Lonely Heart* (1943), a novel of London in the 1930s. After the war he enjoyed to the full the fame and the money that his first novel brought him, and travelled widely, using his imagination and the settings of the countries in which he stopped for a string of novels, none of which recaptured his original fervour.

LLOSA, MARIO VARGAS see VARGAS LLOSA.

LOCHHEAD, LIZ (*b.* 1947) Scottish poet and dramatist, was born in Motherwell, Lanarkshire, the daughter of a local government officer, and was educated at Dalziel High School, Motherwell, and Glasgow School of Art. She went on to teach art at Bishopbriggs High School. Her first book of verse, *Memo for Spring* (1972), celebrates the home and neighbourhood in which she grew up, and the city of Glasgow which she was now discovering. It includes the attractive 'Letter from New England', with its suggestions of irony, a form of statement which she later renounced in favour of greater directness and poems which 'tell a story'. She became a full-time writer after being in 1978 the first recipient of a Scottish/Canadian Writer's Fellowship. In *The Grimm Sisters* (1981) she uses oral tradition and folk and fairy tale material as a basis for an assertion of the feminine role. *Blood and Ice* (1982), her first play, is about MARY SHELLEY, and reflects the 'thrill of terror' which fascinates her. *Mary Queen of Scots Got Her Head Chopped Off* (1989) is a study in dramatic form of different kinds of ambivalence and conflict. She has translated MOLIÉRE's *Tartuffe* into modern Scots (1989), which she herself directed in Edinburgh in 1994. She wrote the version of the York Mystery Plays which was performed in 1996. She is herself a stage performer—*Bagpipe Muzak* (1991) includes recitations and characters. See *Dreaming Frankenstein, and Collected Poems*, new edn 1994.

LOCKE, JOHN (1632–1704) English philosopher, was born in Wrington, Somerset, the son of a land steward, and was educated at Westminster School and Christ Church, Oxford, where he was a life student until the privilege was withdrawn in 1684 on the orders of Charles II. He was attracted by the empiricism of BACON, and studied medicine, which he practised as physician to SHAFTESBURY, who introduced him to leading thinkers and politicians of the day, and gave him a post with the Board of Trade. For reasons of health or political expediency, Locke spent some of the years between 1675 and 1688 on the Continent, where he met philosophers and theologians. Back in England, and in favour, after the accession of William and Mary, he was appointed to several government posts, and ended his days in comfortable retirement. *An Essay Concerning Humane Understanding* (1690) works from a basic premise he had propounded twenty years earlier, which holds that a study of the nature of human understanding is a prerequisite of constructive thought and that knowledge derives from experience. It has become one of the most influential philosophical works in the English language. Other significant studies include *Two Treatises of Government* (1690); a series of 'Letters on Toleration' (1689, 1690, 1692); *Some Thoughts Concerning Education* (1693); and *The Reasonableness of Christianity* (1695), in which he advocates a reunion of the Catholic and Protestant churches. See *Locke on Human Understanding*, ed. I. C. Tipton, 1977 (selected essays); *Political Writings*, ed. David Wootton, 1993; Maurice Cranston, *John Locke*, new edn 1985 (biography); John Dunn, *Locke*, 1984 (introduction to his thought).

LOCKHART, JOHN GIBSON see HOGG; SCOTT, WALTER; WILSON, JOHN.

LODGE, DAVID (*b.* 1935) British novelist and critic, was born in an inner suburb of south London into a lower-middle-class Catholic family of mixed origins, and was educated at St Joseph's Academy, going on at 17 to London University, where he got a first in English. He wrote his first novel, *The Picturegoers* (1960), when he was 18, and his second, *Ginger, You're Barmy* (1962), about a reluctant National Serviceman who inadvertently betrays his best friend, while doing National Service in the Royal Armoured Corps. Afterwards he abandoned the idea of journalism for an academic career, teaching at Birmingham University from 1960, and becoming Professor of Modern Literature in 1976 (on his retirement in 1987 to write full time, he became Honorary Professor). With *The British Museum is Falling Down* (1965) he emerged as a comic novelist, parodist, and satirist. His dualistic vision is ingeniously and wittily expressed in *Changing Places: a Tale of Two Campuses* (1975), in which academic lives, and wives, are swapped and analysed. The same characters recur in *Small World: an Academic Romance* (1984), this time jet-hopping between conferences round the world, with the addition of a naive and out-of-place young Irishman hot in pursuit of the girl of his dreams. In *Nice Work* (1988), one world is academic, the other is industry, as two utterly opposed characters poignantly play out their mutual incomprehension. *Therapy* (1995) is long, for a comic novel, but its excursions into modern middle-age problems, particularly sex, are satisfyingly presented. His first play, *The Writing Game* (1991), echoes his experiences as tutor at residential writing courses. In a note to *Small World*, he refers to the tension between 'the real world' and 'figments of the imagination', which he has discussed in his critical works; these include *The Novelist at the Crossroads and Other Essays on Fiction and Criticism* (1971) and *Working with Structuralism: Essays and Reviews on Nineteenth and Twentieth-Century Literature* (1986). In *After Bakhtin: Essays on Fiction and Criticism* (1990), he discusses the work of the Russian critic and applies it to a wide and diverse range of novelists, with a summary of the current state of academic criticism. *The Art of Fiction* (1992), 'a book for people who prefer to take their Lit Crit in small doses', is based on newspaper articles. See *The Practice of Writing: Essays, Lectures, Reviews and a Diary*, 1997; Bernard Bergonzi, *David Lodge*, 1995 (critical introduction).

LODGE, THOMAS (*c.* 1558–1625) English prose writer and poet, was born in London, the second son of Sir Thomas Lodge (*d.* 1584), merchant, slave trader, and Lord Mayor of London, and was educated at Merchant Taylors' School and Trinity College, Oxford. He began to study for the law at Lincoln's Inn, but abandoned that for literature and Lon-

don literary life, which appears to have infuriated his family. His first work, a defence of poetry and plays (on which his circle largely depended for their living), was an answer to a pamphlet by Stephen Gosson (1554–1624). Probably called *Honest Excuses* and published in 1579, it was suppressed and reissued privately. After further pamphleteering, and service on board a ship voyaging to the Canary Islands in 1588, he published *Scilla's Metamorphosis* (1589), a variation on OVID, pleasantly told in verse, with some other poems, and then the prose fiction work for which he is best known, *Rosalynd: Euphues Golden Legacie* (1590). An elegantly written, well-plotted pastoral romance, interspersed with delicately humorous songs, it is the source of SHAKESPEARE's *As You Like It*. His wanderlust reasserted itself in 1591 when, leaving three lesser pieces of fiction for publication in his absence, he signed up with Sir Thomas Cavendish, at 30 already a veteran of one circumnavigation of the world, for what was presumably intended to be a repeat performance. The expedition only reached the Strait of Magellan (South America), and after suffering tremendous hardships returned in 1593 without its commander, who had died apparently of grief. If Lodge had been seeking at sea what had inspired *Rosalynd*, which had been 'wrought in the ocean when everie line was wet with a surge', he failed. The outcome was merely a collection of only intermittently memorable verses, *Phillis: Honoured with Pastorall Sonnets, Elegies and Amorous Delights* (1593), and a historical romance with some spectacular acts of violence, *A Margarite of America* (1596). *A Fig for Momus, Containing Satires, Eclogues and Epistles* came out in 1595; he also wrote two plays, one of them with ROBERT GREENE. He now had a new faith (Roman Catholicism) and a new career to look forward to, as a doctor of medicine, in which he qualified in Avignon in 1600 and at Oxford in 1602. He then practised in London, and published *A Treatise of the Plague* in 1603.

LOFTING, HUGH (1886–1947) British children's novelist, was born in Maidenhead, Berkshire, of Anglo-Irish parentage. He was educated at a Jesuit boarding school in Derbyshire, at the Massachusetts Institute of Technology, and at the London Polytechnic, after which he worked as a civil engineer in Canada, West Africa, and the West Indies. He married an American in 1912 and settled in New York, but enlisted in the British Army in 1917. While serving in Flanders, rather than send his children news of the front, which would have been censored, he wrote, and illustrated, stories for them inspired by the part that horses were playing in the combat and by the philosophical reflection that 'to develop a horse surgery as good as that of our Casualty Clearing Station would necessitate a knowledge of horse language'. So the unworldly, lovable Dr Dolittle, who *could* talk to animals, was born, and duly appeared in *The Story of Dr Dolittle* (1922) and subsequent tales. Much of the humour stems from the incongruity of animals behaving like humans, and there is satire enough for that essential appeal to adults as well. Lofting himself would have been mortified that his occasional lapse of taste has since been denounced as racism. He was returned from the front line in 1918 with serious wounds, and spent the rest of his life in the USA. After his wife's death in 1927, he married again, only for his wife to die the same year. By his third wife, Josephine Tricker of Toronto, whom he married in 1935, he had a son, for whom the final book in the canon, *Dr Dolittle and the Green Canary* (1951), was written. See Edward Blishen, *Hugh Lofting*, 1968 (critical study).

LOGUE, CHRISTOPHER (*b.* 1926) British poet, dramatist, and actor, was born in Portsmouth, as he explains in 'The Song of Autobiography': 'I came among you in a time of hunger, / Born at daybreak in a dockyard suburb'. He was educated at Portsmouth Grammar School, and served in the Army from 1944 to 1948. He was mainly in Paris until 1956, when he moved into a mews cottage in Notting Hill Gate, London. He began writing professionally when he was 22, and had a book of verse published in Paris in 1953. During the 1960s he and Adrian Mitchell (*b.* 1932) gained cult status with their protest poetry readings. *Songs* (1959), with its effective typographical variations, is still regarded as his best single collection, and contains two particularly impressive longer poems, 'The Story about the Road', a Third World cautionary tale, and his rendering of an extract from HOMER's *Iliad*. This last preoccupation had by 1981 developed into *War Music: an Account of Books 16 to 19 of Homer's Iliad*, which was augmented by *Kings* (1991, staged in 1992), a version of Books 1 and 2, and by *Husbands* (1994), Books 3 and 4. Done from translations, these have a vitality and immediacy which are often lacking from standard renderings. Logue has exercised his satirical bent in contributions to *Private Eye*—see *True Stories from 'Private Eye'* (1973) and other volumes he has edited. As Count Palmiro Vicarion he published a novel, *Lust* (1950), and a book of 'bawdy ballads' (1962) with the Olympia Press, Paris: in contrast to the compilation (under his own name) of *The Children's Book of Comic Verse* (1982), with a more staid publisher in London. See *Selected Poems*, ed. Christopher Reid, 1996.

LONDON, JACK [JOHN GRIFFITH] (1876–1916) American novelist, short-story and prose writer, was born in San Francisco. He was the illegitimate son of Flora Wellman, an itinerant music teacher and lecturer on spiritualism, and of William Henry Chaney, a travelling astrologer, who abandoned her when she was pregnant and, when traced by London in 1897, refused to acknowledge him as his son. Nine months after the birth, Flora married John London, whose surname he was given. A neglected child, he gave up school in 1891 to work in a cannery, and then, with a loan from his former black wet nurse, bought a sloop and became an oyster pirate. When forced out of business by rivals, he joined the Fish Patrol, and used his knowledge to hound them. At 17 he signed on as a seaman on a sealing expedition to the Bering Sea, and won the $25 first prize from the San Francisco *Morning Call* for an article, 'Story of a Typhoon off the Coast of Japan'. In a subsequent job he was exploited by an unprincipled electricity superintendent, and joined the army of tramps, recording in a diary notes he later used in *The Road* (1907), the first major work on the American hobo, for all that it glosses over the harsher realities. After being arrested for vagrancy while visiting Niagara Falls and serving 30 days in the Erie County, New York, Penitentiary, he beat it back home to California, and enrolled for a year at Oakland High School. In 1896, having imbibed on the side the philosophies of DARWIN, ADAM SMITH, SPENCER, NIETZSCHE, and KANT, as well as that of MARX, and been active in the Socialist Labor Party, he went to the University of California, from which he withdrew after one semester because the pace was too slow. He completed his education for authorship in the Yukon in the winter of 1896–97, during the Klondike goldrush, from which he returned with scurvy and a host of experiences.

In 1899 he sold his first story to *Overland Monthly*, and *Atlantic Monthly* sent him $120 for 'An Odyssey of the North'. A book of Alaskan stories, *The Son of the Wolf*, was published in 1900, when, already a veteran of two serious romances, he decided he needed a helpmate, and married Bessie Maddern, by whom he had two daughters. Called by some the 'Kipling of the Klondike' and by others the 'Bret Harte of the Yukon', he was now offered a retainer to write a novel, *A Daughter of the Snows* (1902), which failed. Not so *The People of the Abyss* (1903), a sociological study of the slums of London, to research which he descended into the worst parts of the East End in disguise; and *The Call of the Wild* (1903), which, with the antithetical *White Fang* (1906), explores anthropological issues in a naturalistic canine environment. When Bessie divorced him in 1905, he married the emancipated Charmian Kittredge, five years his senior, who was at the time his secretary. As President of the new Intercollegiate Socialist Society he lectured on the coming revolution throughout the East and Midwest, including Harvard and Yale. He bought a ranch near Glen Ellen, California, and began building his fabulous 45-foot yacht, the *Snark*. In

1907, with Charmian and her uncle as members of an incompetent crew, the unseaworthy craft lurched out of Oakfield harbour, on the first leg of a circumnavigation of the world which was to be for London a practical manifestation of a literary and personal philosophy which pitted man against the elements. As the boat limped westwards, he wrote the semi-autobiographical romance, *Martin Eden* (1908), the death of whose protagonist, by dropping overboard in mid-Pacific, reflected his own disillusionment at a time when he had to return home temporarily to sort out his tangled finances. He finally gave up the voyage in 1909, after succumbing to a multiplicity of tropical and other complaints in the Solomon Islands.

With the money he earned from tales of his adventures in the South Seas and from further novels, including *Burning Daylight* (1910), an idealized romance of a superman, he developed his Beauty Ranch and started building his dream mansion, Wolf House. For adventure, in 1911 he drove with Charmian and a manservant through northern California and Oregon in a four-in-hand. The conflagration that destroyed an almost finished Wolf House in 1913 was probably arson. *John Barleycorn* (1913), his guilt-ridden autobiographical treatise on the dangers of drink, reflected the state of his health as well as of his mind. Whether he died of uremia or by suicide, the body had simply given up. Undeniably a folk hero, he was also a social critic and philosopher, and a storyteller who delighted in uncluttered prose. See *The Portable Jack London*, ed. Earle Labor, 1994; *Novels and Social Writings* and *Novels and Stories*, ed. Donald Pizer, 1982; Andrew Sinclair, *Jack: a Biography of Jack London*, 1978; Earle Labor, *Jack London*, 1974 (critical study).

LONGFELLOW, HENRY WADSWORTH (1807–82) American poet and translator, was born in Portland, Maine, the second of eight children of a lawyer and legislator. 'My Lost Youth' (1855) idealistically reflects aspects of his childhood, during which, at 13, he had a poem printed in the *Portland Gazette*. He was educated at Portland Academy and Bowdoin College, into which he passed when he was 14. Unattracted to the traditional professions of law, medicine, or the ministry, he was trying to persuade his father to let him go on to Harvard and then to become a writer, when Bowdoin offered him a professorship of modern languages, provided he first study in Europe at his own expense. Fluent now in the Romance languages, he took up the post in 1829, and in 1831 married the daughter of a judge.

His first literary work, *Outre-Mer* (1835), published anonymously, is an account of his travels, patterned on IRVING's *The Sketch Book*. He returned to Europe in 1835 to strengthen his command of Germanic languages before becoming Smith Professor of Modern Languages and Belles Lettres at Harvard. His wife died in Rotterdam, after a miscarriage. *Hyperion*, an allegorical prose romance (with which he hoped to press his suit with a reluctant Fanny Appleton, ten years his junior), and his first book of verse, *Voices of the Night*, in which was 'A Psalm of Life', both appeared in 1839. *Ballads and Other Poems* (1841), which included 'The Wreck of the Hesperus', 'The Village Blacksmith', and 'Excelsior', consolidated his reputation. When Fanny finally married him in 1843, her father's gift to them was the historic mansion of Craigie House, Cambridge, Massachusetts. *The Poets and Poetry of Europe* (1845), an anthology of translations, many by himself, was significant in bringing the Old World to the New; so was *Evangeline: a Tale of Acadie* (1847), a North American epic in classical hexameters, in establishing him as a narrative poet.

For whatever reason, he resigned from Harvard in 1854, and pressed on with *The Song of Hiawatha* (1855), an Indian folk legend for which he chose the metre of the Finnish epic, *Kalevala*. Fanny died in 1861, as a result of a bizarre accident while she was sealing packages of her two small daughters' curls. Longfellow, who rushed to her rescue, was badly burned—'The Cross of Snow' (1879) was written later as a memorial to her. To take his mind off the tragedy, he immersed himself in his blank-verse translation of DANTE's *Divine Comedy* (1865–67). In 1868, accompanied by his daughters and other relatives, he visited Europe for the last time. In England he saw his old friend DICKENS, had breakfast with the Prime Minister, dined with the Prince of Wales, and was received at Windsor Castle by Queen Victoria. She commented afterwards: 'I noticed an unusual interest among the attendants and servants. . . . I have since enquired of them, and am surprised and pleased to find that many of his poems are familiar to them. . . . Such poets wear a crown that is imperishable.' Indeed, it has been estimated that, including pirated editions, more copies of Longfellow were sold in Victorian England than of any other living poet, even TENNYSON. He is the only non-British writer whose bust stands in Poets' Corner, Westminster Abbey. See *The Complete Poems*, 1993; *Selected Poems*, ed. Anthony Thwaite, new edn 1993; Arvin Newton, *Longfellow: His Life and Work*, 1962; Cecil B. Williams, *Henry Wadsworth Longfellow*, 1964 (biographical/critical study).

LONGSTREET, AUGUSTUS BALDWIN (1790–1870) American prose writer, lawyer, cleric, and educationist, was born in Augusta, Georgia, of parents of some substance who had migrated from New Jersey. He was educated at the Waddell School, Willington, South Carolina, and Yale, then studied at the law school run by judges Reeve and Gould in Litchfield, Connecticut, being admitted to the Georgia Bar in 1815. In 1817 he married Frances Eliza Peake (1799–1868), and after living with her family in Greensboro the couple bought a 600-acre farm nearby; of their eight children only two daughters reached adulthood. Elected as Greene County's representative to the State Assembly in 1821, and a judge of the Superior Court of Ocmulgee District (a circuit of seven counties) for 1822–25, he stood for Congress in 1824 but withdrew after the death of his mother-in-law and his four-year-old son within two days of each other. He and his wife joined the Methodist Church in 1827 and moved to Augusta, where he opened a law firm. In 1833 the weekly Milledgeville *Southern Recorder* published the first of his realistic, witty sketches of frontier life, *Georgia Scenes*, under the pseudonyms of Hall (a Georgian who had signed the Declaration of Independence) for stories centred on men and Baldwin for those mainly about women. The series continued in the weekly Augusta *States Rights Sentinel*, of which Longstreet was owner and editor 1834–36. There was a collection in volume form, *Georgia Scenes, Characters, Incidents &c., in the First Half Century of the Republic* (1835), 'By a Native Georgian'—a second edition (1840) published by Harper under Longstreet's name, with an introduction by him, further enhanced his national literary reputation. By now, however, he had largely lost interest in this kind of writing.

In 1839 he became a Methodist minister, and was immediately called upon to tend to, and nurse, victims of the yellow fever epidemic. The same year he was appointed President of the Methodist foundation Emory College. His pro-slavery pamphlet, *Letters on the Epistle of Paul to Philemon, or the Connection of Apostolic Christianity with Slavery* (1845), and the volume *A Voice from the South: Comprising Letters from Georgia to Massachusetts* (1847) circulated widely in the South. In 1848, believing he was about to be offered the post of President of the University of Mississippi, he resigned from Emory, only to be passed over. In haste he accepted the presidency of the undistinguished and unruly Centenary College, Louisiana, from which he soon resigned, having consoled himself by exposing the local community in a serialization of the first five chapters of his didactic novel *Master William Mitten: or, A Youth of Brilliant Talents Who Was Ruined by Bad Luck* (serially in full 1859, in volume form 1864). He was now appointed to the University of Mississippi, where he took charge of a disorderly body of students and increased the roll from 76 to 225 in five years. In 1856, to resolve a controversy over his political involvement and real estate speculations, he offered his resignation; it was refused and he was awarded the degree

of DD. Not fully satisfied, he resigned again; to his chagrin there was this time no objection.

Appointed to South Carolina College (now University of South Carolina) in 1857, he publicly encouraged secession from the Union, and in 1860 he withdrew from the International Statistical Conference in London after a speaker warmly acknowledged the presence of a Negro delegate from Canada. His pamphlet *Shall South Carolina Begin the War?* (1861) did not prevent his entire student body leaving to enlist. Now an old man, he retired with his family to Oxford, Georgia, shortly before his house in Oxford, Mississippi, was burned by the Yankees. In 1865 they returned to a cottage in Mississippi. *Stories with a Moral* (1912), edited by his nephew Fitz R. Longstreet, lacks the freshness and humour of *Georgia Scenes*, which stands as a literary monument to the benefits of nature, education, religion, and government. See Kimball King, *Augustus Baldwin Longstreet*, 1984 (biographical/critical study).

LORCA, FEDERICO GARCÍA see GARCÍA LORCA.

LORRIS, GUILLAUME DE (*c*.1212–*c*.1237) French poet, took his name from a village on the Loire above Orleans. He was a priest, who wrote the first 4058 lines of *Roman de la Rose*, an allegorical dream romance in which he set out to describe 'all the Art of love', to which MEUNG provided the continuation in a different vein. It is Lorris's contribution which had the greater effect on English, and Scottish, courtly love poetry, and on the early work of CHAUCER, who is the probable translator of the first part of *The Romaunt of the Rose*, taken from Lorris's portion of the poem. See *Roman de la Rose*, tr. Charles Dahlberg, new edn 1995; *The Romance of the Rose*, tr. and ed. Frances Horgan, 1994.

LOVELACE, EARL (*b*. 1935) Trinidadian novelist and dramatist, was born in Toco, and spent his childhood in Tobago and Port-of-Spain. His first job was as a proofreader with the Trinidad Publishing Company. Subsequently he was a government forestry and agricultural assistant. At the age of 23 he went to the USA to pursue his interest in literature, which, after further study, he taught at Johns Hopkins and other universities. He returned to Trinidad in 1982, joining the Trinidad Folk Theatre, and teaching creative writing at the University of the West Indies. In his first novel, *While Gods are Falling* (1966), the rural existence of Walter's childhood seems preferable to urban life. The contrast between 'being a man' in the village and being submerged in the competitiveness of the city is also reflected in *The Dragon Can't Dance* (1979); in *The Schoolmaster* (1968) and *The*

Wine of Astonishment (1982) the march of progress has eroded old values for those who are left behind in the village. Wider questions of national liberty and government in Trinidad are presented in *Salt* (1996), a panoramic novel which covers the period from 1806 to the present. Human predicaments, dramatic situations, and realistic representation of speech are features, too, of *Jestina's Calypso and Other Plays* (1984) and *A Brief Conversion and Other Stories* (1988).

LOVELACE, RICHARD (1618–57) English poet, was probably born in Holland, the eldest son of Sir William Lovelace of Woolwich, Kent, who was killed at the siege of Groll in 1627. He was educated at Charterhouse and Gloucester Hall, Oxford, where he was a member of the fashionable set. He served in the royalist army in the two inglorious expeditions into Scotland in 1639–40. He then retired to Kent, where he became a justice of the peace, in which capacity he presented to Parliament in 1642 a petition opposing its authoritarian practices. For this presumption he was imprisoned in the Gatehouse, where he wrote the song, 'To Althea, from Prison', with its lines 'Stone Walls doe not a Prison make, / Nor I'ron Bars a Cage'. He was freed on bail after two months, and spent some time in Holland, after penning 'To Lucasta, Going beyond the Seas'. He fought for the French at the siege of Dunkirk in 1646, but there is no evidence for the story that 'Lucasta', having heard a report of his death, married another. Now with the rank of colonel, he was in London in 1647, when he was made a freeman of the Painters' Company, a mark of his aesthetic tastes. In 1648, probably as a precaution, he was again committed to prison, from which he arranged the publication of *Lucasta: Epodes, Odes, Sonnets, Songs, &c.* (1649), containing his immortal lyric, 'To Lucasta, Going to the Warres'. Virtually nothing is known of him after that, but though he was forced to sell Lovelace Place, Bethersden, in 1649, it is unlikely that he died in such a state of poverty as AUBREY suggests. *Lucasta: Posthume Poems* (dated 1659), was edited by his brother, Dudley Posthumus Lovelace, who also published a collection of elegies on the poet (1660). See *Selected Poems*, ed. Gerald Hammond, 1987.

LOWELL, AMY (1874–1925) American poet and critic, a cousin of ROBERT LOWELL, was born in Brookline, Massachusetts, of an old New England family of intellectual distinction. She was brought up on the family estate of Sevenels (which she bought after her parents died when she was in her late twenties) and was educated at local and Boston private schools. Disinclined, and disadvantaged, when it came to marriage, she interested herself in civic affairs and charitable work, until in 1902, while watching a performance by the Italian actress, Eleonora Duse (1859–1924), she conceived her destiny as a poet and identified herself also with the development of the theatre. She published a conventional book of verse, *A Dome of Many-Colored Glass*, in 1912. Her attraction to the Imagist poets and her inclusion in POUND's anthology, *Des Imagistes* (1914), alongside DOOLITTLE and W. C. WILLIAMS, enthused her into appointing herself the leader and promoter of the movement in the USA. *Sword Blades and Poppy Seed* (1914) was significant for containing poems in what she called 'unrhymed cadence' (free verse) and polyphonic prose, and was the first of several collections of a similar nature, for which much inspiration was provided by her relationship with the actress Ada Dwyer (Mrs Harold Russell), who was 11 years her senior—*What's O'Clock* (1925) was posthumously awarded the Pulitzer Prize. She ultimately acknowledged her authorship of the anonymous *A Critical Fable* (1922), a mock-heroic on contemporary literary figures whose model was *A Fable for Critics* by her collateral ancestor J. R. LOWELL, but only after she had accused several others of having written it. Her critical works include *Six French Poets* (1915), *Tendencies in Modern American Poetry* (1917), and a monumental biography of KEATS (1925). See *The Complete Poetical Works*, ed. Louis Untermeyer, 1955; Richard Benvenuto, *Amy Lowell*, 1985 (critical study).

LOWELL, JAMES RUSSELL (1819–91) American poet and critic, was born on the estate of Elmwood in Cambridge, Massachusetts, of a distinguished New England family on his father's side, and of Orcadian descent on his mother's. He was educated locally at William Wells's school, and at 15 went to Harvard, from which, in spite of a scale of monetary incentives from his father for scholastic achievement, he was suspended for a time for absenteeism. After graduating in 1838, he studied law at Dane College, but did not practise. He was soon publishing poetry and prose in journals, including a series of essays on Jacobean drama in the *Boston Miscellany* (1842), as well as volumes of verse, *A Year's Life* (1841) and *Poems* (1844). With a local journalist he founded the *Pioneer*, whose three issues in 1843 contained contributions from E. B. BROWNING, HAWTHORNE, POE, and WHITTIER. Its demise, which personally cost him $1800, was due to genuine misfortune and to unprincipled demands by the publisher. In 1844, after a long engagement, he married Maria White (1821–53), a minor poet and humanitarian activist, under whose influence he contributed articles and poems to the *Anti-Slavery Standard*. Though he continued to publish poetry almost to the end, his reputation was made by, and subsists on, a cluster of works: *The Biglow Papers*, a topical and political lampoon in prose and verse, of which *First Series* appeared in 1848; *A Fable for Critics* (1848), a mock-heroic satire on literary contemporaries which he later claimed to have 'extemporized'; and *The Vision of Sir Launfal*, an Arthurian romance of the Holy Grail, published for the Christmas market in 1848. In 1856 he succeeded LONGFELLOW as Smith Professor of Modern Languages at Harvard, and he was the original Editor (1857–61) of *Atlantic Monthly*. After the deaths of three of his children in infancy, and then of Maria, he married in 1857 Frances Dunlap (*d.* 1885), sister of Maria's closest friend, who had come to look after his surviving daughter. He was US Minister to Spain (1877–80), and to Britain (1880–85), where he acquired a reputation for dining out, but for not much else. See Edward Wagenknecht, *J. R. Lowell: Portrait of a Many-Sided Man*, 1971; Claire McGlinchee, *James Russell Lowell*, 1967 (biographical/critical study).

LOWELL, ROBERT (1917–77) American poet, great-great-nephew of J. R. LOWELL and cousin of AMY LOWELL, was born in Boston. He was educated at St Mark's School, where he had a poet, Richard Eberhart (*b.* 1904), as a teacher, and was 'crushed' not to make the football team; and at Harvard, from which in 1937 he transferred to Kenyon College, where he studied poetry and classics under RANSOM. In 1940 he became a Catholic, and married Jean Stafford (1915–79), the novelist and short-story writer; they divorced in 1948, her 'An Influx of Poets' (1978) being a fictional account of their marriage. In 1943 he served five months of a sentence of a year and a day for refusing army service in World War II on the grounds of his objections to Allied policies. *Land of Unlikeness* (1944) was privately published. *Lord Weary's Castle* (1946), shot with vivid imagery, won the Pulitzer Prize. In 1949 he married Elizabeth Hardwick (*b.* 1916), the critic and novelist. They divorced in 1972; her fictional contribution to the Lowell legend is *Sleepless Nights* (1979). *The Mills of the Kavanaughs* (1951) he described ten years later as 'an obscure, rather Elizabethan, dramatic and melodramatic poem'. *Life Studies* (1959), new poems and a fragmented prose memoir, marked a change in style, and ushered in the confessional mode of poetry of the 1960s. The poems in *Notebook 1967–1968* (1969) were revised for *Notebook* (1970), and then revised again and rearranged into two volumes, *For Lizzie and Harriet* (1973), containing personal poems reflecting the break from his wife and daughter, and *History* (1973), on more general and political issues. *Dolphin* (1973), which won the Pulitzer Prize, is a sonnet sequence celebrating his love for his third wife, the British novelist Caroline Blackwood (Lady Caroline Hamilton-Temple Blackwood, 1931–96), by whom he had had a son in 1971. He died of a heart

attack in a New York taxi. A considerable poet, whose credo was 'revision is inspiration', and whose poetry reflects his ambivalent views towards his ancestry (which also led him to be a formidable but dignified public protester), the tangled, often tormented, nature of his private life, and his recurring manic condition, he was also concerned with integrating visual art into his work: 'Pray for the grace of accuracy / Vermeer gave to the sun's illumination / stealing like a tide across a map / to his girl solid with yearning' ('Epilogue', 1977). *Selected Poems* (1976; rev. edn 1977) is his own choice. See *Collected Prose*, new edn 1990; Ian Hamilton, *Robert Lowell: a Biography*, 1983; Paul Mariani, *The Lost Puritan: a Life of Robert Lowell*, new edn 1996; Steven Gould Axelrod and Helen Deese (eds), *Robert Lowell: Essays on the Poetry*, new edn 1989.

LOWRY, (CLARENCE) MALCOLM (1909–57) British novelist, was born in Birkenhead, Cheshire, the youngest of four children of a wealthy cotton broker and his wife, both staunch Methodists and teetotallers, who sent him away to boarding school in Hertfordshire when he was six, and then to the Leys School, Cambridge. After an eye illness he took to golf, at which he won the Junior Public [Independent] Schools Championship. He also played the ukelele, and composed poetry and jazz. Before going on to St Catherine's College, Cambridge, he persuaded his father to let him sign on as a deckhand in a freighter bound for the China coast—on the return voyage he had to cope with a consignment of seasick wild animals, bound for a zoo. The experience resurfaced in his novel, *Ultramarine* (1933; rev. edn, from his manuscripts, 1963), one of only two books he published in a career of intense industry but little tangible result. He also stayed in Massachusetts with AIKEN—see *Letters of Conrad Aiken and Malcolm Lowry*, ed. Cynthia Sugars (1994)—, who introduced him to Jan Gabrial, in the hope that 'she would take his mind off drinking too much'. They married in 1934 and divorced in 1940. In the meantime they travelled widely, and in Mexico he finished a draft of *Under the Volcano*, the seed of which was a short story of the same name, written in 1936.

In 1940 he married the 35-year-old American mystery writer and former Hollywood starlet, Margerie Bonner, with whom he went to live in a shack in Dollarton, British Columbia, Canada. Here he conceived a Dantesque novel sequence to be called 'The Voyage that Never Ends', of which *Under the Volcano* (1947) was one part. Others were to be the posthumously published *Lunar Caustic* (1968), *Dark as the Grave Wherein My Friend is Laid* (1968), and *October Ferry to Gabriola* (1970), all edited from his manuscript drafts; 'In Ballast to the White Sea' was irrevocably lost when fire destroyed the shack in 1945. The couple finally left Canada in 1954, and settled in Ripe, Sussex, where he died 'by misadventure' of an overdose of drugs and drink. *Under the Volcano*, a symbolic study of the self-destruction of an alcoholic, reflects also the breakdown of values in the 20th century through the parallel tragedy of Mexico. *Hear Us, O Lord, from Heaven Thy Dwelling Place* (1961), a sequence of seven stories which Lowry had prepared for publication, won the Governor General's Award. Poetry written between 1925 and his death is in *The Collected Poetry of Malcolm Lowry*, ed. Kathleen Scherf, with annotations by Chris Ackerley (1992). See Gordon Bowker, *Pursued by Furies: a Life of Malcolm Lowry*, 1995; W. H. New, *Malcolm Lowry*, 1971 (critical study); Ronald Binns, *Malcolm Lowry*, 1984 (critical study).

LU HSÜN (1881–1936) Chinese story writer and essayist, was born Chou Shu-jen in Shaoh-sing, Cheking, the eldest son of a cultured but impoverished family. After being at the Naval Academy, Nanking, he went on a government scholarship to Japan in 1904. There he studied medicine at Sendai until 1906, when he dropped out after seeing news slides of the ignominious decapitation of a countryman in the Russo-Japanese War; instead he chose literature as a way 'to meet the task of spiritual transformation' of China, to which he returned in 1909. After teaching middle-school biology in Hangchow and Shaohsing, in 1912 he accepted a counsellorship in the Ministry of Education of the new Republican administration, which from 1920 to 1926 he combined with lecturing in Chinese literature at the National Peking University. In 1918 he contributed to *New Youth* some poems and a story, ['The Diary of a Madman'] (regarded as the first Chinese Western-style piece of fiction), which, with further stories and critical essays and commentaries, put him in the forefront of the New Culture movement. His first volume of stories and other pieces, [The Outcry] (1923), contained ['The True Story of Ah Q'], a character study with tragic undertones, which began as the first episode of a comic serial, and has achieved international literary status. In 1927 he settled in Shanghai, where he became a reluctant literary pundit, unable to exorcise completely the ghosts of traditionalism. See *Silent China: Selected Writings*, ed. and tr. Gladys Yang, 1973; *Straw Sandals: Chinese Short Stories 1918–1933*, ed. Harold R. Isaacs, 1974.

LUCAN (MARCUS ANNAEUS LUCANUS) (39–65) Roman epic poet, was born in Corduba, Spain, and was educated in Rome. The emperor Nero engineered his political advancement, but then, jealous of his literary precocity, banned him from publishing any more verse. Lucan responded by joining Piso's conspiracy, on the discovery of which he was ordered to commit suicide. The plot was also used as an excuse to get rid of his uncle, SENECA. His only surviving poem, *Pharsalia* (tr. Susan H. Braund as *Civil War*, 1992), is an unfinished epic of the war between CAESAR and Pompey. Dazzling in its wit and epigrammatic style, it lacks the depth of poetic sensibility which he might have achieved in time.

LUCAS, E(DWARD) V(ERRALL) (1868–1938) British journalist, anthologist, and critic, was born in Eltham, Kent, of a Quaker family, which shortly afterwards moved to Brighton. After attending 11 schools, he was at 16 apprenticed to a local bookseller, whom he left after two years to join the staff of the *Sussex Daily News*. In 1892, with a gift of £200 from an uncle, he went to London, where he engaged in a personal study of literature and attended lectures by Professor W. P. Ker (1855–1923) at University College. The following year he became a staff writer for the *Globe*, a London evening paper. Subsequently he was a member of the editorial staff of *Punch*, to which over the years he contributed numerous pieces. He was appointed Chairman of the publishing firm of Methuen in 1924. A voluminous essayist, critic, and travel writer, his aim was to share with his readers the simple joy he took in literature, art, the countryside, romantic places, and cricket. He wrote several light novels, *Over Bemerton's* (1908), set in and above a bookshop, being the most highly regarded. He compiled many anthologies of verse and prose, of which *The Open Road* (1899) contains two of his own poems and some other rare items, and has an especial claim to dubious fame as one of the books cited by the tedious Mr Bast in FORSTER's *Howards End*. Lucas's *The Life of Charles Lamb* (2 vols, rev. edn 1910) is still the standard biography, and though his edition of the Lambs' letters (1935) has been superseded, his capably and copiously annotated *The Works of Charles and Mary Lamb* (6 vols 1912) has not. He was made CH in 1932. See *Reading, Writing and Remembering*, 1932 (reminiscences).

LUCAS, VICTORIA see PLATH.

LUCIE-SMITH, EDWARD (b. 1933) British poet and art critic, was born in Kingston, Jamaica (see 'A Tropical Childhood', 'The Polo Player', 'The Lime-Tree'), and was educated at a preparatory school in England (see 'The Lesson'), at King's School, Canterbury, and at Merton College, Oxford. His first book of verse, published in Oxford in 1954, was written 'in the wake of the Movement' (see CONQUEST). After National Service as an education officer in the Royal Air Force, he became a freelance journalist. *A Tropical Childhood and Other Poems* (1961) was published while he was associated with the Group, later the Writers' Workshop, an anthology of the work of whose members, *A Group Anthology* (1963), he edited with its founder, the poet and critic Philip Hobsbaum (*b.* 1932). As a result of the Group's discussion sessions he began to write longer poems; two dramatic monologues in the style of ROBERT BROWNING, 'Soliloquy in the Dark' and 'Caravaggio Dying', inspired and given extra depth by his understanding of the artist's craft, feature in *Confessions and Histories* (1964). He was a co-founder in 1965 of the specialist publisher, Turret Books, under whose imprint some of his subsequent work appeared. He published a novel, *The Dark Pageant*, in 1977. His studies of art include *Thinking about Art: Critical Essays* (1968), *Eroticism in Western Art* (1972), *Toulouse Lautrec* (rev. edn 1983), *Art in the Seventies* (1980), and *A History of Industrial Design* (1983). *American Realism* (1995) examines painting which reflects 'the ingrained American desire to confront reality directly'. Among his anthologies are *The Penguin Book of Elizabethan Verse* (1965), *The Penguin Book of Satirical Verse* (1967), and *British Poetry since 1945* (1970; rev. edn 1984). See *The Burnt Child: an Autobiography* (1975).

LUCRETIUS (TITUS LUCRETIUS CARUS) (*c.*99–55 BC) Roman philosophical poet, was a devotee of the Greek philosopher, Epicurus (341–270 BC), and dedicated his great poem to Gaius Memmius, a statesman who retired from public life after being impeached for bribery. Otherwise we know nothing about him personally except for the story that he was poisoned by an aphrodisiac, went mad, wrote poetry in his lucid spells, and committed suicide. That he was mad is unlikely: that his work ultimately proved too much for him is possible. *De Rerum Natura* [On the Nature of Things] is the first six books of an unfinished poem unique in Latin and with few equivalents in other literatures (the nearest in English is BRIDGES's *The Testament of Beauty*). It is a work of insight as well as of learning, in which, while subscribing to the Epicurean objection to spiritual gods and their images, Lucretius anticipates the kind of dilemma that modern biologists have had with regard to Christian theology. So he invests Venus with an overall creative power, before explaining the composition of matter and space in atomic terms, and going on to discuss the mind itself, feeling, sex, thought, cosmology, anthropology, meteorology, and geology. *De Rerum Natura* is thus not only a philosophical work, but also a scientific treatise written in the language of poetry. See *On the Nature of Things*, tr. Anthony M. Esolen, 1995.

LURIE, ALISON (*b.* 1926) American novelist, was born in Chicago and graduated from Radcliffe College in 1947. She married Jonathan Bishop in 1948 (divorced 1985). Her first novel, *Love and Friendship* (1962), suggested affinities with AUSTEN for its title, the name of the heroine (Emmy), the restricted canvas (university families), and its wit. In subsequent novels she has continued to investigate relationships in a variety of situations within and outside academia. *Real People* (1969) centres on a writers' colony; the course of *The War Between the Tates* (1974) has parallels with protests against the Vietnam War; in *Only Children* (1979) the adult world is viewed through childrens' eyes; *Foreign Affairs* (1985), which won the Pulitzer Prize, has as its protagonist a middle-aged writer of children's books concerned with her sexuality. *The Truth about Lorin Jones* (1988) is a sustained exploration of the mind (and ambivalence) of a biographer. *Women and Ghosts* (1994) is nine satirical or ironic stories whose structure is provided by a ghost. Lurie began teaching at Cornell University in 1968, and was in 1976 appointed Frederic J. Whiton Professor of English, her subjects including folklore and children's literature. Her critical study, *Don't Tell the Grown-Ups: Subversive Children's Literature* (1990) encourages readers to examine stereotypical works with new eyes.

LUTHER, MARTIN (1483–1546) German theologian, leader of the Reformation, was born in Eisleben. After taking his degree of MA at Erfurt University, he was ordained priest at the Augustinian monastery in Erfurt. In 1513, after becoming Doctor of Theology, he began lecturing at Wittenberg on Psalms, Romans, and Galatians; in 1517 he issued his 95 theses against the sale of indulgences. His three great reform tracts, to the Christian nobility of Germany, on the Babylonian captivity of the Church, and on the freedom of the Christian, appeared in 1520. Threatened with excommunication, he publicly burned canon law, and a copy of the papal bull. While under the protection of the Elector of Saxony at Wartburg, he translated the New Testament into German (1522). In 1525 he married Catherine (Kate) von Bora, a former nun. She had benefited from his plea for the release of young women of aristocratic birth who had been forced into convents by families who could not find suitable matches for them: they had six children. His complete Bible in German was published in 1534, and revised several times in his lifetime. From 1530 until his death he issued an average of twenty publications a year, and wrote numerous letters which survive. About forty songs and a

dozen tunes are all that can definitely be attributed to him as 'father of the German
hymn', a title which he also earned for his
encouragement of congregations to sing together in their native tongue, rather than simply to listen to the Latin of the choir.

LYDGATE, JOHN (c.1370–1449) English
poet, was born in Lydgate, Suffolk, and educated at the Benedictine Abbey of Bury St Edmunds where, according to his poem, 'The
Testament', he was an ill-behaved and inat-
tentive schoolboy. After being a novice, he
became a monk and was ordained priest in
1397. There is a gap in the record until 1415,
when he reappears at Bury, and for several
years after that he was Prior of Hatfield
Broadoak, Essex. He knew London well, and
spent some time in Paris in the 1420s. His significance as a poet depends not so much on
the quality of his writing, which is generally
mundane and muddled, but on its sheer volume. About 145,500 lines survive, evidence of
the influence of patronage on the poetic output of the time and the effect on the preservation of literature of the establishment of the
printing industry in England—before the end
of the 15th century works of his had been
printed by CAXTON, Richard Pynson (d. 1530),
and Wynkyn de Worde (d. c.1535). His major,
or longer, works, all adapted or translated
from the French, include *The Hystorye, Sege
and Dystruccyon of Troye* (known as 'The Troy
Book'), from Guido delle Colonne (d. 1316),
written between 1412 and 1421 at the command of Henry V when Prince of Wales; *The
Siege of Thebes*; *The Pilgrimage of the Life of
Man*, from Guillaume de Deguileville (fl.
1330–58), for the Earl of Salisbury; and *The
Falle of Princis*, done between 1431 and 1438
for the Duke of Gloucester from an enlarged
French version of the Italian of BOCCACCIO.
The best of his shorter poems, many of them
celebrating public or private occasions, can
be found among his religious lyrics. See
Poems, ed. John Norton-Smith, 1966.

LYLY, JOHN (1553/4–1606) English dramatist and prose writer, was born in the Kentish Weald, of an erudite family, and was educated probably at King's School,
Canterbury, and at Magdalen College, Oxford. The appellation 'university wit' has
been applied to him and several of his contemporaries. 'Wit' in this context means 'man
of wits', such as is the hero of Lyly's didactic
prose romance, *Euphues: the Anatomy of Wyt*
(1578), and its sequel, *Euphues and His England* (1580). From the name derives the term
'euphuism' for a style of writing that is orna-
mental but mannered and artistic, reflecting
the humanistic education of its exponents.
During the 1580s Lyly taught at St Paul's
choir school, which was in effect a theatrical
company providing revels for the court of
Elizabeth I in the form of performances by

boys. It is in this light that his eight comedies
must be seen, and his undoubted artifice
judged. They range from the multifarious entertainment of *A Moste Excellent Comedie of
Alexander, Campaspe and Diogenes* (1584), to
the elaborately and minutely constructed
Mother Bombie (1594), and *The Woman in the
Moone* (1597), which was probably intended
also for general audiences, and is the first example of blank verse being used successfully
as the medium of comedy. Lyly is the likely
author of a government-sponsored tract,
Pappe with an Hatchet (1589), supporting the
bishops in the face of a series of subterranean
satirical pamphlets. He was a Member of Parliament from 1597 to 1601. See John Dover
Wilson, *John Lyly*, new edn 1982.

LYNCH, PATRICIA (1898–1972) Irish
children's novelist, was born in Cork and educated at convent schools in Ireland, England, and Belgium. In *A Story Teller's Childhood* (1947), a slightly romanticized re-
creation of her early years, she describes her
relationship with Mrs Hennessy, one of the
genuine travelling storytellers, and the response it wrought in her. She moved with her
mother to England after her father's death,
but in 1916 she was back again in Ireland,
sent by the suffragette Sylvia Pankhurst
(1882–1960) to write about the Easter Rising.
She settled permanently in Dublin after her
marriage to Richard M. Fox, a journalist and
historian, in 1922. Of *The Turf-cutter's Donkey*
(1935), its sequels, and other books in the
same vein, Margery Fisher writes in *Intent
Upon Reading: a Critical Appraisal of Modern
Fiction for Children* (1961): 'To read [her] stories is to be in two worlds at once. . . . Inside
the humble cottage everything is peaceful
and secure, but, once outside, the enchantment is everywhere, sometimes dangerously
alluring, sometimes treated with humorous
disrespect.' Lynch uses legendary material
about Granuaile in *Orla of Burren* (1954), and
about Queen Maeve and Cuchulain in *Fiona
Leaps the Bonfire* (1957), and evokes the person
and times of SWIFT in *The Bookshop on the
Quay* (1956).

**LYNDSAY, (Sir) DAVID, OF THE
MOUNT** (1486–1555) Scottish poet and dramatist, was born on the family estate in Moni-
mail, Fife, and next appears in the records in
1511, when he performed in an interlude at
court, wearing a blue and yellow taffeta
'play-coit'. After the death of James IV at
Flodden in 1513, he became Keeper of the
Kingis Grace's Person. At the beginning of
the personal rule of the young James V in
1529, he was appointed a royal herald, and
undertook the first of several missions to
courts overseas. *The Dreme of Schir David Lyn-
desay* (1628), a political allegory, is addressed
to the King. So are 'An Exhortatioun to the
Kyngis Grace' to be wise, steadfast, and just,

and to eschew lechery, and 'The Complaynt', asking for a loan of 'ane thousand pound or tway' in gold. *The Testament and Complaynt of Our Soverane Lordis Papyngo* (1538) is marginally more subtle and much more fun, as James's pet parrot is made to discourse on topics which the poet feels should be brought to his master's attention. Lyndsay's most spectacular achievement, *Ane Pleasant Satyre of the Thrie Estaitis . . .*, the first great Scottish drama, was performed at Linlithgow Palace on Twelfth Night 1540; in spite of its daring political and ecclesiastical stance and devastating satire, it is reported to have found favour with the King. Certainly its dramatic impact and clever stagecraft made it a potent weapon of reform at the most critical time in Scottish history; it was restaged (in a strengthened form) in 1552, and again in 1554, before Mary of Guise, Queen Regent. In about 1542 Lyndsay was knighted and appointed Lyon King of Arms. He was anticlerical but not anti-reform, and is said to have encouraged KNOX to preach.

LYTTON, EDWARD GEORGE see BULWER-LYTTON.

M

MAC A'GHOBHAINN, IAIN see SMITH, IAIN CRICHTON.

MAC AN T-SAOIR, DONNCHADH BÀN see MACINTYRE.

MACAULAY, ROSE (1881–1958) British novelist and prose writer, was born in Rugby, the second of seven children (none of whom ever married) of a schoolmaster, and spent the years 1887–94 with her parents in Italy. She then went to Oxford High School and Somerville College, Oxford, where nerves prevented her from sitting her finals. She became a writer, living first at home and later in London. Her first novel, *Abbots Verney*, was published in 1906, but it was only with her ninth, *Potterism: a Tragi-Farcical Tract* (1920), a satire on the popular press, that she won public acclaim. *Orphan Island* (1924) revealed her touch for the bizarre situation. Her only historical novel, *They Were Defeated* (1932), is a study of the Civil War in which HERRICK features. In 1943 she spent three months in Portugal, from which she returned fired with enthusiasm. Her affectionate and vivid account of the British experience there over the centuries was published as *They Went to Portugal* (1946), cut by the publisher to half its original length—see *They Went to Portugal Too*, ed. L. C. Taylor (1990) for the rest. A further travel book in a similar bouncy style is *Fabled Shore: From the Pyrenees to Portugal* (1949). Her last novel, *The Towers of Trebizond* (1956), opens: " 'Take my camel, dear," said my aunt Dot, as she climbed down from this animal on her return from High Mass.' Brilliantly witty, it also reflects the private grief of her own 25-year affair with O'DONOVAN, which ended with his death in 1942 and prevented her from practising her strict High Anglicanism. She also published two volumes of verse (1914 and 1919), a biography of MILTON (1934), and a critical study of FORSTER (1938). She was made DBE in 1958. See Jane Emery, *Rose Macaulay: a Writer's Life*, 1991.

MACAULAY, THOMAS BABINGTON (1800–59) British historian, critic, poet, and statesman, was born in Rothley Temple, near Leicester, the eldest child of Zachary Macaulay (1768–1838), the Scottish-born abolitionist, and was brought up in the intellectual, activist atmosphere of London's Clapham Common. He was educated at Aspenden Hall, Hertfordshire, and Trinity College, Cambridge, where he won many prizes and was elected to a fellowship. He was called to the Bar in 1826, and became a celebrity through his critical and topical essays in the *Edinburgh Review*. He was elected to Parliament in 1830, but in 1834 money problems led to his accepting a seat on the Supreme Council of India. In four years there he drafted a new penal code which is the basis of Indian law, and exerted influence to make English the medium of instruction at all levels. He was in 1839 elected Member of Parliament for Edinburgh, which he remained, except for five years, until 1856—his defeat in 1847 is recalled in his poem 'Lines Written in August'. He was Secretary for War 1839–41. *The Lays of Ancient Rome* (1842), with their strong plots, resounding rhythms, and predictable rhymes, were instantly popular.

The first two volumes of *The History of England from the Accession of James II*, which he intended should go up to 1830, were published in 1849. He became ill in 1852, but managed to complete, and see published in 1855, two further volumes. The fifth, up to the death of William III in 1702, was published in 1861 after being finalized from his notes by his sister, who was to be the grandmother of the historian G. M. Trevelyan (1876–1962). Macaulay popularized history by force and pace of narrative, picturesque detail (culled from voluminous and energetic research), sparkling phraseology, and graphic characterization. Some of his portraits, though, are biased or feature contradictory attributes, and some events are distorted by selectivity of facts—he was a Whig politician as well as a historian. He could also be vindictive, as in his essay (1831) on BOSWELL's *The Life of Samuel Johnson*, for which he made partial amends with his article on JOHNSON for *Encyclopaedia Britannica* (1856). He was created Baron Macaulay of Rothley in 1857. He died, fully dressed, sitting in his armchair in the library of his house in Kensington, and was buried in Westminster Abbey. See *Selected Writings*, ed. John Clive and Thomas Pinney, 1972; *Selected Letters*, ed. Thomas Pinney, 1983; George Otto Trevelyan, *The Life and Let-*

ters of Lord Macaulay, new edn 1978; John Clive, *Macaulay: the Shaping of the Historian*, new edn 1987.

MCAULEY, JAMES (1917–76) Australian poet and critic, was born in Lakemba, New South Wales, and educated at Fort Street High School, Sydney, and Sydney University. During World War II he trained members of the New Guinea administration, and after it lectured at the Australian School of Pacific Administration until 1960. He was appointed Reader in Poetry at the University of Tasmania in 1961, subsequently being Professor of English until his death. A poet whose 'constant concern [is] the search for, and the struggle to express, an intuition of the True Form of Man', his first collection, *Under Aldebaran* (1946), illustrated his Australian roots as well as his preference for traditional forms. He had already publicly demonstrated his aversion to modernism by concocting, with his professional colleague and fellow poet Harold Stewart (*b.* 1916), during the course of an afternoon and, in part, from words extracted at random from a variety of standard reference books, a corpus of verse purported to be by 'Ern Malley'. This was accepted and printed by *Angry Penguins* (Autumn 1944), and had a deleterious effect on the development of avant-garde poetry in Australia as well as on the journal, on whose editor, Max Harris (1921-95), injury was added to insult when he was fined £5 for publishing indecent articles—see Michael Heyward, *The Ern Malley Affair* (1993). McAuley's *A Vision of Ceremony* (1956) included 'The Hero and the Hydra', a mythological sequence, and also reflected his conversion to Roman Catholicism. *Captain Quiros* (1964) is a narrative poem in which he develops his quest theme through the exploits of the Portuguese explorer in the southern hemisphere, Pedro Fernandez de Quiros (1563–1614). His critical works include *The Personal Element in Australian Poetry* (1970) and *A Map of Australian Verse: the Twentieth Century* (1975). He was made AM in 1975. See *Collected Poems*, new edn 1994; *Time Given: Poems 1970–1974*, 1976; *The Grammar of the Real: Selected Prose 1959–1974*, 1975; Peter Coleman, *The Heart of James McAuley: the Life and Work of the Australian Poet*, 1980; Lyn McCredden, *James McAuley*, 1992 (critical study).

MCBAIN, ED see HUNTER.

MACBETH, GEORGE (1932–92) Scottish poet and novelist, was born in Shotts, Lanarkshire, the son of an engineer-draughtsman, and moved with his parents to Yorkshire when he was four, though he returned to Scotland for holidays—see *My Scotland: Fragments of a State of Mind* (1973) for reflections on his Scottish upbringing, *A Child of War* (1987) for an account of his first 19 years, and his poem 'The Drawer' for a memory of his

parents' deaths. He was educated at King Edward VII School, Sheffield, and New College, Oxford, where he got a first in Greats. He joined the BBC as a trainee ('I thought if they employed Louis MacNeice they must be interested in poetry') and subsequently became producer/presenter of 'Poetry Now' and 'Poetry Proms', which had a listening audience of 250,000. *A Form of Words* (1954) and *The Broken Places* (1963) contained poems which are violent, but there is nothing insensitive in his continued presentation of horrific images, as he illustrated in *The Garden Cleaver* (1986), a complete sequence of 28 poems of four rhyming triplets on the themes of cruelty, pain, and death, in many forms and circumstances, including blood sports. This post-1970s more formal phase succeeded one in which he experimented with various avant-garde techniques, and with concrete poetry and amusing 'game-poems'. He also wrote some admirable poems about animals, and verses for children as well as about childhood. His first novel was *The Transformation* (1975), and his departure from the BBC in 1976 was partly to enable him to pursue a career as a novelist. *Dizzy's Woman* (1986) is in the form of 24 love letters from the young DISRAELI to Lady Londonderry. *Another Love Story* (1991) is an unashamedly autobiographical account of the breakdown of his brief second marriage, to the novelist Lisa St Aubin de Terán (*b.* 1953), about which he also wrote a series of poems, *Anatomy of a Divorce* (1988). *The Testament of Spencer* (1992), his final, posthumously-published novel, is a modern love story whose elements parallel SPENSER's situation in Ireland exactly 400 years before. *The Patient* (1992) contains poems, poignant but spiritually optimistic, written in the months before his death from motor neurone disease. See *Collected Poems 1958–1970*, 1989.

MACCAIG, NORMAN (1910–96) Scottish poet, was born in Edinburgh and educated at the High School of Edinburgh and Edinburgh University, where he read classics. His father, who owned a drugstore, was from Dumfriesshire and his mother came to Edinburgh from the Outer Hebrides when she was 16, speaking only Gaelic and hardly able to write. According to MacCaig, it was a holiday in his mother's native Scalpay when he was 12 that inspired in him a sense of family and collective history and an acute awareness of sights and sounds (see especially his poems 'Drifter' and 'Return to Scalpay'). Some of his early poetry was published in anthologies of the New Apocalypse (see TREECE), and his first two volumes of verse, which he himself has disregarded, are sometimes held to have followed that trend. *Riding Lights* (1955) heralds the work of the poet he had then become. That and succeeding collections—with a shift of emphasis to free verse in *Surroundings* (1966)—reveal his vivid attention to ordinary things and creatures (his nature poetry embraces pigeons, ducks, frogs, goats, and sheep), and to ordinary activities, such as walking, fishing, playing skittles, and hospital visiting, all expressed with precise language and straightforward images. He is as assured when writing about experiences in Assisi and Manhattan as he is when evoking the essential spirit of northwestern Scotland. His poetry is always accessible, and enjoyable to read even when inflected with sadness. He became a schoolteacher in Edinburgh in 1932. As a conscientious objector during World War II he served 90 days in prison. He retired as a primary school assistant head in 1970, and was Reader in Poetry at Stirling University from 1972 to 1979, in which year he was made OBE. See *Collected Poems*, new edn 1993 of 2nd rev. edn 1990; Marjory McNeill, *Norman MacCaig: a Study of His Life and Work*, 1996.

McCarthy, Mary (1912–89) American novelist, journalist, and critic, was born in Seattle, Washington, the eldest of four children of a Catholic father and a Jewish mother, both of whom died in 1918 in the flu epidemic. She was brought up by relatives—see *Memories of a Catholic Girlhood* (1957)—, at eight won a state prize for an essay on 'The Irish in American History', and was educated at Annie Wright Seminary, Tacoma, and Vassar. A week after graduating she married an actor: they divorced after three years. When she married EDMUND WILSON in 1938 (divorced 1946) she was already reviewing books for the *Nation* and *New Republic*, and was Drama Critic of the *Partisan Review*. At the end of the first week 'he said, "I think you have a talent for writing fiction." And he put me in a little room [and] said, "Stay in there!"' The result was the opening episode of *The Company She Keeps* (1942), a satirical study of the urban set of the 1930s. *The Oasis* (1949; in UK as *A Source of Embarrassment*, 1950) reflects postwar concern about the possibility of a third world conflict; *The Groves of Academe* (1952) has an academic setting, and *A Charmed Life* (1955) that of a provincial artistic community. *The Group* (1963), about eight Vassar graduates, was 'conceived as a kind of mock-chronicle . . . about the idea of progress seen in the female sphere', from the inauguration of President Roosevelt in 1933 to the 1960s. Having decided to end with the inauguration of President Eisenhower in 1952, she finally restricted the action to just eight years. Political journalism is in *Vietnam* (1967) and *Hanoi* (1968); essences of history and place in *Venice Observed: Comments on Venetian Civilization* (1956) and *The Stones of Florence* (1959); drama criticism in *Theatre Chronicles 1937–1962* (1963); and literary studies in *The Writing on the Wall and Other Essays* (1970)—see also *Occasional Prose*

(1985). Her friendship with the German-born philosopher and political activist Hannah Arendt (1906–75) is followed in *In Between Friends: the Correspondence of Hannah Arendt and Mary McCarthy*, ed. Carol Brightman (1995). See Carol Gelderman (ed.), *Conversations with Mary McCarthy*, 1991; Carol Gelderman, *Mary McCarthy: a Life*, 1989.

McClure, S. S. see CATHER.

McCullers, (Lula) Carson (1917–67), née Smith, American novelist and short-story writer, was born in downtown Columbus, Georgia, and began seriously studying music at ten. After contracting rheumatic fever in 1932 she gave up the idea of being a concert pianist, and determined to be a writer. She graduated from Columbus High School in 1933. In New York City in 1934, she lost all her money on the subway and had to take odd jobs to finance her study of creative writing at Columbia University. She married Reeves McCullers in 1937, when she began to write *The Heart is a Lonely Hunter* (1940), a novel of the 'Southern grotesque' school, featuring a deaf-mute. *Reflections in a Golden Eye* (1941), set in an army camp in peacetime, and written as a relaxation, is both graphic and violent. Having divorced Reeves in 1941, she remarried him in 1945 after he returned with combat injuries from serving in Europe in World War II. *The Member of the Wedding* (1946) is an acute study of loneliness, expressed through the longings of a 12-year-old girl. In 1947 the couple were flown home from Paris, both on stretchers, she after suffering a third stroke and he with delirium tremens. Her dramatization of *The Member of the Wedding* opened in 1950 on Broadway, where it ran for 501 performances and won her four awards. The title piece of *The Ballad of the Sad Café and Other Works* (1951) has a hunchback as a protagonist, and a murderous fist fight between a man and his former wife as a climax. In 1953 Reeves tried to talk her into a suicide pact at their home near Paris. She fled back to the USA: he killed himself with a drug overdose in a Paris hotel room. When no longer able to write fiction because of her physical condition, she produced verse for children, published in *Sweet as a Pickle and Clean as a Pig* (1964). See Virginia Spencer Carr, *The Lonely Hunter: a Biography of Carson McCullers*, new edn 1997.

MacDiarmid, Hugh, pseudonym of Christopher Murray Grieve (1892–1978) Scottish poet, was born in Langholm, Dumfriesshire, the elder son of a postman, and was educated at Langholm Academy before becoming a pupil teacher, then a journalist, and serving in World War I as a Royal Army Medical Corps sergeant. His restless and controversial public life thereafter belied his inherently gentle nature. He was at different times expelled from the Scottish National Party and the Communist Party, and he laboured hard and worldwide in pursuit of his political and literary ideals. Initially he wrote poems and stories in English, published in *Annals of the Five Senses* (1923). In the meantime, after at first tinkering playfully in the public library in Montrose with words and phrases from Scots dictionaries, he studied the etymology and development of Lowland Scots, from which he created a literary form, using words from different dialects, which was capable of expressing the experiences and aspirations of modern civilization. His first attempts, attributed to a friend called 'Hugh M'Diarmid', were published in *Sangschaw* (1925) and *Penny Wheep* (1926), and the movement known as the Scottish Renaissance had been launched. His profound influence on Scottish letters is due also to the fact that he was a fine lyrical and philosophical poet, with a gift for rhyme, whose *A Drunk Man Looks at the Thistle* (1926) is a sustained study of national and personal introspection. Also significant were the weeks in 1933 spent on the bare, bleak Shetland island of Whalsay, where he acknowledged the neutrality of the material universe and celebrated the implacable topography of Scotland in verses in both Scots and English, published in *Stony Limits and Other Poems* (1934). See *Complete Poems, Vol. 1*, reissued 1993, *Vol. 2, 1994*, ed. Michael Grieve and W. R. Aitken; *Selected Poems*, ed. Michael Grieve and Alan Riach, new edn 1994; *Selected Prose*, ed. Alan Riach, 1992; *Lucky Poet: a Self-Study in Literature and Political Ideas*, new edn 1994 (autobiographical study); Alan Bold, *MacDiarmid*, new edn 1990 (biography); Roderick Watson, *MacDiarmid*, 1985 (critical introduction).

MACDONAGH, THOMAS see PEARSE.

MACDONALD, ALEXANDER (ALASDAIR MAC MHAIGHSTIR ALASDAIR)(*c.*1695–*c.*1770) Gaelic poet, the son of the Episcopalian Minister of Ardnamurchan, was educated at Glasgow University, which he left early. In 1729 he was a teacher in Ardnamurchan for the Society for Propagating Christian Knowledge, for which in 1741 he produced a Gaelic–English dictionary. He was also an elder of the Kirk. In 1745, having the previous year been reprimanded by his employers for 'composing Galick songs, stuffed with obscene language', he became a Catholic and joined the army of Charles Edward Stuart. It is presumed that he is the Alexander MacDonald who was among the party which greeted the Prince on his arrival off the mainland. Thus it was also he who recited his own poem, 'Charles Son of James', as Charles's standard was unfurled at Glenfinnan and who became the Young Pretender's Gaelic tutor. So many of the poems in his collection, *Ais-eiridh na Sean Chánain Alban-*

naich [Resurrection of the Ancient Scottish Tongue] (1751), were dedicated to the Jacobite cause, or virulently attacked George II or the Campbells (who had supported the Government and were the MacDonalds' traditional enemies), that it is said that a copy was burned in Edinburgh by the public hangman. He was genuinely concerned for the development of Gaelic literature, and composed many intricate and evocative nature poems, as well as a corpus of love poetry, of which the musical 'Praise to Morag' has an amusing twist in its tail. 'The Birlinn of Clanranald', translated into English by MACDIARMID (1935), which describes in heroic and meticulous detail the preparations for a voyage to Ireland, and the adventurous crossing itself, is one of the most outstanding of all sea poems.

MACDONALD, ANSON see HEINLEIN.

MACDONALD, GEORGE (1824–1905) Scottish novelist, poet, and children's writer, was born in Huntly, Aberdeenshire, the second son of the town's leading miller. After being educated locally, he had three months' cramming at Aulton Grammar School, Aberdeen, at 15 and won a bursary to King's College, Aberdeen. During a year away from university for financial reasons, he catalogued a library, probably at Thurso Castle, in which he found in German literature the romance, mysticism, and theology which were to influence his writing. He graduated in 1845, and went to London to be a tutor, but in 1848 enrolled at Highbury College to study for the Congregationalist ministry. He was 'called' to Arundel, Sussex, where he had a lung haemorrhage in 1851, the year of his marriage. In 1852 the deacons responded to charges of 'heresy' against him by members of the congregation by cutting his salary, hoping he would resign. He stuck it for a year, and then gave up, being for the rest of his life a freelance lay preacher, writer, and lecturer, in which capacity he was Professor of English at Bedford College, London 1859–67. *Within and Without: a Dramatic Poem* was published in 1855, but it was with *Phantastes: a Faerie Romance for Men and Women* (1858) that the extent of his mythopoeic art manifested itself. After *David Elginbrod* (1863), in whose Scottish, autobiographical, romantic, theological, and didactic elements are the roots of his other lines of fiction, he had a ready market for his novels.

One of his acquaintances in London at this time was CARROLL, who photographed all the family, and whose earliest child friend was the MacDonald daughter, Mary (1853–78). He was also friendly with RUSKIN, whose traumatic romance with Rose La Touche was the inspiration of *Wilfrid Cumbermede* (1872). He was for two years joint Editor of *Good Words for the Young*, which serialized his classic fairy tale, *At the Back of the North Wind* (1871). After MacDonald was awarded a Civil List pension of £100 a year in 1877, the family, for reasons of Mary's health as well as his, spent some time in Italy. They returned there in 1880, to Bordighera, where friends had provided the funds for a house to be built. In summer he lectured in England and Scotland, where the family touring company performed his version of BUNYAN's *Pilgrim's Progress*, and other plays. In Italy he wrote his most powerful children's story, *The Princess and the Curdie* (1883), and *Lilith: a Romance* (1895), the transition into whose dark, troubled dream-world has been a source of inspiration to later writers, including TOLKIEN and C. S. LEWIS. In 1898 he had a stroke and lapsed into silence. His wife died in 1902, and he was brought back to England, where he died at the home of friends. *George MacDonald: an Anthology*, ed. C. S. Lewis (1946) is a selection of daily readings in Christian thought and feeling, taken from his novels and from *Unspoken Sermons* (3 vols 1867–69). See William Raeper, *George MacDonald*, 1987 (biography); David S. Robb, *George MacDonald*, 1987 (critical study).

MACDONNELL, A. G. see SQUIRE.

McEWAN, IAN (*b*. 1948) British novelist and short-story writer, was born in Aldershot, Hampshire, the only son of an army NCO: 'I was brought up with a strong sense of boundaries. And then we all wanted to kick over the traces.' He was educated at Woolverstone Hall School and the University of Sussex, after which, having cast around for a further degree, he settled for the course in creative writing at the University of East Anglia, supervised by ANGUS WILSON and MALCOLM BRADBURY. 'I was the only applicant. Just me. They pretty much left me alone. . . . I don't think I could have faced a more competitive course.' His first two books, the volumes of short stories, *First Love, Last Rites* (1975) and *In Between the Sheets* (1978), shocked for their principal themes but impressed for the technical command of the medium—see also *The Short Stories* (1995). After two novels which dwelt similarly on sex, death, and hidden perversions, *The Cement Garden* (1978) and *The Comfort of Strangers* (1981), he wrote (having married in 1982 and had children) *The Child in Time* (1987), whose main theme is baby-snatching but whose characters are outwardly more conventional types. Darkness returned with *The Innocent* (1990), a striking novel of sex, death, and espionage in postwar Berlin. The horrifying confrontation in *Black Dogs* (1992) is central to a study of human relationships and ideological differences within a family. *The Imitation Game: Three Plays for Television* (1981) includes 'Solid Geometry', commissioned in 1978 by the BBC, which withdrew it without explanation four days before it was due to be recorded. *The Day-Dreamer* (1994) is a novel for children. See Kiernan Ryan, *Ian McEwan*, 1994 (critical introduction).

McGAHERN, JOHN (*b*. 1934) Irish novelist and short-story writer, was born in Dublin, the son of a police officer, and spent his childhood in Mohill, Co. Roscommon, where he overcame the lack of books at home by having the run of the library in a farmhouse nearby. He was educated at Presentation College, Carrick-on-Shannon, St Patrick's Training College, and University College, Dublin, after which he became a teacher. The depiction of a woman's slow death from cancer in an Irish village in his first novel, *The Barracks* (1963), was highly praised for its sensitivity and revealing credibility. *The Dark* (1965), a study of a youth facing up to the conflicts of a tortured existence, was banned by the Irish Censorship Board, but McGahern refused to allow a protest, which had the support of BECKETT and others, to be mounted. A few months later he was sacked from his teaching post with no reason being given. 'I had no money, I was living in London, and I was doing mostly relief teaching. It was very hard, and I used to feel too tired to write. . . . There are times in my life when I haven't written, though I don't think it has ever gone as long as that, for I didn't write a thing for five or six years.' Eventually he was appointed a Research Fellow at Reading University from 1968 to 1971. Subsequently he lived in Spain and the USA, where he was on several occasions Visiting O'Connor Professor of Literature, Colgate University, New York, before returning with his second wife to a farmhouse near Mohill.

The hero of *The Leavetaking* (1974; rev. edn 1984), having lost his mother from cancer when he was young, falls for an American divorcée; to marry her he has to give up his post in a Catholic school. In *The Pornographer* (1979), the harsher ironies of death, as well as of sex, are dramatically laid bare. *Amongst Women* (1990), with a background of country routines and Catholic rituals in the west of Ireland, reflects the insubstantiality, in the modern world, of the traditions of family life. In his volumes of short stories McGahern often ranges beyond rural Ireland, in particular to Dublin, London, and Spain, while faithfully, often poetically, recording the changes that have taken place in Ireland since the 1950s—see *The Collected Stories* (1992). He was awarded the 1994 Prix de Littérature Étrangère by the Salon du Livre, Bordeaux. See Denis Sampson, *Outstaring Nature's Eye: the Fiction of John McGahern*, 1993 (critical study).

MACGILL-EAIN, SOMHAIRLE see MACLEAN.

McGONAGALL, WILLIAM (c.1825–1902) Scottish versifier, the son of an Irish handloom weaver, was probably born in Edinburgh, and spent his childhood in South Ronaldsay, Orkney. When he was 11, the family moved to Dundee, where he lived for most of the rest of his life. Initially he followed his father's trade. His taste for the stage, which he indulged by being allowed to appear as an amateur actor in performances of touring companies at the Theatre Royal, fostered his preoccupation with the composition of verses which were dramatic in intent, but irredeemably banal in form ('Oh Water of Leith! Oh Water of Leith, / Where the girls go down to wash their teeth'). A local paper published some of them, and he exploited this publicity by printing his works on sheets of paper, which he sold personally throughout central Scotland. Battles and disasters were his stocks in trade, titled dignitaries (especially royalty) his favourite personages. He took to the stage, reciting his own works and energetically (with the help of a naked broadsword) declaiming soliloquies of SHAKESPEARE—he appeared in London in 1880 and New York (expenses paid by a kindly Dundee hotelier) in 1887. He was convinced of his own genius, and usually suffered the baiting of raucous audiences with polite exasperation. William Power (1873–1951), author and critic, who witnessed one such debacle, wrote in *My Scotland* (1934): 'He added to the gaiety of at least one nation, and, as the Ossian of the ineffably absurd, he has entered upon immortality.' *Poetic Gems* was published in 1890; several other collections have appeared since 1962, when new works came to light. See *Collected Poems*, new edn 1992; *The Complete McGonagall*, 1992.

McGOUGH, ROGER (b. 1937) British poet, was born in Liverpool and educated at St Mary's College, Crosby, and Hull University, and qualified as a teacher in 1960. He taught in Liverpool from 1960 to 1964. and was a lecturer at Liverpool College of Art 1969–70, and Poetry Fellow, Loughborough University 1973–75. The appearance of his poems in *The Mersey Sound* (1967; rev. edn 1983), along with those of Adrian Henri (b. 1932) and Brian Patten (b. 1946), his co-performers in the group known as 'The Scaffold', confirmed their reputation and status as the 'Liverpool Poets'. McGough is the more obviously comical of the three, but his laconic style and also compassion make him a sympathetic observer of, and shrewd commentator on, human tragedies as well as frailties, latterly with a touch of domestic romanticism. His collections include *Watchwords* (1969) and *Crocodile Puddles* (1984), and for children, by whom he is equally appreciated, *Sky in the Pie* (1983). See *Selected Poems 1967–1987*, 1989; *You at the Back: Selected Poems 1967–87, Volume 2*, new edn 1993 (for children); *Defying Gravity*, new edn 1993 (subsequent collection).

MACHADO DE ASSIS, JOAQUIM MARIA (1839–1908) Brazilian novelist and poet, was born in Rio de Janeiro and was orphaned when young. He left school at 15 to work as a typesetter and journalist, graduating to being an editor/columnist in 1860. He joined the Ministry of Agriculture, Commerce, and Public Works as a clerk in 1874, retiring in 1908 as Director of Accounts. His early works were plays, produced between 1859 and 1867; he published volumes of verse in 1864 and 1870, and his first novel, *Contos Fluminenses*, in 1872. *Memórias Póstumas de Bráz Cubas* (1881; tr. William L. Grossman as *Epitaph of a Small Winner*, 1953) is a comic narrative of a dead man; *Quincas Borba* (1891; tr. Clotilde Wilson as *The Heritage of Quintas Borba*, 1954) confronts, with 19th-century philosophies; in *Dom Casmurro* (1899; tr. Helen Caldwell, 1953) alternative narratives result logically in two conflicting conclusions. *The Devil's Church and Other Stories*, tr. Jack Schmitt and Lorie Ishimatsu (1977), is a selection from more than two hundred stories. He was Founding President of the Brazilian Academy of Letters 1897–1908.

MACHEN, ARTHUR (1863–1947) Welsh novelist, short-story writer, and translator, was born in Caerleon-on-Usk, the son of a clergyman, and was educated at Hereford Cathedral School. He became a writer after failing his entrance to the Royal College of Surgeons. His earliest works were published at his own expense; his passion for the occult was the motivation for a collection of fantasy pieces, *Thesaurus Incantatus . . .* (1888). An inheritance from his father in 1887 brought him financial independence for 15 years, whereupon he embarked on his translation of the memoirs of CASANOVA (12 vols 1894), and on *The Great God Pan*, a novel of erotic occultism. This was published in 1894 with a second story of diabolism, *The Inmost Light*, by John Lane (1854–1925) in his 'Keynotes' series, which represented the best of the new writers of the Decadent school. *The Hill of Dreams* (1907), the journey of an author into the infernal regions, which anticipates the modern stream-of-consciousness novel, also belongs to this period, during which Machen joined the Order of the Golden Dawn, a society of Christian cabalists of which YEATS was a member. In 1902 he became an actor in the Shakespearian touring company of (Sir) Frank Benson (1858–1939). In 1912 he joined the London *Evening News*, for whom he wrote a topical story, 'The Bowmen', which is the source of the legend of the 'Angels of Mons', who came to the help of the British army. His recognition as a writer of the macabre came when he had turned largely to the composition of personal essays. See *The*

Collected Arthur Machen, ed. Christopher Palmer, 1988; Mark Valentine, Arthur Machen, 1994 (biography).

MACHIAVELLI, NICCOLÒ (1469–1527) Italian statesman, political philosopher, historian, and dramatist, was born in Florence, the son of a lawyer who ensured that from the age of seven he had a humanist education under leading teachers, before going to Florence University. At 29 he became Second Chancellor in the new administration of the Florentine republic, in which capacity he was involved also in diplomatic missions at the highest level and was a member of the military council. In 1513, after the collapse of the regime, he was accused of plotting against the new government, tortured, imprisoned, and fined. Released under a general amnesty after a few months, but unable to get employment, he withdrew to his farm at Sant' Andrea, to consider the political scene objectively and to write. The only work published during his lifetime was Arte della Guerra (1521; tr. Peter Whitethorne as Arte of Warre, 1563, with a dedication to Elizabeth I), in which he pressed the claims of citizen armies. Il Principe [The Prince] (1532), his study of statecraft, was probably completed in 1513, and Discorsi [Discourses] (1531) before 1519. Manuscript translations of both were circulating in England from about 1580, but because of the refusal of a licence for their printing, the first published translations (by Edward Dacres) did not appear until 1640 and 1636 respectively. In the meantime Istorie Fiorentine (1532) had appeared as Florentine Historie, tr. Thomas Bedingfield (1595). La Mandragola (tr. Bruce Penman as The Mandragola in Five Italian Renaissance Comedies, 1978), a well-constructed but rather distasteful comedy, was first performed in Florence and Rome in about 1520. Machiavelli's realistic view of contemporary politics and government and his trenchant precepts have unjustly made his name a byword for guile and unscrupulousness, but his influence on English and Scottish political thought during the 17th century was considerable; he is frequently referred to in Elizabethan and Jacobean drama, and even makes a personal appearance in MARLOWE's The Jew of Malta. See The Portable Machiavelli, ed. Peter Bondanella, 1979; The Prince, tr. Peter Bondanella and Mark Musa, 1984; Sebastian de Grazia, Machiavelli in Hell, new edn 1996 (biography); Quentin Skinner, Machiavelli, 1982 (introduction to his thought).

MacINNES, COLIN (1914–76) British novelist, was born in London, the son by her first marriage of the novelist Angela Thirkell (1890–1961), after whose second marriage he was brought up and educated in Australia. His service as a sergeant in the Intelligence Corps in World War II provided the background to his first novel, To the Victors the Spoils (1950); his second, June in Her Spring (1952), is the story of a romance in the Australian outback. His three London novels, City of Spades (1957), Absolute Beginners (1959), and Mr Love and Justice (1960), are the works for which he is remembered. Racy and articulate, with dialogue which accurately reflects racial and social characteristics, they dissect the teenage subculture of the time and lay bare the attitudes and activities of the underworld. Of his later novels, Westward to Laughter (1969) is an 18th-century pirate adventure story, and Three Years to Play (1970) follows the fortunes of an Elizabethan boy actor. Out of the Garden (1974) is a contemporary thriller with an inbuilt political warning and deft social comment. Out of the Way: Later Essays (1980) is a selection from his contributions to Encounter, New Society, and the Spectator. See Tony Gould, Inside Outsider: the Life and Times of Colin MacInnes, new edn 1996.

MacINTYRE, DUNCAN BAN (DONNCHADH BÀN MAC AN T-SAOIR)(1724–1812) Gaelic poet, was born in Glen Orchy, Argyllshire. He was never able, or could never be bothered to learn, to read and write, and he spoke no English. Because his chief was a Campbell, he reluctantly agreed, for a bribe of 300 merks, to fight as a substitute on the government side during the '45 Rebellion, and took part in the battle of Falkirk, at which he lost the sword he had been lent. Afterwards he became a gamekeeper on the Argyll and Breadalbane lands, composing and committing to memory songs and poems which express his joy in the mountains and rugged moors, and the game with which they were stocked; even on a bad day, such as he recapitulates in 'Song on Missing at Hunting'. In 1768, the year in which a book of his poems (transcribed by the son of the local minister) was published, he was made redundant. He moved to Edinburgh, where he was found work in the City Guard (referred to by FERGUSSON in 'The Daft Days' as 'that black banditti'). While he now needed to celebrate urban topics, which he found in drink and the oddities of local dignitaries, his qualities as a poet and his status as a bard brought him a grant from the London Highland Society, and in the later 1780s he and his wife made a triumphal tour of the Highlands. Incredibly, he joined the Breadalbane Fencibles in 1793, and served for six years as a sergeant. Apart from the sheer gusto of his verse, he was a fine nature poet, whose 'Praise of Ben Dorain' has been translated by Professor John Stuart Blackie (1809–95), and subsequently by MACDIARMID and IAIN CRICHTON SMITH. 'Song of the Foxes' has a poignant ring, as he blesses them for killing 'the grey-faced sheep, who worked our woe' by taking over the hills from the deer.

MCKAY, CLAUDE (1889–1948) Jamaican-born poet and novelist, was born in Sunnyville into a black peasant family, and had no formal education. At about 14 he went to Kingston, became a member of the constabulary, and published two volumes of dialect verse, *Songs of Jamaica* (1911) and *Constab Ballads* (1912). Awarded a medal, and a sum of money, by the Institute of Arts and Sciences, he inaugurated the characteristic exile of Caribbean writers by emigrating to the USA in 1912. After briefly attending Tuskegee Normal and Industrial Institute and Kansas State College, he opened a restaurant in New York, which failed, and then worked as a dining-car attendant. He now began to write again, some of his verse appearing in *The Seven Arts*. After a visit to England, where he was lauded by FRANK HARRIS and was a reporter for a pacifist journal, he was an associate editor of the left-wing *The Liberator* 1919–22. In *Spring in New Hampshire and Other Poems* (1920) and *Harlem Shadows* (1922) Jamaican dialect gave way to archaic poetic diction, and acute observations of Jamaican life to nostalgia and to passionate protests against racial discrimination in America.

Veering towards Communism, as well as active in the Harlem Renaissance, he went as an observer to the 4th Congress of the International in the USSR, where his *Trial by Lynching: Stories about Negro Life in North America* first appeared in a Russian translation (1925; tr. Robert Winter into English, 1975). Possibly to avoid the attentions in New York of his American wife, from whom he was separated, he went on to France, where he remained for ten years. His three novels and a collection of stories, *Gingertown* (1932), reflect black and white conflicts of culture and the problems of adjusting from one to the other. In *Home to Harlem* (1928) a black soldier returns to the USA after serving in France; *Banjo* (1929) features the black cultures which drift to and through the port of Marseilles, which he knew. *Banana Bottom* (1933), in which his early debt to the folklorist Walter Jekyll, author of *Jamaican Song and Story* (1907), is reflected in the character of Squire Gensir, is a study of a rural community and of a young Jamaican woman who is fostered by a white Free Church missionary and his wife after being raped as a child, is sent by them to be educated in Britain, and after returning to her roots asserts her cultural heritage. McKay died in Chicago, having joined the Catholic Church. See *The Passion of Claude McKay: Selected Poetry and Prose 1912–1948*, ed. Wayne F. Cooper, 1973; *A Long Way from Home*, 1937 (autobiographical study); Wayne F. Cooper, *Claude McKay, Rebel Sojourner in the Harlem Renaissance: a Biography*, 1996.

MACKENZIE, (Sir) COMPTON (1883–1972) Scottish novelist, was born Edward Montague Compton in West Hartlepool of a theatrical family, and assumed the name of Mackenzie to emphasize his Scottish ancestry. He was educated at St Paul's School and Magdalen College, Oxford. He chose writing as a career, and published a book of verse and several successful novels, including *Carnival* (1912), a melodramatic romance of the stage, and *Sinister Street* (1913), a vivid study of contemporary adolescence and early manhood, before serving both in action and in the secret service in World War I. His devotion to Scottish issues is reflected in his sequence of six semi-autobiographical novels, published as *The Four Winds of Love* (1937–45). These cover four decades in the many-faceted life of John Ogilvie in various parts of the world according to the points of a compass, from the establishment of the Scottish National Party (of which Mackenzie was a founder member) to 1945. His later novels include the more light-hearted but nevertheless elegantly-written comedies of, and satires on, Scottish life, manners, and superstitions, such as *Whisky Galore* (1947) and *Hunting the Fairies* (1949). A flamboyant but often financially-embarrassed figure, a lover of cats and a staunch supporter of friends and causes he admired, he was knighted in 1952. His life is faithfully and meticulously recorded in his ten-volume autobiography, *My Life and Times* (1963–71). See Andro Linklater, *Compton Mackenzie: a Life*, new edn 1992; and in Cairns Craig (ed.), *The History of Scottish Literature Volume 4: Twentieth Century*, new edn 1989.

MACKENZIE, HENRY (1745–1831) Scottish novelist, essayist, and critic, was born in Edinburgh and educated at the High School of Edinburgh and Edinburgh University, which he left in 1761 without taking a degree to be articled to a King's Attorney in Exchequer. As the Exchequer was governed by English law, he spent two years studying in London, from which he returned in 1768 with some drafts of a novel. *The Man of Feeling* (1771), by which title he himself became known, fulfilled the tenets of sensitivity in the writings of HUME and ADAM SMITH. Short, sentimental, and quirky (it begins at chapter XI), it was the most popular novel in Britain of the 1770s. *The Man of the World* (1773) followed, and later *Julia de Roubigné* (1777), an epistolary novel. In the meantime this shrewd and capable lawyer, who shot game and fished for sport, found another outlet for his literary talents with his heroic tragedy, *The Prince of Tunis* (1773).

In 1779 a group of Edinburgh lawyers who called themselves the Mirror Club established a literary periodical, the *Mirror*; it lasted 16 months, and was succeeded by the *Lounger*, which appeared for two years from February 1785. Both were edited by Mackenzie, who also contributed admirable essays, among them the review (*Lounger*, issue 97) which is the first considerable critique of BURNS. He was the first critic to praise BYRON, having seen a copy of *Poems on Various Occasions* which, as *Hours of Idleness*, had been hammered in the *Edinburgh Review*. In 1788, a paper on German drama which he read to the Royal Society of Edinburgh started WALTER SCOTT on his literary career. They became close literary associates, and in the anonymous dedication to *Waverley* Mackenzie is hailed as 'Our Scottish Addison'. His *Works* (8 vols) were published in 1808, and his life of HOME in 1822. In 1825, at the suggestion of several booksellers and with the encouragement of THOMAS MOORE and Scott, he began his *Anecdotes and Egotisms*. Unpublished at his death, and then bequeathed down several generations, this compendium of character sketches and epigrammatical observations finally appeared (ed. H. W. Thompson) in 1927. Mackenzie was from 1799 until his death Comptroller of Taxes for Scotland. He married, in 1776, the daughter of the Chief of Clan Grant, by whom he had 14 children. There is an appealing description of them and their home in J. G. Lockhart, *Peter's Letters to His Kinsfolk* (1819). See *The Man of Feeling*, ed. Brian Vickers, 1987.

MACKENZIE, KENNETH (IVO) (1913–55) Australian novelist and poet, was born in Perth, Western Australia, and was educated as a boarder at Guildford Grammar School (from which he ran away at 16 and did not return), and at Muresk Agricultural College and the University of Western Australia, from each of which he dropped out after a year. In 1934 he went to Sydney 'to be a writer' and married Kate Loveday (d. 1972). Journalism did not agree with him. A long philosophical poem, *The Earth*, appeared in a limited edition with illustrations by NORMAN LINDSAY in 1937. As Seaforth Mackenzie, the name he used for his novels (Seaforth is a sea-loch in the Isle of Lewis associated with Clan Mackenzie), he published *The Young Desire It* (1937), a delicate treatment of teenage insecurity and sexual attraction, which won the Australian Literature Society's Gold Medal, and *Chosen People* (1938), an immature study of Jewish isolation and complex relationships in an urban setting. He did war service at the prisoner-of-war camp at Cowra, and used the mass break-out of Japanese prisoners from it in 1944 as the basis of *Dead Men Rising* (1951 in UK; banned in Australia until 1969). A collection of poems, *The Moonlit Doorway* (1944), contained many of a personal nature. In 1948 he went to live on his own in the Blue Mountains on an average annual income from his pen of £250, while his wife supported their two children in Sydney. In 1953 he was in hospital, about which he wrote a poetical sequence 'The Hospital—Retrospections'. *The Refuge* (1954) is a further novel of sexual relationships, with the roles reversed. He

drowned in a creek during a visit to Goulburn. See *The Poems of Kenneth Mackenzie*, ed. Evan Jones and Geoffrey Little, 1972.

MACKENZIE, SEAFORTH see MACKENZIE, KENNETH.

MACKINTOSH, ELIZABETH (1896–1952) Scottish novelist and dramatist, was born in Inverness and educated at Inverness Royal Academy, from which she chose to go on to Anstey School of Physical Training, Birmingham, rather than to university or art college. She taught physical education at schools in England, before returning to Scotland on her mother's death to keep house for her father. *The Man in the Queue* (1929), written for a competition as Gordon Daviot, introduced her detective, Alan Grant. Under the same name she wrote several plays, including the successful *Richard of Bordeaux* (1933), which starred (Sir) John Gielgud (b. 1904) as Richard II, and *Queen of Scots* (1934), with the future Lord Olivier (1907–89) as Bothwell, and *Claverhouse* (1937), the standard biography of that charismatic Scottish royalist. As Josephine Tey, the name of her great-great-grandmother, she became one of the most ingenious and respected of modern crime novelists, with titles such as *Miss Pym Disposes* (1946), set in a physical training college, *The Franchise Affair* (1948), a classic modern reworking of an 18th-century cause célèbre, and *Brat Farrar* (1949), a study of an impersonator to an inheritance. Grant, hospitalized after an accident, features again in *The Daughter of Time* (1951); his long-distance investigation of the murder of Richard III's two nephews, the 'Princes in the Tower', stands also as a serious, if partisan, piece of historical scholarship.

MACKLIN, CHARLES (1699–1797) Irish actor and dramatist, was born in Culdaff, Co. Donegal, and learned his craft as a strolling player in the west of England. In 1733 he was playing minor roles in London and living with an actress, Ann Grace (d. 1758), by whom he had that year a daughter, Maria (d. 1781), who also became an actress. During a backstage altercation at Drury Lane in 1735 he thrust a cane through a fellow-actor's eye. The man died, and Macklin was tried for murder. He conducted his own defence, was convicted of manslaughter, and sentenced merely to be branded on the hand, which was done with a cold iron. He and Ann married in 1739. In 1741 he first played Shylock in *The Merchant of Venice*, which had not been seen in its original form since the time of SHAKESPEARE. His immaculate preparation and superlative performance caused George II to lose a night's sleep and to suggest to the Prime Minister that the actor be employed to frighten the House of Commons. In 1746 his own play, *King Henry VII: or, The Popish Im-*

postor, was produced at Drury Lane, and failed, as did several subsequent pieces. In spite of continued appearances in such parts as Iago and Polonius, he retired from the stage in 1753 to become keeper of a tavern, incorporating a 'School of Oratory', at which he lectured on the history of the theatre. He returned to the stage, bankrupt, in 1755.

In 1759, he played Shylock again at Drury Lane, with, as 'afterpiece', his own comedy, *Love à la Mode*, in which he took the part of Sir Archy McSarcasm. In its full version, it still plays well. His much-publicized appearance as Macbeth in 1773 angered the supporters of his rival, David Garrick (1717–79). There were angry scenes in the theatre, and several men were subsequently convicted of 'riot and conspiracy' after a trial at which Macklin personally prosecuted. His *The True Born Scotchman* was premiered at the Smock Alley Theatre in Dublin in 1764. As *The Man of the World* it was twice refused a licence by the Lord Chamberlain: a third version was finally staged in London in 1781, with the aged author as Sir Pertinax Macsycophant. His final performance was as Shylock in 1790, when he forgot his lines. In his insistence on the rights of an author to control his works, for breach of which he several times took offenders to court, he anticipated the efforts of BULWER-LYTTON and others. James Thomas Kirkman (*fl.* 1795–1810), who claimed to be a relation and was held by some to be his illegitimate son, wrote *The Life of Charles Macklin* (1799). See William W. Appleton, *Charles Macklin: an Actor's Life*, 1961.

MACLEAN, ALISTAIR see MONSARRAT.

MACLEAN, SORLEY (SOMHAIRLE MACGILL-EAIN) (1911–96) Gaelic poet, was born on the island of Raasay, and educated in Portree, Skye, and at Edinburgh University, where he got a first in English and began to write poetry. While a teacher in Mull for two years, he observed the barrenness into which the land and the traditional culture had declined, and responded bitterly in verse. At this time, too, he came to know MACDIARMID, whom he helped with his translations of Gaelic verse. He also had an intense and ultimately unhappy love affair, which, with his remorse at not going to fight in the Spanish Civil War, became the tormented themes of his first collection, *Dàin do Eimhir agus Dàin Eile* (1943), translated by IAIN CRICHTON SMITH as *Poems to Eimhir* (1971). He served in the Royal Corps of Signals in World War II, and was severely wounded at the battle of El Alamein in 1943. He returned to teaching afterwards, first in Edinburgh, and then as Headmaster of Plockton Secondary School, Wester Ross 1956–72. His selected poems were published in Gaelic and English in 1977. In his deliberate choice to write in Gaelic rather than in English he denied himself a market but created a modern poetry in an ancient tongue. In this he is in the tradition of 20th-century poets such as YEATS, DAVID JONES, and W. S. GRAHAM, who have sought a poetic language which reflects the standard language of their time, the literary language of the past, and the language of a region or culture. He won the Queen's Gold Medal for Poetry in 1991, the first Gaelic poet to do so. See *From Wood to Ridge / O Choille gu Bearradh: Collected Poems in Gaelic and English*, new edn 1991; and in Cairns Craig (ed.), *The History of Scottish Literature Vol. 4: Twentieth Century*, new edn 1989.

MACLEISH, ARCHIBALD (1892–1982) American poet and dramatist, was born in Glencoe, Illinois, the son of a Scottish merchant philanthropist from Glasgow by his third wife, who was President of Rockford College 1884–88. He was educated at Hotchkiss School and Yale, and married in 1916. A volume of verse, *The Tower of Ivory* (1917), was published while he was serving in the US Army in France in World War I, during which he rose from private to captain. He then graduated as LLB from Harvard, where he taught constitutional and international law before practising in Boston. With his family he spent the years 1923–28 in France, working on his poetry, of which he published several volumes, including the sequence, *The Happy Marriage* (1924). On their return he bought a farm in Massachusetts, wrote *Conquistador* (1932), a Mexican epic inspired by a trip on foot and by mule, which won the Pulitzer Prize, and demonstrated his political and social awareness with the poems of *Frescoes for Mr Rockefeller's City* (1933) and a radio play, *The Fall of the City* (1937). He was Librarian of Congress 1939–44, and as Assistant Secretary of State and subsequently Chairman of Delegation was instrumental in the establishment of the United Nations Educational, Scientific and Cultural Organization in 1946. He was Boylston Professor of Rhetoric and Oratory at Harvard from 1949 until his retirement in 1962. *Panic* (1935), a play based on the financial crisis of 1933, was written in a verse form reflecting the American 'language of accents'. *J. B.* (1958), a 20th-century version of the biblical story of Job, for which he used 'dramatic poetry' as the means of giving 'illusions of the real', was produced on Broadway and won the Pulitzer Prize. See *Collected Poems 1917–1982*, 1985.

MACLENNAN, HUGH (1907–90) Canadian novelist and essayist, was born in Glace Bay, Nova Scotia, the son of a Gaelic-speaking doctor, and was educated at Halifax Academy, Dalhousie University, and (as a Rhodes scholar) at Oriel College, Oxford, where he read Greats. After being rejected by Dalhousie for a teaching post, he continued his classical studies in the USA at Princeton, where he wrote a thesis on a Roman colony in Egypt, *Oxyrhynchus: an Economic and Social Study* (1935). He taught Latin and history at Lower Canada College, Montreal, from 1935 to 1945, when he became a full-time writer and freelance journalist. The focal point of his first novel, *Barometer Rising* (1941), which covers the events of eight dramatic days, is the explosion of the munitions ship in 1917 in Halifax harbour, which he witnessed: catastrophic in its physical effect and cataclysmic in symbolizing the emergence of Canada as a nation. The title of *Two Solitudes* (1945) represents the divide between French- and English-speaking Canadians. Both *The Precipice* (1948) and *Each Man's Son* (1951) reflect the Calvinistic sense of guilt which he inherited from his family. He returned to teaching in 1951, as an associate professor at McGill University, where he was Professor of English 1967–79. In *The Watch That Ends the Night* (1959) he re-creates the agony of a couple coming to terms with the wife's approaching death, in circumstances such as his own first wife had died in 1957. The didacticism detected in all seven novels after his first derives partly from his need, as the first major Canadian novelist, to explore his country's national character, and partly from his natural facility as an essayist. Both his first two collections, *Cross Country* (1949) and *Thirty and Three*, ed. Dorothy Duncan (1954), won the Governor General's Award for non-fiction, which with the fiction awards for 1945, 1948, and 1959 gave him a record five in all. His most lasting examples of this genre are collected in *The Other Side of Hugh MacLennan: Selected Essays Old and New*, ed. Elspeth Cameron (1978). He was given honorary doctorates by 16 Canadian universities (including Dalhousie in 1955), and was made Companion, Order of Canada, in 1967. See Elspeth Cameron, *Hugh MacLennan: a Writer's Life*, 1981; Helen Hoy, *Hugh MacLennan and His Works*, 1990.

MacLEOD, Fiona see SHARP.

MacNAMARA, Brinsley (1890–1963) Irish novelist and dramatist, was born John Weldon in Devlin, Co. Westmeath, one of seven children of the local schoolmaster. Intended for the Excise, he became instead an actor with the Abbey Theatre, Dublin, with whose company he toured the USA in 1911, remaining there afterwards to try and make a career. After a few years he returned to Devlin, where he wrote *The Valley of the Squinting Windows* (1918), a bitter but witty portrayal of the narrowness of village life. The book was burned in Devlin, the school of the author's father was boycotted, and he himself, in fear of his life, was driven to take refuge in Dublin. He continued his exposé of provincial life in *The Clanking of Chains* (1920); in *The Irishman* (as Oliver Blyth, 1920)

he offered an explanation of his literary rationale while satirizing the Irish Literary Revival. *The Mirror in the Dusk* (1921) is by contrast a tragic tale. In 1922, leaving his wife to bring up their child in Co. Clare, he became Registrar of the National Gallery in Dublin, a post he held until shortly before his death. Of his subsequent, and only occasional, novels, *The Various Lives of Marcus Igoe* (1929), a tragicomic fantasy which explores the relationship between fiction and reality, is regarded as the best. He also wrote nine plays which were performed at the Abbey, of which he was a director in 1935—he resigned almost immediately in protest at the staging of O'CASEY's *The Silver Tassie*. Of these, *The Glorious Uncertainty* (1923) and *Look at the Heffernans* (1926) were commercially successful comedies, while *Margaret Gillan* (1933) is a brooding study of female frustration, passion, and revenge.

MacNEICE, (FREDERICK) LOUIS (1907–63) Irish poet, translator, and critic, was born in Belfast, the youngest of three children of a future Anglican bishop, and was educated in England after the death of his mother in 1914 (see his poems 'Carrickfergus' and 'Carrick Revisited'). He went to Marlborough College and Merton College, Oxford, where he got a first in Greats and edited *Oxford Poetry* with AUDEN. His first book of verse, *Blind Fireworks*, was published in 1929. Having obtained a lectureship in classics at Birmingham University in 1929 (see 'Birmingham') he married, against the wishes of his father and her mother, 'Mariette' Ezra, the stepdaughter of the Professor of Classical Archaeology at Oxford. She left him for an American former college football star in 1934, shortly after the birth of their son. He moved to London, where he was a lecturer in Greek at Bedford College, London 1936–39; his verse translation of *The Agamemnon of Aeschylus* (1936) is highly regarded and was successfully staged. *Autumn Journal* (1938), which he described to T. S. ELIOT, his publisher, as 'rapportage, metaphysics, ethics, lyrical emotion, autobiography, nightmare', is regarded as the most moving and best of his long poems. In Manhattan in 1939, he shared a platform with AUDEN and ISHERWOOD, and he returned to the USA later that year to lecture at Cornell University. From 1941 to 1961 he was a producer of radio features for the BBC, for whom he also wrote some outstanding documentaries and dramas—see *The Dark Tower, and Other Radio Scripts* (1947). He combined a full-time career and the distractions of an unsettled family life with his creative impulse, publishing regular volumes of verse and writing critical works, including *Modern Poetry: a Personal Essay* (1938), and his 1963 Clark lectures, *Varieties of Parable* (1965). He died of pneumonia, having caught a severe chill underground while supervising sound effects for a radio programme. He was an inspirational poet, who let the form and content find their own disposition, the ensuing variety of themes and moods being matched by his ear for an exact sound and his eye for a precisely remembered image. In 1942 he married Hedli Anderson, a singer-actress with whom he used to appear on the same cabaret or concert platform. He was made CBE in 1958. See *Collected Poems*, ed. R. R. Dodds, 2nd rev. edn 1979; *Selected Plays*, ed. Alan Heuser and Peter McDonald, 1993; *Selected Literary Criticism*, 1987, and *Selected Prose*, 1990, ed. Alan Heuser; *The Strings Are False: an Unfinished Autobiography*, new edn 1996; Jon Stallworthy, *Louis MacNeice*, new edn 1996 (biography); Peter McDonald, *Louis MacNeice: the Poet in His Contexts*, 1991; Edna Longley, *Louis MacNeice: a Critical Study*, new edn 1996.

MACPHERSON, JAMES (1736–96) Scottish poet, was born in Ruthven, Inverness-shire, the son of a farmer. He was educated as a poor student at King's College, Aberdeen, and studied divinity at Edinburgh University, without taking a degree at either. After teaching in Ruthven he emigrated to Edinburgh, where he published an unremarkable romantic poem, *The Highlanders* (1758). He was encouraged by HOME and others also to publish what he claimed were *Fragments of Ancient Poetry Collected in the Highlands of Scotland and Translated from the Galic or Erse Language* (1760). An excited literary establishment commissioned him to investigate further the oral tradition in the Highlands and to look for lost manuscripts. He duly returned with what he declared was an epic by Ossian, a 3rd-century Gaelic warrior poet, son of the legendary Fingal. His 'Ossian poems', *Fingal* (1761) and *Temora* (1763), were largely if not entirely his own composition, but they appealed enormously to a public which was enthralled by ROUSSEAU's 'noble savage' and avid for tales of primitive passions and heroic action in sublime settings. Not only Scots wanted the poems to be authentic: Napoleon carried them about with him and BYRON thought them splendid. JOHNSON, in an open letter to the press in 1775, called them 'an imposture'. A committee of the Highland Society, chaired by HENRY MACKENZIE, concluded in 1805 that some elements were genuine. Macpherson was secretary to the Governor of Pensacola, West Florida, from 1763 to 1766, when he returned to London and became a political journalist. As agent for the Nabob of Arcot, he made a fortune. In 1784 the Government offered him the lands of his kinsman and clan chief, Ewan Macpherson of Cluny (*d*. 1756), which had been forfeited after the '45 Rebellion, but he insisted that they be restored to Cluny's son. He died on the estate which he had bought in Badenoch, Inver-

ness-shire, and was buried, at his own expense, in Westminster Abbey. See *The Poems of Ossian and Related Works*, ed. Howard Gaskill, 1996 (annotated edition).

MACPHERSON, (JEAN) JAY (*b*. 1931) Canadian poet and critic, was born in England in London, and in 1940 emigrated with her parents to Newfoundland, from which they moved to Ottawa. She went to Carleton College, Ottawa, and Toronto University, where in 1957 she became a member of the English department, and subsequently a professor of Victoria College. *Nineteen Poems* (1952) was published by GRAVES at his Seizen Press, Mallorca. *O Earth Return* (1954), nine short poems under the subtitle 'A Speculum for Fallen Women', was issued by her own small press, Emblem Books, whose third title was LIVESAY's *New Poems* (1955). 'O Earth Return' became the second section of *The Boatman* (1957), an intricate sequence of mythological and biblical allusions in a variety of poetic, often epigrammatic, forms, which won the Governor General's Award. *Welcoming Disaster: Poems 1970–1974* (privately published 1974) is a further sequence in the form of a symbolic quest with, as guide, a teddy bear, whom the poet first discovers 'In a chair, / Filling in for / Him not there'— probably the only teddy in serious poetry outside BETJEMAN. Both books were reprinted in *Poems Twice Told* (1981). She has also published the critical study, *The Spirit of Solitude: Conventions and Continuities in Late Romance* (1982). See Lorraine Weir, *Jay Macpherson and Her Works*, 1994.

MacTHÓMAIS, RUARAIDH see THOMSON, DERICK.

MAETERLINCK, MAURICE (1862–1949) Belgian dramatist, poet, and essayist, was born Mauritius Polydorus Maria Bernardus Maeterlinck in Ghent, the son of a notary. He was educated at the Jesuit College of Sainte-Barbe and Ghent University, where he read law at the request of his parents, whom in 1885 he persuaded that further study in Paris was called for. There, he pursued instead his interest in current literary trends, meeting MALLARMÉ and other Symbolist poets, particularly Villiers de l'Isle Adam (1838–89), a student of the fable and the occult, and publishing a short story as Mooris Maeterlinck (thereafter it was Maurice). He practised law in Ghent, but after a volume of verse, *Serres Chaudes* [Hothouses], and a good critical reception for a Symbolist play, *La Princesse Maleine*, both privately published in 1889 with the connivance of his mother, he accepted both parents' support to live as a writer. He followed *L'Intruse* [*The Intruder*] and *Les Aveugles* [*The Blind*], both performed in Paris in 1891, with another death drama, *Pelléas et Mélisande* (1892; tr. Erving Winslow,

1894), for which he was hailed in London as 'the Belgian Shakespeare' when it was performed there in 1898 with Mrs Patrick Campbell (1865–1904) in the lead; it also became the opera (1902) by Claude Debussy (1862–1918).

In 1895 Maeterlinck met the actress and singer Georgette Leblanc (1876 1941), who was separated from her Spanish Catholic husband. During the fifteen years that they lived together she played many of his heroines and also produced the spectacular version of SHAKESPEARE's *Macbeth*, in his translation, at the 14th-century Abbey of St Wandrille, which they had acquired as a home. His greatest theatrical success was *L'Oiseau Bleu* (tr. A. Texeira de Mattos as *The Blue Bird*, 1909), a creation myth partly inspired by BARRIE's *Peter Pan*. Written in 1905, it was first performed at the Moscow Art Theatre under the direction of Constantine Stanislavsky (1863–1938) in 1909, and in London the following year. At a rehearsal for the French production in 1911 he met an 18-year-old minor actress, Renée Dahon, whom he married in 1919. He was awarded the Nobel Prize for Literature in 1911 for his 'diverse literary activity', which included his essays, of which he went on to publish 12 collections between 1927 and 1942, on entomological and botanical as well as philosophical and mystical themes. He was created Count of Belgium in 1932.

MAHFOUZ, NAGUIB (*b.* 1911) Egyptian novelist, was born of middle-class parents in the ancient quarter of Cairo described in his novel [*Midaq Alley*] (1947; tr. Trevor Le Gassick, rev. edn 1975), from which they moved when he was five to the European-style inner suburb of Abbasiyah, where he went to school. Having taken a degree in philosophy at Cairo University, where he discovered Western fiction, and been for a while a member of the university secretariat, he became a civil servant. He worked in the Ministry of Religious Affairs until 1954, when he married and moved from his mother's house, and then in the Ministry of Culture until his retirement in 1971. His first book, a translation from English, was followed by three pharaonic novels of his own. Having published *Midaq Alley*, his second novel of modern life, and embarked upon, and completed, his 'Cairo Trilogy', he wrote nothing during the five years following the Egyptian Revolution of 1952. The trilogy, a family saga which deals with explosive issues and the hitherto forbidden area of sex, and charts the progress of Egyptian nationalism during the first half of the 20th century, was published in volume form 1956–57, earning him a share of the State Prize for Literature—in English as *Palace Walk*, tr. William M. Hutchins and Olive E. Kenny (1990), *Palace of Desire*, tr. Hutchins, Kenny, and Lorne M. Kenny (1991), and

Sugar Street, tr. Hutchins and Angele Botros Samaan (1992).

Mahfouz broke his silence with [*Children of Gebelawi*] (serialized 1959; tr. Philip Stewart, 1981), in which successive protagonists instinctively re-create in a Cairo alley the lives of Adam, Moses, Jesus, and Muhammad. Still never published in Egypt in volume form, it earned its author a retrospective *fatwa* in 1989, on the grounds that had it been declared at the time, RUSHDIE might have been deterred from writing *The Satanic Verses*—an attempt on Mahfouz's life was made in 1994. In [*Adrift on the Nile*] (1966; tr. Frances Liardet, 1993), Mahfouz explores, in a manner which one critic compared with that of CHEKHOV, the impact of reality on the artificial paradise of a group of bourgeois drug addicts in Egypt in the 1960s. *Arabian Nights and Days* (1982; tr. Denys Johnson-Davies, 1995) is a loose reworking of 13 tales from the *Arabian Nights*, with politico-religious overtones. He was awarded the Nobel Prize for Literature in 1988. See *Echoes of an Autobiography*, tr. Denys Johnson-Davies, foreword by Nadine Gordimer, 1997; Matti Moosa, *The Early Novels of Naguib Mahfooz*, 1994 (critical study).

MAHONY, FRANCES SYLVESTER see PROUT.

MAILER, NORMAN (*b.* 1923) American novelist and prose writer, was born in Long Branch, New Jersey, and was brought up in Brooklyn, New York, 'the most secure Jewish environment in America', where he went to Brooklyn High School. He graduated from Harvard *cum laude* in aeronautical engineering, having in his second year won *Story* magazine's college contest, and latterly driven himself to write three thousand words of fiction a day. He enlisted in the US Army in World War II with the idea of writing 'a short novel about a long patrol'. *The Naked and the Dead* (1948), a long novel about a long patrol, immediately established for him a reputation on which only an extremely ambitious and inventive craftsman could improve. *Barbary Shore* (1951) and *The Deer Park* (1955) were still the works of an apprentice writer, who laid bare his turbulent ego and creative philosophy in the stories and essays in *Advertisements for Myself* (1959). *An American Dream* (1965) is a study of the American consciousness through the persona of a middle-aged 'hipster'. *The Armies of the Night: the Novel as History, History as a Novel* (1968), which won the Pulitzer Prize for non-fiction, is an imaginative reconstruction of the 1967 march on the Pentagon (in which he and ROBERT LOWELL participated) in protest against the Vietnam War, a topic to which he returned metaphorically in his novel, *Why Are We in Vietnam?* (1967). For *The Executioner's Song: a True Life Novel* (1979), which won his second Pulitzer Prize, he fashioned, from a thousand hours of tape-recorded interviews and hundreds of pages of notes, a portrait of Gary Gilmore, a convicted murderer who insisted on his own execution.

The technique of selection and arrangement seemed to desert Mailer when he came to write two enormous novels, *Ancient Evenings* (1983), about ancient Egypt, and *Harlot's Ghost* (1991), a combination of history, biography, literature, basic philosophy, and romance, which is, according to a legend in the book, just the beginning of a saga of the Central Intelligence Agency. *Oswald's Tale: an American Mystery* (1995) is an investigation into the character of President Kennedy's assassin. There is a great deal of the author himself in *Portrait of Picasso as a Young Man: an Interpretative Biography* (1996), for which he draws also on the memoirs (1988) of the artist's first mistress, Fernande Olivier. See Peter Manso, *Mailer: His Life and Times*, rev. edn 1987; Brian Morton, *Norman Mailer*, 1991 (critical study); Michael K. Glenday, *Norman Mailer*, 1995 (critical study).

MAIR, CHARLES (1838–1927) Canadian poet, was born in Lanark, Upper Canada, and studied medicine for a year at Queen's University, which he left to work in the family timber business. In 1868 he published *Dreamland and Other Poems*, in the English Romantic vein, and returned briefly to Queen's before going to Ottawa, where he became a founder of the Anglo-Protestant movement, Canada First. Local Métis took exception to letters he wrote to his brother while paymaster of a government road building project betwen Port Arthur and River Settlement (Winnipeg), which were printed in the Toronto *Globe*. During the Red River Rebellion in 1870 he was imprisoned by the insurgents' leader, Louis Riel (1844–85), and sentenced to death. He escaped, and returned to the fray in 1885 as a quartermaster during Riel's final rebellion, after which he was dubbed the 'warrior poet'. *Tecumseh: a Drama* (1886), which recalls in blank verse the Shawnee chief's support of the British in the War of 1812, is a genuine national play, in which there are some fine descriptive sweeps, notably on the bison. His concern for the preservation of this species is further reflected in the poem 'The Last Bison'. He worked for the federal immigration service from 1898 to 1921. *Through the Mackenzie Basin: a Narrative of the Athabasca and Peace River Treaty Expedition of 1899* (1908) is his record of a mission to negotiate land transfers with the Indians. See *Dreamland and Other Poems and Tecumseh: a Drama*, ed. Norman Shrive, 1974.

MAIS, ROGER (1905–55) Jamaican novelist, was born in Kingston of middle-class parents, and after an early private education spent three years at Calabar High School. At 17 he became a clerk in the Department of Education, which he left after a year. During the next fifteen years he was at different times a banana tallyman, insurance salesman, rice planter, photographer, and reporter on the *Daily Gleaner*. In 1940 he became a staff writer on *Public Opinion*, the journal of the People's National Party, for which he wrote stories—see *Face and Other Stories* (1942) and *And Most of All Men* (1943)—and numerous articles, one of which, decrying Britain's colonial policy, landed him in jail for six months. On his release he took up horticulture, and went back to painting and, eventually, to writing. *The Hills Were Joyful Together* (1953), which BRATHWAITE has called 'the English-speaking West Indies' first ghetto novel', incorporates elements of his prison experiences. In *Brother Man* (1954), drafted in a fortnight in the rainy season of 1951, the tension is between the inhabitants of an urban ghetto and the Rastafarian who is the agent of 'peace an' love'. Mais spent the years 1952–54 abroad, returning to Jamaica ravaged by cancer. *Black Lightning* (1955), in which he explores the place of the artist and human relationships in a rural community, was published posthumously, though he saw an advance copy before he died. See Jean D'Costa, *Roger Mais*, 1978 (critical study).

MAITLAND, (SIR) RICHARD, OF LETHINGTON (1496–1586) Scottish poet and anthologist, described as 'ane valiant, grave and worthy Knight', succeeded to the title and the family estates on the death of his father at the battle of Flodden in 1513. He was educated at St Andrews University, after which he studied law in Paris. He was in the service of James V; of Mary, Queen Regent; of their daughter Mary, Queen of Scots; and of her son James VI. Though now completely blind, he was in 1561 appointed a judge and made Lord Lethington. He was Keeper of the Great Seal from 1562 to 1567, when he resigned in favour of his second son, John (1545–95), later Lord Thirlestane, and retired to devote himself to literature. The Maitland Folio is a collection made by himself of early Scottish poetry, notably of DUNBAR and HENRYSON, with anonymous poems such as *Christis Kirk on the Grene* and *Peblis to the Play*: the Maitland Quarto, made for or by his daughter Margaret, comprises also 16th-century works, including those of JAMES VI and MONTGOMERIE. Both are second only to the collection of George Bannatyne (1545–1608) as authentic sources of Scottish poetry. Maitland's own verse, written later in life, is notable for its tart comments on foibles of the age, as in 'Satire on Town Ladies': 'On claithis they wair [spend] mony a croun; / And all for newfangilness of geir'.

MAJOR, JOHN see BLIND HARRY; BUCHANAN; HOLINSHED.

MALAMUD, BERNARD (1914–86) American novelist and short-story writer, was born in Brooklyn, New York, the elder son of Jewish immigrants from Russia. 'My father was a grocer, my mother, who helped him, after a long illness, died young.' He was educated at Erasmus Hall High School, City College, New York, and Columbia University. He taught for nine years in evening high schools in New York, and then at Oregon State University until 1961, when he went to the Division of Languages and Literature, Bennington College, Vermont. His first novel, *The Natural* (1952), is an allegory featuring the fall and rehabilitation of a baseball player. His treatment of Jewish themes ('I write about Jews, when I write about Jews, because they set my imagination going') begins with *The Assistant* (1957), in which day-to-day existence in a small grocer's store is the setting for a study of Jewish and Gentile assimilation. The title story of *The Magic Barrel* (1958) has become a classic for its blend of humour, poignancy, and use of Jewish tradition. The protagonist of *A New Life* (1961) is a Jewish lecturer at odds with life in a remote West Coast university ('I prefer autobiographical essence to autobiographical history. Events from life may creep into the narrative, but it isn't necessarily my life history.') The very much darker *The Fixer* (1966), which won the Pulitzer Prize, is set in Tsarist Russia. *The Tenants* (1971) is short, brutal, and disturbing; the disintegration of a writer is also the main theme of *Dubin's Lives* (1979). Malamud returned to allegory in *God's Grace* (1982), an appeal for reason before the modern world destroys itself. See *Selected Stories*, new edn 1993; *Talking Horse: Bernard Malamud on Life and Work*, ed. Alan Cheuse and Nicholas Delbanco, 1996 (interviews, essays, and notes).

MALAN, HERMAN see BOSMAN.

MALLARMÉ, STÉPHANE (1842–98) French poet, was born Étienne, in Paris. After his mother's death when he was five, he and his sister (who died in 1858) were brought up by their maternal grandparents. He went to his first boarding school, in Passy, at ten, and was already writing poetry when he left school at 18. His enthusiasm for POE led him to study English seriously. Shortly after marrying a German girl in London in 1863, he began teaching it in Tournon—he later published a translation of 'The Raven' (1875) and of a collection of Poe's verse (1888). While he continued to teach, even after moving to Paris from Avignon in 1871, he experienced in Tournon an emotional crisis during which he lost his religious faith and devoted himself to poetry. He became pre-eminent in a literary circle which included GIDE, VALÉRY, and Paul Claudel (1868–1955), and was a public figure after the publication of HUYSMANS's À Rebours (1884), in which he is cited as the fa-

vourite poet of the embodiment of decadence. A Symbolist in the tradition of BAUDELAIRE, he stated: 'To name an object is to sacrifice three-quarters of that enjoyment of the poem which comes from the guessing bit by bit.' His musical equivalent was Claude Debussy (1862–1918), a frequent visitor to his house in Paris, who set to music the dramatic pastoral poem which was his first book, *L'Après-Midi d'un Faune* [The Afternoon of a Faun] (1876). *Les Poésies* (1887) was first published in a limited edition: cheaper editions followed. The first three 'Poèmes en Prose'—in *Pages* (1891)—were translated by GEORGE MOORE in *Confessions of a Young Man*, where he also warmly recollects Mallarmé's Tuesday evening literary *conversazioni* round the fire. See *Poems*, tr. Brian Coffey, 1990 (bilingual edition); Gordon Millan, *Mallarmé: a Throw of the Dice—the Life of Stéphane Mallarmé*, 1994; Charles Chadwick, *The Meaning of Mallarmé*, 1996 (parallel text translation and critical study).

MALLEY, ERN see MCAULEY.

MALORY, (Sir) THOMAS (*c.*1410–71) prose writer, was of an old Warwickshire family, came into his father's estate at Newbold Revel in about 1433, served in France at the raising of the siege of Calais in 1436, and was Member of Parliament for Warwickshire in 1445, having in the meantime been knighted. Between about 1450 and 1460 he was arrested and imprisoned eight times (and escaped twice) on charges which amount to ambush and intent to murder, aggravated burglary, rape, cattle rustling, and extortion. In 1462 he was with the Earl of Warwick's army in Northumberland, but it would appear that he was soon back in prison, where he died, having completed there in 1469 what he refers to as 'the hoole book of kyng Arthur and of his noble knyghtes of the Rounde Table', which was printed and published in 1485 by CAXTON as *Le Morte Darthur*. This was regarded as the definitive text until the discovery of a fuller contemporary manuscript version in 1943 in the Fellows' Library of Winchester College. Whether one takes the view of Eugène Vinaver—see *Malory: Works* (2nd edn, reissued 1977)—that it comprises eight separate books or that of C. S. LEWIS that it is a conglomerate of many often unfinished or unconnected stories, this remarkable prose romance is the most comprehensive rendering of the legends of King Arthur, told in a racy, descriptive style, with complete balance of dialogue and narrative, and is a landmark, if not an oasis, in the history of English prose. See P. J. C. Field, *The Life and Times of Sir Thomas Malory*, 1993; Elizabeth Archibald and A. S. G. Edwards (eds), *A Companion to Malory*, 1996.

MALOUF, DAVID (*b.* 1934) Australian novelist and poet, was born in Brisbane and educated at Brisbane Grammar School and the University of Queensland. He has since lived in England and in Italy, as well as in Australia, where he was a lecturer at Sydney University from 1968 to 1977. The reminiscent tone of two volumes of verse, *Bicycle and Other Poems* (1970) and *Neighbours in the Thicket* (1974; rev. edn 1980), becomes more reflective and cosmopolitan in *First Things Last* (1980). The boyhood and youth of his poems are to some extent recapitulated in his first novel, *Johnno* (1975). While he has retained in all his subsequent fiction the device of characters of opposite temperaments or circumstances, the situations are extraordinarily varied. *An Imaginary Life* (1978) has an exiled OVID obsessed by a wolf-child. In *Fly Away Peter* (1982), *Harland's Half Acre* (1984), and *The Great World* (1990), which won the MILES FRANKLIN Award, the Commonwealth Writers Prize, and the Prix Femina Étranger in France, he is concerned not only with aspects of 20th-century Australian life and characteristics, but with the effect on them of outside inhumanity, particularly of the wars in Europe and the Far East. *Remembering Babylon* (1993) is a study of the effect on a 19th-century Queensland community of a British youth, cast overboard as a child, who has spent 16 years with an Aborigine tribe—it was in 1996 given the inaugural International IMPAC Dublin Literary Award, the world's most valuable prize for a single work. *The Conversations at Curlow Creek* (1996), set in New South Wales in 1820, describes the relationship and dramatic links between a police officer and an Irishman who has been condemned to be hanged. Though Malouf has latterly divided his time between Australia and Italy, he maintains in his work his presiding theme of home by regarding each journey as a homecoming, whether to the land of his birth or to that which he regards as his cultural home. The linked essays in *12 Edmonstone Street* (1985) develop this theme. He was made AO in 1987. See *Selected Poems 1959-1989*, 1992; Ivor Indyk, *David Malouf*, 1993 (critical study).

MALRAUX, ANDRÉ (1901–76) French novelist and critic, was born in Bondy, just outside Paris, the son of a stockbroker and a baker's daughter. He left school without passing his baccalaureate to work as a bargain hunter for an antiquarian bookseller, published stories and reviews in avant-garde magazines, and, when he was 19, impulsively married the rich, 23-year-old Clara Goldschmidt. On an archaeological expedition in Cambodia in 1923–24 he was convicted of looting a historical monument and released on a technicality. He returned to Indochina in 1925–26, and indulged in political activity in Saigon during the events which form the background to *Les Conquérants* (1928; tr. Winifred Stephens Whale as *The Conquerors*, 1929). *La Condition Humaine* (1933; tr. Haakon M. Chevalier as *Man's Fate*, 1934; tr. Alastair Macdonald as *Man's Estate*, 1948), which won the Prix GONCOURT, covers two days in 1927 during which the Communist insurrection in Shanghai failed. In 1934, after a flight over the Arabian Desert, he announced that he had discovered the legendary city of the Queen of Sheba. He was in Berlin the same year with GIDE, helping the defendants in the trial following the Reichstag fire. *Le Temps du Mépris* (1935: tr. Chevalier as *Days of Wrath*, 1936) reflects his concern about Fascism, as does *L'Espoir* (1937; tr. Stuart Gilbert and Macdonald as *Man's Hope*, 1938), written after he had fought in the Spanish Civil War in 1936–37. During World War II he served in a French tank unit, was captured, escaped, joined the Resistance, and then commanded a brigade in Normandy after the Allied invasion, being awarded both the Croix de Guerre and the Distinguished Service Order. He was Minister of Information 1945–46, and Minister of State for Cultural Affairs 1959–69. An influential if controversial art critic as well as a novelist and man of action, his major work in that field was reissued as *Les Voix du Silence* (1951; tr. Gilbert as *The Voices of Silence*, 1954). He and Clara were finally divorced in 1946, by which time he had had two sons by Josette Clotis, who died in a bizarre railway accident in 1944. He married Madeleine Malraux, his half-brother's widow, in 1948.

MANDEL, ELI(AS WOLF) (1922–94) Canadian poet and critic, was born in Estevan, Saskatchewan, of a Jewish family. He served with the Army Medical Corps in Europe in World War II. He returned to the University of Saskatchewan, after which he taught at Toronto University, Collège Militaire Royal de Saint Jean, Quebec, and the University of Alberta. In 1965 he was appointed to York University, Ontario, where he became a professor of English and humanities in 1967. His first book of verse was *Fuseli Poems* (1960), and in this and other early volumes, of which *An Idiot Joy* (1967) won the Governor General's Award, mythological themes predominate. Images of Jewish suffering recur throughout *Stony Plain* (1973), in which the shock at the horrors of the concentration camps is reflected in the disintegrated prosody of 'On the 25th Anniversary of the Liberation of Auschwitz . . .'. *Out of Place* (1977) is a single poem on Jewish settlement in Saskatchewan. *Life Sentence: Poems and Journals 1976–1980* (1981) reflects his travels in South America and India. Critical essays are collected in *Another Time* (1977), and he edited several significant anthologies, including *Poets of Contemporary Canada 1960–1970* (1972). See *Dreaming Backwards: Selected*

Poetry 1954–1981, 1981; Dennis Cooley, *Eli Mandel and His Works*, 1992.

MANDELSTAM, OSIP (1891–1938) Russian poet and critic, was born in Warsaw of Jewish parents (his father was a leather merchant and his mother a teacher of music), and was brought up in St Petersburg, where only privileged Jews were allowed to live. He was educated at Tenishev School, after which he spent several years travelling and studying in France, Italy, and Germany, followed by a year of philosophy at St Petersburg University. His first book of verse, [*Stone*] (1913; rev. edn 1923; tr. Robert Tracy, 1981), proclaimed him as an Acmeist (see AKHMATOVA) rather than a Symbolist. By the time he returned from weathering out in the south the civil wars following the Revolution of 1917, he had found a distinctive lyrical voice; *Tristia* (1922) owed more to the classical tradition of HOMER, OVID, VIRGIL, and DANTE than to any more localized or contemporary influence. He married Nadezhda Khazina (1899–1980) in 1922. In 1928 he published a book of critical essays, a collection of miscellaneous prose, and a third volume of poetry, incorporating the earlier two and including some more recent poems. It was his last. Later that year, after his personal honour had been publicly impugned in a literary slanging match over a translation he had edited, the couple were spirited out of harm's way to Armenia. [*Journey to Armenia*], tr. Clarence Brown (new edn 1989), comprising a series of impressions which celebrated his recovery from several years of writer's block, was first published in a journal in 1933 in a heavily censored form.

In 1934 the authorities learned from an informer of a short poem making fun of Stalin ('the Kremlin mountaineer') and his taste for executions—see in J. M. Coetzee, *Giving Offense: Essays on Censorship* (1996). Mandelstam was arrested, interrogated, abused, and finally exiled, first to the Urals, where half mad from his treatment, he tried to kill himself, and then to Voronezh—see *Voronezh Notebooks*, tr. Elizabeth and Richard Kane (1994), for poems composed or committed to paper at this time. In 1937 he and his wife (who had insisted on accompanying him the whole time) returned to Moscow, where they were denied anywhere to live and he had two heart attacks. He was arrested while recuperating in a sanatorium, and sentenced to five years' hard labour for 'counter-revolutionary activities'. He was put on a prison train, and died, supposedly of a further heart attack, in a transit camp near Vladivostock. Nadezdha Mandelstam published two memoirs, *Hope Against Hope* (1971) and *Hope Abandoned* (1974), tr. Max Hayward. That two hundred of his later poems survive is due to her dedication and to her memorizing them—see Beth Holmgren, *Women's Work in Stalin's Time: on Lydia Chukovskaia and Nadezhda Mandelstam* (1994) for an account of the literary legacies of two remarkable women. See *Selected Poems*, tr. Clarence Brown and W. S. Merwin, new edn 1989 (verse); *Poems from Mandelstam*, tr. R. H. Morrison, 1990 (prose); *The Collected Critical Prose and Letters*, tr. Jane Gary Harris and Constance Link, new edn 1991; Clare Cavanagh, *Osip Mandelstam and the Modernist Creation of Tradition*, 1995 (critical study); Nancy Pollak, *Mandelstam the Reader*, 1995 (critical study).

MANDER, JANE (1877–1949) New Zealand novelist, was born near Drury, Auckland, the daughter of a first generation New Zealander who had timber milling interests in the Northland, where she grew up and became a pupil teacher in 1892. She turned to journalism in 1902, and worked for her father's *Northern Advocate* and for the *North Auckland Times*. In 1912 she moved to New York, where she attended Columbia University School of Journalism for two years, and where she wrote three novels. *The Story of a New Zealand River* (1920) is inherently a study of conflicts, between the generations, between personal sensitivities and the raw, natural world, and between cultural awareness and the pioneering spirit. In *The Passionate Puritan* (1921), whose protagonist is a teacher, there is a reversal of the accepted gender roles. *The Strange Attraction* (1922) is about a journalist and her romance. All three were condemned in New Zealand for their preoccupation with 'sex problems'. In 1923 she went to London, where she wrote *Allen Adair* (1925), an exploration of relationships in the isolated society of the 'gum country of the north' which is regarded as her best novel, and two others, with New York and London backgrounds. She returned to Auckland in 1932, to look after her elderly father, who died in 1942. She wrote no more fiction.

MANGAN, JAMES CLARENCE (1803–49) Irish poet and translator, was born in Dublin, the son of a grocer, and was well educated at a private school in Saul's Court until forced by his father's bankruptcy to support the whole family. Eccentric in dress as well as in manner, he toiled for seven years as a scrivener and then in a lawyer's office, before being found a job in the Ordnance Survey. He had verses published in almanacs in his teens, and in 1831 he joined the Comet Club, for whose journal he wrote richly ornate but well-crafted poems as Clarence, which he adopted as one of his own names. In 1834 he began contributing to the *Dublin University Magazine*, mainly effective translations from the German, which he knew, but also adaptations of Islamic material from other people's translations. Through his work and contacts in the Ordnance Survey he developed an interest in and a nationalistic passion for Irish material, which he brilliantly reworked in such poems as 'Dark Rosaleen' and 'O'Hussey's Ode to the Maguire', while also compiling original poems on Irish themes. In 1842, when the Ordnance Survey closed down, he began contributing to the *Nation*, whose founder-Editor, (Sir) Charles Gavan Duffy (1816–1903), himself also a poet (and later Prime Minister of Victoria), even paid him a salary, but Mangan's fatal addiction to alcohol made any formal working arrangement impossible. He died in a cholera epidemic, having spent the previous two years in hospital, recovering first from illness and then from an accident. See *Collected Prose*, 1996, and *Collected Poems*, 1997, ed. Martin Van De Kamp and Jacques Chuto; *Autobiography*, ed. James Kilroy, 1968; Brendan Clifford, *The Dubliner: the Lives, Times and Writings of James Clarence Mangan*, 1988; Ellen Shannon-Mangan, *James Clarence Mangan: a Biography*, 1995; Henry J. Donaghy, *James Clarence Mangan*, 1974 (critical study).

MANKOWITZ, WOLF (*b.* 1924) novelist, dramatist, screenwriter, and authority on ceramics, was born in Bethnal Green, London, and educated at East Ham Grammar School and Downing College, Cambridge, where he was a student of LEAVIS. He was for a time a volunteer coal miner in World War II. *A Kid for Two Farthings* (1953), an affectionate, funny, moving celebration of his East End Jewish upbringing, followed *Make Me an Offer* (1952), in which profit-making by any means in the antiques' business is the theme of a quest novella. Jewish life and traditions also feature in several dramatic pieces—see *Five One-Act Plays* (1955). Subsequent novels include *My Old Man's a Dustman* (1956), a study of low-life survival; *Cockatrice* (1963), an exposé of some of the less attractive aspects of the film industry; and two supernatural fantasies of the modern American West, *The Devil in Texas* (1984) and *Exquisite Cadaver* (1990). *A Night With Casanova* (1991), which he announced as being his last book, is a moral fable about mortality, in which CASANOVA, in the last year of his life, meets the Wandering Jew. Volumes of short stories include *The Blue Arabian Nights: Tales of a London Decade* (1973). He received an Oscar for screenplay in 1957, and has been a theatre and film producer, London restaurant owner, antiques and art dealer, and from 1982 to 1986 Adjunct Professor of English at the University of New Mexico. He and his family went to live in the Irish Republic in 1971, when he was also Honorary Consul in Dublin to the Republic of Panama.

MANLEY, (MARY) DELARIVIÈRE (1663–1724) English novelist, dramatist, and political journalist, was a daughter of Sir Roger Manley, historian and royalist soldier, who was Lieutenant Governor of Jersey 1667–74. After his death in 1688, she was persuaded to marry an older cousin, John Manley (*d.* 1714). He was already married, and in due course abandoned her and their child. After living (and quarrelling) with the royal mistress, the Duchess of Cleveland (1641–1709), she wrote two plays, *The Lost Lover: or, The Jealous Husband* and *The Royal Mischief*, which were performed in London in 1696. Now launched on her literary career, she also had several affairs, one of them with the Warden of the Fleet Prison. She edited *The Nine Muses* (1700), elegies to DRYDEN by herself and other women poets. *The Secret History of Queen Zarah and the Zarazians* (1705), in the new vogue of 'scandal story', was also a *roman à clef*, the victim being the Duchess of Marlborough (1660–1744). In *The Secret Memoirs and Manners of Several Persons of Quality, of both Sexes. From the New Atalantis* (1709), she went even further, and was arrested and held in prison. Undeterred, she published further 'Atalantis' exploits (1710 and 1711). In 1711 she took over from SWIFT as Editor of the Tory journal, the *Examiner*. He dined with her in January 1712, and reported to 'Stella' that she was 'very ill of a dropsy and sore leg; the printer tells me he is afraid she cannot live long . . . she is about forty, very homely and very fat'. She recovered, to write *The Adventures of Rivella: or, The History of the Author of the Atalantis* (1714), a source of information about her early life, and *The Power of Love in Seven Novels* (1720), in which she adapts and embellishes her originals. See *A Woman of No Character: an Autobiography of Mrs Manley*, ed. Fidelis Morgan, new edn 1987.

MANN, HEINRICH see MANN.

MANN, THOMAS (1875–1955) German novelist and critic, younger brother of the novelist Heinrich Mann (1871–1950), was born in Lubeck, the second of four children of Senator 'Henry' Mann (1841–91), industrialist, and Julia da Silva Bruhns (1852–1923), whose mother was Portuguese-Creole. He attended the Katharineum, where he repeated his last two grades. He was apprenticed to an insurance company in Munich, to which his widowed mother had moved, when in 1894 he had a story printed in *Die Gesellschaft*. She agreed that he should extricate himself from his apprenticeship provided he enrol for some courses at the local technical high school. He published a volume of stories in 1898. In 1900 he gave up (or was made redundant from) his job as sifter of manuscripts for the satirical journal, *Simplicissimus*, and finished and posted off his first novel. He managed to get himself discharged from military service in the Royal Bavarian Infantry Guards for an 'inflamed flat-foot'. The novel, *Buddenbrooks: Verfall einer Familie* (1901; as *Buddenbrooks: the Decline of a Family*, tr. H. T. Lowe Porter, 1924; tr. John E. Woods, 1993), a study of the effect of a creative talent on several generations of a Lubeck family resembling his own, and published in full after he had refused to cut it by half, sold slowly until its second impression. *Tristan* (1903) contained the story 'Tonio Kröger', in which his alter ego struggles lyrically to find a compromise between artistic freedom and the commonplace elements of daily life. In 1905 he married the talented 19-year-old daughter of the Professor of Mathematics at Munich University, who was the only female student there and shared his passion for cycling: they had six children. After *Königliche Hoheit* (1909; tr. A. Cecil Curtis as *Royal Highness*, 1916), 'a novel of high-life, with a happy ending', he wrote, as World War I threatened, *Der Tod in Venedig* (1912; tr. Lowe-Porter as *Death in Venice*, with *Tonio Kröger*, 1928), a study of an ageing author's fatal attraction for a 13-year-old boy—his own homoeroticism, which his wife and children recognized and indulged, became common knowledge with the release of his diaries in 1977. During World War I Mann fell out with his brother over the way forward for German humanity, which he explored in *Der Zauberberg* (1924; tr. Lowe-Porter as *The Magic Mountain*, 1927), whose theme is the application of art and philosophy to the crises of contemporary existence. Having accepted the Nobel Prize for Literature in 1929, he went into exile in Switzerland when Hitler came to power. Though his works were initially excluded from the Nazi book-burning ceremonies, after his successful proposal for the Nobel Peace Prize of Carl von Ossietzky (1889–1938), who had been in a concentration camp since 1933, he was deprived of his citizenship. In 1939 he and his wife (who was Jewish) sailed for the USA, of which they became citizens in 1944. From there he made 55 anti-Nazi broadcasts to the people of Germany via the British Broadcasting Corporation. He was given a salaried professorship at Princeton and a stipend as a Fellow of the Library of Congress.

Lotte in Weimar (1939; tr. Lowe-Porter as *The Beloved Returns*, 1940), an insight into the GOETHE story, and *Doktor Faustus* (1947; tr. Lowe-Porter as *Doctor Faustus: the Life of the Composer Adrian Leverkühn as Told by a Friend*, 1949), a historical parable of modern Germany, are reflections of his determination to keep alive the cultural traditions of his country, to which he returned for the first time on a visit in 1949. He left the USA for Switzerland in 1952 in the wake of the hysteria over Communism, which he had never supported. He broke off from completing his long-planned comic novel, *Bekenntnisse des Hochstaplers Felix Krull* (1954; tr. Denver Lindley as *Confessions of Felix Krull, Confidence Man*, 1955), of which a fragment had been published in 1922, to write *Die Betrogene* (1953; tr. Williard R. Trask as *The Black Swan*, 1954), a bitter novel reflecting his disillusionment.

Heinrich Mann's engagement with politics was more open than his brother's (he was invited to stand for President of the German Republic in 1932), and his epic satire, *Der Untertan* (1918; tr. Ernest Boyd as *Man of Straw*, 1947) is overtly anti-German. *Professor Unrat* (1905), an impressionistic study of degradation in a small-town setting, was the basis of the film, *The Blue Angel* (1930), with Marlene Dietrich (1904–92) in her first starring role— the novel was translated into English under that title in 1932. He died in California. See Donald Prater, *Thomas Mann: a Life*, 1995; Ronald Hayman, *Thomas Mann: a Biography*, new edn 1997; Nigel Hamilton, *The Brothers Mann*, 1978 (joint biography); Anthony Heilbut, *Thomas Mann: Eros and Literature*, new edn 1997 (critical study).

MANNING, FREDERIC (1882–1935) Australian novelist, was born in Sydney, the fourth son of a four-times lord mayor of the city. Because of chronic asthma he was educated at home, apart from a few months at Sydney Grammar School. At 15 he went to England, where he lived with, initially as his pupil, a family friend who was Vicar of Edenhill, Lincolnshire. Here he wrote poetry—*The Vigil of Brunhild* (1907) and *Poems* (1910)— and prose, including *Scenes and Portraits* (1909), a set of imaginary historical dialogues which anticipated aspects of the poetry of POUND, whom he knew, and T. S. ELIOT. In 1914, though he was over age for service, he enlisted as a private in the King's Shropshire Light Infantry. He served in the fighting on the Somme and Ancre fronts in 1916, and wrote some notable war poems, published in *Eidola* (1917). In 1917 he became an officer in the Royal Irish Regiment in Ireland, where he was charged with insubordination and diagnosed as 'shell-shocked'. In 1918 he returned to his reclusive life as a semi-invalid in Lincolnshire. Some years later he was bullied by an inspired publisher to recount his war experiences as a novel. *The Middle Parts of Fortune* was published anonymously in 1929, and reissued in an expurgated edition as *Her Privates We* (1930) by 'Private 19022'. Graphic and gripping, it is unusual in war fiction for being written by, as well as representing the point of view of, an ordinary soldier. See Verna Coleman, *The Last Exquisite: a Portrait of Frederic Manning*, 1990.

MANNING, OLIVIA (1908–80) British novelist, was born in Portsmouth, the elder child of a retired naval officer by his second marriage to an Irishwoman of American descent. Her childhood was insecure, and money was short. She was educated at Portsmouth Grammar School, and then studied art at Portsmouth Technical College, which she had to leave to earn a living. While a typist in a London store, she sold for a few pounds the copyright in some 'lurid serials', written under the pseudonym of Jacob Morrow (her mother's maiden name). After many attempts, she had *The Wind Changes* (1937) published. In 1939 she married Reginald Smith (*d*. 1985), a British Council lecturer. She went with him to Romania, from which they managed to escape to Greece as war threatened. During World War II she worked as a press officer in Cairo and Jerusalem, where he was posted. In her 'Balkan Trilogy', *The Great Fortune* (1960), *The Spoilt City* (1962), *Friends and Heroes* (1965), her main characters manage always to keep one step ahead of the action of the war. The moving force of her 'Levant Trilogy', *The Danger Tree* (1977), *The Battle Lost and Won* (1978), *The Sum of Things* (posthumously, 1980), is the war itself in the Middle East. Together these six linked novels represent a deliberately intended chronicle of the times. She wrote several other novels, and also volumes of short stories, including *Growing Up* (1948). She was made CBE in 1976.

MANSFIELD, KATHERINE, pseudonym of Kathleen Mansfield Beauchamp (1888–1923) New Zealand short-story writer, was born in Wellington, the third of six children of (Sir) Harold Beauchamp (1858–1938) and Annie Dyer (1864–1918). Between 1893 and 1898 she went to the local village school at Karori, to which her parents had moved. When her father became a director of the Bank of New Zealand, the family returned to Wellington, where she went to Wellington Girls' High School in 1898–99, and to Miss Swainson's School from 1900 to 1902. In 1903 she and her two older sisters enrolled at Queen's College, London, where she met Ida Baker (1888–1978), often referred to as 'LM' (Lesley Moore), who became her lifelong friend. She also fell in love with 'Arnold' (Thomas) Trowell (1889–1966), the musical son of a Wellington musician. In 1906 she returned with her parents to New Zealand, her father having opposed her taking up the cello seriously, 'so my hope for a musical career is absolutely gone'. She opted to be a writer instead (essays and stories had appeared in the *Queen's College Magazine*), and readily slipped into the prevailing mode of the 'vignette', or prose poem, of which three were published in the *Native Companion* in 1907—see *Poems of Katherine Mansfield*, ed. Vincent O'Sullivan (1988), which contains her spasmodic poetic efforts from 1903 to 1922. In 1908 she persuaded her father to give her an allowance and let her return to London, where she immediately had an affair with Garnet Trowell (1889–1947), twin brother of Arnold, to which his parents put a stop. She married George Bowden (1877–1975), a music scholar and singing teacher, in March 1909, but left him the same day, and resumed her liaison with Trowell, by whom she was already pregnant. She miscarried in

Bavaria, where she had gone to have the child.

Back in London, she began to write in *New Age* the black comedy Bavarian sketches published as *In a German Pension* (1911). John Middleton Murry (1889–1957), the young editor of *Rhythm* (later to become an influential literary critic of his time) accepted 'The Woman at the Store' (1911), a harsh story of New Zealand colonial life which was her first to portray her native country, and asked to meet her. He became her lodger and, shortly afterwards, her lover. The flight abroad (to avoid charges of bigamy and fraud) of the publisher both of her book and of *Rhythm* left Murry facing bankruptcy. With a new backer and regular contributions from Mansfield under various names, the magazine struggled on until 1913, having survived for three final issues as the *Blue Review*. The first issue under the new name carried a story by D. H. LAWRENCE, whose wedding to Frieda Weekley they attended in 1914.

In March 1915, alone in the Paris flat of the writer Francis Carco (1886–1958), with whom she had just had a fleeting affair, Mansfield began a novel, to be called 'The Aloe'. She returned to it after her only brother had been killed in action in France, as a New Zealand memorial to him. When revised, cut, and retitled *Prelude*, it was published in 1918 by the WOOLFS, and became the main item in her second collection, *Bliss and Other Stories* (1920). In working on it she had discovered, in the words of C. K. STEAD, that 'a fiction survives, not by leading us anywhere, but by being at every point authentic, a re-creation of life'. In the Burnells she created a New Zealand family whose members recur in 'At the Bay' and 'The Doll's House' and through whom she established the ambience within which another family, the Sheridans, also move, in *The Garden Party and Other Stories* (1922).

In 1917 she was diagnosed as tubercular, and advised to spend winters abroad. Her divorce was finalized in 1918, and she married Murry, a few weeks after a lung haemorrhage. She spent the next four years between London and places in Italy and France, usually accompanied by Murry or Ida Baker, and sometimes by both—Murry was now Editor of the *Athenaeum*, to which initially she contributed regular book reviews. In October 1922 she was admitted to Gurdjieff's Institute for the Harmonious Development of Man, Fontainebleau. She continued to write cheerfully to Murry, who arrived to visit her on 9 January 1923. She died that evening after a sudden haemorrhage. The posthumous *The Dove's Nest and Other Stories* (1923) contained the unfinished 'A Married Man's Story'. This sinister tale marks her final development in the technique of the central character as narrator which effectively began in 1918 with the long story 'Je ne Parle pas Français', loosely based on the visit to Paris in 1913 with Murry during which she first met Carco. See *The Stories of Katherine Mansfield*, ed. Antony Alpers, 1985; *Collected Stories*, 1989; *Selected Letters*, ed. Vincent O'Sullivan, new edn 1990; *The Critical Writings of Katherine Mansfield*, ed. Clare Hanson, 1987; Antony Alpers, *The Life of Katherine Mansfield*, new edn 1982 or rev. edn 1980; Claire Tomalin, *Katherine Mansfield: a Secret Life*, new edn 1988 (biography); Clare Hanson and Andrew Gurr, *Katherine Mansfield* (critical study), 1981; and in C. K. Stead, *In the Glass Case: Essays on New Zealand Literature*, 1981.

MANZONI, ALESSANDRO (1785–1873) Italian novelist, was born on the Manzoni estate near Lake Como, the son of the lively 23-year-old daughter of a prominent writer and (only probably) of the 50-year-old widower to whom she had been married off to avoid a scandal with someone else. At five he was dispatched to boarding school, where his mother did not visit him even before she went off in 1792 to live with a rich Milanese liberal in Paris. He was reunited with her there in 1805, having had an ecclesiastically-oriented education, against which he publicly reacted in 1801 in a poem celebrating the triumph of liberty achieved by Napoleon. Nominally a Catholic, he had a Protestant wedding in 1808 to Henriette Blondel (1791–1833), by whom he had nine children who survived. Both were formally accepted into the Catholic faith in 1810, after which the couple, and his mother, returned to Milan. In about 1812 he embarked on a series of sacred hymns and secular verses, and in 1819 published a historical verse tragedy and a vindication of Catholic morality. It was probably the popularity of WALTER SCOTT which suggested to him the historical novel as a vehicle for his views on religion and society, and on authoritarian government and foreign interference. Set in 17th-century Lombardy during the period of Spanish domination, and invoking historical characters as well as historical incidents, *I Promessi Sposi* (1827; tr. Charles Swan as *The Betrothed Lovers*, 1828; tr. Bruce Penman as *The Betrothed*, 1972) became a national institution even before he published a new version (1840–42) in the modern Tuscan dialect, which was thus confirmed as a more acceptable literary medium than the hybrid Italian of the opposing school of thought. See *On the Historical Novel*, ed. and tr. Sandra Bermann, 1996.

MARCHBANKS, SAMUEL see DAVIES, ROBERTSON.

MARGUERITE DE NAVARRE (1492–1549) French poet and prose writer, was the daughter of the Comte d'Angoulême (*d.* 1496) and elder sister of Francis I, who succeeded to the throne of France in 1515. She was brought up in Cognac, Blois, and Amboise, where she had an excellent education in languages, the Bible, and philosophy. In 1509 she married Charles, Duc d'Alençon. After his death in 1525 she married Henri d'Albret, King of Navarre, by whom she had a daughter, Jeanne (the mother of Henry IV of France). Active in public affairs, patroness of the arts, and protector of the Protestant reformers, she published in 1531 a religious poem, *Le Miroir de l'Âme Pécheresse*, which was condemned as heretical until her brother intervened on her behalf. *Marguerites de la Marguerite des Princesses* and a sequel (both 1547) contained plays and a great number of poems of a personal, reflective, and philosophical nature. The prose work known as *Heptaméron*, first published in 1558, recalls BOCCACCIO in the general background setting to its seventy tales, but though the principal theme is love, she is more concerned with realistically portraying the moral conflicts which it generates in the context of contemporary society. Some of the stories were translated by William Painter (*c.*1540–94) in *The Palace of Pleasure* (1566–67).

MARIVAUX (1688–1763) French dramatist, novelist, and essayist, was born Pierre Carlet in Paris, the son of a civil servant. He studied law but never qualified, having meanwhile had a play performed and a novel published, and begun using the name of Marivaux (or Carlet de Marivaux). He married in 1717, but lost his inheritance in 1720 and his wife in 1723 (his only daughter became a nun in 1746). A writer of considerable versatility, he began contributing essays to *Mercure* in 1717, and from 1721 to 1724 published his own *Spectateur Française*, in the manner of ADDISON and STEELE. Preferring the improvisation and subtlety of the Italian style of acting to the formality of the contemporary French theatre, he wrote, mainly for the Comédiens Italiens, a series of comedies which explore with psychological insight the development of the course of love, notably *La Double Inconstance* (1723) and *Le Jeu de l'Amour et du Hasard* (1730), tr. David Cohen as *Infidelities* and *The Game of Love and Chance* (1980). He finished neither of his major novels, both ingenious studies of middle-class moral sensibilities. Part 1 of *La Vie de Marianne* appeared in 1731; parts 9, 10, and 11, which do not advance the action, were published in 1741. In the meantime he published five parts of *Le Paysan Parvenu* (1735–36; tr. Leonard Tancock as *Up from the Country* in the same volume as the two comedies, 1980), in which the protagonist is male.

MARLOWE, CHRISTOPHER (1564–93) English poet and dramatist, was born in Canterbury, the son of a prosperous shoemaker, and was educated at King's School, Canterbury, and Corpus Christi College,

Cambridge. He graduated as BA in 1584, and as MA in 1587, but only after the Privy Council had mediated with the university authorities, stressing that Marlowe had in the meantime undertaken a confidential mission abroad; this would almost certainly have involved attempting to unearth potential Catholic plots against Elizabeth I. He was probably destined for the Church, but he preferred to pursue the literary career which he had begun at Cambridge. In 1589 he was involved in a sword fight in which his friend Thomas Watson killed a man but was acquitted of murder. In 1592 the constable of Shoreditch sought an injunction to bring Marlowe to justice. On 18 May 1593, a warrant was issued by the Privy Council, on the evidence of KYD, for his arrest for possessing heretical documents. He was never questioned. On 30 May he was killed in a house in Deptford, apparently in a brawl—see Charles Nicholl, *The Reckoning: the Murder of Christopher Marlowe* (1992). He was only 29, the same age as SHAKESPEARE, who was still to write his dark comedies and his tragedies.

Blank verse had first been used in English by SURREY for a translation of VIRGIL in 1557, and was employed by SACKVILLE and Thomas Norton in the first known English tragedy, *Gorboduc* (1561). Marlowe developed the form into what is basically the blank verse of Shakespeare and MILTON. His known plays are six. *The Tragedie of Dido, Queen of Carthage* (performed in 1586, published in 1594), written with NASHE while they were both at Cambridge, is based on VIRGIL's *Aeneid*, Books I, II, and IV. The two parts of *Tamburlaine the Great* (performed 1587, published 1590) tell with massive sweeps of oratory and dramatic visual action the rise to power of the 14th-century Tatar conqueror, Tamerlane. *The Jew of Malta* (performed 1591, published 1633 with a foreword by HEYWOOD) follows the fall to and escape from ignominy of a Jewish merchant, who wreaks awful and indiscriminate revenge, betrays the island to the Turks, is rewarded with the governorship, and himself meets an end as ingeniously violent as any in the play. *Edward II* (performed 1592, published 1594) is a telescoped account of an uneasy reign of the King's passion for his favourite, Gaveston, concentrating on the characters and achieving dramatic tension by quick and frequent changes of scene. *The Massacre at Paris* (performed 1593, published 1594), which exists only in a corrupt and truncated text, covers 17 years of contemporary events from the St Bartholomew massacre of the Huguenots to the deaths of the Duke of Guise and Henry III of France in 1589. *The Tragical History of Dr Faustus* (performed 1594, published 1604, but 1616 with a better text) is a classic version of the tale of the man who sold his soul to the devil, based on the apparent exploits of a 16th-century itinerant German wizard called

Faust. Marlowe invests the story with genuine tragic overtones, even if the middle portion of the play, representing the 24 years between Faustus's bargain and his death, tends to lapse into a series of knockabout conjuring routines. While these, or some of these, may have been the work of a collaborator, for whom Samuel Rowley (*d*.?1633) is the least unlikely candidate, Marlowe presumably conceived the play, and certainly wrote the crucial scenes. Poetry known to have been written by him comprises a translation of some of OVID's *Amores* and of LUCAN's *Pharsalia*, Book I; the famous lyric 'Come live with me and be my love'; and the first two sestiads (books) of the mythological cautionary tale of forbidden love, *Hero and Leander*, which was completed by CHAPMAN.

In the course of a short and turbulent life, Marlowe earned respect among his contemporaries and a place in literary posterity. He was a fine poet, some of whose lines are not just memorable, but familiar: 'Who ever loved that loved not at first sight' (*Hero and Leander*); the amassing of wealth by means of precious stones, thus enclosing 'Infinite riches in a little room' (*The Jew of Malta*); 'The sweet fruition of an earthly crown' (*Tamburlaine*); 'Was this the face that launched a thousand ships?' and 'See, see where Christ's blood streams in the firmament' (*Dr Faustus*). He inherited the metre of blank verse, with its almost uniform end-stopped line, and by varying the stresses and the position of the stops forged it into something quite new and potent, so that JONSON could acknowledge, in his poem to the memory of Shakespeare, 'Marlowe's mighty line'. He was also the first English dramatist consistently to display an understanding of dramatic action, and of conflict and suspense as essential components of drama. See *Complete Plays and Poems*, ed. E. D. Pendry, rev. edn 1976; *Doctor Faustus and Other Plays*, ed. David Bevington and Eric Rasmussen, 1995 (A and B Texts, *Tamburlaine, The Jew of Malta, Edward II*); Harry Levin, *Christopher Marlowe: the Overreacher*, 1965 (critical study); Roger Sales, *Christopher Marlowe*, 1991 (critical study); Thomas Healy, *Christopher Marlowe*, 1994 (critical introduction).

MARQUAND, JOHN P(HILLIPS)

(1893–1960) American novelist, was born in Wilmington, Delaware, and educated at Newburyport High School, Massachusetts, and Harvard, where he majored in chemistry. He served in the National Guard on the Mexican border in 1916, and then in France as an intelligence officer with the US Army 77th Artillery in 1917–18 in World War I. After a year on the New York *Herald-Tribune* he went into advertising to earn more money, and worked on the Lifebuoy soap campaign. With $400 saved, he retired to an old mill and wrote *The Unspeakable Gentleman* (1922), a historical cloak-and-dagger romance. He emerged to settle in Cambridge, Massachusetts, after his marriage (the first of three) in 1922. After writing several novels for the popular market, he travelled for the *Saturday Evening Post* in China and the Far East, which provided the background of several novels, including those about the polite Japanese, Mr Moto. *The Late George Apley* (1937), gently satirical of Boston society, was the first of his novels to be taken seriously by the critics, and won the Pulitzer Prize. *H. M. Pulham Esq* (1941) takes a wider look at the same stratum of New England life. Marquand returned to army intelligence in World War II, during which he travelled extensively in the Pacific. *So Little Time* (1943) and *B. F.'s Daughter* (1946; in UK as *Polly Fulton*, 1947) explore the effect of the war on American society. In *Melville Goodwin, USA* (1951), the inner characters of a two-star general and a journalist are revealed during the course of an extended interview. The protagonist of what he announced beforehand as his last novel, *Women and Thomas Harrow* (1958), has affinities with its creator and his past.

MÁRQUEZ, GABRIEL GARCÍA see GARCÍA MÁRQUEZ.

MARQUIS, DON(ALD ROBERT PERRY) (1878–1937) American humorist, poet, short-story writer, and dramatist, was born in Walnut, Illinois, son of a doctor with a love of nature and literature. After high school and a variety of jobs, including chicken-plucker, he briefly attended Knox College, Galesburg, in 1898. He then worked as a county schoolteacher and on the railroad before joining the staff of a weekly county newspaper, for which he wrote a regular column, filling unused space with sonnets of 13 lines, the capacity of the typesetter's composing stick. After a spell at the Census Bureau in Washington and working for various newspapers there and in Philadelphia, he settled in Atlanta, where he was an associate editor on the *Atlanta News* and then on J. C. HARRIS's *Uncle Remus's Magazine*, and met and married a journalist, Reina Melcher. In 1909 he moved to New York, where he and Reina supported themselves by freelancing—his first book, the novel *Danny's Own Story* (1912), was finished then. Their life changed in 1912, when he was taken on to write a daily column in the New York *Evening Sun*.

In 1908 he had written in *Uncle Remus's Magazine* about 'Literary Cockroaches'. In his 'Sun Dial' column on 29 March 1916, he introduced Archy, a philosophical as well as a literary cockroach, whose contributions were found each morning in the typewriter: 'i with the gift of a homer / must smile when a mouse calls me pal / tumble bugs are my familiars / this is the punishment meted / because I have written vers libre'—the lack of capitals was due to Archy's inability to manage the shift key. As companion and foil Marquis invented the cat Mehitabel; the pair first appeared as a book in *archy and mehitabel* (1927), and subsequently in other volumes— see also *archyology: the long lost tales of archy and mehitabel*, ed. Jeff Adams (1996), uncollected stories. Though remembered, as he feared he would be, as the 'creator of a goddam cockroach', he used other comic personae, such as Hermione—see *Hermione and Her Little Group of Serious Thinkers* (1917), monologues in free verse satirizing upper-class pretentiousness. Clem Hawley, the 'Old Soak', 'whose devotion to alcoholic fellowship and endearing generosity of spirit superseded the practical concerns of work and family support', and who personified Marquis's opposition to Prohibition, inspired *The Old Soak's History of the World* (1924) and a play, *The Old Soak* (1922), which ran for 423 performances on Broadway. This was his greatest dramatic success: his greatest and most demoralizing failure was his play about the Crucifixion, *The Dark Hours* (published 1924), which ran for only eight performances in 1932.

In 1925, having written a daily column for 13 years, the last three for the *Herald Tribune*, he gave up his '23-inch grave'. Now without a regular salary, he tried Hollywood for a time. To this period belong a novel of Hollywood, *Off the Arm* (1930), the volumes of short stories *When the Turtles Sing and Other Unusual Tales* (1928) and *A Variety of People* (1929), and *Love Sonnets of a Caveman and Other Poems* (1928). His life was dogged by tragedy. His 5-year-old son died in 1921, Reina in 1923, and their 13-year-old daughter in 1931. In 1926 he married Marjorie Vonnegut, who died suddenly in 1936, shortly after he had suffered a third stroke, which left him helpless. See *The Best of Don Marquis*, ed. Christopher Morley, 1946; Edward Anthony, *O Rare Don Marquis*, 1962 (biography); Lynn Lee, *Don Marquis*, 1981 (biographical/critical study).

MARRYAT, FREDERICK (1792–1848) British novelist and seaman, was born in Westminster. Having several times tried to run away to sea from school, he was in 1806 entered as a midshipman in the *Impérieuse*, commanded by the dashing Lord Cochrane (1775–1860). He served in the West Indies and off the North American coast, becoming a lieutenant in 1814, and a commander in 1815, when he was invalided home. He was back at sea in 1820, commanding the sloop which guarded Napoleon's escape routes from St Helena. He was Senior Naval Officer in Rangoon in 1824, and in 1825 commanded the daring expedition against the Burmese up the Bassein River, and was promoted to captain. He served in the Atlantic from 1828 to 1830, when he resigned for 'private' reasons.

He was awarded a gold medal in 1818 for saving life at sea, was elected a Fellow of the Royal Society in 1819 for his work on signalling, and was made CB in 1826. Now he became a novelist, having already written at sea *The Naval Officer: or, Scenes and Adventures in the Life of Frank Mildmay* (1829). The father of the English sea story, he usually centres his action on a boy growing into manhood, as in *Mr Midshipman Easy* (1836) and *Percival Keene* (1842), in which an illegitimate youth serves under his father and brings him round to a sense of responsibility for him. He also wrote children's novels, notably *The Children of the New Forest* (1847), a Civil War romance. In 1847, eager for a change, he applied to the Admiralty for a posting at sea. In his anger at being refused, he broke a blood vessel. His death was hastened by the loss at sea of his eldest son. His daughter Florence (1838–99) wrote over seventy books, including novels with such titles as *A Scarlet Sin* (1890). See Oliver Warner, *Captain Marryat: a Rediscovery*, 1953.

MARSH, NGAIO (1895–1982) New Zealand novelist and theatrical producer, was born in Christchurch 'of what the Victorians used to call poor but genteel parentage', and was educated at St Margaret's College and Canterbury University School of Art. Her ambition to be a painter, as which she was one of a notable Christchurch group, was diverted when an actor-manager turned down a romantic play she had written, but took her on as an actress. After several years as a producer, she joined a friend in an interior-decorating business in London, where one rainy day she started writing a detective novel. *A Man Lay Dead* (1934) was the first of 31, all of which feature as detective the urbane Roderick Alleyn, named after the founder of her father's school, Dulwich College. She returned home in 1932, after which she divided her time between England, where she was fêted as a novelist, and New Zealand, where she lived in the wooden house built by her father in the Cashmere Hills above Christchurch, and 'intellectual friends tactfully avoid[ed] all mention of my published work'. In New Zealand, however, she exercised her talent as a producer, especially of SHAKESPEARE, and worked for the establishment of a professional theatre. In her last novel, *Light Thickens* (1982), she combined her two interests with a murder mystery centred on a performance of Shakespeare's *Macbeth*. It was probably diffidence which prevented her from writing the 'serious novel about New Zealand' which she contemplated. Her autobiography, *Black Beech and Honeydew* (rev. edn 1981), is wholly reticent about her writing. She was made OBE in 1948 and DBE in 1966. See Margaret Lewis, *Ngaio Marsh: a Life*, new edn 1992; Kathryne Slate McDorman, *Ngaio Marsh*, 1991

(critical study); Rahn, B. J. (ed.), *Ngaio Marsh: the Woman and Her Work*, 1995.

MARSTON, JOHN (1576–1634) English poet and dramatist, was born in Oxfordshire, the son of a well-to-do lawyer and of the daughter of an Italian physician. He was educated at Brasenose College, Oxford, and for a career in the law at the Middle Temple, where his father had rooms. He preferred the company and example of the literary coterie of the time, and in 1598 published *The Metamorphosis of Pigmalions Image, and Certaine Satyres* (the title piece has been variously read as a poor attempt at erotic verse, a seduction poem, and a parody), and *The Scourge of Villanie*, in which he continued his attacks on the literary prelate, Joseph Hall (1574–1656). It seems that he was already working on his didactic satirical comedy, *Histriomastix*, for the child actors of St Paul's to perform in 1599, when an edict inspired by John Whitgift (c.1530–1604) effectively banned the publication of verse satires and epigrams. All Marston's plays were written for boys' companies, but they vary in form. *Jack Drum's Entertainment* (1600) is a farce; *Antonio and Mellida* and *Antonio's Revenge* (both 1602) are Italianate tragic burlesques. In *The Malcontent* (1604) and *Parasitaster: or, The Fawne* (1606) the plots turn on the disguise motif. In 1605 he collaborated with JONSON and CHAPMAN to write *Eastward Hoe*, for which Jonson anyway was imprisoned; in *The Dutch Courtezan* (1605) he similarly exploits character contrasts and the balance between comedy and tragedy. *The Wonder of Women: or The Tragedie of Sophonisba* (1606) is an out-and-out tragedy (after SENECA), in which the poetry shines through. In 1608 he was briefly imprisoned for a reason which is obscure, but immediately afterwards he sold his share in the Blackfriars' company, and studied for the Anglican priesthood at St Mary's Hall, Oxford, being ordained in 1609. He was Rector of Barford St Martin, Wiltshire, until 1616, and of Christ Church, Hampshire 1616–31. See *Selected Plays*, ed. P. Jackson Macdonald and Michael Neill, 1986; Anthony Caputi, *John Marston, Satirist*, 1961 (critical study).

MARTIAL (MARCUS VALERIUS MARTIALIS) (c.40–104) Roman epigrammatic poet, was a Spaniard from Bilbilis who came to Rome in 64, and was taken up by his fellow-countrymen SENECA and LUCAN, until they were purged by Nero. Initially he lived in a third-floor flat on the slope of the Quirinal Hill, and scraped a living by writing short verses to order. He went on to publish several books of them, and to own a farm in the country as well as a house in Rome. He was a hack, a parasite, and, when it suited him (as when writing about the emperor Domitian), an unctuous flatterer. He was, however, almost always witty and frequently poetic, and pioneered a form of literature which has had many exponents. See *The Epigrams*, tr. James Michie, 1978 (includes Latin texts); *Martial in English*, ed. John Sullivan and Anthony Boyle, 1996.

MARTIN, THEODORE see AYTOUN.

MARTIN, VIOLET see SOMERVILLE.

MARTINEAU, HARRIET (1802–76) British novelist, essayist, and educationist, was born in Norwich, the sixth of eight children of a manufacturer of cloth and bombazine. She received a good Unitarian education at home and at a local school, but began to go deaf in her teens—she already had no sense of smell. When she was 24, her fiancé, a Unitarian minister, became insane, and her father died. In 1829 her family was destitute, and she took financial responsibility for them. Unable to teach because of her deafness, she wrote, and came to earn more money by her pen than any woman before her. *Illustrations of Political Economy* (1832–34), stories exemplifying economic principles, sold phenomenally and made her famous. She moved to London, and toured America, where she fearlessly condemned slavery and promoted women's rights. *Deerbrook* (1839), her best and most conventional novel, is a didactic study of provincial life. In 1846 she built herself a house in Ambleside, in the Lake District, from which she wrote to E. B. BROWNING that 'here [sensual vice] is beyond anything I could ever have looked for', and where she was visited by CHARLOTTE BRONTË, GEORGE ELIOT, and other literary luminaries. WORDSWORTH, her neighbour, thought her 'a dangerous companion', and particularly deprecated her proselytizing zeal for mesmerism, which she claimed had cured her of a near-fatal illness—the publication of *Letters on Mesmerism* (1845) suggested to many others that she had abandoned her rationalist stance. In 1847 she visited the Middle East. She wrote numerous crusading works, and from 1852 to 1869 contributed leading articles to the *Daily News*. Outspoken, eccentric, and frequently ill, she declared, 'I long ago came to the conclusion that . . . I am probably the happiest single woman in England.' See *Autobiography*, new edn 1983; *Selected Letters*, ed. Valerie Sanders, 1991; Robert K. Webb, *Harriet Martineau: a Radical Victorian*, 1960; Shelagh Hunter, *Harriet Martineau: the Poetics of Moralism*, 1996 (critical study).

MARVELL, ANDREW (1621–78) English poet and satirist, was born in Winestead-in-Holderness, Yorkshire, the son of the vicar, who moved his family to Hull in 1624. He was educated at Hull Grammar School and Trinity College, Cambridge; in 1637 verses of his in Latin and Greek were published in a

volume celebrating the birth of a child to the King. In about 1639 he had a brief association with Catholicism, but was recalled to Anglicanism and Cambridge by his father, who was drowned in the Humber in 1641. He travelled abroad between 1642 and 1647, and flexed his poetic muscles in the satire, 'Flecknoe, an English Priest at Rome'—Richard Flecknoe (*d. c.*1678) priest, traveller, and dud poet, was in Rome during Lent in 1645 and 1646, and reappears in DRYDEN's *Mac Flecknoe*. In 1650 Marvell wrote 'An Horatian Ode upon Cromwell's Return from Ireland', the first of several tributes to the Lord Protector, but significant in that he is equally fair to Charles I, who even when on 'the tragic scaffold', 'He nothing common did or mean / Upon that memorable scene'. From 1650 to 1652 he was tutor to the daughter of Lord Fairfax (1612–71), the Parliamentary general, at Nun Appleton House in Yorkshire, where it is presumed he wrote most of his lyrical poems, including 'Bermudas', as well as some very pleasing examples of local and pastoral verse, such as 'Upon Appleton House', 'Upon the Hill and Grove at Bilbrough', 'The Garden', and the 'Mower' pieces. For a time in 1656, and again between 1662 and 1665, he was abroad on political or undercover business of state. In 1657, on the recommendation of MILTON, he was appointed Latin Secretary to the Council of State, and it is said that he supported Milton at the time of the Restoration of the Monarchy in 1660. He was elected Member of Parliament for Hull in 1659, and sat until his death. *The Last Instructions to a Painter*, written in 1667, is a standard form of attack on the licence of the court, and less inspired than his anonymous prose satire against religious intolerance, *The Rehearsal Transpros'd* (1672). None of his early poems were printed in his lifetime. *Miscellaneous Poems* (1681) was published from manuscripts found by a 'Mary Marvell', who claimed to be his wife but appears to have been his housekeeper, Mary Palmer.

Marvell's lyric themes are conventional and at first sight their treatment is almost commonplace, but his intellectual capacity and command of rhythm, rhyme, phrase, and wit endow them with extraordinary quality. 'On a Drop of Dew' begins as a nature poem but expands effortlessly into an analogy of the soul. 'The Nymph Complaining for the Death of Her Faun' incorporates a whole range of additional emotions. 'To His Coy Mistress' is rightly famous for its treatment of, and scholarly but delightful variations on, HERRICK's exhortation to 'Gather ye rosebuds while ye may': typified by his attribution in a single phrase of both wings and chariot to Time, 'Time's wingéd chariot', and the aptness of his metaphors. In his political and satirical poems, he looks forward to and often does not suffer by comparison with DRYDEN.

See [*Works*], ed. Frank Kermode and Keith Walker, 1991; *The Complete Poems*, ed. George deF. Lord, 1993; [*Selected Verse*], ed. Frank Kermode and Keith Walker, 1994; Robert Wilcher, *Andrew Marvell*, 1986 (critical study); Annabel Patterson, *Andrew Marvell*, 1994 (critical introduction).

MARX, KARL (1818–83) German political philosopher, was born in Trier, the son of a Jewish lawyer who had nominally converted to Protestantism to enable him to practise. He was educated at the gymnasium in Trier and at Berlin University, having transferred from Bonn after being jailed for drunkenness and wounded in a duel. A doctoral thesis was accepted in 1841, but when no academic post materialized, he took to journalism, writing on social and political affairs for *Rheinische Zeitung*, which he edited in 1842 until it was banned. In 1843 he married his childhood sweetheart, Jenny von Westphalen (*d*. 1883), to whom he had been engaged for seven years. They settled in Paris, where he met Friedrich Engels (1820–95) and began to collaborate with him in writing pamphlets. Expelled from Paris, he went to Brussels, where he signed a contract for a study of economics and politics, which he did not deliver—the first of many deadlines missed by *Das Kapital*. Following the congress of the newly established Communist League in London in 1847, he and Engels produced the celebrated Communist manifesto (1848; ed. David McLellan, 1992), outlining his theory of politics. After further expulsions and participation in revolutionary activities in Cologne, he and his family took refuge in London, where he spent the rest of his life. *Zur Kritik der politischen Ökonomie* (1859; tr. N. I. Stone as *A Contribution to the Critique of Political Economy*, 1904) was only a portion of what was intended to be a wider work. In 1864, at the inaugural meeting of the International Workingmen's Association (later First International), he was elected to its general council. The first volume of *Das Kapital* was published in 1867. He never completed the second or third volumes, which were prepared for press after his death by Engels and first published in English (tr. Samuel Moore and Edward Aveling) in 1887. See *Selected Writings*, ed. David McLellan, 1977; David McLellan, *Karl Marx: a Biography*, 3rd edn 1996; Frank E. Manuel, *A Requiem for Karl Marx*, 1995 (critical biography).

MASEFIELD, JOHN (1878–1967) British poet, novelist, children's writer, and dramatist, was born in Ledbury, Herefordshire, the third of six children of a country solicitor. His mother died in 1885, and in 1888 he went as a boarder to King's School, Warwick, from which he was removed three years later on the death of his father. He continued his edu-

cation in the school-ship HMS *Conway*, and sailed for South America as an apprentice merchant seaman in 1894, but was sent home after being ill. He returned to sea a year later, but deserted ship in New York, spending three years working in a carpet factory in Yonkers and doing other jobs, while reading the English poets and starting to write. Back in England, he was a bank clerk for three years, during which he recovered his health. He also met YEATS, and published *Salt-Water Ballads* (1902) and two further volumes, containing such popular poems as 'Sea Fever' and 'Cargoes', as well as evocations of the land ('Tewkesbury Road' and 'Twilight'). Such poems gave him a reputation as a kind of maritime KIPLING, an influence Masefield denied. He married in 1903 and for a time worked for the *Manchester Guardian*, before increasing his literary range and output with some excellent adventure stories, including *Lost Endeavour* (1910) and *Jim Davis* (1911), and plays, of which *The Tragedy of Nan* (1908), a domestic tragedy set in the early 19th century, is praised by Professor Allardyce Nicoll in *British Drama* (4th edn 1947) for its 'unflinching realism'. The same attribute could be applied to the narrative poem, *The Everlasting Mercy* (1911), some of whose scenes and language shocked the literary world but, according to Frank Swinnerton in *The Georgian Literary Scene* (1935), 'made the general public read what he had written'. In *Dauber* (1913), written in rhyme royal, the conflict between the artist and his environment is set within a stirring narrative of the sea. Masefield served with the Red Cross in France and the Dardanelles in World War I, immediately after which he published *Reynard the Fox* (1919), a narrative poem about a fox hunt which is redolent of the English countryside.

He and his wife (she died in 1960) now settled in Boar's Hill, Oxford, where he built a small theatre next door. While continuing to write poetry and plays, including *The Coming of Christ* (1928), he became a noted children's author, whose fantasies *The Midnight Folk* (1927) and *The Box of Delights* (1935), and rousing costume thrillers, *Dead Ned* (1938) and *Live and Kicking Ned* (1939), are still read and admired. *The Nine Days Wonder* (1941) is a prose account of the retreat from Dunkirk, written without the deliberate romanticism of his equivalent work of World War I, *Gallipoli* (1916). He was appointed Poet Laureate in 1930, a post which he undertook seriously and assiduously, and he was awarded the OM in 1935. See *Collected Poems*, 1929; *Selected Poems*, ed. Donald E. Stanford, 1984; *So Long to Learn: Chapters of an Autobiography*, 1966; Constance Babington-Smith, *John Masefield: a Life*, new edn 1985; Muriel Spark, *John Masefield*, new edn 1992 (biographical/critical study); Margery Fisher, *John Masefield*, 1963 (study of his children's books).

MASON, A(LFRED) E(DWARD) W(OODLEY) (1865–1948) British novelist and dramatist, was born in Camberwell, London, and was educated at Dulwich College and Trinity College, Oxford, after which he went on the stage, touring in the provinces. In 1894, though he was in the first production of C. B. SHAW's *Arms and the Man*, he could get no other part in London, and turned to writing novels instead. His aptitude for cloak-and-dagger intrigue was confirmed by his second novel, *The Courtship of Morrice Buckler* (1896), for the tale of adventure by *Miranda of the Balcony* (1899), and for historical romance by *Clementina* (1901), about the mother of Charles Edward Stuart. A trip to the Sudan after the battle of Omdurman (1898) gave the setting for *The Four Feathers* (1902), an adventure story which is also a psychological study of heroism in several forms. *At the Villa Rose* (1910) introduced the French detective, Inspector Hanaud, who reappears in subsequent novels, notably *The Prisoner in the Opal* (1928). Mason was Liberal Member of Parliament for Coventry 1906–10, and as a major in the Royal Marine Light Infantry in World War I was a secret agent in Spain, Morocco, and Mexico. Latterly he returned to the historical novel with *Fire Over England* (1936), *Königsmark* (1938), and *Musk and Amber* (1942). Of his plays, *The Witness for the Defence* (produced 1911) has most merit. *At the Villa Rose* (1920) and *Running Water* (1922), from his own novels, had mixed success, the former running for 126 performances, very good for that time, and the latter for only 28. Deservedly popular for his versatility as well as for his skill, he refused a knighthood as being an irrelevance to a childless, unmarried man. See Roger Lancelyn Green, *A. E. W. Mason: the Adventures of a Story Teller*, 1952.

MASON, BOBBIE ANN (b. 1940) American short-story writer and novelist, was born in Kentucky and brought up against 'the sheltered and isolated background' of a farm near Mayfield. After graduating from the University of Kentucky, she took further degrees in English at the State University of New York, Binghamton, and the University of Connecticut, after which she taught English and journalism at Mansfield State College, Pennsylvania, for seven years. Her first two books were critical studies: *Nabokov's Garden: a Guide to Ada* (1974) and *The Girl Sleuth: a Feminist Guide to the Bobbsey Twins, Nancy Drew, and Their Sisters* (1975). When she discovered her true métier, 'to write about my roots and the kinds of people I'd known, but from a contemporary perspective', she produced, in *Shiloh and Other Stories* (1982), a set of portraits of small-town society whose distinction is in their being presented without irony or sentimentality. A further volume of stories is *Love Life* (1989). *In Country* (1985) is a novel which is both comic and poignant, as a young woman whose father died in the Vietnam War tries to make sense of it and of her relationship with her uncle, who survived the same conflict. It was followed by *Spence + Lila* (1988), a study primarily of the erosion by economic change of an ageing couple's traditional rural livelihood, and *Feather Crowns* (1993), in which, in 1900, the wife of a western Kentucky tobacco farmer bears quintuplets and becomes a celebrity.

MASON, BRUCE (1921–82) New Zealand dramatist, was born in Wellington, brought up in Takapuna, and educated at Wellington College. He spent a year at Wellington Teachers Training College, where his one-act play, *Focus*, written when he was 19, was performed in 1941. During World War II he was a naval sublieutenant, serving on Russian convoy duties. He then became a research assistant and a curator of manuscripts, had his first short story published ('The Glass Wig', *Landfall* 1947), and began an association with the Unity Theatre, Wellington, which between 1948 and 1960 he served as President, Secretary, and committee member. He was a co-founder of the Downstage Theatre, Wellington, for which, to ensure continuity of production, he also wrote, directed, and performed. The first two of his quartet of domestic plays, *The Bonds of Love* and *The Evening Paper*, were produced at the Unity Theatre in 1953. *The Pohutukawa Tree* (produced 1957, published 1960) was the first of a sequence of five plays with Maori themes. Frustrated at the lack of opportunities for the production of indigenous drama, he presented and performed in 1960 the first of his solo pieces, *The End of the Golden Weather*, a boyhood reverie—see in *Bruce Mason Solo* (1981). Latterly he returned to the drama of social issues with *The Blood of the Lamb* (1981). He died after surviving several operations for cancer. He was made CBE in 1980. See David Dowling, *Introducing Bruce Mason*, 1982.

MASON, R(ONALD) A(LISON) K(ELLS) (1905–71) New Zealand poet, was born in Penrose, Auckland, and educated at Auckland Grammar School and Auckland University College. Apart from visits to Samoa, Tonga, Australia, and China, his working life was spent almost entirely in Auckland, as public works foreman, trades union secretary, landscape gardener, and part-time college coaching tutor and schoolteacher. In 1923 he circulated in manuscript a collection of his poetry, under the title of *In the Manner of Men*. *The Beggar* (1924), a selection of poems all written before he was 19, and published by himself in book form in brown paper covers, is regarded as the first manifestation of an original and gifted New Zealand poetic voice. The commercial publication of a limited edition of *No New Thing: Poems 1924–1929* (1934), in whose opening poem he describes his 'bitter verses' as 'sponges steeped in vinegar / useless to the happy-eyed / but handy for the crucified', was fraught with production problems, and only a few copies reached the public. *This Dark Will Lighten: Selected Poems 1923–1941* (1941), for which he rearranged the typography of earlier poems and dispensed with conventional punctuation, was adequately marketed but revealed how little he had composed since his initial burst of enthusiasm. He also wrote dramas and was an active political journalist with Marxist leanings. See *Collected Poems*, introduction by Allen Curnow, 1990; J. E. Weir, *R. A. K. Mason*, 1977 (critical study).

MASSINGER, PHILIP (1583–1640) English dramatist, was born in Salisbury, the son of Arthur Massinger (*d.* 1606), a man of standing in the academic and political fields, and was educated at St Alban Hall, Oxford, without taking his degree. He collaborated with DEKKER and TOURNEUR, and regularly with JOHN FLETCHER. His own tragedies, which include *The Duke of Millaine* (printed 1623) and *The Roman Actor* (1629), fall in time between those of SHAKESPEARE and the more decadent horrors of JOHN FORD, and though there is a superficial structure, the characters fail to inspire emotion. The same lack of vitality affects his romantic tragicomedies, of which *The Bondman: an Antient Story* (1624) and *The Maid of Honour* (1632) are nevertheless interesting examples of their kind. It is with his two out-and-out comedies, *A New Way to Pay Old Debts* (1633) and *The City Madam* (licensed 1632), that he emerges as worthy to stand with JONSON; though they are nearer to the comedy of CONGREVE, over forty years ahead, in their dependence on intrigue and in their memorable portraiture of hypocrisy in the forms of Sir Giles Overreach, based on a real-life villain, and Luke Frugal, the servile brother turned monster when he believes the head of the household is out of the way. Massinger died suddenly one night in his house in Southwark, and his body, accompanied by actors, was taken to the nearby church of St Saviour's and, according to one account, buried in the same grave as Fletcher. See *Selected Plays*, ed. Colin Gibson, 1978.

MASTERS, EDGAR LEE (1868–1950) American poet, dramatist, and novelist, was born in Garnett, Kansas, and was brought up in Illinois, where he graduated from Lewistown High School, and was admitted to the Illinois Bar in 1891. He had already published *A Book of Verse* (1898) and *Maximilian: a Play in Five Acts* (1902) when he went into law partnership with Clarence Darrow (1857–

1938), who in 1925 was to make the famous (and initially unsuccessful) defence of the Tennessee science teacher, John T. Scopes, charged with teaching the doctrine of evolution. The partnership broke up in acrimony in 1911 and Darrow later represented Masters's first wife in her divorce proceedings. *Songs and Sonnets*, by 'Webster Ford', was published in two volumes 1910–12. A study of *Selected Epigrams from the Greek Anthology* (1890), edited and translated by J. W. Mackail (1859–1945), gave him the inspiration and poetic form for *Spoon River Anthology* (1915), an ingenious arrangement of epigrammatic statements from the grave, revealing the lives and inner thoughts of a whole small-town community, much extended in *The New Spoon River* (1924). He gave up the law in 1920 and moved to New York, where he wrote extensively: novels in the *Spoon River* vein, biographies, including those of VACHEL LINDSAY (1935), WHITMAN (1937), and TWAIN (1938), and an autobiography, *Across Spoon River* (1936), as well as more verse and plays. He never matched, still less transcended, the creativity which made the *Spoon River* poems influential in the depiction of communities and in the development of the short story.

MATHER, COTTON (1663–1728) American prose writer, scholar, and Puritan divine, was born in Boston, eldest son of Increase Mather (1639–1723), cleric and writer, and grandson of Richard Mather (1596–1669) and John Cotton (1584–1652), English-born pioneers of New England Congregationalism. He entered Harvard College at the age of 12, already able to write and speak Latin, to read New Testament Greek, and to understand Hebrew. He graduated in 1678 and, feeling that his childhood stammer disqualified him from preaching, decided to be a physician. He overcame his handicap, however, took his MA degree at Harvard in 1681, and was in 1685 installed as his father's colleague at the Second Church of Boston, where he remained for the rest of his life. Passed over as President of Harvard, he played a part in many political and social issues. He actively supported the rebellion in 1689 against the Governor of New England, Sir Edmund Andros (1637–1714), who was captured, imprisoned, and returned to England. His genuine interest in witchcraft, about which he wrote *Memorable Providences Relating to Witchcraft and Possessions* (1689), and his pronouncements on the influence of the Devil in undermining religious stability, led him to be held partly responsible for the witchcraft trials of Salem in 1692. He did, however, recommend caution in the acceptance of evidence; his fault was that he did not speak out against the miscarriage of justice. He also advocated schools for the children of slaves. Having in 1714 been one of the very few Americans elected to the Royal Society in London before

1750, he studied the effects of smallpox inoculation some time before he championed the practice; he was strenuously opposed and had a bomb thrown through the window of his house.

His first wife, Abigail Philips, died in 1702 after 16 years of marriage. In 1703 he married Elizabeth Hubbard, a widow, who died in 1713. His third wife, Lydia George, whom he married in 1715, went mad. Of his 15 children by his first two marriages, only six lived beyond childhood, and only two survived him. Throughout traumas in his personal life, and the performance of pastoral as well as public duties, he continued to research and write—in a library which numbered several thousand volumes.

The most impressive of his numerous works, which embraced almost every known kind of non-fiction and for which he employed a variety of styles, is *Magnalia Christi Americana: or, The Ecclesiastical History of New England from Its First Planting, in the Year 1620, unto the Year of Our Lord, 1698* (London, 1702). In seven volumes (800 large-format pages), and incorporating some of his previously published works, it comprises a history of the colony, of Harvard College, and of the Congregational Church, biographies of governors, ministers, and Harvard graduates, and accounts of God's workings. *Bonifacius: an Essay Upon the Good, that is to be Devised and Designed . . .* (1710), later known as *Essays to Do Good*, whose relevance to succeeding generations was acknowledged by BENJAMIN FRANKLIN, is a study of Christian civic responsibility with practical suggestions for exercising it. In *The Christian Philosopher* (1721), Mather summarized aspects of scientific knowledge and argued for a reconciliation of science and religion. *The Political Fables* (unpublished in his lifetime but circulated in manuscript in about 1692) is unique in early American literature and reflects the precision and style of English prose masters of the time. See *Selections from Cotton Mather*, ed. Kenneth B. Murdock, new edn 1960; Kenneth Silverman, *The Life and Times of Cotton Mather*, 1984; David Levin, *Cotton Mather: the Young Life of the Lord's Remembrancer 1663–1703*, 1978.

MATSUO BASHŌ see BASHŌ.

MATURIN, CHARLES ROBERT (1782–1824) Irish novelist and dramatist, was born in Dublin and educated at Trinity College, Dublin. He became Curate of Loughrea, and later of St Peter's, Dublin. In 1809 his father, who had been helping him financially, was wrongfully dismissed from his government post. Though he was subsequently reinstated, the family suffered in the meantime, and Maturin set up a school in his house to augment his stipend. He was also writing novels: *Fatal Revenge: or, The Family of Mont-*

orio (1807), a prentice Gothic tale, which WALTER SCOTT praised in the *Quarterly Review; The Wild Irish Boy* (1808), in which ROUSSEAU's and WORDSWORTH's philosophy of nature is brought to bear on Irish nationalism and the Irish character; and *The Milesian Chief: a Romance* (1812). Disaster struck when he lost his house, and with it his school, from standing surety for a friend. In desperation, he sent the manuscript of a tragedy to Scott, who sent him £50 and passed the play on to BYRON, who also contributed £50, and persuaded Edmund Kean (1787–1833) to stage it at Drury Lane. *Bertram: or, The Castle of St Aldobrand* (1816) did moderately well: not so *Manuel* (1817) and *Fredolfo* (1819), and Maturin went back to fiction. After *Women: or, Pour et Contre* (1818), came *Melmoth the Wanderer* (1820), a compelling Gothic horror novel (some regard it as the most sublime of the genre), whose protagonist sells his soul to the devil in return for a longer life, and regrets it—WILDE, who was related to Maturin through his mother, assumed the name Sebastian Melmoth after his release from prison. A man whose penchant for extravagance and show was tempered by eccentricity and a brooding morbidity, all of which are reflected in his single masterpiece, it is said Maturin's death was accelerated by his taking the wrong medicine. See Robert E. Lougy, *Charles Robert Maturin*, 1975 (critical study).

MAUGHAM, W(ILLIAM) SOMERSET (1874–1965) British novelist, short-story writer, and dramatist, was born in Paris, the youngest son of the legal adviser to the British Embassy. He lived in France until at ten he was orphaned and put into the care of an uncle, the Vicar of Whitstable, Kent. He was educated at King's School, Canterbury, and later spent a year at Heidelberg University without taking a degree. At his own insistence, he became a medical student at St Thomas's Hospital, and managed while studying to read voraciously and to observe human life. His first novel, *Liza of Lambeth* (1897), was published the year he qualified as MRCS LRCP, whereupon he abandoned medicine for literature and travelled in Spain. The failure of subsequent novels and the rejection of several plays almost made him reverse his decision. His first play to be performed was a one-act piece in German, *Schiffbrüchig* (1901). *A Man of Honour* was put on by the Stage Society in 1903. In 1907 *Lady Frederick*, a traditional comedy of manners, was staged at the Royal Court Theatre as a stopgap. It ran for 422 performances; within a year he had three other plays also running in the West End. He continued to write plays until 1933, in a variety of styles and moods, his cynical comedies *The Circle* (1921), some of whose cast were lustily booed for inaudibility on its first night, and *The Constant Wife* (1927) being the most highly regarded.

In 1911, now more comfortably off, he began his most lasting literary work, the semi-autobiographical *Of Human Bondage* (1915), whose depressive realism did not at first appeal to a country involved in World War I. During the war he served in the Intelligence Department, his experiences being reflected later in *Ashenden: or the British Agent* (1928). In 1916 he married Syrie Wellcome, the daughter of the philanthropist Thomas Barnado (1845–1905): they were divorced in 1927. Meanwhile he visited the East with his secretary/companion Gerald Haxton (1892–1944); published *The Moon and Sixpence* (1919), based on the life of Paul Gauguin (1848–1903), the French postimpressionist painter; and absorbed the basic social atmosphere which he used most effectively in the many of his short stories set in that region, of which the most famous is 'Rain' (1921). In 1928 he settled in a villa at St Jean, Cap Ferrat, where he wrote *Cakes and Ale* (1930), a novel in which he gently takes revenge on the English literary establishment. Having escaped from France in a coal boat, he spent the war years in the USA, from which he returned to France, after publishing *The Razor's Edge* (1944), which reflects his interest in Indian mysticism. He founded the Somerset Maugham Award in 1947, to enable promising young British writers to travel. He was appointed CH in 1954. See *Short Stories*, 4 vols, new edns 1990; *Selected Plays*, new edn 1991; *The Summing Up*, 1938 (autobiographical study); *A Writer's Notebook*, new edn 1991 (extracts from journal); Robert Calder, *Willie: the Life of W. Somerset Maugham*, new edn 1992; Bryan Connon, *Somerset Maugham and the Maugham Dynasty*, 1996 (family history); John Whitehead, *Maugham: a Reappraisal*, 1988.

MAUPASSANT, GUY DE (1850–1893) French short-story writer and novelist, was born at Château de Miromesnil, near Dieppe, and grew up in Étretat, Normandy, after his parents separated in about 1856. He was educated at the seminary in Yvetot, and for a year at Collège Impérial, Rouen. His study of law was interrupted by service in the Franco-Prussian War, after which he entered the Ministère de la Marine in 1872 as a clerk, subsequently transferring to the Ministère de l'Instruction Publique. A countryman and sportsman by inclination, to whom city streets were anathema, he published his first short story in 1875, as Joseph Prunier. Through FLAUBERT, who was a friend of his mother, he met novelists such as DAUDET and ZOLA, to whose collection of stories, *Les Soirées de Médan* (1880), subsidized by Zola as a means of publicizing his literary philosophy of Naturalism, he contributed 'Boule de Suif' [Ball of Fat]. It was a literary sensation. He resigned from the civil service and published in quick succession two collections of stories,

La Maison Tellier (1881) and *Mademoiselle Fifi* (1882), and a novel, *Une Vie* (1883). These were followed by more of the same kind as well as by books about his travels. Of his six novels, *Pierre et Jean* (1888; tr. Clara Bell as *Pierre and Jean*, 1890; tr. Leonard Tancock, 1979), a study of family rivalries and discontents, prefaced by some general comments on the novel as an art form, has lasted best. His natural, and developed, gift, however, was for the short story, which he imbued with truth as well as style—see *A Day in the Country and Other Stories* (1990) and *Mademoiselle Fifi and Other Stories* (1993), tr. David Coward. The first symptoms of syphilis manifested themselves before he was 30. His mind began to go in 1889, and in 1892 he tried to commit suicide. He died in a private asylum.

MAURIAC, FRANÇOIS (1885–1970) French novelist, dramatist, and critic, was born in Bordeaux, where after his father's death in 1887 he and his three talented brothers were brought up by their mother in accordance with strict Catholic tenets. He was educated at the local lycée and university, after which he entered the École Nationale des Chartres, Paris, in 1906, though attendance at classes was secondary to his development as a writer. He served as a hospital orderly during World War I until invalided out in 1917 after contracting malaria in Salonika. He found a true literary voice with his fifth novel, *Le Baiser au Lépreux* (1922; tr. James Whittal as *The Kiss to the Leper*, 1923; tr. Gerard Hopkins as *A Kiss for the Leper*, 1950), an account of a disastrous arranged marriage; in the wake of Catholic protests at his pessimism, after *Génetrix* (1923; tr. Hopkins, 1950) he adopted a more naturalistic stance in his depiction of family conflicts. *Thérèse Desqueyroux* (1927; as *Thérèse* tr. Eric Sutton, 1928; tr. Hopkins, 1947), the self-discovery of a woman acquitted of attempting to poison her husband, was in part a personal protest which culminated in a crisis of faith, from which he emerged a calmer writer, more concerned with matters of salvation. He was awarded the Nobel Prize for Literature in 1952.

MAUROIS, ANDRÉ (1885–1967) French novelist and biographer, was born Émile Herzog in Elbeuf, of a family of Jewish industrialists, and was educated at the Lycée Corneille, Rouen, and Caen University. At the end of his year's army service he went into his father's cloth factory until World War I, in which he served at the front as a liaison officer with the British Army. His first novel, *Les Silences du Colonel Bramble* (1918; tr. Thurfrida Wake as *The Silence of Colonel Bramble*, 1919), caught the tone of an English officers' mess, observed through the eyes of a Frenchman. In the course of a career in which he continued to interpret the French to the English, the

English to the French, and both to the Americans, he wrote a history of England (tr. 1937) as well as of France (tr. 1949); and perpetuated, with *Ariel* (1923; tr. Ella D'Arcy, 1924), his life of P. B. SHELLEY, a form of biography of which he said that the writer 'might and should arrange his authentic materials in the manner of a novel and give his reader the feeling of a hero's progressive discovery of the world, which is the essence of romance'. *The Oxford History of English Literature* calls it 'of little value', but, in 1935, as the first of the initial ten Penguin titles, it was sold alongside fiction by CHRISTIE, HEMINGWAY, and SAYERS (at 6d each). He also wrote biographical studies of DISRAELI (tr. 1927), BYRON (tr. 1930), VOLTAIRE (tr. 1932), DICKENS (tr. 1934), PROUST (tr. 1950), DUMAS (tr. 1957), and BALZAC (tr. 1965). During World War II he was a liaison officer in France until the country fell, when he went to the USA. He enlisted again in 1943 when France officially re-entered the war, and served in north Africa and Italy. He was made Honorary KBE in 1938. See *Memoirs 1885–1967*, tr. Denver Lindley, 1970.

MAVOR, O. H. see BRIDIE.

MAXWELL, GAVIN see RAINE, KATHLEEN.

MAYAKOVSKY, VLADIMIR (VLADIMIROVICH) (1893–1930) Russian poet and dramatist, was born in Bagdadi (now Mayakovsky) and was brought up and went to school in Moscow, where he joined the Bolshevik party and was imprisoned in 1909–10. At the Moscow Institute of Painting, Sculpture, and Architecture in 1911–14, he became associated with the Futurist literary movement, under whose banner he began to publish his egocentric verse and drama, including the tragedy *Vladimir Mayakovsky* (1913). Having stated in 1917 that there was no problem in his acceptance of the Revolution, he set about becoming a poet of the masses without, seemingly, any clear notion as to how this might be achieved; he was torn between attempting to 'democratize' his style, as he did in his memorial poem to Lenin (1924), and waging an all-out war against the aesthetics of art, in pursuit of which he helped to found and edit the periodicals *Lef* (1923–25) and *New Lef* (1927–28). Two further plays, [*The Bedbug*] (1929) and [*The Bathhouse*] (1930), failed to appeal to the public. As unfortunate in love as he was confused in his destiny, he shot himself: only to be rehabilitated by Stalin in 1935 as 'the most talented poet of our Soviet epoch' and, according to PASTERNAK, compulsorily propagated 'like potatoes in the reign of Catherine the Great', which was, he added wryly, 'his second death'. See *Poems*, ed. Herbert Marshall, 1965; *The Complete Plays*, tr. Guy Daniels, 1968;

Wiktor Woroszylski, *The Life of Mayakovsky*, tr. Boleslaw Taborski, 1972.

MEHTA, VED (*b.* 1934) Indian prose writer, was born in Lahore. After being blinded by meningitis at the age of three, he was sent by his father, a public-health officer, to be trained at Dadar School for the Blind, an orphanage in Bombay. He was subsequently educated at Emerson Institute for the Blind, Lahore, and learned to type and to read Braille at the St Dunstan's centre for army personnel in Delhi. At 15 he went to Arkansas School for the Blind and then to Pomona College in the USA, after which he studied history at Balliol College, Oxford—see *Up at Oxford* (1993)—, and Harvard. He became a staff writer on the *New Yorker* in 1961, and a US citizen in 1975. *Face to Face*, an account of his life which he later saw as 'a sort of outline' for 'a large autobiographical work', was published in 1957. *Walking the Indian Streets* (1960), like most of his books composed of material first published in the *New Yorker*, was his version of a return visit to India after ten years away, made with MORAES, who wrote it up as *Gone Away: an Indian Journey* (1960). The two accounts differed so markedly that Mehta issued a revised edition, with an explanatory introduction (1971). The 'autobiographical work', spanning the years up to 1949 and set against the disturbed Indian political background of the times, duly manifested itself as four classic accounts, *Daddyji* (1972), *Mamaji* (1979), *Vedi* (1982), and *The Ledge Between the Streams* (1984). *Fly and the Fly-Bottle* (1963; 2nd edn 1983) and *The New Theologians* (1966) are interviews with historians, philosophers, and theologians. He has also published historical studies, notably *A Family Affair: India under Three Prime Ministers* (1982), and a comic novel, *Delinquent Chacha* (1967).

MELVILLE, HERMAN (1819–91) American novelist and poet, was born Melvill (the 'e' was added in the 1830s) in New York, the third of eight children of a couple of Scottish and Dutch-Colonial descent respectively. In 1830 his father, a dry goods merchant, went bankrupt and took a job in Albany, where he died insane in 1832. The family financial situation was not helped by the fact that an illegitimate daughter of Mr Melvill and her mother now made a claim on his inheritance from the estate of his own father. Melville was taken out of Albany Academy, did clerical jobs and a bit of teaching, and took a course in surveying and engineering at Lansingburgh Academy; none of which, in the aftermath of the 1837 Depression, led to anything. In 1839 he signed on as a deck hand in a packet ship to Liverpool and back, an experience which he re-created later in *Redburn: His First Voyage* (1849). Having still failed to land a job, in January 1841 he sailed as a seaman in the whaler *Acushnet*, bound for the South Seas, 'my Yale College and my Harvard'. In spite of the boat being new (it carried a library), and its owners acquaintances of the family, he and a colleague deserted in the Marquesas Islands in 1842, and spent four weeks with a Taipi tribe. Taken off by an Australian barque, he got involved in a mutiny, and after a period of somewhat ludicrous confinement in Tahiti, shipped in another whaler to Hawaii, where he enlisted as an ordinary seaman in a US warship, which deposited him in Boston in October 1844. As he later wrote to HAWTHORNE (1851): 'From my twenty-fifth year I date my life. Three weeks have scarcely passed, at any time between then and now, that I have not unfolded within myself.'

Melville's fictional account of his sojourn with the natives was taken by his elder brother Gansevoort (1816–1846), Secretary of the American Legation in London, and shown to John Murray (1808–92), the son of BYRON's publisher. It appeared as *Typee: a Peep at Polynesian Life, During a Four Months' Residence in a Valley of the Marquesas* (1846), and was published in New York in an expurgated version under a slightly different title—the discrepancy between the 'Four Months' and the four weeks he actually stayed enabled him to include anthropological observations from other accounts. A sequel, *Omoo* (1847), recounting with good humour his subsequent adventures among the mutineers and in Tahiti, was equally well received, and he promptly married Elizabeth Knapp Shaw, whose father was the Chief Justice of Massachusetts. *Mardi: and A Voyage Thither* (1849), begun as the third in the sequence, became, in the hands of its quixotic author, a satirical romantic fantasy, packed with literary allusions. He restored his reputation as a narrator with *Redburn* and *White-Jacket: or, The World in a Man-of-War* (1850), loosely based on the last lap of his voyage but with elements from other sources and from his imagination. *Journal of a Visit to London and the Continent 1849–1850* (ed. Eleanor Melvill Metcalf, 1948) records a momentous trip, primarily to arrange for the publication of *White-Jacket* in the face of the lack of copyright protection afforded in Britain to American authors.

In 1850 he moved with his family to Pittsfield, Massachusetts, a few miles from the home of Hawthorne, whose wife found him 'a person of great ardor & simplicity. He is all on fire with the subject that interests him. It rings through his frame like a cathedral bell.' *Moby-Dick* (1851; in Britain as *The Whale*), his epic novel of a quest for the white whale which symbolizes a whole range of aspirations, was described seventy years later by FORSTER (*Aspects of the Novel*) as 'an easy book, as long as we read it as a yarn or an account of whaling interspersed with

snatches of poetry. But as soon as we catch the song in it, it grows difficult and immensely important.' Its importance was belied by its sales, which during the last 25 years of Melville's life averaged an annual 22 copies. *Pierre: or, The Ambiguities* (1852), a weird amalgam of styles and genres, found even less favour with the public—it was effectively refused by his British publisher. *The Isle of the Cross* was rejected by his American publisher and was probably destroyed. He now felt himself for a time reduced to writing anonymous stories for magazines, among which were 'Bartleby, the Scrivener' (1853) and 'Benito Cereno' (1855). *Israel Potter: His Fifty Years of Exile* (1855), about a rejected hero of the American War of Independence, was more straightforward; but the reception of *The Confidence-Man, His Masquerade* (1857), a study of evil with allegorical implications, published while he was on a European tour for his health, made it the last novel to appear during his lifetime. He did the lecture circuit for three years, and then moved to New York to look for a job, his depression and the reaction to a carriage accident making him so difficult that his family thought he was going insane.

In 1866 he was appointed an inspector of customs, which he remained until 1885. He was now writing poetry: *Battle-Pieces and Aspects of the War* (1866), Civil War verse which ranks with WHITMAN's *Drum-Taps*; *Clarel: a Poem and Pilgrimage in the Holy Land* (1876); and *John Marr and Other Sailors* (privately published 1888)—see *Selected Poems of Herman Melville*, ed. Hennig Cohen (1991). And in 1888 he began the story, *Billy Budd* (discovered after his death and published in 1924), his final statement on good and evil. In this (to return to Forster), 'after the initial roughness of his realism—[he] reaches straight back into the universal, to a blackness and sadness so transcending our own that they are indistinguishable from glory'. The year before he died Melville received from the British Museum what was almost certainly a request for biographical information for a monograph: his reply indicated that he was astonished, because he had thought that his books were long forgotten! See Leon Howard, *Herman Melville: a Biography*, 1951; Laurie Robertson Lorant, *Melville: a Biography*, 1996; Hershel Parker, *Herman Melville: a Biography, Volume 1 1819–1851*, 1996; David Kirby, *Herman Melville*, 1994 (critical biography); A. R. Humphreys, *Melville*, 1962 (critical study); Tyrus Hillway, *Herman Melville*, 1985 (critical study).

MENCKEN, H(ENRY) L(OUIS)

(1880–1956) American journalist and critic, was born in Baltimore, where he lived all his life, and was educated at Knapp's Institute and Baltimore Polytechnic Institute. When he announced that he wanted to be a newspaperman and not go to college, his father consigned him to the family cigar factory. He took a correspondence course in writing, and was commended for using 'conversational style and colloquial expressions that prevail in the purlieus of a large city'. After his father's sudden death in 1899, he became a reporter on the Baltimore Herald, for which he worked in various capacities, including drama critic. In 1906 he became Editor of the Sunday Sun, for whose group he worked until 1941. His life's work as literary critic began seriously in 1908, when he became Literary Editor of Smart Set, of which he was Editor from 1914 to 1923 with George Jean Nathan (1882–1958). They founded the detective magazine, the Black Mask (1920), and the American Mercury (1924), a journal of literature and opinion; as Editor of the latter until 1933, he actively engaged in battle against puritanism, which he defined as 'the haunting fear that somewhere, someone may be happy'. His first book was Ventures into Verse (1903); his first two prose works were studies of the plays of G. B. SHAW (1905) and of the philosophy of NIETZSCHE (1908). The American Language (1919), several times revised and enlarged (the last in 1949), is a formative study of the development and usage of this separate stream of English. He published an anthology of his writings as A Mencken Chrestomathy (1949): he prepared a further collection, only recently discovered in manuscript, A Second Mencken Chrestomathy, ed. Terry Teachout (1995). Of Happy Days (1940), the first of three autobiographies, followed by Newspaper Days (1941) and Heathen Days (1943), he once remarked: 'I should say it is about eighty per cent truth. The rest consists of icing on the cake.' Further volumes of autobiography were embargoed for 35 years after his death: My Life as Author and Editor, ed. Jonathan Yardley (1993), was finished in 1948, just before a severe stroke cost him his ability to read and write—see also Thirty-Five Years of Newspaper Work, ed. Fred Hobson, Vincent Fitzpatrick, and Bradford Jacobs (1994). See Fred Hobson, Mencken: a Life, new edn 1995.

MEREDITH, GEORGE (1828–1909) British novelist, poet, and critic, was born in Portsmouth, the son of a naval tailor. After the death of his mother in 1833 and the departure of his father to London and then to Cape Town, he was brought up by aunts, and educated locally and at the Moravian school at Neuwied on the Rhine, and was then articled to a solicitor in London. He married the widowed daughter of PEACOCK in 1849, but she eloped in 1858 with the artist Henry Wallis (1830–1916), who had used Meredith as the model for his famous painting of the death of CHATTERTON—a sequence of events imaginatively recalled by ACKROYD in his novel, Chatterton (1987). A second marriage

in 1864 was happier. Meredith preferred to be known as a poet, but it was as a novelist that he became (with HARDY) regarded as a grand old man of literature, though without tangible reward, to which his tendency to play out his own misfortunes with an overwrought intensity contributed. The title poem of Modern Love, and Poems of the English Roadside, with Poems and Ballads (1862) is a sonnet-like sequence, recording incidents in a broken marriage. After two early prose fantasies, he published 12 novels, and his continuous experimentation with form justifies his influential status. In The Ordeal of Richard Feverel (1859), a runaway wife leaves a father to care for his son. A father/son relationship is also the theme of The Adventures of Harry Richmond (1871). The Egoist (1879), intellectually his most satisfying novel, is a practical exposition of his lecture 'On the Idea of Comedy and the Uses of the Comic Spirit' (1877). His most successful novel was Diana of the Crossways (1885), based on a contemporary scandal, and again featuring an erring wife. See Lionel Stevenson, The Ordeal of George Meredith, 1954; V. S. Pritchett, George Meredith and English Comedy, 1970.

MERES, FRANCIS see KYD; SHAKESPEARE.

MERRILL, JAMES (1926–95) American poet, was born in New York City, son of Charles E. Merrill (1885–1956), the financier and broker, and his second wife. He was brought up in some style, and was educated at Lawrenceville School and Amherst College, where his father had been. 'Broken Home' (1966) reflects the break-up of the marriage in 1937–38 and his feelings for his mother at a time when he 'found it difficult to believe in the way my parents lived'—he recreated his family as the Tannings in his novel The Seraglio (1957). At Amherst, where his stay was interrupted by service in the US Army, he graduated summa cum laude, having submitted a thesis on PROUST, whose subsequent influence on Merrill's writing was profound. 'When it came to sex,' he said in an interview, 'I had to face it that the worst iniquity my parents (and many of my friends) could imagine was for me a blessed source of pleasure and security—as well as suffering, to be sure.' His homosexuality, like that of Proust and CAVAFY, another writer with whom he identified, is a recurring theme in his poetry—the life and early death from leukemia of his close friend, the young Dutch poet Hans Lodeizen (1924–50), are frequently alluded to.

His first two books of verse were privately printed, though he included much of the second, The Black Swan (1946), in his first commercially-published collection, First Poems (1951), in which he introduced an alter ego, Charles, who reappears in several later poems. With *The Country of a Thousand Years of Peace* (1959), which incorporated many of the poems in *Short Stories* (1954), he had come to the choice of self, in many personifications and settings, as the dominant theme in his art. His canvas was extended by travel, and from 1959 for twenty years he and his companion, David Jackson (*b.* 1922), wintered in Greece from their spectacular home in Stonington, on Long Island Sound. Both environments feature in *Nights and Days* (1966), which won the National Book Award. Images of fire link the sequence of memories in *The Fire Screen* (1969); in *Braving the Elements* (1976) the view is cosmic. *The Divine Comedies* (1976), incorporating 'The Book of Ephraim', won the Pulitzer Prize. A trilogy with *Mirabell: Books of Number* (1978), winner of the National Book Award, and *Scripts for the Pageant* (1980), the whole was reissued with an epilogue, 'Coda: the Higher Keys', as *The Changing Light at Sandover* (1982). 'Ephraim' is a spirit originally contacted by Merrill and Jackson in 1955 through the medium of an Ouija board, whose intimations are used as the basis for the poet's exploration of three 'other worlds'—key figures are his friends AUDEN and Maria Mitsotáki (1907–74). His final collection, *A Scattering of Salts* (1995), is one of his most reflective, and includes 'The Ring Cycle', which looks back both to 'Matinees' (1969) and to the long-term effects of the opera by Richard Wagner (1813–83), which he first saw when he was 12, on his subsequent emotions. Shorter poems are in *From the First Nine: Poems 1946–1976* (1982). Prose is in *Recitative* (1986). See *Selected Poems*, 1996; *A Different Person: a Memoir*, 1993; Ross Labrie, *James Merrill*, 1982 (biographical/critical study); Stephen Yenser, *The Consuming Myth: the Work of James Merrill*, 1987 (critical study).

MERWIN, W(ILLIAM) S(TANLEY)

(*b.* 1927) American poet, dramatist, and translator, was born in New York City, son of a Presbyterian minister. He was brought up in Union City, New Jersey, and Scranton, Pennsylvania—recollections of an austere childhood occur in poems in *The Drunk in the Furnace* (1960) and *The Moving Target* (1963). His studies at Princeton were interrupted by service in the US Navy Air Corps. He graduated in Romance languages, after which he did a year's postgraduate study. He then spent two years as a tutor in France, Portugal, and Majorca, where his pupil was a son of GRAVES, one of his earlier models along with POUND, YEATS, and AUDEN, who published his first book of verse, *A Mask for Janus* (1952), in the Yale Younger Poets. In London (1951–54) he worked as a translator of French and Spanish classics for the BBC. *Darkling Child*, a verse play written with Dido Milroy, who in 1963 became his second wife, was performed at the Arts Theatre in London in 1956. He was

Playwright-in-Residence, Poet's Theatre, Cambridge, Massachusetts 1956–57, where his *Favor Island* was produced in 1957. He was Poetry Editor of *The Nation* 1961–63. In his poetry he now adopted a new style and form, blunter in language and deeper in thought. He accepted the Pulitzer Prize for *The Carrier of Ladders* (1970) but gave away the prize money on the grounds that his country's attitude to international politics made him 'too conscious of being an American'. *The Miner's Pale Children* (1970) and *Houses and Travelers* (1977) are volumes of prose poems in the form of fictional narratives, fables and folk tales, parables, and personal recollections. In the collection of verse, *The Rain in the Trees* (1988), he is primarily concerned with ecological matters and the erosion of language and belief. The poems in *The Vixen* (1996), in which Merwin dispenses not only with punctuation (using just a capital letter to indicate the beginning of direct speech) but also largely with the line break as a poetic device, are laments for the extinction of ancient culture in rural southwest France, a region in which he has lived and which he depicted in the prose *The Lost Upland: Stories of Southwest France* (1992). *Lament for the Makers* (1996) is a series of elegies on poets who have influenced him.

Merwin's first published volume of translation was the Spanish epic *The Poem of the Cid* (1959). He began translating 'with the idea that it could teach me something about writing poetry. . . . It is love, I imagine, more that learning that . . . will impel me to be wary of any skill coming to shadow and doctor the source.' As well as translating from Latin and from the Romance languages, including NERUDA (1969), GARCÍA LORCA, and JIMÉNEZ, he has collaborated with a native speaker or scholar to produce versions of Sanskrit love poetry (1977) and of MANDELSTAM (1973)—see also *Selected Translations 1948–1968* (1968), *Selected Translations 1968–1978* (1979), and *Four French Plays* (1985).

Unframed Originals: Recollections (1982) comprises prose reminiscences; *Regions of Memory: Uncollected Prose 1949–1982* (1987) includes autobiographical essays and comment on the art of poetry. See *The First Four Books of Poems*, new edn 1989; *The Second Four Books of Poems*, 1993; *Selected Poems*, 1988; Cheri Davis, *W. S. Merwin*, 1981 (critical study); Mark Christhilf, *W. S. Merwin, the Mythmaker*, 1986 (critical study).

MEUNG, JEAN (CLOPINEL) DE

(*c.*1240–1305) French poet and translator, probably came from the village of Meung-sur-Loire. He was educated in Paris in the seven liberal arts, and there or elsewhere in philosophy and theology, while also interesting himself in law and medicine. A scholar before a cleric, who led an unclerical life, he wrote the 17,722-line continuation of *Roman* *de la Rose* of LORRIS, but in a different style—satirical, often cynical, with excursions into social, theological, and philosophical issues of the times. It is his tone and outlook which CHAUCER absorbed by the time he came to write *The Canterbury Tales*. Among other works, Meung translated into French *De Consolatione Philosophiae* of BOETHIUS, the topography of Ireland of GIRALDUS, and the letters of ABÉLARD and Héloïse.

MEW, CHARLOTTE (1869–1928) British poet, was born in Bloomsbury, London, the daughter of an architect; she was educated at Lucy Harrison's School for Girls, and attended lectures at University College, London. Of the four children who survived infancy, two became insane and had to go into asylums, and the family finances were further crippled by the father's death in 1898. Her grim story, 'Passed', appeared in 1894 in an early issue of *The Yellow Book*, and some money came in from the publication of critical articles, poems, and stories in literary journals—'The Fête' was published by POUND in *The Egoist* in 1914. 'The Farmer's Bride', a pathetic little cameo of female frigidity and fear, also provided the title of a volume of 17 of her poems published in 1916 (2nd enlarged edn 1921). A Civil List pension was procured for her in 1923, at the instigation of HARDY and other literary figures, but her mother died that same year, and her sister, with whom she lived, in 1927. Shortly after that she committed suicide in a nursing home by drinking disinfectant. A further volume of her verse, *The Rambling Sailor*, was published in 1929. The ineffable sadness of her life is reflected in her poetry, which dwells on childhood, grief, passion, and, of course, death, and is expressed, often in the form of a dramatic monologue, with control, restraint, precision, and a fine attention to rhythm. See *Collected Poems and Prose*, ed. Val Warner, 1982; Penelope Fitzgerald, *Charlotte Mew and Her Friends*, new edn 1989.

MEYNELL, ALICE (1847–1922), née Thompson, British poet and critic, was born in Barnes, Surrey, and was educated at home and in France and Italy by her father, who was a friend of DICKENS. Following her mother's example, she became a Roman Catholic in 1872, which brought her into contact with the circle of DE VERE. Through him she met TENNYSON, who encouraged her to publish her poetry. *Preludes* (1875) was much admired. In 1877 she married Wilfrid Meynell (1852–1948), with whom she edited several journals, including the *Weekly Register* and *Merry England*, and discovered and cared for FRANCIS THOMPSON. Beginning with *The Rhythm of Life* (1893), she published several volumes of critical essays, almost all of them reprinted from the many journals for which she wrote. Although there are nine volumes

of verse from her first to *The Last Poems* (1923), her output was small and her range limited, comprising in the main carefully constructed observations of small things and analyses of inner and religious emotions. Her literary judgment was usually sound, and expressed with subtlety and authority. Among her eight children were Viola Meynell (1886–1956), novelist and poet, and Sir Francis Meynell (1891–1975), typographer and founder of the Nonesuch Press. See June Badeni, *The Slender Tree: a Life of Alice Meynell*, 1981.

MICKIEWICZ, ADAM (1798–1855) Polish poet, was born near Novogrodek, Lithuania, and was educated at Vilna University, after which he became a teacher in Kovno, and in 1822–23 published a two-volume book of verse. In 1823 he was arrested by the Russian authorities and was forced to live in Russia until 1829. He then travelled and lived in western Europe, being Professor of Latin at Lausanne University (1839–40) and of Slavonic Literature at Collège de France (1840–44) in Paris, from which he was dismissed for bringing nationalist politics into his lectures. As active a patriot as he was an ardent patriotic poet, whose romanticism was influenced by BYRON, he died in Constantinople trying to raise a Polish battalion to fight against Russia in the Crimean War. His main works are *Konrad Wallenrod* (1828), a narrative poem of Poland's struggle against Russia, *Dziady* (1823–32), a tripartite dramatized poem of national consciousness, and *Pan Tadeusz* (1834; tr. Kenneth Mackenzie, 1966), an epic poem of the liberation of Poland and Lithuania by Napoleon on his ill fated march to Moscow in 1811–12.

MIDDLETON, THOMAS (1580–1627) English dramatist, was born in the City of London, the son of a prosperous 'citizen and bricklayer', was educated at The Queen's College, Oxford, without apparently taking a degree, and by 1601 is recorded as 'daily accompanying the players' in London. Shortly after this he married the sister of an actor, having now published *The Wisdom of Solomon Paraphrased* (1597), *Micro-Cynicon: Six Snarling Satires* (1599), and *The Ghost of Lucrece* (1600), a continuation of SHAKESPEARE's poem with lengthy lamentations. He collaborated with DEKKER on *The Honest Whore, Part I* (1604), and then wrote several comedies for boys to perform to middle-class audiences. More sophisticated dramas followed the decline of the boys' companies. In *Women Beware Women* (performed *c.*1621), a tragedy with ironic twists and two plots, Bianca, a Venetian girl married to a Florentine, finds herself out of place in whatever social station she seeks. *A Chaste Maid in Cheapside* (1613) is a comical skit on contemporary attitudes to sex and money. *A Game at Chesse* (1624), a very popular, brilliantly staged, satire on international politics, was so topical that it was prosecuted. *The Changeling*, written with ROWLEY and performed in 1622, is a skilfully constructed tragedy of the effects of lust and evil, with a depth of feeling rare for the times outside Shakespeare. *The Revenger's Tragedy* (1607) has been attributed to Middleton but, following T. S. ELIOT and other critics, is here regarded as by TOURNEUR. See *Five Plays*, ed. Bryan Loughrey and Neil Taylor, 1988; *A Mad World, My Masters, and Other Plays*, ed. Michael Taylor, 1996 (comedies).

MILL, JOHN STUART (1806–73) philosopher and practical reformer, was born in London, the eldest son of James Mill (1773–1836), Scottish philosopher, journalist, historian of India, and official (from 1830 Head) of the administration of the East India Company in London. James personally undertook the education of his son, which was in accordance with the principles of his friend BENTHAM and included a year in France. In 1823 Mill began, under his father, a career in India House. He was a regular contributor to the *Westminster Review* from its inception in 1824, in which year he was arrested for distributing copies of a pamphlet on birth control by throwing them into basement areas where maidservants worked. He suffered a nervous breakdown in 1826, probably caused by the intellectual tension imposed upon him from childhood. At a dinner party in 1830 at which MARTINEAU was also present, he met Harriet Taylor (1807–58), the bored and brilliant wife of a pharmacist. Their common interests, notably in women's rights, drew them together; their wildly indiscreet romance lasted until 1851, two years after the death of her complaisant husband, when they married and set up home together in Blackheath Park. After Harriet's death, her daughter, Helen Taylor (1831–1907), who had had a brief career on the stage, became Mill's secretary, housekeeper, and intellectual helpmeet.

In 1858 Mill retired from India House, having in the meantime been proprietor and Editor of the amalgamated *London and Westminster Review* from 1837 to 1840, and published *A System of Logic* (1843), which revived interest in the subject, and *Principles of Political Economy* (1848), which owed something to his friend David Ricardo (1772–1823), as well as to the writings of ADAM SMITH and Thomas Malthus (1776–1834). *On Liberty* (1859) is regarded as one of the finest expressions of political and social freedom, upon which he enlarged, in the context of the practical workings of the administration, in *Considerations on Representative Government* (1861). In 1865 he agreed to be put up as Member of Parliament for Westminster on a Liberal ticket. He condescended to visit the constituency only twice, but was elected and served for three years. In 1867, in a carefully prepared but weakly presented speech, he proposed an amendment to the Reform Bill, involving the substitution of 'person' for 'man', which would open suffrage to properly qualified women. It was defeated, but not so disastrously as he expected. Paradoxically, *The Subjection of Women* (1869), with its controversial, but inconclusive, proposals for divorce, had more influence on the women's rights movement overseas than it did immediately in Britain. Having suffered for some years from tuberculosis, Mill died as a result of an attack of erysipelas in Avignon, where he was buried. Helen edited his *Autobiography* (1873), which had been largely drafted in 1853–54 under Harriet's guidance, and also *Three Essays on Religion* (1874). See *On Liberty and Other Essays*, ed. John Gray, 1991; *Autobiography*, ed. John M. Robson, 1989; Michael St John Packe, *The Life of John Stuart Mill*, 1954; Josephine Kamm, *John Stuart Mill in Love*, 1977 (biographical study); William Thomas, *Mill*, 1985 (introduction to his philosophy).

MILLAY, EDNA ST VINCENT (1892–1950) American poet and dramatist, was born in Rockland, Maine, the eldest of three daughters of a couple who divorced when she was eight. Her mother, who worked as a nurse, encouraged her in music and poetry, and in 1912, three years after she left Camden High School, her poem 'Renascence' was published in *The Lyric Year*. With the support of a benefactor she went to Vassar, where she starred in her own play, *The Princess Marries the Page* (published 1932), one of three she wrote while she was there. *Renascence, and Other Poems* (1917) was published in the year she graduated, after which she lived in poverty in Greenwich Village, New York, had affairs, wrote for magazines, and acted with the Provincetown Players, for whom she directed her *Aria da Capo* (published 1920), an enigmatic combination of harlequinade and pastoral. *A Few Figs from Thistles* (1920; enlarged edns 1921, 1922) just failed to win the Pulitzer Prize, which was awarded to her in 1923 for 'the best verse published in 1922'; she was the first woman to receive it for poetry. *The Harp-Weaver, and Other Poems* (1923), much of it reflecting disillusionment or grief, was published on her return to the USA after two years in Europe. *Distressing Dialogues* (1924) includes satirical pieces written as Nancy Boyd while she was abroad. *Wine from These Grapes* (1934) marked a change from the cynicism and open sexuality of her love poetry to philosophical objectivity; this is also displayed, with a political awareness, in the Platonic dialogue in verse, *Conversation at Midnight* (1937), which she rewrote after the manuscript was destroyed in a hotel fire. One of the leading poets of her time, and an active feminist (and feminist poet), she published *Collected Sonnets* in 1941, and *Collected Lyrics* in 1943. In 1923 she married Eugen Jan Boissevan (*d.* 1949), an importer, with whom she lived on a farm in Austerlitz, New York. See *Collected Poems,* new edn 1992; *Selected Poems,* ed. Colin Falck, introduction by Richard Eberhart, 1991; Norman A. Brittin, *Edna St Vincent Millay,* rev. edn 1982 (critical study).

MILLER, ARTHUR (*b.* 1915) American dramatist, was born in Manhattan, New York, the second son of an Austrian Jewish immigrant who, though almost illiterate, built up a clothing business employing a thousand workers, which collapsed in the crash of 1929. 'The impact [of the Depression] was incalculable. . . . America is hope, even when it doesn't work. America is promises. . . . I don't think America ever got over the Depression.' The family moved to Brooklyn. After graduating from high school, he saved $13 of his weekly wage of $15 from an auto-parts warehouse for his college tuition, and in 1934 persuaded the University of Michigan to ignore his low school grades and to admit him to study journalism. With his confidence boosted by winning the Avery Hopwood Award for his first play, *Honors at Dawn* (produced 1936), written in four days from minimal theatrical know-how (he won it again the following year for his second, *No Villains*), he graduated as BA in 1938, and married in 1940. By the time *The Man Who Had All the Luck,* set in a small Midwest town, was produced on Broadway in 1944, he had written a number of plays for radio programmes, done an extraordinary variety of jobs (including mouse attendant in a laboratory), and collected material for a film script on a tour of army camps in World War II, about which he published a journal, *Situation Normal* (1944). The play failed. He published a novel, *Focus* (1945), and then had his first success. *All My Sons* (1947), after a deliberately slow start, representing 'undisturbed normality', introduces all sorts of revelations and conflicts, albeit with the help of stock devices. *Death of a Salesman* (1949), subtitled 'Certain Private Conversations in Two Acts and a Requiem', which won the Pulitzer Prize, also ends with a suicide, but in this case it is a dramatic consummation of the delusions with which men like Loman are affected, and which are then inflicted on their families. In the Congressional hysteria in the 1950s about the infiltration of Communism he found parallels with the Salem witch trials in the 17th century. *The Crucible* (1953) is so firmly set in its own context, that a critic of just one of its revivals at various centres in the UK in 1990 could comment: 'Miller's play is as timeless as it was in the "new times" of the 1950s.' In 1954 he was refused a passport to go to Brussels for the Continental premiere, on the grounds that he was 'believed to be supporting members of the Communist movement'. In 1956 he refused to identify to the Committee on Un-American Activities people he had seen at writers' meetings. His conviction of contempt, with a fine of $500 and a 30-day suspended prison sentence, was quashed on appeal.

After the Fall (1964) was seen at the time as an autobiographical reflection of his divorce in 1956 and subsequent marriage to the film star Marilyn Monroe (1926–62). After she miscarried he wrote a screen play, *The Misfits* (1961), for her as a gift—the story on which it is based appeared in *I Don't Need You Any More: Stories* (1967). By the time the film was shot the marriage was over. They were divorced in 1961, but her life and mysterious death have continued to excite public susceptibility. In its inherent expression of guilt feelings about the Holocaust, *After the Fall* is also a preface to Miller's deeper study of 'the randomness of victimization', *Incident at Vichy* (1964). *The Price* (1968) represents a return to the subject of father/son relationships and recriminations. With *The Ride Down Mt Morgan* (1991), seven years in the writing, he sprang another surprise on the public, with a comic play about retribution, in this case inflicted upon a bigamist. *The Last Yankee* (1992), a further minor piece, which plays for 90 minutes, is a study of contrasting middle-class mores, in the setting of the psychiatric ward of a New England hospital. The elusive Jewishness which pervades *Broken Glass* (1994) reflects his own feelings: 'If there weren't any anti-Semitism, I wouldn't think of myself as Jewish.' *Plain Girl* (1995), 52 pages long, is a novel in which the daughter of Jewish immigrants looks back over a life which began for her among the left-wing intellectual circles of 1930s' New York. Miller was Cameron Mackintosh Visiting Professor of Contemporary Theatre at Oxford 1994–95. In 1962 he married the photographer Ingeborg Morath (*b.*. 1923), with whom he has produced several topographical studies. See *Collected Plays,* 5 vols 1988–95; *The Theater Essays of Arthur Miller,* ed. Robert A. Martin, new edn 1994; *Timebends: a Life,* new edn 1995 (autobiography); Matthew C. Roudane (ed.), *Conversations with Arthur Miller,* 1987; Neil Carson, *Arthur Miller,* new edn 1989 (critical study); Alice Griffin, *Understanding Arthur Miller,* 1996.

MILLER, HENRY (1891–1980) American novelist and prose writer, was born in New York City, the only child of German-American lower-middle-class parents, and was brought up in Brooklyn, where he went to Eastern District High School. He dropped out of the City College of New York after two months, travelled, worked in his father's tailor's shop, married, and then had his only steady job, as messenger and then messenger employment manager for Western Union from 1921 to 1924. He then, while aspiring to be a writer, reverted to occasional labour, ran a speakeasy, and begged. In 1930 he went, without money or, initially, his second wife, who recurs as the enigmatic Mona/Mara figure in his works, to Paris, where he lived for ten years. During this time he established an intellectual relationship of some intimacy with NIN, and wrote the semi-autobiographical, unashamedly exhibitionistic *Tropic of Cancer* (1934) and *Tropic of Capricorn* (1939), and the fictionalized sketches of *Black Spring* (1936), all of which were banned in the USA until the 1960s. A sojourn in Greece in 1939 resulted in *The Colossus of Maroussi: or, The Spirit of Greece* (1941), an interesting and lively variation on the standard travelogue. In 1946 he settled in Big Sur, California, where he wrote the autobiographical fantasy, 'The Rosy Crucifixion': *Sexus* (1949), *Plexus* (1953), and *Nexus* (1960), all published in Paris. He married for the fifth time in 1967. See *A Henry Miller Reader*, ed. John Calder, 1985; Mary V. Dearborn, *The Happiest Man Alive: a Biography of Henry Miller*, new edn 1992.

MILLER, HUGH (1802–56) Scottish prose writer, journalist, and geologist, was born in Cromarty, the son of a sea captain who went down with his ship and all hands off the east coast in 1807. In his philosophical autobiographical study, *My Schools and Schoolmasters* (1854), he tells the story of his life up to 1840, when he accepted an invitation to edit the evangelical weekly, the *Witness*, which became the voice of the Free Church after the Disruption in 1843. An imaginative and bookish boy who reacted against the discipline of school, he worked as a stonemason, which inspired his pursuit of geology and the ultimate publication of several beautifully-written studies, including *The Old Red Sandstone* (1841), which ran him into difficulties when he tried to reconcile his own scientific observation with the teaching of his Church about the Creation. In 1825 the stone dust in his lungs forced him to leave Edinburgh for Inverness, where he married and wrote a variety of works, including *Poems, Written in the Leisure Hours of a Journeyman Mason* (1829), *Letters on the Herring Industry* (1829), and *Scenes and Legends of the North of Scotland* (1835). He was an accountant in the Commercial Bank of Scotland from 1834 until his appointment in Edinburgh to the *Witness*, in which capacity he condemned the Clearances, and advocated the education of the working classes, but opposed Chartism as being too radical. He shot himself in a fit of depression brought on by overwork and illness. See *Hugh Miller's Memoir: from Stonemason to Geologist*, ed. Michael Shortland, 1995; George Rosie, *Hugh Miller, Outrage and Order: a Biography and Selected Writings*, 1981.

MILLIN, SARAH GERTRUDE (1889–1968), née Liebson, South African novelist, was born in Zagar, Lithuania, of Jewish parents, who brought her to South Africa when she was five months old. At first they were the only European family at the Vaal River diamond diggings, near Kimberley, where she was educated. Her father came to own 'trading rights, ferry rights, waterworks, and a farm, here and there along the river'. Though on her ability she could have gone to college, she preferred to write. She lived in Johannesburg after her marriage to Philip Millin (1888–1952), a barrister who became a Supreme Court judge. She published 15 novels, of which the early ones, beginning with *The Dark River* (1919), were naturalistically based on her observation of life along the Vaal. For its treatment of, and her attitude to, miscegenation, the family saga *God's Stepchildren* (1924) was vigorously publicized by the Nazis. It is, though, a poignant as well as a tragic novel by a talented writer, of which David Rabkin in his comparative study with PLOMER's *Turbott Wolfe*—in Kenneth Parker (ed.), *The South African Novel in English* (1978)—concludes: 'The importance of these writers in the development of the South African novel lies . . . in their identification of the colour question as the central moral issue of South African society.' She also wrote biographies of Cecil Rhodes (1933) and General Smuts (1936). See *The Night is Long*, 1941 (autobiography); Martin Rubin, *Sarah Gertrude Millin: a South African Life*, 1977.

MILLS, MARTIN see BOYD, MARTIN.

MILNE, A(LAN) A(LEXANDER) (1882–1956) British dramatist, novelist, journalist, and children's writer, was born in Hampstead, London, and educated at Westminster School and Trinity College, Cambridge, where he played cricket, edited *Granta*, and got a third in mathematics. In 1906, after struggling as a freelance writer, he became Assistant Editor of *Punch*, for which he also regularly wrote sketches. Though a pacifist, he served creditably on the Somme in 1916 as a signals officer, being invalided home with trench fever. A comedy, *Wurzel-Flummery*, was performed in London in 1917 and led to a successful career as a writer of light plays which lasted into the 1930s and included *Mr Pim Passes By*—published in *Second Plays* (1921)—and *The Dover Road*—in *Three Plays* (1923). *The Red House Mystery* (1922) is a model detective novel, which two months after its publication ISHERWOOD dramatized for an end of term House Supper at school. Intoxicated by the infancy of his son, Milne produced two volumes of verse for children, *When We Were Very Young* (1924) and *Now We Are Six* (1927), and two books of stories about the child's toy animals, *Winnie-the-Pooh* (1926) and *The House at Pooh Corner* (1928). These earned him the immortality which he craved, but imposed an inescapable, and unwelcome, typecasting on his literary reputation. The stories succeed for their depiction of a uniquely-imagined world in which the child/adult roles are reversed in an idyllic setting. *Peace with Honour* (1934), a denunciation of war, reflected public opinion at the time. His son, Christopher Milne (1920–96), served, and was wounded, in the Italian campaign in World War II, married a cousin, and in 1951 settled in Devon, where he opened a bookshop. In two elegant autobiographical works, *The Enchanted Places* (1974) and *The Path through the Trees* (1979), he describes his search for a true identity and for psychological independence from the persona foisted upon him by his father. See Ann Thwaite, *A. A. Milne: His Life*, new edn 1991; and in Alison Lurie, *Don't Tell the Grown-Ups*, 1990.

MILOSZ, CZESLAW (*b.* 1911) Lithuanian-born poet, novelist, and critic, was born in Szetejnie and went to school and university in Vilnius, taking a degree in jurisprudence in 1934—see *Beginning with My Streets: Baltic Reflections*, tr. Madeline G. Levine (1992). He worked for Polish National Radio before World War II, during which he was a member of the Resistance. He was in the Polish Diplomatic Service in Washington, D.C., and Paris from 1945 to 1950, when his disenchantment with Communism caused him to break away from his roots. After living in Paris, he went to California, where from 1961 to 1978 he taught Slavic languages and literature at Berkeley, becoming a US citizen in 1970. After publishing several books of verse in Poland, and others subsequently in Paris, he achieved international recognition with a collection of essays, [*The Captive Mind*] (1953; tr. Jane Zielonko, 1953), in which he explored the reaction of Polish intellectuals to Communism. In an autobiographical study, [*Native Realm: a Search for Self-Definition*] (tr. Catherine S. Leach, 1968), he set out his approach to poetry: 'Instead of thrusting the individual into the foreground, one can focus attention on the background, looking upon oneself as a sociological phenomenon.' English translations of his poetry began to be published in the 1970s, with *Bells in Winter*, a selection translated by himself and Lillian Vallee, appearing in the USA in 1978—see also *The Collected Poems 1931–1987* (1988), *Provinces: Poems 1987–1991*, tr. the author and Robert Hass (1991), and *Facing the River: New Poems*, tr. the author and Hass (1995). His novels include [*The Issa Valley*] (1955; tr. Louis Iribarne, 1981), a semi-autobiographical evocation of an undisturbed childhood in rural Lithuania. He has also written *The History of Polish Literature* (1969), and is an unusually gifted translator who has rendered SHAKESPEARE, MILTON, and T. S. ELIOT into Polish, and Polish poets into English—see his *Postwar Polish Poetry: an Anthology* (rev. edn 1983). He was awarded the Nobel Prize for Literature in 1980.

MILTON, JOHN (1608–74) English poet and prose writer, was born in London, the eldest son of a wealthy Protestant scrivener and minor composer, who destined him 'from a child to the pursuits of literature'. He was educated at St Paul's School and Christ's College, Cambridge, where he was dubbed, according to AUBREY, 'the lady of Christ's College', for his fair complexion. He graduated as MA in 1632, having demonstrated his skill at Latin verse and composed the considerable poems 'On the Morning of Christ's Nativity', 'L'Allegro', and 'Il Penseroso'. Until 1638 he studied on his father's estate at Horton, Buckinghamshire, accepting commissions to write the masques *Arcades* and *Comus*, for performance with music by Henry Lawes (1596–1662)—see the sonnet 'To My Friend Mr Henry Lawes' (1646). *Comus*, performed at Ludlow Castle on 29 September 1634 for the inauguration of the Earl of Bridgewater (1579–1649) as Lord President of Wales, contains genuine conflict within a traditional form of entertainment. The elegy 'Lycidas' was written in 1637 in memory of a former fellow-student. In 1639 Milton cut short a study tour of Italy and Greece because of the impending English Civil War. He then rented a house in London and took in pupils, starting with his own nephews, while involving himself in the arguments for a reformation of the Protestant Church. To this end he wrote several notable pamphlets in support of Puritanism, including *The Reason of Church-Government Urg'd against Prelatry* (1641), in which he also suggested his personal responsibilities as a poet. In 1642 he married Mary Powell, the 16-year-old daughter of an Oxfordshire squire. She went home after a few weeks, which may or may not have induced him to write *The Doctrine and Discipline of Divorce* (1643), in which he advocates incompatibility as grounds for divorce. He countered the growing threat of censorship with *Areopagitica* (1644), an impassioned plea for the freedom of the press. He published *Poems, both English and Latin* in 1645, the year in which Mary returned to him—she died in 1652, having had three daughters who survived. A few weeks after the execution of Charles I in January 1649, Milton defended the revolution in *The Tenure of Kings and Magistrates*, and was then appointed Latin Secretary to the Council of State. He was already going blind, and by 1652 was entirely so, though he continued in public office. He recorded his feelings in the sonnet 'When I consider how my light is spent', but was more resigned to his state when he wrote 'Cyriack, this three years' day these eyes . . .' (1655).

In 1656 he married Katharine Woodcock, who had a daughter in 1657, but died the following year, being remembered in the sonnet 'Methought I saw my late espoused saint' (1658). In spite of Cromwell's death in 1658, he courageously produced further pamphlets in support of that regime, including *The Readie & Easie Way to Establish a Free Commonwealth* (1660). He was thus in deep trouble at the Restoration of Charles II in May 1660, but thanks to the intervention of his friends escaped with a brief prison sentence and a pardon. In 1663 he married Elizabeth Minshull (1638–1727), a cousin of Nathan Paget (1615–79), his friend and probably also his doctor, who had recommended her to the poet. At his house in Bunhill Fields he now used his family and others as amanuenses to help him complete the great epic poem he had been contemplating for years, and had probably begun in about 1658. *Paradise Lost* was published in 1667, and in a revised version in 12 books in 1674—in 1680 his widow sold the copyright for £8. It is notable less for its encompassment of the war in Heaven and projections of world history than for the representation of Satan and the graphic and sympathetic account of the Fall of Man. During the plague of 1665–66 the family moved to a cottage in Chalfont St Giles, Buckinghamshire, which still survives, but they returned to London in time to endure the Great Fire of 1666. Milton continued to write and to publish: the lesser and shorter epic, *Paradise Regain'd*, and the biblical dramatic poem, *Samson Agonistes*, together in 1671; and a new edition of his poems in 1673; as well as prose works, including *History of Britain* (1670), in the unfinished form in which he had abandoned it in 1659. He died of gout.

Doubts about the validity of the poetic influence exerted by *Paradise Lost*, as well as its portrait of God—see LEAVIS in his *The Common Pursuit* (1952) and EMPSON, *Milton's God* (rev. edn 1981), where issue is taken with C. S. LEWIS in his *A Preface to Paradise Lost* (reissued 1960)—are secondary to the fact that it is the most noble poem in the language. See *Complete English Poems, with 'Of Education' and 'Areopagitica'*, ed. Gordon Campbell, new edn 1993; [*Selected Verse*], ed. Stephen Orgel and Jonathan Goldberg, new edn 1994; *John Milton: Selected Prose*, ed. C. A. Patrides, 1974; A. N. Wilson, *The Life of John Milton*, new edn 1996; William Riley Parker, *Milton: a Biography*, 2nd edn 1996, and *Milton: a Biographical Commentary*, 2nd edn 1996, ed. Gordon Campbell; Peter Levi, *Eden Renewed: the Public and Private Life of John Milton*, 1996; E. M. W. Tillyard, *Milton*, rev. edn 1966 (critical biography); Lois Potter, *A Preface to Milton*, new edn 1986; Dennis Danielson (ed.), *The Cambridge Companion to Milton*, 1989.

MISHIMA YUKIO (1925–70) Japanese novelist, short-story writer, and dramatist, was born in Tokyo, where he graduated from the Peers' School in 1944 with a citation from the Emperor. He took a degree in jurisprudence at Tokyo University in 1947, and published his first novel (and third book) the following year. The first to be published in the West was [*The Sound of Waves*] (1954; tr. Meredith Weatherby, 1956), a tale of rural love, followed by [*Confessions of a Mask*] (1949; tr. Weatherby, 1958), a semi-autobiographical case history of the development of a sado-masochistic homosexual. Similar preoccupations inform [*Forbidden Colours*] (1951–53; tr. Alfred H. Marks, 1968) and [*The Sailor Who Fell from Grace with the Sea*] (1963; tr. John Nathan, 1965). His distaste for the spiritual desolation of modern Japan compared with the traditions of its imperial past led him to raise a private army and to mount a coup in support of the Emperor. When it, predictably, failed, he disembowelled himself in ceremonial fashion, in the same way as does the hero of his story, ['Patriotism'] (tr. Geoffrey W. Sargent in *Death in Midsummer*, 1967), after the attempted coup in 1936. *Acts of Worship*, tr. John Bester (1991) comprises seven stories spanning his literary career.

MITCHELL, ADRIAN see LOGUE.

MITCHELL, JAMES LESLIE see GIBBON, LEWIS GRASSIC.

MITCHELL, MARGARET (1900–49) American novelist, was born in Atlanta, Georgia, the second child of an attorney and of a dedicated suffragette. She was educated at Washington Seminary, Atlanta, and studied medicine for a year at Smith College, Massachusetts, before returning home to keep house for her widowed father and making a dramatic, if unconventional, impression on local society. Her marriage in 1922 to 'Red' Upshaw lasted less than a year, and she then became a feature writer and reporter on the Atlanta *Journal* Sunday magazine. In 1925 she married John R. Marsh, an advertising executive, and the following year resigned from her job after an ankle injury. For the next ten years she worked on the manuscript of her novel about the American Civil War which would take up the challenge thrown at Southern women: 'They don't deserve to survive because they won't fight—don't know how to fight.' She reluctantly agreed to allow a Macmillan editor, Harold S. Latham (1887–1969), to read it, and then asked for it to be returned. He refused. *Gone with the Wind* (1936) won the Pulitzer Prize, and sold over a million copies in its first six months. After the world premiere in Atlanta of the technicolor film (1939), she retired into hiding, and impersonators were reported in various parts of the country. Her only other work of fiction, *Lost Laysen*, was discovered many years later and published in 1996. A premonition that she would die in a car accident was duly vindicated when she was run over and killed while crossing the street. After her husband's death the estate passed to her brother, Stephens Mitchell (*d.* 1983), who authorized a sequel to *Gone with the Wind*. Alexandra Ripley's *Scarlett* (1991) was a financial but not a critical success. In 1994 the executors of the Mitchell estate commissioned a further sequel from EMMA TENNANT, which was ultimately rejected by the American publisher who had contracted to publish it. See Darden Asbury Pyron, *Southern Daughter: the Life of Margaret Mitchell*, 1992.

MITCHELL, W(ILLIAM) O(RMEROD) (*b.* 1914) Canadian novelist, was born in Weyburn, Saskatchewan, but after contracting bovine tuberculosis was taken by his widowed mother to St Petersburg, Florida, where he went to St Petersburg High School. His further studies at Manitoba University, where he won a gold medal for philosophy in 1934, were interrupted by a recurrence of illness; they were resumed several years later at the University of Alberta, where he graduated in education in 1942, having in the meantime travelled in North America and Europe and worked as a seaman and salesman. He taught in Alberta schools until 1944, when, having had stories published in *Maclean's*, Toronto, he became a full-time writer. His first novel, *Who Has Seen the Wind* (1947), the development from infancy to self-realization of a boy in Saskatchewan, is also his most famous. The protagonists in his weekly comic sketches on radio, 'Jake and the Kid' (1949–57), rematerialized in a book of short stories, *Jake and the Kid* (1961), which won the Stephen LEACOCK Medal for Humour—see also *According to Jake and the Kid: a Collection of New Stories* (1989). Other radio and stage plays are in *The Dramatic W. O. Mitchell* (1982), which includes his stage adaptation (produced 1981) of his second novel, *The Kite* (1962), an extended anecdote featuring a 111-year-old Calgary man with a fertile memory and a mind of his own. He returned to the theme of the vulnerability of youth in *How I Spent My Summer Holidays* (1981). He was made Officer, Order of Canada, in 1973. See Dick Harrison, *W. O. Mitchell and His Works*, 1994.

MITFORD, MARY RUSSELL (1787–1855) British prose writer, poet, and dramatist, was born in Alresford, Hampshire, the only child of a doctor who preferred gambling to work; as a result the family was reduced to living in lodgings in London when she was ten. On a visit with him to the lottery office, she chose a number which, when he had bought up other shares in the ticket, won them £20,000. She now spent four years at a school in Hans Place, London, and her father built them a Georgian mansion in the country. Between 1810 and 1813 she published five volumes of verse. By 1820 the family was

again in straits, and had to move to a cottage at Three Mile Cross, near Reading, 'a series of closets, the largest of which may be about eight feet square'. Here she buckled down to support her mother, who died in 1829, and her feckless father, on whose death in 1842, still in debt, she declared, 'Everybody shall be paid, if I sell the gown off my back or pledge my little pension' (£120 a year from the Civil List, which she had been awarded in 1837). She wrote plays, of which *Julian: a Tragedy* (1823) was one of several to be staged in London. Some pieces on country life, published in the *Lady's Magazine* in 1819, grew into *Our Village* (5 vols 1824–32). The detailed observation of nature, sympathetic character sketches of the social spectrum, and lively descriptions of rural activities and recreations (she is the first woman to write knowledgeably about cricket), have proved irresistible to readers ever since. *Recollections of a Literary Life* (1852) incorporates quotations from literature. Her correspondents included LAMB, LANDOR, RUSKIN, and E. B. BROWNING, to whom she gave the famous Flush, a puppy of her own cocker spaniel. See Vera Watson, *Mary Russell Mitford*, 1949 (biography).

MITFORD, NANCY (1904–73) novelist and biographer, was the eldest of seven children of David Freeman-Mitford (1878–1958), who became 2nd Baron Redesdale in 1916, and whom she caricatured mercilessly, but with little exaggeration, in her novels, notably *The Pursuit of Love* (1945). Because he did not believe in his daughters having any education, she received little except what she learned at finishing school, at art college, and subsequently in France, from which she returned to three seasons of debutante socializing. She left home at 24, subsisted precariously by writing for magazines, and published several satirical novels of upperclass life, of which the first was *Highland Fling* (1931). She married the Hon. Peter Rodd in 1933. They were finally divorced in 1958. During World War II she was an Air Raid Precautions driver in London, and was assistant in and then manager of a West End bookshop. With *The Pursuit of Love*, which also celebrates her own love for an officer in the Free French forces, she achieved popular success, which she consolidated with *Love in a Cold Climate* (1949). *Don't Tell Alfred* (1960) mocks the Diplomatic Service. Her only play, *The Little Hut* (1951), adapted from André Roussin (1911–88), was successful also as a film. From 1947 she lived in Paris, where she wrote graceful biographical studies of Mme de Pompadour (1954), VOLTAIRE (1957), Louis XIV (1966), and Frederick the Great (1970), which are full of social and domestic detail. An article in *Encounter* in 1955—reprinted in *A Talent to Annoy: Essays, Journalism, and Reviews 1929–1968*, ed. Charlotte Mosley (1988)—sparked off the controversy about the distinction between U[pper class] and non-U. She was made CBE in 1972. See *Love from Nancy: the Letters of Nancy Mitford*, ed. Charlotte Mosley, 1993; Selina Hastings, *Nancy Mitford*, new edn 1986 (biography).

MITTELHOLZER, EDGAR (1909–65) Guyanese novelist, was born in New Amsterdam of a middle-class family with European origins on both sides—see his early autobiography, *A Swarthy Boy* (1963). He was educated at Berbice High School, failing his Senior School Certificate after writing a short story in place of the English composition essay. In 1928 he began bombarding English publishers with stories and novels, but it was not until 1939, when he was 'doing odd jobs for the customs', that *Corentyne Thunder* (1941) was accepted, the first novel of peasant life in British Guiana. Shortly afterwards he went to Trinidad, where he set *A Morning at the Office* (1950), and from which he emigrated to England in 1948, the first West Indian of his generation to do so in order to make a career as a writer. This he achieved with twenty further novels which reflect his preoccupation with the Caribbean divided identity as well as his own divided mind. The most sensational of these are the quartet, *Children of Kaywana* (1952; in two volumes, the second entitled *Kaywana Heritage*, 1976), *The Harrowing of Hubertus* (1954; as *Kaywana Stock*, 1968), and *Kaywana Blood* (1958), the saga of a Guyanese family of mixed race origins during three hundred years of history. Mittelholzer committed suicide by burning himself to death in a field in Sussex.

MOIR, DAVID MACBETH (1798–1851) Scottish novelist, poet, and doctor, was born in Musselburgh, and was apprenticed to a doctor when he was 13. After qualifying in Edinburgh, he returned to his home town to practise. Under the cryptogram 'Δ' (the Greek character 'Delta') he contributed sketches, essays, and poems to *Blackwood's Edinburgh Magazine*; through the journal he was an associate of JOHN WILSON and met GALT, whose friend he became and a memoir of whom he later wrote (1841). *The Life of Mansie Wauch, Taylor in Dalkeith* (1828) began as a serial in the magazine. These small-town sketches lack the imagination and irony of Galt, and in their unsophisticated comedy presage the Kailyard novelists (see BARRIE). *Domestic Verses* (1843) commemorates the deaths of three of his children and of several of those of the Blackwood's coterie. He also wrote *Outlines of the Ancient History of Medicine* (1831), the first instalment of a fuller study which he never completed owing to pressure of work, and several papers on cholera, an epidemic of which he observed at first hand in Musselburgh in 1832. He edited the poems of HEMANS (7 vols 1839; one vol. 1848). His health was undermined in 1844 by his sit-

ting up all night in damp clothes at the bedside of a patient, and by a carriage accident in 1846. He died after a fall sustained when dismounting from his horse. His *Poetical Works*, ed. Thomas Aird, was published in 1852.

MOLESWORTH, (MARY LOUISA), MRS (1839–1921), née Stewart, British novelist and children's writer, was born in Rotterdam, the daughter of a Scottish merchant. She was brought up in Manchester—*The Carved Lions* (1895) incorporates some of her childhood memories—and was educated at home and at a boarding school in Switzerland. In 1861 she married Major Richard Molesworth (*d.* 1900), whose violent temper (the result of a head wound in the Crimea) was ultimately the cause of their separation in 1879. They had four children, after the deaths of the eldest and youngest of whom she wrote *Lover and Husband* (1869), under the pseudonym of Ennis Graham. She began to write for children in 1875, and though the moral of *Carrots: Just a Little Boy* (1876) is aimed at adults, the story is realistic and the child's mental processes convincing. *The Cuckoo Clock* (1877) is a fantasy involving a real child and a magical, but crotchety, cuckoo. Like *The Tapestry Room* (1879), her seventh book of many and the first to be published under her own name, it leaves the discerning reader to decide whether the adventures happened or are the imaginings of the characters. See Roger Lancelyn Green, *Mrs Molesworth*, 1961 (critical study).

MOLIÈRE (1622–73) French dramatist, was born Jean-Baptiste Poquelin in Paris, the son of a prosperous upholsterer who arranged in 1637 that the honorary post at court which he had bought was vested in his son. He was educated at the Jesuit Collège de Clermont, and studied law at Orleans. In 1643 he renounced everything, including the post at court, assumed his pseudonym, and set up the Illustre-Théâtre with the theatrical family of Béjart. The eldest daughter, Madeleine (1618–72), is assumed to have been his mistress; the youngest (or according to some, Madeleine's daughter), Armande-Grésinde-Claire-Elisabeth (1642–1700), became his wife in 1662 and subsequently the female lead in most of his plays. In 1646, after he had been imprisoned for debt and bailed out by his father, he and the company took to the provinces, from which they returned to Paris in 1658. A short farce of his composition amused the young Louis XIV and led to the company being installed in the hall of the Petit-Bourbon under the patronage of the King's brother, the Duc d'Orléans, and subsequently in the Palais-Royal. *Les Précieuses Ridicules* (1659) was a popular success; *L'École des Femmes* (1662) gave notice of a comic talent which was concerned also with deeper, if controversial, issues. *Tartuffe* (1664; tr. M. Medbourne, 1670), a study of a religious hypocrite, caused an outrage, and was banned for several years, despite the personal support of its author by the King, who stood as godfather to his first child (a son who only lived a few weeks), and in 1665 appointed the company Troupe du Roi. *Le Misanthrope* (1666) and *L'Avare* (1668; tr. and adapted by Thomas Shadwell as *The Miser*, 1672) are further explorations of men with obsessions.

Ballet master and deviser of musical occasions, as well as actor and dramatist, Molière presented many entertainments at court, of which *Le Bourgeois Gentilhomme* (1670) is also one of his best-known plays, and was revived (in a new English version by Nick Dear) in London in 1992. By a supreme stroke of dramatic irony, he was taken ill while playing the lead in *Le Malade Imaginaire* (1673) and died soon afterwards. His plays, some in verse and some in prose, usually consist of five acts and observe the traditional dramatic unities of action, setting, and time. They were borrowed or plundered by the English dramatists of the times, even by DRYDEN. Sometimes, as in the case of *The Citizen Turn'd Gentleman* (1672) by Edward Ravenscroft (1644–1704), two plays were amalgamated where a single French comedy was not regarded as substantial enough to make one English play. There are modern translations of Molière by John Wood (1953, 1968), Richard Wilbur (1982), and George Gravely and Ian Maclean (1989).

MOMADAY, N(AVARRE) SCOTT (*b.* 1934) American novelist and poet, was born in Lawton, Oklahoma, of a Kiowa father and a part-Cherokee mother, both of whom were artists and teachers. He was brought up in New Mexico and Arizona, attending reservation, mission, and public schools, and a military high school in Virginia. He graduated from the University of New Mexico in 1958, and in 1963 became a PhD of Stanford University, where his tutor in literature was the poet-critic Yvor Winters (1900–68). He subsequently taught at the universities of California (Santa Barbara and then Berkeley), and Stanford, being appointed Professor of English and Comparative Literature at the University of Arizona in 1980 and Regents Professor of English Literature in 1985. His first novel, *House Made of Dawn* (1968), which won the Pulitzer Prize, is held to have initiated the Native American Literary Renaissance—see also ERDRICH and ORTIZ. In it a mixed-blood veteran of World War II vainly, as it transpires, tries to effect a cultural compromise. In *The Ancient Child* (1989) an artist does succeed, with the help of his Kiowa lover, in crossing a spiritual divide. Kiowa folk material in *The Journey of Tai-me* (privately published, 1967) was incorporated in *The Way to the Rainy Mountain* (1969), a quest for a tribal

heritage from its beginnings to final decline, in prose and verse, with commentary and typographical effects. He has also published several volumes of verse, beginning with *Angle of Geese and Other Poems* (1974)—see also *In the Presence of the Sun: Stories and Poems 1961–1971* (1992). See *The Names: a Memoir*, new edn 1987; Matthias Schubnell, *N. Scott Momaday: the Cultural and Literary Backgrounds*, 1985 (critical study).

MONSARRAT, NICHOLAS (1910–79) British novelist, was born in Liverpool, the fourth child of a surgeon of French descent and of the daughter of a former Lord Mayor of Nottingham, and was educated at Winchester College and Trinity College, Cambridge. After two years articled to a Nottingham solicitor he went to London to be a writer, and gave notice of his pacifist views by participating in public demonstrations. With his fourth novel, *This Is the Schoolroom* (1939), he achieved some notice in the USA as well as in Britain. Inclined by his conscience to join the St John's Ambulance Brigade at the beginning of World War II, he changed his mind in the dark days of 1940 and answered an advertisement for 'gentlemen with yachting experience' to be officers in the Royal Naval Volunteer Reserve. He served at sea throughout the rest of the war, at the end of which he was commanding a frigate with the rank of lieutenant commander. From 1946 to 1953, while continuing to write novels, he was Director of the UK Information Service in Johannesburg, from which he transferred to Ottawa as British Information Officer. He became a full-time writer in 1956. *The Cruel Sea* (1951), which he was three years writing, is the British maritime novel of World War II, admired for its depth of character as well as for the action. It outgunned its nearest rival and successor, *H.M.S. Ulysses* (1955) by Alistair Maclean (1922–88), though Maclean, with his more limited range (the adventure thriller), had the greater popular success thereafter. Monsarrat's subsequent novels included several particularly strong stories, notably *The Story of Esther Costello* (1953), about the exploitation of a girl who is blind, deaf, and dumb, *The Tribe that Lost Its Head* (1956) and its sequel, *Richer than All His Tribe* (1968), set in an emerging African state, and *The Kapillan of Malta* (1973), which he researched on the spot. See *Life is a Four-Letter Word*, 2 vols, new edns 1969–72 (autobiography).

MONTAGU, ELIZABETH see MORE, HANNAH.

MONTAGU, LADY MARY WORTLEY (1689–1762) British prose writer and poet, was born in Covent Garden, London, the eldest daughter of Evelyn Pierrepont (*c.*1665–1726), soon to become 5th Earl and later 1st

Duke of Kingston, and Lady Mary Fielding (*d.* 1692). She supplemented, and countered, her governess's educational methods by her own precociousness and passion for learning, which she indulged in her father's libraries, and by 13 had secretly taught herself to read and write Latin fluently. She was a pretty and high-spirited girl, and in 1710, without her father's permission, began to correspond with Edward Wortley Montagu (1678–1761), a rising Member of Parliament, whom she had met through his sister. They eloped and were married two years later, her father only being reconciled in 1714, after the birth of their son. In 1715–16 she collaborated with POPE and GAY in a literary escapade; her contribution was six satirical 'Eclogues' for private circulation, in one of which she describes her anguish at contracting smallpox, which left her face severely pitted. In 1716 her husband was appointed Ambassador to Turkey, and during their two years in Constantinople she kept a journal from which she later compiled her colourful 'Embassy Letters', published in 1763 after her death—see *Turkish Embassy Letters*, ed. Malcolm Jack, introduction by Anita Desai (1993).

Back in England, with houses in Covent Garden and Twickenham, she enhanced her reputation as a wit, poet, intellectual, and journalist—*The Nonsense of Common-Sense*, a political weekly which appeared in 1737–38, was written by her. She was also instrumental in the introduction into Britain of inoculation against smallpox, which she had seen practised in Turkey. In 1739, for reasons of which probably only one was her romantic attachment to a talented, bisexual, Italian charmer, Count Francesco Algarotti (1712–64), she abandoned her husband, family, and friends for the Continent, where she lived in Venice, Avignon, Brescia, and Padua. During this time she wrote a number of short pieces of fiction which survived as drafts and fragments; these have now been published as *Romance Writings*, ed. Isobel Grundy (1996). She returned to England in June 1762, after Edward's death, and herself died six months later. Knowing that her daughter and son-in-law, with their aristocratic antipathy towards the book trade, would not favour anything of hers being published, she prudently left a manuscript of her letters from Turkey with a clergyman in Rotterdam, 'to be disposed of' as he thought 'proper'. He took the hint. *Works* (1803) contained the rest of her voluminous and entertaining correspondence which survived. See *Complete Letters of Lady Mary Wortley Montagu*, ed. Robert Halsband, 3 vols 1965–67; *Essays and Poems: and 'Simplicity', a Comedy*, ed. Robert Halsband and Isobel Grundy, new edn 1993; Robert Halsband, *The Life of Lady Mary Wortley Montagu*, new edn 1961.

MONTAGUE, JOHN (*b.* 1929) Irish poet, was born in Brooklyn, New York (see 'The Cage'), but spent his childhood in Co. Tyrone and was educated at St Patrick's College, Armagh, and University College, Dublin. He has been a journalist as well as a teacher, in which capacity he was Associate Professor of English, University College, Cork. His first book of poetry was *Forms of Exile* (1958), and he published a volume of short stories in 1964. His themes are Ireland, love, and nature. His Catholic background, unusual for an Ulster poet, finds expression in *The Rough Field* (1972), which spans the history of the province and the lives of some of his family, in *A Slow Dance* (1975), in which the current violence is invoked and deplored, and in *The Dead Kingdom* (1984), a personal and mythic journey from Cork to Fermanagh. *The Figure in the Cave and Other Essays*, ed. Antoinette Quinn (1989), includes statements about his poetic development and philosophy. See *Collected Poems*, 1995; *Selected Poems*, 1982; *New Selected Poems*, 1990.

MONTAIGNE, MICHEL (EYQUEM) DE (1533–92) French prose writer, was the eldest of eight children of a lawyer and landowner in Bordeaux and Montaigne and of a wealthy Jewess of Spanish or Portuguese descent. He went to Collège de Guienne, Bordeaux, when he was six, to the university there at 13, and to Toulouse University at 16. He was appointed to a legal position in Perigueux in 1554, and in Bordeaux in 1557. He served at court in 1561–62, after which he returned to Bordeaux, where he married in 1565 (only one of his six daughters lived for more than a few months). On his father's death in 1568 he inherited the estates of Montaigne. His first literary work (1569) was a translation from the Latin of the 'Natural Theology' of Raymond Sebond, a Catalan who taught medicine and theology in Toulouse in the 1420s—see also Montaigne's *Apology for Raymond Sebond*, tr. M. A. Screech (1987). In 1571 he went into semi-retirement in the library in a tower of his country house, and coined the literary term *essai* [trial] to denote his personal response to and his opinions on any one of a range of historical, social, philosophical, and literary topics which together comprise an autobiographical study. After publishing the first two volumes of *Essais* (1580), he went to Germany and Italy to seek a cure for his gallstones, being recalled in 1581 by the news that he had been elected Mayor of Bordeaux. After a second term of office, and a revision of his great work (1583), he took his family away to avoid the plague, returning in 1586 to add a third volume (1588). His adopted daughter, Marie de Gournay, edited a definitive edition (1595), the first English translation being that

MONTGOMERY, L(UCY) M(AUD)

of John Florio (1603)—see also *The Essays: a Selection*, tr. M. A. Screech (1993).

MONTALE, EUGENIO (1896–1981) Italian poet, critic, and translator, was born in Genoa, left school at 14, studied opera singing, and served in the trenches as an infantry officer in World War I. With others he founded in Turin in 1922 the literary journal *Primo Tempo*, which he co-edited for its life of eight issues. His first book of verse, *Ossi di Seppia* (1925; tr. William Arrowsmith as *Cuttlefish Bones*, 1990), reflected both political concern and an awareness of the natural world. In 1927 he became Curator of the Vieusseux Library in Florence, where he remained after losing his post in 1938 for refusing to join the Fascist party. The sharper language of *Le Occasioni* (1939; tr. Arrowsmith as *The Occasions*, 1987) carried messages of coming chaos, analysed, alongside occasional, topographical, and personal poems, in *La Bufera e Altro* (1956; tr. Arrowsmith as *The Storm and Other Things*, 1985). In 1948 he moved to Milan, where he was for many years a contributing editor of the literary section of *Il Corriere della Sera*. His translations include poetry by SHAKESPEARE (also plays), EMILY DICKINSON, HARDY, and T. S. ELIOT, and fiction by MELVILLE, STEINBECK, and ANGUS WILSON. He was awarded the Nobel Prize for Literature in 1975. See *Selected Poems*, ed. Glauco Cambon, 1965 (bilingual edn).

MONTESQUIEU, (SECONDAT, CHARLES LOUIS DE), BARON DE (1689–1755) French social and political philosopher, was born at his father's seat of La Brède, near Bordeaux, lost his mother when he was seven, and was educated by the Oratorians at Tuilly, near Paris, after which he studied law at Bordeaux. In 1714 he was appointed counsellor to the parliament at Bordeaux, and in 1716 succeeded to his uncle's office as its president and also to his uncle's title. He was more interested, however, in scientific research and in literature. Having published anonymously *Lettres Persanes* (1721; as *Persian Letters* tr. Mr Ozell, 1722; tr. C. J. Betts, 1973), a social satire in the form of letters between two Persian princes and their friends, multiple wives, lovers, and eunuchs, and some minor works, he sold his office in 1726 and moved to Paris, where at the second attempt he was elected to the Académie Française. In England in 1729–31, he became the friend of CHESTERFIELD, studied the House of Commons in action, and was elected to the Royal Society. He returned to La Brède, where he prepared *L'Esprit des Lois* (1748; tr. Thomas Nugent as *The Spirit of the Laws*, 1750), a systematic treatise on politics, based on historical facts and published anonymously, of which he was able to acknowl-

edge that 22 editions were printed within a short time.

MONTGOMERIE, ALEXANDER (*c.*1545–*c.*1598) Scottish poet, was a son of the Laird of Hessilheid, and was through his mother distantly related to JAMES VI, himself no mean poet, whose teacher he became. In 1583 the King granted him a pension, chargeable against certain rents of the archbishopric of Glasgow, which led to a protracted lawsuit, and the loss of the pension. In the meantime Montgomerie was active in the Catholic interest, and was imprisoned. He was further implicated in a Catholic plot in 1597, after which he disappears from the records. 'The Flyting betwixt Montgomerie and Polwart [Sir Patrick Hume of Polwarth, Master of the Royal Household]', a spirited, coarse, highly alliterative piece of extended invective, was probably first spoken in public in about 1582. *The Cherrie and the Slae*, published in Edinburgh in 1597, is a traditional allegorical poem, but its interest is in the interpretation of the two forces as Catholicism (the sweet, refreshing cherries in the tree) and Protestantism (the bitter but more accessible sloes on the bush), in the metrical form (probably his own invention), and in the opening realistic rather than stylized scene of nature. He also wrote some neat love sonnets, of which 'To His Mistress' and 'The Tender Snow of Granis Soft and Quhyt . . .' are particularly delightful. Until FERGUSSON and BURNS rediscovered it as a literary form, he was the last notable poet to write in Scots. See Helena M. Shire, *Alexander Montgomerie: a Selection from His Songs and Poems*, 1960; R. D. S. Jack, *Alexander Montgomerie*, 1985 (critical study).

MONTGOMERY, L(UCY) M(AUD) (1874–1942) Canadian novelist, was born in Clifton, Prince Edward Island, 'of Scotch ancestry, with a dash of English, Irish and French'. Her mother died when she was a baby, and she was brought up by her maternal grandparents in Cavendish, where she went to the district school and at 15 had a poem printed in a local paper. She did a teacher training course at Prince of Wales College, Charlottetown, and then studied at Dalhousie University. She taught for three years before returning to care for her now widowed grandmother, who died in 1911. That year she married a Presbyterian minister, Rev. Ewan MacDonald, with whom she was in rural Ontario parishes until she retired to Toronto in 1936. Her first and most famous novel, *Anne of Green Gables* (1908), which is still enjoyed by children, began as an idea jotted down in a notebook and eventually utilized for a short serial in a Sunday School magazine: 'Elderly couple apply to orphan asylum for a boy. By mistake a girl is sent them.' Its humour and genuine charm are less evident in the series of romanticized sequels, culminating in *Anne of Ingleside* (1939), in which the heroine is now materfamilias. More down to earth, and more autobiographical, are *Emily of New Moon* (1923), about a struggling writer, who reappears in *Emily Climbs* (1925) and *Emily's Quest* (1927). She was made OBE in 1937. There are editions of her correspondence (1960, 1980) and of her journals (1986, 1987, 1993). See Catherine M. Andronik, *Kindred Spirit: a Biography of L. M. Montgomery*, 1993.

MONTHERLANT, HENRI DE (1896–1972) French novelist and dramatist, was born in Paris of an ancient Catalonian family. He became interested in bullfighting at the age of nine, and killed his first bull when he was 15. In 1912 he was dismissed from the École Sainte-Croix de Neuilly, but passed his baccalaureate. After World War I, in which he was badly injured by a shell, he devoted himself to sport (particularly athletics and soccer), and to writing. *Le Songe* (1922; tr. Terence Kilmartin as *The Dream*, 1962), is a novel in which his recurring motif of universal manhood has a background of the war; *Les Olympiques* (1924) is a celebratory amalgam of prose, poetry, and drama with an athlete as linking protagonist. The novel *Les Bestiaires* (1926; tr. Peter Wiles as *The Matador*, 1957) is a lyrical, sometimes mystical, exaltation of bullfighting, in which he himself had ceased to participate after being gored in 1925. *Les Célibataires* (1934; tr. Kilmartin as *The Bachelors*, 1961) is a study of the futility of faded nobility. *Les Jeunes Filles* (1936; tr. Thomas McGreevy as *Young Girls*, 1937) is the first novel of a tetralogy (tr. Kilmartin 1968) in which he explores the reactions of selected types of women to the monstrous egocentricity and nihilism of his non-hero. After World War II he turned more to the theatre—see *The Master of Santiago and Four Other Plays*, tr. Jonathan Griffin (1951).

MONTROSE, (GRAHAM, JAMES), 5TH EARL AND 1ST MARQUIS OF (1612–50) Scottish royalist soldier and poet, was born in Montrose, succeeded to his father's title in 1626, and was educated at St Andrews University. In 1629 he married Magdalen (d. 1648), the youngest of six attractive daughters of Lord Carnegie (1575–1658). Initially a supporter of the National Covenant, he changed his allegiance out of disaffection with those who sought to control Scotland, especially the Earl (later Marquis) of Argyll (1598–1661). At the outset of the Civil War in 1642 he threw his support behind Charles I—his poem 'My dear and only love . . .' is a moving expression of his political loyalty and noble ideals. He was created Marquis in 1644, and in an astonishing campaign in Scotland over the succeeding 12 months he smashed the army of the Cove-

nant. Glasgow was at his mercy, but his Highland troops melted away on personal business. With only six hundred men left he was defeated by an army of six thousand sent from England. He escaped to Europe, from which he returned to the Highlands in 1650, hoping to raise an army for Charles II. His rudimentary force was overwhelmed at Carbisdale, and he was handed over to his enemies by a laird from whom he had sought, and expected, shelter. He was taken to Edinburgh, where the death sentence had already been passed. With incredible dignity, he faced his accusers in Parliament, and on his last night composed the sadly prophetic lines 'Let them bestow on every airth a limb . . .'. He was hanged, and his limbs were cut off and distributed among the chief towns of Scotland. All the bits that could be found were reassembled for his state funeral in 1661, after the Restoration of the Monarchy. See John Buchan, *Montrose*, new edn 1996 (biography).

MOODIE, SUSANNA (1803–85), née Strickland, Canadian prose writer and novelist, the youngest sister of the biographers, Agnes (1796–1874) and Elizabeth (1794–1875) Strickland, and of TRAILL, was born in England at Stowe House, near Bungay, Suffolk, the daughter of an importer and London dock manager. In 1808 the family moved to Reydon Hall, near Southwold, where she was educated by her father until his death in 1818 in restricted circumstances, and then by her sisters. Her first novel, *Spartacus: a Roman Story* (1822), written when she was 13, was followed by 'a series of children's tales', and by articles, stories, and poems (some signed 'Z. Z.' or 'Sophia Sandys') in journals and annuals. In 1831 she published *Enthusiasms, and Other Poems*, and two anonymous anti-slavery pamphlets for PRINGLE, who introduced her to a Scot recently returned from South Africa, John W. Dunbar Moodie (1797–1869), whom she married the same year. Dunbar having succumbed to 'Canada mania', they emigrated in 1832 with their first child to Upper Canada and bought a cleared farm in Newcastle district. In 1834 they moved to the unbroken land in Douro, Peterborough, which had been granted to them, near the Traills. The experiences of these terrible pioneer years, during which she had four more of their seven children, and which included the rebellion of 1837, are recounted with refreshing frankness and remarkable good humour in *Roughing It in the Bush* (1852), to which she added a sequel, *Life in the Clearings, Versus the Bush* (1853). Dunbar was appointed Sheriff of the county of Hastings in 1839, and the family moved thankfully to Belleville. She was a major contributor to the *Literary Garland*, Montreal, for the whole of its, for those days, long existence from 1838 to 1851, and in 1847–48 she and Dunbar edited and largely wrote *Victoria Magazine*, Belleville, a periodical designed to educate farmers and mechanics. She also wrote several sentimental novels of sensation and intrigue, and *Flora Lyndsay: or, Passages in an Eventful Life* (1854), a semi-autobiographical novel which chronologically precedes *Roughing It in the Bush*. Dunbar, who had already published *Ten Years in South Africa* (1835), and who had to resign from his post in 1863 after being accused of 'farming of offices' and wrongly convicted on a technicality, added to the canon with *Scenes and Adventures of a Soldier and Settler* (1868). After his death Moodie lived in Toronto. See *Letters of a Lifetime*, ed. Carl Ballstadt, Elizabeth Hopkins, and Michael Peterman, 1985 (correspondence with biographical commentary); John Thurston, *The Work of Words: the Writing of Susanna Strickland Moodie*, 1996 (critical study).

MOORE, BRIAN (b. 1921) Irish-born Canadian novelist, was born in Belfast, the fourth of nine children of a surgeon who married at 50 and died when the boy was 18. He went to St Malachy's Diocesan College, Belfast, which reappears in all its grimness in *The Feast of Lupercal* (1957) as an indictment of the Catholic education of the time. Unable to go to university, as his parents wanted, because of a failing in mathematics, he joined the Air Raid Precautions service from school, a period of his life which is reflected in *The Emperor of Ice-Cream* (1965), his most autobiographical novel. In 1943 he left Ireland to work for the Ministry of War Transport, which he served as a civilian in Algiers, Naples, and Marseilles. After the war he was with the UN Relief and Rehabilitation Administration in Poland for a year, and then worked as a freelance journalist in Scandinavia and France. In 1948 he went to Canada in pursuit of a young woman he admired. The quest was in vain, but he stayed, and became a Canadian citizen. He was a proofreader and then a reporter on the *Montreal Gazette* until 1952, after which the earnings from four thrillers (written for the American market as Michael Bryan) enabled him to live while he wrote serious fiction, which he began to do during several months in a log cabin in the Laurentian Mountains. *Judith Hearne* (1955; in USA as *The Lonely Passion of Judith Hearne*, 1956), a compelling portrait of an ageing Belfast spinster, was followed by *The Feast of Lupercal* and *The Luck of Ginger Coffey* (1960), a much lighter study of an Irish immigrant in Montreal who has put his Catholicism aside, which won the Governor General's Award. In 1959 he settled in the USA, where he wrote a film for Alfred Hitchcock (1899–1980), became in 1976 a professor in creative writing at the University of California, Los Angeles, and settled with his second wife in Malibu. *The Doctor's Wife* (1976) completed a quartet of novels in which Belfast is the backdrop to citizens' private lives. Having in *The Colour of Blood* (1987) examined in an Eastern European setting the clash between Church and State which leads to terrorism, he returned to the milieu of Belfast with *Lies of Silence* (1990), a suspense thriller whose aim is to reflect the views of the 'silent majority'.

A writer who excels at the portrayal of female protagonists but who has stressed, 'It's boring when a novelist is totally in love with the central character. The minor ones must become vivid,' he defies categorization because of the variety of his themes, settings, and moods: *The Great Victorian Collection* (1975), winner of his second Governor General's Award, is a fantasy of academia which moves between California and Canada; *The Mangan Inheritance* (1979; in USA as *Family Album*, 1979) is an excursion into the Gothic in the form of a failed writer's search for self through links with his reputed ancestor, MANGAN; *No Other Life* (1993) is ostensibly a straightforward adventure novel in the vein of GRAHAM GREENE (in that the setting and background political situation resemble those of Haiti in recent times), but it carries alarming undercurrents of eschatological and other fears. *The Statement* (1995) investigates Catholic sympathy with Nazis and anti-Semites during and after the Occupation of France during World War II. See Jo O'Donoghue, *Brian Moore*, 1990 (critical study).

MOORE, GEORGE (AUGUSTUS) (1852–1933) Irish novelist, dramatist, and critic, was born at the family seat of Moore Hall, Ballyglass, Co. Mayo, the eldest son of the politician, landowner, and owner and breeder of racehorses, George Henry Moore (1811–70), and was educated at Oscott College, Birmingham. After the death of his father, and on his coming of age, he went to Paris to be a painter, but having failed to make the grade, turned to literature. His first published works were two volumes of verse in the style of BAUDELAIRE—*Flowers of Passion* (1878) and *Pagan Poems* (1881)—and *Martin Luther: a Tragedy in Five Acts* (1879). In 1880, the money from his Irish rents having dried up, he went to London, where he wrote two novels whose social realism verges on the naturalistic: *A Modern Lover* (1883), later rewritten as *Lewis Seymour and Some Women* (1917), and *A Mummer's Wife* (1885), the prissy attitude to which on the part of the circulating libraries moved him to issue a trenchant pamphlet, *Literature at Nurse* (1885). His ambivalent feelings towards the Irish surfaced in *A Drama in Muslin* (1886), in which the plight of the tenants is contrasted with the frivolities, and domestic realities, of the well-to-do. After several further novels which he later suppressed, he produced *Esther Waters* (1894), a striking English novel which concentrates on a seduced serving girl and her subsequent struggles, against a background of the racing world which he knew well. In 1900, disillusioned with England, he moved to Dublin and joined YEATS in managing the Irish Literary Theatre and in generating a new Irish literature. They collaborated in a bizarre fashion on the play *Diarmuid and Grania* (1901); it was written by Moore in French, translated into English, then into Irish, back again into English, and finally polished by Yeats. More lasting manifestations of this Irish phase are the deliberate harshness and directness of the stories in *The Untilled Field* (1903) and the melodic line he created for *The Lake* (1905).

He returned to London in 1911, and settled in Ebury Street, from which distance he published three mischievous autobiographical exposés of the Irish Literary Revival and of Irish Catholicism, under the general title of *Hail and Farewell* (1911–14; new edn. ed. Richard Allen Cave, 1985). Always concerned with improving what he had written, he developed an idea in his play about St Paul, *The Apostle* (1911), into the novel *The Brook Kerith* (1916), for which he adopted a rationalistic stance, rewriting the New Testament story as though Jesus was secretly taken from the cross and saved. It succeeds because he did not set out to shock and he had first journeyed through Palestine to absorb the atmosphere of the terrain. Held in equal regard is *Heloïse and Abelard* (1921), in which the lovers stand out from a canvas of dreamlike settings, crowded with colourful medieval characters. He was a respected critic, some of his essays being collected in *Impressions and Opinions* (1891) and *Avowals* (1924; privately printed 1919). To recapture the essence of meetings which make up *Conversations in Ebury Street* (1924), he dictated it to a secretary. *Modern Painting* (1893) was instrumental in extending the reputation of the French Impressionists. See Tony Gray, *A Peculiar Man: a Life of George Moore*, 1996; Richard Allen Cave, *A Study of the Novels of George Moore*, 1978.

MOORE, JOHN (1729–1802) Scottish novelist, travel writer, and doctor, was born in Stirling, and educated at the Grammar School of Glasgow and Glasgow University, where he studied literature and philosophy while being also apprenticed to a surgeon. He served as an assistant army surgeon in Europe, and was for a time doctor to the British Ambassador in Paris. He was then in practice in Glasgow until 1772, when he embarked on a five-year European tour with his charge, the young 8th Duke of Hamilton (1756–1837); the outcome was *A View of Society and Manners in France, Switzerland and Germany* (1779), and a similar work on Italy (1781). His first novel, *Zeluco* (1789), a study of sheer wickedness in the person of a Sicilian noble, with humorous interludes, was admired by BYRON, who in the preface to *Childe Harold* refers to his hero as 'the sketch of a modern Timon, or a poetical Zeluco'. It was also praised by BURNS in the course of a correspondence with Moore. *Edward* (1796) is, by contrast, the story of a thoroughly good man. *Mordaunt* (1800) is an epistolary novel in three incongruent parts, comprising a travelogue, an account of the terrors in France, and a series of character sketches. After its publication he moved for his health from Clifford Street, Mayfair, to Richmond, where he died. He also wrote *Medical Sketches* (1786), in which he uses the effect of eating ice cream to illustrate the transference of senses between nerves; *A View of the Causes and Progress of the French Revolution* (1795), whose royalist stance offended Burns; and a memoir of his friend SMOLLETT (1797). His eldest surviving son was Sir John Moore (1761–1809) of Corunna, remembered in 'The Burial of Sir John Moore' by Charles Wolfe (1791–1823), 'Not a drum was heard . . .'.

MOORE, MARIANNE (1887–1972) American poet and critic, was born in Kirkwood, Missouri, where she and her elder brother were brought up by their mother in her parents' home: their father, an engineer, having had a nervous breakdown after failing to build a smokeless furnace, retired to his parents in Ohio. After a move to Carlisle, Pennsylvania, she was educated at Metzger Institute schools and Bryn Mawr, where she had poetry published in college magazines. She graduated in 1909, took a secretarial course at Carlisle Commercial College, and taught at the US Indian School in Carlisle. Her professional publication began in 1915 with a poem in the *Egoist* in London, and five in the influential Chicago journal, *Poetry: a Magazine of Verse*. During World War I and the early 1920s she regularly contributed to 'little' magazines which promoted the work of the 'new poets', including AIKEN, STEVENS, and W. C. WILLIAMS, among whose group she was also admired for 'Titian hair, a brilliant complexion, and a mellifluous flow of polysyllables'—see Robin G. Schulze, *The Web of Friendship: Marianne Moore and Wallace Stevens* (1996).

In 1918 she and her mother (who lived with her until her death in 1947) moved to New York, where for four years she was a part-time assistant in her local branch library. *Poems* (1921), a selection of 24 made by DOOLITTLE from those which had appeared in magazines, and published in London without Moore's knowledge, included 'Poetry', her enigmatic, often revised, critical statement, in which the function of poets is to be 'literalists of the imagination' and to present 'imaginary gardens with real toads in them'. The occasion brought her out of her innate reticence, and she reprinted 21 of the poems among the 53 in *Observations* (1924), published in New York by Dial Press, whose international literary journal, the *Dial*, she edited from 1926 until it ceased publication in

1929. For the next three decades she worked as a freelance writer and critic, increasing her reputation with *Selected Poems* (1935) and *Collected Poems* (1951), which won the Pulitzer Prize, the National Book Award, and two further honours. Her celebrity status was such that the Ford Motor Company invited her to propose a name for a new car, her move from Brooklyn to Manhattan in 1966 provoked a controversy in the press, and in 1968 she threw the first ball of the new baseball season at the Yankee Stadium. This was achieved in spite of her reputation as a 'poet's poet', who used complex and subtle means to illustrate paradoxes. See *The Complete Poems of Marianne Moore*, ed. Clive Driver and Patricia C. Willis, 2nd rev. edn 1984; *The Complete Prose of Marianne Moore*, ed. Patricia C. Willis, 1987; Charles Molesworth, *Marianne Moore: a Literary Life*, new edn 1991; Bernard F. Engel, *Marianne Moore*, rev. edn 1989 (critical study); Cristanne Miller, *Marianne Moore: Questions of Authority*, 1996 (critical study).

MOORE, THOMAS (1779–1852) Irish poet and biographer, was born in Dublin of Catholic parents (his father was a grocer), and was educated at a private grammar school in Dublin and at Trinity College, Dublin. He read for the Bar in London, where his fine voice and musical ability made him a welcome guest of the aristocracy. *Odes of Anacreon* (1800), a metrical translation done at college, was followed by the pseudonymous but only faintly improper *The Poetical Works of the Late Thomas Little, Esq* (1801). In 1803 he was appointed Admiralty Registrar in Bermuda, but in 1804 he left the post to a deputy, travelled in America, and returned to London, where he published *Epistles, Odes and Other Poems* (1806). *Irish Melodies*, with 'symphonies and accompaniments', appeared in instalments (1807–1834) and confirmed his reputation as a lyricist and Irish national bard. *Lalla Rookh* (1817), verse tales with linking prose, was a fully-researched attempt to satisfy the vogue for the oriental, but while it was popular throughout Europe, only the songs have lasted. In 1818 his Bermuda deputy decamped with the official funds. Moore was declared bankrupt, and had to spend several years abroad, during which he visited BYRON in Italy, who presented him with his 'Memoirs', written between 1818 and 1821. In 1822 Moore's debt to the Admiralty was paid off and he returned to London. On Byron's death, he was persuaded to consent to the destruction of the 'Memoirs' and in their place to write and edit *Letters and Journals of Lord Byron: with Notices of His Life* (1830). He also wrote a perceptive life of SHERIDAN (1825). His versatility as a writer is further demonstrated by the satirical verse collection, *The Fudge Family in Paris* (1818), and a novel of the Irish situation, *Memoirs of Captain Rock* (1824). See *The Journals of Thomas Moore 1818–1841*, ed. Peter Quennell, 1964; *The Letters of Thomas Moore*, ed. Wilfred S. Dowden, 2 vols 1964; Terence de Vere White, *Tom Moore, the Irish Poet*, 1977.

MORAES, DOM(INIC) (*b.* 1938) Indian poet, was born in Bombay, the son of Frank Moraes (*d.* 1974), Editor of *The Times of India* and later of the *Bombay Express*, with whom he travelled extensively as a child, and of a doctor. He had a book on cricket published when he was 13. While at Jesus College, Oxford, he published a book of verse, *A Beginning* (1957), for which he became the first non-British winner of the Hawthornden Prize for a work of imaginative literature. About this time, having lent FORSTER some of his poems and received the comment, 'I'll write to you about them', he responded courteously, 'I do not wish you to write about them, I wish you to read them.' He was one of three Commonwealth poets (with PETER PORTER and WALCOTT) among those invited to contribute to *15 Poems for William Shakespeare* (1964). *John Nobody* (1965) and *Poems 1955–1965* (1966) concluded his early period of verse, in which mystical and personal elements and the social effects of modern political oppression predominate. He was a roving reporter for the *New York Times Sunday Magazine* from 1968 to 1971, Managing Editor, *Asia Magazine*, Hong Kong 1971–73, and Chief Literary Consultant, United Nations Fund for Populations, in India 1973–77. *Absences* (1983) represented a return to verse writing after 17 years, marked especially by poems in which the exploits of mythical characters ('Gabriel', 'Gladiator', 'Merlin', and others) illuminate the tragedies inherent in modern society. He has published several books on his travels, as well as studies of the stateswoman Mrs Gandhi (1980) and the cricketer Sunil Gavaskar (1987). See *Collected Poems 1957–1987*, 1987; *My Son's Father*, new edn 1991; and *Never at Home*, new edn 1994 (autobiography).

MORAVIA, ALBERTO, pseudonym of Alberto Pincherle (1907–90) Italian novelist and short-story writer, was born in Rome, the son of a Jewish architect and of the daughter of a Catholic civil servant. After contracting a tubercular infection of the leg bones when he was eight, which left him with a permanent limp, he never returned to school, but acquired a wide knowledge of literature through reading and with the help of a succession of English, French, and German governesses. Sent at 16 to a sanatorium in the Dolomites, he began and for five years worked on *Gli Indifferenti* (1929; tr. Aida Mastrangelo as *The Indifferent Ones*, 1932; tr. Angus Davidson as *The Time of Indifference*, 1953), a forerunner of the existentialist novel, originally published in Milan at his father's expense. During the 1930s he travelled, mainly to distance himself from the Fascist regime, of which he finally fell foul with the satirical *La Mascherata* (1941; tr. Davidson as *The Fancy Dress Party*, 1947). After the German occupation in 1943 he and his novelist wife sheltered in the Abruzzi mountains, an experience which opened his eyes to the daily realities of life among the poor and inspired *La Ciociara* (1957; tr. Davidson as *Two Women*, 1958). Many aspects of the lower life of Rome, to which he moved in 1954, feature in two hefty volumes of stories (1954, 1959), a selection from which is in *Roman Tales*, tr. Davidson (1988). With *Io e Lui* (1971; tr. Davidson as *Two: a Phallic Novel*, 1972), a lively dialogue between a scriptwriter and his sexual organ, he dropped all pretence of keeping eroticism within bounds. Film critic, travel journalist—see *A Quale Tribù Appartieni?* (1972; tr. Davidson as *Which Tribe Do You Belong To?*, 1974), literary philosopher, and social activist, he was in 1984 elected to the European Parliament as a representative of the independent left. After separating from his wife and living for many years with a prominent feminist writer, he married, in his 80th year, a 34-year-old Spanish divorcée who was a press officer at his publisher. See Thomas Erling Peterson, *Alberto Moravia*, 1996 (biographical/critical study).

MORE, HANNAH (1745–1833) British poet, dramatist, and prose writer, was born in Stapleton, near Bristol, the fourth of five daughters of a dictatorial headmaster who was determined that they should all become teachers, as he could not afford dowries. She was educated at home and then at the school set up by her eldest sister in Bristol, at which she became a teacher. In 1767 she became engaged to a wealthy estate owner twenty years her senior, who jilted her after seven years of vacillation, offering an annuity of £200 as compensation. Vowing never to marry, she refused the money, which was then accepted on her behalf without her knowledge. On annual visits to London she moved in literary circles, became very close to the actor-manager David Garrick (1717–79) and his wife, and through Elizabeth Montague (1720–1800), the essayist and letter writer, became a member of the Bluestocking Circle, an informal society of women who met for intelligent and intellectual conversation.

Her first literary exercise, *Search after Happiness: a Pastoral Drama* (1773), was written for her pupils, as was *The Inflexible Captive* (1774), which with an epilogue by Garrick was performed at the Theatre Royal, Bath. *Sir Eldred of the Bower, and The Bleeding Rock*, comprising two lush ballads, was published in 1776. *Ode to Dragon, Mr Garrick's House-Dog at Hampton* (1777) laments the retirement from the stage of Garrick, with whose encouragement she wrote two melodramatic tragedies, *Percy* (1778) and *The Fatal Falsehood* (1779). She became more inclined to good

works, and was entangled with Ann Yearsley (1752–1806), the 'poetical milkwoman', whose poems she edited (1784) but from whom she got no thanks. Now living in Cowslip Green, Somerset, she met William Wilberforce (1759–1833), the abolitionist and Evangelical reformer, wrote *Slavery, a Poem* (1788), and at his instigation established a local Sunday School, which, with the help of her sisters, was the first of many in the Cheddar area. *Village Politics* (1793) was a tract for the poor intended to counter the radicalism that had sparked off the French Revolution. Her 49 'Cheap Repository Tracts' (1795–97) led to the foundation of the Religious Tract Society in 1799. *Coelebs in Search of a Wife* (1809), her only real novel, suggests the Evangelical ideal of wifehood. Her last sister died in 1819, after which she was terrorized and cheated by her servants in the house in Wrington which they had bought in 1802, until persuaded to move to Clifton in 1828. See *Selected Writings*, ed. Robert Hole, 1996; Mary Gwladys Jones, *Hannah More*, 1952 (biography).

MORE, (Sir) THOMAS (1478–1535) English prose writer and statesman, was born in the City of London, the son of a judge, and was educated at Canterbury Hall, Oxford. He was called to the Bar but chose to spend four years in retreat, from which he emerged to resume a brilliant legal career, to enter Parliament, and to marry. He was knighted by Henry VIII in 1521 and held several posts of state, the last, which he accepted reluctantly, being Lord Chancellor. He resigned in 1532, unable to accept the King's divorce from Catharine of Aragon so that he could marry Anne Boleyn. When Henry appointed himself head of the English Church in 1534, More twice refused to accept his supremacy over the Pope, and was beheaded. He was canonized in 1935. *Utopia*, one of the finest statements of humanism, partly written while on a diplomatic mission to Flanders, was published in Latin in 1516, and translated into English by Ralph Robynson (1551). The ideal, but in some respects idyllic, state is contrasted with English social, corporate, and religious life in the early 16th century seen by an imaginary traveller. *History of King Richard the Thirde*, written in English and Latin in about 1513, became via the chronicles of Grafton and Hall (see HOLINSHED) the source of SHAKESPEARE's *Richard III*. While awaiting execution, More wrote the moving *A Dialoge of Comfort against Tribulacion* (1553). His friendship with ERASMUS, whom he first met in 1499, led to a correspondence between them which upholds the Renaissance ideal of immortality through the preservation of personal letters. His son-in-law, William Roper (1496–1578), wrote *The Mirrour of Vertue: or the Life of More* (1625). See *A Sir Thomas More Reader*, ed. Rudolph E. Habenicht, 1996; R. W.

Chambers, *Thomas More*, new edn 1982; Anthony Kenny, *Thomas More*, 1983 (introduction to his thought).

MORGAN, CHARLES (1894–1958) British novelist, was born in Bromley, Kent, the younger son of a distinguished civil engineer of Welsh origin who had been born and brought up in Australia. He was educated at the Royal Naval College, Dartmouth, and served in the Atlantic and on the China station, but resigned in 1913, hoping to go to Oxford and become a writer. He rejoined in 1914, and was with the Naval Brigade of the Royal Naval Volunteer Reserve at Antwerp, during the retreat from which he was interned in Holland. Here he remained, on parole, until 1917, imbibing European culture and writing a novel, based on his naval experiences, *The Gunroom* (1919), which he had to rewrite in England after the ship carrying his baggage home was sunk by a mine. He was at Brasenose College, Oxford, from 1918 to 1922, and was President of the Oxford University Dramatic Society, through which he became Assistant Drama Critic of *The Times* in 1921; he was Drama Critic 1926–39. *Portrait in a Mirror* (1929), an exploration of the inspiration of the artist, brought him recognition also in France, where it won the Prix Fémina-Vie Heureuse Anglais. *The Fountain* (1932), a wartime love story set in Holland and told with poetic intensity, is a study also of the search for spiritual freedom in the contemporary world, a theme to which he returned in *The Voyage* (1940) and his impressionistic play, *The Flashing Stream* (1938). He served in the Admiralty in World War II, during which articles by him were secretly circulated in Occupied France, and he was one of the first British civilians to enter Paris after its liberation in 1944. *Epitaph on George Moore* (1935) is a fine essay on the novelist. His volumes of essays include *The Writer and His World* (1960). See H. C. Duffin, *The Novels and Plays of Charles Morgan*, 1959.

MORGAN, EDWIN (*b*. 1920) Scottish poet, critic, and translator, was born in Glasgow, the son of a clerk with a firm of iron and steel scrap merchants who later became a director of it. He was educated at Glasgow High School and Glasgow University, serving in the Royal Army Medical Corps, mainly in the Middle East, during World War II—'Morgan ate sand, slept sand at El Ballah / while gangrened limbs dropped in the pail', he writes in *Sonnets from Scotland* (1984). He returned to Glasgow University, afterwards, as a teacher, and was Titular Professor in English 1975–80. Some of his most persistent themes were already apparent in his first book of verse, *The Vision of Cathkin Braes* (1952). Since then he has used his acute comic sense and talent for enthusiasm particularly to express his conviction that in change there is hope,

employing a variety of forms including concrete/visual poetry, sometimes with a judicious use of Scots. Glasgow often features as a launching pad for his observations. His translations embrace *Beowulf* as well as BRECHT, NERUDA, PASTERNAK, TSVETAYEVA, MAYAKOVSKY, and YEVTUSHENKO. Critical studies include *East European Poets* (1976) and *Crossing the Border: Essays in Scottish Literature* (1990). See *Collected Poems*, new edn 1996; *Nothing Not Given: Reflections on His Life and Work*, ed. Hamish Whyte, 1991.

MORGAN, (SYDNEY), LADY (*d*. 1859), née Owenson, Irish poet and novelist, the daughter of Robert Owenson (1744–1812), a Protestant actor-manager of Catholic descent, and his Methodist wife from Shrewsbury, was born either on board the Irish packet in 1776 or in Dublin in 1783. She was educated at a Huguenot school in Clontarf, and became a governess after her father's failure as a producer. She published *Poems* in 1801, followed by *St Clair: or, The Heiress of Desmond* (1803), a novel of Platonic friendship in romantic surroundings. *The Wild Irish Girl* (1806), Ossianic in its romanticism, didactic in its exposition of traditional Irish life and culture, and Messianic in its approach to Irish nationalism, made her reputation, which she exploited in character in Regency salons, singing sad Irish songs to her own harp accompaniment. She became a member of the household of the Deputy Lord-Lieutenant, 1st Marquis of Abercorn (1756–1818), whose personal doctor, Sir Charles Morgan (1783–1843), she married in 1812. She wrote three further flamboyant Irish novels—notably *The O'Briens and the O'Flahertys* (1827)—whose understanding of the problems of the times contributed to the Catholic Emancipation Act of 1829. She lived in London from 1837, when she was awarded by the Prime Minister, Lord Melbourne (1779–1848), an annual pension of £300, the first woman to receive such an honour for services to literature. She travelled in Ireland and on the Continent, and wrote historical and contemporary studies of France and Italy, as well as a biography of the 17th century Italian painter, Salvator Rosa (1840), and a well-researched historical and sociological survey, *Woman and Her Master* (1824). See Mary Campbell, *Lady Morgan: the Life and Times of Sydney Owenson*, 1988; James Newcomer, *Lady Morgan the Novelist*, 1990.

MORRIS, JULIAN see WEST, MORRIS.

MORRIS, WILLIAM (1834–96) British poet, prose writer, book designer, and craftsman, was born in the London suburb of Walthamstow, the son of a city businessman, and was educated at Marlborough College and Exeter College, Oxford. He gave up the idea of the Church, was articled to an architect, and then became a professional painter on the advice of D. G. ROSSETTI, with whom and others he formed an interior decorating firm. In 1859 he married Jane Burden (1840–1914), a groom's daughter who was a much-painted Pre-Raphaelite model. His enthusiasm for the freedom of the craftsman from the constrictions of capitalism and the dangers of mass production was instrumental in his founding the Socialist League in 1884; in 1890 he set up the Kelmscott Press to produce fine books. *The Defence of Guenevere and Other Poems* (1858) revealed a flair for romantic narrative verse in easy rhythm and rhyme, especially in the title poem, a striking treatment of scenes from MALORY, and 'The Haystack in the Floods'. *The Life and Death of Jason* (1867) and *The Story of Sigurd the Volsung* (1877) are verse retellings of classical and Norse myth. In *The Earthly Paradise* (1868–70) he used CHAUCER's storytelling framework effectively to combine Greek, Germanic, Norse, and Celtic folklore. *A Dream of John Ball* (1888) and *News from Nowhere* (1890) are prose romances in which his socialist doctrines are interwoven with forward and backward time slips. He also wrote historical novels based on north European legend, of which *A Tale of the House of the Wolfings* (1889) is a good example. See *Selected Poems*, ed. Peter Faulkner, 1992; *William Morris by Himself: Designs and Writings*, ed. Gillian Naylor, new edn 1996; Fiona MacCarthy, *William Morris: a Life for Our Time*, new edn 1995; Paul Thompson, *The Work of William Morris*, new edn 1993 (critical biography); Peter Stansky, *William Morris*, 1983 (introduction to his ideas).

MORRISON, TONI (*b.* 1931) American novelist, was born Chloe Anthony Wofford in Lorain, Ohio, and graduated as BA from Howard University (1953) and MA from Cornell University (1955). She taught English at Texas Southern University and then at Howard, where she met Harold Morrison, a Jamaican architect, whom she married. They separated in 1964, when she became an editor for a New York publishing house while bringing up her two sons. Her exploration of black consciousness in a white society began with *The Bluest Eye* (1970), centring on the rape by her father of a girl who prays for 'the blue eyes of a little white girl'. In her third novel, *Song of Solomon* (1977), the search for a family's past throws light on mysterious and repressed situations in the present. The basis of *Tar Baby* (1981) is a culture clash between a sophisticated African-American and her black lover from the rural South. In the mid-19th-century setting of *Beloved* (1987), which won the Pulitzer Prize, a runaway slave has killed her children rather than return them to the fate which she had tried to escape. The qualities of individuality and unpredictability underscore the harsher aspects of the black experience of the 1920s in *Jazz* (1992). Morrison was appointed to the Albert Sch-

weitzer Chair at New York State University in 1984, and to the Robert F. Goheen Chair at Princeton in 1989. She has also published *Playing in the Dark: Whiteness and the Literary Imagination* (1992). She was awarded the Nobel Prize for Literature in 1993. See Trudier Harris, *Fiction and Folklore: the Novels of Toni Morrison*, new edn 1993; Linden Peach, *Toni Morrison*, 1995 (critical study); Jan Furman, *Toni Morrison's Fiction*, 1996.

MORROW, JACOB see MANNING, OLIVIA.

MORTIMER, JOHN (*b.* 1923) British dramatist and novelist, was born in Hampstead, London, and educated at Harrow and Brasenose College, Oxford. Unfit for war service, he progressed from 'fourth assistant director' to scriptwriter for the Crown Film Unit. He was called to the Bar in 1948, and became QC in 1966, and Master of the Bench, Inner Temple, in 1975. 'The best playwright ever to have defended a murderer at the Central Criminal Court', as he describes himself, began with 'The Dock Brief' and other short plays—see *Five Plays* (1970)—in which the comedy and dialogue are usually more prominent than characterization or message. Of his full-length plays, *Two Stars for Comfort* (1962) has unsympathetic as well as lovable characters, and a realistic ending. *A Voyage Round My Father* (1970) is a portrait of a barrister who, like his own father, went blind but continued his career and family life regardless. His first novel, *Charade* (1957), was written during the war and resuscitated later. Latterly, his novels have tended to begin as, or be developed alongside, television serials or series, such as *Paradise Postponed* (1985), featuring a monstrously awful politician, and *Summer's Lease* (1988), a satire on the English abroad with elements of suspense and mystery. Horace Rumpole, the outspoken legal hack who first rose to cross-examine in *Rumpole of the Bailey* (1978), has subsequently, through many volumes of short stories, become a national institution—see also *The Best of Rumpole* (1993). A libel case is a feature of *Dunster* (1992), in which the mystery of the ultimate responsibility for a tragedy in World War II is gradually resolved. Mortimer married, as his first wife, Penelope Mortimer (*b.* 1918), whose frank novels analysing the less attractive aspects of marriage, notably *The Pumpkin Eater* (1963), influenced the genre—her autobiography, *About Time Too 1940-1978* (1993), records the slow break-up of their marriage. He was made CBE in 1986. See *Clinging to the Wreckage: a Part of Life*, new edn 1995; *Murderers and Other Friends: Another Part of Life*, new edn 1995 (autobiography).

MORTIMER, PENELOPE see MORTIMER.

MOSCHUS see THEOCRITUS.

MOTLEY, WILLARD (1912–65) American novelist, was born into a middle-class black family in Chicago, where he went to high school. Bored with the neighbourhood in which he was brought up, he moved into the slums in search of an identity, and then worked his way throughout the USA by whatever means, and doing whatever work, came to hand, living where he could; and where he could not, serving a 30-day sentence for vagrancy in Wyoming. In the 1940s he worked as a photographer, radio scriptwriter, and interviewer for the Chicago Housing Authority, and then as a writer for the Office of Civilian Defense. He was concerned with social rather than racial issues, his first novel, *Knock on Any Door* (1947), exploring the effect of environment on the son of an Italian family in Chicago, through juvenile delinquency to his execution for murder at the age of 21. *We Fished All Night* (1951) focuses on the conditions in the Chicago slums which bred political racketeers as well as gangsters. In 1951 he moved to Mexico, where he found similar deprivations to account for cultural and moral degeneration, which he described in *Let Noon Be Fair* (1966).

MPHAHLELE, EZEKIEL (or **ES'KIA**) (b. 1919) South African novelist and critic, was born in Cape Location, Pretoria, and brought up in the village of Maupaneng, Transvaal, and then in a two-room house (in which there were several children and some eight adults) in the black location of Marabastad, Pretoria. He was educated at St Peter's School, Johannesburg, and trained as a teacher at Adams College, Durban, after which he worked as a clerk and typing instructor at an institute for the blind. In 1945 he married, and was appointed English and Afrikaans Master at Orlando High School, Johannesburg, only to be banned from teaching in 1952 because as Secretary of the Transvaal African Teachers' Association he opposed the introduction of Bantu education. He taught for a year in Basutoland, did odd jobs, and then joined the editorial staff of *Drum*. In 1957, having studied at the University of South Africa by correspondence, and graduated as MA in English with distinction, he went into exile in Nigeria, where he lectured for Ibadan University. He surrendered his passport for a British one in 1959. During the next fifteen years he was Director of the African Programme of the Congress for Cultural Freedom, in Paris, under whose auspices he set up the Chemchemi Creative Centre in Nairobi, and taught at the universities of Denver, Zambia, and Pennsylvania.

In 1976 he attended a conference in South Africa on a temporary visa, and applied for his passport to be restored. He returned permanently in 1977, when he changed his first name to its African equivalent. He became an inspector of education in Transvaal when his application for the chair of English at the University of the North was blocked. He was appointed Senior Research Fellow at the African Studies Institute, Witwatersrand University, in 1979, subsequently becoming Professor of African Literature. His *Man Must Live and Other Stories* was published in Cape Town in 1947, and *The Living and Dead and Other Stories* in Nigeria in 1961, by which time his ghetto sketches had become more vitriolic in their protest. He received the degree of PhD at Denver University for the manuscript of his semi-autobiographical novel of exile, *The Wanderers* (1972). *Chirundu* (1979) is about a politician in a new African state. A permanent place in literature is more likely, however, for the first volume of his autobiography (1959), and for his critical study of African writing and writing about Africans, *The African Image* (1962), the 1974 edition of which incorporates parallels with Afro-American literature. See *Down Second Avenue*, new edn 1971 (autobiography), *Afrika My Music: an Autobiography 1957–1983*, new edn 1995; N. Chabani Manganyi, *Exiles and Homecomings: a Biography of Es'kia Mphahlele*, 1983.

MTSHALI, OSWALD (MBUYISENI, formerly **JOSEPH)** (b. 1940) South African poet, was born in Vryheid, Natal, and educated at Inkamana High School. His ambition to go to Witwatersrand University foundered when the separate universities' legislation was introduced. He refused to attend a 'tribal college', and became a driver and delivery man in Johannesburg. Verses which appeared in various journals were collected as *Sounds of a Cowhide Drum*, published in Johannesburg (1971), and also in London (1972) and New York (1972). A further volume, *Fireflames* (1980), was banned in South Africa. In a paper presented at the University of Iowa in 1975 he explains: 'I write in English for my present state of reality or unreality and I write in Zulu to establish my identity which will be translated by posterity.' Critics are not unanimous about the poetic quality of lines such as 'Pneumatic drills / roar like guns in a battlefield / as they tear the street. / Puffing machines swallow the red soil / and spit it out like a tuberculotic's sputum.'; but he was the first black South African for twenty years to publish a book of verse in that country, and the first who wrote in that country to have one published abroad. He obtained a degree in creative writing at Columbia University, and after his return was appointed deputy headmaster of a privately-funded commercial college in Soweto.

MUGGERIDGE, MALCOLM (1903–90) British prose writer, journalist, and sage, was born in Croydon, Surrey, the son of a lawyer's clerk who later became a Labour Member of Parliament. He was educated at Selhurst Grammar School and Selwyn College, Cambridge, where his state school education and socialist upbringing gave him a sense of isolation. After teaching at the Union Christian College, Alwaye, in southern India, he married a niece of BEATRICE WEBB, and sailed for Egypt, where he lectured at Cairo University. In 1930, with the encouragement of RANSOME, he joined the editorial staff of the *Manchester Guardian*, whose Moscow correspondent he was for nine months in 1932–33. The upshot of the experience, to which the attitude of Western visitors to the evils perpetrated in the name of Communism contributed, was disillusionment with the system, expressed in his novel, *Winter in Moscow* (1934). *The Thirties: 1930–1940 in Great Britain* (1940) is a cynical study of the decade, reflecting the chaos which follows a loss of faith. During World War II, in which he was a member of the Intelligence Corps and then of MI5, he spent much of his time as an agent in Mozambique. In 1944, shortly after its liberation, he was sent to Paris, where in the course of his duties he secured the release of WODEHOUSE and his wife, who had been arrested and interrogated by the police. After serving on the *Daily Telegraph* as leader writer, Washington Correspondent, and Deputy Editor, he was Editor of *Punch* from 1952 to 1957, while developing a reputation as a skilled, if somewhat anarchic, broadcaster and interviewer. During his latter years, which he spent in rural Sussex, he wrote *The Green Stick* (1972) and *The Infernal Grove* (1973), two volumes of sparkling memoirs, intended as part of an unfinished autobiographical sequence, 'Chronicles of a Wasted Time'. While his attitude to religion changed over the years (he became a Catholic in his late seventies), his preoccupation with it is reflected in much of his later writing. See Richard Ingrams, *Malcolm Muggeridge: the Biography*, new edn 1996; Gregory Wolfe, *Malcolm Muggeridge: a Biography*, new edn 1996.

MUIR, EDWIN (1887–1959) Scottish poet, novelist, critic, and translator, was born in Deerness, Orkney, the youngest of six children of a farmer, and attended Kirkwall Grammar School irregularly. When he was 14, the family was evicted and moved to Glasgow: within five years both his parents and two brothers were dead. After working as a clerk, he married in 1919 a Scottish academic, Willa Anderson (1890–1970), who later wrote two novels under her own name and published translations as Agnes N. Scott. They settled in London. A near-breakdown was averted by psychoanalysis, and a European tour was made possible by the publication in the USA of *We Moderns* (1918), a collection of aphorisms under the pseudonym of Edward More. On their return he pub-

lished *First Poems* (1925), and three novels. His income at that time came from reviews and critical articles—see P. H. Butter (ed.), *The Truth of Imagination: a Collection of Reviews and Essays by Edwin Muir* (1988)—and from translating European literature (notably KAFKA) with his wife. He was British Council Director in Prague 1945–48 and Rome 1949–50, and Warden of Newbattle Abbey College 1950–55. In 1946 he wrote, 'I've been trying for some years to write poetry that was both simple and unexpected', and much of his best verse was written after he was 50. Unsensational, reflective, plainly stated, it often reaches back to his childhood and beyond into history, and forward to a time when confusion and destruction will have been exorcized. He advocated a Scottish national literature in English, which caused him to fall out with his friend MACDIARMID. He was made CBE in 1953. See *The Complete Poems of Edwin Muir*, ed. P. H. Butter, 1992; *Selected Prose*, ed. George Mackay Brown, 1989; *An Autobiography*, new edn 1993; Willa Anderson, *Belonging: a Memoir*, 1968; P. H. Butter, *Edwin Muir: Man and Poet*, new edn 1977; Margery McCulloch, *Edwin Muir: Poet, Critic and Novelist*, 1993 (critical study).

MUKHERJEE, BHARATI (*b.* 1940) novelist and short-story writer, was born in Calcutta of a Bengali Brahmin family (her father was a chemist and businessman), and went to schools in England and Switzerland, and then to Loreto House, Calcutta, and the universities of Calcutta, Baroda, and Iowa. On the creative writing course at Iowa in 1961 she met the Canadian novelist and academic, Clark Blaise (*b.* 1940): 'I had never been alone in a room with a man who was not a relative and now, for the first time, my body was speaking and making decisions for me. I became an "accidental immigrant".' They married in 1963, and had two sons. She taught English at several Canadian universities between 1964 and 1978, becoming a Canadian citizen in 1971. *The Tiger's Daughter* (1972) and *Wife* (1975) reflect her own ambivalent situation, which is further examined in *Days and Nights in Calcutta* (1977), comprising separate accounts by her and her husband of a year spent in India in 1973.

They left Canada because of 'the persistent effects of racial prejudice against people of my national origin', and in 1980 took up permanent residence in the USA, where she became a teacher at the University of California, Berkeley. Regarding herself now as an American writer in the tradition of those whose families were immigrants within recent memory, she has in the collections *Darkness* (1985) and *The Middleman and Other Stories* (1988) explored the attitudes of illegal as well as of rightful incomers to 'the tyranny of the American dream'. In *Jasmine* (1989), a young woman's hazardous odyssey from the Punjab to Iowa, and from being the dowerless widow Jyoti to Jane Ripplemeyer, also represents the workings of fate, the universal challenges of society, and the role of the individual. *The Holder of the World* (1993) incorporates time-slips in a progression from a Puritan colony in Massachusetts to a Moghul court. She became a US citizen in 1988. 'I'm not interested in preserving, in an artificial way, the Indianness I arrived with in 1961. My dress reflects my personal style. My accent reflects all the places in which I have lived. I have a right to refashion myself, to think of myself as American in my own, special Bengali way.' See Alam Fakrul, *Bharati Mukherjee*, 1996 (biographical/critical study).

MULDOON, PAUL (*b.* 1951) Irish poet, was born in Co. Armagh. He was educated at St Patrick's College, Armagh, and Queen's University, Belfast, and worked in Belfast as a BBC Talks Producer. His first book of verse, a pamphlet, was published when he was 20, and his first collection proper, *New Weather* (1973), in which the Irish climate is a medium through which the world may be seen in a new light, two years later. His collections since *Mules* (1977) have often begun with a group of short poems anticipating aspects of the longer poem or sequence which follows. He now lives and teaches in the USA, where he has entertainingly re-created himself as an American writer, while retaining his Irish relish for linguistic exuberance. The short poems in *Quoof* (1983), some reflecting his childhood, which he sets beside the present in the title poem, are prefaced by an extract from Eskimo folklore, and succeeded by an American extravaganza, 'The More a Man Has the More a Man Wants'. In *Madoc: a Mystery* (1990) the main narrative poem is a teasing excursion into American folk history, with references to the Pantisocratic commune imagined by SOUTHEY and COLERIDGE, but never realized. *Shining Brow* (1993) is a libretto for an opera about a traumatic decade in the life of the American architect, Frank Lloyd Wright (1869–1959). *The Annals of Chile* (1994), his seventh collection, celebrates, among other events, the birth of a daughter, and includes 'Yarrow', a long poem incorporating a whirl of incidents, images, and personal recollections, which has been referred to as 'a new kind of elegy, an elegy for the unborn and the dead alike'. See *New Selected Muldoon*, 1996; Tim Kendall, *Paul Muldoon*, 1996 (critical study); Clair Wills, *Paul Muldoon*, 1996 (critical study).

MULGAN, JOHN (1911–45) New Zealand novelist, was born in Christchurch, the son of the journalist Alan Mulgan (1881–1962), who wrote one novel, *Spur of Morning* (1934), and an autobiography, *The Making of a New Zealander* (1958). John Mulgan was educated as a boarder at Wellington College, and then at

Auckland Grammar School and Auckland University College, where he excelled at sport. Having failed to be nominated as a Rhodes Scholar at Oxford, he made his own way there, and got a first. He then worked for the Clarendon Press in Oxford, indulged in journalism, and collaborated with DAVIN on *An Introduction to English Literature* (1947). In 1938 he wrote a novel, *Man Alone* (1939), the experiences of an English drifter from his arrival in New Zealand in 1919, through the economic troubles and the Auckland riots in 1932, to his participation in the Spanish Civil War. Mulgan enlisted in 1939 before the beginning of World War II. He served in the North African desert, and was then parachuted into occupied Greece, where he fought as a guerrilla until the German withdrawal, winning the Military Cross and, in the same way as the hero of his novel, proving himself to be a man 'you can't kill'. As a lieutenant colonel, he returned to Greece in 1945 in command of the force established to help Greeks who had suffered in the Allied cause. The reasons for his suicide in Cairo have never adequately been explained. His autobiographical *Report on Experience*, 'only the draft and outline of a book I'd like to write', was published posthumously (ed. J. A. W. Bennett, 1947), with a new edition in 1985. See Paul Day, *John Mulgan*, 1977 (critical study); and in C. K. Stead, *In the Glass Case: Essays on New Zealand Literature*, 1981.

MULOCK, DINAH MARIA see CRAIK.

MULTATULI, pen name of Eduard Douwes Dekker (1820–87) Dutch novelist, was born in Amsterdam, the son of a sea captain, and at 12 entered the Latin School to study for the ministry. He left after three years, worked in the office of a textile business, and at 18 sailed in his father's ship for Indonesia, where he became a clerk in the Auditor-General's office. In 1842 he was made a district officer in Sumatra, but was suspended a year later for an irregularity in the books and transferred to a series of similar posts. In 1856, after three years' leave in Holland, during which his infallible system for playing roulette completely failed him, he returned to Indonesia bankrupt, and became Assistant Resident in Lebak, Java. Within four months he had amassed sufficient evidence of malpractice and oppression of the people on the part of one of the native princes to justify a formal charge. When the Resident asked him to withdraw it, and the Governor General refused to support him, he resigned. After a year unemployed, he returned to Europe, and wrote *Max Havelaar*, a semi-autobiographical indictment of the Dutch colonial system in Java, in which his first wife, Everdine, Baroness van Wijnbergen, appears as Tina. It was published in 1860 through the offices of the writer and lawyer Jakob van

Lennep (1802–68), who then fraudulently acquired the copyright and in deference to government sensibilities radically changed the text. Even so, according to a member of the Dutch parliament it 'sent a shiver through the country'. Dekker, however, was never reinstated in the Foreign Service, one of his aims in writing the book; it was published in its original form, with notes, in 1875. See *Max Havelaar: or, The Coffee Auctions of the Dutch Trading Company*, tr. Roy Edwards, new edn 1987.

MUNDAY, ANTHONY (1553–1633) English dramatist, ballad writer, and pamphleteer, was born in London and in 1576 was apprenticed to a stationer, from whom he broke away two years later to go abroad. After some months in Rome he returned with messages and holy relics for Catholics in England. He wrote ballads and also pamphlets, including *A Second and Third Blast of Retrait from Plays and Theatres* (1580), the 'first blast' having been delivered by Stephen Gosson (1554–1624) as *The School of Abuse* (1579). He turned his Italian experiences to profit as an informer against the Jesuits (some of them acquaintances from the English College in Rome), who were executed and then horribly mutilated in 1582—he wrote an eye-witness account, *A breefe and True reporte of the Executions of certaine Traytours at Tiborne* (1582). One of the condemned priests volubly, but fruitlessly, protested his innocence on the scaffold, as a result of which an unseemly argument took place, in which Munday was involved. To justify his status as an expert on such matters, he wrote *The English Romayne Life* (1582), a vivid account of his time in Rome and of the things he saw there. His attitude to the theatre changed, or else his opposition to it had been an example of brazen hackwork, and he wrote several semi-historical pieces, including *John a Kent and John a Cumber* (c.1594) and *The Downfall of Robert, Earle of Huntingdon* (1598), a version of the Robin Hood legend. He also wrote pageants for the City of London, and translated popular romances. He was a friend of the antiquary John Stow (1525–1605), a new edition of whose *Survey of London* he edited in 1618. He outlived all his more famous literary contemporaries. A monument erected to his memory in St Andrews Church described him as 'Citizen and Draper'.

MUNRO, ALICE (*b.* 1931), née Laidlaw, Canadian short-story writer, was born in Wingham, Ontario, the eldest child of a struggling silver fox and turkey farmer (a descendant of HOGG), who in his seventies wrote a novel (posthumously published) on the basis, 'If Alice can do it, so can I.' She was educated locally, read avidly, being particularly impressed by MONTGOMERY's 'Emily' stories and, at 13, by EMILY BRONTË's *Wuther-*

ing Heights ('not the romanticism but the things that she did about the farm, the house, the fields'). She began writing short stories seriously when she was 18. She studied English for two years at the University of Western Ontario, which she left in 1951 to marry James Munro. They went to Vancouver, and then in 1963 to Victoria, where they opened a bookstore. She had a story printed in *Mayfair* in 1953, and 'dribbles' in magazines and on radio during the ensuing decade, during which she brought up three daughters. Her first collection, *Dance of the Happy Shades* (1968), won the Governor General's Award. She was highly praised in the *Manchester Guardian*; the *Wingham Advance Times* castigated her for having a 'warped mind', drawing attention to sex, and using 'bad language'.

The stories in *Lives of Girls and Women* (1971), her only book classified as a novel, follow the development of Del Jordan through childhood and adolescence to the point at which she decides to leave her rural small town. A protagonist also links the stories in *Who Do You Think You Are?* (1978; in UK 1980, and USA 1982, as *The Beggar Maid: Stories of Flo and Rose*). In a radio interview—see in Graeme Gibson (ed.), *Eleven Canadian Novelists* (1972)—she said: 'I'm not an intellectual writer. I'm very, very excited by what you might call the surface of life . . . things about people, the way they look, the way they sound, the way things smell, the way everything is that you go through everyday.' A chronicler of people and situations in rural Ontario (to which she returned in 1976 with her second husband, Gerald Fremlin), she has become increasingly concerned with personal relationships of all kinds, and the moment at which they can break apart, such as she describes in *The Progress of Love* (1986), with which she won her third Governor General's Award. In *Friend of My Youth* (1990), which evokes society in the region over the past fifty years, the disintegrator is often death, in any of its manifold guises. *Open Secrets* (1994) won the W. H. Smith Literature Award in the UK. See *Selected Stories*, 1996; Judith Miller (ed.), *The Art of Alice Munro: Saying the Unsayable*, 1984 (includes interview); Hallvard Dahlie, *Alice Munro and Her Works*, 1984; Catherine Sheldrick Ross, *Alice Munro: a Double Life*, 1992 (biographical/critical study).

MUNRO, H. H. see SAKI.

MUNRO, NEIL (1864–1930) Scottish novelist, short-story writer, and journalist, was born in Inveraray, Argyllshire, of a distant line of the family of the Munros of Foulis said to have descended from a survivor of the battle of Flodden in 1513. He began work in a lawyer's office but switched to journalism, being Editor of the *Glasgow Evening News* from 1918 to 1927. *The Lost Pibroch and Other Shieling Stories* (1896), the first of several collections, ostensibly belongs to the Celtic Twilight school of writing, but he employs a twinkling (and in later books sometimes tragic) irony, which is well illustrated in 'The Sea-Fairy of French Foreland'. *John Splendid* (1898), *Doom Castle* (1901), and *The New Road* (1914) are thoughtfully conceived, colourfully executed Highland historical adventures. Paradoxically, for his interest in Celtic lore and culture was genuine and his qualifications for re-creating them impeccable, he is best remembered for the richly comic stories and sketches about the Clyde 'puffer' (tugboat) and her crew, under skipper Para Handy, conceived as journalistic pieces. First published in book form as *The Vital Spark* (1906) by 'Hugh Foulis' (he would not use his real name), they were collected in *Para Handy and Other Tales* (1931)—*Para Handy: the Collected Stories . . .* , ed. Brian Osborne and Ronald Armstrong (1992), includes 18 previously unpublished tales. *Poetry* (1931), edited by BUCHAN, is a collection of his verse, much of it of a spirited romantic nature. See *The Brave Days*, 1931 (memoirs).

MURDOCH, IRIS (*b.* 1919) British novelist, philosopher, and dramatist, was born in Dublin and educated at Badminton School, Bristol, and Somerville College, Oxford. She worked as an assistant principal in the Treasury from 1942 to 1944, and then as an administrative officer with the UN Relief and Rehabilitation Administration until 1946. She was a Fellow of St Anne's College, Oxford, and university lecturer in philosophy from 1948 to 1963. Her first novel, *Under the Net* (1954), established her as a writer with a distinctive style and purpose, the philosophical implications and symbolism being submerged (except for those who wish to uncover them) in an entertaining and comic, but often complicated and grotesque, plot with many incidents, in which the characters are motivated by chance or contingency as well as by their search for love, knowledge, and freedom. Among her subsequent novels, which embrace a wide variety of settings, *The Sandcastle* (1957), *The Bell* (1958), and *A Severed Head* (1961) are particularly notable; after a slight falling-off the vein of inventiveness was rediscovered in *The Nice and the Good* (1968), *The Sea, the Sea* (1978), which won the Booker prize for fiction, and *Nuns and Soldiers* (1980). Later works, such as *The Green Knight* (1993) and *Jackson's Dilemma* (1995), tend towards the mystical and the philosophical. *The Three Arrows, and The Servants and the Snow* (1973) contains the two plays she has written apart from adaptations of her own novels—also published, with *The Black Prince*, in *Three Plays* (1989). Among her other works are *Sartre: Romantic Realist* (1953); a collection of essays, *The Sovereignty of Good* (1971); *A*

Year of the Bird: Poems (1978); and *Acastos: Two Platonic Dialogues* (new edn 1987). PLATO provides the background to her philosophy, which she expounds in *Metaphysics as a Guide to Morals* (1992), a mapping of associated subjects through which readers are encouraged to find their own way. She married the scholar and critic John Bayley (*b.* 1925) in 1956. She was created DBE in 1987. See Richard Todd, *Iris Murdoch*, 1984 (critical study); A. S. Byatt, *Degrees of Freedom: the Early Novels of Iris Murdoch*, 2nd rev. edn 1994.

MURRAY, CHARLES (1864–1941) Scottish poet, was born in Alford, Aberdeenshire, educated at Gallowhill School, and apprenticed in 1881 to a firm of civil engineers in Aberdeen. He emigrated to South Africa in 1888, became manager of a gold mine in 1899, and served as a lieutenant in the Railway Pioneer Regiment in the Boer War. From Deputy-Inspector of Mines for Transvaal in 1901, he rose through Under-Secretary for Public Works, and then Chief Engineer and Secretary, to be Secretary of Public Works for the Union of South Africa in 1910. He was made CMG in 1922, and on his retirement returned to Scotland. At a dinner in his honour in Aberdeen in 1912, he explained that his poems were written for his father, and that it was 'simply inevitable' that 'they should be written in the vernacular', i.e. the northeastern dialect of Scots. They also portray as well as reflect a whole way of life. Twelve copies only of *A Handful of Heather* (1893) were printed in Aberdeen for private circulation. Thirteen of the 40 poems he saved and revised, and these were reprinted, with 21 new ones, in *Hamewith* (1900), of which an enlarged edition, with an introduction by LANG, was published in London in 1909. Among the new poems in 1909 were 'The Whistle' ('He cut a sappy sucker from the muckle roddentree . . .'), and seven couthie translations from HORACE. His range, and his remarkable sense of characterization and feeling, as well as of irony, were further demonstrated in *A Sough o' War* (1917), poems which had their inspiration in situations of World War I at the front ('Fae France') and at home in Buchan ('Dockens afore His Peers'). See *Hamewith: the Complete Poems of Charles Murray*, introduced by Nan Shepherd, 1979.

MURRAY, LES(LIE) A(LLAN) (*b.* 1938) Australian poet, was born and grew up on the dairy farm at Bunyah, between Forster and Gloucester on the coast of New South Wales, to which he returned to live in 1986. He was educated at Taree High School and Sydney University, to which he went back later to obtain his degree, and was a technical translator at the Australian National University from 1963 to 1967. He gave up full-time employment for writing in 1971, and was co-Editor of *Poetry Australia* 1974–80. His first book of verse, *The Ilex Tree* (1965), was a joint publication with Geoffrey Lehmann (*b.* 1940), a former fellow-student. His literary philosophy is based on the distinction between the 'Athenian' social system, centred on the ruling city (illustrated in Australian terms in his poem 'Sydney and the Bush'), and the 'Boeotian', in which urban and rural traditions are interdependent. Thus in *The Weatherboard Cathedral* (1969) and *Poems Against Economics* (1972) traditional values predominate, while in *Lunch and Counter Lunch* (1974) an even broader, and more unusual range of topics, including the police, is subjected to his inventive scrutiny. *Ethnic Radio* (1977) includes 'Five Gaelic Poems' (the validity of the Scottish oral tradition is another of his poetic preoccupations) and 'The Buladelah—Taree Holiday Song Cycle', based on an Aboriginal song and celebrating the annual Christmas migration of modern urban families back to their roots in the country. *The Boys Who Stole the Funeral* (1979) is a 'novel sequence' in verse in which a violent plot is used to symbolize the search for or return to rural values, and conversation is uncannily rendered within the rhythm of the verse.

At around the time of publication of *The Daylight Moon* (1987) Murray suggested in an interview that 'what really distinguishes Australian poetry is the land of Australia itself, and the kind of endless detailed rehearsal . . . of Australian peculiarities that goes into it'. The book itself embodies numerous illustrations of the breadth of the 'peculiarities', while in *Dog Fox Field* (1991) the range of forms is wider still, and themes are related to the international scene. The poems in *Translations from the Natural World* (1993) are divided according to their subjects: travel, and also displacement; the personae of animals, fish, and plants; and home. Collections of his prose pieces are *The Peasant Mandarin* (1978), *Persistence in Folly* (1984), and *The Paperbark Tree: Selected Prose* (1992). He edited *The New Oxford Book of Australian Verse* (1986). He was made AO in 1989. See *Collected Poems*, new edn 1992; *Subhuman Redneck Poems*, 1996 (T. S. Eliot Prize); Lawrence Bourke, *A Vivid Steady State: Les Murray and Australian Poetry*, 1992.

MURRY, JOHN MIDDLETON see MANSFIELD.

MUSIL, ROBERT (1880–1942) Austrian novelist, was born in Klagenfurt and educated at military cadet schools until 1898, after which he studied engineering in Brno and philosophy at Berlin University, where he wrote a PhD thesis on the physicist/philosopher Ernst Mach (1838–1916). Except for the war years 1914–18, when he served in the Austrian army, employment took second place to writing, which, after a novel of adolescent homosexuality, *Die Verwirrungen des*

Zöglings Törless (1906; tr. Ernst Kaiser and Eithne Wilkin as *Young Törless*, 1955), two volumes of short stories (1911 and 1924), and two plays (1921 and 1923), centred on *Der Mann ohne Eigenschaften*, a novel sequence which he never finished and of which three volumes were published (1930, 1933, and 1942; as *The Man Without Qualities*, tr. Kaiser and Wilkin, 1953–60; tr. Sophie Wilkin and Burton Pike, 1995). Intellectually wide-ranging, witty and challenging, it explores the predicament of the individual in contemporary European society. His works were banned in Germany after the annexation of Austria in 1938, when he escaped to Switzerland, where he continued to work on his novel until his death. See *Selected Writings*, ed. Burton Pike, 1992; *Precision and Soul: Essays and Addresses*, tr. Burton Pike and David S. Luft, 1990.

MUSSET, ALFRED DE (1810–57) French poet, dramatist, and novelist, was born in Paris, was educated at Collège Henri IV, and published a translation of DE QUINCEY's *Confessions of an English Opium Eater* when he was 18. A precocious collection of verses in the manner of BYRON, *Les Contes d'Espagne et d'Italie* (1830), gave him the entrée to HUGO's circle of literary acquaintances, whom he soon abandoned in pursuit of a less restrictive lyric philosophy, demonstrated in *Poésies Complètes* (1840) and *Poésies Nouvelles* (1852). The failure of his play, *La Nuit Vénitienne* (1830), put him off the theatre, but not drama itself, which he began to publish for readers only in *Un Spectacle dans un Fauteuil* [Armchair Theatre] (1833–34) and continued in *Comédies et Proverbes* (1840), though several of these plays have since become staple repertory comedies—see *Three Plays*, tr. Declan Donnellan and Peter Meyer (1993), *Five Plays: The Moods of Marianne, Fantasio, Lorenzaccio, Don't Play with Love, Caprice*, ed. Claude Schumacher, tr. Donald Watson and others (1995), and *Comedies and Proverbs*, ed. and tr. David Sices (1994). He re-created aspects of an unfortunate liaison with SAND in a novel, *La Confession d'un Enfant du Siècle* (1836; tr. Kendall Warren as *The Confession of a Child of the Century*, 1892): her version of the affair is *Elle et Lui* (1859), to which his brother Paul responded with *Lui et Elle* (1860). In 1838 Musset became Librarian of the Ministry of the Interior, and though his health began to give way shortly afterwards, he continued to write and to echo his varied experience.

MYERS, L(EOPOLD) H(AMILTON) (1881–1944) British novelist, was born in Cambridge, the elder son of the writer Frederic Myers (1843–1901), who was a co-founder of the Society for Psychical Research. He was educated at Eton and then spent a year in Germany (where he had an enjoyable affair with a working-class girl) before going to Trinity College, Cambridge, which he left on his father's death to look after his distraught mother. They went to America, where Frederic had promised to meet his wife posthumously. The encounter did not materialize, but Myers had some kind of mystical experience in a Chicago hotel bedroom, and met his future wife in Colorado—she was nine years his senior and refused to marry him until 1908. Helped by a legacy, he had a leisurely, rich life, and wrote *Arvat* (1908), a play in blank verse expressing discontent. Unfit for service in World War I, he worked as a clerk in the Foreign Office. *The Orissers* (1922), his first novel, at which he had worked since 1909, is about spiritual and material conflicts over a country estate. Its reception propelled him into literary society, though privately he reacted against what he saw as the self-regard of the Bloomsbury Group (see VIRGINIA WOOLF). After *The 'Clio'* (1925), lighter and set in a steam yacht on the Amazon, he began his sequence, *The Near and the Far* (1929), *Prince Jali* (1931), and *Rajah Amar*, published together as *The Root and the Flower* (1935), to which *The Pool of Vishnu* (1940) is a conclusion. Historical only in the sense that the setting is 16th-century India, they represent a search into values and responsibilities. Latterly he was disturbed that his intellectual view of Communism could not be reconciled with the facts. He killed himself with an overdose of veronal.

MYLES NA GCOPALEEN see O'BRIEN, FLANN.

N

NABOKOV, VLADIMIR (1899–1977) American novelist, short-story writer, poet, critic, and translator, was born in St Petersburg, Russia, the eldest of five children of Vladimir Dmitrievich Nabokov (1870–1922), jurist and statesman, who died by an assassin's bullet on a platform in Berlin while shielding the lecturer, and of Elena Ivanovna Rukavishnikov (1876–1939). At five he recognized himself in POTTER's Squirrel Nutkin: bold, bad, and tricksy, which he largely remained all his life. At seven his passion for butterfly collecting began, in which he is credited with several discoveries, including Nabokov's Pug. He went to Tenishev School, and at 17 published a book of verse. After the Bolshevik coup in 1919, the family went to the Crimea, where his father acted as Regional Minister of Justice, and from there to voluntary exile in Berlin, to which Nabokov returned in 1922 after taking his degree at Trinity College, Cambridge. He married Véra Slonim (1902–90) in 1925; a son, Dmitri, later the co-translator of some of his Russian novels, was born in 1935. Having moved to Paris in 1937, he took his family to the USA in 1940, and became an American citizen in 1945. He was Lecturer in Russian at Wellesley College, Massachusetts 1941–48, concurrently holding a research fellowship at the Museum of Comparative Zoology at Harvard. He was then Professor of Russian Literature at Cornell University until 1959, when the success of Lolita enabled him to retire to Montreux, Switzerland, to devote himself to writing and to a final pursuit of lepidoptera.

Beginning in 1926, he published in Russian, as V. Sirin, nine novels. The most significant of them are [The Defence] (1930; tr. 1964), reflecting his interest in chess; [Invitation to a Beheading] (1938; tr. 1959), a dystopian reaction to the political state of eastern Europe; and [The Gift] (serialized 1937–38, published 1952; tr. with Michael Scammell, 1963), the longest and most profound of them—after finishing it, he was in such financial straits that he wrote, 'It is a mystery to me how I exist at all.' Having already translated [Laughter in the Dark] (1932; tr. 1938) himself, he now embarked on his first book in English, The Real Life of Sebastian Knight (1941), a quest novel with chess imagery, written in winter in an unheated Paris flat on a suitcase propped across the bidet. Writing in English for a new audience was, he wrote, 'exceedingly painful—like learning anew to handle things after losing seven or eight fingers in an explosion', and he often mourned his native language. Many of the stories in The Stories of Vladimir Nabokov, ed. Dmitri Nabokov (1995) were originally written in Russian for an audience primarily of emigrés in Berlin and Paris.

In the USA he first wrote a critical biography of GOGOL (1944). Bend Sinister (1947), the work of a mind troubled by news from Europe, and Nine Stories (1947) were inadequate harbingers of the sensational Lolita (Paris 1955; in USA 1958), a seriocomic, often tender, treatment of an utterly taboo subject, the sexual abuse of a complaisant 12-year-old 'nymphet', which is also a stylistic and linguistic triumph. The protagonist of Pnin (1957) is a St Petersburg-born professor of Russian at a provincial college in America, an amiable academic in a world which is totally alien. American academia also features obliquely in Pale Fire (1962), a 999-line poem by a recently murdered academic, with foreword, notes, commentary, and index by an exiled European who was his neighbour. Nabokov's last major novel was Ada, or Ardor: a Family Chronicle (1969), in which linguistic legerdemain offsets a political allegory. In an interview in 1967 he commented: 'I shall be remembered by Lolita and my work on Eugene Onegin'—his monumental edition of PUSHKIN's verse novel (4 vols, rev. edn 1976). He added, 'Lolita is famous. Not I. I am an obscure, doubly obscure, novelist with an unpronounceable name.' Speak Memory: an Autobiography Revisited (1966) is a revised and expanded version of Conclusive Evidence: a Memoir (1951). See Brian Boyd, Vladimir Nabokov: the Russian Years and Vladimir Nabokov: the American Years, 2 vols new edns 1993; Andrew Field, The Life and Art of Vladimir Nabokov, new edn 1992; Tony Sharpe, Vladimir Nabokov, 1991 (critical study); Michael Wood, The Magician's Doubts: Nabokov and the Risks of Fiction, new edn 1996 (critical study).

NAIDU, SAROJINI (1879–1949), née Chattopadhyaya, Indian poet and politician, was born in Hyderabad of a talented Bengali Brahmin family. At 16, her parents, horrified at her attraction to a doctor of a lower caste and different region, packed her off to England to study at King's College, London, and Girton College, Cambridge. While there she wrote some romantic verse which caught the attentions of ARTHUR SYMONS and of GOSSE, who suggested that she should apply her literary ability to giving 'some revelation of the heart of India'. On her return there in 1889 she immediately married the doctor, and in due course had four children, and published *The Golden Threshold* (1905) and several further volumes of sentimental verses. A meeting in 1914 with the statesman Mohandas (*Mahatma*) Gandhi (1869–1948) led to a close association with him and with the cause of women's education and rights (especially with regard to purdah), and with Indian nationalism, in pursuit of which she travelled in Africa, the USA, and Canada, and was several times imprisoned in India. She chaired the Indian National Congress in 1925 (the first woman to do so), and on India's independence in 1947 was appointed Governor of Uttar Pradesh.

NAIPAUL, SHIVA(DHAR SRINI-VASA) (1945–85) Trinidadian novelist, the younger brother of V. S. NAIPAUL, was born in Port-of-Spain and educated at Queen's Royal College and St Mary's College. He won an island scholarship to University College, Oxford, where he switched from psychology, philosophy, and physiology to Chinese. His first novel, the seriocomic *Fireflies* (1970), charting the decline and disintegration of two branches of an influential Indian family in Port-of-Spain, won three British awards. *The Chip-Chip Gatherers* (1973) centres on a family whose recent origins are in a primitive rural outpost stuck in a sea of sugar cane, the unhealthy influence of which continues to pervade the characters' lives. During the 1970s he journeyed from his London home to the Caribbean; to India; to East Africa, about which he wrote an outspoken travelogue, *North of South* (1978); and to the USA, where he wrote a background study of the mass suicide in Guyana of the American sect, the People's Temple, *Black and White* (1980). His third novel, *A Hot Country* (1983), was also his last. He died of a heart attack. Articles and stories are in *Beyond the Dragon's Mouth* (1984) and *An Unfinished Journey* (1986).

NAIPAUL, (Sir) V(IDIADHAR) S(UR-AJPRASAD) (*b.* 1932) Trinidadian novelist, was born in Chaguanas, Trinidad, the eldest son of a Brahmin Hindu journalist, Seepersad Naipaul (1906–53), whose privately published *Gurudeva and Other Indian Tales* (1943; in UK 1976) was in the vanguard of local East Indian fiction. He was educated at Queen's Royal College, where 'in the fourth form I wrote a vow on the endpaper of my *Kennedy's Revised Latin Primer* to leave [Trinidad] within five years. I left after six.' Disturbed by the tension between those of Indian and African descent as much as by the prevailing attitude to talent in Trinidad, after studying at University College, Oxford, he settled in London, where for two years he edited the BBC radio programme, 'Caribbean Voices'. In *Finding the Centre: Two Narratives* (1984) he describes the discovery of a valid starting point for his first book (the third to be published), *Miguel Street* (1959), in which sketches of childhood are organized round a place. In *The Mystic Masseur* (1957), the focus is on an eccentric misfit; *The Suffrage of Elvira* (1958) centres on an event, a weird election in 'the smallest, most isolated and most neglected of the nine counties of Trinidad', where 'things were crazily mixed up'. In their comedy, sharp satire, and convincing detail, they presage Naipaul's master work, and the finest novel of the Caribbean experience, *A House for Mr Biswas* (1961). Covering three generations, and featuring the convergent (and mixed) fortunes of two families, it lays bare, with pathos, rich humour, and gentle irony, a whole society caught within a tenuous social structure. A second phase as a novelist began with *Mr Stone and the Knights Companion* (1963), an English story, and continued in a grimmer mood. *The Mimic Men* (1967), set in England and the Caribbean, is a study of political power; the tripartite *In a Free State* (1971), which won the Booker prize for fiction, focuses on isolation, exile, and expatriation in the USA, England, and East Africa; *Guerrillas* (1975) deals with disillusionment in the face of post-colonial chaos. In *A Bend in the River* (1979) he explores the reactions of different traditional and modern societies to the political and social implications of dictatorship in a central African state.

Naipaul considers his non-fiction to be an integral part of his work, and in another passage in *Finding the Centre* explains that he travels 'to discover other states of mind . . . so while, when I travel, I can move only according to what I find; I also live as it were, in a novel of my own making, moving from not knowing to knowing, with person interweaving with person and incident opening into incident'. This attitude generated and shaped *The Middle Passage: Impressions of Five Societies . . . in the West Indies and South America* (1962), in which is some of the background to *A House for Mr Biswas* and *The Mimic Men*, and informed his trilogy, *An Area of Darkness: an Experience of India* (1965), *India: a Wounded Civilization* (1977), and *India: a Million Mutinies Now* (1990), in which country he found clues to his own Trinidadian background.

Guerrillas contains elements of a real murder, a study of which is in *The Return of Eva Perón, with The Killings in Trinidad* (1980), where he states: 'An autobiography can distort; facts can be realigned. But fiction never lies: it reveals the writer totally.' At the same time he has been concerned about the form of the modern novel, of which he said in an interview in 1990: '[It] no longer seems to bring back truth. Writers used to put those disclaimers at the beginning of their books, "all these characters are false"—and I suppose that is what I find wrong with it.' *The Enigma of Arrival* (1987), published as a novel but described by himself as 'a synthesis of the worlds and cultures that made me', is the most complete but by no means the only autobiographical work of Naipaul that we have. A similar blend of memoirs, fantasies, historical reflections, and social and political commentary, largely in a Trinidadian context, distinguish *A Way in The World: a Sequence* (1994). In 1955 he married Patricia Ann Hale (1932–96) an Oxford contemporary, who in the 1960s resigned from being a history teacher to spend more time with him and to travel with him. They had no children. In 1996 he married Nadira Khannum, a 38-year-old Pakistani journalist, whom he had met in Lahore five months before. He was knighted in 1990. In 1993 he was the inaugural winner of the (£30,000) David Cohen Prize for British Literature. See Peter Hughes, *V. S. Naipaul*, 1988 (critical study); Bruce King, *V. S. Naipaul*, 1993 (critical study); Fawzia Mustafa, *V. S. Naipaul*, 1995 (critical study).

NAIRNE, (CAROLINA), BARONESS (1766–1845), née Oliphant, Scottish poet, was born at Gask, the family estate in Perthshire. Named after Charles Edward Stuart, she was the daughter of Laurence Oliphant (1724–92), a prominent Jacobite, who even after being allowed back to Scotland from Europe in 1763, stoutly refused to recognize the House of Hanover. In 1806 she married her cousin, Major William Nairne, who in 1824 was restored by George IV to his hereditary title of Baron Nairne, which had been forfeited after the '45 Rebellion. On his death in 1830, she moved from Edinburgh to Bristol with her son, whose education she personally supervised and with whom she travelled abroad until his death from flu in Brussels in 1837. In 1843 she returned to Gask to live with her nephew and his wife. Known for her looks when young as the 'Flower of Strathearn', she took a great interest in BURNS's reworking of Scottish songs, and in about 1792 began, in secret, composing her own, to traditional airs. These included the well-known Jacobite songs, 'The Hundred Pipers an A'', 'Charlie is My Darling', and the lament for his departure, 'Will Ye No' Come Back Again', and also the neat poem of street-cries, 'Caller Herrin'' and the romantic 'Land o' the Leal'. Not even her husband knew of her literary efforts, which she published anonymously or as Mrs Bogan of Bogan. Only just before her death did she agree to the publication of an anonymous volume of her poems. It appeared posthumously as *Lays from Strathearn* 'by Carolina, Baroness Nairne', permission for its contents finally to be attributed to her having been given by her sister.

NARAYAN, R(USIPURAM) K(RISH-NASWAMI) (*b.* 1907) Indian novelist, was born in Madras and brought up by his grandmother and an uncle in Mysore, where he was educated at the Collegiate High School and Maharaja's College, from which he only graduated after spending an extra year there. He was briefly a teacher, and then became a reporter on a Madras newspaper, while honing his fiction technique by studying the stories of BENNETT, DOYLE, JACOBS, and WODEHOUSE in *Strand Magazine*. In the semi-autobiographical *Swami and Friends: a novel of Malgudi* (1935), to which *The Bachelor of Arts* (1937) and *The English Teacher* (1945) are sequels, he introduced the microcosmic, middle-class milieu which is the almost invariable setting of his gently humorous, universally admired studies of an Indian society whose ancient traditions keep clashing, but sometimes merging, with those introduced by the British. He is often concerned with a cycle of life in which the moment of truth for the protagonist is a mystical revelation, culminating in a return to the status quo, as in *The Dark Room* (1938), *The Financial Expert* (1952), and *The Painter of Signs* (1976), or in a withdrawal into an alternative world, as in *The Guide* (1958), *The Sweet-Vendor* (1967), and *The Man Eater of Malgudi* (1961). The protagonist of *A Tiger for Malgudi* (1983) is the tiger himself, representing, through the Hindu doctrine of reincarnation, the turbulent nature of India. In *Waiting for the Mahatma* (1955) Narayan involves his unworldly hero, who is in love with one of Gandhi's followers, in the wider issues of the campaign for independence. *The Grandmother's Tale* (1993) contains three novellas, of which the title story is an autobiographical account of an aspect of his family roots. He has also published *A Writer's Nightmare: Selected Essays 1958–1988* (1988), and condensed versions in modern prose of *The Ramayana* (1972) and *The Mahabharata* (1978). See *My Days: a Memoir*, new edn 1989; William Walsh, *R. K. Narayan: a Critical Appreciation*, 1983.

NASH, OGDEN (1902–71) American poet, was born in Rye, New York, and educated at St George's School, Newport, and (for a year) at Harvard, from which he dropped out after his 69-year-old father lost his job as a naval stores executive. He tried teaching, the stock market (he sold one bond in eighteen months, to his godmother), selling, and advertisement copywriting, before joining the publisher Doubleday Doran, initially as an advertising assistant. The *New Yorker* printed two of his poems in 1930, of which 'Hymn to the Sun and Myself' reappeared alongside other reflections (e.g. 'Candy / Is dandy / But liquor / Is quicker') in *Hard Lines* (1931), which quickly reprinted. In 1931, after the briefest of tenures as Managing Editor of the *New Yorker*, he joined Farrer & Rinehart as an assistant editor; and after an extended courtship, during which he wrote over 350 letters, married Frances Leonard. In 1933, having been offered a contract by the *Saturday Evening Post* for 26 verses a year at $100 each, he went freelance and settled with his wife and two daughters in Baltimore. Ill-health cut short a final attempt in 1941 to become a Hollywood screenwriter, but the musical show written with PERELMAN, *One Touch of Venus* (1943), was a smash hit on Broadway. By 1958, when he had the first of three operations for a complaint that was never fully diagnosed, he had published a dozen books of verse, including *The Private Dining Room and Other New Verses* (1952), with its devastatingly observed 'Middle-aged life is merry and I love to lead it, / But there comes a time when your eyes are all right but your arm isn't long enough to hold the telephone book where you can read it'. He explained his philosophy: 'I made up my mind a long time ago that I would rather be a great bad poet than a bad good poet.' See *Candy Is Dandy: the Best of Ogden Nash*, ed. Linell Smith and Isabel Eberstadt, introduction by Anthony Burgess, new edn 1994.

NASHE, THOMAS (1567–1601) English prose writer, was born in Lowestoft, Suffolk, and educated at St John's College, Cambridge, as a sizar. He was in London in 1588 where, inspired by the courageously printed and amusingly written 'Marprelate' pamphlets attacking the Anglican establishment, he entered the literary lists with *The Anatomie of Absurditie* (1589), a long, ill-organized, but well-phrased and witty attack on a range of topics from women to Euphuistic writers. *Pierce Pennilesse his Supplication to the Devill* (1592), analysing each of the deadly sins in terms of London society types, is all the more effective for being better constructed, but he chose to insert a few pages of colourful invective at the expense of Gabriel Harvey (c.1549–1630), critic and friend of SPENSER, and his brother Richard (1560–1623), a writer on astrology. This initiated a literary Armageddon which, on Nashe's part, continued through *Strange News . . .* (1593), which also includes a defence of his late friend ROBERT GREENE, and *Have with You to Saffron-Walden* (1596), in both of which he displayed a violent and outrageous technique of satire which contrasts strongly with that later employed by DRYDEN. The form, and also the satire, of *The Unfortunate Traveller: or, The Life of Jacke Wilton* (1594) are different. This loosely-constructed chronicle, incorporating picaresque elements and literary parodies, is recognizable as a novel, in which historical figures are involved in

sensational and sinister fictional events. He had a hand in the lost play, *The Isle of Dogs*, for which JONSON was imprisoned in 1597. His lodgings were searched and he thought it prudent to retire for a while to Yarmouth, whose hospitality and history he celebrated in *Nashes Lenten Stuff, with the Praise of the Red Herring* (1599), which includes a burlesque on MARLOWE's 'Hero and Leander'. In the summer of that year an edict called for all his books (and those of 'Dr Harvey') to be seized, and banned the printing of any further works by them. Nashe was only 31. Two years later he was dead. See *The Works of Thomas Nashe*, ed. R. B. McKerrow, rev. edn, ed. F. P. Wilson, 5 vols 1958; Charles Nicholl, *A Cup of News: the Life of Thomas Nashe*, 1984; G. R. Hibberd, *Nashe: a Critical Introduction*, 1962.

NATHAN, GEORGE JEAN see MENCKEN.

NATSUME SŌSEKI (1867–1916) Japanese novelist, was born Natsume Kinnosuke in Tokyo, the youngest, unexpected, child of a 53-year-old hereditary ward chief whose position disappeared with the Imperial Restoration in 1868. He was adopted by a childless couple, but at eight was returned home when they divorced. He had the statutory training in classical Chinese, and after completing college in 1890 entered the newly-established English department of Tokyo University, from which he graduated in 1893 and took a post at Tokyo Normal College. In 1895 he surprisingly left for the provinces, teaching first in the small castle town of Shikoko and then at Kumamoto, where he made an arranged marriage with the daughter of the chief secretary of the House of Peers. In 1900 he was offered, and told he must accept, a government scholarship to England to study the language, without any instructions or guidance as to how to go about it. He spent the time reading furiously, alone in a succession of increasingly cheaper lodgings in London (including 6 Flodden Road, Camberwell). He returned to his wife and child in 1903, and took up the teaching post (in succession to HEARN) at Tokyo Imperial University which was a condition of his scholarship—his autobiographical novel [*Grass on the Wayside*] (1915; tr. 1969) covers this period. In 1904 he produced for a magazine editor a short story, which was rejected, rewritten, and published as ['I Am a Cat'] (1905). The response was such that ten further episodes were added, comprising eventually a three-volume, humorous, cat's-eye view of upper-middle-class manners (1905–07; tr. Aiko Itō and Graeme Wilson, 1972). He resigned from the university in 1907 at the earliest possible moment, and became Literary Editor of *Asahi Shimbun*, in which several of his novels were serialized. With Shimazaki Tōson (1872–1943) he created the modern Japanese novel, inspired by Western models but Japanese in identity and vision. *Sanshiro* (1909; tr. Jay Ruben, 1977), [*And Then*] (1909; tr. Norma Moore Field, 1978), and *Mon* (1911; tr. Francis Mathy, 1972) constitute a trilogy in which different relationships are explored in the context of the period after the Russo-Japanese War of 1904–05.

NEILSON, JOHN SHAW (1872–1942) Australian poet, was born in Penola, South Australia, the eldest child of John Neilson (1844–1922), who had emigrated from the Scottish Highlands when he was nine, and who had verse published in local and national Australian journals. The boy had spent a year at the state school in Penola when his impoverished family moved, as settlers, to Minimay, Victoria, where there was no school at the time. He read at home (especially COLERIDGE, BURNS, and THOMAS HOOD), and found consolation in nature for the barrenness of the land (see 'The Poor, Poor Country'). In 1889 the family moved by waggon to Dow Well, near Nhill, where both he and his father were forced to be contract labourers. Some of his verses were printed in the *Nhill Mail* in 1894, and his work began to appear in the *Bulletin* in 1896, the year he branched out on his own as an itinerant labourer. In his thirties he contracted severe eye trouble, often having to dictate to his mates what he had composed during the day's work. Further poems appeared from 1911 in the resuscitated *Bookfellow*, which had printed 'Old Granny Sullivan' in 1907 and issued it as a separate leaflet in 1916. The *Bookfellow* also published three volumes of his poetry: *Heart of Spring* (1919), replacing *Green Days and Cherries*, which got no further than proof copy stage; *Ballad and Lyrical Poems* (1923); and *New Poems* (1927). In 1928 he was found a quiet billet as a messenger with the County Roads Board in Melbourne. Though he was happy there, city life stifled his poetry, the surviving bulk of which had already been affected by the ravages of mice at Chinkapook, during the mouse plague of 1917. He retired from his post in 1941, still unmarried. He has been called a mystic pastoralist. He is a fine lyrical poet, the depth of meaning of whose 'The Orange Tree' continues to occupy critics; he also wrote some atmospheric ballads in the Scottish as well as Australian tradition. See *The Poems of Shaw Neilson*, ed. A. R. Chisholm, 1965; *Selected Poems*, 1992; Hugh Anderson and L. J. Blake, *John Shaw Neilson*, 1972 (critical biography).

NERUDA, PABLO (1904–73) Chilean poet, was born Ricardo Eliecer Neftalí Reyes de Basoalto in Parral—he assumed his pseudonym in 1920 and formally adopted it as his name in 1946. His mother died during his infancy, and his father (a train driver) took him to Temuco, where he went to school. He then attended the Instituto Pedagógico, Santiago. Before he was 20 he had published two books of verse, of which *Veinte Poemas de Amor y Una Canción Desesperada* (1924; tr. W. S. Merwin as *Twenty Love Poems and a Song of Despair*, 1969), 'a book of love-sadness, of love-pain', which was regarded at the time as erotic, by his own account sold 'almost two million copies' world wide by 1970—see also *Los Versos del Capitán: Poemas de Amor* (1952; tr. Brian Cole as *The Captain's Verses*, 1994). He was appointed to the Diplomatic Service in 1927, serving in Southeast Asia, Argentina, Spain, and Mexico. He returned to Chile in 1943, and was in 1945 elected to the Senate as a Communist; he was exiled for his views in 1948. While he was abroad he completed *Canto General* (1950; tr. Jack Schmitt, 1991), a Marxist-oriented epic of Chile, with autobiographical sections. He returned to Chile in 1952, and published *Odas Elementales* . . . (3 vols 1954–57; tr. Margaret Sayers Peden as *Elemental Odes*, bilingual edn 1991), in which he abandoned gloomy passions and epic modes for verse which spoke to the people about more everyday matters. He stood for the presidency of Chile in 1969, but, to avoid a party split, withdrew after four months hard campaigning in favour of Salvador Allende (1908–73), after whose election he was appointed Ambassador to France. He was awarded the Nobel Prize for Literature in 1971. See *Selected Poems*, ed. Nathaniel Tarn, tr. Anthony Kerrigan, W. S. Merwin, Alastair Reid, and Nathaniel Tarn, new edn 1993; *Selected Odes*, tr. Margaret Sayers Peden, 1990; *Memoirs*, tr. H. St Martin, new edn 1994.

NERVAL, GÉRARD DE (1808–55) French poet and prose writer, was born Gérard Labrunie in Paris, the son of a doctor in Napoleon's army whose wife died in 1810 following him on the Russian campaign. He was educated at Collège Charlemagne. At 18 he published six books of political and satirical verse, and at 20 a translation of GOETHE's *Faust* which was set to music in 1829 by Hector Berlioz (1803–69). He studied medicine, but gave it up in 1834 after inheriting 30,000 francs from his grandfather, with which, after some time travelling, he founded the review *Le Monde Dramatique*. Its failure a year later bankrupted him, but he still pursued the precarious calling of freelance journalist. He wrote the lyrics for, and collaborated with HUGO to produce, the musical play *Piquillo* (1837), starring Jenny Colon (d. 1842), who was for him the embodiment of perfect womanhood and of his fascination with the stage—she married someone else in 1838. Having published his early work as Gérard, he began in about 1840 to assume 'de Nerval', a family paddock in Valois and also an anagram of his mother's maiden name. After an attack of insanity in 1841, he set out to re-establish his career by taking an extended trip through Egypt, Lebanon, and Turkey; he wrote up his accounts in visionary style and finally shaped them into volume form as *Voyage en Orient* (1851; ed. and tr. Norman Glass as *Journey to the Orient*, 1972). *Les Filles du Feu* (1854; tr. James Whitall as *Daughters of Fire*, 1923), a spiritual autobiography in the form of prose narratives, including the largely pastoral romance, 'Sylvie', to which was appended his mystical sonnet sequence, 'Les Chimères' (tr. Peter Jay as *The Chimeras*, 1984), appeared shortly before he underwent his fifth course of treatment for mental instability. Five months later he was found hanged from a lamp post in Rue de la Vieille-Lanterne. See *Selected Writings*, ed. and tr. Geoffrey Wagner, new edn 1968.

NESBIT, E(DITH) (1858–1924) British poet, novelist, and children's writer, was born in London, the youngest daughter of an agricultural chemist who died in 1862. She was educated at an Ursuline convent in France, and at boarding schools in Germany and Brighton, from which she escaped in the holidays to her own room in the family home in Kent, where she dreamed of being a great poet. The insecurity, and sometimes poverty, that she experienced as a child continued during her unconventional life with Hubert Bland (*d.* 1914), a political journalist, whom she married in 1880. She accepted his socialist principles, and with him was one of the founders of what in 1884 became the Fabian Society. She also accepted, and brought up with her own, three children of his various liaisons, while herself having young lovers. To earn money, she wrote verse—*Lays and Legends* (1886, 2nd series 1892)—and magazine stories, and tried giving public recitals and even colouring Christmas cards by hand. It was perhaps Bland's loss of his capital through an absconding partner that gave her the theme for her first children's novel, *The Story of the Treasure Seekers* (1899), in which Mr Bastable suffers the same fate and his children try all kinds of strategems to revive the family finances, but the sure touch, and deft characterization and dialogue are entirely her own. The Bastables reappear in two more stories, after which she embarked on her domestic fantasies—*Five Children and It* (1902), *The Phoenix and the Carpet* (1904), and *The Story of the Amulet* (1906). *The Railway Children* (1906) marked a return entirely to the real world and is an excursion into sentiment. She was awarded a Civil List pension in 1915, and married a marine engineer in 1917. See Julia Briggs, *A Woman of Passion: the Life of E. Nesbit*, new edn 1989; Anthea Bell, *E. Nesbit*, 1960 (critical study).

NEWBOLT, (Sir) **HENRY** (1862–1938) British poet, was born in Bilston, Staffordshire, the elder son of the Vicar of St Mary's by his second marriage, and was educated at Clifton College and Corpus Christi College, Oxford. He was called to the Bar in 1887 and practised for 12 years, during which he contributed to the *Law Digest* while also answering the call of literature. He wrote a Napoleonic tale, *Taken from the Enemy* (1892), and a tragedy in blank verse, *Mordred* (1895). In 1896 LANG published six of his poems in *Longman's Magazine*, and the *St James's Gazette* printed 'Drake's Drum' (with its refrain, 'Capten, art tha' sleepin' there below'), which BRIDGES and YEATS admired. *Admirals All* (1897), containing 12 similarly spirited poems, went through four impressions in a fortnight. The titles alone of *The Island Race* (1898) and *Drake's Drum, and Songs of the Sea* (1914) reflect the wholesome, patriotic fervour of the times and of the author of such poems as 'He Fell among Thieves' and 'Vitaï Lampada' ('There's a breathless hush in the Close tonight . . .'). He was appointed Professor of Poetry of the Royal Society of Literature in 1911, and served in the Admiralty during World War I, after which he wrote the concluding two volumes of the official account of naval operations. He was knighted in 1915, and made CH in 1922. See *Selected Poems*, ed. Patric Dickinson, 1981.

NEWBY, P(ERCY) H(OWARD) (*b.* 1918) British novelist, was born in Crowborough, Sussex, and educated at Hanley Castle Grammar School, Worcester, and St Paul's (Teacher Training) College, Cheltenham. He served in the Royal Army Medical Corps in France and Egypt from 1939 to 1942, when he became until 1946 a lecturer in English at Fouad I University, Cairo. In 1949 he joined the BBC, being Controller of the Third Programme 1958–71, Director of Radio Programmes 1971–75, and Managing Director of Radio 1975–78. He was Chairman of the English Stage Company 1978–84. What he terms 'the relationship between innocence and knowledge' is particularly reflected in his Middle East and Mediterranean novels such as *Agents and Witnesses* (1947), *The Picnic at Sakkara* (1955), *Revolution and Roses* (1957), and *Something to Answer For* (1968), the first winner of the Booker Prize for fiction. These are farces in which an English traveller generally ends a series of disastrous confrontations in the same state of incomprehension as at the beginning. In his novels with British settings he analyses middle- and lower-middle-class life, sometimes balancing farce with serious introspection into the psychological differences between characters, as in *A Season of England* (1951), *One of the Founders* (1965), and *Coming in with the Tide* (1990). *The Retreat* (1953) reflects his experience of teacher training, and *Feelings Have Changed* (1981) of working for the BBC. *Something about Women* (1995), his 28th book, is primarily a parable; the linking character is an Anglo-Catholic clergyman whose vision of women changes during the course of the events described. He was made CBE in 1972.

NEWMAN, JOHN HENRY (1801–90) British theologian, was born in the City of London, the eldest child of a banker, and was educated at a private school in Ealing and at Trinity College, Oxford. He was elected a Fellow of Oriel College in 1822, was ordained in 1824, and was Vicar of the university church of St Mary's 1828–43—see *Newman's University Sermons* (1970). His disillusionment with the Church of England is charted precisely and persuasively (and when demolishing his antagonist, ironically) in *Apologia pro Vita Sua* (1864), which began as a response to KINGS-LEY's anonymous attack in a review, and became a literary and spiritual prose classic. He became a Catholic in 1845, and founded the Oratory in Birmingham in 1848. *The Idea of a University Defined and Illustrated* (1873), which he regarded as one of his most artistically perfect works, was based on *Discourses on the Scope and Nature of University Education* (1852) and on his experience as Rector from 1854 to 1858 of the new Catholic University in Dublin. The last of his numerous theological works was *An Essay in Aid of a Grammar of Assent* (1870), an examination of belief. In the early 1830s he contributed over a hundred sacred poems, including 'Pillar of the Cloud' (better known as the hymn 'Lead, Kindly Light') to the *British Magazine*, which were reprinted, with others by members of the Oxford Movement, as *Lyra Apostolica* (1834). He returned to poetry later, when ill and envisaging death, to write *The Dream of Gerontius* (1866), a journey of the soul, later made into an oratorio by Edward Elgar (1857–1934). He also wrote two anonymous novels, *Loss and Gain: the Story of a Convert* (1848) and *Callista: a Sketch of the Third Century* (1856). He was created Cardinal of San Giorgio in Velabro in 1879. See Ian Ker, *John Henry Newman: a Biography*, new edn 1990; Sheridan Gilley, *Newman and His Age*, 1994; Owen Chadwick, *Newman*, 1983 (introduction to his thought).

NEWTON, (Sir) **ISAAC** (1642–1727) philosopher, mathematician, and physicist, was born at Woolsthorpe, Lincolnshire, the posthumous son of a minor landowner, and was educated at Grantham Grammar School and, as a sizar, at Trinity College, Cambridge. He was elected a Fellow of the college in 1667, Lucasian Professor of Mathematics in 1671, and in 1672 a Fellow of the Royal Society, of which he was President from 1703 until his death. He propounded the laws of gravity, on which he had been working since 1665, in a series of university lectures in 1684 under the title of 'De Motu Corporum' [On the Movement of Bodies], which formed the first part of his great treatise, *Philosophiae Naturalis Principia Mathematica* (1687), translated into

English by Andrew Motte in 1729. Newton's other major scientific works are *Opticks* (1704) and *Arithmetica Universalis* (1707). He also published several writings on theological subjects. He twice represented Oxford University in Parliament, and was Master of the Mint from 1699. He was knighted in 1705. At times a sick and frequently a bitter and quarrelsome man, his contribution to English literature lies less in the manner in which he wrote (which was frequently in Latin), than in his ability to reconcile advanced scientific discoveries with Christian beliefs, and in his exposition of his 'Newtonian' philosophy, which had a profound influence on the Enlightenment, and is reflected in the work of such poets as POPE and JAMES THOMSON (1700–48). WORDSWORTH, who first read *Opticks* when he was at school, rearranged his Cambridge room so that, from his bed, he could see the top of the chapel window of Trinity College under which stood the statue 'Of Newton with his prism and silent face, / The marble index of a mind for ever / Voyaging through strange seas of Thought, alone' (*Prelude* III, 61–63). See Richard Westfall, *The Life of Isaac Newton*, new abridged edn 1994 of *Never at Rest: a Biography of Isaac Newton*, new edn 1983; John Fauvel, and others (eds), *Let Newton Be!: a New Perspective on His Life and Works*, new edn 1989.

NGŨGĨ WA THIONG'O (*b.* 1938) Kenyan novelist, dramatist, and critic, was born James Ngugi in Kamirithu, Limuru, to one of the wives of a peasant farmer. He was educated at a Gikuyu independent school, and then at Alliance High School and Makerere University College, where he read English. In his second year he stopped, on impulse, a final year student who was involved in the creative activities of the campus, and asked if he could send him a story to read. When written, and later retitled, it became 'Mugumo'—see *Secret Lives and Other Stories* (1975), which he refers to as his 'creative autobiography over the past twelve years'. He also wrote at this time a play, *The Black Hermit* (performed by the Uganda National Theatre 1962, published 1968), and two novels. *Weep Not Child* (1964), the first published novel in English by an East African, explores the effect on ordinary villagers of the Mau Mau war for independence. *The River Between* (1965), which was written first, goes back to the quarrels with the missionaries in the 1930s, and establishes the traditional right of the Gikuyu people to their land. After a year as a reporter on the Nairobi *Daily Nation*, he studied on a British Council scholarship at Leeds University. During this time he wrote *A Grain of Wheat* (1967), which centres on the close of the colonial era while questioning the motives and actions of the new independent regime.

On his return in 1967 he changed his name

to its traditional form, and took up a teaching post at Nairobi University College. He was in 1972 appointed Chairman of the Department of Literature, Nairobi University, where he consolidated 'a syllabus which would have oral literature at the centre, then written African literature from East Africa, from Africa and from the Caribbean, from Afro-America and so on, and then the literature of Europe . . .'. In *Petals of Blood* (1977), the involvement in a triple murder of four suspects is the linking theme of a study of the background to the continued unrest among the sections of society to whom independence had not brought freedom. Responding to a demand from the community, and with communal cooperation, he wrote (with Ngugi wa Mirii) *Ngaahika Ndeenda*, a play in Gikuyu (translated as *I Will Marry When I Want*, 1982). It was produced in the open as a village drama with actors from the community at Kamirithu in October 1977, but a month later the licence to perform it was withdrawn by the authorities. In December Ngũgĩ was arrested at his home and held without charge or trial for a year in the maximum security prison of Kamiti—see *Detained: a Writer's Prison Diary* (1981).

In *Devil on the Cross* (1982), translated by himself from the Gikuyu version which he wrote in prison on carefully secreted leaves of lavatory paper, he employs the biblical language with which his original readers were familar as well as oral tradition in a further study of political and economic exploitation. He went into exile in Europe in 1982, and then to the USA, having decided to use Gikuyu for all subsequent creative works. These have included a symbolic novel, tr. Wangui wa Goro as *Matigari* (1989), and a series of children's adventure stories about the fight for Kenyan independence, seen through the eyes of his character Njamba Nene. After teaching at Yale and other universities, he was appointed Professor of Comparative Literature and Performance Studies at New York University. His critical works include *Homecoming: Essays on Africa and Caribbean Literature, Culture and Politics* (1972) and *Decolonising the Mind: the Politics of Language in African Literature* (1986), the ideas in which are developed in the collection of essays, *Moving the Centre: the Struggle for Cultural Freedoms* (1993)—see also *Writers in Politics* (1996). See G. D. Killam, *An Introduction to the Writings of Ngugi*, 1980; David Cook and Michael Okenimpke, *Ngugi wa Thiong'o: an Exploration of His Writings*, 2nd edn 1996; and in Jane Wilkinson (ed.), *Talking with African Writers*, 1992.

NICHOL, BP see ONDAATJE.

NICHOLS, GRACE (*b.* 1950) Guyanese poet and novelist, was born in a coastal village and moved with her family to Georgetown when she was eight. She left high school at 16 to earn her own living, later taking a diploma in communications. After teaching in primary school from 1967 to 1970, she became a journalist, and in 1977 emigrated to Britain. She works in both English and Creole, tending 'to want to fuse the two tongues because I come from a background where the two were continually interacting'. *I Is a Long Memoried Woman* (1983), which won the Commonwealth Poetry Prize, is a poem cycle reflecting women's aspects of the search for an Afro-Caribbean identity. In *The Fat Black Woman's Poems* (1984) and *Lazy Thoughts of a Lazy Woman* (1989), some striking and some ironic poems compensate for some overambitious feminine metaphors—see also *Sunrise: New Poems* (1996). She has also written a semi-autobiographical novel of youth in Guyana, *A Whole of a Morning Sky* (1986), and stories and poems for children.

NICHOLSON, NORMAN (1914–87) British poet and dramatist, the son of a shopkeeper, was born in the terrace house in Millom, Cumbria, in which he lived all his life. He was educated at Millom Grammar School, but in 1930 was diagnosed as having tuberculosis. He returned home after 15 months in bed in a Hampshire sanitorium, unfit for a job or for university, and became a writer. He also, having been brought up as a Methodist, returned to the Anglican faith in which he had been baptized, and which pervades much of his poetry and drama. In his earlier work, collected in *Five Rivers* (1944), *Rock Face* (1948), and *The Pot Geranium* (1954), he is concerned with expressing universal issues in terms of his environment and of the changing circumstances of Millom. Its inhabitants, with members of his own family, feature in *A Local Habitation* (1972), from which a more colloquial tone emerges. In *Sea to the West* (1981), by which time Millom had ceased to be an industrial town, his concern is with the elemental world from which it originally sprang. His verse plays include *The Old Man of the Mountains* (rev. edn 1950) and *Birth by Drowning* (1960), in which he relocates Old Testament prophets in modern Cumbria. He also wrote two novels, *The Fire of the Lord* (1944) and *The Green Shore* (1947), Cumbrian topographical works, and studies of COWPER (1951, 1960) and WELLS (1950). In 1956 he married a teacher, Yvonne Gardner (*d.* 1982). In 1965 he was finally pronounced free of tuberculosis. He was made OBE in 1981. See *Selected Poems 1940–1982*, 1982; *Collected Poems*, ed. Neil Curry, 1994; *Wednesday Early Closing*, 1975 (autobiography).

NICOLSON, (Sir) HAROLD (1886–1968) British critic and biographer, was born in Tehran, the son of the British Chargé d'Affaires, Arthur Nicolson (1849–1928), later Lord Carnock, and spent his childhood following his parents around their postings abroad or with relatives in Ireland. He was educated at Wellington College and Balliol College, Oxford, where he only obtained a pass degree, though in 1909 he passed brilliantly into the Diplomatic Service. In 1913 he married SACKVILLE-WEST—see *Vita and Harold: the Letters of Vita Sackville-West and Harold Nicolson*, ed. Nigel Nicolson (1992). He worked in London on diplomatic duties during World War I, after which he was a member of the British delegation which co-managed the Treaty of Versailles. He began his literary career with *Paul Verlaine* (1921), the first of several critical biographies of literary figures, among whom were TENNYSON (1923), BYRON (1924), and SWINBURNE (1926). He served in Tehran in 1925–27, his recall to London and demotion following, but not necessarily being connected with, the publication of *Some People* (1927), a series of witty semi-autobiographical essays—the studies of his ancestors, *Helen's Tower* (1937) and *The Desire to Please* (1943), are also indirectly autobiographical. He resigned from the service in 1929 after spending two years in Berlin. He was National Labour Member of Parliament for West Leicester 1935–45. His official biography of George V was published in 1952. Other significant historical works include *Peacemaking, 1919* (1933) and *The Congress of Vienna* (1946). *Marginal Comment* (1939) and *The English Sense of Humour* (1944) demonstrate his skill as a writer of essays constructed on classically circular lines. In 1956 he stood for election as Professor of Poetry at Oxford, and lost to AUDEN by only 24 votes. He was knighted in 1953. See *Diaries and Letters 1930–1962*, ed. Nigel Nicolson, 3 vols new edn 1969–71; *Diaries*, ed. Nigel Nicolson, 1996.

NIETZSCHE, FRIEDRICH WILHELM (1844–1900) German philosopher and critic, was born in Rocken, the son of a Lutheran pastor. His career at the universities of Bonn and Leipzig was so spectacular that at 25 he was appointed Professor of Classical Philology at Basel, where he remained until 1879. *Die Geburt der Tragödie* (1872; as *The Birth of Tragedy*, tr. Wm A. Haussmann, 1909; tr. Shaun Whiteside, ed. Michael Tanner, 1993) was dedicated to Richard Wagner (1813–83), the protagonist of whose opera *Siegfried* he saw as embodying his superman, but with whom he fell out for what he termed the composer's 'histrionic self-deception'. In *Also sprach Zarathustra* (1883–85; tr. R. J. Hollingdale as *Thus Spoke Zarathustra*, 1961) he further developed his vision of man either declining into the 'last man', or 'overcoming' himself and giving birth to the 'overman'. YEATS, who was first introduced to his work in 1902 and returned to it in the 1930s, referred to him as 'that strong enchanter' and cites him by name in his didactic poem, 'The Phases of the Moon' (1918). Nietzsche went

mad in 1889 and spent the rest of his life in his mother's house in Weimar. His evil genius was his sister, Elisabeth Förster-Nietzsche (1846–1935), who in 1886 founded with her husband Nueva Germania, an Aryan homeland in Paraguay, and who obtained Nietzsche's papers after his death and misrepresented his views as Nazi propaganda. See Ronald Hayman, *Nietzsche: a Critical Life*, new edn 1995; Robert C. Holub, *Friedrich Nietzsche*, 1995 (biographical/critical study); Michael Tanner *Nietzsche*, 1997 (critical study); Michael Tanner, *Nietzsche*, 1994 (introduction).

NIN, ANAÏS (1903–77) American novelist and diarist, was born in Neuilly, France, the eldest of three children of a concert pianist of Spanish origin, and of a singer of French–Danish parentage eight years older than her husband, both of whom were born in Cuba. After her husband's final desertion, mother and children moved to Barcelona in 1914. From there they sailed for New York; en route Nin began her diary, in the form of letters to her father, with whom she was reunited in an incestuous relationship in 1933 (he died in 1949). After dropping out of Wadleigh High School (she later took a few courses at Columbia University), she worked as an artist's model, and in 1923 married, in Cuba, Hugh Guiler, later known as Ian Hugo, engraver and film maker. By 1931 she was installed in a house in Louveciennes, a suburb of Paris, writing *D. H. Lawrence: an Unprofessional Study* (1932), which had a mark of class, and was embarking on an affair with HENRY MILLER; she also supported him financially and they gave each other creative encouragement. In 1932 she began psychoanalysis, which she practised as a lay analyst in New York.

In 1936 she bought a houseboat on the Seine, and published *The House of Incest*, a surrealist, introspective prose poem, through her own press, Siana (Anaïs reversed). She returned to New York in 1939, and in 1942 established, in Greenwich Village, Gemor Press to print a revised version of *The Winter of Artifice* (1939), three linked novellas developing the theme of a father/daughter relationship; *This Hunger* (1945); and *Under a Glass Bell* (1944), short stories. Subsequent novels were published commercially but uneconomically. She made her debut as a film actress in 1946, and her reputation as a writer and literary figure finally in 1966, with the publication of *The Diary of Anaïs Nin: 1931–1934*. Nine volumes covering the years 1914–74, three of them published posthumously, represent only about a quarter of her total autobiographical text, which she revised regularly. It includes fragments of two posthumously published volumes of erotica, *Delta of Venus* (1977) and *Little Birds* (1979), originally written in the 1940s for a private collector, whose other suppliers included Miller and BARKER. Unexpurgated sections of the diaries have appeared as *Henry and June* (1986) and *Incest* (1993). At the age of 52 Nin bigamously married a man of 36, with whom she lived in California, while jetting back and forth also to stay with Guiler in New York, both husbands being unaware of each other's existence until she was dying. See Deirdre Bair, *Anaïs Nin: a Biography*, new edn 1996; *Recollection of Anaïs Nin: By Her Contemporaries*, ed. Benjamin Franklin, 1997; Nancy Scholar, *Anaïs Nin*, 1984 (critical study).

NIVEN, FREDERICK (1878–1944) Canadian novelist, was born in Valparaiso, Chile, of Scottish parents, who brought him back to Glasgow when he was five. He was educated at Hutchesons' Grammar School and Glasgow School of Art. He worked in the cloth trade, and as an assistant in circulating libraries, and then, in British Columbia, in construction camps, returning from there on a cattle boat, an experience which he later recreated in his novel, *S.S. Glory* (1915). His first novel, *The Lost Cabin Mine* (1908), is an adventure story of the Canadian West. He returned to Canada as a freelance journalist in 1912–13, and, with his wife, as an immigrant in 1920, having because of a heart condition spent World War I as a civil servant in London. As well as fiction, he published two volumes of poetry, several descriptive works on Canada, and an autobiographical sketch, *Coloured Spectacles* (1938). His thirty novels include, from his early period, several potboilers, written to keep himself and his wife in funds. The rest have Scottish (often Glasgow) or Canadian settings and themes; among the former are the significant examples of Scottish realistic fiction, *Justice of the Peace* (1914) and *The Staff at Simson's* (1937). His most notable contribution to Canadian literature is the trilogy, *Mine Inheritance* (1940), *The Flying Years* (1935), and *The Transplanted* (1944), whose basic theme is settlement and Scottish immigration in British Columbia from the beginning of the 19th into the 20th century.

NKOSI, LEWIS (*b.* 1936) South African critic and dramatist, was born in Durban and educated there at the Zulu Lutheran High School, being brought up as an orphan by his grandmother. He became a journalist, first on a Durban Zulu newspaper, and then as a chief reporter for *Drum* in Johannesburg, where he lived in the Sophiatown ghetto. On his acceptance of a year's fellowship in journalism at Harvard, he was issued with a one-way exit permit and banned from returning. His play about racism, *The Rhythm of Violence* (1964), was reportedly the first play by a black South African to have been published for nearly forty years. GORDIMER has described his volume of critical essays, *Home and Exile* (1965), as 'unique in South African literature' in that 'simultaneously he is a young black who has a foot in the white liberal world, while holding his place in the black proletariat of the "township"'. He lived in London for some years, and travelled as a journalist, subsequently returning to Africa as a senior lecturer in English at the University of Zambia. Later works include the essays *The Transplanted Heart* (1975) and *Tasks and Masks: Themes and Styles of African Literature* (1981).

NOONAN, ROBERT see TRESSELL.

NORRIS, (BENJAMIN) FRANK(LIN) (1870–1902) American novelist, was born in Chicago, and studied art in Paris, English literature at the University of California, and then creative writing at Harvard for a year, during which he wrote parts of two novels, *McTeague* and *Vandover and the Brute*. Travelling in South Africa in 1895, he ran up against the Uitlander insurrection against the Boers, which he reported for the San Francisco *Chronicle*. Having been captured by the Boers and deported, he joined the editorial staff of the *Wave*, which serialized his novel, *Moran of the Lady Letty* (1898), an adventure story with a female protagonist. In 1898 he went to Cuba to report the Spanish–American War for *McClure's Magazine*. He then became a reader for Doubleday McClure, which published his *Blix* (1899), the love story of a struggling newspaper reporter, and *McTeague: a Story of San Francisco* (1899). While the latter, a study of a brute man's degeneration, owes much to the influence of ZOLA, and its ending is pure sensation, it was a genuine contribution to the American naturalistic novel. Norris died after an appendicectomy, having written two novels of a projected trilogy, 'The Epic of Wheat': *The Octopus: a Story of California* (1901) and *The Pit: a Story of Chicago* (1903). *Vandover and the Brute*, the final degradation of whose protagonist is the condition of werewolf, was thought too strong for publication at the time, but it finally appeared in 1914, after the manuscript had been lost in the San Francisco earthquake of 1906, and rediscovered. Norris's theories about naturalistic writing are in *The Responsibilities of the Novelist and Other Essays* (1903). See Franklin Walker, *Frank Norris: a Biography*, 1963; Donald Pizer, *The Novels of Frank Norris*, 1966.

NORTH, CHRISTOPHER see WILSON, JOHN.

NORTH, THOMAS see PLUTARCH.

NORTJE, ARTHUR (1942–70) South African poet, was born in Oudtshoorn, Cape Province. As a child he was brought by his mother to Port Elizabeth, where he was educated at Government High School, being taught by BRUTUS, who was a great influence on his early writing of poetry. He then attended the segregated Western Cape University, where he read English and psychology, and got a teaching qualification. He went to Oxford on a scholarship in 1965, and chose not to return to South Africa after taking his degree. He taught for two years at Hope High School in Columbia, Canada, before returning to Oxford in 1970 as a postgraduate. He died of an overdose of drugs shortly before he was due to be deported to South Africa. The several hundred of his published and unpublished poems reflect his dedication to traditional English poetic forms and the changing circumstances and disturbed pattern of his life. See *Dead Roots*, 1973 (poems); and in Christopher Heywood (ed.), *Aspects of South African Literature*, 1976.

NORTON, THOMAS see SACKVILLE.

NOSTRADAMUS (MICHEL DE NO-TREDAME or NOSTREDAME) (1503–66) French astrologer, was born of Jewish descent in St Remy, and studied philosophy at Avignon and medicine at Montpellier. He practised as a physician in Agen, Salon, and Lyons, being especially commended for his service during outbreaks of the plague. He began making prophecies in about 1547, and published a book of them in rhyming quatrains, *Centuries* (1555; enlarged edn 1558). He was now received by the nobility and appointed physician to Charles IX. His fame, and the controversies inherent in the interpretation of his enigmatic predictions, have outlived him by centuries. *The True Prophecies or Prognostications of M. Nostradamus*, tr. T. de Garençière, was published in London in 1672. See Francis King, *Nostradamus*, 1993 (biography).

NOYES, ALFRED (1880–1958) British poet, novelist, dramatist, and critic, was born in Wolverhampton, son of a grocer who later became a teacher, and had a good grounding in classics at schools in Aberystwyth. He went to Exeter College, Oxford, for which he was a formidable oarsman, but failed to take his degree because he was too preoccupied with arranging the publication of his first book of verse, *The Loom of Years* (1902). His predilection for traditional forms and metres, and a melodious gift, won him a wide audience and a permanent niche in school anthologies. Poems such as 'The Barrel-Organ' (1904), with its refrain, 'Go down to Kew in lilac-time . . .', and 'The Highwayman' (1907) are worthy of critical attention, but his epic poem, *Drake* (2 vols 1906–08), and other imitations, have an artificial ring. *Forty Singing Seamen* appeared in 1907. In 1913, having married an American, he gave a series of lectures at the Lowell Institute in Boston on 'The Sea in English Poetry'. He occupied the visiting chair of Modern English Literature at Princeton from 1914 to 1923. A visit to Mount Wilson Observatory inspired a three-volume, 10,000-line epic, *The Torch-Bearers* (1922–30), in which he sought to reconcile the work of scientists with Christian thought. Controversial as well as anti-modernist, he stopped the public auction of a privately-owned copy of JOYCE's *Ulysses*, and ordered HUGH WALPOLE from his house for recommending the book to his young daughter. Having become a Roman Catholic in 1927, he offended the clergy with his study of VOLTAIRE (1938). His failing sight moved him to write several especially poignant poems, including 'Look down on us gently who journey by night' and 'Spring, and the Blind Children'. He was made CBE in 1918. See *Collected Poems*, new edn, 1963; *Two Worlds for Memory*, 1953 (autobiography).

OAKLEY, BARRY (*b.* 1931) Australian dramatist and novelist, was born in Melbourne and educated at the Christian Brothers College, St Kilda, and Melbourne University, after which he was a secondary school teacher until 1962. He was then until 1973 successively a lecturer at the Royal Melbourne Institute of Technology, an advertising copywriter, and a journalist with the federal Department of Trade and Industry, living in Melbourne with his wife and six children. In 1955 he began to contribute stories to magazines and newspapers, some of which are reprinted in *Walking Through Tigerland* (1977). His first novel, *A Wild Ass of a Man* (1967), in which a fanatic meets an improbable and ironic end, was published in the same year that his first play, *From the Desk of Eugene Flockhart*, was read at the Emerald Hill Theatre. In two further picaresque novels, *A Salute to the Great McCarthy* (1970), about an Australian Rules football star, and *Let's Hear It for Prendergast*, about 'the tallest poet in the world', society, even at its most absurd, proves too much for innocent ambition. *Witzenhausen Where Are You?* (1968) and *A Lesson in English* (1969) were among the first experimental plays performed at the La Mama Theatre, Carlton. He has written many other plays: satirical, such as *The Feet of Daniel Mannix* (1971); farcical, such as the study of HORNE, *The Ship's Whistle* (1979); and comic but sympathetic, such as *Scanlan* (1978), whose subject is KENDALL. The most often performed, and possibly the most Australian, is *Bedfellows* (1975), whose theme of marital, and extra-marital, relationships is explored with broad humour, but also with penetrating and sometimes painful realism. See *The Great God Mogadon and Other Plays*, 1980; *Scribbling in the Dark*, new edn 1993 (reminiscences).

OATES, JOYCE CAROL (*b.* 1938) American novelist, short-story writer, poet, and critic, was born in Millersport, New York, grew up on her grandparents' farm in Erie County, and went to high school near Buffalo. She graduated with considerable distinction in English and philosophy from Syracuse University in 1960, having during the course of her creative writing studies produced a novel each semester. While doing further study at the University of Wisconsin, she met Raymond J. Smith, an English professor, whom she married in 1961. Progress towards the degree of PhD was abandoned when she discovered that a story of hers was included in *Best American Stories* (1961), after which she went on to combine teaching—at the universities of Detroit (1961–67) and Windsor (1967–78), and as Writer-in-Residence at Princeton from 1978—with co-editing (with her husband) the *Ontario Review*, and writing a formidable amount of fiction, poetry, and criticism. Of the size of her output she has said: 'Productivity is a relative matter. And it's really insignificant: what is ultimately important is a writer's strongest books.' Though from early on criticized for a 'high dosage of violence', she has responded that in the context of 'the number of pages I have written, and the "violent" incidents dispersed through them, I rather doubt that I am a violent writer in any meaningful sense of the word'; and that from KAFKA she learned 'to make a jest of horror'.

A volume of short stories, *By the North Gate* (1963), and a novel, *With Shuddering Fall* (1964), opened a canon in which she has offered insights into the American psyche through a range of fictional forms. These include Gothic romance—*Bellefleur* (1980); satire—*Unholy Loves* (1979); fantasy—*Childwold* (1976); political parable—*Black Water* (1992); and sheer but brutal realism—*them* (1969), which won the National Book Award, *You Must Remember This* (1987), in which she demonstrates her understanding of the sport of boxing, and *Foxfire: Confessions of a Girl Gang* (1993), a further novel about the 1950s. *What I Lived For* (1994), her 24th novel, is a study of a rough-hewn man of contradictions haunted ultimately by a sense of a destiny for which he is not entirely responsible. She has written several thrillers as Rosamond Smith. Subsequent volumes of short stories include *The Wheel of Love* (1970), *A Sentimental Education* (1981), and *Last Days* (1984). For her poetry, which began in volume form with *Women in Love and Other Poems* (1968), see *Invisible Woman: New and Selected Poems 1970–1982* (1982) and *The Time Traveler: Poems 1983–1989* (1990). Critical and other essays are in *The Edge of the Impossibility: Tragic Forms in Literature* (1972), *Contraries* (1981), *The Pro-*

fane Art (1983), and *Woman Writer: Occasions and Opportunities* (1988). She compiled and contributed critical notes to *The Oxford Book of American Short Stories* (1993). See Eileen Teper Bender, *Joyce Carol Oates: Artist in Residence*, 1987 (critical study); Greg Johnson, *Understanding Joyce Carol Oates*, 1989.

O'BRIEN, CONOR CRUISE (*b.* 1917) Irish critic and historian, was born in Dublin and educated at Sandford Park School and Trinity College, Dublin, his PhD study being published as *Parnell and His Party 1880–1890* (1957). He entered the Department of External Affairs in 1944, at which time he was also contributing (as Donat O'Donnell) articles to literary magazines which were collected as *Maria Cross: Imaginative Patterns in a Group of Modern Catholic Writers* (1952). He was a member of the Irish delegation to the United Nations from 1956 to 1960, and was appointed UN Representative in Katanga in 1968. *To Katanga and Back* (1962) describes his dramatic intervention in local affairs and subsequent resignation from the UN; *The United Nations: Sacred Drama* (1967) rehearses his views on the organization itself. His experiences in Africa also inspired his play, *Murderous Angels* (1968). He was Vice-Chancellor, University of Ghana 1962–65, and Albert Schweitzer Professor of Humanities, New York University 1965–69. He was elected a Labour Member of the Irish Parliament in 1969, and was Minister for Posts and Telegraphs 1973–77, in the ruling coalition with Fine Gael. He represented Dublin University in the Senate 1977–79. He was Editor-in-Chief of the *Observer* 1978–81, after which he returned to teaching in the USA. Volumes of essays include *Herod: Reflections on Political Violence* (1978), comprising studies in various forms of violence in Ulster; *Writers and Politics* (1965); and *Passion and Cunning and Other Essays* (1988), whose lead piece is 'An Essay on the Politics of W. B. Yeats' (1965), the argument of which has continued to be a subject of controversy. Recent studies are *Ancestral Voices: Religion and Nationalism in Ireland* (1994), a synthesis of history and autobiography, *On the Eve of the Millenium: the Future of Democracy through an Age of Unreason* (1996), and the controversial *The Long Affair: Thomas Jefferson and the French Revolution* (1996). He has also written books on CAMUS (1969) and on BURKE (1992). Kate Cruise O'Brien (*b.* 1948), short-story writer and novelist, is his daughter. See Donald Harman Akenson, *Conor: a Biography of Conor Cruise O'Brien— Volume One: Narrative, Volume Two: Anthology*, 1994.

O'BRIEN, EDNA (*b.* 1932) Irish novelist, short-story writer, and dramatist, was born in rural Tuamgraney, Co. Clare, the youngest of four children in a home without books. 'My mother was extremely suspicious of litera-ture because she thought it was bad and could lead to sin. My father wasn't interested in books. His reading was confined to the *Irish Field* and bloodstock manuals.' She was educated at the National School, Scariff ('a bit shambolical') and, much more strictly, at the Convent of Mercy, Loughrea, going on to the Pharmaceutical College of Ireland, and qualifying as a pharmacist. She married a writer, from whom she was divorced in 1967. Since 1959 she has lived in London, with frequent visits to Ireland. Her trilogy, *The Country Girls* (1960), *The Lonely Girl* (1962, reissued 1964 as *Girl with Green Eyes*), and *Girls in Their Married Bliss* (1964), which tells of girls maturing, being initiated into love, and being disappointed, has strong autobiographical echoes. Love in its infinite variety is the main-spring of her work, whether it is love for an older man or a younger man or (frequently) the wrong man, or for a woman or one's mother or one's son, and her settings are usually London and Co. Clare.

House of Splendid Isolation (1994), her 14th novel, represents her imaginative view of the Troubles, at the heart of which is the unusual relationship between an elderly widow in a mouldering mansion and an IRA terrorist in search of a safe house. The model for the latter was Dominic 'Mad Dog' McGlinchy, whom O'Brien interviewed at length during his ten-year prison sentence—he was shot dead by the INLA in 1994. Even more topical is *Down by the River* (1996), inspired by the notorious Irish case of a 14-year-old repeatedly abused and made pregnant by a family friend. O'Brien has been praised both for her lyricism and her frankness, though to some critics her stronger work is in her short stories, of which *Lantern Slides* (1990) is the sixth collection. (She has described the short story as 'a quick, short shaft of prose, [which] must have the effect and the after-effect of a flash of lightning'.) She has adapted several of her novels for the stage, for which she has also written *Virginia* (rev. edn 1985), from VIRGINIA WOOLF's diaries, and *Madame Bovary* (1987). *Mother Ireland* (1976) places her writing in the context of her upbringing and of Ireland.

O'BRIEN, FLANN, one of the many pseudonyms of Brian O'Nolan (1911–66) Irish novelist and journalist, was born in Strabane, Co. Tyrone, the third of 12 children of an Irish-speaking officer of the Customs and Excise. He was educated at Blackrock College and University College, Dublin, where he studied English, Irish, and German literature, and wrote a thesis on Irish poetry. He worked for the Irish Civil Service from 1935 until he retired in 1953. His first novel, *At Swim-Two-Birds* (1939), is experimental in form and gaily satirical of attitudes to Gaelic culture in intent. A second, *The Third Policeman*, darker and rather disturbing, was rejected, and only published in 1967 after his death. He then wrote, in Irish, *An Bèal Bocht* (1941; tr. Patrick Power as *The Poor Mouth*, 1973), part parody of and part devastating attack on the Irish-speaking establishment. His next, and last two, novels, *The Hard Life: Exegesis of Squalor* (1961) and *The Dalkey Archive* (1964), followed the reissue by a London publisher in 1960 of *At Swim-Two-Birds*. From 1940 to 1966 he entertained the public three times a week with his column, in Irish and English, in the *Irish Times*, 'Cruiskeen Lawn' [full little jug] under the byline of 'Myles na gCopaleen' [Myles of the Ponies], a character from GRIFFIN. In the words of A. Norman Jeffares in *Anglo-Irish Literature* (1982), it 'provided a suitable métier for his idiosyncratic castigation of cultural confusion or pretension, and through it runs an irresistible sense of humour, ranging from the deadpan to the free play of an exceptionally sharp associative mind'. See Anthony Cronin, *No Laughing Matter: the Life and Times of Flann O'Brien*, new edn 1990; Sue Asbee, *Flann O'Brien*, 1991 (critical study).

O'BRIEN, KATE (1897–1974) Irish novelist and dramatist, was born in Limerick and educated at Laurel Hill Convent, Limerick, and University College, Dublin. She began to write while a governess in Spain, and after a brief marriage to a Dutch journalist (it lasted a year), she settled in England and was for a time on the staff of the *Manchester Guardian*. Her first works were plays, *Distinguished Villa* (1926) and *The Bridge* (1927); she turned to the novel as a form of individual expression which did not involve contributions by others. *Without My Cloak* (1931), a portrait of three generations of an Irish family, won both the Hawthornden and James Tait Black Memorial prizes. While she wrote from, and of, a Catholic background, the conflicts which ensue when the heroine breaks away from traditional constrictions to realize herself resulted in both *Mary Lavelle* (1936) and *The Land of Spices* (1941) falling foul of the Irish censors. A similar act of liberation informs *As Music and Splendour* (1958), which has a lesbian theme. *That Lady* (1946), a more romantic piece, is set in the charged atmosphere of the court of Philip II of Spain. She also wrote two beautifully observed topographical, social, and cultural studies, *Farewell Spain* (1937) and *My Ireland* (1962), and a biography, *Teresa of Avila* (1951). After living in England for twenty years, she returned to Ireland, before finally coming back to England in 1965. See *Presentation Parlour*, new edn 1994 (reminiscences); Lorna Reynolds, *Kate O'Brien: a Literary Portrait*, 1987.

O'CASEY, SEAN (1880–1964) Irish dramatist, was born John Casey in Dublin, the youngest of 13 children of poor Protestant parents of whom five survived. Because of a disease of the eyes, he had little schooling, and appears to have taught himself to read, while living with his mother and remaining brother in a tenement after his father's death when he was six. He worked as a casual labourer from the age of 14, educating himself from books he bought, borrowed, and sometimes stole, and revelling particularly in the language and stagecraft of SHAKESPEARE and other Elizabethan dramatists. In about 1910 he was caught up in the Irish political scene, and at various times joined the Gaelic League, the Irish Socialist Party, the recently-formed Irish Transport and General Workers Union, and the Irish Citizen Army, though he did not participate in the 1916 Rising. By this time he was writing plays. After four rejections, *The Shadow of a Gunman* was put on at the Abbey Theatre in 1923 (O'Casey was working as a cement mixer at the time); the following year *Juno and the Paycock* ran for two weeks, the first Abbey play ever to do so. The political turbulence and violence of the times and the language and atmosphere of the tenements had been brought resoundingly to the stage, and female characters represented as more heroic than the men. With £25 royalties in his pocket, O'Casey became a full-time writer. Enraged patriots rioted in response to his treatment of the 1916 Easter Rising in *The Plough and the Stars* (1926), and when six weeks later he was invited to London to receive the Hawthornden Prize for *Juno and the Paycock*, he decided to remain permanently in England. His self-imposed exile became complete when in 1928 his anti-war play about a disabled footballer, *The Silver Tassie*, with its symbolic second act, was rejected for the Abbey by YEATS, though it was produced in London in 1929 and has since received critical acceptance.

From 1938 O'Casey lived in Devon, and continued to experiment with expressionism. *Purple Dust*, published in 1940 but not performed in England until 1945, is an Irish fantasy, played out between two English plutocrats, Stoke and Poges, their mistresses, and sundry builders' mates. The semi-autobiographical *Red Roses for Me*, produced in 1946, has a stylized Dublin setting. At this time he was also writing the six autobiographies which begin with *I Knock at the Door* (1939) and conclude with *Sunset and Evening Star* (1954)—reissued together as *Autobiographies* (1963; in two volumes, new edn 1992). The early volumes at least, before the querulousness obtrudes, are outstanding works of prose as well as graphic reconstructions of the life of an extraordinary man. He was a playwright with a gift of rich language, whom J. C. Trewin describes in his introduction to *Three More Plays* (1965) as 'an Elizabethan out of time'. In 1927 he married the actress Eileen Reynolds, who died in 1995 at the age of 95—see her biography of him, *Sean* (1971). See Gary O'Connor, *Sean O'Casey: a*

Life, new edn 1989; James Simmons, *Sean O'Casey*, new edn 1984 (critical study); and in Raymond Williams, *Drama from Ibsen to Brecht*, rev. edn 1987.

O'CONNOR, FLANNERY (1925–64) American short-story writer and novelist, was born in Savannah, Georgia, into a devoutly Catholic family. At five, she trained a chicken to walk backwards (a feat recorded by Pathé News), which led her ultimately to acquire an unusual menagerie of domestic birds (including peacocks), and inspired some of the freakish creatures which inhabit her fiction. In 1938 the family moved to Milledgeville, where her father died three years later of disseminated lupus at the age of 45. She was educated at Peabody High School and Georgia State College for Women, after which she attended the Writer's Workshop, University of Iowa, graduating as Master of Fine Arts in 1947. 'The Geranium', one of the stories which was a part of her thesis, was published in *Accent* in 1946. She had her first major attack of lupus in 1950, after which she lived with her mother on a farm near Milledgeville, from 1955 able to get around only on crutches. Her two novels, *Wise Blood* (1952) and *The Violent Bear It Away* (1960), are both tragic odysseys of country preachers; one of them finds a form of revelation in self-destruction, and the other, a 14-year-old boy, is bound by religious forces from which he has unsuccessfully tried to extricate himself. *A Good Man is Hard to Find and Other Stories* (1955) and the posthumous *Everything That Rises Must Converge* (1965) contain 19 of the 31 stories which comprise her main oeuvre. A religious intensity motivates the strange visions which underlie her tragicomic situations and invests with dark humour the grotesque elements in her Southern characters. See *The Complete Stories*, new edn 1991; Miles Orvell, *Flannery O'Connor: an Introduction*, 1991.

O'CONNOR, FRANK, pseudonym of Michael O'Donovan (1903–66) Irish short-story writer, critic, and poet, was born in Cork of a poor family and left school at 12. He was imprisoned during the Civil War (1922–23) for his Republican activities, which are reflected in his first volume of stories, *Guests of the Nation* (1931). For the next twenty years he was prominent in Irish literary life, contributing reviews and articles to the *Irish Statesman* and *The Bell*, and being a director of the Abbey Theatre from 1935 to 1939. He also published short stories; two novels; *Three Old Brothers, and Other Poems* (1936); *The Big Fellow* (1937), a biography of Michael Collins, the politician and Sinn Fein leader; and *The Fountain of Magic* (1939), a collection of translations from Irish poetry. He lived in the USA during the 1950s. His stories, of which there are several collections, are fine examples of

the narrative art, in which human experience, especially that of young people, is explicitly revealed. His literary criticism is incisive and straightforwardly expressed, and includes *The Lonely Voice: a Study of the Short Story* (1963) and *The Backward Look: a Survey of Irish Literature* (1967). His contribution to the rediscovery, through translation, of traditional Irish literature can be seen in his *Kings, Lords and Commons: an Anthology from the Irish* (1959). See *Short Stories*, 2 vols 1990; *An Only Child*, new edn 1996, and *My Father's Son*, new edn 1994 (autobiography); James Matthews, *Voices: a Life of Frank O'Connor*, 1983; Maurice Wohlgelernter, *Frank O'Connor: an Introduction*, 1977.

ODETS, CLIFFORD (1906–63) American dramatist, was born in Philadelphia of a hard-working Jewish-American family which prospered with his father's elevation from machine feeder to owner of a printing business in New York City, to which they moved in 1912. He dropped out of Morris High School after two years as 'a waste of time', tried printing, but could not resist the call of the stage. After playing minor roles in travelling repertory, he settled in New York, where in 1929 he understudied Spencer Tracy (1900–67) on Broadway. In 1930 he became a founder member of the Group Theatre, a collective enterprise. He was a member of the Communist Party for eight months in 1934, during the depths of the Depression. *Waiting for Lefty* (1935), a proletarian protest drama which reflected the Group's philosophy of putting social content before dramatic structure, brought the houses down with its final rallying call of 'STRIKE, STRIKE, STRIKE!!!'; by the middle of the year it had been played throughout the USA by 32 Theatre League groups, and been banned in seven cities. *Awake and Sing!* (1935), a study of conflicts within a Jewish family, and *Till the Day I Die* (1935), of the threat of Nazism from a German Communist angle, increased his potential value as a Hollywood screenwriter; but having turned down $4000 a week, he had to settle for $2500 after the failure of *Paradise Lost* (1935). *Golden Boy* (1937), a melodrama about a violinist turned boxer which was his biggest commercial success, has elements of the cinema in it, as has *The Country Girl* (1950), in which characterization and social relationships replace his earlier political idealism. See Gerald Weales, *Odets: the Playwright*, 1985 (critical study).

O'DONOVAN, GERALD (1871–1942) Irish novelist, was born Jeremiah O'Donovan in Co. Down, the son of a builder from Cork who travelled round to work on the erection of piers. He was educated for the priesthood, entering St Patrick's College, Maynooth, in 1889, and being ordained in 1895. As a curate and then administrator in Loughrea, he was able to express his liberal and progressive views, and in 1901 he even invited a theatrical company to come from Dublin to perform. He joined the Irish Agricultural Organization Society, to whose committee he was elected as a representative for Connaught in 1901. He was also prominent in the Gaelic League. In 1904, after difficulties with his new bishop, for whose post it appears he may have been chosen locally, but rejected by the Vatican, he left the priesthood and went to Dublin, and from there to London, now calling himself Gerald. He married in 1910, and in 1913 published the first of his six novels, *Father Ralph* (1913), which reflects his own experiences as a modernist in the priesthood. *Waiting* (1914) treats the delicate but potentially explosive subject of intermarriage between faiths. He worked in the Department of Propaganda in World War I, during the course of which he met, and established a long-standing relationship with, ROSE MACAULAY, who appears as Grace in *The Holy Tree* (1922). It was his last novel. What he did for a living thereafter is apparently not clear even to his children. He fractured his skull in an accident in 1939 while on holiday in the Lake District with Rose Macaulay, though his death three years later was from cancer.

O'DONOVAN, MICHAEL see O'CONNOR, FRANK.

O'FAOLAIN, SEAN (1900–91) Irish short-story writer, novelist, critic, and biographer, was born John Whelan in Cork, the son of a constable in the Royal Irish Constabulary, and was educated at the Christian Brothers secondary school and University College, Cork, changing his name to its Irish equivalent in sympathy with his political convictions. After serving with the Irish Republican Army, and being an educational publisher's representative, he continued his education on a Commonwealth Fellowship (sponsored by GEORGE RUSSELL) at Harvard, and was then a lecturer in English at Strawberry Hill Teachers' Training College, Middlesex. He returned to Dublin in 1933, having published his first book and been promised £200 a year for three years by the publisher to write more. *Midsummer Night Madness and Other Stories* (1932) was largely experimental in form and style, and elusively romantic. Subsequent collections contain more compassion and humour, while evoking exactly an atmosphere of place or setting, and covering a broad canvas of situations inherent in the contemporary climate of Ireland. His three novels, *A Nest of Simple Folk* (1933), *Bird Alone* (1936), and *Come Back to Erin* (1940), enabled him to develop in each case a single character in revolt against a central orthodoxy.

Among his biographies are *De Valera* (1939) and *Newman's Way: the Odyssey of John Henry Newman* (1952). His most effective criticism is in *The Short Story* (1948) and *The Vanishing Hero: Studies in the Novelists of the Twenties* (1956). As founder-Editor of *The Bell* 1940–46, he encouraged young, and older, Irish writers to express themselves freely, and gave them, and contemporary Irish letters, a firmer stepping stone in the mainstream of modern literary thought and values. In 1928 he married Eileen Gould (1900–88), writer of children's books and folk tales. Their daughter is the novelist and short-story writer Julia O'Faolain (b. 1932). He had three fairly momentous affairs: with BOWEN, with a British journalist who came to Dublin as assistant editor of *The Bell* in 1945, and with an American socialite whom he had originally met at Harvard. See *Collected Stories*, 3 vols 1980–82 (Vol. 1 as *Midsummer Night Madness*, 1989); *Vive Moi!*, revised edn 1994, foreword by Julia O'Faolain, of his 1964 autobiography; Maurice Harmon, *Sean O'Faolain: a Life*, 1994; Maurice Harmon, *Sean O'Faolain: a Critical Introduction*, 1984.

O'FLAHERTY, LIAM (1896–1984) Irish novelist and short-story writer, was born in Inishmore in the Aran Islands, and was educated at Blackrock College and, for a year, at University College, Dublin, after which he joined the Irish Guards in 1915 and served at the front. In 1921, at the head of a group of dockers, he seized the Rotunda in Dublin for the Communists, and he was an active Republican during the Civil War. His first two published novels, *Thy Neighbour's Wife* (1923) and *The Black Soul* (1924), have backgrounds of Aran and the cultural contrasts that exist even within a small community. He returned there with *Skerrett* (1932), which charts the progress of a reforming schoolmaster to revolutionary and ultimately to self-destruction, and *Famine* (1937), in which he uses folkore and history vividly to re-create the dispersal of the community in the 1840s. From 1927 almost until his death he was constantly on the move; his own restlessness is reflected in the pursuit of self-discovery on the part of the main characters in his novels, and in his autobiographical works, *Two Years* (1930), *I Went to Russia* (1931), and *Shame the Devil* (1934). The best of his many short stories are those in which he records with pity, but also with humour, the harsh realities of the vanished Aran way of life—and death. In these stories in particular, but also in his work as a whole, the speech patterns and oral traditions of the Gaelic civilization are near the surface. See *Short Stories*, new edn 1996; *Letters of Liam O'Flaherty*, ed. A. A. Kelly, 1996; A. A. Kelly, *Liam O'Flaherty the Storyteller*, 1976.

OGOT, GRACE (b. 1930), née Akinyi, Kenyan novelist and short-story writer, was born in Butere, Central Nyanza District, and educated at Ng'iya Girls' School and Butere High School, after which she trained as a nurse in

Uganda and studied midwifery at St Thomas's Hospital, London. She was a nursing sister and tutor in midwifery at Maseno Hospital in 1958–59, and then for 15 months a scriptwriter and broadcaster for the BBC Overseas Service. She married a historian in 1959. Since then she has had four children; has been Community Development Officer at Kisumu and engaged with the Student Health Service at Makerere University College; and has worked as an airline public relations officer. She was a delegate to the United Nations in 1975, and to Unesco in 1976, and was subsequently elected to Parliament. She was a founder member of the Writers' Association of Kenya, and its President 1975–80. Though her first experience with the East African Literature Bureau was discouraging ('They really couldn't understand how a Christian woman could write such stories . . .'), she became the first woman to have fiction published by the East African Publishing House. Her novel, *The Promised Land* (1966), explores the traditional role of the woman in marriage. The duty of women and attitudes to medicine feature strongly in her short stories, of which the first of several volumes was *Land Without Thunder* (1968). A further novel, *The Graduate*, appeared in 1980. She is also concerned with the continuation of the culture and language of Luo, in which she has written two novels and a book of short stories.

O'GRADY, STANDISH (JAMES) (1846–1928) Irish folklorist, novelist, and historian, was born in Castletown Berehaven, Co. Cork, and educated at Trinity College, Dublin, after which he practised law in Dublin. A reading of Irish history by Sylvester O'Halloran (1728–1807) and Eugene O'Curry (1796–1862) stimulated him to produce his two-volume study, *History of Ireland: the Heroic Period* (1878) and *History of Ireland: Cuculain and His Contemporaries* (1880), to which the complementary *History of Ireland: Critical and Philosophical* (1881) was intended as a corrective on factual matters. In *Finn and His Companions* (1892) and a trilogy about Cuchulain (1894, 1901, 1920) he attempted to rewrite legend in the form of historical adventure, which is neither easy nor often successful. Better as adventure stories are some historical novels, notably *Red Hugh's Captivity* (1889) and *The Flight of the Eagle* (1897). He supported the Unionist cause, and in *Toryism and the Tory Democracy* (1886) advanced a theory of cooperation between landlord and rural tenant. In pursuit of his ideals he founded and edited the *All-Ireland Review*, which lasted from 1900 to 1907. He left Ireland in 1918, and died in the Isle of Wight. For the genuine excitement he inspired in contemporary writers simply by his discovery of genuine material, rather than for the way he presented it, he is regarded by many

as the founder of the Irish Literary Revival, and there are echoes of his phraseology in the poetry of YEATS. His cousin, Standish Hayes O'Grady (1832–1915), who spent thirty years as an engineer in the USA, was also interested in Irish oral literature, from which he translated *Silva Gadelica* (1892).

O'HARA, FRANK (1926–66) American poet, dramatist, and art critic, was born in Baltimore, and grew up in Worcester, Massachusetts. He was educated at the New England Conservatory of Music and, after naval service in the South Pacific, at Harvard and the University of Michigan. He joined the staff of the Museum of Modern Art, New York, in 1951, and, after resigning to give more time to writing, rejoined it in 1955. *City Winter and Other Poems* (1952) and *Oranges* (1953) were published by the Tibor de Nagy art gallery. He was at the centre of the 'New York Poets', who included Kenneth Koch (*b.* 1925) and James Schuyler (1923–91), and used the city as a backdrop for personal, often personalized, expressions which reflect the immediacy of a moment, sensation, or train of thought. He was an editor and reviewer for *Art News*, and wrote plays of an avant-garde nature. He died from injuries after being struck at night by a beach buggy on Fire Island. See *The Collected Poems*, ed. Donald Allen, introduction by John Ashbery, 1995; *Selected Poems*, ed. Donald Allen, new edn 1993.

O'HARA, JOHN (1905–70) American novelist and short-story writer, was born in Pottsville, Pennsylvania, the eldest of eight children of a leading local doctor, whose horse sleigh the boy used to drive on emergency calls. He was expelled from Keystone State Normal School and Fordham Preparatory School for breaking rules, and finally graduated from Niagara Preparatory School in 1924. Accepted by Yale, he withdrew when his father died, and worked as a reporter on the Pottsville *Journal* and Tamaqua *Courier*. In 1927 he went to New York, and between then and 1933, when he went freelance, held various journalistic and editorial posts, often briefly, on newspapers and magazines, including the *Herald Tribune* and *Time*, and had a first marriage, which lasted two years. His sketches and stories began to appear in the *New Yorker* and other magazines in 1928. *Appointment in Samarra* (1934), his first novel, established him as a storyteller with a feel for the development of character. *Butterfield 8* (1935) was based on the revelations of the scandalous past of a society girl whose body was washed up on Long Island in 1931. *Hope of Heaven* (1938) and *The Big Laugh* (1962) are novels of Hollywood. In *Ten North Frederick* (1955) and *From the Terrace* (1958) disillusionment is the price of ambition. A short-fiction writer whose range varied between the one-page monologue and the novella, he published some fifteen volumes from 1935 onwards. *Pal Joey* (1940), a sequence of 'letters' from an irrepressible, second-rate nightclub performer, was turned into a realistic musical comedy (1940). See Frank MacShane, *The Life of John O'Hara*, new edn 1987; Matthew J. Bruccoli, *The O'Hara Concern: a Biography of John O'Hara*, new edn 1996.

OKARA, GABRIEL (*b.* 1921) Nigerian poet and novelist, was born in Bumoundi in the Niger delta, the son of an Ijaw chief, and was educated at Government College, Umuahia, and Yaba Higher College, Lagos. He trained as a bookbinder, moved on to publishing and, after studying journalism at Northwestern University, Illinois, became Principal Information Officer, Eastern Regional Government, Enugu. During the civil war of 1967–69 he was Director of the Cultural Affairs Division, Biafran Ministry of Information. He became Director of the Rivers State Publishing House, Port Harcourt, in 1972. As a writer, his linguistic credo is unusual: 'The only way to use [African ideas, philosophy, folklore, and imagery] effectively is to translate them almost literally from the African language native to the writer.' His poems began to appear in literary journals in the 1950s, and were anthologized, especially 'The Call of the River Nun' and 'The Snow Flakes Sail Gently Down' (of a winter in the USA), and also translated. In *The Voice* (1964), a symbolic quest novel, he weaves Ijaw syntax and expressions into English poetic prose. *The Fisherman's Invocation* (1978), a slim collection of his verse, was joint winner of the 1979 Commonwealth Poetry Prize.

O'KEEFFE, JOHN (1747–1833) Irish dramatist, was born in Dublin and educated there in Saul's Court and then at an art school. He was more drawn to the theatre, and from 1762 to 1774 was a member of the Smock Alley company. His *Tony Lumpkin in Town*, a sequel to GOLDSMITH's *She Stoops to Conquer*, was performed in Dublin in 1773, and was a resounding success in London in 1778. After a similar reception for a comic opera, *The Son-in-Law* (1779), and the collapse of his marriage to a Protestant actress, he moved to London, hoping to find regular work as an actor. Instead he became a prolific writer of farces with songs ('Amo Amas I Love a Lass', 'I am a Friar of Orders Grey') and of comic operas and plays, of which *The Prisoner at Large* (1788) and *The Wicklow Mountains* (1796) have serious Irish themes, and *The Agreeable Surprise* (1781) and *Wild Oats* (1791) some lasting merit—the latter, a pacy tragicomedy of blunders in situation and character, written in a hurry to replace a dramatization of the fall of the Bastille which was cancelled because of anti-French senti-

ment, was successfully revived in London in 1976 and 1995. In 1797 the blindness with which he had been afflicted since he was 23 became total and he fell into financial straits, to which the outright sale of many of his copyrights had contributed. At a Covent Garden charity performance for him of his *Lie of a Day* (1796), attended by the Prince of Wales, he was led on stage to deliver a poetical address he had written. In about 1815 he moved to Hampshire, where he composed his 'Recollections' (1826). From 1788 he was devotedly attended by his only daughter, Adelaide O'Keeffe (1776–1855), a versatile writer in her own right, whose first novel, *Llewellin*, an ingenious historical tale, was written in 1795 and published anonymously in 1799. She wrote children's verses, of which 'The Kite' appeared in *Original Poems: Calculated to Improve the Mind of Youth* (1808), one of several volumes of her poems. Her *Dudley* (1819) is an epistolary novel.

OKIGBO, CHRISTOPHER (1932–67) Nigerian poet, was born in Ojoto, a village near Onitsha, the son of a Catholic schoolteacher, and was educated at Government College, Umuahia, and University College, Ibadan, where he read classics, and wrote music and performed as an accompanist. He was Private Secretary to the Federal Minister of Research and Information 1956–58, after which he taught Latin at Fiditi Grammar School for two years, and was then a university librarian at Nsukka and Enugu. In 1962 he became West African representative of the Cambridge University Press. He was also West African editor of the literary journal *Transition*, Kampala, which 'publishes anybody who cares to write for [it], black or white. We do not discriminate' (a reference to *Black Orpheus*, Ibadan). Never having fired even an air rifle in his life, he joined the Biafran army at the beginning of the civil war in 1967, and went as a major to the front, where he learned to use a gun. He was killed in action three months later. He began seriously to write poetry, instead of music, in 1957. He published two collections, *Heavensgate* (1962), 'an Easter sequence [which] later grew into . . . an offering to Idoto, the village stream of which I drank . . .', and *Limits* (1964), in which the poet is also prophet. *Labyrinths, with Path of Thunder* (1971), published posthumously but planned and with an introduction by Okigbo, contains the definitive versions of both books, with notable additions, such as 'Lament of the Silent Sisters' (1962) and 'Lament of the Drums' (1964), choral poems in whose message, he said in an interview in 1965, 'there might be some political tinge'. His voice is personal, and distinctive, and dedicated to his conviction that 'there is no such thing as Negro art' (he refused to accept the poetry prize of the Dakar Festival of Negro Arts 1966), or even 'African literature'.

Thus he felt free, in one of his last poems, 'Lament of the Masks' (1965), for the YEATS centenary, to eulogize the Irish poet in lines adapted from a Yoruba royal praise song, and elsewhere consciously to echo T. S. ELIOT, HOPKINS, POUND, and even 'Little Bo Peep'.

OLDHAM, JOHN (1653–83) English poet, was born in Shipton Magna, Gloucestershire, the son of a Nonconformist clergyman who, after being ejected from his post in 1662, was able to make a comfortable living from his estate and by keeping a school. The boy was educated at home, at the grammar school at Tetbury, and at St Edmund Hall, Oxford, where his provisional degree was withdrawn when he failed to comply with its conditions. He returned home, taught for his father, and composed occasional verses, with which he hoped to impress the local gentry, and a Pindaric elegy on his college friend, Charles Morwent, who died in 1675. In 1676 he became an assistant master at Whitgift School, Croydon, where in July of that year he wrote a satirical poem (later called 'A Satyr Against Vertue'), which earned him a congratulatory visit from ROCHESTER. He first appeared in print with the ode *Upon the Marriage of the Prince of Orange with Lady Mary* (1677). In 1679 he became tutor at Reigate to the grandson of Sir Edward Thurland (1606–83), former Solicitor General to the King. Further public recognition came with *Satyrs Upon the Jesuits* (1681), the success of which encouraged him to give up his job, but a year later he was a tutor again in Essex. He was rescued by an offer from William Pierrepont (*d.* 1690), later 4th Earl of Kingston, to live at his mansion near Nottingham. Oldham's talents now blossomed with a string of satires in heroic couplets such as '. . . Dissuading the Author from the Study of Poetry' and imitations of JUVENAL and BOILEAU, which moved DRYDEN to begin 'To the Memory of Mr Oldham': 'Farewell, too little and too lately known, / Whom I began to think and call my own'. He died of smallpox. See *The Poems of John Oldham*, ed. Harold F. Brooks, 1987; Paul Hammond, *John Oldham and the Renewal of Classical Culture*, 1983.

OLIPHANT, CAROLINA see NAIRNE.

OLIPHANT, MARGARET (1828–97), née Wilson, Scottish novelist, biographer, historian, and journalist, was born in Wallyford, Midlothian, the youngest child of an excise clerk, who, after moves to Lasswade and Glasgow, settled with his family in Liverpool in 1838. At 16 she took to writing fiction, as an alternative to needlework, while attending her sick mother—her disreputable brother Willie (*d.* 1885) purloined her first effort and published it later under his own name as *Christian Melville* (1856). Willie did, however, take *Passages in the Life of Mrs Margaret Mait-*

land of Sunnyside (1849) to a London publisher, who sent her a contract, and published it and two historical romances. And it was at Willie's, where she was acting as housekeeper, that she met her cousin, Francis Wilson Oliphant (1818–59), a stained-glass window designer, whom she married in 1852. She continued to write novels and became a regular contributor to *Blackwood's Edinburgh Magazine*, which paid the bills. In 1859 the family went to Italy in the hope of improving Francis's tuberculosis. He died in Rome, leaving her with the two surviving of their five children, and pregnant with another.

The rest of the life of this remarkable woman ('I don't think I have ever had two hours undisturbed . . . during my whole literary life') was a catalogue of periodic misery and of unrelenting toil; she had not only to educate her own children (all of whom died before her) and those of her brother Frank (*d.* 1875), but also to support two brothers. She spent the terrible winter of 1860–61 in Edinburgh, where Blackwood's tactfully discouraged her ('myself all blackness and whiteness in my widow's dress') from writing a further novel for serial publication. Nettled rather than rattled, that night, when she had put the children to bed, she began the 'Carlingford Series' of domestic novels, the earliest of which were serialized and published by Blackwood's in volume form. They run from *The Rector and the Doctor's Family* (1863) and *Salem Chapel* (1863) to *Phoebe, Junior: a Last Chronicle of Carlingford* (1876). In all she wrote almost a hundred novels, fifty short stories—see especially *Selected Stories of the Supernatural*, ed. Margaret K. Gray, 1985—innumerable articles and reviews, travel books, historical and topographical works, and biographies (including that of CHALMERS). She also wrote the official history of Blackwood's (1897). See *Autobiography*, ed. Elisabeth Jay, 1990; Elisabeth Jay, *Mrs Oliphant: 'A Fiction to Herself': a Literary Life*, 1995; Merryn Williams, *Margaret Oliphant: a Critical Biography*, 1986; Jenni Calder, *Margaret Oliphant*, 1992 (biographical/ critical study).

OLSON, CHARLES (1910–70) American poet and critic, was born in Worcester, Massachusetts, and while young moved with his parents to Dogtown, Gloucester, a community of twenty people. He went to Wesleyan University, and then to Yale and to Harvard, where he did research in American studies. In the meantime, and subsequently, he had various jobs, including fisherman, mailman, teacher (at Clark University and Harvard), and political worker. In the late 1940s he was invited to replace his friend DAHLBERG as an instructor at Black Mountain College, near Asheville, North Carolina, an experimental teaching institute founded in 1933, of which he was Rector from 1951 until it closed in 1956. His first book, *Call Me Ishmael* (1947), a

critical study of MELVILLE, was as unorthodox in its exposition as it was influential in
its discussion of what he termed 'MYTH . . .
SPACE . . . TRAGEDY' in *Moby Dick*. In a further significant critical work, the essay 'Projective Verse' (in *Poetry New York*, 3. 1950)—as
Projective Verse Vs the Non-Projective (1959)—,
he postulated: 'Verse now, 1950, if it is to go
ahead, if it is to be of *essential* use, must, I
take it, catch up and put into itself certain
laws and possibilities of the breath, of the
breathing of the man who writes as well as of
his listenings.' The Black Mountain Poets
were not so much a poetic movement as a
group of like-minded individuals who included CREELEY, LEVERTOV, Paul Blackburn
(1926–71), and Joel Oppenheimer (b. 1930).

Olson, 6' 9" tall, was also an amateur archaeologist, who 'hunted among stones' for
the original inspirations of art, especially
among the Mayas, in the same way as he
looked for the 'kinetics' whereby a 'poem is
energy transferred from where the poet got
it', a concept he explored further in the poem
'The Kingfishers' (1949). His life work was
the Maximus poems, a grand design first
conceived in 1945. *The Maximus Poems 1–10*
were published in 1953, with subsequent
continuations; the whole, ed. George F. Butterick, appeared posthumously in 1983. Inspired partly by W. C. WILLIAMS's *Paterson*,
and modelled in format on the *Cantos* of
POUND, it is his response to his own criteria
in the form of a sequence of three hundred
varied poems in which he distils, through the
persona of the 2nd-century Platonic philosopher Maximus of Tyre (a projection of himself), the history, geology, and social environment of the town of Gloucester. See *The
Collected Poems*, ed. George F. Butterick, 1992;
Selected Writings of Charles Olson, ed. Robert
Creeley, new edn 1971; *Selected Poems*, ed.
Robert Creeley, new edn 1993; Paul Christen-
sen, *Charles Olson: Call Him Ishmael*, 1979
(critical study).

OMAR KHAYYÁM, more properly Umar-i-
Khayyám [Umar, son of the tent-maker]
(1048–1131) Persian mathematician, astrono-
mer, philosopher, and poet, was born in Nis-
hapur. He wrote a treatise on algebra in his
twenties and, having been among those summoned by the Sultan in 1074 to build a new
observatory, was instrumental also in the revision of the Muslim calendar. A manuscript
of his secular *rubáiyát* (rhyming quatrains),
private thoughts for private circulation only,
was acquired eight hundred years later in
Calcutta by the Ipswich-born oriental
scholar, Edward Cowell (1826–1903), and
sent to EDWARD FITZGERALD, whom he had
originally encouraged to learn Persian. Fitz-
Gerald arranged 75 of Omar's verses into a
sequence (1859), expressing their spirit in a
metrical pattern not dissimilar to that of the
medieval Latin hymn, 'Dies Irae', and pub-

lished various revised editions during his
lifetime. Subsequent verse translations include those by GRAVES and Omar Ali-Shah
(1967) (unrhymed), and by Peter Avery and
HEATH-STUBBS (1979).

ONDAATJE, MICHAEL (b. 1943) Canadian poet and novelist, was born in Colombo,
Ceylon (Sri Lanka), the fourth child of a
charming and eccentric alcoholic and of a
beautiful drama teacher. After his parents'
divorce he joined his mother in England,
where he was educated at Dulwich College.
He went to Canada in 1962, studied there at
Bishop's, Toronto, and Queen's universities,
and wrote a thesis on MUIR. He joined the English department at York University, Toronto,
in 1971. His eye for the bizarre was demonstrated in his first book of verse, *The Dainty
Monsters* (1967). His third, *The Collected Works
of Billy the Kid: Left Handed Poems* (1970),
which won the Governor General's Award, is
an evocative amalgam of sketches of the life,
and violent death, of the outlaw, William
Bonney (1859–81), employing a variety of
graphic techniques. It was produced on the
stage in 1973. His second Governor General's
Award was for *There's a Trick with a Knife I'm
Learning to Do: Poems 1963–1978* (1979; in UK
as *Rat Jelly and Other Poems 1963–1978*, 1980).
Coming Through Slaughter (1976) is an impressionistic novel about the life, and death in a
state mental hospital, of the jazz musician
Buddy Bolden (1876–1931).

His fictional philosophy is enshrined in *In
the Skin of a Lion* (1987), a brutal foundation-
myth of the building of Toronto: 'The first
sentence of every novel should be: "Trust me,
this will take time, but there is order here,
very faint, very human." ' *The English Patient*
(1992), a study of the minds and motives of
an intriguing foursome in Tuscany in 1945 in
a battered villa which is surrounded by unex-
ploded mines, took six years to complete and
went through ten separate drafts (with a
fountain pen, 'because it's more personal'). It
was joint winner of the Booker prize for fiction with *Sacred Hunger* (1992) by Barry Unsworth (b. 1930), and won the Governor General's Award in Canada. Ondaatje has
directed films, including *Sons of Captain
Poetry* (1971), on the Canadian concrete poet,
bp Nichol (b. 1944). On return visits to Sri
Lanka in 1978 and 1980 he investigated his
colourful family background, evoked in *Running in the Family* (1982), a prose study in
sketches and conversations, with a verse interlude. See *The Cinnamon Peeler: Selected
Poems*, new edn 1992; Ed Jewinski, *Michael
Ondaatje: Express Yourself Beautifully*, 1994
(critical introduction); Nell Waldman, *Michael
Ondaatje and His Works*, 1992.

O'NEILL, EUGENE (1888–1953) American dramatist, was born in a hotel room in
New York City, the younger son of an Irish-

born actor who believed he had ruined his career by touring for years on end in the title role in a dramatization of DUMAS's *The Count of Monte Cristo*. His mother, who came from a respectable business background, could never reconcile herself to following her husband around, or forgive herself for the death of a second son from measles, and became a morphine addict. After attending Catholic and nonsectarian boarding schools, the boy went to Betts Academy, Stamford, from which he graduated in 1906. His career at Princeton was terminated at the end of one year after he threw a rock through the stationmaster's window. He drifted, and in 1909 secretly married a girl whom he had got pregnant; he immediately left on a gold prospecting expedition to Honduras, from which he returned empty-handed. (The marriage was terminated in 1912: the child, Eugene O'Neill Jr, killed himself in 1950.)

When not living in a New York waterfront bar called 'Jimmy the Priest's', he succumbed to the lure of the sea, sailing as a seaman from Boston to Buenos Aires, to Durban and back in a cattle-steamer, and then to New York, from where he did a round trip to England. The posthumously performed *Long Day's Journey Into Night* picks up his own situation (he calls himself Edmund, the name of his dead brother) and that of his parents and elder brother in 'August 1912', being the actual month in which he was diagnosed as tubercular. When he was 'discharged as arrested' from a sanitorium, he had determined to become a dramatist: 'I read about everything I could lay hands on: the Greeks, the Elizabethans—practically all the classics—and of course all the moderns. Ibsen and Strindberg, especially Strindberg . . .'. He had already begun to write plays when he enrolled for a year on Harvard's play-writing course, run by George Pierce Baker (1866–1935). *Bound East for Cardiff*, set in the hold of a British tramp-steamer in mid-Atlantic, and *Thirst* (published 1914) were staged by the Provincetown Players in their wharfside converted fish-house in Cape Cod in 1916; *Before Breakfast* was produced in their winter headquarters in Greenwich Village, New York, the same year. Three further one-act plays involving the crew of the steamer, *Moon of the Caribbees*, *The Long Voyage Home*, and *In the Zone*, were performed in 1917–8—the four, which are regarded as the best of the twenty one-act plays he wrote at this time, were revived and performed in the USA as a chronological sequence in 1993. In 1918 he married Agnes Boulton, from whom he separated in 1927. He later disowned both their children— Shane (*b.* 1919) for his aimless dissolute life (he finally committed suicide), and Oona (1925–91) for marrying, at 18, the film star/ director (Sir) Charles Chaplin (1889–1977).

Beyond the Horizon (1920), his first signifi-

cant full-length play, a realistic representation of the mixed fortunes and troubled aspirations of a farming family, was produced on Broadway. *The Emperor Jones* (1920) is an experiment in expressionism, which he extended in *The Hairy Ape: a Comedy of Ancient and Modern* (1922). The symbolism in *Anna Christie* (1921), which was originally staged in an unsatisfactory form in 1920 as *Chris Christopherson*, serves to strengthen the illusion, as the father and an admirer each finds and then loses the girl, who is not what she seems. In *Desire Under the Elms* (1924), set in a New England farm in 1850, he used his study of FREUD to investigate conflicts and earthy relationships in an unstable family. *Strange Interlude* (1928) is a modern tragedy, the action of which covers 25 years and is presented in two parts. At the end of the first part the pattern is established; during the second it breaks into pieces. In the trilogy *Mourning Becomes Electra* (1931)—*Homecoming*, *The Hunted*, and *The Haunted*—he relocates the *Oresteia* of AESCHYLUS in 19th-century New England. *The Iceman Cometh* (produced in 1946, but written in 1939) develops dramatically from a conversation piece peopled by habitués of a bar resembling 'Jimmy the Priest's', and moves easily along the comic side of the line between that and tragedy.

At the same time O'Neill was working on two cycles, one about an Irish family in America from 1755, and the other of one-act dramas; only one play from each survived. He was also planning and writing an autobiographical sequence, of which he completed three works out of the nine. The first to be finished, in 1940, was *Long Day's Journey Into Night*, which he instructed should not be published for 25 years after his death; he changed his mind after the suicide of Eugene Jr. He described it as an attempt to face the dead and to write 'with deep pity and understanding for all the four haunted Tyrones' (as he called his family in the play). It was produced in 1956, after his death in 1953 of bronchial pneumonia had brought to an end a decade during which his hands had become so paralysed from a neurological disorder that he could not write. This study of a family's excoriation of each of the other three members in turn, moves from breakfast-time calm to midnight's painful realization that life will never be the same for any of them. It gained him his fourth Pulitzer Prize. He won the Nobel Prize for Literature in 1936, the only writer solely a dramatist ever to have done so. See *Complete Plays*, 2 vols 1988; *Selected Letters of Eugene O'Neill*, ed. Travis Bogard and Jackson R. Bryer, new edn 1994; Arthur and Barbara Gelb, *O'Neill*, new edn 1995 of rev. edn 1973 (biography); Travis Bogard, *Contour in Time: the Plays of Eugene O'Neill*, rev. edn 1988.

ONETTI, JUAN CARLOS (1909–1994) Uruguayan novelist, was born in Montevideo. He did not finish his secondary education, but after going to Argentina became a successful journalist. In 1939 he published his first novel, *El Pozo*, a grim look at Uruguay, to which he returned to work briefly in 1942, and permanently in 1955, becoming a municipal librarian in 1957. *Tierra de Nadie* (1941; tr. Peter Bush as *No Man's Land*, 1994), his second novel, is a study of Buenos Aires society in the early 1940s, after the signing of the Nazi–Soviet pact. Most of his subsequent novels, existentialist in approach, experimental in style, and disillusioned in tone, are set in Argentina. For *La Vida Breve* (1950; tr. Hortense Carpentier as *A Brief Life*, 1976) and *El Astillero* (1961; tr. Rachel Caffyn as *The Shipyard*, 1968) he created his fictional city of Santa María. In the early 1980s he fell foul of the army regime and emigrated to Spain. He took a final look at Santa Maria in his last book, *Past Caring?* (1993; tr. Bush, 1994). Stories are in *Goodbye and Stories*, tr. Daniel Balderston (1990) and *Onetti's Short Stories*, tr. Peter Turton (bilingual edition 1994).

O'NOLAN, BRIAN see O'BRIEN, FLANN.

OPIE, AMELIA (1769–1853), née Alderson, English novelist and poet, was born in Norwich, the only child of a doctor of Unitarian principles, whose housekeeper she became when her mother died in 1784. She learned French and music, sang her own ballads, had a novel, *The Dangers of Coquetry*, published anonymously in 1790, and acted locally in her own tragedy, *Adelaide*. Society visits to London began in 1794, and in 1798 she married the self-taught painter, John Opie (1761–1807), who was recently divorced. He encouraged her literary career, and she helped him to write the lectures he gave in 1807 as Professor of Painting at the Royal Academy. *The Father and Daughter* (1801), to which was appended a selection of her verses, is typical of her 'tales', which, though they often have as background events and issues of the day, centre on a family separation culminating in reconciliation or death—*Adeline Mowbray* (1805) is subtitled 'The Mother and Daughter'. *Poems* (1802) contained several poetical variations on the same theme. After her husband's death she returned to Norwich, but made forays to London, where she mixed with the literary set (including BYRON, WALTER SCOTT, SHERIDAN, and STAËL) and evaded offers of marriage. In 1825, just before her father's death, she became a Quaker. She had already, after the publication of *Madeline* (1822), renounced fiction, and was furious with her publisher for announcing (and obtaining orders for) a novel which she had begun and irrevocably abandoned. She now devoted herself to good works, tracts, and poems of a morbid nature, with social interludes in Paris and London. She attended the Great Exhibition of 1851 in a wheelchair, and challenged an 88-year-old in a similar vehicle to a race.

O'RANE, PATRICIA see DARK.

ORCZY, (EMMA MAGDALENA ROSALIA MARIE JOSEPHA BARBARA), BARONESS (1865–1947) novelist, was born at Tarnaörs, Hungary, the daughter of Baron Felix Orczy, who took up his first love of music when his peasants, suspicious of his modern farming methods, burned the place down. She attended convent schools in Brussels and Paris, and, after the family settled in London, studied painting at the Heatherley School of Art, where she met Montague Barstow (d. 1943). They were married in 1894. Though she knew no English until she was 15, she wrote fiction for magazines, of which the best received were a series of armchair detective stories, later published in volume form as *The Old Man in the Corner* (1909). *The Scarlet Pimpernel*, featuring the dandy, Sir Percy Blakeney, as the daring organizer of escapes from the terrors of the French Revolution, was written in 1902 and rejected by more than a dozen publishers. It was finally published in 1905 to coincide with the London production of a stage version which she had written with her husband. She wrote many more historical romances, including several 'Pimpernel' sequels, among which are *I Will Repay* (1906) and *The Elusive Pimpernel* (1908). She inherited Tarnaörs in 1906, but never lived there. At the end of World War I she and her husband settled in Monte Carlo, which they were prevented from leaving at the outset of World War II. See *Links in the Chain of Life*, 1947 (autobiography).

ORTEGA Y GASSET, JOSÉ (1883–1955) Spanish philosopher and critic, was born in Madrid and educated at a Jesuit school in Malaga, Deusto University, and Madrid University, where he studied philosophy and received his doctorate in 1904. After further study in Germany, and some publishing ventures, he was in 1910, at the age of 27, appointed Professor of Metaphysics at Madrid University. His first book, *Meditaciones del Quijote* [Meditations on Quixote] (1914) looks at the destiny of Spain in terms of what he regarded as its greatest spiritual work. In *España Invertebrada* (1921; tr. Mildred Adams in *Invertebrate Spain . . .*, 1937) he investigated the nature of Spain and its people; in *El Tema de Nuestro Tiempo* (1922; tr. James Cleugh as *The Modern Theme*, 1931) he reaffirmed his metaphysical stance. Having founded *El Espectados*, a journal of articles and essays written entirely by himself, eight issues of which appeared between 1916 and 1934, he established *Revista de Occidente* (1923), a monthly literary, political, scientific, and philosophical review. In *La Rebelión de la Masas* (1929; tr. as *The Revolt of the Masses*, 1932) he advocated a united European civilization as an answer to the control and development of the aspirations of 'mass-man'. He left Spain in 1936 at the outset of the Civil War. He returned in 1948, when he was refused permission to restart publishing *Revista de Occidente*, but allowed to set up and manage the Instituto de Humanidades, only for it to be shut down by the government in 1950.

ORTIZ, SIMON J. (*b.* 1941) American poet, was born in Albuquerque, New Mexico, the son of a stonemason/woodcarver, and was educated on the Acoma Reservation in Bureau of Indian Affairs schools. After service in the US Army he went to the universities of New Mexico and (as International Writing Fellow) Iowa. He has been a public relations consultant to cultural organizations and has taught at several universities. A poet who can say, in 'A Designated National Park', 'This morning / I have to buy a permit to get back home', he writes 'because Indians always tell a story. . . . The only way to continue is to tell a story'. His first book of verse was *Naked in the Wind* (1970); *A Good Journey* (1977) is a particularly significant collection. Subsequent volumes are *Woven Stone* (1992) and *After and Before the Lightning* (1994). Short fiction is in *Fightin': New and Collected Stories* (1983).

ORTON, JOE (1933–67) British dramatist, was born in Leicester, the eldest child of a gardener. After failing his eleven-plus examination from primary school, he took a secretarial course. An interest in amateur dramatics led to his winning a scholarship to the Royal Academy of Dramatic Art in 1951. Here he met and began a homosexual relationship with Kenneth Halliwell (*b.* 1926), who suggested he should write, rather than act, which Orton had found too restricting an activity. Living in bedsitters, doing temporary jobs to keep themselves, they wrote several unpublished novels together; in 1962 they were imprisoned for six months for defacing (artistically and amusingly) book jackets in public libraries. After six years of nothing but rejections of his own novels and plays, the BBC accepted Orton's radio play, *The Ruffian on the Stair*. It was broadcast in 1964, three months after the stage première of *Entertaining Mr Sloane* (published 1964). During the next three years he adapted his radio play for the stage (1966), and wrote three further one-act plays and two more full-length plays, *Loot* (1965), which won the *Evening Standard* award for the best play of the year, and *What the Butler Saw* (produced 1969). In these he made sick comedy, often

black farce, out of hitherto taboo situations, and reinvented the art of the stage epigram. In August 1967 Halliwell, who resented Orton's success, battered him to death with a hammer in their Islington flat, and then killed himself with sleeping tablets. See *Complete Plays*, 1990; John Lahr, *Prick Up Your Ears: the Biography of Joe Orton*, new edn 1987; Maurice Charney, *Joe Orton*, 1984 (critical study).

ORWELL, GEORGE, pseudonym of Eric Blair (1903–50) British novelist, essayist, and critic, was born in Bihar, India, the son of a peripatetic agent in the opium department of the Indian government. In 1904 his mother brought him and his elder sister back to England, where they settled in Henley-on-Thames. At eight he was sent away to a boarding school on the Sussex coast, as he recorded in an autobiographical sketch, 'Such, Such Were the Joys' (a quotation from BLAKE), probably written in 1940, but for reasons of libel not published until 1968. The outbreak of war in 1914 inspired his first published work, a poem 'Awake! Young Men of England', in the *Henley and South Oxfordshire Standard*. In 1917 he took up the scholarship he had won at Eton, and after five years there, instead of following his contemporaries to Oxford, for which he would have needed a further scholarship, he joined the Indian Imperial Police and served in Burma. In 1927, on his first home leave, he resigned. It was not just that he wanted to write and had grown to hate the idea of the Empire, but he objected to doing the work that imperialism involved. He now felt he must establish a new identity as well as seek a different social environment. He spent some time visiting the poor in London's East End, and then took a room in a working-class district of Paris, where he did menial jobs, gave English lessons, and tried to get his work published. Finally, having had pneumonia, he had to return home to his parents in Suffolk when his money ran out. He now completed an account of his recent experiences which, after two rejections, was accepted by Victor Gollancz (1893–1967) and published as *Down and Out in Paris and London* (1933) by 'George Orwell'—the surname is a river in Suffolk. During the next few years he did some teaching and reviewing, worked in a bookshop, and published three novels, of which the first, *Burmese Days* (1934), based on his military experiences, came out initially in New York because of libel fears in Britain.

Early in 1936 Gollancz commissioned him to write a book about the conditions of the unemployed in the north of England. He spent several months researching it, then moved into a Hertfordshire cottage, which he reopened as the village store. The account of his investigations, *The Road to Wigan Pier*, appeared in 1937. In the second half of the book he took a revolutionary socialist stance which opposed Marxism and embarrassed members of the Left Book Club, of which it was a choice. When it was published, however, he was in Spain, fighting on the Republican side in the Civil War. From this experience and his analysis of the politico-historical background came *Homage to Catalonia* (1938). After an illness, he wrote (in Morocco) a further novel, *Coming Up for Air* (1939), in which nostalgia for the Henley of his childhood is mixed with social philosophy presented through the persona of an insurance salesman. Unfit for service in World War II, he earned money from journalism, worked for the BBC, and was Literary Editor of *Tribune* 1943–45. His anti-revolutionist political satire, *Animal Farm*, which in time did much to discredit the Soviet system, was finished early in 1944, but because of doubts in the minds of publishers was not published until August 1945. Four months earlier his wife, Eileen O'Shaughnessy, had died from heart failure during a routine operation, worrying about money to the last. With their two-year-old adopted son, he settled in Jura, off the west coast of Scotland, in 1946, and between bouts of tuberculosis wrote his last novel, the frightening forecast of totalitarianism, *Nineteen Eighty-Four* (1949). In 1949 he was moved from a sanatorium in the Cotswolds to University College Hospital, London, where in October he married Sonia Brownell (1918–80) from his bed. He died three months later.

His critical essays include studies of DICKENS, KIPLING, WELLS, YEATS, and SWIFT ('Politics and Literature: an Examination of *Gulliver's Travels*'), as well as of boys' comics, pornography, and obscenity. In 'Why I Write' (1946) he expounds his personal history and philosophy as an author. The penetrating essay, *The Lion and the Unicorn: Socialism and the English Genius*, was originally published as a slim hardback in 1941. In the end he was no nearer resolving the discrepancies within the various branches and shades of socialism than he had been at the beginning, but he succeeded in illuminating the enigmas for those who wanted to perceive them and to accompany him on his journeys towards a revelation. See *Collected Essays, Journalism and Letters of George Orwell*, ed. Sonia Orwell and Ian Angus, 4 vols new edn 1970; Bernard Crick, *George Orwell: a Life*, rev. edn 1992; Michael Shelden, *Orwell: the Authorised Biography*, new edn 1992; Valerie Meyers, *George Orwell*, 1991 (critical study); Raymond Williams, *Orwell*, new rev. edn 1991 (introduction to his work and thought).

OSBORNE, DOROTHY (1627–95) English letter writer, was born at the family seat of Chicksands, Bedfordshire, the daughter of Sir Peter Osborne (1584–1653), Governor of Guernsey. Her father hastily retreated to Guernsey at the outset of the Civil War to hold the garrison for the King, and remained there, besieged, for four years. He then lived in exile in St Malo until 1649, when on payment of a vast fine he returned to Chicksands. On a visit to him in 1648 Dorothy had met TEMPLE, who delayed his onward journey to Paris until angry messages from his father forced him to proceed. Her family, probably for financial reasons, were equally opposed to any match between them. The love letters that she wrote from March 1652 to October 1654 are elegantly but colloquially expressed, and full of news and good sense as well as of longing. They also chart the course of their romance, during which their infrequent meetings often served to increase her sense of insecurity and hopelessness, so that in October 1653 she ends a brief note explaining her behaviour, 'Tell me what you will have me do.' Her father died in March 1654. In June she insisted that they announce their engagement, and in October she came to London to prepare for her wedding. A week before it, she went down with smallpox. Temple was constantly with her, and she recovered, but with the loss of her looks. They were married on Christmas Day. The rest of her life was bound up with her husband's. They had six children, of whom just one reached adulthood, only to drown himself in 1689 in a fit of insanity. See *Letters to Sir William Temple*, ed. Kenneth Parker, 1987; and in David Cecil, *Two Quiet Lives*, new edn 1989 (with THOMAS GRAY).

OSBORNE, JOHN (1929–94) British dramatist, was born in Fulham, London, into a family which, according to him, suffered from a sense of having 'Come Down in the World'. His parents, having separated after his birth, came together again in 1936, and lived in Surrey. Osborne went to local schools and, after his father's death, to Belmont College, Devon. After working on trade magazines, notably *Gas World*, he became a stage manager and actor in repertory, before himself writing plays. *Look Back in Anger* (1956, published 1957), brought to public notice by a review by KENNETH TYNAN, revolutionized attitudes to the theatre in that its hero, Jimmy Porter, spoke for and was of an educated working-class generation which had become disaffected, like many other young people, by middle-class values and ineffective government. Osborne became the focus of a literary movement known as the Angry Young Men (AMIS was another), and the term 'kitchen-sink drama' was applied to the style of realistic working-class family conflict typified by *Look Back in Anger*, and reflected also in the plays of Shelagh Delaney (b. 1939) and some of those of WESKER. *The Entertainer* (1957) starred Laurence Olivier (1907–89) as a pathetic relic of the old music hall. *Luther* (1961) presents the founder of Protestantism, with fair historical accuracy and with dramatic intensity, as yet another articulate opponent of established order. *Inadmissible Evidence* (1964) is an experiment in style and form, and in later plays, including *The Hotel in Amsterdam* (1968) and *A Sense of Detachment* (1972), Osborne employed a variety of stage techniques to enforce his characters' controversial statements, which are often delivered as though they were monologues. *Déjà Vu* (1991; staged as *Déjàvu*, 1992) resuscitates Jimmy Porter, 36 years on, as an unappealing whiner, who speaks with the voice of his creator. *Damn You, England: Collected Prose* (1994), containing some of his most lively as well as vituperative writing, was, according to him, put together by his fifth wife and a publisher's editor, without his ever seeing it. His last work to be performed was *England, My England* (Christmas Day 1995), a television musical drama of the life of the composer Henry Purcell (1659–95), for which he wrote the screenplay with Charles Wood (b. 1933). See *Plays, One*, new edn 1996; *A Better Class of Person: an Autobiography 1929–1956*, new edn 1991; *Almost a Gentleman: an Autobiography, Vol. II 1955–1966*, new edn 1992; Ronald Hayman, *John Osborne*, 3rd edn 1976 (critical study).

O'SULLIVAN, VINCENT (*b.* 1937) New Zealand poet, short-story writer, and critic, was born in Auckland and educated at Auckland University, after which he studied at Lincoln College, Oxford. He taught at the universities of Victoria and Waikato, and was then a freelance writer, returning later to Victoria University as Professor of English. In his introduction to *An Anthology of New Zealand Poetry* (1970) he argued, 'Europe is the closest that a New Zealander has to an extensive birthright. . . . And what at first appears to be a cultural penalty may in fact be construed as rigorous liberty.' In his own verse, the first collection of which was *Our Burning Time* (1965), he tends to rework, often intricately, themes from classical and other mythologies, or to present aspects of personal day-to-day experience or autobiographical recollections—see *Selected Poems* (1992). The same preoccupation with reverie informs many of his short stories, collected in *The Boy, The Bridge, The River* (1978), *Dandy Edison for Lunch and Other Stories* (1981), *Survivals and Other Stories* (1985), and *The Snow in Spain* (1990). He has edited the poems (1988) and, with Margaret Scott, the collected letters (1984–) of MANSFIELD. Latterly he has turned to drama, of which *Shuriken* (1985) signalled a notable debut.

OTWAY, THOMAS (1652–85) English dramatist and poet, was born in Trotton, Sussex, the son of the curate of the parish, and was educated at Winchester College and Christ Church, Oxford, which he abandoned for London in 1671, to try to scrounge a living as a poet and actor. A disastrous attack of stage fright while appearing in BEHN's *The Forc'd Marriage* finally convinced him to give up acting. Instead he wrote *Alcibiades* (1675), a heroic drama in heroic couplets. It was not a success, but in its cast was Elizabeth Barry (1658–1713), mistress of ROCHESTER, on her way to becoming the finest tragic actress of her generation. The story of Otway's unrequited passion for her has been current ever since six love letters, purportedly from him to her, were included in the 1712 edition of his *Works*. Whatever the truth, after the well-deserved reception of the tragedy *Don Carlos, Prince of Spain* (1676), Rochester appears as the dedicatee and Barry as one of two actresses in Otway's double bill, *Titus and Berenice* (1677), from RACINE, and *The Cheats of Scapin* (1677), from MOLIÈRE. Still unable to make ends meet, he volunteered as an officer in Flanders in 1678, but was back in London in June 1679, when he challenged John Churchill (1650–1722), later Duke of Marlborough, to a duel in the Duke's Theatre 'for beating an orange wench', and got the better of him. For Barry he now created the name part of Monimia in *The Orphan* (1680), a domestic drama of extreme pathos. She also starred as Belvedira in *Venice Preserv'd, or, The Plot Discover'd* (1682), a deep tragedy of torn loyalties, the plotting and counter-plotting of which recalled the current situation at Charles II's court. Otway died in extreme poverty in a house on Tower Hill. See *The Works of Thomas Otway*, ed. J. C. Ghosh, 2 vols new edn 1968.

OUIDA, pen name of Marie Louise De La Ramée (1839–1908) British novelist, was born in Bury St Edmunds, Suffolk, the daughter of Louis Ramé, a brilliant teacher of French who gave her an excellent education at home. In 1859, in London, she was introduced to AINSWORTH, who promptly printed 17 of her stories of society and military life in *Bentley's Miscellany*, in which also appeared her first novel, 'Granville de Vigne'. This was published in volume form as *Held In Bondage* (1863), for which she adopted the style of Ouida, a childish pronunciation of her second name, Louise. *Under Two Flags* (1867) is regarded as the best of her novels in her original vein, but she also wrote some witty social fantasies, notably *Princess Napraxine* (1884) and *Othmar* (1885), and acutely observed and sympathetic tales of Italian peasant life, including *A Village Commune* (1881). Impractical in financial matters as well as extravagant, from 1874 she lived permanently in Italy, latterly in a state of penury only partially relieved by a Civil List pension, which she first refused but was finally persuaded to accept in 1906. She had through the years been alternately resented and patronized by CORELLI, who now publicly proposed the establishment for her of a relief fund, to which she contributed an opening £25. A humiliated Ouida, whose permission had not been sought, sent a telegram forbidding any use of her name. She died in utter squalor in Viareggio. She was an intellectual and clever writer with a refreshingly European rather than simply a British outlook. Her essays for various journals were collected in *Views and Opinions* (1895) and *Critical Studies* (1900).

OVID (PUBLIUS OVIDIUS NASO) (43 BC–AD 18) Roman elegiac poet, was born in Sulmo, of an ancient and high-ranking family, and studied rhetoric and law in Rome. He held minor official posts, but never practised law, preferring the life of a literary philanderer. *Heroides* [Heroines], a series of imaginary letters to faithless lovers in mythology, was written between *Amores* [Love Poems] and *Ars Amatoria* [The Art of Love]. These were not so much erotic as irresponsible in that they appeared to condone adultery, a criminal offence, on which the emperor Augustus was rather touchy: he had banished his daughter, Julia, for just that. In AD 8, Julia's daughter went, too, for the same offence, and Ovid, now in his fifties, was banished to Tomi, on the bleak coast of the Black Sea, for what he calls 'a poem' and 'an error'. He was never allowed back, even after the death of Augustus, though he kept writing pleading letters—and poetry. Whereas his earlier works had been deftly and wittily composed in elegiac couplets, he turned to hexameters for *Metamorphoses*, a broadly-based collection of myths and legends with a common theme of transformation, which was widely drawn upon by later writers, including CHAUCER and GOWER. Ovid was married early and twice divorced, his third wife remaining devoted to him to the last. See *Metamorphoses*, new edn 1987, and *The Love Poems*, new edn 1990, *Sorrows of an Exile (Tristia)*, tr. A. D. Melville, ed. E. J. Kenney, new edn 1995; *The Poems of Exile*, tr. Peter Green, 1994; *Heroides*, tr. Harold Isbell, 1990.

OWEN, WILFRED (1893–1918) British poet, was born in Oswestry, Shropshire, on the border with Wales (both his parents were probably of Welsh origin), and was educated in Birkenhead, where his father was a stationmaster, and at Shrewsbury Technical College. After failing to get into university, he responded to the training of his deeply religious mother, and worked unpaid in the parish of Dunsden, near Reading. In 1913 he became an English teacher in Bordeaux, where he began to write verse. He enlisted in 1915, and was commissioned in the Manchester Regiment in January 1917 and posted to France. In June he was sent home with shell shock to Craiglockhart Hospital, Edinburgh, where he met and was encouraged by SASSOON. He returned to the front in September 1918, won the Military Cross, and was killed

near Ors on 4 November, a week before the end of hostilities. He is regarded as the finest poet of World War I, but he is a war poet only in that all his best verse was written under its influence. His distinction is in his choice of language and the way he uses it in different metrical forms, with assonance and alliteration, as well as rhyme, pararhyme, and half-rhyme, to heighten the horror and compassion of his view, as in the last verse of 'Exposure' (completed September 1918): 'To-night, this frost will fasten on the mud and us, / Shrivelling many hands, puckering foreheads crisp. / The burying-party, picks and shovels in shaking grasp, / Pause over half-known faces. All their eyes are ice, / But nothing happens.' Only four of Owen's poems were published during his lifetime, all in periodicals. Seven more were printed by EDITH SITWELL in *Wheels* (1919), and collections of his verse were edited by Sassoon (1920) and (with a memoir) BLUNDEN (1931). See *The Poems of Wilfred Owen*, ed. Jon Stallworthy, new edn 1990; *Selected Letters*, ed. John Bell, 1986; Jon Stallworthy, *Wilfred Owen: a Biography*, new edn 1988; Dominic Hibberd, *Wilfred Owen: the Last Year 1917–1918*, new edn 1993.

OZICK, CYNTHIA (*b.* 1928) American novelist, short-story writer, poet, critic, and essayist, was born in New York City. Her parents, who had emigrated from Russia and were of Lithuanian-Jewish tradition, ran a drugstore; her maternal uncle was the Hebrew poet Abraham Regelson. To her grandmother, who insisted on her being accepted at religion school (normally a boys' prerogative) at the age of 5½, she owes her introduction to feminism and to Yiddish. After unhappy experiences at a Bronx primary school ('I am still hurt. . . . I had teachers who . . . made me believe I was stupid and inferior'), she had a fruitful academic career at Hunter College High School, Manhattan, and New York University, and then wrote a thesis on HENRY JAMES at Ohio State University. She married Bernard Hallote, a lawyer, in 1952; they had a daughter in 1965. A full-time career writer, with a brief experience as a teaching assistant on a stipend and as a department store advertising copywriter, she began and after several years abandoned a philosophical novel, and wrote poetry ('Apocalypse' was published in *Commentary* in 1959) and articles. In her first published novel, *Trust* (1966), on which she spent 6½ years (it is over 600 pages long and she refused to accept her editor's suggestions for cuts), she sets lust against law, and paganism against religion, between 1930 and 1957, in American and European settings and situations that variously recall James, SHAKESPEARE, and other writers. By her own admission, while researching and writing it, she changed from being an American writer to a Jewish writer, having been particularly influenced by reading the German scholar and Jewish leader, Rabbi Leo Baeck (1873–1956). In 1964–65 she had several poems published in the journal *Judaism*.

The Pagan Rabbi and Other Stories (1971), in which the title story has a supernatural element, included 'Envy: or Yiddish in America', whose underlying theme is the conflict between traditional and modern culture and which caused some controversy in Jewish circles. *Bloodshed and Three Novellas* (1976) contained 'An Education', her first story, written in 1964, about a young woman, a brilliant classical scholar, who ultimately exchanges her youthful lost illusions for a mind of her own. After a third collection, *Levitations: Five Fictions* (1982), Ozick published her second novel, *The Cannibal Galaxy* (1983), in which she uses traditional Jewish narrative techniques and a Jewish day school to explore the nature of genius. In *The Messiah of Stockholm* (1987) she returned to one of her more predominant themes, redemption through literature. *The Shawl* (1989) is two stories centred on the Holocaust.

Though, as she asserts, 'I stopped writing my own poetry at around age 36,' she has recreated herself as a translator of Yiddish poetry, notably in Irving Howe and Eliezer Greenberg (eds), *A Treasury of Yiddish Poetry* (1969) and Irving Howe, Ruth Wisse, and Khone Shmeruk (eds), *The Penguin Book of Yiddish Verse* (1987). Highly regarded as a fiction writer who draws on Jewish textual tradition, she sees a writer as 'someone born with a gift. An athlete can run. A painter can paint. A writer has a facility with words. A good writer can also think.' To her, 'Jewish history is intellectual history and . . . can become the content of a writer's mind; but it isn't equal to a writer's mind.' Literary, sociological, and political essays are in *Art & Ardor* (1983), *Metaphor and Myth* (1989), and *Portrait of the Artist as a Bad Character: and Other Essays on Writing* (1994). *Fame and Folly* comprises 17 essays on writers and their works, and on the war between life and art. See *A Cynthia Ozick Reader*, ed. Elaine M. Kauvar, 1996 (poems, fiction, essays); Joseph Lowin, *Cynthia Ozick*, 1988 (biographical/critical study); Sanford Pinsker, *The Uncompromising Fiction of Cynthia Ozick*, 1987 (critical study).

P

PAGE, P(ATRICIA) K(ATHLEEN)
(*b.* 1916) Canadian poet and painter, was
born in England in Swanage, Dorset, and emigrated to Canada with her parents in 1919.
She was educated at St Hilda's School, Calgary, after which she worked in St John, New
Brunswick, as a sales assistant and radio actress, and wrote a short symbolic novel; it
was published several years later as *The Sun
and the Moon* (1944) by 'Judith Cape', and reissued under her own name in *The Sun and
the Moon, and Other Fictions* (1973). During
the 1940s she worked in Montreal as a filing
clerk and historical researcher, and then in
Ottawa as a writer for the National Film
Board. Her first book of verse was *As Ten as
Twenty* (1946). She married William Arthur
Irwin in 1950, and from 1953 to 1964 accompanied him on his postings as High Commissioner in Australia, and Ambassador to Brazil and then Mexico. *The Metal and the Flower*
(1954) won the Governor General's Award.
Though while she was away from Canada
she concentrated on drawing and painting
(as P. K. Irwin), to this period belong some
particularly evocative poems of temporary
exile, such as 'Cook's Mountains', 'Brazilian
Home', and 'Storm in Mexico'. *Evening Dance
of the Grey Flies* (1981) is her only subsequent
collection of new poems. *The Glass Air: Selected Poems* (1985) includes nine atmospheric
drawings and two essays: on the relationship
between writing and painting, and on the effect of visual images see also *The Glass Air:
Poems Selected and New* (1991). *Brazilian Journal* (1987) is an account of her time in that
country. She was made Officer, Order of Canada, in 1977. See John Orange, *P. K. Page and
Her Works*, 1994.

PAINE, THOMAS (1737–1809) British radical journalist, was born in Thetford, Norfolk,
the son of a Quaker corset maker, and was
educated at Thetford Grammar School. He
had a variety of jobs—corset maker, seaman
in a privateer, tobacconist, schoolmaster, and
exciseman. He was dismissed from the last
of these in 1774 after being commissioned to
write a pamphlet agitating for better pay and
conditions for excisemen. He went to
America and there published *Common Sense*
(1776), advocating independence from Britain, and a series of pamphlets under the gen-

eral title of *The Crisis*. After being rewarded
with a number of posts of state, he returned
to England in 1787, and wrote *Rights of Man:
Being an Answer to Mr Burke's Attack on the
French Revolution* (1791–92) in two parts: in
the second he took a broader view and proposed several far-reaching reforms. He was
forced, however, to take refuge in France,
where he was first elected to the National Assembly, and then imprisoned for 11 months
for proposing that Louis XVI should be given
asylum in America. Eventually, disgruntled
with French politics, he returned to America
in 1802, having in the meantime published
The Age of Reason (1794–95), a treatise on
deism, the anti-Christian aspects of which offended even his most fervent American supporters. He died in New York. In contrast to
BURKE's easy eloquence and close argument,
Paine's style is rather that of a crusading
journalist, plainer and more resounding. See
Thomas Paine Reader, ed. Michael Foot and
Isaac Kramnick, 1987; *Collected Writings*, ed.
Eric Foner, 1995; Jack Fruchtman, Jr, *Thomas
Paine: Apostle of Freedom*, new edn 1996 (biog-
raphy); John Keane, *Thomas Paine: a Political
Life*, new edn 1996; Gregory Claeys, *Thomas
Paine: Social and Political Thought*, 1989.

PALEY, GRACE (*b.* 1922), née Goodside,
American short-story writer, was born in
New York City of Jewish immigrant parents
from Russia, and grew up in the Bronx in a
home in which Russian and Yiddish were
spoken. She was educated at Evander Childs
High School and for a year at Hunter College;
she married Jess Paley when she was 19, and
had two children. She has taught English at
Sarah Lawrence College and City College,
New York. A 'political person', who has lived
in Chile and visited Vietnam, Nicaragua, and
China to observe conditions, and has been
closely involved in the Women's Pentagon
Action and other movements, she admits to
'writing about ordinary political people: I
think they've been abandoned in many ways,
as though they don't exist'. *The Little Disturbances of Man: Stories of Men and Women at
Love* (1959) introduces two (for much of their
time) single-parent narrators, Faith and Virginia, whose reappearances add a structural
dimension to her oeuvre, which she extended
with *Enormous Changes at the Last Minute*

(1974) and *Later the Same Day* (1985). Of the novel as a form, she has said: 'I can't write longer things—I try to write everything the right size, length and width—and depth, for what it is.' 'What it is' always demonstrates an understanding of children and adults of all ages and kinds, Gentile as well as Jew, an ear for dialogue, and a sense of comedy. Poetry is in *Begin Again: New and Collected Poems* (1992). She married Robert Nichols in 1972. See *The Collected Stories*, new edn 1995.

PALMER, VANCE (1885–1959) Australian novelist, short-story writer, and critic, was born in Bundaberg, Queensland, and educated at Ipswich Boys' Grammar School, after which he became a journalist. He freelanced for two years in London, returning to Australia via Finland, Siberia, and Japan, and then resorted to a variety of jobs in his home state. He went again to London, from which he returned in 1915 having married Janet Higgins, who as Nettie Palmer (1885–1964) became not only a helpmeet and sometimes the family breadwinner, but also a considerable literary critic in her own right. Palmer's philosophy, first publicly stated in an article in 1905, was the development of a national literature which would express the 'spirit' of Australia, and this he assiduously fostered through articles, reviews, and broadcasts. He was instrumental, with ESSON, in the establishment of the Pioneer Players in Melbourne in 1921–22, and himself wrote several notable one-act plays—see *The Black Horse and Other Plays* (1924)—as well as full-length comedies. His first published books were *The Forerunners* (1915), verse, and *The World of Men* (1915), short stories, a medium in which he excelled particularly when evoking the encroachment of the adult world on the consciousness of youth. His early novels, beginning with *The Shantykeeper's Daughter* (1920), were romances of station life or (as Rann Daly) of the South Seas. Latterly, with *The Passage* (1930), *The Swayne Family* (1934), and the 'Golconda' trilogy, culminating in *The Big Fellow* (1960), he succeeded in illuminating the Australian character in the context of its environment. See Vivian Smith, *Vance and Nettie Palmer*, 1975; Harry Heseltine, *Vance Palmer*, 1970 (critical study); and in David Walker, *Dream and Disillusion: a Search for Australian Cultural Identity*, 1976.

PARKER, DOROTHY (1893–1967), née Rothschild, American short-story writer, poet, and journalist, was born in West End, New Jersey, of an American-Jewish garment manufacturer and his Scottish wife, who died when she was in infancy. She was educated at a private school in New Jersey and at the Blessed Sacrament Convent, New York City. She started by composing captions for fashion pictures, and graduated to writing drama criticism for *Vanity Fair*, which sacked her for being too caustic in her reviews. She married a stockbroker, Edwin Pond Parker II, in 1917: they separated in 1919 and divorced in 1928. As 'Constant Reader' in the *New Yorker*, she found a regular outlet for her critical sense and outrageous wit from 1925 to 1927, when she went completely freelance. *Enough Rope* (1926) was the first of three collections of tart verses about brittle situations; underlying the humorous side is an essence of despair—she herself twice attempted suicide. In two volumes of short stories, *Laments for the Living* (1930) and *After Such Pleasures* (1933), she made especially effective use of the dramatic monologue. In 1933 she married a failed film actor, Alan Campbell (1905–63): they divorced in 1947, and remarried in 1950. During the 1930s they wrote together 15 successful Hollywood films, from which it is estimated they earned $500,000. Her alignment with Communism, in whose name she opposed Fascism and Nazi Germany, rebounded when she and her husband were blacklisted in the 1950s for un-American activities. She died as she had often been in her life, alone and in financial dificulties. Her put-downs are legendary and, many of them, timeless in their wit: 'Go to the Martin Beck Theatre and watch Katharine Hepburn [in Norman Macowan's *The Lake*] run the gamut of emotion from A to B' (1933). See *The Collected Dorothy Parker*, introduction by Brendan Gill, new edn 1989; Marion Meade, *Dorothy Parker: What Fresh Hell Is This?*, new edn 1991 (biography).

PASCAL, BLAISE (1623–62) French scientist and philosopher, was born in Clermont, lost his mother when he was three, and was educated by his father, a lawyer and civil servant, in Paris and Rouen. He is said to have worked out for himself at the age of 12 several of the geometrical propositions of Euclid (*fl. c.*300 BC). At 16 he published a treatise on conic sections; at 19 he invented a calculating machine; at 24 he became the first to describe the properties of the vacuum. In November 1654 he had a religious revelation, details of which he inscribed on parchment and wore round his neck for the rest of his life. He now began regular retreats at the Jansenist monastery, Port-Royal, whose differences of opinion with the Jesuits he supported in a series of 18 anonymous pamphlets, *Lettres Provinciales* (1656–57; tr. 1657). He died after a period of intense pain, probably caused by a congenital malformation of the skull. Notes for a defence of the Christian religion were collected and published by his friends as *Pensées* [Thoughts] (1669; tr. J. Walker, 1688; tr. A. J. Krailsheimer, 1966), which subsequent editors have arranged according to various plans—see also *Pensées and Other Writings*, tr. Honor Levi, ed. Anthony Levi (1995).

PASTERNAK, BORIS (LEONIDOV-ICH) (1890–1960) Russian poet, novelist, critic, and translator, was born in Moscow of Jewish parents, his father being a painter (and illustrator of TOLSTOY) and his mother a musician. After gymnasium he read law at Moscow University, from which he took a year off to study philosophy at Marburg University. Initially a Futurist poet, he published a collection, [Twin in the Clouds], in 1914, and another, [Above the Barriers], in 1917, when, unfit for army service because of a leg broken in childhood, he was working in a chemical factory in the Urals. He was then an apolitical poet, whose first significant collection, [My Sister—Life] (1922; tr. Mark Rudman with Bohdan Boychuck, 1983), included poems of love and of nature composed in 1917 and 1918 while the nation was at its most disorderly—long poems of revolutionary awareness written during the 1920s are far less poetically inspired. He published a volume of stories in 1925, and in 1931 an autobiographical sketch, [Safe Conduct] (tr. Beatrice Scott in Prose and Poems, ed. Stefan Schimanski, rev. edn 1959), which concludes with the death of MAYAKOVSKY. His fifth collection of verse, [Second Birth] (1932), in which he celebrated his meeting his second wife, was his last new original work to appear for ten years, during which he conducted what he termed his 'long silent duel' with Stalin, and earned his living by translation, including some distinguished versions of plays of SHAKESPEARE.

Latterly he put all his literary effort into his poetic novel, [Dr Zhivago], an expression of resurrection after destruction, even of a man's belief in himself, which covers the period before, during, and after the Revolution of 1917; it ends with the poems of his protagonist, reflecting his own personal view of the events. It was published in Italy in 1957, and in English (tr. Manya Harari and Max Hayward) in 1958, when he was awarded the Nobel Prize for Literature. In the political uproar and campaign of personal vilification which followed, including his expulsion from the Writers' Union, he declined the award. See Selected Poems, tr. Jon Stallworthy and Peter France, new edn 1991; An Essay in Autobiography, tr. Manya Harari, with Poems 1955–1959, 1990; Peter Levi, Pasternak, new edn 1991 (biography); Evgeny Pasternak, Boris Pasternak: the Tragic Years 1930–1960, tr. Michael Duncan, poetry tr. Ann Pasternak Slater and Craig Raine, new edn 1991.

PASTON, JOHN (1421–66) English gentleman and letter writer, the son of a judge, was probably born on the family estate in Norfolk, and was educated at Trinity Hall and Peterhouse, Cambridge. He then studied law, which he used to good effect in many property deals and other legal ploys, including the administration of the estate of the wealthy Sir John Fastolf (c.1378–1459), to which he also claimed to be the heir. He was twice elected Member of Parliament for Norfolk, and three times committed to the Fleet prison in London. He married the heiress Margaret Mautly (d. 1484); their two eldest sons were (Sir) John (1442–1479), courtier, and (Sir) John (1444–1503), soldier. The collection of letters between the four of them especially, but also to and from other members of the family, friends, business acquaintances, estate managers, clerks, and their womenfolk, was begun by John Paston, who kept files of them for business purposes. After the death in 1732 of William Paston, 2nd Earl of Yarmouth and last of the line, the correspondence passed through various hands until it was acquired by the antiquary Sir John Fenn (1739–94), who published a selection in 1787. Most of the letters were written between 1460 and 1480; they reveal not only the liveliness and clarity of expression with which both men and women of the time corresponded, but also the hazards of keeping hold of one's property in the face of lawless usurpers, the details of the day-to-day management of estates, the complexities and strains of family life, and the protracted negotiations required to secure a favourable marriage or avert an unfavourable one. See Norman Davis (ed.), The Paston Letters, 1983 (selection in modern spelling); H. S. Bennett, The Pastons and Their England, new edn 1990.

PATER, WALTER (1839–94) British critic and novelist, was born in Shadwell, east London, the son of a doctor, who died when the boy was five. His mother died soon after he entered King's School, Canterbury, and the four children were put in the charge of an aunt—'The Child in the House' (1878), his first published short story, may reflect his own homesickness when young. He went to The Queen's College, Oxford, intending to become a clergyman, and was persisting with the idea even after a loss of faith, when a friend denounced him to the Bishop of London. He read classics, and studied German philosophy on his own account, after which, though his degree was only second class, he was in 1864 elected a Fellow of Brasenose College. From 1869, when he was not in Oxford (and sometimes when he was meant to be) or travelling abroad, he lived with his two sisters in London. The end of an anonymous article on MORRIS in the Westminster Review, including the injunction, 'To burn always with this hard gem-like flame, to maintain this ecstasy, is success in life', appeared as the 'Conclusion' to his Studies in the History of the Renaissance (1873), and caused quite a stir. There was less controversy about, and much to admire in, the rest of the work, in which occurs the memorable description of the 'Mona Lisa' of Leonardo da Vinci (1452–1519), which YEATS printed as poetry as the opening item in *The Oxford Book of Modern Verse* (1936). *Marius the Epicurean* (1885), a novel tracing the spiritual progress of a young Roman, was to be the first of three philosophical romances, but only part of a second, 'Gaston De Latour', was written. *Imaginary Portraits* (1887) comprises four fictionalized projections of his ideas. *Appreciations* (1889) is a collection of his critical articles in literary periodicals. As teacher as well as critic, he was a reluctant but respected leader of the artistic taste of his times. See *Essays in Literature and Art*, ed. Jennifer Uglow, new edn 1990; Denis Donoghue, *Walter Pater: Lover of Strange Souls*, 1995 (critical biography); Laurel Brake, *Walter Pater*, 1995 (critical introduction).

PATERSON, A(NDREW) B(ARTON), 'BANJO' (1864–1941) Australian poet, was born on Narramba station, near Molong, New South Wales. He was educated at Sydney Grammar School, and qualified as a solicitor of the Supreme Court of New South Wales. He had already published, as 'The Banjo', some popular bush ballads of his own composition, including 'Clancy of the Overflow' and 'The Man from Snowy River', when in 1892 LAWSON, who took a more realistic view of the outback, challenged him to a verse contest in the *Bulletin*. *The Man from Snowy River and Other Verses* (1895) extended his reputation (the first impression sold out within a week), from which point the fabulous ethos of his verse was reflected in his personal life. He went hunting, shooting, and pearl diving. As war correspondent in 1901 he covered the opening shots of the Boer War in South Africa, then travelled to China to write up the Boxer Rebellion. He edited the Sydney *Evening News* from 1904 to 1906, and the *Town and Country Journal* in 1907–08. When he was unable (now being in his fifties) to get to the front as a correspondent in World War I, he returned to Australia and then served in Egypt, with the rank of major, as remount officer to the Australian Light Horse. His *Saltbush Bill, J. P.* (1917), which included 'Waltzing Matilda', an Australian national song, was issued to Australian soldiers as recreational reading. After the war he edited the Sydney *Sportsman*, and pursued his sporting passions, notably for the turf, about which he wrote authoritatively and well. He also published two novels, *An Outback Marriage* (1906) and *The Shearer's Colt* (1936), as well as *Three Elephant Power, and Other Stories* (1917). His compilation, *The Old Bush Songs, Composed and Sung in the Bushranging, Digging and Overlanding Days* (1905; rev. edn 1930), testifies to the research which informs his own verse. He was made OBE in 1939. See *Singer of the Bush* and *Song of the Pen*, ed. Rosamund Campbell and Philippa Harvie, 1983 (complete works); *The Penguin Banjo Paterson*, ed. Clement Semmler, 1993; Clement Semmler, *The Banjo of the Bush: the Work, Life and Times of A. B. Paterson*, 2nd edn 1984; Colin Roderick, *Banjo Paterson: Poet by Accident*, 1993 (biography).

PATMORE, COVENTRY (1823–96) British poet and critic, was born in Woodford, Essex, and educated privately without any thought to a career, though his journalist father was unable to support him at university. *Poems* (1844) contained several narrative works which impressed members of the Pre-Raphaelites. In 1846 his father's speculations failed, and he obtained a post in the printed book department of the British Museum, feeling sufficiently comfortable in 1847 to marry. The union inspired two sequences of narrative poems extolling married love in a Victorian upper-middle-class milieu: *The Betrothal* (1854) and *The Espousals* (1856), published together as *The Angel in the House*. Some of the main characters reappear in two further verse novels, *Faithful for Ever* (1860) and its sequel, *The Victories of Love* (1863). His wife died in 1862, after having had six children, and in 1864 he married again and became a Catholic. After the death of his second wife, he married his children's governess. In *The Unknown Eros, and Other Odes* (1877), a tendency towards mystical eroticism becomes religious eroticism. There are a number of his poems, notably 'Departure' and 'The Toys', in which he records, without symbolism, normal human reactions to domestic crises, the emotions being enhanced by the metrical form he devised for his odes, in which longer and very short lines are supported by an irregular rhyme scheme. Though he admired the work of TENNYSON, and ROBERT BROWNING and RUSKIN were close friends, his criticism and reviews, collected in *Principle in Art* (1889) and *Religio Poetae* (1893), suffer from an inability to appreciate fully anyone's work but his own—see also *Bow in the Cloud: Selected Essays*, ed. Antony Matthew, (1996).

PATON, ALAN (1903–88) South African novelist, was born in Pietermaritzburg, the eldest child of a Scottish Christadelphian shorthand writer to the Supreme Court and of a teacher of English descent. He was educated at Maritzburg College and Natal University College, after which he taught at Ixopo High School and then at Maritzburg College. In 1935, after nearly dying of salmonella poisoning, he became Principal of Diepkloof Reformatory, Johannesburg, where he remained until he resigned in 1948 to write full time. In 1946, on a mission to examine prison conditions in Sweden, he took time off to see the country of HAMSUN, where a chance visit to Trondheim Cathedral inspired *Cry, the Beloved Country* (1948), the first chapter of which he wrote before dinner that evening. This lyrical and powerful novel, suggesting a Christian resolution of the problem of race, was as influential within South Africa as it was in promoting an awareness abroad of the country's political policies. *Too Late the Phalarope* (1953) explores the essence of the Afrikaner upbringing and the tragic consequences of one man's natural proclivities. In 1953 he resigned as Honorary Commissioner in South Africa for Toc H, to which he had devoted much of the previous 25 years, for its refusal to give up its colour bar. In the same year he helped to found the nonracial Liberal Party, of which he was President from 1958 until it was banned in 1968. He continued to advocate individual freedom and racial equality. He published a book of short stories, *Debbie Go Home* (1961). Among his non-fiction works are *Kontakion for You Departed* (1969), a moving examination of his relationship with his first wife, who died in 1967, and of the structure of marriage; *Instrument of Thy Peace: Meditations Prompted by the Prayer of St Francis* (1968), a series of religious reflections; and substantial biographies of Jan Hofmeyer (1964) and Archbishop Clayton (1973). See *Knocking on the Door: Shorter Writings*, ed. Colin Gardner, 1975; *Towards the Mountain*, new edn 1986, and *Journey Continued*, new edn 1989 (autobiography); Peter F. Alexander, *Alan Paton: a Biography*, new edn 1996.

PATTEN, BRIAN see MCGOUGH.

PATTERSON, ORLANDO (b. 1940) Jamaican-born novelist and sociologist, was born in Westmoreland, Jamaica, and educated at Kingston College and the University of the West Indies, after which he studied sociology at the London School of Economics. He was appointed a professor of sociology at Harvard University in 1971, and is now an American citizen. In his first, and most significant, novel, *The Children of Sisyphus* (1964), the plight of the inhabitants of a Kingston slum and the search for a viable existence are seen alongside Rastafarian idealism. There is an existential theme also to *An Absence of Ruins* (1967). *The Sociology of Slavery: an Analysis of the Origins, Development, and Structure of Negro Slave Society in Jamaica* (1967), a study of the forces behind the society which evolved, can be read as background to his and other Jamaican novels. *Freedom, Volume One: Freedom in the Making of Western Culture* (1991) won the US National Book Award: the second volume, *Freedom in the Modern World*, was published in 1992.

PAUSANIAS see DOBSON; LEVI; FRAZER.

PAVESE, CESARE (1908–50) Italian novelist, poet, critic, and translator, was born in Santo Stefano Belbro and educated at the Liceo Massimo d'Azeglio, Turin, and Turin University, where he wrote a thesis on WHITMAN. His preoccupation with American literature continued with translations of SINCLAIR LEWIS, MELVILLE, ANDERSON, DOS PASSOS, and STEIN, and is reflected in the conversational style of his first book of verse (1936), published while he was confined by the Fascists in Calabria for having a girlfriend who was a Communist. At the end of World War II, during which he worked for the publisher Einaudi in Turin, he joined the Communist Party, without being able to reconcile his commitment with his creative instincts. The latter prevailed in the social realism of the novels *Il Compagno* (1947; tr. W. J. Strachan as *The Comrade*, 1959) and *La Casa in Collina* (1949; tr. Strachan as *The House on the Hill*, 1956), and in short stories set in and around contemporary Turin—see *The Leather Jacket: Stories*, ed. Margaret Crosland, tr. Alma Murch (1980). His most complete statement of the conflict between traditional innocence and modern values, *La Luna e i Falò* (1950; tr. Louise Sinclair as *The Moon and the Bonfire*, 1952), set in a Piedmontese country environment which has survived the war unchanged, was also his last. He was caught up in yet another disastrous love affair, this time with an American actress, for whom he wrote some fine verse—see *Selected Poems*, tr. Crosland (1971). When other things went wrong, too, he killed himself in a hotel room near Turin station.

PAZ, OCTAVIO (b. 1914) Mexican poet and critic, was born in Mexico City, the son of a lawyer, from whom he inherited his interest in social and political causes. Educated by French Marist fathers, he had his first poem published when he was 17, and his first book of verse, in an edition of 65 copies, in 1933. In 1936 he gave up his studies at the University of Mexico and went to Yucatan, where he set up a school in a poor rural area. The following year, at the invitation of NERUDA, he visited Spain, where what he witnessed of the Civil War led him to question his views on Marxism. Back in Mexico in 1938 he founded the literary review *Taller*, of whose group of poets he was the most prominent, and edited the journal *El Hijo Pródigo* from 1943 to 1945. He then joined the Diplomatic Service, his first posting being as cultural attaché in Paris, where he became associated with the Surrealist movement. He subsequently served as Chargé d'Affaires in Japan, and as Ambassador to India from 1962 to 1968, when he resigned in protest at his government's suppression of the student demonstration before the Olympic Games in Mexico. He then held visiting professorships at Cambridge and Harvard.

His first books to appear in English were *Piedra de Sol* (1957; tr. Muriel Rukeyser as *Sun Stone*, 1963), an elaborately structured exploration of cosmological, personal, and social philosophies, and *Selected Poems*, tr. Rukeyser (1963). He was awarded the Nobel Prize for

Literature in 1990, for 'his impassioned writing with wide horizons, characterized by sensuous intelligence and humanistic energy', not only in verse, but also in prose—mention was made of *El Laberinto de la Soledad* (1950; tr. Lysander Kemp in *The Labyrinth of Solitude and Other Essays*, 1962), in which he explores his identity as a Mexican 'and in a broader meaning as a Latin American'. Further critical essays are in *On Poets and Others*, tr. Michael Schmidt (1987), and *The Other Voice*, tr. Helen Lane (1992). *The Double Flame: Essays on Love and Eroticism*, tr. Lane (1996) began, he explains, in 1965 as a little volume on love, when he had fallen into the condition in India. It was finally completed in 1993 as a study of the context of human love and the soul ('eroticism'). *Selected Poems* (1979) contains translations by BISHOP and TOMLINSON. See *Collected Poems 1957–1987*, ed. Eliot Weinberger, new edn 1994 (bilingual edn).

P'BITEK, OKOT (1931–82) Ugandan poet and critic, was born in Gulu, Acoli, the son of a schoolmaster, and was educated at Gulu High School, King's College, Budo (where he composed and produced a full-length opera), and Government Teacher Training College, Mbarara. At 22 he published a novel in the Luo language of Acoli, and began 'Wer pa Lawino' [Song of Lawino], a protest poem in the persona of an Acoli wife abandoned for a 'modern' woman. An athlete as well as a scholar, he toured Britain with the Ugandan national soccer team in 1956, and stayed on to take a certificate of education at Bristol University and a degree in law at the University of Wales; he then obtained the degree of BLitt at Oxford with a thesis, 'Oral Literature and Its Background among the Acoli and Lango' (1963). Back in Uganda he lectured in sociology at Makerere University College, published an English version of *Song of Lawino* (1966), completed the Luo version (published 1969), and became Director of the Uganda National Theatre and Cultural Centre, Kampala. Dismissed from his post (apparently for political implications in *Song of Lawino*), he went to Kenya, where he taught at the University College of Nairobi and in 1968 founded the Kisumu Arts Festival. He died shortly after taking up the post of Professor of Creative Writing at Makerere University. For *Song of Lawino*, which is both pungent and witty, he invented a form of verse based on the oral tradition. It was reissued (1984) with *Song of Ocol* (1970), a male response. *Two Songs: Song of a Prisoner, Song of Malaya* (1971) are more overtly political. His critical works include the trenchant *African Religions in Western Scholarship* (1970), and a collection of equally outspoken essays, *Africa's Cultural Revolution*, introduction by Ngugi Wa Thiong'o (1973). See G. A. Heron, *The Poetry of Okot p'Bitek*, 1976.

PEABODY, ELIZABETH see HAWTHORNE; THOREAU.

PEACOCK, THOMAS LOVE (1785–1866) British novelist and poet, was born in Weymouth, Dorset, the son of a London glass merchant, who died in 1788. The boy and his mother went to live in Surrey with her father, Captain Love. He was educated privately until he was 13, after which he followed his own disposition. He had published four books of verse when in 1812 he met P. B. SHELLEY and became a close friend and member of his circle, handling Shelley's affairs when he left England in 1818, and being joint executor with BYRON on his death. 1818 was the year, too, in which *Nightmare Abbey* appeared, the third—after *Headlong Hall* (1816, anonymously) and *Melincourt* (1817)—of his strain of satirical conversation pieces lightly veiled as novels. Also in 1818 he at last found a congenial job, with the East India Company, where he became Assistant to the Examiner of Correspondence, and ultimately Chief Examiner in succession to MILL's father. In 1829 he outlined a proposal for sending the India mail by steamship to Syria, overland to the Upper Euphrates, by paddle-steamer to Basra, and then by steamship again. He retired in 1856, having informed a House of Commons Select Committee on Steam Navigation that he was 'not aware that it would be any benefit to the people of India to send Europeans amongst them' because of the potentially destructive effect on Indian morals and domestic habits. He wrote two further satirical novels, *Crotchet Castle* (1831) and *Gryll Grange* (1861), and two amusing historical romances. He was only a minor poet, but a fine versifier. *The Four Ages of Poetry* (1820), an ironical detraction of the Romantics, prompted Shelley's *Defence of Poetry*. Peacock's *Memoirs of Percy Bysshe Shelley* (1858–62) contains a vivid re-creation of the poet. In 1819, remembering a young woman he had met on a trip to Wales in 1811 but had had no contact with since, he wrote to her proposing marriage. She accepted, and he became in due course MEREDITH's father-in-law. See *The Complete Peacock*, ed. David Garnett, new edn (with foreword by Lord Blake) 1989; Marilyn Butler, *Peacock Displayed: a Satirist in His Context*, 1979.

PEAKE, MERVYN (1911–68) British novelist, poet, and artist, was born in Kuling, China, the son of a Congregationalist medical missionary, and was educated at Tientsin Grammar School, and then Eltham College, Kent, and the Royal Academy Schools. He taught life drawing at the Westminster School of Art from 1935 to 1939, and in 1937 married the artist, Maeve Gilmore, who subsequently wrote a biography of him (1970) and edited collections of his writings and drawings. A nervous breakdown during

World War II led to his being invalided out of the Army and appointed a war artist. In 1949, after three years in Sark, which is the setting of his novel, *Mr Pye* (1953), he returned to England with his family, whom he supported precariously by teaching part time and by writing, painting, and illustrating, until he became incapacitated by the onset of Parkinson's disease at the age of 46. The first of several volumes of his poetry was *Shapes and Sounds* (1941). His major literary work is the trilogy, *Titus Groan* (1946), *Gormenghast* (1950), and *Titus Alone* (1959), in which he projects a fantastical, grotesque, and symbolic world, full of fears and horrors, whose people respond in different ways to the ancient rituals which dominate them. Part of the experience which led to the creation of such a setting and situation was the visit he was commissioned to make to Belsen concentration camp shortly after its liberation. Among his most memorable illustrations are those for CARROLL's *The Hunting of the Snark* and COLERIDGE's *The Rime of the Ancient Mariner*.

PEARSE, PATRICK (1879–1916) Irish poet and patriot, was born in Dublin and educated by the Christian Brothers in Westland Row, and at University College, Dublin, qualifying also as BL in 1901. He was Editor of the Gaelic League's weekly journal from 1903 to 1909, when he gave up the post to concentrate on St Enda's School, which he had founded in 1908. He continued, as a journalist and public speaker, to campaign for Irish to be more widely used and for the development of Gaelic as a medium of modern literature. To this end he also wrote plays (mainly for performance by St Enda's), short stories, and poetry. The Gaelic lyrics in *Suantraidhe agus Goltraidhe* [Songs of Sleep and Sorrow] (1914) are regarded as superior to his English poems, of which 'The Rebel' and 'The Fool' in particular have a relevance to the forthcoming explosion of violence, just as 'Renunciation' refers to the inevitability of its outcome for him. He saw force as the only means by which Ireland could become separate, and as President of the Republic's provisional government read out its proclamation on the steps of the General Post Office in Dublin at the time of the Easter Rising in 1916. He was executed by a British firing squad, as were also two other promising poets, Thomas MacDonagh (1878–1916) and Joseph Mary Plunkett (1887–1916). See *The 1916 Poets: the Collected Poetry of Padraic H. Pearse, Thomas MacDonagh and Joseph M. Plunkett*, ed. Desmond Ryan, new edn 1995; Ruth Dudley Edwards, *Patrick Pearse: the Triumph of Failure*, new edn 1990.

PEARSON, BILL [WILLIAM HARRISON] (b. 1922) New Zealand novelist and critic, was born in Greymouth and educated at Greymouth Technical High School, Canterbury University College, and Otago University. After serving with the New Zealand forces in the Far and Middle East and in Europe during and immediately after World War II, and beginning a career as a teacher, he went to London, where he studied for a PhD degree at King's College and taught for a year in London County Council schools. While he was there, he wrote for *Landfall* (September 1952) a trenchant piece, 'Fretful Sleepers: a Sketch of New Zealand Behaviour and its Implications for the Artist'—reprinted in his collection, *Fretful Sleepers and Other Essays* (1974). In the course of it he cites MEYNELL's condescension to colonials in an article in *Merry England* (October 1891), and concludes: 'The solution for us is to look to the here and now . . . , to concentrate on the very things she might have called vulgar, and develop them to the point where they mean something to people outside New Zealand, to make a meaning out of the drives and behaviour of common people.' In his only work of fiction, *Coal Flat* (1963; rev. edn 1970), he did precisely that. Set in 1947 in a West Coast mining town whose activities centre on the school, the pub, the mine, and the dance hall, it is a bleak, pessimistic, but enthralling study of a self-contained society. See also *Six Stories* (1991). Pearson was Lecturer in English, Auckland University 1954–66, and Associate Professor from 1970 to his retirement, having in the meantime been Senior Research Fellow, Australian National University. Other prose works are *Henry Lawson among Maoris* (1968) and *Rifled Sanctuaries: Some Views of the Pacific Islands in Western Literature to 1900* (1984). See article by CURNOW, 'Coal Flat Revisited' (1975), in Cherry Hankin (ed.), *Critical Essays on the New Zealand Novel*, 1982.

PEELE, GEORGE (1556–96) English dramatist and poet, was born in London, the son of James Peele, Clerk of Christ's Hospital, who wrote books on accountancy and city pageants. After being a free scholar at Christ's Hospital, he was educated at Broadgates Hall and Christ Church, Oxford, graduating as MA in 1579. An Oxford friend commented (in Latin) on his propensity for mixing serious matters with lively jokes or japes, which would appear to be justified by the publication in 1607 of *Merrie Conceited Jests of George Peele*, in the manner of such books of the time, which should not be regarded as autobiographical. In 1579 the governors of Christ's Hospital ordered Peele senior to 'discharge his house of his son George'. Further details about his life are mainly speculative, but he was clearly one of the university wits who brought a sense of form, as well as poetry and passion, to Elizabethan drama, and whatever his personal characteristics, Peele was a bold and versatile dramatist. *The*

Araygnement of Paris (printed 1584) is a Greek pastoral with a surprising, and topical, climax. *The Battell of Alcazar* (performed *c*.1589) is a historically-inspired romantic tragedy. *The Famous Chronicle of King Edwarde the First* (printed 1593) was in the new tradition of the English chronicle play. *The Love of King David and Fair Bethsabe* (performed *c*.1593) has been termed 'a kind of mystery play'. *The Old Wives Tale* (printed 1595) has recently emerged from its designation as a mangled fragment to be seen as a thoroughly ingenious piece of lyrical stagecraft. Outside his plays, much of Peele's verse was written to order, for pageants and other occasions. He is believed to have died destitute. See *The Life and Works of George Peele*, ed. D. H. Horne, F. S. Hook, and John Yoklavich, 3 vols 1952–70.

PENNANT, THOMAS see WHITE, GILBERT.

PEPYS, SAMUEL (1633–1703) English diarist, was born in the City of London, the son of a tailor, and was educated at St Paul's School and Magdalene College, Cambridge. He came of modest immediate family (his father was the third son of a third son and had married a London washmaid), but his father's first cousin, Edward Montagu (1625–1672), later Lord Sandwich, gave him a post in his household. Through this, and by his own abilities, he rose to positions of great influence in the country, including Treasurer to Tangier 1665–79, Secretary to the Admiralty 1673–79, Member of Parliament for Harwich 1685–89, King's Secretary for Naval Affairs 1684–89, and President of the Royal Society 1684–86. His diary runs from 1 January 1660 (the year of the Restoration of the Monarchy) to 31 May 1669, when he discontinued it because of eyestrain, from which he recovered. Written largely in shorthand, it was first deciphered in 1825, but was not published in full until edited by Robert Latham and William Matthews (11 vols 1970–83). It complements EVELYN's diary in that it is a very personal (and frank) narrative, written up from rough notes (but always within a few days of the events), and not revised. Racy and colloquial, it is the richest possible record not just of a tumultuous age, an exciting society, and the minutiae of private and public life, but of a brilliant and likable man's activities and interests and his huge enjoyment of them. His lively but long-suffering wife Elizabeth, the daughter of a Huguenot refugee, whom he had married in 1655 when she was 15, died in 1669. They had no children, and he never remarried. See Richard Ollard, *Pepys: a Biography*, new edn 1993 of rev. edn 1991.

PERCY, THOMAS (1729–1811) British antiquary, poet, and cleric, was born in Bridgnorth, Shropshire, the son of a grocer and, according to BOSWELL, was indubitably of direct descent from the family of Percy, earls of Northumberland. He was educated at Bridgnorth Grammar School and Christ Church, Oxford, and was in 1753 presented with the college living of Easton Maudit, Northumberland, where he remained for 29 years, collecting also the posts of chaplain to the Duke of Northumberland and to the King, and in 1778 becoming Dean of Carlisle. His literary interests and enquiring mind led him to publish in 1761, as 'a curious specimen of Chinese literature', *Hau Kiou Choaan: or, The Pleasing History*, the first appearance in a European language of a Chinese novel. Done from translations, it had voluminous apparatuses, compiled by himself. *Five Pieces of Runic Poetry Translated from the Islandic Language* (1763) was done so carefully and exactly that he avoided the suspicions which were now being attached to MACPHERSON's 'Ossian'. In about 1758 he received from a friend a priceless folio manuscript volume of ballads. With the encouragement and advice of authorities such as WARTON, he used this as the basis of *Reliques of Ancient English Poetry* (1765), which reflects his judgment and literary flair and exercised considerable influence on contemporary taste, as well as popularizing the ballad form. In 1782 he was appointed Bishop of Dromore, Ireland, where he did his job vigorously and spent the rest of his long life. Of him, JOHNSON wrote in 1778, in an open letter of apology for an unintentional affront: 'He is a man very willing to learn, and very able to teach; a man out of whose company I never go without having learned something.'

PERELMAN, S(IDNEY) J(OSEPH) (1904–79) American humorist, journalist, and dramatist, was born in Brooklyn of Russian-Jewish immigrant parents. He was brought up in Providence, Rhode Island, where his father became a poultry farmer after several business failures, one of which had been to back a Yiddish musical version of WALTER SCOTT's *The Heart of Midlothian*. He won first prize in a national essay contest sponsored by *American Boy* in 1917, the year he entered the Classical High School, Providence. At Brown University he met NATHANAEL WEST, whose sister Laura (*d.* 1970) he married in 1929. *Dawn Ginsbergh's Revenge* (1929), a collection of prose and cartoons, carried a quote from Groucho Marx (1890–1977): 'From the moment I picked up your book until I laid it down, I was convulsed with laughter. Someday I intend reading it.' *Strictly from Hunger* (1937) was the first of several collections of pieces from the *New Yorker*, to which he began contributing in 1931. In common with many writers, he rented his talents to Hollywood, initially as co-author of the Marx brothers' film, *Monkey Business* (1931), the first (subsequently rejected) script of which he was called upon to read to the four brothers, their wives and appendages (all just arrived in Los Angeles after four days in a train), sundry hangers-on, and five dogs. The starting points of his essays are most frequently daily life and the hazards of house ownership; the theatre and film worlds; travel, of which he became an inveterate and veteran exponent; and other people's commercial or literary writings—one of his most subtle pieces, 'Anna Trivia Pluralized', in *Baby, It's Cold Outside* (1970), is a parody of JOYCE and Joycean scholarship. See *The Most of S. J. Perelman*, introduction by Dorothy Parker, new edn 1991; *The Last Laugh*, 1981 (unfinished autobiography and sketches).

PÉREZ GALDÓS, BENITO (1843–1920) Spanish novelist and dramatist, was born in Las Palmas, Canary Islands, and went to Colegio San Agustin. When he was 19, his mother sent him to study law at Madrid University to keep him apart from the illegitimate daughter of her brother's American ex-mistress, with whom he had fallen in love. From university, he joined the editorial staff of *La Nación*, which in 1868 printed his translations of DICKENS's *Pickwick Papers*. He published his first novel in 1870, thereafter classifying his extensive fictional oeuvre under 'Episodios Nacionales'—five sequences of historical novels from the battle of Trafalgar (1815) to the restoration of the Bourbon dynasty in Spain (1874); and 'Novelas Español Contemporáneas'—socially-orientated explorations of aspects of 19th-century Spain comprising idealistic, psychological, and naturalistic novels. In the naturalistic vein is *Fortunata y Jacinta* (1886–87; tr. Agnes Moncy Gullón as *Fortunata and Jacinta*, 1973), a study of sexual mores and class distinctions, which is regarded as his greatest work. Some of his most successful plays were adaptations of his own novels. The petty antagonism that he evoked in his own country culminated in his nomination for the Nobel Prize for Literature in 1912 being set aside by the committee. The award, which he had earned, would have resolved some of his personal financial difficulties (he abjured marriage as an incitement to infidelity, and instead preached, and practised, free love), and alleviated the blindness from which he suffered for the last eight years of his life.

PERKINS, MAXWELL see ROTH, HENRY; WOLFE, THOMAS.

PESSOA, FERNANDO (1888–1935) Portuguese poet, was born in Lisbon and (his father having died) was brought up in South Africa, where his stepfather was a Portuguese consul and where he went to Durban High School. After returning to Lisbon when he was 17 and studying for a year at Lisbon University, he continued for a time to write in English, in which he published *Antinous*, 35

Sonnets (1918). He earned a modest living by writing letters in English and French for Lisbon businesses, involved himself in literary affairs, and wrote poetry. His inspirational breakthrough came in 1914, when he invented three alternative personae, Ricardo Reis, Alberto Cueiro, and Álvaro de Campos, under each of which, and his own name, he freely composed Portuguese verses of a different nature. In spite of a cooperative output of several hundred complete poems, the only book of verse in his native language to be published in his lifetime was *Mensagem* [Message] (1934), 44 patriotic pieces. He died of cirrhosis. See *A Centenary Pessoa*, ed. Eugénio Lisboa and L. C. Taylor, tr. Keith Bosley and others, 1995; *Selected Poems*, tr. Jonathan Griffin, new edn 1996.

PETRARCH (FRANCESCO PETRARCA) (1304–74) Italian poet and scholar, was born in Arezzo, where his father, a notary, had settled after being exiled from Florence in 1302, a few months after DANTE. From there he moved to Carpentras in France, near the papal court at Avignon, which was effectively the focus of the medieval world and, until 1353, the point from which Petrarch began his many journeys. He studied law at Montpellier University from the age of 12, and at Bologna from 1320 to 1326, when he returned to Avignon, took minor orders, and embarked on a literary career, subsidized by patrons and by the income from benefices. One of his earliest tasks was to reconstruct LIVY's history of Rome, of which his is the first critical edition. In 1337 he made his own contribution to Roman history, *De Viris Illustribus* [On Famous Men], and, after discovering CICERO's letters in Verona, embarked on an equivalent corpus of correspondence in Latin. In 1333 he conceived an epic poem after the style of VIRGIL, *Africa*, celebrating the exploits of Scipio Africanus (234–183 BC), which he later abandoned. He was, however, still at the beginning of his career, and had written only a few poems in Italian (at that time not considered a suitable vehicle for literature), when in 1341 he was formally crowned in Rome (with a laurel wreath) as poet laureate. His Latin works, which include philosophical treatises and dialogues, brought him international renown, especially after the development of printing in the 1460s.

Petrarch's local fame and confirmed position in literary posterity spring from his sighting, in the church of St Clare in Avignon on 6 April 1327, the lady he appropriately calls Laura, who died, by his own account, at precisely the same time on the same day of the same month, 21 years later. Whether she existed or not, and she has been identified with Laure, wife of Hugo de Sade (a remote ancestor of SADE), who died of the plague in 1348, having had 11 children, she is the subject of the 366 lyrics of *Canzoniere*, originally known as *Rerum Vulgarium Fragmenta* [Vernacular Fragments] (tr. R. M. Durling as *Petrarch's Lyric Poems*, 1976; tr. Mark Musa, 1996), and the further inspiration for the six longer poems comprising *Trionfi* (tr. Ernest H. Wilkins as *The Triumphs of Petrarch*, 1962); all first printed together in 1470. The metrical sequence within *Canzoniere* is the source of the English sonnet form introduced by WYATT, and Elizabethan poetry abounds in the kind of conceit which Petrarch used in proclaiming the virtues and beauties of his love. Latterly he abandoned Avignon and his estate at Vaucluse for Milan. After 1361 he lived in Venice, Pavia, and Padua, channelling his literary energies into the composition of further letters, in which (as in all his work) the personal and the universal are linked, and he complains variously about his private condition and the state of the world. From these he selected 128 for posterity, to add to those he had written earlier. He died in a house he had built in Arqua, having made provision in his will to be buried in the seven different places in which he reckoned he might die. See *Selections from the Canzoniere and Other Works*, tr. Mark Musa, 1985; Nicholas Mann, *Petrarch*, 1984 (introduction to the man and his works).

PETRONIUS, GAIUS (*d.* 66) Roman novelist, was proconsul of Bithynia and then consul in Rome (62), before becoming organizer of Nero's personal revels, in which capacity he was also known as Petronius Arbiter, from his job title of *Elegantiae Arbiter* [Judge of Taste]. *Satyricon* is the original picaresque novel, a bisexual odyssey of two men and their boy round the towns of southern Italy. Only fragments survive, including 'Trimalchio's Dinner Party', which splendidly exhibits the manners of the nouveaux riches. Petronius, victim of one of Nero's periodic purges, died in style. According to TACITUS he bled himself slowly to death, while making conversation, eating, and sleeping, having written down 'a classified list of Nero's most disgraceful acts with male as well as female partners, and their names, which he sent to the emperor under seal'. T. S. ELIOT's *The Waste Land* has as its epigraph a quotation from the *Satyricon* about the Sibyl of Cumae. See *Satyrica*, tr. R. Bracht Branham and Daniel Kinney, 1996; *The Satyricon*, tr. P. G. Walsh, 1996.

PHILIPS, AMBROSE (1674–1749) British poet, was born in Shropshire and educated at Shrewsbury School and, as a sizar, at St John's College, Cambridge, of which he was a Fellow from 1699 to 1708. He was then employed for a time in Denmark, from which he addressed 'Epistle to the Earl of Dorset' (1709). Back in London he became a member of ADDISON's set which met at Button's Cof-

fee House. Before the first performance of his adaptation of RACINE's *Andromaque, The Distrest Mother* (1712), a whole issue of the *Spectator* was devoted to hyping it. In a series of articles in STEELE's *Guardian*, his *Pastorals* (1710) came in for high praise, which so nettled POPE that he submitted an ironic article (*Guardian*, 40) comparing Philips with himself, which appeared, but only on the surface, to favour the former. JOHNSON observes (*Lives of the Poets*) that 'from that time Pope and Philips lived in a perpetual reciprocation of malevolence'. On the accession of George I in 1714 Philips was made a justice of the peace for Westminster, and in 1717 a commissioner for the lottery. He published, and largely wrote, the twice-weekly journal, the *Freethinker*, from 1718 to 1721. In 1724 he went to Ireland as secretary to his friend Hugh Boulter (1672–1742), the new Archbishop of All-Ireland. He was elected to the Irish Parliament in 1727, and became a judge of the Prerogative Court in 1734. He returned to London in 1748. The term 'namby pamby' was coined to describe his poems to children, of which 'To Miss Margaret Pulteney' (1727) begins: 'Dimply damsel, sweetly smiling, / All caressing, none beguiling . . .'.

PHILIPS, KATHERINE (1631–64), née Fowler, English poet, known as 'the matchless Orinda', was born in London, the daughter of a wealthy merchant, who died in 1642. She was educated at a boarding school in Hackney, and according to AUBREY was very religious as a child, praying for an hour at a time and taking down sermons verbatim. In 1647 she married the 54-year-old James Philips MP, of Cardigan, who had previously been married to a daughter of her mother's new husband. She divided her time between Cardigan, where she knew VAUGHAN, who was practising in the next county, and London, where she adopted the pseudonym 'Orinda' and gave other fanciful names to her circle of friends, which included TAYLOR. Some of her verses were prefixed to the 1651 edition of Vaughan, some to the collected plays (1651) of William Cartwright (1611–43), and others were circulated in manuscript. In 1662 she went to Dublin on business connected with her husband's Irish properties. While she was there she wrote *Pompey* (1663), translated from CORNEILLE, which was performed with great success in Dublin and published there and in London. A London bookseller brought out an unauthorized volume of her *Poems* (1664), which she forced him to withdraw. She died in London of smallpox shortly afterwards. An authorized edition was published in 1667. Her reputation, rather than the quality of her verse, gives her the claim to be the first genuine English poetess, though to be fair her work was much admired by KEATS, who in a letter (1817) quotes the whole of a poem to her bosom friend 'Rosannia', and compares another to JOHN FLETCHER. See Patrick Thomas, *Katherine Philips*, 1988 (critical study).

PILKINGTON, LETITIA see SWIFT.

PINDAR (*c.*520–*c.*440 BC) classical Greek lyric poet, was born of a noble Spartan family in Cynoscephalae, a village near Thebes. His earliest poem celebrates the win in a running race of a member of a distinguished Thessalian family at the Pythian games in 498. Praise for a victory at athletics is the keynote of most of his poems and fragments which have survived. They are tempered with psychological and philosophical sensibility, illuminated with deft mythological parallels, and written with technical assurance in a variety of complex metres. His reputation in the ancient world was such that, according to PLUTARCH, Alexander the Great, when he destroyed Thebes in 335 BC, killed or sold into slavery the whole population, except those who had openly supported the Macedonians and descendants of the family of Pindar. And though his works were intended to be sung and danced in chorus, COWLEY's use of the term 'Pindarique' to describe some of his own verses began a trend which, JOHNSON comments, 'immediately overspread our books of poetry; all the boys and girls caught the pleasing fashion, and they that could do nothing else could write like Pindar'. See *Odes*, tr. Richmond Lattimore, 2nd rev. edn 1976.

PINERO, (Sir) **ARTHUR WING** (1855–1934) dramatist, was born in Islington, the son of a solicitor. After some education in private schools he worked in his father's office while still very young, and was then employed by another solicitor in Lincoln's Inn Fields. At 15, he enrolled in the elocution class at Birkbeck Scientific and Literary Institution (now Birkbeck College), which fired his interest in the stage. In 1874 he got himself taken on as 'utility man' at the Theatre Royal, Edinburgh. When that theatre burned down, he went to Liverpool, and then to London, where he became a member of the Lyceum Company in 1876, and of the Haymarket Theatre in 1881. When he left the Haymarket in 1844 (his final stage role was Sir Anthony Absolute in SHERIDAN's *The Rivals*), he was an emerging dramatist, having written 16 plays, mainly farces, of which the first was *£200 a Year* (1877). The light comedies, *The Magistrate* (1885), *The Schoolmistress* (1866), and *Dandy Dick* (1887), gave notice of an independent and unusual talent, which was confirmed with *The Profligate* (1889), a drama so serious that he was compelled to supply an alternative, happy, ending. It was the prelude to his development in the middle years of his career of the 'problem play', of which he was a pioneer. In particular he depicted the predicament of women in Victorian society, as with *The Second Mrs Tanqueray* (1893), which startled its first-night audience, and the powerful *Mid-Channel* (1909). During the same period he wrote *Trelawny of the 'Wells'* (1898), a romantic piece about the decay of Sadler's Wells Theatre. He was a stickler for adherence to his text, even when a play was being performed in America. He was knighted in 1909. See *Plays by A. W. Pinero*, ed. Russell Jackson, 1986; *Trelawny of the 'Wells' and Other Plays (The Magistrate, The Schoolmistress, The Second Mrs Tanqueray)*, ed. Jacky Bratton, 1995; John Dawick, *Pinero: a Theatrical Life*, 1993.

PINTER, HAROLD (*b.* 1930) British dramatist and poet, was born in London, the son of a Jewish tailor, and was educated at Hackney Downs Grammar School, before becoming an actor. Of his first play, the one act *The Room*, produced at Bristol University in 1957, he says: 'I went into a room one day and saw a couple of people in it. . . . I started off with the picture and let them carry on from there.' His first full-length play to be performed, *The Birthday Party* (1958), established his idiosyncratic style, whereby he develops an initial situation in a charged atmosphere through dialogue whose inconsequence and apparent illogicality are nearer to real colloquial conversation than had been usual in the modern theatre except in the plays of BECKETT and BRECHT. Pinter's settings, though, are realistic. *The Caretaker* (1960), also inspired by a real situation, is set in a broken-down flat: three shorter plays, *The Collection* (1962), *The Dwarfs* (1963), and *The Lover* (1963), all first performed on television, have multiple sets representing middle-class homes. In *The Homecoming* (1965) a bizarre household plays out its sexual and general frustrations and fantasies. *Landscape* and *Silence*, first staged as a double bill in 1969, are even more experimental, and static. In *Old Times* (1971) and *No Man's Land* (1975)—in which Pinter himself played the lead in the 1992 revival—the action as well as the dialogue are discontinuous. *Mountain Language* (1989) is a 20-minute play expressing the agony of political imprisonment. It was presented in 1992 in a double bill with *Party Time* (1991), the two representing respectively Pinter's images of 'base' and 'superstructure' (a vacuous social world which ignores the existence of political prisoners). In *The New World Order* (1991), another brief and menacing drama, two interrogators discuss a prisoner, in his presence. The familiar Pinteresque mixture of lunatic formality and menace overlies a study of a dying man in *Moonlight* (1993), his first full-length (80 minutes) play for 15 years. His next play, *Ashes to Ashes* (1996), a 40-minute confrontation between a male and a female character, confirmed his continued dedication to the language and dramatic world which he first exploited in the 1950s.

Pinter's only novel, *The Dwarfs* (1990), was originally written between 1952 and 1956; parts of it were subsequently used for the stage play. In 1995 he was the second recipient of the David Cohen Prize for British Literature of £30,000. He married the biographer and novelist Lady Antonia Fraser (*b.* 1932), née Pakenham, in 1980. See *Plays*, 4 vols new edns 1996; *Collected Poems and Prose*, 1995; Michael Billington, *The Life and Work of Harold Pinter*, 1996; Martin Esslin, *Pinter the Playwright*, 5th edn 1992; Susan Hollis Merritt, *Pinter in Play: Critical Strategies and the Plays of Harold Pinter*, new edn 1995; Ronald Knowles, *Understanding Harold Pinter*, 1995 (critical study); Ronald Knowles, *Harold Pinter*, 1993 (critical introduction).

PIRANDELLO, LUIGI (1867–1936) Italian dramatist and novelist, was born in Agrigento, Sicily, the second of six children of a sulphur mine proprietor, and went to school in Palermo at Sant' Agata Militello. He studied literature and law for a year at Palermo University, transferring to Rome, and then to Bonn, where he graduated in 1891, having submitted a doctoral thesis on the phonetic development of the Agrigento dialect. He embarked on a career as a writer in Rome, and though he had had a book of verse printed in Palermo in 1889, in 1893 he listed in a letter 21 unpublished stories, novels, plays, and books of poetry. In 1894 he made an arranged marriage with 22-year-old Antonietta Portulano, the daughter of a business associate of his father; he managed to raise three children on fees for short stories, a volume of which was published in 1894, a salary as a teacher in a training college, an allowance from his father, and the income from his wife's dowry. In 1903 his father lost his own money and the dowry in the failure of a mine exploitation. On hearing this, Antonietta had a physical and nervous breakdown, from which she never recovered. Pirandello took in private pupils and stepped up his literary output, one profitable outcome of which was the novel *Il Fu Mattia Pascal* (1904; tr. Arthur Livingston as *The Late Mattia Pascal*, 1923). In 1915, with the encouragement of the Sicilian National Theatre, he became a serious dramatist: *Liolà* (1916), a traditional drama originally written in Sicilian, is a landmark in Italian theatrical history. In *Così È (se Vi Pare)* (1917; tr. Livingston as *And That's the Truth*, 1925; tr. Frederick May as *Right You Are! (If You Think So)*, 1947) he first consciously explored the nature of personality and the relationship between reality and illusion. In 1919 Antonietta was inveigled into a mental clinic, from which she refused ever to return home—she survived until after World War II. *Sei Personnagi in Cerca d'Autore* (1921; tr. May as *Six Characters in Search of an Author*, 1954),

an ingenious inversion of stage conventions in which the characters insist on being the arbiters of their own fates, which is the first of a trilogy, achieved an international reputation. Delusion, and then insanity which has an appalling logic, the theme of *Enrico IV* (1922; tr. Edward Storer as *Henry IV*, 1925), stem from a man's fall from his horse during an historical pageant. With these plays Pirandello introduced a new kind of theatre.

In 1924, having, as he later claimed, 'been a fascist for 30 years', he formally joined the Fascist party, but his attitude to politics became contradictory and his nominal allegiance ended in 1935 with his public praise of Mussolini for assenting to the establishment of the State Theatre. Latterly he enjoyed the friendship of Marta Abba, a young Milanese actress who joined his Arts Theatre company in 1924 and to whom he left the copyright in all the plays he wrote after meeting her—see *Pirandello's Love Letters to Marta Abba*, ed. and tr. Benito Ortolani (1994). See *Collected Plays*, tr. Robert Rietty and others, 4 vols 1987–96; *Six Characters in Search of an Author and Other Plays*, tr. Mark Musa, new edn 1995; A. Richard Sogliuzzo, *Luigi Pirandello, Director: the Playwright in the Theatre*, 1982.

PITTER, RUTH (1897–1992) British poet, was born in Ilford, Essex, of parents who were both teachers and who, she writes, 'loved poetry and were determined to impart it to their children'; one of their methods was to bribe her to learn it by heart, at rates of between 1d and 6d (according to length) for each poem in F. T. Palgrave's *The Golden Treasury*. She was educated at Coborn School for Girls, east London, and was a clerk in the War Office during World War I. She commented: 'I am not even a professional writer, just a poet; the occupations of my life other than this have been simply to gain a subsistence, and I have usually worked with my hands.' This she did first by painting pottery in Suffolk, and then from 1930 as a partner in a Chelsea craft workshop. *First Poems* was published in 1920, but she discounted the worth of any of her verse before *A Mad Lady's Garland* (1934). Her work has a musical simplicity, with which she 'tried to be faithful to delight, to beatitude, being unable to see what else can be absolutely significant. For what else can God be supposed to exist?'. She also had a lively sense of humour, especially when writing about cats—*On Cats* (1947)—or gardening—*The Rude Potato* (1941). The death in the early 1970s of the friend with whom she lived in Buckinghamshire turned her into a recluse, from which state she was rescued in 1984 by a new neighbour. She never married, observing, 'One might be very fond of [men], but it would have been cruelty to animals to marry them.' In 1955 she was the first woman to receive the Queen's Gold Medal for Poetry, and she was made CBE in 1979. See *Collected Poems*, new edn 1996.

PLAATJE, SOL(OMON) T(SHEK-ISHO) (1876–1932) South African novelist, was born in Boshof, Orange Free State, and educated at Pniel Lutheran Mission School. He was interpreter to the Court of Summary Jurisdiction during the siege of Mafeking in 1899–1900, and then served as a war correspondent—see *Mafeking Diary: a Black Man's View of a White Man's War*, ed. John Comaroff (1990). He was a founder member in 1912 and the first General Secretary of the African National Congress. *Native Life in South Africa* (1916) is a political and social study particularly opposing the Natives Lands Act of 1913. To celebrate his 50th birthday, a group of Bantu, coloured, and Indian supporters started a fund through which his house was bought and presented to him in appreciation of his unpaid work for non-Europeans. *Mhudi: an Epic of South African Native Life a Hundred Years Ago*, written in about 1918 and first published in 1930 (ed. T. J. Couzens, 1975), is the first African novel written in Africa by a black African. It is also a significant political novel in that historical events provide a model for the situation in his own times, and he presents the coming of the Boers in the context of the interaction between the black peoples who were already there. *Sechuana Proverbs with Literal Translations and their European Equivalents* (1916) highlights links between the language usage of pastoral nations. He also translated SHAKE-SPEARE into Sechuana. See *Selected Writings*, ed. Brian Willan, 1997; Brian Willan, *Sol Plaatje: South African Nationalist 1876–1932*, 1988.

PLATH, SYLVIA (1932–63) American poet, was born and brought up in Boston, Massachusetts, the elder child of a distinguished German entomologist and his American–Austrian wife. Her father's death of gangrene when she was eight, the result of his failing to get treatment for a diabetic condition, left her with feelings of guilt and, ultimately, of hostility. Tenacious in her fixation to succeed as a writer ('I will slave and slave until I break into those slicks'), she was already publishing stories and poems in magazines when she entered Smith College in 1950. After a breakdown in 1953 she attempted suicide; 'But they pulled me out of the sack, / And they stuck me together with glue' ('Daddy', 1962). After graduating *summa cum laude* in 1955, she went as a Fulbright scholar to Newnham College, Cambridge; while she was there she met TED HUGHES, whom she married in 1956. They spent two years in the USA, where she taught at Smith and attended ROBERT LOWELL's poetry seminars at Boston University. They then settled in a small flat in London, where

she wrote, as Victoria Lucas, *The Bell Jar* (1963), an autobiographical novel in which the re-creation of her own mental state at college reflects the confusion about the role of women which prevailed in the 1960s.

The Colossus: Poems was published in the UK in 1960, and in 1961 the couple bought an old country house in Devon. They separated in December 1962, when, after making a bonfire of manuscripts of both of them, she took their two small children to London. There, in a bleak and freezing flat, she wrote, in an astonishing burst of creative energy, the stark, angry poems which became *Ariel* (1965). And there, she gassed herself after taking sleeping pills. Though her work contains some appealing poems about her children and the natural world, much of it reflects the darker side of daily domestic life, infused with a romantic view of death. Posthumous collections of verse are *Crossing the Water* (1971) and *Winter Trees* (1971), and of stories and prose, *Johnny Panic and the Bible of Dreams: and Other Prose Writings* (1977). *Collected Poems*, ed. Ted Hughes (1981) won the Pulitzer Prize. A 130-page manuscript of an unfinished novel, 'Double Exposure', disappeared after her death. *The It-Doesn't-Matter Suit* (1996) is a children's fantasy recently discovered by her family. *Letters Home: Correspondence 1950–1963* (1975) was edited by her mother, Aurelia Schober Plath. Biographical studies have prompted bitter controversy. See Charles Newman (ed.), *The Art of Sylvia Plath: a Symposium*, 1970; Linda Wagner (ed.) *Critical Essays on Sylvia Plath*, 1984.

PLATO (*c.*427–*c.*347 BC) philosopher and classical Greek prose writer, was born in Athens of an aristocratic family. At about twenty he became a disciple of the philosopher, Socrates (469–399), on whose execution (by drinking hemlock) for subversive teaching, he retired with other Socratics to Megara. He then travelled, and in 390–88 paid the first of three extended visits to Syracuse, during which, at the instigation of the cultured Dion (*d.* 353), he tried unsuccessfully to introduce some ideas of rational government. In 388 he founded near Athens, in an olive grove sacred to Academus, his 'Academy', effectively the first university, to which he admitted women as equals. Whereas Socrates deplored the written word as a medium of exposition, Plato circumvented its disadvantages by presenting philosophical argument through a dialogue, in which he never speaks in his own person. By this means Socrates lives as a personality, and participates in the discussions forming some of Plato's most influential and sublime works: *Protagoras*, on the science of life; *Phaedo*, on the nature of death and the immortality of the soul; *Republic*, on the nature of the ideal state; and *Symposium* (which means a drinking party or banquet, the venue of this discussion), in which is expressed the concept of Platonic love. His 'Theory of Ideas', which is one of his principal contributions to philosophical thought, derives from the notion of the Good, towards which the philosopher ascends through definitions collected from particulars. See David J. Melling, *Understanding Plato*, 1987.

PLAUTUS, TITUS MACCUS (254–184 BC) Roman dramatist, was born in Sarsina, a small village in Umbria, and left home early to come to Rome. He worked as a stage propman and, with the money he earned, set himself up in the same kind of business. When it failed, he took a job turning a baker's handmill, which he was able to give up after writing his first three plays. Of 130 attributed to him, about twenty have survived, a sure measure of their popularity. Though based on Greek models, they have a raw freshness of their own. There is little characterization, but he was adept at varying his plots and settings, and at verbal fireworks. His stock devices are the generation gap, twin heroes/heroines, and pert slaves. The chief character in *Miles Gloriosus* [*The Braggart Soldier*] is the prototype of the Elizabethan stage boaster, whose manifestation in *Ralph Roister Doister* (c.1553) by Nicolas Udall (1505–56) marks the first English comedy written for public performance. SHAKESPEARE's *Comedy of Errors* is taken from Plautus's *Menaechmi*. See *The Comedies*, 4 vols, ed. David R. Slavitt and Palmer Bovie, tr. Constance Carrier and others, 1995; *Four Comedies*, tr. Erich Segal, 1996.

PLINY 'THE ELDER' (GAIUS PLINIUS SECUNDUS) (23–79) Roman scientist and historian, was born at Como of a wealthy and influential family, practised at the Bar in Rome, had several military postings (during one of which, in Germany, he began a 22-book history of the German wars), and probably went to ground during the reign of Nero. He returned to public life on the accession of Vespasian in 70, and between then and his death held senior government posts, including that of deputy governor of Spain, while writing thirty more works of Roman history and the 37 books of his 'Natural History'. This, his only surviving work, covers many subjects, including physics, geography, ethnology, physiology, zoology, botany, medicine, and metallurgy, with digressions into anything else which interested him. He drew his material from written sources (when he was not reading himself or writing or dictating, he had someone read aloud), and from his own observations. He was in command of the naval station at Misenum when Vesuvius erupted. He went ashore on the beach, taking notes all the time, and was asphyxiated by the fumes or buried under falling rocks. Pliny 'the Younger', Gaius Plinius Caecilius Secundus (61–c.113),

public servant, philanthropist, and writer of letters, was his nephew and adoptive son.

PLOMER, WILLIAM (1903–73) British novelist and poet, was born in Pietersburg, Transvaal, of English parents (his father was in the British administration), and was educated at Rugby School until he was withdrawn because of poor eyesight when he was 15. For this reason, instead of going to university, he was apprenticed to a farmer in the Stormberg Mountains, and then joined his parents in a trading venture in Zululand. He used these experiences in *Turbott Wolfe*, written when he was 19 but not published until 1925, when it caused a storm of protest for its treatment of miscegenation. (In the meantime he had worked with ROY CAMPBELL and VAN DER POST on the short-lived journal, *Voorslag*.) He now went to Japan, and after three years there, to London. He returned to South Africa only once, in 1956. He wrote poetry, further novels, and short stories, and was for many years literary consultant to the firm of Jonathan Cape, to which he brought KILVERT and IAN FLEMING. While as a poet he is best known for his sometimes horrific and farcical modern ballads and his sarcastic character sketches, most critics prefer his straight, descriptive, African poems. He also wrote librettos for the composer Benjamin (later Lord) Britten (1913–76). While readers especially of his novel *Sado* (1931) can hardly be unaware of his homosexuality, as he wrote in a letter to a friend: 'I think blatant homosexuality, like other forms of blatancy, can be tiresome and uncivilized.' From 1953 he lived a reticent existence on a Sussex housing estate, first in Rustington and then in Hassocks. He was awarded the Queen's Gold Medal for Poetry in 1968, and was made CBE in 1968. See *Collected Poems*, rev. edn 1973; *Autobiography*, with a postscript by Simon Nowell-Smith, 1975; Peter F. Alexander, *William Plomer: a Biography*, new edn 1990.

PLUNKETT, JAMES, pseudonym of James Plunkett Kelly (*b.* 1920) Irish novelist and short-story writer, was born in Dublin, of which he has written, 'Despite its tensions and its tragedies, [it] was a good city to grow up in.' He was educated at the Christian Brothers school in Synge Street, and also studied the violin and viola at Dublin College of Music. He left school at 17 and worked for seven years as a clerk in the Gas Company, after which he was a branch secretary of the Workers' Union of Ireland from 1946 to 1955. His first stories had appeared in *The Bell*, under the editorship and guidance of O'FAOLAIN, in 1942. *The Trusting and the Maimed, and Other Irish Stories* (1955) was significant for its technical brilliance and its balance of vision, from childhood to old age—see also *Collected Short Stories* (1977). He was also writing radio plays, of which he subsequently adapted *Big Jim* (1954) for the stage as *The Risen People* (performed in London 1959, published 1978). After working for Radio Eireann from 1955 to 1960, he joined Irish Television as a producer-director, being a senior producer from 1974 until his retirement in 1985. His novel *Strumpet City* (1969), a panorama of Dublin between 1907 and 1914, ranges over a wide social spectrum, but is a particularly vivid realization of working-class life. The semi-autobiographical *Farewell Companions* (1977) takes up the story in the 1920s, and covers the period until the mid-1940s. He uses techniques of multiple narration and movements back and forth in time again in *The Circus Animals* (1990), in which he confronts Irish political and religious issues of the 1950s. *The Gems She Wore: a Book of Irish Places* (1972) is an imaginative and personal guide. He was President, Irish Academy of Letters 1980–82.

PLUNKETT, JOSEPH MARY see PEARSE.

PLUTARCH (*c.*46–*c.*120) Graeco-Roman philosopher and biographer, was born in Chaeronea, Boeotia, where he held various municipal offices. He was an influential member of the college of priests at neighbouring Delphi, and taught the locals Platonist philosophy, which he had studied in Athens in his twenties. He also lectured in Rome, where he found favour with the emperor, Domitian, by whose successors, Trajan and Hadrian, he was rewarded with an honorary consulship and a post as a procurator of Greece. His surviving works, which are considerable in volume, are of two kinds. *Moralia* is a collection of ethical, antiquarian, and miscellaneous essays, whose general approach provided a model for writers such as BACON, MONTAIGNE, and TAYLOR—see *Essays*, ed. Ian Kidd, tr. Robin Waterfield (1992). For his 'Parallel Lives', he matched a biographical sketch of the career of a notable political figure in Greek history with that of a similar Roman personage, for example DEMOSTHENES and CICERO. He had a gift for narrative and for the telling detail or anecdote, and it was largely through his eyes that Renaissance writers viewed classical history. The *Lives* were translated into French by Jacques Amyot (1513–93), and from French into English in 1579 by Sir Thomas North (1535–*c.*1601), in which form it was the source of SHAKESPEARE's *Julius Caesar*, *Antony and Cleopatra*, and *Coriolanus*.

POE, EDGAR ALLAN (1809–49) American poet, short-fiction writer, and critic, was born Edgar Poe in Boston. He was the second of three children of David Poe, actor son of a Baltimore family from Ireland, and of Elizabeth Arnold (1787–1811), an actress of English parentage who married him in 1806

after the death of her first husband, another actor in the company. In 1810 David Poe apparently deserted his wife; after her death in Richmond, Virginia, Edgar was fostered by John Allan (1780–1834), a Scottish-born local tobacco merchant, and became Edgar Allan Poe. In 1815 the Allans took him to England, where he boarded at Manor House School, Stoke Newington. In 1820 they returned to Richmond, where he went to private schools, and fell for a school friend's mother, whom he later immortalized in 'To Helen' (1831), in which occurs '. . . the glory that was Greece, / And the grandeur that was Rome'. After her death in 1824 he addressed his attentions to the 15-year-old daughter of a neighbour, Elmira Royston, to whom he became secretly engaged. Letters he wrote to her from the University of Virginia were intercepted by her father, and by the time his university career had ended in 1826 after eight months, Allan having refused to pay his gambling debts of $2000, she was engaged to someone else. He left home in a huff for Boston, where he privately printed *Tamerlane, and Other Poems* (1827), 'By a Bostonian', and enlisted in the army under the name of Edgar A. Perry. After Mrs Allan died in 1829 he was reconciled to his foster father, who enabled the now Sergeant Major Perry to obtain an honourable discharge, and supported his application to enter West Point as an officer cadet. Allan was not so keen on Poe's poetry, however, and they fell out again after the publication of *Al Aaraaf, Tamerlane, and Minor Poems* (1829), and Allan's remarriage in 1830. Without any means of support, Poe engineered his dismissal from West Point, having secured enough subscriptions from his fellow cadets to finance the publication of *Poems* (1831), in which were 'To Helen', 'Israfel', and 'The Doomed City' (later 'The City in the Sea').

He now went to live in Baltimore with his widowed aunt, Maria Poe Clemm, and her family, which included her daughter Virginia, then aged seven. He was writing stories, of which 'Mezengerstein' and others appeared anonymously in the Philadelphia *Saturday Courier* in 1832, and 'MS Found in a Bottle' won a $50 prize offered by the Baltimore *Saturday Visiter*. He returned to Richmond in 1835 as assistant editor to the owner of the *Southern Literary Messenger*. In 1836 he married Virginia, now 13, whose mother came to live with them. He left his job in 1837, one of the reasons being his drinking, though it is probable that his continuing drink problem was due not so much to the amount he drank as to his having a weak head for it. In 1838 the trio went to Philadelphia, where they subsisted on the breadline while he wrote further stories, did miscellaneous journalism, and was successively, until he resigned or was fired, Literary Editor of *Burton's Gentleman's Magazine* and *Graham's*

Magazine, for which he wrote the famous review of *Twice-Told Tales* which enhanced the reputation of HAWTHORNE. *Tales of the Grotesque and Arabesque* (1840) earned nothing. In 1842 the unfortunate Virginia broke a blood vessel while singing, and was never the same again. By the time the family arrived in New York in 1844, however, Poe had written several of the stories which established him as a master of the macabre and of terror, and the principal progenitor of the detective story and the tale of deduction—'The Tell-Tale Heart' (1843), 'The Black Cat' (1843), 'The Premature Burial' (1844), 'The Murders in the Rue Morgue' (1841), 'The Purloined Letter' (1841), and 'The Gold Bug' (1843). He was now also the most famous, and feared, literary critic in the country.

After working for the *Evening Mirror*, he joined the *Broadway Journal*, of which he became owner in 1845. 'The Raven', first published in the *Evening Mirror*, which had pirated it from the *American Review*, became the title piece of *The Raven and Other Poems* (1845). The *Journal* failed in 1846; Virginia died in 1847. His final two years were marked by violent swings of mood. He delivered lectures: *Eureka*, a prose poem on the universe, was published in 1848, and 'The Poetic Principle' from his manuscript in 1850. He was briefly engaged to the widowed poet from Providence, Sarah Helen Whitman (1803–78), the subject of a second 'To Helen'; he was at the same time passionately pouring out his heart to Annie Richmond, the 28-year-old wife of a wrapping paper manufacturer. In Richmond in the summer of 1849 he called on Elmira, now a rich widow, and it seems that they became engaged again. His movements between leaving Richmond on 27 September and being admitted unconscious on 3 October to a Baltimore hospital, where he died four days later in a delirium, have never satisfactorily been explained. See *The Complete Tales and Poems*, new edn 1987; *Poems and Essays on Poetry*, ed. C.H. Sisson, 1995; *Selected Poems and Essays*, ed. Richard Gray, new edn 1993; Kenneth Silverman, *Edgar A. Poe: Mournful and Never-Ending Remembrance*, new edn 1993 (biography); Julian Symons, *The Tell-Tale Heart: the Life and Works of Edgar Allan Poe*, 1978; Jeffrey Meyers, *Edgar Allan Poe: His Life and Legacy*, 1992.

POLYBIUS (*c*.202–*c*.120 BC) Greek historian, was born in Megalopolis, Arcadia, and followed his father into a prominent political and military position in the Achaean League. After the final Roman defeat of Macedonia in 168, the victors, suspicious of the neutrality of the League during the conflict, deported to Rome a thousand of its members, including Polybius. He became the tutor, and ultimately the close friend, of the Roman general, Scipio Aemilianus (*c*.185–129), whom he accompanied to the siege of Carthage in 146.

After the destruction of Corinth that same year, he was involved in the reorganization and administration of the new Roman settlement. He thus had first-hand knowledge of the Roman character, and of Roman methods of making war and extending and maintaining an empire, which he used in writing his political and military 'History' of the growing decadence of Greece and the emergence of the unifying influence of Rome. With LIVY he is the main source of information about the period. See *The Rise of the Roman Empire*, tr. Ian Scott-Kilvert, 1979.

POPE, ALEXANDER (1688–1744) British poet, critic, and translator, was born in London, the son of a linen merchant who soon afterwards, respecting the new law forbidding Catholics to live within ten miles of London, rented a house in Hammersmith and in 1700 bought Whitehall House, Binfield, by Windsor Forest. The boy had a little schooling at home, in Hampshire (from where he was removed after lampooning the head), and in London, but was prevented by his faith from going to university. At 15, he went to London at his own request to learn French and Italian. These, with his Latin and Greek, enabled him to read even more widely, though by this time Pott's disease had set in, permanently stunting his growth and giving him severe curvature of the spine. In his teens he frequented Will's Coffee House, Russell Street, the haunt of the London literary set. In 1707 Jacob Tonson (*c*.1656–1736) offered to publish some of his poetry, and the four 'Pastorals' appeared in *Poetical Miscellanies, Part VI* (1709). In *An Essay on Criticism* (1711) Pope put into sparkling heroic couplets the general views of the time on critical taste and methodology. *Windsor Forest* (1713) starts out as a traditional pastoral, though all the more effective in that Pope knew and loved the setting, but praise of the retired life is extended to incorporate a splendid vision of universal peace following the Treaty of Utrecht in 1713. In 1712 a first version appeared of *The Rape of the Lock*, inspired by an upper-class prank in which Arabella Fermor lost to an admirer one of the delectable curls at the back of her neck. A second version was published in 1714, enlarged from two cantos to five by the addition of supernatural 'machinery', notably the guardian sylphs, one of whom gets too close at the critical moment: 'Fate urg'd the sheers, and cut the Sylph in twain / (But airy substance soon unites again) . . .' (III, 150–51). This mock-heroic masterpiece also succeeded in calming tempers frayed by the original incident.

Pope now announced his plan to translate HOMER's *Iliad*, for which he relied heavily on earlier translations. The first four books were published in 1715, two days before a rival version by Thomas Tickell (1686–1740). The rest followed at intervals until 1720. *The*

Works of Mr Alexander Pope appeared in 1717. For the next ten years he concentrated on Homer, with the official assistance of two friends in the translation of the *Odyssey* (1725–26), and on his edition of SHAKE-SPEARE's *Works* (1725). His painstaking but occasionally misplaced labour to restore the texts of the plays makes him the first genuine Shakespearian scholar, but his failings were pilloried by Lewis Theobald (1688–1744), a more serious and pedantic editor, who was preparing his own edition. Pope was now living in Twickenham with his widowed mother (she died, much to his grief, in 1733). Here his friend SWIFT encouraged him to write the satirical poem which appeared anonymously as *The Dunciad* (1728), with Theobald as the chief butt. *The Dunciad Variorum* (1729) is supplied with spoof footnotes and other critical apparatus, while in the final version (1743) CIBBER appears as 'hero'. Pope published his philosophical poem, *An Essay on Man* (1733–34), anonymously, hoping thus to avoid malicious criticism—the device succeeded and he was soon glad to acknowledge the work as his own. *Imitations of Horace* appeared from 1734 to 1739, and when published together in the complete works of 1751, edited by William Warburton (1698–1779), were prefaced with *Epistle to Dr Arbuthnot* (1734), a lively apologia for the profession of satirist. By devious means, because it was not etiquette to do so, he succeeded in 1735 in publishing edited versions of some of his private correspondence, which though selective, are nevertheless revealing about his mental process.

As a man, this diminutive (4' 6") twisted creature was loved by some and hated and feared by many—he revenged himself on the notorious publisher Edmund Curll (1675–1747) by dosing his wine with a particularly violent emetic. His women friends included MONTAGU; Martha Blount (1690–1762), to whom he addressed 'Epistle II, to a Lady: Of the Characters of Women'; and the poet Anne Finch (1661–1720), Countess of Winchilsea—see in Barbara McGovern, *Anne Finch and Her Poetry* (1992). He could be a bitter versifier, but he was also a great poet, whose correctness of style was a model for succeeding generations, and of whom COWPER could write in 1781, 'Then Pope, as harmony itself exact, / In verse well disciplin'd, complete, compact, / Gave virtue and morality a grace . . .' (*Table Talk*, 646–49). In his dealings with his publishers Pope was an innovator in book design—see David Foxon, *Pope and the Early Eighteenth-Century Book Trade*, rev. and ed. James McLaverty (1991). See [*Works*], ed. Pat Rogers, 1993 (chronological selection, including prose); [*Selected Verse*], ed. Pat Rogers, 1994; Maynard Mack, *Alexander Pope: a Life*, new edn 1988; Bonamy Dobrée, *Alexander Pope*, 1951 (critical biography); Geoffrey

Tillotson, *On the Poetry of Pope*, 2nd edn 1950; Ian Gordon, *A Preface to Pope*, 2nd edn 1994.

PORTER, HAL (1911–84) Australian novelist, short-story writer, poet, and dramatist, was born in the Melbourne suburb of Albert Park, the eldest of six children of a privately-educated sporting enthusiast who worked as an engine driver. He was educated at Bairnsdale High School, and at 13 won a literary competition sponsored by the *Bairnsdale Advertiser*, which he joined as a cub reporter on leaving school at 16. After a year he went into teaching, which he enjoyed and to which he returned several times. Shortly after his marriage in 1939 he was knocked down by a car and so badly injured that war service was out of the question, making him for the rest of his life conscious of not having shared that experience with others of his generation. His decision to give all his available time to the essentially isolated pursuit of writing was instrumental in his divorce in 1943, after which he remained a bachelor. Though he had had verse and stories published in journals during the 1930s, his only book during this period was *Short Stories* (1942), printed for private circulation. He taught at private schools during the war, and afterwards was variously cook, hotel manager, and hospital orderly in between further periods of teaching, the last of which was at the school for children of Australian and American servicemen in Kure, Japan, in 1949–50. On his return he was Director of the National Theatre, Hobart 1951–53, and then Chief Librarian, Bairnsdale and Shepparton until 1961, when he finally felt confident enough to become a full-time writer.

His first commercially published book was *The Hexagon* (1956), poems in traditional forms but with intricate word-play, such as were also collected in two subsequent volumes (1968 and 1973). His first novel, *A Handful of Pennies* (1958), was written on a grant from the Commonwealth Literary Fund to re-create his Japanese experiences. He wrote just two more: *The Tilted Cross* (1961), a tale of dark romance and conflicting societies in colonial Van Diemen's Land, based on sound documentation; and *The Right Thing* (1971), a study of family relationships. His volume of short stories, *A Bachelor's Children* (1962), included 'Revenge', written when he was 20 and already proclaiming him as a craftsman, the development of whose vision, variety of mood and style, and mastery of character and setting, places him alongside those who have achieved worldwide recognition in this field. *Selected Stories*, ed. Leonie Kramer (1971) contains stories from that collection and from two later ones. He wrote plays much as relaxation but with sound theatrical understanding, *The Professor* (published 1966) being an effective tragedy of the clash between Australian and Japanese cultures. His literary reputation has been enhanced by his autobiographies, *The Watcher on the Cast-Iron Balcony* (1963), *The Paper Chase* (1966), and *The Extra* (1975). He was made AM in 1982.

PORTER, KATHARINE ANNE (1890–1980) American short-story writer, was born Callie Russell Porter in a log cabin in Indian Creek, Texas. After the death of their mother in 1892, the four children were cared for by their paternal grandmother in Kyle. When she died in 1901, their father took them to San Antonio, where Porter attended the Thomas School for a year, and then with her sister opened a 'studio of music, physical culture and dramatic reading'. At 16 she made the first of four unhappy marriages, the last three to men considerably younger than herself. In 1917, after two years in hospital with tuberculosis, she became a reporter on the Fort Worth *Critic*, owned by a fellow patient. After a spell on the *Rocky Mountain News*, Denver, and a brush with death during the 1918 flu epidemic, she moved to New York. Between 1920 and 1930 she made several visits to Mexico, the setting of her first significant story, 'María Concepción' (1922), and of other stories, notably 'Flowering Judas' (1929)—these two were among the six published as *Flowering Judas* (1930; enlarged edn 1935). She lived in Berlin in 1931–32, and Paris 1933–36. *Pale Horse, Pale Rider: Three Short Novels* (1939) contained 'Old Mortality', one of several stories whose heroine, the child Miranda Gay, is clearly a reflection of herself. After *The Leaning Tower and Other Stories* (1944), she took up again her self-imposed task of writing an enormous allegorical novel, which had started simply as a logged record of her sea voyage to Europe in 1931. As *Ship of Fools* (1962), a densely packed artifice of linked incidents and character studies, it became a popular success. *The Collected Stories of Katharine Anne Porter* (1965) won the Pulitzer Prize. See Janis P. Stout, *Katharine Anne Porter: a Sense of Our Times*, 1995 (critical biography); Willene Hendrick and George Hendrick, *Katharine Anne Porter*, rev edn 1988 (critical study).

PORTER, PETER (*b.* 1929) Australian poet, was born in Brisbane and educated at the Church of England Grammar School and Toowoomba Grammar School, being deeply affected by the traumas of boarding school and by the early death of his mother. After having some training in journalism, he went to England in 1951, and settled in London, working as a clerk, a bookseller, and an advertising copywriter until 1968, when he became a freelance writer, reviewer, and broadcaster. His first poem was published when he was 28, and the first of his many books of poetry, *Once Bitten, Twice Bitten* (1961), when he was 32. An expatriate who wrote of Aus-

tralia in *The Times Literary Supplement* (1971) that 'nobody has any natural talent and the Great Supervisor fails me over a whole range of Anglo-Saxon virtues', he remained away for 23 years before returning for the Adelaide Festival, though he has since held visiting posts at several universities, including Melbourne, of which he is DLitt. An often satirical poet with a penchant for reflecting on the work of European writers as diverse as AUDEN, CHAPMAN, DOSTOEVSKY, JOYCE, MARSTON, DOROTHY OSBORNE, Simon Raven (*b.* 1927), and MARTIAL—see especially *After Martial* (1972)—he excels at the expression of the day-to-day doings, and ageing, of the modern cosmopolitan European, and at the epigrammatic line, and has found inspiration especially in the land and people of Italy. In the collections *The Chair of Babel* (1992) and *Millenial Fables* (1994) he takes an admonitory and satirical look at what he sees as the corporate madness of the final years of the millenium. See *Collected Poems*, 1984; *A Porter Selected*, 1989; Bruce Bennett, *Spirit in Exile: Peter Porter and His Poetry*, 1991; Peter Steel, *Peter Porter*, 1993 (critical study).

PORTER, WILLIAM SIDNEY see HENRY.

POTTER, BEATRIX (1866–1943) children's writer and illustrator, was born in South Kensington, London, of wealthy and over-protective parents. She was educated by governesses at home, where she secretly introduced into her third-floor nursery a menagerie of small mammalia and amphibia, which she studied and drew. This continued as a mere pastime until she was 27, when she wrote and illustrated stories about her animals, initially to amuse a sick child. Unable to find a publisher for them, she had finally resorted to printing privately *The Tale of Peter Rabbit* (1900) and *The Tailor of Gloucester* (1902), before the firm of Frederick Warne undertook commercial publication of her work. In 1905, in the face of strong parental opposition, she became engaged to Norman Warne, the son of the firm's founder, an event of which she later wrote in a letter, 'I thought my story had come right, with patience and waiting, like Anne Elliot's did [in AUSTEN's *Persuasion*]'. Within a few months, Norman was dead. Her resilience was such that she took the opportunity of escaping from home by buying with her earnings a small mixed farm at Sawrey, in the Lake District, where she learned the craft of farming and continued to produce her uniquely imagined little books. At the age of 47, again against the wishes of her parents, she married William Heelis, a local solicitor who had advised her on land purchases. They were very happy, and she became an expert breeder of hill-sheep and an active conservationist. Her success as both writer and illustrator is due not just to her story-telling ability, but also to her shrewd characterization and ecological accuracy—she was also a noted botanical artist. See Leslie Linder, *A History of the Writings of Beatrix Potter including Unpublished Work*, new edn 1987; Ruth K. MacDonald, *Beatrix Potter*, 1986 (critical study).

POUND, EZRA (1885–1972) American poet, translator, and critic, was born in Hailey, Idaho, the son of a Land Office registrar who took up a post as assistant assayer at the US Mint in Philadelphia in 1887. He was educated at Cheltenham Military Academy, Cheltenham Township High School, and the University of Pennsylvania, by which time he had resolved that at thirty he would know more about poetry than any man alive; 'In this search I learned more or less of nine foreign languages, I read Oriental stuff in translations, I fought every university regulation and every professor who tried to make me learn anything except this . . .'. In 1903 he transferred to Hamilton College, returning to Pennsylvania in 1905 to take the degree of MA and to do postgraduate studies. His post as head of French, Spanish, and Italian at Wabash College, Indiana, was terminated probably for a variety of reasons besides his 'Continental' ways, culminating in his giving hospitality in his rooms to a 'lady-gent impersonator'. In 1908 he left the USA for Europe, privately printing in Venice one hundred copies of a 72-page book of verse, *A Lume Spento* (1908), before settling in London. There he published in quick succession several further volumes of poetry and a critical study, *The Spirit of Romance* (1910). He did some teaching and reviewing, and without himself making an impression on the general public, except for his colourful appearance, was generous in his help to others: notably YEATS, to whom he gave the same kind of editorial inspiration which T. S. ELIOT received from him a few years later, and JOYCE, on whose behalf he successfully petitioned publishers and potential benefactors.

In 1914 he married Dorothy Shakespear (1886–1972), the daughter of a close friend, Olivia Shakespear, the periodic mistress and frequent correspondent of Yeats. During this period he began work on his 'Cantos', of which there were ultimately 116, written over fifty years and published serially in draft and in finished versions, beginning in *Poetry: a Magazine of Verse* in 1917, and continuing through successive volumes until 1969. Collected editions appeared in 1948, 1964, 1970, and 1976. The intention was to offer a total, coherent expression of his thought and reading, incorporating reflections on the circumstances of his life. Before leaving England for the Continent, where he settled in Rapallo as a neighbour (and tennis partner) of BEER-BOHM, he published *Hugh Selwyn Mauberley* (1920), with its ironic subtitle, 'Life and Con-

tacts', a lyrical affirmation of disillusionment. In 1923 he met, in Paris, Olga Rudge (1895–1996), a talented violinist and musicologist. They had a daughter in 1925. Subsequently he lived alternately with Olga and his wife, who had a son in 1926. The three co-habited uneasily in Italy during the exigencies of World War II.

In 1941 he broadcast in English on Italian radio a series of talks which were generally pro-Fascist and explicitly anti-Semitic. Failing to get back to the USA after America entered the war, he resumed his broadcasts, was indicted in his absence for treason, and was arrested in Italy in May 1945. For six months he was held in the American Disciplinary Training Centre at Pisa, initially in a barbed-wire cage in the open. After suffering a mental breakdown he was moved into a tent, where he composed the first draft of the 'Pisan Cantos' (LXXIV–LXXXIV). Flown back to the USA in handcuffs, he was adjudged 'insane and mentally unfit for trial, and in need of care in a mental hospital'. He was committed to St Elizabeth's Hospital, a Federal asylum for the insane, where he remained for over twelve years. *The Pisan Cantos* (1948) received the Library of Congress inaugural Bollingen Prize for poetry, sparking off a moral as well as a literary public controversy. His release in 1958 without being tried was finally engineered with the help of T. S. ELIOT, FROST, HEMINGWAY, and MACLEISH. He returned to Italy, living with Dorothy until 1962, and then with Olga in Venice, where he died. See *The Cantos*, new edn 1996; *Collected Shorter Poems*, new edn 1984; *The Translations of Ezra Pound*, ed. Hugh Kenner, enlarged edn 1970, *Literary Essays*, ed. T. S. Eliot, new edn 1954; Humphrey Carpenter, *A Serious Character: the Life of Ezra Pound*, 1988; Hugh Kenner, *The Poetry of Ezra Pound*, new edn 1986 (critical study); Peter Wilson, *A Preface to Ezra Pound*, 1997.

POWELL, ANTHONY (*b.* 1905) British novelist and critic, was born in London and educated at Eton and Balliol College, Oxford. His first novel, *Afternoon Men* (1931), hovers between satire and sheer comedy, and introduces the social milieu (upper-middle- and upper-class/artistic and professional) which he continued to dissect for the rest of his writing life. His fifth, *What's Become of Waring* (1939), which follows a hunt for the person of a mysterious author, is the most timeless of his prewar novels. After World War II, in which he served with distinction in the Intelligence Corps, he recharged his creative impulse with a study of the antiquary, *John Aubrey and His Friends* (1948). He then embarked consciously on a sequence of novels (at first six but then 12) in which ideas could be connected and characters thoroughly developed, beginning with *A Question of Upbringing* (1951) and ending with *Hearing Secret Har-*

monies (1975), and having a chronological framework corresponding to Powell's own experience and times. These originally appeared under the overall title of *The Music of Time*, a reference to the painting 'A Dance to the Music of Time', by Nicolas Poussin (1594–1665), which subsequently became the title of the series. Compared with his prewar novels, the style is more relaxed, and the dialogue, though still sharp, is less elusive. The characters and the interplay between them contribute the basis of the blend of the comic and tragic which is Powell's hallmark. Outside the canon once again are *O, How the Wheel Becomes It!* (1983), a study of the self-realization of a second-rate author, and *The Fisher King* (1986). *Miscellaneous Verdicts: Writings on Writers 1946–1989* (1990) was followed by *Under Review: Further Writings on Writers 1946–1989* (1992). He was made CBE in 1956, and CH in 1988. See *A Dance to the Music of Time*, 4 vols new edns 1995; *Journals 1982–1986*, new edn 1996; *Journals 1987–1989*, new edn 1997; *To Keep the Ball Rolling*, 5 vols 1976–82, one vol. (abridged) 1983 (memoirs); Neil McEwan, *Anthony Powell*, 1991 (critical study); Hilary Spurling, *Invitation to the Dance: Handbook to Anthony Powell's 'Dance to the Music of Time'*, new edn 1992; Isabelle Joyau, *Investigating Powell's 'A Dance to the Music of Time'*, 1994 (critical study).

POWERS, J(AMES) F(ARL) (*b.* 1917) American novelist and short-story writer, was born in Jacksonville, Illinois, of a professional and artistic Catholic family—see his autobiographical story 'Jamesie' (1947) for some early experiences. After an undistinguished career at Quincy Academy, he did not consider becoming a priest, but found what work he could in Chicago: as a department store assistant, insurance salesman, and chauffeur. In 1938 he became an editor of the Chicago Historical Records Survey and enrolled for night classes on the Chicago campus of Northwestern University. He had to give up the classes when the survey finished in 1941. He then worked for Brentano's bookshop, from which he was dismissed for declining to purchase war bonds. At this time he wrote his first short story, 'He Don't Plant Cotton' (1943), about Negro humiliation. Early in 1943 he attended a priests' seminar in Minnesota, and experienced an intensification of his faith. He went into personal retreat in an orphanage near Pittsburgh, after which he wrote his first story on a Catholic theme, 'Lions, Harts, Leaping Does' (1943). Having refused to report for military service, he was in September 1943 sentenced to three years in prison, from which he was paroled in November 1944, and worked as a hospital orderly. In 1946 he married Betty Wahl, a student at St Benedict's, Minnesota, whom he had met five months earlier when he was persuaded by one of her teachers to read the

manuscript of her novel—some of her short stories were published in the *New Yorker* from 1947. His own first book, *Prince of Darkness and Other Stories* (1947), contained 11 stories; his next collection, *The Presence of Grace*, only nine. In between times he taught at Marquette University, Milwaukee, for two years ('When things get really tough I take a job, usually teaching'), and with his family lived for two years in County Wicklow, Ireland. During 1957–61 ('I seldom do more than one page a day'), he worked in Dublin and St Cloud, Minnesota, on his satirical novel of the Catholic clergy, *Mort d'Urban* (1962), chapters of which had already appeared as short stories. It won the National Book Award.

Shortly afterwards he stated that at the careful pace he worked, he would probably not publish more than two or three more novels in his lifetime. *Look How the Fish Live*, short stories, was published in 1975, and his second novel, *Wheat that Springeth Green*, a more comic view of the priesthood, in 1988. Powers is a writer of the mores of the Midwest who came to combine the satire of WAUGH (he has also cited ALDOUS HUXLEY, TROLLOPE, BEERBOHM, and LARDNER in this category) with the craftsmanship such as he found in F. S. FITZGERALD, JOYCE, and K. A. PORTER (over whose *Ship of Fools* he won the National Book Award). He regards himself as a Catholic writer only in the sense that MAURIAC or GRAHAM GREENE are Catholic writers; he is primarily a *writer*. See John V. Hagopian, *J. F. Powers*, 1968 (biographical/critical study).

POWYS, JOHN COWPER (1872–1963) British novelist and prose writer, was of Welsh origin by his father, and was collaterally descended from DONNE and COWPER on his mother's side. The eldest of 11 children, he was born at his father's vicarage in Shirley, Derbyshire, and from 1879 was brought up in the West Country. He was educated at Sherborne School and Corpus Christi College, Cambridge, after which he got a job as a peripatetic lecturer at several girls' schools on the Sussex coast. He had some poems published (1896 and 1899), and in 1896, with some misgivings due to a neurosis about sex, married Margaret Lyon (*d.* 1947), from whom he was later separated. From 1898 to 1909 he travelled the country lecturing for the Oxford University Extension Delegacy, and in 1911, under the management of G. Arnold Shaw (*d.* 1937), he undertook the first of many winter tours of the USA. The last of these was in 1934, after which he and Phyllis Playter (*d.* 1982), an American he had met and fallen in love with in 1921, set up house together in Wales, first in Corwen and then in Blaenau Ffestiniog. His first novel, *Wood and Stone: a Romance*, was published in the USA in 1915, but he only achieved recognition with his fourth, *Wolf Solent* (1929), the first of four

West Country stories, of which *A Glastonbury Romance* (1933) best illustrates his central theme of self-fulfilment. *Owen Glendower: an Historical Novel* (1940) and *Porius: a Romance of the Dark Ages* (1951) have Welsh backgrounds; the latter, cut at the insistence of its original publisher from 1589 pages of typescript to 999, and then rejected, was reissued in full in 1994, ed. Wilbur T. Albrecht.

He also published several collections of philosophical essays, and studies of DOROTHY RICHARDSON (1931), DOSTOEVSKY (1947), and RABELAIS (1948). *Confessions of Two Brothers* (1916), written with Llewellyn Powys (1884–1939), novelist, travel writer, and obsessive lover, was originally intended to be 'Confessions by the Six Brothers Powys', but the others did not complete the assignment or, in the case of T. F. POWYS, did not do so in time. See *Autobiography*, new edn 1994; *Petrushka and the Dance: the Diaries of John Cowper Powys 1929–1939*, ed. Morine Krissdóttir, 1995; Richard Perceval Graves, *The Brothers Powys*, new edn 1984 (joint biography of J. C., T. F., and Llewellyn); Glen Cavaliero, *John Cowper Powys: Novelist*, 1973 (critical study).

POWYS, LLEWELLYN see POWYS, JOHN COOPER.

POWYS, T(HEODORE) F(RANCIS) (1875–1953) British novelist and short-story writer, brother of J. C. POWYS, was born in Shirley. He was at Sherborne 'Prep' from 1885 to 1889, but instead of going on to the senior school he was sent to a private boarding school in Aldeburgh, Suffolk, and was at 15 apprenticed to a farmer. Two years later his father set him up in an isolated farm at Sweffling, Suffolk, which he tried hard to make pay, when he was not buried in a book. In 1901, having suffered fits of depression, he gave up the farm and settled into an eremitic existence in Dorset, from which novels and stories eventually began to emerge. In 1905 he married Violet Dodds (d. 1966), an 18-year-old 'girl of the earth'. *The Soliloquy of a Hermit* (1916) was gladly accepted by an American publishing house which had already rejected his two brothers' 'Confessions', which it was originally intended to complement. His novels and collections of stories, beginning with *The Left Leg* (1923), are rooted in the soil and in the characteristics of those who work or depend on it, and are usually 20th-century fables in which sins are exposed and different traits contrasted. His stories—see *Mock's Curse: Nineteen Stories* (1995)—are more highly regarded than his novels, of which *Mr Tasker's Gods* (1925) has a savage theme. *Mr Weston's Good Wine* (1927), his most popular work, is a parable of wickedness and virtue in a rural setting, told with ironic humour. See William Hunter, *The Novels and Stories of T. F. Powys*, new edn 1976.

PRAED, ROSA (1851–1935), née Murray-Prior, Australian novelist, was born on a country station in Queensland, the eldest daughter of a grazier who later became a politician and Postmaster General of the state. She was largely self-educated, and with her brothers and sisters wrote, and printed, a family magazine. She had experienced the social and political life of Brisbane when she married Arthur Campbell Praed, the son of a London banker, in 1872. For three years they lived in the greatest discomfort on his station on Port Curtis Island, before thankfully finding a buyer and going to England. Her first novel, *An Australian Heroine* (1880), re-creates the conditions and station life in general, which also recur as background in *The Head Station* (1885) and *The Romance of a Station* (1889). Of her forty novels, half deal wholly or in part with Australia, and for all their colonial leanings reveal an understanding of the politics and local snobberies of the time; her English heroes, such as Hardress Barrington in *Policy and Passion* (1881), are often bounders. She also wrote novels with themes drawn from a study of psychology, beginning with *Nadine* (1882), and, with Justin MacCarthy (1860–1936), three English political novels. In 1899 she met Nancy Harward (c.1865–1927), with whom she lived after separating from her husband. She believed Nancy to be the reincarnation of a Roman slave-girl, whose story she recounted in *Nyria* (1904). Her daughter was born deaf and consigned to a lunatic asylum; of her three sons, one was killed in a car crash, one was gored to death by a rhinoceros, and the other, a cancer sufferer, committed suicide. See *My Australian Girlhood*, 1902 (autobiography); Colin Roderick, *In Mortal Bondage: the Strange Life of Rosa Praed*, 1948.

PRATT, E(DWIN) J(OHN) (1882–1964) Canadian poet, was born in Western Bay, Newfoundland, the son of a Methodist minister. After attending St John's Methodist College, he was for four years a teacher and student minister in remote communities, and was in due course ordained. After extensive studies at Victoria College, Toronto University, where he became PhD in theology while also lecturing in psychology at University College, he accepted a post to teach English at Victoria College, where he remained until 1953, when he was appointed Emeritus Professor. His stern Newfoundland background or the crisis of faith which led him to abandon the ministry, and sometimes both, are reflected in much of his verse, which he did not begin to publish until he was 35. *Newfoundland Verse* (1923), the first of several collections of shorter poems of which *The Fable of the Goats and Other Poems* (1937) won the Governor General's Award, included a continuation of *Rachel: a Sea Story of Newfoundland* (privately printed 1917). *The Witches' Brew*

(1925) is a mock-heroic on an experiment to assess the effect of alcohol on fish. 'The Cachelot' and 'The Great Feud: a Dream of a Pliocene Armageddon', which make up *Titans: Two Poems* (1926), use primeval creatures as protagonists in tremendous encounters which foreshadow narrative poems in which humans battle with the elements and with obstacles imposed by authoritarianism or ignorance. Such in particular are *The Titanic* (1935), *Brébeuf and His Brethren* (1940), a re-creation of the martyrdom of the Jesuits in Huronia in the 17th century, and *Towards the Last Spike: a Verse Panorama of the Struggle to Build the First Canadian Trans-continental . . .* (1952), an epic account, which gained him a third Governor General's Award for poetry, of the epic fight against nature, time, and imminent backrupcy to complete the 2500-mile Canadian Pacific Railway in 1871–75. See *The Complete Poems*, ed. Sandra Djwa and R. G. Moyles, 2 vols 1989; David G. Pitt, *E. J. Pratt: the Truant Years 1882–1927*, 1984, and *E. J. Pratt: the Master Years 1927–1964*, 1987.

PRAZ, MARIO (1896–1982) Italian critic and essayist, was born in Rome, and after his father's death when he was four was brought up in Florence, where he attended the Ginnasio-Liceao Galileo. He went on to the universities of Bologna, Rome, and Florence, where he became PhD in English, having arrived at that subject after switching from law to classics, and then quarrelling with his professor. He pursued his study of the Metaphysical poets in the British Museum, qualifying as *libero docente* in English literature, and then taught Italian studies at the universities of Liverpool (1924–32) and Manchester (1932–34), before returning to Rome as Professor of English Language and Literature (Emeritus from 1966). His marriage in 1934 to an Englishwoman broke up in 1945 because, he has confessed, of his 'passion for Empire furniture'. Best known in Italy as an essayist, it is as a critic of English and comparative literature that he made his international reputation, beginning with his study of 'decadent' writers and artists, *La Carne, la Morte e il Diavolo nella Letteratura Romantica* (1930; tr. Angus Davidson as *The Romantic Agony*, 1933; reissue of 2nd edn, with introduction by Frank Kermode, 1970). Another seminal work is *The Flaming Heart: Essays on Crashaw, Machiavelli, and Other Studies of the Relations between Italian and English Literature from Chaucer to T. S. Eliot* (1958). *La Casa della Vita* (1958; tr. Davidson as *The House of Life*, 1964) comprises autobiographical essays. He was made Honorary KBE in 1962.

PRÉVOST, (ANTOINE-FRANÇOIS), ABBÉ (1697–1763) French novelist and translator, was born in Hesdin, and was educated in Paris and La Fleche for the Jesuit priesthood, which he abandoned to join the army. In 1720 he began a second novitiate, with the Benedictines, taking his vows at the abbey of Jumieges in 1721. He worked as a monk in Normandy and Paris, sublimating his natural proclivities into writing romantic novels anonymously. The scandal broke with the publication in 1728 of volumes III and IV of *Les Memoires et Aventures d'un Homme de Qualité*. He took refuge in England, where he was tutor to the son of the Lord Mayor of London, gathered material for a fifth volume of 'Man of Quality', and possibly had the experiences which went into a final volume (1731). He also began *Le Philosophe Anglais: ou, Histoire de M. Cleveland, Fils Naturel de Cromwell, écrite par lui-même* (1731; tr. as *The Life and Entertaining Adventures of Mr Cleveland, natural son of Oliver Cromwell, written by himself*, 1734–35). After a period in Holland, and a further visit to England, where he was implicated in a charge of forgery, he was reconciled with the Church in France, only to be exiled again. He finally returned to spend the last twenty years of a hectic life as secular priest and freelance writer, in which capacity he translated SAMUEL RICHARDSON's *Clarissa* (1751) and *Sir Charles Grandison* (1755–58). He also prepared a definitive edition (1753) of *Histoire du Chevalier Des Grieux et de Manon Lescaut* (as *Manon Lescaut* tr. 1738; tr. L. W. Tancock, 1950). Originally the last volume of 'Man of Quality', it is the classic story of a young man's obsessive, and faithful, love for a teenage adventuress.

PRICE, (EDWARD) REYNOLDS (b. 1933) American novelist, short-story writer, poet, translator, and critic, was born in Macon, North Carolina, into a close family whose conversation shaped his dialogue, and whose real or imagined suffering at the time of his childhood during the Depression underlies much of his fiction. 'Hopeless in sports' and miserable as an adolescent, he went from high school in Raleigh to Duke University, where he graduated *summa cum laude*, having already experimented in the writing of fiction. As a Rhodes Scholar at Merton College, Oxford 1955–58, he studied under the literary scholars Lord David Cecil (1902–86) and Helen Gardner (1908–86), did a BLitt thesis on MILTON, and wrote several short stories, of which 'A Chain of Love' (introducing the Mustian family) was published in *Encounter* (see SPENDER) in 1958. He became a member of the faculty of Duke in 1958, being elected James B. Duke Professor in 1977. A writer who also teaches, he has aimed to achieve in his life the Christian solitude whose dialogue with love is central to his literary endeavours. His first novel, *A Long and Happy Life* (1962), was also published in its entirety in *Harper's Magazine*—his dramatized version was, as *Early Dark*, published in 1977 and performed in New York in 1978. Like his second novel, *A Gener-*

ous Man (1966), and *Good Hearts* (1988), it deals with incidents in the lives and metaphorical quests of the Mustian family. *The Surface of the Earth* (1975) and *The Source of Light* (1981) comprise a family saga in which the protagonist, as the normal circles of life are played out, seeks his own identity and assuagement of the guilt he feels about his dead father; it concludes with *The Promise of Rest* (1996). Short stories are in *The Names and Faces of Heroes* (1963) and *Permanent Errors* (1970)—see also *The Collected Stories* (1993).

Much of his verse, of which *Vital Provisions* (1982) and *The Laws of Ice* (1986) are collections, further reflects his Christian commitment, as do his translations from the Bible: *A Palpable God* (1978) contains versions from both the Old and New Testaments, undertaken as part of a process towards the 'purification' of his language, with an essay, 'The Origins and Life of Narrative'. Critical essays are in *Things Themselves: Essays and Scenes* (1972) and *A Common Room: Essays 1954–1987* (1989). *Clear Pictures: First Loves, First Guides* (1989) is a memoir. See Jefferson Humphries (ed.), *Conversations with Reynolds Price*, 1991; Constance Rooke, *Reynolds Price*, 1983 (biographical/critical study).

PRICHARD, KATHARINE SUSAN-NAH (1883–1969) Australian novelist and journalist, was born in Fiji, the daughter of the Editor of the *Fiji Times*. She was brought as a child to Tasmania—see her autobiographical children's story, *The Wild Oats of Han* (1928; rev. edn 1968)—and then to Melbourne. She went to South Melbourne College, whose founder and headmaster, J. B. O'Hara (1862–1927), himself a poet, encouraged her to write. Because of reverses in the family fortunes (her father subsequently committed suicide), she gave up the idea of university, and was a governess in Gippsland, and a teacher and then a journalist in Melbourne. In 1908 she went to London as a freelance journalist for the Melbourne *Herald*, whose 'Women's Work' column she then edited until 1912, when she returned to London. What she saw as a journalist of war conditions in France appalled her as much as had the living conditions of the poor in London. Her first novel, *The Pioneers* (1915), a period tale, won the Australian section of the Hodder and Stoughton All-Empire competition, and with the prize of £250 she went back to Melbourne. In 1919 she married Captain Hugo Throssell VC, and went to live in Greenmount, Western Australia. She was a founder member of the Communist Party of Australia, and wrote some political studies, including *Marx: the Man and His Work* (1922). With *The Black Opal* (1921), about an opal mining operation, she entered the political and documentary phase of her career as a novelist. She lived among the workers in the karri forests for *Working Bullocks* (1926), and

spent time on a cattle station for *Coonardoo: the Well in the Shadow* (1929), the first novel realistically to portray an Aboriginal (and a woman, too) in a leading role. She toured with a circus for *Haxby's Circus: the Lightest, Brightest Little Show on Earth* (1930).

In 1933 she embarked on a tour in the USSR, on the way back from which she had news that her husband had killed himself. The reason was almost certainly financial problems, but she feared that he had read the manuscript of her next novel, *Intimate Strangers*, in which the financially-embarrassed husband commits suicide, leaving his wife to her lover. She did not publish it until 1937, with the denouement altered, the suicide averted, and the couple reconciled. Her trilogy, *The Roaring Nineties: a Story of the Goldfields of Western Australia* (1946), *Golden Miles* (1948), and *Winged Seeds* (1950), traces (through the life of Sally Gough) industrial growth, depression, and unrest up to the 1940s, while reflecting her views on female independence and her political awareness. She also published two volumes of poetry (1913 and 1932), and several of short stories, and wrote a number of plays. Of these, *Brumby Innes*, a raw cattle-station drama, won the *Triad* magazine award in 1927, but was not produced until 1972, when it was greeted with critical acclaim. See *Child of the Hurricane: an Autobiography*, 1963; Ric Throssell, *Wild Weeds and Wind Flowers*, 2nd rev. edn 1990 (biography); Richard Nile, *The Making of a Really Modern Witch: Katharine Susannah Prichard 1919–1969*, 1990; Jack Beasley, *A Gallop of Fire: the Work of Katharine Susannah Prichard*, new edn 1993 of *The Rage for Life*, 1964.

PRIESTLEY, J(OHN) B(OYNTON) (1894–1984) British novelist, dramatist, essayist, and literary and social critic, was born in Bradford, Yorkshire, the son of a schoolmaster, and was educated at Belle Vue Grammar School, Bradford, which he left at 16 of his own choice to work for a wool merchant while preparing to be an author. He was blown up during service in the trenches in World War I, after which he went to Trinity Hall, Cambridge, before settling in London with wife and child, and £50 capital. After several books of essays and literary criticism, he published in 1927 two apprentice novels, *Adam in Moonshine* and *Benighted*. *The Good Companions* (1929), the adventures of a touring theatre company, established his reputation as a novelist, which was confirmed with *Angel Pavement* (1930), a saga of lower life in London. Later novels have similarly varied settings, and include *Festival at Farbridge* (1951) and *The Image Men* (1968). His equally long career as a successful dramatist began with *Dangerous Corner* (1932)—also in *Three Time Plays* (1947)—and included *An Inspector Calls* (1947), and *The Linden Tree* (1948), an understanding assessment of postwar moods of young and old. *Literature and Western Man* (1960) is less an historical survey than a critique of the current situation. Of his collections of essays, *Thoughts in the Wilderness* (1957) has proved most influential. His enlightening Sunday broadcasts after the nine o'clock news during the first summer of World War II were published as *Postcripts* (1940). His first wife died in 1925. In 1953, after a divorce from his second wife, he married Jacquetta Hawkes (1910–1996), née Hopkins, the archaeologist and mythologist, with whom he wrote two plays. He was awarded the OM in 1977. See *Margin Released*, 1962 (literary reminiscences); Vincent Brome, *J. B. Priestley*, 1988 (biography).

PRINGLE, THOMAS (1789–1834) Scottish poet of South Africa, was born in Teviotdale, Roxburghshire, the son of a farmer. An accident as a child left him on crutches all his life. He was educated at Kelso Grammar School and Edinburgh University, and entered the Register Office, Edinburgh, in 1811 as a copyist. In 1817 he and James Cleghorn (1778–1838) became editors of the new *Edinburgh Monthly Magazine*, published by William Blackwood (1776–1834). After three issues they were given notice, having, in the words of a contemporary, 'failed in their engagements and otherwise treated [Blackwood] unhandsomely', and were succeeded by HOGG and JOHN WILSON. After two more editorial disasters, WALTER SCOTT, who had been impressed by his poems, *The Autumnal Excursion, or Sketches in Teviotdale* (1817), recommended a grant of land for him and a party of settlers in the Neutral Territory of Cape Colony from which the Xhosa had been expelled. There Pringle adapted his pastoral expression to African situations: 'First the brown Herder with his flock / Comes winding round my hermit-rock / His mien and gait and vesture tell, / No shepherd he from Scottish fell'. His Border upbringing enabled him to understand, rather than deprecate, the cattle-raiding habits of the Xhosa. 'Pringle writes about the non-white with humanitarian feeling,' says MPHAHLELE. To which GORDIMER has added: 'He anticipated, astonishingly, themes that were not to be taken up again by any writer in South Africa for a hundred years, and longer' (among them miscegenation). He moved to Cape Town, where he worked in the public library, and published a journal whose Whig politics and outspokenness on controversial matters caused it to be suppressed by the Governor and to his leaving the country in 1826. In 1827 he was appointed Secretary of the Anti-Slavery Society, in which capacity he signed in 1834, shortly before his death, a document announcing the abolition of slavery in British colonies. *African Sketches, Narrative of a Residence in South Africa* (1834) contains his most significant verse. See June Meiring, *Thomas Pringle: His Life and Times*, 1968.

PRIOR, MATTHEW (1664–1721) British poet, was born in Dorset, of Nonconformist parents (see 'An Epistle to Fleetwood Shephard Esq'), and went to Westminster School, from which he was removed on his father's death to work for his uncle, the proprietor of the Rhenish Wine House in the City of London. The Earl of Dorset (1638–1706), finding the boy reading HORACE in the bar, invited him to translate a piece. This became a customary diversion for the clientele, and Dorset arranged for his return to Westminster, from which he went on to St John's College, Cambridge. While there, he wrote with Charles Montagu (1661–1715), later Earl of Halifax, *The Hind and the Panther Transvers'd to the Story of The Country Mouse and the City Mouse* (1687), a burlesque on DRYDEN. He became secretary to the Ambassador in The Hague, taking part in the negotiations leading to the Treaty of Ryswick (1697), for which he received a bonus of 200 guineas. He also found time for relaxation (see 'Written in the Year 1696', also known as 'The Secretary'). After serving in Paris, he became an under-secretary of state; in 1700 he succeeded LOCKE as Commissioner for Trade. The volume of 17 of his poems published in 1707 was unauthorized. *Poems on Several Occasions* (dated 1709) contained 51.

During the reign of Queen Anne Prior changed his political allegiance from the Whigs to the Tories, on whose behalf he secretly instigated negotiations in Paris leading to the Treaty of Utrecht (1713), which became jocularly known as 'Matt's Peace'. With the Whigs back in power in 1715, he suffered a year's house arrest in the home of a Parliamentary official. On his release, Robert Harley (1661–1724), Earl of Oxford, formerly Tory leader of the Government (see also DEFOE), initiated the publication by subscription of the 1818 edition of *Poems on Several Occasions* (111 poems, of which Prior spent a year producing definitive versions). He also paid half the purchase price of Down Hall, Essex, where the poet spent the rest of his life. Prior was a master of light and colloquial verse, the best of which embraces the bawdy denouements of 'Hans Carvel' and 'The Ladle', the only marginally indelicate 'An English Padlock' and 'To a Young Gentleman in Love', the tribute to his maidservant/mistress 'Jinny the Just', and the songs, especially 'To Phillis' and 'Chloe Beauty has and Wit'. Of his longer works, 'Solomon on the Vanity of the World' is of greater intellectual than literary interest; 'Alma: or, the Progress of the Mind', drafted while he was under arrest, illustrates as well as ridicules the various systems of philosophy. See *The Literary Works of Matthew Prior*, ed. H. Bunker Wright and Munroe K. Spears, 2nd edn 1971.

PRITCHETT, (Sir) V(ICTOR) S(AW-DON) (1900–97) British short-story writer, novelist, travel writer, and critic, was born in Ipswich, Suffolk, and educated at Alleyn's School, Dulwich, which he was forced to leave at 16 to work in the leather trade. After four years he went to Paris, where he became a photographer's assistant. He was correspondent of the *Christian Science Monitor* in Ireland and Spain from 1923 to 1926, when he became a freelance reviewer in London, especially for the *New Statesman*, of which he was appointed a director in 1946. His first book, *Marching Spain* (1928), records his travels in that country, which remained a chief interest. The best of his five novels is held to be *Mr Beluncle* (1951), a comedy of characterization in which a man's compulsive fantasy takes over his life. His finest work is in his short stories, the first collection of which was *The Spanish Virgin and Other Stories* (1930). In an interview in 1988, Pritchett described himself as a craftsman, not an aesthete, preferring 'the plotless story where there's plenty of action, plenty of drama, but much of it internal'. His critical works include *The Living Novel* (1946), *George Meredith and English Comedy* (1970), the subject of his Clark Lectures at Cambridge the previous year, and *Lasting Impressions* (1990), essays on other writers, when writing about whom his tone was always generous, but firm. He also wrote biographies of BALZAC (1973), TURGENEV (1977), and CHEKHOV (1988). He was made CBE in 1968, knighted in 1975, and appointed CH in 1993. See *The Complete Collected Stories*, new edn 1992; *The Complete Essays*, 1991; *A Cab at the Door: Childhood and Youth 1900–1920*, 1968, and *Midnight Oil*, 1971 (autobiography, published together new edn 1994).

PROPERTIUS, SEXTUS (c.50–c.15 BC) Roman elegiac poet, was born near Assisi. His father died when he was young, and the family was dispossessed in the proscriptions following the death of CAESAR, but his mother sent him to Rome to be educated for the law. Instead he turned to poetry, and published in about 26 BC a book of elegies, which brought him fame and an introduction to literary circles. Resisting persuasion to write patriotic verse, he published three more books in the same vein before his early death from an unknown cause. Most of his poems describe his love for Cynthia, who in real life was called Hostia and was a freed-woman or a courtesan. They are peppered with academic allusions and pervaded with melancholy, but the emotions read as though they are sincerely expressed and the poetry is rich in sound. See *The Poems*, tr. Guy Lee, introduction by Oliver Lyne, new edn 1996.

PROUST, MARCEL (1871–1922) French novelist and critic, was born in Paris of a Catholic father, who was a doctor, and a Jew-ish mother. When he was nine he had his first severe attack of asthma, which played havoc with the rest of his life. He was educated at the Lycée Condorcet and, after military service, at the École des Sciences Politiques, after which he infiltrated high society. He began contributing to reviews in 1892, fought a duel in 1897 with an author whose work he had criticized, and worked on a novel, *Jean Santeuil*, not published until 1952 (tr. Gerard Hopkins, 1955), which is a preliminary sketch for *À la Recherche du Temps Perdu*. His preoccupation with the work of RUSKIN led to critical articles on that author in 1900, and to copiously annotated translations of *The Bible of Amiens* (1904), a spiritual as well as an architectural guidebook, and of *Sesame and Lilies* (1906). In 1909 he virtually abandoned his social life and retired to his cork-lined bedroom to devote himself to *À la Recherche*; he published the first volume, *Du Côté de chez Swann* [*Swann's Way*] (1913), extracts from which had appeared in *Le Figaro* at his own expense after several publishers had turned it down. In 1914 his adored chauffeur/secretary, Alfred Agostinelli, died when he crashed his plane into the sea on his first solo flight: to be transformed into Albertine, the fickle mistress in subsequent volumes of the sequence, of which the second, *À l'Ombre des Jeunes Filles en Fleurs* [*Within a Budding Grove*] (1918) won the Prix GONCOURT. The seven volumes constitute a deeply significant, quasi-autobiographical study of people and a society, in which the protagonist, Marcel, assumes a variety of roles before ultimately regaining his lost vocation as a writer. The sequence has been reissued as *In Search of Lost Time* (1992) in a revised translation in five volumes, tr. C. K. Scott Moncrieff and Terence Kilmartin, vol. 5 rev. D. J. Enright, with a sixth volume, *Time Regained: a Guide to Proust*, compiled by Terence Kilmartin, rev. Joanna Kilmartin. See *Against Sainte-Beuve and Other Essays*, tr. John Sturrock, new edn 1994: *On Art and Literature 1896–1919*, tr. Sylvia Townsend Warner, new edn 1996; George D. Painter, *Marcel Proust: a Biography*, new edn 1996 of two vols 1956, 1965; Derwent May, *Proust*, 1984 (introduction to his thought).

PROUT, FATHER, pen name of Frances Sylvester Mahony (1804–66) Irish journalist, was born in Cork, the second son of a woollen manufacturer, and was educated at Clongowes Wood, Co. Kildare, by the Jesuits, whose order he decided to enter. He studied in France, where he demonstrated a fine facility in Latin and Greek, and in 1830 he returned to Clongowes Wood as Prefect of Studies. A drunken outing with students led to his resignation, and to his subsequent dismissal from the Order, but after further studies he was ordained a priest, and assigned to Cork, where he gave selfless service during the cholera epidemic. In 1834, presumably having been relieved of his duties, he turned up in London, where he established himself as a journalist. For two years he regaled the readers of *Fraser's Magazine* with monthly instalments of the posthumous writings of 'Father Prout', whom he introduced as the son of SWIFT and Stella. Scholarly, entertaining, and often interspersed with his own lyrics (notably 'The Shandon Bells') and verse parodies, they were collected as *The Reliques of Father Prout* (1836). His most glorious spoof was to accuse THOMAS MOORE of having plagiarized some of his songs, in proof of which he offered the 'originals' in Greek, Latin, and Old French. He contributed also to DICKENS's *Bentley's Miscellany* and *Daily News*, of which he was Rome correspondent in 1846–47. He ended his days in Paris, from which he sent an inaugural ode for THACKERAY's *Cornhill Magazine* in 1860.

PRUNIER, JOSEPH see MAUPASSANT.

PULCI, LUIGI see BYRON; ARIOSTO.

PURCHAS, SAMUEL see HAKLUYT.

PURDY, AL(FRED WELLINGTON) (*b.* 1918) Canadian poet, was born in Wooller, Ontario, two months after the munitions' explosion at Trenton, where he was brought up by his strictly religious mother after his father's death in 1920. He left Albert College, Belleville, without completing grade 10, and had a variety of occasional jobs before serving in the Royal Canadian Air Force in northern British Columbia during World War II. In 1944 he paid a Vancouver printer $200 to produce 500 copies of a book of verse, *The Enchanted Echo*. While working in a mattress factory in the early 1950s he was persuaded by a friend to read modern poetry, which fired him to become a full-time poet. He built a house on Roblin Lake, Prince Edward County, where he wrote while his wife earned their keep. In his fourth and fifth volumes, the aptly named *The Crafte So Longe to Lerne* (1959) and *Poems for All the Annettes* (1962), a mature writer emerged with a voice of his own and a penchant for making poetry out of everyday activities and observations. *The Cariboo Horses* (1965) won the Governor General's Award, as later did his collected poems. His first novel, *A Splinter in the Heart* (1990), covers a 16-year-old's summer in Trenton in 1918, the year of the Trenton Disaster. He edited *I've Tasted My Blood: Poems 1956–1968* (1969) by Milton Acorn (1923–85), whom his Toronto contemporaries named 'the people's poet'. Purdy was made Member, Order of Canada, in 1982. See *Collected Poems*, ed. Russell Brown, with an afterword by Dennis Lee, 1986; Louis MacKendrick, *Al Purdy and His Works*, 1994.

PUSHKIN, ALEXANDER (SERGEEVICH) (1799–1837) Russian poet, novelist, and dramatist, was born in Moscow of a former boyar family; his mother was descended from a slave, an Ethiopian aristocrat acquired by Peter the Great as a child, who later became a military engineer. He began writing poetry at the lycée at Tsarskoe Selo, near St Petersburg, and continued to do so while working unenthusiastically in the city as a civil servant, one of his more delightful efforts being the mock-heroic ['Ruslan and Lyudmilla'] (tr. Nancy Dargel as *Ruslan and Ludmilla: a Novel in Verse*, 1994). He was also generally living it up and participating in the activities of a politically-orientated literary debating club, some of the members of which were associated with the Decembrists, whose revolt in 1825 against the new Tsar, Nicholas I, led to the execution of five of them. Pushkin's contribution to club proceedings was purely literary, but his liberal-minded verses came to the notice of the authorities. In 1820 he was compulsorily 'transferred' to the south, where he was inspired by the environment to write the romantic narrative poems ['The Prisoner of the Caucasus'] and ['The Fountain of Bakchisarai']; and to begin ['The Gypsies'], a more thoughtful example of the genre, and his celebrated 'novel in verse', *Eugene Onegin*.

In 1824 he was dismissed altogether from the civil service and ordered to live under police supervision on his mother's estate at Mikhailovskoye in the northwest. His parents, furious at his irresponsibility, departed to St Petersburg, leaving Pushkin on his own. It was an opportunity of creative solitude which he celebrated by writing *Boris Godunov* (1831; tr. Alfred Hayes, 1918), his notable verse tragedy after the style of SHAKESPEARE. Nicholas I was more favourably inclined to him than his predecessor had been, and Pushkin was given his freedom. In 1831, after visiting his brother in the Caucasus in an attempt to join the army there, he married Natalia Goncharova, a 20-year-old beauty whom he had been pursuing for three years. The arrival of two children did nothing to ease the family budget. Pushkin's appointment as a gentleman of the chamber at court was irksome to him in the light of the fact that the Tsar clearly fancied his wife; so, unfortunately, did Baron D'Anthès, the French-born adopted son of the Dutch ambassador. Goaded by anonymous letters and the well-meant comments of his friends, Pushkin wrote a provocative letter to the ambassador, and was challenged by D'Anthès to a duel, in which he was mortally wounded. He died two days later. Natalia received a pension from the Tsar and later remarried. D'Anthès was invited to leave the country and eventually returned to France, where he lived until 1895, apparently unrepentant to the last at having killed Russia's greatest poet. Apart from *Boris Godunov*, *Eugene Onegin* (1833; tr. Charles Johnston, rev edn, introduction by

John Bayley, 1979; tr. James E. Falen, 1995), and the story ['The Queen of Spades']—see in *Complete Prose Tales*, tr. Gillon R. Aitken (1978) and *Complete Prose Fiction*, tr. Paul Debreczeny (1983)—he wrote some of the finest lyrics in the Russian language, while ['The Bronze Horseman'] is a narrative poem of extraordinary imaginative power and historical understanding—see *The Bronze Horseman and Other Poems*, tr. D. M. Thomas (1982). See *Alexander Pushkin*, ed. A. D. P. Briggs, 1997 (selection); Robin Edmonds, *Pushkin: the Man and His Age*, 1995.

PYM, BARBARA (1913–80) British novelist, was born in Oswestry, Shropshire, the daughter of a solicitor, and was educated at Liverpool College, Huyton, a boarding school, and at St Hilda's College, Oxford, where she got a second in English and had numerous romantic adventures. She then lived at home, writing, doing housework, and fending off propositions of marriage. During World War II she worked as a postal censor in Bristol (and had an unhappy love affair), and from 1943 served in the Women's Royal Naval Service, becoming a third officer and being posted to Naples. After the war she joined the International African Institute, for which she worked until her retirement in 1974. She had written an unpublished novel when she was 16. A further novel, begun in 1934, finally appeared as *Some Tame Gazelle* (1950), under the imprint of the publishing firm which had rejected it 14 years earlier. Between 1952 and 1961 she published five more domestic novels distinguished by their gentle irony. The next, and several ideas for further novels, were consistently rejected over the ensuing 16 years, until she was nominated by LARKIN and Lord David Cecil (1902–86) in a survey in *The Times Literary Supplement* as the most underrated writer of the century. This nudged the firm to which it was on offer to publish *Quartet in Autumn*

(1977). For three years she was able to enjoy her new-found cult status, but she died of cancer just before the publication of the last book she wrote, *A Few Green Leaves* (1980). Latterly she lived with her sister in the tiny Oxfordshire village of Finstock. See *A Very Private Eye: an Autobiography in Letters and Diaries*, new edn 1994; Hazel Holt, *A Lot to Ask: a Life of Barbara Pym*, new edn 1992; Michael Cotsell, *Barbara Pym*, 1989 (critical study).

PYNCHON, THOMAS (*b.* 1937) American novelist, was born in Glen Cove, New York. At Cornell University he first read engineering physics, but after service in the US Navy, he returned to graduate in English, of which one of his teachers was NABOKOV. While there he published his first story in the *Cornell Writer*. He was an editorial writer for the Boeing Corporation in Seattle, subsequently living in Mexico before settling in California. That is about all that has been discovered about a writer the only known photograph of whom was taken in 1955. *V* (1963), *The Crying of Lot 49* (1966), and *Gravity's Rainbow* (1973) are acknowledged as brilliantly evoked, surreal, often parabolical or parodical manifestations of an exuberant mind; each has a tenuous thread of interest from which are generously dispensed clues to the author's general meaning. Situations include a secret society for the subversion of the US postal system, an international cartel controlling the supply of light bulbs, alligators breeding in the sewers of New York, and the symbolically phallic flight of a V2 rocket. *Gravity's Rainbow* shared the National Book Award with a book of stories by SINGER; was selected for the Pulitzer Prize but thrown out by the advisory board as being 'obscene' and 'unreadable'; and won the Howells Medal, which the author refused. After a 17-year silence, broken only by a collection of early short stories, *Slow Learner* (1984), *Vineland* (1990) proved a critical disappointment. See Molly Hite, *Ideas of Order in the Novels of Thomas Pynchon*, 1983.

Q

QUARLES, FRANCIS (1592–1644) English poet and prose writer, was born at the family manor in Romford, Essex, the son of Elizabeth I's Surveyor-General of naval victualling, who died soon after the boy's birth. He was educated at Christ's College, Cambridge, and then studied law, after which he went abroad as cupbearer to the Princess Elizabeth on her marriage to the Elector Palatine (from whom the present British Royal Family is descended). On his return he was for a time secretary to James Ussher (1581–1656), Archbishop of Armagh, in Ireland. He also wrote *A Feast for Worms, Set Forth in a Poem of the History of Jonah* (1620) and several other equally gloomy biblical narrative poems. In 1635, now retired to Essex, he produced *Emblems*, in five volumes, each of which contained 15 symbolic pictures (many, according to the custom of the time, copied from other books), to which he appended pious verses. It is said to have been the most popular book of verse in the 17th century. He was appointed Chronologer of the City of London in 1640, in which year he wrote *The Virgin Widow* (published 1649), a comic allegorical dramatic piece. He now confined his literary activities to prose, of which *Enchyridion* (1640; enlarged edn 1641), a collection of religious and moral aphorisms, was especially admired and often reprinted. He died a pauper, leaving a widow and the nine surviving of their 18 children, the eldest of whom, John Quarles (1624–65), became an impecunious poet and died in London of the plague.

QUENEAU, RAYMOND (1903–76) French novelist and poet, was born and went to school in Le Havre, then studied philosophy at Paris University. After military service he got a job with the Comptoire National d'Escompte, mixed with but did not see eye to eye with the Surrealist poets, and embarked on a study of *fous littéraires*. His first novel, *Le Chiendent* (1933; tr. Barbara Wright as *The Bark-Tree*, 1968), reflected his preoccupation with spoken language and experimental narrative forms. His long poem *Chêne et Chien* [Oak and Dog] (1937) is a personal exploration of the line between unhappiness and happiness for which he drew on his experience of psychoanalysis. Depths and patterns of meaning underlie the novels *Un Rude Hiver* (1939; tr. Betty Askwith as *A Hard Winter*, 1948) and *Pierrot Mon Ami* (1942; tr. J. Maclaren-Ross as *Pierrot*, 1950), the latter published during the Occupation of France. The zany heroine let loose on Paris in *Zazie dans le Metro* (1959; tr. Wright as *Zazie in the Metro*, 1960) was more to the public taste. In *Exercises de Style* (1947; tr. Wright as *Exercises in Style*, 1958) the same incident is related in 99 different styles. Unlimited, if finite, possibilities attend *Cent Mille Milliards de Poèmes* (1961; tr. John Crombie as *One Hundred Million Million Poems*, 1983), the pages of the book being cut into horizontal strips so that each line of ten sonnets can be combined with lines from any of the others. This was a practical demonstration of the philosophy of Ouvroir de Littérature Potentielle (Oulipo), a literary subgroup (formed by himself) of the Collège de Pataphysique, an organization devoted to pataphysics, a science created by the French writer and dramatist, Alfred Jarry (1873–1907), which in its pursuit of imaginary solutions can also be regarded as the science of the absurd—see *Oulipo Laboratory: Texts from the Bibliotheque Oulipienne*, tr. Harry Matthews, Iain White, and Warren Motte (1995).

QUEVEDO, FRANCISCO DE see GONGORA.

QUILLER-COUCH, (Sir) **ARTHUR** (1863–1944) British novelist, poet, and critic, usually known as 'Q', was born in Bodmin, Cornwall. He was educated at Clifton College and Trinity College, Oxford, about which he composed his best-known poem, 'Alma Mater' (1896), and where he wrote his first novel, *Dead Man's Rock* (1887). Having stayed on for one year as a lecturer in classics, he spent the next five in London, working as a freelance journalist and also for a publisher, to whose Liberal weekly, *The Speaker*, he contributed a story a week from 1890, as well as articles and reviews. During this time he was supporting his widowed mother, two brothers, a wife (from 1889), and a son (from 1890), while also trying, gallantly and ultimately successfully, to wipe off family debts which he was under no obligation to pay. In 1892 his health broke down and on medical advice he went to live by the sea, at Fowey, Cornwall, the 'Troy Town' of his novels. He continued to support himself and family by his pen, producing on average two books a year. As well as fiction, he wrote serious verse, light verse, such as the hilarious mishmash of sporting terms, 'The Famous Ballad of the Jubilee Cup' (1897), and parodies, such as 'A New Ballad of Sir Patrick Spens' (1898), and compiled anthologies, most notably *The Oxford Book of English Verse* (1900; rev. edn 1939). In 1912, to his surprise, he was appointed King Edward VII Professor of English Literature at Cambridge, in which capacity he gave several series of memorable lectures, collected as *On the Art of Writing* (1916), *Studies in Literature* (1918, 1922, 1929), and *On the Art of Reading* (1920). As a novelist, his talents lay in historical adventure and Cornish romanticism—he was commissioned to complete STEVENSON's *St Ives* (1897), and another Cornish novelist, DAPHNE DU MAURIER, did the same for his *Castle Dor* (1962). He was knighted in 1910. See *Memories and Opinions: an Unfinished Autobiography*, ed. S. C. Roberts, 1944.

R

RABELAIS, FRANÇOIS (c.1490–1553) French prose writer, was born in Chinon, was educated probably at the Benedictine monastery of Seuilly and at the University of Angers, and became a Franciscan friar in 1520. Thwarted by his superiors' opposition to his reading the New Testament in Greek, he joined the Benedictines, and then in about 1528 became a secular priest. In 1530 he enrolled in the Faculty of Medicine at Montpellier University, becoming BM after only three months. He set up in practice in Lyons, published translations of the Greek physicians Hippocrates (c.460–c.357 BC) and Galen (c.130–c.199), and entered into correspondence with leading humanists, including ERASMUS. The popular success of a chapbook chronicling the deeds of the 'monstrous giant Gargantua' moved him to produce a follow-up of his own (under the anagram 'Alcofribas Nasier'), *Horribles et Espouvantables Faictz et Prouesses du Très Renommé Pantagruel, Fils du Grant Géant Gargantua* (1532), which was promptly condemned as obscene by Paris University. Rabelais responded with *Vie Inestimable du Grant Gargantua . . .* (1534), a satirical pre-sequel in which he aired his views on education, the morality of war, and theologians. Predictably, it too was proscribed, with such vehemence that he was forced to go into hiding.

He was rescued by Cardinal Du Bellay (1492–1560), who took him to Italy, and then secured him a post as physician in a monastery, until his fellow canons objected to his presence. After taking his doctorate at Montpellier, he was for a time attached to the court. A third book (1546), chauvinistically male but theologically unobjectionable, suffered the same fate as the others, and attacks on him were now mounted also by CALVIN and a monk calling himself Putherbus. To an incomplete fourth book (1548) he added some lively anti-papal allusions, but shortly after the complete version was published (1552), the new King, Henry II, made up his differences with the Pope, and the volume was banned. Indeed, it is said that Rabelais was imprisoned; certainly he renounced the emoluments Du Bellay had granted him as absentee incumbent of two parishes. A fifth book, in two instalments (1562–64), is not regarded as being entirely genuine. The whole work, however, for its zest, erudition, wit, and comic invention, is one of the world's most notable literary entertainments, whose disciples range from SWIFT and STERNE to JOYCE. URQUHART's creative translation (1653–93) of the first three books was continued (1694) rather less felicitously by Peter Motteux (1660–1718), an unremarkable dramatist of Norman origin who died in a London brothel—see *Gargantua and Pantagruel*, tr. Urquhart and Motteau, introduction by Terence Cave (1994). See *The Histories of Gargantua and Pantagruel*, tr. Burton Raffel, new edn 1992.

RABINOVITZ, SOLOMON see SHALOM ALEICHEM.

RACINE, JEAN (1639–99) French dramatist, was born in La Ferté-Milon. His mother died in 1641 giving birth to his sister, and his father, after a brief second marriage, died in 1643. He was brought up by his maternal grandmother and was educated as a boarder at the grammar school at Beauvais and at the progressive school of Port-Royal des Champs (whose religious beliefs PASCAL was supporting), after which he studied philosophy at Collège d'Harcourt, Paris. Failing, in spite of nepotism, to gain a benefice in the diocese of Uzèr, he returned to Paris, where in 1664 he offered a tragedy after the Greek, *La Thébaïde*, to MOLIÈRE, whose company presented it that summer. *Alexandre le Grand* (1665) was put on first by Molière and two weeks later by Montfleury (c.1600–67), and caused a breach with Port-Royal, to whose adherents 'a man who writes plays is a public poisoner'. In November 1667, the day after a private preview in the Queen's apartments in the Louvre, *Andromaque* opened at the Hôtel de Bourgogne. Racine's mistress, Mlle Du Parc (1633–68) was in the title role: in a court disposition during a series of sorcery trials in 1679 he was accused of poisoning her in order to enjoy the services of Mlle Champnesle (1642–98), who played several of his tragic heroines. The subject of *Bérénice* (1670) was suggested to him by Henrietta (1644–70), Duchesse d'Orléans, sister of the King of England (Charles II) and sister-in-law of Louis XIV; she also proposed the same theme to CORNEILLE. Both plays were performed within a week of each other five months after her sudden death, with Racine's outlasting its rival. In 1677, after several further successes, particularly *Iphigénie* (1674) and *Phèdre et Hippolyte* (1677), further explorations of themes from Greek mythology, he made a sensible but loveless marriage with 25-year-old Catherine de Romanet, renounced the theatre, and was appointed (with BOILEAU) Historiographer Royal.

He wrote nothing more for the stage until persuaded by Mme de Maintenon (1635–1719), mistress and (from 1683) secret wife of Louis XIV, to compose two plays for her school for impoverished young ladies at St-Cyr. Two biblical plays resulted, *Esther* (1689; publicly performed 1721) and *Athalie* (1691). The latter, one of his strongest works, fell flat when played by schoolgirls and had small success when published, but was recognized as a masterpiece when it was finally put on at the Comédie Française in 1716. Racine was a tragic dramatist of the highest order, whose observance of the unities of action, setting, and time enabled him all the more effectively to develop a situation from the point at which it is about to burst open. The poetry of his rhyming alexandrines is the perfect match for his dramatic plan—it is said that he wrote the second line of each couplet first, in order to avoid any suggestion of artifice. See *Andromache, Britannicus, Berenice*, new edn 1967, and *Iphigenia, Phaedra, Athaliah*, new edn 1970, tr. John Cairncross; *Britannicus, Phaedra, Athaliah*, tr. C. H. Sisson, 1987.

RADCLIFFE, ANN (1764–1823), née Ward, British novelist and poet, was born in London, the daughter of a tradesman who through his and his wife's family had connections in artistic and court circles. When she was 23 she married, in Bath, William Radcliffe, a lawyer who later became Editor of the *English Chronicle*. After a short novel, *The Castles of Athlin and Dunbayne* (1789), she published *A Sicilian Romance* (1790), which WALTER SCOTT regarded as the first English poetical novel. She followed it with *The Romance of the Forest* (1791), which quickly went through several editions, was dramatized by John Boaden (d. 1839), and was translated into French and Italian. Her reputation in modern times rests on *The Mysteries of Udolpho, a Romance Interspersed with Some Pieces of Poetry* (1794), for which her publisher paid the then unprecedented sum of £500 for the first edition. The 'poetry' is puerile, but the novel itself is one of the most famous examples of the Gothic genre, being all the more impressive in that even the most bizarre manifestations have rational explanations. Such was its success that she received £800 for *The Italian, or the Confessional of the Black Penitents* (1797), a romance of the Inquisition. Having written a travel book about her carriage trip through Holland and Germany, she retired

from the literary scene so completely that in 1816 an anonymous compiler, thinking she was dead, published a book of her verses, with the addition of some of his or her own. See Robert Miles, *Ann Radcliffe: 'The Great Enchantress'*, 1995 (critical biography); J. M. S. Tompkins, *Ann Radcliffe and Her Influence on Later Writers*, 1980; John Andrew Stoler, *Ann Radcliffe: the Novel of Suspense and Terror*, 1980.

RADCLYFFE-HALL, MARGUERITE see HALL, RADCLYFFE.

RAINE, CRAIG (*b.* 1944) British poet and critic, was born in Bishop Auckland, Durham, the son of a one-time 'painter and decorator, plumber, electrician, publican and boxer, but when I was growing up, he was a Spiritualist and a faith healer'—see the memoir 'A Silver Plate' in *Rich* (1983; trade edn 1984). He was educated at Barnard Castle School and Exeter College, Oxford. During the 1970s he was a lecturer successively at Exeter and Lincoln colleges and Christ Church, Oxford. He was Poetry Editor at Faber & Faber, a post originally created by T. S. ELIOT, from 1981 to 1991, when he became a Fellow of New College, Oxford. His poetry, which is spare, tight, and expressive of a wide range of emotions and situations, often has a literary, a historical, or simply an erotic starting point. His books of verse before *Rich* were *The Onion, Memory* (1978) and *A Martian Sends a Postcard Home* (1979). The collection *Clay: Whereabouts Unknown* (1996) records his reactions over ten years to the births of two sons and the deaths of relatives and friends. *History: the Home Movie* (1994) is a historical chronicle in verse, with fictional episodes, comprising 87 poems in three-line stanzas, which reflects the links between his family and that of PASTERNAK—Raine's wife Ann, whom he met in 1972 when they were both research students at Oxford and married a few weeks later, is the daughter of the Russian poet's sister and of Raine's uncle. *'1953'* (1996) is a strong verse play based on *Andromaque* of RACINE, transformed to a 1950s' scenario in which the Axis powers have won World War II. *Haydn and the Valve Trumpet: Literary Essays* (1990)—the title is a reference to a reviewer's anachronism—is a substantial collection of his literary journalism.

RAINE, KATHLEEN (*b.* 1908) British poet and critic, was born in Ilford, Essex, but spent part of her childhood as an evacuee in Northumberland, where she places her 'poetic roots'. She was educated at the County High School, Ilford, and at Girton College, Cambridge, where she read natural sciences and was the only female member of the 'Cambridge Poets', who included EMPSON. *Stone and Flower: Poems 1935–1943* (1943) was distinctive for its precise awareness and observation of natural phenomena. Since then she has quietly pursued the policy she expressed in the introduction to *The Collected Poems of Kathleen Raine* (1956): 'The ever-recurring forms of nature mirror eternal reality; the never-recurring productions of human history reflect only fallen man, and are therefore not suitable to become a symbolic vocabulary for the kind of poetry I have attempted to write.' She was a Research Fellow at Girton from 1955 to 1961. Her critical works include several studies of BLAKE—notably *William Blake* (1951; rev. edn 1969)—and of DAVID JONES and YEATS. She was a co-founder in 1981 of the journal, *Temenos*, 'to re-affirm values which we regard as essential if the arts are to recover from their present decline'. Her series of spiritual and literary autobiographies, *Farewell Happy Fields* (1973), *The Land Unknown* (1975), and *The Lion's Mouth* (1977)—reissued in one volume as *Autobiographies* (1991)—is also a record of her intense but unfulfilled relationship with Gavin Maxwell (1914–69), the travel writer, naturalist, and author of *Ring of Bright Water* (1960)—see Douglas Botting, *Gavin Maxwell: a Life* (1993). After his death she wrote the poetical sequence, *On a Deserted Shore* (1973). See *Collected Poems 1935–1980*, 1981; *The Presence: Poems 1984-1987*, new edn 1994; *Living with Mystery: Poems 1987–1991*, 1992; *Selected Poems*, 1989.

RALEGH (or **RALEIGH**), (Sir) **WALTER** (1552–1618) English poet, prose writer, man of war, and adventurer, was born in Hayes Barton, Devonshire, a younger son of a country gentleman, and spent a year or so at Oriel College, Oxford, before fighting in Europe and Ireland as a volunteer to the Protestant cause. By 1580 he had become a favourite of Elizabeth I, in whose honour he composed several poems (addressed to 'Cynthia'), and on whose behalf he harried the Spaniards and discovered and colonized Virginia. He was knighted on his return. His plain, racy account of the naval action in which the *Revenge* went down (TENNYSON based his ballad 'The Revenge' on it) was published anonymously in 1591. The next year he fell out of favour because of his affair with a maid-of-honour, whom he later married (their first sexual encounter is entertainingly described by AUBREY). His reputation revived after his exploration of Guiana, of which he published in 1596 a basically accurate description. Accused in 1603 of conspiracy against James I (James VI of Scotland), he was sentenced to death but was instead imprisoned for life in the Tower of London, where he wrote *The History of the World* (1614), a well-written and well-arranged account of biblical, Greek, and Roman history which breaks off at the end of the Third Macedonian War in 168 BC . He was released in 1616 to find a gold mine in Guiana. The expedition was a disaster, and on his return the

original sentence of beheading was carried out, which he awaited calmly, writing verses. There was no authenticated edition of his poetry until that edited in 1875 by John Hannah (1818–88), Archdeacon of Lewes. See *Selected Writings*, ed. Gerald Hammond, new edn 1986; Stephen Coote, *A Play of Passion: the Life of Sir Walter Ralegh*, new edn 1994; Walter Oakeshott, *The Queen and the Poet*, 1960.

RAMANUJAN, A(TTIPAT) K(RISHNASWAMI) (1929–93) Indian poet, was born in Mysore and educated at D. Bhanumaiah's High School and Maharaja's College, becoming PhD in linguistics at the University of Indiana, USA, in 1963. He taught English literature at several Indian universities between 1950 and 1958. In 1962 he became a member of the teaching staff of Chicago University, where he was appointed professor of Dravidian studies and linguistics in 1972. His first book of verse, *The Striders* (1966), was a Poetry Society recommendation. He explained that 'English and my disciplines (linguistics, anthropology) give me my "outer" forms . . . and my first thirty years in India . . . , my personal and professional preoccupations with Kannada and Tamil, the classics and folklore give me my substance'. He also published volumes of verse, and a novel, in Kannada. See *The Collected Poems of A. K. Ramanujan*, 1995.

RAMSAY, ALLAN (1684/5–1758) Scottish poet, dramatist, and anthologist, was born in Leadhills, Lanarkshire, the son of a factor who died shortly afterwards. His mother married a local farmer, who educated him at the parish school and in 1700 apprenticed him to an Edinburgh wig-maker. Ramsay became a master wig-maker and was elected a city burgess in 1710. In 1724 he finally abandoned the wig trade for the book trade, and in 1725 founded the first circulating library in Britain. In *Poems* (1721) he employed a variety of verse forms, including the epistle and what he termed the 'standard habbie', a six-line rhyming stanza ending with a short punch line (see SEMPILL). He wrote both in English and in Scots, which had ceased to be a poetic medium since JAMES VI's court moved to London in 1603. He further revived interest in Scottish literature with *The Ever Green* (1724), an anthology of early poetry, and several collections of ballads and songs, *The Tea-Table Miscellany* (1724–37). His verse play, *The Gentle Shepherd* (1725), which has good songs and excellent characterization, was the first notable Scottish drama for almost two hundred years. In 1736 he built in Carubber's Close the first regular theatre in Edinburgh. He was forced to close it almost immediately in the aftermath of the Licensing Act of 1737, in effect banning unauthorized performances outside London; Ramsay appealed against it unsuccessfully in verse to the Court of Session. A genuine pastoral and satirical poet, he created an atmosphere in which FERGUSSON could write in Scots and from which BURNS took his inspiration. His son Allan (1713–84), the portrait painter, designed for his father's retirement a house on Castle Hill, Edinburgh, which the poet, alarmed at the expense, altered while it was being built, giving it, according to the judge Lord Milton (1692–1766), the likeness of a goose pie. See *Poems by Allan Ramsay and Robert Fergusson*, ed. Alexander Manson Kinghorn and Alexander Law, new edn 1985; Burns Martin, *Allan Ramsay: a Study of His Life and Works*, new edn 1973; and in Andrew Hook (ed.), *The History of Scottish Literature Vol. 2: 1660–1800*, new edn 1989.

RANSOM, JOHN CROWE (1888–1974) American poet and critic, was born in Pulaski, Tennessee, the son of a Methodist minister who gave him his early education. After graduating from Vanderbilt University in 1909, he read Greats as a Rhodes Scholar at Christ Church, Oxford, and returned to Vanderbilt in 1914 as a member of the English faculty. He was a 1st lieutenant in the US Army Field Artillery in France in World War I, during which he wrote *Poems About God* (1919). Back at Vanderbilt, a literary group had been formed locally which came to include, in addition to himself and his colleague Donald Davidson (1893–1968), their students ALLEN TATE and WARREN. It also published *The Fugitive* (1922–25), a poetry journal reflecting its members' opposition to Southern romanticism and to industrialization, whose other contributors included HART CRANE, GRAVES, and Laura Riding (1901–91). *Chills and Fever* (1924) presaged a marked change in Ransom's attitude to his own poetry; a selection from it and from *Poems About God* was published by the WOOLFS in London as *Grace After Meat* (1924). After *Two Gentlemen in Bonds* (1927), he published only a handful of new poems, though he continued to revise his earlier work, and to reissue it as *Selected Poems*, the 1969 edition of which won the National Book Award. He was from 1937 to 1958 Carnegie Professor of Poetry at Kenyon College, where he founded in 1939, and edited until 1959, the *Kenyon Review* as a voice of the New Criticism. His critical works include *The World's Body* (1938), essays; *The New Criticism* (1941); and *Beating the Bushes: Selected Essays 1941–1970* (1972). See Thomas D. Young, *Gentleman in a Dustcoat: a Biography of John Crowe Ransom*, 1976.

RANSOME, ARTHUR (1884–1967) British journalist and children's writer, was born in Leeds, the eldest child of a history professor who died, unnecessarily, after an accident incurred while fishing on a family holiday, when the boy was 13. He was educated at Rugby School and studied science for two terms at Yorkshire College (later Leeds University) before, at 17, going to London, where he scraped a living as a hack journalist. When he could, he spent holidays with the Collingwood family in the Lake District. In 1913, to escape an unhappy marriage and the effects of being sued (albeit unsuccessfully) by Lord Alfred Douglas (1870–1945) for statements in a commissioned book about WILDE, he went to Russia. He became a correspondent for the *Daily News*, taught himself the language, and studied the folklore, which he re-created in *Old Peter's Russian Tales* (1916). He remained in Russia until 1919, becoming friendly with leaders of the Revolution, about which he wrote in *The Crisis in Russia* (1921). He also met Evgenia Shelepin (d. 1975), who had been secretary to Leon Trotsky (1879–1940), and whom he married in 1924 after his divorce. During the 1920s he was a reporter on the *Manchester Guardian*, for which he went to Egypt and China in 1924–26. He gave his other time to fishing, about which he wrote *Rod and Line* (1929), and sailing—*'Racundra's' First Cruise* (1923) recounts a Baltic trip in a ketch of his own design. In 1928, now living in the Lake District, he taught the Collingwood grandchildren to sail. The experience inspired *Swallows and Amazons* (1930) and its long line of holiday adventures, with their sense of place and attention to constructive detail. He was made CBE in 1953. See *The Autobiography of Arthur Ransome*, ed. Rupert Hart-Davis, new edn 1985; Hugh Brogan, *The Life of Arthur Ransome*, new edn 1992; Peter Hunt, *Approaching Arthur Ransome*, 1992 (critical study).

RAO, RAJA (b. 1908) Indian novelist and short-story writer, was born in Hassan, Mysore, and educated at Madarasa-e-Aliya School, Hyderabad, for a year at Aligarh Muslim University, and then at Nizam College, Hyderabad, from which he graduated in English in 1929. He then studied in France at Montpellier University and the Sorbonne. He spent many of the ensuing years in France (his first wife, whom he married in 1931, was French), and subsequently divided his time between India, Europe, and the USA, where he became a part-time professor of philosophy at the University of Texas, Austin, in 1965. In *Kanthapura* (1938), which FORSTER held to be the best Indian novel written in English, he traces the emergence of a revolt against a local plantation manager, describing the village, its inhabitants, and their day-to-day activities in a language which reflects their speech and cultural characteristics. *The Serpent and the Rope* (1960)—the title refers to the symbols of illusion and reality in Indian tradition—moves between India, France, and Britain, reflecting through its main characters his personal situation in the 1930s and also his philosophical and spiritual sensitivities, in the exposition of which he draws on several ancient cultures. *The Cat and Shakespeare: a Tale of India* (1965), an exploration of individual destiny, and *Comrade Kirillov* (1976, but written in the 1940s), in which Marxist and Hindu philosophies are compared, are novellas. *The Policeman and the Rose* (1978) includes stories from *The Cow of the Barricades and Other Stories* (1947).

RATTIGAN, (Sir) **TERENCE** (1911–77) British dramatist, was born in Kensington, London, the second son of a diplomat, Frank Rattigan (1878–1952), who in 1922, when Acting High Commissioner in Constantinople, had to resign from the service because of his affair with Princess Elisabeth of Romania, lately become Queen of Greece. The two boys were taken by their mother for a holiday in a cottage rented from a drama critic. The only books in it were plays, which Rattigan read right through and as a result formed his life's ambition. He won a scholarship to Harrow, and another to Trinity College, Oxford. After writing (with a friend, Philip Heiman) *First Episode*, a play about Oxford which was performed in London in 1933, he left university, with his father's grudging consent and on condition that he live at home for two years. At the end of this time, having written six plays without an acceptance, he took a job as a scriptwriter with Warner Brothers. *French Without Tears*, a comedy based on a French crammer he had attended in 1921 at his father's instigation, was finally staged in November 1936, after a last-minute change of denouement and a disastrous dress rehearsal. It ran for 1030 performances. In 1941, on the advice of a psychiatrist whom he had consulted about his writer's block, he volunteered for the Royal Air Force, in which he became an air gunner with the rank of flight lieutenant. *Flare Path* (1942), about the strain affecting RAF officers, was written while he was on active service, and was his second successful play.

After the war he capitalized on his craftsmanship and ability to treat dramatic situations powerfully with *The Winslow Boy* (1946), *The Browning Version* (1948), *The Deep Blue Sea* (1952), and *Separate Tables* (1954). A misguided reference to 'Aunt Edna', personifying his intended audience, which he inserted in the preface to his second volume of collected plays (1953), returned to haunt him, especially in the light of the reception of the new wave of avant-garde dramatists. Latterly, his consistent touch faltered, but *Cause Célèbre* (1977), completed while he was dying of cancer, was described by the *Sunday Times* critic as 'theatrical in the best sense of the word'. In addition to film scripts of his own plays, Rattigan wrote those for *The Way to the Stars* (1945), *The Final Test* (1953), and *Goodbye Mr Chips* (1969). He was made CBE in 1958 and was knighted in 1971. See *Plays*, 2 vols 1982, 1985; Geoffrey Wansell, *Terence Ratti-*

gan, 1995 (biography); Michael Darlow and Gillian Hodson, *Terence Rattigan: the Man and His Work*, new edn 1983.

RAVENSCROFT, EDWARD see MO-LIÈRE; TATE, NAHUM.

RAWLINGS, MARJORIE KINNAN (1896–1953) American novelist, was born in Washington, and in 1907 won $2 in a story competition in the *Washington Post*. She was educated at Western High School and the University of Wisconsin, after which she was a publicist for the Young Women's Christian Association in New York. She married journalist and yachtsman Charles Rawlings in 1919; they were divorced in 1933. During the 1920s she was a staff writer on the *Louisville Courier Journal* and *Rochester Journal*, and wrote syndicated verses ('Songs of a Housewife'). After settling on an orange grove in Cross Creek, Florida, she had a series of sketches and a story published in *Scribner's Magazine* in 1930–31. Though she stated in an address in 1939, 'I don't hold any brief for regionalism and I don't hold with the regional novel as such', it was as a novelist of the Florida backwoods where she lived that she began her career with *South Moon Under* (1933); and had her greatest success, with *The Yearling* (1938), about a boy, the fawn he rears, and the betrayal wrought by man and nature, which won the Pulitzer Prize. In 1941 she married Norton Baskin, a hotel owner, who once replied to a visitor who had exclaimed at seeing 'the fine hand of Marjorie Kinnan Rawlings' in the decor: 'You do *not* see Mrs Rawlings' fine hand in this place. Nor will you see my big foot in her next book. She writes. I run a hotel.' The years 1943–47 were largely spent defending a suit for libel brought by a friend who claimed she had suffered 'great pain and humiliation' from passages in *Cross Creek* (1942), a topographical autobiography. The case finally went against Rawlings on appeal to the Florida Supreme Court, which ordered her to pay damages of $1.

READ, (Sir) **HERBERT** (1893–1968) British critic and poet, was born in Kirbymoorside, Yorkshire, the eldest son of a farmer, after whose death in a riding accident the boy was sent at the age of nine to the Crossley and Porter Endowed School for orphans in Halifax. He left at 16 to work as a savings bank clerk, but persuaded an uncle to advance a small legacy, on which he went to Leeds University. As an officer in the Green Howards, he won both the Distinguished Service Order and the Military Cross in World War I, during and after which he wrote a number of war poems—*The End of a War*, a trio of poems about an appalling incident in France, appeared in 1933. After a brief spell in the Treasury, he worked at the

Victoria and Albert Museum, and was then Professor of Fine Art at Edinburgh University 1931–33. He was Editor of the *Burlington Magazine* from 1933 to 1939, during which time he also published some formative works of art criticism, including *Art and Society* (1937). He was a co-founder of the Institute of Contemporary Arts in 1947. Though he championed novelty in art, his literary criticism centred on the Romantics—see *Collected Essays in Literary Criticism* (1938). He wrote one novel, *The Green Child* (1935), an allegorical fantasy of modern times. Like its chief protagonist, he retired to rural Yorkshire in 1950, an event celebrated in the title poem of *Moon's Farm and Poems Mostly Elegaic* (1955). While he wished to be regarded primarily as a poet, it is as a champion of the visual arts that he is remembered. TREECE comments in *Herbert Read: an Introduction to His Work by Various Hands* (1944): 'The ultimate attraction of Read's work, and of his character . . . lies in the enigma, paradox, and perfectly wedded opposites.' He was knighted in 1953. The novelist Piers Paul Read (*b.* 1941) is his son. See *Collected Poems*, new edn 1992; *Collected Essays*, ed. Piers Paul Read, 1992; *The Innocent Eye*, new edn 1996 (early autobiography); *The Contrary Experience: Autobigraphies*, new edn, foreword by Graham Greene, 1973; James King, *The Last Modern: a Life of Herbert Read*, 1990.

READE, CHARLES (1814–84) British novelist and dramatist, was born at Ipsden House, Oxfordshire, the youngest of 11 children of a country gentleman, and was educated privately and at Magdalen College, Oxford, where, in spite of only a third class degree in Greats, he was elected to a fellowship and subsequently became Vice-President. He was called to the Bar in 1853, but instead chose to write. The Theatres Act (1843) paved the way for the opening of many new theatres (subject only to their obtaining a licence) and for the staging of original plays; as a result the standard melodrama could now take on a more literary aspect. His most successful play was the comedy, *Masks and Faces* (1852), written with Tom Taylor (1817–80), which he then turned into a novel, *Peg Woffington* (1853), a romanticized study of the Irish actress (*c.*1718–60) which presents her as more moral than she appears to have been. Some of the research he had put into *Gold* (1853) was utilized in the novel, '*It Is Never Too Late to Mend*' (1856), exposing prison conditions and the treatment of criminals, from which he made another play in 1865. Further crusading novels were *Hard Cash* (1863), revealing the iniquities of private lunatic asylums, and *Put Yourself in His Place* (1870), on dubious trades-union practices. His passion for research led also to the novel for which he is universally remembered, *The Cloister and the Hearth* (1861), an extraordi-

nary panorama of medieval European life and customs, based on a study by ERASMUS and expanded from his own short story, 'A Good Fight', which appeared in the journal *Once a Week* in 1859. He never married, but he fathered an illegitimate son, whom he made his heir. He lived with the actress Laura Seymour from 1855 until her death in 1879. See *Plays*, ed. Michael Hammett, 1986.

REANEY, JAMES (*b.* 1926) Canadian poet and dramatist, was born in South Easthope, Ontario, and educated at the Central Collegiate Vocational Institute, Stratford, and University College, Toronto, after which he taught English at the University of Manitoba, returning to Toronto to write a PhD thesis on the influence of SPENSER on YEATS. He married the poet Colleen Thibaudeau (*b.* 1925) in 1951. In 1960 he became a professor of English at Middlesex College, University of Western Ontario, where he founded the art and literary 'little magazine', *Alphabet*, which he edited (and often himself printed) for the whole of its existence (1960–71). *The Red Heart* (1949), a collection of lyrics in which a child-figure/poet seeks to come to terms with provincial society, and *A Suit of Nettles* (1958), a suburban eclogue whose structure is based on Spenser's *The Shepheardes Calender*, each won the Governor General's Award; so did his third volume of verse, *Twelve Letters to a Small Town* (1962), in the same year as his *The Killdeer and Other Plays* (1962) won it for drama. In that and a further collection of plays, *Masks of Childhood*, ed. Brian Parker (1972), the image of childhood features as a symbol of innocence. His most ambitious dramatic achievement, involving a variety of stage techniques and forms, is the sequence based on the massacre of an immigrant Irish family in Ontario in 1880: *Sticks and Stones* (produced 1973), *The St Nicholas Hotel* (1974), and *Handcuffs* (1975), published as *The Donnellys: a Trilogy* (1983). See *Selected Shorter Poems*, 1975, and *Selected Longer Poems*, 1976, ed. Germaine Warkentin; Richard Stingle, *James Reaney and His Works*, 1994.

REDGROVE, PETER (*b.* 1932) British poet and novelist, was born in Kingston, Surrey, and educated at Taunton School and Queen's College, Cambridge, where he read science, after which he worked as a scientific journalist and editor. He was a founder-member of the Group (see LUCIE-SMITH), and published his first volume of verse, *The Collector and Other Poems*, in 1960, since when he has regularly brought out new collections. After being Gregory Fellow in Poetry at Leeds University 1963–65, he was from 1966 to 1983 Poet-in-Residence at Falmouth School of Art in Cornwall. The local terrain appears as a background in many of his poems, in which love and science often feature. From the start his work was particularly concerned with the continuum between the imagination when dreaming and when awake, and between the real and surreal worlds. His novels include *In the Country of the Skin* (1972), which won the *Guardian* award for fiction, and *The Beekeepers* (1980). He has also written several books with his wife, the poet and novelist Penelope Shuttle (*b.* 1947), including a novel of the occult, *The Terrors of Dr Treviles* (1974), a study of attitudes and the creative impulse, *The Wise Wound: Menstruation and Everywoman* (1978), and *Alchemy for Women: Personal Transformation through Dreams and the Female Cycle* (1995)—her own collections include *Building a City for Jamie* (1996), which records the coming of middle age and the growing up of their daughter. Redgrove was awarded the Queen's Gold Medal for Poetry in 1996. See *The Moon Disposes: Poems 1954–1987*, new edn 1989; *Book of Wonders: the Best of Peter Redgrove's Poetry*, ed. Jeremy Robinson, 1996; *The Cyclopean Mistress: Selected Short Fiction*, 1993 (prose poems); *Sex-Magic-Poetry-Cornwall: a Flood of Poems*, ed. Jeremy Robinson, 2nd rev. edn 1995; *Assembling a Ghost*, 1996 (subsequent collection).

REEVE, CLARA (1729–1807) British novelist, was born in Ipswich, the eldest of eight children of the perpetual Curate of St Nicholas, who, she claimed, taught her all she knew. On his death in 1755, she moved with her mother and two sisters to Colchester, where she began her literary career with *Original Poems on Several Occasions* (1769). She translated from Latin the political romance, *Argenis* by John Barclay (1582–1621), which was published as *The Phoenix* (1772). In 1777 she had *The Champion of Virtue: a Gothic Story*, 'by the Editor of the PHOENIX', privately printed by a local printer. After some revisions undertaken at the suggestion of her friend Martha Bridgen, second daughter of SAMUEL RICHARDSON, she sold the copyright in what was now called *The Old English Baron* to a London bookseller for £10. It was published under her name in 1778. 'The literary offspring of *The Castle of Otranto*, written upon the same plan', as she admits in the preface, differed from that book in that it was concerned less with supernatural violence than with the 'manners of true life' and with the emotions of the characters—HORACE WALPOLE, predictably, commented in a letter (1778), 'It is so probable that any trial for murder at the Old Bailey would make a more interesting story.' Only in *The Exiles: or, The Memoirs of the Count de Cronstadt* (1788) did she again generate any romantic excitement. She wrote three moralizing contemporary novels, a historical story, and 'Castle Connor', the manuscript of which was lost in transit on the Ipswich to London coach. *The Progress of Romance Through Times, Countries and Manners* (1785) is a treatise, in the form of a dialogue, on the English novel and ancient romance. She died in Ipswich, unmarried. See *The Old English Baron*, ed. James Trainer, 1967.

REID, FORREST (1875–1947) Irish novelist, was born in Belfast, the son of a business manager who had previously been a bankrupt shipowner, and was educated at the Royal Academical Institution. He wrote his first novel, *The Kingdom of Twilight* (1904), while an apprentice with a Belfast tea-importer. In 1905 he received a legacy, with which he took himself to Christ's College, Cambridge, shortly after the publication of his second book, *The Garden God* (1905). Like most of his other novels a study of adolescence and male friendships, it has a scene in which the hero encourages his friend to pose naked on the rocks during a swimming expedition. Reid, in his innocence, not only sent a copy to HENRY JAMES, but dedicated the book to him. James was appalled. FORSTER read his third, *The Bracknels* (1911; rev. edn, as *Denis Bracknel*, 1947), about a Belfast lad misunderstood by his family, and wrote an appreciative letter. This was the start of a lifelong friendship, even though Reid was shocked by parts of *Maurice*, claiming not to have realized that its author was homosexual. Reid rewrote *Following Darkness* (1912) as *Peter Waring* (1937), in which form it presents a balanced picture of confused adolescence in the 1890s. In his trilogy, *Uncle Stephen* (1931), *The Retreat* (1936), and *Young Tom* (1944), he takes his chief protagonist gradually back to adolescence and childhood. Reid lived all his life in Belfast, unmarried, but pursued several interests, especially croquet, which he often played in England at championship level. He also wrote significant critical works on YEATS (1915) and DE LA MARE (1929), and two memorable autobiographical studies, *Apostate* (1926) and *Private Road* (1940). See Brian Taylor, *The Green Avenue: the Life and Writings of Forrest Reid 1875–1947*, 1980.

REID,   V(ICTOR)   S(TAFFORD) (1913–87) Jamaican novelist, was born, was educated, and lived in Jamaica, having been a journalist and newspaper foreign correspondent, and run a publishing and printing company. His first novel, *New Day* (1949), is significant in the immediate postwar development of West Indian literature in following the growth of Jamaican nationalism from the Morant Bay Rebellion of 1865 to the establishment of the new constitution in 1944. Further, these recollections of an 87-year-old, middle-class, white farmer of Afro-European ancestry make it the first West Indian novel in which the narration is in Jamaican dialect. Reid also broke new ground in his only other adult novel, *The Leopard* (1958), in which he pursued his theme of Afro-Caribbean relationships through a study of colonial tension during the Mau Mau rebellion in Kenya. He also wrote fiction for children.

REMARQUE, ERICH MARIA (1898–1970) German novelist, was born in Osnabruck of French Catholic descent, and went to the local gymnasium. Drafted into the army at 18, he was wounded five times during the campaign in World War I in which a whole generation of his countrymen was destroyed, while the newspapers recorded 'Im Westen nichts Neues' [No news in the west]. After the war he tried being a teacher, stonecutter, and test driver, before becoming a journalist. *Im Westen nichts Neues* (1929; as *All Quiet on the Western Front* tr. A. W Wheen, 1929; tr. Brian Murdoch, 1995) was by an extraordinary coincidence published in the same month that SHERRIFF's *Journey's End* had its West End premiere in London. Brutally realistic, written in the first person, but intended as 'neither an accusation nor a confession', though it asks pertinent questions of its readers, it sold 2¹/₂ million copies world wide in 18 months. In 1932 he left Germany for Switzerland in disillusionment at the Nazi regime, which banned the book in 1933 as 'defeatist' and deprived him of his citizenship. In 1939 he went to the USA, of which he became a citizen in 1947. He published several popular novels, of which *The Three Comrades*, tr. Wheen (1937) was made into a film (1938) with screenplay by F. S. FITZGERALD. See Christine R. Barker and R. W. Last, *Erich Maria Remarque*, 1979 (critical study).

RENDELL, RUTH (*b.* 1920), née Grasemann, British novelist and short-story writer, was born in London. Both her parents were teachers; her mother was Swedish but was brought up in Denmark. She was educated at Loughton High School. She worked on a newspaper from 1948 to 1952. She and her journalist husband, Donald Rendell, married in 1950, divorced in 1975, and remarried two years later. They live in a 16th-century house in Suffolk whose whereabouts are a closely-guarded secret. There are three distinct strands to her novel writing. The 14 detective stories (in an interview in 1990 she claimed that this was the definitive canon) involving Inspector Wexford began with *From Doon with Death* (1964) and are also distinctive for the attention given to the private lives and domestic traumas of Wexford and his faithful associate, Burden—she subsequently added a 15th, *Kissing the Gunner's Daughter* (1992), and a 16th, *Simisola* (1994). Her individual thrillers usually have multi-layered plots and urban settings, and depend on some criminal maladjustment for the development of the main situation. Beginning with *A Dark-Adapted Eye* (1986), she has also written, as Barbara Vine, novels which, while mainly concerned in some way with crime, delve deeper into psychology and motivation; in *The Brimstone Wedding* (1996) she interweaves the stories of two very different women, each with a secret. The Rendell/Vine distinction became finally blurred with *The Keys to the Street* (1996), an exploration of love and loss to which murders and mystery provide the background, published under her real name. *Collected Stories* appeared in 1988; subsequent collections have included *The Copper Peacock and Other Stories* (1991) and *Bloodlines: Long and Short Stories* (1995). She was made CBE in 1996.

RHYS, JEAN, pseudonym of Ella Gwendolen Rees Williams (1890–1979) British novelist and short-story writer, was born at Roseau, Dominica, the daughter of a Welsh doctor and a white Dominican, and was educated there at the convent school until she was 16. She then spent one term at the Perse School, Cambridge, and one at Tree's School of Dramatic Art (later RADA), after which she became a chorus girl and found the first of a series of middle-aged lovers. She married a Dutch writer in 1919, and lived with him in Paris until he was imprisoned. Some of her 'sketches' of Paris were published by FORD MADOX FORD in the *transatlantic review* in 1924. They had an affair, and he wrote an enthusiastic foreword to *The Left Bank and Other Stories* (1927). The four novels she then wrote, *Postures* (1928), *After Leaving Mr Mackenzie* (1931), *Voyage in the Dark* (1934), and *Good Morning, Midnight* (1939), closely reflect her own somewhat alarming experiences between 1914 and 1937. Their spare style, which was so distinctive for the time, may have contributed to the obscurity into which they and their author now drifted. Divorced in 1932, she married an Englishman, who died in 1945. In 1947 she married Max Hamer (*d.* 1964), after whose imprisonment for embezzlement the impoverished couple were found in a derelict cottage in Devon. She was traced there at the time of the BBC broadcast of *Good Morning, Midnight* in 1957, after several reports of her death.

Wide Sargasso Sea (1966) is only 55,000 words long, but such was the care with which she pared it down, and such the pain and labour that it cost, that she had only been prevented from destroying the manuscript by the local vicar, who plied her with whisky and encouragement until it was finished. It is the story of the mad Creole wife of CHARLOTTE BRONTË's Mr Rochester in *Jane Eyre*, from her childhood in Jamaica to the moment of truth of the conflagration at Thornfield Hall. Stark, but intensely vivid, it is a splendid work of creative imagination, and also a major contribution to West Indian literature. Jean Rhys was made CBE in 1978. See *The Collected Short Stories*, 1990; *Letters 1931–1966*, ed. Francis Wyndham and Diana Melly, new edn 1995; *Smile, Please: an Unfinished Autobiography*, ed. Diana Athill, new edn 1990; Carole Angier, *Jean Rhys*, new edn 1992 (biography); Cheryl Alexander Malcolm and David Malcolm, *Jean Rhys*, 1996 (biographical/critical study); Coral Ann Howells, *Jean Rhys*, 1991 (critical study).

RICH, ADRIENNE (*b.* 1929) American poet and critic, was born in Baltimore, 'Split at the root, neither Gentile nor Jew, / Yankee nor rebel' ('Readings of History', 1960). She was the daughter of a Jewish doctor and of a Southern Protestant musician, who taught her at home until she was nine. She then went to Roland Park Country School and Radcliffe College, graduating in the year in which *A Change of World* (1951), with a preface by AUDEN, was published in the Yale Series of Younger Poets. In 1953 she married Alfred Conrad, a Jewish lecturer in economics, and quickly had three sons, who were brought up Jewish. In *Snapshots of a Daughter-in-Law: Poems 1954–1962* (1963) she began to express the social, political, and personal concerns to which much of her creative energy has since been devoted. She and her husband separated in 1966: he died in 1970. The title of *The Will to Change: Poems 1968–1970* (1971) reflected her attitude to active involvement in the process of political and social change. In a paper in 1976 she explained: 'It is the lesbian in us who drives us to feel imaginatively, render in language, grasp, the full connection between woman and woman . . . [and] who is creative, for the dutiful daughter of the fathers is only a hack.' *Twenty-One Love Poems* (1976) is a sequence of lesbian lyrics. She has taught English at several universities, being appointed at Stanford in 1986. Collected poetry is in *The Fact of a Doorframe: Poems Selected and New 1950–1984* (1984) and *Collected Early Poems 1950–1970* (1993)—see also *An Atlas of the Difficult World: Poems 1988–1991* (1992) and *Dark Fields of the Republic: Poems 1991–1995* (1995); essays are in *On Lies, Secrets, and Silence: Selected Prose 1966–1978* (1979), *Blood, Bread, and Poetry: Selected Prose 1979–1985* (1986), and *What is Found There: Notebooks on Poetry and Politics* (1995). See *Selected Poems 1950–1995*, 1996.

RICHARDS, FRANK, pseudonym of Charles Hamilton (1876–1961) British children's writer, was born in Ealing, Middlesex, the sixth of eight children of a journalist who died when the boy was seven. He was educated at various church and private schools and, according to his own account, sold his first story when he was 17. He began to concentrate on writing for boys' papers, especially the *Gem* (founded 1907) and the *Magnet* (1908); on the title page of the issue of March 1908 of the latter was the first illustration of Billy Bunter of the Remove, looking comparatively slim. The stories about Greyfriars School (written under the Frank Richards name which Hamilton in due course as-

sumed as his own) proliferated, and Bunter gradually put on more weight, becoming the Fat Owl, in which form, with the other four chief characters and their academic establishment, he remained fossilized. The stories reappeared after World War II in hard covers, and Bunter and Co. took on a further lease of life through television, for which Richards wrote the scripts. The last book of all was *Bunter's Last Fling* (1965), published alongside J. S. Butcher, *Greyfriars School: a Prospectus* (1965), a comprehensive guide to activities, curriculum, and buildings, which is a skit on the real thing. The continued popularity of the series was due to the very familiarity of the setting, plots, and situations, as well as of the characters. Richards, who was said in his heyday to turn out 1½ million words a year (on one occasion 18,000 words in one day), created innumerable schools, about which he wrote under many names, including Hilda Richards, author of stories about Bessie Bunter at Cliff House. He never married. *The Autobiography of Frank Richards* (1952) is deficient on the subject of his early years.

RICHARDSON, DOROTHY M(ILLER) (1873–1957) British novelist, was born in Abingdon, Berkshire, and educated at Southborough House, Putney. While her father dissipated his inheritance (he went bankrupt in 1893), she taught in Germany, and was then a governess in England. After her mother's suicide in 1895, she became a Harley Street dentist's receptionist, and mixed in progressive circles. She began earning some money from journalism in 1908, and from translation in 1913. An independent and early exponent of the stream-of-consciousness technique in fiction (see also MAY SINCLAIR), she began, with *Pointed Roofs* (1915), a sequence of 12 autobiographical novels (in which WELLS, with whom she had an affair in 1907, appears as Hypo Wilson), finally published together as *Pilgrimage* (1938). It was further extended by *March Moonlight* and reissued posthumously in 1966–67. VIRGINIA WOOLF, who wrote to a friend that she had been 'bribed by very large sums of money to do what of all things I have come to detest—write reviews for the *Nation* [and *Athenaeum*]', said in her review of *Revolving Lights* (1923) that its author had 'developed and applied to her own uses, a sentence which we might call the sentence of the feminine gender'. In 1917 Richardson married an artist, Alan Odle, 15 years younger than she was; he died of tuberculosis in 1948. See Gloria G. Fromm, *Dorothy Richardson: a Biography*, new edn 1994; John Rosenberg, *Dorothy Richardson, the Genius They Forgot: a Critical Biography*, 1973; Jean Radford, *Dorothy Richardson*, 1992 (critical study); Carol Watts, *Dorothy Richardson*, 1995 (critical introduction).

RICHARDSON, HENRY HANDEL, pen name of Ethel Florence Lindesay Robertson (1870–1946), née Richardson, Australian novelist, was born in Melbourne, the elder daughter of Walter Lindesay Richardson (1825–79), an Irish doctor who emigrated in 1852, and Mary Bailey (1836–95), who had been sent out from England to join her brother when she was 14. Dr Richardson, having retired and taken his family travelling in Europe, was forced by the collapse of his investments to practise again, in Hawthorn, then Chiltern, then Queenscliffe, where he developed signs of madness and was removed to a Melbourne asylum. His wife managed to get a job as postmistress in upcountry Koroit, where Richardson, since 'Mother had an unconquerable prejudice against State Schools', had lessons with the parson's daughters at the rectory, and where her father spent his last months. Mrs Richardson was promoted to a better post in Maldon, and her daughter boarded for four years at the Presbyterian Ladies' College, Melbourne, where she was 'considered odd and unaccountable'. After an unhappy spell as a morning-governess in a private school in Toorak, she and her sister left Australia with their mother for a trip 'home'. She never returned, 'save for a flying six-weeks' visit [in 1912], to test my memories'.

In 1887 her mother took her to Leipzig to study music, at which she had shown some skill. Here she realized that she did not have the talent to become a concert pianist, but discovered a métier in her desire to contribute to European literature. She also found a husband, John G. Robertson (d. 1933), later Professor of Germanic Studies at London University, whom she married in 1895. For her first novel, *Maurice Guest* (1908), on which she had worked since 1897, she chose a male pen name, as GEORGE ELIOT had done. Heavy and brooding, it uses the heady atmosphere of the Leipzig Conservatorium as the milieu for a study of sexual infatuation and the nature of genius. *The Getting of Wisdom* (1910) 'contained a very fair account of my doings at school'. Light and intended to amuse, and with the intensity of her own relationship with an older girl toned down, this classic child's-eye view so offended the school that when she tried to revisit it during her brief trip two years later, she was refused admittance. In *Australia Felix* (1917), *The Way Home* (1925), and *Ultima Thule* (1929), reissued as *The Fortunes of Richard Mahony* (1930), she used aspects of her father's life to explore the tensions in a marriage; and employed the realities and vagaries of Australian life in the decades following 1850 to illustrate the psychological pulls exercised by the old and the new countries. The first two books of the trilogy sold so badly that their publisher, Heinemann, rejected the third, which was published at her husband's expense. It was taken up by Heinemann after a rapturous reception, and its author was nominated for the Nobel Prize for Literature in 1932. She published *The End of a Childhood and Other Stories* (1934), and just one more novel, *The Young Cosima* (1939), a historical study of musical genius which lacks the depth with which she was able to treat themes from her own experience. From the time the couple moved from Strasbourg to London in 1903, Richardson lived much in her own world, visited by acquaintances, and attended devotedly first by her husband, and then, in Sussex, by her secretary-companion, Olga Roncoroni. See *The End of a Childhood: the Complete Stories of Henry Handel Richardson*, ed. Carol Franklin, 1992; *Myself When Young*, 1948; Dorothy Green, *Henry Handel Richardson and Her Fiction*, 1986 (rev. edn of *Ulysses Bound*, 1973).

RICHARDSON, JOHN (1796–1852) Canadian novelist, was born in Queenston, Upper Canada, of United Empire Loyalist and Indian descent. He fought for the British in the War of 1812, and served in the British Army in the West Indies from 1816 to 1818, after which he settled in London. For his epic poem *Tecumseh: or, The Warrior of the West in Four Cantos with Notes* (1828), he employed the mock-heroic metrical form of BYRON's *Don Juan*, and had a failure. His novel, *Écarté: or, The Salons of Paris* (1829), reflects his own rakish experiences in France. *Wacousta: or, The Prophecy* (1832), the first Canadian novel by a native Canadian, is an extraordinary, Gothic-style romance of revenge set in the 1760s—there is a modern edition, ed. Carl Klinck (1967), and a dramatization by RE-ANEY (1979). After serving as a major on the royalist side in 1835 in the Spanish civil war, he returned to Canada as a correspondent for *The Times*, from which he was removed for his critical attitude to the administration of the country. He wrote a sequel to *Wacousta*, *The Canadian Brothers: or, The Prophecy Fulfilled* (1840; reissued in USA, with diplomatic excisions, as *Matilda Montgomerie*, 1851). He was publisher of *The New Era: or, The Canadian Chronicle*, Brockville. After its failure he established *The Canadian Loyalist and Spirit of 1812*, Kingston, which had an equally truncated existence, as did his appointment as a superintendent of police on the Welland Canal in 1845. In 1849 he went to New York, where he died in extreme poverty. He wrote other novels of a sensational kind, and accounts of his experiences in Spain and Canada set against the events of the time. See David Beasley, *The Canadian Don Quixote: the Life and Works of Major Richardson, Canada's First Novelist*, 1977; Dennis Duffy, *John Richardson and His Works*, 1983.

RICHARDSON, SAMUEL (1689–1761) British novelist and printer, was born in Derbyshire, one of nine children of a craftsman carpenter. Though intended for university and the Church, he does not appear to have had a particularly good education (his understanding of Latin and Greek was poor), though he was early on commissioned independently by three local young ladies to write love letters on their behalf. When family financial difficulties threatened, he was apprenticed at 17 to a London printer, and in 1719 opened his own business, first in Fleet Street and then in Salisbury Court, where he became the official printer of the *Journals* of the House of Commons. In 1739 two booksellers invited him to write a handbook of model letters covering various situations, to help 'country readers' to compose their own. *Letters Written to and for Particular Friends on the Most Important Occasions* duly appeared in 1741, but in the meantime the initial idea had further blossomed into a full-blown novel.

Pamela: or Virtue Rewarded (1740, dated 1741) was written largely at his country house, North End in Hammersmith, in the three months November 1739 to January 1740. It was significant in that its 15-year-old heroine, who successfully defends her virginity throughout, is a serving girl. The device of letters written shortly after the events they describe gives an immediacy to each episode and heightens the suspense, as does the enormous detail with which the situations are embellished. The book's success, which coincided with the beginnings of the circulating libraries, can be judged from the fact that someone immediately brought out a spurious *Pamela in High Life*, which induced Richardson to add two further volumes (1741), constituting a less impressive continuation. It also inspired HENRY FIELDING to enter the field of comic fiction. *Clarissa* (1747–48) has a similar theme but a tragic end, and is more successful as a novel in that there are four correspondents, who supplement each other's accounts and extend the book's range. *The History of Sir Charles Grandison* (1754) has a more complex but equally sensational love interest with, on this occasion, a hero, who vacillates most honourably between the attractive Harriet Byron and an Italian inamorata of his past. AUSTEN was so impressed that she dramatized episodes from it, probably for performance by her family.

Richardson was a moralist who specialized in divided minds and in females in psychological as well as sometimes physical distress. In 1755 he published *A Collection of the Moral and Instructive Sentiments . . . Contained in the Histories of Pamela, Clarissa, and Sir Charles Grandison*. He was a considerable artist in both his crafts. In 1754 he was elected Master of the Stationers' Company, and in 1760 he bought a half share in the business of law printer to the King. He died of apoplexy. He was married twice, each wife bearing him six children, of whom only four daughters survived him. See T. C. Duncan Eaves and Ben D. Kimpel, *Samuel Richardson: a Biography*, 1971; Mark Kinkead-Weekes, *Samuel Richardson: Dramatic Novelist*, 1973; Jocelyn Harris, *Samuel Richardson*, 1987 (critical study).

RICHLER, MORDECAI (b. 1931) Canadian novelist, was born in the St Urbain Street district of Montreal—see *The Street: Stories* (1969)—the son of a Jewish junk dealer. He went to Baron Byng High School, which he renamed Fletcher's Field High in his autobiographical stories ('Under the jurisdiction of the Montreal Protestant School Board, [it] had a student body which was nevertheless almost a hundred per cent Jewish'). He left Sir George Williams University after two years, having become 'quite frightened that if I got a BA, I'd get an MA, and then I might try for a PhD, and that would be the end of me'. After two years in Paris, he returned to Montreal, where he worked for the Canadian Broadcasting Corporation. In 1954, having been sent £100 advance by a British publisher for his first novel, he left for England. *The Acrobats* (1954), 'a mixture of Hemingway and Sartre and all the other writers I had read', he now rejects. His fourth, *The Apprenticeship of Duddy Kravitz* (1959), has become the archetypal story of the Jew who pushes himself out of the modern ghetto to material success, by any means. *Cocksure* (1968), a bawdy satire on London society and the communications' business, won the Governor General's Award, which also went that year to his *Hunting Tigers Under Glass: Essays and Reports* (1968), and then to his next novel, *St Urbain's Horseman* (1971), in which the Jewish experience is realistically and symbolically played out through two overlapping lives. In 1972, having used up his English experience, he returned to Montreal, made a brief foray to Hollywood, taught creative writing for two years at Carleton University, Ottawa, and was a selector for the American Book-of-the-Month Club (1972–88). *Solomon Gursky Was Here* (1989), the outcome of eight years of research and writing, is a labyrinthine family saga in which Canadian history and the innate Jewish ability to stir things up are inventively combined. His political commitment is demonstrated in *Oh Canada! Oh Quebec!: Requiem for a Divided Country* (1992). He is the compiler of *Writers on World War II: an Anthology* (1992). See *This Year in Jerusalem*, new edn 1996 (autobiographical study).

RIDER HAGGARD, H. see HAGGARD.

RIDING, LAURA see CAMERON; GRAVES; RANSOM.

RILKE, RAINER MARIA (1875–1926) German poet, was born in Prague, the son of a railway official whose military career had been cut off by illness. He was educated at the Piarist School, Prague, from 1882 to 1884, when his mother went to live with her lover in Vienna. He then attended the military academies at Sankt Polten and Mahrisch-Weisskirchen until 1891, when his parents accepted that the regime was making him ill. He went to the Commercial Academy in Linz, after which he studied for a year each at the universities at Prague, Munich, and Berlin. In 1898 he began an affair with Lou Andreas-Salomé, who was 36 and married. He went to Russia with her and her husband in 1899, and again, with her alone, in 1900, which was the inspiration for *Das Stunden-Buch* (1905; see *Poems from the Book of Hours*, tr. A. L. Pick, 1961), his first significant contribution to literature. He married Clara Westhoff, a sculptor, in 1901: they had a daughter, but effectively lived separate lives from 1907. Fascinated by the conflict, 'I do not want to sunder art from life; I want them, somehow or somewhere, to be of one meaning', he travelled, and stayed, in many parts of Europe in his pursuit of a conjunction. He associated with intellectuals such as FREUD, TOLSTOY, and the French sculptor, Auguste Rodin (1840–1917), as whose secretary he acted in 1905; and tangled emotionally with Magda von Hattingberg ('Benvenuta') and Baladine Klossowska ('Merline'). *Neue Gedichte* (1907; as *New Poems*, tr. J. B. Leishman, 1964; tr. Stephen Cohn, 1992) reflected his isolation of self through the representation of individual objects as self-sufficient, and the acceptance of life and death as part of the same thing. He returned triumphantly to these themes in *Duineser Elegien* (1923; tr. Leishman and Stephen Spender as *Duino Elegies*, rev. edn 1948) and *Die Sonette an Orpheus* (1923; as *Sonnets to Orpheus*, tr. Leishman, 1936; tr. Leslie Norris and Alan Keele, 1991)—see also *Duino Elegies, Sonnets to Orpheus*, tr. David Young (1978). His death from leukaemia was hastened by an infection caused by a scratch from the thorn of a rose, one of his favourite symbols. See *Selected Poems*, tr. Albert Ernest Flemming, 2nd edn 1986; *Uncollected Poems*, tr. Edward Snow, 1996 (bilingual edition); *Letters to a Young Poet*, tr. M. D. Herter Norton, new edn 1993 of rev. edn 1954; Donald Prater, *A Ringing of Glass: the Life of Rainer Maria Rilke*, new edn 1994; Ralph Freedman, *Life of a Poet: Rainer Maria Rilke*, 1996.

RIMBAUD, ARTHUR (1854–91) French poet, was born in Charleville, the second of four children who survived of an army officer who abandoned his family in 1860. He had already published poems in Latin and French when the local school suspended its operations in 1870 because of the Franco-Prussian War. Having then run away from home three times, he was at the invitation of VERLAINE packed off to Paris with his mother's blessing, taking with him 'Le Bateau Ivre' [The Drunken Boat], an extraordinary

poetic vision in 25 quatrains of rhyming alexandrines. An intense relationship ensued, culminating, after two trips to London, in Brussels, where Verlaine shot him in the hand and was sentenced to two years' imprisonment. Rimbaud worked at the 16 prose poems and verses comprising *Une Saison en Enfer*, which was printed in Brussels in 1873 but never distributed, for though his mother had paid the deposit he was unable to meet the final bill. That was his last attempt at publication, though Verlaine edited *Illuminations* (1886; tr. Enid Rhodes Pescel with *A Season in Hell*, 1973), an enigmatic fusion of free verse and poetic prose which some critics regard as the first manifestation of Surrealism. In 1880, after several years of international vagrancy, he arrived in Harar, Ethiopia, which was the base from which he conducted for the rest of his life a career of dubious dealing in arms and other commodities. He died of cancer in Marseilles, where his right leg had been amputated six months earlier, after he had been carried by litter to Aden, and gone from there by sea to France. See *A Season in Hell: the Psychological Autobiography of Arthur Rimbaud*, tr. Patricia Roseberry, new edn 1995; *A Season in Hell and Other Poems*, tr. Norman Cameron, new edn 1994; *Poems*, tr. Paul Schmidt, ed. Peter Washington, 1994.

RIVE, RICHARD (1931–89) South African short-story writer, was born in District Six, Cape Town, the son of an American seaman and a 'coloured' South African, and won a scholarship to high school. He graduated in English at Cape Town University in 1949, and then taught English and Latin, initially at Hewat Training College. In 1962 he toured Africa and Europe on a Fairfield Foundation scholarship. His first volume of short stories of urban slum life, *African Songs*, was published in East Berlin in 1963. He wrote two novels: *Emergency* (1964) covers the three days between the Sharpeville massacre and the imposition of a state of emergency; *Buckingham Palace: District Six* (1987) explores the characters and attitudes of a community driven out of their homes to make a 'whites only' area. He studied at Columbia University, New York, in 1965–66; as a Junior Research Fellow at Magdalen College, Oxford 1971–74, he wrote a thesis on SCHREINER, the first volume of whose letters he edited (1988). In an interview in 1963 he said that 'a body of literature is emerging from South Africa which is going to be a South African literature regardless of the participants or the colour of their skins. . . . I am urban South African, and I do not wish to be anything else.' He was one of the few black writers of his generation to live and write in South Africa. He was murdered in his home in District Six, Cape Town. The perpetrator or perpetrators have never been brought to justice. See *Ad-*

vance, Retreat: Selected Short Stories, 1990; *Writing Black*, 1981 (autobiographical study).

ROBBE-GRILLET, ALAIN (*b.* 1922) French novelist, was born in Brest of 'extreme right-wing anarchists', and was educated at lycées there and in Paris, and at the Institut National Agronomique. He spent some time in Nuremberg under the German forced labour scheme during World War II, after which, having obtained his *agrégation d'agronomie*, he did agricultural research in Morocco, French Guinea, and Martinique. He became a full-time writer after being sent home in 1951 for health reasons, and in 1955 was made literary adviser to Éditions de Minuit, his publisher. An early exponent of what came to be known as the *nouveau roman*, he has stated his position in the essays in *Pour un Nouveau Roman* (1963; tr. Barbara Wright in *Snapshots and Towards a New Novel*, 1965). His first novel to be published in English was *Le Voyeur* (1955; tr. Richard Howard as *The Voyeur*, 1958), in which a travelling watch salesman on a visit to the island of his birth is surprised and relieved not to be charged with a murder and rape which he may, or may not, have committed. *La Jalousie* (1957; tr. Howard as *Jealousy*, 1959)—the French title is a pun—centres on a husband's obsession that his wife is having an affair. *Dans le Labyrinthe* (1959; tr. Christine Brooke-Rose as *In the Labyrinth*, 1960) is a further exploration of consciousness, with distinct echoes of KAFKA. His best-known work is the film *L'Année Dernière à Marienbad* (1961), for which he wrote the script and dialogue, before turning it into a novel (1961; tr. Howard as *Last Year at Marienbad*, 1962). The series of three novels termed 'Romanesques'—*Le Miroir Qui Revient* (1984; tr. Jo Levy as *Ghosts in the Mirror*, 1991), *Angélique ou l'Enchantment* (1988), and *Les Derniers Jours de Corinthe* (1994)—are postmodernist autobiographical studies.

ROBERTS, (Sir) CHARLES G(EORGE) D(OUGLAS) (1860–1943) Canadian poet, novelist, and short-story writer, was born in Douglas, New Brunswick, the son of an Anglican minister, and spent his childhood in a country parish by the Tantramar marshes—see his nostalgic poem, 'The Tantramar Revisited' (1886). He was educated at the Collegiate School, Fredericton, and the University of New Brunswick. He graduated in 1881, having already published the innovative *Orion and Other Poems* (1880), the first of numerous collections spanning sixty years. He is the most notable of the Confederation Poets, all born in the 1860s, who constitute the first school of Canadian verse—see also CARMAN, LAMPMAN, and D. C. SCOTT. As a further measure of his influence, the title poem of *The Iceberg and Other Poems* (1934) marks one of the earliest effective uses of free verse in Canadian poetry. After a brief spell

as Editor of the *Week*, Toronto, he taught English, French, and economics at King's College, Windsor, from 1885 to 1895. *Earth's Enigmas* (1896) is his first incursion into a field of modern fiction of which, with SETON, he was an innovator, and which includes, in *The Heart of the Ancient Wood* (1900), one of several distinctive expressions of the difficult art of fabulizing the human–wild animal relationship without sentiment. In 1897 he left his wife and family to be a freelance writer and editor in New York, from which he went to England in 1908. He enlisted as a private in the British Army in 1914, transferring to the Canadian Army, in which he became a major. He was subsequently attached to the Canadian War Records Office in London. He returned to Toronto in 1925, and was knighted in 1935 for his services to Canadian literature. Theodore Goodridge Roberts (1877–1953), the poet and author of historical romances and novels of adventure, was his younger brother. See *The Collected Poems of Sir Charles D. G. Roberts: a Critical Edition*, ed. Desmond Pacey and Graham Adams, 1985; Terry Whalen, *Charles D. G. Roberts and His Works*, 1994.

ROBERTSON, ETHEL FLORENCE LINDESAY see RICHARDSON, HENRY HANDEL.

ROBINSON, EDWIN ARLINGTON (1869–1935) American poet, was born in Head Tide, Maine, and grew up in Gardiner (the 'Tilbury Town' of his verse). He dropped out of Harvard in 1893 after his father's death and the loss of the family fortune, and returned home to be a professional poet. Poems from *The Torrent and the Night Before* (privately printed 1896) reappeared in *The Children of the Night* (1897), a gloomy volume, mainly in the lyrical style. After his mother's death in 1896 he went to New York City, and was a subway inspector until President Theodore Roosevelt (1858–1919), who admired his work, obtained for him a sinecure in the New York Custom House, which he held until the change of administration in 1909. *The Man Against the Sky* (1916) was written after he had discovered the MacDowell Colony, a creative retreat in Peterboro, New Hampshire, founded in memory of the composer Edward A. MacDowell (1861–1908), to which he then returned every summer. *Collected Poems* (1921) won the Pulitzer Prize, as did *The Man Who Died Twice* (1924) and *Tristram* (1927), the last of a trilogy of Arthurian romantic narrative poems. Obsessed with failure, financially embarrassed, and periodically alcoholic, he was essentially the Miniver Cheevy of his own poem, who '. . . loved the Medici, / Albeit he had never seen one; / He would have sinned incessantly / Could he have been one' (1910). See Ellsworth Barnard, *Edward Arlington Robinson: a Critical Study*, 1952.

ROBINSON, LENNOX (1886–1958) Irish dramatist, was born in Douglas, Co. Cork, the son of a Church of Ireland cleric, and had little formal education because of ill health. He became interested in the stage after seeing the Abbey Theatre company on tour in Cork in 1907. In 1908 his first play, *The Clancy Name*, a rural piece, was performed in Dublin at the Abbey Theatre, of which he was appointed Manager in 1909. He resigned in 1914 after an unsuccessful American tour, and was succeeded by ERVINE. He returned to the company in 1919, and was in 1923 made a director, in which capacity he voted with YEATS for the rejection of O'CASEY's *The Silver Tassie*. He was a prolific dramatist, whose best plays reflect his versatility. *The Whiteheaded Boy* (performed 1916), *The Round Table* (1922), *The White Blackbird* (1925), and *The Bird's Nest* (1938) are domestic comedies of family attitudes. In *Church Street* (1934) and *Drama at Inish* (1934), the touch is still light, but the messages are social ones. In *The Lost Leader* (1918) he explores what might have been if the Irish political leader, Charles Stewart Parnell, had not died in 1891 at the age of 45. He also wrote an autobiographical novel, *A Young Man from the South* (1917), and *Ireland's Abbey Theatre: a History, 1899–1951* (1951). See Michael J. O'Neill, *Lennox Robinson*, 1964 (critical study).

ROCHESTER, (WILMOT, JOHN), 2ND EARL OF (1647–80) English poet, was born in Ditchley, Oxfordshire, the son of a famously hard-drinking Cavalier general, to whose title he succeeded in 1658. He was educated at Burford Grammar School and Wadham College, Oxford, after which he travelled in Europe. In 1664 he appeared at the court of Charles II, where his wit, looks, and dissipation earned him a reputation, and his outspokenness several periods of exclusion from the royal presence. In 1665 he abducted the heiress Elizabeth Malet, for which he was sent to the Tower of London for three weeks. He married her in 1667 and had four children by her (she died of apoplexy in 1681), and one by the actress Elizabeth Barry (1658–1713). He was converted on his deathbed by Gilbert Burnet (1643–1715), later Bishop of Salisbury, who wrote *Some Passages of the Life and Death of the Right Honourable Earl of Rochester* (1680). As it was to be with BURNS, Rochester's early death, his amorous exploits, and the obscenity of some of his verse overshadowed his gift for lyrical and satirical poetry. His work has the ring of truth, as in the song 'My Dear Mistress Has a Heart . . .', and at times a tenderness ('A Song of a Young Lady to Her Ancient Lover'). The philosophical tone ('Upon Nothing', 'Plain Dealing's Downfall') recurs in *A Satyr against Mankind Written by a Person of Honour* (1679), a study of the human condition as well as of contemporary society. See *The Complete Poems*, ed. David M. Vieth, new edn 1975; *The Complete Works*, ed. Frank H. Ellis, 1994; Vivian de Sola Pinto, *Enthusiasm in Wit: a Portrait of John Wilmot Earl of Rochester*, rev. edn 1962 of *Rochester*, 1935; Marianne Thormählen, *Rochester: the Poems in Context*, 1993.

ROETHKE, THEODORE (1908–63) American poet, was born in Saginaw, Michigan, of a Prussian family who came to the USA in 1872 and established a thriving greenhouse business. The greenhouse reappears as a continuing motif in the volumes which constitute his spiritual autobiography: *The Lost Son, and Other Poems* (1948), *Praise to the End!* (1951), and *The Waking: Poems 1933–1953* (1953), which won the Pulitzer Prize. In 1922 his father, Otto Roethke, sold his share in the business to his brother Charles, whom he had discovered was embezzling company funds. Charles committed suicide in 1923; Otto died of cancer three months later. Theodore, after graduating from Arthur Hill High School, insisted on going on to the University of Michigan, Ann Arbor, after which he did a year's postgraduate study at Harvard. Poems he showed to Robert Hillyer (1895–1961), a poet and a member of the faculty, were submitted to literary journals, and published. At Lafayette College, Pennsylvania, where he was an English lecturer and tennis coach, he established his vocation as a 'teacher poet'. While at Michigan State College in 1935 he experienced a drug- and drink-induced mystical union with nature, was hospitalized for several months, and was then made redundant. He went on to Pennsylvania State College, and while there published his first book of poetry, *Open House* (1941). He was appointed to the University of Washington, Seattle, in 1947. *Words for the Wind* (1957) and *The Far Field* (1964) contained, in such poems as 'I Knew a Woman', 'The Far Field', and 'The Meadow Mouse', haunting reflections on love and on nature. See *The Collected Poems of Theodore Roethke*, new edn 1985; *On the Poet and His Craft: Selected Prose of Theodore Roethke*, ed. Ralph J. Mills, 1965; Jay Parini, *Theodore Roethke: an American Romantic*, 1980 (biography); Peter Balakian, *Theodore Roethke's Far Fields: the Evolution of His Poetry*, 1989.

ROGERS, SAMUEL (1763–1855) British poet, was born in Stoke Newington, and received a fine education at private schools in north London. Instead of becoming a Presbyterian minister, he was persuaded to enter the bank in Cornhill of which his father was a partner. Gradually he came into the whole family share in the business, and an annual income of £5000. He began his poetical vocation with *An Ode to Superstition* (1786). *The Pleasures of Memory* (1792) is significant for its time in that it is based on the philosophical theory of association of ideas, but it is the work of a dilettante, who felt bound to burden his exposition with footnotes. *The Voyage of Columbus* (1810) is an excursion into romanticism, and *Jacqueline* (1814, in the same volume as BYRON's *Lara*) a simple country tale; he resumed his reflective persona in *Human Life* (1819). In *Italy: a Poem* (2 vols 1822 and 1828) he roughly followed, in blank verse and prose, the progress of Byron's Childe Harold. Like all his works except *Jacqueline*, it was published at his own expense, which he could easily afford. He was thus able to destroy the unsold copies and reissue it in one volume in 1830, with sumptuous engravings by J. M. W. Turner (1775–1851) and Thomas Stothard (1755–1834). A connoisseur of art, with which he filled his house overlooking Green Park, he knew everybody, to the extent that on the death of WORDSWORTH he was offered the Poet Laureateship, which he declined, leaving it for TENNYSON. His breakfasts were famous. WALTER SCOTT commented, of one he attended in 1826 in the company of his daughters and son-in-law: 'R. was exceedingly entertaining, in his dry, quiet, sarcastic manner.' Rogers's *Table-Talk* was first published in 1856 (ed. Alexander Dyce).

ROJAS, FERNANDO DE (1475/6–1541) Spanish novelist, was born in La Puebla de Montalban, Toledo, of a family which had been forcibly converted from Judaism. He became a Bachelor of Law at Salamanca University in 1498 or 1499, by which time he had written the first version of what is usually called *La Celestina*. Published as *Comedia de Calisto y Melibea* (1499), this 16-act romantic novel in dialogue ends with the death of Calisto in a fall and the suicide of Melibea, whom he has just successfully seduced, by jumping off the roof. An enlarged version, in 21 acts, with an extended denouement and additional characters, was published between 1502 and 1504 as *Tragicomedia de Calisto y Melibea*. In both, Celestina, the superior procuress, is murdered by Calisto's servants, with whom she has refused to share her fee. In about 1507 Roja moved from his home town to Talavera, where he practised law, served for a number of years as Lord Mayor, and in about 1517 married Leonor Alvarez, whose Jewish-born father, Alvaro de Montalbán, was in 1525 refused permission to be represented by Rojas when being interrogated by the Inquisition. *La Celestina* was first translated into English by the Spanish scholar James Mabbe (1572–1642) as *The Spanish Bawd Represented in Celestina* (1631). See *La Celestina, the Spanish Bawd*, tr. J. M. Cohen, 1964.

ROLFE, F(REDERICK) W(ILLIAM) (1860–1913) British novelist, who claimed to be Baron Corvo and also used the appellation Fr Rolfe, was born in Cheapside, London, of a piano-manufacturing family. He left North London Collegiate School for Boys at 14, and from 1878 to 1886 taught at various schools. Having been converted to Catholicism, he studied at St Mary's College, Oscott, and then for the priesthood at Scots College, Rome, from which he was expelled in 1890. His earliest stories appeared in *The Yellow Book*, and were collected as *Stories Toto Told Me* (1898) and *In His Own Image* (1901). *Chronicles of the House of Borgia* (1901) is both a learned and a colourful pageant of the times. In *Hadrian the Seventh* (1904), a riotous autobiographical projection in which the hero is summoned to be Pope in reparation for his rejection as priest, he attempted to get his own back on the Catholic Church, and largely succeeded. In 1908, having mercilessly and ungratefully battened on friends and well-wishers in London, he left for Venice, where he continued to sponge on them from a distance. Sinister, embittered, and depraved, he left various works of fiction which have been published posthumously, including the semi-autobiographical *The Desire and Pursuit of the Whole: a Romance of Modern Venice* (1934; ed. Andrew Eburne, with cuts restored, 1993) and *Nicholas Crabbe: or, The One and the Many* (1958). There have been several collections of his letters. See A. J. A. Symons, *The Quest for Corvo: an Experiment in Biography*, new edn 1993 (biography).

ROLLE, RICHARD (*c*.1300–49) English mystic, was born in Thornton Dale, near Pickering, Yorkshire. He was for a time at Oxford, which he left when he was 18 to return home to be a hermit. Having devised an appropriate outfit from clothes that were to hand, he went off by himself, and was given shelter, and his own room, by the Dalton family. Here he composed some of his earlier works. Subsequently he had a cell in the archdeaconry of Richmondshire, and then at Hampole, where it is presumed he died of the plague. He was the first English mystic to write in the vernacular, into which quite early in his vocation he translated the Psalter and accompanying commentary from Latin. Latterly he wrote epistles in English for the encouragement and edification of holy women: the most attractive of these, *The Form of Living*, is addressed to his 'chosen pupil', Margaret Kirkby, a young anchoress at East Layton. His more significant religious works are in Latin, and include *Incendium Amoris* (as *The Fire of Love*, tr. Clifton Wolters, 1972; tr. H. C. Backhouse, new edn 1992), and *Melos Amoris*, ed. E. J. F. Arnould (1957). See Frances M. M. Comper, *The Life of Richard Rolle. together with an edition of his English lyrics*, new edn 1969.

RONSARD, PIERRE DE (1524–85) French poet, was born in Chateau de la Poissonière, near Couture-sur-Loir, the sixth and youngest child of a cultivated soldier who built his manor house on the site of the feudal home. After being tutored at home, he was sent at nine to Collège de Navarre of Paris University, which he soon left to become a page at court. He went to Scotland in 1537 in the train of Madeleine, the daughter of Francis I, who had married James V of Scotland; she survived the local climate for only two months. A year learning martial arts at the Écuries of the Duc d'Orléans came to nothing when he returned from accompanying a diplomatic mission to Germany with otitis, which affected his hearing for the rest of his life. Instead, in 1543 he took minor orders (sufficient to qualify for one or more benefices from patrons), and studied under the classical scholar Jean Dorat (1508–88). When Dorat was appointed head of Collège de Coqueret in 1547, he went too. Here he and DU BELLAY formed a group of poets called the 'Brigade', whose inner circle, named the 'Pléiade' from about 1553, comprised themselves, Dorat, Antoine de Baïf (1532–89), Rémy Belleau (1528–77), Étienne Jodelle (1532–73), and Pontus de Tyard (1521–73). His benefices, of which the major ones were St Cosme-lez-Tours (1565) and Croixval (1566), and a court pension (he was appointed almoner to the young King Charles IX in 1559), supported his literary endeavours, for which he is the most significant French poet of the 16th century. He made the alexandrine the medium of serious verse, using it for the thoughtful utterances in *Hymnes* (1555–56) and for his patriotic reflections on the poor state of the country, which he began with *Discours sur les Misères de ce Temps* (1562).

His lyrics foreshadow the Romantic movement two hundred years later. Besides exalting Mary, Queen of Scots, his love poetry conferred immortality on several less distinguished ladies: among them are Cassandre Salviati (c.1531–1609); Marie Dupin, a country girl whom he encountered in 1554 when she was 15; and the final love of his life and the object of 142 'Sonnets pour Hélène' (1578), Hélène de Surgères, maid of honour at court, whom he first met in 1566 when she was 19. DRAYTON, DRUMMOND, MONTGOMERIE, and SPENSER are among the 16th- and early 17th-century English and Scottish poets who benefited from his influence. See *Poems of Love*, 1975, and *Odes, Hymns and Other Poems*, 1977, ed. and tr. Grahame Castor and Terence C. Cave.

ROS, AMANDA M'KITTRICK, pseudonym of Anna Margaret M'Kittrick (1860–1939) Irish novelist and poet, was born near Ballynahinch, Co. Down, trained at Marlborough Training College, Dublin, and was appointed to a teaching post in Larne, whose stationmaster, Andrew Ross (*d.* 1917), she married in 1887. As a tenth wedding anniversary present, he gave her the money to pay for the publication of her novel, *Irene Iddesleigh* (1897). With the proceeds from its sales, she built them a new house. A second, much longer, novel, *Delina Delaney*, was published in 1898. The absurdity and artificiality of their plots is only exceeded by the extravagance of the language and the oddity of the style, of which alliteration and hanging participles are conspicuous features: 'Putting on her little sailor hat, Father Guerdo stood facing the rustic ruby, then moved forward and locked the door of his menial menage of misery.' Lengthy legal wrangling over a limekiln, which she inherited from a friend in 1908, left her as embittered with lawyers as she already was with critics. Since prose fiction did not seem to be a sufficiently effective medium of retribution, she burst into verse, with *Poems of Puncture* (1913) and *Fumes of Formation* (1933). After Ross's death, she married a farmer, who died in 1933. She left an unfinished novel, *Helen Huddleson* (ed. and completed by Jack Loudan, 1969). She had her own appreciation society, founded at Oxford University in 1907, to read aloud extracts from her work. See *Amanda McKittrick Ros Reader*, ed. Frank Ormsby, 1988; Jack Loudan, *O Rare Amanda!*, new edn 1969 (biography).

ROSENBERG, ISAAC (1890–1918) British poet, was born in Bristol of a Russian-Jewish immigrant family, and was brought up in London's East End, where he attended board schools. At 14 he was apprenticed to an engraver in Fleet Street. Thanks to Jewish philanthropy, he was able to study at the Slade School of Art, where he won several prizes, and exhibited his paintings at the Whitechapel Gallery. He published privately a pamphlet of verse, *Night and Day* (1912), followed by *Youth* (1915). Diagnosed as having weak lungs, he went to South Africa in 1914 to stay with his sister. Though medically unfit for war service, he returned in 1915 and enlisted in the army, to earn money for the family. He was in the Bantam Regiment and then the King's Own Royal Lancasters, and suffered considerably from blistered feet and other privations, including being forbidden to send poetry home from France because the censor could not be bothered to read it. Still a private, he was killed in action near Arras. SASSOON saw in him 'a fruitful fusion between English and Hebrew culture'. Though he would have been (and was) a poet anyway, the main body of his work has associations with the war. It ranges from 'On Receiving the News of the War' and 'August 1914', to graphic re-creations of its grim horrors and private repulsions in 'Marching', 'Louse Hunting', and 'Dead Man's Dump', and to brief lyrical moments in 'Break of Day in the Trenches' and 'Returning, We Hear the Larks'. Images of war occur in poems based on classical or biblical themes, and in the unfinished *Moses; a Play* (1915). See *The Collected Works of Isaac Rosenberg: Poetry, Prose, Letters, Paintings, and Drawings*, ed. Ian Parsons, rev. edn 1979; Joseph Cohen, *Journey to the Trenches: the Life of Isaac Rosenberg 1890–1918*, new edn 1992.

ROSS, ALAN (*b.* 1922) British poet, prose writer, and editor, was born in Calcutta and spent his infancy in Bengal, being brought back to England when he was seven. He was educated at Haileybury and St John's College, Oxford, and served in destroyers and minesweepers during World War II, having already published a book of verse, *Summer Thunder* (1941). He has since displayed many talents: travel writer; cricket and soccer, and briefly North African, correspondent of the *Observer*; children's author; critic; anthologist; and publisher. In 1961, when JOHN LEHMANN gave it up, he became Editor and proprietor of the *London Magazine*, whose scope and influence he single-handedly increased. He has also owned steeplechase and flat-race horses. His poetry is marked by its graphic quality, and its accessibility. Arguably the best cricketer also to have published poetry of distinction, his accounts of tours abroad, most notably *Australia 55: a Journal of the MCC Tour* (2nd edn 1983), are in a class of their own. His autobiographical studies, *Blindfold Games* (1986), *Coastwise Lights* (1988), and *After Pusan* (1995), are interspersed with poems written at the time or out of the experiences he describes. They also feature a most colourful collection of endearing literary and artistic eccentrics, to whom he has been a valued friend. He was made CBE in 1982. See *Poems 1942–1967*, 1968; *The Taj Express: Poems 1967–1973*, 1973.

ROSS, MARTIN see BOWEN; SOMERVILLE.

ROSS, SINCLAIR (*b.* 1908) Canadian novelist and short-story writer, was born on a farm in Shellbrook, Saskatchewan, and after high school worked for the Union (later Royal) Bank of Canada in local townships until 1933, when he was transferred to Winnipeg. He served in the Canadian Army in England during World War II, after which he returned to the bank in Montreal until his retirement in 1968. He then lived in Greece and Spain until 1980, when he came back to Canada. Pre-eminent as a chronicler of Canadian prairie life, his first novel, *As For Me and My House* (1941), is set, as are many of his stories, during the Depression of the 1930s, and reflects through the diary of the repressed wife of a minister the stultifying isolation as well as the hardships. In both *The Well* (1958) and *Whir of Gold* (1970), which have Saskatchewan–Montreal settings, honesty ultimately prevails over criminal instincts. The experimental form of *Sawbones Memorial* (1974), in which the action is represented through a mosaic of dialogues, memories, and speeches at a retirement party, adds a fresh dimension to the literature of the Canadian small town. *The Lamp at Noon and Other Stories* (1968) has an introduction by LAURENCE. See Morton Ross, *Sinclair Ross and His Works*, 1994.

ROSS, WILLIAM (UILLEAM ROS) (1762–90) Gaelic poet, was born in Skye and educated on the mainland at the grammar school in Forres. The family moved to Gairloch in Wester Ross, and he joined his father as an itinerant pedlar. On one of their trips he met and fell in love with Marion Ross in Stornoway, but in 1782 she married a sea captain, became Mrs Clough, and went to live in Liverpool. In 1786 Ross became the schoolmaster at Gairloch. It is said that Marion was unhappy in her marriage and wrote to Ross, asking him to come to her. He got as far as Stirling before deciding that discretion was wiser than ardour, and returned home, catching on the way the chill which aggravated his tubercular condition, and killed him. While he wrote poems of a conventional nature, to Charles Edward Stuart, to his homeland, to the seasons, and to whisky, he also expressed his unrequited love for Marion in a number of poems which are most unusual of their kind, and which have been translated into English by IAIN CRICHTON SMITH and DERICK THOMSON. In their poetic form they reflect the poetry of BURNS and of the elegists of classical times, with both of which he was familiar, and in their personal intensity there is nothing to match them in Gaelic literature until MACLEAN.

ROSSETTI, CHRISTINA (1830–94) British poet, sister of D. G. ROSSETTI, was born in London, the youngest of four children of an Italian academic, a poet and freedom fighter, who arrived in England as a refugee in 1824. She was educated at home by her mother, her strict religious upbringing being in line with the Anglicanism of the Oxford Movement. Ill for most of her teens, she remained at the various family homes, caring for her father until his death in 1854, her mother until she died in 1886, and then two aunts. She never married, though on religious grounds she broke off one engagement and rejected a proposal from a man with whom she was in love. At the age of 17, at the instigation of her brother, she submitted two poems to the *Atheneum*, which were published. She contributed seven poems to the Pre-Raphaelite journal, *The Germ*, in 1850. With the help of her brother, who also supplied two woodcuts as illustrations, she got published *Goblin Market and Other Poems* (1862), whose narrative title poem is a parable of love and death in the Pre-Raphaelite ethos. With *The Prince's Progress and Other Poems* (1866), it gained her a reputation among the literary élite which her shyness made it difficult for her to enjoy.

Through a prolonged period of family sorrows she continued to write, both poetry—including *Sing-Song: a Nursery Rhyme Book* (1872) and *A Pageant and Other Poems* (1881)—and devotional prose. The conflict between her intellectual background and religious inclination, the depths of feeling she experienced in her personal life, and her technical brilliance in conventional verse forms, notably the sonnet, rondeau, and ballad, give her a distinctive, and sensuous, poetic voice. See *Poems and Prose*, ed. Jan Marsh, 1994; *Selected Poems*, ed. C. H. Sisson, 1984; *Selected Prose of Christina Rossetti*, ed. David A. Kent and Paul Stanwood, 1996; Kathleen Jones, *Learning Not to Be First: the Life of Christina Rossetti*, new edn 1992; Jan Marsh, *Christina Rossetti: a Writer's Life*, 1995.

ROSSETTI, DANTE GABRIEL (1828–82)

British poet and painter, was born in London and educated at King's College School and the Royal Academy. With several other artists he founded the Pre-Raphaelite Brotherhood, which aimed to recapture the essence, colour, and detail of pre-Renaissance art. Their journal, *The Germ*, lasted four issues in 1850 under the editorship of Rossetti's younger brother William (1829–1919), who was to become the uncle of FORD MADOX FORD. A passionate friendship with his model, Elizabeth Siddal (*b. c.*1834), was finally consummated when he married him in 1860. She died of a drug overdose two years later, and in 1870 he retrieved from the coffin the poems he had buried with her. His other great love was Jane, the wife of MORRIS, who appeared unperturbed by the relationship. (Warmth and sex were for many years provided by Fanny Cornforth.) The reception in some circles of his verse translations, *The Early Italian Poets 1100–1300* (1861), reissued as *Dante and His Circle* (1874), led him to publish *Poems* (1870). It included the 50 'House of Life' sonnets which (with the unnecessary expurgation of 'Nuptial Sleep') were repeated in sequence in *Ballads and Sonnets* (1881); 'The Blessed Damozel', which had originally appeared in the second issue of *The Germ* and which particularly symbolizes the Pre-Raphaelite mood; the contemporary but romanticised 'Jenny'; and the ballad-like 'Troy Town' and 'Sister Helen'.

Rossetti the poet tries partly to reflect his artistic aims in a literary form, and partly to reconcile the body, the spirit, and love. He became a virtual recluse in his house in Cheyne Walk, Chelsea, after 1872, never recovering from a breakdown brought on by drugs, alcohol, and the climax of a long-running literary feud (which appears to have been begun by his brother William). It was intensified by an attack by 'Thomas Maitland'—the poet and journalist Robert Buchanan (1841–1901)—on 'The Fleshly School of Poetry' in the *Contemporary Review* of October 1871. Rossetti replied with 'The Stealthy School of Criticism' in the *Athenaeum* in December, but the psychological damage to him had been done. See *Selected Poems and Translations*, ed. Clive Wilmer, 1991; Oswald Doughty, *A Victorian Romantic: Dante Gabriel Rossetti*, new edn 1960 (biography); Joan Rees, *Modes of Self-Expression: the Poetry of Dante Gabriel Rossetti*, 1981.

ROSSETTI, WILLIAM see FORD, FORD MADOX; ROSSETTI, D. G.; WHITMAN.

ROTH, HENRY (1906–1995)

American novelist, was born in Tysmenitz, Galicia, and was brought to New York in 1908. The family moved from the Lower East Side to Harlem in 1914, first to the Jewish and then (because his mother wanted a better view) to the Irish quarter. He went to De Witt Clinton High School and the City College of New York, where he was when in 1927 he left home and moved in with the much older New York University professor, Eda Lou Walton, a poet with a bohemian lifestyle. She encouraged him to write and complete *Call It Sleep* (1934), a cross-sectional view of Jewish East Side life, seen mainly through the eyes of the child David Schearl between the ages of 6 and 8. It had moderate reviews. Maxwell Perkins (1884–1947) commissioned a second novel for Scribner's which, though it featured a Communist proletarian and Roth had joined the Communist Party and 'dedicated my creativity to the portrayal of proletarian virtue', was never finished. Instead he suffered if not necessarily the most profound then certainly the longest recorded attack of writer's block, for which several explanations, none of them conclusive, are suggested in the collection of his essays, correspondence, diaries, and interviews, *Shifting Landscape*, ed. Mario Materassi (1987).

In 1938, at an artists' retreat to which he had gone in search of release, he met Muriel Parker (*d.* 1990), a pianist and composer, whom he married in 1939. From New York the couple moved with their two sons to Boston, where Roth worked as a toolgrinder, and then to Maine, where he was a supply teacher, psychiatric assistant in a mental hospital, and then a duck and goose farmer, while also offering private tuition in Latin and mathematics. His anonymity was broken after *Call It Sleep* was reissued in 1960 and then published in paperback in 1964. It was hailed as a masterpiece for its contribution to Jewish writing, social history, and the literature of the psychology of childhood, and for its uncanny recreation of different forms of dialogue. With the help of his wife, who for a period became a schoolteacher to support the family, the bonds of the blockage were eventually loosened. In 1979, never having given up trying, Roth began a six-volume novel, *Mercy of a Rude Stream*, of which the first, *A Star Shines Over Mt Morris Park* (1994) is largely a recycling of his childhood experiences; the second, *A Diving Rock in the Hudson* (1995), is revealing about aspects of his youth which he had erased from his memory when writing his two previous novels; the third, *From Bondage* (1996), recalls the circumstances of his life in the 1930s.

ROTH, PHILIP (*b.* 1935) American novelist and short-story writer, was born in Newark, New Jersey, of Jewish immigrant parents, and was educated at Weequahic High School; Newark College, Rutgers University; and Bucknell University. After a year's postgraduate study at Chicago University, he did army service and then returned to Chicago to teach English for two years. 'Goodbye, Columbus', published in the *Paris Review* 1958–59, was reprinted in his first book, *Goodbye, Columbus, and Five Short Stories* (1959), which won the National Book Award. The voice was unmistakably Jewish and irreverent, and the dialogue was vibrant, and funny. It was not until his fourth book, and third novel, *Portnoy's Complaint* (1969), that he managed to absorb his 'ideas about sex, guilt, childhood, about Jewish men and their Gentile women' into 'an overall fictional strategy'. It also proved shocking to some. *The Great American Novel* (1973) enabled him to combine his mockery of that genre with his childhood preoccupation, baseball. The trilogy, *The Ghost Writer* (1979), *Zuckerman Unbound* (1981), and *The Anatomy Lesson* (1984)—published with *The Prague Orgy* (1985) as *Zuckerman Bound* (1985)—demonstrates the truism that the line between autobiography and fiction can be both marginal and perplexing. He then produced a coda, *The Counterlife* (1987), followed by *The Facts: a Novelist's Autobiography* (1988), which purports to fill 'the gap between the autobiographical writer that I am thought to be and the autobiographical writer that I am'.

He returned to fiction, but still with a preoccupation with the author's other self, in *Deception* (1990). *Operation Shylock: a Confession* (1993) is a further basis for sharp speculation about the nature of self and the place of the Jew in the modern world. Mickey Sabbath, the protagonist of *Sabbath's Theater* (1995), is a battered 64-year-old Jewish Falstaff who advertises himself as having an affinity with King Lear. His monstrous fortunes and priapic escapades represent wild laughter in the face of death. *Patrimony: a True Story* (1991) is a worried attempt by Roth to come to terms with memories of his father. Roth married Margaret Martinson in 1959. They separated in 1962; she was killed in a car crash in 1968. His second marrriage, in 1990, was to the British actress Claire Bloom (*b.* 1931); they divorced in 1995—her autobiography is *Leaving a Doll's House* (1996). Critical essays by Roth are in *Reading Myself and Others* (1975). See *Philip Roth Reader*, 1980; George J. Searles (ed.), *Conversations with Philip Roth*, 1992; Hermione Lee, *Philip Roth*, 1982 (critical study); Jay Halio, *Philip Roth Revisited*, 1992 (critical study).

ROUSSEAU, JEAN-JACQUES (1712–78) social philosopher and prose writer, was born in Geneva. His mother died a few days later, and in 1722 his father, a Protestant watchmaker, disappeared after being involved in a fight. Apprenticed to a lawyer and then to an engraver, he too left town in 1728 when he was unable to return from a walk because the city gate was locked. He was converted to Catholicism in Turin, and for twelve years, when he was not wandering in Italy, Switzerland, or France, he lived mainly with Mme de Waren (*c.*1702–64), whose lover he became in 1733. He settled in Paris in 1742, failed to interest the Academy of Sciences in a new form of musical notation, and began a long relationship with Thérèse le Vasseur (1721–1801), their several children being consigned to the Foundling Hospital. In 1749, while walking to visit DIDEROT, who was under house arrest at Vincennes after being released from jail, he read in a magazine he was carrying an announcement of a prize offered by the Academy of Dijon for an essay on whether the progress of the arts and sciences had contributed to the purification of morals. Deciding that it had not, he advanced in his winning entry, *Discours sur les Sciences et les Arts* (1750; tr. R. Wynne, 1752), his theme of the 'noble savage', happier in a natural state than in a civilized one, which had a remarkable influence on European culture and put the English Lakes, and the Lake Poets, on the map. He intensified his views in an essay on inequality (1755), having returned to Protestantism and begun a fruitful creative period during which he lived rent free in cottages on the estates of wealthy patrons. One of these was Mme d'Epinay, with whom he ultimately fell out because of his passionate affair with her sister-in-law, Sophie d'Houdetot, who already had a husband and a lover. Romantic sensibilities in form the unlikely rural *ménage à trois* which is the ultimate theme, but not the final outcome, of his novel, *Julie: ou, La Nouvelle Héloïse* (1761; tr. William Kenrick as *Eloisa*, 1761). He presented his views on education in the form of a further novel, *Émile: ou, De l'Éducation* (1762; tr. Kenrick as *Emilius and Sophia: or, A New System of Education*, 1762–63), and on liberty in the essay *Du Contrat Social* (1762; tr. as *A Treatise on the Social Compact*, 1764). Threatened with arrest in France, and with both books banned in Geneva, where *Émile* was publicly burned, he settled in the region of Neuchatel under the protection of Frederick (the Great), King of Prussia, assumed Armenian costume, and renounced his Genevan citizenship.

In 1766, at the invitation of DAVID HUME, he took refuge in England, where he began to compose his *Confessions* (1782–89; tr. 1783–91; tr. J. M. Cohen, 1953), an autobiography which is a model of readability and frankness. Persecution mania drove him back to France, where after further attempts at self-justification, he finally resigned himself to calmer reflections, manifested in *Les Rêveries du Promeneur Solitaire* (1782; tr. Peter France as *Reveries of the Solitary Walker*, 1979), which inspired THOMAS GRAY's *Elegy*. . . . The simplicity and modesty of his last years belie his reputation as one of the earliest embodiments of what CARLYLE termed 'the hero as man of letters' (1840). See Maurice Cranston, *Jean-Jacques: the Early Life of Rousseau*, new edn 1987, *The Noble Savage: Jean-Jacques Rousseau 1754–1762*, new edn 1993, and *The Solitary Self: Jean-Jacques Rousseau in Exile and Adversity 1762–1778*, 1996.

ROWE, NICHOLAS (1674–1718) British dramatist and poet, was born in Little Barford, Bedfordshire, the son of a prominent lawyer, and was educated at Westminster School, from which he went straight to the Middle Temple, being called to the Bar in 1696. The first of his blank-verse tragedies, *The Ambitious Step-Mother*, was performed in 1700; that and *Tamerlane* (1701), which was regularly revived on the anniversary of the landing of the Protestant William and Mary in 1688, moved a contemporary critic to suggest, 'considering the degeneracy of our present Poets, Mr Roe has the fairest Pretence to succeed *Dryden* in *Tragedy* of any of his Brethren'. *The Fair Penitent* (1703), the first of what he termed his 'she-tragedies', is significant also in that its 'melancholy tale of private woes' began a resurgence of the domestic drama. He then wrote a comedy, *The Biter* (1704), at which he was one of the few members of the audience to laugh. He did not repeat the experiment. His edition of *The Works of Mr William Shakespear* (1709), in six volumes with a biography and critical notes, makes him the first serious Shakespearian editor. His search for public employment now brought him the post of secretary to the Duke of Queensberry, after whose death in 1711 he wrote his first play for seven years, *The Tragedy of Jane Shore* (1714), the public success of which was enhanced by clever pre-production publicity. With the accession of George I in 1714, he found regular preferment at last, becoming Land Surveyor to the Customs, Poet Laureate (1715), and Clerk of the Presentations (1718). His final play was *The Tragedy of Lady Jane Grey* (1715). His last days were chronicled by the press, and he was buried in Westminster Abbey 'over-against Chaucer'. LUCAN's *Pharsalia*, the great translation in verse on which he had been working for twenty years, was published in 1719, and earned his widow a pension of £40

a year from the King. See *Three Plays*, ed. J. R. Sutherland, 1929.

ROWLEY, SAMUEL see MARLOWE.

ROWLEY, WILLIAM (c.1585–c.1642) English dramatist, not to be confused with Samuel Rowley (d. ?1633), who may have had a hand in MARLOWE's *Dr Faustus*, is one of the more shadowy of those who wrote in collaboration for the Jacobean theatre. A leading stage comedian, he appears to have written unaided the comedy *A Shoe-Maker a Gentleman* (performed 1609), the tragedy *All's Lost by Lust* (c.1619), which PEPYS records seeing in 1661, and two revisions of earlier plays whose first performances there is no record, *A Woman Never Vexed* and *A Match at Midnight*. With MIDDLETON he wrote *A Faire Quarrell* (1617) and *The Spanish Gipsie* (1621), as well as the profound tragedy, *The Changeling* (1622). He also collaborated at different times with DEKKER, JOHN FORD, HEYWOOD, and WEBSTER, and with Dekker, Ford, and Webster wrote the lost *The Late Murder in Whitechapel*.

ROWSON, SUSANNA (1762–1824), née Haswell, American novelist and dramatist, was born in England in Portsmouth, the daughter of a naval officer who took her as a child to Massachusetts, where he had been appointed to the customs: she described the sinking of their ship outside Boston harbour in her novel, *Rebecca: or, The Fille de Chambre* (1792). The family returned to England in 1778 after being interned as loyalists. In 1786 she married William Rowson, a hardware merchant (and trumpeter in the royal horse guards). She also published a novel, *Victoria* (1786); *Poems on Various Subjects* (1788); two more novels; and then *Charlotte: a Tale of the Truth* (1791), a melodramatic story of seduction, betrayal, and ruination, set in Britain and New York City during the War of Independence (1775–81). When her husband's business failed, the couple went on the stage (she as singer and dancer as well as actress). After performing in Edinburgh they undertook an American tour to Philadelphia, Baltimore, Annapolis, and Boston, where they settled. The publication in America of *Charlotte* (in some editions as *Charlotte Temple*) in 1794 made her the first American best-selling novelist. She was also writing plays, of which the topical musical comedy *Slaves in Algiers: or, A Struggle for Freedom* (1794) gave dramatic expression to her feminism: 'Women were born for universal sway, / Men to adore, be silent, and obey.' In 1797 she opened an academy for young ladies in Boston, where she taught until 1822, adding to her varied canon textbooks on history, geography, and spelling.

ROY, GABRIELLE (1909–83) French-Canadian novelist and short-story writer, was born in Saint-Boniface, Manitoba, the youngest of 11 children. She was educated there at St Joseph Academy, and at Winnipeg Normal School, after which she taught in local schools until 1937, when she went to England to study drama at the Guildhall School of Music and Drama. She returned to Canada at the outbreak of World War II, and worked as a journalist until the publication of her first novel. *Bonheur d'Occasion* (1945; tr. Hannah Josephson as *The Tin Flute*, 1947; tr. Alan Brown, 1980), a study of how war can ironically ease the problems of urban unfortunates, won the Governor General's Award in its English translation, and the Prix Fémina in the original, the first Canadian novel to win a major French literary award. Three collections of linked stories reflect her childhood and early adult experiences in Manitoba: *La Petite Poule d'Eau* (1950; tr. Harry Binnse as *Where Nests the Water Hen*, 1950), *Rue Deschambault* (1955; tr. Binnse as *Street of Riches*, 1957, winner of the Governor General's Award), and *La Route d'Altamont* (1966; tr. Joyce Marshall as *The Road Past Altamont*, 1966). Each of the four stories in *La Rivière Sans Repos* (1970) examines an aspect of the clash of cultures affecting the Eskimo civilization—one of them was published separately as *Windflower* (tr. Marshall, 1970). A different child from a prairie outpost or a Winnipeg slum features in each of the stories in *Ces Enfants de Ma Vie* (1977; tr. Brown as *Children of My Heart*, 1979), for which she was given her third Governor General's Award, this time in the original French. *Fragiles Lumières de la Terre: Écrits Divers 1942–1970* (1978, tr. Brown as *Fragile Lights of Earth*, 1982) contains journalism as well as autobiographical and literary essays. Roy married Dr Marcel Carbotte in 1947, in which year she also became the first woman Fellow of the Royal Society of Canada. She was made Companion, Order of Canada, in 1967.

RUBENS, BERNICE (*b.* 1928) British novelist, was born in Cardiff, the third of four children of a Lithuanian refugee who worked as a tallyman for a shilling a week. She was educated at Cardiff High School for Girls and the University College of South Wales, and married Rudi Nassauer in 1947, the year in which she graduated. After teaching for a year, she became a writer and director of documentary films for the United Nations and other organizations. Her first novel was *Set on Edge* (1960); her fourth, *The Elected Member* (1969), won the Booker prize for fiction. She has commented: 'My first four novels were essentially on Jewish themes in a Jewish environment, for in that environment I felt secure.' Her broad territory, in these and subsequent books, is the desperation of the loveless and the rejected, and her range embraces sheer comedy, comedy of manners, tragicomedy, and tragedy, without ever jettisoning her essential, often sly, verbal wit. Her observation of family relationships is especially acute, and her situations are varied, and unusual. A male transvestite heads the cast of *Sunday Best* (1971); a foetus keeps a diary in *Spring Sonata* (1979); a rapist is at large among genteel widows on a cruise in *Birds of Passage* (1981). *Brothers* (1983) is a Russia to Israel Jewish family chronicle of four generations; in *Kingdom Come* (1990) she charts the coming, the career, the doubts, and the inevitable rejection of a 17th-century Messiah. While some of her characters may verge towards the psychotic, the protagonist of *A Solitary Grief* (1991) is a psychiatrist, whose attitude to his handicapped child causes rather than relieves his suffering. *Mother Russia* (1992), described by one critic as 'the mother of all blockbusters', had contradictory reviews. Rubens returned to her roots with *Yesterday in the Back Lane* (1995), a realistic blend of love, death, guilt, and atonement which begins in Cardiff during the bombing in World War II.

RUDD, STEELE, pseudonym of Arthur Hoey Davis (1868–1935) Australian fiction writer, was born in Drayton on the Darling Downs, Queensland, the son of a Welsh blacksmith who in 1870 selected land at Emu Creek, where the family moved in 1875 and where the boy went to the state school until he was 12. After working in shearing sheds and as a stock rider, he became a civil service clerk in Brisbane, transferring to the Sheriff's Offfice in 1889, and being appointed Under-Sheriff in 1902. He was made redundant in 1904, by which time, as Steele Rudd, he had become a notable humorist. ('Steele' stood for STEELE, and 'Rudd' was a contraction of 'Rudder', under which he had written rowing skits in the Brisbane *Chronicle* in the early 1890s.) From 1895 he contributed to the *Bulletin* sketches based on the experiences of his own family, published as *On Our Selection* (1899) and *On Our New Selection* (1903). He now founded *Steele Rudd's Magazine*, which folded in 1907 but was subsequently revived three times under different guises. After trying farming on the Darling Downs, he finally returned to city life in about 1917. The original Rudd family characters, and their comic attempts to make order out of disarray, became enshrined in Australian mythology, thanks partly to their manipulation by their creator, in whose *Green Grey Homestead* (1934) they make a final appearance, and partly to their exploitation through other media. Bert Bailey (1868–1939), with Edmund Duggan (1862–1938), adapted *On Our Selection* for the stage in 1912, and himself played the part of Dad for many years; there have been numerous film, radio, and strip cartoon spin-offs. See *A Steele Rudd Selection*, ed. Frank Moorhouse, 1986.

RUKEYSER, MURIEL see WALKER.

RUNYON, (ALFRED) DAMON (1880–1946) American journalist and short-story writer, was born Runyan (the change of spelling is said to have been due to a compositor's error in a by-line) in Manhattan, Kansas. He was left alone with his father, a typesetter, in Pueblo, Colorado, after the death of his mother from consumption in 1889. He left Hindale Elementary School at 12, worked as an errand boy for local newspapers, and in 1895 was taken on as a reporter. He served in the 13th Minnesota Volunteers in the Spanish-American War (1898–1900). He then reported for Colorado newspapers, graduating to writing on sport for the San Francisco *Post* and on crime, politics, and business for the *Rocky Mountain News*, whose social editor he married. In 1911 he was hired as a sportswriter by the New York *American*, owned by William Randolph Hearst (1863–1951), for whose conglomerate he wrote in various capacities most of the ninety million published words with which he is credited. With 'Romance in the Roaring Forties' (*Cosmopolitan Magazine*, 1929) he initiated a long line of stories, many of which first appeared in the *Saturday Evening Post*. He made lovable caricatures of the people with whom he mixed (gangsters, murderers, tarts), and invented, or recorded, a fractured English dialect, depending on the use of the historic present for the narrative, which was described as 'Runyonese' in a serious correspondence which developed in journals in England in the 1930s. The title of the first of many collections, *Guys and Dolls* (1931), was also that of the successful musical based on his characters (1952). Admired but not liked by his fellow journalists ('Damon would throw a drowning man both ends of the rope'), he ignored his children and his wife, after whose death he married his mistress, a 26-year-old Mexican dancer. See Jimmy Breslin, *Damon Runyon: a Life*, 1992.

RUSHDIE, SALMAN (*b.* 1947) British novelist, was born in Bombay of a Muslim family and had a bilingual upbringing in English and Urdu. His family emigrated to Pakistan in 1964. He was educated in England at Rugby School and King's College, Cambridge. After a year as a professional actor with a multi-media theatrical group, he subsidized his novel writing by working part time as an advertising copywriter. His first novel, *Grimus* (1975), is a fantasy whose ultimate source is a 12th-century Sufi narrative poem called *The Conference of Birds*. In the richly inventive, and often comic, *Midnight's Children* (1981), which won the Booker prize for fiction and two other awards, and in *Shame* (1983), the narrator in each case is a character who, like Rushdie himself, is on the borderline between cultures. *The Satanic Ver-*

ses (1988), which is in part an attack on the Thatcherite regime in Britain, gave offence for remarks put into the mouth of its characters. On 14 February 1989 the Ayatollah Khomeini issued a *fatwa* (legal ruling) declaring Rushdie an apostate who should be killed for insulting the Prophet Muhammad. Rushdie went into hiding. In December 1990, he made a statement in which he embraced Islam and formally disassociated himself from the sentiments of the characters in his novel. *Haroun and the Sea of Stories*, a fable with a child as chief character, was written in hiding and published in 1990. *Imaginary Homelands: Essays and Criticism 1981–1991* (1991) includes 'In Good Faith', his dignified article written just before the *fatwa*, 'Is Nothing Sacred', the Herbert Read Memorial Lecture which was read out in his absence by PINTER, and 'Why I Have Embraced Islam'. A new edition (1992), published on the third anniversary of the declaration of the *fatwa*, has the paper he delivered in person at Columbia University, New York, in December 1991. In 1992 he was enabled to visit Denmark, Spain, Norway, Germany, Sweden, Canada, and Ireland, to drum up support for the cancellation of the *fatwa*. He wrote in an article in February 1993: 'I suspect that because I have not been killed many people think that there is nobody trying to kill me.'

His second book written in hiding was *East and West* (1994), nine short stories of various genres, illustrating the theme of 'Home', 'such a scattered, damaged, various concept in our present travails'. It was followed by his first novel since *The Satanic Verses*, *The Moor's Last Sigh* (1995), a parable of good and evil tracing the course of a family's, and India's, upheavals before and after Independence. By 1996 Rushdie was making public appearances, still under police protection. He visited Australia and New Zealand in 1995, and the Leipzig Book Fair early in 1996: afterwards a militant Muslim leader (since deceased) in the UK confirmed that the *fatwa* remained in place. In its name the publishers or translators of the Japanese, Italian, Norwegian, and Turkish editions of *The Satanic Verses* have been wounded or killed. See Catherine Curdy, *Salman Rushdie*, 1996 (critical study).

RUSKIN, JOHN (1819–1900) British prose writer, art critic, and social philosopher, was born in London, the only child of a wealthy wine merchant, and was educated by his mother and by tutors until he went to Christ Church, Oxford, where at the third attempt he won the Newdigate Prize for poetry. *Modern Painters* (1843–60) began as a vindication of J. M. W. Turner (1775–1851), and became an artistic and spiritual guide to the history of Europe, which Ruskin knew from frequent tours with his parents. *The Seven Lamps of Architecture* (1849) offended architects but brought reason and eloquence to bear on the relationship between virtue and art, which he elaborated in *The Stones of Venice* (1851–53). He was one of the founders of the Working Men's College in 1854. This was the start of a phase of social and political awareness, exemplified by *Unto This Last: Four Essays on the First Principles of Political Economy* (1862—the essays were originally published in *Cornhill Magazine* in 1860), which was regarded as absurd in its time, and *Sesame and Lilies* (1865), on the position of women in society. In 1870 he became the first Slade Professor of Fine Art at Oxford. His review of the Grosvenor Gallery exhibition in 1877, in the course of which he accused the American painter James Abbott McNeill Whistler (1834–1903) of 'flinging a pot of paint into the public's face', was the subject of a libel action; Whistler was awarded damages of one farthing.

Ruskin's classic and urbane fairy tale, *The King of the Golden River* (1851), was written in 1841 for 12-year-old Euphemia ('Effie') Chalmers Gray, who was to become his unfortunate partner from 1848 to 1854 in an unconsummated marriage, on the annulment of which she married the painter, John Everett Millais (1829–96). In 1866 he proposed unsuccessfully to 18-year-old Rose La Touche, whom he had known since she was nine and who died insane in 1875. On his father's death in 1864 he had inherited a small fortune; when his mother died in 1871 he bought a house on Coniston in the Lake District. From here, in 1880, moved by the illustrations by Kate Greenaway (1846–1901) for her *Under the Window* (1878), he initiated a correspondence with her, the prime object of which was to secure a private source of pictures of little girls. Soon afterwards the mental instability which had affected his life became periodic insanity. See *Selected Writings*, ed. Kenneth Clark, new edn 1991; *Praeterita*, ed. Kenneth Clark, new edn, ed. A. O. J. Cockshut, 1994 (autobiography); Joan Abse, *John Ruskin: the Passionate Moralist*, 1980 (biography); Timothy Hilton, *John Ruskin: the Early Years 1819–1859*, 1985; George Landow, *Ruskin*, 1985 (introduction to his theories).

RUSSELL, BERTRAND, (3RD EARL RUSSELL) (1872–1970) philosopher, was born in Trelleck, Monmouthshire, the younger son of Viscount Amberley. He was a godson of MILL, and grandson of the 1st Earl Russell (1792–1878), and succeeded to the title in 1931. His mother having died in 1874 and his father in 1876, he was brought up by his grandmother, and was educated by tutors until he went to Trinity College, Cambridge, of which he was elected a Fellow in 1895. His first major work was *Principles of Mathematics* (1903). *Introduction to Mathematical Philosophy* (1919) was written in prison, to which he was sentenced for six months for a seditious article. With his second wife he founded a progressive school in Hampshire

in 1927. His appointment to a chair at the City College of New York in 1940 was abruptly terminated by litigation, the authorities being successfully sued for employing an atheist who practised free love. *A History of Western Philosophy* (1945) finally brought him financial security. *Human Knowledge: Its Scope and Limits* (1948) was the last of a long line of philosophical works through which he became publicly recognized as an outstanding logician. An active opponent of nuclear warfare, and founder of the Committee of 100, he was in 1961, with his fourth wife, sentenced to prison for his part in demonstrations, but served only a week because of his age. His Whig aristocratic background and his remarkable intelligence instilled in him a conviction that whatever he thought was right, even on matters about which he knew nothing. The first of numerous objects of extramarital desire was Lady Ottoline Morrell (1873–1938), who addressed to him some 1500 letters. He was awarded the OM in 1949, and the Nobel Prize for Literature in 1950. See *Portraits from Memory and Other Essays*, new edn 1995, and *Autobiography*, new edn 1985; Caroline Moorehead, *Bertrand Russell*, new edn 1993 (biography); Ray Monk, *Bertrand Russell: the Spirit of Solitude*, 1996 (critical biography); A. C. Grayling, *Russell*, 1996 (introduction to his logic and philosophy).

RUSSELL, GEORGE WILLIAM (1867–1935) Irish poet, painter, editor, economist, and journalist, who wrote under the pseudonym of Æ (a contraction of æon), was born in Lurgan, Co. Armagh, and educated at Rathmines School, Dublin, and the Metropolitan School of Art, where he met YEATS, who especially awakened in him a sense of mystic communication with an idealistic Celtic past. *Homeward: Songs by the Way* (1894) promised more by way of poetic vision than he later achieved, but he had other ways of expressing his interest in the development of modern Irish literature and his concern for the Irish political scene. In 1897 he gave up his job as a draper's clerk to work for the Irish Agricultural Organisation Society, whose journal, the *Irish Homestead*, he edited from 1906 to 1923, when it amalgamated with the *Irish Statesman*, of which he was Editor until 1930. His play *Deirdre* was performed in 1902, and he was associated with the Irish National Theatre Society and the United Arts Club, while his support of the Irish Literary Society led to his compiling *New Songs* (1904), which included the work of some of the best of the younger writers whose talents he had spotted. His political writing is best seen in *The National Being* (1916), and his imaginative prose in *The Interpreters* (1920). See *Collected Works*, ed. Henry Summerfield, 3 vols 1978–84; Henry Summerfield, *That Myriad-Minded Man: a Biography of G. W. Russell—'Æ'*, 1975.

RUTHERFORD, MARK, pseudonym of William Hale White (1831–1913) British novelist, was born in Bedford, the son of a Dissenting bookseller who later became a doorkeeper at the House of Commons, from which vantage point he wrote parliamentary sketches. He was educated at Bedford Modern School, from which, after a process of conversion, he went to New College, St John's Wood, to study for the Independent ministry. With two others, he was expelled in 1852 for unorthodox biblical views, towards which he was almost certainly impelled by reading WORDWORTH's *Lyrical Ballads*. He did some work for the *Westminster Review*, at whose offices he met GEORGE ELIOT. In 1854 he passed into the civil service, working first as a clerk in Somerset House, and from 1858 in the Admiralty, where he rose to be Assistant Director of Contracts until his retirement on a pension in 1891. For *The Autobiography of Mark Rutherford, Dissenting Minister* (1881) and *Mark Rutherford's Deliverance, Being the Second Part of His Autobiography* (1885; rev. edn 1888) he invented not only a pseudonymous author, but also Reuben Shapcott, who was supposed to have edited them after Rutherford's death. Essentially they are lucid accounts of his own spiritual progress and of the sensibilities of the Nonconformist community. Rutherford also wrote four other novels, of which *Clara Hopgood* (1896) was accused of immorality on account of the determination of Clara's sister not to marry the man by whom she is pregnant. Sir William Hale-White (1857–1949), the physician, was his eldest son.

RYMER, THOMAS (1641–1713) English critic, was born in Yorkshire and educated at Northallerton Free School and Sidney Sussex College, Cambridge. In 1664 his father was convicted of planning an uprising against the monarchy, and was hanged, drawn, and quartered. Thomas went from Cambridge to Gray's Inn, and was called to the Bar in 1673. In 1674 he appeared in print as the (anonymous) translator of *Reflections on Aristotle's Treatise of Poesie* by the contemporary French critic, René Rapin. In his own *The Tragedies of the Last Age* (1678), written in the form of a letter to Sir Fleetwood Sheppard (1634–98), he brings what he calls 'common sense' as well as 'the practice of the ancients' to bear particularly on three plays of BEAUMONT and FLETCHER. He also coined the term 'poetical justice' for the function of the poet (or tragedian) to 'see justice exactly administered, if he intended to please'. His heroic tragedy in rhyming verse, *Edgar, or the English Monarch*, was also published in 1678, but was never performed. He returned to the attack on sacred dramatic cows in *A Short View of Tragedy* (1693), devoting a third of it to SHAKE-SPEARE's *Othello*, which he had left out of his previous book for want of space. His views on that play, whose 'tragical part is, plainly none other, than a Bloody farce, without salt or savour', could be held outrageous were they not in places so witty. On SHADWELL's death in 1692, the posts of Poet Laureate and Historiographer Royal were separated, the latter going to Rymer. In this capacity he also edited all treaties made by the English government since 1101; at his death, 15 volumes of *Foedera* had been published, partly at his own expense. See *The Critical Works of Thomas Rymer*, ed. Curt A. Zimansky, 1956.

SÁBATO, ERNESTO (*b.* 1911) Argentinian novelist, was born in Rojas of Italian immigrant parents, and completed his secondary schooling in La Plata, where he also attended the university, at which he studied physics. In his youth an anarchist, he became a leader of the Young Communists in 1931, when he went underground for a while, living incognito, to avoid oppression. After being awarded a research scholarship to study radiology in Paris, he transferred his research to the Massachusetts Institute of Technology. He was appointed a professor of theoretical physics at the Teachers' Training College, La Plata, in 1940. He lost his post in 1945 after protesting against the prevailing regime, though he had already determined on a literary career. In a series of collections of essays and critical works published from 1945, he addresses literary, philosophical, linguistic, and social issues. His novels *El Túnel* (1948; tr. Harriet Onis as *The Outsider*, 1950; tr. Margaret Sayers Peden as *The Tunnel*, 1988) and *Sobre Héroes y Tumbas* (1961; tr. Helen R. Lane as *On Heroes and Tombs*, 1990) are powerful studies of artistic psychopaths, in which present-day and historical Argentina are reflected by the use of a variety of modernist techniques. As novelist, observer, chronicler, and a character in his own book, he examines in *Abaddón el Exterminador* (1974; tr. Andrew Hurley as *The Angel of Darkness*, 1991) the total state of mankind in Argentina in the 1970s.

SACKVILLE, THOMAS (1st Earl of Dorset) (1536–1608) English poet and dramatist, was born at Buckhurst in Withyham, Sussex, the only son of Sir Richard Sackville (*d.* 1566), who as Under-Treasurer of the Exchequer and Chancellor of the Court of Augmentations amassed so much wealth that after his death he was known as 'Fillsack'. He joined the Inner Temple in 1555 and was called to the Bar. With a fellow student, Thomas Norton (1532–84), who was at about that time translating CALVIN's *The Institution of Christian Religion* (1561), he wrote *Gorboduc*, first performed before Elizabeth I, his second cousin, on 18 January 1561. It was published in 1565, and was brought out in a revised edition as *The Tragedie of Ferrex and Porrex* (1570). Previously, performances of tragedy had

been largely adaptations or translations of SENECA and other classical authors. *Gorboduc* is both the first English tragedy and the first English play in blank verse. As in classical tragedy, the action of this sad tale of kingly indecision is offstage; after the main protagonists are dead, the moral is driven home in a curious fifth act in which the perils of there being no legitimate heir to a throne are propounded. Sackville contributed to the second part of *A Myrroure for Magistrates* (1563) the dramatic poem on Henry, Duke of Buckingham, and also 'The Induction', in which flashes of genuine poetry illumine a suitably gloomy prologue to the tales of woe. He inherited his father's fortune in 1566, and was created Lord Buckhurst in 1567. He was much in demand for diplomatic missions, one of which, in 1586, was to inform Mary, Queen of Scots, that she had been condemned to death. Under her son, James I (VI of Scotland), he was made Lord Treasurer for life and Earl of Dorset. He died suddenly at the council table.

SACKVILLE-WEST, VICTORIA (or **VITA**) (1892–1962) British novelist and poet, was born at Knole, Kent, which had been granted to SACKVILLE by Elizabeth I in 1566. Her father became 3rd Baron Sackville in 1908. She was educated mainly by governesses at Knole, where she read prodigiously and began to write. Foreign travel broadened her experience. In 1913 she married NICOLSON—their remarkable relationship and her affair with Violet Trefusis (1894–1972), the daughter of Edward VII's mistress, Alice Keppel (1869–1947), is described in Nigel Nicolson, *Portrait of a Marriage* (1973). Among her earlier published books were *Knole and the Sackvilles* (1922), a historical account of the house and its inhabitants; *The Land* (1926), a long poem in the style of VIRGIL's *Georgics*; and *The Edwardians* (1930), a record, in the form of a novel, of Edwardian high society and country living. In 1930 she and her husband bought the derelict Sissinghurst Castle, Kent, whose garden, which they themselves created, in his words, to combine 'the element of expectation with the element of surprise', has become a national heritage. In all she published over forty books; other notable ones are the precisely-expressed, elegant novel, *All Passion Spent* (1931), and the joint biography, *The Eagle and the Dove: St Teresa of Avila, St Thérèse of Lisieux* (1943). A volume of *Collected Poems* was published in 1933. Articles on gardening which she wrote for the *Observer* from 1946 to 1961 were collected in several books; a recent reprint is *In Your Garden* (1996). She was made CH in 1948. See Victoria Glendinning, *Vita: the Life of Victoria Sackville-West*, new edn 1992.

SADE, (DONATIEN ALPHONSE-FRANÇOIS), MARQUIS DE

(1740–1814) French novelist and prose writer, was born in Paris and educated at Collège d'Harcourt, being then commissioned in the army. He served in the Seven Years War, at the end of which in 1763 he was discharged, whereupon his father forced him into a dynastic marriage with Renée-Pélagie de Montreuil (1741–1810)—see Margaret Crosland, *Sade's Wife: the Woman Behind the Marquis* (1995). His mildly deviant behaviour with bevies of prostitutes, some of whom complained of rough treatment, got him into trouble with the police: in 1772 he was condemned to death for sodomy, but reprieved. His mother-in-law now obtained a *lettre de cachet*, on the strength of which he was put away without trial. While in solitary confinement, latterly in the Bastille in Paris, from which he was moved in 1789 a few days before its sack marked the beginning of the French Revolution, he amused himself by writing up his sexual fantasies. He also wrote a philosophical novel, *Aline et Valcour*, published in eight volumes in 1795, and a number of tales in the Gothic or picaresque tradition, 11 of which were published as *Les Crimes de l'Amour* (1800), the first work to carry his name—see *The Crimes of Love*, tr. Crosland (1996).

On the abolition by the people's government of *lettres de cachet*, he was freed and was for a time a judge of a revolutionary tribunal, in which capacity he demonstrated such leniency to his mother-in-law's family, and to others, that he nearly went to the guillotine himself. He was imprisoned again in 1801, for publishing obscene works, principally *Justine* (1791). In 1803 his ungrateful in-laws had him permanently incarcerated in the lunatic asylum at Charenton, where he lived comfortably, attended by two mistresses: a middle-aged actress and a teenager. His wife remained loyal to him until 1810, when she divorced him. As a philosopher he held that human beings are fundamentally bad and that the physical and sexual exploitation of others is a natural expression of sensual gratification—see *The Misfortunes of Virtue and Other Early Tales*, ed. and tr. David Coward (1992). In 1767 he had succeeded to his father's title of Comte, which he declined to use. See *The Passionate Philosopher: a Marquis de Sade Reader*, ed. Margaret Crosland, new edn 1993; Donald Thomas, *The Marquis de Sade*, new edn 1993 (biography); Maurice Lever, *Marquis de Sade: a Biography*, tr. Arthur Goldhammer, new edn 1994.

SAGAN, FRANÇOISE,

pseudonym (after PROUST) of Françoise Quoirez (*b.* 1935) French novelist, was born in Cajarc of a bourgeois Catholic Parisian family. At the end of the German Occupation they returned to Paris, where she went to the Couvent des Oiseaux et du Sacré Coeur. After a year at a mountain school recovering from anaemia, she was enrolled in a progressive course of study, and failed her baccalaureate and then her foundation course at the Sorbonne. Just 18, she had a tiff with her mother on holiday and went back alone to the family apartment, where she wrote, in two-and-a-half months, *Bonjour Tristesse* (1954; tr. Irene Ash, 1955), a sparely told novel of the self-discovery of a teenage girl who is obsessed with the status quo. She was two years mulling over her second, *Un Certain Sourire* (1956; tr. Anne Green as *A Certain Smile*, 1956), the story of the conflicts in her love life of a student at the Sorbonne, which she then wrote as quickly as her first. The two are said to have sold over two million copies in the USA alone. She has continued to write stylish, witty novels of situation which require no specialized knowledge of France on the part of the reader. She has also written plays, a ballet, and several well-known songs. Her hobby is sports cars—she became notorious for fast driving, and had a bad accident on the road in 1957.

SAHGAL, NAYANTARA

(*b.* 1927), née Pandit, Indian novelist and journalist, was born in Allahabad, the second of three daughters of an actively political couple—the title of her first volume of autobiography refers to an incident at the age of three, when her father was hauled off to prison while the family was at tea. She was the niece of Jawaharlal Nehru (1889–1964) and thus the first cousin of Mrs Indhira Gandhi (1917–84). She was educated at the local convent and then, her father having heeded 'Gandhiji's call to boycott British and government-aided institutions', at the American school of Woodstock, Mussooree. In 1943 she was sent to Wellesley College, Massachusetts, where she graduated as BA in history in 1947. Her father having died in 1944, and her mother (Vijayalakshmi Pandit) now serving abroad as Indian Ambassador to the USSR (she was later Ambassador to the USA, and High Commissioner in London), Sahgal then lived for a time at the residence of Nehru, now Prime Minister. Describing herself as 'Indian—by blood, nationality, upbringing and conviction—and Western by virtue of my English medium education', her novels, unsurprisingly, 'have a political background or political ambience'. The first, *A Time to be Happy* (1958), is set during the struggle for independence between 1932 and 1948. *This Time of Morning* (1965) is a study of political power in the ensuing period, and *Storm in Chandigarh* (1969) of the background to the partition of the Punjab. In *The Day in Shadow* (1971) the focus shifts to personal relationships; events during two critical episodes in recent history are the basis of *A Situation in New Delhi* (1977) and *Rich Like Us* (1985). *Plans for Departure* (1985) and *Mistaken Identity* (1989) are historical novels of the Raj in the 20th century. Sahgal is also a distinguished political journalist (and was a member of the Indian delegation to the United Nations in 1978), her *Indhira Gandhi: Her Road to Power* (1982) is an outspoken as well as shrewdly analytical account of a regime. She married Gautam Sahgal, a businessman, in 1949 (divorced 1967), and E. N. Mangat Rai, a civil servant, in 1979. See *Prison and Chocolate Cake*, 1954, and *From Fear Set Free*, 1962 (autobiography).

SAINT-EXUPÉRY, ANTOINE DE (1900–44) French novelist, prose writer, and airman, was born in Lyons, one of five children whose father died in 1904. He was educated at Notre Dame de Saint Croix, Le Mans, and Villa Saint-Jean, Fribourg, Switzerland, where he passed his baccalaureate. He then entered the Lycée Saint-Louis, Paris, to prepare for the École Navale, and, after two years study, he failed his oral exam. During military service in 1921–23 he obtained a military pilot's licence, and in 1929 he became Director of Aeroposta Argentina, personally pioneering some of the initial flights, for which he was made a member of the Legion of Honour in 1930 (he became Officer in 1938). This provided the background of two poetic novels, *Courrier Sud* (1929; tr. Stuart Gilbert as *Southern Mail*, 1933) and *Vol de Nuit* (1931; tr. Gilbert as *Night Flight*, 1932). After the collapse of the holding company, he was briefly a test pilot, and then reluctantly accepted a public relations post with Air France after being nearly drowned in a submerged seaplane. He also patented aeronautical inventions, the first of which was a landing device, and undertook journalistic assignments in Russia and Spain. Having acquired his own plane, he attempted in 1935 to break the speed record from Paris to Saigon. He crashed in the desert just east of the Nile valley, and with his mechanic walked for five days without food or water until they came across a Bedouin caravan; he re-created the experience in *Terre des Hommes* (1939; as *Wind, Sand and Stars* tr. Lewis Galantière, 1939; tr. William Rees, 1995).

Pilote de Guerre (1942; as *Flight to Arras* tr. Galantière, 1942; tr. Rees, 1995) is primarily a philosophical meditation on flying and the role of the pilot in World War II. Until the German occupation of France he flew reconnaissance missions over enemy territory, for which he was awarded the Croix de Guerre.

After three years in the USA, he returned to active service in Algiers, and flew American Lightning aircraft until grounded for overshooting the runway. In 1944 he managed to get permission to make five reconnaissance flights from Sardinia. He disappeared without trace on the tenth. *Le Petit Prince* (1943; tr. Katherine Woods as *The Little Prince*, 1944), with his own illustrations, is an allegorical story for children, in which he explored many of his personal philosophical convictions. Remaining officially married to Consuelo Gomez Carrillo (*d.* 1979), who was half his height and as childish, romantic, and unfaithful as he was, and with whom he could not bear to live, he addressed long, reproachful letters to her, while indulging in numerous platonic and sexual relationships with other women. See Paul Webster, *Antoine de Saint-Exupéry: the Life and Death of the Little Prince*, new edn 1994; Stacy Schiff, *Saint-Exupéry: a Biography*, new edn 1996.

SAINT-JOHN, HENRY see BOLINGBROKE.

SAINT-JOHN PERSE, pen name of Marie-René-Alexis Saint-Léger Léger (1887–1975) French poet and diplomat, was born in Saint-Léger-les-Feuilles, Guadaloupe, of ancient local descent on both sides. The family moved to Pau in 1899, and after passing his baccalaureate at the local lycée, he studied law at Bordeaux University. His first book of verse, *Éloges* (1911; tr. Louise Varèse as *Éloges and Other Poems*, 1944), written when he was 21, records his emotional development as a child. In 1914 he entered the Foreign Service. While Secretary of Legation in Peking, he travelled in Manchuria, Mongolia, and the Gobi Desert, and wrote, in a disused Taoist temple which he rented, *Anabase* (1924; tr. T. S. Eliot as *Anabasis*, 1938), a narrative poem evoking the ancient migrations of the East. While Cabinet Director (1925–32) and Secretary-General (1933–40) of Foreign Affairs, he published nothing, so as not to compromise his position. Removed from his post in 1940, he took refuge in the USA: in Paris the collaborationist government deprived him of his citizenship and the Gestapo wrecked his flat and destroyed his unpublished manuscripts. *Exil* (1942; tr. Denis Devlin in *Exile and Other Poems*, 1949), written in a Long Island beach house loaned by friends, is one of a series of poems of self-discovery in a foreign land. *Vents* (1946; tr. Hugh Chisholm as *Winds*, 1953), largely written after his rights and privileges had been restored, is an epic meditation on the future of the civilization of Europe; *Amers* (1957; tr. Wallace Fowlie as *Seamarks*, 1958), is a celebration of man's destiny. An honorary member of the British orders KCVO (1927), GBE (1938), and KCB (1940), he was also Grand Officer, Legion of

Honour, and received the Nobel Prize for Literature in 1960.

ST OMER, GARTH (*b.* 1931) St Lucian novelist, was born in Castries and educated at St Mary's College and, after seven years teaching in the eastern Caribbean, at the University of the West Indies, Jamaica, where he graduated in French. He taught in France and Ghana, before devoting the years 1966–69 to writing. In 1975 he joined the English department of the University of California. His fictional vision is the alienation of the educated West Indian in his own land, a subject explored in three novels and in the two novellas in *Shades of Grey* (1968), of which *The Lights on the Hill* was published separately in 1986. The protagonist of *A Room on the Hill* (1968) finally decides to stay where he is, puzzling over his motives, accepting ultimate despair. In *Nor Any Country* (1969) a return to St Lucia exercises a partial rehabilitation but offers only a partial solution, which is cheerlessly analysed in *J——, Black Bam and the Masqueraders* (1972).

SAKI, pen name (from a line in EDWARD FITZGERALD's *Rubaiyat*, 4th edn) of Hector Hugh Munro (1870–1916) British short-story writer, was born in Akyab, Burma, the son of a Scottish army officer who was Inspector General of Police. After the death of his mother, he was at the age of two shipped to England with his brother and sister and brought up in Devon by two terrifying aunts. After four terms at Bedford Grammar School, he travelled abroad with his father. He joined the Burma Police in 1893, but returned home after suffering seven attacks of fever in 13 months. He wrote political satire for the *Westminster Gazette*, collected as *The Westminster Alice* (1902). His first book was *The Rise of the Russian Empire* (1900), on the strength of which he became correspondent for the *Morning Post* in the Balkans in 1902, and then in Warsaw, St Petersburg, and Paris. He returned in 1908 to resume a freelance career. His first volume of short stories, *Reginald* (1904), was followed by three more, the last of which was *Beasts and Super-Beasts* (1914). Satirical, especially when describing society living, epigrammatic, and often with a touch of cruelty leavened by his sharp wit, they feature paradoxes and incongruities of a kind which have lasting parallels. *The Unbearable Bassington* (1912) is a book-length story in the same vein. *When William Came: a Story of London Under the Hohenzollerns* (1914) postulates the aftermath of a successful invasion by Germany. At 44 he enlisted as a private in the 22nd Royal Fusiliers, and was sent to France in 1915, having refused a commission. He was shot through the head by a sniper near Beaumont Hamel. See *The Complete Saki*, introduction by Noël Coward, new edn 1982; A. J. Langguth, *Saki: a Life of Hector Hugh*

Munro, with Six Stories Never Before Collected, 1982.

SALINGER, J(EROME) D(AVID) (*b.* 1919) American novelist and short-fiction writer, was born in New York City, the younger child of a Jewish ham importer and of a Gentile of Scottish–Irish parentage. After two years at McBurney School, Manhattan, he went to Valley Forge Military Academy, from which he graduated in 1936. He attended a summer session at New York University in 1937, went to Austria and Poland, and then enrolled at Ursinus College, Pennsylvania, which he left during his first year to attend the short-story writing class at Columbia University, New York. In 1941 he had work published in *Collier's Magazine* and *Esquire*, and the *New Yorker* bought a story about a mixed-up teenager called Holden Caulfield, which was not published until 1946. In the meantime he served as a staff sergeant in counterintelligence with the US Army 4th Division in Europe in World War II, and had stories published also in the *Saturday Evening Post*. In 1948 he landed a contract with the *New Yorker*, which published 'For Esmé—With Love and Squalor' in 1950. *The Catcher in the Rye* (1951), the novel he finally achieved out of the character of Caulfield (he had withdrawn an earlier version in 1946), received mixed notices, and though it reached fourth place in the *New York Times* best-seller list, it did not achieve cult status until the publication of the paperback (1953) and of *Nine Stories* (1953; in UK as *For Esmé— With Love and Squalor, and Other Stories*). Salinger now went into retreat in Cornish, New Hampshire, from which his public utterances have been confined to lawsuits. *Franny and Zooey* (1961) was originally two stories in the *New Yorker* about the Glass family, whose saga he continues tantalizingly in *Raise High the Roofbeam, Carpenters and Seymour: an Introduction* (1963). 'Hapworth 16, 1924', a further and presumably final instalment in the Glass saga, was published in the *New Yorker* on 19 June 1965. Ian Hamilton's *In Search of J. D. Salinger* (1988) is a study of trying to write a biography. The rest is silence, except from the writers of critical studies. See Jack Salzman (ed.), *New Essays on 'Catcher in the Rye'*, 1992.

SALKEY, ANDREW (*b.* 1928) Jamaican novelist, poet, and children's writer, was born in Colon, Panama, and educated at St George's College, Kingston, Munro College, St Elizabeth, and London University. He taught English for two years in a London comprehensive school, and wrote radio scripts and conducted interviews for the BBC External Services until 1976, after which he divided his time between London and Massachusetts, where he had been appointed Professor of Creative Writing at Hampshire College. In *A Quality of Violence* (1959), set in rural Jamaica during the drought of 1900, the conflict is between the black followers of the cult of Pocomania and the brown landowning minority. *Escape to an Autumn Pavement* (1960) examines the plight of the middleclass Jamaican in London, and *The Late Emancipation of Jerry Stover* (1968) the roots from which the exodus occurred. In later novels exiles consider a return to what Salkey summarizes in his political and sociological poem sequence, *Jamaica* (1973), 'Is the lan' I want / an' is the lan' / I out to get'. His two studies, *Havana Journal* (1971) and *Georgetown Journal* (1972), record his personal reactions to the way in which political developments in Cuba and Guyana were affecting cultural attitudes in the Caribbean.

SAND, GEORGE, pseudonym of Baronne Dudevant (1804–76), née Amantine-Lucille-Aurore Dupin, French novelist, was born in Paris and after her father's death was brought up and educated at her grandmother's estate at Nohant, which she later inherited. She went to the Couvent des Anglaises, Paris, from 1817 to 1820, and in 1822 married Baron Dudevant (*d.* 1871), by whom she had two children before they finally separated in 1836. In 1831 she went to Paris to be a writer, contributed to *Le Figaro* and *Revue des Deux Mondes*, and mixed in artistic society, from whose ranks she chose a succession of lovers. The first was Jules Sandeau (1811–83), with whom she wrote a novel, *Rose et Blanche* (1831), and from whose name she derived her pseudonym. Others included MUSSET and the composer Frédéric Chopin (1810–49). Her affairs, as well as her marriage, provided some of the material for, and the outlook of, her earlier novels, notably *Lélia* (1833). During the 1840s she concentrated on social themes, as in *Consuelo* (1842–43). In about 1848 she retired to Nohant, where she indulged primarily in tales of country life, publishing one or more novels almost every year until her death. HENRY JAMES, reviewing *Mademoiselle Merquem* (1868), commented: 'The time was when Madame Sand's novels were translated as fast as they appeared, and circulated, half surreptitiously, as works delightful and intoxicating, but scandalous, dangerous, and seditious.' They were read in French by the Victorian *littérateurs*; the effect of the novels of her first phase are traceable in CHARLOTTE and EMILY BRONTË, of the second in GEORGE ELIOT, and of the third in HARDY—see Patricia Thomson, *George Sand and the Victorians* (1977). CARLYLE coined the term 'George Sandism' to sum up what he saw as 'in the world . . . few sadder, sicklier phenomena . . . than George Sand and the response she meets with'. His wife, however, frequently refers in her letters to the excitement Sand's novels aroused in her, though, 'having still some sense of decency remaining', she used the name 'Erasmus Darwin' when borrowing them from the London Library.

SANDBURG, CARL (1878–1967) American poet, was born in Galesburg, Illinois, the eldest child of an immigrant Swedish ironworker who could read Swedish but never learned to write. The boy, whose early autobiography, *Always the Young Strangers* (1953), was published on his 75th birthday (designated 'Carl Sandburg Day' in Chicago), left school at 13, and did numerous odd jobs, including shining shoes in a barber's shop. After serving in Puerto Rico in 1898 in the Spanish-American War, he enrolled in Lombard College, which he left in 1902 to go wandering, without bothering to take his degree. In 1904 his former professor printed on a hand press 50 copies of Sandburg's pamphlet, *In Reckless Ecstasy*, and two other prose items. After being a district organizer for the Wisconsin Social-Democrats, and marrying Lillian ('Paula') Steichen, a teacher and the sister of Edward Steichen (1879–1973), the photographer, he went to Milwaukee, where he worked as a newspaper reporter, and then in 1912 to Chicago. 'Chicago' ('Hog Butcher for the World, / Tool Maker, Stacker of Wheat . . .') was one of his nine poems on local themes published in *Poetry: a Magazine of Verse* in 1914. With *Chicago Poems* (1916), *Cornhuskers* (1918), and *Smoke and Steel* (1920) he became the laureate of the industrialized working class. He gave up newspaper work in 1920, and became a lecturer and performer, reading his poetry and singing folk songs to his own guitar accompaniment. *The American Songbag* (1927) and *The People, Yes* (1936) reflected his researches into American folk tradition, and in his monumental biography, *Abraham Lincoln: the Prairie Years* (2 vols 1926) and *Abraham Lincoln: the War Years* (4 vols 1939), which won the Pulitzer Prize for history, he celebrated an archetypal American folk hero. *Remembrance Rock* (1948), originally commissioned by Metro-Goldwyn-Mayer as 'a biographical novel of American life, manners, and morals', was never filmed. *Complete Poems* (1950) won the Pulitzer Prize. See *The Complete Poems*, rev. and expanded edn 1969; *The Selected Poems*, ed. George and Willene Hendrick, 1996; Penelope Niven, *Carl Sandburg: a Biography*, new edn 1994; Gay Wilson Allen, *Carl Sandburg*, 1972 (critical study).

SANTAYANA, JORGE ('GEORGE') (1863–1952) Spanish philosopher and critic, was born in Madrid of Spanish parents, and was taken to Avila when he was two. In 1872 his father left him in Boston, USA, with his wife, who had promised her first husband, an American, that she would bring up their three children there. In 1886 he graduated *summa cum laude* at Harvard, where in 1889 he was appointed a professor of philosophy.

He followed a book of verse (1894) with *The Sense of Beauty* (1896), a significant study of aesthetics based on one of his courses: as was *Three Philosophical Poets* (1910), on LUCRETIUS, DANTE, and GOETHE, to which T. S. ELIOT, a graduate student of Santayana in 1908, acknowledges a debt in his criticism of Dante. *The Life of Reason* (5 vols 1905–06) contains the essence of Santayana's moral philosophy, in the realms especially of common sense, society, art, and religion. His mother's death in 1912 left him without a base in Boston at a time when his close friends and relatives were in Europe. He resigned from Harvard, and never returned to the USA, in spite of numerous offers of academic posts. For a time he lived a secluded life of study and writing in Oxford, stoutly refusing to be formally attached to any college. In 1919 he settled on the Continent, where he took permanent rooms in the Hotel Bristol, Rome, from which he travelled to other countries. In *Realms of Being* (4 vols 1928–40) he elaborated on his personal philosophical system. *The Last Puritan* (1935), 'a memoir in the form of a novel', was a critical and popular international success, being regarded by the American public less as the testament of a philosopher than as a comedy of mannners about Boston society. During World War II he remained in Rome as a paying guest in a Catholic nursing home. *Persons and Places*, his autobiography, was published in three volumes in 1944, 1945, and 1953. See *Selected Critical Writings*, ed. Norman Henfrey, 2 vols 1968; Noel O'Sullivan, *Santayana*, 1992 (critical study).

SAPPHO 7th-century BC Greek lyric poet, was born in the Aegean island of Lesbos, which she left at some point to live in Sicily because of some political disturbances. To judge from the fragments of her work which are all that we have out of the nine books of verse which did not survive the Middle Ages, she was a skilful composer of tender, sometimes passionate, simply-worded expressions of love, or about love, for the female sex. She was also in demand as a writer of wedding songs, and was herself married, and had a daughter. The apochryphal story that she threw herself over a cliff after being rejected by a boatman of legendary beauty was reworked by POPE in his youthful poetical exercise, 'Sappho to Phaon'. See *Sappho of Lesbos: the Poems*, tr. Terence DuQuesne, 1990 (with Greek texts and textual notes); in *Seven Greeks*, tr. Guy Davenport, 1995; Margaret Williamson, *Sappho's Immortal Daughters*, 1995 (investigation of her life and culture).

SARGESON, FRANK (1903–82) New Zealand short-story writer, novelist, and critic, was born in Hamilton and educated at Hamilton High School, and studied law extramurally at Auckland University College.

Having qualified as a solicitor in 1926, he spent a year in England and on the Continent, and on his return found work as an estates clerk in a government department in Wellington. A chance encounter in a bar with an eccentric KEATS enthusiast led him back to the poet's work and letters, and to a reconsideration of his own literary efforts. A nearbreakdown in 1929 was averted when he went to live at Okahakura with his easygoing uncle, who allowed him to write in the mornings in return for help on the land in the afternoons. In 1931, having had his first novel rejected, he moved near Auckland into the Takapuna property which was to remain his headquarters for the rest of his life. During the Depression he subsisted on the dole of nine shillings a week, did odd jobs in gardens and kitchens, and wrote stories and articles, only a few of which were published. As he continued to work towards 'an appropriate language to deal with the material of New Zealand life', matters looked up. He published *Conversation with My Uncle and Other Stories* (1936) and contributed to *Tomorrow* and other journals. Surgical tuberculosis prevented war service, and after a further volume of stories, *A Man and His Wife* (1940), he completed, in his 39th year, the novel he felt himself now able to write. It was very short; having been serialized in JOHN LEHMANN's *New Writing* it became the title story of *That Summer and Other Stories* (1946). His first published novel was thus *I Saw in My Dream* (1949), a progress from youth to emancipation; his most highly regarded is *Memoirs of a Peon* (1965), the ironic, picaresque exploits of an Auckland CASANOVA. *Wrestling with the Angel* (1964) contains his two plays, *A Time for Sowing* (1961) and *The Cradle and the Egg* (1962). See *The Stories of Frank Sargeson*, 1982; *Conversation in a Train and Other Critical Writing*, ed. Kevin Cunningham, 1985; *Once is Enough: a Memoir*, 1973, *More than Enough: a Memoir*, 1975, *Never Enough! Places and People Mostly*, 1977 (reissued 1981 in one volume as *Sargeson*); H. Winston Rhodes, *Frank Sargeson*, 1969 (critical study).

SAROYAN, WILLIAM (1908–81) American short-story writer, novelist, and dramatist, was born in Fresno, California, the youngest of four children of Armenian immigrants. When their father died in 1911, they were all put into an orphanage in Oakland for four years, until their mother could support them. Saroyan was educated in Fresno, while doing different kinds of jobs, especially telegraph boy, out of school, from which he dropped out before graduating. He worked in San Francisco as a telegraph operator and then branch manager, but after publishing a story in *Overland Monthly and Outwest Magazine* in 1928 he decided to be a professional writer. *The Daring Young Man on the Flying Trapeze and Other Stories* (1934)—the title story is about a starving writer—gave notice of an unusual if enigmatic talent. After several further collections, of which *Three Times Three* (1936) was published by a student cooperative in Los Angeles, where he was working on Hollywood scenarios for SCHULBERG's father, he began assembling his stories by theme or, as with *My Name is Aram* (1940), by setting and character. He adapted a story in *Three Times Three* as a one-act play (1938) and then as a full-length sentimental comedy, *My Heart's in the Highlands* (1939), which ran for six weeks on Broadway. *The Time of Your Life* (1939), set in a San Francisco waterfront honky-tonk and much more experimental, was awarded the Pulitzer Prize, which he refused. None of his numerous subsequent plays, in which he attempted to put truth before artifice, has quite the same verve. *The Human Comedy* (1943), his first novel, dedicated to his mother, 'who cannot read and enjoy English as well as you read and enjoy Armenian', is a semi-autobiographical story, transferred to the time of World War II, of a small-town telegraph boy, which began as a film scenario. *Rock Wagram* (1951) is a novel of self-discovery, *The Laughing Matter* (1953) of isolation and ironic desolation. In 1943, while serving in the Signal Corps during World War II he married Carol Marcus (later Matthau), with whom he had had a relationship since she was 16. They divorced in 1949, remarried in 1951, and divorced again in 1952. *The Bicycle Rider in Beverly Hills* (1952), *Here Comes / There Goes / You Know Who* (1961), *Not Dying* (1963), and *Short Drive, Sweet Chariot* (1966) are autobiographical studies.

SARTRE, JEAN-PAUL (1905–80) French philosopher, novelist, and dramatist, was born in Paris, the son of a naval officer who died in 1906. He was brought up in his grandparents' home in Meudon and then in Paris, where in 1915 he went to the Lycée Henri IV, returning there in 1920 after three years at the coeducational lycée in La Rochelle, where his mother had moved when she remarried. When he started to specialize in philosophy at the École Normale Supérieure, he had already published in *La Revue sans Titre* under a pseudonym a story, 'L'Ange du Morbidi' [Angel of Morbidity], and several chapters of a novel which he never finished (a fate which attended many of his subsequent works). In 1928 he failed his *agrégation*; in his resit in 1929 he came first, with BEAUVOIR second. Their lifelong affair, whose ramifications defy belief, began shortly afterwards. After military service, he taught philosophy in schools in Le Havre, Laon, and Neuilly, and published *L'Imagination* (1936), an extended philosophical essay, *La Nausée* (1938; tr. Lloyd Alexander as *Nausea*, 1949), an intellectual novel, and a volume of short stories (1939). Called up in 1939 as an

artillery meteorologist, he was taken prisoner when the Germans overran France. In 1941 he escaped in disguise from Stalag XIID at Trier, where he had directed and acted in his own Christmas mystery play, *Bariona* (published 1962). The experience inspired further symbolic dramas, of which *Les Mouches* (1943; tr. Stuart Gilbert as *The Flies*, 1946) and *Huis Clos* (1944; tr. Gilbert as *In Camera*, 1946) were produced during the Occupation.

In 1944 Sartre gave up teaching for writing, travelling, lecturing, and political activism, while editing with Beauvoir the avant-garde monthly, *Les Temps Modernes*. His trilogy of novels, 'Les Chemins de la Liberté' [Paths of Freedom] (1945–49; tr. Eric Sutton and Gerard Hopkins, 1947–50), gave concrete expression to the existentialist views he had expounded in *L'Être et le Néant* (1943; tr. Hazel Barnes as *Being and Nothingness*, 1956). In *Critique de la Raison Dialectique* (1960; tr. Alan Sheridan Smith as *Critique of Dialectical Reason*, 1976) he set out criteria which he applied in *L'Idiot de la Famille* (1971; tr. Barnes as *The Idiot of the Family*, 1982), an exhaustive but ultimately unfinished study of FLAUBERT. He published an autobiography, *Les Mots* (1963; tr. Bernard Frechtman as *The Words*, 1964), shortly before he was awarded the Nobel Prize for Literature, which he refused on the grounds that it was an award only for Western or for Soviet dissident writers. He never married, but in 1965 he formally adopted as his daughter Arlette Elkaïm, a 28-year-old Algerian Jewess who had been one of his bedmates for nine years. See Annie Cohen-Solal, *Sartre: a Life*, new edn 1988; Arthur C. Danto, *Sartre*, 2nd edn 1991 (introduction to his thought).

SASSOON, SIEGFRIED (1886–1967) British poet and prose writer, was born in Weirleigh, Kent, of Jewish origin. His father left home when the boy was seven and died in 1895. He was educated at Marlborough College and Clare College, Cambridge, which he left without a degree to indulge his passions for playing cricket, writing verse, and hunting the fox. In 1915 he was commissioned in the Royal Welch Fusiliers and served in France, where he won the Military Cross, was recommended for the Victoria Cross, and was severely wounded in 1917. While convalescing in England he wrote and made public a searing attack on the conduct of the war. He was pronounced to be suffering from shell shock, and was returned to the front in 1918, where he was wounded in the head. In the meantime his graphic, brutal, but compassionate war poems, published in *The Old Huntsman* (1917) and *Counter-Attack* (1918), had established him as a considerable war poet, an identity which belied his subsequent development as a writer of satirical, reflective, and spiritual poetry, and of evocative prose. *Memoirs of a Fox-Hunting Man* (1928) perfectly epitomizes a whole social ethos and was the first of three volumes of fictionalized experience which were published together as *The Complete Memoirs of George Sherston* (1937). He retraced Sherston's steps in his autobiographies, *The Old Century and Seven More Years* (1938), *The Weald of Youth* (1942), and *Siegfried's Journey* (1945). He was made CBE in 1951. See *Collected Poems 1908–56*, 2nd edn 1961; Michael Thorpe, *Siegfried Sassoon: a Critical Study*, 1966.

SAVERY, HENRY (1791–1842) British-born novelist, was born in Butcombe, near Bristol, the son of a banker. In 1815 he married in Bristol, where he is listed as a sugar-refiner in 1817, and a bankrupt in 1819. He returned to the same trade in 1822, having in the meantime edited the *Bristol Observer and Gloucester, Monmouth, Somerset and Wiltshire Courier*. In 1824 he overstretched himself, resorted to forging bills, panicked, and tried to escape to America. The ship was delayed off Cowes, and Savery, seeing his partner approach in a rowing boat with a constable, jumped overboard. He was picked up and charged. In a dramatic trial, he pleaded guilty as advised, and then, the judge having donned the fatal black cap, argued: 'I was not aware that to forge the names of persons not in existence was criminal.' The sentence of death was commuted to transportation for life only hours before it was due to be carried out. In Tasmania, his education secured him clerical posts, but his devious business activities on the side caused him problems. He applied for his wife and son to join him, but when she found out that he was still a convict, they quarrelled, he attempted suicide, and she sailed back home. While in prison for debt, he amused himself by writing, as Simon Stukeley, a series of sketches for the *Colonial Times and Tasmanian Advertiser*, which, when published in volume form as *The Hermit in Van Diemen's Land* (1829), became the first Australian book of essays. On his release he wrote anonymously a fictional autobiography, *Quintus Servintus* (1831), the first Australian novel, which ends with the convict hero, now 41, receiving a pardon. Its author was not so lucky. He was given a conditional pardon in 1838, but was subsequently convicted of forgery again, and died in the prison hospital.

SAYERS, DOROTHY L(EIGH) (1893–1957) British novelist and dramatist, was born in Oxford, the daughter of a clergyman, and was educated at the Godolphin School and Somerville College, Oxford, where she got a first in modern languages. She then published two books of verse, and had two short spells as a teacher and one in publishing, before becoming in 1921 an advertising copywriter for S. H. Benson Ltd, with whom she remained until 1931. *Whose Body?* (1923), the first of what have been described as 'detective novels of manners', introduced Lord Peter Wimsey, detective extraordinary, for whom she went on to provide a *Who's Who* entry and other biographical evidence. The varied backgrounds of her novels are filled in with scholarly precision, especially the Oxford setting of *Gaudy Night* (1935), in which Lord Peter undergoes a subtle character change under the influence of an even more vividly realized creation, Harriet Vane, who first appeared in *Strong Poison* (1930), on trial for the murder of her lover. After *Busman's Honeymoon* (1937) Sayers turned her attention to religious drama, of which she wrote for radio *The Man Born to Be King* (1943), a play-cycle in prose on the life of Christ. She was President of the Modern Language Association 1939–45, and a co-founder in 1949, and then President, of the Detection Club. She published a translation, with commentary, of DANTE's *Inferno* (1949) and *Purgatorio* (1955). In 1924, on the rebound from a passionate but unconsummated romance with the Russian-born novelist and journalist, John Cournos (1881–1966), she had a brief affair with a car salesman/mechanic; the baby that resulted, a son, was put out to a cousin to be brought up. In 1926 she married Captain Oswald A. Fleming (d. 1950), a journalist. The boy was now given the name Fleming, and was at the age of ten instructed to regard Sayers as his adoptive mother. See *The Letters of Dorothy L. Sayers 1899–1936: the Making of a Detective Novelist*, ed. Barbara Reynolds, new edn 1996; Ralph E. Hone, *Dorothy L. Sayers: a Literary Biography*, 1979; Barbara Reynolds, *Dorothy L. Sayers: Her Life and Soul*, new edn 1994.

SCANNELL, VERNON (*b.* 1922) British poet and novelist, was born in Spilsby, Lincolnshire, and educated at Queen's Park School, Aylesbury. During World War II he served in the Gordon Highlanders in the Middle East and in Normandy, where he was wounded. At one time a professional boxer and from 1955 to 1962 a teacher of English, he published his first book of verse, *Graves and Resurrections*, in 1948; his third, *The Masks of Love* (1960), won the Heinemann prize for literature. He has described his main poetic themes as 'violence, the experience of war, the "sense of danger" which is part of the climate of our times . . .'. Along with recollections of the war, and poems, such as 'Any Complaints', in which war images occur, there are studies of situations, incidents, and people in the contemporary world which are often brutal, generally sympathetic, and usually expressed with a dry wit, as well as reflections of a more personal nature—in *A Time for Fires* (1991), his 13th collection, he writes fiercely but with painful simplicity about growing old. His novels reflect similar themes, with *The Fight* (1953), his first, *The*

Big Time (1965), and *Ring of Truth* (1983) being set in the world of boxing. His critical works include *Edward Thomas* (1963) and *Not Without Glory: Poets of the Second World War* (1976), and he has compiled *Sporting Literature: an Anthology* (1987). *A Proper Gentleman* (1977) is an account of his unusual, and ultimately violent, experiences in the role of Resident Poet in the newly-created village of Berinsfield, Oxfordshire, in 1975–76. In *The Tiger and the Rose* (1971), *Argument of Kings* (1987), and *Drums of Morning: Growing Up in the Thirties* (1992) he has told his life story in reverse order. See *Collected Poems 1950–1993*, 1994.

SCHILLER, (JOHANN CHRIST-OPH) FRIEDRICH (von) (1759–1805) German dramatist, poet, and critic, was born in Marbach-am-Neckar and educated at the Duke Karl Eugen's Military Academy, where he studied law and then medicine. His first poem was published in 1777, and his third attempt at a medical dissertation was accepted by the examiners in 1780, when he qualified as a regimental doctor and was posted to Stuttgart. Having been put under 14 days' arrest for taking absence without leave to attend a performance in Mannheim of his first play, *Die Raüber* [*The Robbers*] (1792), a drama of the *Sturm und Drang* [Storm and Stress] school, and further displeased the duke by having written it, he chose to flee Wurttemberg for Mannheim, where he was offered a year's contract to write three plays. Without employment afterwards, he founded his own literary and critical journal, *Rheinische Thalia* (subsequently *Thalia* and, from 1792, *Neue Thalia*), in which much of his work first appeared. 'An die Freude' [Ode to Joy] was one of the poems he wrote during the next four years, a period which culminated in the publication and premiere of *Don Carlos* (1787; tr. G.H. Noehden and J. Stoddart, 1798), which marks the beginning of his exploration of political and moral issues through the medium of historical drama, and his change from prose to a flexible form of blank verse. He moved to Weimar, and was in 1789 appointed a professor of history at Jena University. He was recommended for the post by GOETHE, whom he first met at the home of his future wife, Charlotte von Lengefeld (they married in 1790). A serious illness in 1791 caused him to resign from the university and delayed the completion of the substantial *Geschichte des dreissigjährigen Krieges* (1793; tr. Captain Blaquiere as *The History of the Thirty Years War in Germany*, 1799).

After the publication of his major treatise on aesthetics (1795; tr. E. M. Wilkinson and L. A. Willoughby as *On the Aesthetic Education of Man*, 1967), he returned to creative writing with 'Die Macht des Gesanges' [The Power of Song] and other poems. Discussions with Goethe on epic and dramatic poetry led to them both experimenting with the ballad form, and to Schiller moving towards a more symbolic historical drama within the framework of the European tragic tradition. The sombre plays of the *Wallenstein* trilogy (tr. F. J. Lamport with *The Robbers*, 1979) were performed in 1798–99, published in 1800, and immediately translated into English by COLE-RIDGE (1800). In *Maria Stuart* (1800; as *Mary Stuart*, tr. J. C. Mellish, 1801; tr. Stephen Spender, 1959; with *Don Carlos*, tr. Hilary Collier Sy-Quia, adapted by Peter Oswald, introduction by Lesley Sharpe, 1996) he further explored the dichotomy between political and spiritual freedom, contrasting the situations of Elizabeth I of England and her cousin, and enemy, Mary, Queen of Scots. Subsequent plays, notably *Die Jungfrau von Orleans* (1801; tr. J. E. Drinkwater as *The Maid of Orleans*, 1835) and *Wilhelm Tell* (1804; tr. Samuel Robinson as *William Tell*, 1825), are more experimental in technique as well as in historical perspective. He received a patent of nobility in 1802. He died of pneumonia ten months after the birth of his fourth child. CARLYLE's *The Life of Schiller* (1825) is the first English biography of any significant German writer. BULWER-LYTTON translated *The Poems and Ballads of Schiller* (1844). See Lesley Sharpe, *Friedrich Schiller; Drama, Thought and Politics*, 1991 (critical study); T. J. Reed, *Schiller*, 1991 (introduction).

SCHMITZ, ETTORE see SVEVO.

SCHOPENHAUER, ARTHUR (1788–1860) German philosopher, was born in Danzig (now Gdansk, Poland), the son of a trader of Dutch descent, and was brought up in Hamburg, where he went to a private school until he was 15. He then accompanied his parents on a two-year trip abroad, which included three months' boarding at a school in Wimbledon. On their return he was put into a mercantile office, where he stayed, even after his father's death, until 1807, when he took himself off to school in Gotha and then Weimar to study classics. When he received his father's inheritance, he enrolled at Göttingen University, from which he transferred to Berlin to study philosophy, finally presenting his doctoral thesis at Jena. He lived with his mother in Weimar until 1814, when they quarrelled and he walked out, never to see her again. From then until 1818 he lived in Dresden, where he wrote *Die Welt als Wille und Vorstellung* (1819; 3rd edn 1859; tr. R. B. Haldane and J. Kemp as *The World as Will and Idea*, 1883–86), a pessimistic interpretation of Christianity which proposes that there is no need to reconcile the evil of the world with the existence of God. It received little attention. Appointed a professor of philosophy at Berlin, he obtusely chose to lecture at the same time as the more senior, and more distinguished, Georg Wilhelm Friedrich Hegel

(1770–1831), and failed to attract an audience. He published nothing more until 1836, having in 1831 fled the cholera epidemic in Berlin, in which Hegel died, and settled in Frankfurt, where he lived alone and for the rest of his life followed an identical daily routine. He received scant recognition in his lifetime until the publication of *Parerga und Paralipomena* (1851; ed. and tr. R. J. Hollingdale as *Essays and Aphorisms*, 1970). See Christopher Janaway, *Schopenhauer*, 1994 (introduction).

SCHREINER, OLIVE (1855–1920) South African novelist and social reformer, was born at Wittebergen mission station, on the edge of Basutoland, the sixth surviving child of a German Wesleyan missionary and his English wife. She was self-educated and became a freethinker at an early age; a loan of SPENCER's *First Principles* in 1871 introduced her to scientific naturalism. While a governess, and plagued with asthma, she worked on three novels, for one of which she determined to find a publisher when she went to England in 1881 to try for a career in medicine. Nothing came of the latter, but after several rejections her book was taken by Chapman and Hall, whose reader was MEREDITH, and published as *The Story of an African Farm* (1883) by 'Ralph Iron'. The identity of the author quickly became known. She was lionized, had an intense relationship with Havelock Ellis (1859–1939), the sexologist—see *'My Other Self': the Letters of Olive Schreiner and Havelock Ellis 1884–1920*, ed. Yaffa Claire Draznin (1993)—, and became involved in public discussions on women's rights. She returned to South Africa in 1889, taking up residence in Matjesfontein in the Karoo, where she was visited and consulted by the eminent. *Dreams* (1890) is a collection of allegories. In 1894 she married Samuel Cronwright, an ostrich farmer eight years her junior, who changed his name to Cronwright-Schreiner, and later became a politician. A daughter, born in 1895, only lived for 16 hours. Schreiner's need to be identified with a cause, which was her rationale as a novelist, led her to write the fictional *Trooper Peter Halket of Mashonaland* (1897), an outspoken and ironic attack on the political ambitions of Cecil Rhodes (1853–1902), and to take the side of the Boers against the British. *Women and Labour* (1911), a major feminist study, was just part of what for years she had referred to as her 'sex book', the manuscript of which she claimed had been destroyed. She was a prominent member of the Women's Enfranchisement League, but resigned when it transpired that its aims only referred to whites.

Marooned in England during World War I, she was unpopular for her opposition to hostilities, and was asked to leave her lodgings because of her German name. She became so changed by illness that when her husband joined her after a separation of five years, he did not recognize her. She returned, without him, to the Cape, and died five months later at Wynberg, being reinterred, as she had requested, on Buffels Kop in the Karoo. Her husband arranged for the publication of the unfinished novel about prostitution and other matters of female concern, *From Man to Man: or, Perhaps Only . . .* (1926), and the romantic semi-autobiographical *Undine* (1928). These were the two other novels on which she had worked in the 1870s, neither of which she wanted published. In their presentation of intelligent womanhood challenging conventions they have a similar theme to *The Story of an African Farm*, whose significance today is the lasting impression made by its evocation of the South African landscape and of the ethos of the time, and in the lead she gave to novelists such as GEORGE MOORE and D. H. LAWRENCE by delving into forbidden subjects. See Ruth First and Ann Scott, *Olive Schreiner: a Biography*, new edn 1990; and in Kenneth Parker (ed.), *The South African Novel in English*, 1978.

SCHULBERG, BUDD (*b*. 1914) American novelist and screenwriter, was born in New York City, the son of a motion picture pioneer, and grew up in Hollywood. He was educated at Los Angeles High School, Deerfield Academy, and Dartmouth College, after which he became 'a sort of apprentice screenwriter for movie producers David O. Selznick and Walter Wanger'. One of the Hollywood short stories he published in national magazines gave the title to his first novel, *What Makes Sammy Run?* (1941), an account of the meteoric rise from poverty to motion picture mogul which is archetypal in the uncompromising irony of its Jewish and Hollywood backgrounds. He served as a US Navy lieutenant in Strategic Services during World War II, in the aftermath of which he was in charge of photographic evidence for the Nuremberg War Crimes Tribunal. The doomed protagonists of *The Harder They Fall* (1947) and *The Disenchanted* (1950) are respectively a heavyweight boxer on the way up and a heavyweight novelist on the way down, the latter having affinities with F. S. FITZGERALD. *Waterfront* (1955), adapted from his own screenplay, is a brutal exposé of New York waterfront life. See also *Love, Action, Laughter and Other Sad Tales* (1990). See *Moving Pictures: Memories of a Hollywood Prince*, 1981 (reminiscences).

SCHUYLER, JAMES see O'HARA, FRANK.

SCHWARTZ, DELMORE (1913–1966) American poet, short-story writer, and critic, was born in Brooklyn, New York, the elder son of middle-class Jewish parents who immigrated as children, and who separated when he was young. He was educated at George Washington High School and New

York University, after which he did postgraduate studies in philosophy at Harvard without taking a further degree, though his grades were excellent. *In Dreams Begin Responsibilities* (1938) comprised verse in various forms from lyric to long poem, short stories, and drama. In 1940 he was appointed to teach composition at Harvard—he resigned in 1947, possibly out of dissatisfaction. In 1943 he became an editor of the *Partisan Review*, which he remained until 1955. The short stories of *The World is a Wedding* (1948) especially evoke Jewish disillusionment in America in the 1920s. During the 1950s he held visiting lectureships at various universities, and also several editorial posts. *Summer Knowledge: New and Selected Poems 1938–1958* (1959) won the Library of Congress Bollingen Prize. He separated from his second wife in 1957. Latterly, though he was a visiting professor of English at Syracuse University from 1962 to 1965, his sense of intellectual alienation gave way to delusions of persecution. He died of a heart attack in a seedy New York hotel. *Selected Essays of Delmore Schwartz*, ed. Donald A. Dike and David H. Zucker (1970) contains his critical writings. Correspondence between him and the publisher of the avant-garde journal *New Directions* is in Delmore Schwartz and James Laughlin, *Selected Letters*, ed. Robert Phillips (1993).

SCOTT, ALEXANDER (*c.*1515–83) Scottish poet, is believed to be the same who played the fife in a tableau in Paris in 1540, organized by the Knights of the Round Table of the King of the Basoche, and who was musician and organist at the Priory of Inchmahome in the Lake of Menteith in 1548: his poem, 'The Lament of the Maister of Erskine', commemorates the death at the battle of Pinkie in 1547 of the elder brother of John Erskine (*d.* 1572), later Regent Mar, who was at the time the licensor of the Priory. In 1549 his two sons were legitimized, which probably means that he had now married their mother. That it was an unsuccessful marriage is suggested by the comment, 'Quod Scott, quhen his wife left him', written by the manuscript collector, George Bannatyne (1545–1608), beside the poem, 'To luve unluvit it is ane pane'. By 1562 Scott had become some form of Protestant, and his 'Ane New Yeir Gift to the Quene Mary, quhen scho come first Hame' contains some severe remarks about the licence of the Catholic establishment in Scotland. In 1565 he was receiving income as a canon of the priory at Inchaffray, and in 1567 and 1570 he made substantial purchases of lands in Fife and Perthshire. Most of his surviving poetry comprises love lyrics—sophisticated, intricate, technically varied, and often crying out to be sung, especially 'Lo, quhat it is to lufe! / Lerne, ye that list to prufe, / be me, I say, that no ways may / the grund of greif remufe, /

bot still decay both nycht and day. / Lo, quhat it is to lufe!' See John MacQueen (ed.), *Ballattis of Luve*, 1970.

SCOTT, DUNCAN CAMPBELL (1862–1947) Canadian poet and short-story writer, was born in Ottawa, the son of an itinerant Methodist minister who encouraged him in 'every evident talent' and whose sojourns in various towns in Quebec gave him the background of his stories. He was educated at Smith Falls High School, Ontario, and Wesleyan College, Stanstead, Quebec. Lacking the funds to go on to medical school, he became a clerk third class in the Indian Branch (later Department of Indian Affairs), Ottawa, rising in 1909 to Superintendent of Indian Education, and in 1923 to Deputy Superintendent General, which he remained until his retirement at 70. With the encouragement of LAMPMAN, whose literary executor he became and whose poems he posthumously edited (1900), he began to write. *The Magic House, and Other Poems* (1893) was conventionally Romantic. In *Labor and the Angel* (1898) he brought his poetic ability to bear on his experience of the Indian culture; he went on to produce poems such as 'The Forsaken' and 'On the Way to the Mission'—in *New World Lyrics and Ballads* (1905). 'At Gull Lake: August 1910' appeared in *The Green Cloister: Later Poems* (1935). In the stories in *In the Village of Viger* (1896) and *The Witching of Elspie* (1923)—see also *In the Village of Viger and Other Stories*, ed. S. L. Dragland, 1973—he presented French Canada with a sense of realism, and sometimes with irony and a reflection of the supernatural, making him the most significant Canadian short-story writer of his time. He was made CMG in 1934. See *Selected Poetry*, ed. Glenn Clever, 1974; *Selected Stories*, ed. Glenn Clever, 1987.

SCOTT, F(RANCIS) R(EGINALD) (1899–1985) Canadian poet, translator, lawyer, and social philosopher, was the son of (Ven.) Frederick George Scott (CMG DSO) (1861–1944), known as the 'poet of the Laurentians'. He was born in the rectory of St Matthew's, Quebec, and was educated at Quebec High School, Bishop's College, Lennoxville, and (as a Rhodes scholar) at Magdalen College, Oxford. He then read law at McGill University, to which, having been called to the Quebec Bar, he returned to teach in 1928, being Macdonald Professor of Law 1955–67 and Dean of the Faculty of Law 1961–64. National Chairman of the Cooperative Commonwealth Federation from 1942 to 1950, and an authority on constitutional law, he was leading counsel in several significant civil rights cases before the Supreme Court of Canada between 1956 and 1964, and was appointed QC in 1961. His first Governor General's Award was for *Essays on the Constitution: Aspects of Canadian Law and Politics*

(1977). In his youth a composer of light verse, in 1925 he founded with A. J. M. SMITH the *McGill Fortnightly Review* as a forum for modern poetry; he subsequently edited other literary journals, *Canadian Mercury* (1928–9), *Canadian Forum* (1936–39), *Preview* (1942–44), and *Northern Review* (1945–47). His own first volume of verse was *Overture* (1945); to his social and political satire he added poems expressive of a humanistic attitude to nature and society, demonstrated especially in *The Dance is One* (1973). *The Collected Poems of F. R. Scott* (1981), which won the Governor General's Award, includes some of his translations of French-Canadian poets, notably HE-BERT; he also compiled and translated the influential anthology, *Poems of French Canada* (1977). He was made Companion, Order of Canada, in 1967. See Sandra Djawa, *The Politics of the Imagination: a Life of F. R. Scott*, 1989.

SCOTT, PAUL (1920–78) British novelist, was born in Southgate, London, and educated at Winchmore Hill Collegiate School until he was 14, when he and his elder brother were removed because of the collapse of their father's business as a fashion artist. A job was found for him with an accountant, and an introduction to poetry came through a relationship with a homosexual estate agent and, more decorously, with a literary-minded couple who lived next door. Called up by the Army in 1940, he won a stripe (was promoted to lance corporal) and then lost it through some sexually-orientated misdemeanour, married a nurse six years older than he was, and published an opaque poem, *Gerontius* (1941). In 1943 he was commissioned in the Royal Indian Army Corps, in which he served in India and Malaya in the provision of air supplies. His knowledge of accountancy got him a job in publishing after the war, and his experience of both fields a partnership in a literary agency, where he guided the ascendancy of BRAINE, FOWLES, and MORRIS WEST. He resigned in 1960 to further his own literary career. His earlier novels, *Johnnie Sahib* (1952), *The Alien Sky* (1953), and *The Mark of the Warrior* (1958), and to a greater extent *The Chinese Love Pavilion* (1960) and *The Birds of Paradise* (1962), all of which are set in the East, earned some critical acclaim but not enough money to live on. The 'Raj Quartet', *The Jewel in the Crown* (1966), *The Day of the Scorpion* (1968), *The Towers of Silence* (1972), and *A Division of the Spoils* (1975), took ten years to write, wrecked his health and his marriage, and was only completed with the help of extra advances from his publisher and frequent recourse to the bottle. Massive and intricate, it is a largely successful attempt by a man with a deeply divided nature to explain the divisions from which modern India emerged. *Staying On* (1977), no more than a coda to the major work, won the Booker prize for fiction, five

months before his death and several years before the television adaptation of the 'Raj Quartet' (as *The Jewel in the Crown*) made him famous as a writer. See Hilary Spurling, *Paul Scott: a Life*, new edn 1991; Robin Moore, *Paul Scott's Raj*, 1990 (critical study).

SCOTT, (Sir) WALTER (1771–1832) Scottish novelist, short-story writer, poet, historian, folklorist, dramatist, editor, and critic, was born in Edinburgh's insanitary Old Town, ninth child of a solicitor. He was permanently lame from infantile paralysis contracted when he was about eighteen months old; as a result he spent some years recuperating in the Borders and in Bath, before rejoining his family, now removed to the New Town. Between bouts of further illness he went to the High School of Edinburgh and Edinburgh University, becoming an apprentice in his father's firm in 1786, and being called to the Scottish Bar in 1792. He married Charlotte Carpenter (1770–1826), of French birth, in 1797; they were to have two sons and two daughters. In 1799 Scott was appointed Sheriff-Depute of Selkirkshire, where he completed his collection of oral ballads, published as *Minstrelsy of the Scottish Border* (1802–03). He now turned to composing his own historical ballad-epics, *The Lay of the Last Minstrel* (1805), *Marmion: a Tale of Flodden Field* (1808), and *The Lady of the Lake* (1810).

From 1806 to 1812 he was a clerk of the Court of Session, while at the same time involving himself financially with the publishing and printing company of Ballantyne. He had a town house in North Castle Street and a country seat at Abbotsford, Melrose, which over the years he extended into the Gothic mansion which can be visited today. In 1813, while searching there in an old desk for some fishing tackle, he found part of a novel which he had abandoned in 1805. When he had finished it, *Waverley: or, 'Tis Sixty Years Since* (1814) became the first of a long line of enormously popular historical novels which included *Guy Mannering* (1815), *Rob Roy* (1817), *The Heart of Midlothian* (in *Tales of My Landlord*, 1818), and *Redgauntlet* (1824), known collectively as the 'Waverley Novels'. They were all published anonymously, possibly because he felt them beneath him as an official of the law, but probably because he did not want to appear to be leading so many lives. The secret was publicly revealed at a charity dinner in 1827, by which time he had much enjoyed being the cause of what was a mystery to all except close friends and perceptive critics.

He was largely responsible for the rediscovery in Edinburgh Castle in 1818 of the Scottish crown jewels, which had been missing for 111 years. In 1819 he received a baronetcy from the hand of George IV, whose visit to Edinburgh in 1822 the now 'Sir' Walter Scott brilliantly stage-managed, initiating in the process the revival of the Scottish tartan tradition. His business affairs, however, had been in trouble as far back as 1813, and when in 1826 the general economic depression caused the collapse of his partners, he was declared bankrupt. Though already suffering from recurring illness, he refused his friends' help in settling with his creditors, declaring proudly—according to the reminiscences of Lord Cockburn (1779–1854), *Memorials of His Time* (1856)—'No! this right hand shall work it all off!'. *The Journal of Sir Walter Scott 1825–32* (1890) contains his own account of the events of that year (including the death of his wife four months after the disaster), and of the rest of his life, during which he drove himself to write wide-ranging works, including *St Valentine's Day: or, The Fair Maid of Perth* (1828), three series of *Tales of a Grandfather* (1828–30), and *Letters on Demonology and Witchcraft* (1830). In 1830 he had the first of a series of cerebral haemorrhages. The Government put a frigate at his disposal for the winter of 1831–32, but he had to be rushed back from Naples to Abbotsford, where he died. His trustees had then paid off 11 shillings in the pound of his original debts of over £100,000.

As a very successful Romantic poet who wrote in English on Scottish themes, Scott spread Scottish culture far and wide—see *Selected Poems*, ed. James Reed (1992). He was a worthy founder of the historical novel in that he was fair to both sides in a conflict, and he represented historical characters and events with intelligence and insight, while having an eye to comedy and the effective representation of Scottish speech. He was also an originator of the genre of the short story, of which he wrote several particularly powerful tragic and supernatural examples—see *The Two Drovers and Other Stories*, ed. Graham Tulloch (1987). In all this he was instrumental in propagating, for better or for worse, the romantic view of Highland history which still popularly pertains today. He edited the works of DRYDEN (1808) and SWIFT (1814). His elder daughter Sophia married John Gibson Lockhart (1794–1854), whose admirable biography of Scott was published in seven volumes in 1837–38 (abridged edn 1848). See Edgar Johnson, *Sir Walter Scott: the Great Unknown*, 1970 (biography); John Sutherland, *The Life of Sir Walter Scott: a Critical Biography*, new edn 1997; Robin Mayhead, *Walter Scott*, 1973 (critical study); David Brown, *Sir Walter Scott and the Historical Imagination*, 1979.

SEDGES, JOHN see BUCK.

SEDLEY (or **SIDLEY**), (Sir) **CHARLES** (1639–1701) English poet and dramatist, was born posthumously in Aylesford, Kent, and succeeded to the title in 1656 on the death of his brother, whose widow he married the following year. He went to Wadham College, Oxford, without taking a degree. PEPYS records some of the rowdiest excesses of this Restoration court poet, who was in 1633 tried before the Lord Chief Justice and fined £650 for indecent exposure and lewd behaviour on the balcony of Oxford Kate's, a Covent Garden tavern, witnessed by a crowd of a thousand. He wrote two comedies, *The Mulberry Garden* (1668), whose opening is based on MOLIÈRE's *L'École des Maris*, and *Bellamira: or, The Mistress* (1687), a reworking of TERENCE's *The Eunuch*. His tragedy in heroic couplets, *Antony and Cleopatra* (1677), was probably superseded that same year by *All for Love*, by his friend DRYDEN. In 1668 he was elected Member of Parliament for Romney, in which capacity he often spoke in the House. In 1680 his skull was fractured when the roof of the tennis court in the Haymarket collapsed while he was playing. He was instrumental in promoting the Revolution which brought William and Mary to the throne in 1689, albeit that his only daughter, Catherine (1657–1717), Duchess of Dorchester, was James II's mistress. *The Miscellaneous Works* (1702), including poems, translations, and speeches in Parliament, was edited by Captain Ayloffe, nephew of Sedley's mistress, Ann Ayscough, with whom he had gone through a form of marriage in 1672, though his wife was still alive, but insane. See *The Poetical and Dramatic Works of Sir Charles Sedley*, ed. V. de Sola Pinto, 2 vols 1928.

SEFERIS, GEORGE, pen name of Giorgos Seferiades (1900–71) Greek poet, critic, and diplomat, was born in Smyrna, Turkey. In 1914 he went to Athens, where he attended classical gymnasium and Athens University, after which he studied law at the Sorbonne in Paris and English in London. He entered the Greek Ministry of Foreign Affairs in 1926, serving in London (1931–34) and Albania (1936–38). During World War II he worked for the Free Greek government in Crete, South Africa, Italy, and Egypt; in Alexandria he first properly encountered the work of CAVAFY, whom he succeeded as the second modern Greek poet to achieve international fame. Subsequently he was Ambassador in Lebanon (1953–56) and in London (1957–62). He translated a selection of T. S. ELIOT into modern Greek in 1936, at a time when he was particularly concerned with using rather than following the classical literary tradition; as he shows in 'The Exile's Return', in which he emphasizes the bleakness of the political situation in 1938 by denying the reader the expected revelation of the homecoming of Odysseus. His later poetry is imbued with a lyrical pessimism. *On the Greek Style: Selected Essays in Poetry and Hellenism*, tr. Rex Warner and Th. D. Frangopoulos (1966) contains enlightening studies of the place of tradition in contemporary literature. He was awarded the Nobel Prize for Literature in 1963. See *Com-*

plete Poems, tr. Edmund Keeley and Philip Sherrard, 2nd edn 1995.

SELVON, SAMUEL (1923–94) Trinidadian novelist, was born in the small village of Barataria, the son of a dry goods merchant of Indian and Scottish descent, and left Naparima College at 16 to go to work. He wrote stories during war service as a naval wireless operator, and was then a journalist on the *Trinidad Guardian*. In 1950 he went to London, where he was 'swept up by exaltation. It was so vivid as a period of time, so very much alive.' He took a room in Notting Hill and worked at the Trinidad High Commission until becoming a full-time writer in 1954 after the publication of his first novel. *A Brighter Sun* (1952), to which *Turn Again Tiger* (1958) is a sequel, heralded the heyday of the Trinidadian novel. A story of the growing self-determination of a young labourer in Trinidad, it is notable also for its humour and for the deft mixture of English narrative and Creole dialogue. A form of Trinidadian dialect is the medium of narration of *The Lonely Londoners* (1956), for its pathos as well as its wit and lyricism regarded as among the very best novels of exile. Some of its characters, in fresh situations for which Selvon creates new stylistic and descriptive devices, reappear in *The Housing Lark* (1965), *Moses Ascending* (1975), and *Moses Migrating* (1983). After living in London for thirty years he settled in Canada. He was twice married. See in Bruce King (ed.), *West Indian Literature*, 2nd edn 1995.

SEMPILL, ROBERT, OF BELTREES (*c.*1595–*c.*1665) Scottish poet, not to be confused with Robert Sempill (*c.*1530–95), ballad writer, was the elder son of Sir James Sempill of Beltrees (1566–1625), author of an anti-Catholic satirical drama, *A Picktooth for the Pope: or, The Packman's Paternoster* (published 1669). Little is known about his life beyond his education at Glasgow University and his marriage to a daughter of Lyon of Auldbar. Several poems attributed to him appeared in *Choice Collection of Comic and Serious Scottish Poems* (1706–11), compiled by the Edinburgh printer James Watson (*d.* 1722). Among them is 'The Life and Death of the Piper of Kilbarchen, or the Epitaph of Habbie Simpson'. The six-line verse form which he used for this, rhyming *aaabab*, with the fourth and last lines having only two stresses, was triumphantly resuscitated by RAMSAY, who christened it the 'standard habbie', and was used to excellent effect by FERGUSSON and BURNS. Sempill and his son, Francis (*c.*1616–82), were neither of them great poets, but they are significant in that being of the educated lesser gentry, they represent a new kind of author. They also provide a link between the Scots verse of the 16th century and its revival in the 18th century.

SENECA, LUCIUS ANNAEUS (*c.*4 BC–AD 65) Roman philosopher and dramatist, was born in Corduba, Spain, the second son of Seneca 'the Elder' (*d. c.*37), writer and teacher of rhetoric. He was brought to Rome at an early age, and was influenced by the Stoics. He climbed the political ladder, being consul in 56. His pretensions to be a practising philosopher are questionable. He condoned various dynastic murders, and was banished for eight years under suspicion of having an affair with one of the sisters of the mad emperor Caligula. From his return until his retirement in 62 he was tutor to Nero, and while he undoubtedly but only temporarily curbed the worst excesses of his pupil, he grew rich in the process. He died, as did his nephew LUCAN, in the purge following the Pisonian conspiracy. In addition to a number of philosophical treatises and essays, which include several investigations of natural phenomona, he left a wicked skit on the dead emperor Claudius, *Apocolocyntosis*. His nine verse tragedies (a tenth is thought to be by a later hand) were almost certainly designed to be read aloud or recited, rather than performed. Their melodrama and rhetoric were imitated by early English tragic dramatists such as SACKVILLE and KYD, at a time when the plays of AESCHYLUS, EURIPIDES, and SOPHOCLES, on which Seneca drew, were less well known, Latin being more treasured as a language than Greek. See *The Tragedies*, tr. David R. Slavitt, 2 vols 1995.

SENGHOR, LÉOPOLD (SÉDAR) (*b.* 1906) Senegalese poet, philosopher, and statesman, was born of Serere stock in the village of Joal, fifth child by an out-of-town wife of a groundnut merchant who became a Catholic convert. Having learned no French until he was seven, he was educated at a local Catholic missionary school, and in Dakar at an ecclesiastical seminary and then a lycée. He won a scholarship (the first ever awarded by Senegal) for higher education in Paris, at the Lycée Louis-le-Grand and then the Sorbonne, where he became in 1935 the first African to achieve the degree of *agrégation*. He taught in lycées, embraced *négritude* (the cultural contribution of the Black African to humanity), and wrote the lyric poetry which was to appear as *Chants d'Ombre* [Songs of Shadow] (1945). *Hosties Noires* [Black Hostages] (1948) contained verses written while a German prisoner during World War II, after he had survived a Nazi firing squad. His anthology of black African verse, *Anthologie de la Nouvelle Poésie Nègre et Malgache* (1948), with a preface by SARTRE, became a seminal work. A further volume of his own is *Nocturnes* (1961; tr. John Reed and Clive Wake, 1969), a sequence of love poems. Deputy for Senegal in the French National Assembly from 1946 to 1959, he was, on the independence of the country of his birth in 1960, elected its first President, in which capacity he served until his retirement in 1980. See *Selected Poems*, 1964, and *Prose and Poetry*, 1976, ed. and tr. John Reed and Clive Wake; *The Collected Poetry*, tr. M. Dixon, 1992; Janet G. Vaillant, *Black, French, and African: a Life of Léopold Sédar Senghor*, 1990.

SEROTE, MONGANE WALLY (*b.* 1944) South African poet and novelist, was born in Sophiatown and taken shortly afterwards to the Johannesburg township of Alexandra, where 'compared to many people, I came from a well-to-do family. My mother was a nurse, my father a mechanic.' He was educated for 18 months in Lesotho, and then at Alexandra Secondary School and Morris Isaacson High School, Soweto. He became a freelance journalist, selling local stories to whichever papers would buy them. In about 1965 he began working for the underground movement of the African National Congress. He was arrested in 1969 and after spending nine months in solitary confinement was released without charge. His books of verse include *Yakhal'inkomo* (1972), *Tsetlo* (1974), and *Behold Mama, Flowers* (1978). GUY BUTLER has observed about him and MTSHALI that 'their very lack of formal instruction in European eloquence has left them freer to employ African modes of expression'. In his political poems Serote seems to argue for a form of separatism in which the black dictates terms. *To Every Birth Its Blood* (1981), a novel set in Alexandra Township, has a sharp, allusive style. Serote was a Fulbright scholar at Columbia University, USA, graduating in 1979, after which he settled in Gaberone, Botswana, attached to the Medu Arts Ensemble. In 1986 he moved to London to work there for the ANC. He subsequently returned to South Africa. *Third World Express* (1992), a long poem, won the 1993 Noma Award for Publishing in Africa. See *Selected Poems*, ed. Mbulelo Vizikhungo Mzamene, 1982; and in Jane Wilkinson (ed.), *Talking With African Writers*, 1992.

SERVICE, ROBERT W(ILLIAM) (1874–1958) Scottish poet of the Canadian north, was born in England in Preston, the eldest of ten children of a Scottish bank teller, and at the age of four went with a younger brother to live for several years with his father's relatives in Kilwinning, Ayrshire. The family reconvened in Glasgow, where he went to Hillhead High School. After being a clerk in the Commercial Bank of Scotland, he emigrated in 1895 to British Columbia, worked his way down the west coast to Mexico and back, and in 1903 resumed his banking career with the Canadian Bank of Commerce, which posted him to the Yukon in 1904. Here he observed the aftermath of the Klondike gold rush, in which he set his highly coloured narrative verses such as 'The

Shooting of Dan McGrew' ('A bunch of the boys were whooping it up in the Malamute saloon . . .') and 'The Cremation of Sam McGee', published in *Songs of a Sourdough* (1907), which was followed by *Ballads of a Cheechako* (1909). A novel, *The Trail of '98* (1911), was not such a success, and after the publication of *Rhymes of a Rolling Stone* (1912), he left Canada, initially to cover the Balkan War in 1912 for the Toronto *Star*. Service as a war correspondent and stretcher-bearer in France in World War I provided the background for *The Rhymes of a Red-Cross Man* (1916). From 1913 he lived successively in Paris, Nice, Los Angeles, and Monte Carlo, enjoying a huge income and continuing to write popular verse and negligible romantic novels. At 39 he decided to marry: someone French, for that was where he was living, but like his mother who 'would be willing to black my shoes of a morning . . . spitting on them to make the blacking go further . . . a wee Scotch lassie who would respect the bawbees [pennies]'. He appears to have had no trouble finding a suitable partner. He wrote two autobiographies; the title of the second, *Harper of Heaven: a Record of Radiant Living* (1948), sums up his later years while belying his engagingly modest attitude to his triumphs: 'For God-sake, don't call me a poet, / For I've never been guilty of that.' See *Collected Poems of Robert Service*, 1993; *The Best of Robert Service*, ed. Anne Watts, new edn 1995; James Mackay, *Vagabond of Verse: Robert Service, a Biography*, new edn 1996.

SETON, ERNEST THOMPSON (1860–1946) naturalist and fiction writer, was born Ernest Thompson in South Shields, and later added the name 'Seton' to reflect his descent from the Scottish aristocratic family, a branch of whom were earls of Winton. In 1866 his family emigrated to Canada, where he was educated at Toronto Grammar School and won a scholarship to the Royal Academy in London. Back in Canada in 1881, he studied animal and bird life and habits, made an international name as an illustrator, and was in 1892 appointed official naturalist to the Government of Manitoba, one of the fruits of which was *Life Histories of Northern Animals: an Account of the Mammals of Manitoba* (2 vols 1909). *Wild Animals I Have Known* (1898) was the first, and is the most famous, of many collections of nature stories based on his observations and instinct. In 1896 he settled in the USA, where he founded a boys' organization, the Woodcraft Indians, the basis of whose philosophy was enshrined in his children's novel, *Two Little Savages: Being the Adventures of Two Boys who Lived as Indians and What They Learned* (1903). That and other writings were subsumed into the official handbook of the Boy Scouts of America, which he established in 1910 with the movement's founder, Sir Robert (later Lord) Baden-Powell (1857–

1941), and of which he was appointed Chief Scout. In 1915, having repeatedly and, as recent research has shown, with some justification, charged the administration with militarism, he was expelled from the organization on the grounds that he was not an American citizen—he became one in 1931, shortly after settling in New Mexico. While he certainly humanized nature in his animal stories, he was a far better naturalist than ROBERTS and others whose anthropomorphism came under attack from scientists. AT-WOOD, in her critical study of Canadian literature, *Survival* (1972), cites his work as illustrating the Canadian inclination to identify with a hunted prey. Anya Seton, author of *Dragonwyck* (1944), *Katherine* (1954), and other meticulously researched 'bodice rippers', who died in 1990 without ever divulging her date of birth, was a daughter by his first wife, whom he married in 1896. See Betty Keller, *Black Wolf: the Biography of Ernest Thompson Seton*, new edn 1988; Lorraine Mc-Mullen, *Ernest Thompson Seton and His Works*, 1994.

SEXTON, ANNE (1928–75), née Harvey, American poet, was born in Newton, Massachusetts, the third daughter of a woollen manufacturer. She was educated at a boarding school in Lowell and at Garland Junior College, Boston, from which she eloped when she was 19 and married Alfred 'Kayo' Sexton II—the marriage lasted 26 years. At the age of 27, after the birth of her second daughter, a long period of emotional instability culminated in a complete mental breakdown and a suicide attempt. A therapist encouraged her to write about her experiences. She attended ROBERT LOWELL's poetry seminars at Boston University, where she met and became close to PLATH, after whose suicide she wrote, in 'Sylvia's Death' (1963): 'Thief!— / how did you crawl into, / crawl down alone / into the death I wanted so badly, and for so long . . .'. Death, guilt, insanity, sex, and incest haunt her work, for which 'confessional' is an even more apt term than when applied to that of others of her contemporaries. *To Bedlam and Part Way Back* (1960) was followed by *All My Pretty Ones* (1962), the title being a reference to the deaths of both her parents in their fifties within three months of each other. *Live or Die* (1966) won the Pulitzer Prize. *Love Poems* (1969) records a protracted affair: *The Death Notebooks* (1974) contains further reflections on suicide. She won several grants, awards, and travelling fellowships; was Crawshaw Professor of Literature at Colgate University in 1972; and taught creative writing at Boston University from 1972 to 1974. She killed herself by inhaling carbon monoxide. Diane Wood Middlebrook, *Anne Sexton: a Biography* (1991) draws on tapes and other records of her psychotherapy sessions. See *The Complete Poems*, 1990; *The Selected Poems of Anne Sexton*, ed. Diane Middlebrook and Diana Hume George, 1991; *No Evil Star: Selected Essays, Interviews, and Prose*, ed. Steven Colburn, 1985.

SHADBOLT, MAURICE (*b.* 1932) New Zealand short-story writer and novelist, was born in Auckland and educated at Te Kuiti High School, Avondale College, and Auckland University. He worked as a journalist, and was then a documentary scriptwriter and director for the National Film Unit, before becoming a full-time writer in 1957. He has said that 'as a man of my time and place, I have simply tried to make sense of both'. The main title of *The New Zealanders: a Sequence of Stories* (1959) aptly reflects his subsequent exploration of his country's environment and history, and the personalities of its peoples. This he has conducted in further short stories—see *Figures in Light: Selected Stories* (1978); in novels, beginning with the almost statutory saga of rebellious youth, *Among the Cinders* (1965; rev. edn 1984); in *The Presence of Music: Three Novellas* (1967), studies of the place of the artist in society and in terms of personal relationships; and in a play, *Once on Chunuk Bair* (1982), centring on the Gallipoli campaign in 1915. Latterly, as in the trilogy *Season of the Jew* (1986), *Monday's Warriors* (1990), and *House of Strife* (1993), he has used historical events, and historical characters, as a means of focusing attention on present discontents. In the account of his family, *One of Ben's: a Tribe Transported* (1993), he states that for him there is 'only one reason to write, and it is not to serve literary fashion or scholarly fads. It is . . . to get a grip on our existence . . . flag it down for a moment as it flies past. If we also win a little harmony from the human bedlam, that is serendipity.' He was made CBE in 1989.

SHADWELL, THOMAS (1642–92) English dramatist and poet, was probably born at Santon Hall, Norfolk, and was educated at King Edward VI Free Grammar School, Bury St Edmunds, and for a year at Gonville and Caius College, Cambridge, before studying law at the Middle Temple, of which his father was a member. He married an actress, and in 1668 his first play, *The Sullen Lovers*, a comedy of humours in the manner of JONSON, was performed with great success. He was a professional dramatist who aimed to please the audience rather than the critics, and over the next 24 years he wrote a dozen more comedies. They include the rather vulgar *Epsom Wells* (1672); a satire on the new scientific vogue, *The Virtuoso* (1676); and an exposé of London low life, *The Squire of Alsatia* (1688). These three in particular rank him next after ETHEREGE and WYCHERLEY among comic dramatists of the time. His reputation, however, has suffered ever since *MacFlecknoe: or a Satyr upon T. S.* (1682), later freely acknowledged as the work of the Poet Laureate, DRYDEN. It was unfair, but it was witty ('The rest to some faint meaning make pretence, / But Shadwell never deviates into sense'), and whatever the cause of its being written, it has survived as a poem which succeeds in its aim of diverting its readers. There was some compensation for Shadwell. On the accession of William and Mary in 1689, he addressed to them two excruciatingly flattering 'congratulatory poems', and later that year he was appointed to the posts Dryden had had to relinquish for his political and religious principles, Poet Laureate and Historiographer Royal. It is believed that he died of an overdose of opium, which he had been taking for some years to relieve pain. See Albert S. Borgman, *Thomas Shadwell: His Life and Comedies*, new edn 1969.

SHAFFER, PETER (*b.* 1926) British dramatist, was born in Liverpool, twin brother of Anthony, the author of a successful stage play which is a parody of detective fiction, *Sleuth* (1970). They were both at St Paul's School. After being conscripted as coal miners during World War II (Peter passed his hours down the pit mentally rehearsing the roles of SHAKESPEARE's tragic heroes), they went to Trinity College, Cambridge. From 1951 to 1954 Peter worked in the acquisitions department of New York Public Library. His first play, *Five Finger Exercise* (1958), far from being in the current 'Angry Young Men' stream (see JOHN OSBORNE), is a tense, middle-class domestic drama in the style of PINERO or RATTIGAN. His next success, *The Royal Hunt of the Sun* (1965), is a panoramic epic of 16th-century Peru. *Black Comedy* (1967), the idea for which came from a sketch he saw performed by the Peking Opera in 1955, is a farce which turns on the reversal of light and dark. There is darkness of a different kind in *Equus* (1973), which explores the case of a stableboy who has deliberately blinded six horses with a spike. In *Amadeus* (1979), the dying Mozart accuses his rival of poisoning him. *Lettice and Lovage* (1987) is a penetrating study of two women. If there is a link between Shaffer's varied themes and moods, it is a concern with modern psychology, and with man's destructive need for vengeance, further explored in *The Gift of the Gorgon* (1993). Stylistically he favours the impassioned monologue as a dramatic device. His success both with the critics and the public is a measure of his versatility. He was made CBE in 1987.

SHAFTESBURY, (COOPER, ANTHONY ASHLEY), 3RD EARL OF (1671–1713) English philosopher and critic, was born at Exeter House, the London residence of his grandfather, who features in DRYDEN's *Absalom and Achitophel*. His early education was supervised by LOCKE, on whose recommendation he was looked after from the age of three by a governess who spoke fluent Latin and Greek. He went to Winchester College from 1683 to 1686, and was then taken on an educational tour of Europe, during which he learned perfect French. He was elected Member of Parliament for Poole in 1695, and succeeded to his title in 1699, after which he attended debates in the House of Lords when his health allowed. Plagued by asthma, he suffered particularly in the London smog; he died in Naples, where he had retired in 1711. His philosophical and literary views were encompassed in *Characteristicks of Men, Manners, Opinions, Times* (1711). Here he propounded the theory of benevolence, maintaining the existence of a moral sense and of a perfect universe. As a critic, he supported ridicule as a test of truth, and argued that goodness, beauty, and truth are synonymous.

SHAKESPEARE, WILLIAM (1564–1616) English dramatist and poet, the elder son of a glover and dealer in leather goods and wool, was baptized in Stratford-upon-Avon Parish Church on 26 April 1564. A bond was issued on 28 November 1582 for his marriage to Anne Hathaway, eight years his senior. Their daughter Susanna was baptized on 26 May 1583, and twins on 2 February 1585. That is virtually all that is known about Shakespeare's early life, though almost certainly he attended the local grammar school. In 1592 he is spitefully alluded to in ROBERT GREENE's *A Groats-worth of Wit Bought with a Million of Repentance*, as 'an upstart crow beautified with our feathers'. After the plague of 1592–94 had disrupted the London theatrical scene, he surfaces as a member of the Lord Chamberlain's Men, becoming a partner in the establishment of the new Globe Theatre in 1599. The company became the King's Men in 1603, and in 1610 Shakespeare retired to his Stratford house of New Place, a considerable property which he had bought in 1597.

During the plague epidemic he wrote, and published, his two narrative poems, *Venus and Adonis* (1593) and *Lucrece* (1594), both dedicated to the young Earl of Southampton (1573–1624). Francis Meres (1565–1647) refers to both poems in *Palladis Tamia* (1598), and also to the circulation by Shakespeare of 'his sugred Sonnets among his private friends'. These were published, mysteriously dedicated to a 'Mr W. H.', by an adventurous bookseller in 1609, without their author's permission. There are 153 sonnets, No. 126 being merely 12 lines of rhymed verse. They appear to be addressed to an unknown young man who is the poet's favoured friend and is being urged to marry, to a rival poet who has ingratiated himself with the young man, and to the poet's mistress (the famous Dark Lady), who between times has been having an affair with the poet's friend. Their quality varies, but Nos 18, 87, 89, 97, 98, 116, 130, 144, and 146 in particular are among the finest of their kind. The intensity which burns through the sequence suggests firmly that it is autobiographical, which would seem to be confirmed by the fact that it was never reissued in the poet's lifetime.

Shakespeare cared little about the publication of his plays. What are known, from their format, as the Quartos are largely pirated editions written down during a performance—the first recorded one is *Titus Andronicus* (1594). The First Folio edition, ed. John Heminge (*d.* 1630) and Henry Condell (*d.* 1627), actors and both of them friends of Shakespeare, was published in 1623. Internal and external evidence, including the dates of quartos, suggests that among his earlier plays, written between about 1587 and 1592, are *The Comedy of Errors* and *Richard III*. At about the same time as *Venus and Adonis* and *Lucrece*, he produced the lyrical comedy *A Midsummer Night's Dream*, the tragedy *Romeo and Juliet*, and the play which hovers in between the two categories, *The Merchant of Venice*. From 1596 to 1599 was his age of history—*Richard II*, the two parts of *Henry IV*, and *Henry V*. They were followed by the high fantasies, *Much Ado About Nothing*, *As You Like It*, and *Twelfth Night or What You Will*. The committal to the Tower of London of his erstwhile patron Southampton, after the rebellion of the Earl of Essex in 1601, probably had a greater effect on the progression of Shakespeare's dramatic art than the accession of James I (JAMES VI of Scotland) two years later: it is to this period that the 'dark comedies' or 'bitter comedies' belong—*All's Well That Ends Well*, *Troilus and Cressida*, and *Measure for Measure*. His even darker phase, the period of the great tragedies, had already begun in 1599 with *Julius Caesar*, in which the character of Brutus presages that of Hamlet. The source of the play of *Hamlet*, which dates from about 1601, is a tale of revenge from Norse folklore, but in Shakespeare's hands it becomes a penetrating study of man's attitude to and ambiguous relationship with life and death. In *Othello*, *Macbeth*, *King Lear*, *Timon of Athens*, *Coriolanus*, and *Antony and Cleopatra*, he poured out his messages of poetic pessimism, depicting in turn each of the major vices: jealousy, lust for power, vanity, ingratitude (also cruelty), pride, and sexuality. To his final period belong the fairy tales (and some of his sweetest poetry) of *The Winter's Tale* and *The Tempest*, both performed in 1611. Probably the last play in which he had a hand (JOHN FLETCHER is the most likely collaborator) literally brought down the house, as an errant cannon in *Henry VIII* demolished the Globe in 1613 during the play's third or fourth performance. See *The Complete Works*, ed. Stanley Wells, 1988; Samuel Schoenbaum, *William Shakespeare: a Compact Documentary*

Life, 2nd edn 1987; Stanley Wells, *Shakespeare: a Dramatic Life*, 1994 (historical study of his art); C. T. Onions, *A Shakespeare Glossary*, 3rd edn 1986; and critical studies by Harley Granville-Barker, G. B. Harrison, John Dover Wilson, F. E. Halliday, E. M. W. Tillyard, and G. Wilson Knight in particular.

SHALOM ALEICHEM [Hebrew: 'Peace be with you' or 'How do you do?'], pseudonym of Solomon Rabinovitz (1859–1916) Yiddish novelist, short-story writer, and dramatist, was born in Pereyaslev, Ukraine, the son of a grain and lumber merchant who fell on hard times and became an innkeeper. After leaving gymnasium in 1876, he taught in local schools and then in 1877 became tutor in the home of a Jewish landowner, who dismissed him when he was discovered to be in love with the daughter of the house. The pair married in 1883, the year he left his post as government-appointed rabbi at Lubuy and decided to abandon Hebrew as a literary medium and to write stories and sketches in Yiddish, which was considered bad form—hence the pseudonym. In 1888 he founded *Di Yidishe Folksbibliotek* [The Yiddish Popular Library] to raise the status of Yiddish, but he went bankrupt after the publication of the second annual volume, and had to reside abroad until his mother-in-law settled his debts. With the advent of Yiddish daily newspapers in eastern Europe, he became able to support himself and his growing family by his pen, but the pogroms of 1905 set him on a series of wanderings: first to the USA, where he was disheartened by his reception, and then through Europe, giving public recitations of his works, and taking refuge in resorts and spas for his tuberculosis. When World War I broke out he was forced to return to the USA, where in spite of his misgivings being realized about the lack of financial returns, on the day of his funeral most of the Jewish businesses in New York stopped work. A humorist with a profound insight into the Jewish talent for survival, he has been translated into many languages, including Hebrew, Russian, and English; the musical *Fiddler on the Roof* (1964) is based on a dramatization of one of his stories. *The Great Fair*, tr. Tamara Kahana (1958) is an autobiographical novel of childhood and youth of unusual charm. See *The Best of Shalom Aleichem*, ed. Irving Howe and Ruth R. Wisse, new edn 1991.

SHAMS UD-DIN MUHAMMAD see HAFIZ.

SHAPCOTT, THOMAS (*b.* 1935) Australian poet and novelist, was born in Ipswich, Queensland, one of identical twin boys. He left Ipswich Grammar School at 15 to work in his father's accounting firm, of which he became a partner in 1972, having in 1968 graduated in art at Queensland University. He was a public accountant from 1972 to 1978. In two early books of verse, *Time on Fire* (1961) and *The Mankind Thing* (1964), he deliberately sublimated his instinct to experiment, which he has done since in a variety of forms while being 'concerned with exploring ways of balancing essentially lyrical expression with the cadence of lyric speech'. A notable collection is *Shabbytown Calendar* (1975), in which he examines his origins and gives rein to his sense of place. His fiction has followed similar lines of development. *Flood Children* (1981) was published for young adults. *The Birthday Gift* (1982) is a study of a pair of unidentical twin boys from Ipswich who grow up, and apart, together. In *White Stag of Exile* (1984), even more experimental in form, the emigration to Australia in the 19th century of the Director of the Hungarian National Gallery of Art is the basis of an exploration of national and intellectual links. Short stories are in *Limestone and Lemon Wine* (1988) and *What You Own* (1991). The demonstration of cultural links also informs his anthology, *Contemporary American and Australian Poetry* (1976). He was in 1973 one of the original members of the Australia Council Literature Board, of which he was Director from 1983 to 1990, when he became Executive Director of the National Book Council. In 1982 he married as his second wife the poet Judith Rodriguez, née Green (*b.* 1936). He was made AO in 1989. See *Selected Poems 1956–1988*, rev. edn 1989; *Biting the Bullet: a Literary Memoir*, 1990 (essays, reviews, reflections).

SHARP, WILLIAM ('Fiona Macleod') (1855–1905) Scottish poet and novelist, was born in Paisley and educated at Glasgow Academy and Glasgow University. After teaming up with a group of gypsies, he was placed in a lawyer's office by his father, on whose death in 1876 he took an extended trip to Australia, which he found too rough for him. He obtained a post in a London bank, which he gave up in 1881 to combine a literary career with travelling. In 1884, having spent five months studying art in Italy, he married a first cousin, to whom he had been unofficially engaged for nine years. During his first burst of activity he produced several books of verse, two novels, and studies of D. G. ROSSETTI (of whose circle he had been a member), P. B. SHELLEY, HEINE, and ROBERT BROWNING, besides editing the 'Canterbury Poets' and 'Biographies of Great Writers' series. In 1889 he went to the USA and Canada, and thence, via Scotland, to Rome, where he spent the winter of 1890–91, and wrote a group of poems, *Sospiri di Roma* (1891), in which he re-creates the romantic image of the ancient past. He also assumed an alternative, feminine, persona, whom he called Fiona Macleod. As this lady, whom he claimed was a reclusive cousin and for whom he compiled an entry in *Who's Who*, he wrote several novels, beginning with *Pharais: a Romance of the Isles* (1894), and volumes of shorter pieces, including *The Sin-Eater and Other Tales* (1895); two verse dramas; and a corpus of poetry, collected in *From the Hills of Dream: Mountain Songs and Island Runes* (1896). The ancient culture which he depicts never existed, but he is in the Celtic Twilight tradition for his visionary and musical qualities, and for his presentation, in Highland settings, of the ancient rituals of love, and war, and death.

SHAW, GEORGE BERNARD (1856–1950) Irish dramatist, novelist, essayist, and critic, was born in Dublin of Protestant parents. His father's drinking habits barred the family from genteel society, and when Shaw was 16 his headstrong but musical mother left for London, taking his two sisters with her. After four years at Wesley School, he became a clerk in a firm of land agents in 1871, being soon promoted to cashier when the incumbent of that post decamped with some rents. He appeared in print in 1875 in *Public Opinion*, with a letter acutely analysing the influence of the American evangelists, Dwight Moody and Ira Sankey. In 1876 he threw up his job and moved to London, where he lived with his mother in an uncomfortable house off Fulham Road. Here he wrote five novels, of which the last, *An Unsocial Socialist*, was the first to be published (1884 as a serial, 1887 as a book), and the first, *Immaturity*, was not published until 1930. After reading MARX in French, he became an active socialist, forced himself to be an accomplished public speaker, and became an executive council member of the Fabian Society, for whom he edited *Fabian Essays in Socialism* (1889). He was a book reviewer for the *Pall Mall Gazette* 1885–88, and Music Critic for the *Star* (as 'Corno di Bassetto') 1888–89 and for the *World* 1890–94. From this experience derived two admirable critical works, *The Quintessence of Ibsenism* (1891) and *The Perfect Wagnerite* (1898).

In response to the challenge of the modern theatre offered by IBSEN, he resuscitated and rewrote a play he had begun in 1885 with William Archer (1856–1924): *Widowers' Houses* (performed 1892) was a new kind of play in that different sides of a social problem are presented and argued out upon the stage. *Mrs Warren's Profession* (written in 1893 but banned from public performance until 1926) has a similar intention. At the start, Shaw's future as a dramatist seemed no more profitable than it had been as a novelist, though *The Devil's Disciple*, a historical drama based on the exploits of General Burgoyne (1722–92), was financially successful when it was staged in New York in 1897. His prestige was enhanced, however, by his work as Dramatic Critic of the *Saturday Review* from 1895 to 1898, as was his political and economic experience by service as a local government councillor for Saint Pancras (1897–1903). In 1898 he broke new ground when he published *Plays Pleasant and Unpleasant*, including *Mrs Warren's Profession*, *Arms and the Man*, and *Candida* (the first of a line of plays with remarkable heroines). Shaw was convinced that plays should be read in the same way as novels, and he provided explicit and graphic stage directions and also prefaces, which are rather postscripts, or treatises, on the play's theme. *Three Plays for Puritans* (1901) included *Caesar and Cleopatra*, an enjoyable if imaginary representation of the famous historical romance. From now on his plays were regularly produced as well as read, and he particularly demonstrated the breadth of his social awareness and the control of his medium and of dialectics, as well as his sense of comedy, in *Man and Superman* (published 1903), *Major Barbara* (1907), *The Doctor's Dilemma* (1911), *Androcles and the Lion* (1914), *Pygmalion* (1916), and *Saint Joan* (1924). *Back to Methuselah* (1921), his 'metabiological pentateuch', is in effect five plays spanning a philosophical existence from the Garden of Eden to 'as far as thought can reach'. His most notable prose works of the interwar period are *The Intelligent Woman's Guide to Socialism and Capitalism* (1928) and *The Adventures of a Black Girl in Her Search for God* (1932). The latter, an ironic parable, was written in Africa, where he had to extend his stay after an accident, caused by his putting his foot on the brake of a hired car instead of on the accelerator.

In 1898 overwork caused him to collapse. An acquaintance of his own age, the Irishborn heiress Charlotte Payne-Townshend, went to his home (he was still living with his mother, but now in Fitzroy Square) and was so horrified by the conditions that she insisted on removing him to the country. To avoid scandal, he proposed marriage, and was accepted. His mother died in 1913. After the death of his wife in 1943, he lived on at the house in Ayot St Lawrence, Hertfordshire, which he had bought in 1906. He was a prolific letter writer, whose correspondence with Ellen Terry was published in 1931, with Mrs Patrick Campbell in 1952, and with Harley Granville-Barker in 1956. He was awarded the Nobel Prize for Literature in 1925. See *The Bodley Head Collected Plays with Their Prefaces*, 7 vols 1970–75; *Bernard Shaw Theatrics: Selected Correspondence of Bernard Shaw*, ed. Dan H. Laurence, 1995; Hesketh Pearson, *Bernard Shaw: a Biography* new edn 1987; Michael Holroyd, *Bernard Shaw: the Search for Love 1856–1898*, new edn 1990, *Bernard Shaw: the Pursuit of Power 1898–1918*, new edn 1993, *Bernard Shaw: the Lure of Fantasy 1918–1950*, new edn 1993, *Bernard Shaw: the Last Laugh 1950–1991*, new edn 1993, and *The Shaw Companion*, 1992; Desmond MacCarthy, *Shaw: the Plays*, new edn 1973.

SHAW, IRWIN (1913–84) American novelist, short-story writer, and dramatist, was born in New York City and educated at Brooklyn public schools and Brooklyn College, from which he graduated in English in 1934, having been rusticated for a year for failing calculus as a freshman. While writing radio serials, he composed a one-act semi-expressionistic play, *Bury the Dead*, set in the 'second year of the war that is to begin tomorrow night'. Its powerful pacifist message and spectacular stagecraft made it a notable theatrical event when it was moved to Broadway in 1936 after two performances at the left-wing New Theatre League. After having had four more plays produced in New York, he served in the US Army Signal Corps in World War II in North Africa, the Middle East, France, and Germany, becoming a warrant officer. In his eagerly-awaited first novel, *The Young Lions* (1948), three individuals, an intellectual liberal, a Jew, and a German, present the moral issues inherent in the war which had just ended. *Rich Man, Poor Man* (1970) is typical of most of his subsequent novels, big, disjointed, and sociologically-orientated; an exception is *Lucy Crown* (1956), a study of the effect of a broken marriage on an only child. Critics regard his best fiction as being in his short stories, 63 out of the total of 84 being collected in *Five Decades* (1978), of which he says: 'In a novel or a play you must be a whole man. In a collection of stories you can be all the men or fragments of men, worthy and unworthy, who in different seasons abound in you.' Many of his stories are about expatriates in Paris or elsewhere on the Continent (he himself lived in Europe from 1951); a recurring motif is the moment of truth, the point when the eyes of the protagonist, or the reader, are opened to the underlying reality of the situation. See James R. Giles, *Irwin Shaw*, 1991 (biographical/critical study).

SHELLEY, MARY (WOLLSTONE-CRAFT) (1797–1851), née Godwin, British novelist, was born in London, the daughter of GODWIN and WOLLSTONECRAFT, who died a few days after the birth. Brought up by a stepmother who was uncongenial even to her own children, and by a highly intellectual but distant father, she revelled in the freedom she experienced during two extended visits between 1812 and 1814 to Tayside, near Dundee, where she stayed with a family whose son worked with Mary's stepbrother, Charles Clairmont, in the Edinburgh publishing house of Constable. She appears to have met P. B. SHELLEY properly for the first time in May 1814, and in July of that year they left England together, with her 16-year-old stepsister Claire in tow—see Robert Gittings and Jo Manton, *Claire Clairmont and the Shelleys*

1798–1879 (1992). All three of them, with Mary's infant son by Shelley, returned to Switzerland in 1816, where they joined forces with BYRON, by whom the assembled company was challenged, as morning broke one day, to write a 'ghost story'. Only one was completed, Mary's *Frankenstein, or the Modern Prometheus* (published anonymously in 1818), the initial situation of which, as she explains in the introduction to the acknowledged (much changed) 1831 edition, came to her in a nightmare. What was perhaps more extraordinary than finishing her story of horror was that this quiet, shy, 19-year-old unmarried mother had conceived, in the form of a synthetic being which haunts its creator, a character which would subsequently inspire numerous books, films, and other flights of the imagination, and in doing so had written the first science fantasy. (Research published in 1996 suggesting that the original inspiration for the character came from her visit with Shelley in 1814 to the ruined Castle Frankenstein, birthplace of Konrad Dippel (1673–1734), a physician notorious for his experiments with corpses, does not detract from the imaginative use she made of it.)

She and Shelley were finally married in London on 30 December 1816. After his death, she stayed for the winter in HUNT's uncomfortable household, returning to England in 1823. Between 1840 and 1843 she and her son travelled on the Continent, about which she wrote *Rambles in Germany and Italy* (1844). She also did journalistic work, and wrote short stories and several further novels, of which *Lodore* (1835) and *Falkner* (1837) retrace elements of her life with Shelley, and *The Last Man* (1826), a story of the future in which disaster strikes Europe, is a forerunner of a popular genre. She edited her husband's poetry (1839) and prose (1840). See *The Mary Shelley Reader*, ed. Betty T. Bennett and Charles E. Robinson, 1991; *The Journals of Mary Shelley*, ed. Paula R. Feldman and Diana Scott-Kilvert, 2 vols new edns 1995; *Selected Letters*, ed. Betty T. Bennett, 1995; Muriel Spark, *Mary Shelley*, 2nd rev. edn 1993 of *Child of Light: a Reassessment of Mary Wollstonecraft Shelley*, 1951.

SHELLEY, PERCY BYSSHE (1792–1822) British poet and essayist, was born at Field Place, Horsham, Sussex, the eldest son of Timothy Shelley (*d.* 1844), a Member of Parliament who succeeded to his father's baronetcy in 1815. He was educated at Sion House Academy, Isleworth, and Eton. By the time he left school he had published *Zastrozzi: a Romance* (1810), was making arrangements for a second novel, and had written, with his sister Elizabeth, *Original Poetry by Victor and Cazire* (1810). In 1810 he went up to University College, Oxford, where he became a close friend of Thomas Jefferson Hogg (1792–1862), his future biographer. Between

them they concocted and (in February 1811) distributed an anonymous pamphlet, *The Necessity of Atheism*. Shelley made no attempt to conceal his authorship, and the pair were expelled for refusing to answer questions. That summer he rescued Harriet Westbrook, a pretty 16-year-old school friend of his sisters, from what he saw as the tyranny of her family by eloping with her to Edinburgh, where they went through a form of marriage. The union was not a success. While they were living together he wrote *Queen Mab: a Philosophical Poem with Notes*, which was published privately in 1813, and in subsequent unauthorized editions became a Chartist handbook.

In 1814 he fell for Mary (MARY SHELLEY), the 16-year-old daughter of GODWIN and WOLLSTONECRAFT, and went off with her to Switzerland, accompanied by her even younger stepsister, Jane (or Claire) Clairmont—see also *The Journals of Claire Clairmont*, ed. Marion Kingston Stocking (1968). The title poem of *Alastor: or the Spirit of Solitude, and Other Poems* (1816) was written when he was back in England. It reflects his depression at being hounded by creditors and by the unfortunate Harriet, by whom he now had two children, and being cast out even by that apostle of free love, Godwin, who still expected Shelley's financial support, especially after the death of the poet's grandfather in 1815 gave him a regular income. In 1816 the unusual trio returned to Lake Geneva, where BYRON joined them. A pregnant Harriet was found drowned in the Serpentine in Hyde Park in December, whereupon Shelley and Mary married in London. In 1817 he published a romantic epic in Spenserian metre in support of revolution, *Laon and Cythna*, which was suppressed and reissued in a bowdlerized form later that year as *The Revolt of Islam*.

In 1818 the Shelleys took their two children to Italy, where the death of their daughter inspired the beautiful 'Lines Written Among the Euganean Hills', whose assurance is a measure of the artistic confidence which enabled him to complete *Prometheus Unbound* (1820), an idealistic, allegorical drama with much soaring poetry. *The Cenci* (1819), a melodramatic verse play composed for the theatre but regarded at the time as too strong to be staged, was written after the death of their son in 1819. The incomparable 'Ode to the West Wind' belongs to this period too. Later that year Mary had a further boy, Percy Florence (1819–89), who inherited the baronetcy in 1844. They moved permanently to the region of Pisa in 1820, where they were joined by several devotees, and where Shelley wrote *Adonais: an Elegy on the Death of John Keats* (1821). The discovery of a gorgeous Italian girl, Emilia Viviani, holed up in a nearby convent while her mother had an affair, rekindled Shelley's knight-errant visions, which he embodied in *Epipsychidion* (1821). Less Platonic was his admiration for Jane, the common-law wife of Edward Williams (she had been abandoned by her army officer husband), to whom he wrote several lyrics in 1822. He was also working on 'The Triumph of Life'. This philosophical poem, in which the poet is guided by ROUSSEAU through a series of visions, shows a strong influence of DANTE's *Divine Comedy*, which Shelley had closely studied. Its central event is based on the *Triumphs* of PETRARCH, and the verse form (*terza rima*) is that of both the *Triumphs* and the *Divine Comedy*. He had completed 544 lines when, early in July, he and Williams sailed his new boat to Leghorn to see HUNT. On the return journey the boat capsized in a squall, and they were both drowned. The bodies were later washed ashore, where in deference to the quarantine laws they were burned, in the presence of Byron and Edward Trelawny (1792–1881), who described the scene in *Records of Shelley, Byron and the Author* (1878). Mary herself edited *The Poetical Works of Percy Bysshe Shelley* (1839).

In the light of the charisma attached to Shelley's rebellious nature, moral nonconformity, continuous questing after a personal religion, Neo-Platonism of language and thought, and his youth (he was not yet 30 when he died), some critical hostility is perhaps inevitable. He had an extraordinary command of form and metre, and an intellectual capacity which belied his unfinished education. He produced many political pamphlets and essays, of which 'A Philosophical View of Reform' (1820) and 'A Defence of Poetry' (1821) are particularly notable. The latter was provoked by PEACOCK's *The Four Ages of Poetry*, and is an affirmation, based on the experience of history, of the moral and social contribution of the poet. See *The Complete Poetical Works*, ed. Thomas Hutchinson, rev. G. M. Matthews, 1995; *Shelley's Prose*, ed. David Lee Clark, preface by Harold Bloom, new edn 1988; Richard Holmes, *Shelley: the Pursuit*, new edn 1995 (biography); Earl R. Wasserman, *Shelley: a Critical Reading*, new edn 1977; Michael O'Neill, *The Human Mind's Imaginings: Conflict and Achievement in Shelley's Poetry*, 1989.

SHEPARD, SAM (*b.* 1943) American dramatist, was born Samuel Shepard Rogers in Fort Sheridan, Illinois, the son of a serviceman, and was educated at Duarte High School, California. There are conflicting accounts of his upbringing, but in 1963 he arrived in New York City, where his first play, *Cowboys*, was performed Off Off Broadway the following year. Further short plays followed in quick succession, based mainly on the notion of capturing the movement of the characters' minds, in much the same way as was happening in popular music. Shepard has played in groups and bands, and in his first full-length play, *The Tooth of Crime* (1972), two rock stars confront each other in a metaphorical contest for survival. It was first produced in London, where he and his family spent the years 1970–74 and where he had experience of stage direction. Subsequently many of his plays have been projections of family discord through which he suggests links and explores (but does not necessarily resolve) conflicts with aspects of American life and popular culture; as he does in particular in the trilogy, *Curse of the Starving Class* (1976), *Buried Child* (1978), which won the Pulitzer Prize, and *True West* (1980).

In the 1980s he developed a talent for film acting, and won an Oscar nomination for his role in *The Right Stuff* (1983). His last full-length play for some time was *A Lie of the Mind* (1985), in which the fractured language reflects the broken life of a woman in thrall to love. Before the opening of *Simpatico* (1994), he publicly expressed his concern about commercialism in the theatre: 'There is always this marketing aspect that seems to leap on top of everything like a vampire. You don't have the luxury of learning from your mistakes. You just get the axe.' The play, a strongly-developed psychological thriller with surprisingly sympathetic characterization, much of it written in his head while driving his Dodge across country, was excellently received in New York and London. Stories are in *Motel Chronicles and Hawk Moon* (1985). *Cruising Paradise* (1996) comprises 39 autobiographical and semi-autobiographical pieces. See *Seven Plays*, new edn 1997; *Plays*, 2 vols 1996; Joseph Chaikin and Sam Shephard, *Letters and Texts 1972–1984*, new edn 1995 (diaries, journals, letters); Martin Tucker, *Sam Shepard*, 1993 (critical biography); Carl Rosen, *Sam Shepard*, 1993 (critical study).

SHERIDAN, FRANCES see SHERIDAN.

SHERIDAN, RICHARD BRINSLEY (1751–1816) Irish dramatist and British politician, was born in Dublin, the second son of Thomas Sheridan (1719–88), actor-manager of the Theatre Royal and biographer of SWIFT (1784), and Frances, née Chamberlaine (1724–66)—his grandfather, Thomas Sheridan (1687–1738), was a minor poet and a friend of Swift. A theatre riot in 1754 caused the parents to leave Ireland, the boy joining them in England in 1759. In spite of Thomas's success as an elocutionist and Frances's with her novel, *Memoirs of Miss Sidney Bidulph* (1761)—recently assessed as 'a cult-of-distress and sentimental classic, a love story of great moral complexity . . . at the centre of many important currents in the 18th-century novel'—, and with a comedy, *The Discovery* (1763), the couple had to take refuge from creditors in France in 1764, leaving Sheridan as a boarder at Harrow. In 1770, after Frances's death, Thomas, back in England and in funds, took his son to Bath, where Sheridan was so struck by a young singer, Elizabeth Linley (1754–92), that he accompanied her, and a chaperon, to France, where she hoped to get away from sexual harassment by an importunate suitor. On their return, having gone through an invalid form of marriage, they were separated, though Sheridan had to fight two duels with one of her suitors, in the second of which he was wounded. They were properly married in 1773. Their son, Tom (1775–1817), became a theatre manager; the daughter born in 1792 was not Sheridan's.

Sheridan, having given up his law studies at the time of the marriage, of which his father still disapproved, wrote a play at the suggestion of the manager of Covent Garden Theatre to earn some money. *The Rivals*, which drew on his personal life, was withdrawn in January 1775 after two disastrous performances. It was put on again ten days later in a cleaned-up and tightened form, and was a hit, the characters of Sir Anthony Absolute and Mrs Malaprop passing into English dramatic heritage. A short farce, *St Patrick's Day*, was followed by a comic opera, *The Duenna* (1775), which, with *The Rivals*, moved JOHNSON to observe that Sheridan 'has written the two best comedies of his age'. In 1776 he borrowed heavily to become principal manager of Drury Lane Theatre, for which he wrote *A Trip to Scarborough* (1777), adapted from VANBRUGH's *The Relapse*; *The School for Scandal* (1777, first published in Dublin 1780), his masterpiece of anti-sentiment; and *The Critic* (1779, published 1781).

In 1780 he was elected to Parliament, representing Stafford, Westminster, and Ilchester between then and 1812. For most of this time he was a prominent and eloquent member of the opposition—he supported BURKE in the motion to impeach Warren Hastings in 1788, speaking on all four days, of which EDWARD GIBBON commented: 'At the close [he] sank into Burke's arms—a good actor; but I called this morning, he is perfectly well.' He also served in office three times, being Treasurer of the Navy and Privy Councillor 1806–07, and an adviser to and spokesman for the Prince of Wales—the notable actress Mrs Dora Jordan (1761–1816), whom Sheridan regularly employed when she was not completely incapacitated by her numerous royal pregnancies, was the mistress of the Prince's brother, the Duke of Clarence, later William IV, who pursued her after being rejected by Elizabeth Sheridan. Apart from *Pizzaro* (1799), a hastily composed adaptation of a German drama which contradicted his own tenet not to mix politics and the theatre, Sheridan wrote no more for the stage, but he maintained his association with Drury Lane until 1809, when he watched its destruction by fire, replying to a friend who remarked on his equanimity, 'A man may surely be allowed to take a glass of wine by his own fireside.' He was a chronic alcoholic, whose policy of 'borrow and fear not' contributed to his ending his life in the most wretched circumstances. Three years after Elizabeth's death he had wooed and married the young daughter of the Dean of Winchester, Hester Jane ('Hecca') Ogle (1771–1817), who was already afflicted with cancer when he died. *The School for Scandal*, written when Sheridan was 25, is the most glittering of English comedies, restoring rather than disturbing its audience's faith in human nature. See *Plays*, ed. Cecil Price, 1975; Linda Kelly, *Richard Brinsley Sheridan: a Life*, 1997; James Morwood, *The Life and Works of Richard Brinsley Sheridan*, 1985; James Morwood and David Crane (eds), *Sheridan Studies*, 1995 (essays on Sheridan as a dramatist, theatrical manager, and politician).

SHERRIFF, R(OBERT) C(EDRIC) (1896–1975) British dramatist and novelist, was born in Hampton-Wick, Surrey, and educated at Kingston Grammar School, after which he joined an insurance company. He served as a captain in World War I, being severely wounded at Passchendaele in 1917. Back in insurance, he wrote plays for his local rowing club, of which he was an active member, to perform for funds. *Journey's End* began as a novel, but with the denouement and the whole action transferred to the Western Front, was reluctantly put on by the English Stage Society in 1928, and only just managed to get a public airing in January 1929. It ran for 594 performances and by the autumn it was also playing on Broadway, New York (485 performances), and in 17 foreign languages in Europe. Somehow, 11 years after the war, the tide against its depiction on the stage had turned, and the play's sheer realism spoke directly about things which up till then had not been openly discussed, still less shown. Sherriff's next play, *Badger's Green* (1930), a pleasant English rural comedy, failed, and he determined to become a schoolmaster, entering New College, Oxford, to read for a history degree. He never sat it, having taken time off to go to Hollywood to write the screenplay of WELLS's *The Invisible Man*, and concluded that he was not up to the work. He wrote other screenplays (notably *The Dam Busters*), and more stage plays, of which the most popular were the mysteries, *Miss Mabel* (1949) and *Home at Seven* (1950). Of several novels, the unpretentious, episodic, seaside holiday story, *The Fortnight in September* (1931) was the most successful, but *The Wells of St Mary's* (1962), a black comedy, has survived best. See *No Leading Lady: an Autobiography*, 1968; York Notes on *Journey's End*, 1991.

SHIMAZAKI TŌSON see NATSUME SOSEKEI.

SHIRLEY, JAMES (1596–1666) English dramatist and poet, was born in London and educated at Merchant Taylors' School, St John's College, Oxford, and Catherine Hall, Cambridge. He took orders and was Headmaster of Edward VI Grammar School, St Albans 1623–25, but after his conversion to Catholicism moved to London and became a dramatist. He prospered under royal patronage, and between 1636 and 1640 made several trips to Dublin, where his plays were staged at the new public theatre in Werburgh Street and at the castle of the Lord Deputy. The Act of Parliament in 1642 suppressing the stage ended his career when it was at its height, and his affairs were further put in hazard by his natural support of the royalist cause during the Civil War. He published his *Poems* (1646), returned to teaching, and wrote masques for private performance, including *The Contention of Ajax and Ulysses* (published 1659), in which are the lines: 'The glories of our blood and state / Are shadows, not substantial things. / There is no armour against fate, / Death lays his icy hand on Kings.' He and his wife are said to have died on the same day of exposure and other privations, having lived in the open for two months after the Great Fire of London. More of his tragicomedies survive than of any other author except JOHN FLETCHER, but he was at his best in the contemporary comedy, of which *The Wittie Faire One* (1632) looks back to JONSON and forward to WYCHERLEY and FARQUHAR, and *The Lady of Pleasure* (1635) has a heroine who could well grace a Restoration comedy of manners. His tragedies, which include *The Traytor* (1631) and *The Cardinal* (1641), are full of the lust, bloodthirstiness, and casual attitude to murder which had become features of such dramas.

SHOLOKHOV, MIKHAIL (ALEKSANDROVICH) (1905–84) Russian novelist, was born in Kruzhilin, a Cossack village on the Don, and was educated in Moscow and Voronezh. At 15 he was serving in the Bolshevik army, at 18 he was married, and at 20 he was publishing realistic stories of social and political conflicts in Cossack rural society—see *One Man's Destiny: and Other Stories, Articles and Sketches 1923–1963*, tr. H. C. Stevens (1967). At the same time he was beginning his four-volume epic novel cycle (1928–40; tr. Stephen Garry as *And Quiet Flows the Don*, 1934, and *The Don Flows Home to the Sea*, 1940), a rich panoramic exploration of the Cossack culture and character in the years between 1912 and 1922—see also *Quiet Flows the Don*, tr. Robert Daglish, rev. and ed. Brian Murphy (1996). His subsequent work, which includes [*Seeds of Tomorrow*] (1932; tr. Garry, 1935) and a sequel, dealing with the advent of collectivization in the same region, suffers considerably in comparison. He was elected to the Supreme Soviet in 1937, and became a member of the Central Committee of the Communist Party in 1961. Accusations of plagiarism, which were current in the 1920s and resurfaced in the 1970s at the instigation of SOLZHENITSYN, have never fully been substantiated. He was awarded the Nobel Prize for Literature in 1965.

SHORTHOUSE, JOSEPH HENRY (1834–1903) British novelist, was born in Birmingham of a Quaker family. His education locally and at Grove House, Tottenham, was hampered by his excruciating stammer and, in 1842, by a virulent attack of typhus. At 16 he went into the family chemical factory. At meetings of a Friends' Essay Society, he overcame his hesitant manner and met his future wife, whom he married in 1857. Both became Anglican in 1861. An epileptic attack in 1862 left him permanently a semi-invalid. In 1867 he began writing *John Inglesant*, of which he would read one or two paragraphs a night to his wife. It was finally finished in 1876, but after it had been rejected by several publishers, he put the manuscript away. In 1880 he had one hundred copies privately printed and bound in vellum, one of which WARD sent personally to Alexander Macmillan (1818–96), who published it in 1881. It sold 10,000 copies in the first year. Parts of this novel of a spiritual quest in 17th-century England and Italy were forty years later found to have been painstakingly stitched together from sources of the times, but it is still an impressive feat of the imagination, and it had enormous influence, especially among those who found their own religious dilemmas reflected in it. The author was lionized, and went on to write five further, but only minor, novels. He died in Edgbaston, from which he had hardly ever been farther away than London, having for the previous three years been unable to do much more than read and pray.

SHUTE, NEVIL, pen name of Nevil Shute Norway (1899–1960) British novelist, was born in Ealing, Middlesex, and went to Shrewsbury School, and then to the Royal Military Academy with a view to being commissioned in the Royal Flying Corps. He returned to civilian life when he failed his final medical because of his stammer, and served at home in the Suffolk Regiment at the end of World War I, before going to Balliol College, Oxford. From there he went into the de Havilland aircraft company, learned to fly, and in 1924 joined the Airship Guarantee Co., becoming in 1929 deputy chief engineer to (Sir) Barnes Wallis (1887–1979) on the R100, in which he flew to and from Canada. The crash of its government-sponsored rival, the R101, in 1930 put an end to the project, and he founded his own construction company, Airspeed. He resigned in 1938 to write full time, having had several novels published, beginning with *Marazan* (1926). During World War

II he served as an officer in the Royal Naval Volunteer Reserve on the construction of secret weapons, wrote a best-selling novel, *Pied Piper* (1942), and went as a government correspondent on the Normandy landings in 1944 and to Burma in 1945. *No Highway* (1948) deals with the problems from metal fatigue which he foresaw in the aircraft passenger business. In 1948 he flew himself to Australia, where he decided to settle in 1950. In *A Town Like Alice* (1950), a young English woman, who has with her group suffered incredible privations in Malaya during World War II at the hands of the Japanese, uses an inheritance to transform a depressed settlement in the Australian Gulf country into 'a town like Alice [Springs]'. *On the Beach* (1957) projects conditions after a global nuclear holocaust. *Slide Rule* is an autobiography up to 1938.

SHUTTLE, PENELOPE see REDGROVE.

SIDLEY, CHARLES see SEDLEY.

SIDNEY, (Sir) **PHILIP** (1554–86) English poet, prose writer, and critic, was born at Penshurst Place, Kent, the eldest son of a famous family, though his means were modest for the whole of his life and his knighthood in 1583 was not for merit, but for reasons of protocol, so that he could stand as proxy at a court ceremony. He was educated at Shrewsbury School and Christ Church, Oxford, without taking a degree—he did not return after the plague had closed the university in 1571. Between 1572 and 1575 he travelled on the Continent and met prominent intellectuals, after which he spent some months with his father, Sir Henry Sidney (1529–86), Lord Deputy of Ireland. Like so many bright young men, he fell in and out of favour with Elizabeth I, his only appointment for the present, in spite of the efforts of his uncle, the Earl of Leicester (*c.*1532–88), being as an ambassador to the courts of Rudolph, Emperor of Germany, and William of Orange in 1577. His strong literary interests led to a close friendship with SPENSER, who dedicated *The Shepheardes Calender* to him in 1579. In about 1580, during a period of unemployment, he was staying with his sister Mary (1561–1621), Countess of Pembroke, later a notable literary patron and a less notable minor poet. Here he began for her amusement a romance, which he never finished, but which was published in 1590 in a truncated version as *The Countesse of Pembrokes Arcadia*, and more fully and with revisions in 1593. For this he combined the Menippean form of prose interspersed with verse used in *Arcadia* (1501), by the Italian Jacopo Sannazaro (1458–1530), with the kind of action in the prose epic *Aethiopica* of the 4th-century Greek writer Heliodorus, which had been translated (from a Latin version) in 1569 by Thomas Underdowne (*fl.* 1566–87). At about this time, too,

he wrote his critical essay on the current state of English poetry, published in 1595 both as *The Defence of Poesie* and as *An Apologie for Poetrie*.

He was elected to Parliament for his father's former constituency of Kent in 1581, the year in which Penelope Devereux (1562–1607), to whom he had formerly been engaged, married Lord Rich. He now addressed to her the first considerable English sonnet sequence, comprising 108 sonnets and several songs, which was published in 1591 as *Astrophel and Stella*. He was himself married in 1583 to Frances Walsingham, by whom he had a daughter who became Countess of Rutland. In 1585 he was appointed Governor of Flushing, to pursue, under Leicester, the Dutch war against Spain. After one brilliant military exploit, he was mortally wounded by a bullet in an attack near Zutphen, handing the bottle of water, which was brought to him, to a dying soldier with the immortal words, 'Thy necessity is yet greater than mine.' He died four weeks later in Arnhem, attended by his very pregnant wife, whose baby was to be stillborn.

The Defence of Poesie is the most considerable work of English criticism at least until DRYDEN. In his *Arcadia* Sidney experimented with, stretched, and embellished the new literary medium of English prose. Of *Astrophel and Stella*, c. s. LEWIS observes in *English Literature in the Sixteenth Century* (1954): 'Considered historically . . . and in relation to his predecessors, Sidney is one of our most important poets.' A sidelight on the subject of women and romance in Renaissance times, as well as on the status of Sidney, is provided by Anna Weamys, who may have been the daughter of a prebendary of Westminster Abbey and was likely to have been in her early twenties when she wrote *A Continuation of Sir Philip Sidney's 'Arcadia'* (1651; ed. Patrick Colborn Cullen, 1995). See [*Selected Verse*], ed. Katherine Duncan-Jones, 1994; *Selected Poems*, ed. Catherine Bates, 1994; Albert C. Hamilton, *Sir Philip Sidney: a Study of His Life and Works*, 1977; John Buxton, *Sir Philip Sidney and the English Renaissance*, 3rd edn 1987.

SIENKIEWICZ, HENRYK (1846–1916) Polish novelist, was born in Wola Okrzejska and went to gymnasium and university in Warsaw. A freelance journalist and writer, he travelled in Europe, the East, and Africa, and in 1876–78 visited America to seek a site for a settlement in California. All his novels were originally written as serials, the historical trilogy of 17th-century Polish political and social upheavals (1884–88) being published in English as *With Fire and Sword* (1890), *The Deluge* (1891), and *Pan Michael* (1893), tr. Jeremiah Curtin. *Quo Vadis?* (1896; tr. Curtin, 1896), his richly-patterned story of the conflict between Christianity and the ancient religions in

Rome at the time of Nero, has been translated into numerous languages and was made into a Hollywood epic film (1951). He was officially presented with an estate in Poland in 1900, and he was awarded the Nobel Prize for Literature in 1905.

SILKIN, JON (b. 1930) British poet and editor, was born in London, was evacuated during World War II to Wales, and was educated at Dulwich College and Leeds University, of which he was later Gregory Fellow in Poetry (1958–60). His first book of verse, *The Portrait and Other Poems* (1950), was published at the beginning of a period during which he worked as a manual labourer and as a teacher of English to foreign students. Latterly he has taught writing and poetry at universities in England, the USA, Australia, and Israel. Much of his own poetry is rooted in Northumberland, where he has lived for many years, and in the ferment of his Jewish background. He is particularly moving in his treatment of death, most of all in the autobiographical 'Death of a Son', whose theme is taken up and extended in his dramatic poem, 'The People'. *The Lens-Breakers* (1992) resumes his concerns with the horror of violence and with the fragility of life. He was a co-founder in 1952 of *Stand*, of which he has been the principal editor ever since. Of the editorial policy of this, the most enduring and influential of postwar 'little magazines', he wrote in 1991: 'I believe art is needed even more now, now that the contagion of indifference to one's brother or sister human appears to have reached an unparalleled condition.' His critical works include *Out of Battle: the Poetry of the Great War* (1972), and he is editor of *The Penguin Book of First World War Poetry* (rev. edn 1981) and co-editor, with Jon Glover, of *The Penguin Book of First World War Prose* (1990). See *Selected Poems*, 3rd rev. edn 1994.

SILLITOE, ALAN (b. 1928) British novelist, short-story writer, and poet, was born in Nottingham, the son of a worker in a bicycle factory. He was educated locally, leaving school at 14 also to work in a cycle factory. He was a radio operator in the Royal Air Force from 1946 to 1949, part of his service being in Malaya. He then lived in France and Spain for several years, during which he wrote most of the poems later published in *The Rats and Other Poems* (1960), in which he expresses his impatience with society. A similar exasperation with authority, asserted with raw fury, informs his first novel, *Saturday Night and Sunday Morning* (1958), and also motivates the working-class heroes in the title story of *The Loneliness of the Long-Distance Runner* (1959) and in *A Start in Life* (1970). In other novels the search is for a more complete life, as in *Key to the Door* (1961); the trilogy about Frank Dawley which concludes with

The Flame of Life (1974); and *Her Victory* (1982). In both *The Lost Flying Boat* (1983) and *Last Loves* (1990) the quest involves a return by ex-servicemen, motivated in one case by greed and in the other by nostalgia, to sites where they once operated. *Raw Material* (rev. edn 1978) is a series of memoirs in fictional form in which he outlines his family background and explores the philosophy behind his fiction. He has continued to publish poetry—see *Collected Poems* (1993)—which he uses to 'express emotions that can't be expressed in any other medium'. He married the American-born short-story writer and poet Ruth Fainlight (b. 1931) in 1959. See *Collected Stories*, new edn 1996; *Life Without Armour*, new edn 1996 (autobiography to 1958).

SIMENON, GEORGES (1903–89) Belgian novelist, was born in Liège and educated at the the Institut St André and at a military school, which he left at 15. After abandoning two jobs and coming into contact with the criminal world, he was offered a trial by the *Gazette de Liège*, for which he then wrote a daily piece signed 'Georges Sim', the name under which he wrote his first novel (1921). He moved to Paris in 1922, and married an artist in 1923. He was soon writing forty popular novels a year under 24 registered pseudonyms, having heeded the advice of COLETTE, who rejected two of his stories for *Le Matin* as 'too literary', and established his literary credo of brevity and readability, imposing upon himself a vocabulary of 2000 words. The first Maigret detective novels, 11 of them, appeared under his own name in 1931. What he called his 'hard novels' attracted the attention of critics such as GIDE and MAURIAC, and he announced in 1937 that he would win the Nobel Prize for Literature in ten years' time. He never did (he later denounced the judges), though *La Veuve Couderc* (1942; tr. John Petrie as *Ticket of Leave*, 1954) and *La Neige Était Sale* (1948; tr. Louis Varèse as *The Snow Was Black*, 1950) are regarded as especially evocative of the darker side of everyday existence. He served as Commissioner for Belgian refugees in La Rochelle during World War II, after which he sailed for the USA with his wife and young son, leaving behind his wife's maid, who had been his mistress for 15 years. On the voyage he met a 25-year-old French-Canadian woman who joined his new household in Canada, and married him in 1950. There were also 10,000 (according to him), 1200 (according to his second wife), other women with whom he had sexual relations. In 1957 he took an extensive chateau in Switzerland, where he continued to write several novels a year until 1973, when he announced his retirement, only to buy a tape recorder, on which he dictated 25 volumes of unreliable but entertaining memoirs. See Patrick Marnham, *The Man*

Who Wasn't Maigret: a Portrait of Georges Simenon, new edn 1994.

SIMPSON, LOUIS (*b.* 1923) American poet and critic, was born in Kingston, Jamaica, the younger son of a lawyer of Scottish descent and of a Polish-born Jewess whose family had emigrated to New York. He remained with his father when his parents divorced, and went to Munro College. After his father's death in 1940 he joined his mother in New York, and entered Columbia University, from which he was drafted into the US Army in 1942. He served in the 101st Airborne Division in Europe during World War II, winning the Bronze Star and two Purple Hearts for his action in combat; in a corpus of notable war poems, the poignant 'Carentan O Carentan' 'describes the first actual battle experience of the company in which I served'. He graduated at Columbia University in 1948, and then spent two years in France, during which he attended classes at Paris University and assembled and published at his own expense *The Arrivistes: Poems 1940–1949* (1949). After taking a higher degree in English at Columbia University, he spent four years as a publisher's editor before returning to Columbia as an instructor; he was appointed a professor of English at the University of California in 1959, and at the State University of New York in 1967.

At the End of the Open Road (1963), his third commercially-published volume of verse, which won the Pulitzer Prize, marked a change from traditional forms to 'irregular, unrhymed lines—I was attempting to write verse that would sound like speech', and demonstrated a greater depth of vision. In *Searching for the Ox* (1976) and subsequent collections he explores his childhood and his mother's memories of hers, and depicts the everyday details of daily American life. *Riverside Drive* (1962) is an autobiographical novel. *North of Jamaica* (1972; in UK as *Air with Armed Men*, 1972) is autobiography. His critical works include joint studies of POUND, T. S. ELIOT, and W. C. WILLIAMS (1975) and of DYLAN THOMAS, GINSBERG, PLATH, and ROBERT LOWELL (1978), *A Company of Poets* (1981), and *The Character of the Poet* (1986). *Ships Going Into the Blue: Essays and Notes on Poetry* (1995) includes autobiographical reflections. See *Collected Poems*, new edn 1990; *There You Are*, 1995 (subsequent collection).

SINCLAIR, 'MAY' [MARY AMELIA ST CLAIR] (1863–1946) British novelist, was born in Rock Ferry, Cheshire, the sixth and youngest child, and only daughter, of a shipowner, after the collapse of whose business in 1870 her parents separated. She lived with her mother in somewhat straitened circumstances until the latter's death in 1901, and seems to have been largely self-educated, apart from the formative year 1881–82, spent

at Cheltenham Ladies College. She contributed to the school magazine, despite the editorial censorship of the school's redoubtable founder, Dorothea Beale (1831–1906), who subsequently wrote affectionate letters to her and introduced her to the idealist philosophy of T. H. Green (1836–82). Her first published work was *Nakiketos and Other Poems* (1886) and an article of philosophical criticism in an American journal—she was still propounding theories based on Green's in *The New Idealism* (1922). Of her earliest novels, the first being *Audrey Craven* (1897), Beatrice Harraden (1864–1936), another former pupil, commented cattily in a letter to Miss Beale which was largely about her own popularity as a novelist: 'I see May Sinclair from time to time. For your sake I have tried in many ways to help her; but she is extremely "difficile". . . . I much fear that she has not the special gifts which make for success in fiction, though she is so clever and writes so well. . . . Her last book though so well reviewed as a clever piece of work, was quite unsuccessful. I believe Mr Blackwood spoke of only two hundred copies sold.'

The Divine Fire (1904), about the artist in modern society, *was* successful, particularly in the USA, where Sinclair then toured. An active suffragette, she drove an ambulance on active service during World War I, recounting her experiences in *A Journal of Impressions in Belgium* (1915). She has been credited with the first use in a literary context, in a review of DOROTHY RICHARDSON in the *Egoist* (1918), of the term 'stream of consciousness', coined by William James (see HENRY JAMES). Though her later novels, which include the autobiographical *Mary Olivier: a Life* (1919) and its converse, *Life and Death of Harriet Frean* (1922), are modernist in narrative technique, they are also increasingly concerned with psychoanalytical factors. See Theophilus E. M. Boll, *Miss May Sinclair, Novelist: a Biographical and Critical Introduction*, 1972.

SINCLAIR, UPTON (1878–1968) American novelist, was born in Baltimore and moved with his family to New York in 1888. Kept at home until he was ten, he went through eight grammar school grades in two years, and entered the City College of New York at 13. After graduating, he financed himself as a special student at Columbia University by writing novelettes of military academy life as Lieutenant Frederick Garrison and Ensign Clarke Fitch. After several rejections, he privately printed his first novel, *Springtime and Harvest: a Romance* (1901): it was taken up commercially and reissued as *King Midas* (1901). This was the beginning of a long career that spanned over forty novels and numerous political and polemical prose works. With the proceeds from *The Jungle* (1906), a naturalistic exposé of the Chicago meat-packing trade, he established a cooperative socialist community, the Helicon Home Colony, in New Jersey. In 1934 he founded EPIC (End Poverty in California), on whose ticket he stood as Democratic candidate for the state governorship, and was only narrowly defeated. With *World's End* (1940), which begins at a music festival in Germany, he inaugurated a long sequence of novels about Lanny Budd, covering the international scene from 1911 to 1950; *Dragon's Teeth* (1942) won the Pulitzer Prize and was the basis of his nomination by G. B. SHAW for the Nobel Prize for Literature. See *The Autobiography of Upton Sinclair*, 1963.

SINGER, ISAAC BASHEVIS (1904–91) short-story writer, novelist, and children's writer in Yiddish, was born in Radzymin, Poland, and grew up in Warsaw, where his father was a rabbi, and where he went to the Tachkemoni Rabbinical Seminary. He worked as a proofreader on a literary journal and in 1926 began publishing stories in Hebrew, from which he switched to Yiddish, the living language of his childhood. He edited the magazine *Globus*, which in 1935 serialized his first novel (tr. Jacob Sloan as *Satan in Goray*, 1958). In 1935 he joined his brother, the novelist Israel Joshua Singer (1893–1944), in New York, where he became a prolific, valued, and lifetime contributor to the *'Jewish Daily Forward'*. He continued to write fiction, too, in Yiddish: 'I like to write ghost stories and nothing fits a ghost better than a dying language . . . ghosts love Yiddish, and as far as I know, they all speak it.' [*The Family Moskat*] (tr. A. H. Gross, 1950) was his first book to appear in English. Like [*The Manor*] (tr. Elaine Gottlieb and Joseph Singer, 1967) and [*The Estate*] (tr. Singer, Gottlieb, and Elizabeth Shub, 1969) it is a chronicle novel; together the three of them cover family life in Poland from 1863 to 1939. The publication in a translation by BELLOW of his story 'Gimpel the Fool' (*Partisan Review*, 1953), in which simple faith and innocence prevail, led to *Gimpel the Fool and Other Stories* (1957). In this and several subequent volumes, the last of them written when he was 84, he re-creates the lost world of Polish Jewry through humorous situations and poignant characters, with a dash of the supernatural, sometimes transposing his milieu to the New World— see *The Collected Stories* (1982).

He was concerned with recording Jewish society rather than trying to change it, and his innate exuberance particularly surfaces in [*The Fools of Chelm and Their History*] (tr. the author and Shub, 1973) and other notable children's books. 'I believe in story telling. . . . The events must speak for themselves,' he explained: and on another occasion, 'Asking the author for an interpretation of his books is like asking a chicken what chemicals it used when it laid an egg.' [*The Certificate*] (serialized 1967; tr. Leonard Wolf, 1993), the second of his works posthumously published in

book form, is a fictional counterpart to his autobiographical studies about his early struggles as an author and with his faith, and his disillusionment with Warsaw city life. He published several of these, notably *In My Father's Court* (tr. Channah Kleinerman-Goldstein and others, 1966), and *Love and Exile: the Early Years—a Memoir* (1984), incorporating three earlier volumes. He became an American citizen in 1943, and was awarded the Nobel Prize for Literature in 1978 for his 'impassioned narrative art which, with roots in a Polish-Jewish cultural tradition, brings universal conditions to life'. See Janet Hadda, *Isaac Bashevis Singer: a Life*, 1997; Lester Goran, *The Bright Streets of Surfside: the Memoir of a Friendship with Isaac Bashevis Singer*, 1994; Edward Alexander, *Isaac Bashevis Singer*, 1980 (biographical/critical study); Lawrence S. Friedman, *Understanding Isaac Bashevis Singer*, 1988.

SINGH, KHUSHWANT (*b.* 1915) Indian novelist, short-story writer, and historian, was born in Hadali (now in Pakistan) and educated in New Delhi at the Modern School and St Stephen's College, graduating from Government College, Lahore, in 1934. He then studied law at King's College, London, and was called to the English Bar in 1938. He practised in the High Court in Lahore until 1947, after which he became a press attaché to the Indian Foreign Service in London and Ottawa. He was a visiting lecturer at Oxford and at several universities in the USA between 1965 and 1969, when he became Editor of the *Illustrated Weekly of India*, Bombay. He subsequently held leading editorial posts on other national journals, and was elected to the Indian Parliament in 1980. His first book was *The Mark of Vishnu and Other Stories* (1950), a form of fiction in which he has played the part of an ironic observer—see *The Collected Short Stories* (1989). *Train to Pakistan* (1956, also known as *Mano Majra*), a short, tersely expressed, documentary novel of a village in the Punjab during the mass racial killings and counter-killings that followed Partition, is all the more effective because of the detached nature of the narrative. *I Shall Not Hear the Nightingale* (1959) is a much weaker account of some of the less attractive aspects of the national character. *Delhi* (1990), on which he worked for over twenty years, is a rich, exuberant, panoramic view of six hundred years of the history of the city, and especially of the Sikhs, ending on a note of tragedy with the aftermath of the assault on the Sikh temple at Amritsar.

SIRIN, V. see NABOKOV.

SISSON, C. H. see HEATH-STUBBS.

SITWELL, EDITH (1887–1964) British poet, anthologist, biographer, and critic, the elder sister of OSBERT and SACHEVERELL SIT-

WELL, was born in Scarborough and brought up at the family seat of Renishaw Hall, Derbyshire, where her early taste for literature and music, and her striking but unconventional looks, clashed with her parents' interests and ideals. She found no outlet for her talents until she left home in 1914 and published a volume of poetry, *The Mother* (1915). As a counterblast to what she saw as the reflectively rural nature of contributions to the series, *Georgian Poetry* (see RUPERT BROOKE), she edited annually from 1916 to 1921 *Wheels*, in each issue of which there appeared poems by all three Sitwell siblings, and in 1919 seven by OWEN. Her penchant for abstract phraseology and effects created by unusual vocal and tonic rhythms was made widely known by the public performance in 1923 of her poem-sequence, *Façade*, set to music by William Walton (1902–83). The verbal virtuosity stayed with her, but her subsequent poetry is equally concerned with symbolic contrasts, as in the long poem *Gold Coast Customs* (1929), in *Street Songs* (1942), and in *Green Song and Other Poems* (1944). Her critical and historical works include *Alexander Pope* (1930), *Aspects of Modern Poetry* (1934), *The English Eccentrics* (1933), and *The Queens and the Hive* (1962), on Elizabeth I. She was awarded honorary doctorates by four universities (and insisted on three suffixes of Hon. DLitt and one of Hon. LittD after her name) and was made DBE in 1954. See *Collected Poems*, new edn 1993; *Selected Letters*, ed. Richard Greene, 1997; Victoria Glendinning, *Edith Sitwell: a Unicorn among Lions*, new edn 1993 (biography); Maurice Bowra, *Edith Sitwell*, new edn 1982 (critical study).

SITWELL, (SIR) OSBERT, (5TH BARONET)(1892–1969) British poet, novelist, short-story writer, and prose writer, was born in London and educated at Eton. Having deliberately failed his entrance to military staff college, he was nevertheless persuaded to enter the Army in 1911, and served in France in World War I as an officer in the Grenadier Guards, from which he resigned in 1919. In the same year he published *The Winstonburg Line*, three satirical, pacifist poems. His satiric vein persisted in a further volume of verse, *Argonaut and Juggernaut* (1919), in three novels, *Before the Bombardment* (1926), *The Man Who Lost Himself* (1929), and *Miracle on Sinai* (1933), and in his first book of short stories, *Triple Fugue* (1924). Satire is tempered with compassion in *Dumb-Animal and Other Stories* (1930), and in three verse portraits, *England Reclaimed: a Book of Eclogues* (1927), *Wrack at Tidesend* (1952), and *On the Continent* (1958). His travel books, notably *Winters of Content* (1932) and *Escape with Me* (1939), are a judicious blend of description and art appreciation. His master-work is his autobiographical pageant of characters, observations, and experiences, published between 1944 and 1950 under the titles of *Left*

Hand, Right Hand!, *The Scarlet Tree*, *Great Morning!*, *Laughter in the Next Room*, and *Noble Essences*; with a postscript, *Tales my Father Taught Me* (1962). He succeeded to his father's title in 1943, and was made CBE in 1956, and CH in 1958. See *Collected Short Stories*, introduction by Francis King, 1974; John Pearson, *Façades: Edith, Osbert and Sacheverell Sitwell*, new edn 1989.

SITWELL, (SIR) SACHEVERELL, (6TH BARONET) (1897–1988) British poet, prose writer, and critic, was born in Scarborough and educated at Eton and Balliol College, Oxford, serving in the Grenadier Guards in World War I. His first book of verse, *The People's Palace*, was published in 1918. Subsequent volumes provided the basis of *Collected Poems* (1936) and *Selected Poems* (1948), after which, and until *An Indian Summer: 100 Recent Poems* (1982), it seemed that his crisp, linguistically intricate but descriptive style was out of fashion. His travels took him to almost every country of the world (in 1960 he was made a freeman of the city of Lima, Peru); he wrote revealingly as well as elegantly about many of them. His wide critical interests are demonstrated in his numerous books on art, architecture, music, and social history, and in philosophical and bibliographical works. He was the only one of the three Sitwell siblings to marry, which he did in 1925. He inherited his brother's title in 1969, and was made CH in 1984. See *All Summer in a Day: an Autobiographical Fantasia*, 1926; *For Want of a Golden City*, 1973 (autobiographical study); Sarah Bradford, *Sacheverell Sitwell: Splendours and Miseries*, 1993 (biography).

SKELTON, JOHN (*c.*1460–1529) English poet, went to Oxford and Cambridge universities, to both of which he was official poet. He took holy orders in 1498, when tutor to the future Henry VIII. From about 1502 to 1511 he was Rector of Diss, Norfolk, where, if we are to believe the jest-book, *Merie Tales Newly Imprinted and Made by Master Skelton* (1567), he had a fairly wild time and kept a mistress, by whom he had a child. Back at court, he was appointed Henry's poet laureate. His earliest works were translations from the Latin, after which he wrote *The Bowge of Courte* [Court Rations], a satirical poem in the form and metre of a dream allegory. Of the same period is *Magnificence*, a morality drama performed before Henry VII at Woodstock. Skeltonic verse has no consistent rhythm or line structure, only an irregularly imposed rhyme. In this jerky form he composed *Philip Sparrow*, a dirge for a pet bird which C. S. LEWIS in *English Literature in the Sixteenth Century* (1954) calls 'our first great poem of childhood', and *The Tunning of Elinor Rumming*, a somewhat coarse exposé of life in an alehouse presided over by a female publican whose real-life counterpart was in 1522 charged with overpricing and with serving short measures. He used rhyme royal for *Speak, Parrot*, but reverted to Skeltonics for *Colin Clout* and *Why Come Ye Not to Court*, all of which so lampooned Cardinal Wolsey (c.1475–1530) that the poet had to seek sanctuary. He emerged to make amends by dedicating to the prelate the poem known as *The Garland of Laurel* (1523), ostensibly an allegorical review of medieval poetry, which ends with seven lyrics addressed to various ladies of his acquaintance.

SKELTON, ROBIN (b. 1925) Canadian poet, critic, and editor, was born in England in Easington, Yorkshire, and educated at Pocklington School, York, Christ's College, Cambridge, and Leeds University. He lectured in English at Manchester University until 1963, when he emigrated to Canada and joined the English department of the University of Victoria, British Columbia, where he was Chairman, Department of Creative Writing 1973–76. A versatile poet whose first collection, *Patmos and Other Poems* (1955), and the four which followed were published in London, and *Selected Poems 1947–1967* (1968) initially in Toronto, he has become regarded as a significant writer of poetic exile. He has also contributed to the development of Canadian literature by his association with *Malahat Review* as co-founder and joint Editor (1967–71), and Editor (1972–83). His critical works include *The Poet's Calling* (1975), *Poetic Truth* (1978), and *Celtic Contraries: Selected Essays* (1990); among his many anthologies are *Poetry of the Thirties* (1964), *Poetry of the Forties* (1968), and *Two Hundred Poems from the Greek Anthology* (1971), which he also translated. See *The Collected Shorter Poems 1947–1977*, 1981; *The Collected Longer Poems*, 1985.

SLESSOR, KENNETH (1901–71) Australian poet and journalist, was born Schloesser (the family changed the name during World War I) in Orange, New South Wales, the son of a mining engineer and of the daughter of Scottish immigrants. He was educated at Sydney Church of England Grammar School, after which he became a journalist. In 1927 he joined the staff of the satirical *Smith's Weekly* in Sydney, becoming Editor in 1938. *Earth-Visitors* (1926) contained several poems which had appeared in the limited edition of *Thief of the Moon* (1924). It was followed by *Cuckooz Contrey* (1932) and *Five Bells: XX Poems* (1939), whose often-anthologized title poem is an elegy to a friend drowned in Sydney Harbour. Light verse written for *Smith's Weekly* appeared in *Darlinghurst Nights and Early Morning Glories* (1933). During World War II he was an official Australian war correspondent—see *War Diaries* (1985) and *War Despatches* (1987) ed. Clement Semmler—until his resignation after departmental criticism of his account of the

fighting in New Guinea. *One Hundred Poems 1919–1939* (1944) constituted all that he wanted preserving: he wrote only three more, which were incorporated in a revised edition, *Poems* (1957). He was a chief leader writer and Literary Editor of the Sydney *Sun* 1944–57, Editor of the literary journal *Southerly* 1956–61, and a leader writer for the Sydney *Daily Telegraph* 1957–69. 'Five Visions of Captain Cook' (1931) proved an influential poem on the themes of the voyager and discovery, and he is unequalled as a poet of the city of Sydney. *Bread and Wine: Selected Prose* was published in 1970, and further light verse in *Backless Betty from Bondi*, ed. Julian Croft (1984). He was made OBE in 1959. See Geoffrey Dutton, *Kenneth Slessor: a Biography*, 1991; Adrian Caesar, *Kenneth Slessor*, 1996 (biographical/critical study); Herbert C. Jaffa, *Kenneth Slessor: a Critical Study*, new edn 1977.

SMART, CHRISTOPHER (1722–71) British poet, was born in Shipbourne, Kent, the son of a steward to the Vane estates in that county. After his father's death in 1733, he was educated at Durham School and, thanks to an annuity from the Duchess of Cleveland, mother-in-law of Henry Vane, at Pembroke Hall, Cambridge, of which he became a Fellow. In 1749 debts, drink, and restlessness took him to London, where he lived as a hack writer. In spite of publishing *Poems on Several Occasions* (1752) and *The Hilliad* (1753), a satire on a medical quack, and winning the Seatonian prize at Cambridge for religious verse five times, his financial state was such that he is said in 1775 to have signed a 99-year lease on his exclusive services to the periodical, *Universal Visiter*. He developed symptoms of religious mania and was confined to various asylums between 1756 and 1763, during which time he was writing *Jubilate Agno* (not published until 1939), a rich amalgam of personal thoughts and devotions, in which occurs the minutely observed portrait of his cat ('For I will consider my Cat Jeoffry . . .'). *A Song to David* (1763), one of the most outstanding religious lyrical poems in the language, contains 86 rhyming stanzas, intricately arranged and crammed with strange and romantic images, and joyfully rising and falling to end with a triumphant climax. For the rest of his life he published translations, psalms, religious lyrics, and hymns, but in April 1770 he was committed as a debtor to the King's Bench prison, where he died. See *The Poetical Works*, ed. Marcus Walsh and Karina Williamson, 4 vols 1980–87; *The Religious Poetry of Christopher Smart*, ed. Marcus Walsh, 1972.

SMART, ELIZABETH see BARKER.

SMITH, A(RTHUR) J(AMES) M(ARSHALL) (1902–80) Canadian poet, anthologist, and critic, was born in West-mount, Montreal, of English immigrant parents. He was educated at Westmount High School and McGill University, where he initially did a BSc course, edited a literary supplement to the *McGill Daily*, and with F. R. SCOTT founded the *McGill Fortnightly Review*. He spent the years 1927–29 at Edinburgh University, where he wrote a thesis on the Metaphysical poets. Unable to find an academic job in Canada during the Depression, he went to the USA. In 1936 he found a permanent post at Michigan State University, where he remained until 1972, latterly as Poet-in-Residence as well as a professor of English. He became a US citizen, while retaining a home in Canada. With a group of poets who included Scott, KLEIN, and PRATT, he edited *New Provinces: Poems of Several Authors* (1936); he was persuaded to drop his preface criticizing and mocking older and more conventional Canadian poets. *The Book of Canadian Poetry* (1943; rev. edns 1948, 1957) gave a further fillip to Canadian poetry. Though his own verse had been widely published in journals since the 1920s, his first volume was *News of the Phoenix and Other Poems* (1943), which won the Governor General's Award. A skilful and versatile writer, whose range covers the bawdy as well as the austere, he was as constructively critical of his own work as of that of others; his five collections, of which the last was *The Classic Shade: Selected Poems* (1978), contain in all fewer than two hundred poems. Collections of prose are *Towards a View of Canadian Letters: Selected Critical Essays 1928–1971* (1973) and *On Poetry and Poets: Selected Essays of A. J. M. Smith* (1977). See Michael Darling, *A. J. M. Smith and His Works*, 1994.

SMITH, ADAM (1723–90) Scottish political economist, was born in Kirkcaldy, the posthumous son of the local customs controller, and was, it is said, kidnapped by gypsies when he was three, but quickly rescued. He was educated at the burgh school, Glasgow University, and Balliol College, Oxford, to which he won an exhibition. He then set up as a freelance lecturer in Edinburgh until his appointment in 1751 at Glasgow University as Professor of Logic, from which he transferred to the chair of Moral Philosophy the following year. In *The Theory of Moral Sentiments* (1759), which has elements of the doctrines of DAVID HUME, he made observations also about the state of English poetry. JOHNSON remarked, on hearing that BOSWELL had been a student of Smith at this time: 'Sir, I was once in company with Smith, and we did not take to each other; but had I known that he loved rhyme as much as you tell me he does, I should have hugged him.' In 1764 Smith resigned his post in favour of a life annuity of £300 a year to act as tutor to the young Duke of Buccleuch (1746–1812) on an

extended European tour. In 1766 he retired to Kirkcaldy to continue writing *An Inquiry into the Nature and Causes of the Wealth of Nations* (1776), an enormously influential and wide-ranging work in which he skilfully examined the forces contributing to world development. In 1778 he returned to Edinburgh as a commissioner of customs, living in the Canongate with his mother (who died in 1794 at the age of 89) and two cousins. *Essays on Philosophical Subjects* (1795), published posthumously, had a 'Biographical Memoir' by the philosopher, Professor Dugald Stewart (1753–1828). See *The Essential Adam Smith*, ed. Robert L. Heilbroner, 1986; Ian Simpson Ross, *The Life of Adam Smith*, 1995; D. D. Raphael, *Adam Smith*, 1985 (introduction to his work).

SMITH, ALEXANDER (1830–67) Scottish poet and prose writer, was born in Kilmarnock, the son of a lace-pattern designer, and was educated at a school in John Street in Glasgow, to which his parents had moved. Unwilling to go into the Church, he followed his father's trade. In 1846 he joined the Addisonian Literary Society, to which he contributed essays on literary and philosophical topics. His poems were printed in the *Eclectic* and *Critic*, and he came to the notice of the critic, Rev. George Gilfillan (1813–78), who wrote an effusive article in the *Critic* on 'A New Poet in Glasgow', and recommended his works to the students of Glasgow University. Assured now of an audience, Smith published *A Life-Drama and Other Poems* (1853), which in all sold the unprecedented number for a first book of poetry of nearly eleven thousand copies. With his earnings, this homely-looking young Scot took a trip to England, met MARTINEAU in the Lakes and SPENCER in London, and on his return spent a week at Inveraray Castle as the guest of the Duke of Argyll. Influential friends obtained for him the post of Secretary to Edinburgh University in 1854. *City Poems* (1857) had some merit, but his poetic reputation had been undermined by AYTOUN's satirical 'Firmilian'. *Edwin of Deira* (1861), a historical poem about the 7th-century King of Northumbria, suffered in comparison with TENNYSON's *The Idylls of the King*, and its author received just £15.5s.3d for his four years' labour. His prose works have proved more lasting, notably *Dreamthorp: a Book of Essays Written in the Country* (1863) and *A Summer in Skye* (1865), which has some graphic comparisons between industrial Glasgow and the natural beauties of the Isle of Skye. He died of typhoid.

SMITH, CHARLOTTE (1749–1806), née Turner, British novelist and poet, was born in London. Her mother died when she was three, and she was educated at boarding schools until she was 12. She married the son of a West India merchant in 1765; her first child died, and her second was born, when she was 17. More children followed, her husband was jailed for debt, and in 1784, to earn money, she published at her own expense *Elegiac Sonnets, and Other Essays*, of which there were further editions, with an additional volume in 1797. She then joined her degenerate husband in a decrepit chateau in France, where he had gone to escape his creditors. She left him in 1787 and returned to England. With eight children to support, she became a novelist with a sharp eye to middle-class tastes and a colourful sense of grievance against elements of society, notably lawyers, at whose hands she had herself suffered. After *Emmeline, the Orphan of the Castle* (1788), she produced in the next ten years nine more novels; *The Emigrants* (1793), a blank-verse poem on victims of the French Revolution; and several works for children. *The Old Manor House* (1793), which is regarded as her best novel, features her favourite theme (and personal anathema), a withheld inheritance, and is enhanced by lovers' separation, social satire, and loving descriptions of the English countryside. COWPER, who had heard her read extracts at the home of William Hayley (1745–1820), commented in a letter to a friend of the acquisition of a cask of gin and the expectation of a printed copy: 'How happy wouldst thou find thyself in the enjoyment of both these articles at once!' Though latterly afflicted by illness and family crises, she continued to send money to her husband. See *The Poems of Charlotte Smith*, ed. Stuart Curran, new edn 1995.

SMITH, IAIN CRICHTON (*b.* 1928) Scottish poet, novelist, and short-story writer, who also writes in Gaelic as Iain Mac a'Ghobhainn, was born in the Isle of Lewis and educated at the Nicolson Institute, Stornoway, and Aberdeen University. He taught English at Oban High School from 1955 to 1977. While his bilingualism has not elicited any dichotomy in his work (he has translated into English the poetry of MACINTYRE and MACLEAN, as well as his own short stories and verse), it has highlighted the conflicts between the Calvinistic discipline of the Free Kirk and the comparative freedom of his youth—reflected in the titles of his early collections of verse, *Thistles and Roses* (1961) and *The Law and the Grace* (1965)—and between the ancient Gaelic culture and the baseless culture of modern Scotland. *Ends and Beginnings* (1994) concludes with a long poem, written in the 'conspicuous phraseology' of the Old Testament, voicing his feelings about Christianity and its dogma. In his first novel, *Consider the Lilies* (1968), an elderly woman experiences the traumas of the Clearances in the 19th century—he frequently returns to the portrayal of old age in his fiction and verse, for example in the poem 'Old Woman'.

The Last Summer (1969) and *My Last Duchess* (1971) are in essence autobiographical novels, while in *The Dream* (1990) he explores the different reactions on the part of a Glasgow couple to the island of their birth and to the Highland tradition. The telling spareness in his capturing of images and situations is as effectively demonstrated in his short stories as it is in his poetry. He was made OBE in 1980. See *Collected Poems*, new edn 1995 (includes translations of his own poetry in Gaelic); *Listen to the Voice: Selected Stories*, introduction by Douglas Gifford, 1993; *A Life*, 1986 (verse autobiography).

SMITH, JOHNSTON see CRANE, STEPHEN.

SMITH, PAULINE (1882–1959) South African short-story writer, was born in Oudtshoorn, the daughter of an English resident physician to a predominantly Afrikaans area of Little Karoo, and his Scottish wife. She was educated by governesses, briefly at the Girls' High School, and sporadically, owing to illness, in Scotland and England. The sudden death in 1898 of her father, whose companion she had been on excursions to see patients, affected her deeply and cut her off from her childhood roots, though she revisited South Africa several times. Some of the items in *Platkops Children* (1935), a book of children's stories and verses, were written in her teens; sketches of Scottish life appeared in the *Aberdeen Free Press* under a pseudonym. When she was 26 she met BENNETT in Switzerland while travelling with her mother. A year later he records (in *Journals*, 13 October 1909): 'In the evening I got Pauline Smith to talk about her novel, but I think I mentioned it first. Sheer magnanimity and obstinacy mingled.' His faith in her ability slowly overcame her diffidence and countered the effect of a serious illness. In 1923, when she was living in Dorset, he put into Poole Harbour in his yacht and persuaded her to come for a sail. She showed him her story 'The Pain'. He sent it to the *Adelphi* magazine, which printed it and several more. Eight were published in *The Little Karoo* (1925; new edn, with the addition of 'Desolation' and 'The Father', 1930). For their depiction of the desolate existence of the poverty-stricken Afrikaner and for the craft of their writing, they represent an outstanding and unusual contribution to literature in English. Her novel, *The Beadle* (1926), demonstrates her depth of understanding of human nature in that a love story which has echoes of D. H. LAWRENCE is set within the broader framework of Afrikaner society. See *Stories, Diaries and Other Unpublished or Out-Of-Print Work*, ed. Ernest Deveira and Sheila Scholten, 1983; and in Kenneth Parker (ed.), *The South African Novel in English*, 1978.

SMITH, ROSAMOND see OATES.

SMITH, 'STEVIE' [FLORENCE MARGARET] (1902–71) poet and novelist, was born in Hull, the younger daughter of a consultant engineer who, when his business failed, left his family and went to sea. She was brought up in Palmers Green (then a country village outside London) by her mother and by an aunt, who features in her writing as the 'Lion' and with whom she later lived. After three years of tuberculosis, she was educated at Palmers Green High School and the North London Collegiate School. She then took a secretarial course at Mrs Hoster's and joined the publishing house of Newnes, where she worked until 1953. After trying to get some of her poems published and being advised instead to 'go away and write a novel', she did just that, typing it in the firm's time on the firm's 'very yellow' carbon-copy paper. *Novel on Yellow Paper* (1936), an autobiographical exercise in the free association of ideas and experience, was followed in the same vein by *Over the Frontier* (1938) and *The Holiday* (1949). Collections of her verse, with her spiky illustrations, began with *A Good Time Was Had by All* (1937), and include *Not Waving But Drowning* (1957), whose title poem begins: 'Nobody heard him, the dead man, / But he still lay moaning: / I was much further out than you thought / And not waving but drowning.' Her poetry, which often sprang from a news item, one of her own drawings, or a fleeting vision (as the incongruous sight of a cat on the London underground), can be grave or gay, kind or unkind, and frequently reflects the tensions in her own make-up. She died of a brain tumour, having several times contemplated, and at least once attempted, suicide. She was awarded the Queen's Gold Medal for Poetry in 1969. See *The Collected Poems of Stevie Smith*, ed. James MacGibbon, new edn 1985; *Selected Poems: a New Selection*, 1994; Frances Spalding, *Stevie Smith: a Critical Biography*, new edn 1990.

SMITH, SYDNEY GOODSIR (1915–75) Scottish poet, was born in Wellington, New Zealand, the son of (Sir) Sydney Smith (1883–1969), then a medical officer in the New Zealand Army Corps, and his Scottish wife. He was educated at Malvern College and, after an abortive attempt to read medicine at Edinburgh University, where his father was now Professor of Forensic Medicine, at Oriel College, Oxford. Unfit for military service, he taught English to Polish servicemen in Scotland during World War II. His first book of verse, *Skail Wind* (1941), contained several poems in Scots, including 'Epistle to John Guthrie', in which he justifies his use of that language: '. . . ye jist maun dree / My Scots; for English, man, 's near deid, / See the weeshy-washy London bree / An tell me then whaes bluid is reid!' The publication of *The Deevil's Waltz* (1946) coincided with the action of the group of Edinburgh poets called the Makars Club to rationalize the spelling of Scots, in which he is the principal poet of the Scottish Renaissance alongside MACDIARMID. His distinctive, often uproarious, and sometimes tender approach is best seen in *Under the Eildon Tree* (1948), 24 linked celebrations of love, evoking figures from classical and Celtic legend and history (as well as 16-year-old Sandra, picked up in an Edinburgh pub). Variously a freelance journalist, radio writer, and art critic for the *Scotsman*, he also wrote, in Scots, a verse play, *The Wallace* (1960), and a rambling, inventively expressed, comic novel of Edinburgh, *Carotid Cornucopia* (1947). See *Collected Poems 1941–1975*, introduction by Hugh MacDiarmid, 1975.

SMITHYMAN, KENDRICK (b. 1922) New Zealand poet and critic, was born in Te Kopuru, Auckland, and educated at Seddon Memorial Technical College, Auckland Teachers College, and Auckland University College. He served in the New Zealand forces in World War II, after which he taught in primary schools until 1963, when he became a senior tutor in the English department, Auckland University. *Seven Sonnets* (1946) was followed by *The Blind Mountain and Other Poems* (1950), and then by several further collections including *The Seal in the Dolphin Pool* (1974), in whose 'A Chip of Marble' he confesses, 'I could not get the hang / of evocation'. This belies one of the chief attributes of a poet whose realism is in the tradition of the 1930s, whose inventiveness reflects the American poetic influence of the immediate postwar period and his travel in Britain and North America, whose wit illuminates aspects of daily life, and whose voice, with that of BAXTER and CURNOW, is regarded as a central feature of postwar poetry in New Zealand. *A Way of Saying* (1965) was the first full-length study of New Zealand poetry. See *Selected Poems*, ed. Peter Simpson, 1990; *Auto/Biographies: Poems 1987, 1988, 1989*, 1993.

SMOLLETT, TOBIAS (1721–71) Scottish novelist, was born on his grandfather's estate in the Vale of Leven, Dunbartonshire, and was educated at Dumbarton Grammar School and Glasgow University, where he acquired a medical qualification. In 1740 he set out for London to find a producer for his verse tragedy, *The Regicide, or James I of Scotland*. When he failed to do so, he signed on as a ship's surgeon for the chaotic expedition against the Spanish in the West Indies. He was subsequently stationed in Jamaica, where he found his future bride, the Creole daughter of an English planter. He returned to England in 1744, having resigned his commission. An outspokenness towards his patients militated against his establishing a profitable practice but was an asset in journalism, which he exercised with two fairly ferocious Juvenalian satires, *Advice* (1746) and *Reproof* (1747), and other unmemorable topical verses. Then, as it were out of the blue, he produced an anonymous novel, *The Adventures of Roderick Random* (1748), a semi-autobiographical account, told with vivid detail, of a much put-upon Scot who joins the Navy, serves in the West Indies, and finally retrieves his lost fortunes. So good was it that it was thought to be the work of HENRY FIELDING, under whose name it was translated into French. Smollett responded in 1749 by resuscitating *The Regicide* and publishing it as 'by the author of Roderick Random'. Even after the success of *The Adventures of Peregrine Pickle* (1751), for which he had visited Paris in pursuit of first-hand material for its hero's Grand Tour, money problems loomed. Having obtained a medical degree from St Andrews University, he tried to set up practice in Bath, but the nearest he got to medical recognition, before devoting himself entirely to literature, was to assist Dr William Smellie (1697–1763), the celebrated obstetrician, with the revision of his *Treatise on Midwifery* (1752).

Typically, his next two novels, *The Adventures of Ferdinand, Count Fathom* (1753), an early terror story, and *The Adventures of Sir Launcelot Greaves* (1762), with a latter-day Don Quixote as hero, failed because of his determination to experiment. He had meanwhile translated (1755) the original *Don Quixote* of CERVANTES, and other Continental works. He also wrote a disconcertingly minatory travel guide, *Travels through France and Italy* (1766), which moved STERNE to dub him 'Smelfungus', and *A Complete History of England to 1748* (1757–58). He was Editor of the *Critical Review* 1756–63 (being imprisoned for three months in 1759 for impugning the courage of an admiral), the *British Magazine* 1760–67, and *The Briton* 1762–63. His last novel, *The Expedition of Humphry Clinker* (1771), in which a party of travellers wander through England and Scotland (revisited by him in 1766), is in letter form, with ever-changing points of view, frequent but forgivable prejudices, and superb humour and narrative timing. He never really recovered from the death of his 15-year-old daughter in 1763, and he spent much of the rest of his life abroad for his health, tended by his wife and by those foreign doctors whom he did not mistrust. He died at the villa they had taken near Livorno (Leghorn)—he was an advocate of the climate of the Mediterranean in the treatment of tuberculosis, from which he suffered. See Lewis M. Knapp, *Tobias Smollett: Doctor of Men and Manners*, new edn 1963; Paul-Gabriel Boucé, *The Novels of Tobias Smollett*, tr. Antonia White, 1976; and in Andrew Hook (ed.),

The History of Scottish Literature Vol. 2: 1660–1800, new edn 1989.

SNORRI STURLUSON (1179–1241) Icelandic poet and historian, was born on the estate of Hvamm, the son of a chief, and had a cultured upbringing at Odin, in the household of the learned Ion Loptsson. He was president of the Althing 1215–18 and 1222–31, having spent two of the intervening years in Norway and Sweden. In the end he meddled too much in international affairs and was assassinated by emissaries of Haakon IV of Norway. He is the author of two highly significant works: *Heimskringla* [Orb of the World], a collection of 17 sagas comprising a history of the kings of Norway from mythical times to 1177; and the *Prose Edda*, whose three parts constitute respectively a collection of Norse mythology, a study (with examples) of different forms of skaldic verse, and a treatise on Norse metre. The anonymous *Egil's Saga* (c.1230) has been attributed to him, in that it offers an overview of early Scandinavian and English history similar in conception to that of *Heimskringla*, with which it also shares an understanding of human character.

SNOW, (Sir) **C(HARLES) P(ERCY)** (1905–80) British novelist and critic, was born in Leicester, the son of a clerk in a shoe factory. He was educated at Alderman Newton's Grammar School and, for a career in science, at University College, Leicester. He went on to research in physics at the Cavendish Laboratory, Cambridge, becoming a Fellow of Christ's College in 1930, and being a college tutor from 1935 to 1945. When the results of his own research failed to confirm his expectations, he turned his attention to scientific administration and to the exposition of current scientific achievements, in which he saw himself being a social critic as well as a writer, though his first novel, *Death Under Sail* (1932), was a light detective story. During World War II he was Technical Director, Ministry of Labour, and from 1945 until his resignation from the civil service in 1960 he was a commissioner for the government recruitment of scientists. As a member of the House of Lords, he was Parliamentary Secretary, Ministry of Technology 1964–66. In 1935, after publishing *The Search* (1934), which centres on the vagaries of a scientific career, he conceived the idea for a sequence of novels which would reflect contemporary English society and issues. *Strangers and Brothers* (1940; reissued as *George Passant* in 1973, to allow the original title to be used for the series) is the first of 11 novels which draw on Snow's professional and personal experiences over the years, and in which Lewis Eliot, informed observer or sometimes chief protagonist, is his alter ego. *The Masters* (1951) and *The Affair* (1960) are exposures of university politics; nuclear scientists and moral dilemmas feature in *The New Men* (1954), and politicians in *Corridors of Power* (1964). His lectures at Cambridge, *The Two Cultures and the Scientific Revolution* (1959; introduction by Stephan Collini, 1993), reflecting upon the barriers of misunderstanding and ignorance between practitioners in science and the arts, provoked a fierce response from LEAVIS on the definition of 'culture'. Snow was made CBE in 1943, was knighted in 1957, and in 1964 became a life peer with the title of Baron Snow. In 1950 he married, as her second husband, the novelist Pamela Hansford Johnson (1912–81), whose main works are her first, *This Bed Thy Centre* (1935), and *The Unspeakable Skipton* (1959), based on the life of ROLFE.

SNYDER, GARY (*b*. 1930) American poet and essayist, was born in San Francisco and 'grew up in a rural family in the state of Washington. . . . I came here by a path, a line, of people that somehow worked their way from the Atlantic seaboard westward over 150 years. One grandfather ended up in the territory of Washington, and homesteaded in Kitsap County. My mother's side was railroad people down in Texas, and before that they'd worked the silver mines in Leadville, Colorado.' He was educated at Lincoln High School, Portland, Oregon, and Reed College, where he read anthropology. After studying linguistics at Indiana University, he returned West, and was associated with GINSBERG, KEROUAC (who portrayed him in *The Dharma Bums*), and other members of the San Francisco Renaissance, while at the same time reading classical Chinese at the University of California, Berkeley. Subsequently he judiciously combined the active with the contemplative. He has been a seaman on a South Pacific tanker, a logger, a timber scaler, and a forest-fire watcher on Sourdough Mountain, Alaska. In Japan between 1959 and 1968 he studied Buddhism under Zen teachers. His poetry, which includes tender expressions of eroticism, has reflected the life he was leading at the time. *Riprap*, his first collection—the term is one used by foresters—, was published in Japan in 1959, and subsequently incorporated in *Riprap, and Cold Mountain Poems* (1965). In *Myths and Texts* (1960) he used Native American folk material such as has informed his continuing interest in 'ethnopoetics', the recovery and transmission of tribal/oral poetry—see also *The Old Ways: Six Essays* (1977). *Earth House Hold* (1969) and *The Practice of the Wild* (1990) are influential volumes of essays on political and ecological issues. His collection of verse, *Turtle Island* (1974), won the Pulitzer Prize. In the subsequent collections *Axe Handles* (1983) and *Left Out in the Rain: New Poems 1947–1985* (1986) he further explores the validity of the cultural rehabilitation of the natural world. *Mountains and Rivers Without End* (1996) has been de-

scribed as an 'American epic poem'. Snyder became a professor at the University of California, Davis, in 1985. See Bob Steuding, *Gary Snyder*, 1976 (critical study); Patrick D. Murphy, *Understanding Gary Snyder*, 1992 (critical study).

SOLZHENITSYN, ALEXANDER (ISAYEVICH) (*b*. 1918) Russian novelist, was born in Kislovodsk in the northern Caucusus, the posthumous son of a student who had enlisted in the army and been killed six months previously, and of a shorthand typist. He was brought up in Rostov-on-Don, where he took a diploma in mathematics and physics at the university, while also completing a correspondence course at the Institute of Philosophy, Literature, and History in Moscow. In 1941 he was called up from his post as a physics teacher to be a driver of horse-drawn vehicles, from which he graduated to the artillery, serving as the commander of a gun position and becoming a twice-decorated captain. On 9 February 1945 he was arrested and stripped of his rank and medals for criticizing Stalin in a private letter to a friend. Having served five years' imprisonment in Moscow and then three years in a labour camp in Kazakhstan, where he developed stomach cancer, he was released into exile, from which he returned in 1956 to settle as a teacher in Ryazan, some two hundred kilometres south of Moscow. His first published work was [*One Day in the Life of Ivan Denisovich*] (1962; tr. Ralph Parker, 1963; tr. H. T. Willetts, 1991), a stark study of survival in a labour camp. In [*Cancer Ward*] (1968; tr. Nicholas Bethell and David Burg, 1969) and [*The First Circle*] (1968; tr. Michael Guybon, 1968), both first published outside the USSR, he explored, through the medium of his own experiences, philosophies of destiny and choice. Having been expelled from the Writers' Union in 1969, and awarded the Nobel Prize for Literature in 1970, he was in 1974 deported after the publication in Paris of the first two parts of his meticulous history of the Soviet penal system, [*The Gulag Archipelago*] (1973–76; tr. Thomas P. Whitney, 1974–78), following the suicide of his former assistant who, after five days of interrogation by the KGB, had revealed where she had hidden a copy of the complete work. See Michael Scammell (ed.) *The Solzhenitsyn Files*, tr. Catherine A. Fitzgerald and others (1995) for documents relating to his harassment by the Soviet authorities.

In 1976 he settled with his second wife and children in the USA, on an estate in the mountains near Vermont, where he gave the place the aspect of a labour camp, and lived an ascetic existence in a hut in the grounds. Here he continued his projected novel cycle of modern Russian history, ['The Red Wheel'], which began with [*August 1914*] (1971; tr. Michael Glenny, 1972), employing a variety of additional narrative techniques drawn from non-fiction writing, newspaper journalism, and film making. He returned permanently to Russia in 1994, to a tumultuous reception from the general public. [*The Oak and the Calf*] (1975; tr. Willetts, 1980) is an autobiographical study of literary life in the USSR. [*Invisible Allies*] (1991; tr. Alexis Klimoff and Michael Nicolson, 1996) is an account of the underground network which supported his opposition to the Soviet establishment, written in Zurich before he came to the USA. *'The Russian Question' at the End of the Twentieth Century*, tr. Yermolai Solzhenitsyn (1995), written just before his return, is a historical essay centring on the rules of the tsars.

SOMERS, JANE see LESSING, DORIS.

SOMERVILLE,   E(DITH)   O(E-NONE) (1858–1949) Irish novelist, was born in Corfu, where her father, a colonel in the Buffs, was stationed. She was educated by governesses at the family seat of Drishane, Castletownshend, Co. Cork, and briefly at Alexandra College, Dublin. She studied painting in Dusseldorf and Paris in 1884. In 1886, while working at home on a commission to illustrate three serials for the *Graphic*, she first met her second cousin, Violet Martin (1862–1915), who, as 'Martin Ross', became her literary collaborator. Out of their unique rapport, the nature of which has never satisfactorily been explained, came *An Irish Cousin* (1889), a curious blend of Irish Gothic and social comment. Their third joint venture into fiction, *The Real Charlotte* (1894), for its depiction of society, its subtle narrative and dialogue, and its characterization, especially of the eponymous anti-heroine, is regarded as the finest Irish novel of that period. The stories in *Some Experiences of an Irish R. M.* (1899) were conceived in response to a request from *Badminton Magazine*, and were largely written while Martin was severely incapacitated after a fall while hunting. Nevertheless this and its sequels, *Further Experiences of an Irish R. M.* (1908) and *In Mr Knox's Country* (1915), are comic masterpieces of misunderstandings and sporting occasions, as an ex-Indian army officer from England adjusts to being a resident magistrate in rural Ireland. Martin's name as co-author, and her spiritualistic intervention, were still attributed after her death to several novels, of which *The Big House of Inver* (1925), a story of family social and economic decline, is the most notable. Somerville, having been Master of the West Carbery Fox Hounds 1903–08 and 1912–19, reverted to her secondary occupation of painting, of which she held several exhibitions in London and two in New York. She continued to live at Drishane until 1946, when with her sister she moved to a house in the village appropriately called 'Tally-Ho'.

See *Selected Letters*, ed. Gifford Lewis, 1989; Gifford Lewis, *Somerville & Ross: the World of the Irish R. M.*, 1985 (biography); Hilary Robinson, *Somerville and Ross: a Critical Appreciation*, 1980.

SOPHOCLES (496–406 BC) classical Greek dramatist, was born in Colonus, near Athens, and defeated Aeschylus for the drama prize in 468. His some 120 plays, the last of which, *Oedipus at Colonus*, was finished just before his death, included 18 prize-winning tetralogies. As well as making the action depend more on the will of the characters than of the gods, he introduced the third actor, and was the first to use a scene-painter. Only seven tragedies survive. Of these, *King Oedipus*, in which the truth is revealed that Oedipus has slain his father and married his mother, and *Antigone*, whose heroine stands up for her rights, live on particularly in the modern imagination and demonstrate to the full the ability of Sophocles to illustrate human suffering and emotions. His influence on English literature, and on Western thought as a whole, is considerable. MILTON was steeped in his work, and *Samson Agonistes* particularly recalls aspects of *Oedipus at Colonus*. ARNOLD is probably thinking of the same play when he refers to Sophocles in 'Dover Beach'. SWINBURNE's *Atalanta in Calydon* is a tribute to the classical Greek dramatists, and its popular success at the time is a reflection of the poetic quality of the choral odes of Sophocles. From his reading of Sophocles FREUD derived the term 'Oedipus complex' as the basis of his theory of infant sexuality. YEATS wrote, from various translations, poetically and dramatically effective versions of the two Oedipus plays, whose intensity was such that during a performance in 1927 the barking of a phantom dog was heard. POUND and HEANEY are other modern poets who have produced versions of the plays in English. Sophocles was a popular personage in his own time, and was in 440 elected one of the ten generals deputed to sort out the troublesome Samians. As a founder-member of the guild or college of Asclepius, he was effectively responsible for introducing to Athens the craft of medicine. See *The Theban Plays: Oedipus the King, Oedipus at Colonus, Antigone*, ed. David Grene and Richard Lattimore, 1994.

SORLEY,   CHARLES   HAMILTON (1895–1915) Scottish poet, was born in Aberdeen, the second child and elder twin son of Professor William Sorley (1855–1935), who in 1900 moved with his family to Cambridge, where he had been appointed to the chair of Moral Sciences. He was educated at Marlborough College, where he gained a reputation as a fearless literary critic and a precocious poet. Having won a scholarship to University College, Oxford, he spent the first few months of 1914 with a family in Mecklen-burg, and then enrolled for a term at the uni-versity at Jena. He was on a walking tour in the Moselle when Austria-Hungary declared war on Serbia, and with a friend was impris-oned for several hours as a spy. Back in En-gland, he enlisted and was straightaway com-missioned in the Suffolk Regiment. Though he was one of the first officers in the newly-formed 'Kitchener's Army', his attitude to war, fostered by his months in Germany, was ambivalent—expressed in the plea for mu-tual understanding of 'To Germany' and in the irony of 'All the Hills and Vales Along'. His battalion was posted to France in May 1915, and was moved into the support trenches in July, and into the front line at the beginning of the battle of Loos, by which time he had been promoted to captain. Towards the end of October, overdue for leave, he was killed by a sniper's bullet. The sonnet beginning 'When you see millions of the mouthless dead / Across your dreams in pale battalions go . . .' was found in his kit when it was returned to England. GRAVES, re-cording the fact of his death in *Goodbye to All That*, refers to him as 'one of the three poets of importance killed in the war', the others being OWEN and ROSENBERG. See *The Poems and Selected Letters of Charles Hamilton Sorley*, ed. Hilda D. Spear, 1978.

SOUSTER, RAYMOND (*b.* 1921) Cana-dian poet, was born in Toronto, of which he has said: 'Toronto has a flavour all its own. . . . My roots are here; this is the place that tugs at my heart when I leave it and fills me with quiet relief when I return to it.' He was edu-cated at Toronto University schools and for a year at the Humberside Collegiate Institute, after which, except for war service in the Royal Canadian Air Force, he worked for the Canadian Bank of Commerce in Toronto until 1984. He published his first 'little magazine', *Direction*, while in the Air Force, and his first book of verse, *When We Are Young*, in 1946. A significant offshoot of *Contact*, which he founded in 1952, and which survived until 1954, was Contact Press, which he ran with DUDEK and LAYTON as a literary publishing house from 1952 to 1967. Described as an urban imagist, his best poetry, which is spread through many collections, of which *The Colour of the Times* (1964) won the Gover-nor General's Award, is to be found among his shorter lyrics. See *Collected Poems 1940–1988*, 7 vols 1980–92; Bruce Whiteman, *Raymond Souster and His Works*, 1985.

SOUTAR, WILLIAM (1898–1943) Scot-tish poet, was born in Perth, the son of a joiner, and was educated at Perth Academy until 1916, when he was conscripted into the Royal Navy. Symptoms appeared of what in 1924 was diagnosed as the spine disease which was to cripple and kill him, but after

demobilization he took a degree in English at Edinburgh University, having in 1923 pub-lished anonymously a book of poems, *Glean-ings by an Undergraduate*. An operation in 1930 failed to halt his condition, and he noted in his diary that 3 November of that year was the last day on which he was able to get out of bed. His father extended his ground-floor bedroom, and for 13 years he carried on a he-roic existence, dispassionately recorded, to-gether with his views on poetry, politics, and metaphysics, in a series of remarkable jour-nals—see *Diaries of a Dying Man*, ed. Alexan-der Scott (1954). He was now writing also in Scots, about which he stated to MACDIARMID, 'If the Doric is to come back alive, it will come first on a cock-horse.' True to his con-viction, he produced *Seeds in the Wind: Poems in Scots for Children* (1933; rev. edn 1943) which, together with *Riddles in Scots* (1937) and the posthumously published 'Whigma-leeries', constitute the most significant collec-tion of verse for children in the language. All his poems are short, and to the point. He wrote better in Scots than in English (though some of his English poems about World War II have a neat, sardonic ring), and by continu-ous experiment he enriched the language and its poetic range, not least through his 'Themes and Variations', for which he would use English poems and translations from many languages as starting points for new poems in Scots. See *Poems of William Soutar: a New Selection*, ed. W. R. Aitken, 1988.

SOUTHALL, IVAN (*b.* 1921) Australian children's novelist, was born in Canterbury, Victoria, and left Box Hill Grammar School at 14 to work for the Melbourne *Herald* as an engraver. He joined the Royal Australian Air Force in 1942, and served in England in Coastal Command, captaining a Sunderland flying boat and winning the Distinguished Flying Cross for an action in which a U-boat was sunk—see his short personal account of the war, *Flying West* (1974). In 1960, having been freelance since 1947 and written nine adventure stories for boys about the exploits of a RAAF pilot, he 'woke up one morning determined never to write another book for children. The dear little darlings could go jump in the lake.' Then, there being a delay in the research for his next adult documentary book, he embarked on a novel, which 'began to look like the source of a story that might involve children of the ordinary kind'. *Hills End* (1962) was the first of several books in which a group of children face up to an exter-nal disaster. Subsequent novels, of which *Josh* (1971) won the British Library Association's Carnegie Medal, have tended to concentrate on the joys and agonies of a single character, and particularly on the traumas of growing up and seeking a personal identity. He was made AM in 1981. See *A Journey of Discovery: Writing for Children*, 1975 (essays).

SOUTHERN(E), THOMAS (1660–1746)
Irish dramatist, was born in Oxmantown, near Dublin, and educated at Trinity College, Dublin, after which, in 1678, he entered the Middle Temple to study law. In his first play, the tragedy *The Loyal Brother* (1682), for which DRYDEN supplied a prologue and epilogue, the virtuous prince represents the Catholic Duke of York, later James II. *The Disappointment* (1684) is a domestic drama. In 1685 he joined the Army as an ensign, but after he had quickly risen to command a company, his military prospects were dashed by the abdication of James II. He now reverted to his literary career, and produced a comedy, *Sir Anthony Love* (1690), whose popularity he acknowledged was due mainly to the fact that the name part was written for and played by the talented Mrs Mountfort (1667–1703). A less successful, but better, comedy is *The Wives Excuse: or, Cuckolds Make Themselves* (1692). The best of all his works are the tragedies *The Fatal Marriage* (1694) and *Oronooko* (1696), both based on stories by BEHN. By all accounts a highly respected man, to whom Dryden entrusted the revision and completion of his tragedy, *Cleomenes* (1692), he managed his affairs better than most of his calling, being described by POPE as 'Tom, whom Heaven sent down to raise / The price of prologues and of plays'. See *The Works of Thomas Southerne*, ed. Robert Jordan and Harold Love, 2 vols 1988; John W. Dodds, *Thomas Southerne, Dramatist*, new edn 1970.

SOUTHEY, ROBERT (1774–1843) British
poet and prose writer, was born in Bristol, the son of a draper, but was largely brought up by an eccentric maiden aunt in Bath. Having been expelled from Westminster School for publishing a magazine, the *Flagellant*, which denounced flogging, he was accepted by Balliol College, Oxford, where he wrote a lot of bad verse, went on the river, and thought up ways of getting out of going into the Church, which his family expected him to do. The 'Pantisocracy', the self-governing, self-reliant society in America which he devised with COLERIDGE, came to nothing, but after he left Oxford in 1794 without taking his degree, he rather established a small commune in a cramped Bristol flat. In 1795, having published *Poems* with Robert Lovell (1770–96), and sold *Joan of Arc: an Epic Poem* (1796), he secretly married his fiancée, Edith Fricker, from whom he parted on the same day to go with his uncle to Lisbon. On his return he made an attempt to study law, but was unable to go along with it. He now became a full-time writer and journalist. *Poems* (2 vols 1797–99) was followed by *Thalaba the Destroyer* (1801), the first of several narrative poems based on his voluminous reading. In 1803 he was finally persuaded to join the Coleridge household at Greta Hall, Keswick, where he remained for the rest of his life,

supporting his family, and some of the Coleridges as well, by the prodigious output of his pen.

In 1813 WALTER SCOTT turned down the Poet Laureateship on the grounds that he already held two crown appointments as a lawyer, and recommended Southey as being more needful if not more deserving of the post. Southey's acceptance, and his subsequent support of moves to eradicate sedition and public dissent, turned to embarrassment when *Wat Tyler*, a product of his radical youth, the manuscript of which he had presumed lost, was published in 1817 without his permission. Though he was in his day something of a poetic innovator, apart from a few poems, such as 'Inchcape Rock', 'My days among the Dead are passed . . .', and 'The Battle of Blenheim' (with its ironic refrain, 'But 'twas a famous victory'), and his succinct *The Life of Nelson* (1813), he is remembered as the faithful friend of Coleridge and WORDSWORTH, and the butt of BYRON'S *The Vision of Judgement*. Edith died, insane, in 1837, and with his own mind now failing, he married Caroline Bowles (1786–1854), a very minor poet with whom he had corresponded for twenty years. See Mark Storey, *Robert Southey: a Life*, 1997.

SOYINKA, WOLE (AKINWANDE OLUWOLE SOYINKA) (b. 1934) Nigerian dramatist, poet, novelist, and critic, was born of a Yoruba family in Abeokuta, Western Nigeria, the son of the Headmaster of St Peter's School and of the founder of the local Women's Union group; he calls her the 'Wild Christian' in his affectionate early reminiscences, *Aké: the Years of Childhood* (1981). He was educated at St Peter's, Abeokuta Grammar School, Government College, Ibadan (to which he won a scholarship at his second attempt), and University College, Ibadan, after two years at which he went to England, graduating in English at Leeds University in 1957. He was already writing plays. He himself produced *The Swamp Dwellers* as an entry for the London University Drama Festival in 1958; it was performed at the Arts Theatre, Ibadan, with his *Lion and the Jewel* in 1959. He was now a script reader at the Royal Court Theatre, London, where in 1959 he presented his own programme of readings, songs, and a nightmarish one-act political satire on South Africa, *The Invention*. Back in Nigeria he wrote a one-act comedy, *The Trials of Brother Jero* (produced 1960), to which *Jero's Metamorphosis* (1973) is a sequel. He also completed, directed, and acted in his ambitious symbolic drama, *A Dance of the Forests*, presented by his own company, the 1960 Masks, for the celebration of Nigerian independence in October 1960, at which it won the prize offered by the British literary journal, *Encounter*. Then came his three tragedies: *The Strong Breed* (1964), with its scapegoat theme; *Kon-*

gi's *Harvest* (1964), which is also a satire on the contemporary political scene; and *The Road* (1965), in which he uses sharp action, a variety of styles of dialogue, and elements of Yoruba culture in an exploration of the essence of death. In 1965 he published his first novel, *The Interpreters*, a study of the relationship between human personality and fate. He was also in police custody for several weeks, on a charge of substituting a tape of a spoof election broadcast for the official one; he was acquitted for lack of evidence. The image of the road as an altar upon which lives are senselessly sacrificed in the interests of progress recurs in and informs the first collection of his poetry, *Idanre and Other Poems* (1967), in which is none of his earlier, satirical verse.

In 1967 he was appointed Head of the Department of Dramatic Arts at Ibadan University, but before he could take up the post he was hunted by the military authorities and the secret police for his public denunciation of the civil war and for his efforts to avert it. He was held without trial for 26 months, 23 of them in solitary confinement—see his account, *The Man Died: Prison Notes* (1972)—, during which he wrote fragments of verse, drama, and prose between the lines of books smuggled in to him. The poems are collected in *A Shuttle in the Crypt* (1972), which includes the two which he managed to smuggle out, published as *Poems from Prison* (1969). Other writings drafted during his incarceration include the allegorical drama of evil, *Madmen and Specialists* (published 1971), and a second novel, *Season of Anomy* (1973). In 1970 he gave up his post at Ibadan to devote his time to writing, and went into exile to avoid being involved in political debate. He returned after the fall of the prevailing regime in 1975 to be Professor of Comparative Literature and Head of the Department of Dramatic Arts, Ife University, where he founded a roving company, the Guerrilla Theatre, to present his 'shot-gun sketches' of political satire.

Ogun Abibimañ (1976) is a long poem inspired by Mozambique's stand against Rhodesia. It celebrates, through the intervention of Ogun, Yoruba god of iron, war, and hunting, a union of African divisions which will liberate South Africa, a theme to which *Mandela's Earth and Other Poems* (1988) is also devoted. He retired from Ife in 1985 and returned to Abeokuta, subsequently going into voluntary exile again as a result of the continuation of military rule in Nigeria—in *The Open Sore of a Continent: a Personal Narrative of the Nigerian Crisis* (1996) he explores the history of and future for his country. *The Beatification of an Area Boy*, first performed in Leeds in 1995, is a comedy about modern Nigeria at whose heart lies a chilling realism. In *Isarà: a Voyage around 'Essay'* (1989) he constructs an imaginative biography of his father (whose nickname was 'Essay', standing for his ini-

tials), using as starting points documents he found in an old tin box. His critical works include *Essays on Literature and Culture*, ed. Biodun Jeyifo (1988). He was awarded the Nobel Prize for Literature in 1986. See *Collected Plays 1*, 1973, and *2*, 1974; *Six Plays*, 1984; *Ibadan: the Penkelemes Years—a Memoir 1945–1967*, new edn 1995; Eldred D. Jones, *The Writing of Wole Soyinka*, rev. edn 1988; and in Jane Wilkinson (ed.), *Talking with African Writers*, 1992.

SPARK, MURIEL (*b.* 1918), née Camberg, British novelist, short-story writer, poet, and critic, was born in Edinburgh of a Jewish father (her mother was English), and was educated at James Gillespie's School for Girls, Edinburgh, and Heriot Watt College, where she sought to complete her 'education in English prose' while studying technical subjects. She was a teacher in a boys' school in return for being taught shorthand and typing, and then worked in an exclusive Princes Street department store. Having concluded that 'in order to write about life as I intended to do, I felt I had first to live', she became engaged to a teacher 13 years her senior, and joined him in Southern Rhodesia (Zimbabwe), where they were married in 1937. The marriage collapsed, and in 1944 she returned to Britain, where an enthusiasm for the work of COMPTON-BURNETT landed her a secretarial job in the political intelligence department of MI6. She was General Secretary of the Poetry Society and Editor of *Poetry Review* 1947–49. At this time she was writing critical and biographical works and poetry—see *Collected Poems* (1967)—but she turned to writing fiction after winning the *Observer* short-story competition in 1951.

She became a Catholic in 1954, which superimposed an intellectual pattern on the conflicting elements of her upbringing and earlier years. She established her distinctive novel-writing process from a conviction that 'any good novel, or indeed any composition which called for a constructional sense, was essentially an extension of poetry'. Her first novel, *The Comforters* (1957), established her motif of the social or cultural misfit, or loner in a society of misfits, which recurs especially in *The Ballad of Peckham Rye* (1960), *The Driver's Seat* (1970), *Loitering with Intent* (1981), and *A Far Cry from Kensington* (1988). In her most widely-publicized novel, *The Prime of Miss Jean Brodie* (1961), a strong-willed but obtusely arrogant schoolmistress is the architect of her own destruction. Sinister figures hover round the bizarre dinner party guests in *Symposium* (1990), one of whom is a witch. In her 20th novel, a further black comedy, *Reality and Dreams* (1996), a film director's art and his life become confused in 'the tract of no-man's land between dreams and reality'. Muriel Spark's dialogue has the precision of a poet and the wit of a skilled satirist, while her eye for the bizarre and her skill as a short-story writer—see *The Collected Stories* (1994)—enable her to crystallize a character, a situation, or a complete milieu in a few paragraphs, or even words.

In 1963, life in London became 'impossible. I felt that I had lost my privacy, my freedom.' She moved to New York, where the Editor of the *New Yorker*, in which much of her work has first appeared, gave her an office overlooking Times Square. In 1967 she transferred to Rome, getting herself 'admitted to the Salvator Mundi hospital' when she needed the privacy in which to finish a book. Since the 1980s she has lived permanently in a 14th-century priest house in Tuscany. She was made OBE in 1967, and DBE in 1993. Winner of David Cohen Prize for British Literature in 1977. See *Curriculum Vitae*, new edn 1994 (autobiography to 1957); Norman Page, *Muriel Spark*, 1990 (critical study); Judy Sproxton, *The Women of Muriel Spark*, 1992 (critical study).

SPENCER, ELIZABETH (*b.* 1921) American novelist and short-story writer, was born in Carrollton, Mississippi, into a family which on both sides had farmed in Carroll County since the 1830s. As a child she spent much time at the family plantation owned by her mother's father, a former county sheriff. A lifelong storyteller, she was educated at J. Z. George High School, Carrollton, and Belhaven, the Presbyterian college for women in Jackson, after which she did a MA thesis on YEATS at Vanderbilt University, where her tutor was the poet-critic Donald Davidson (1893–1968). After two years as a schoolteacher, she became a reporter on the Nashville *Tennessean*, while taking an evening course in short-story writing. She resigned in 1946 to work full time on a novel, *Fire in the Morning* (1948), a story of dark secrets, family hatreds, and reconciliation. She was a member of the English faculty of the University of Mississippi from 1948 to 1953, during which time she wrote *This Crooked Way* (1952). In 1953 she went to Italy on a Guggenheim Fellowship and met John Rusher (*b.* 1920), an Englishman who was director of a language school in Rome; they were married in Cornwall, UK, in 1956. *The Voice at the Back Door* (1956), about 'the confrontation of races on the local level' is her final fictional statement in the Southern literary tradition and her strongest novel. Its publication marked a watershed in her life. In 1957 the *New Yorker* published her short story, 'The Little Brown Girl', which it had rejected in 1947—her only published story had been 'Pilgrimage' (1950). In 1958 she and her husband settled in Montreal, Canada. In *The Light in the Piazza* (1960), published also in the *New Yorker* in its entirety, she turned to a female protagonist and an international setting, as she did again in *No Place for an Angel* (1967) and *The Snare*

(1972). Male protagonists, complex relationships, and the Mississippi coast after the 1969 hurricane, are features of *The Salt Line* (1985).

In the meantime Spencer developed her shorter fiction, a recurrent theme of which she has described as 'liberation and the regret you have when you liberate yourself'. Her first collection, *Ship Island and Other Stories* (1968), was reprinted with *Knights and Dragons* (1965), a novella about a guilt-ridden American woman in Italy, in *The Stories of Elizabeth Spencer* (1981)—see also *Jack of Diamonds and Other Stories* (1988) and *On the Gulf* (1991). *Marilee* (1981) comprises three stories of a young woman growing up in the South who has affinities with Spencer had she stayed in Mississippi and not become a writer. See Peggy Whitman Prenshaw, *Elizabeth Spencer*, 1985 (biographical/critical study).

SPENCER, HERBERT (1820–1903) British philosopher, was born in Derby, the eldest and only survivor of eight children of a teacher of mathematics. He was educated locally until he was 13, when he was sent to an uncle, Thomas Spencer (1796–1853), the social reformer, who was perpetual Curate of Hinton Charterhouse, near Bath. After literally running away (he did the 120-mile journey home on foot in three days), he was sent back, and stayed for three years. In 1837 he became a civil engineer on the railways, but was made redundant in 1841 when the line on which he was working was completed. After dabbling in political and technical journalism, he was in 1848 appointed a subeditor on the *Economist*, with free accommodation and tickets to the theatre and opera, of which he was the journal's critic. He now wrote his first book, *Social Statics, or the Conditions Essential to Human Happiness Specified . . .* (1850). 'Human happiness', to him, did not include marriage to Marian Evans (GEORGE ELIOT), whom he much admired for her intellect, and who probably would have married him, but her lack of 'physical beauty' (as he later explained to friends) disqualified her. In 1853, having been left £500 by his uncle, he gave up his job and went on the Continent. He returned complaining of 'signs of an enfeebled action of the heart', which enabled him to act the eccentric hypochondriac for the rest of his bachelor life. In his monumental 'System of Synthetic Philosophy' (announced in 1860, published 1862–96), *First Principles, The Principles of Biology, The Principles of Psychology* (originally published in 1855, but now revised), *The Principles of Sociology*, and *The Principles of Ethics*, he attempted a synthesis of human knowledge according to the laws of evolution.

SPENDER, (Sir) STEPHEN (HAROLD) (1909–95) British poet, critic, editor, and translator, was born in London (half German and 'at least one quarter Jewish'), and spent his childhood 'in a style of austere comfort against a background of calamity'. He was educated at University College School and University College, Oxford, where he was a friend of MACNEICE and was approved of by AUDEN. 'Still at the stage of putting my money on an appearance of madness in my poems', in 1928 he produced on a small hand press editions of about thirty copies each of *Nine Experiments* 'by S. H. S.' and *Poems* by Auden. He left Oxford after two years without finishing his degree, and from 1930 to 1933 spent half the year in Germany, where he was caught up in the political and social unrest of the times, which along with his personal uneasiness is reflected in *Poems* (1933) and in the critical work, *The Destructive Element: a Study of Modern Writers and Beliefs* (1935)—his experiences in Germany were also reflected in *The Temple*, a novel written at this time but not published until 1988 on the grounds of indecency and potential libel.

With the experience also of the Spanish Civil War (1936–39)—expressed in his collection *The Still Centre* (1939)—he is regarded primarily as a poet of the 1930s, to which many of his best-known and most memorable poems belong: 'A Stop Watch and an Ordnance Map', 'The Express', 'Two Armies', 'An Elementary School Classroom', and 'The Pylons', from which derived the name of the Pylon school of poets, whose work was concerned with modern industrial development. He was founder-Editor with CONNOLLY of the literary magazine *Horizon* 1934–41, and co-Editor of *Encounter* 1953–66, in which many new authors were brought to public notice, and contemporary literary controversies were aired. As translator as well as poet, he enabled the work especially of GÁRCIA LORCA and RILKE to be read in English. He was in 1966 the first non-American to be appointed Consultant in Poetry to the Library of Congress. He was Professor of English Literature, University College, London 1970–77. He was awarded the Queen's Gold Medal for Poetry in 1971, made CBE in 1962, and knighted in 1983. An unauthorized biography published in 1992 raised questions of the morality as well as of the dangers of writing about living people who wish to preserve their privacy. While Spender was unsuccessful in his attempt to get that book suppressed, a novel published shortly afterwards, to which he objected on the grounds that it breached the copyright in his autobiography, *World Within World* (1951), was withdrawn before the case came to court, only to be reissued in 1996 after the poet's death. See *Collected Poems 1928–1985*, new edn 1989; *Dolphins*, 1993 (subsequent collection); *World Within World*, new edn 1991, and *The Thirties and After: Poetry, Politics, People (1933–1975)*, 1978 (memoirs); *Journals 1939–1983*, ed. John Goldsmith, new edn 1992.

SPENSER, EDMUND (1552–99) English poet, was born in London and educated at Merchant Taylors' School from its foundation in 1561 until 1569, when he went to Pembroke Hall, Cambridge, as a sizar, graduating as MA in 1576. Gabriel Harvey (c.1549–1630), a Fellow of the college and a teacher of rhetoric, introduced him to the Earl of Leicester (c.1532–88), a favourite of Elizabeth I, and to Leicester's nephew, SIDNEY, to whom Spenser dedicated *The Shepheardes Calender* (1579). This series of 12 eclogues, one for each month of the year, in which the poet appears as Colin Clout, represents a return to pastoral verse and to the language of CHAUCER; it also contradicts the correspondence between Spenser and Harvey published in 1580 (*Three Proper, and Wittie, Familiar Letters* and *Two Other Very Commendable Letters*), in which among observations about earthquakes is an exploration of the use of Latin and Greek metres for English poetry. In 1579 Spenser married Machabyas Childe, by whom he had two children. In 1580 he went to Ireland as secretary to the new Governor, Lord Grey of Wilton (1536–93). His administrative career flourished, and he collected various posts and sinecures after Grey's recall in 1582, being in 1590 formally assigned the estate and castle of Kilcolman, Co. Cork.

Spenser had begun writing *The Faerie Queen* in 1580, but it was not until 1589, on a visit to London, that he found a publisher for the first three books, which appeared under his own name in 1590, with a dedication to Elizabeth I, who responded by awarding him a pension for life of £50 a year. The same publisher, William Ponsonbie (c.1546–1604), 'dwelling in Paules Churchyard at the figure of the Bishops Head', issued in 1591 *Daphnaïda: an Elegie upon the Death of . . . Douglas Howard* (daughter of Lord Howard), and *Complaints*, a collection of splendid longer poems (including 'The Ruines of Time', 'Virgil's Gnat', and 'Mother Hubberds Tale') which had to be withdrawn as two of them contained unkind allusions to the Lord Treasurer, Lord Burleigh (1520–98). *Colin Clouts Come Home Againe* (1595) was written in 1591 and is prefaced by a letter to RALEGH, who had sponsored Spenser's London trip. This autobiographical eclogue rehearses the excursion, describes the court, and concludes with an appreciation of a return to a pastoral existence and to the poet's love, Rosalind. Machabyas must have died some years earlier, for Rosalind was an English girl, Elizabeth Boyle, who had settled in Ireland with her brother. The couple were married in 1594. Spenser records his courtship in a sonnet sequence, *Amoretti* (1595), published with 'Epithalamion', a gorgeous wedding hymn which is as unusual in the striking range of its musical verse, its detail, and its wit, as it is in the fact that it is the bridegroom's own gift to his bride. By contrast, *Prothalamion*

(1596), written for the 'double marriage' of Lady Elizabeth and Lady Katharine Somerset, daughters of the Earl of Worcester, is merely a great poem. *The Second Part of the Faerie Queen*, books IV to VI, was also published in 1596, and completes all we have of the planned 12 books, apart from 'Two Cantos of Mutabilitie', presumed to belong to one of the further books and included in the edition of 1609.

In 1596 Spenser prepared a report, *A View of the Present State of Ireland*, advocating even tougher measures against terrorists in particular (he also proposed that all Irish poets should be put to death for their 'lewd love of libertie'). It was circulated in manuscript, but publication was shelved pending 'further authority'. In September 1598 he was appointed High Sheriff of Cork, but the following month the rebel patriot, the Earl of Tyrone (*c*.1540–1616), having previously routed the English army near Armagh, invaded Munster. The province erupted, and Kilcolman was razed. Spenser escaped with his family, and was sent to London with dispatches for the Government, among which he took a personal memorandum about the situation for the Queen, written by himself. He was taken ill shortly after his arrival, died on 13 January, and was buried in Westminster Abbey.

Whether Spenser wrote more than we have of *The Faerie Queen* is not known, but the scheme of the complete work and the incident which precipitates the action of the first book are described in the poet's letter to Ralegh dated 23 January 1589. The effect of this epic dream romance, which also has myriad allegorical depths, is heightened by the stanza form he invented for it: eight iambic pentameters rhyming *ababbcbc*, followed by a triumphant Alexandrine rhyming *c*. See *The Poetical Works*, ed. J. C. Smith and E. de Selincourt, new edn 1970; *Selected Shorter Poems*, ed. Douglas Brooks-Davies, 1995; W. L. Renwick, *Edmund Spenser: an Essay on Renaissance Poetry*, new edn 1964; Graham Hough, *A Preface to the Faerie Queen*, 1962; C. S. Lewis, *Spenser's Images of Life*, ed. Alastair Fowler, new edn 1978.

SPINOZA, BENEDICT (formerly **BARUCH) DE** (1632–77) Dutch philosopher, was born in Amsterdam, one of two children who survived to adulthood of the six by three wives of Michael de Spinoza (*d.* 1654), a Spanish Jew who probably came to the Netherlands as a child in the emigration of the *marranos*. He studied for the rabbinate under Manasseh ben Israel (1604–57)—who in 1655 petitioned Cromwell to readmit Jews to England—but was sidetracked by contact with those who found extensions of their intellectual being in unorthodox Christianity, modern science, the philosophy of DESCARTES, and the Latin language. In 1656, unable to justify Judaism on the basis of the theophany at Sinai, he was formally expelled from the synagogue and was for a time banished by the civil authorities as a freethinker. On his return he lived by giving private lessons in philosophy and by grinding optical lenses. In the secluded village of Rijnsburg from 1660 to 1663, he received learned visitors, including Henry Oldenburg (*c*.1615–77), first Secretary of the Royal Society in London, and wrote, in Latin, his exposition of Cartesian philosophy (1663), the only book he published under his own name. The anonymous *Tractatus Theologico-Politicus* [Theologico-Political Treatise] (1670) was condemned by the Reformed Church in 1673 and banned in 1674. In 1673 he undertook a fruitless peace mission to the French forces ensconced in Utrecht. Later the same year he was offered a professorship at Heidelberg by the Elector Palatine, provided that he did not 'disturb the religion publicly established'. He refused, choosing instead to eke out his retirement in The Hague.

Spinoza died of consumption, probably aggravated by dust from the lens grinding. Friends gathered together parts of his correspondence and unpublished and unfinished works, and issued them in an anonymous volume in 1677. It included *Ethica* [Ethics], which he had withheld from publication. In five parts, it incorporates his theory that God is immanent throughout the world, not an external ruler, and that absolute knowledge is obtainable through reason. Predictably, the book was banned—after it had sold out. Spinoza is the greatest Jewish philosopher, whose writings, though influenced by Judaism, belong in the mainstream of European philosophy. He wrote in Latin because, of all the languages he knew, it was capable of responding to the intricacy of his philosophical and scientific argument. He never married; he did sketching for a hobby, smoked a pipe, and enjoyed a mug of beer. See Roger Scruton, *Spinoza*, 1986 (introduction to his thought and works).

SPRAT, THOMAS see COWLEY.

SQUIRE, (Sir) **J(OHN) C(OLLINGS)** (1884–1958) British poet, critic, and journalist, was born in Plymouth, and educated at Blundell's School and St John's College, Cambridge. After working as a freelance journalist and publishing *Poems and Baudelaire Flowers* (1909), he became in 1913 Literary Editor of the *New Statesman*. *The Survival of the Fittest, and Other Poems* (1916) was a protest against the war. In 1919 he founded the monthly literary magazine, the *London Mercury*, which he edited until 1934 and in which he made a point of encouraging poets, though his active promotion of those who were for convenience termed the Georgians led them also to be called the 'Squirearchy'. He was Chairman of the Architecture Club

1922–28, and of the English Association 1926–29; and was a governor of the Old Vic Theatre from 1922 to 1926. Between the wars he managed his own cricket club, the Invalids, of which BLUNDEN was at one time President—Squire and a typical Invalids eleven are hilariously but affectionately portrayed by the Scottish novelist A. G. Macdonnell (1895–1941) in *England Their England* (1933). Regarded even in his own time less as a serious poet than as a skilled parodist—see *Collected Parodies* (1921)—he was able occasionally to grip the heart, as in 'Winter Nightfall' and the chilling 'The Stockyard', written after a visit to Chicago. He published several volumes of short stories and collections of critical essays and reviews, and edited *A Book of Women's Verse* (1921) and *The Cambridge Book of Lesser Poets* (1927). He was knighted in 1933. See *Collected Poems*, introduction by John Betjeman, 1959; *The Honeysuckle and the Bee*, 1937 (autobiography).

STAËL, MME DE (1766–1817), née Germaine Necker, French novelist, prose writer, and critic, was born in Paris, the only child of Jacques Necker (1732–1804), politician and financier, and of Suzanne Churchod (1737–94), who had once been engaged to EDWARD GIBBON. She was educated at home, and after several years of negotiations was in 1786 married to Baron de Staël (1749–1802), the Swedish Ambassador. They formally separated in 1800; of her children, only the first, a daughter who died at 20 months, was his. She aired her theory of freedom in *Lettres sur . . . Jean-Jacques Rousseau* (1788; tr. as *Letters on the Works and Character of J. J. Rousseau*, 1789). At the onset of the French Revolution in 1792 she left for Coppet, the castle and barony on the Lake of Geneva which her father had bought in 1784. From there she went on to England, and acted as chatelaine of the *émigré* colony at Juniper Hall (where BURNEY met her future husband). She returned when a state of war was declared with France. *De la Littérature . . .* (1800; tr. as *A Treatise on Ancient and Modern Literature, 1803*), a formidable study of the European situation in which she expressed the essence of romanticism, was published shortly before Napoleon, contrary to her hopes, re-established his position at the battle of Marengo. After the publication of *Delphine* (1802; tr. 1803, tr. Avriel I I. Goldberger, 1995), a novel with political as well as feminist implications, he forbade her to come within ten leagues of Paris. She was well received in Germany and Italy, and made Coppet a centre of active liberal thought and literary discussion. She wrote two further novels (1802, 1807); a study of Germany (printed in 1810, destroyed by the police, and first published in 1813, in England); and other historical and critical works. In 1816, a few days after offering to achieve a reconciliation between BYRON and

his wife, she married John Rocca (1788–1818), invalided out of the army at 22, to whom she had been formally but secretly betrothed in 1811, and by whom she had a son in 1812. See *Major Writings of Germaine de Staël*, ed. Vivian Folkenflik, 1992; Madelyn Gutwirth, *Madame de Staël, Novelist*, 1978 (critical study).

STAFFORD, JEAN see LOWELL, ROBERT.

STANHOPE, PHILIP DORMER see CHESTERFIELD.

STANISLAVSKY, CONSTANTINE see CHEKHOV; MAETERLINCK.

STANYHURST, RICHARD (1547–1618) Irish prose writer and translator, was the eldest son of James Stanyhurst (d. 1573), Recorder of Dublin and Speaker of the Irish House of Commons. He was educated at Peter White's School at Kilkenny, and at University College, Oxford, after which he studied law in the Inns of Court. He then returned home, accompanied, as his tutor, by (St) Edmund Campion (1540–81). Using the elder Stanyhurst's library, Campion wrote in ten weeks a history of Ireland, which was revised by Stanyhurst and published in 1577 in HOLINSHED's *Chronicles* with his own *Treatise Containing a Plaine and Perfect Description of Ireland*. While he was not particularly complimentary to the Irish, he is one of the earliest Irish authors of note who wrote in English. As a critic he inveighed against contemporary poets who lacked a classical education, and as a poet wrote love songs to a girl 'in body fine fashioned, a brave Brounette'. She was too anxious for marriage, however, and instead he married Janet Barnwell, who died in childbirth in 1579 at their Knightsbridge home, aged 19. He now settled in Leyden, where in 1593 he published a curious, lumbering translation into English hexameters of the first four books of VIRGIL's *Aeneid*, into which he introduced words of his own coinage. Though he made a second marriage to an English Catholic, he never returned either to England or Ireland.

STARK, FREYA (1893–1993) British traveller and prose writer, was born in Paris, the elder daughter of a sculptor and of a painter; her parents commuted between Montmartre and Asolo, near Venice, a Renaissance town recommended to them by Pen Browning (see ROBERT BROWNING), whom she remembered as having a face which reminded her of an orange. (Her home in Asolo for many years was opposite the lodgings where in 1889 Robert Browning finished *Asolando*.) She was brought up in the west of England and in Italy, and was educated at home by governesses and by reading on her own, having been able to speak German and Italian, as well as English, since she was five. At 13 she suffered a horrifying accident in the Piedmont silk factory which her mother managed, being half scalped when her loose waist-length hair was sucked by the draught of an electric loom into the workings of a vertical spindle, which then whirled her round and round off the ground. She spent the years 1912–14 as a day student at Bedford College, London University, where she came under the influence of Professor W. P. Ker (1855–1923), the Scottish scholar and teacher of English, who became her adoptive godfather—his death occurred while they were climbing together on Monte Rosa in the Alps. She subsequently studied for a year at the School of Oriental Studies before a brave gamble on the Stock Exchange made it possible for her to travel in the East, on which she was determined despite several years of debilitating illness. The course of her journeys can be followed from her books about them and the regions she traversed: they began with *Baghdad Sketches* (1932; in UK 1937), and included *The Southern Gates of Arabia* (1936), *Letters from Syria* (1942)—one of the territories in which she was engaged in government service during World War II—, *Beyond Euphrates* (1951), *The Coast of Incense* (1953), *Riding to the Tigris* (1959), *The Minaret of Djam* (1970), and *Rivers of Time* (1982), which contains a wide selection from her unique range of photographs of aspects of the Middle East. *Traveller's Prelude* (1950) is an autobiography of the years 1893–1927. In 1947 she married Stewart Perowne (*d.* 1989), from whom latterly she lived apart. She was made CBE in 1953 and DBE in 1972. Molly Izzard, *Freya Stark: a Biography* (1993), published on Dame Freya's one hundredth birthday, has been criticized for its controversial attitude to its subject and for its structure. See Alexander Maitland, *A Tower in the Wall: Conversations with Dame Freya Stark*, 1982.

STEAD, C(HRISTIAN) K(ARLSON) (*b.* 1932) New Zealand poet, novelist, short-story writer, and critic, was born in Auckland and educated at Mount Albert Grammar School and Auckland University. After teaching at the University of New England, New South Wales, he became a member of the staff of Auckland University in 1959, being Associate Professor 1964–68, and Professor of English 1969–86. He has said, 'Poetry is made of words', a proposition he demonstrated in *Whether the Will is Free: Poems 1954–1962* (1962), in which was 'Pictures in a Gallery Undersea', voted by subscribers the most popular poem in *Landfall* in 15 years of publication. The long title sequence of *Quesada: Poems 1972–1974* (1975) reflects the quest of CERVANTES's Quixote. Subsequently 'a very large *subject* forced its way into my poems', American involvement in Vietnam and New Zealand's support of it, the manifestation of which was *Walking Westward* (1979). *Between*

(1988) includes among examples of poetic deftness several witty variations on CATULLUS. *Voices* (1990), commissioned by the Government to mark the sesquicentenary, presents a series of self-portraits of typical New Zealand characters, in history and today. Events feature, too, in his first novel, *Smith's Dream* (1971; rev. edn 1973), a political fable. Later ones include *All Visitors Ashore* (1984), sharply recounted reveries of a disappointed academic, *Sister Hollywood* (1989), and *The End of the Century at the End of the World* (1992), an evaluation (in the 1990s in New Zealand) of a past love affair in the form of a series of literary exercises. His critical studies *The New Poetic* (1964; rev. edn as *The New Poetic: Yeats to Eliot*, 1987) and *Pound, Yeats, Eliot and the Modernist Movement* (1986) are relevant also to his own practice as a poet and to poetry in New Zealand. Reviews, lectures, and critical essays are collected in *In the Glass Case: Essays on New Zealand Literature* (1981) and *Answering to the Language: Essays on Modern Writers* (1989). He was made CBE in 1985.

STEAD, CHRISTINA (1902–83) Australian novelist, was born in Rockdale, Sydney, the daughter of a distinguished naturalist with socialist principles, by whom she was largely brought up after her mother's death when she was two, and whose children by a second marriage in 1907 she helped to raise. She was educated at Sydney Girls' High School and Sydney Teachers' College, after which she administered tests instead of being a class teacher, because of her weak voice. She then worked as a secretary, scrimping and saving up for the fare to Europe. In London, where she had gone principally in pursuit of an Australian university lecturer with whom she had fallen in love, she met William (Bill) Blake (Blech) (1893–1968), an economist and Marxist who had been brought up in the USA, the son of German-Jewish immigrants. He gave her a job and in 1929 they went together to Paris. 'Dear Bill said to me once in the beginning of things he would like to be to me what G. H. Lewes was to George Eliot. . . . I was not very pleased, because G. E. was not a pretty girl.' They finally married in 1952 after his divorce.

Her first novel, *Seven Poor Men of Sydney* (1934), is modernist in technique, comprising a series of loosely-connected character studies. It was published after *The Salzburg Tales* (1934), 50 stories and sketches with linking commentary, cobbled together to provide a more conventional introduction to her work. *House of All Nations* (1938) is a long, riveting tale of skulduggery in the banking business. *The Man Who Loved Children* (1940), with its grim, melodramatic ending, is an exploration of her own adolescent experience, with the setting transferred to America; *For Love Alone* (1944), set in Sydney and London, reflects her own self-imposed privations and the circumstances of the years before she left Sydney. The couple lived in the USA from 1937 to 1947, and then largely in England. After three lesser novels with New York backgrounds, Stead produced, after a gap of 14 years, *Dark Places of the Heart* (1966; in UK as *Cotters' England*, 1967), a study of poverty in postwar Britain, followed by *The Puzzleheaded Girl: Four Novellas* (1967). After Blake's death she visited Australia in 1969 and then returned permanently in 1974, subsisting (it is said) on a diet of steak tartar and red vermouth, and quarrelling with her long-suffering family and even with her literary admirers, who included PATRICK WHITE. She wrote two further novels: *The Little Hotel* (1973), a black comedy of ongoings in a Swiss hotel, and *Miss Herbert (The Suburban Wife)* (1976), a feminist cautionary tale. *I'm Dying Laughing* (1986), posthumously published in a form edited by her literary executor, is a study, tragic and comic in turns, of Hollywood radicalism, corruption, and greed in the early 1940s. See Chris Williams, *Christina Stead: a Life of Letters*, 1990 (biography); Hazel Rowley, *Christina Stead: a Biography*, new edn 1995; Susan Sheridan, *Christina Stead*, 1988 (critical study); Jennifer Gribble, *Christina Stead*, 1994 (critical study).

STEELE, (Sir) **RICHARD** (1672–1729) British essayist and dramatist, was born in Dublin, the son of an attorney, and was educated at Charterhouse and Merton College, Oxford, which he left suddenly to join the Guards. Erratic as well as extravagant, in 1701 he published *The Christian Hero*, a treatise advocating sound Christian behaviour, and wrote the first of three comedies of sentiment (*The Funeral: Or, Grief à-la-Mode*, *The Lying Lover: Or, The Ladies Friendship*, and *The Tender Husband: Or, the Accomplished Fools*), none of which was successful. A brief marriage to an elderly heiress was followed by a more permanent one to Mary Scurlock (*d.* 1730), addressed as 'Dear Prue' in his correspondence (published 1787), whom he had met at his first wife's funeral. In 1709 he founded the thrice-weekly periodical the *Tatler* which, with ADDISON's continuing help, was succeeded by the *Spectator*. His own daily journal, the *Guardian*, ran for 175 issues in 1713. He was elected to Parliament in 1713, and expelled in 1714 for seditious libel. He returned to grace in 1715, when he was appointed Inspector of the Royal Stables and Commissioner for Drury Lane Theatre, and knighted. His last comedy, *The Conscious Lovers*, staged in 1722, takes a more realistic and romantic view of marriage than had been usual in Restoration drama. He had more charm and humour than Addison (he remarked of Lady Elizabeth Hamilton in the *Tatler*, 49, that '. . . to behold her is an immediate check to loose behaviour; to love her is a liberal education'), and was a more dedicated political journalist; but it was their combined talents and shrewd awareness of their public that brought them lasting acclaim. See *The Tatler*, ed. Donald F. Bond, 3 vols 1987; Willard Connely, *Sir Richard Steele*, 1934.

STEIN, GERTRUDE (1874–1946) American novelist, poet, dramatist, and critic, was born in Allegheny, Pennsylvania, the youngest of five surviving children of wealthy Jewish parents, who took them to Europe in 1875 after there had been devastating floods and a fire in the region—see Linda Wagner-Martin, *'Favored Strangers': Gertrude Stein and Her Family* (1995). They returned five years later to settle in East Oakland, California, where she was educated at local schools and by governesses at home. Her mother died in 1888 and her father in 1891. When her brother Leo (1872–1947) went to Harvard, she followed him to Radcliffe College, where she read philosophy and psychology under William James (1842–1910), brother of HENRY JAMES; and then to Johns Hopkins University, where she studied medicine half-heartedly before joining him in Paris in 1903. They collected modern art and a salon of modern painters whose techniques of perception she determined to reproduce linguistically: the book was eventually published as *Matisse, Picasso and Gertrude Stein* (1933). Her first published work was *Three Lives* (1909), in which she tried to represent the consciousness and speech rhythms of three ordinary women. *The Making of Americans: Being a History of a Family's Progress*, a cubist novel of the sensibility of Americans, was written in 1906–08, but did not find a publisher until 1925 (in USA 1926). In 1909 Alice B. Toklas (1877–1967), a Californian, joined the household, and became Stein's typist, editor, housekeeper, cook, and 'wife'—for an account of their relationship see Diana Souhami, *Gertrude and Alice* (1992). Leo, who did not appreciate her writing, now divided the art collection with her and left for Austria —see Brenda Wineapple, *Sister, Brother: Gertrude and Leo Stein* (1996).

Tender Buttons: Objects, Food, Rooms (1914) reflected her theory 'that nouns made poetry but in prose I no longer needed the help of nouns and in poetry did I need the help of nouns'. Thus 'Salmon' becomes: 'It was a peculiar bin a bin fond in beside.' Because of the difficulty of getting published, Stein sold the painting 'Girl with a Fan' by Pablo Picasso (1881–1973) and set up Toklas as her publisher under the imprint of Plain Edition, which issued several of her books, including *Operas and Plays* (1932)—see also *Selected Operas and Plays*, ed. John Malcolm Brinnin (1993) and *Last Operas and Plays*, ed. Carl van Vechten (1995). For *The Autobiography of Alice B. Toklas* (1933), an inverted memoir of herself and their artistic and literary set in Paris, she at last achieved public recognition, and in 1934 she did a lecture tour to American universities and other institutions. *Everybody's Autobiography* (1937) and *Wars I Have Seen* (1945) are autobiographical studies in a more experimental, less playful vein. The couple were in England when World War II broke out. They immediately returned to Paris; after its fall in 1942 they went to their house in the south of France, where they remained, despite the potential danger from their being Jewish. Stein died of cancer in Paris, her last words reportedly being: 'What is the answer?', and when there was none, 'Then what is the question?'. See *Gertrude Stein Companion*, ed. Bruce Kellner, 1988; *A Stein Reader*, ed. Ulla E. Dydo, new edn 1993; Linda Simon (ed.), *Gertrude Stein Remembered*, 1995; Renate Stendhal, *Gertrude Stein: in Words and Pictures*, 1994.

STEINBECK, JOHN (1902–68) American novelist and short-story writer, was born in Salinas, California, the third of four children, and the only son, of parents of German and Irish descent. His father managed a flour mill and was Treasurer of Monterey County; his mother was a teacher. The family bookshelves contained a wealth of standard authors. After graduating from Salinas High School in 1919, he attended Stanford University as a special student, with marine biology as his main subject. He left without taking a degree, much of his time having been spent earning money to support himself at a variety of jobs, including waiter, ranch hand, clerk, and 'breaking army remounts for officers' gentle behinds' at $30 an animal. Determined to be a writer, he worked his way to New York aboard a freighter, but found no outlet for his stories. He returned west by the same means after a year, during which he had worked on a building site and been fired from a post as a reporter. He supported himself by temporary work, as estate caretaker, driver of a mail coach, and on a fish farm, where he met his first wife, who was on holiday in the area. They began married life staying rent free in the family summer cottage, on an allowance from his father and on what she could earn from occasional work. *Cup of Gold* (1929), a fictional life of the 17th-century buccaneer, Sir Henry Morgan, found a publisher after seven rejections, but made no money. A breakthrough came when the New York literary agency of (Mavis) McIntosh and (Elizabeth) Otis offered to handle his work, but it was only with his fourth novel, *Tortilla Flat* (1935), that he began to make an impact. This warm, earthy, episodic treatment of the lives of the local *paisanos* also reflected his passion for Arthurian legend: 'For Danny's house was not unlike the Round Table, and Danny's friends were not unlike the knights of it.' *In Dubious Battle* (1936) describes the exploitation of fruit pickers, both by management and by unscrupulous strike leaders. His reportage of the conditions of immigrant workers after a visit to a camp near Sacramento in 1936, and his fears of a revolt, caused such controversy that a friend wrote from New York expressing concern about his personal safety.

Of Mice and Men (1937), a novel of compassion rather than protest, the only draft of which was half-destroyed by a playful puppy and had to be rewritten, sold 117,000 copies in its first month. He successfully adapted it for the stage the same year. The plight of the migrant workers, personified by the Joad family from Oklahoma, is the theme of *The Grapes of Wrath* (1939), a novel of strong social protest about which he felt so ambivalent that he advised, 'This will not be a popular book. And it will be a loss to do anything except print a small edition . . .' (it was 850 pages long). It was also so naturalistic that he was begged to tone down the language (he agreed) and to alter the controversial ending (he refused). It won the Pulitzer Prize and is the key novel in his canon. During World War II he was a war correspondent in the European sector for the New York *Herald Tribune*—see Roy S. Simmonds, *John Steinbeck: The War Years 1939–1945* (1996). When the film *Lifeboat* (1944), which he had written for Alfred Hitchcock (1899–1980) to direct, was released, he was so appalled at distortions of his original script that he demanded that his name be removed from the credits: his request was not granted.

In 1948 his second marriage broke up and the death occurred in a car accident of his closest friend, Edward Ricketts, a marine biologist with whom he had collaborated on research, and who has affinities with Doc, the immaterialistic modulator of *Cannery Row* (1945). He married again in 1950. *East of Eden* (1952), loosely based on the biblical story of Cain and Abel, covers three generations of discord in the Salinas Valley. *The Winter of Our Discontent* (1961) is a study of conscience in a small-town setting. Having in 1959 returned to the King Arthur legend (if he had ever left it), he spent almost a year in England working on a version of MALORY, which he never completed. His published non-fiction includes *Sea of Cortez* (1941), a philosophical and scientific meditation written with Ricketts; *A Russian Journal* (1948), first-hand political observations; and *Travels with Charley in Search of America* (1962) and *America and Americans* (1966), sociological reportage—see Warren French, *John Steinbeck's Nonfiction Revisited* (1996). He insisted on paying McIntosh and Otis commission on the monetary award from the Nobel Prize for Literature, which he won in 1962. See Elaine Steinbeck and Robert Wallstein (eds), *Steinbeck: a Life in Letters*, new edn 1994; Jackson J. Benson, *The True Adventures of John Steinbeck, Writer*, new edn 1990 (biography); Jay Parini, *John Steinbeck: a Biography*, new edn 1996; Howard Levant, *The Novels of John Steinbeck: a Critical Study*, new edn 1983; R. S. Hughes, *Beyond the Red Pony: a Reader's Companion to Steinbeck's Complete Short Stories*, 1987.

STENDHAL, pseudonym of Marie-Henri Beyle (1783–1842) French novelist and critic, was born in Grenoble, the son of a lawyer. His mother died when he was seven. He was educated at the École Central, Grenoble, and passed into the École Polytechnique, Paris, which he never attended, instead accepting an offer from a cousin of a clerical job in the Ministry of War. He held staff positions in Napoleon's army in Italy, Germany, Austria, Hungary, and Russia, and in 1814 was assisting in the organization of the southeast frontier when Napoleon was exiled to Elba. He went to Italy and wrote, under his pseudonym, a history of Italian painting, lives of musicians, and a travel guide. In 1818 he fell in love with Mathilde Viscontini Dembowski (1790–1825), an ardent patriot. He left in 1821 because of her indifference to his suit, and because he was suspected by the Austrian police of being connected with the Carbonari. In Paris he published a philosophical treatise expressing his feelings for Mathilde (referred to as Métilde), *De l'Amour* (1822; tr. Gilbert and Suzanne Sale as *Love*, 1957), followed by two critical pamphlets, *Racine et Shakespeare* (1823, 1825), in which the classical regularity of the former is unfavourably contrasted with the free creativity of the latter. His first novel, *Armance* (1827), revealed him in practice as more of a realist than a Romantic. The title of *Le Rouge et le Noir* (1830; tr. Catherine Slater as *The Red and the Black*, introduction by Roger Pearson, 1991) refers to the red coats of the military and the black garb of the priesthood, which has regained the ascendancy after the era of Napoleon, and through which Julien Sorel moves to material triumphs and ultimately to murder.

After the revolution in 1830, Stendhal obtained the consulship in Trieste, but had to accept Civitavecchia instead when the Austrian government blocked the appointment. He wrote *La Chartreuse de Parme* (1839; tr. Margaret R. B. Shaw as *The Charterhouse of Parma*, 1958), his masterly tale of destiny, in 52 days. Based on an old manuscript, with the setting brought forward to the period of Waterloo, it incorporates a memorable account of the battle itself in the course of a series of intrigues and secret passions. He had an apoplectic stroke in 1841 and returned to Paris, where he died suddenly of a further seizure. *Vie d'Henri Brulard* (posthumously published 1890; tr. John Sturrock as *The Life of Henry Brulard*, 1995), written in 1835–36, is a masterly exercise in self-exploration, taking Stendhal's life up to his 17th year, with some anticipations of subsequent experiences. See Jonathan Keates, *Stendhal*, new edn 1995 (biography).

STEPHEN, LESLIE see THACKERAY; WOOLF, VIRGINIA.

STEPHENS, JAMES (1882–1950) Irish novelist and poet, was born in Dublin. At an early age he was placed in an orphanage, where he got a firm grounding in Protestantism but little else, and from which he ran away, living rough and depending on people's kindness. It was probably his tiny stature which enabled him to empathize particularly with the fairies and other small beings of Irish mythology, just as, by his own account, he used as a child to squat beside a dog, or cat, or even a bush, and practise projecting himself into it. His first volume of verse, *Insurrections* (1909), was more concerned with highlighting the conditions of the Dublin poor, but latterly his poetry became more mystical in outlook, matching the surer development of his prose. He was a protégé of G. W. RUSSELL, who recommended the publication of his novel of urban idealism, *The Charwoman's Daughter* (1912). His most lasting work is *The Crock of Gold* (1912), a philosophical fairy tale with modern implications. His sense of comedy is more evident in *Deirdre* (1923) and in *In the Land of Youth* (1924), in which he attempts to reconcile heroic Irish mythology with simple rural delights. He was Registrar of the Irish National Portrait Gallery from 1915 to 1924, after which he divided his time between Paris and London, where he became an outstanding broadcaster of his own, idiosyncratic, scripts, published as *James, Seamus and Jacques* (1964). See *Collected Poems*, 2nd edn 1954; Hilary Pyle, *James Stephens: His Works and an Account of His Life*, 1965.

STERNE, LAURENCE (1713–68) British novelist, was born in Clonmel, Ireland, the son of an English army officer whose family followed him around. They went back to England, and then to Ireland again: to Wicklow, near which the boy fell unhurt through a millrace, to Dublin, where in 1721 he learned to write, and to Carrickfergus. From 1723 until his father's death in Jamaica in 1731 (having survived being run through in a duel with a fellow officer in Gibraltar), Sterne was settled in a school in Halifax. In 1733 a cousin offered to support him at Jesus College, Cambridge; he graduated as BA in 1736, and took holy orders in 1738. From then until 1759 he lived the life of an eccentric Yorkshire country parson. He was frequently ill with consumption, and his wife, whom he had married in 1741 on learning that she had bequeathed him her property, proved as much a trial to him as he clearly was to her. A dispute among the clergy of York Minster suggested to him the plot of a comic novel, *A Political Romance*, which was regarded as so unsuitable for publication that it did not appear until 1769; it was often reissued as *The History* *of a Good Warm Watch Coat.* The success it achieved among his friends, among whom it had been privately circulated in 1759, determined him to become a novelist. He wrote the first two books of *The Life and Opinions of Tristram Shandy, Gentleman*, which he arranged to be printed in York at a friend's expense, after they had been turned down by the London publishing firm of Robert Dodsley (1703–64), to which Sterne had offered them for £50. The reaction of the international literary world was phenomenal. Sterne moved to London to capitalize on his new reputation. Dodsley's brother James (Robert having retired) was now only too pleased to reissue the first two books (1760), to commission the author to supply a further volume every year for the rest of his life, and to publish a collected edition of his sermons as *The Sermons of Mr Yorick* (7 vols 1760–69). In spite of recurrent illness, Sterne plunged enthusiastically into the fashionable life of London and France, while keeping to his contract for *Tristram Shandy* (the ninth book was published in 1767), and writing *A Sentimental Journey through France and Italy* (1768), though Italy remained unvisited by the whimsical traveller. During the spring of 1767 he indulged in an energetic but Platonic affair with Eliza Draper, a 23-year-old charmer, until she sailed to join her husband in India. For her he wrote *The Journal to Eliza*, discovered in 1851.

'Digressions, incontestably, are the sunshine,' wrote Sterne in *Tristram Shandy* (I, 22), but along with his quirkish typographical devices and punctuation, and non sequiturs which are rather associations of ideas on the principles of LOCKE, they are integral to a unique construction by a comic genius and in part anticipate the stream-of-consciousness technique. By the time he came to write *A Sentimental Journey*, more feeling and decorum had set in, but even if he did intend to complete the odyssey, the book's present conclusion is sheer perfection. See Arthur H. Cash, *Laurence Sterne: the Early and Middle Years* and *Laurence Sterne: the Later Years*, new edns 1992.

STEVENS, WALLACE (1879–1955) American poet, was born in Reading, Pennsylvania, the second of five children of a lawyer who wrote some poetry, and went to school locally. In 1897 he enrolled as a special student at Harvard, where he published several poems in the *Harvard Advocate*; he left in 1900 to pursue a literary career in New York City. After a brief spell as a journalist, he went instead to law school, and was admitted to the New York Bar in 1904. Several jobs failed before he became a member of the legal staff of the American Bond Co. In 1909 he married Elsie Moll (1886–1963), whom he had met in Reading in 1904, and whom he had courted from a distance with poems and

gaily-phrased letters. 'Carnet de Voyage', a group of eight poems, was published in *Trend* in 1914, his first appearance in print since Harvard. In 1916 he joined the Hartford Accident and Indemnity Co. as a claims investigator, and moved to Hartford, Connecticut. In 1934 he became a vice president of the company, for which he was still working shortly before his death. He was 44 when his first volume of verse, *Harmonium* (1923), appeared. It included several of his most frequently anthologized, and most self-critical, poems, 'Sunday Morning', 'The Comedian as the Letter C', and 'Peter Quince at the Clavier'; and some of his most effective excursions into comedy, such as 'Cortege for Rosenbloom' and 'The Emperor of Ice-Cream'. There was no further book until *Ideas of Order* (1935), after which there were regular collections until 1950. Just as he recognized, as in 'The Idea of Order at Key West' (1936), the role of the poet in making order out of chaos, so, in the title poem of *The Man with the Blue Guitar and Other Poems* (1937) and elsewhere, he posited the relationship between nature and art. *Notes Toward a Supreme Fiction* (1942) is a long poem defining the art of poetry—his lectures on the subject were published in *The Necessary Angel: Essays on Reality and the Imagination* (1951). *The Collected Poems of Wallace Stevens* (1954) won the National Book Award and the Pulitzer Prize. See *Letters of Wallace Stevens*, ed. Holly Stevens, new edn 1996; Joan Richardson, *Wallace Stevens: the Early Years, 1879-1923*, 1986, and *Wallace Stevens: the Later Years, 1923-1925*, 1988 (biography); Susan B. Weston, *Wallace Stevens: an Introduction to the Poetry*, 1977; Frank Kermode, *Wallace Stevens*, 2nd rev. edn 1989 (critical study).

STEVENSON, ROBERT LOUIS (1850–94) Scottish novelist, short-story writer, poet, essayist, and travel writer, was born Robert Lewis Balfour Stevenson in Edinburgh, the only child of Thomas Stevenson (1818–87) of the famous family of lighthouse engineers, and Margaret Balfour (1829–97), a minister's daughter. Constant illness disrupted his education, of which the years 1861–63 were spent at Edinburgh Academy. His first published work, paid for by his father, was a novel of the last days of the Covenanters, *The Pentland Rising* (1866). The following year he went to Edinburgh University to read engineering, but on explaining to his father in 1871 that he wanted to make writing his career, he was persuaded at least to study law for the time being, and he qualified as an advocate in 1875. Meanwhile he had shocked his parents by expressing agnostic sympathies. There is evidence also that he frequented brothels; research in 1996 largely confirms the theory of DAICHES in his study of RLS (1947) that Kate Drummond, an Edinburgh prostitute with whom Stevenson appears to have had a romantic relationship, was the inspiration for Catriona Drummond in *Catriona*.

A meeting with HENLEY in 1874 resulted in their writing four poor plays together, but also gave Stevenson access to outlets for reviews and essays, of which he made several collections, the first being *Virginibus Puerisque* (1881). Foreign expeditions for his health, by unusual means, gave him the material for *An Inland Voyage* (1878) and *Travels with a Donkey in the Cévennes* (1879). In 1879 he went to California to persuade a woman he had met in France, Fanny Osbourne (1840–1914), ten years his senior and just divorced, to marry him—see Alexandra Lapierre, *Fanny Stevenson: a Romance of Destiny*, tr. Carol Cosman (1995) for a fully researched but partly fictionalized account of her life. Back in Europe and still travelling, he completed his first full-length novel, *Treasure Island* (1883), published initially in *Young Folks' Magazine* and particularly memorable for its subtle narrative technique. In *Kidnapped* (1886), its sequel *Catriona* (1893; in USA as *David Balfour*, 1893), and *The Master of Ballantrae* (1889), he is concerned with personal conflicts, and Scottish history and topography, as well as with adventure. Conflict in the form of a dual personality is the theme of *Strange Case of Dr Jekyll and Mr Hyde* (1886), according to his own account, 'conceived, written, rewritten, re-written, and printed inside ten weeks', to resolve problems of tradesmen's bills. *Not I, and Other Poems* (1881) contained several poems expressing the anguish of youth. *A Child's Garden of Verses* (1885) is a nostalgic recapitulation of the pleasures and fantasies of childhood. On the whole, however, his poetry is mild stuff beside the supernatural short stories 'Thrawn Janet' (1881) and 'Markheim' (1886), which were published in *The Merry Men, and Fables and Other Tales* (1887).

In 1887 he and his wife sailed for America and chartered a racing schooner to take them to the South Seas in a final search for a congenial climate for him. They found it in Samoa, where they built a house on the estate of Vailima. Here he wrote with his stepson, Lloyd Osbourne (1868–1947), two tales of violent adventure, *The Wrecker* (1892) and *The Ebb-Tide* (1894). He also completed nine chapters of *Weir of Hermiston*, which for depth of character, insight into a confrontation between father and son such as he had himself experienced, and power of style, exceeds anything else he wrote— the fullest version is ed. Catherine Kerrigan, 1996, as the first volume in the Centenary Edition of the works. The unfinished historical adventure, *St Ives*, has been completed (1897) by QUILLER-COUCH and (1990) by Jenni Calder (*b.* 1941), the elder daughter of DAICHES. Stevenson died of a cerebral haemorrhage. His significance to English literature lies more in what he promised to achieve than in what he wrote during his short life: in terms of Scottish literature, he was in several ways a true successor to WALTER SCOTT. See *Collected Poems, Vol. 1*, ed. John Manning and Elizabeth Waterston, 1996; *The Complete Short Stories*, ed. Ian Bell, 1993; Jenni Calder, *RLS: a Life Study*, new edn 1990; Frank McLynn, *Robert Louis Stevenson: a Biography*, new edn 1994; R. C. Terry (ed.), *Robert Louis Stevenson: Interviews and Recollections*, 1996; Robert Kiely, *Robert Louis Stevenson and the Fiction of Adventure*, 1964; J. R. Hammond, *A Robert Louis Stevenson Companion: a Guide to the Novels, Essays and Short Stories*, 1984.

STEWART, DOUGLAS (1913–85) Australian poet, dramatist, and critic, was born in Eltham, Taranaki, New Zealand, of an Australian father, and was educated at New Plymouth Boys' High School and Victoria University College. When a staff position as light verse writer on the *Bulletin* in Sydney did not materialize, he returned to New Zealand, where he privately published a book of verse, *Green Lions* (1936). He finally joined the *Bulletin* in 1938, and was Literary Editor 1940–61. He was then Literary Adviser (1961–72) to Angus and Robertson, the main publisher of Australian poetry at that time. Two slim volumes of wartime verse were followed by *The Dosser in Springtime* (1946), Australian-orientated poems in which he extended his range to include ballads. In the ballad sequence *Glencoe* (1947), the government-inspired massacre in the Scottish Highlands in 1692 is the basis of a 'protest against barbarity, cruelty and violence'. Further poetic developments were highlighted in *Sun Orchids* (1952), which contained significant nature poems and a sequence evoking an incident during the Antarctic expedition in 1914 led by Sir Ernest Shackleton (1874–1922). Discovery of a different nature inspired the long title poem of his last collection, *Rutherford, and Other Poems* (1962), in the course of which the New Zealand-born physicist appears as 'the great sea-farer of science'. *The Fire on the Snow*, his major verse drama, written 'under blind compulsion' without any experience as a dramatist or of 'the technicalities of radio playwriting', was broadcast in 1941 and published in 1944. Tense and moving, it covers the final assault on the South Pole in 1912 by Captain Scott (1868–1912) and the deaths of all five members of the party. A folk hero of a different kind, the bushranger Ned Kelly (1855–80), features in *Ned Kelly*, written for the stage but first publicly aired on radio in 1942 (published 1943). *Four Plays* (1958) includes also *The Golden Lover* (broadcast 1943) and *Shipwreck* (produced 1948). Reviews and other critical articles are collected in *The Broad Stream: Aspects of Australian Literature* (1975). He was made OBE in 1960. See *Collected Poems 1936–1967*, 1967; *Selected Poems*, 1992; *Springtime in Taranaki: an Autobiography of*

Youth, new edn 1991; Clement Semmler, *Douglas Stewart: a Critical Study*, new edn 1977.

STEWART, HAROLD see MCAULEY.

STEWART, J(OHN) I(NNES) M(ACKINTOSH) (1906–94) Scottish novelist and critic, was born in Edinburgh, and educated at Edinburgh Academy and Oriel College, Oxford, where he got a degree with first class honors in English. A meeting with (Sir) Francis Meynell (1891–1975) led to a commission to edit for the Nonesuch Press *Montaigne's Essays: John Florio's Translation* (1931), largely on the strength of which he obtained a lectureship at Leeds University. On the way out to take up the post of Jury Professor of English at Adelaide University in 1935, he wrote his first mystery story under the pen name of Michael Innes, *Death at the President's Lodging* (1936). Ten similar novels followed during his ten years there, 'the South Australian climate [being] just right for authorship of this sort'. Witty and of an intellectual nature, they continued to come thereafter. He was a Fellow of Christ Church, Oxford 1949–73, and Reader in English Literature 1969–73. His first work of fiction under his own name was *Mark Lambert's Supper* (1954), which, like several of his subsequent novels, involves a quest for an artistic work. 'A Staircase in Surrey' is the overall title of a sequence about growing up and Oxford life, beginning with *The Gaudy* (1974). He also published volumes of short stories, both as J. I. M. Stewart and as Michael Innes. His critical works, noted, like his novels, for their wit as well as their erudition, include studies of KIPLING (1966), CONRAD (1968), and HARDY (1971), and the volume in the Oxford History of English Literature, *Writers of the Early Twentieth Century* (1963; reissued 1990 with this title).

STEWART, JOHN, OF BALDYNNEIS see FOWLER.

STOKER, BRAM [ABRAHAM] (1847–1912) Irish novelist, was born in Dublin, the second son of a civil servant and of a self-styled social reformer of a somewhat erratic nature. Unable to stand upright until he was seven, he nevertheless had a distinguished athletic as well as academic career at Trinity College, Dublin, where he also developed a passion for the work and personality of WHITMAN. In 1870 he became a civil servant at Dublin Castle, where he wrote his first book, *The Duties of Clerks of Petty Sessions in Ireland* (1879). From 1871 he doubled as unpaid drama critic of the *Evening Mail*. His passion for the stage was such that he volunteered to do the publicity in Dublin for the tour in the autumn of 1876 of the actor (Sir) Henry Irving (1838–1905). In 1878 he married

Frances Anne Balcombe, who was said to be one of the three most beautiful women in London and who had been courted also by WILDE. The honeymoon was cut short when Irving asked him to become his manager and secretary (in which capacity he estimated that over the years he wrote half a million letters). He remained with Irving until the actor dropped dead in a Bradford hotel after playing in TENNYSON's *Becket*—his *Personal Reminiscences of Henry Irving* (1906) is a valuable theatrical record.

Latterly, to his wife's delight, he studied for the Bar; he never practised, but she made certain that he was always referred to as a barrister rather than a man of the theatre or of the pen. Although he published several novels, of which the first was *Under the Sunset* (1882), and non-fiction works, including *Famous Imposters* (1910), in which he postulates that Elizabeth I was a man, he is remembered just for one book, *Dracula* (1897). While owing something to a story by LE FANU, it has become the archetypal vampire story, with a touch of the Ruritanian as well as the Gothic about its gruesome goings-on. His wife sold the film rights of *Dracula* in 1930 for $40,000 to Universal Pictures, who made the first sound version. There have been numerous other films since; on the occasion of the release of the 1992 version, the original novel featured on the American best-seller lists. See Daniel Farson, *The Man Who Wrote 'Dracula': a Biography of Bram Stoker*, 1975; Barbara Belford, *Bram Stoker: a Biography of the Author of 'Dracula'*, 1996.

STOPPARD, TOM (*b.* 1937) British dramatist, was born in Zlin, Czechoslovakia, taken by his parents to Singapore just before World War II, and then sent with his mother to India to avoid the Japanese invasion, in which his father died. After the war, his mother married an Englishman, whose name he took. He was educated at Pocklington School, Yorkshire. He worked as a newspaper journalist in Bristol from 1954 to 1960, when he went freelance to write for the theatre, though his first published works were short stories and a comic novel, *Lord Malquist and Mr Moon* (1966). His first play, *A Walk on the Water*, was produced on television in 1963, and in a revised form as *Enter a Free Man* on the London stage in 1968. The central theme of *Rosencrantz and Guildenstern Are Dead* (first staged in Edinburgh in 1966), as of many of his plays, is the powerlessness of man in the face of fate and external forces, in this case seen through the eyes of two of SHAKESPEARE's minor characters. In *Jumpers* (1972), regarded as his best play, the predicament of the moral philosopher in a pragmatic world is highlighted by the invasion of his privacy by public events on a vast television screen. *Travesties* (1974), a comedy of ideas reflecting the collapse of modernism under critical scrutiny, was revived in a revised form in 1993. *Professional Foul* (1978), written for television, is a philosophical drama of human rights set in Czechoslovakia.

The Real Thing (1982) starred Felicity Kendal (*b.* 1946) as an actress who falls in love with a playwright—they married in 1992. In *Arcadia* (1993), his first new stage play for five years, the Stoppard mix of elements incorporates the chaos theory in science, landscape gardening, BYRON, and literary detective work. Similar transitions in time and space are a feature of *Indian Ink* (1995), expanded from a radio drama of 1991, which offers Stoppard's interpretation of the last days of Anglo-India. He uses theatrical and technical devices as well as verbal gymnastics to amuse, and startle, his audience, and what may sometimes appear derivative is intentional parody. His radio plays, often extensions of a single, bizarre situation, have been published in *The Plays for Radio 1964-1991* (1994); see also *The Real Inspector Hound, and Other Entertainments* (1993). See *Plays, Volume One*, new edn 1996; *The Television Plays 1965-1984*, 1993; Ronald Hayman, *Tom Stoppard*, 4th edn 1982 (critical study); Anthony Jenkins, *The Theatre of Tom Stoppard*, 2nd edn 1989.

STOREY, DAVID (*b.* 1933) British novelist and dramatist, was born in Wakefield, Yorkshire, the third son of a miner. He was educated at Queen Elizabeth Grammar School, Wakefield, and Wakefield Art School, after which he subsidized his studies at the Slade School of Fine Art in London by travelling back and forth to play as a professional for Leeds Rugby League Club. Rugby league football is the background of his first novel, *This Sporting Life* (1960), in which, as in *Flight into Camden* (1960), the focus is on the conflict between working-class origins and modern aspirations, just as it is in BRAINE's *Room at the Top*, published a few years earlier. In *Radcliffe* (1963), the difference is one of class itself, while *Pasmore* (1972) and *A Temporary Life* (1973) explore the conflicts which can lead to mental breakdown. *Saville* (1976), which won the Booker prize for fiction, is a more straightforward, semi-autobiographical story of a boy's development to manhood and independence. In *A Prodigal Child* (1982), various areas of conflict in earlier novels are brought together in one. His first play, *The Restoration of Arnold Middleton* (1967), was written in 1959 for the Royal Court Theatre in London, but first performed seven years later by the Traverse company in Edinburgh. To many critics, it remains the most entertaining of his several disturbing or farcical conversation pieces, some of which reflect elements or incidents in the novels—see *Plays One: 'Home', 'Stages' and 'Caring'* (1992). Trained as an artist, and now a spare-time painter, Storey has no illusions about the con-

flicts within the writer's craft, as he explained in an interview in 1990: 'Basically I like writing something every day even if it is rubbish, just to prove I can do it.' See also *Storey's Lives: Poems 1951-1991* (1992).

STOW, JOHN see MUNDAY.

STOWE, HARRIET BEECHER (1811–96) American novelist and writer of short fiction, essays, and instructional works, was born in Litchfield, Connecticut. She was the youngest daughter and the seventh of nine children of Lyman Beecher (1775–1863), preacher and prose writer, and his first wife, Roxana Foote (*d.* 1816), and sister of Catherine Beecher (1800–78), educationist and reformer, and Henry Ward Beecher (1813–87), clergyman, prose writer, and editor. She was educated at her sister's school, Hartford Female Seminary, and taught there and at Catherine's next foundation, the Western Female Institute in Cincinnati, where their father was President of Lane Theological Seminary. In 1833 the sisters published *Primary Geography for Children*, described as a 'very capital little book' in the *Western Monthly Magazine*, to which Harriet began contributing stories anonymously in 1834, winning a prize for 'New England Sketch'. On 6 January 1836 she married, as his second wife, Calvin Stowe (1802–86): twin girls were born on 29 September. During the next 14 years she had five further difficult pregnancies, but retained a measure of independence by travel and by contributing to other journals, the Cincinnati *Chronicle* and *Journal*, and the New York *Evangelist*. *The Mayflower: Sketches of Scenes and Characters among the Descendants of the Pilgrims* (1843) was a collection of 15 such pieces.

In 1850 the family moved to Brunswick, Maine, where Calvin Stowe had been appointed to the faculty of Bowdoin College. The cumulative effect of items in the anti-slavery *National Era* (founded 1847), the death from cholera in 1849 of an infant son, and the passing of the Fugitive Slave Act (1850), moved her to an ultimate gesture of resentment against the repressions in her own life. 'Uncle Tom's Cabin: or, The Man that was a Thing', began serialization in the *National Era* in June 1851. As *Uncle Tom's Cabin: or, Life among the Lowly* (1852), it follows alternately, in Victorian literary fashion, two groups of characters to make up a composite picture of a society. It sold 350,000 copies in its first year. Stowe responded to inevitable attacks from anti-abolitionists by issuing *A Key to Uncle Tom's Cabin* (1853), which was not so much a justification of her argument, or a parade of authoritative sources, as a defence of her personal integrity. In 1852 Calvin Stowe was appointed to Andover Theological College, and in 1853 she made the first of three visits to Europe, during which she mixed with the British aristocracy and literary set—see *Sunny Memories of Foreign Lands* (1854). She went on writing abolitionist material, including *Dred: a Tale of the Great Dismal Swamp* (1856), until the Emancipation Proclamation of 1862.

Her money-making career continued without her ever recapturing the apocalyptic vision of *Uncle Tom's Cabin*; though *The Pearl of Orr's Island* (1862), a New England idyll, and *Oldtown Folks* (1869), a Massachusetts melodrama, have literary merit. She was one of the original contributors to *Atlantic Monthly* (founded 1857), for which she wrote, as Christopher Crowfield, regular articles on home-making and related topics, published as *House and Home Papers* (1865), *Little Foxes* (1866), and *The Chimney-Corner* (1868). Her fascination with the work of BYRON prompted 'The True Story of Lady Byron's Life' (*Atlantic Monthly*, 1869), the sensational tone of which caused an immediate 12.5 per cent drop in the journal's circulation. Undeterred, she enlarged the article into *Lady Byron Vindicated* (1870). While a form of personal emancipation brought her satisfaction, she was much disturbed by the drowning in 1857 of her eldest son, Henry, without his having been formally 'saved', and by the action for adultery brought against Henry Ward Beecher in 1874 by his friend, and her sometime editor, Theodore Tilton (1835–1907), and the subsequent protracted trial. She began to go senile in about 1884. See Joan D. Hedrick, *Harriet Beecher Stowe: a Life*, new edn 1995; John R. Adams, *Harriet Beecher Stowe*, rev. edn 1989 (biographical/critical study).

STRACHEY, (GILES) LYTTON (1880–1932) British critic and biographer, was born at Stowey House, Clapham Common, London, the 11th of 13 children of General Sir Richard Strachey (1817–1908) by his second wife, and was educated at Leamington College, at Liverpool University (for two distressing years), and at Trinity College, Cambridge. He wrote regular articles for the *Spectator* and other literary journals, and was a prominent member of the Bloomsbury Group (see VIRGINIA WOOLF). His first (and, to some, his most balanced) book was *Landmarks in French Literature* (1912). At the time of World War I, during which he was a conscientious objector, he devised a technique of biography demonstrated in *Eminent Victorians* (1918), in which he aims by elegant prose and judicious selection and presentation of detail to reveal illustrious figures as less virtuous than they had seemed hitherto. Though heavily criticized, the book made his reputation. His attempt to repeat the formula in *Queen Victoria* (1921) foundered in that he could not dent the heroic mould of his subject, but resulted in a fairer exposition. *Elizabeth and Essex: a Tragic History* (1928) contains a greater extent of speculation but is even more readable. From 1916 Strachey lived in close relationship with the painter Dora Carrington (1893–1932) and, after her marriage in 1921, with her husband too. She committed suicide after Strachey's death from cancer. While unable to bring much understanding of psychology to his biographical studies, he invented a literary form which, for better or for worse, led to the fictionalized biography. *The Shorter Strachey* (1980), selected and introduced by Michael Holroyd and Paul Levy, comprises 30 of his critical, autobiographical, and biographical essays. See Michael Holroyd, *Lytton Strachey: a Biography*, new edn of 2nd rev. edn, 1995.

STRATEMEYER, EDWARD see ALGER.

STRICKLAND, AGNES and **ELIZABETH** see MOODIE.

STRINDBERG, (JOHAN) AUGUST (1849–1912) Swedish dramatist and novelist, was born in Stockholm, the fourth of 12 children of a shipping agent and his former maidservant, who married four months before he was born—the father went bankrupt in 1853 and in 1863, after the death of his wife, married his young housekeeper. Strindberg went to Uppsala University in 1867; failed his examinations in 1869; failed in his attempt to become an actor; and wrote two plays that were rejected. [*In Rome*] (1870) had a few performances and earned him a bursary from Karl XV to return to university to study modern languages and political science; he left in 1872 after the payments dried up. He now wrote a historical drama, [*Master Olof*], which was not staged for nine years; tried journalism, then librarianship (cataloguing Chinese manuscripts); and fell in love with the bisexual Siri von Essen, wife of Baron Wrangel, a Guards officer, who in due course divorced her, ostensibly so that she could go on the stage. Strindberg married her in 1877 after she had become pregnant. [*The Red Room*] (1879; tr. Ellie Schleussner, 1913), an autobiographical novel, established his name as an author, but further plays had only transitory success, and his politico-historical studies and satires were attacked. In 1883 he took his family abroad for six years, to France, Switzerland, Germany, and Denmark, returning to Sweden briefly in 1884 to face a charge of blasphemy (of which he was acquitted) arising from a collection of autobiographical stories, [*Marriage*] (1884). [*The Father*], the first of several half-length, single-set, naturalistic dramas, was first performed in Copenhagen in 1887, having been rejected in Sweden. A bowdlerized [*Miss Julie*] was published in Sweden in 1888, but the play was banned in Denmark the day before it was due to open, its world premiere being a private performance at Copenhagen University Students' Union on 14 March 1889—

Strindberg himself saw it for the first time in 1908, at a private showing just for himself, G. B. SHAW, and Mrs Shaw.

He and Siri were divorced in 1891, after which he went to Germany, where he met and married Frida Uhl, a young Austrian journalist. He left her in 1894 and settled in Paris, where, in spite of having at one time six plays running concurrently, he lapsed into poverty and near-insanity, conducting pseudo-scientific experiments and dabbling in alchemy in his lodgings—*Inferno* (1897; tr. Mary Sandbach with *From an Occult Diary*, 1979), written in French, is an account of these years. Back in Sweden, he embarked on a mystical drama trilogy, [*To Damascus*] (1898–1904) and, inspired by SHAKESPEARE'S history plays, began to build up a corpus of dramas about Sweden's past. In 1900 he met, and in 1901 (after his divorce from Frida had been formalized) married, Harriet Bosse, a Norwegian actress 29 years his junior. She left him the same year, with their baby daughter: they were divorced in 1904. In 1907, having written no play for three years, he established in Stockholm his own Intimate Theatre, for which, until its failure three years later, he wrote four 'Chamber Plays', the only one of which to have lasted is [*The Ghost Sonata*] (1908), the most obscure of all his dramas. He died of stomach cancer, having become engaged to an 18-year-old actress, Fanny Falkner, who could not bring herself to marry him but who looked after him with her mother in the flat in their house into which he had moved. He is Sweden's greatest writer, whose influence can be traced in the plays of O'NEILL and has been acknowledged by JOHN OSBORNE, and whose pioneering work in staging dream worlds which are compatible with modern psychological thinking is a direct source of the Theatre of the Absurd. See *Plays*, tr. Michael Meyer, 6 vols 1980–87; *Selected Essays*, ed. and tr. Michael Robinson, 1996; Michael Meyer, *Strindberg: a Biography*, new edn 1992.

STRONG, L(EONARD) A(LFRED) G(EORGE) (1896–1958) Irish novelist and poet, was born near Plymouth, Devon. His father, an agricultural industrialist, was half-Irish and his mother wholly so, and family holidays were spent with her parents near Dublin. He won scholarships to Brighton College and Wadham College, Oxford. A spinal condition made him unfit for service in World War I. Beginning with *Dublin Days* (1921), he published several books of verse and two of short stories during the 1920s, while teaching at the Oxford private school, Summer Fields. The reception of his first novel, *Dewer Rides* (1929), a story of Dartmoor, encouraged him to become a full-time writer in 1930. Two novels, *The Garden* (1931) and *Sea Wall* (1933), are distinguished evocations of the Irish landscape and of Irish life.

His best poetry is polished and epigrammatic—see *The Body's Imperfection: the Collected Poems of L. A. G. Strong* (1957). Among many non-fiction works, he wrote a biography of THOMAS MOORE (1937) and a critical study of JOYCE (1949); there are portraits of SYNGE and YEATS in *Personal Remarks* (1953), and reflections on his profession in *The Writer's Trade* (1953). He was a director of the publishing house of Methuen from 1938 to 1958, and was both a member of the Irish Academy of Letters and a Fellow of the Royal Society of Literature. See *Green Memory*, 1961 (autobiography).

STUART, FRANCIS (*b.* 1902) Irish novelist, was born in Queensland, Australia, the son of an Irish sheep farmer, on whose death a year later he was brought to Ireland. He was educated in England at Rugby School, and shortly afterwards, when he was 18, he married Iseult Gonne (1894–1954), to whom, and to whose mother, YEATS had frequently and unsuccessfully proposed. Yeats, now himself married, was not best pleased, and later wrote, rather unfairly, of having known 'A girl that knew all Dante once / Live to bear children to a dunce'. Stuart fought on the Republican side in the Irish Civil War, was captured, and was interned until November 1923. His first book, the volume of verse, *We Have Kept the Faith* (dated 1923), was highly praised, even by Yeats, but he turned to fiction as a more appropriate medium for experimentation and the expression of his dissident outlook and general philosophy. *Women and God* (1931), in which he developed the connection between sex and religion, was the first of 11 novels written before World War II. In 1940 he went to Berlin University, where he lectured throughout the war on English and Irish literature. He was arrested by the French occupation forces in 1945, and imprisoned for a time, though no formal charges were laid against him—like WODEHOUSE he had broadcast from Berlin to listeners in a neutral country. He lived in Germany and France until 1951, and then in London until 1958, when he returned to Ireland. He had been separated from Iseult, on whose death he married a German woman whom he had met during the war. *The Pillar of Cloud* (1948) and *Redemption* (1949) are spiritual reflections on the position of Irishmen in wartime Germany. *Black List, Section H* (1971 in USA; 1975 in UK) is more overtly autobiographical. A second volume of verse, *We Have Kept the Faith: Poems 1918–1992*, was published in 1992. See Geoffrey Elborn, *Francis Stuart: a Life*, 1990.

STUKELEY, SIMON see SAVERY.

STYRON, WILLIAM (*b.* 1925) American novelist, was born in Newport News, Virginia, the son of a marine engineer, and was educated at Christchurch Preparatory School and Davidson College, from which he transferred in 1943 to Duke University as a member of the Marine Corps unit. There he was encouraged to write short stories; after graduating in 1947, he enrolled for a course in short-story writing at the New School for Social Research, New York. Recalled as a reservist 1st lieutenant in 1950 during the Korean War, he participated in a 36-mile route march such as is the subject of his second novel, *The Long March*, published in *Discovery* in 1953 and in volume form in 1956. His first, *Lie Down in Darkness* (1951), which appeared shortly after his discharge, focuses on a Southern man whose daughter has committed suicide in New York. *The Confessions of Nat Turner* (1967), a study of the psychological development of the literate slave leader and preacher who organized a rebellion in the Upper South in 1831, won the Pulitzer Prize but met with some hostility from those concerned about race relations. In *Sophie's Choice* (1979), his reflection on 'human institutions; humanly contrived situations which cause people to live in wretched unhappiness' centres on the Holocaust. While acknowledging the concern of Jewish intellectuals, notably the philosopher and critic George Steiner (*b.* 1929), that 'It's not clear that those who were not themselves fully involved should touch upon these agonies unscathed,' Styron justified his stance as an artist and his creation of a victim who is Polish but not Jewish: 'I wanted to show that the Nazis were out to get the whole human race.' *Darkness Visible: a Memoir of Madness* (1990) is an autobiographical study of his own brush with chronic depression after becoming allergic to alcohol. *A Tidewater Morning* (1993), prefaced with an epigram from THOMAS BROWNE, 'The long habit of living indisposeth us for dying', comprises three stories centring on fear of personal disintegration in which the narrator and the settings reflect the author's own life. *This Quiet Dust and Other Writings* (1982) is a collection of essays.

SUCKLING, (Sir) JOHN (1609–41) English poet and dramatist, was born in Twickenham, Middlesex, the eldest son of a wealthy statesman, Sir John Suckling (1569–1627). He was educated privately and at Trinity College, Cambridge, after which he served in military capacities and studied on the Continent, being knighted on his return in 1630. The foremost wit and poet of the court of Charles I, he was a notorious gambler ('so that,' according to AUBREY, 'no shopkeeper would trust him for 6*d*'), and a formidable opponent in the bowling alley and at the card table (he was possibly the inventor of the game of cribbage). Also an enthusiastic but inglorious soldier, he fled to France after participating in a royalist army plot to free the King's adviser, the Earl of Strafford

(1593–1641), from jail, and probably committed suicide there. That he was an effective writer in prose is shown by his political thesis advising the King on his public relations image, in the form of a letter to 'Mr Henry German'—Henry Jermyn MP (*d.* 1684), later Earl of St Albans—, and his tract on Socianism addressed to Edward Sackville (1591–1652), 4th Earl of Dorset and a member of the Privy Council, *An Account of Religion by Reason* (written in 1637, published 1646). He wrote four unremarkable plays, of which *Aglaura* (1638) has alternative tragic and tragicomic fifth acts. His literary reputation rests on his comic verse, notably 'A Ballade Upon a Wedding', and on his lyrics, largely unpolished but memorable for their inventiveness of language. His famous song, 'Why so pale and wan, fond lover, / Prithee, why so pale?', occurs in *Aglaura*, IV. ii. See *The Works of Sir John Suckling: the Non-Dramatic Works*, ed. Thomas Clayton, 1971, and *The Plays*, ed. L. A. Beaurline, 1971.

SUETONIUS (GAIUS SUETONIUS TRANQUILLUS) (*c.*69–*c.*140) Roman biographer, was probably born in Algeria. His family was of the class of knights and his father was a regular army officer. He studied and briefly practised law, before holding a succession of palace posts, becoming director of the imperial libraries and then chief of Hadrian's personal secretariat, through which he had access to archive material on earlier reigns. It appears that he was one of those dismissed in 122, on Hadrian's return from Britain, for showing disrespect to the empress, but he may later have been reinstated. The only one of his numerous biographical and antiquarian works which have survived intact is his series of racy and anecdotal lives of the Caesars. We also have his studies of HORACE, LUCAN, and TERENCE. See *The Twelve Caesars*, tr. Robert Graves, rev. Michael Grant, 1979.

SURREY, (HOWARD, HENRY), EARL OF (*c.*1517–47) English poet, was born probably at Kenninghall, Norfolk, and was given his courtesy title when his father became Duke of Norfolk in 1524. He was well educated at home, and in 1529 became companion to Henry Fitzroy (1519–36), Duke of Richmond, who was the illegitimate son of Henry VIII by a lady-in-waiting to the Queen, and who married Surrey's sister Mary in 1533. Surrey was married in 1532 to Frances Vere (*d.* 1577), daughter of the Earl of Oxford. His professional life comprised military service in England and France (his ability was questionable, but not his bravery) and court favour (he was elected Knight of the Garter in 1541), interspersed with bouts of violence and law-breaking (he was twice imprisoned). He was finally beheaded for treason. His distinction is in his being an innovative and technically skilful poet, who owed much to the inspiration of WYATT, with whom he shares the credit for introducing into English the Petrarchan sonnet, in which medium his themes are love, friendship, and chivalry. There are two revealing poems of polite complaint about his incarceration: one of them from Windsor, and the other a satire against the citizens of London for misinterpreting his 'protest', which took the form of breaking their windows. He also translated Books II and IV of VIRGIL's *Aeneid*, described by their first printer (*c.*1554) as 'drawne into a straunge metre', in other words the first example of English blank verse. Other poems were first published in *Songes and Sonettes by Surrey and Other* (1557), edited by Richard Tottel (*c.*1530–94)—known as 'Tottel's Miscellany'. See *Selected Poems*, ed. Dennis Keene, 1985.

SURTEES, ROBERT SMITH (1803–64) British novelist, was born at Hamsterley Hall, Co. Durham (which he inherited on his father's death in 1838), and was educated at Durham Grammar School and for a career in the law, which he abandoned in 1831 to become co-founder and, until 1836, Editor of the *New Sporting Magazine*. He published *The Horseman's Manual, Being a Treatise on Soundness, the Law of Warranty, and Generally on the Laws Relating to Horses* in 1831. He contributed to his own journal a serial, published in 1838 with 12 illustrations by Phiz—Hablot K. Browne (1815–82)—as *Jorrocks' Jaunts and Jollities, or the Hunting, Racing, Driving, Sailing, Eating, Eccentric and Extravagant Exploits of that Renowned Sporting Citizen, Mr John Jorrocks of Great Coram Street*. Further adventures of Jorrocks, who is said to have given DICKENS the idea for *Pickwick Papers*, appeared in *Handley Cross, or Spa Hunt: a Sporting Tale* (1843), illustrated by John Leech (1817–64). More novels in a similar didactic but predominantly satirical vein include *Hillingdon Hall, or the Cockney Squire: a Tale of Country Life* (1845), his best-constructed work, and *Mr Sponge's Sporting Tour* (1853). Surtees had a skilled novelist's perception of situation and character, and a feeling for enjoyable language. He was also the first to write about hunting and its social ethos. He was averse to seeing his name in print, and all his novels appeared anonymously. He was High Sheriff of Durham in 1856. See Leonard Cooper, *R. S. Surtees*, 1952 (biography); Robert L. Collison, *A Jorrocks Handbook*, 1964; Norman Gash, *Robert Surtees and Early Victorian Society*, 1993.

SUTCLIFF, ROSEMARY (1920–92) British novelist and children's writer, was born in West Clandon, Surrey, the only child of a naval officer. The crippling arthritic condition which she suffered since childhood and made progress between wheelchair, dining-room chair, and bed painful and exhausting, and writing a laborious process, restricted her education to home and to a short period at Bideford School of Art. Just as five somewhat inchoate children's books in the early 1950s gave no hint of the lasting impact she was to make on the historical novel for young readers, so, after two romantic period novels, *Lady in Waiting* (1957) and *The Rider of the White Horse* (1959), the publication of *Sword at Sunset* (1964) was a revelation, as well as a landmark in literature about the Dark Ages. A similar insight illuminates *The Mark of the Horse Lord* (1965), published for children, and other novels for that market, notably *Warrior Scarlet* (1958) and her clutch of stories about Roman Britain, *The Silver Branch* (1957), *The Lantern Bearers* (1959), and *Frontier Wolf* (1981), which demonstrate also her understanding of military history and tactics, as well as her habitual, often mystical, sense of place. In spite of the fact that her condition seriously affected the bones of her hands, she was a member of the Royal Society of Miniature Painters. *Blue Remembered Hills* (1983) is an autobiographical sketch of her earlier years which casts little light on the nature of her creative inspiration. She was made OBE in 1975 and CBE in 1992.

SUTHERLAND, EFUA (*b.* 1924), née Morgue, Ghanaian dramatist, was born in Cape Coast, where she grew up with a Christian family and was educated at St Monica's School and Teacher Training College. She then studied education at Homerton College, Cambridge, and linguistics at the School of Oriental and African Studies, London University. She returned to Ghana in 1951, and in 1954 married an American, William Sutherland, with whom she set up a school in the Transvolta. After Ghana's independence in 1956 and the formation of the Arts Council of Ghana, she founded a writers' society, primarily to encourage writing for children, and then, as a further boost to budding authors, the Ghana Drama Studio, Accra, to whose experimental theatre programme she contributed her first two full-length plays. *Edufa* (published 1967), is her version of the Alcestis story of EURIPIDES. *Foriwa* (1967), intended for open-air performance, explores in a constructive and optimistic manner the imposition of new ways on old traditions. An outcome of the Drama Studio was the establishment of the School of Drama, University of Ghana, Legon, with which she and DE GRAFT became closely associated. She also, from 1963, undertook research into African literature and drama at the university's Institute for African Studies. Her espousal of the play within the community, and in particular village theatre, is seen in *The Marriage of Anansewa: a Storytelling Drama* (1975), a folk play with audience participation. *Vulture! Vulture! and Tahinta: Two Rhythm Plays* (1968) is drama for children.

**SUTHERLAND, ROBERT GARI-
OCH** see GARIOCH.

SVEVO, ITALO, pen name of Ettore
Schmitz (1861–1928) Italian novelist, was
born of Jewish parents in Trieste, and was at
12 sent to a commercial school at Segnitz-am-
Main. His first published piece was an article
in a Trieste newspaper, derived from HEINE,
absolving SHAKESPEARE from anti-Semitism
in *The Merchant of Venice*: a few weeks before,
he had been rejected for a job because he was
Jewish. He worked as a bank clerk in Trieste
from 1880 to 1899, and after his first novel,
Una Vita (1892; tr. Archibald Colquhoun as *A
Life*, 1963), published at his own expense,
sank without trace, he taught part time at the
local college of commerce and economics. A
similar fate attended his second novel, *Seni-
lità* (1898; tr. Beryl de Zoete as *A Man Grows
Older*, 1932), a further study of a man's inability to cope with his professional and personal
lives. In 1899 he went into business with his
father-in-law. Needing to brush up his English, in 1907 he took private lessons from
JOYCE, who was most impressed by his pupil's literary endeavours. Schmitz the industrialist prospered during World War I as a
manufacturer of paints for ships; only after
his retirement did Svevo return to writing,
with *La Conscienza di Zeno* (1923; tr. de Zoete
as *The Confessions of Zeno*, 1930). Apparently
written in a fortnight, it significantly and in
an original fashion developed his stock
theme of male inadequacy and demonstrated
the efficacy of psychoanalysis. Even so, it
needed some pressure from Joyce for the
book to be accepted in critical circles, and
Svevo died in a car crash without finishing
the sequel. He also wrote some short stories—see *La Novella del Buon Vecchio e della
Bella Fanciulla* (1930; tr. L. Collison-Morley as
*The Nice Old Man and the Pretty Girl, and Other
Stories*, 1930). See John Gatt-Rutter, *Italo
Svevo: a Double Life*, 1988 (biography).

SWIFT, JONATHAN (1667–1745) Irish
prose writer, poet, and cleric, was born in
Dublin of English parents after his father's
death and was educated at Kilkenny College
and Trinity College, Dublin. After living with
his mother in Leicester (her home town), he
became in 1689 secretary to TEMPLE, with
whom the Swift family had connections, at
Moor Park, Surrey. Here he met and was
tutor to eight-year-old Esther Johnson
(whom he much later dubbed 'Stella'), the
daughter of the companion to Temple's widowed sister. He was also writing poetry, including 'Ode to the Athenian Society', about
which (according to JOHNSON) DRYDEN pronounced, 'Cousin Swift, you will never be a
poet.' In 1694 he took holy orders in the Anglican Church, after which he spent two
years in Ireland, returning to Moor Park in
1696. Here he wrote his first two prose sat-

ires, *A Tale of a Tub*, a burlesque on the religious disagreements of the times with digressions into current philosophy and learning,
and *An Account of a Battel Between Antient and
Modern Books in St James' Library* ('The Battle
of the Books'), a mock-heroic account of a literary controversy involving Temple—the two
were published together in 1704.

On Temple's death, he returned to Ireland
as chaplain to the 2nd Earl of Berkeley (*d.*
1710), on his appointment as a lord justice; in
1701 he became a prebendary of St Patrick's
Cathedral and Vicar of Laracor, Co. Meath,
and received his DD. At his suggestion, Esther, with her close friend Rebecca Dingley as
chaperon, moved to Dublin. They met constantly but never alone, and the suggestion
that at some point they secretly married is as
perplexing as the reason why they may never
have married at all. From 1710 to 1714 he was
mainly in London on political business for
the Church, becoming a valued friend of and
an active propagandist for the ruling Tory
party, after abandoning his allegiance to the
Whigs for their indifference to the interests of
Anglicans in Ireland and to the Test Act. The
letters he wrote to Esther during this period,
partly in code and with excursions into baby
talk, offer a fascinating, informal, and often
thoroughly indiscreet insight into London social and political life. They were first published in 1766–68, and from 1784 have been
known as *Journal to Stella*.

Queen Anne opposed his preferment in
England, but through the good offices of the
Duke of Ormonde (1665–1745) he was appointed Dean of St Patrick's in 1713. He reconciled himself to Dublin, and became an
able church administrator and a thorn in the
flesh of the British Government. He also had
a problem with another, and younger, girlfriend, Esther Vanhomrigh, whose attentions
he had unsuccessfully tried to divert by his
witty poem, 'Cadenus and Vanessa' (*c.*1712).
She pursued him to Ireland and remained
there, dying in 1723 from, it is said, shock at
Swift's reaction to her letter to Stella asking
point-blank whether she and Swift were married. Under the pseudonym of M. B. Drapier,
he published in 1724 *A Letter to the Whole People of Ireland*, inflaming the country to boycott
a proposed new coinage. The Government
imprisoned the printer and offered £300 for
information about the author. Everyone
knew it was Swift, but no one came forward
with proof, or claimed the reward. The coinage was abandoned. He was acclaimed a national hero, and his return to Dublin from a
visit to London in 1726 was greeted with
bells and bonfires. The occasion for the visit
had been the publication of *Travels into Several Remote Nations of the World by Lemuel Gulliver* ('Gulliver's Travels'). While it contains
allusions to contemporary events and attitudes, it is of continued universal appeal for
its satirical insight into human behaviour. In

1727 he made his last visit to England. He was deaf, an extension of the vertigo he had long suffered (now thought to have been Menière's syndrome), but he continued to write. To these years belong his most notorious piece of satirical pamphleteering, *A Modest Proposal for Preventing the Children of Poor People from Being a Burthen* . . . (1729)—his remedy was to eat them, for which he offered several recipes—, and some occasional verse which is notable for its vigorous use of ordinary language. His brain began to fail in 1738, and in 1740 trustees took over his affairs. He was buried in St Patrick's next to his beloved Stella, who had died in 1728.

Apart from the driving *saeva indignatio* [fierce indignation] which he attributed to himself, and the playfulness with which he often exercised it, Swift's distinction lies in his prose—simple, controlled, and concrete. He inspired the love of literary and political friends (notably POPE), as well as of women, not the least devoted of whom was Letitia Pilkington (1712–50), whose *Memoirs* (1748) are a valuable source of information about his personal habits. See *Selected Works*, ed. Angus Ross and David Woolley, 1984; *Selected Poems*, ed. Pat Rogers, 1993; *Selected Poems*, ed. A. Norman Jeffares, new edn 1996; *Swift's Irish Pamphlets: an Introductory Selection*, ed. Joseph McMinn, 1991; David Nokes, *Jonathan Swift: a Hypocrite Reversed*, new edn 1987 (critical biography); Joseph McMinn, *Jonathan Swift: a Literary Life*, 1991.

SWINBURNE, ALGERNON CHARLES

(1837–1909) British poet, dramatist, and critic, was born in London, the eldest child of Admiral and Lady Jane Swinburne. He was educated at Eton, where he arrived clutching a bowdlerized edition of SHAKESPEARE (a present from his mother when he was six), and at Balliol College, Oxford. He was rusticated in 1860, having that same year published two verse plays (*The Queen-Mother* and *Rosamond*), and was finally expelled for time wasting. He was of ambiguous sexual inclinations, though an emotional romance with a cousin, broken off because of their consanguinity, inspired his fine lyrical poem, 'The Triumph of Time'. While at Oxford he became associated with the Pre-Raphaelites and he was for a time a member of D. G. ROSSETTI's ménage. In 1862 he had poetry and essays published in the *Spectator*, including a defence of MEREDITH's *Modern Love*. The following year he completed *Chastelard* (1865), the first of three dramas about Mary, Queen of Scots, of which the other two are bogged down by historical fact. *Atalanta in Calydon* (1865), a verse drama structured like a Greek tragedy, won the praise of the critics and the applause of young men about town, who chanted to each other the melodic rhyming choruses, of which the most memorable is 'When the hounds of spring are on winter's

traces . . .'. *Poems and Ballads* (1866) caused a sensation for what were seen as the expressions of 'the libidinous laureate of a pack of satyrs', a charge he rebutted in *Notes on Poems and Reviews* (1866). Renouncing for the moment freedom of speech in favour of the liberation of man, he followed his political poem, *A Song of Italy* (1867), with *Songs before Sunrise* (1871), in which he used his poetic talent and versatility to support Italian republicanism. *Poems and Ballads: Second Series* (1878) lacked some of the excitement of its predecessor, but contained some of his best poems, including 'A Forsaken Garden' and 'Ave Atque Vale'. He had by this time written most of 'Tristram of Lyonesse' (published in 1882), an uneven but thoughtful and sometimes powerful treatment of medieval romance (composed as a counterblast to TENNYSON), but his faculties were being destroyed by periods of chronic alcoholism. In 1879 Theodore Watts (1832–1914), later Watts-Dunton, a solicitor turned literary critic and novelist, took official charge of him in his Putney house, where Swinburne lived on for thirty years, and continued to write, though in a subdued fashion. There is a vivid and sympathetic portrait of them both at home under the title 'No 2 The Pines' in BEERBOHM's *And Even Now* (1920).

Swinburne's poetry is notable for its emotional appeal and almost shameless glorying in language. His plays, however, lack the dramatist's art. His early study, *William Blake: a Critical Essay* (1868), is a significant contribution to the interpretation of BLAKE's 'Prophetic Books', and modern critics generally confirm the underlying soundness of his judgments on other poets too. He also wrote *Love's Cross-Currents*, an epistolary novel originally published in 1862 in serial form as *A Year's Letters*, and fragments of *Lesbia Brandon* (published in 1952). See *Selected Poems*, ed. Len M. Finlay, 1987; *The Swinburne Letters*, ed. Cecil Y. Lang, 6 vols 1959–62; Jean Overton Fuller, *Swinburne: a Critical Biography*, 1968; Jerome J. McGann, *Swinburne: an Experiment in Criticism*, 1972.

SYMMES, ROBERT EDWARD see DUNCAN.

SYMONS, A. J. A. see SYMONS, JULIAN.

SYMONS, ARTHUR (1865–1945) British

poet, critic, translator, and editor, was born in Milford Haven, Pembrokeshire, of Cornish parents. His father, a Methodist minister, served on nine different circuits during the boy's upbringing. He was educated until he was 16 at private schools, and at 19 was editing volumes in the 'Shakespeare Quarto Facsimiles' series. His first book, a critical introduction to ROBERT BROWNING, was published in 1886, and the first of several of his volumes of verse, *Days and Nights*, in 1889. He contributed critical articles to the *Athenaeum* and *Saturday Review*, and became Editor of the *Savoy* in 1896. Visits to France brought him in touch with contemporary European creative development, which he propounded in *The Symbolist Movement in Literature* (1899). In 1893 he had become involved with a 19-year-old ballet dancer known as Lydia. They had a passionate affair, which was briefly resumed after her marriage in 1896. Symons was still writing poems to her at the end of his life. He himself married Rhoda Bowser (1874–1936), daughter of a Newcastle shipping magnate, in 1901. Overwork had already contributed to his being in a disturbed state when they visited Italy in 1908. They had an argument and she returned to England. Shortly afterwards he had a complete breakdown in Ferrara and was picked up by the police and put in jail, from which he was rescued by the British Ambassador. He analysed that experience, and the subsequent two years of incarceration in asylums in Italy and England, in *Confessions: a Study in Pathology* (1930). While he recaptured his ability to work, his acute critical sense tended to remain directed towards writers of the 1890s and immediately after. See Karl Beckson, *Arthur Symons: a Life*, 1987.

SYMONS, JULIAN (1912–94) British novelist and critic, was born in London, the younger brother of A. J. A. Symons (1900–41), biographer of ROLFE and bibliographer, whose biography he wrote (1950). The family's fortunes fluctuated, and he was educated at state schools, after which he worked from 1929 to 1941 as a shorthand typist and secretary with an engineering firm. During this time he published *Confusions about X* (1939), the first of several books of verse. ('From the age of 16 I regarded myself primarily as a poet. It was only later, some time at the start of the 1950s, that I realized I wasn't a good one.') He also founded, and edited from January 1937 until the outbreak of World War II, the magazine *Twentieth Century Verse*, which was a platform for younger English, and American, poets. He served in the 57th Tank Regiment during the war. While working afterwards as an advertising copywriter, he 'dug out of a dusty drawer a near-comic detective story'. Published as *The Immaterial Murder Case* (1945), it was the first of his many crime novels, a form of expression which paid the bills and enabled him 'to show the violence that lives behind the bland faces most of us present to the world'— *Playing Happy Families* (1994) came out shortly before his death. In 1947 he was enabled to devote himself to writing when OR-WELL persuaded the *Manchester Evening News* to take him on as his successor on its literary pages at £10 a week. He was a co-founder in 1953 of the Crime Writers' Association, and President of the Detection Club 1976–85. His critical works include studies of DICKENS (1951), CARLYLE (1952), POE (1978), DOYLE (1979), and HAMMETT (1985), and *Bloody Murder: From the Detective Story to the Crime Novel* (2nd rev. edn 1992).

SYNGE, J(OHN) M(ILLINGTON) (1871–1909) Irish dramatist and poet, was born in Newtown Little, Dublin, the youngest of five children of a barrister who died when Synge was one year old. He was educated privately and at Trinity College, Dublin, where he studied Irish and Hebrew. From an early age he took a great interest in natural history, and it was reading DARWIN at 14 which led him soon afterwards to renounce religion. His first choice of career was to be a musician, for which he studied in Germany for two years. In 1895, however, he decided to become a writer, and for the next seven years spent each winter in Paris. Here he met YEATS, who introduced him to Maud Gonne's Young Ireland Society (from which he soon resigned on political grounds), and who suggested he should visit the then remote Aran isles (where Yeats's great-uncle had been rector) to further his knowledge of Irish traditional life. He returned there time and again, recapturing its landscape and peasant society in his prose account, *The Aran Islands* (1907; with his own photographs, 1979). His personal experience of a romance blighted on religious grounds inspired his first, rejected, play, 'When the Moon Has Set', and much of his early poetry. Thereafter his plays are redolent of the lore and customs of the country people of Aran or of Wicklow, the language reflecting Gaelic syntax and incorporating in a natural way words, phrases, and speech rhythms which he had absorbed on his travels. *The Shadow of the Glen* (performed 1903) and *Riders to the Sea* (1904) are one-act tragedies based on folk tales. At about the same time as he was writing them, he embarked on *The Tinker's Wedding*, which (after six complete drafts) was published in 1907, but not performed. In 1904 he became a co-director with Yeats and GREGORY of the Abbey Theatre, which staged his *The Well of Saints* (1905), in which the folklore has a supernatural element and the setting an equivalent remoteness.

The Playboy of the Western World (1907) opened to an unpredicted, if perhaps predictable, storm. The first-night audience erupted at the image of 'chosen females standing in their shifts', and on the second night the police had to be called in to calm rioters who saw the portrayal of the peasantry as an insult to Irish nationalism. This sparkling play goes at a great pace, moving effortlessly between tragedy, comedy, and farce to, at the end, pathos. Synge's relationship with the 19-year-old Abbey actress, Molly Allgood, is reflected in some of the poems he wrote at this time, such as 'Is it a month . . .' and 'The Meeting'; so is the imminence of death, for he had Hodgkin's disease. When he died he was still revising *Deirdre of the Sorrows* (1909), an enduring and intricate excursion into Irish mythology. He was a meticulous craftsman, who was able to exercise simultaneously an unusually high standard of both dramatic and poetic expression. See *Collected Plays, Poems and The Aran Islands*, ed. Alison Smith, 1996; *The Playboy of the Western World and Other Plays*, ed. Ann Saddlemyer, new edn 1995; *Poems and Translations*, new edn 1972; *Autobiography*, ed. Alan Price, 1965; D. H. Greene and E. M. Stephens, *J. M. Synge 1871–1909*, 1959 (biography); David M. Kiely, *J. M. Synge: a Biography*, 1995; Robin Skelton, *The Writings of J. M. Synge*, 1971.

T

TACITUS, CORNELIUS (*c.*55–*c.*117) Roman historian, was probably born in Gaul, and studied law in Rome. He was an excellent speaker, and published a book on the subject in his twenties. He became a senator, and was consul in 97, and governor of Asia in 112. He married the daughter of the distinguished soldier and governor of Britain, Agricola (37–93), whom he believed had been poisoned on the orders of the emperor Domitian, and of whom he wrote an elegant and flattering memoir. We have just a few books of his two series of histories covering the reign of Tiberius to that of Domitian, which are known as the 'Histories' and the 'Annals'. He also wrote a graphic report on the land and people of Germany. He was a literary stylist as well as a shrewd observer and commentator, and an upholder of the ancient virtues of his nation. See *The Agricola and The Germania*, tr. Harold Mattingley, rev. S. A. Handford, 1970; *The Annals of Imperial Rome*, tr. Michael Grant, rev. edn 1971; *The Histories*, tr. Kenneth Wellesley, rev. edn 1975; Ronald Mellor, *Tacitus*, new edn 1995 (biographical/critical study).

TAGORE, RABINDRANATH (1861–1941) Indian poet, fiction writer, dramatist, and philosopher, was born in the family mansion at Jorasanko, Calcutta, the youngest of 14 children of an enlightened Hindu scholar who required his children, when they read SHAKESPEARE'S *Macbeth* at home, to translate it into Bengali verse. He was educated mainly at home by tutors (school irked him), and at 16 had published stories, essays, literary criticism, and dramatic pieces, and regularly gave public recitals of his poetry. In 1880 he gave up studying law at University College, London, and returned home. In 1883 he married Mrinalini Devi (*d.* 1902). In 1890 his father dispatched him to look after the family estates in East Bengal, where he came into close contact with the 'little people' who feature so stimulatingly in his stories. Having determined to educate his five children himself, in 1901 he established at Santiniketan, Bolpur, a riverside site which his father had bought as a religious retreat, an open-plan school, which he kept going by selling his wife's jewellery and the copyright in his collected works up to that time. (In 1918 he re-dedicated it as Vsiva-Bharati University, to be an international institution of learning and understanding.) In 1912 he accompanied his son to London, partly to recuperate from an illness, during which he had translated into free English verse (as his first literary efforts in English) poems from his Bengali *Gitanjali* (1910). With a few more from other volumes of his lyrics, they were taken up by the India Society as its annual publication for 1912. And with editorial help (and an enthusiastic introduction) by YEATS, the book was published by Macmillan in 1913 as *Gitanjali (Song Offerings)*, for which Tagore was awarded the Nobel Prize for Literature. Further volumes were *The Gardener* (1913), *Fruit-Gathering* (1916), and *Lover's Gift and Crossing* (1918). *Glimpses of Bengal*, sketches of life extracted from his letters and translated by his nephew Surendranath Tagore, appeared in 1921.

During the last twenty years of his life Tagore made nine foreign tours, in spite of ill health, to North and South America, Europe, Russia, China, and Japan, as well as three trips to Ceylon. In 1930 he took up painting as a hobby, and became so good at it that exhibitions were mounted in Berlin, Munich, Moscow, Paris, and New York. He was knighted in 1915, but resigned from the Order in 1919 in protest at the British action in Amritsar during the riots in the Punjab. See *Selected Short Stories of Rabindranath Tagore*, ed. Andrew Robinson, tr. Krishna Dutta and Mary Lago, introduction by Anita Desai, 1991; *Collected Poems and Plays*, 1990; *Selected Poems*, tr. William Radice, new edn 1990; *My Reminiscences*, new edn (tr. Andrew Robinson) 1991; Krishna Dutta and Andrew Robinson, *Rabindranath Tagore: the Myriad-Minded Man*, 1995 (biography); Mary M. Lago, *Rabindranath Tagore*, 1976 (critical study).

TANIZAKI JUN'ICHIRO (1886–1965) Japanese novelist, was born and brought up in Tokyo, the grandson of a printer/publisher, and while at primary school attended part-time private academies to study classical Chinese and English—see [*Childhood Years: a Memoir*] (serialized 1955–56; tr. Paul McCarthy, 1988), in which are the sources of emotions and sensations that recur as themes in his fiction. At middle school he wrote most versatily for the school magazine. During his time at high school he was dismissed from his post of tutor/houseboy (to earn his keep) for having an affair with a maid of the household. He went to Tokyo University in 1908 to study Japanese literature, only to be expelled after two years for non-payment of fees. By 1911 literary magazines were printing his work, and his first novel, unconventional in theme but classical in style, had appeared. His first major work to be published in the West was [*The Makioka Sisters*] (1948; tr. Edward G. Seidensticker, 1957), an upperclass family saga looking back to the pre-militarism of the early 1930s, serialization of which had been halted by the militaristic government during World War II. Written just before it was [*A Cat, a Man, and Two Women*] (1937; tr. McCarthy, 1990), a comic variation on the eternal triangle. The works of his later period, such as [*The Key*] (1956; tr. Howard S. Hibbert, 1960) and [*Diary of a Mad Old Man*] (1962; tr. Hibbert, 1965), reflect in theme the ageing of their author while confirming his penchant for wit and eroticism. [*In Praise of Shadows*] (1933; tr. Thomas J. Harper and Seidensticker, 1991) is a sequence of meditations on the passing of the Tokugawa period, which ended in 1868.

TASMA, pen name of Jessie Couvreur (1848–97), née Huybers, Australian novelist, was born in Highgate, London, the daughter of a Dutch merchant who emigrated with his family to Hobart in about 1852. At 18 she married 25-year-old Charles Fraser, but six years later took off with her mother and several brothers and sisters on a two-year tour of Europe. On her return in 1875, relations between them were strained. She spent most of the next few years in England and on the Continent, supporting herself by journalism and lecturing on Australia. She divorced Fraser in 1883, and in 1885 married Auguste Couvreur, a member of the Belgian parliament and Brussels correspondent of *The Times*. The *Australasian* printed some of her short stories, and began in January 1888 the serialization of *Uncle Piper of Piper's Hill*, which on its publication in book form in 1889 the *Spectator* called 'only the third work of fiction possessing remarkable merit that has come to us from the Antipodes' (the others being MARCUS CLARKE's *For the Term of His Natural Life* and BOLDREWOOD's *Robbery Under Arms*). It succeeds especially for its portrait of urban society, its characterization, and the contrast between the settled Pipers and the immigrant Cavendishes. Her five further novels, while reflecting the taste for the 'sex problem' generated by SCHREINER's *The Story of an African Farm*, are also reworkings of her experiences as Mrs Fraser. On her husband's death in 1894, she took on his job with *The Times*. She died of heart failure and was cremated at her own wish, having been, in an article in 1878, one of the first Australians publicly to advocate the practice. See Patricia Clarke, *Tasma: the Life of Jessie Couvreur*, 1994.

TASSO, TORQUATO (1544–95) Italian poet, was born in Sorrento, the third child of Bernardo Tasso (1493–1569), poet, and Porzia de' Rossi (*d.* 1556). In 1554, after two years at a Jesuit school in Naples, he joined his father in exile, first in Rome, then at the court of Urbino, and then in Venice. He read law at the universities of Padua and Bologna, and then, having already published *Rinaldi* (1562), a long romance in verse, studied poetry and philosophy for a year in Padua at the Accademia degli Eterei. In 1565 he entered, as ARIOSTO had done, the service of the Este family, initially with Cardinal Luigi d'Este. In 1572 he came back to Ferrara as resident poet to the Cardinal's brother, Duke Alfonso II, for whose court he composed the pastoral play *Aminta*. It was performed in 1573, and published in 1581 in a pirated edition. It was in print in England before 1585 in a Latin version, which was then translated into English in 1587 by Abraham Fraunce (*fl.* 1587–1633), who revised it alongside the Italian and reissued it as *The Countess of Pembroke's Yvychurch* (1591)—SPENSER alludes to it and its 'sweet Poets verse' in *The Faerie Queen* (III. vi, 45).

Tasso also worked on his epic poem of tribute to his patrons, *Gerusalemme Liberata* [Jerusalem Delivered], which he set at the time of the First Crusade, weaving mythical and romantic elements into his account of the relief of Jerusalem by Godfrey of Bouillon (*c.*1060–1100). Regrettably, instead of publishing it, he submitted it in manuscript to the scrutiny of friendly, and unfriendly, critics, whose contrary, and contradictory, comments so confounded him that while making revisions he had a nervous breakdown, and set off disguised as a peasant for Sorrento, where he had a sister. He returned to Ferrara in 1579, only to be put into the hospital of Sant' Anna as insane. An incomplete pirated edition of his epic was printed in 1580 as *Il Goffredo*, followed by various editions under the original title. In 1585 he was released into the custody of Prince Vincenzo Gonzaga, Duke of Mantua, and wrote a tragedy in the classical Greek mould, *Il Re Torrismondo* [Torrismondo the King] (tr. Maria Pastore Passaro, 1996). He then embarked on a restless tour of towns and friends' establishments, in the course of which he published a hopelessly botched revision of his epic as *Gerusalemme Conquistata* (1593). Invited to Rome in 1594 by Pope Clement VIII to be crowned laureate, he was regarded on arrival as too ill to receive the honour and was admitted to the monastery of Sant' Onofrio, where he died.

His total oeuvre comprises nearly two thousand lyrics and poems in other forms, numerous letters, and a body of prose dialogues and discourses, including several on poetry—see *Discourses on the Heroic Poem*, ed. and tr. Mariella Calvachini and Irene Samuel (1973). An English translation by Richard Carew (1555–1620) of the first five cantos of *Gerusalemme Liberata* appeared in 1594. The complete work, done, like the original, into *ottava rima* by Edward Fairfax (1568–1635), illegitimate son of Sir Thomas Fairfax of Denton (*d.* 1600), was published as *Godfrey of Bulloigne: or, The Recoverie of Jerusalem* (1600), in which form it has long held its own as a translation. Tasso's life story is the subject of a lost play which DEKKER was paid for emending in 1604. SHELLEY intended to write a tragedy about him; BYRON, in 'The Lament of Tasso', refers to his hypothetical romance with Princess Leonora, which GOETHE immortalized in his play, *Torquato Tasso* (1790).

TATE, (JOHN ORLEY) ALLEN (1899–1979) American poet, biographer, and critic, was born in Clarke County, Kentucky, and had a disrupted childhood and early education after the family business interests were lost in 1907. In 1918 he entered Vanderbilt University where, with his teacher, RANSOM, and his roommate, WARREN, he actively participated in the founding of *The Fugitive*, to whose first issue in 1922 he contributed two poems as Henry Feathertop. In 1924 he married Caroline Gordon (1895–1981), novelist and short-story writer: they were divorced in 1959. The arrangement of *Mr Pope and Other Poems* (1928), under the categories of 'Space', 'Time', and 'History', reflected early on his preoccupation with the stable order of things; the poems 'To the Lacedemonians' and 'Ode to the Confederate Dead' illustrate his view of the present in terms of the past. His reading of T. S. ELIOT, whom he met in London in 1928, added a religious intensity to his poetry; he became a Roman Catholic in 1950. *Collected Poems 1919–1976* was published in 1977. He taught English at the University of Minnesota from 1951 until his retirement in 1968. As a critic, he was a proponent of the New Criticism—see *Collected Essays* (1959) and *Essays of Four Decades* (1968). He wrote two biographies, *Stonewall Jackson: the Good Soldier* (1928), and *Jefferson Davis: His Rise and Fall* (1929), and a Civil War novel, *The Fathers* (1938).

TATE, NAHUM (1652–1715) Irish poet and dramatist, was born in Dublin, the second son of a Puritan clergyman called Faithful Teate, and was educated at Trinity College, Dublin. His *Poems* was published in London in 1677 (enlarged edn 1684), and his first tragedy, *Brutus of Alba: or, The Enchanted Lovers*, based on the story of Dido and Aeneas, was performed in 1678. In all he wrote some nine plays, including an adaptation of SHAKESPEARE's *King Lear* (1681), in which the Fool makes no appearance and Cordelia lives, and marries Edgar; it was the standard theatre version for almost two hundred years. It is customary to decry his work, but Allardyce Nicoll in *British Drama* (4th edn 1947) cites *A Duke and No Duke* (1684) and *Cuckolds-Haven: or, An Alderman No Conjurer* (1685) in nominating Tate and Edward Ravenscroft (1644–1704) as dramatists to whom 'more than any others we owe the development and establishment of English farce'. Tate wrote, with DRYDEN, the second part of *Absalom and Achitophel* (1682), and in 1692 succeeded SHADWELL as Poet Laureate. He was reappointed on the accession of Queen Anne in 1702, when he was also made Historiographer Royal. His only original poem of any note is *Panacea: a Poem upon Tea* (1700). He collaborated with Nicholas Brady (1659–1726) in producing *A New Version of the Psalms* (1696), and wrote the libretto for *Dido and Aeneas*, the only true opera by Henry Purcell (1659–95), first performed at a girls' school in Chelsea in 1689. It appears that he died while hiding from his creditors. See Christopher Spencer, *Nahum Tate*, 1972 (critical study).

TAYLOR, JEREMY (1613–67) English prose writer and cleric, was born in Cambridge, the son of a barber, and was educated at the Perse School and Gonville and Caius College, Cambridge, becoming a Fellow and taking holy orders before he was 21. Archbishop Laud (1573–1645) had him transferred to Oxford, where he became a Fellow of All Souls and in 1642 was made DD by royal mandate—he was a chaplain to Charles I. In 1645 he was captured and imprisoned by the Parliamentary army. On his release he was given protection by the 2nd Earl of Carbery (*c.*1600–86), the royalist peer, at whose seat, Golden Grove in Carmarthenshire, he spent much of the next ten years. After the Restoration of the Monarchy in 1660 he was appointed Bishop of Down and Connor, and Vice-Chancellor of Dublin University. A liberal churchman, it is for the baroque splendour of his exposition that he is remembered, and especially for his extended similes, often prefaced with, 'So I have seen . . .'. His style can be readily appreciated in *The Rule and Exercises of Holy Living* (1650) and *The Rule and Exercises of Holy Dying* (1651), while his religious stance is best illustrated by *The Liberty of Prophesying* (1647). More unusual is *A Discourse of the Nature, Offices and Measures of Friendship, with Rules of Conducting It* (1657), addressed to KATHERINE PHILIPS, among whose circle he was known as Palaemon. Taylor was twice married. He died in Lisburn of a fever caught from a patient to whom he was ministering. See C. J. Stranks, *The Life and Writings of Jeremy Taylor*, new edn 1978.

TAYLOR, PETER (HILLSMAN) (1917–94) American short-story writer and novelist, was born in Trenton, Tennessee. In 1926–32 the family lived in St Louis, where his father, who had served as a circuit attorney general, was President of the Missouri State Life Insurance Co. He was educated at Memphis Central High School, Tennessee, but after a family row walked out on a scholarship to Columbia University and worked his passage on a New Orleans transatlantic freighter. After one semester at Southwestern College, he enrolled at Vanderbilt University, from which he dropped out and sold real estate after RANSOM moved to Kenyon College, where Taylor finally settled in 1938, becoming an enthusiastic member of the literary elite—the first-person narrative of '1939' (1955) contains close autobiographical parallels. He had two stories published in *River* in 1937, and in 1940, the year he graduated, WARREN accepted three more for *Southern Review*. During World War II he was at Fort Oglethorpe, Georgia, and Tidworth Camp, Wiltshire, UK, as a sergeant in the Rail Transportation Corps. In 1943 he married, in Tennessee, Eleanor Ross (*b.* 1920), whose verse collection *Wilderness of Ladies* (1960), had an introduction by their friend JARRELL.

In 1946 he began his teaching career at the Woman's College of the University of North Carolina; it finished when he retired from the University of Virginia, Charlottesville, where he became a member of the English faculty in 1967. *A Long Fourth and Other Stories* (1948), *The Widows of Thornton* (1954), and *Happy Families Are All Alike: a Collection of Stories* (1959), contained in all 26 stories. *Miss Leonora When Last Seen and Fifteen Other Stories* (1963) and *The Collected Stories of Peter Taylor* (1969), which have ten stories in common, are compilations from the earlier books with some new pieces. Subsequent collections are *In the Miro District and Other Stories* (1977), *The Old Forest and Other Stories* (1985), and *The Oracle at Stoneleigh Court* (1993). *A Woman of Means* (1950) is a novella. His novel *A Summons to Memphis* (1986) won the Pulitzer Prize. In his introduction to *A Long Fourth and Other Stories* Warren suggested that Taylor's basic themes were 'the disintegration of families . . . the attrition of loyalties, the breakdown of old patterns, and the collapse of old values'. A writer particularly concerned with form, Taylor continued to explore these themes while also illustrating new aspects of Southern culture in the urban centres and among the expatriate communities in the cities of the Midwest. See James Curry Robison, *The Short Stories of Peter Taylor*, 1988 (critical study).

TEMPLE, (Sir) **WILLIAM** (1628–99) English essayist and statesman, was born in London, the eldest son of Sir John Temple (1600–77), Master of the Rolls in Ireland. He was educated at Bishop Stortford School and Emmanuel College, Cambridge, which he left in 1648, without taking a degree, to finish his education on the Continent. On the way there, he met DOROTHY OSBORNE, with whom he corresponded until their marriage in 1655. After several years in Ireland, during which he sat in the Irish Parliament, he embarked on a career in diplomacy, in the course of which he negotiated the Triple Alliance of England, Holland, and Sweden (1668), was twice Ambassador to The Hague, and contrived the marriage between William of Orange and the Princess Mary. He was made a baronet in 1666. He refused a secretaryship of state from Charles II in 1679, and again from (the now) King William in 1689, when, disillusioned by 'the uncertainty of princes, the caprices of fortune, the corruption of ministers, the violence of factions, the unsteadiness of counsels, and the infidelity of friends', he went into retirement. He moved from Sheen to the greater seclusion of Moor Park, Farnham, engaged SWIFT as secretary, and applied himself to literature and to his garden. He published *Observations upon the United Provinces of the Netherlands* (1673) and *Miscellanea* (1680), which included 'Upon the Original and Nature of Government' and other political and personal essays. A second part of *Miscellanea* appeared in 1690, and a third (edited by Swift) in 1701. His essays are distinctive, for their time, for their unadorned, rhythmical style, and for the confidence with which he pursued any topic or line of argument which took his fancy, even if this policy occasionally led him into trouble with academics.

TENNANT, EMMA (*b.* 1937) British novelist, was born in London, the eldest child by his second marriage of the 2nd Baron Glenconner (1899–1983), and grew up in Scotland. She was educated at St Paul's Girls' School and at a finishing school in Oxford, came out as a debutante, and studied art history in Paris. She published her first novel, *The Colour of Rain* (1964), as 'Catherine Aydy', a name she claims to have got from a Ouija board. In *The Time of Crack* (1973), a geological disaster is the inspiration for black comedy and the reversal of the gender roles, a topic to which she frequently returns and which dominates her work. *The Bad Sister* (1978) is an imaginative feminist reworking of HOGG's *The Confessions of a Justified Sinner*. In *Queen of Stones* (1982), schoolgirls comprise the group which is, as in BALLANTYNE and GOLDING, isolated from the adult world. Her message is at its most explicit in *Sisters and Strangers: a Moral Tale* (1990), in which the fate of a modern Eve is held up as a warning; it is at its most extreme in the TV screenplay, *Frankenstein's Baby* (1990), in which a male pregnancy is engineered. Political satire motivates *The Last of the Country House Murders* (1974) and *Black Marina* (1985). *Faustine* (1992) is a modern feminist version of the Faust legend of MARLOWE in a Gothic setting, in which the consumer society is remorselessly analysed. In *Tess* (1993) she uncovers some of the sidelights on HARDY's relations with and attitudes to women within a structure derived from *Tess of the d'Urbervilles*. *Pemberley* (1993) and *An Unequal Marriage* (1994) are sequels to AUSTEN's *Pride and Prejudice*, and *Emma in Love* (1996) to that author's *Emma*. Tennant was founder-Editor of the literary magazine *Bananas* 1975–78, and is Editor of the Viking/Penguin series, 'Lives of Modern Women'.

TENNANT, KYLIE (1912–88) Australian novelist, was born in Manly, New South Wales, and was educated there at Brighton College. In 1932 she married the social historian Lewis Rudd (*d.* 1979). Her first novel, *Tiburon* (1935), a study of rural poverty in New South Wales during the Depression, was praised as social realism, a judgment which did not fully take into account the satire and sheer comedy with which she continued to invest the circumstances and activities of the groups of society that people her novels, in which the city often symbolizes despair. Not that the experiences she describes are undocumented: she lived in a Sydney slum for *Foveaux* (1939); journeyed on the road and worked with travellers for *The Battlers* (1941), and with itinerant bee-keepers for *The Honey Flow* (1956); built boats for *Lost Haven* (1946); and contrived to spend a week in jail before writing *The Joyful Condemned* (1953; complete version as *Tell Morning This*, 1968). Her play, *Tether a Dragon* (1952), which highlights aspects of the life and career of the federal Prime Minister, Alfred Deakin (1856–1919), won the Commonwealth Jubilee competition, though better dramatic work is in her one-act plays for young people. She also wrote biographical and popular historical works. She was made AO in 1980. See *The Missing Heir*, 1986 (autobiography).

TENNYSON, ALFRED (1st Baron Tennyson) (1809–92) British poet and dramatist, was born in Somersby, Lincolnshire, the sixth of 12 children of an elder son who had been passed over in his wealthy father's will and had reluctantly entered the Church. The boy was educated at Louth Grammar School and by his father, and went to Trinity College, Cambridge, in 1827, about fifty of his poems having already been published in the anonymous compilation, *Poems by Two Brothers*—actually by three, the others being Frederick (1807–98) and Charles (1808–79). Of the brilliant young men he now met, he became especially close to Arthur Hallam (1811–33), with whom he spent two idyllic holidays on the Continent, and who became engaged to Tennyson's sister, Emily (1811–89). In 1829 he won the Chancellor's Gold Medal for poetry with a piece on the set subject of 'Timbuctoo', which encouraged him to publish *Poems, Chiefly Lyrical* (1830), whose main interest lies in the rhythmical and disturbing 'Mariana'

and the impassioned 'The Ballad of Oriana'. In 1831 Mr Tennyson died, and the poet abandoned Cambridge to help look after the family. Though on the whole *Poems*, dated 1833 but published in December 1832, showed more promise than the earlier volume, it was coolly received, which is understandable in that memorable poems such as 'The Lady of Shalott', 'The Lotus Eaters', and 'Oenone' were not yet in their definitive versions. In September 1833 Hallam died suddenly in Vienna of a ruptured blood vessel. The shock to Emily was catastrophic: the effect on Tennyson was profound. On top of family and financial problems, he had lost not only someone closer than brother or mere friend, but the prop whose recognition of his artistic genius was essential at a time when his professional confidence was waning (as 'The Two Voices', written largely before the tragedy, demonstrates).

For two years he wrote little, and it was another seven before he published again, but in the meantime he had found his own voice. *Poems* (2 vols 1842) contained rewritten versions of 16 earlier poems; the memorable blank-verse dramatic monologue, 'Ulysses'; 'Morte d'Arthur' and 'Sir Galahad', his first excursions into Arthurian legend; 'Locksley Hall', an attempt at social protest; and the classic lament, 'Break, Break, Break'. In 1845 he was granted a Civil List pension of £200 a year for life, which relieved his immediate financial worries and enabled him to travel. In 1847 he published *The Princess: a Medley*, an over-idyllic novella in verse supporting women's rights, punctuated (in the third edition in 1850) with some of his finest lyrics, including 'Now sleeps the crimson petal . . .'. On 1 June 1850 *In Memoriam A. H. H.* appeared. There had been a trial run printed for his friends in March, and now it was published anonymously, but there was no doubt in the minds of the public as to the author's identity. This tribute to Hallam in the form of a sequence of 131 poetic reminiscences, elegies, and reflections, pronounced Tennyson not just the foremost poet of his age, but also a scientist and philosopher. On 13 June he married Emily Sellwood (1813–96), whom he had known for twenty years—see Ann Thwaite, *Emily Tennyson: the Poet's Wife* (1996). They had been engaged once before, but the match had been broken off because of his poor health and limited prospects. And in November he was appointed Poet Laureate in succession to WORDSWORTH, a post he assumed with characteristic thoroughness, dignity, and (occasionally) immortality, as with *Ode on the Death of the Duke of Wellington* (1852) and 'The Charge of the Light Brigade' (1854), which was, according to him, written 'in a few minutes'. This second period of poetic output closed with *Maud* (1855), a series of dramatic monologues (later called a 'monodrama') whose violent story incorporates some outspoken social criticism.

The Idylls of the King (1859), a series of Arthurian narratives, was the culmination of years of study, meditation, and practice. Expanded versions of the original four appeared at intervals; further episodes were published in *The Holy Grail, and Other Poems* (1870), and as *Gareth and Lynette*, with 'The Last Tournament' (1872). The final order is that of the 1889 edition. The descriptive writing is fine and the poetry ripples along, but the characters are unconvincing on both an allegorical and a realistic plane. The lack of a driving dramatic sense is evident, too, in the verse plays that he wrote between 1875 and 1892. There was no slackening in his output of occasional, lyrical, narrative, and meditative verse, and it is to his later years that 'The Revenge', 'Rizpah', 'The Voyage', and 'Crossing the Bar' belong. He was created a baron in 1884, becoming Alfred, Lord Tennyson. The Tennysons had two sons. The younger, Lionel (1854–86), who wanted to be an actor, died of malaria shortly after arriving in India, where he had gone instead at his mother's behest to join the staff of the Viceroy. The elder, Hallam (1852–1928), 2nd Baron Tennyson, wrote a sanitized biography, *Alfred Lord Tennyson: a Memoir* (2 vols 1897), on the completion of which he and his mother destroyed all letters, journals (including her own), and other papers which might suggest that the poet was other than a Christian gentleman. See *The Poems of Tennyson*, ed. Christopher Ricks, 3 vols, 2nd rev. edn 1987; *Selected Poems*, ed. Christopher Ricks and Aiden Day, 1991; *The Letters of Alfred Lord Tennyson*, ed. Cecil Y. Lang and Edgar F. Shannon Jr, 3 vols 1981–90; Robert B. Martin, *Tennyson: the Unquiet Heart*, new edn 1983 (biography); Christopher Ricks, *Tennyson*, 2nd edn 1989 (critical biography); Roger Ebbatson, *Tennyson*, 1988 (introduction).

TERENCE (PUBLIUS TERENTIUS AFER) (185–159 BC) Roman dramatist, was brought to Rome as a slave, probably from Africa, and was educated by his owner, Terentius Lucanus, who gave him his freedom and from whom Terence took his name. It is said that he submitted his first comedy, *Andria*, to the curule aediles (in their capacity as municipal entertainments' officers), who referred him to the dramatist, Caecilius (*c*.219–*c*.166). Caecilius, who was at dinner, was so impressed that he invited Terence to eat and to share his couch of honour. The play was performed in 166, and Terence wrote five more before he died in a shipwreck, or of disease, on a trip to Greece to look for plots. He was only 26, but his plays are better constructed than those of PLAUTUS and the originals he adapted. CONGREVE, in a preface to *The Way of the World*, extols 'the Purity of his

Stile, the Delicacy of his Turns, and the Justness of his Characters'. DIDEROT suggested that of all comic dramatists only Terence and MOLIÈRE had the gift of individualizing their characters in a timeless way. See *The Comedies*, tr. Betty Radice, 1976; *The Comedies*, tr. Palmer Bovie, Constance Carrier, and Douglass Parker, 1995.

TERESA (OF AVILA), ST (1515–82) Spanish religious reformer and prose writer, was born Teresa Sánchez de Cepeda y Ahumada, of mixed Jewish and Christian descent, near Avila. After her mother's death when she was 11, she consorted, by her own account, with a frivolous cousin, and was finally sent to board at a local Augustinian convent. She became a Carmelite nun when she was about twenty, but it was not until 1555, after many years of illness, that her reading of AUGUSTINE's *Confessions* encouraged her to examine her own experiences and, helped by her intellectual and mystical visions, to begin the reform of the Order. The first convent of the Discalced ('Barefooted' or Reformed) Carmelites was that of San José in Avila, the process of its foundation in 1562 being fully described in *Vida*, her autobiography, which she had begun to write in the 1550s and which she completed in 1565 at the request of her confessors. *Libro de las Fundaciones* [The Foundations] describes her subsequent journeys and the establishment of 16 further religious houses. *El Castillo Interior* [The Interior Castle], also called *Las Moradas* [The Mansions], is an analysis of her spirituality, written in 1577 after a mystical vision in the convent in Toledo in which she had been confined by orthodox Carmelites who were at the time trying to get her deported to South America. From 1567 she had the practical support of her protégé, JOHN OF THE CROSS. She was canonized in 1622, and was in 1814, at a time of national crisis, proclaimed the patron saint of Spain. See *The Life of Saint Teresa*, tr. J. M. Cohen, new edn 1987.

TEY, JOSEPHINE see MACKINTOSH.

THACKERAY, WILLIAM MAKEPEACE (1811–63) British novelist and journalist, was born in Calcutta, the only child of the Collector of Alipore, and was sent back to England after his father's death in 1816. He was educated at Charterhouse and Trinity College, Cambridge, from which he removed himself because he felt his studies would be of no practical use. In the expectation of a considerable legacy under his father's will, he travelled on the Continent and then studied law. When his inheritance did not materialize owing to the collapse of the Indian Bank, he became a journalist. In 1836 he married Isabella Shawe (1816–94) in Paris, where he was correspondent to the *Constitutional*.

The paper failed six months later, and the couple returned to England, where he contributed regularly to *Fraser's Magazine*, as well as to other periodicals. A daughter, the novelist Anne Thackeray Ritchie (1837–1919), was born the following year, but after the birth in 1840 of their third child ('Minny', first wife of Leslie Stephen, the father of VIRGINIA WOOLF), Isabella had a mental breakdown from which she never recovered. In a variety of forms and under several pseudonyms (of which Fitzboodle and Titmarsh were the most famous), Thackeray now worked towards the novel of realism told with irony that became his hallmark, of which the first was *The Luck of Barry Lyndon*, serialized in 1844. He also wrote *The Snobs of England* (1846–47) and a collection of parodies, *Punch's Prize Novelists* (1847). *Vanity Fair: a Novel without a Hero* (1847–48) was published in *Punch* in 20 monthly parts under his own name and with his own illustrations. This long novel of society love, life, and death during the Napoleonic wars is especially notable for its time not only for its broad scope, but also for the depth and consistency of the characterization, qualities which have enabled it to endure as much as any novel by his friend DICKENS, whose success he was so anxious to emulate. *The History of Pendennis* (1849–50) concentrates on a single character from feckless youth to maturity.

In 1850 Thackeray received a generous offer from CHARLOTTE BRONTË's publisher for his next novel. *The History of Henry Esmond* (1852) is a dramatic historical study of a young man whose melancholy and misfortune were reflected in an unhappy incident in the author's own life, when he was warned off the talented Jane Brookfield (*d.* 1896) by her husband, the cleric and inspector of schools, William Brookfield (1809–74), with whom Thackeray had been at Cambridge. *The English Humourists of the Eighteenth Century* (1853) and *The Four Georges* (1860) were based on lectures he gave in the USA in 1852–53 and 1855–56. Between visits he wrote *The Newcomes* (serialized 1853–55), a family saga. His last major novel, *The Virginians* (1857–59), is set in England and America. In 1860 he became the first Editor of *Cornhill Magazine*, in which appeared his two further novels and a fragment of *Denis Duval*, left unfinished on his sudden death from a spasm. He imbued the English novel with a wider vision than it had had before, piecing together the action from the points of view of several characters. See *Selected Letters of William Makepeace Thackeray*, ed. Edgar F. Harden, 1996; Gordon N. Ray, *Thackeray: the Uses of Adversity 1811–1846*, 1955, and *Thackeray: the Age of Wisdom: 1847–1863*, 1958 (biography); Ann Monserrat, *Thackeray: an Uneasy Victorian*, 1980 (biography); John Carey,

Thackeray: Prodigal Genius, new edn 1980 (critical biography).

THEOBALD, LEWIS see POPE.

THEOCRITUS (*c.*310–*c.*250 BC) Hellenistic pastoral poet, was born in Syracuse, and probably spent several years studying in the island of Cos under the poet and critic, Philetas. In 274 he appealed to Hiero, the Syracusan general, for patronage (see Idyll XVI). Unsuccessful, he went to Alexandria, where for several years he found favour at the court of Ptolemy Philadelphus. Pastoral poetry begins with Theocritus, in the poems in which his rustics meet, often exchange rude jokes, and vie with each other in the composition of songs. And the lament for the shepherd-poet 'Daphnis', which is sung by Thyrsis in Idyll I, is the prototype of the pastoral elegy. The form recurs in the 1st century BC in Bion's moving lament for 'Adonis', and Moschus's for 'Bion', and is very effectively employed later in MILTON's 'Lycidas', SHELLEY's *Adonais* (for KEATS), and ARNOLD's 'Thyrsis' (for CLOUGH).

THEROUX, PAUL (*b.* 1941) American novelist, short-story writer, and travel writer, was born in Medford, Massachusetts, the younger brother of novelist Alexander Theroux (*b.* 1939) and one of six other children of a French-Canadian leather salesman and an Italian-born teacher. He was educated at Medford High School and the University of Massachusetts, after which he trained for the Peace Corps at Syracuse University. Posted to Nyasaland in 1963, he taught at Soche Hill College, wrote anodyne articles for the *Christian Science Monitor*, and more politically-oriented pieces for *Atlantic Monthly* and other journals. After the country became independent in 1964 as Malawi, he was deported for subversive activity and expelled from the Peace Corps. He returned to Africa to teach at Makerere University, Uganda, where he came across V. S. NAIPAUL, 'the first good writer I had ever met', of whom he wrote a critical study (1972). *Waldo*, a novel of adolescent rebelliousness, was published in 1967, when he married a young English woman in Kampala.

ENRIGHT initiated his appointment in 1968 to teach Jacobean drama at Singapore University, where he wrote about Africa—*Jungle Lovers* (1971) reflected political horrors, after the private nightmares in *Girls at Play* (1969). He settled in England as a full-time writer in 1971. Double images are a feature of *Picture Place* (1978), and double lives of *Doctor Slaughter* (1984) and *Chicago Loop* (1990). He brings the scene-building and dialogue-writing techniques of a novelist to his travel books, which have often been about journeys by train ('I sought trains; I found passengers'), as in *The Great Railway Bazaar: By Train through Asia* (1975) and *The Old Patagonian Express: By Train through the Americas* (1979). *The Happy Isles of Oceania: Paddling the Pacific* (1992) records an uncomfortable odyssey undertaken as therapy, after which, having separated from his wife, he settled in Hawaii. *Millroy the Magician* (1993), which he called a 'companion piece' to *The Mosquito Coast* (1982), was followed by a further travel book, *The Pillars of Hercules: a Grand Tour of the Mediterranean* (1995). *My Other Life: a Novel* (1996), in which the narrator is called Paul Theroux, is intended as a riposte to those who said of *My Secret History* (1989), 'That's not really a novel—that's your autobiography.' *The Collected Stories* (1997) contains *Half Moon Street: Two Short Novels* (1984), a selection from *Sinning with Annie* (1972) and *World's End* (1980), and four uncollected tales.

THIBAUDEAU, COLLEEN see REANEY.

THIRKELL, ANGELA see MACINNES.

THOMAS (OF BRITAIN) see GOTTFRIED.

THOMAS À KEMPIS (1380–1471) German prose writer, was born Thomas Haemarken of humble parentage in Kempen, near Dusseldorf. He was educated at the local grammar school until he was 13, when he joined his elder brother at the Congregation of the Common Life, a brotherhood founded at Deventer in 1376 by Gerhard Groote (1340–84). In 1399 he entered the monastery of Mount S. Agnes, Zwolle, of which his brother was now Prior, and where he remained for the rest of his life. He was elected Sub-Prior in 1425, was Master of the Novices, and kept the monastery's chronicle. In addition to copying the Scriptures and other holy books, he himself wrote in Latin several biographies, including one of Groote, and numerous devotional works, of which *De Imitatione Christi* (tr. Leo Sherley-Price as *The Imitation of Christ*, 1952), in four books, is of universal appeal for its literary quality and the directness of its teaching about the philosophies embodied in the Light of Truth and the Life of Grace. The first complete translation into English was in 1556 by Richard Whytford (*c.*1475–*c.*1557), a canon of Syon House, London.

THOMAS OF ERCELDOUNE (or **THOMAS THE RHYMER**) (*d. c.*1297) Scottish poet and seer, was born and lived in Erceldoune (Earlston) in Berwickshire. His second sight is referred to by BARBOUR, writing shortly after his death. Among the numerous prophecies attributed to him are the death of Alexander III, the Scottish defeats at the battles of Flodden and Pinkie, the accession and lineage of JAMES VI, and the bridging of the River Tweed. The source of his re-

markable inspiration is explained in the ballad 'Thomas the Rhymer' ('True Thomas lay on Huntlie bank . . .'), to which WALTER SCOTT, in *Minstrelsy of the Scottish Border*, added a second part 'from the printed prophecies vulgarly [commonly] ascribed to the Rhymer', and a third part of his own composition. Scott also edited (1804) a metrical romance, *Sir Tristrem*, which he claimed is the one which Thomas's contemporaries accredited to him.

THOMAS THE RHYMER see THOMAS OF ERCELDOUNE.

THOMAS, AUDREY (*b.* 1935), née Callahan, Canadian novelist, was born in the USA in Binghamton, New York, and has recorded the charged atmosphere of her upbringing in *Songs My Mother Taught Me*, her first novel (not published until 1973). She was educated at a New Hampshire boarding school, at the Mary Burnham School, and at Smith College, Northampton, with a year in the UK at St Andrews University. In 1958 she married Ian Thomas, with whom she emigrated to Canada, where she began a family of three daughters while studying for a further degree in English at the University of British Columbia, Vancouver. They spent the years 1964–66 in Ghana, where he was teaching at the University of Science and Technology, Kumasi. The opening story in *Ten Green Bottles* (1967) reworks her own experiences in a Ghanaian hospital during which she had a miscarriage, reflected also in the traumas of the protagonist of her first published novel, *Mrs Blood* (1967). The novellas, *Munchmeyer, and Prospero on the Island* (1972), and the epistolary *Latakia* (1979) capture the feeling of the island home she made after separating from her husband (they were divorced in 1979) and of a subsequent sojourn in Crete. Her novels, in which the chief characters are in a sense reflections of a single persona, and many of her short stories express women's ambivalence towards independence and the wish for attachment. The collection *The Wild Blue Yonder* (1990) has an accessibility and attention to descriptive detail which are not features of her earlier, more experimental, fiction. See Barbara Godard, *Audrey Thomas and Her Works*, 1994.

THOMAS, D(ONALD) M(ICHAEL) (*b.* 1935) British novelist, poet, and translator, was born in Redruth, Cornwall, and was educated at Redruth High School, University High School, Melbourne, and New College, Oxford. He taught at Teignmouth Grammar School from 1959 to 1963, and was Senior Lecturer in English, Hereford College of Education 1964–78. His verse, first published in volume form in *Personal and Possessive* (1964), began with the erotic, verged into science fiction, and developed and broadened into themes reflecting family relationships, origins, and emotions—see *The Puberty Tree: New and Selected Poems* (1992). Some of the same preoccupations inform his novels, of which the first, *The Flute-Player* (1979), is set in an undefined city which has degenerated into totalitarian-induced chaos. *The White Hotel* (1981) draws for its startling effect on the sexual hysteria of an imaginary patient of FREUD and the Babi Yar massacre of Jews in 1941. The five novels *Ararat* (1983), *Swallow* (1984), *Sphinx* (1986), *Summit* (1987), and *Lying Together* (1990), comprise the sequence 'Russian Nights', in which modern history and international politics, and the forces of fantasy and the unconscious, are intricately layered in the interests of bitter comedy. *Flying to Love* (1992) is a reworking of the circumstances of the assassination of President John F. Kennedy in 1963, constructed in the form of a fantasy. A dying Freud appears as the unnamed protagonist of *Eating Pavlova* (1994), reflecting Thomas's assertion in his memoirs, *Memories and Hallucinations* (1988), that 'art is the Oedipal crossroads where dreams, love and death meet'. Among his translations is the poetry of AKHMATOVA, PUSHKIN, and YEVTUSHENKO.

THOMAS, DYLAN (1914–53) Welsh poet and prose writer, was born in Swansea, the only son of the English master at Swansea Grammar School, where he was educated. He was an undistinguished scholar, except in English, but he edited and contributed to the school magazine with some flair. For a year after leaving school in 1931 he worked as a reporter for the *South Wales Daily Post*. Then he became a professional poet. His first poem in the national press was published in 1933 by the *Sunday Referee*, which then awarded him its major literary prize and financed the publication of his first book, *18 Poems* (1934), in which the authentic voice of the frustrated teenager speaks out. In November 1934 he moved to London, returning periodically to Swansea, where he completed *Twenty-Five Poems* (1936); these are more derivative and on the whole more obscure, but 'This bread I break . . .' and the sequence of ten poems of which the first begins 'Altar-wise by owl-light . . .' express the Christian feeling which imbues much of his subsequent verse. In 1937 he married Caitlin (1914–94), daughter of the Irish writer Francis MacNamara (1884–1916)—see Paul Ferris, *Caitlin: the Life of Caitlin Thomas* (1993). They settled in Laugharne on the Carmarthenshire coast. Thomas was unfit for service in World War II, which he spent in Wales, visiting London to see friends, publishers, and the BBC. What he called his 'war-work' involved writing screenplays for government propaganda films, of which the most notable was *Our Country*; he later wrote scripts for Gainsborough and Paramount, of which the horror film *The Doctor and The Devils* (1986) was one of the very few ever to be made—see *The Filmscripts*, ed. John Ackerman (1996).

Portrait of the Artist as a Young Dog (1940) is a series of humorous and compassionate autobiographical prose sketches. *Deaths and Entrances* (1946), his most considerable volume of poetry, contained several poems of a celebratory, nostalgic nature which were more accessible to the general reader than much of his earlier verse and were of immediate popular appeal. Such are 'Poem in October' ('It was my thirtieth year to heaven . . .'), 'Poem on His Birthday' ('In the mustardseed sun . . .'), 'Fern Hill' ('Now as I was young and easy under the apple boughs . . .'), and 'In the White Giant's Thigh' ('Through throats where many rivers meet, the curlews cry . . .').

After several nomadic postwar years, the family returned to Laugharne. He was now a much sought-after broadcaster, some of whose radio scripts are preserved in *Quite Early One Morning* (1954), the title piece of which is the seed of *Under Milk Wood*. In 1950 he made the first of four lecture tours in the USA to earn money—as an earner he was improvident rather than unsuccessful. *Collected Poems* (1952) contained just 89 poems that he wished at that time to keep, including one of the last he wrote, 'Do Not Go Gentle into that Good Night', inspired by the tragic spectacle of his father's lingering death. *Under Milk Wood: a Play for Voices*, a topographical mood poem in prose with songs in verse, was first heard at the Young Men's Hebrew Association in New York in May 1953, with the poet reading First Voice and Rev. Eli Jenkins. He died of alcohol poisoning on a return visit later that year. The first broadcast of *Under Milk Wood* was made by the BBC on 25 January 1954. Though Thomas did not know the Welsh language, his poetic music and verbal extravagance are essentially Welsh, and at his best he is a poet of great feeling and originality. See *Collected Poems 1934–1953*, ed. Daniel Jones, new edn 1996; *The Collected Stories*, ed. Walford Davies, 1993; *The Dylan Thomas Omnibus: Poems, Stories, and Broadcasts*, 1995; *The Collected Letters* ed. Paul Ferris, 1985; Paul Ferris, *Dylan Thomas: a Biography*, rev. edn 1985; George Tremlett, *Dylan Thomas: In the Mercy of His Means*, new edn 1993 (biography); John Ackerman, *Dylan Thomas: His Life and Work*, 3rd rev. edn 1996; William York Tindall, *A Reader's Guide to Dylan Thomas*, 1996.

THOMAS, (PHILIP) EDWARD (1878–1917) British poet and prose writer, was born in Lambeth, London, and educated at St Paul's School and Lincoln College, Oxford. He married while still an undergraduate. Having no inclination towards a permanent job, and with a book, *The Woodland Life* (1897), already written, he became a professional author. Between 1902 and 1915 he published 25 books, all prose—essays, travel and topography, literary criticism (including a study of SWINBURNE), biography, myths and legends, and a novel, *The Happy-go-Lucky Morgans* (1913). Many are simply literary hackwork, but some, such as *The Heart of England* (1906) and *The Icknield Way* (1913), contain the germs and some of the main themes of his verse, which he did not begin to compose until he was 36, and then only at the express encouragement of FROST. Even so, he chose to write poetry under the pseudonym of Edward Eastaway, and he only lived to see in print what he published privately as *Six Poems* (1916). He was commissioned in the Artists' Rifles in World War I, and was killed in the battle of Arras. The war features only obliquely in his poems, which are particularly concerned with the English countryside and often have a wry, melancholic taste, with recurrent images of search and self-analysis. See *The Collected Poems of Edward Thomas*, ed. R. George Thomas, new edn 1981; *Selected Letters*, ed. R. George Thomas, 1996; R. George Thomas, *Edward Thomas: a Portrait*, new edn 1989; Andrew Motion, *The Poetry of Edward Thomas*, new edn 1991.

THOMAS, R(ONALD) S(TUART) (*b.* 1913) Welsh poet and critic, was born in Cardiff and educated in Holyhead and at University College, Bangor, followed by a period of training for the ministry at St Michael's College, Llandaff. He was ordained in 1936 and served the Church of Wales as rector or vicar of country parishes until his retirement in 1978. He learned Welsh early on in his career in order to fulfil his vocation properly, and was impressed in the 1940s by the example of MACDIARMID and others in attempting to recapture the true essence of Scottish poetry. The expression of Welsh literary nationalism in his first two (privately published) volumes of verse gave way in the 1950s to the themes of Welsh pastoral care of both flocks and souls. More recently he has written about the nature of poetry itself, as in 'Poetry for Supper', in which he also employs one of his favourite motifs, the persona (often a peasant farmer) through whom he speaks to the reader or argues the opposite poles of a case. In spite of the graphic bleakness of his landscapes and the perfectly characterized indifference of so many of his parishioners, there are statements, and indeed whole poems, of redemption, compassion, and hope, forthcoming still in *Mass for Hard Times* (1992). He was awarded the Queen's Gold Medal for Poetry in 1964, and edited *The Penguin Book of Religious Verse* (1963), and selections of GEORGE HERBERT, EDWARD THOMAS, and WORDSWORTH. See *Collected Poems 1945–1990*, new edn 1995; *No Truce with the Furies*, 1995 (subsequent collection); *Autobiographies*, tr. from Welsh by Jason Walford Davies, 1997;

Justin Wintle, *Furious Interiors: R. S. Thomas, God and Wales*, 1996 (biography); J. P. Ward, *The Poetry of R. S. Thomas*, 1992.

THOMPSON, FLORA (1876–1947), née Timms, British prose writer and novelist, was born in Juniper Hill, a hamlet on the border between Oxfordshire and Northamptonshire, the daughter of a stonemason. She left school at 14 to work in the village post office at Fringford, first of several such jobs which eventually took her to Grayshott, Surrey, in 1897. She and her husband began their married life in Liphook, Hampshire, where they ran the post office, and where she wrote 'small sugared love stories' to supplement the family income (there were three children), as well as accomplished nature essays. A volume of verse, *Bog Myrtle and Peat*, appeared in 1921. They moved to Devon in 1928. Her celebrated autobiographical evocation of rural life, in which the observer and chief protagonist, Laura, grows up in the period between the 1870s and 1890s, *Lark Rise* (1939), *Over to Candleford* (1941), and *Candleford Green* (1943), was reissued as *Lark Rise to Candleford* in 1945. Not only a sensitive study of childhood to womanhood, it is also a rich source of social history and a chronicle of community life, from hamlet to village to market town. A fictionalized version, *Still Glides the Stream*, was posthumously published in 1948, and *A Country Calendar and Other Writings*, ed. Margaret Lane, in 1979. See Gillian Lindsay, *Flora Thompson: the Story of the Lark Rise Writer*, new edn 1991.

THOMPSON, FRANCIS (1859–1907) British poet and critic, was born in Preston, the son of a doctor. He was brought up in the Catholic faith, and was educated at Ushaw College and, at his father's wish, as a medical student at Owens College, Manchester. After failing his examinations several times, he left home in 1885 to try and earn a living in London as a writer—his mother's gift of DE QUINCEY's *Confessions of an English Opium Eater* may have influenced this decision and encouraged his addiction to opium. After two years living homeless in the streets, he was taken up by Wilfrid and Alice MEYNELL, to whose *Merry England* he had submitted two poems and an article on scraps of paper. They cared for him, arranged his 'drying out' periods at a Welsh monastery, and organized his literary career. Three volumes of his poetry were published in his lifetime: *Poems* (1893), *Sister Songs* (1895), and *New Poems* (1897). In his mystical vision and symbolism, combined with ornate style and poetic diction, Thompson looks back to the Metaphysical poets. This is particularly true of his greatest poem, 'The Hound of Heaven', which represents the conflict between human and divine love in terms of Catholic dogma. He also wrote poems of lyrical simplicity, including 'Cheated Elsie', the sequence 'A Narrow Vessel', and 'At Lord's', the finest poem about cricket. His reviews are collected in *Literary Criticisms of Francis Thompson*, ed. T. L. Connolly (1948). See Brigid M. Boardman, *'Between Heaven and Charing Cross': the Life of Francis Thompson*, 1988.

THOMSON, DERICK (RUARAIDH MACTHÓMAIS) (*b.* 1921) Gaelic poet, was born in Stornoway, Isle of Lewis, and was educated there at the Nicolson Institute, and at Aberdeen and Cambridge University, and the University College of North Wales. He taught at the universities of Edinburgh, Glasgow, and Aberdeen before returning to Glasgow in 1963 as Professor of Celtic. He has explained: 'I was writing in Gaelic and English from my early teens, but finally settled down to using Gaelic only from my mid-twenties. But there was already some demand for English versions of Gaelic poems, and this has continued.' His poetry reflects the island life of his childhood and the modern life of the town, as well as his cultured and sophisticated view of nationalism, which embraces Europe and the world beyond. He was founder-Editor of the Gaelic quarterly, *Gairm*, in 1952, and Chairman of the Gaelic Books Council 1968–91. His critical works include *An Introduction to Gaelic Poetry* (rev. edn 1989). See *Creachadh na Clàrsaich / Plundering the Harp: Collected Poems 1940–1980*, 1982; *Smeur an Dòchais / Bramble of Hope: Poems*, 1992.

THOMSON, JAMES (1700–48) Scottish poet, was born in Ednam, Roxburghshire, the son of a minister who died in 1716 while exorcizing a ghost. He was educated in Jedburgh and at Edinburgh University, which he left for London after his prose exercises had been adversely criticized. He never returned to Scotland. His long, blank-verse poems, *Winter* (1726), *Summer* (1727), and *Spring* (1728), were collected with 'Autumn' in *The Seasons* (1730), to which he added a deistic 'Hymn on the Seasons'—he revised and enlarged them over the next 16 years. *The Seasons* is less a forerunner of the Romantics than a trendsetter in nature poetry, and Thomson's observation of and obvious delight in the minutiae of the natural world look back to an earlier Scottish tradition. His other major work, *The Castle of Indolence: an Allegorical Poem. Written in Imitation of Spenser* (1748), contains more poetic invention than its subtitle would suggest. It probably began as a political exercise, but he took so long over it (contemporaries joked that he was too indolent) that its point was lost. Among shorter pieces, 'Hymn on Solitude' and 'To the Memory of Sir Isaac Newton' are notable. He also wrote five moderate stage tragedies, and with David Malloch (*c.*1705–65) *Alfred: a Masque* (1740), in which is the poem (and the

words of the song), 'Rule Britannia'. His literary activities earned him the sinecures of Secretary of Briefs in the Court of Chancery (1732–37) and Secretary General of the Leeward Islands (1744–46), and a pension from the Prince of Wales. At 42 he met a lady whom he pursued in writing and in person for four years, until she married a sailor who later became a vice admiral. Thomson died at his home in Richmond after catching a chill on the Thames. See *The Seasons and The Castle of Indolence*, ed. James Sambrook, new edn 1983; James Sambrook, *James Thomson 1700–1748: a Life*, 1991.

THOMSON, JAMES (1834–82) Scottish poet, was born in Port Glasgow, the son of a seaman, who returned from a voyage in 1840 with paralysis of body and mind. The family moved to London, the mother died, and the boy was found a place at the Royal Caledonian Asylum in Hertfordshire. In 1850 he entered the Royal Military Asylum, Chelsea, to train as an army schoolmaster. During 18 months' teaching practice in Ireland, he fell in love with and became engaged to 14-year-old Matilda Weller. She died in 1853, to be remembered for the rest of his life in his poems, letters, diary, and conversation. In 1858 he began contributing poems and critical articles to the *London Investigator* and *Tait's Edinburgh Magazine*, and in 1860 to the radical *National Reformer*, edited by his friend Charles Bradlaugh (1833–91), the social philosopher, who was later barred from taking his seat in the House of Commons for six years for refusing to take the parliamentary oath. From 1859 he signed pieces 'B. V.': 'Bysshe' for P. B. SHELLEY, and 'Vanolis', an anagram of 'Novalis', pseudonym of the German romantic poet, Friedrich Hardenberg (1772–1801), another whose teenage fiancée had died. After being discharged from the army for insubordination in 1862, Thomson lived for four years with the Bradlaughs in countrified Tottenham, where he wrote some of his more cheerful verse, including 'Sunday at Hampstead', 'Sunday Up the River', and the autobiographical 'Vane's Story', and subsided into alcoholism. He translated works of LEOPARDI, and wrote the narrative poem 'Weddah and Om-el-Bonain' (published 1871–72), while living on his own in Pimlico. He also wrote the grim, episodic 'City of Dreadful Night' (1874), in which the real and a symbolic London are the background to a hopeless spiritual quest for relief from despair.

In 1872 a business venture took him to America on behalf of the Champion Gold and Silver Company, but he was soon recalled. An assignment as correspondent in Spain for the *New York World* ended in disaster when he collapsed. *The City of Dreadful Night, and Other Poems* was published at last in 1880, with another book of verse five months later, and *Essays and Phantasies* in 1881. Latterly he subsisted on hack journalism, and alcohol, in dingy lodgings near University College Hospital, suffering from chronic depression and insomnia, about which in 1882 he wrote his last good poem. See Tom Leonard, *Places of the Mind: the Life and Work of James Thomson ('B. V.')*, 1993; Imogen B. Walker, *James Thomson (B. V.): a Critical Study*, new edn 1970.

THOREAU, HENRY DAVID (1817–62) American essayist, natural history writer, and social philosopher, was born in Concord, Massachusetts, and christened David Henry. He was educated at Concord Academy and Harvard, and then took a teaching post at the local Centre School. After a fortnight a member of the school committee insisted that he flog his pupils to maintain order. Thoreau took a ruler to six of them, one of whom was a maid in his own house, and then resigned in protest. After working in his father's pencil factory, where he invented a better method of processing the graphite, he opened a school with his elder brother, John, in the former Concord Academy building; to general surprise they ran it without corporal punishment. During the summer vacation in 1839 they travelled in a boat of their own design and construction by river to Hooksett, New Hampshire, and then climbed Mount Washington. Shortly afterwards, first John and then Henry proposed to Ellen Sewall, the elder sister of one of their pupils. She rejected them both because of their liberal principles. When the school had to close because of John's ill health, Henry, who had now had essays and poems published in the Transcendentalist journal, the *Dial*, accepted an invitation from EMERSON to be a handyman in his home. In 1842 John cut himself while shaving, and died of lockjaw several days later: Henry was so upset that he developed psychosomatic symptoms of the disease. He returned to the pencil factory in 1844, and on a fishing expedition accidentally set fire to a substantial part of the Concord woods. To avoid public embarrassment, and to achieve the privacy to write, he built himself a log cabin on the shore of Walden Pond, where he lived for two years.

Here, while experimenting with self-sufficiency, he wrote the account of the trip with John, *A Week on the Concord and Merrimack Rivers*, and began *Walden: or, Life in the Woods*, his philosophical masterpiece of observation of nature and of self. In 1846 he opted for the local jail rather than pay his poll tax, and was furious to be released after one night when an anonymous donor (probably an aunt) paid it for him. The experience, however, inspired the more effective protest of his essay 'Resistance to Civil Government' (1849), in a volume published by Elizabeth Peabody (1804–94), HAWTHORNE'S sister-in-law. In

1848 he began a career as a lecturer, while also advertising his services as a surveyor. He was forced to publish *A Week on the Concord* at his own expense in 1849, and then to buy back much of the edition four years later: 'I have now a library of nearly nine hundred volumes, over seven hundred of which I wrote myself.' Nettled by this failure, he put *Walden* through seven different drafts, incorporating the feedback from lectures at which he read extracts. Published commercially in 1854, it sold well and established him as a celebrity.

Thoreau's search for a wilder kind of nature than Concord could offer took him several times to Maine and to Cape Cod—collections of his essays, often written in the form of travelogues, were posthumously published as *The Maine Woods* (1864) and *Cape Cod* (1865), and poetry as *Poems of Nature* (1895). Always a fervent abolitionist (the Thoreau family home was a staging point on the underground railroad), he was outraged by the Fugitive Slave Act (1850), but did not publicly speak out until 4 July 1854, when he delivered the address 'Slavery in Massachusetts', first published on 21 July in the *Liberator*. Later he defended the actions of the anti-slavery crusader John Brown (1800–59), who was hanged after the doomed attack on Harper's Ferry. In 'A Plea for Captain John Brown' (published 1860) he suggested: 'I do not wish to kill or to be killed, but I can foresee circumstances in which both these things would be to me unavoidable' (scholarly opinion is divided as to whether he knew about Brown's earlier exploit in Kansas in 1856, when he murdered five pro-slavery men in cold blood). On his father's death in 1859 Thoreau took over the pencil factory, the atmosphere of which damaged his already suspect lungs. He died of consumption in a bed which he had himself made. See *Political Writings*, ed. Nancy L. Rosenblum, 1996; *In the Woods and Fields of Concord: Selections from the Journal of Henry David Thoreau*, ed. Walter Harding, 1984; *Faith in a Seed: 'The Dispersion of Seeds' and Other Late Natural History Writings*, ed. Bradley P. Dean, introduction by Robert D. Richardson, Jr, 1994; *Wood-Notes Wild: Walking with Thoreau*, ed. Mary Kullberg, 1995 (selection); *The Days of Henry Thoreau: a Biography*, 2nd rev. edn 1993; Richard J. Schneider, *Henry David Thoreau*, 1987 (biographical/critical study); Joel Myerson (ed.), *The Cambridge Companion to Henry David Thoreau*, 1995 (critical essays).

THUCYDIDES (*c*.460–*c*.400 BC) classical Greek historian, was an Athenian whose family owned gold mines in Thrace. He embarked on a history of the Peloponnesian War (431–404), he says, 'at the moment that it broke out, believing that it would be a great war, and more worthy of being described than any that had preceded it. This belief was not without foundation.' In 430 he was among the countless Athenian citizens struck down with the plague, whose symptoms he graphically recounts. In 424 he was one of the ten generals elected to go north and keep Amphipolis from falling into Spartan hands. It was lost, and he went into exile until the end of the war. His account breaks off in mid-flight in 411. Thucydides is the greatest historian of the ancient world, and the first to study man's political behaviour and to pursue truth—in contrast, for example, to HE-RODOTUS, there are no supernatural agencies. His analysis of the causes of the war is scientific and his rendering of its course dispassionate. He quotes official documents. Over one-fifth of the work is in the form of speeches, of which he says that he never introduces any unless there is evidence that one was made at the time, and that he has endeavoured in each case to reproduce its substance.

THURBER, JAMES (1894–1961) American humorist, essayist, and short-story writer, was born in Columbus, Ohio, and at six lost an eye when he was shot by his elder brother while playing at William Tell. He was educated at East High School and Ohio State University, which he left without taking his degree and worked as a code clerk for the State Department in Washington and Paris. In 1920 he returned to Columbus, where he was a newspaper reporter and wrote and directed musical comedies at the university. In 1925 he went to France, at the urging of his first wife, to write a novel about his school days, which did not get beyond the first chapter. Back in New York, he bombarded magazines with stories, sketches, and poems. In 1927 he took up an introduction to E. B. WHITE, whose sister he had met on board ship, and went to see him at the offices of the *New Yorker*. There he met the magazine's founder, Harold Ross (*d*. 1952), who, thinking he was an old friend of White, hired him as managing editor. He soon managed to get himself reduced to mere staff writer—his memoir, *The Years with Ross* (1959), caused some offence to former colleagues; see also Thomas Kinkel, *Genius in Disguise: Harold Ross of the 'New Yorker'* (1995). *Is Sex Necessary?* (1929), written with White, is a skit on the psychiatry of marriage. His first collection of sketches, *The Owl in the Attic and Other Perplexities*, was published in 1931, when his first cartoons appeared in the *New Yorker*. *My Life and Hard Times* (1933), with his own incomparable drawings, contained 'The Night the Bed Fell In', 'The Dog that Bit People', and other pseudo-autobiographical expressions of unworldliness such as became his literary motif. The tables are turned in 'The Unicorn in the Garden', in *Fables for Our Time* (1940); his story 'The Secret Life of Walter Mitty', in *My World and Welcome to It* (1942),

gave to the language a new term to describe a person who has grandiose fantasies. A series of operations on his remaining eye in 1940 left him with minimal vision. Within a few years he was almost blind, though he continued to write by composing stories in his head, and played the role of himself in *A Thurber Carnival* for 88 performances in 1960. See *Writings and Drawings*, 1996; Neil A. Grauer, *Remember Laughter: a Life of James Thurber*, new edn 1996; Harrison Kinney, *James Thurber: His Life and Times*, 1995.

THWAITE, ANTHONY (*b*. 1930) British poet and critic, was born in Chester and educated at Kingswood School, Bath, and Christ Church, Oxford, where he was Editor of *Isis*. His first book of verse was published while he was an undergraduate, and his second, *Home Truths*, in 1957. He lectured at Tokyo University from 1955 to 1957. He was a BBC radio producer 1957–62, Literary Editor of the *Listener* 1962–65, Assistant Professor of English, University of Libya 1965–67, Literary Editor of the *New Statesman* 1968–72, and co-Editor of *Encounter* 1973–85. His fascination with the past is particularly reflected in *The Stones of Emptiness* (1967), many of the poems in which were written in Libya, and in *Victorian Voices* (1980), a series of dramatic monologues from the mouths of real or imaginary 19th-century characters. His critical works include *Poetry Today: a Critical Guide to British Poetry 1960–1984* (1985) and *Twentieth-Century English Poetry* (1978), and he has compiled (with Geoffrey Bownas) *The Penguin Book of Japanese Verse* (1964) and edited the poems (1988) and letters (1992) of LARKIN. He met at university, and married in 1955, Ann Thwaite (*b*. 1932), née Harrop, children's novelist and biographer of BURNETT, (1974), GOSSE (1984), MILNE (1990), and Emily TENNYSON (1996). See *Poems 1953–1988*, 1989; *The Dust of the World*, 1994 (later collection).

THYNNE, FRANCIS see HOLINSHED.

TIRSO DE MOLINA, pen name of Fray (Friar) Gabriel Téllez (1580/1–1648) Spanish dramatist, was born in Madrid and was received into the Order of Our Lady of Mercy (Mercedarians) in 1601, after which he studied arts and theology at Salamanca, Toledo, Guadalajara, and Alcala. He began to write for the theatre when he was in Madrid in 1610. *El Vergonzoso en Palacio* [The Shy Man at Court], the first of his comedies which can be dated, was performed in 1611, when he moved to Toledo. *Don Gil de las Calzas Verdes* [Don Gil of the Green Breeches] introduced a favourite motif, the cross-dressed heroine wooing her rival in love—he complained that its initial failure was due to the age and girth of the actress playing the part. He assumed his pen name in 1616, and resumed his literary activities after spending the next two years on a mission with his Order in Santo Domingo (Haiti). *Los Cigarrales de Toledo* [The Country Houses of Toledo] (1624) is a miscellany of stories, verses, plays, and critical commentary, within a fictional framework in the manner of BOCCACCIO. In 1625, most probably at the instigation of a literary rival, he was accused by the Committee for Reform of the Council of Castile of writing 'profane plays', and posted by his Order to Trujillo as *Commendador* of its monastery there. He returned in 1629, to pursue a largely clerical career, being appointed *Definidor* in the province of Castille in 1632. As the official chronicler of the Mercedarians, he spent seven years rewriting and completing their history, which was then suppressed by the general of the Order and was not published until 1973–74. He wrote about four hundred plays of different kinds, of which five authorized volumes appeared in his lifetime. While a personality with the characteristics of Don Juan existed in medieval literary tradition, his play, *El Burlador de Seville* [The Trickster of Seville], is the source of the modern representation and of the opera *Don Giovanni* of Wolfgang Amadeus Mozart (1756–91).

TOCQUEVILLE, ALEXIS DE (1805–59) French political scientist and historian, was born in Paris of an aristocratic family, at whose chateau at Verneuil he spent his childhood and with his elder brothers was taught by the family priest. He attended the lycée at Metz and then studied law, becoming, through his father's influence, a magistrate in the government court at Versailles when he was 21. After the July Revolution in 1830 he took the oath of loyalty to Louis-Philippe: 'I am at war with myself,' he wrote to Mary Mottley, his English fiancée, whom he met at Versailles in 1828 and married in 1836. 'How simple the path would have been if duty had accorded with all the susceptibilities of honour.' After being required to take the oath again two months later, he and his friend Gustave de Beaumont (1802–66) applied for official leave to study American prison reforms. They arrived in Newport in May 1831 after an uncomfortable voyage of 5$^{1}/_{2}$ weeks, and spent nine months in the USA—see George Wilson Pierson, *Tocqueville in America*, abridged by Dudley C. Lunt (rev edn 1996). Their report (1833) was published on both sides of the Atlantic. In 1833 Tocqueville visited England and Ireland—see *Journeys to England and Ireland*, tr. George Lawrence and K. P. Mayer (1958)—, where he was able to put his thoughts on the functioning of a democracy further into perspective; he also met MILL, on whose subsequent philosophy his views were of some influence. The first two volumes of Tocqueville's *De la Démocratie en Amérique* were issued by a reluctant Paris publisher in 1835; they were immediately translated by the young English man of letters Henry Reeve (1813–95) for publication in Britain and the USA as *Democracy in America*. For the first time the French public had a full account of the working of a modern democracy, and Americans a clear and not uncritical analysis of their political and legal systems which benefited from its European perspective. Two further volumes followed in 1840—see *Democracy in America*, tr. Lawrence, ed. J. P. Mayer and Max Lerner (1966). Beaumont's contribution was *Marie: ou, L'Esclavage aux États-Unis; Tableau de Moeurs Americaines* (1835; tr. Barbara Jackson as *Marie, or Slavery in the United States, a Novel of Jacksonian America*, 1958).

In 1839 Tocqueville was elected to the Chamber of Deputies, in which he represented Valognes until the end of the Second Republic in 1848. He was then re-elected and appointed to the Constitutional Committee. Though he opposed Louis-Napoleon's principles he served as his Foreign Minister for five months in 1849. When Louis-Napoleon dissolved the constitution in 1851, Tocqueville retired to his estates and, though suffering from the onset of tuberculosis, worked at his *Souvenirs* (1893; tr. Lawrence as *Recollections*, 1970), and at his classic study of political cause and effect, *L'Ancien Régime et la Révolution* (1856; tr. M. W. Patterson, 1933).

TOLKIEN, J(OHN) R(ONALD) R(EUEL) (1892–1973) British novelist, philologist, and literary scholar, was born in Bloemfontein, Orange Free State. He was brought to England, but was orphaned when he was 12 and put in the care of a Catholic priest. He was educated at King Edward's School, Birmingham, and Exeter College, Oxford. After serving in World War I, in which he contracted trench fever, he worked on the *New English Dictionary*. He was Reader in English Language at Leeds University (1920–25), then Professor of Anglo-Saxon (1925–45) and of English Language and Literature (1945–59) at Oxford. From 1917 until his death he worked on a series of tales of 'Middle-Earth' through which he sought to express his theological and philosophical beliefs, posthumously collected into *The Silmarillion*, ed. Christopher Tolkien (1977). He drew on this imaginative storehouse for a children's fantasy, *The Hobbit* (1937). The 'sequel' for which the publisher then asked was not published for nearly twenty years, by which time it had grown into the richly-original adventure saga of *The Lord of the Rings*, comprising *The Fellowship of the Ring* (1954), *The Two Towers* (1954), and *The Return of the King* (1955), for which he created a complete mythology. His contributions to literary scholarship are best illustrated by his essays on Beowulf, Gawain, and fairy stories in *The Monsters and the Critics, and Other Essays*, ed.

Christopher Tolkien (1983). He was made CBE in 1972. See *Letters*, ed. Humphrey Carpenter and Christopher Tolkien, new edn 1995; Humphrey Carpenter, *J. R. R. Tolkien: the Authorized Biography*, 1993; C. W. R. D. Moseley, *J. R. R. Tolkien*, 1996 (critical introduction).

TOLSTOY, LEO (COUNT LEV NI- KOLAEVICH TOLSTOY) (1828–1910) Russian novelist, was born on the family estate of Yasnaya Polyana, Tula, south of Moscow, and after the deaths of both parents was educated by private tutors in Moscow and Kazan, where he entered the university in 1844. After a year he transferred from Eastern languages to law, and then returned to Yasnaya Polyana when he inherited it in 1847. He sat his final examinations at St Petersburg University in 1849, but withdrew after passing the first two subjects. In 1851 he visited the Caucasus, where his brother was stationed, and the following year joined up as a NCO. He was already writing stories, but his first published work was the autobiographical study [*Childhood*] (1852), which he followed in due course with [*Boyhood*] (1854) and [*Youth*] (1857). In 1854 he was promoted to ensign and posted to the Crimea, where he served in action at Sebastopol, and wrote a series of uncompromising sketches of the war (1855–56). Having met leading literary figures in St Petersburg, he resigned his commission in 1856, and finally settled back at Yasnaya Polyana, where in 1859 he established a school for peasant children.

In 1862 he finished his novel [*The Cossacks*] (1863), which he had begun some nine years earlier and which became in 1878 (tr. E. Schuyler) his first work to be published in English. Also in 1862 he married Sonya Behrs (1844–1918), the first of their 13 children being born in 1863—see William L. Shirer, *Love and Hatred: the Troubled Marriage of Leo and Sonya Tolstoy* (1994). [*War and Peace*] (1869; tr. Clara Bell from French, 1886; tr. Louise and Aylmer Maude, ed. Henry Gifford, 1991), his massive novel of Russian life during and after the Napoleonic wars, of which his wife laboriously wrote out the fair copy from his numerous drafts, began serialization in 1863. The seed of *Anna Karenina* (1878; tr. Nathan Haskell Dole, 1886; tr. Rosemary Edmonds, 1954; tr. Louise and Aylmer Maude, 2nd edn, ed. W. Gareth Jones, 1995), his penetrating study of a young wife's affair which leads to her destruction, was the suicide of a woman who threw herself under a train near his home; the inspiration to begin writing it was a PUSHKIN story in which the reader is plunged *in medias res*. the novel began monthly serialization in 1873, the last part, due for publication in 1877, being rejected by the journal's editors, who did not agree with its sentiments.

A spiritual crisis caused by his questioning the whole moral basis of contemporary existence led to such philosophical works as [*A Confession*] (1879–80), ['What Men Live By'] (1881), and ['What I Believe'] (1882), and to the novel, [*The Kreutzer Sonata*] (1890), and the play, [*The Dominion of Darkness*] (1886), the performance of which was banned by the censor. In 1891 he renounced all rights in his works after 1881, and the following year divided his property and possessions among his wife and children. His philosophy, based on non-resistance to evil, regeneration without benefit of Church, and abolition of government, is reflected in his final major novel, [*Resurrection*] (1899; tr. Louise Maude, 1901; tr. Edmonds, 1966). Written to help finance the exodus of the fundamentalist peasant sect, the Doukhobors, to Canada, it also caused him to be excommunicated from the Russian Orthodox Church. His moral stance and thinking brought pilgrims to Yasnaya Polyana, but his asceticism caused family ructions. He finally left home secretly with his youngest daughter, but died of a chill ten days later at the railway station at Astoporo. See Henri Troyat, *Tolstoy*, tr. Nancy Amphoux, new edn 1987 (biography).

TOMLINSON, CHARLES (*b.* 1927) poet, critic, and translator, was born in Stoke-on-Trent and educated at Longton High School and Queen's College, Cambridge. After further study at London University, he became a lecturer in English at Bristol University, being appointed Reader in 1968, Professor in 1982, and Emeritus Professor of English Poetry in 1992. He has also held visiting academic posts at several American universities. His experience as a painter (exhibitions of his works have toured Britain) and translator has contributed to the discipline of his verse, in which his absorption of French and modern American poetry is also reflected and which is often concerned with the evocation of landscapes and the passage of time. His original models included W. C. WILLIAMS, PAZ, and CREELEY, and he ultimately chose to write poetry where 'space represented possibility and where self would have to embrace that possibility somewhat self-forgetfully, putting aside the more possessive claims of personality'. His first collection was *Relations and Contraries* (1951). In *The Way In* (1974) he examines his childhood: religion is the main theme of *Annunciations* (1989). With the nature poems in *The Door in the Wall* (1992) are reflections on political commitment. His Clark lectures at Cambridge were published as *Poetry and Metamorphosis* (1983). *Some Americans* (1981) includes interviews with and studies of MARIANNE MOORE, POUND, and Williams. He edited and translated selected poems of PAZ (1979), and compiled *The Oxford Book of English Verse in Translation* (1980).

See *Collected Poems*, expanded edn 1987; *Translations*, 1983.

TONE, (THEOBALD) WOLFE (1763–98) Irish patriot and prose writer, was born in Dublin, the son of a coach builder, who was determined that his son should go to Trinity College, Dublin, for which he prepared reluctantly at Rev. William Craig's school in Stafford Street. At 16 he concluded that a military 'red coat and cockade, with a pair of gold epaulets' would be an advantage when approaching women, but in 1785, while still at college, he eloped with and married 16-year-old Martha Witherington (*d.* 1849). After graduating, he cursorily studied law in London, where he subsidized himself by journalism, and was called to the Irish Bar in 1789. He was one of the founders of the United Irish Society in 1791. The following year, though a Protestant, he was appointed a secretary of the Catholic Committee, in which capacity he helped to bring about the act giving the vote to Catholics (1793). With the United Irishmen still bent on revolution, and documents having been seized which implicated him as being in correspondence with the French, he sailed with his family to America, where he made plans to settle as a farmer. An impassioned plea from Ireland, however, sent him to France, where he negotiated for the dispatch of a fleet (with himself as adjutant general), which was dispersed by a hurricane. He embarked with a further expedition in 1798, but was captured, tried, and sentenced to hang as a traitor. When his request as a soldier was refused, he cut his own throat in prison with a penkife, and died of the wound a week later. His journals and reminiscences, incorporated in *Life of Theobald Wolfe Tone* (1826), with their sharply observed detail and dry wit, are the work of an accomplished writer. See Marianne Elliott, *Wolfe Tone: Prophet of Irish Independence*, new edn 1991.

TOOMER, (NATHAN) JEAN (1894–1967) American novelist, short-story writer, and poet, was born Eugene Pinchback Toomer in Washington DC. He was the son of a reputedly rich Georgian planter, who vanished before the baby was born, and of Nina (1868–1909), daughter of P. B. S. Pinchback (1837–1921), a notable black politician who was acting Governor of Louisiana during the Southern reconstruction following the Civil War. He went to M Street High School, Washington. After trying agriculture and then physical training, he enrolled at the University of Chicago to read biology as a prelude to medicine, dropped out to study sociology at New York University, but changed to history at the City College of New York. When he was rejected for war service in 1917 because of a sports' injury, he sold cars in Chicago, taught physical education in Mil-

waukee, and then returned to New York to pursue law. In 1918 he finally decided that his life lay in literature. He was introduced into literary society by the poet Lola Ridge (1883–1941), an editor of *Broom*, and met the critic Waldo Frank (1889–1967), who became a lifelong friend. While temporary head of a black industrial college in Sparta, Georgia, in 1921 he conceived the basis of a work which would transcend white prejudice against black writing, using modern literary techniques to emphasise lyrical aspects of the primitive life and the universal theme of the search for and reassertion of one's roots, in which he received encouragement from ANDERSON.

Cane (1923), a composite work in three parts comprising stories, sketches, poems, and a dramatized piece ('Kabnis'), elements of which he had already published in literary magazines, was favourably received but went out of print after its original edition and a small reprint (1927) sold out. While he continued to write, apart from two religious pamphlets the only other book published in his lifetime was the privately-printed collection of aphorisms, *Essentials* (1931). For some years, until scandal overtook the group, he promoted the beliefs of the Russian mystic George Ivanovich Gurdjieff (1877–1949). In 1931, listing himself as white on the licence, he married Margery Bodine Latimer (1899–1932), a novelist, who died in childbirth the following year. In 1934 he married Marjorie Content, the widow of a Wall Street banker, who survived him. In 1939 he went to India in search of a philosophy of life; the following year he and and his wife became Quakers. His health began to fail in 1950, and he spent much of his last ten years in nursing homes. *Cane* was finally reprinted in 1967 and in paperback in 1969, to take its place in the Harlem Renaissance and to coincide with the Second Renaissance of Afro-American literature. See *A Jean Toomer Reader: Selected Unpublished Writings*, ed. Frederik L. Rusch, 1995; *Collected Poems*, ed. Robert B. Jones and Margery Toomer Latimer, 1988; Nellie Y. McKay, *Jean Toomer, Artist: a Study of His Literary Life and Work 1894–1936*, new edn 1987; Brian Joseph Benson and Mabel Mayle Dillard, *Jean Toomer*, 1980 (biographical/critical study).

TOTTEL, RICHARD see SURREY; WYATT.

TOURNEUR, CYRIL (*c.*1575–1626) English poet and dramatist, was secretary to Sir Francis Vere (1560–1609), commander in the Netherlands in the Spanish wars, and may well have been the author of 'A Funerall Poem Upon the Death of the Most Worthy and True Soldier Sir Francis Vere' (1609). He certainly wrote 'The Transformed Metamorphosis' (1600), a satirical allegory whose meaning is obscure, and *The Atheist's Tragedy* (printed 1611), a revenge drama with ghoulish goings-on in a graveyard and an unusual denouement—D'Amville, the villain, unwittingly brains himself with the axe while acting the executioner. The authorship of *The Revenger's Tragedy* (1607) has never categorically been established, and because it is a better constructed and more poetic play, it has been thought unlikely to be by the same hand as the apparently later *The Atheist's Tragedy*, though a number of critics still assign it to Tourneur. The chief character, Vindice, is concerned not just to avenge the poisoning of his fiancée by the Duke, but to eradicate the Duke's court and the corruption it stands for, and is himself finally punished for taking too far the practical expression of his moral passion. In 1625 Tourneur was Secretary to the Council of War of Viscount Wimbledon (1572–1638) during the ill-fated expedition to seize Spanish treasure ships off Cadiz. The fleet turned back, and he was one of the sick men put ashore at Kinsale, Ireland, where he died.

TRAHERNE, THOMAS (1637–74) English poet and prose writer, was born in Herefordshire, the son of a shoemaker. He was brought up by his father's brother (who was twice mayor of Hereford), and was educated at Brasenose College, Oxford. He was parish priest of Credenhill from 1661 to 1669, when he became chaplain to Sir Orlando Bridgeman (c.1606–74), Keeper of the Seals. The only work published during his lifetime was *Roman Forgeries* (1673), a study of the authenticity of certain documents relating to Catholicism, though *Christian Ethicks* (1675) was probably ready for printing. His poems, many prepared for press by his brother Philip, did not come to light until 1896, when an unsigned manuscript book was discovered on a London bookstall. Subsequent research revealed an unfinished prose work, *Centuries of Meditations* (published 1908), a series of spiritual guidelines which offer parallels with childhood. The experience and innocence of childhood run through his verse, as in 'Wonder', 'My Spirit', 'Dreams', 'Poverty', and 'Shadows in the Water', which perfectly captures a child's fascination with and puzzlement at the 'other world' of reflections. This recall of a child's-eye view of the surroundings and of God, as well as the variety of his stanza forms, give Traherne's verse an unusual charm which outweighs his limited range, often abstract vocabulary, and the inconclusive endings of so many of his poems. See *Selected Poems and Prose*, ed. Alan Bradford, 1991.

TRAILL, CATHARINE PARR (1802–99), née Strickland, Canadian prose writer, children's author, and naturalist, elder sister of MOODIE, was born in England in Kent, and with *The Tell Tale* (1818), a collection of pieces, was the first of the literary Strickland siblings to be published. Several didactic juveniles followed, of which *Little Downey: or, The History of a Field Mouse* (1822) gave notice of her interest in natural history, and *The Young Emigrants: or, Pictures of Canada. Calculated to Amuse and Instruct the Minds of Youth* (1826) foreshadowed her future. In 1832 she married a Scot (and friend of Moodie's husband), Lieutenant Thomas Traill (1793–1859). Three months later the couple emigrated to Douro, near Peterborough, where they took up his military land grant next to the property of her brother Samuel (1805–67), author of *Twenty-Seven Years in Canada West* (1853). They moved to Peterborough in 1839, she during the intervening pioneering years having had four of their seven children (out of nine in all) who reached adulthood, and written her most significant work, *The Backwoods of Canada: Being Letters from the Wife of an Emigrant Officer; Illustrative of the Domestic Economy of British America* (1836). For the next twenty years, during which they moved in 1846 to Rice Lake, she largely supported the family by writing for journals. She also compiled *The Female Emigrant's Guide, and Hints on Canadian Housekeeping* (1854), and wrote children's books, among them *The Canadian Crusoes: a Tale of the Rice Lake Plains* (1852), in which three children survive in the wild for two years. After her husband's death she lived in Lakeford, Ontario, where she wrote the text for *Canadian Wild Flowers* (1868) and compiled the authoritative *Studies of Plant Life in Canada: or, Gleanings from Forest, Lake and Plain* (1885), both illustrated by Moodie's second child, Agnes Fitzgibbon (1833–1913). See *I Bless You in My Head: Selected Correspondence*, ed. Carl Ballstadt, 1996.

TREECE, HENRY (1911–66) British poet, historical novelist, children's writer, and critic, was born in Wednesbury, Staffordshire, and educated at Wednesbury High School and Birmingham University, where he was university boxing captain. Except for war service in the Royal Air Force, he was from 1938 until his early death Senior English Teacher at Barton-on-Humber Grammar School. With the Scottish poet J. F. Hendry (1912–86) he founded in the 1930s the New Apocalypse: 'In my definition, the writer who senses the chaos, the turbulence, the laughter and the tears, the order and the peace of the world in its entirety, is an Apocalyptic writer.' In the words of FRASER, the movement 'in a sense derives from Surrealism, and one might even call it a dialectical development of it, the next stage forward': it also served as a fraternity of like-minded young poets, most of them living outside London, who welcomed this chance to meet and correspond with each other. DYLAN THOMAS was drawn into this group, and Treece's *Dylan Thomas: Dog Among the Fairies*

(1949; rev. edn 1956) was the first critical study of him. Treece published six volumes of his own verse, the last of which was *The Exiles* (1952). He now embarked on a new literary career as a historical novelist. His themes are the crossroads of history and the conflicts of cultures, and he is at his best when writing about the Dark Ages and more ancient times, as in *The Dark Island* (1952), *The Golden Strangers* (1956), and *Electra* (1963). He applied the same qualities and objectives to his books for children, by whom his Viking novels in particular are still widely read, and who still respond to the last book he wrote, the intriguing *The Dream-Time* (1967). See *How I See Apocalypse*, 1946; Margery Fisher, *Henry Treece*, 1969 (mainly on the children's books, but including his 'Notes on Perception and Vision').

TRESSELL, ROBERT, pen name of Robert Noonan (1870–1911) British novelist, was born in Dublin, educated there or in London, married in 1890, left his wife in 1893, and lived in South Africa for two years. From 1902 he worked as a house painter and sign writer in Hastings, Sussex, where he died of tuberculosis. Between 1907 and 1910, to give his only daughter, Jessie Pope, some financial security, he wrote a novel. *The Ragged Trousered Philanthropists: Being the story of twelve months in Hell, told by one of the damned, and written down by Robert Tressell* was published in 1914 in a version bowdlerized and drastically edited by Jessie. Even in that form it powerfully, satirically, and graphically reflects the attitudes of the 'philanthropists' (the working class) towards their capitalist exploiters. In its full version, ed. Frederick C. Ball (1955), what had been regarded as a social documentary and the outstanding working-class novel of its time, is seen also as a 20th-century fable. See Jack Mitchell, *Robert Tressell and the Ragged Trousered Philanthropists*, 1969 (critical study).

TREVELYAN, G. M. see MACAULAY, THOMAS BABINGTON.

TREVOR, WILLIAM, pseudonym of (William) Trevor Cox (*b.* 1927) Irish novelist and short-story writer, was born in Mitchelstown, Co. Cork, of mixed south/north parentage, and spent his childhood there and in 'Youghal by the sea, and Skibbereen which people said was at the back of beyond'. He was educated at St Columba's College and Trinity College, Dublin, after which he taught history in Northern Ireland and art in England. For five years, during which he published a novel, *A Standard of Behaviour* (1958), he was then a professional sculptor, but gave up a potentially profitable practice in 1960 because 'I couldn't get the people in my head into the sculpture. I had to write short stories to bring them to life.' To finance his writing,

he worked as an advertising copywriter (in the same company as LUCIE-SMITH and EWART) until 1964, when he published a second novel, *The Old Boys*, which won the Hawthornden Prize for a literary work by an author under 41.

His first volume of short stories was *The Day We Got Drunk on Cake and Other Stories* (1967). Living in Devon, he feels, gives him the distance he requires from which to conjure up the essence of his native Ireland, as he has done in *Mrs Eckdorf in O'Neill's Hotel* (1969), *Fools of Fortune* (1983), and in *Reading Turgenev*, the first of the two complete novels in *Two Lives* (1991); but his forte is the creation and manipulation of characters, often bizarre, always believable, and the setting is wherever they can most effectively weave their odd ways. Two worlds chillingly collide in *Felicia's Journey* (1994), a study of a pregnant Irish girl preyed upon by a pervert in the English Midlands, which won Trevor his third Whitbread Award.

Of the short story, he said in an interview in 1992: 'It's a very, very difficult form. . . . Novels can be ragbags and go wandering off, but a good short story should not have an unnecessary word in it. . . . Because of its brevity and compression, a story must leave behind a smear or dob of paint on the mind from which the reader has to do the rest of the work'—see *Collected Stories* (1992), *Selected Stories* (1995), and *After Rain* (1996). He has also written plays for the stage, for radio, and for television, for which he has adapted his own stories. A member of the Irish Academy of Letters, he was made Honorary CBE in 1977. See *Excursions in the Real World*, 1994 (autobiographical essays); Gregory A. Schirmer, *William Trevor: a Study of His Fiction*, 1990; Kristin Morrison, *William Trevor*, 1993 (critical study).

TRILLING, LIONEL (1905–75) American critic and novelist, was born in New York City of Jewish immigrant parents, and was educated there at public schools and at Columbia University. After teaching at Hunter College, he returned in 1932 to Columbia, where he became Woodberry Professor of Literature and Criticism in 1965 and University Professor in 1970. His first published work was a story in *Menorah Journal* in 1925; his first book was his doctoral dissertation on ARNOLD (1939; rev. edn 1949). Subsequently he published a study of FORSTER (1943; rev. edn 1965). The re-emergence of the *Partisan Review* in 1937 gave him a critical outlet in which both modernism and leftism were fused. He founded no school of criticism, but his belief in the power of literature to 'transform, elevate and damage' (*New Republic*, March 1976) influenced many. Significant books are *The Liberal Imagination: Essays on Literature and Society* (1950) and *Beyond Culture: Essays on Literature and Learning* (1965), in which he draws particularly on the thinking of FREUD, on whom he wrote *Freud and the Crisis of Our Culture* (1955). His novel, *The Middle of the Journey* (1947), reflected the communist/liberal literary split of the 1930s and anticipated the political controversy in the 1950s. His wife Diana, née Rubin (1905–96), essayist and critic, whom he married in 1929, wrote an account of their lives: *The Beginning of the Journey: the Marriage of Diana and Lionel Trilling* (1993). See William M. Chace, *Lionel Trilling: Criticism and Politics*, 1980 (critical study).

TROLLOPE, ANTHONY (1815–82) British novelist and short-story writer, was born in London, the fourth son of an improvident and irascible barrister, and was educated at Harrow, Winchester College, and then Harrow again when the family fortunes began to fail. His mother, Frances Trollope (1780–1863), née Milton, returning from America after the collapse of one of her husband's madder financial schemes, determined to support the family by writing, and produced *Domestic Manners of the Americans* (1832) and many more travel books, as well as novels—see Teresa Ransom, *Fanny Trollope: a Remarkable Life* (1995). When her husband was declared bankrupt in 1834, she took the family to Belgium, having obtained for the 19-year-old Trollope a position as clerk with the Post Office in London. After seven unhappy years he volunteered for a transfer to Ireland, where he became a good administrator, took up hunting, and in 1844 married Rose Heseltine (1821–1917), the daughter of a Yorkshire bank manager after whose retirement in 1852 it was discovered that he had been fiddling the books.

In Ireland, Trollope began also to write. *The MacDermots of Ballycloran* (1847) was followed by a second Irish novel, and then by *La Vendée: an Historical Romance* (1850). All failed. From 1851 to 1853 he was charged with reorganizing postal services in southwest England and the Channel Isles, in the course of which he invented the pillar box; in 1854 he was appointed Surveyor of Mail Coaches. He resigned in 1867, having made several foreign tours on business, and become a leading literary figure. He edited *St Paul's Magazine* from 1867 to 1870, and in 1868, as a Liberal, came bottom in the poll for the parliamentary constituency of Beverley, though the election was later declared invalid because of bribery and the borough disenfranchised. His own reckoning was that by 1879 he had earned a total of £68,959.17s.6d from his books. He settled in a Hampshire village in 1880, and died of a seizure which struck him while laughing at a book during a family dinner party in London. For the past 22 years he had nursed a romantic attachment for the American actress, journalist, and feminist, Kate Field (1838–96)—her other literary admirers included ROBERT BROWNING and LANDOR, who at 83 undertook to teach her Latin and wrote a poem about being kissed by her.

Trollope was a prolific but subtle writer. His fourth novel, *The Warden* (1855), was a success and inaugurated the 'Barsetshire' sequence of social comedies, the others being *Barchester Towers* (1857), *Doctor Thorne* (1858), *Framley Parsonage* (1861), *The Small House at Allington* (1864), and *The Last Chronicle of Barset* (1867). Set in an imaginary county in the west country, they deal with the interplay between mainly ecclesiastical figures and with domestic events and issues. His strength is the delineation and development of character, which he employs with equal effect in the 'Palliser' series of novels of politicians and aristocrats: *Can You Forgive Her?* (1864–65), *Phineas Finn, the Irish Member* (1869), *The Eustace Diamonds* (1873), *Phineas Redux* (1874), *The Prime Minister* (1876), and *The Duke's Children* (1880). Of his many other novels, the love-tangled *The Claverings* (1867) and the satirical *The Way We Live Now* (1875) are of most interest today. He published five volumes of short stories, many of which are set in foreign parts—see *The Collected Shorter Fiction*, ed. Julian Thompson (1992), and *Early Short Stories* and *Later Short Stories*, ed. John Sutherland (1995)—, several books on his travels, and lives of THACKERAY (1879), CICERO (1880), and Lord Palmerston (1882). See *An Autobiography*, ed. John Skilton, 1996; Richard Mullen, *Anthony Trollope: a Victorian in His World*, new edn 1992 (biography); N. John Hall, *Trollope: a Biography*, new edn 1993; Victoria Glendinning, *Trollope*, new edn 1993 (biography); Richard Mullen, *The Penguin Companion to Trollope*, 1996.

TROLLOPE, FRANCES see TROLLOPE.

TSVETAEVA, MARINA IVANOVNA (1892–1941) Russian poet and critic, was born in Moscow, the daughter of a philologist and art critic who founded what is now the Pushkin Museum of Fine Arts. Her mother, a musician, having contracted tuberculosis in 1902, took her two daughters with her through Europe in her search for treatment, and died in 1906. Tsvetaeva then went to school in Moscow, did an informal course in Old French at the Sorbonne, and in 1910 privately published a volume of over a hundred lyrics. At an artistic community in the Crimea she met Sergey Efron (1893–1939), whom she married in 1912, the year her second volume of verse was commercially published. Sergey volunteered for the army at the beginning of World War I, and was an officer in 1917 when at the onset of the Revolution he went to fight for the White Army. In 1922, not having seen or heard from him for five years, during which she had subsisted in Moscow largely on the charity of friends, she got permission to join him in Berlin; from there they moved to Prague, and then in 1925 to Paris. Though she continued to write poetry, and also prose, the collection published in Paris in 1928, [After Russia], was her last book to appear during her lifetime. In 1937 Sergey was involved in the assassination near Lausanne of a Soviet defector and was spirited back to Moscow, where she joined him in 1939. A few months later both he and their daughter were arrested. She never saw them again. Shunned by the literary establishment and effectively homeless, she chose in 1941 to be evacuated with her 16-year-old son, and took a Volga steamship for Kazan. They were refused permission to disembark until the boat reached Yelabuga, in the Tatar Republic, where, after failing to find any work, she hanged herself.

Deeply affected but totally repelled by the Revolution, and during her lifetime unable to reach a dedicated readership either in Russia or outside, she has only latterly been recognized as a poet of passionate insight and linguistic innovation. Her sister Anastasia, who died in Moscow in 1993 at the age of 98, dedicated herself, on her release in the 1950s from over twenty years in Stalinist prison camps, to retrieving Marina's work, which had been banned. Selections of the poetry have been translated by FEINSTEIN (1971; rev. edn 1993) and David McDuff (1987; 2nd edn 1991); criticism is in *A Captive Spirit: Selected Prose*, tr. J. Marin King (1980). See Viktoria Schweitzer, *Tsvetaeva*, ed. Angela Livingstone, tr. H. T. Willetts and Robert Chandler, poetry tr. Peter Norman, new edn 1995 (biography); Lily Feiler, *Marina Tsvetaeva: the Double Beat of Heaven and Hell*, 1995 (biography); Marina Razumovsky, *Marina Tsvetayeva: a Critical Biography*, tr. Aleksey Gibson, 1995.

TU FU see LI PO.

TURBERVILLE, GEORGE (*c*.1544–*c*.1597) English poet and prose writer, was the second son of a branch of the ancient Dorset family, the D'Urbervilles of HARDY's *Tess*. He was educated at Winchester College and New College, Oxford, which he left in 1562 without taking a degree. He entered the Inns of Court to study law, and became a member of a lively set of minor literary figures. In 1567 he published translations of *Heroides* of OVID (some parts in the new metre of blank verse) and the Latin *Eclogues* of Mantuan— Baptista Mantuanus (1448–1516)—and a collection of short, unremarkable verses of his own, *Epitaphes, Epigrams, Songs and Sonets*. In 1568 he was appointed secretary to Thomas Randolph (1523–90), whom he accompanied to Russia on his mission to the court of Ivan the Terrible to secure privileges for English merchants. Three epistles in doggerel verse, written to friends from Moscow, appeared in *Epitaphes and Sonnettes* (*c*.1574), and were re-

printed (without the lines recounting the Russian penchant for homosexuality) by HAKLUYT. Also in *Epitaphes and Sonnettes* is an epistle announcing his marriage, through which he appears to have acquired property at Shapwick in Dorset. *Epitaphes and Sonnettes* was published as an annex to *Tragical Tales* (earliest publication unknown, reissued in 1587), which he translated from the Italian (chiefly of BOCCACCIO), according to the title page 'in time of his troubles', a reference to an attack on his life. It was dedicated to his elder brother, who was himself murdered in 1580. Turberville also wrote prose treatises on falconry and on hunting, both published in 1575, after which he seems to have ceased to write. See John E. Hanking, *The Life and Works of George Turberville*, new edn 1973.

TURGENEV, IVAN (1818–83) Russian novelist, short-story writer, and dramatist, was born in Orel and brought up on the family estate of Spasskoe and then in Moscow. He entered Moscow University in 1833, transferring to St Petersburg in 1834, the year his father died. After graduating in 1837, he spent three years in Europe, where he attended philosophy lectures at Berlin University and mixed with radical thinkers. In 1842 he passed his examinations for MA at St Petersburg, but did not complete his dissertation. He worked briefly for the civil service, but having in 1843 published a narrative poem and a romantic drama set in Spain, he gave up employment for literature. He also became infatuated with Pauline Viardot (1821–1910), née Garcia, the mezzo-soprano and composer, and accompanied her and her husband to France. All this displeased his mother, who cut off his allowance, which until her death in 1850 forced him to write for a living, mainly verse and plays—his one dramatic masterpiece, [*A Month in the Country*] (tr. Richard Freeborn, 1991), the first notable Russian drama in which the conflict is internal, was written in 1850, published in 1855, but not performed until 1872. With [*A Sportsman's Sketches*] (1852), a series of rural observations and speculations which he believed was instrumental in the abolition of serfdom in 1863, he found an effective fictional form and voice, which was silenced when he was arrested for a politically incorrect obituary of GOGOL. He spent a month in jail and was then exiled to Spasskoe under police supervision.

From 1856, when he published *Rudin*, the first of three novels exploring contemporary society, of which [*Home of the Gentry*] (1859; tr. W. R. S. Ralston as *Liza*, 1869; tr. Freeborn, 1970) and [*On the Eve*] (1860; tr. C. E. Turner, 1871) are interesting also as descriptions of Russian liberalism, he spent an increasing amount of time abroad. [*First Love*] (1860; in *First Love and Other Stories*, tr. Freeborn, 1989, and *First Love and Other Stories*, tr. Isaiah Berlin and Leonard Shapiro, 1994), the most passionate of his works, was inspired by an incident in his youth, when he fell for an older girl, only to discover that she was his father's mistress. In his finest novel, [*Fathers and Sons*] (1862; tr. 1867; tr. Freeborn, 1991), he presented a nihilist as capable of human feeling and subject to the workings of fate, a reading which appealed neither to conservatives nor radicals. The ensuing controversy drove him finally to settle abroad with the Viardots, with whom he jointly bought an estate near Paris in 1875. Though now out of touch with Russian life and thus no longer a writer of the times, he continued to produce novels which, to quote HENRY JAMES, 'began almost always with the vision of some person or persons, who hovered before him, soliciting him, as the active or passive figures, interesting him and appealing to him, just as they were and by what they were'. He died of cancer, the agonies of his final days being such that he threw an inkwell at Pauline. See Henri Troyat, *Turgenev: a Biography*, tr. Nancy Amphoux, new edn 1991.

TURNER, ETHEL (1872–1958) Australian children's novelist, was born in England in Doncaster, the younger daughter of George Burwell and sister of Lilian Turner (1870–1956), also a children's writer. Burwell died shortly afterwards, and their mother married Henry Turner, whose name they assumed. In 1881, after his death, Mrs Turner took them to Australia, where she married again. Her daughters were educated at Sydney Girls' High School; soon after leaving they edited together a magazine for schoolgirls, *Iris*. Ethel wrote many novels and stories for young people, of which *Seven Little Australians* (1894) has achieved the status of a classic for its characterization and for its philosophy: 'In Australia a model child is—I say it not without thankfulness—an unknown quantity. . . . There is a lurking spirit of joyousness and rebellion and mischief in nature here, and therefore in children.' (Not that ingenious pranks and horseplay on the part of the six children of an army officer and his dead first wife, and the one of his new girl-wife, go without fatherly retribution.) *The Family at Misrule* (1895) is a sequel; in *Little Mother Meg* (1902) the eldest girl, now married, has new problems to face, as does the second girl. Turner married Herbert C. Curlewis, later a judge of the District Court of New South Wales, in 1896. Their daughter, Jean Curlewis (1899–1930), was a children's novelist of a more romantic nature than her mother, with whom she wrote *The Sunshine Family: a Book of Nonsense for Boys and Girls* (1923). After her daughter's death from tuberculosis, Turner wrote no more.

TUTUOLA, AMOS (*b.* 1920) Nigerian story writer, was born in Abeokuta, and at seven was put out to work as a servant in return for being sent to school. He went to Lagos High School, and then, having refused to return to his master because of the wife's brutality, to the Anglican Central School, Abeokuta, until the fees dried up on his father's death in 1939. Having failed to earn enough from the family farm to continue his education, he trained as a blacksmith, as which he served with the Royal Air Force in Lagos from 1943 to 1946. While a messenger in the Department of Labour, and 'still in hardship and poverty', he responded to a magazine advertisement and wrote a novel 'within a few days successfully because I was a story-teller when I was in school', which he sent to the United Society for Christian Literature, who passed it on to the London house of Faber & Faber. *The Palm-Wine Drinkard and His Dead Palm-Wine Tapster in the Deads' Town* (1952), a seemingly artless blend of Yoruba folklore and rudimentary English, was hailed by DYLAN THOMAS in the *Observer* as 'brief, thronged, grisly and bewitching. . . . Nothing is too prodigious or too trivial to put down in this tall, devilish story.' While British and American readers saw him as one of the first black African writers to achieve international recognition, in West Africa he was criticized for his poor English and for retelling tales that were well known. In 1956 he became a stores officer with the Nigerian Broadcasting Corporation, Ibadan, from which he retired in the late 1970s and established a bakery. He continued to write in the same vein, with a gap between *Ajaiyi and His Inherited Poverty* (1967) and *The Witch-Herbalist of the Remote Town* (1981), becoming recognized even by his fellow Nigerians for his unique contribution to the preservation of the Yoruba oral tradition by employing the colonial language which had threatened to destroy it.

TUWHARE, HONE (*b.* 1922) New Zealand poet, was born in Kaikohe, and educated at Berestord Street School and Seddon Memorial Technical College, Auckland. He served in the Maori Battalion in 1945, and then in the New Zealand Second Divisional Cavalry. He worked as a boilermaker, and was active in the affairs of several trades unions, as well as being a member of his district executive of the Communist Party of New Zealand. Through *No Ordinary Sun* (1964), published when he was in his forties, and further collections in 1970, 1972, 1974, 1978, and 1982, he became the first Maori writing in English to gain a national reputation as a poet. It is not just for their authenticity, but also for their natural intensity, that poems which reflect his geographical and social roots, such as 'Burial', 'Time and the Child', 'Not by Wind Ravaged', and the ironic 'To a Maori Figure Cast in Bronze . . .', are regarded as his most significant. He has also published short stories and a play. See

Mihi: Collected Poems, 1987; *Deep River Talk: Collected Poems*, 1994.

TWAIN, MARK, pseudonym of Samuel Langhorne Clemens (1835–1910) American humorist, novelist, children's writer, and journalist, was born in Florida, Missouri, the fifth child of John Marshall Clemens (*d*. 1847), of Virginia, and Jane Lampton (*d*. 1890), of Kentucky. They moved to Hannibal, on the west bank of the Mississippi, in 1839. He had a literary and, from his mother, Calvinistic upbringing, and from the age of 4¹/₂ attended private schools, latterly J. D. Dawson's school for young ladies and a few boys of 'good morals'. His father went bankrupt shortly before dying of pneumonia, and in 1848 he started work for a local printer. In 1851 he was taken on by his brother Orion (1825–98), publisher of the *Western Union* (later the *Journal*), into whose columns of typesetting he introduced items of his own composition, especially when Orion was away. He then worked in St Louis and Keokuk, from where, having fortuitously discovered a $50 bill in the street, he set out for the Amazon, making a deal with the *Keokuk Post* to write a series of humorous letters on his travels. En route on the Mississippi, he changed his mind and got himself apprenticed as a pilot. He was licensed in 1859, and operated on the St Louis to New Orleans stretch until it was closed in 1861 at the outbreak of the Civil War. After a few weeks playing at soldiers, he went west with Orion, who had been appointed secretary of the territory of Nevada. After losing his savings in timber claims and silver prospecting, he struck lucky when the Virginia City *Territorial Enterprise*, to which he had submitted humorous letters, offered him a job. He first signed himself 'Mark Twain' (probably a reference to the river boat leadsman's call, 'By the mark, twain', i.e. two fathoms, signifying 'safe water below') in 1863, in the course of a two-year stint during which he wrote nearly two thousand local items. Many were hoaxes, and after a particularly scandalous one he quietly left town. At the request of the comic lecturer and humorous writer Artemus Ward—Charles Farrar Browne (1834–67)—he wrote 'Jim Smiley and His Jumping Frog', an imaginative rendering of a folk tale which 'set all New York in a roar' when published in the *Saturday Press* (1865). It became the title story of his first book, *The Celebrated Jumping Frog of Calaveras County, and Other Sketches* (1867), and the mainstay of his own initial reputation as a public performer.

Letters written as roving correspondent for the San Francisco *Alta California* on a Mediterranean excursion to Europe and the Holy Land, bolstered by other material, were the basis of *The Innocents Abroad* (1869); he wisely, on the advice of STOWE's brother, Henry Ward Beecher, negotiated a 5 per cent royalty instead of a $10,000 outright payment. In 1870 he married Olivia Langdon (1845–1904), 'the most beautiful girl I ever saw . . . & the *best*'. She was the daughter of a New York coal and lumber dealer, who bought and furnished for them a house in Buffalo, where until 1871 Twain was an editor and, with a loan from his father-in-law, part-owner of the *Express*. They had a son, who died in infancy, and three daughters.

Now America's leading humorist, he accepted a 7.5 per cent royalty for *Roughing It* (1872), an autobiography-cum-travel book on his experiences in the West and on a subsequent visit to the Sandwich Islands. He gave lectures based on it to packed houses in London for two months. In 1874 the family moved into the 'part cathedral, part cuckoo clock' in Hartford, designed from his own sketches. He had already begun, but put aside, *The Adventures of Tom Sawyer* (1876) when he wrote a series of nostalgic sketches for *Atlantic Monthly*, 'Old Times on the Mississippi', which eventually became chapters 4–17 of *Life on the Mississippi* (1883). Encouraged by HOWELLS, he went back to it, but restricted the action to Tom's boyhood, though he originally maintained that 'it is only written for adults'. It was issued as a book for boys; its chief significance is that it is the source of the protagonist of *The Adventures of Huckleberry Finn* (London, 1884; New York, 1885), on which he worked on and off for eight years. Written entirely in a carefully fashioned vernacular, it stands up to criticism as a classic representative of any of the genres of fiction which have been attributed to it.

In 1894, Webster, the publishing firm he had established for his wife's nephew, went bankrupt, and the following year he had to admit that the typesetting machine in whose development he had been investing since 1880 was unmarketable. Over $100,000 in debt, he turned to potboilers—*The Tragedy of Pudd'nhead Wilson* (1894) being an honourable exception—and to a round-the-world lecture tour, to retrieve his fortunes and his respect. He returned with both restored, but the effort had exhausted him. He predicted: 'I came in with Halley's comet in 1835. It is coming next year. . . . The Almighty has said, no doubt: "Now here are these two unaccountable freaks; they came in together, they must go out together." ' True to the mercurial character of its author, to whom art was everything, *The Autobiography of Mark Twain*, ed. Charles Neider (1959), begun in 1877, contains fiction as well as fact. See Bernard de Voto, *The Portable Mark Twain*, 1977; *Selected Writings of an American Skeptic*, ed. Victor Doyno, 1995; *Tales, Speeches, Essays and Sketches*, ed. Tom Quirk, 1995; *The Complete Humorous Sketches and Tales of Mark Twain*, ed. Charles Neider, new edn 1996; John C. Gerber, *Mark Twain*, 1988 (biographical/critical study); Henry B. Wonham, *Mark Twain and the Art of the Tall Tale*, 1993 (critical study); Shelley Fisher Fishkin, *Lighting Out for the Territory*: Reflections on Mark Twain and American Culture, 1996; R. Kent Rasmussen, *Mark Twain A to Z: the Essential Reference to His Life and Writings*, 1996.

TYLER, ANNE (b. 1941) American novelist, was born in Minneapolis and educated at Duke University, from which she graduated in 1961. Having married in 1963 (she has two daughters), she worked as a university librarian until 1965, when the family settled in Baltimore, the setting of many of her novels. Beginning with her first, *If Morning Ever Comes* (1964), a recurring motif is the sympathetic treatment of the eccentric, rebellious, non-communicative, or simply independently-minded individual in the context of traditional family conventions. Tyler herself has nominated her fifth, *Celestial Navigation* (1974), a bleak account of a brilliant but pathologically shy artist who brings himself to propose marriage but then fails as a husband, as her earliest work of genuine quality. Unfulfilled belonging is one of the manifold features of her ninth, *Dinner at the Homesick Restaurant* (1982), which, with its several narrative strains, marked a high point in her development of the serio-comic novel. Subsequent novels have been more accessible: *The Accidental Tourist* (1985), in which a tragedy accentuates a family rift and helplessness prevails; *Breathing Lessons* (1988), winner of the Pulitzer Prize; *Saint Maybe* (1991), a tangle of births and deaths eventually resolved; and *Ladder of Years* (1995), her 13th, in which a bored mother and housewife successfully manufactures her disappearance. Short stories have appeared in various journals, including the *New Yorker*. See Alice Hall Petry, *Understanding Ann Tyler*, 1990 (critical study); Dale Salwak (ed.), *Anne Tyler as Novelist*, 1995.

TYNAN, KATHARINE (1861–1931) Irish poet, novelist, and journalist, was born in Co. Dublin, one of the 11 children who lived past infancy of a gentleman dairy farmer, and was brought up in the comfortable surroundings of Whitehall, Clondalkin. An ulcerated eye infection as a child left her with a permanent condition which she referred to as 'purblind'. She was educated at the Dominican Convent of St Catherine of Siena at Drogheda until she was 14, shortly after which she became her father's official companion and hostess. In 1885 she published *Louise de la Vallière and Other Poems*, mainly conventional and fashionable, but expressing her Catholicism and feminine outlook. She also met YEATS, who was influential in furthering her career, and she his. In 1893 she married Henry A. Hinkson, a barrister who also wrote novels, and settled in London. She contributed literary reviews and crusading articles to Irish, English, and American journals, and wrote historical romances and sensational (but decorously expressed) novels of protest, often with Irish settings. In several volumes of verse, culminating with *Innocencies* (1905), she confirmed her status as a significant poet of the Irish Literary Revival, especially with her poems of nature and of motherhood. *The Holy War* (1916) and *Herb O'Grace* (1918) were extremely popular for their reflections from an unusual angle on World War I, in which two of her sons were fighting. The family had returned to Ireland in 1911 when Hinkson was appointed Resident Magistrate for Co. Mayo. After his death in 1919 she became even more dependent on her literary efforts, while at the same time travelling extensively in Britain and western Europe, with her daughter as guide. The political chaos which she witnessed during three long stays in Cologne is described in *Life in the Occupied Area* (1925), one of several volumes of memoirs; the others are *Twenty-Five Years* (1913), *The Middle Years* (1916), *The Years of the Shadow* (1919), *The Wandering Years* (1922), and *Memories* (1924). Her daughter, Pamela Hinkson (1900-82), was a novelist under her own name and that of 'Peter Deane', as whom she wrote a notable novel of World War I, *The Victors* (1925). See *Poems*, ed. Monk Gibbon, 1963; Marilyn Gaddis Rose, *Katharine Tynan*, 1974 (critical study).

TYNAN, KENNETH (1927–80) British dramatic critic, was born in Birmingham, the illegitimate son of Sir Peter Peacock (1872–1948), six times mayor of Warrington, and Rose Tynan (1888–1961), with whom Sir Peter lived as Peter Tynan for five days of the week. He was educated at King Edward's School, Birmingham, and Magdalen College, Oxford. He started writing sophisticated drama criticism when he was 17, and published his first collection of pieces, *He that Plays the King*, in 1950. When he came down from Oxford in 1951 he was both actor and director before becoming Drama Critic of the *Spectator* (1951–52), *Evening Standard* (1952–53), and *Daily Sketch* (1953–54). Of his standing in 1954, when he joined the *Observer*, Lord Olivier (1907–89) wrote in *Confessions of an Actor* (1982): 'His destructive weapons were deadly, strengthened by the scintillating quality of his writing. His praise was equally impressive.' In 1963 he accepted Olivier's invitation to be Literary Manager of the National Theatre, in which capacity he brought STOPPARD to the London stage, and persuaded the management to commission, advertise, and sell tickets for SHAFFER's *Black Comedy* before a word of it had been written. He resigned in 1969, after a dispute with the governors over *Soldiers*, a play by Rolf Hochhuth (b. 1931) in which allegations are made about WINSTON CHURCHILL's actions during World War II. He was joint producer of *Sol-*

diers when it was staged at another London theatre in 1968. He devised and partly wrote the popular, but critically disparaged, 'evening of elegant erotica', *Oh! Calcutta!* (1969, published 1988). His collected criticism is in *A View of the English Stage 1944–1963* (new edn 1984). *Profiles*, ed. Kathleen Tynan and Eddie Eban (1990) contains 50 telling studies of performers and performances. In 1951 he married the American novelist Elaine Dundy (*b*. 1927), in whose *The Dud Avocado* (1958) he appears thinly disguised as a photographer. His second wife, Kathleen (1938-1995), whom he married in 1967, became his biographer. See Kathleen Tynan, *The Life of Kenneth Tynan*, new edn 1995; *The Kenneth Tynan Letters*, ed. Kathleen Tynan, 1996.

U

UDALL, NICOLAS see PLAUTUS.

UNGARETTI, GIUSEPPE (1888–1970) Italian poet, was born in Egypt in Alexandria, and educated in Paris at Collège de France and the Sorbonne. After serving in the infantry in World War I, he was a journalist before being Professor of Italian Literature, Sao Paulo University 1936–42, and Professor of Modern Italian Literature, Rome University 1942–59. *Il Porto Sepolto* [The Buried Port] (1916) effectively established the hermetic mode of poetry, distinctive for the absence of conventional punctuation and metre, which he employed compellingly in the earlier volumes of 'La Vita d'un Uomo' [The Life of a Man] sequence, notably *Il Dolore* [Sorrow] (1947). He also translated into Italian sonnets of SHAKESPEARE and the 'Visions' of BLAKE. See *Selected Poems*, ed. and tr. Patrick Creagh, 1971.

UNSWORTH, BARRY see ONDAATJE.

UPDIKE, JOHN (*b.* 1932) American novelist, short story writer, poet, and critic, was born in Shillington, Pennsylvania. His father, a high school mathematics teacher of modest means, was of Dutch–American descent: his mother, a would-be writer, of German ancestry. Of himself when young: 'He saw art—between drawing and writing he ignorantly made no distinction—as a method of riding a thin pencil out of Shillington, out of time altogether, into an infinity of unseen and even unborn hearts. He pictured this infinity as radiant. How innocent!' He was educated at local public schools and Harvard. In 1954 he graduated *summa cum laude*, and had a story, 'Friends from Philadelphia', published in the *New Yorker*—'The acceptance reached me at my parents' farm, where my mother and I had both so often plodded out to the tin mailbox to reap our rejection slips.' After a year in England at the Ruskin School of Art, Oxford, he was a *New Yorker* staff writer until 1957, when he settled with his first wife and family in Ipswich, Massachusetts, where he rented an office above a restaurant in which to write. *The Carpentered Hen and Other Tame Creations* (1958; in UK as *Hoping for a Hoopoe*, 1959) was a collection of verse, a form of expression by means of which, through *Mid-*point and Other Poems* (1969) to *Facing Nature* (1985), he has demonstrated a neat touch and a reflective consciousness—see also *Collected Poems 1953–1993* (1993), in two sections: poetry and light verse.

The Same Door (1959) comprised *New Yorker* stories, some of them revised; *The Poorhouse Fair* (1959), his first novel, is a futuristic study of elderly people in a setting remembered from his childhood. With *Rabbit, Run* (1960), written during a personal religious crisis, he embarked on a chronicle of revelations of American fears and dreams through four decades, followed by *Rabbit Redux* (1971), *Rabbit is Rich* (1981), which won the Pulitzer Prize, as did *Rabbit at Rest* (1990). In *The Centaur* (1963), which won the National Book Award, themes from Greek mythology have their parallels in incidents which reflect his own family life in the 1940s. *Couples* (1968) focuses on suburban sexual relationships, a topic which recurs in *Marry Me* (1976). Issues of both theology and sexuality are explored in *A Month of Sundays* (1975), *Roger's Version* (1986), and *S* (1988), three linked novels in which situations in HAWTHORNE's *The Scarlet Letter* are re-created in contemporary American terms. James Buchanan (1791–1868), US President from 1857 to 1861, during which the first secession from the Union occurred, is the subject of Updike's play, *Buchanan Dying* (1974), and also of a biography being written by the sexually hyperactive protagonist of *Memories of the Ford Administration: a Novel* (1992), in which the earlier and later administrations counterpoint one another and back up a further stylish exploration of modern mores. Updike combined his talents as a critic of Latin American fiction and his experience of travel in *Brazil* (1994), an excursion into magic realism. *In the Beauty of the Lilies* (1996) is a saga, linked with the history of the movies, of four generations of a family, which also reflects his religious beliefs.

He has published, according to his own account, about two hundred short stories: 'More closely than my novels, more circumstantially than my poems, these efforts each hold my life's incidents, predicaments, crises, joys.' *The Afterlife and Other Stories* (1994) is a recent collection of pieces written between 1986 and 1994. *Self-Consciousness: Memoirs* (1989), written in his 57th year, contains autobiographical essays and reflections. Other collections are *Just Looking: Essays on Art* (1990), *Odd Jobs: Essays and Criticism* (1991), and *Golf Dreams: Writings on Golf* (1996). See Robert Detweiler, *John Updike*, rev. edn 1984 (critical study); Donald J. Grenier, *John Updike's Novels*, 1984; Judie Newman, *John Updike*, 1988 (critical study).

UPWARD, EDWARD see ISHERWOOD.

URQUHART, (Sir) **THOMAS, OF CROMARTY** (1611–1660) Scottish prose writer and translator, Chief of Clan Urquhart, was the eldest son of Sir Thomas Urquhart (1582–1642). He was educated at King's College, Aberdeen, which he entered at the age of 11 and left without a degree to go abroad. In 1637 he and a younger brother were accused of locking up their father, who was clearly losing control of his financial affairs. Urquhart and his clan took part in the royalist victory over the Covenanters at Turriff in 1639, the first battle of the Civil War. In London in 1641 he was knighted by Charles I, and published a uniformly dull volume of verses, *Epigrams: Divine and Moral*. He returned home on his father's death, assigned some of his rents to the creditors of the estates, and went abroad. When he got back in 1645, the creditors were still there, and continued to hound him in his 15th-century fortress. He had in the meantime published *The Trissotetras* (dated 1645), a largely impenetrable thesis on trigonometry. On the execution of Charles I in 1649, Urquhart was one of those who raised the standard for Charles II and captured Inverness. After Charles's Scottish coronation at Scone in 1651, he accompanied the royalist army, with the rank of colonel, to Worcester. He was captured in the total rout, and lost most of his manuscripts, which he had brought with him in three vast 'portmantles'. He was released on parole after a month in the Tower of London and then in Windsor Castle, one of those who were to forfeit their estates unless they could prove that their services were in the interests of the commonweal. He responded by publishing three remarkable works with fanciful pseudo-Greek titles. In *Pantochronochanon: or, A Peculiar Promptuary of Time* (1652), he traced his ancestry back through 152 generations to Adam. *Ekskubalauron: or, The Discovery of a Most Exquisite Jewel* (1652) is a lively plea for a universal language, with digressions, one of which comprises his famous character sketch of the 'Admirable Crichton', James Crichton (1560–82). In *Logopandekteision* (1653) he detailed his proposals for his universal language. His most lasting work, however, is his version of the *Gargantua and Pantagruel* of RABELAIS (books 1 and 2, 1653; book 3, 1694), one of the great translations in terms of rendering the spirit of the original. Latterly Urquhart lived abroad, where it is said he died of laughter after hearing of the Restoration of Charles II. The chiefship of Clan Urquhart passed to his brother, on whose death it devolved on the Urquharts of Craigfintry. See *The Admirable Urquhart: Selected Writings*, ed. Richard Boston, 1975; *The Jewel*, ed. R. D. S. Jack and R. J. Lyall, 1983.

V

VALÉRY, PAUL(-AMBROISE) (1871–1945) French poet and critic, was born in Cette (Sète) of a Corsican father and an Italian mother. He was educated at Collège de Sète (now Collège Paul-Valéry), the lycée in Montpellier, to which the family had moved, and Montpellier University, where he read law. With the encouragement of MALLARMÉ he began to publish verse in 'little magazines' in 1890. In October 1892 he went through some kind of intellectual crisis during a stormy night in Genoa, and renounced literature for the cultivation of his mind. He finally broke 25 years' silence, during which he had worked in the War Office, become in 1900 secretary to the Director of Agence Havas, the press association, and .published only prose, with *La Jeune Parque* (1917), an obscure, 500-line poem with echoes of RACINE. The appearance of *Charmes: ou Poèmes* (1922), written after 1917, established him as the ultimate Symbolist. He was appointed to the newly established chair of poetics at Collège de France in 1937. He is buried in the seaside cemetery at Sète which is the subject of his best-known poem, 'Cimitière Marin'. His collected works have been issued in English translation, ed. Jackson Mathews, 15 vols 1956–75.

VANBRUGH, (Sir) **JOHN** (1664–1726) British dramatist and architect, was born in London, the son of a sugar baker and grandson of Gillis Van Brugg (d. 1646), a refugee Flemish merchant, and was probably educated at Chester Grammar School. He had some architectural training in France between 1683 and 1685, and was commissioned in the Earl of Huntingdon's regiment in 1786. In 1790 he was imprisoned in France for two years (apparently for travelling without a passport), after which he resumed his military career, achieving the rank of captain. Two of his earliest plays, *The Relapse: or Virtue in Danger* (1697) and *The Provok'd Wife* (1697), are also his most original. Though the former contains within two plots the standard devices of Restoration comedy (temptation, seduction, impersonation, and reconciliation), the latter is of one piece and has a genuinely, and still at the end unresolved, unhappy marriage motivating the plot. More than other writers of his time, he came to rely on the development of comic situations rather than on dialogue or the expression of fanciful humours, as he demonstrated in *The Country House* (1704), adapted from a play by the French dramatist, Florent Carton Dancourt (1661–1725). *The Provok'd Husband* was left unfinished and was completed by CIBBER. Vanbrugh was appointed Comptroller of the Royal Works in 1702, and was knighted in 1714. He designed Castle Howard and Blenheim Palace, the cost of which so appalled the Duchess of Marlborough that at one point she refused to pay the suppliers' bills. See Laurence Whistler, *Vanbrugh: Architect and Dramatist*, new edn 1978.

VAN DER POST, (Sir) **LAURENS** (1906–96) South African novelist, explorer, and anthropologist, was born near Philippolis, the 13th of 15 children of parents of Dutch descent, and was educated at Grey College, Bloemfontein. He served in a whaling ship, the experience of which is recaptured in his novel, *The Hunter and the Whale: a Tale of Africa* (1967). He worked on *Voorslag* with ROY CAMPBELL and PLOMER, hurriedly went to Japan—see *Yet Being Someone Other* (1982)—and was then variously a journalist and farmer in South Africa and England. His only prewar book, the novel *In a Province* (1934), was significant for its time in seriously questioning the rule of white law in South Africa. He enlisted in the British Army in 1939, and was taken prisoner in 1942 while commanding a small guerrilla unit in the Far East—see his account, *The Night of the New Moon* (1970), in USA as *The Prisoner and the Bomb*. He stayed in the East in 1945, being Military Attaché, with the rank of colonel, to the British Minister in Batavia until 1947, when he was made CBE. *A Bar of Shadow* (1956) was reprinted in *The Seed and the Sower* (1963), three stories reflecting his experiences in action and as a prisoner-of-war. In other novels he has examined the position of the exiled artist—*The Face Beside the Fire* (1953)—and created an extended saga of survival which begins with the destruction of a South African farm—*A Story Like the Wind* (1972) and *A Far-Off Place* (1974).

Venture to the Interior (1952) is his account, enhanced by reflective passages, of his mission on behalf of the British Government to explore the region of Mount Mlanje (the inspiration of HAGGARD's *People of the Mist*). Subsequent expeditions provided the basis of *The Lost World of the Kalahari* (1958) and *The Heart of the Hunter* (1961), as distinguished for their insight into the civilization, and mind, of the Bushman as for their contribution to the literature of travel and adventure. *Journey into Russia* (1964) describes what he calls 'perhaps the longest single journey through the Soviet Union undertaken since the war by someone who is not a communist'. He was knighted in 1981. See *Feather Fall: an Anthology*, ed. Jean-Marc Pottiez, new edn 1995; *The Admiral's Baby*, 1996 (postwar memoir).

VAN DRUTEN, JOHN see ISHERWOOD.

VAN VECHTEN, CARL see HUGHES, LANGSTON.

VARGAS LLOSA, MARIO (*b.* 1936) Peruvian novelist, was born in Arequipa—his father, having abandoned his wife when she was five months' pregnant and remained incommunicado for 11 years, reappeared after the boy had all the time been led to believe he was dead. In 1952, when his father discovered that he was writing verses instead of attending to his school work, he was sent to Leoncio Prado Military Academy, in the courtyard of which copies of his first novel were later publicly burned. He went on to the University of San Marcos, Lima. In 1955 he eloped with his aunt-by-marriage Julia, ten years his senior. Aspects of his courtship are interwoven into the fictional plot of *La Tía Julia y el Escribidor* (1977; tr. Helen R. Lane as *Aunt Julia and the Scriptwriter*, 1982). For his aunt's version of the story of their marriage, see Julia Urquidi Illanes, *My Life with Mario Vargas Llosa*, tr. C. R. Perricone (1988)—they divorced in 1964 so that he could marry her niece (and his first cousin). He did further study at the University of Madrid, after which he was a journalist and broadcaster in France, and taught at Queen Mary and King's colleges, London University, and at universities in the USA and Puerto Rico. He returned permanently to Peru in 1974, and unsuccessfully contested the presidential election in 1990—*El Pes en el Agua* (1993; tr. Lane as *A Fish in the Water*, 1994) is a record of his political campaign, interspersed with telling accounts of his earlier life.

He published a book of short stories in Spain in 1959, followed by the novel *La Ciudad y los Perros* (1963; tr. Lysander Kemp as *The Time of the Hero*, 1966), in which the mixed social backgrounds and wild behaviour of cadets and staff at the military academy at which he studied represent a microcosm of Peruvian society. With *La Casa Verde* (1965; tr. Gregory Rabassa as *The Green House*, 1968) it reveals a consistent scepticism at a time when he advocated Marxism. Similarly

textured in narrative technique is *Conversación en la Catedral* (1969; tr. Rabassa as *Conversation in the Cathedral*, 1975), a study of political strife in Peru in the 1950s. In *El Hablador* (1987; tr. Lane as *The Storyteller*, 1990) the strands of narrative are mixed to bring an ancient culture in conflict with the present, and to unravel the mystery of the fate of a charismatic friend of the writer. In *Lituma en los Andes* (1993; tr. Edith Grossman as *Death in the Andes*, 1996) he offers a metaphor for a vision of Peruvian society which is part mystery, part political allegory. Vargas Llosa has also written major critical studies in Spanish of GARCÍA MARQUEZ (1971) and FLAUBERT (1975). *A Writer's Reality*, introduction by Myron Lichtblau (1991), is a series of personal essays on his craft, in English. A further selection, ranging from 1962 to 1994, is *Making Waves*, ed. and tr. John King (1996), which includes journalism on topical and political issues as well as critical essays.

VAUGHAN, HENRY (1622–95) Welsh poet (he called himself 'Silurist', i.e., man of south Wales), a cousin of AUBREY, was born in Llansaintffraed, Breconshire. With his twin brother, Thomas (*d.* 1666), he was educated by a local rector and at Jesus College, Oxford, after which he studied law and then medicine. They both fought for the royalists in the Civil War, and were captured and imprisoned. Afterwards, Henry practised as a physician at Newton-by-Usk; Thomas studied and wrote treatises on magic and mysticism. Henry's first book, *Poems, with the Tenth Satyre of Juvenal Englished* (1646), is in the secular mode of the tavern poets, notably DONNE and JONSON, and the form is repeated in *Olor Iscanus* [Swan of Usk]: *Select Poems and Translations* (1651), which was published without his consent. For in the meantime, following the inspiration of GEORGE HERBERT, he had turned to religious poetry, published in *Silex Scintillans* [Sparks from the Flint]: *Sacred Poems and Private Ejaculations* (1650; enlarged edition 1655). The best of these poems, which include 'The Retreat', 'Peace' ('My soul there is a country . . .'), 'The World' ('I saw eternity the other night . . .'), and 'Man', sparkle with brilliant lines, and have a mystical depth and an understanding of the natural world. *The Mount of Olives: or Solitary Devotions* (1652) comprises meditations in prose. See *The Complete Poems*, ed. Alan Rudrum, 1981; Stevie Davies, *Henry Vaughan*, 1995 (critical biography).

VEGA CARPIO, LOPE DE (1562–1635) Spanish dramatist, poet, and novelist, was born in Madrid, and studied Latin and Spanish under the novelist Vicente Espinel (1550–1624) from 1572 to 1574, when he went to a Jesuit school. From 1576 to 1578 he was in the household of Bishop Mansique de Lara and attended Alcala University. He then entered the service of the Marquis of Las Navas, studied at Salamanca University, and in 1583 enlisted in the expedition sent to put down a rebellion in the Azores. Already an up-and-coming playwright, he embarked on his return on a torrid affair with Elena Osorio, married since 1576 to a strolling actor. When she left Vega Carpio for the wealthy nephew of a cardinal, he responded by circulating two ribald poems about her and her family, for which he was jailed for libel and exiled for seven years. (He recorded the course of the affair in *La Dorotea*, a novel in prose and verse, written soon afterwards but not published until 1632.)

He settled in Valencia, married in 1588 (by proxy) 17-year-old Isabel de Urbino, of a prominent Madrid family, and immediately left with the Spanish Armada on its disastrous expedition against England, which he and his ship survived. Isabel died in childbirth in 1594. After his return to Madrid he set up house with Micaela de Luján, an actor's wife, the 'Lucinda' of his poetry, by whom he had several children whose paternity was ascribed to her husband until his death in 1603, after which they were baptized as 'parents unknown'. In 1598 he published *La Dragontea*, an epic in ten cantos vilifying the English hero of the Armada fiasco, Sir Francis Drake (c.1540–96), and married Juana de Guardo, the daughter of a wealthy butcher/fishmonger. In 1604, by which time he was said to have written three hundred plays, he published the first of 25 volumes of his collected works, *Las Comedias*, and set up two households in Toledo, one with his wife and one with Micaela, who went her own way in 1607. Juana died in 1613, and he was living with Jerónima de Burgos, a married actress, when in 1614 he became a priest. The last of his numerous loves was Marta de Nevares ('Amarilis'), the unhappy young wife of a businessman, after whose death they lived together until she died, blind and insane, in 1632. In 1634, their 17-year-old daughter, who had become Vega Carpio's secretary/companion, was seduced and abducted by a Madrid hidalgo, and he never saw her again. He took to repenting daily for his misdeeds and to scourging himself every Friday. During the course of his state funeral, which lasted nine days, there were more than a hundred and fifty orations.

Vega Carpio's total output of plays has been estimated at over fifteen hundred, of which he claimed to have written a hundred in less than a day each. About five hundred survive, justifying his position as the founder of a Spanish national theatre and creator of the *comedia* (a three-act verse play); he was also a lyric poet of considerable skill and feeling. *Fuente Ovejuna*, his compelling portrayal of a peasant uprising, was presented (tr. Adrian Mitchell) in London in 1989 by the National Theatre, and revived in 1992. *Arte Nuevo de Hacer Comedias* [The New Art of Writing Plays], the amusing verse treatise which he read to a literary society in Madrid in 1609, is (tr. W. T. Brewster) in Brander Matthews (ed.), *Papers on Playmaking* (1957). See *Five Plays*, tr. Jill Booty, introduction by R. F. D. Pring-Mill, 1961; *Two Plays: Madness in Valencia, The Idiot Lady*, tr. David Johnston, 1995.

VERGA, GIOVANNI (1840–1922) Italian novelist, was born in Catania of a Sicilian landowning family, and was educated privately and at Catania University, where he read law. He lived in Florence from 1865 to 1870, and then in Milan, writing romantic novels of what he later called 'elegance and adultery'. The distinctive exception was *Nedda* (1874), a tale of an unmarried mother of the Sicilian peasantry, the realism of which presaged his initiating the mode of *verismo*. Even before he abandoned Milan for Sicily in 1885 he had spent more and more of his time there, finding his subject matter in the daily lives and temperament of the peasants and fishermen, and representing the Sicilian dialect by adapting standard Italian usage. His most notable works in this vein are two volumes of stories which D. H. LAWRENCE translated as *Little Novels of Sicily* (1925) and *Cavalleria Rusticana, and Other Tales of Sicilian Life* (1928), and the novels *I Malavoglia* (1881; tr. M. A. Craig as *The House by the Medlar Tree*, 1890) and *Mastro-don Gesualdo* (1889; tr. Craig, 1893; tr. D. H. Lawrence, 1923). Verga was made a life senator on his 80th birthday.

VERLAINE, PAUL (1844–96) French poet, was born in Metz, the son of a captain in the Engineers, and was educated at the Institution Landry and the Lycée Bonaparte in Paris, after which he worked as a civil servant in the Hôtel de Ville, a source of income of which many young poets availed themselves. *Poèmes Saturniens* (1866), a melancholy, musical reflection of the Parnassian credo, and collections in 1869 and 1870, contain most of what is lasting in his work. In 1870 he married the 17-year-old Mathilde Mauté. In 1871 he got involved with the insurrectionist Communards, and RIMBAUD arrived in his life. Their association led to his being sentenced to two years' hard labour after he had shot Rimbaud in the hand. While in prison he read SHAKESPEARE, brushed up his English generally, and wrote and arranged the publication of the curious *Romances Sans Paroles* (1874), of which not one copy of the edition was sold. Mathilde obtained a judicial separation in 1874 (she was one of the first to take advantage of the legalization of divorce ten years later), which led to his return to the Catholic faith. In the double state of emotion which ensued, he wrote some fine religious verse, and vowed to give up absinthe. On his release from jail in 1875 he went to England, where he taught in a village school in Stick-ley, Lincolnshire, and then at St Aloysius College, Bournemouth. Attempts at farming in France failed, and the death from typhoid of Lucien Létinois (1861–83) prompted the gradual deterioration of his existence. He returned to absinthe and was in 1884 sentenced to a month in jail and a fine of 500 francs for making violent threats to his mother. Much of what he now wrote was recycled from earlier work, published in order to maintain a bizarre lifestyle between three different women. See *Selected Poems*, ed. and tr. Joanna Richardson, 1974.

VERNE, JULES (1828–1905) French novelist, was born on Ile Feydeau in the Loire at Nantes, the son of a lawyer, and became a boarder at the seminary of St Donatian in 1837. Thwarted in an unpremeditated attempt to run away to sea when he was 11, he commented: 'After this I shall travel only in my imagination.' He left school at 16, and after working in his father's office went to Paris to further his law studies. He passed his examinations while also trying to establish himself as a writer, at which he had some minor success with pieces for the stage. In 1856 he set up as a stockbroker, and the following year married a young widow. A trip to Scotland in 1859 inspired a taste for romance and for spectacular landscapes. At 34, still without any position as a man of letters, he combined the prevailing preoccupations with ballooning and Africa into an adventure story. After being rejected by several publishers, *Cinq Semaines en Ballon* (1863; tr. as *Five Weeks in a Balloon*, 1869) was enthusiastically accepted, subject to revisions, as a children's story. It was the first of a stream of similar amalgams of fact and imaginative and scientific fiction, of which *Voyage au Centre de la Terre* (1864: tr. as *A Journey to the Centre of the Earth*, 1873), *Vingt Milles Lieues sous les Mers* (1870; tr. as *Twenty Thousand Leagues under the Sea*, 1874), and *Le Tour du Monde en Quatre-Vingts Jours* (1873; tr. G. M. Towle as *Around the World in Eighty Days*, 1874) still have the power to excite. In 1872 he was awarded a prize by the Académie Française. Fame and wealth enabled him to entertain lavishly, to have a sea-going yacht, and to travel: until in 1886 he was forced into retirement when he was shot, for no reason, by a demented nephew, the bullet permanently lodging in his leg. Comparing Verne's work with his, WELLS wrote (1933): 'He helped the reader to imagine [actual possibilities of invention and discovery] done and to realize what fun, excitement or mischief would ensue. Many of his inventions have "come true". But [my stories] do not pretend to deal with possible things; they are exercises of the imagination in a quite different field.' Written in 1863, rejected by his publisher that year or in 1864, and never published until 1994 is Verne's *Paris au XXe Siècle*, ed. Piero Gondolo della

Riva, tr. Richard Howard as *Paris in the Twentieth Century* (1997), part satire on the state of society at the time, part cultural autobiography, and part astonishing foresight into the technology and sociology of the 1960s. See Brian Taves and Stephen Michaluk, Jr, *The Jules Verne Encyclopaedia*, 1996.

VICENTE, GIL (*c*.1465–*c*.1537) Portuguese dramatist, was born in rural Portugal, possibly near Serra da Estrela, and was attached to the court as goldsmith in about 1490, becoming national overseer of gold and silver craft in 1509, and being Master of the Royal Mint 1513–17. From 1502 he was also court dramatist, writing in Spanish as well as in Portuguese, and sometimes both in the same play. In spite of the fact that most of his plays were written for court and state occasions, he was able to invest his comedies with lyricism and depth of characterization, and effectively to establish a Portuguese tradition in religious drama, while blending elements from a variety of sources. Luis, his son born in about 1520 of a second marriage, was responsible for the compilation of his collected works, published in Lisbon in 1562, in which stage directions are included.

VIDAL, GORE (*b*. 1925) American novelist, dramatist, and essayist, was born at West Point, New York, where his father was an instructor in aeronautics; his mother was a daughter of the blind Senator Thomas Pryor Gore (1870–1949). After going to Phillips Exeter Academy, he served in the US Army during World War II, becoming a warrant officer and finding himself acting as first mate in a supply ship in the Aleutian Islands. At sea he wrote *Williwaw* (1946), a war novel set in an army supply ship in the Aleutian Islands. Bent on becoming a man of letters, he wrote his third novel, *The City and the Pillar* (1948; rev. edn 1965; new edn with introduction and seven short stories, 1995), in Guatemala. After the publication of this exploration of an all-American lad's homosexuality, he left the USA again, to spend two years in North Africa and Europe (his family had come from Venice in the 1860s). *The Season of Comfort* (1949), a portrait of a young man and his mother, represents a further venture into fictionalized autobiography. *A Search for a King: a Twelfth Century Legend* (1950) initiated a significant historical phase, which included *Julian* (1964), a study of the Roman emperor known as the 'Apostate', who ruled from 361 to 363. The phase continued with *Washington D.C.* (1967), the first of a series of six novels culminating with *Hollywood* (1990), in which he offers a panorama of American history. A more acid, witty taste informs *Myra Breckenridge* (1968) and *Myron* (1974), whose protagonist undergoes a sex change and a reversal, and then experiences fantasies in both roles. *Live from Golgotha* (1992), told with a sense of history and a plethora of jokes, transplants biblical events into the television age. He has written detective novels as Edgar Box. There have been several collections of his elegant, erudite, savage, and witty essays on literary, historical, and political subjects, including *A View from the Diner's Club: Essays 1987–1991* (1991)—the title is a reference to his declining membership of the National Institute of Arts and Letters on the grounds that he was already a member of the Diners Club. *United States: Essays 1952-1992* (1993) won the National Book Award. *Palimpsest* (1995) is an anecdotal, discursive autobiography. See Jay Parini (ed.), *Gore Vidal: Writer against the Grain*, new edn 1994 (critical study).

VIGNY, ALFRED DE (1797–1863) French poet, was born in Loches and educated at the Lycée Bonaparte, Paris, after which he became a sublieutenant in the Gendarmes du Roi. He left the army in 1827 as a captain, having spent most of his service on garrison duty. In the meantime he had published *Cinq-Mars* (1826), a historical novel of the 17th century in which symbolism plays a large part; *Poèmes* (1822), reflecting classical and biblical themes; *Eloa: ou, La Soeur des Anges* [The Sister of the Angels] (1824), a verse mystery play of the redemption of Satan, involving a female angel and drawing on MILTON, BYRON, and THOMAS MOORE; and *Poèmes Antiques et Modernes* (1826), effectively his collected verse, whose final (1837) edition comprised just 20 poems, illustrating a romantic but pessimistic moral philosophy—a posthumous volume appeared in 1864. In 1825, in Pau, he married an English woman, Lydia Bunbury (*d.* 1862). He was a devoted if not dutiful husband. For the actress Marie Dorval (1798–1850), with whom he had a seven-year affair, he wrote his three original plays, which include *Chatterton* (1835), in which she played the young poet's fictional mistress who comes to a spectacular end. He also adapted for the French stage SHAKESPEARE's *Othello* (1829) and *The Merchant of Venice* (1839). *Servitude et Grandeur Militaires* (1835; tr. Marguerite Barnett as *The Military Condition*, 1964) comprises three stories in different moods, in which values are explored in military contexts.

VILLON, FRANÇOIS (1431–after 1462) French poet, was born François de Montcorbier in Paris, and took his surname from his guardian, Guillaume de Villon, chaplain of Saint-Benoit-le-Bétourné and a teacher at Paris University, from which Villon graduated as MA in 1452. In 1455 he killed a priest in a brawl. Pardoned in 1456, he then participated in a robbery of gold coins from the Chapel of the College of Navarre, and left Paris in a hurry when an accomplice confessed. At the end of a fairly wild odyssey through various towns, he was in 1462 imprisoned for the theft, but released when he undertook to repay the money. He was rearrested for taking part in yet another street brawl, and condemned to death: the sentence was commuted to banishment, but not before he had composed his own 'Epitaph', in which he graphically described what would happen to his corpse and those of 'five or six' others alongside whom he expected to be hanged. Autobiographical details occur throughout 'Le Lais' [The Legacy], written in 1456 before he went on the run, and 'Le Testament', a sequence or collection of poems in a variety of moods (including bawdy and satirical), probably finalized in 1461–62, in which appears the famous *ballade* with the refrain, 'Mais où sont les neiges d'antan'. D. G. ROSSETTI, SWINBURNE, and ROBERT LOWELL are among those who have translated individual poems into English verse. See *Selected Poems*, ed. and tr. Peter Dale, new edn 1978.

VINE, BARBARA see RENDELL.

VIRGIL (PUBLIUS VERGILIUS MARO) (70–19 BC) Roman epic, pastoral, and didactic poet, was born near Mantua in Cisalpine Gaul. He was educated in Cremona and Milan, and went on to higher education, probably in Naples and Rome. He was never very fit, which may be why he then returned to the family farm to write. After the civil unrest in 41, during which the farm was confiscated but then restored to him on appeal, he went to live in Campania. His *Eclogues*, a series of bucolic episodes in the manner of THEOCRITUS, was published in 37. His patron Maecenas (*c.*70–8 BC) encouraged him to write the *Georgics*, on which he spent the next seven years. These four books of didactic verse describe the activities of a farming year, with emphasis on traditional agricultural industries, on a return to the old forms of worship, and on communal working.

Augustus, now emperor in all but title and name, felt that an epic poem glorifying his achievements would be appropriate. Maecenas (as honorary minister of arts) approached several writers, all of whom turned down the idea. Virgil accepted it on his own terms, and was still working on his account of the mythological antecedents of Rome in the year 19, when he met Augustus in Athens. Instead of going on a tour of Greece and the east as he had intended, he accompanied the emperor back to Italy. On the way, he caught a fever, and died at Brundisium a few days after landing, having asked his friends to burn the manuscript. With commendable sense, they did no such thing. The *Aeneid* is unfinished in that it was to be revised and polished. The story is complete and ends on a dramatic climax. It is the national epic of the Roman empire, and the most famous and influential poem of the Roman era. Virgil always wrote in hexameters, a form he perfected, and his mastery of which no one ever equalled. In DANTE's *Divine Comedy*, Virgil, personifying Human Reason, is the poet's guide to the Gates of Paradise. TENNYSON, in 'To Virgil', calls him 'Wielder of the stateliest measure / ever moulded by the lips of man'. See *The Aeneid*, tr. Robert Fitzgerald, new edn 1993 (verse), tr. David West, 1991 (prose); *The Eclogues and Georgics*, tr. C. Day Lewis, new edn 1983, introduction and notes by R. O. A. M. Lyne (verse); *Virgil in English*, ed. K. W. Gransden, 1996; Jasper Griffin, *Virgil*, 1986 (introduction to the works).

VITTORINI, ELIO (1908–66) Italian novelist, translator, and critic, was born in Sicily in Syracuse, the son of a railway station employee who lived on the job. He left school at 17 after five years of primary education and three at a business school, and worked on a road-building gang. He was also writing stories, a volume of which was published in 1931. While working as a proofreader on a Florentine daily, he learned English, and when he was forced to give up his job because of lead-poisoning, earned a precarious living by translating D. H. LAWRENCE, POE, FAULKNER, and STEINBECK. *Conversazione in Sicilia* (1941; tr. Wilfrid David as *Conversation in Sicily*, 1948), a poetic novel of a search for a meaningful reality through a recall of childhood, caused him to fall out with the Fascist party (of which he was not a member), and in 1943 he was imprisoned until the German occupation, during which he went underground. A similar literary style informs *Il Garofano Rossi* (1948; tr. Anthony Bower as *The Red Carnation*, 1953), an exploration of adolescent reaction to Fascism, several chapters of which had been published in 1933–34 in *Solaria*, a small Florentine cooperative venture. Postwar social problems feature in *Il Sempione Strizza l'Occhio al Fréjus* (1949; tr. Cinina Brescia as *The Twilight of the Elephant*, 1951). Vittorini founded the critical journals *Il Politecnico* (1945–47) and *Il Menabò* (1959–67) for the study of cultural directions in the current environment. As literary adviser to Mondadori, he rejected the dying LAMPEDUSA's manuscript as 'rather old-fashioned', 'essayish', and 'unbalanced'.

VOLTAIRE, pseudonym of François-Marie Arouet (1694–1778) French novelist, dramatist, poet, prose writer, and philosopher, was born in Paris, the son of a notary, and was educated as a boarder at the Jesuit College of Louis-le-Grand. His irresponsible attitude to studying law offended not only his father, who tried to obtain a *lettre de cachet* against him, but also the authorities, who consigned him briefly to the Bastille in 1717 for writing scurrilous verses. While there, he composed *La Ligue* (1723; as *La Henriade*, 1728; tr. John Lockman as *Henriade*, 1732), an epic poem on

the religious conflicts associated with the accession of Henry IV, the first Bourbon King of France. *Oedipe*, adapted from the Greek legend, the first of his numerous verse tragedies, ran exceptionally for 45 performances in 1718. With a pension from the Regent, a third of his father's fortune, and the profits from his business deals, Voltaire was now on the way to being rich. Insulted by a nobleman for his middle-class background, and then beaten up by the man's servants, he made noises threatening a duel, and was in 1726 arrested and put once more in the Bastille, from which the authorities released him when he expressed a wish to visit England. The most tangible outcome of his three-year stay is *Lettres Philosophiques* (1734; tr. Lockman, 1733; tr. Leonard Tancock as *Letters on England*, 1980); his depiction of England (for all its amusingly described foibles) as a land of freedom, toleration, and progress was taken by the French as criticism of their institutions—see *Letters Concerning the English Nation*, ed. Nicholas Crook (1994) for Voltaire's English text, in which he largely wrote the book. In *Zaïre* (1732; tr. as *The Tragedy of Zara*, 1736), reminiscent of SHAKESPEARE's *Othello*, love overcomes the tenets of religion, a theme to which he often returned. In 1733 he began an affair with the Marquise du Chatelet (1706–49), which was condoned by her husband, in whose chateau in Lorraine, remodelled by Voltaire to suit his convenience, they all lived together.

In 1736 he started his celebrated correspondence with Frederick the Great of Prussia, at whose court he spent the years 1750–53 (he was now having an affair with his widowed niece, whom Frederick refused to allow to accompany him). His historical work, *Le Siècle de Louis XIV* (1751; tr. as *The Age of Lewis XIV*, 1752) was first published in Berlin. Still *persona non grata* in Paris, and having quarrelled with Frederick, in 1755 he bought an estate near Geneva, where he published *Candide* (1759; tr. as *Candid*, 1759; tr. John Butt as *Candide*, 1947), his satirical fable in the form of a picaresque novel, in which his philosophical message underlies the agony and farce. In 1759 he moved to Ferney, a smaller estate in Lorraine, and first proclaimed his battle cry of '*écrasez l'infâme*' [crush infamy], with which he campaigned vigorously against the evils and atrocities undertaken in the name of religion, and against travesties of justice. Under his stewardship Ferney became an industrial town famous for Swiss watches and silk stockings. He finally returned to Paris in triumph at the age of 83, but the excitement and the stream of distinguished visitors took their toll. He died three months later, his mummified body being smuggled out of Paris to the monastery of Scellières, whose prior had agreed to give it a Christian burial. See *Selected Writings*, ed. Christopher

Thacker, 1995; A. J. Ayer, *Voltaire*, 1986 (bio-graphical/critical study).

VONNEGUT, KURT, JR (*b*. 1922) Amer-ican novelist, dramatist, and essayist, was born in Indianapolis of German descent. His father was an architect and his mother took to writing stories after her family's brewing fortune disappeared during the Depression: 'She was a good writer, but she had no talent for the vulgarity the slick magazines re-quired. Fortunately, I was loaded with vul-garity, so, when I grew up, I was able to make her dream come true.' He went to Shortridge High School and Cornell Univer-sity, from which he went to serve in the US Army Infantry in World War II. Captured by the Germans, he was incarcerated in an un-derground meat locker during the Allied bombardment which destroyed Dresden in 1945. What happened to the city that night affected his view of humanity and was re-created in his novel *Slaughterhouse-Five: or, The Children's Crusade* (1969). After the war he enrolled at Chicago University to read an-thropology ('It confirmed my atheisim'), keeping himself as a police reporter for the Chicago City News Bureau. He took no de-gree—it was mailed to him twenty years later when his department read *Cat's Cradle* (1963). After working in public relations for General Electric, he became a freelance writer in 1950. He is a pessimist whose jokes are a way of combating despair, and whose first two nov-els, *Player Piano* (1952) and *The Sirens of Titan* (1959), resemble science fiction. From *Break-fast of Champions: or, Goodbye, Blue Monday* (1973), he has offered an underlying form of moral instruction. In *Hocus Pocus* (1990), the awful image of an America of the near future is the setting for an autobiographical narra-tive, in a variety of outrageous forms, of an extraterrestrially manipulated existence. *Fates Worse than Death: an Autobiographical Collage of the 1980s* (1991) is a non-fictional re-flection of his attitudes towards modern soci-ety. See Stanley Schatt, *Kurt Vonnegut*, 1976 (critical study).

WACE, ROBERT see GEOFFREY OF MON-
MOUTH.

WADDELL, HELEN (1889–1965) Irish
scholar and novelist, was born in Tokyo, the
youngest of ten children of a Presbyterian
missionary. Her mother died when she was
two. Her father subsequently married a
cousin, and brought the family back to Ulster, where he died soon afterwards. She was
educated at Victoria College and Queen's
University, Belfast. Until her stepmother's
death in 1919 she looked after her, writing
bible stories for a weekly journal and a play,
The Spoiled Buddha (performed 1915), and
publishing *Lyrics from the Chinese* (1913). In
1920 she went to Somerville College, Oxford,
to do a research degree, and also lectured on
medieval mime at St Hilda's College. A travelling scholarship took her to Paris for two
years, after which she published *The Wandering Scholars* (1927), a study of the French
medieval culture which inspired 'Carmina
Burana', for which she became the first
woman Fellow of the Royal Society of Literature. *Medieval Latin Lyrics* (1929) is as much a
work of poetic creation as of translation. Her
only novel, *Peter Abelard* (1933), is a poetic,
spare, scholarly retelling of the love of the
12th-century theologian for Héloïse (see ABE-
LARD). In the 1930s Waddell was much in demand as a lecturer and was showered with
honorary degrees, while publishing further
translations and educational and scholarly
works. During World War II she was Assistant Editor of *The Nineteenth Century*, and suffered in the bombing. Her last contribution to
literature was a lecture at Glasgow, *Poetry in
the Dark Ages* (1948). Soon after its publication she declined into mental paralysis, as a
result of which for the last years of her life
she could recognize no one and nothing. See
Dame Felicitas Corrigan, *Helen Waddell: a Biography*, new edn 1990.

WAIN, JOHN (1925–94) British novelist,
poet, and critic, was born in Stoke-on-Trent
and educated at the High School, Newcastle-
under-Lyme, and (during World War II, in
which he was unfit to serve) at St John's College, Oxford, where he was a pupil of C. S.
LEWIS. In 1947 he became a lecturer in English at Reading University, whose School of

Art published his first book, *Mixed Feelings:
Nineteen Poems* (1951). A further volume of
verse, *A Word Carved on a Sill*, was published
commercially in 1956. He gave up teaching
for writing after the publication of *Hurry on
Down* (1953), a picaresque comic novel reflecting the social conflicts of the times. *Strike
the Father Dead* (1962) is an elaboration of a
similar theme, told in turn by three different
protagonists. The contemporary saga which
begins at Oxford in the 1930s with *Where the
Rivers Meet* (1988) is continued, still at Oxford, in the 1950s with *Comedies* (1990) and
Hungry Generations (1994). From being originally associated with the Movement (see
CONQUEST), his poetry diversified along epigrammatic and then more adventurous
lines—see *Poems 1949–1979* (1981). His non-
fiction includes *A House for the Truth: Critical
Essays* (1972), *The Living World of Shakespeare:
a Playgoer's Guide* (rev. edn 1979), and a biography of JOHNSON (rev. edn 1980). He edited
selections of Johnson and HARDY, and compiled many anthologies, including *The Oxford
Library of English Poetry* (1988). He was Professor of Poetry at Oxford 1973–78, and was
made CBE in 1984. See *Sprightly Running:
Part of an Autobiography*, 1962.

WALCOTT, DEREK (b. 1930) St Lucian
poet and dramatist, born in Castries, has
written, 'To be born on a small island, a colonial backwater, meant a precocious resignation to fate.' His father, a senior civil servant
with artistic leanings, died when he was one,
and he and his twin brother were brought up
by their mother, an infant school headmistress who took in sewing to keep them at
school. Part-white, and from an early age impressed by the English language, whereas the
common speech of the island was a French
patois, he was further 'estranged . . . from the
common life of the island' by being a Methodist in a predominantly Catholic community. He was educated at St Mary's College,
the administration of which was during his
time taken over by the Presentation Brothers
of Cork, through whom he was introduced to
the work of MANGAN, SYNGE, YEATS, and even
JOYCE. Another influence was Harold Simmons (1914–66), a professional artist who
recognized that Walcott's talent as a painter
was a secondary consideration beside his

huge potential as a poet, and who read GEORGE CAMPBELL's *First Poems* aloud to him. Walcott's *25 Poems* (1948) was privately published but went into a second edition; his first play, *Henri Christophe*, was performed in 1950. That year, having been awarded a scholarship to the University of the West Indies, Jamaica, by the British government organization assisting in the rehabilitation of the island after fire destroyed Castries in 1948, he finally left St Lucia. In 1959 he founded the Trinidad Theatre Workshop, which he directed until 1976—see Bruce King, *Derek Walcott and West Indian Drama: Not Only a Playwright but a Company—The Trinidad Theatre Workshop 1959–1993* (1995). He now divides his time between Trinidad, where he lives, and the USA, where he was appointed Visiting Professor at Boston University in 1985.

In a Green Night: Poems 1948–1960 (1962), *Selected Poems* (1964), *The Castaway and Other Poems* (1965), and *The Gulf and Other Poems* (1969) represent a continuous process of absorption rather than rejection of literary influences, of development of metre and form, of experiment with dialect, and of revision; they evoke, in particular, history and the Caribbean landscape, the creative process, love, and friendship. The commissioning by ALAN ROSS of an article, 'Leaving School' (*London Magazine*, September 1965), inspired him to extend the piece into a St Lucian autobiography, which became instead the autobiographical poem, *Another Life* (1973)—see Edward Baugh's critical study of it, *Derek Walcott: Memory as Vision* (1978). In *Sea Grapes* (1976), *The Star-Apple Kingdom* (1979), and subsequent collections, he has attained a poetic strength and a maturity of vision, without jeopardizing his conscious search for simplicity. *Omeros* (1990), which won the W. H. Smith Literary Award, in its re-examination of the themes of identity, exile, and suffering, its fusion of sources, and its critical, often self-critical, attitude to the obligations of the artist, is far more than a parade of Homeric materials in a Caribbean setting. The collection *Bounty* (1997) is an elegy for his mother, for CLARE, and for his colonial background.

In the 1960s GRAVES wrote that Walcott 'handles English with a closer understanding of its inner magic than most (if not any) of his English-born contemporaries'. In 1987 BRODSKY called him 'the best poet the English language has today'. In 1988 he became the first Commonwealth writer to be awarded the Queen's Gold Medal for Poetry, and in 1992 he was awarded the Nobel Prize for Literature for his poetic works 'of great luminosity, sustained by a historical vision, the outcome of a multicultural commitment'.

While his many plays include naturalistic dramas, notably *Remembrance* (1978), his main themes stem from the folklore of St Lucia, often expressed in terms of God and justice, as well as of good and evil. In *The Odyssey* (1992), commissioned by the Royal Shakespeare Company and staged in Stratford in an exciting production, he presents the essence of HOMER's epic in hexameters, transposing some of the situations into what he sees as their modern equivalents. *Dream on Monkey Mountain and Other Plays* (1971) is prefaced by an essay on the West Indian creative imagination, in which he postulates, 'The future of West Indian militancy lies in art.' See *Collected Poems 1948–1984*, new edn 1990; Robert D. Hammer, *Derek Walcott*, 1981 (critical study).

WALKER, ALICE (*b.* 1944) American novelist, short-story writer, and poet, was born in Eatonton, Georgia, the eighth child of a sharecropper, and was educated at Spelman College, Atlanta, from which she transferred to Sarah Lawrence College, New York. Poems of reflection on Africa, which she had visited, and her native Georgia, written at a time of acute personal distress, were passed on to an agent by her teacher, Muriel Rukeyser (1913–80), the poet and political activist, and published in *Once* (1968), the first of her several books of verse—see *Her Blue Body Everything We Know: Earthling Poems 1965–1990 Complete* (2nd rev. edn 1992). She graduated in 1965 and, instead of taking up a fellowship to write in Africa, became a social worker and then participated in the voter registration drive in Mississippi. In 1967 she married Melvyn Leventhal, a white activist civil rights lawyer (divorced 1976). After teaching at several colleges, she was appointed a professor of English at Yale in 1977. Her first novel, *The Third Life of Grange Copeland* (1970), written while she was at college, is an exploration of black responsibility in a white society. *Meridian* (1976) focuses on activism. In *The Color Purple* (1982), which won the Pulitzer Prize, an epistolary vernacular technique is the medium for a quest for identity. One of its characters reappears as the protagonist of *Possessing the Secret of Joy* (1992), a polemical novel exposing the iniquities of female circumcision. *The Complete Short Stories* (1994) comprises the collections *In Love and Trouble* (1973) and *You Can't Keep a Good Woman Down* (1979). *In Search of Our Mothers' Gardens: Womanist Prose* (1983) and *Living By the Word* (1988) include autobiographical essays and literary criticism; *The Same River Twice: Honoring the Difficult* (1996) is an autobiographical study of recent years.

WALKER, KATH (OODGEROO NOONUCCAL) (1920–93) Australian poet, was born Kathleen Jean Mary Ruska, the daughter of a member of the Noonuccal tribe, and grew up in Stradbroke Island in Mceton Bay, Queensland. She was educated at primary level and at 13 went into domestic service in Brisbane. Rejected for training as a nurse because she was Aboriginal, she served in the Australian Women's Army Service. She married Bruce Walker, a Brisbane docker of Aboriginal descent, in 1942. She began writing verse in the 1950s, when she was becoming increasingly involved in activities for Aboriginal rights and progress. The title and title poem of *We Are Going* (1964) strike a note of warning: '. . . They came here to the place of their old bora ground / Where now the many white men hurry about like ants. / Notice of estate agent reads: "Rubbish May Be Tipped Here".' Dedicated to the Federal Council for the Advancement of Aboriginal and Torres Strait Islanders, of which she was state secretary, it is the first book by an Aboriginal woman, and the first example of contemporary black Australian writing to be published. It was followed by *The Dawn is at Hand* (1966). *My People: a Kath Walker Collection* (1970) includes poems from both books. *Stradbroke Dreamtime* (1972) is a collection of stories for children. In 1988 she renounced her award of MBE and her name in revulsion at the celebrations of the bicentenary of white settlement, becoming Oodgeroo, 'paper bark tree'. See Ulli Beier, *Quandamooka: the Art of Kath Walker*, 1985.

WALLACE, EDGAR (1875–1932) British novelist, short-story writer, dramatist, and journalist, was born in Greenwich, London, the illegitimate son of a widow, Polly Richards (1843–1903), née Blair, an actress. Neither the father, Richard Horatio Edgar, nor his mother, Miss Alice Marriott (1824–1900), the theatrical manager and celebrated female Hamlet, who was Polly's employer, ever knew of the birth. He was brought up by a family called Freeman, and went to Reddins Road School, Camberwell, playing truant to sell newspapers in Ludgate Circus, at a spot where a memorial plaque to him was later mounted. He left school at 12, and worked in a printing house, a shoe shop, and a rubber company, and as a ship's cook and milk delivery boy, before enlisting in the Royal West Kent Regiment. He transferred to the Medical Staff Corps in 1896, and served in South Africa, where he became known as the 'Soldier Poet'. He bought his discharge in 1899, and became war correspondent of the *Daily Mail*, and then Editor of the new *Rand Daily Mail*. After quarrelling with his proprietor in 1903 he returned to London and rejoined the *Daily Mail* as a reporter. In 1905 he wrote, and himself published, *The Four Just Men*, the first of an astonishing output of popular novels and volumes of stories which appeared at an average of between five and six a year. Among thrillers the stories in *The Mind of Mr J. G. Reeder* (1925), and among adventures those in *Sanders of the River* (1911) and sequels, have some lasting merit. He was also a successful dramatist, whose crime play *The Ringer*,

based on his own novel, *The Gaunt Stranger* (1925), ran for 410 performances in 1926. As editor, reporter, and racing columnist—see *Winning Colours: Selected Racing Writings of Edgar Wallace*, ed. John Welcome (1991)—he remained all his life closely associated with journalism. With the help of two secretaries, a dictaphone, and numerous cigarettes and cups of sweet, milky tea, he would turn out forty thousand words a week, all his own work—in the course of a libel action against an author who had accused him of plagiarism he publicly pledged £5000 to anyone who could prove he used other writers. He died in New York, where he had been writing the script which was filmed as *King Kong*. See *People: a Short Autobiography*, 1926; Margaret Lane, *Edgar Wallace, Fleet Street's Shallow Genius: Reinventing the Thriller*, new edn 1992 of *Edgar Wallace: the Biography of a Phenomenon*, rev. edn 1964.

WALLACE-CRABBE, CHRIS(TOPHER) (*b.* 1934) Australian poet and critic, was born in Richmond, Victoria, and educated at Scotch College and Melbourne University. He was Harkness Fellow at Yale from 1965 to 1967, and became a senior lecturer in English at Melbourne University in 1968, subsequently being appointed to a personal chair. He became Director of the university's Australian Centre in 1989. He has summed up his poetic philosophy as being 'resistant to fashionable notions of defeatism'; 'Somewhere deep down, I do believe that against all odds one can make, build, do—that the burden is finally and absolutely on one's own shoulders.' Since his early books of verse, *No Glass Houses* (1956) and *The Music of Division* (1959), he has come 'to seek more supple rhythms and more autonomous images. . . . And a poetry which questioned the English language.' Later volumes include *Selected Poems: 1955–1972* (1973), *I'm Deadly Serious* (1988); *Action Shots* (1988), prose poems; *For Crying Out Loud* (1990); and *Rungs of Time* (1993), in which he speculates in areas of science and philosophy. His critical works include *Melbourne or the Bush: Essays on Australian Literature and Society* (1973), *Three Absences in Australian Writing* (1983), and *Falling into Language* (1990), essays. Among his several anthologies is (with Peter Pierce) *Clubbing of the Gunfire: 101 Australian War Poems* (1984), on the general topic of which his own 'The Shapes of Gallipoli' is a significant contribution.

WALLER, EDMUND (1606–87) English poet, was born at the manor house of Coleshill, Hertfordshire. His father died in 1616, leaving him a fortune. He was educated at Eton and King's College, Cambridge, but took no degree. When he entered Lincoln's Inn in 1622, he was already a Member of Parliament. In 1631 he married a rich heiress, who died in childbirth in 1634. Shortly after this he met Lady Dorothy Sidney (1617–84), later Countess of Sunderland, who in his affections and his poetry progressed from being addressed by her own name ('On my Lady Dorothy Sidneyes Picture') to that of 'Sacharissa'. It was probably at this time, too, that he wrote 'On a Girdle' and the song 'Go lovely Rose . . .'. Though a member of the Long Parliament, and a cousin of John Hampden (1594–1643), he was in 1643 involved in the plot to seize London for Charles I, who was sitting things out in Oxford. Called upon to plead for his life at the Bar of the House of Commons, he implicated others who were in the plot. He was banned from Parliament for life and imprisoned, awaiting trial, in the Tower of London, from which he wrote offering to pay a fine of £10,000. It was accepted, and he was banished. In 1651 he was pardoned, and returned from France to his home in Beaconsfield and to his second wife, whom he had married just before he went away. He was re-elected to Parliament after the Restoration of the Monarchy in 1660. A teetotaller, he had a long if largely uninspired poetical career, during which he happily wrote panegyrics both to Cromwell and to Charles II. His celebration of the escape from drowning at sea of Charles I when Prince of Wales is one of the earliest uses of the heroic couplet. *Poems &c.* was published in 1645, and *The Second Part of Mr Waller's Poems* in 1690.

WALPOLE, HORACE (or **HORATIO**) (1717–97) novelist and prose writer, was born in London, the youngest son by 11 years of Sir Robert Walpole (1676–1745; Prime Minister 1721–42) and his first wife. He was educated at Eton and King's College, Cambridge, and then toured Europe for two years with GRAY. He was a Member of Parliament from 1741 to 1767. In 1748 he bought a house on the Thames at Twickenham, which he refashioned inside and out into a Gothic castle and named Strawberry Hill. Here he established a private press, whose first product was *Gray's Odes* (1757), followed by Walpole's own gossipy compilation, *A Catalogue of the Royal and Noble Authors of England* (1758). He also printed his *Anecdotes of Painting in England* (1762–71), a pioneer among histories of British art. In 1746 he was moved by the lonely and romantic atmosphere of his house to write *The Castle of Otranto* (1765), initially published anonymously as a translation of an Italian book printed in 1529. This, the first Gothic novel, is full of terrible sights and sounds, with at least one tremendous climax in each chapter. Walpole's memoirs were at his request kept sealed for 20 years after his death, but it is his voluminous correspondence, largely written for publication, which best reveals him and his times. On the death of his nephew in 1791, he became 4th Earl

of Orford. He never married, but in his latter years much enjoyed the company of women, especially that of the literary sisters Mary (1763–1852) and Agnes (1764–1852) Berry, 'the best informed and most perfect creatures I ever saw at their age', whom he first met in 1788—see their correspondence, *The Grace of Friendship: Horace Walpole and the Misses Berry*, ed. Virginia Surtees (1995). In Timothy Mowl, *Horace Walpole: the Great Outsider* (1996) it is suggested that on his youthful European tour he had a homosexual affair with Henry Fiennes Clinton, 9th Earl of Lincoln (1720–94). See *Selected Letters*, ed. W. S. Lewis, 1973 (the full correspondence was published in 48 vols, 1937–83); R. W. Ketton-Cremer, *Horace Walpole: a Biography*, 3rd edn 1964.

WALPOLE, (Sir) **HUGH** (1884–1941) British novelist, was born in Auckland, New Zealand, the eldest child of the Canon of St Mary's Cathedral (later Bishop of Edinburgh). He was educated at King's School, Canterbury, and Emmanuel College, Cambridge. After realizing that he had a vocation neither for the kind of work he experienced at the Mercy Mission to Seamen nor for teaching, which he tried briefly at Epsom College, he became a full-time writer in London, where he published his first novel, *The Wooden Horse* (1909), written when he was an undergraduate. With his reputation boosted by a long article in *The Times Literary Supplement* by HENRY JAMES, who was a close friend, he published five more novels before World War I, including *Mr Perrin and Mr Traill: a Tragi-Comedy* (1911), a strong story of obsession in a public (i.e. independent) school staff room. During the war he served with the Red Cross in Russia, being awarded the Order of St George for his rescue of a wounded man under fire, and then in the British propaganda bureau in Petrograd; out of these experiences he wrote *The Dark Forest* (1916) and *The Green Mirror* (1918). As a popular novelist, he was a complete all-rounder. *Jeremy* (1919), *Jeremy and Hamlet* (1923), and *Jeremy at Crale* (1927) comprise a semi-autobiographical trilogy from childhood to schooldays. *Portrait of a Man with Red Hair: a Romantic Macabre* (1925) is one of his psychological thrillers. 'The Herries Chronicle' of six novels (1930–43) is a long, romantic family saga, set in the Lake District, where he had his bachelor country house. He founded the influential, but informal, book trade fraternity, the Society of Bookmen, in 1921. He was made CBE in 1918 and was knighted in 1937. See Rupert Hart-Davis, *Hugh Walpole: a Biography*, new edn 1985.

WALTON, ISAAK (1593–1683) prose writer and biographer, was born in Stafford and apprenticed to a London ironmonger, being made a freeman of the Ironmongers' Company in 1618. As a member of the congregation of St Dunstan's-in-the-West, of which DONNE was made Vicar in 1624 as an additional appointment, he got to know the poet and, through him, Sir Henry Wotton (1568–1639), Provost of Eton and a poet in his own right. On Donne's death in 1631, Wotton undertook to write his biography, but he died without making much progress. Walton, who had acted as his researcher, was appalled at the thought of the great 1640 edition of Donne's sermons lacking a biographical introduction, and wrote it himself—it was also published separately in an enlarged version as *The Life and Death of Dr Donne* (1658). His simple piety and his lucid, unadorned prose made such an appeal that he was prevailed upon to write lives of Wotton (1651), HOOKER (1665), and GEORGE HERBERT (1670). In the meantime, probably influenced by the defeat at Marston Moor in 1644 of the royalists, to whom he was wholly sympathetic, he had taken early retirement, to indulge in his hobby of coarse fishing; though after the final defeat of Charles II at Worcester in 1651, he was entrusted with one of the crown jewels, which he safely delivered to London. His best-known work, *The Compleat Angler, or the Contemplative Man's Recreation* (1653), a leisurely guide, as well as a literary experience, in the form of a dialogue interspersed with verse, anecdotes, and folklore, was reissued in 1676 as *The Universal Angler*, with a section on fly-fishing by his friend Charles Cotton (1630–87). Walton was twice married: in 1626 to Rachel Floud (*d.* 1640), whose seven children all died in infancy, and in about 1646 to Anne Ken (*d.* 1662)—their surviving son Isaac (1651–1719) became a prebendary of the diocese of Salisbury.

WARD, (MARY), MRS HUMPHRY

(1851–1920), née Arnold, British novelist and social campaigner, was the granddaughter of 'Arnold of Rugby' and the niece of ARNOLD. She was born in Hobart, Tasmania, where her father, a school administrator, made a spectacular conversion to Catholicism; he returned with his family to Britain in 1856. One of eight children, she was educated at the Ambleside school of Jemima Clough (1820–92), the younger sister of CLOUGH, and at other boarding schools until she was 16, when her father's reconversion to Anglicanism enabled him to obtain a teaching post at Oxford, where the family reconvened. In 1872 she married Thomas Humphry Ward (1845–1926), Fellow of Brasenose College and later an art critic, by whom she had three carefully-spaced children. In 1881 they moved to London, where she published her first novel, *Miss Bretherton* (1884). She was a long time writing and finding a publisher for *Robert Elsmere* (1888), which expresses as well as reflects the ideological confusions of the times. Arguably the most popular novel of the century, it sold over half-a-million copies

in the USA, from which she earned £100. For the American rights of her next, *The History of David Grieve* (1892), she was paid £7000, the USA having in 1891 become a party to international copyright.

She now bought, as a second home, a house and estate in Hertfordshire. She developed the working people's centre she had established in Gordon Square, Bloomsbury, in 1890 into the Passmore Edwards Settlement (1897), now the Mary Ward Centre, where she pioneered special schooling for handicapped children. Crippled by a conglomeration of physical and neurological disorders, she continued to write novels reflecting social and religious issues. Though they were reviled at the time by younger critics such as BENNETT, STRACHEY, VIRGINIA WOOLF, and REBECCA WEST (who described her literary career as 'one long specialization in the *mot injuste*'), some of them have merit as novels of the Victorian era. On a lecture tour in the USA in 1908 she met Theodore Roosevelt (1858–1919). At his instigation and with the support of the British Government she wrote *England's Effort: Six Letters to an American Friend* (1916); the first-hand research took her into the trenches in France, and the book was said to have hastened American intervention in World War I. She was an active campaigner against votes for women, and founded the Women's National Anti-Suffrage League in 1908. Two months before her death she was appointed one of the first seven women magistrates. See John Sutherland, *Mrs Humphry Ward: Eminent Victorian, Pre-Eminent Edwardian*, new edn 1991.

WARNER, REX

(1905–86) British novelist, poet, and translator, was born in Birmingham, the son of a clergyman, and was brought up in the Gloucestershire countryside. He was educated at St George's School, Harpenden, and Wadham College, Oxford, where he read classics and English. He then became a teacher, leaving a post in England, after a disagreement of principle with the Head, to go to Egypt, from which he returned to Frensham Heights School, Farnham. *Poems* (1937) was reissued in a revised edition as *Poems and Contradictions* (1945). While contemporaries tended to use poetry as the medium of expressing their political concern, Warner, as ORWELL was to do, used fiction. Of his three allegorical novels, *The Wild Goose Chase* (1937), *The Professor* (1938), and *The Aerodrome* (1941), the last is particularly impressive for its subtle picture of the destruction of a society in the names of freedom and efficiency. He was Director of the British Institute in Athens 1945–47, and a professor of English, University of Connecticut 1964–74. His historical novels, *The Young Caesar* (1958), *Imperial Caesar* (1960), *Pericles, the Athenian* (1963), and *The Converts* (1967) are works also of classical scholarship. His versions of Greek mythology, *Men and Gods* (1950) and *Greeks and Trojans* (1951), have a seamless as well as a timeless quality. His translations include works of AESCHYLUS, EURIPIDES, PLUTARCH, THUCYDIDES, and XENOPHON.

WARNER, SYLVIA TOWNSEND (1893–1978) British novelist, short-story writer, and poet, was born in Harrow, the only child of a master at the school, and was educated at home. She worked in a munitions factory during World War I, after which she was until 1928 a member of the editorial team responsible for the ten-volume *Tudor Church Music*. *The Espalier* (1925) was the first of several volumes of verse—see *Collected Poems*, introduction by Claire Harman (1982). Her first novel, *Lolly Willowes* (1926), a blend of fantasy and light reality about a liberated woman who becomes a witch, was the first American 'Book of the Month'. In 1927 she went to New York as guest critic of the New York *Herald-Tribune*. *Mr Fortune's Maggot* (1927) is a study of homosexual passion. When she was 36, having had a long and secret affair with the much older and married musicologist, Percy Buck (1871–1947), she was introduced by T. F. POWYS to Valentine Ackland (1906–68), a poet and short-story writer, with whom she had an intense and permanent lesbian relationship, which survived Ackland's faithlessness in the 1940s and conversion to Catholicism in the early 1950s—*Whether a Dove or Seagull: Poems* (1934) is the work of them both. They went together to Spain in 1930 to work for the Red Cross, and in 1935 they joined the Communist Party, to which Warner remained committed all her life. She was a versatile novelist, whose oeuvre also includes the fanciful *The True Heart* (1929), the satirical *After the Death of Don Juan* (1938), and the historical novels *The Corner That Held Them* (1948), about life in a medieval nunnery, and *The Flint Anchor* (1954), based on a genealogical mystery in her own family. Her short stories, of which more than 140 first appeared in the *New Yorker*, illustrate her delicate touch. Though she never finished the biography of Powys on which she worked for many years, she wrote one of T. H. WHITE (1967), whom she never met. See Claire Harman, *Sylvia Townsend Warner: a Biography*, 1995; *The Diaries of Sylvia Townsend Warner*, ed. Claire Harman, new edn 1995.

WARREN, ROBERT PENN (1905–89) American novelist, short-story writer, poet, and critic, was born in Guthrie, Kentucky, of bookish parents, and was educated at Clarksville High School, Tennessee, and, after an eye accident while hunting made him physically unfit for a naval career, at Vanderbilt University, where 'all kinds of people wrote poems . . . [and] freshmen were buying the *New Republic* or the *Nation*, to get the new

poem by Yeats or Hart Crane'. Described by his teacher as 'a prodigy whom at birth the Muse had apparently invested with a complete literary equipment', he shared rooms with ALLEN TATE, and had poems published in *The Fugitive*. He did postgraduate study at the University of California, at Yale, and (as a Rhodes Scholar) at Oxford. He received a commission to write his first book, *John Brown: the Making of a Martyr* (1929), and also the story 'Prime Leaf' (1931), about the tobacco wars in the South, which he later developed into his first novel, *Night Rider* (1939). In the meantime he taught English at Vanderbilt and at Louisiana State University; published *Thirty-Six Poems* (1935); and founded in 1935, as a forum for the New Criticism, the quarterly *Southern Review*, with Cleanth Brooks (1906–94), with whom he also wrote the textbooks *Understanding Poetry* (1938) and *Understanding Fiction* (1943)—see also Mark Royden Winchell, *Cleanth Brooks and the Rise of Modern Criticism* (1996). He taught English at the University of Minnesota (1942–50); and was a professor of playwriting (1950–56), and of English (1961–73) at Yale.

He first conceived, and wrote, *All the King's Men* (1946), his third novel, as a verse play, *Proud Flesh* (produced 1946). This powerful study of Southern political power and corruption won the Pulitzer Prize, and was staged in his own adaptation in 1959. Of his subsequent novels, *World Enough and Time* (1950), *Band of Angels* (1955), and *Wilderness: a Tale of the Civil War* (1961) are imaginative historical reconstructions of Southern history; *The Cave* (1959), *Flood: a Romance of Our Time* (1964), and *Meet Me in the Green Glen* (1971) reflect the experience of his part of the South from the 1940s onwards. *A Place to Come To* (1977) transcends his usual unities of time, setting, and theme to record the rags-to-riches rise of an Alabama lad to international academic renown and to recount the natural history of a love affair. After *Selected Poems 1923–1943* (1944), he wrote, and published, little verse until *Promises: Poems 1954–1956* (1957), which won both the Pulitzer Prize and the National Book Award. *Audubon: a Vision* (1969), a long, significant poem loosely based on a violent incident in the life of the 19th-century naturalist, expresses the poet's preoccupation with identity and his yearning for truth and serenity. He continued to publish collections of verse up to *New and Selected Poems 1923–1985* (1985), which includes *Audubon*. His critical studies address historical and political issues, as in *Segregation: the Inner Conflict in the South* (1956), *The Legacy of the Civil War* (1961), and *Who Speaks for the Negro?* (1965), as well as literature, as in *Democracy and Poetry* (1975). He was in 1985 appointed the USA's first Poet Laureate. In 1952 he married, as his second wife, the novelist Eleanor Clark (b. 1913). See Joseph Blotner, *Robert Penn Warren: a Biography*, 1996;

Charles Bohner, *Robert Penn Warren*, rev. edn 1981 (critical study).

WARTON, THOMAS (1728–90) British poet and critic, was the son of Thomas Warton (1688–1745), Professor of Poetry at Oxford 1718–28, and the younger brother of Joseph Warton (1722–1800), poet and Headmaster of Winchester College. He was born in Basingstoke, Hampshire, and educated at Winchester College and Trinity College, Oxford, of which he became a Fellow in 1751, and where he remained all his life. In 1757 he was elected Professor of Poetry, an office he held until 1767. He was the anonymous editor of the miscellany of university wit, *The Oxford Sausage* (1764 and 1772). *The Pleasures of Melancholy* (1747), a pleasing derivative poem in blank verse, was written when he was 17. *Poems* (1777), largely lyrics and nature poems, went through three further editions in his lifetime. In 1785 he was appointed Camden Professor of Ancient History, and on 14 April of that year, on the death of William Whitehead (1715–85), he was made Poet Laureate. His greatest contribution was as a critic. He edited *Milton's Poems upon Several Occasions* (1785), and wrote *The History of English Poetry, from the Close of the Eleventh Century to the Commencement of the Eighteenth Century* (3 vols 1774–81), completed up to 1600; it was the first study of its kind, which also illuminates contemporary manners as well as contempory critical criteria. BURNEY, who met the brothers Warton at a dinner party in 1783, commented: 'Dr [Joseph] Warton made me a most obsequious bow. . . . He is what Dr Johnson calls a rapturist, and I plainly saw he meant to pour forth much civility into my ears. . . . Mr Tom Warton, the poetry historiographer, looks unformed in his manners, and awkward in his gestures. He joined not one word in the general talk, and, but for my father, who was his neighbour at dinner . . . he would never have opened his mouth after the removal of the second course.'

WARUNG, PRICE, pen name, a combination of his mother's maiden name (Price) and the Aboriginal word for Sydney, of William Astley (1855–1911) Australian short-story writer. He was born in Liverpool and brought by his parents to Melbourne when he was four. He was educated at Melbourne Model School, where he was encouraged in his ambition to be a writer. After working as a bookseller, he was a founding editor of the *Richmond Guardian*, and then edited the *Riverine Herald*, after which he had a nervous breakdown. On his recovery in 1880 he returned to journalism. In about 1890 he moved to Sydney, where he was a regular contributor to the *Bulletin*, whose editorial policy at the time was sympathetic to his socialist principles and anti-British sentiments. In particu-

lar he wrote about ninety highly-coloured stories of convict life, in which the whole range of convicts is presented as more sinned against than having sinned. Some of them were published in *Tales of the Convict System* (1892) and *Tales of the Early Days* (1894), in which he introduces the Ring, a convict Mafia dedicated to circumventing the 'System'. He fell out with the *Bulletin* in 1893, and was then briefly Editor of the *Australian Workman*, after which he lapsed into periods of mental instability and drug addiction. He published two further volumes of convict tales and one of sketches based on his early experiences on the River Murray at Echuca, *Half-Crown Bob and Tales of the Riverine* (1898). See Barry Andrews, *Price Warung (William Astley)*, 1976 (biographical/critical study).

WASHINGTON, BOOKER T(ALIAFERRO) (1856–1915) American social reformer and prose writer, was born in Hale's Ford, Virginia, the son of an unknown white man and a slave, and was brought up in Malden, West Virginia, taking his stepfather's first name as his surname. He attended makeshift night schools while working as a salt packer, coal miner, and houseboy, and in 1872 made the 500-mile journey to Hampton Normal and Agricultural Institute, through which he worked his way (as a janitor) to honours. He returned there to run an experimental programme for native American students, and was in 1881 appointed the first Principal of Tuskegee Institute, Alabama, to train black people for trades and as teachers. Invited to speak to an audience of two thousand at the Atlanta Exposition in 1895, he delivered an address advocating opportunity for blacks and peaceful coexistence in return for the surrender of certain civil rights. It was reprinted in his autobiography, *Up from Slavery* (1901), as significant a document in its argument as in the simplicity of its language. In 1901 he organized the National Negro Business League in Boston, and through public appearances, and private consultations, exerted influence as a thinker as well as an orator, though his conciliatory tone offended DU BOIS. His biography of DOUGLASS (1906) is a pioneering work in that field. See Louis R. Harlan, *Booker T. Washington: the Making of a Black Leader, 1856-1901*, 1972 and *Booker T. Washington: the Wizard of Tuskegee, 1901-1915*, new edn 1987.

WATEN, JUDAH (1911–85) Australian novelist, was born of a Jewish family in Odessa and brought by them to a small town in Western Australia in 1914. He was educated at the Christian Brothers College, Perth, and University High School in Melbourne, to which the family moved in 1926. In 1930 he edited the avant-garde magazine, *Strife*, which expressed the intention of the proletarian novelist to 'work with facts'. During the 1930s he spent some time in England, where he took part in one of the hunger marches, and was imprisoned for three months for political activism. Writing took second place at this time to politics, and it was only when he determined to 'write about people I knew, real people as it were, not changing them into other people', that his career as a novelist was launched. From *Alien Son* (1952), a collection of sketches based on his childhood experiences, which is unusual in its depiction of an immigrant Jewish community in an Australian country town, he proceeded to *The Unbending* (1954), a documentary novel which features communist political aspirations as well the problems of Jewish assimilation. Other novels with Jewish themes include *Distant Land* (1964), set at the time of World War II, and *So Far No Further* (1971); *Scenes from Revolutionary Life* (1982), set in the 1930s, is partly autobiographical. Further autobiographical stories and sketches are in *Love and Rebellion* (1978). *From Odessa to Odessa: the Journey of an Australian Writer* (1969) is an account of a visit to the USSR in which he also explores his family roots. He was made AM in 1979.

WATKINS, VERNON (1906–67) Welsh poet, was born in Maesteg, of Welsh-speaking parents, and was educated at Repton School and Magdalene College, Cambridge. Apart from the war years, during which he served in the Royal Air Force, he worked as a bank clerk in Swansea from 1925 to 1965. The poetry of YEATS was a guiding influence, as was the personal encouragement of DYLAN THOMAS—see *Dylan Thomas: Letters to Vernon Watkins* (1957). His first volume of verse, *Ballad of the Mari Lwyd, and Other Poems* (1941), contained many simple evocations of Welsh childhood. In eight further significant collections, he developed his vision of the nature of time (images of the sea, fountains, and trees recur) and of artistic inspiration (which he saw as a religious gift), particularly in the poems in which he uses the persona of the Welsh mythical bard Taliesin. Watkins called himself 'a Welsh poet writing in English', using what he regarded as the rich satisfaction of the language in a way that frequently resounds with musical rhythms and Welsh intonations, which are especially evident in his ballads. His translations, notably from the German of HEINE and HÖLDERLIN, were for him a natural expression of his poetic craft, and are collected in *Selected Verse Translations, with an Essay on the Translation of Poetry*, ed. Ruth Pryor (1977). See *Collected Poems*, 1986; Leslie Norris (ed.), *Vernon Watkins 1906–67*, 1970 (essays and tributes by various hands).

WATSON, JAMES see SEMPILL.

WATSON, SHEILA (*b.* 1909), née Doherty, Canadian novelist and short-story writer, was born in New Westminster, British Columbia, where the family lived in the grounds of the Provincial Mental Hospital, of which her father was Superintendent. She was educated at the convent schools of the Sisters of Sainte Anne, the Convent of the Sacred Heart, Vancouver, and the University of British Columbia, where she qualified as a teacher. During the 1930s she taught in elementary schools, including a one-room establishment at Dog Creek, whose ambience she recaptured later in her novel. In 1941 she married the experimental poet and dramatist, Wilfred Watson (*b.* 1911). After further teaching assignments, she wrote *The Double Hook* (1959), an elliptically presented work with dramatic action and changes of fortune, which is regarded as a forerunner of the modernist Canadian novel. In 1965 she completed for Toronto University the PhD thesis on WYNDHAM LEWIS which she had begun in 1957. She was a member of the English department of Alberta University from 1961 to 1975, and with her husband and others published the literary journal, *White Pelican*, from 1971 to 1978. Her shorter fiction has been published as *Four Stories* (1979).

WATTS, ISAAC (1674–1748) British poet and hymn writer, was born in Southampton, the eldest of nine children of a shoemaker who was at the time of the birth in the local jail for his religious opinions, but who later ran a flourishing boarding school. He was educated at Southampton Grammar School and Stoke Newington Dissenting Academy. After two years studying and writing at home, he worked as a private tutor, and in 1702 became Pastor of the Independent Congregation at Mark Lane, London. In 1712, after recurrent bouts of illness, he was offered houseroom by a member of the congregation, Sir Thomas Abney (1640–1722). Watts lived with him, and then his widow, for the rest of his life, first at Theobalds, Hertfordshire, and then at Abney House, Stoke Newington, from which he would be driven in to preach on Sundays when his health allowed. His verse was published in *Horae Lyricae: Poems Chiefly of the Lyric Kind* (1706; 'much enlarged' edn 1709); *Hymns and Spiritual Songs* (1707; 'corrected and much enlarged' edn 1709); *Divine Songs Attempted in Easy Language for the Use of Children* (1715), some of which CARROLL parodied in *Alice's Adventures in Wonderland*; and *The Psalms of David Imitated* (1719). He was not simply the writer of such famous hymns as 'Our God, our help in ages past' and 'Jesus shall reign . . .'. He was the adventurous poet of 'The Day of Judgement', and an authority on, and expert in, the metre of blank verse. He also wrote philosophical and sociological, as well as theological, works in prose. Of the award of honorary degree of DD by Edinburgh University in 1728, JOHNSON commented in *Lives* *of the Poets*: 'Academical honours would have more value, if they were always bestowed with equal judgement.'

WAUGH, EVELYN (1903–66) British novelist, biographer, journalist, and travel writer, the younger brother of the novelist Alec Waugh (1898–1981), was born in Hampstead, London, of parents of Scottish descent. He was educated at Lancing College—his brother's novel about his school days, *The Loom of Youth* (1917), making it impossible to follow him at Sherborne—and Hertford College, Oxford. He taught in three private schools in as many years before deciding that he would rather study carpentry. After his first book, *Rossetti: His Life and Works* (1928), he wrote a novel to earn money with which to get married—the marriage, to Evelyn Gardner (1903–93), lasted barely a year. *Decline and Fall* (1928), which draws on his experiences at Oxford and after, was an immediate success for its ironic, often bitter, treatment of quite serious matters. In *Vile Bodies* (1930), he satirized the contemporary manners of young people in a recognizable but equally fantasized setting. A cruise in 1929 was the basis of *Labels: a Mediterranean Journal* (1930); attendance as a reporter at the coronation of Haile Selassie gave him the material for *Remote People* (1931) and the background of a further novel, *Black Mischief* (1932). Similarly, a tough safari produced *Ninety-Two Days: the Account of a Tropical Journey through British Guiana and Part of Brazil* (1934) and the tropical sequences in *A Handful of Dust* (1934); an assignment to cover the Italian-Abyssinian war for the *Daily Mail* resulted in *Waugh in Abyssinia* (1936) and *Scoop: a Novel about Journalists* (1938).

Waugh became a Catholic in 1930, and in 1937, his first marriage having been annulled, he married Laura Herbert (*d.* 1973). He saw active service with the Royal Marines and the Commandos in Dakar and Crete in 1940–41, and finished World War II as a member of the British Mission in Yugoslavia. *Brideshead Revisited: the Sacred and Profane Memories of Captain Charles Ryder* (1945) is both his most substantial novel and the first in which the characters are drawn as real people rather than as figures of fun or pity. *The Loved One: an Anglo-American Tragedy* (1948) is an excursion into the macabre. *Men at Arms* (1952), *Officers and Gentlemen* (1955), and *Unconditional Surrender* (1961), republished together as *Sword of Honour* (1965), draw heavily on his wartime experiences as the background to dark military and social satire.

The Ordeal of Gilbert Pinfold (1957) is less a novel than a surrealist narrative, in which its disturbed hero, who bears an uncanny resemblance to the author, comes through self-revelatory hallucinations to comparative peace of mind. Even at his most disturbing, Waugh is essentially a comic writer, trying to come to terms with the contradictions he found in life. And throughout his novels the Catholic Church often appears symbolically as an oasis in prevailing chaos. Other biographies are *Edmund Campion: Jesuit and Martyr* (1935) and *Ronald Knox* (1959). *Evelyn Waugh: a Little Order*, ed. Donat Gallagher (1977) is a selection from his journalism. His friendship with NANCY MITFORD is recorded in *The Letters of Nancy Mitford and Evelyn Waugh*, ed. Charlotte Mosley (1996). He had six children, of whom, when they were young, he wrote to his wife: 'I can't afford to waste on them any time which could be spent on my own pleasures. I have sent them some kippers as compensation.' Auberon Waugh (*b.* 1939), the novelist, journalist, and critic, is his eldest son. See *A Little Learning*, new edn 1983 (early autobiography); *The Diaries of Evelyn Waugh*, ed. Michael Davie, new edn 1995; *The Letters of Evelyn Waugh*, ed. Mark Amory, new edn 1995; Martin Stannard, *Evelyn Waugh: the Early Years 1903–1939*, new edn 1988, and *No Abiding City: Evelyn Waugh 1939–1966*, new edn 1993; Selina Hastings, *Evelyn Waugh: a Biography*, new edn 1995; Jacqueline McDonnell, *Evelyn Waugh*, 1988 (critical study).

WEAMYS, ANNA see SIDNEY.

WEBB, (MARTHA) BEATRICE (1858–1943), née Potter, British economist, was born at Standish House, Gloucestershire, the eighth of nine daughters of an industrialist, and was educated at home. A reluctant socialite, she became a socialist through her friendship with SPENCER, which led her to investigate conditions in London's East End (sometimes disguised as a working girl), and to write up her findings in articles and reports. Through the Fabian Society she met Sidney Webb (1859–1947), whom she married in 1892. Their first biographer, Mary Agnes Hamilton (1884–1962), records: 'At the time, to many of her friends and his, there was something strange in the alliance of the tall, handsome, brilliantly gifted woman, who was pre-eminently a member of the governing class, and the undersized little man who, although purely English, looked, with his beard and eyeglasses, like a foreigner, and spoke like a cockney. Those who saw it so, saw the surface only.' 'The firm of Webb', as Beatrice called it, travelled the world in the interests of research into political and social systems, served on numerous royal commissions (she was the dominant force behind, and on, that which investigated the Poor Laws in 1905–09), and was instrumental in founding the London School of Economics. Though their joint writings can hardly be reviewed as literature, books such as *The History of Trade Unionism* (1894), *Industrial Democracy* (1897), and *The Decay of Capitalist Civilization* (1923) have influenced creative writers whose works bear on sociology. For reasons of political expediency Sidney Webb was created Baron Passfield in 1929, but Beatrice refused to be known as Lady Passfield. Her diaries, ed. Norman and Jeanne Mackenzie (4 vols 1982–85) are a valuable source of social and economic history.

WEBB, FRANCIS (1925–74) Australian poet, was born Francis Charles Webb-Wagg in Adelaide, and was brought up by his father's parents after his mother's death when he was two. He was educated at Christian Brothers' schools in Chatswood and Lewisham, and trained in Canada as a wireless air gunner during World War II (see 'The Gunner'). After a year at Sydney University, during which he won the university mile (an experience reflected in 'The Runner'), he returned to Canada, where he worked as a publisher's reader. *A Drum for Ben Boyd* (1948), a poem in 15 sections in which the Scottish merchant adventurer is viewed through the eyes of different characters, had been published in the *Bulletin* in 1946. The voyager theme, through the exploits of the Prussian explorer, Ludwig Leichhardt (who disappeared in 1848), recurs in 'Leichhardt Pantomime', an analysis of characters and motivation, published in the *Bulletin* in 1947, and revised and included with some shorter poems in *Leichhardt in Theatre* (1952). In 1950 he returned to Australia via England, where he had the first of his recurrent mental breakdowns. He spent the years 1953–59 in England, mainly in Norfolk or in a Birmingham psychiatric hospital, the experience of which is re-created in 'A Death at Winson Green' and 'Hospital Night'. He still managed to write another heroic voyager sequence, 'Eyre All Alone', published in *Socrates and Other Poems* (1961) along with some fine lyrics, including 'Bells of St Peter Mancroft' and the Nativity poem, 'Five Days Old', expressing his wonderment at being allowed to hold a tiny child. The poems in *The Ghost of the Cock* (1964) were largely composed before the first of several spells in Callan Park mental hospital, where he died. They include 'Ward Two', an eight-part sequence which incorporates 'Harry' ('It's the day for writing that letter, if one is able . . .') and 'Around Costessey', in which the focus of his search for artistic, mental, and spiritual salvation is a Norfolk village. See *Collected Poems*, 1969; *Cap and Bells: the Poetry of Francis Webb*, ed. Michael Griffith and James McGlade, 1991 (annotated collection); Michael Griffith, *God's Fool: the Life and Poetry of Francis Webb*, 1991.

WEBB, MARY (1881–1927), née Meredith, British novelist, was born in Leighton-under-the-Wrekin, Shropshire, the daughter of a schoolmaster. She was brought up among swarms of bees, which recur in her best-known novel, *Precious Bane* (1924), as does, in the form of the heroine's hare-lip, the disfigurement she herself suffered as a result of Graves's disease. She was educated at home and for two years at a finishing school in Southport. In 1912 she married a schoolmaster, with whom she lived, not altogether happily, in Weston-super-Mare, Lyth Hill near Shrewsbury (where they had a market garden), and, from 1921, Hampstead (London). She wrote essays, poetry, and short stories—see *Collected Prose and Poems*, ed. Gladys Mary Coles (1977)—in addition to the five novels published during her lifetime, of which the first was *The Golden Arrow* (1916). Intense, passionate, and predominantly simplistic evocations of rural life, they went largely unremarked until the Prime Minister, Stanley Baldwin (1867–1947), sang their posthumous praises at a Royal Literary Fund dinner in 1928. To meet the resulting demand, all five were reprinted in a uniform edition, with a volume of essays and poems (introduced by DE LA MARE), *The Spring of Joy*, and an unfinished historical romance, *Armour Wherein He Trusted*, in 1929. The appearance, and continued popularity with a more discerning readership, of *Cold Comfort Farm* (1932) by Stella Gibbons (1902–89), a rural parody suggested by *Precious Bane*, was only a temporary setback to Webb's reputation. See Gladys Mary Coles, *Mary Webb*, 1990 (biography).

WEBB, PHYLLIS (*b.* 1927) Canadian poet, was born in Victoria, British Columbia, and at 22, in the year she graduated from the University of British Columbia, stood unsuccessfully as a Co-operative Commonwealth Federation candidate for the provincial parliament. She went on to do further study in English at McGill University, and lived in London and Paris before teaching at the University of British Columbia from 1961 to 1964. Contact Press (see DUDEK) published a selection of her verse, with that of LAYTON and the Scottish-born Gael Turnbull (*b.* 1928), in *Trio* (1954). A volume of her own, *Even Your Right Eye*, largely written on her travels, followed in 1956. She was a programme organizer and producer for the Canadian Broadcasting Corporation from 1964 to 1969. After a spell of isolation in Saltspring Island, British Columbia, she emerged to teach again at the University of British Columbia, and then to lecture in creative writing at Victoria University. Her poetic preoccupations with distress, death, and suicide became subsumed into the spare feminist lyrics of *Naked Poems* (1965); interest in the Russian anarchist movement led to the unfinished sequence, 'The Kropotkin Poems'. Latterly she has experimented with, while redefining the direction of, the Persian lyric form, the *ghazal*—see HAFIZ—, published in *Water and Light: Ghazals and Anti Ghazals* (1985). *The Vision Tree: Selected Poems*, ed. Sharon Thesen (1982) won the Governor General's Award. A subsequent collection is

Hanging Fire (1990). *Talking* (1982) is a collection of critical essays and broadcasts. See John F. Hulcoop, *Phyllis Webb and Her Works*, 1994.

WEBSTER, JEAN see CRAPSEY.

WEBSTER, JOHN (*c*.1580–1638) English dramatist, is said to have been by virtue of his birth a freeman of the Merchant Taylors' Company, but the first reference proper to him is in 1602, as a playwright for the Admiral's Men. After working with DEKKER, HEYWOOD, and others on some largely lost plays, he surfaces as Dekker's collaborator in two city comedies for the boy actors of St Paul's, *West-Ward Hoe* and *North-Ward Hoe* (both published 1607). *The White Devil—The White Divel, or the Tragedy of Paulo Giordano Ursini, Duke of Brachiano, with the Life, and Death, of Vittoria Corombona, the Famous Venetian Curtizan* (1612)—is based on historical events some thirty years earlier. After an arresting opening it moves through scenes of horror, gore, and ghostly appearances to an improbable end, enlivened by some splendid lines of poetry. *The Duchess of Malfi*—published as *The Tragedy of the Dutchesse of Malfy* (1623)—was first performed in 1614, and is based on an English translation of a story of Matteo Bandello (*c*.1490–1561). Less well-constructed than *The White Devil*, and with an even more improbable plot, it nevertheless has passages of profound theatre, notably the death of the Duchess which occupies Act IV, and lines whose effect is heightened by irregular metre, such as 'I am the Duchess of Malfi still' and 'Cover her face; mine eyes dazzle; she died young'. In his later plays Webster neither attempted nor achieved anything like this. See *The Duchess of Malfi and Other Plays*, ed. René Weiss, new edn 1996; Clifford Leech, *Webster: a Critical Study*, new edn 1982.

WEDDE, IAN (*b*. 1946) New Zealand poet, novelist, and short-story writer, was born in Blenheim, and spent part of his childhood in East Pakistan and England. He went to Auckland University, after which he travelled widely, spending 1969–70 as a British Council teacher in Amman, Jordan, the source of several stark poems, including 'Land-mine Casualty . . .'. He subsequently worked in a variety of lowly-paid outdoor and factory jobs, but also as an art critic. He has suggested that 'what *creates* the artist-writer is not the ideas (experiences, perceptions) he has . . . but the fact that he gives them a form in writing. . . . The butcher, the baker, and the candlestick maker (after all) have ideas and experiences too.' His first substantial book of verse was *Earthly: Sonnets for Carlos* (1975), addressed to his first-born child, and comprising a sequence of unrhymed sonnets whose movement and flow are enhanced by judicious typography and the originality of

his verbal approach. He has also written a novella, *Dick Seddon's Great Dive* (1976), and the novels *Symme's Hole* (1986) and *Survival Arts* (1988), as well as for radio, the theatre, and cabaret. See *Driving into the Storm: Selected Poems*, 1988; *Tendering: New Poems*, 1989; *The Drummer*, 1994 (subsequent collection).

WEDDERBURN, ROBERT (*c*.1510–57) Scottish poet and prose writer, the son of a Dundee merchant, was educated at St Leonard's College, St Andrews University. He took holy orders as a priest, embraced Protestant doctrines, and became Vicar of Dundee. His two illegitimate sons were legitimized by royal favour in 1553. He had two older brothers. James (*d*. 1553) worked for their father, and wrote dramatic entertainments, among which, according to the historian, David Calderwood (1575–1650), were a tragedy about the beheading of John the Baptist and a comedy, *Historie of Dionysius the Tyranne*, 'wherein he likewise nipped the Papists'. For his assaults on the Catholic Church James was declared a heretic and banished to France, where he died. John (*d*. 1556), who entered the priesthood in 1528, was also exiled for his beliefs. Together, the three compiled, rewrote, or translated from German the contents of *Ane Compendious buik of godlie Psalmes and spirituall Sangis*, a notable and lively collection celebrating the Protestant Reformation, 'with diveris otheris Ballatis changeit out of prophane Sangis in godlie sangis, for avoyding of sin and harlatrie'. More commonly known as *The Gude and Godlie Ballatis*, it was first published anonymously in 1567, after all three were dead, but the name of Wedderburn was soon associated with it by popular report. The authorship of *The Complaynt of Scotland* (1549), a scholarly prose allegory of the condition of Scotland, was first firmly attributed to Robert Wedderburn by David Laing (1793–1878), in his introduction to the reprint (1868) of the 1578 edition of *The Gude and Godlie Ballatis*.

WELDON, FAY (*b*. 1931), née Birkinshaw, British novelist, short-story writer, dramatist, and critic, was born in Alvechurch, Worcestershire, and grew up in New Zealand, to which her parents had migrated—her father was a doctor. Her early education was at the Girls' High School, Christchurch. After her parents' divorce, she and her sister were brought back by their mother to England, where she went to Hampstead Girls' High School, London, and St Andrews University, reading economics and psychology. She left the Foreign Office having had a baby, and subsequently became a journalist and an advertising copywriter. She married Ron Weldon, jazz musician, in 1963—their divorce became official eight hours after his death in 1994. Her first novel, *The Fat Woman's Joke* (1967), began as a television play, transmitted in 1966. A variety of forms and idiosyncratic devices mark her pursuit of the feminine point of view from different angles. There is the story within a story of *Words of Advice* (1977), *Praxis* (1978), *The President's Child* (1983), and *Darcy's Utopia* (1990). Diabolical but straight revenge is the moving force of *The Life and Loves of a She-Devil* (1983), and supernatural revenge of *Remember Me* (1976). The conflagration in *Life Force* (1992) constitutes yet another act of arson committed by a vengeful heroine. The reproductive process and the psychology of pregnancy feature in *Puffball* (1980) and *The Cloning of Joanna May* (1989); therapists are the main target in *Affliction* (1994). Throughout her novels and short stories—see *Wicked Women: a Collection of Short Stories* (1995)—woman may be pitched against woman, but the men who exploit them are usually worsted. Her critical works include *Letters to Alice: On First Reading Jane Austen* (1984) and a study of REBECCA WEST (1985).

WELLS, H(ERBERT) G(EORGE)

(1866–1946) novelist, British short-story writer, and historian, was born in Bromley, Kent, the third son and youngest child of a shopkeeper (and professional cricketer) and a lady's maid. He was educated at Bromley Academy, which he left at 14 to become a draper's assistant; later, at his own initiative, he studied at the Normal School of Science of London University. In 1889–90 he taught at Henley House, the school owned by MILNE's father. He published two scientific textbooks in 1893, and in 1894 left his wife of three years and eloped with one of his students at the University Tutorial College, whom he subsequently married (she died in 1927). His first novel, *The Time Machine: an Invention* (1895), is a fantasy of the future; *The Island of Doctor Moreau* (1896), *The Invisible Man* (1897), and *The War of the Worlds* (1898) equate more to the modern genre of science fiction, with the addition of some implied social comment. At the same time he was writing short stories with a variety of themes and moods. The social milieu of his youth is reflected in the light novels *Love and Mr Lewisham* (1900), *Kipps: the Story of a Simple Soul* (1905), and *The History of Mr Polly* (1910). *Tono-Bungay* (1908) exposes the brittleness of society, exemplified also by the accusation of 'immorality' levelled at *Ann Veronica: a Modern Love Story* (1909). The model for this novel about an early 20th-century feminist was Amber Reeves (1887–1981), later a novelist and prose writer, by whom he had an illegitimate child, as he did five years later by REBECCA WEST. His advocacy of free love, world government, and genocide is rehearsed in Michael Coren, *The Invisible Man: the Life and Liberties of H. G. Wells* (1993), though some of his more extreme views were shared by other intellectuals of the times. He was above all,

however, a remarkable story teller, whose vision and popular appeal are evident also in *The Outline of History: Being a Plain History of Life and Mankind* (1919–20). See *The Complete Short Stories*, new edn 1987; *Experiment in Autobiography*, 2 vols new edn 1984; Norman and Jeanne MacKenzie, *The Time Traveller: the Life of H. G. Wells*, rev. edn 1987; Michael Foot, *H. G.: the History of Mr Wells*, new edn 1996; Peter Kemp, *H. G. Wells and the Culminating Ape*, new edn 1996 (critical study).

WELTY, EUDORA

(*b.* 1909) American short-story writer and novelist, was born in Jackson, Mississippi, of a family which was successful in the insurance business, and was educated at the Central High School, Jackson, Mississippi State College for Women, and the University of Wisconsin. After studying advertising for a year at Columbia Business School, and finding no work in New York, she returned home and did a variety of publicity and journalistic jobs, including taking photographs round the state. A New York gallery exhibited her unposed studies of black people in 1936, and in her collection of these, *One Time, One Place: Mississippi in the Depression* (1971) she explains the link between them and her development as a writer. Her first published story was 'Death of a Travelling Salesman' (1936); others appeared in the *Southern Review* (see WARREN) and *Atlantic Monthly*, with a collection, *A Curtain of Green and Other Stories*, in 1941. A short novel in the form of a fantasy, *The Robber Bridegroom* (1942), was followed by *The Wide Net and Other Stories* (1943), by *Delta Wedding* (1946), a study of the breaking down of Southern society barriers, and by *The Golden Apples* (1949), a short-story cycle set in a fictitious Mississippi community. *The Ponder Heart* (1954), with its hilarious courtroom scene, is a long story which first appeared in the *New Yorker*.

Losing Battles (1970), 15 years in the writing, is her longest and most complex work, and was the first to feature on the best-seller lists. The narrative, which explores the clan feuds and home truths of a hill country family during the Depression, is meticulously structured in choral form almost entirely in dialogue, with episodes of sheer farce predominating. *The Optimist's Daughter* (1972), a short, essentially tragic, novel, won the Pulitzer Prize. *One Writer's Beginnings* (1984) is a search for her literary persona, reflecting events not chronologically but as a 'continuous thread of revelation'.

A regional writer in that her settings and characters are Southern, as are those of FAULKNER, K. A. PORTER, and Warren, she is more readily identified with fiction writers whose concern is with revealing the inner self. Her book reviews, written between 1942 and 1984 mainly for the *New York Times Book Review*, are in *A Writer's Eye: Collected Book Re-*

views, ed. Pearl Amelia McHaney (1994). See *The Collected Stories of Eudora Welty*, new edn 1996; *Selected Stories of Eudora Welty: a Curtain of Green and Other Stories*, new edn 1992; Paul Binding, *The Still Moment: Eudora Welty, Portrait of a Writer*, 1994; Ruth M. Vande Kieft, *Eudora Welty*, rev. edn 1987 (critical study).

WENDT, ALBERT (*b.* 1939) Samoan novelist and poet, was born in Apia, Western Samoa, where he went to primary school. 'I am Samoan with a "dash" of German . . . New Zealand is a second home which I treasure.' He won a government scholarship there in 1952, and was educated at New Plymouth Boys' High School, Ardmore Teachers' College, and Victoria University. He won the *Landfall* short story competition for writers under 25 in 1963. He returned to Western Samoa in 1965, and was Principal of Samoa College 1969–73. In 1974 he joined the teaching staff of the University of the South Pacific, becoming Professor of Pacific Literature and, in 1978, Director of the South Pacific Centre in Western Samoa. He was appointed Professor of New Zealand and Pacific Literature, Auckland University, in 1988. Of *Sons for the Return Home* (1973), the first published novel by a Samoan, he wrote: 'I suppose in some ways it is an attempt to write out of my system part of my New Zealand experience; to show what it is like being Samoan and being Samoan in another culture.' The book had been written some years earlier, and by the time he came to write *Pouliuli* (1977) and *Leaves of the Banyan Tree* (1979), powerful studies of Samoan culture and society, he had also written and published a body of verse—see *Inside Us the Dead: Poems 1961 to 1974* (1976), and also *Shaman of Visions* (1984). After several years of virtual silence he brought out an ambitious novel, *Ola* (1991), which had a mixed reception. *Flying-Fox in a Freedom Tree* (1974) and *The Birth and Death of the Miracle Man* (1986) are collections of short stories.

WESKER, ARNOLD (*b.* 1932) British dramatist and short-story writer, was born in London's East End of Jewish immigrant parents, and was educated at Upton House School, Hackney. After National Service in the Royal Air Force, he did many different jobs before having three linked plays performed in Coventry—*Chicken Soup with Barley* (1959), *Roots* (1959), and *I'm Talking about Jerusalem* (1960)—, which were staged in London in 1960 as the 'Wesker Trilogy' (published 1960 as *The Wesker Trilogy*). There are political undertones in them as ordinary families face the realities of life in postwar Britain and gravitate between extremes of hope and despair. The main characters are from contrasting working-class backgrounds (metropolitan Jewish and rural Norfolk), and the dialogue captures exactly the appropriate

accents and dialects. *The Kitchen* (1959), written originally for television, is a play of conflicts set in a restaurant kitchen which, to Wesker, also represents the world. In *Chips with Everything* (1962) confrontations between National Servicemen and regular RAF officers are used as a microcosm of what he saw as growing political control over freedom of thought. Later plays have won less recognition, but include *The Merchant* (1976), in which SHAKESPEARE's *The Merchant of Venice* is re-presented as an exercise in racial integration. In 1960 Wesker's commitment saw the establishment of Centre 42, which aimed during its short life to exploit trades-union support for the arts. Collections of short stories include *Love Letters on Blue Paper* (1974), the title story of which was published as a play in 1978. See *Plays*, 3 vols new edns 1976–80; *Wild Spring and Other Plays*, 1995; *As Much as I Dare: an Autobiography (1923–1959)*, new edn 1995; Glenda Leeming, *Wesker the Playwright*, 1983.

WESLEY, JOHN (1703–91) British theologian and diarist, the founder of the Methodist Church, was born at Epworth Rectory, Lincolnshire, the 15th child and second surviving son of the rector. He was educated at Charterhouse and Christ Church, Oxford, and was ordained priest in 1728. In 1729 he returned to Oxford as a Fellow of Lincoln College, and joined his brother Charles (1707–88), later the hymn writer, in a group for religious study and help to others, whose systematic ('methodic') approach earned its members the name 'Methodists'. In 1735, when his *Journal* begins, he embarked on a mission to Georgia, and was briefly associated with the Moravians. After his return, he established the first Methodist chapel in Bristol in 1739. He journeyed unceasingly for the next fifty years, during which he travelled 250,000 miles, preached forty thousand sermons, and organized innumerable societies within the Church of England. He also wrote copiously: commentaries, histories, treatises, translations, as well as hymns. The stark style of the entries in his journal, which he kept until 1790, vividly reflects the pain as well as the passion of his triumphant but often dangerous progress. See *The Journal of John Wesley*, ed. Elisabeth Jay, 1987.

WEST, MORRIS (*b.* 1916) Australian novelist, was born in St Kilda, Melbourne, and educated at St Mary's College and Melbourne University. A member of the Christian Brothers, he taught in schools in New South Wales and Tasmania, but left the Order in 1939 before taking his final vows. He was a cipher officer in the South Pacific during World War II, after which he was for a time secretary to the former Prime Minister, William Morris Hughes (1862–1952). He then worked in radio, and founded and became

Managing Director of Australian Radio Productions. In 1955 he left Australia to be a freelance film, dramatic, and feature writer, subsidizing himself by writing novels, having already, as Julian Morris, published the semiautobiographical *Moon in My Pocket* (1945). *Children of the Sun* (1957), a factual study of the street children of Naples, brought him worldwide attention. *The Devil's Advocate* (1959), his seventh novel if one written as Michael East is also included, launched him into the international bestseller lists; *The Shoes of the Fisherman* (1963) is a further novel featuring Vatican politics. In much the same way as GRAHAM GREENE, West has an instinct for the treatment of newsworthy international issues, such as those in *The Ambassador* (1965) and *The Tower of Babel* (1968), and for universal themes. *The World is Made of Glass* (1983) is a different kind of documentary, being a psychological case study of the psychoanalyst Carl Jung (1875–1961) and a patient. The effects of manic depression are explored in *Vanishing Point* (1996), as a financier manipulates others and is himself manipulated into bleak chaos. West returned to Australia in 1983, and was made AO in 1985.

WEST, NATHANAEL (1904–40) American novelist, was born Nathan Weinstein in New York City of Lithuanian Jewish immigrants, his father being a successful building contractor. Having attended De Witt Clinton High School irregularly, he got into Tufts College on a forged school record, dropped out during his first term, and transferred to Brown University, using someone else's grades. He graduated in English in 1924, worked desultorily for his father, legally changed his name, and spent three months in Paris. In 1927 relatives got him a job as night manager of a small Manhattan hotel. His youngest sister, to whom he was very close, married PERELMAN in 1929. He heavily revised a burlesque confessional novel, written during his college days, which was published as *The Dream Life of Balso Snell* (1931). In 1930, again through family influence, he was appointed manager of the Sutton Hotel, New York, where he stayed for two years. Preliminary drafts for *Miss Lonelyhearts* (1933), a savage social satire centring on the efforts of an advice columnist to live his masquerade, were published in 1932 in a short-lived revival of *Contact*, which he edited with w. c. WILLIAMS. *A Cool Million: the Dismantling of Lemuel Pitkin* (1934) is a comic study of failure in the context of American idealism. From 1936 he was employed on and off as a Hollywood scriptwriter, a milieu he remorselessly parodied in *The Day of the Locust* (1939). In 1940 he married Eileen McKenney, a 27-year-old divorcée of bohemian tendencies. Returning from a hunting trip in Mexico, he drove through a stop sign in California. Both died

in the collision with another vehicle. *My Sister Eileen*, the dramatization of the family memoir (1938) by Eileen's sister, Ruth McKenney (1911–72), opened on Broadway a few days later. *The Complete Works of Nathanael West* (1957) has a long introductory essay by ALAN ROSS.

WEST, REBECCA, pseudonym of Cicily Fairfield (1892–1983) British novelist, critic, and journalist, was born in Paddington, London, the third daughter of an Irish journalist and entrepreneur, who abandoned his family in 1901. She was educated in her mother's native Edinburgh at George Watson's College, after which she spent a year at the Royal Academy of Dramatic Art. In 1911 she joined the journalistic staff of the *Freewoman*, choosing as a pseudonym the name of the strong-willed heroine of IBSEN's *Rosmersholm*. She was soon also writing political articles and reviews for the *Clarion* and other periodicals—see *The Young Rebecca: Writings of Rebecca West 1911–1917*, ed. Jane Marcus (1982). A provocative review in 1912 of WELLS's *Marriage* led to a meeting, and to a stormy ten-year affair, during which she gave birth to a son, the novelist Anthony West (1914–87)—see his outspoken *H. G. Wells: Aspects of a Life* (1984). Her first book was a critical study of HENRY JAMES (1916). Her first novel, *The Return of the Soldier* (1918), a story of the war with the emphasis on the woman's angle, was followed by the melodramatic feminist cautionary tale, *The Judge* (1922).

In 1930 she married Henry Andrews (d. 1968), with whom she made several visits to Yugoslavia, which inspired her wide-ranging study of the country and its people, *Black Lamb and Grey Falcon* (1942). Attendance as a reporter at war crimes' and treason trials after World War II led to *The Meaning of Treason* (1947): the first edition was 'to give the public information which would otherwise not have reached it', and a second (1951) 'to protect the public from misinformation which was being given it by both hands'. It was republished as *The New Meaning of Treason* (1964), a further revised edition (1956) having been withdrawn. The last two novels published during her lifetime, *The Fountain Overflows* (1957) and *The Birds Fall Down* (1966), both mature studies of growing up before World War I, are regarded as her best. An unfinished novel, on which she worked sporadically for twenty years, is the title piece of *The Only Poet and Other Stories*, ed. Antonia Till (1992). She was made CBE in 1949, and DBE in 1959. See *Family Memories: an Autobiographical Journey*, ed. Faith Evans, new edn 1992; Victoria Glendinning, *Rebecca West: a Life*, new edn 1996; Carl Rollyson, *Rebecca West: a Saga of the Century*, 1996 (biography).

WESTMACOTT, MARY see CHRISTIE.

WHARTON, EDITH (1862–1937), née
Jones, American novelist, short-story writer,
poet, and travel writer, was born in New York
City, the third child and only daughter of a
prominent city landowner, who in 1866 took
his family to France for six years. She was educated at home by governesses. At 14 she
wrote a novel, 'Fast and Loose'; when she
was 16 a selection of 29 of her verses were
privately published as *Verses* (1878)—
HOWELLS printed one of them in *Atlantic
Monthly* in 1879. And at 17 'Pussy' Jones
made her social debut. Her father died in
1882; in 1885, after a broken engagement and
a brief romantic attachment, she married Edward Wharton (1849–1928), a Boston socialite. When not in New York or travelling in
Europe, they lived initially in a cottage on her
mother's estate in Newport, Rhode Island,
with an entourage which included an Alsa-
tian housekeeper, an English butler, and a
swarm of small dogs. An Aegean cruise was
an inspirational experience; a legacy from a
distant cousin made her financially secure.
Scribner's Magazine accepted her poem, 'The
Last Giustiniani' (1889), and a story, 'Mrs
Manstey's View' (1890). In 1893 Scribner's
proposed a collected volume of stories,
which in the light of society's, and her mother's, distrust of professional writers, precipitated an identity crisis and a nervous breakdown, to which her troubled marriage also
contributed. Her first book after her recovery
was *The Decoration of Houses* (1897), written
with a young architect, Ogden Codman. The
stories finally appeared as *The Greater Inclination* (1899), followed by a novella, *The Touch-
stone* (1900), and a further collection of stories, *Crucial Instances* (1901).

Her first meeting with HENRY JAMES,
whom she had long admired from a distance,
took place in England in 1904 and was the
beginning of a firm friendship—see *Henry
James and Edith Wharton: Letters 1900–1915*,
ed. Lyall Powers (1990). *The House of Mirth*
(1905) affirmed her in the public eye as a novelist of the conflicts of social manners, particularly in the setting of New York.

In 1907 she set up a home in Paris, where
in 1909 her husband confessed to having
speculated with her capital, and also to using
it to buy an apartment in Boston for his mistress—Wharton finally divorced him in 1913.
In the meantime she had been having an affair with an American journalist, Morton Ful-
lerton (1865–1952), an experience reflected in
'Life' and the sonnet sequence 'The Mortal
Lease', which were included in *Artemis to Ac-
taeon, and Other Verse* (1909). In *Ethan Frome*
(1911), a New England novel written after the
end of the affair, a botched suicide leaves the
lovers in the care and at the mercy of the
woman from whom they had tried to escape.

There are echoes of her own anti-self in the
ruthless heroine of *The Custom of the Country*
(1913), who sails through several marriages
before returning to her first husband, now a
billionaire, in a progression which is a commentary on the effect of the new values on
the old. She won the Pulitzer Prize for *The
Age of Innocence* (1920), a mellower satire than
earlier works, in which convention triumphs
over desire, and which is the last of her major
novels, though by no means the last of all.
For her work in France during World War I,
especially towards the relief of tuberculosis
among the military and civilians, she was in
1916 appointed Chevalier of the Legion of
Honour; in 1919, after giving her only a
minor award during the war, the King of Belgium made her Chevalier of the Order of Leopold—see Alan Price, *The End of the Age of
Innocence: Edith Wharton and the First World
War* (1996). *Edith Wharton Abroad: Selected
Travel Writings, 1888–1920*, ed. Sarah Bird
Wright, preface by Shari Benstock (1995) covers her travels in Europe in a custom-built
chauffered car, mainly with James as companion, and cruises in a chartered yacht
along the coast of North Africa. An autobiography, *A Backward Glance* (1934), is a suitably
selective account of her life and her creative
process. See R. W. B. Lewis, *Edith Wharton: a
Biography*, new edn 1993; Shari Benstock, *No
Gifts from Chance: a Biography of Edith Wharton*, new edn 1995; Cynthia Griffin Wolff, *A
Feast of Words: the Triumph of Edith Wharton*,
1977 (critical study); Millicent Bell (ed.), *The
Cambridge Companion to Edith Wharton*, 1995
(critical essays).

WHEATLEY, PHILLIS (c.1753–1784)
American poet, was born in West Africa,
probably in Senegal, and was shipped to Boston as a slave in 1761. She was bought by a
well-to-do tailor, John Wheatley (d. 1778), for
his wife Susannah (d. 1773). According to her
master, 'Without any assistance from School
Education and by only what she was taught
in the Family' (the Wheatleys had two children), 'she, in sixteen Months Time . . . attained the English Language . . . to such a
degree as to read the most Difficult Parts of
the Sacred Writings.' She began writing verse
at about 13, by which time she had also, it is
clear from her writings, imbibed from classical mythology and the poetry of MILTON,
POPE, and THOMAS GRAY. She wrote 'To the
University of Cambridge, in New England',
comprising 15 heroic couplets, the verse form
she usually employed, in 1768. When she was
16, she joined the Old South Church of Boston: her elegy on the death of the English revivalist preacher Rev. George Whitefield—
see also EDWARDS—was her first poem to be
published (1770). In 1770, partly for reasons
of her health, she was taken to England,
where among those who warmly received

her, and admired her charm and conversation, was Selina Hastings (1707–91), Countess of Huntingdon, whose chaplain Whitefield had been. *Poems on Various Subjects, Religious and Moral* (1773), 'By Phillis Wheatley, Negro Servant to Mr John Wheatley', with a prefatory note by the Governor of Massachusetts testifying to their authenticity, and a portrait of the author, was published in London while she was there, and distributed also by a bookseller in Boston—the first American edition was in 1777.

She was called back to Boston by the illness of Mrs Wheatley, who died shortly afterwards. After the death of John Wheatley, Phillis, now freed, married another freed slave, John Peters, who appears to have been well read and to have studied law. He was disapproved of by the Wheatley family—he may have been a black activist. Certainly he was unable to provide for his wife and two children who died in infancy. He was imprisoned for debt in 1784, probably at the same time as Phillis died, in great poverty, with their third child lying ill beside her. Poems of her latter years included 'To His Excellency General Washington' (1776) and *Liberty and Peace* (1784), printed as a pamphlet under her married name of Peters. *Memoir and Poems of Phillis Wheatley* was published in 1834, and her letters in 1864. See *The Collected Works of Phillis Wheatley*, ed. John C. Shields, new edn 1990.

WHITE, E(LWYN) B(ROOKS) (1899–1985) American humorist, essayist, and children's writer, was born in Mount Vernon, New York, and educated at Mount Vernon High School and Cornell University, where he edited the *Cornell Daily Sun*. After turning down a teaching post at the University of Minnesota, he tried a few journalistic jobs, and then with a friend set out across country in his Model T Ford. Six months later they ended up in Seattle, Washington, where he became a reporter on the *Seattle Times*. Concluding that he 'was not quick enough or alert enough—I was always taking the wrong train going in the wrong direction', he boarded a steamer to Alaska, voluntarily giving up his first-class passenger status to work as a crew member. His first piece for the *New Yorker*, 'Defense of the Bronx River', appeared in 1925, and from 1927 until 1938 he was a full-time member of staff, writing 'Notes and Comments', poems, stories, captions, and reviews. Most of his adult works are collections: *The Lady is Cold* (1929), his first book, of light verse; *Ho-Hum* (1931), of the inimitable tag-lines with which he embellished newsbreaks, a *New Yorker* speciality; *Quo Vadimus?* (1939), of sketches; and *One Man's Meat* (1942, enlarged edn 1944) and *The Points of the Compass* (1962), of articles and essays written after he had left New York to live on his farm in Maine. In 1945 he covered for the *New Yorker*

the San Francisco Conference at which the United Nations was born—see *The Wild Flag* (1946). *Stuart Little* (1945), about a mouse whose parents are humans, and *Charlotte's Web* (1952), whose protagonist is a spider, are children's fantasies of rare imagination and wit. See *Writings from the New Yorker 1927–1976*, ed. Rebecca Dale, 1992.

WHITE, GILBERT (1720–93) British naturalist, the eldest son of a barrister, was born in his grandfather's house, Selborne Vicarage, Hampshire, and was brought up in 'Wakes', a house on the opposite side of the village square (now the Gilbert White Museum). He was educated at the grammar school in Basingstoke and at Oriel College, Oxford. After being awarded his degree, when he was presented with an autographed copy of POPE's *Iliad*, he was elected a Fellow of the college, and took holy orders. He was a temporary curate in several parishes, and in 1755 settled in Selborne, from which he administered the curacy of Faringdon. He finally became Curate of Selborne in 1784—he could never be the vicar because the living was in the hands of Magdalen College, Oxford, and he was an Oriel man. In 1767 he wrote the first of his published letters to the Welsh traveller and naturalist, Thomas Pennant (1726–98), and two years later he was corresponding also with the Hon. Daines Barrington (1727–1800), Recorder of Bristol, who had devised a system of recording data called 'The Naturalist's Journal'. These vivid letters of a self-trained, acute observer of nature, enlivened by verses and shrewd and often amusing comment, were published by his brother Benjamin (1725–94) in *The Natural History and Antiquities of Selborne* (dated 1789)—the 'Antiquities', a series of historical reports which are often omitted from modern editions, lack the spontaneity of his letters to fellow naturalists. At the age of 72 he was taken seriously ill after officiating at the funeral of a young girl, and died a fortnight later. The modern environmental movement is based on the same balance between man and nature which he pioneered. See *The Natural History of Selborne*, ed. Paul Foster, 1993; Richard Mabey, *Gilbert White*, new edn 1993 (biography).

WHITE, PATRICK (1912–90) Australian novelist and dramatist, the son of a wealthy grazier whose grandfather had settled in Hunter Valley in 1826, was born in London, where his parents happened to be on holiday. He spent his early years on stations in New South Wales, of which he wrote in an autobiographical sketch, 'The Prodigal Son' (1958): 'Whatever has come since, I feel that the influences and impressions of this strange, dead landscape predominate.' He was sent to England to Cheltenham College, which he loathed, especially the team games.

He then spent three years as a jackaroo on sheep stations, and wrote some 'immature' novels, as well as a drawing-room comedy and a one-act play which he later suppressed, but which were produced at the Playhouse, Sydney, in 1933. In 1932 he went to King's College, Cambridge, to read history, but switched to modern languages. In 1935 he published *The Ploughman and Other Poems*, and went to London, where he wrote sketches and lyrics for revues, and had his first story, 'The Twitching Colonel', printed in the *London Mercury* (1937). Of his first novel, *Happy Valley* (1939), a saga in an Australian mountain town, the *Adelaide Mail* commented: 'Surely a little hope, a little looking toward the future, might be advisable.' Of his second, *The Living and the Dead* (1941), a harsh English novel of the 1910s to 1930s, MUIR wrote in the *Listener*: 'Mr White has a passionate spirit of exploration, in his dealing with experience, which is given only to writers to whom imagination is a calling.' During World War II White served with the Royal Air Force in the Middle East and Greece as an intelligence officer. Afterwards, not without vacillation, he returned to Australia, and with his male partner, Manoly Lascaris, settled on a former duck farm outside Sydney, where they grew olives and citrus fruit, and bred Saanen goats and Schnauzer dogs.

The Aunt's Story (1948), the odyssey of a spinster in search of reality, established him as a major novelist. *The Tree of Man* (1955), the struggles of a small farmer told not without humour, and *Voss* (1957), a mystical epic of the pioneer days of exploration, were quickly acknowledged as Australian classics (the latter winning the W. H. Smith Literary Award as well as the MILES FRANKLIN Award). The spiritual and physical journeys of a German Jew, an English housewife, and an Aboriginal artist end in the garden of an Australian woman in *Riders in the Chariot* (1961). It brought him his second Miles Franklin Award, in a year in which he was the subject of a dramatic parochial furore. The Board of the Adelaide Festival of Arts overruled its advisers and rejected his powerful, idealistic play, *The Ham Funeral*, which he had developed in London in 1947 from a painting and an idea of (Sir) William Dobell (1899–1970). It was staged instead by the Adelaide University Theatre Guild; so were *The Season at Sarsaparilla* (1962) and *Night on Bald Mountain* (1964), both written, as was *A Cheery Soul* (1963), within the next year—see *Collected Plays*, Vol. 1 (1985); Vol. 2 was published in 1994. The fictional suburb of Sarsaparilla reappears as the setting of *The Solid Mandala* (1966), a version of the Cain and Abel story, which was his own favourite among his novels. *The Vivisector* (1970) and *The Eye of the Storm* (1973) reflect the city of Sydney itself, into which White and Lascaris moved in

1964, 'wet, boiling, superficial, brash, beautiful, ugly Sydney, developing during my lifetime from a sunlit village into this present-day parvenu bastard'. *A Fringe of Leaves* (1976) is a study of redemption through understanding, based on the survival of a white woman among Aborigines after a shipwreck in 1836. *The Twyborn Affair* (1979) is an exploration of the problems of ambiguous sexuality. White himself obtrudes into his last novel, *Memoirs of Many in One, by Alex Xenophon Demirjian* (1986), another study of indefinite gender roles, but also of old age.

Latterly he wrote further plays for the experimental theatre, *Big Toys* (published 1978), *Signal Driver* (1983), and *Netherwood* (1983). His short fiction is in *The Burnt Ones* (1964), *The Cockatoos* (1974), and *Three Uneasy Pieces* (1981). *Patrick White Speaks* (1990), a collection of utterances on various issues, illustrates the obligation he felt to speak out on matters of public anxiety. His notorious cantankerousness has been identified as a theatrical protective cloak, and his forbidding expression with a reluctance to reveal his false teeth. He was awarded the Nobel Prize for Literature in 1973: with the proceeds he established the annual Patrick White Award for an older Australian author whose work may not have received the acclaim or financial return that it deserves (the first winner was CHRISTINA STEAD). He was made AC in 1975, but resigned from the Order the following year in protest at governmental policies. See *Flaws in the Glass: a Self-Portrait*, new edn 1983; *Patrick White Letters*, ed. David Marr, new edn 1996; David Marr, *Patrick White: a Life*, new edn 1992; Martin Gray (ed.) *Patrick White, Life and Writings: Five Essays*, 1991; Brian Kiernan, *Patrick White*, 1980 (critical study); Simon During (ed.), *Patrick White*, 1996 (critical study).

WHITE, T(ERENCE) H(ANBURY)

(1906–64) British novelist, was born in Bombay, the son of a district superintendent. From 1911 he was brought up in a more settled family atmosphere by his grandparents in England. He was educated at Cheltenham College and Queen's College, Cambridge, where, after a year off (subsidized by a group of dons) to recover from tuberculosis, he got a brilliant first in English. After teaching for two years at a preparatory school, and in 1929 publishing two books of verse, he was in 1932 appointed Head of English at Stowe School. Having now published several unproductive novels, he resigned in 1936 and went to live in a gamekeeper's cottage on the Stowe estate. *England Have My Bones* (1936), a 'scissors and paste' job compiled from his hunting, shooting, and flying diaries, with his own woodcuts, sold well enough for its publisher to offer him £200 a year against a book a year. He responded with *The Sword in the Stone* (1938), a 'Book of the Month' in the USA and the first of what became a quartet of novels, finally published as *The Once and Future King* (1958), though the last book, *Candle in the Wind*, had been finished in 1941; a fifth, *The Book of Merlyn*, which was delivered at the same time, did not appear until 1977. Selectively based on MALORY, in whom White saw as a central theme 'to find an antidote to war', it is a superbly inventive, and funny, Arthurian saga, whose underlying purpose is to celebrate the land, people, and mythology of Britain. He lived in Ireland during World War II, and then in the Channel Islands. Other notable novels are *Mistress Masham's Repose* (1946), in which a girl living in Stowe finds descendants of SWIFT's Lilliputians, and *The Master: a Adventure Story* (1957). See Sylvia Townsend Warner, *T. H. White*, new edn 1989 (biography).

WHITE, WILLIAM HALE see RUTHER-FORD.

WHITMAN, WALT(ER) (1819–92) American poet and journalist, was born in West Hills, New York, one of nine children of English–Dutch descent of Walter Whitman (*d.* 1855), a carpenter/builder and small-time farmer, and Louisa Van Velsor (*d.* 1873), who was barely literate. In 1823 the family moved to Brooklyn, where he attended public schools until he was 11, when he went to work as a lawyer's office boy (the proprietor paid for him to join a circulating library) and then as a printer's apprentice (he was allowed to contribute 'sentimental bits' to the paper). Having qualified as a journeyman, he returned to Long Island in 1836, did some school teaching, founded and for a year wrote, printed, and distributed his own weekly paper, and then worked for the *Long Island Democrat*. Back in New York in 1841, he edited and contributed to newspapers and journals, had stories published in the *Democratic Review*, and wrote a temperance novel, *Franklin Evans: or, The Inebriate* (1842). He then edited the Brooklyn *Daily Eagle*, and wrote its literary pages, until his resignation on political grounds. He found a job on a new daily paper in New Orleans, where he spent three steamy months and got the inspiration for the evocative poem 'I Saw in Louisiana a Live-Oak Growing' (1860). He then briefly edited the Brooklyn *Weekly Freeman*, before spending five mysterious years in the building trade, studying and forging rough friendships (he also used to visit sick horse-bus drivers in hospital); from this experience he emerged as a poet of outstanding originality.

The privately published ('for the convenience of private reading only') *Leaves of Grass* (1855), a 96-page volume with no author's name on the title page (though there was a frontispiece engraving of himself in working men's clothes), comprised 12 untitled poems in unrhymed, free verse (the first being called 'Song of Myself' in the 1881 edi-

tion). It carried an 8000-word, eccentrically punctuated preface in which he set out his literary credos and offered a vision of an American national poetry. Into its nine editions, the last of which (1891), 438 pages, he corrected shortly before his death, he worked all his verse—the preface was dropped after the first edition, but became a source of several subsequent poems. The reception of the original edition did not match the startling nature of the contents, though EMERSON sent him an enthusiastic letter, and there were complimentary anonymous or pseudonymous reviews, some of them written by Whitman himself. The second edition (1857), containing Emerson's letter and a reply, was a financial disaster. He now got a job as Editor of the Brooklyn *Daily Times*, which he held for two years. Things looked up in other directions, too. It seems that he had now come to terms with his homosexuality; the *Saturday Press* printed 'A Child's Reminiscence' ('Out of the Cradle Endlessly Rocking') in its Christmas issue 1859; a Boston publisher offered to bring out the third edition of *Leaves of Grass* (1860), in which Whitman, in spite of Emerson's admonitions, insisted on including the sexually outspoken sequence later known as 'Children of Adam'.

In 1862, reading that his younger brother George had been wounded in action in Virginia in the Civil War, he set out to find him. The injury turned out to be slight, but the sight of the more severely wounded moved him to take a clerical job in the Paymaster's office in Washington, where he spent the rest of his time until the end of the war in 1865 visiting and helping them. The experience inspired 'The Wound-Dresser' and other poems in *Drum-Taps* (1865), to which, after the assassination of President Abraham Lincoln (1809–65), he added as an appendix the elegy 'When Lilacs Last in the Dooryard Bloom'd'. Having transferred to the office of the Department of the Interior, he was dismissed when it was realized that he was author of the 'obscene' *Leaves of Grass*, but his friends got him a similar post the next day in the Attorney General's office. Two of them also rallied round with books in his defence: W. D. O'Connor, *The Good Gray Poet: a Vindication* (1866) and John Burroughs, *Notes on Walt Whitman as Poet and Person* (1867). *Poems of Walt Whitman*, a selection made by William Michael Rossetti (1829–1919), younger brother of D. G. ROSSETTI, was published in Britain in 1868. It generated a series of fan letters from Anne Gilchrist (1828–85), the widow of the biographer of BLAKE and herself a minor writer and literary critic, who offered marriage but had to settle for friendship, which in 1876 she came to America to enjoy in person, accompanied by her children. In *Democratic Vistas* (1871), essays on 'Democracy', 'Personalism', and 'Literature', Whitman developed some of the arguments in the 1855 Preface. The suppression of the seventh (1881) edition of *Leaves of Grass* in Boston was good for sales elsewhere: publication was transferred to Philadelphia. He was now able to buy a modest house in Camden, New Jersey, where he was visited by the great, British as well as American, and tended by a housekeeper and a personal BOSWELL, Horace Traubel (1858–1919), who recorded his every word for posterity, and published three volumes of *With Walt Whitman in Camden* (1906–14). Whitman had a stroke in 1873, and another in 1888. See Gay Wilson Allen, *The Solitary Singer: a Critical Biography of Walt Whitman*, new edn 1985, and *A Reader's Guide to Walt Whitman*, new edn 1991; Bettina Knapp, *Walt Whitman*, 1994 (critical biography); David S. Reynolds, *Walt Whitman's America: a Cultural Biography*, new edn 1996; Gay Wilson Allen and Ed Folsom (eds), *Walt Whitman and the World*, 1995; Ezra Greenspan (ed.), *The Cambridge Companion to Walt Whitman*, 1995 (critical essays).

WHITTIER, JOHN GREENLEAF

(1807–92) American poet and journalist, the second child and eldest son in a Quaker family, was born in the farmhouse near Haverhill, in the Merrimack valley, Massachusetts, which his great-great-grandfather built. He attended district schools, was early on enthused by the work of BURNS, and in 1826 had two poems accepted for the *Newburyport Free Press* by William Lloyd Garrison (1805–79), who persuaded Whittier's parents that he should go to college. In 1827 he enrolled in Haverhill Academy, but withdrew during his second year and went to Boston, unwilling to be educated 'on the charities of others'. While editing successively the *American Manufacturer*, *Haverhill Gazette*, and *New England Weekly Review*, he turned out a lot of journalism himself, and published *Legends of New-England* (1831), which he later suppressed. Back at home after a nervous breakdown, he was cared for by his mother and his sister, Elizabeth (1815–64), some of whose verses were later included in collected editions of his work; he also wrote a long poem, *Moll Pitcher* (1832; rev. edn, including 'The Minstrel Girl', 1840).

He was elected a delegate to the Anti-Slavery Convention in Philadelphia in 1833, and as a member of the Massachusetts Legislature from 1835 to 1837 was subjected to public violence. He was also writing abolitionist verses, and edited the *Pennsylvania Freeman* from 1837 to 1839, after which he settled in a cottage in Amesbury. *Lays of My Home, and Other Poems* (1843), the first authorized collection of his verse, was published, as were succeeding ones, in Boston; *Ballads and Poems* (1844) was issued in London. *Leaves from Margaret Smith's Journal in the Province of Massachusetts Bay, 1678–1679* (1849) is an imaginative reconstruction of the times in prose, as

seen through the eyes of an English visitor. His attitude to the Civil War (1861–65) was that of a sad patriot awaiting the triumph of right which would 'mould anew the nation': with the exception of 'Barbara Frietchie' there was little to stir the blood in *In War Time and Other Poems* (1864). In 1856, J. R. LOWELL, as editor of *Atlantic Monthly*, had written to him: 'I shall not let you rest until I have got a New England pastoral out of you.' *Snow-Bound: a Winter Idyl* was finally written in 1864–65, and published in volume form in 1866, when it matched the success of LONGFELLOW's *Hiawatha*. Whittier was seriously ill in 1867, but he lived on, writing and receiving honours. The respect in which he was held was marked by an *Atlantic Monthly* dinner for his 70th birthday, and his popularity by national celebrations on his 80th.

WIEBE, RUDY (b. 1934) Canadian novelist

and short-story writer, was born in a one-room log cabin in a small Mennonite community in Fairholme, Saskatchewan, of Low German-speaking parents who had emigrated from the USSR in 1930, and did not speak English until he went to school. After World War II his parents moved to another community at Coaldale, Alberta. He was educated at Alberta Mennonite High School and the University of Alberta, from which he won a Rotary scholarship to study for a year at Tubingen University, West Germany. He then took a theology degree at the Mennonite Brethren Bible College, Winnipeg, where he was the first Editor of the Mennonite Brethren *Herald*; he resigned after 18 months during what he calls the 'fantastic ruckus' following the publication of his first novel. After teaching English at Goshen College, Indiana, for four years, he went back to the University of Alberta, becoming a professor of English in 1977. In an interview with MANDEL in 1974 he said: 'If you don't know where you are and where you come from you're more or less like an animal that has no memory.' In his fiction, which began with the *Bildungsroman*, *Peace Shall Destroy Many* (1962), he has brought his Mennonite background, strong Christian faith, and instinctive knowledge of what it is like to be a stranger in a land to bear on his investigation of the roots of the Canadian experience. He often re-creates historical events and personages, as in *The Blue Mountains of China* (1970), *The Temptations of Big Bear* (1973), *The Scorched-Wood People* (1977), and *The Mad Trapper* (1980). Affinities between Mennonite and Indian enable him to write with especial understanding of the attitudes and problems of a culture in conflict with modern society, which he has also done in short stories, in *Where Is the Voice Coming From* (1974) and *Alberta: a Celebration* (1979). See W. J. Keith, *Epic Fiction: the Art of Rudy Wiebe*, 1981.

WIESEL, ELIE (*b.* 1928) novelist and historian, was born of Jewish parentage in Sighet, Transylvania, and was at 16 transported to Auschwitz, where his mother and sister were gassed, and then to Buchenwald, where his father died of starvation and dysentery. He contracted blood poisoning from food given to him by the Americans who liberated the camp in 1945. He attended the Sorbonne in Paris from 1948 to 1951, after which he worked as an international journalist. Of writing about the Holocaust, he has said: 'On the one hand, [a survivor] feels he must. On the other hand, he feels . . . if only I didn't have to.' He cut down his 900-page account ('it's testimony'), originally written in Yiddish, to 160 pages. It was translated into French and then (by Stella Rodway) into English as the novel *Night* (1960)—published in one volume (1974) with *L'Aube* (1960; *Dawn*, 1961) and *Le Jour* (1961; *The Accident*, 1962). Subsequently he has written 'all kinds of novels and books on all kinds of subjects in order not to write about the Holocaust . . . about the Bible, Hasidism, Russian Jews'. His wife Marion has translated much of his work into English from the original French. After a near-fatal accident when he was hit by a taxi in New York while reporting on the United Nations, he stayed in the USA, of which he became a citizen in 1963. He was appointed Andrew W. Mellon Professor in the Humanities at Boston University in 1976, and was awarded the Nobel Peace Prize in 1986.

In January 1995 he spoke at Auschwitz on the occasion of the 50th anniversary of the camp's liberation: 'I speak to you as a man who fifty years ago had no name, no hope, no future and was known only by a number. . . . Close your eyes, my friends, and listen, listen to the silent screams of terrified mothers, listen to the prayers of anguished old men and women, listen to the tears of children. . . . Look and listen as the victims quietly walk towards dark flames so gigantic that the planet itself seemed in danger . . .' See *From the Kingdom of Memory: Reminiscences*, new edn 1995; *All Rivers Run to the Sea: Memoirs Vol. 1 1928–1969*, (France 1994) 1996.

WIGGLESWORTH, MICHAEL (1631–1705) American poet and Puritan divine, was born in England in Yorkshire, and emigrated in 1638 with his family, who settled in New Haven, Connecticut. At 16, he entered Harvard College to study medicine. He graduated first in his class in 1651, and stayed on to teach undergraduates while studying for MA. In 1656 he was called to the church of Malden, Massachusetts, where he ministered to souls and bodies for the rest of his long life, plagued by real illnesses and imaginary ones (including syphilis), and being married three times, on the second occasion to his teenage serving girl. To offset his unpopularity in the pulpit he wrote didactic verse, of which *The Day of Doom: or, A Description of the Great and Last Judgment* (1662) is regarded as the first American best seller. The epitome of Puritan belief, its 224 eight-line stanzas in common hymn metre were committed to memory by those who responded to its fearful, comforting, and stirring images, and by their children. A new edition of his diary (ed. Edmund S. Morgan) was published in 1970.

WILBUR, RICHARD (*b.* 1921) American poet and translator, was born in New York City; his father was a painter and his maternal grandfather and great-grandfather were newspaper editors. He had a rural childhood in a house on an estate in New Jersey. At Amherst College (1938–42) he toyed with being a journalist and spent summer vacations touring 'most of the 48 states by freight-car'. He married in 1942. He began seriously to write poetry while serving as a sergeant in the 36th Infantry Division in Europe: 'One does not use poetry for its major purposes, as a means of organizing oneself and the world, until one's world somehow gets out of hand.' Seven poems in his first book, *The Beautiful Changes and Other Poems* (1947), and several more in his second, *Ceremony and Other Poems* (1950), reflect his war service; others deal with nature, the senses, and odd experiences. At this time he said of his craft: 'Rhyme seems to me an invaluable aid in composition. It creates difficulties which the utterance must surmount by increased resourcefulness. . . . The use of strict poetic forms, traditional or invented, is like the use of framing and composition in painting. . . . Limitation makes for power: the strength of the genie comes of his being confined in a bottle.' *The Poems of Richard Wilbur* (1963) was a selection from his first four collections, of which *Things of the World* (1956) won the Pulitzer Prize. He has further exploited his natural precision of language and his wit to translate from the French poems of LA FONTAINE, ADAM, BAUDELAIRE, and VALÉRY, and several comedies of MOLIÈRE, notably *The Misanthrope* (1955) and *Tartuffe* (1963)—see also *Molière: Four Comedies* (1982). A poet who aims to be in touch with people, he taught English at Harvard (1947–54), Wellesley College (1955–57), and Wesleyan University (1955–57), and was Writer-in-Residence at Smith College 1977–86. In 1958 he was appointed General Editor of the Dell Laurel Poetry Series. He was US Poet Laureate 1987–88. See *New and Collected Poems*, new edn 1989; *Responses: Prose Pieces 1953–1976*, 1976; *On My Own Work*, 1983; Rodney Stenning Edgecombe, *A Reader's Guide to the Poetry of Richard Wilbur*, 1995.

WILDE, OSCAR (FINGAL O'FLAHERTIE WILLS) (1854–1900) Irish dramatist, novelist, short-story writer, critic, and poet, was born in Dublin, the younger son of the surgeon and writer on Irish archaeology and topography, Sir William Wilde (1815–76), and Jane, née Elgee (1826–96), who ran a literary salon and wrote revolutionary verse under the name of 'Speranza'—see Joy Melville, *Mother of Oscar: the Life of Jane Francesca Wilde* (1994). He was educated at Portora Royal School, Trinity College, Dublin, and Magdalen College, Oxford, where he won the Newdigate Prize for poetry with *Ravenna* (1878), came under the artistic influence of RUSKIN and PATER, and got a first in Greats, having in the meantime toured Italy and Greece. He burst into London society, to which he preached the doctrine of aestheticism with wit and conversational skill. *Poems* (1881) is mainly derivative, but a few later verses stand out, such as 'The Harlot's House', 'On the Sale by Auction of Keats' Love Letters', and 'Symphony in Yellow'— see *Selected Poems*, ed. Malcolm Hicks (1992).

After a lecture tour of the USA in 1882, he married Constance Lloyd (*d*. 1896), by whom he had two sons. He wrote *The Happy Prince, and Other Tales* (1888), a collection of witty and compassionate fairy stories for children (and their parents), and critical essays, of which 'The Decay of Lying' (1889) and 'The Critic as Artist' (1890) are notable. More fiction followed in 1891: *Lord Arthur Savile's Crime, and Other Stories* and *The Picture of Dorian Gray*, his only novel, a study of decadence and self-destruction. His early works for the theatre were sombre: *Vera, or the Nihilists* (produced in the USA 1882); a verse tragedy, *The Duchess of Padua* (1883); and the uncomfortable *Salomé* (written in French in 1891, published 1893, performed in Paris 1896, but banned in Britain until 1905; English translation by Lord Alfred Douglas published 1894). Now came a string of successful social comedies. *Lady Windermere's Fan* (produced 1892, published 1893), *A Woman of No Importance* (produced 1893, published 1894), and *An Ideal Husband* (produced 1895, published 1899) are beneath their veneer of wit concerned with human nature and tinged with sentiment. *The Importance of Being Earnest* (produced 1895, published 1899), however, continues to delight as a comedy of manners whose lightness of style, brilliant dialogue, and skilled construction carry along a series of absurd paradoxes.

In 1895 the libel action Wilde brought against the Marquis of Queensberry—father of Lord Alfred Douglas (1870–1945)—, who had accused him of being a homosexual, failed. Wilde was then himself arrested, tried, and sentenced to two years' hard labour. In prison he wrote *De Profundis* (not published in full until 1949), a prose apologia for his conduct. His poetic reputation largely rests on *The Ballad of Reading Gaol* (1898), an understandably overwrought but moving account of prison experience. Shunned by society, he left England after his release. Under the

name of Sebastian Melmoth (after MATURIN's character), he lived wretchedly on the Continent for three years until his death in Paris, having lost his ability to write. See *Plays, Prose Writings and Poems*, ed. Anthony Fothergill, new edn 1996; *The Importance of Being Earnest and Other Plays* (*Lady Windermere's Fan, Salome, A Woman of No Importance, An Ideal Husband*), ed. Peter Raby, 1995; *The Writings*, ed. Isobel Murray, 1989 (selection); *Complete Shorter Fiction*, ed. Isobel Murray, 1980; *Selected Letters*, ed. Rupert Hart-Davis, new edn 1989; Richard Ellmann, *Oscar Wilde*, new edn 1988 (biography).

WILDER, THORNTON (1897–1975) American novelist and dramatist, was born in Madison, Wisconsin, the son of a newspaperman who was American Consul General to Shanghai and Hong Kong from 1905 to 1909, when the family returned to Berkeley, California. He was educated at Thacher School, Ojai, Oberlin College, where he read classics, and Yale. Of the 16 of his three-minute plays published as *The Angel That Troubled the Waters* (1928), some were written as early as 1915; his first full-length play, *The Trumpet Shall Sound*, was serialized in the *Yale Literary Magazine* in 1919–20. After graduating, he spent a year studying archaeology at the American Academy in Rome, and in 1922 went to teach French at Lawrenceville School, New Jersey. *The Cabala* (1926), his first novel, is a non-realistic revelation of Italian artistic society. In *The Bridge of San Luis Rey* (1927), which won the Pulitzer Prize, the collapse of a Peruvian bridge in 1714 is the background to an investigation of the five people who went down with it, and of the fate that chose them to die. His third, *The Woman of Andros* (1930), is based on a plot of TERENCE. Having now started 'with the purely fantastic twentieth-century Rome, then Peru, then Hellenistic Greece, I began, first with *Heaven's My Destination* [(1934)] to approach the American scene'. In this satirical novel, a not-so-innocent Baptist preacher brushes with various facets of society.

He gave up schoolmastering in 1928 to write. In 1931 he accepted an invitation to teach at Chicago University, where he stayed for five years, and invited STEIN to give a series of lectures in 1935. She convinced him of the superiority of drama over fiction as an art form, because the audience can actually see 'pure existing'. *Our Town* (1938) won the Pulitzer Prize. Played entirely without scenery, it centres on ordinary life, and natural death, in a small town, and on the tragedy inherent in the failure to see the human condition in the context of all other human beings. *The Merchant of Yonkers* (1939), revived as *The Matchmaker* at the Edinburgh Festival in 1954—it later became the hit musical, *Hello Dolly!* (1963)—, is a farcical satire set in the 1880s. *The Skin of Our Teeth* (1942), for which he won a third Pulitzer Prize, draws on JOYCE's *Finnegans Wake* to express, with comedy and satire, Wilder's theory of the survival of man in the face of catastrophe. During World War II he served in North Africa and Italy in the Intelligence Corps of the US Air Force, in which he rose to lieutenant colonel. His first book afterwards was *The Ides of March* (1948), a fictional study of dictatorship through the character of CAESAR. *The Eighth Day* (1967), in which the 'enormous tapestry' of history is brought to bear on an event in the present, won the National Book Award.

WILDING, MICHAEL (*b.* 1942) British novelist, short-story writer, and critic, was born in Worcester, and educated at Royal Grammar School, Worcester, and Lincoln College, Oxford. Having briefly been a primary school teacher, he went to Australia where, except for the years 1969–72, when he was a senior lecturer at Birmingham University, he has taught ever since at Sydney University, being appointed Reader in English in 1972 and Professor of English in 1993. He is an experimental writer whose collection of short stories, *Aspects of the Dying Process* (1972), and *Living Together* (1974), his first novel, were, like his subsequent fiction, published first in Australia. They enshrine his vision of the urban culture of the 1970s, during which, as a character observes in his second novel, *The Short Story Embassy* (1975), the coming of the Pill provided 'a whole different anthropology' for the writer. In his short stories in particular—see *The Man of Slow Feeling: Selected Short Stories* (1985) and *Great Climate* (1990)—the onus of constructing meaning from the combination of highly visual images is on the reader. His critical works include *Political Fictions* (1980), *Dragon's Teeth: Literature in the English Revolution* (1987), *Social Visions* (1994), critical essays, and studies of MARCUS CLARKE. He edited *Tabloid Story*, an ingeniously marketed forum for new short fiction, from its inception in 1972 to 1976. He was a co-founder, with Pat Woolley (*b.* 1947), and a director (1974–79) of the alternative publishing house, Wild and Woolley, and in 1971 became Australian Editor of *Stand* (see SILKIN).

WILKES, JOHN see CHURCHILL, CHARLES.

WILKINSON, ANNE (1910–61), née Gibbons, Canadian poet, was born in Toronto, and was (on her mother's side) a member of the notable Osler family, whose story and contribution to Canada's development she later traced in *Lions in the Way: a Discursive History of the Oslers* (1956). Her childhood was spent between London, Ontario; her grandfather's mansion of Craigleigh, Toronto; a summer home on Lake Simcoe; and a seaside house in Santa Barbara, California,

where her mother went for the winters. She was educated at home by tutors and at progressive schools in the USA, England, and France. She married F. R. Wilkinson, a surgeon, in 1932: they had three children, and were divorced in 1952. She published just two volumes of verse, *Counterpoint to Sleep* (1951) and *The Hangman and the Holly* (1955), comprising 94 pages in all. Nevertheless she made a lasting impact for the intellectual and sensual quality of her poetry, and for its range, from the reminiscent, through the descriptive, to the philosophical. She was, from its establishment in 1956 until her death from cancer, a member of the editorial board and a patron of the *Tamarack Review*. See *Collected Poems, and a Prose Memoir*, ed. A. J. M. Smith, 1968.

WILKINSON, IRIS GUIVER see HYDE, ROBIN.

WILLIAMS, CHARLES (1886–1945) British poet, novelist, and critic, was born in Holloway, London, the only son of a clerk, and was brought up in St Albans, where he went to the Abbey School. In 1902 he won a county scholarship to University College, London, from which he withdrew two years later for financial reasons. He took a job with the Methodist Bookshop, Holborn, enrolled at the Working Men's College, and in 1908 joined Oxford University Press in London as a proofreader, from which he progressed to editor and literary adviser. His first book was *The Silver Stair* (1912), a sonnet sequence inspired by meeting his future wife, whom he married in 1917. Lectures he gave at the City of London Literary Institute were the basis of two critical works, *The English Poetic Mind* (1932) and *Reason and Beauty in the Poetic Mind* (1932). His allegorical fantasy, *The Place of the Lion* (1931), was to have a profound influence on C. S. LEWIS, who read it at the same time as Williams, as editor, was reading the manuscript of Lewis's *The Allegory of Love*. At the outbreak of World War II, Williams moved to Oxford with the London staff of the Press, leaving his wife in London. He was drafted in as a university lecturer in English, and became a member of the exclusive literary drinking circle, the Inklings, to which Lewis and TOLKIEN belonged. Having concentrated on writing theology for several years, he combined both theological and poetic intelligence in his study of DANTE, *The Figure of Beatrice* (1943). He was also a historical biographer and a verse dramatist—see *Collected Plays*, introduction by John Heath-Stubbs (1963). His most lasting work is likely to be the two poetic sequences in which he uses Arthurian legend as a basis for his own exploration of the 'Matter of Britain', *Taliessin Through Logres* (1938) and *The Region of the Summer Stars* (1944). See Glen Cavaliero,

Charles Williams: Poet of Theology, 1983 (critical study of his whole oeuvre).

WILLIAMS, (GEORGE) EMLYN

(1905–87) Welsh dramatist and actor, was born in Mostyn, Flintshire, the son of an iron-worker who became an innkeeper, and of a strict Puritan who regarded a youth who studied as a drudge on the housekeeping purse. He spoke Welsh until he went to school at eight, and hardly heard English spoken until he was 11. At Holywell County School his French teacher, Yorkshire-born Miss Sarah Cooke, then 33, spotted his ability, gave him new boots, had him coached in languages with a view to his becoming a teacher, and later, as mental therapy, lent him her golf clubs—the relationship is re-created in his most lasting play, *The Corn is Green* (1938). With her encouragement he won a scholarship to Christ Church, Oxford, where he was a leading member of the Oxford University Dramatic Society and decided instead on the theatre as a career. He made his London stage debut in 1927, and his name as a dramatist with *A Murder Has Been Arranged* (1930), a thriller set on a stage which is presumed to be haunted. He played the key role of the sinister house boy in his *Night Must Fall* (1935). Of his Welsh plays in addition to *The Corn is Green*, *The Druid's Rest* (1944) has a lighter theme and is rich in local colour, and *The Wind of Heaven* (1945) is a 19th-century parable of the birth of Christ. Eclipsed as a dramatist in the postwar trend away from orthodox drama, he resuscitated the Victorian art of the one-man recital, which he launched in 1951 as *Emlyn Williams as Charles Dickens*. Subsequently he performed a dramatic reading of DYLAN THOMAS, *A Boy Grows Up* (1955). He was made CBE in 1962. See *The Collected Plays*, 1961; *George: an Early Autobiography 1905–1927*, new edn 1976; *Emlyn: an Early Autobiography 1927–1935*, new edn 1982; James Harding, *Emlyn Williams: a Life*, new edn 1996.

WILLIAMS, RAYMOND (1921–88)

Welsh novelist and critic, was born in Llanfihangel Crocorney, the son of a railway signalman, and was educated at Henry VIII Grammar School, Abergavenny, and (with an interval for World War II, when he served as an anti-tank captain in the Guards Armoured Division) at Trinity College, Cambridge. After teaching literature for the Oxford University Delegacy for Extra-Mural Studies, he was elected a Fellow of Jesus College, Cambridge, in 1961, becoming Reader in 1967, and being Professor of Drama 1974–83. In his trilogy of Welsh novels, the working-class domesticity of *Border Country* (1960) gives way to shop-floor politics and broader socialist issues in *Second Generation* (1964), and to international economics in *The Fight for Manod* (1979). In about 1980 he began work on 'an unusual kind of historical novel in which the continuity is not of people but of place'. Posthumously published as *The People of the Black Mountains: Vol. 1, The Beginning* (1989), *Vol. 2, The Eggs of the Eagle* (1990), its stories illustrate his commitment to the view that though walls, or geographical borders, restrict cultural development, they also encourage the reassessment of readings of the past. Of many critical works, the most influential have proved to be *Culture and Society 1780–1950* (1958), in which he challenges LEAVIS's view of culture and argues the case for writers being a part of history, not its governors, *Drama from Ibsen to Eliot* (1952; republished as *Drama from Ibsen to Brecht*, rev. edn 1987); and *Marxism and Literature* (1977), an examination of the place of literature within Marxist cultural theory. See Fred Inglis, *Raymond Williams: His Life and Times*, 1995; Stephen Regan, *Raymond Williams*, 1995 (critical study).

WILLIAMS, TENNESSEE (1911–83)

American dramatist, novelist, and short-story writer, was born Thomas Lanier Williams in Columbus, Mississippi, the son of a travelling salesman and of the daughter of an Episcopalian minister. The family moved to St Louis in 1918. He attended the University of Missouri, but left when his father withdrew his financial support, and worked in a shoe warehouse, writing at night. After a nervous breakdown, to which his mother's puritanism and his father's tyranny contributed, he recuperated at the home of his grandparents. Then, with a renewed determination to write, he took himself to Washington University, St Louis, from which he transferred to the playwriting course at the University of Iowa, where he graduated in 1938. The source of *The Glass Menagerie* (1944), his first dramatic success, is a story, 'Portrait of a Girl in Glass', which 'grew out of the intense emotions I felt [at that time] seeing my sister's mind begin to go'—Rose later had a prefrontal lobotomy, and spent most of the rest of her life in institutions. In 1939 he was in New Orleans, had had six plays produced in provincial theatres (the first in Memphis in 1936), and had acquired the name 'Tennessee'. It was a 'happy period . . . I came out in the gay world. I didn't think of it as coming out. I thought of it as a new world.' *The Glass Menagerie*, a 'memory play' in which a family of misfits suffer a collapse even of their most grotesque fantasies, 'ended that period and new problems developed with success'.

The destruction of the faded Southern belle, Blanche, in *A Streetcar Named Desire* (1947) is physical and brutal, yet she maintains her fantasies to the end. The play shocked with its power, and won the Pulitzer Prize. For the next two decades Williams regularly turned out new plays, of which some have lasted particularly well. Love returns to the grieving heroine of *The Rose Tattoo* (1948), who erupts at any suggestion that her husband, shot dead by rival drug-runners, was ever unfaithful. In *Cat on a Hot Tin Roof* (1955), his other Pulitzer Prize winner, 'Maggie the Cat' manipulates a Mississippi plantation family to her advantage and to a possible reconciliation with her feckless husband. The setting of *The Night of the Iguana* (1961) is a dingy hotel on the Mexican coast. The characters are in transit or are running away from something; the theme is the permanence of pain.

During the 1960s Williams's dependence on drink and drugs increased, until in 1969, after an accident in a new kitchen which was being built in his home in Key West, his brother had him 'immediately converted to Roman Catholicism' and committed to a hospital psychiatric ward. Thereafter he still managed to keep writing, though his attempts at experimentation were less appreciated than his former work. He died alone in a New York hotel, choking to death on the cap of a nasal spray that he was using as a cup for pills. He also published two volumes of poetry, and several of short stories—see *Collected Stories*, ed. Gore Vidal (1985). For his novel *The Roman Spring of Mrs Stone* (1950) he received through the post in 1981 an Italian literary prize, which puzzled him, as when the book (and the film) appeared, the Italians had been upset by this story of a Roman gigolo and an older woman. *Memoirs* was published in 1975, and *Where I Live: Selected Essays*, ed. Christine R. Day and Bob Woods, in 1978. See *The Theatre of Tennessee Williams*, 7 vols 1971–81 (plays); Lyle Leverich, *Tom: the Unknown Tennessee Williams*, new edn 1996 (biography to 1945); Signi L. Falk, *Tennessee Williams*, new edn 1985 (critical study).

WILLIAMS, WILLIAM CARLOS (1883–1963) American poet, novelist, short-story writer, dramatist, and critic, was born in Rutherford, New Jersey, of an English-born father and a mother of Basque and Dutch-Jewish descent who had grown up in Puerto Rico. In 1898, after being at local public schools in Rutherford, he and his younger brother went with their mother for two years to Europe, where he attended the Château de Lancy, Geneva, and the Lycée Condorcet, Paris. From Horace Mann High School, New York City, he went to the University of Pennsylvania, graduating in medicine, to which he had switched from dentistry. Here he met DOOLITTLE, with whom he discovered 'the wonder of *Aucassin and Nicolette*', and POUND, who became a close friend and poetic mentor. He did his internship in New York City at French Hospital and at the Nursery and Child's Hospital, from which he resigned after finding skulduggery in the accounts. In 1909 he privately printed *Poems* ('bad Keats, nothing else—oh well, bad Whitman too'), proposed to and was accepted by Florence

(Floss) Herman, the sister of his brother's former fiancée, and went to Europe to study paediatrics in Leipzig. He married in 1912, and in 1913 the couple moved into 9 Ridge Road, Rutherford, his home for the rest of his life, and the place where he held his general practice. The experimental poems in *Al Que Quiere!* (1917) and prose in *Kora in Hell: Improvisations* (1920) developed, in *Spring and All* (1923), into a voice distinctly American in its contexts, which he further explored in the historical character sketches in *In the American Grain* (1925).

His activity was as astonishing as his inventiveness. While keeping up his practice until the 1950s, when after a series of strokes he handed it over to his elder son, and holding a consultancy in paediatrics at the Passaic General Hospital, he produced 36 further books and two translations. *Collected Poems 1921–1931* (1934), which had a preface by STEVENS, was followed by *The Complete Collected Poems 1906–1938* (1938), *The Collected Later Poems* (1950; rev. edn 1963), and *The Collected Earlier Poems* (1951). His long poem, *Paterson*, an autobiographical epic exploring the essence of America, in which he carried to its ultimate degree his search for the ideal poetic line, remained unfinished after the publication of five books (1946–58; in one volume, ed. C. J. MacGowan, 1992). For his last collection, and final book, *Pictures from Brueghel and Other Poems* (1962), he was posthumously awarded the Pulitzer Prize. His novels include the trilogy, begun in 1927, *White Mule* (1937), *In the Money* (1940), and *The Build-Up* (1952), which follows a family from the birth of a daughter (Floss) to 1917, when America entered World War I. *The Farmers' Daughters* (1961) is a collection of stories, and *Many Loves* (1961) of his plays. *The Selected Essays* (1954) incorporates some of his criticism. *The Autobiography of William Carlos Williams* (1951) is a selective account, complemented by *Yes, Mrs Williams* (1959), a memoir of his unusual mother. See *Collected Poems, Vol. 1 1909–1939, Vol. 2 1939–1962*, ed. A. W. Litz and C. J. MacGowan, new edns 1992; *Selected Poems*, ed. Charles Tomlinson, new edn 1990; *The Collected Stories*, introduction by Sherwin B. Nuland, new edn 1996; James Laughlin, *Remembering William Carlos Williams*, 1996; James E. B. Breslin, *William Carlos Williams: an American Artist*, new edn 1986 (critical study).

WILLIAMSON, DAVID (*b.* 1942) Australian dramatist, was born in Melbourne, the elder son of a bank official, and was brought up in Bairnsdale. He graduated in mechanical engineering at Monash University, and was a designer engineer with General Motors before being a teacher of thermodynamics and social psychology at Swinburne College of Technology from 1966 to 1972. His first play, *The Coming of Stork*, was performed at the La Mama Theatre, Carlton, in 1970; it was published in 1974 with two other plays examining 'the collisions caused by inescapable differences between individuals playing themselves out within a tight social context', *Jugglers Three* (1972) and *What If You Died Tomorrow* (1973). As illustrations of what he described in an interview in 1972 as an 'awful Australian uniqueness', they and *Don's Party* (1971), a comic conversation piece, present a middle-class educated, but somewhat foul-mouthed and promiscuous, society in unusual and amusing situations. *The Removalists* (1971) explores an ugly incident in which two policemen kill a wife-beater in his own home. *The Department* (published 1976) and *The Club* (1978) are studies of power struggles in an academic department and the committee room of an Australian Rules football club respectively. Marital differences, never fully resolved but at least aired and ultimately tolerated, are the subject of *The Perfectionist* (1983). In *Emerald City* (1987), as it was with *Travelling North* (1979), climatic differences have a symbolic bearing on the spiritual journeys undertaken by the main characters. Sex, power, and greed, in the family, at work, or in society as a whole, are variously treated in *Top Silk* (1989), *Siren* (1991), *Money and Friends* (1992), and *Brilliant Lies* (1993), while in *Dead White Men* (performed in UK 1996) Williamson returns to academia with a biting satire on contemporary literary studies. See *Collected Plays*, 2 vols 1986, 1993; Brian Kiernan, *David Williamson: a Writer's Career*, 1990.

WILLIAMSON, HENRY (1895–1977) British novelist, was born in Brockley, Kent, the son of a bank clerk, and was educated at Colfe's Grammar School, Lewisham, after which he served as an officer in the Bedfordshire Regiment at the front in World War I. The spontaneous Christmas truce in 1914, after which the troops who had fraternized in No Man's Land went back to killing each other, affected him for life. After the war, only 23, he eked out his war pension by being a motorcycle correspondent, until a reading of JEFFERIES encouraged him to retire to an Exmoor cottage, and write. The four novels which comprise the 'Flax of Dream' sequence, *The Beautiful Years* (1921; rev. edn 1929), *Dandelion Days* (1922; rev. edn 1930), *The Dream of Fair Women* (1924; rev. edn 1931), and *The Pathway* (1928), recount, through the persona of Willie Madison, aspects of and idealistic reflections on his own childhood, boyhood, youth, and early manhood. *Tarka the Otter: His Joyful Water-Life and Death in the Two Rivers* (1927), which won the Hawthornden Prize for a novel by an author under 41, was inspired by the loss of a real otter which he had reared. *Salar the Salmon* (1935) reveals a similar expertise as a naturalist and commitment as a conservationist. His fear of the outcome of a recurrence of international hos-

tilities led him to support the fascism of Sir Oswald Mosley (1896–1980) and even openly to praise Hitler's social policies, as a result of which he was briefly interned at the beginning of World War II, and then allowed to return to his Norfolk farm. His 15-book postwar sequence, 'A Chronicle of Ancient Sunlight', begins in late-Victorian London with *The Dark Lantern* (1951), and traces the life of Willie's cousin, Phillip. In a sense both these novel sequences are autobiographical, but he also wrote three volumes of autobiography, *The Children of Shallowford* (rev. edn 1959), *The Story of a Norfolk Farm* (1941), and *A Clear Water Stream* (1958). He died in a London hospital, on the very day that the death scene of Tarka was being filmed at the exact spot which he describes in the novel. See *Collected Nature Stories*, 1995; *Notebooks of a Nature Lover*, 1996; Anne Williamson, *Henry Williamson: Tarka and the Last Romantic*, 1995 (biography).

WILSON, A(NDREW) N(ORMAN) (b. 1950) British novelist, biographer, critic, and journalist, was born in Stone, Staffordshire, into a home which has been said to be identified with that in his novel, *Incline Our Hearts* (1989), which, with *A Bottle in the Smoke* (1990), *Daughters of Albion* (1991), *Hearing Voices* (1995), and *A Watch in the Night* (1996), constitute the 'Lampitt Papers' sequence following the saga of an intellectual and aristocratic dynasty. He was educated at Rugby School and New College, Oxford, where in 1971 he won the Chancellor's Essay Prize and married one of his tutors. He studied for the priesthood at St Stephen's College, Oxford, from which he withdrew after a year. He taught for a year at Merchant Taylors' School, London, before returning to Oxford to be a lecturer in English at St Hugh's College (and also New College) from 1976 to 1982. He was Literary Editor of the *Spectator* 1981–3. *The Healing Art* (1980) and *Wise Virgin* (1983) are the more highly regarded of his satirical novels, in which observations are often acerbic and sometimes arch, but which demonstrate also a compassionate understanding of a character's predicament. To some readers, better work is to be found in his critical biographies of WALTER SCOTT (1980), MILTON (1983), BELLOC (1984), TOLSTOY (1988), for which he first learned Russian, and C. S. LEWIS (1990), in which he proves that to be iconoclastic it is not necessary also to be unsympathetic. In *Jesus* (1992) he attempts to reconcile New Testament theology with Christian scholarship. He is a prolific and provocative journalist, whose work has appeared in journals and newspapers as varied as *The Times Literary Supplement*, *New Statesman*, *Daily Mail*, and London *Evening Standard*—see *Penfriends from Porlock: Essays and Reviews 1977-1986* (1988).

WILSON, (Sir) **ANGUS** (1913–91) British novelist, short-story writer, and critic, was born in Bexhill, Sussex, the sixth and very much the youngest son of a Scot who spent most of his time, and his income, gambling. As a result much of his childhood was spent in genteel poverty in hotels or boarding houses. He was educated at Westminster School and Merton College, Oxford. During World War II he was engaged in secret work in the Foreign Office. He was Deputy Superintendent of the Reading Room, British Museum 1949–55, and Professor of English Literature, University of East Anglia 1966–78, where he established with MALCOLM BRADBURY the MA course in creative writing among whose students have been MCEWAN and Kazuo Ishiguro (b. 1954), whose The Remains of the Day (1989) won the Booker prize for fiction.

In 1946, as therapy for crippling attacks of nervous anxiety, Wilson began to write short stories. In his first two books, The Wrong Set and Other Stories (1949) and Such Darling Dodos and Other Stories (1950), a realistic situation often verges towards farce or a bizarre act of violence. In that they are usually episodic, he carried over the short-story technique to his novels, the first three of which, Hemlock and After (1952), Anglo-Saxon Attitudes (1956), and The Middle Age of Mrs Eliot (1958), are otherwise traditional in form. His analysis of character is deft and satirical, and done with a blend of cruelty and compassion, while he is often concerned with laying bare the private guilt behind the public appearance. In The Old Men at the Zoo (1961), which marks the beginning of a period in which he experimented with pastiche, he projects into the future the moral predicament of a conscientious public servant in a society at war and then in defeat. Late Call (1964), No Laughing Matter (1967), and Setting the World on Fire (1980) are more concerned with family relationships and attitudes. His critical works include studies of ZOLA (1952), DICKENS (1970), and KIPLING (1977); Diversity and Depth in Fiction: Selected Critical Writings (1983); and The Wild Garden: or, Speaking of Writing (1963), in which he describes the background to his fiction. He was made CBE in 1968 and was knighted in 1980. See Margaret Drabble, Angus Wilson: a Biography, 1996; Jay Halio, Angus Wilson, 1964 (critical study).

WILSON, COLIN (b. 1931) British novelist and critic, was born in Leicester and educated at Gateway Secondary Technical School. After National Service in the Royal Air Force, and various jobs in London and Paris, he became a full-time writer in 1954. His first book, The Outsider (1956), a study of alienation in terms of creative genius, with examples from both art and literature, instigated a form of 'new existentialism', upon which he enlarged in a number of subse-

quent philosophical works. The Craft of the Novel (new edn 1986) is based on a series of lectures he gave at Rutgers University, New Jersey. His novels, of which the first was Ritual in the Dark (1960), based on the exploits of 'Jack the Ripper', embrace various genres, and in the main explore further the darknesses of the mind and soul. A man who sees writing primarily as a medium to clarify his philosophy about the business of living—and he has written more than ninety books—, he expressed his confidence in an interview in 1996: 'It's the job of writers and thinkers to try to create a synthesis for the rest of the human race, whether it's a steam engine or a philosophical idea. My steam engine is almost ready.' See Nicolas Tredell, The Novels of Colin Wilson, 1982.

WILSON, EDMUND (1895–1972) American critic, novelist, poet, dramatist, and journalist, was born in Red Bank, New Jersey, and educated at the Hill School, Pottstown, Pennsylvania, and Princeton, where he became a friend of F. S. FITZGERALD. After a year as a reporter on the New York Evening Sun, he served in France during World War I, first in a base hospital, and then as a sergeant in the US Army Intelligence Corps. Having edited Vanity Fair for a year, he became in 1921 Drama Critic for the New Republic, with which he was associated for twenty years. In 1923 he made the first of four marriages, of which the third (1938–46) was to MCCARTHY. His first play, The Crime in the Whistler Room, was performed by the Provincetown Players in 1924—see in Five Plays (1954). In 1929 he published a book of verse, Poets, Farewell!, and a novel of Greenwich Village, I Thought of Daisy, in which MILLAY appears as Rita. A subsequent excursion into fiction, Memoirs of Hecate County (1946), a sequence of six stories, was banned for the eroticism of one of them. The US Supreme Court finally upheld the publisher's conviction after a 4–4 tied vote, and the book was not reissued until 1959.

Wilson's most influential work was done as a literary critic, in such books as Axel's Castle (1931), essays mainly about symbolism; and as a political and historical philosopher, in To the Finland Station (1940) and Patriotic Gore: Studies in the Literature of the American Civil War (1962). The breadth of his scholarship is evident also in The Scrolls of the Dead Sea (1955). He published several volumes of essays and reviews, including The Bit between My Teeth: a Literary Chronicle of 1950–1965 (1965), and a collection of personal essays, A Piece of My Mind: Reflections at Sixty (1956).

His meticulously-kept journals and recollections have been published as Upstate, Prelude, The Twenties, The Thirties, The Forties, The Fifties (1967–75), ed. Leon Edel, and The Sixties: the Last Journal 1960–1972, ed. Lewis M. Dabney (1993). The Nabokov–Wilson Letters:

the Correspondence Between Vladimir Nabokov and Edmund Wilson 1940–1971, ed. Simon Karlinsky (1979) records a literary friendship which at one point degenerated into an unseemly wrangle over the translation of PUSHKIN. See *From the Uncollected Edmund Wilson*, ed. Janet Groth and David Castronovo, 1995 (essays on aspects of contemporary literature); Jeffrey Meyers, *Edmund Wilson: a Biography*, 1995; Janet Groth, *Edmund Wilson: a Critic for Our Time*, 1989.

WILSON, ETHEL (1888–1980), née Bryant, Canadian novelist, was born in South Africa, the only child of a British Methodist missionary. After the death of her mother in 1889 and her father in 1898, she lived with her maternal grandmother in Vancouver, being educated at a Methodist boarding school in England and at Vancouver Normal School, where she obtained a teacher's certificate. She taught in schools in Vancouver until 1920, and in 1921 married Dr Wallace Wilson (*d.* 1966), later President of the Canadian Medical Association. Though she had short stories printed in Britain in the *New Statesman and Nation* in the 1930s—see *Mrs Golightly and Other Stories* (1961)—, she did not publish her first novel, *Hetty Dorval*, a study of youthful innocence and experience, until 1947. She used some of her own family history in *The Innocent Traveller* (1949), which follows the life of a centenarian from the English Midlands to Vancouver. *The Equations of Love: Tuesday and Wednesday, Lilly's Story* (1952) comprises two novellas of situation in a lower-middle-class environment. The theme of escape to a new life among the natural landscapes of British Columbia distinguishes *Swamp Angel* (1954). *Love and Salt Water* (1956) darkly explores aspects of emotional and physical pain.

WILSON, JOHN (1785–1854) Scottish essayist, critic, and poet, was born in Paisley, the eldest son of a wealthy gauze manufacturer, and was educated at the grammar school in Paisley, privately by the Minister of Mearns, and at Glasgow University. He went on in 1803 to Magdalen College, Oxford, where he was known as a prodigious long-jumper and drinker, and won the Newdigate Prize for poetry. With his inheritance from his father, he bought the estate of Elleray in the Lake District, and in 1809 took WORDSWORTH off for a week's fishing. In 1810 he wrote to his Glasgow University contemporary, John Smith (1784–1849), the bookseller, offering a volume of poems. His proposal having been accepted, he wrote again in April 1811 to ask if Smith would buy part of his library, as he was about to marry and was short of ready money. *The Isle of Palms and Other Poems*, largely turgid and obscure, was published in 1812. A second volume, *The City of the Plague*, which Smith wisely declined,

was finally published in 1816 by Archibald Constable (1774–1827), who went bankrupt in the recession of 1826.

In 1815 bad stewardship on the part of an uncle caused the loss of most of Wilson's capital. He gave up Elleray and with his wife joined his mother's extended household in Edinburgh, where they remained for several years. In 1817 he, HOGG, and J. G. Lockhart (1794–1854) took over the editorship of the *Edinburgh Monthly Magazine*. The first issue (in October) of the new journal, renamed *Blackwood's Edinburgh Magazine*, was also nearly the last, as it contained a vicious attack on COLERIDGE and an even more scurrilous assault on HUNT, as well as the notorious 'Chaldee MS', a devastating skit on Edinburgh society. Wilson continued to write for *Blackwood's* for over twenty years, during which he contributed essays and reviews, a series of stories, published in volume form as *Lights and Shadows of Scottish Life* (1822), and from 1822 to 1835, under the name of Christopher North, the witty and satirical dialogues, 'Noctes Ambrosianae'—see *The Noctes Ambrosianae*, ed. J. H. Alexander (1992), a critical selection. In 1820, after what he described as 'a contest of a most savage nature', he was elected by the Tory-dominated Town Council to the vacant chair of Moral Philosophy at Edinburgh University, for which he was hardly qualified academically. With the help of friends, he managed to compile and safely to negotiate his first course of lectures, after which, until his resignation on health grounds in 1851, his ability as a natural communicator stood him in good stead.

WODEHOUSE, (Sir) P(ELHAM) G(RENVILLE) (1881–1975) novelist, short-story writer, and dramatist, was born in Guildford, Surrey, the third son of a Hong Kong magistrate; he was of ancient English families on both sides, and was educated at Dulwich College. He spent two years in Hong Kong as a bank clerk, which he gave up for journalism while at the same time writing boys' school stories, in which features which distinguish his later novels are already apparent. From 1904 onwards he was frequently in New York, where on the day World War I broke out he married the twice-widowed, but still young, Ethel Rowley (*d.* 1984); he adopted her daughter Leonora (1904–1944), whom he addressed in letters as 'Snorkles'. He was made Hon. DLitt at Oxford in 1939, but settled in the USA after World War II, during which he was interned in Europe and while in German hands agreed to broadcast to America, causing much offence in Britain—the texts are in *Performing Flea*, ed. William Townsend (1953). He became a US citizen in 1955, his final rehabilitation in official British circles coming with his being made KBE in 1975.

While unfairly overshadowed by his ability to amuse and entertain, his skill at constructing plots, creating and sustaining characters (and a complete world within which to manipulate them), and producing visual and verbal effects with astonishing economy of language and injections of literary and classical allusions, has never been in doubt. The accusation of repeating himself in his novels can be offset against the subtlety with which he varies the pace and the situations in his many short stories, and though his characters people a semi-mythical upper crust of society, the differences between the American and British ethos are lovingly recorded and satirized. The inane Bertie Wooster and the imperturbable Jeeves, and many of their dicta, have passed into English literary tradition. Only marginally less memorable are Ukridge and Psmith, Aunt Agatha and Lord Emsworth, and the parade of rich characters who hack, bludgeon, finesse, or cleave, as the case may be, their way round the course in his inimitable golfing stories—see numerous omnibus volumes. Wodehouse also wrote, on his own account and with others, over thirty plays and musical comedies. See *Wodehouse on Wodehouse*, new edn 1981 (contains *Bring on the Girls, Performing Flea, Over Seventy*); *Yours, Plum: the Letters of P. G. Wodehouse*, ed. Frances Donaldson, new edn 1992; Barry Phelps, *P. G. Wodehouse: Man and Myth*, 1992 (biography); R. B. D. French, *P. G. Wodehouse*, 1966 (critical study).

WOLFE, THOMAS (1900–38) American novelist and short-story writer, was born in Asheville, North Carolina, the youngest of eight children of a stonecutter, who was a great reader, and his third wife, who first met him when she called on him as a book agent. He was educated at North State (a private school), and at the University of North Carolina, where he did a playwriting course, starred in his own play, *The Return of Black Gavin*, edited the student newspaper, and won a philosophical essay prize. After doing postgraduate study in drama and literature at Harvard, he got a teaching post at Washington Square College, New York University, which apparently enabled him to take time off to write and to travel. Returning from Europe in 1925, he met, as the boat was landing, Aline Bernstein (1881–1955), rich, beautiful, married, and a talented stage and costume designer, who had read one of his plays. He joined her in England in 1926, when he decided to abandon drama for fiction. With her encouragement, financial support, and provision of a place in which to live and work, he completed a 1000-page manuscript in 1928. Maxwell Perkins (1884–1947), Editor-in-Chief at Scribner's, showed interest; with his help it was reorganized and cut by a third, and published as *Look Homeward, Angel* (1929), a lyrical account of youth in which Eugene

Gant is Wolfe himself. With an advance on a second novel, Wolfe gave up his teaching post and, his finances boosted also by a Guggenheim grant, went to Europe, where he was pursued by cables and letters from Mrs Bernstein, threatening suicide—see *My Other Loneliness: Letters of Thomas Wolfe and Aline Bernstein*, ed. Suzanne Stutman (1983).

In due course he delivered an enormous manuscript, 'The October Fair', of which a reworked part, taking Eugene's life up to his meeting with Esther Jack/Aline Bernstein, was published as *Of Time and the River* (1935). A continuation of the story was shelved when Aline threatened legal action—Wolfe was prone to lawsuits, the most damaging of which was brought against him in 1936 for alleged libel in a story in *From Death to Morning* (1935), which was settled out of court. A breach with Scribner's (though he appointed Perkins administrator of his estate) led in May 1938 to his depositing with the firm of Harper, who had offered an advance of $10,000 unconditionally, what was by one account an eight-foot-high pile of manuscript. In July, after a car trip through the National Parks, he contracted pneumonia in Seattle. On 12 September he was admitted to the Johns Hopkins Hospital in Baltimore, where he died three days later, an operation having revealed incurable miliary tuberculosis of the brain. The manuscript, which contained several versions of many incidents, was made into two novels, *The Web and the Rock* (1939) and *You Can't Go Home Again* (1940), in which Gant has become George Webber, but Esther retains her name and her identity—see Leslie Field, *Thomas Wolfe and His Editors: Establishing a True Text for the Posthumous Publications* (1987). Further portions were included in a collection of short pieces, *The Hills Beyond* (1941)—see also *The Complete Short Stories of Thomas Wolfe*, ed. Francis E. Skipp (1987). Wolfe was a huge man, whose voracious appetite for experience reflected the vast sweeps of language with which he evoked his personal vision of his times. See *The Autobiography of an American Novelist*, ed. Leslie Field, 1983; David Herbert Donald, *Look Homeward: a Life of Thomas Wolfe*, 1987; John Lane Idol, *A Thomas Wolfe Companion*, 1987.

WOLFE, TOM (THOMAS KENNERLY WOLFE, JR) (*b.* 1931) American novelist and journalist, was born in Richmond, Virginia, edited his local high school newspaper, read English (and pitched for the baseball team) at Washington and Lee University, and then did five years' postgraduate study in American studies at Yale. He went into journalism, working on the *Washington Post* and then the New York *Herald-Tribune*, for whose weekend magazine, and later in *Esquire* and *Harper's Bazaar*, he developed his version of the 'New Journalism', investing hard fact with personal emotion, expressed in spectacular graphic style. *The Kandy-Ko-lored Tangerine-Flake Streamline Baby* (1965), with his own drawings, was the first of his collections of apocalyptic pieces—subsequent ones have had equally pyschedelic titles. *The Electric Kool-Aid Acid Test* (1968) is a weird travelogue. *The Right Stuff* (1980) is nearer the non-fiction novel in its depiction of the world of the US astronaut. *The Bonfire of Vanities* (1987), his first novel proper, is a richly-textured romp of New York City. His account of how he prospected, researched, and wrote it is in his controversial article in *Harper's* (1989), 'Stalking the Billion-Footed Beast: a Literary Manifesto for the New Social Novel'. See William McKeen, *Tom Wolfe*, 1995 (critical study).

WOLFRAM VON ESCHENBACH (*fl. c.*1195–1225) German poet, was a roving knight who alludes to himself as Bavarian, and probably operated over a broad area with Eschenbach at its centre. The 25,000 lines of *Parzival* (tr. A. T. Hatto, 1980) comprise a retelling, with an ending, of the 'Perceval' of CHRÉTIEN, in which the Grail is now a stone. The unfinished *Willehalm* (tr. Marion E. Gibbs and Sidney M. Johnson, 1984), also in rhyming couplets, describes two great battles between the Franks and the Saracens, and the outcomes of the carnage. He also left some lyric verse and a fragment of 'Titurel', an elaboration of the love story of two of the characters in *Parzival*.

WOLLSTONECRAFT, MARY (1759–97) British prose writer and journalist, was born in Spitalfields, London, the second of seven children of the son of a prosperous handkerchief weaver and his Irish wife, whom he had met when he was an apprentice in the family business. In 1765 the family moved into the country, then to Beverley, Yorkshire, where Wollstonecraft attended a local day school, and in 1774 back to the London suburb of Hoxton, where she received an education from neighbours, in whose house she met Fanny Blood (1757–85). In 1781 she gave up her job as a lady's maid to look after her mother, after whose death she lived for a time with the Bloods; she left them to help her sister Eliza escape (leaving her baby behind) from an unacceptable marriage. She ran a school (with her sisters and Fanny) in Islington and then in Newington Green, where she found congenial the company and outlook of the local Rational Dissenters (Unitarians). Fanny went to Lisbon in 1785 to marry; Wollstonecraft sailed to see her later in the year and found her dying in childbirth. The school failed in her absence, and she gladly accepted an advance of £10 from the radical publisher, Joseph Johnson (1738–1809), to write a book.

Thoughts on the Education of Daughters (1787), like all her writings done at great speed, established the facts about female employment. She became governess to the expanding family of the Irish peer Robert King (1754–99), Earl of Kingsborough, and his wife Caroline, but was dismissed. She exacted retribution in *Mary* (1788), a realistic novel ('I have drawn from Nature'), in which romantic love and feeling as a guide to behaviour are emphasized but adultery is never (quite) condoned, and the Countess of Kingsborough is recognizable as the unhappy materfamilias. Johnson now set her up in a house of her own and paid her keep in return for her undertaking to work for him, in particular as an editor of and contributor to the first British literary and scientific journal for the general public, the monthly *Analytical Review*, which consisted almost entirely of book reviews. *A Vindication of the Rights of Men* (1790), published anonymously, was (in spite of its title) the first refutation of BURKE's *Reflections on the Revolution in France* to be published; a second edition carried her name, which now became well known. In November 1791, at one of Johnson's dinner parties, she met GODWIN, who had not read any of her works. Also present was PAINE, who may have encouraged her to embark on *A Vindication of the Rights of Woman: with Strictures on Political and Moral Subjects* (1792), a crusading journalistic work whose passion outweighs its lack of structure.

In November 1792, when the artist and critic, Henry Fuseli (1741–1825), and his new wife, an artists' model, both rejected her offer to make up a *ménage à trois*, she went to Paris. Shortly after the declaration of hostilities between the French Republic and Britain, she met and was seduced by Gilbert Imlay (*c.*1754–1826), an American soldier and adventurer, and author of *Topographical Description of the Western Territory of North America* (1792); their child, Fanny Imlay (1794–1816), was born in Le Havre. After publishing *An Historical and Moral View of the Origin and Progress of the French Revolution* (1794), Wollstonecraft returned to London, attempted suicide by swallowing (not quite enough) laudanum, and then agreed to go to Scandinavia, with baby and a maid, to attend to Imlay's business interests. In October 1795, having discovered that Imlay had another girlfriend, she jumped off Putney Bridge into the Thames, but was fished out and revived.

Six months later she called on Godwin uninvited to seek professional help; in due course they became lovers. Their marriage in March 1797 was against the principles of both, but within a few days they settled into domesticity in a new house he had bought for them, with separate rooms in which to work. She died six months later, after giving birth to MARY SHELLEY. See *The Works of Mary Wollstonecraft*, ed. Janet Todd and Marilyn Butler, 7 vols 1989; *Selected Letters*, ed. Betty Bennett, 1995; *Political Writings*, ed. Janet

Todd, 1994; Claire Tomalin, *The Life and Death of Mary Wollstonecraft*, 2nd rev. edn 1992; Jane Moore, *Mary Wollstonecraft* 1996 (critical introduction).

WOOD (or **À WOOD**), **ANTHONY** see AUBREY.

WOOD, ELLEN (MRS HENRY WOOD) (1814–87), née Price, novelist, was born in Worcester, the eldest daughter of a glove manufacturer, but lived as a child with her maternal grandmother. Her retentive memory is legendary, and she is said to have been able at 13 to repeat most of SHAKE-SPEARE's plays by heart. In 1836 she married Henry Wood (*d.* 1866), a banker and shipping magnate, with whom she spent much of the next twenty years in France. *Danesbury House* (1860), written in a month, won a prize of £100 from the Scottish Temperance Society for a novel extolling its principles. She had suffered from curvature of the spine from childhood; paralysis of the hands, from which she never fully recovered, set in while she was writing *East Lynne* (1861). This novel of both sensation and situation is the one for which she is remembered; even if the immortal words, 'Dead—and never called me Mother', belong not to the book itself but to one of the many stage adaptations which immediately followed (for which she received nothing). *Mrs Halliburton's Troubles* (1862) and *The Channings* (1862) have less freshness and more sententious gloom. In 1867 she followed the example of BRADDON, and became Editor and proprietor of *Argosy*, in which much of her subsequent work first appeared. It was not until 1879 that she admitted to the authorship of the 'Johnny Ludlow' stories (based, in the manner of GASKELL, on the Worcester of her youth), which began to appear in 1868 and were published in two series of three volumes (1874–80). For all its melodrama and implausible plotting, *East Lynne* is a contribution to the regional novel of realism, and in this and subsequent novels Wood colourfully depicted a stratum of society in which legal machinations feature prominently.

WOODCOCK, GEORGE (1912–95) Canadian poet, critic, editor, and prose writer, was born in Winnipeg of unsuccessful British immigrant parents, who returned to Shropshire, England, a few months after his birth. He went to Sir William Borlase's School, Marlow. Unable to take up a half-fees scholarship at Oxford, until World War II, during which he was a conscientious objector and edited a radical literary journal, *Now*, he worked in London as a clerk for the Great Western Railway; expressed anarchist tendencies; infiltrated the literary coterie of ROY CAMPBELL, ORWELL, READ, and DYLAN THOMAS; and wrote youthful verse which reflected

SQUIRE's 'Georgian-orientated anthologies', a collection of which he published as *The White Island* (1940). After the war he became a freelance writer, returning to Canada in 1949, the year in which for reasons inherent in 'Black Rose' (1976) he largely gave up writing poetry until the 1960s, when he published *Selected Poems* (1967). From 1956 to 1963 he taught English at the University of British Columbia, where in 1959 he founded (and edited until 1977) *Canadian Literature* as a forum for critical discussion. He is the author of travel books of a discursive but informative nature on his journeys to Asia and South America, as well as of historical and sociological works on Canada. He wrote critical and biographical studies of GODWIN (1946), BEHN (1948), WILDE (1950), ORWELL—*The Crystal Spirit* (1966), which won the Governor General's Award—MACLENNAN (1969), RICHLER (1970), ALDOUS HUXLEY (1972), and READ (1972), as well as, among more general works, *Odysseus Ever Returning: Essays on Canadian Writers and Writing* (1970), *Northern Spring: the Flowering of Canadian Literature* (1987), and *George Woodcock's Introduction to Canadian Fiction* and . . . *to Canadian Poetry* (both 1994). *Collected Poems* (1983), which is divided into ten wide-ranging thematic groups, with an additional section of translations, he described as 'nearer to an autobiography than it is to an ordinary collection of verse'. *Taking It To the Letter* (1981) is a selection of correspondence which illustrates the relationship between editor and author. *Letter to the Past* (1983) is an autobiography—see also *Walking through the Valley: an Autobiography* (1994).

WOODFORDE, (Rev.) JAMES (1740–1803) British diarist, was born in Ansford, Somerset, the son of the rector of the parish, and was educated at Winchester College and New College, Oxford, being elected a Fellow in 1761, and ordained in 1764. He held several curacies before returning to New College in 1773 as Sub-Warden. He was appointed an assistant proctor (university disciplinary officer) the following year, at the end of which he was elected rector of a college living, Weston Longeville, Norfolk, though he continued to live in college until 1776. Thereafter he remained at Weston Longeville parsonage until his death. He never married, though in 1774 he proposed to Betsy White, of Shepton Mallet. 'She was not averse to it at all,' he records, but shortly afterwards she jilted him for 'a Gentleman of Devonshire by name Webster, a man reputed to have 500 P^d per annum, 10,000 P^d in the Stocks, beside expectation from his Father'. His niece Nancy Woodforde (1757–1830) came to live with him in 1779, and stayed for the rest of his life. The inventory of his will shows assets of £437, against debts of £250. His diary runs from his undergraduate days to ten weeks before his death.

It is precisely because he was an obscure country parson whose life was outwardly tranquil that it is such a treasure house of local and social lore, and of the minutest detail of the daily routine, gargantuan meals, and household and other expenses of a man in his position, while objectively illustrating the national character during an almost continuous state of international crisis. It is equally revealing about individual characteristics: 'Had but an indifferent night of Sleep, Mrs Davie and Nancy made me up an Apple Pye Bed . . .' (3 February 1781). See *The Diary of a Country Parson 1758–1802*, ed. John Beresford, 1981; Roy Winstanley, *Parson Woodforde: the Life and Times of a Country Diarist*, 1996.

WOOLF, LEONARD (1880–1969) British novelist, prose writer, and publisher, the husband of VIRGINIA WOOLF, was born in Kensington, London, the second son of Reform Jewish parents. His father, Sidney Woolf QC, died in 1892 leaving a widow and nine children. The boy won scholarships to St Paul's School and Trinity College, Cambridge, after which he joined the Colonial Service. He was posted to Ceylon in 1904, and in 1908 was appointed administrative and judicial officer of the region of Hambantota—his novel *The Village in the Jungle* (1913) is an understanding and admirably evoked representation of the local experience. In 1912 his marriage and doubts about the ethics of imperialism led to his resignation from the service. He became a socialist and a member of the Fabian Society in 1913, and, being unfit for war service, threw himself energetically into studying and writing about international affairs, besides establishing and masterminding the activities of the Hogarth Press—see J. H. Willis Jr, *Leonard and Virginia Woolf as Publishers: the Hogarth Press 1917–1941* (1992). He was joint Editor of the *Political Quarterly* 1931–59 and Literary Editor of the *Nation* 1923–30. Among his political works are *The Intelligent Man's Way to Prevent War* (1933) and *Barbarians at the Gate* (1939). His memorial, however, especially now that the Hogarth Press has been several times subsumed, is his five-volume autobiography: *Sowing* (1960), *Growing* (1961), *Beginning Again* (1964), *Downhill All the Way* (1967), and *The Journey Not the Arrival Matters* (1969). Elegantly written, wryly humorous, and brimming with acutely observed portraits of literary figures of his time, it was reissued in two volumes, ed. Quentin Bell, in 1980.

WOOLF, (ADELINE) VIRGINIA (1882–1941) novelist and critic, was born in London, the third child of (Sir) Leslie Stephen (1832–1904), Editor of the *Dictionary of National Biography*, and his second wife, who died in 1895. She was educated at home by her parents and tutors. On her father's death, she, her elder sister Vanessa (1879–1961),

later married to the art critic, Clive Bell (1881–1962), and her two brothers, set up house in Gordon Square WC1, which became the centre of the Bloomsbury Group, an informal association of intellectuals wishing to free art and society from Victorian restrictions—see *The Bloomsbury Group: a Collection of Memoirs and Commentary*, ed. S. P. Rosenbaum (1994). In 1905 she began to contribute reviews and articles to *The Times Literary Supplement* and other journals, while teaching evening classes of working men and women at Morley College. She married LEONARD WOOLF in 1912. They moved to Hogarth House, Richmond, in 1915, the year of her most violent recurrence of mental instability and of the publication of her first novel, *The Voyage Out*, conventional in pattern, which she had written between 1906 and 1913. In 1917 the couple bought a hand press, on which they printed, as the first publication of the Hogarth Press, *Two Stories*—'The Mark on the Wall' by Virginia and 'Three Jews' by Leonard. *Night and Day* (1919), written mainly as a recuperative exercise, was deliberately a less intense novel than her first. *Jacob's Room* (1922), in which she first demonstrated her distinctive impressionistic technique, was published by the Hogarth Press, which had now become a commercial operation. In 1924 the firm, and the Woolfs, moved to Tavistock Square, Bloomsbury—see Richard Kennedy, *A Boy at the Hogarth Press* (1972) for a first-hand, illustrated account of working there.

In her essays, 'Modern Fiction' (1919) and 'Mr Bennett and Mrs Brown' (1924), Woolf propounded a new novelistic genre which became the literary element of Modernism and her own medium of expression. She first used the stream-of-consciousness technique (pioneered by JOYCE and DOROTHY RICHARDSON) in *Mrs Dalloway* (1925). In *To the Lighthouse* (1927), her exploration of various themes through psychological insight into the minds of her characters is at its most assured and poetic. With *The Waves* (1931), *The Years* (1937), and *Between the Acts* (1941) she took innovation and experiment even further. Her slighter novels, *Orlando: a Biography* (1928), a literary fantasy whose bisexual protagonist is SACKVILLE-WEST—see Suzanne Raitt, *Vita and Virginia: the Work and Friendship of V. Sackville-West and Virginia Woolf* (1993)—, and *Flush: a Biography* (1933), about E. B. BROWNING's dog, were written in between times as a means of restoring her mental equilibrium. Shortly after finishing *Between the Acts* (1941), originally called 'Pointz Hall', she drowned herself in the river by their country cottage, Monk's House, Sussex, fearful that her mental condition was irreversible.

A Room of One's Own (1929) is a trenchant and witty plea for the recognition of women writers. Two volumes of her enlightening literary criticism were published in her lifetime,

The Common Reader, First Series (1925), and *Second Series* (1932). See *Collected Essays*, ed. Leonard Woolf, 1966–67; *Essays*, 4 vols, ed. Andrew McNeillie, 1986–94; *Selected Essays*, 2 vols, ed. Rachel Bowlby, 1992–93; *Selected Short Stories*, ed. Sandra Kemp, 1993; *A Moment's Liberty: the Shorter Diary of Virginia Woolf*, ed. Anne Olivier Bell, 1990; *Congenial Spirits: the Selected Letters of Virginia Woolf*, ed. Joanne Trautmann Banks, new edn 1993; Quentin Bell, *Virginia Woolf: a Biography*, new edn 1996 of 2nd rev. edn 1990; Lyndall Gordon, *Virginia Woolf: a Writer's Life*, new edn 1986; James King, *Virginia Woolf*, new edn 1995 (biography); Hermione Lee, *Virginia Woolf: a Biography*, 1996; Joan Bennett, *Virginia Woolf: Her Art as a Novelist*, rev. edn 1975; Hermione Lee, *The Novels of Virginia Woolf*, 1977.

WORDSWORTH, DOROTHY see WORDSWORTH.

WORDSWORTH, WILLIAM (1770–1850) British poet, was born in Cockermouth, Cumberland, the second son of the business manager to the local magnate. After his mother's death in 1778 (his father died in 1783) he was sent to Hawkshead Grammar School, boarding with a family, where he indulged freely in the outdoor life and began to write poetry. In 1787 he went as a sizar to St John's College, Cambridge. His lack of enthusiasm for a career as an academic or in the Church gave him a detached attitude to his studies; he was more interested in walking tours in France, Switzerland, Germany, and Wales. After graduating as BA (without honours) in 1791, he spent several months absorbing the atmosphere of London before being attracted to France in the throes of the Revolution. There he was converted to republicanism and had a love affair with Annette Vallon (1766–1841), but had to return to London in December 1792 because his money had run out and his guardians would not advance him any more. A few days later his daughter Caroline was born in Orleans. In 1793 he published, in separate volumes, *An Evening Walk*, addressed to 'a Young Lady'—his sister Dorothy (1771–1855)—and *Descriptive Sketches Taken During a Pedestrian Tour in the Alps*, regarded by the critics as showing promise and by COLERIDGE, who heard them read aloud at a literary club meeting, as the work of 'an original poetic genius'.

For two years he moved uneasily about England, staying with friends, disturbed by his separation from France, by the excesses of the Revolution, and by the declaration of war between the two countries. His mental state and immediate future were saved by a legacy from a 21-year-old friend with the instructions that it should be used to further his poetic career. He and Dorothy were now offered a rent-free cottage in Racedown, Dorset. In 1797 they rented Alfoxden House, near Stowey, to be near Coleridge, whom Wordsworth had met in 1795. Free from worries, inspired by the proximity to nature, and encouraged by Coleridge, he was able both to think about poetry and to write it. In 1798 he and Coleridge published jointly, but anonymously, *Lyrical Ballads, with a Few Other Poems*, of which Wordsworth wrote in a short 'Advertisement' that 'the majority . . . are to be regarded as experiments' in using conversational language in poetry. In the second, enlarged edition, published in January 1801, this had grown into a preface in which he justifies the employment in poetry of 'language really used by men' and discusses the nature of poetry and the creative process by which it is produced—in a third edition (1802) he extended his arguments about metre and poetic diction and developed his definition of a poet as 'a man speaking to men'.

On their return in 1799 from a stay in Germany, the Wordsworths settled in the Lake District parish of Grasmere, at Dove Cottage (to 1808)—see Dorothy Wordsworth, *The Grasmere Journals*, ed. Pamela Woof (1993)—, Allan Bank (to 1811), and the Rectory (to 1813). In August 1802 they spent four weeks with Annette and Caroline in Calais—Caroline married in 1816 and had three daughters, the eldest of whom was called Dorothée. In October 1802 Wordsworth married Mary Hutchinson, an old friend, who moved into the cottage with her new husband and sister-in-law—they had five children, of whom two died in 1812, and a third, the poet's beloved eldest daughter, Dora, in 1847. *Poems in Two Volumes* (1807), the culmination of Wordsworth's poetic development and of five fruitful years of writing, included 'Ode on Intimations of Immortality', 'Resolution and Independence' (originally called 'The Leech-Gatherer'), 'Ode to Duty', 'Sonnets Dedicated to Liberty and Order', and some good poems inspired by a tour of Scotland in 1803 with Dorothy, during which they met WALTER SCOTT—see Dorothy Wordsworth, *Recollections of a Tour Made in Scotland*, ed. J. C. Shairp (1874; new edn 1974).

In 1813 the family moved to Rydal Mount, and from then until 1842 Wordsworth held the post of Distributor of Stamps for Westmoreland, which involved the collection of Inland Revenue duties. He was appointed Poet Laureate in 1843. At his death, his creative and spiritual autobiography, the most sustained and original feat of English poetry since MILTON's *Paradise Lost*, remained unpublished. *The Prelude* (1850), of which he wrote two 'parts' before the end of 1799, and a further 11 books between 1801 and 1805, was originally intended as an introduction to 'The Recluse', an unfinished philosophical poem, part of which was published in 1814 as *The Excursion*. He revised it at intervals until 1839; the final version, in 14 books, was published by his executors three months after his death. The title was given to it by his widow, who died in 1859 at the age of 89. Dorothy, who had lived with them throughout their marriage but whose mind had given way in 1835, survived her brother by five years. Her *Journals* (first published in 1897) are a valuable source of information about the poet's creative instincts and personality, as well as being excellent literary records of social life, people, and places. See *Poetical Works*, ed. Thomas Hutchinson, rev. Ernest de Selincourt, new edn 1969; *Poetical Works*, ed. Paul D. Sheats, 1978; *Selected Poems*, ed. Sandra Anstey, 1990; [*Selected Verse*] ed. Stephen Gill and Duncan Wu, 1994; *The Prelude: Four Texts (1798, 1799, 1805, 1850)*, ed. Jonathon Wordsworth, rev. edn 1995; *The Letters*, ed. Alan G. Hill, 1984; *The Letters of Dorothy Wordsworth*, ed. Alan G. Hill, new edn 1991; *The Journals of Dorothy Wordsworth*, ed. Paul Hamilton, 1992; Stephen Gill, *William Wordsworth: a Life*, new edn 1990; Robert Gittings and Jo Manton, *Dorothy Wordsworth*, new edn 1988 (biography); John Purkis, *A Preface to Wordsworth*, rev. edn 1986; Jonathon Wordsworth, *William Wordsworth: the Borders of Vision*, rev. edn 1984 (critical study).

WOUK, HERMAN (*b.* 1915) American novelist and dramatist, was born of Jewish parentage in New York, where he was educated at Townsend Harris Hall and Columbia University, after which he was for six years a radio scriptwriter, mainly for the comedian Fred Allen (1894–1956). During World War II he served in the US Navy, spending three years at sea in the Pacific, latterly as executive officer in a destroyer-minesweeper. *Aurora Dawn* (1947), his first novel, is a satire centring on the advertising business; *The City Boy* (1948) is a story of youth. *The Caine Mutiny* (1951), for which he won the Pulitzer Prize, is one of the most interesting novels of World War II in that the action at sea is the means by which the ultimate climax is approached, not an end in itself. In *Marjorie Morningstar* (1955), a study of the moral development of an ambitious Jewess, traditional values are somehow upheld yet again. *The Winds of War* (1971) and its sequel, *War and Remembrance* (1978), follow the fortunes of a naval officer and his family through World War II. *Inside, Outside* (1986), which depicts a different kind of career progress, is funny and very Jewish. *The Hope* (1993) is a novelized account of the first twenty years of the State of Israel; *The Glory* (1994) covers the next twenty. His plays include *The Traitor* (1949), a study of atomic espionage, and *The Caine Mutiny Court-Martial* (1954). He has also written *This Is My God: the Jewish Way of Life* (rev. edn 1973).

WRIGHT, DAVID (1920–94) British poet, was born in Johannesburg, South Africa, with which he maintained cultural links. Deaf from the age of seven after scarlet fever, he was educated in England at Northampton School for the Deaf, from which he went on to Oriel College, Oxford. In 1942 he took a flat in London, joined the staff of the *Sunday Times*, and became a member of the bohemian drinking set to which ROY CAMPBELL, PATRICK KAVANAGH, and DYLAN THOMAS belonged. In 1948 he went into isolation in Cornwall; after his return he published *Poems* (1949). 'Deafness can be a stimulus. I do not notice more but I notice differently. . . . Like an eccentrically-sited camera taking angle-shots that distort but may often reveal otherwise masked lineaments of truth, the deaf person watches from the unexpected and unguarded quarter.' While some of his verse reflected his attitude to his disability, as in *Monologue of a Deaf Man* (1958), he was also a sensitive poet of romantic, and more mundane, places, and of animals and birds, and a composer of conversational epistles and poetic journals. *Elegies* (1990) is a collection of graceful and rhythmical poems for old friends. In 1959 he founded and until its demise in 1962 edited the influential underground literary and arts journal *X* with his friend, the painter Patrick Swift, whose widow he married in 1987, after the death in 1985 of his first wife—he compiled *An Anthology from X* (1988). He edited several anthologies of prose and verse, and published prose translations of *Beowulf* (1957) and CHAUCER's *The Canterbury Tales* (1964), of which he did a further translation, in verse, with introduction and notes (1985). See *Selected Poems*, 1988; *Deafness: an Autobiography*, new edn 1994 of 2nd rev. edn 1990.

WRIGHT, JAMES (ARLINGTON) (1927–80) American poet and translator, was born just before the Depression in Martins Ferry, Ohio, 'where one slave / To Hazel-Atlas Glass became my father. / He tried to teach me kindness' ('At the Executed Murderer's Grave'). He went to Martins Ferry Senior High School, where an imaginative teacher rescued him from a vocational course and introduced him to the Russian writers and to classical Latin poetry—HORACE was an especial influence on him. He then did two years army service, part of it with the occupational forces in Japan. In 1948, on the GI Bill, he was accepted by Kenyon College (according to him the only one which did not reject his application); he was the first member of his family to go to college. There he was taught by RANSOM and won the Robert FROST Poetry Prize. In 1952 he graduated, had his first poem published, was awarded a Fulbright scholarship at the University of Vienna, and got married—there were two sons, born in 1953 and 1958. He then did a postgraduate English course at the University of Washington, Seattle, where his creative-writing tutor was ROETHKE; he subsequently wrote a PhD thesis on DICKENS. He was appointed to the English Department of the University of Minnesota in 1957, and later taught at Macalester College (1963–65) and Hunter College, New York (1966–80).

His first two collections of verse were *The Green Wall* (1957) and *Saint Judas* (1959). There followed an unsettled period, compounded of job dissatisfaction, marriage break-up (there was divorce in 1962), and artistic frustration. He received encouragement from the poet Robert Bly (*b.* 1926), with whom he translated (1962) the Austrian surrealist poet Georg Trakl (1887–1914) and (1968) NERUDA—see also *Neruda and Vallejo: Selected Poems* (1993). The collection that finally emerged, *The Branch Will Not Break* (1963), was a breakthrough in terms of form, vision, and originality. In 1967 he married (Edith) Anne Runk, a nursery school educationist whose support and inspiration are celebrated especially in *Two Citizens* (1974)—*The Summers of James and Annie Wright* (1980) comprises 11 prose pieces of which she wrote four.

Collected Poems (1971), which won the Pulitzer Prize, comprised, in addition to 33 new poems, most of *The Green Wall*, and all of his other three collections. The latest of these was *Shall We Gather at the River* (1968), which was almost finished when he met Anne and includes the 'Jenny Poems'—Jenny has been identified variously as an Ohio prostitute and a composite fictional muse. Having already translated the poetry of HESSE (1970), he exorcized some of the conflict with his elder son Franz by translating with him Hesse's philosophical work in verse and prose, *Wandering* (1972). The death of his mother in 1974 a year after that of his father, who had dropped out of school to be a wage earner and had worked, except when laid off, for fifty years for the glass factory, precipitated a nervous breakdown. He and his wife visited Europe, especially Italy, several times in the 1970s. Wright died of cancer of the tongue. The last volume of poetry published during his lifetime was *To a Blossoming Pear* (1977), less bitter and more subtle than earlier collections, and marking a more ambivalent and optimistic attitude to the country of his birth. *This Journey* (1982) was finished in manuscript just before he entered hospital for the last time. See *Above the River: the Complete Poems*, new edn 1992; *Collected Prose*, ed. Anne Wright, 1983; David C. Dougherty, *James Wright*, foreword by Anne Wright, 1987 (biographical/critical study).

WRIGHT, JUDITH (*b.* 1915) Australian poet and critic, was born in Armidale, New South Wales, the eldest child of a pastoralist whose family had arrived in Australia in 1828 and established the property of Dalwood in the Hunter Valley. She studied by correspondence and, after her mother's death when she was 12, boarded at New England Girls' School, Armidale, where an English teacher encouraged her poetry writing. After her first year at Sydney University she abandoned the formal course in English to read more eclectically. At 22, she and a cousin went on a series of walking tours in Austria, Germany, Hungary, and Scotland, from which a Jacobite ancestor had escaped to France after the '45 Rebellion (the family subsequently settled in Cornwall, changing its name from the clan appellation of MacGregor, which had been proscribed, to Wright). On her return she lived in Sydney, subsidizing her writing, much of which she immediately destroyed, by taking temporary secretarial jobs. During World War II she went back for a time to her father's property of Wallamumbi to help out. From this experience, which encouraged her to recapture the circumstances of her childhood, she wrote the metaphysical 'The Moving Image', and other notable poems whose starting point is the land or its people, such as 'South of My Days', 'For New England', 'Northern River', and 'Bullocky'. During the years 1944–46 she worked as a clerk for the Australian Universities Commission, Brisbane, and in the evenings assisted in editing *Meanjin Papers*, whose Editor, Clem Christesen (*b.* 1911), having taken the journal to Melbourne, published her first book of poetry, *The Moving Image* (1946). She was a statistical officer at the University of Queensland from 1946 to 1949, during which time she met and married the novelist, dramatist, and philosopher, Jack McKinney (1891–1966). Latterly they lived on the plateau of Mount Tamborine.

She has said: 'I started off being called a "nature poet", a silly classification because after all you are a person, not a piece of nature. Anything I have ever written has had its human meaning even if it started from the natural.' Supporters of the 'nature poet' theory, especially male readers, were startled by poems in *Woman to Man* (1949), such as 'Woman to Man', 'Woman's Song', and 'Woman to Child', in which the love act, reproduction, and the physical process of birth are frankly explored and precisely realized. To her, 'Language is the creative element in man, and poets work in this material that is almost impossible to work in because every word you use is a poem in itself.' This preoccupation, and the search for its satisfactory resolution, also inform poems celebrating her love for her husband and for her daughter, Meredith, poems on the environment (as an active conservationist she has tramped through the corridors of power as well as along the routes of protest marches), and the fine explorer poem, 'Two Sides of a Story'; they are evident, too, in the jolly rhymes and vividly expressed observations of *Birds* (1962), written for Meredith.

She has published a book of short stories, *The Nature of Love* (1966), and several novels for children. In *The Generations of Men* (1959) she traces the lives, times, and struggles with the land of her grandparents, May and Albert Wright, whose diaries she also used as the basis of *The Cry for the Dead* (1981), an indictment of those who destroyed the land and oppressed the Aborigines. Her critical works include the significant *Preoccupations in Australian Poetry* (1965); *Because I Was Invited* (1975), essays and reviews; and studies of individual Australian poets. She is Hon. DLitt of five Australian universities, and was awarded the Queen's Gold Medal for Poetry in 1992, the first Australian to be so honoured. See *Collected Poems 1942–1985*, 1994; Shirley Walker, *Flame and Shadow: a Study of Judith Wright's Poetry*, new edn 1996; Jennifer Strauss, *Judith Wright*, 1996 (critical study).

WRIGHT, RICHARD (1908–60) American novelist, was born near Natchez, Mississippi, the elder son of an illiterate sharecropper who deserted his schoolteacher wife in 1914. His early years were spent in misery and poverty, travelling round to relatives, his mother becoming partially paralysed by a stroke. After five years at the Smith-Robinson Public School, Jackson, and in reaction against his family's religious convictions, he went to Memphis, and from there to the black ghetto of Chicago. While doing a variety of menial jobs he 'was seriously contemplating a literary career', which took on more of a reality when in 1932 he joined the John Reed Club for the use of art for revolutionary ends. He had poems, of which 'I Have Seen Black Hands' (1934) is typical, and stories published in left-wing journals. He joined the Communist Party in 1933. Now a central figure in the South Side Writers' Group and having had his story 'Big Boy Leaves Home' (1933) published in a national anthology, he split with the Chicago branch of the party and went to New York, where he became Harlem Editor of the *Daily Worker*. *Uncle Tom's Children: Four Novellas* (1938), his first published book, was reissued later that year with a fifth story and an autobiographical essay, 'The Ethics of Living Jim Crow'.

Native Son (1940), an explosive novel about a young criminal which explores the background to his consciousness, brought Wright to the notice of the literary establishment and the reading public. The text was altered in proof in deference to the Book-of-the-Month Club—a critical version is in *Works, Vol. 1*, ed. Arnold Rampersad (1991). After a very brief marriage to a dancer, he achieved personal stability through his second wife, also white, whom he married in 1941, and by whom he had two daughters. *Black Boy* (1945) is his autobiography to 1927: a second part, also written in 1943–44, was published posthumously as *American Hunger* (1977). From 1947 his home base was in France, where unlike BALDWIN, whose mentor he was and who lived there to try and come to terms with his own identity, he was drawn into French intellectual life. He wrote three more novels, of which *The Outsider* (1953) is an existentialist study of misery and freedom in an American context. While some questions have been aired about the suddenness of his death in Paris, it is generally accepted that it was due to a heart attack. Of several other posthumously published works, *Rite of Passage*, afterword by Arnold Rampersad (1994), written in 1945 while Wright was waiting for *Black Boy* to be published, is a long story about a gang of black teenagers living underground in Harlem. See Michel Fabre, *The Unfinished Quest of Richard Wright*, tr. Isabel Barzun, 2nd edn 1993 (critical biography); Robert Felgar, *Richard Wright*, 1980 (biographical/critical study).

WRIGHTSON, PATRICIA (*b.* 1921), née Furlonger, Australian children's novelist, was born in Lismore, New South Wales, and was educated through the State Correspondence School and at St Catherine's College, Stanthorpe. She married in 1943 (divorced 1953). She was Secretary and Administrator of the Bonalbo District Hospital 1946–60, and of the Sydney District Nursing Association 1960–64. She was Assistant Editor (1964–70) and Editor (1970–75) of the New South Wales Department of Education's *School Magazine*. In the five children's novels she published between 1955 and 1965, she tackled a range of themes including growing up, the exercise of responsibility, and the changing relationship of the land and its two peoples. She developed the first two of these in a highly imaginative and novel way in *'I Own the Racecourse!'* (1968). The third recurs in *An Older Kind of Magic* (1972) and subsequent novels in which she has used Aboriginal lore in an increasingly ambitious fashion, culminating in the trilogy, *The Book of Wirrun* (1983). She won the international Hans Christian ANDERSEN Award in 1986, and was made OBE in 1978.

WYATT, (Sir) THOMAS (1503–42) English poet, was born at Allington Castle, Kent, the son of a councillor of Henry VII, and was educated at St John's College, Cambridge. He was appointed Clerk of the King's Jewels in 1529, and served Henry VIII in various capacities abroad. He was imprisoned three times: in 1534 for brawling, in 1536 on a charge of adultery with Anne Boleyn (he was knighted on his release in 1537), and in 1541 for treason, of which he was acquitted. He introduced into English from Italian, and passed on to SURREY, the sonnet form of PETRARCH, which for all his irregularities of metre he often did better than his protégé (cf. 'The long love that in my thought doth harbour . . .' with Surrey's version of the Petrarchan original, 'Love that reigneth and liveth within my thought . . .'). For all his travel abroad, his songs and lyrics are in the English tradition. His technique is best seen in 'My lute awake . . .'; 'They flee from me . . .'; 'What rage is this . . .'; 'Perdie, I said it not . . .'; and 'In eternum . . .' and 'Blame not my lute . . .', where he effectively uses a simple refrain at the end of each stanza gradually to build up to a final climax. The general tone of his verse, however, is gloomy and resentful. None of it was published in his lifetime, but a volume of translations of 'certayn psalmes chosen out of the psalter of David' was printed in 1549. Of the attributed poems in 'Tottel's Miscellany' (1557), 97 are by Wyatt, as against 40 by Surrey. See *Complete Poems*, ed. R. A. Rebholz, 1981; *Selected Poems*, ed. Hardiman Scott, 1996; Kenneth Muir, *The Life and Letters of Sir Thomas Wyatt*, 1963.

WYCHERLEY, WILLIAM (1640–1716) English dramatist and poet, was born in Clive, Shropshire, the son of a country gentleman who educated him at home and when he was 15 sent him to France for five years. On his return he was briefly attached to The Queen's College, Oxford, which he left to study law in London. His poem *Hero and Leander in Burlesque* was published anonymously in 1669. The comedy *Love in a Wood, or, St James's Park* was performed in 1671, and led to a fortuitous meeting, described with relish by John Dennis (1657–1734), the dramatist and critic. As the King's mistress, the Duchess of Cleveland (1641–1709), about whom PEPYS admits to having erotic fantasies, passed Wycherley in the opposite direction in Pall Mall, she leant out of her carriage and called him 'a son of a whore'. When he had recovered from his surprise, recognizing the remark as an allusion to a song in the play, he ordered his carriage to be turned round. He caught up with the lady and invited her to attend that night's performance, where, from the pit under the King's Box, 'he entertained her during the whole play'. Needless to say, the published version (1672) has an unctuous dedication to her. Three more comedies followed: *The Gentleman Dancing-Master* (1673), *The Country-Wife* (1675), and *The Plain-Dealer* (1677).

Wycherley's reputation and his position at court were ruined by a disastrous marriage in 1681 to the Countess of Drogheda—after her death the following year her will was disputed and he spent several years in prison for debt. Restored to favour if not to funds, he published *Miscellany Poems* (1704), the subsequent editions of which incorporated revisions made on the advice of the 16-year-old POPE. He remarried in 1715, and died 11 days later, leaving his young widow £400 a year, which his nephew had to pay. His first three plays are in the Restoration format of rakes, fops, and amorous intrigues, though they are much better constructed and characterized, and more honestly vulgar than most, and have underlying hints of outrage. This satirical streak is more evident in *The Plain-Dealer*, whose hero (suitably named Manly) mistrusts mankind and is brought to his senses by a devoted female admirer. See *The Country Wife and Other Plays*, ed. Peter Dixon, 1996; P. F. Vernon, *William Wycherley*, 1965 (critical introduction).

WYCLIFF, JOHN (c.1328–84) English cleric and philosopher, was born near Richmond, Yorkshire, went to Oxford in about 1345, and became Master of Balliol College, from which he resigned in 1361 to take up the first of several ecclesiastical offices. In the early 1370s he was in the service of the Crown, whose representatives, notably John of Gaunt (1340–99), generally supported him in his opinions on the relative authority of Church and State, which he expounded in two treatises in Latin, *De Dominio Divino* and *De Civili Dominio*. When he attacked the doctrine of transubstantiation, however, even this support melted away. He retired to his parish of Lutterworth, Leicestershire, where he died after suffering several strokes. In the meantime a court summoned by the Archbishop of Canterbury had formally condemned his views and instigated the persecution of the followers of his teachings, known as Lollards. After his death many of his writings were destroyed, and in 1428 his bones were dug up and thrown into the River Swift. Because of the difficulty of ascribing particular works in English to him personally, such writings are usually referred to as Wycliffite.

WYLIE, ELINOR (1885–1928), née Hoyt, American poet and novelist, was born in Somerville, New Jersey, the eldest of five children in a distinguished Philadelphia family—her father was appointed Solicitor General of the USA in 1897. She was educated at the exclusive Mrs Flint's school, Philadelphia, travelled Europe with her grandfather, and made her social debut. In 1905 she married Philip Hichborn, an admiral's son, by whom she had a son in 1907. In 1910 she left her son with an aunt and eloped with Horace Wylie, a married lawyer 15 years her senior. They went to England, where they lived in the New Forest as 'Mr and Mrs Waring' for three years, during which she had a volume of verse, *Incidental Numbers* (1912), privately published in London. After Hichborn's suicide and Wylie's divorce they returned to the USA, married, and settled in Washington, where she became acquainted with SINCLAIR LEWIS and William Rose Benét (1886–1950), the poet and editor, who suggested she should submit her verse to literary journals. The reception of *Nets to Catch the Wind*

(1921), whose contents had a distinctly 19th-century flavour, encouraged her to think of herself as a potential literary figure. She left Wylie and moved to New York, where she was for a time Poetry Editor of *Vanity Fair*. In 1923, after her divorce, she married Benét, who was a widower with three children. A second volume of verse, *Black Armour*, and her first novel, *Jennifer Lorn: a Sedate Extravaganza*, set in 18th-century England and the Orient, were published in 1923. Her personal literary coterie organized a 'Jennifer Lorn Dinner', the dishes being mentioned in the book or in BECKFORD's *Vathek*. A conscious professional as well as an artist, she followed up with two more novels: *The Venetian Glass Nephew* (1925), a romantic fantasy, and *The Orphan Angel* (1926; in Britain as *Mortal Image*, 1927), her only novel with an American setting, in which she fantasizes the survival from drowning of SHELLEY, and his subsequent allegorical quest for Silver La Croix. In 1926 she took to spending summers alone in England. A third book of poems, *Trivial Breath*, and a fourth novel, *Mr Hodge & Mr Hazard*, an 'everyday fable' in which a Victorian philistine clashes with 'the last Romantic poet', were published in 1928. In the autumn she had a stroke in New York, and died the day after finalizing the texts of her sonnet sequence, *Angels and Earthly Creatures* (1929; limited edn, printed in England, 1928). Benét edited *The Collected Poems of Elinor Wylie* (1932). See Judith Farr, *The Life and Art of Elinor Wylie*, 1983.

WYNDHAM, JOHN, pseudonym of John Wyndham Parkes Lucas Beynon Harris (1903–69) British novelist and short-story writer, was born in Knowle, Warwickshire, the eldest son of a barrister, and was educated at Bedales School. He tried various careers before, encouraged by a small private income, he turned to writing. He published science-fiction stories in American magazines as John Beynon Harris, and then, in 1935, broke into the English market with a serial in *Passing Show*, written under the name of John Beynon. During World War II he worked first as a censor in the civil service, and then in a cipher office as a corporal in the Royal Corps of Signals. His first novel, *The Day of the Triffids* (1951), written as John Wyndham, established his name as well as a new, postwar, genre in science fiction; in this case, the human race is pitched against both blindness and a monstrous strain of virulent and mobile plant life. A global disaster of a different kind features in *The Kraken Awakes* (1953), while in *The Chrysalids* (1955) and *The Midwich Cuckoos* (1957) children are affected with strange powers. Of his volumes of short stories, *The Seeds of Time* (1956) and *Consider Her Ways and Others* (1961) have survived the test of time in the same way as have most of his novels.

X

XENOPHON (*c*.430–*c*.355 BC) Greek historian, was an Athenian. In 401 he accompanied the ten thousand Greek mercenaries recruited by Cyrus to help him wrest the throne of Persia from his brother, Artaxerxes II. When Cyrus was killed near Babylon and the Greek generals lured into a trap and beheaded, Xenophon took charge, and in an epic march brought the army back to the sea—see his account of the exploit, *Anabasis*, tr. Rex Warner as *The Persian Expedition* (new edn 1972). Shortly afterwards he was formally banished from Athens, and appears as a member of the Spartan forces against the Persians in 396, and against Athens in 394. The Spartans granted him an estate near Olympia, where he lived comfortably with his family for the next twenty years until ejected in a local rising, and moving to Corinth. His banishment was lifted in about 365, but he probably did not return to Athens. *Hellenica*—tr. Rex Warner as *A History of My Times* (new edn 1979)—is his continuation of the story of the Peloponnesian War from 411, when THUCYDIDES breaks off, to its end in 404, with an additional five books of rather rambling memories of the succeeding period to 362, when Theban domination collapsed. He also wrote treatises on horsemanship, hunting, and household management; recollections of the philosopher, Socrates (469–399), whom he knew; and a fictional account of the education and career of Cyrus the Great, founder of the Persian empire.

Y

YEATS, W(ILLIAM) B(UTLER)
(1865–1939) Irish poet, dramatist, and prose
writer, was born in Sandymount, Dublin, the
eldest child of the artist John Butler Yeats
(1839–1922) and brother of the artist Jack Butler Yeats (1871–1957)—for Yeats's relations
with his two hardworking younger sisters
see Joan Hardwick, *The Yeats Sisters* (1996).
The family moved to London in 1867, but in
1880 returned to Dublin, where he went to
the High School, Harcourt Street, and then to
the School of Art. His first published poem
appeared in the *Dublin University Review* in
1885. After the family settled in London once
more, he made frequent visits to Ireland, and
in 1888 edited an anthology of contemporary
poetry, *Poems and Ballads of Young Ireland*,
which contained four of his own poems.

In 1889 he published in London *The Wanderings of Oisin and Other Poems*, whose title
poem, based on elements he had found in
translations of Gaelic mythology, marks the
beginning of the Irish Literary Revival. He
also met Maud Gonne (1866–1953), as beautiful as an actress as she was fervent as an Irish
nationalist. He fell hopelessly in love and
proposed to her unsuccessfully on many occasions—see *The Gonne–Yeats Letters 1893–
1938*, ed. Anna McBride White and A. Norman Jeffares (2nd edn 1993). His first play,
The Countess Cathleen (1892), which was composed in prose and then reworked in verse,
was written for her. So was a group of poems
under the heading of 'The Rose', published
in *The Countess Kathleen and Various Legends
and Lyrics* (1891) and subsequently in *Poems*
(1895), which comprised a selection of what
he wanted preserved. The rose, signifying
eternal beauty, was one of the many symbols
which he drew from Irish mythology and occult lore to illustrate his poetic themes. In the
stories in *The Secret Rose* (1897), occultism is
overlaid with Pre-Raphaelite detail, and
poems reflecting his obsession with Maud
occur also in *The Wind Among the Reeds*
(1899), *In the Seven Woods* (1903), and *The
Green Helmet, and Other Poems* (1910). He had,
in addition, a sporadic affair with Mrs Olivia
Shakespear (1863–1938), who became his lifelong correspondent and confidante, and
whose daughter married POUND—see John
Harwood, *Olivia Shakespear and W. B. Yeats*
(1989).

In 1897 the second of his many visits to
Coole Park, Co. Galway, the home of GREG-
ORY, led to the establishment of the Irish Literary Theatre, with GEORGE MOORE, Edward
Martyn (1859–1923), and Yeats as directors.
It was replaced in 1902 by the Irish National
Dramatic Society, with himself as President.
An early production was his *Cathleen Ni Hou-
lihan* (1902), a symbolic play about the struggle for Irish independence, in which Maud
played an electrifying role. In 1905 he became
a co-director, with Lady Gregory and SYNGE,
of the Abbey Theatre, where his *Deirdre*, a
tragedy from the heroic sagas, was first performed in 1906. Later, he experimented with
other dramatic forms: a series derived from
the Japanese Noh plays was published as
Four Plays for Dancers (1921).

In 1916 Maud's husband, John MacBride,
whom she had shocked Yeats by marrying in
1903, was executed for his part in the Easter
Rising. The next year, having been turned
down yet again by Maud, and also several
times by Iseult (1894–1954)—see also STU-
ART—, Maud's illegitimate daughter by a
Frenchman, he married Georgie Hyde Lees
(1895–1968), a young English woman who
had mediumistic powers. His wife's attempts
to draw him out of his obvious unhappiness
by automatic handwriting resulted, much to
her surprise, in *A Vision* (1925), an exploration into the cyclical view of history and of
human experience. It also revived his poetic
impulse, leading to his collections *The Tower*
(1928) and *The Winding Stair, and Other Poems*
(1933), in which a philosophical attitude to
old age, wit, scorn, sensuality, and a sense of
panic about the world's future predominate.
Although he had often been ill, he was writing plays and fine poetry to the last. He died
while wintering in the Riviera. He was in-
terred in Roquebrune and reburied in Sligo
in 1948. Besides being an experimental dramatist in a variety of forms, he was a poet of
many moods and skills whose work has had
a dominant effect on much modern poetry.
He was instrumental in founding an Irish national literary and, perhaps even more significantly, dramatic movement. His *Essays
1931–1936* was published in 1937, and he was
Editor of *The Oxford Book of Modern Verse
1892–1935* (1936). From 1922 to 1928 he was
an active senator of the Irish Free State. He

refused a knighthood in 1915. He was awarded the Nobel Prize for Literature in 1923. See *Yeats's Poems*, ed. A. Norman Jeffares, 1989; *Selected Poems*, ed. Robert Gill, 1993; *Collected Plays of W. B. Yeats*, 1952; *Autobiographies*, new edn 1988; A. Norman Jeffares, *W. B. Yeats: a New Biography*, new edn 1990; R. F. Foster, *W. B. Yeats: a Life, Volume 1—the Apprentice Magi 1865–1914*, 1997; Edward Malins and John Purkis, *A Preface to Yeats*, 2nd edn 1994; A. Norman Jeffares, *A New Commentary on the Poems of W. B. Yeats*, 1984; A. S. Knowland and A. Norman Jeffares, *A Commentary on the Collected Plays of W. B. Yeats*, 1975.

YERBY, FRANK (1916–92) American novelist, was born in Augusta, Georgia, of mixed parentage: 'Do not call me Black. I have more Seminole than Negro blood in me.' He was educated at Paine College, Augusta, and Fisk University, going on to postgraduate study at Chicago University, after which he taught in Louisiana. In 1941, having married one of his students, he gave up teaching to become a laboratory technician with the Ford Motor Co. in Michigan. His early literary work was of social protest against the treatment of contemporary black Americans, and included the short stories 'Health Card' (1944) and 'Homecoming' (1946), and a novel which no one would publish. According to his account, he cynically analysed the market for popular fiction, and came up with *The Foxes of Harrow* (1946), set in the American South; it was the first of numerous historical novels (he preferred the term 'costume dramas') which, an obituarist suggests, 'were not so much bodice-rippers as accounts of bodices being voluntarily undone by strong-willed heroines with, or without, the cooperation of heroes more interested in action than in gentle wooing'. Other backgrounds include the Crusades, in *The Saracen Blade* (1952), said to have sold ten million copies; the French Revolution, in *The Devil's Laughter* (1953); and early Christian times, in *Judas, My Brother: the Story of the Thirteenth Disciple* (1969). Novels in which he addresses more serious issues include *Speak Now* (1969) and *The Dahomean* (1971; in UK as *The Man from Dahomey*). In 1953 he visited Spain, where he met, and, after his divorce, married, his second wife, and settled in Madrid.

YEVTUSHENKO, YEVGENY (ALEKSANDROVICH) (*b.* 1933) Russian poet, was born in Zima, Siberia, and was brought up in Moscow after his geologist parents (his mother also sang, to entertain the troops) separated in 1941. At 15 he had a poem printed in *Soviet Sport*; he was 19, and a student at the Institute of World Literature, when his first collection was published. The death of Stalin in 1953 was a contribution to the liberation of minds, and he found a me-

tier in the realization that 'poetry was mobile . . . a poem was much quicker to write than a novel, and it could be read in public even before it came out in print'. His emergence as a public poet came with ['Zima Junction'] (1956), a long autobiographical poem, a major theme of which is his fascination with his own consciousness and emerging identity. From 1960 he travelled abroad, performing in public, composing instant verses, and generally cosmopolitanizing the Soviet Union. 'Babiy Yar' (1961), an impressive poem commemorating the German massacre (with the assistance of some Ukrainians) of the Kiev Jews, and written, by his own account, in two hours as an attack on anti-Semitism within the Soviet Union, was first read at the Moscow Polytechnic after he had given a talk about Cuba. By 1963 he could draw an audience of fourteen thousand at a Moscow stadium. While Western critics have pointed to the unevenness of his work and the decline in his reputation as a poet, there has been no shortage of translations. *A Precocious Autobiography*, tr. Andrew R. MacAndrew (1963) is an impressionistic study of his first thirty years. *Don't Die Before You're Dead*, tr. Antonia W. Bouis (1995) is an autobiographical novel of the attempted revolution in Moscow in 1991. See *The Collected Poems 1952–1990*, ed. Albert C. Todd, 1992.

YONGE, CHARLOTTE M(ARY) (1823–1901) British novelist, was born in Otterbourne, Hampshire, an area which she hardly left all her life except for visits to relatives and one business trip to France in 1869, to stay with the family of the historian, François Guizot (1787–1874). She was educated in classics and mathematics by her overbearing father, and in modern languages by tutors; from the age of seven until her death she taught in the village Sunday School. She is quoted as having 'no hesitation in declaring my full belief in the inferiority of women', to whose moral and religious improvement she dedicated her literary talents. In this she was encouraged by her mentor, Rev. John Keble (1792–1866), founder of the Oxford Movement in the Church (and also Professor of Poetry at Oxford 1831–41), who became her local vicar in 1836; it was her family's decision that any earnings should be devoted to good causes. Her best-known book, *The Heir of Redclyffe* (1853), long and tedious as it may be to modern readers, is, perhaps surprisingly, a romantic novel. *The Daisy Chain: or, Aspirations, a Family Chronicle* (1856), £2000 of her earnings from which went to a missionary college in New Zealand, and other similarly-based works, are significant prototypes of the modern family novel for young people so soon to be immortalized by ALCOTT, the heroine of whose *Little Women* (1868) is found in chapter 3 in the attic 'eating apples and crying over *The Heir of Redclyffe*'. Yonge was the sole Editor from its foundation in 1851 to 1890 of the *Monthly Packet*, a girls' magazine designed to imbue them with the spirit of the Oxford Movement; she also edited the *Monthly Paper of Sunday Teaching* from 1860 to 1875, and *Mothers in Council* from 1890 to 1900. Between times she wrote some hundred novels and many educational books, and translated historical works from the French. See Margaret Mare and Alicia C. Percival, *Victorian Best-seller: the World of Charlotte M. Yonge*, 1948; Alethea Hayter, *Charlotte Yonge*, 1996 (introduction).

YORKE, HENRY VINCENT see GREEN.

YOUNG, ANDREW (1885–1971) Scottish poet and naturalist, was born in Elgin and educated at the High School of Edinburgh and Edinburgh University, being ordained in the United Free Church in 1912. In 1918 he became Minister of the English Presbyterian Church in Hove, Sussex. During the 1930s he was converted to the Church of England, and was Vicar of Stonegate in Sussex from 1941 until his retirement in 1959. He was made a canon of Chichester Cathedral in 1948. His first book of verse, *Songs of Night* (1910), was published privately, and it was only after the appearance of seven volumes in all that he reached a significant audience with a selection of his poems, *Winter Harvest* (1933). His themes are inspired by a minute observation and knowledge of nature and the landscape (as in 'The White Blackbird', 'Ploughing in Mist', 'Mountain View', 'The Snowdrop', 'Daisies', and the curious 'Hibernating Snails'), and by profound religious meditation. His most sustained poem is *Out of the World and Back* (1958), the journey of a soul— the first part was published as *Into Hades* (1952). He also wrote a verse mystery play, *Nicodemus* (1937), and several botanical and topographical prose works, including *A Prospect of Flowers* (1945) and *The Poet and the Landscape* (1962). He was awarded the Queen's Gold Medal for Poetry in 1952. See *Poetical Works*, ed. Edward Lowbury and Alison Young, 1985.

YOUNG, DOUGLAS (1913–73) Scottish poet and classicist, was born in Tayport, Fife, and spent his childhood in India, where his father worked for a Dundee jute company. He was educated at Merchiston Castle School and St Andrews University, which he favoured over Oxford and Cambridge, to which he also passed, for its golf courses. He subsequently won an open exhibition to New College, Oxford, where he read Greats. In 1938 he became assistant to the Professor of Greek at Aberdeen. An active and impressive member of the Scottish National Party, he refused to be conscripted in World War II (though he would probably have been rejected as unfit), on the grounds that the act

was contrary to Scottish law. He was imprisoned for a year, during which he supervised the publication of *Autran Blads: an Outwale o Verses* (1943). This erudite and enjoyable volume contained some of his best-known poems in Scots, such as 'Sabbath in the Mearns' and 'Sang by the Sea', and translations into Scots from Gaelic, Latin, and Greek, and into Greek from Scots. After the war he taught classics at University College, Dundee, and St Andrews University, becoming Senior Lecturer in 1960. He was appointed Professor of Classics at McMaster University, Ontario, in 1968, and to the new chair in Greek at the University of North Carolina in 1970. He died suddenly at his desk, with his HOMER in front of him. He translated the *Oresteia* of AESCHYLUS into English verse (1974); his versions in Scots of *The Frogs* and *The Birds* of ARISTOPHANES, as *The Puddocks* (1957) and *The Burdies* (1959), were both later performed at the Edinburgh Festival. *A Clear Voice: Douglas Young, Poet and Polymath*, ed. Clara Young and David Murison (n.d.), contains a selection of his writings and a memoir.

YOUNG, EDWARD (1683–1765) British poet and dramatist, was born in Upham, Hampshire, the son of the rector, who became Dean of Salisbury. He was educated at Winchester College, going on at the advanced age of 19 to New College, Oxford, on the death of whose warden, with whom he was lodging, he transferred to Corpus Christi College. He was nominated to a law fellowship at All Souls, and graduated as DCL in 1719, having in the meantime become a minor light in London literary circles, and published some occasional and commemorative poems. Two tragedies, *Busiris, King of Egypt* (1719) and *The Revenge* (1721), owe more to the poetic than the dramatic art. At this time he was tutor to the young Marquis of Wharton (1698–1731), who was a somewhat erratic patron—Young had to apply to the courts to settle a financial disagreement between them. *Love of Fame: or, The Universal Passion* (1725–28) is a collection of satires on types of people. In about 1727 he took holy orders and withdrew his third play, *The Brothers*, while it was in rehearsal. He was appointed a royal chaplain in 1728, and Rector of Welwyn, Hertfordshire, in 1730. In 1731 he married Lady Elizabeth Lee, the widowed daughter of the Earl of Lichfield. Her death in 1740, following those of her daughter and son-in-law, prompted *The Complaint: or, Night-Thoughts on Life, Death, & Immortality* (1742–46), an influential blank-verse poem in nine 'Nights' which is the most sustained example of 18th-century graveyard poetry. In 1753 he resuscitated *The Brothers*, which was staged on behalf of the Society for the Propagation of the Gospel. When the takings fell short of what he had anticipated, he paid the balance himself. His prose treatise, *Conjectures on Original Composition* (1759), contains some useful observations.

YOUNG, FRANCIS BRETT (1884–1954) British novelist and poet, was born in Halesowen, Warwickshire, the son of a doctor, and was educated at Epsom College and Birmingham University; he qualified as MB in 1907, and set up in practice in Devon. The following year he married a concert singer (he often acted as her accompanist). His first published book was a critical study of BRIDGES (1913), some of whose poems he set to music. Beginning with *Deep Sea* (1914) he published several novels during World War I, in which he served in East Africa in the Royal Medical Corps; he recorded some of his experiences in *Marching on Tanga* (1917). Severely and permanently affected by malaria, he was invalided out in 1918 with the rank of major, and was never able to resume his medical career. In 1919 he published *The Young Physician*, a semi-autobiographical novel, and *Poems 1916–1918*. He and his wife lived in Capri until 1929, in a house which it is said was built for them in exchange for his translating the architect's stories into English. They then spent three years in the Lake District, before settling near Evesham, Worcestershire. Equally adept at visualizing harsh or romantic settings on land or at sea, he was up to World War II able to write a novel a year, with a range of themes and in different moods; the most highly regarded are *Cold Harbour* (1924), *Portrait of Clare* (1927), *My Brother Jonathan* (1928), and the unfinished South African trilogy, *They Seek a Country* (1937) and *The City of Gold* (1939). The Battle of Britain in 1940 inspired him to compose *The Island* (1944), a verse saga in a variety of poetic forms, recalling high and low points in British history. He died in Cape Town, where he had gone on medical advice.

YOURCENAR, MARGUERITE (1903–87) French novelist, poet, and critic, was born Marguerite de Crayencour in Brussels, of two ancient and wealthy Flemish families; she assumed the approximate anagram of her name in the 1920s, and adopted it legally in 1947. Her mother died ten days after the birth, and Yourcenar spent her childhood on the family estate near Lille. She was educated privately, and travelled widely with her father until his death in 1929 and the loss of the family fortune in the Wall Street crash. She published two books of verse before she was 20; *Feux* (1936; tr. Dori Katz as *Fires*, 1981), prose poems, was written after a crisis of love. In 1937 in Paris she met Grace Frick (1903–79), an American academic, with whom in 1939 she settled in the USA. She became an American citizen in 1947, though she continued to write in French. *Mémoires d'Hadrien* (1951; tr. Grace Frick as *Memoirs of Hadrian*, 1954), her first novel to be published in English, and also her best known, is the epistolary revelations of the Roman emperor, in which the past, and eternal personal predicaments, are vividly brought to life. Others include *Le Coup de Grâce* (1939; tr. Frick as *Coup de Grâce*, 1957), a slight story of an inverted love triangle whose elegance reflects the classical French tradition; and *L'Oeuvre au Noir* (1968; tr. Frick as *The Abyss*, 1976; reissued as *Zeno of Bruges*, 1994), about the 16th-century alchemist.

She also wrote plays based on the Greek tragedians; and published several collections of critical essays—see *That Mighty Sculptor, Time*, tr. Walter Kaiser (1992). Among her translations into French are VIRGINA WOOLF's *The Waves* (1937) and HENRY JAMES's *What Maisie Knew* (1947). Her French citizenship was restored in order that she might accept membership of the Académie Française in 1980, the first woman ever to be elected. Her last fiction to appear in English is *A Blue Tale and Other Stories*, tr. Alberto Manguel (1995), three early pieces, though the title story was not published in French until 1993. *Souvenirs Pieux* (1974; tr. Maria Louise Ascher as *Dear Departed*, 1992), a family history whose recurring theme is the ecology movement, is the first of three discursive and aphoristic memoirs, the last of which is unfinished. See Josyane Savigneau, *Marguerite Yourcenar: Inventing a Life*, tr. Joan E. Howard, 1993 (biography).

Z

ZAMYATIN, YEVGENY IVANOVICH
(1884–1937) Russian novelist and short-story
writer, was born in Lebedyan, Tambov, and
studied naval engineering at the Polytechnic
Institute, St Petersburg, where he lived illegally after being imprisoned in 1905 and exiled to his home town for political activity.
He spent 1916–17 in England as a naval architect at Newcastle upon Tyne, supervising the
construction of ten icebreakers for the Tsarist
government. Now a lapsed Bolshevik, he returned to Russia just before the October Revolution, as a result of which there were no
more new ships and no proper job for him. A
short novel, [*The Islanders*] (1918), satirizing
the English, had some success, however, and
he was able to survive as a lecturer in creative
writing, editor, and official of the Writers'
Union, while himself writing stories—see *The
Dragon and Other Stories*, tr. Mirra Ginsburg
(1975)—and translating such writers as SHER-
IDAN, HENRY, LONDON, and WELLS, on whom
he published two critical essays. He was also
indebted to the 'new and entirely original
species of literary form' created by Wells 'in
his novels of socio-fantasy' for his anti-Uto-
pian novel of life in a totalitarian state, [*We*]
(tr. Guilbert Guerney, introduction by Michael Glenny, 1970). Originally translated
into English by Gregory Zilboorg and first
published in New York (1924), it was translated from English into Czech (1926), and
from Czech back into Russian, in which extracts were published in Prague in an émigré
magazine (1927). This was the signal for the
persecution of its author and the banning of
all his work in the Soviet Union. His personal
appeal to Stalin in 1931 to be allowed, with
his wife, to leave the country 'for medical
treatment' was granted with the support of
GORKY, and he settled in Paris, where he died.
In its political implications as well as its
theme, [*We*] is a worthy forerunner of OR-
WELL's *Nineteen Eighty-Four*. See *A Soviet Heretic: Essays by Yevgeny Zamyatin*, ed. and tr.
Mirra Ginsburg, 1974; Alex M. Shane, *The Life
and Works of Evgenij Zamjatin*, 1968.

ZANGWILL, ISRAEL (1864–1926) British
novelist and dramatist, was born in London,
the son of an impoverished Russian-Jewish
refugee, and was educated at the Jews' Free
School and London University. He taught for
a few years at his former school, and then became a full-time writer. After having had several stories published, he was commissioned
by the Jewish Publication Society of America
to write a 'big' Jewish novel. *Children of the
Ghetto* (1892) is a vivid, compassionate, moving, and often very funny expression of Jewish life in the East End of London. Attempts
to repeat the formula, *Ghetto Tragedies* (1893)
and *Ghetto Comedies* (1907), were less successful. His other memorable work is *The King of
the Schnorrers* (1894), a collection of stories
which had first appeared in the humorous
journal, the *Idler*. Zangwill became a prominent member of the Jewish community and a
leading spokesman for Zionism (he founded
the Jewish Territorial Organization for the
Settlement of Jews Within the British Empire), though in his personal life he displayed
an ambivalence towards his faith. See Joseph
H. Udelson, *Dreamer of the Ghetto: the Life and
Works of Israel Zangwill*, 1990; and in Chaim
Bermant, *What's the Joke: a Study of Jewish Humour Through the Ages*, 1986.

ZOLA, ÉMILE (1840–1902) French novelist
and critic, was born in Paris, the only child of
an Italian civil engineer (who died when the
boy was seven) and his much younger working-class French wife. He was educated at
Collège d'Aix, where his close friend was
Paul Cézanne (1839–1906), though it was
Zola who used to win the school drawing
prize, and at the Lycée Saint-Louis, Paris. He
passed the written but not the oral test for his
baccalaureate in 1858, and failed completely
the following year. After working as a clerk
in the Excise Office, he was taken on by the
publishing house of Hachette, graduating
from dispatch to advertising, which was useful experience when it came to the promotion
of his first book, *Contes à Ninon* (1864), a collection of stories. In 1865 he joined the daily
newspaper *L'Événement* as arts columnist, in
which capacity he defiantly supported the
Impressionist school of Cézanne, Edouard
Manet (1832–83), and Claude Monet (1840–
1926). *Thérèse Raquin* (1867; tr. Leonard Tancock, 1972), a study of guilt, was his first successful attempt to match in fiction the
Impressionists' interpretations of contemporary life, though the 'Naturalism' to which he
laid claim had more to do with realism than

with its scientific connotation. He now embarked on what became a sequence of 20
novels, under the general heading of 'Les
Rougon-Macquart', exploring the destructive
influences of heredity on members of the
same family during the Second Empire
(1851–70). Of these, *L'Assommoir* (1877; tr.
Tancock, 1970), *Nana* (1880; tr. George
Holden, 1972), and *La Bête Humaine* (1890; tr.
Tancock as *The Beast in Man*, 1977; tr. Roger
Pearson, 1996) in particular brought him notoriety as well as fame and wealth, while also
establishing him as a champion of the working classes. In 1870 he married Alexandrine-
Gabrielle Meley (1839–1925), the orphaned
love-child of a teenage liaison: they had no
children. In 1888 he began an affair with the
20-year-old Jeanne-Sophie-Adèle Rozerot, his
wife's sewing maid, who used to pose for
him in his exercise of the new art of photography. He set her up in a Paris apartment:
they had a daughter (*b.* 1889) and a son (*b.*
1891).

The first (carefully bowdlerized) translation of Zola into English was *Nana* (1884), negotiated by GEORGE MOORE on behalf of the
London publisher, Henry Vizetelly (1820–
94). In 1888 Vizetelly offered no defence
against the prosecution of *Nana* and two
other 'obscene libels' in the form of novels by
Zola, and was fined and bound over for a
year, during which he issued further translations. He was tried again, pleaded guilty on
the advice of his counsel, and was sentenced
to three months in jail. Notwithstanding, in
1893 Zola paid a visit to Britain as the guest
of the Institute of Journalists, the highlight of
which was a ball at the Guildhall, at which
four thousand guests clapped his arrival. In
1897 he was involved in the case of Alfred
Dreyfus (1859–1935), in whose defence he
deliberately courted prosecution with an article in *L'Aurore* under the headline 'J'Accuse'
(1898)—see *The Dreyfus Affair: 'J'Accuse' and
Other Writings*, ed. Alain Pagès, tr. Eleanor
Levieux (1996). His appeal against a sentence
of a year's imprisonment for libel was upheld
on a technicality, and a new trial ordered. To
keep the Dreyfus affair alive, Zola fled to England, outside the jurisdiction of French law,
where Jeanne and the children joined him.
He returned a year later, when the Appeal
Court upheld a petition for the retrial of
Dreyfus. Zola died of carbon monoxide poisoning, caused by a faulty flue in his bedroom. See Frederick Brown, *Zola: a Life*, 1996.